CHAMBERS & PARTNERS
LEGAL PUBLISHERS

Chambers Student Guide

CAREERS IN THE LAW

2010

Published by Chambers and Partners Publishing
(a division of Orbach & Chambers Ltd)
23 Long Lane, London EC1A 9HL
Tel: (020) 7606 1300 Fax: (020) 7600 3191
email: info@ChambersandPartners.co.uk
www.ChambersandPartners.com

Our thanks to the many students, trainees, pupils, solicitors, barristers and graduate recruitment personnel who assisted us in our research. Also to the researchers of *Chambers UK 2010* from which all firm rankings are drawn.
Copyright © 2009 Michael Chambers and Orbach & Chambers Ltd

ISBN: 978-0-8551-312-1

Publisher: Michael Chambers
Editor: Anna Williams
Deputy Editor: Richard Simmons
Writers: Alex Hocking, Arjun Harindranath, Colin Warriner, Grant Cohen, Hayley Furminger, Kate Monson, Marion Volondat, Samantha Rose
Database: Andrew Taylor, Robert Bailey
A-Z Co-ordinator: Gemma Buckle
Production: Jasper John, John Osborne, Paul Cummings, Pete Polanyk, Robert Howe
Business Development Manager: Brad D. Sirott
Business Development Team: Bianca Maio, Lennie Sarkis, Liz Brennan, Neil Murphy, Richard Ramsay
Proofreaders: John Bradley, Nicholas Widdows, Sally McGonigal
Printed by: Butler Tanner & Dennis

So you want to be a lawyer...

Welcome to the 2010 edition of the *Chambers Student Guide* to careers in the law. We've written this book to give you the information, tools and confidence to help you make a sound career decision.

This guide is the only publication to offer these three key ingredients:

- The True Picture: an insight into the training schemes at 125 law firms, based on in-depth interviews with hundreds of trainees. The trainees were selected by us, not by their law firms, and they spoke to us freely and frankly under the protection of anonymity.
- Chambers Reports: a look at life inside 24 barristers chambers. These reports were written after visits to each of the sets and interviews with pupils, barristers and clerks.
- Law School reviews: compiled after feedback from students who have completed courses at each of the schools, plus interviews with course directors.

Chambers and Partners publishes guides to the legal professions around the world. You will benefit enormously from using our *Chambers UK* guide to refine your search for a law firm or chambers to train with. The best performing firms and sets in over 65 areas of practice are identified by way of league tables in *Chambers UK*, and you can get all this information online, for free, by visiting www.chambersandpartners.com.

All the guides we publish have one thing in common – they are independent. In a market flooded with publications for law students we take great pride in this fact. No one's money influences what we say about them.

This book could be the most useful thing you read this year, so get stuck in and we wish you great success for your future career.

The Student Guide team
September 2009

Contents

> • **This guide, if used properly, can greatly ease the process of pursuing a career in the law**

1: Becoming a Lawyer

Calendar of events and deadlines — 9
Avoid missing law fairs and crucial application deadlines for training contracts and vacation schemes

What kind of lawyer do you want to be? — 15
- Do you want to become a solicitor or a barrister?
- Learn about the different types of law firms
- The recruitment market summarised
- Other types of legal practice and alternative career paths
- What do recruiters really want?

Useful work experience — 35
- Pro bono activities and volunteering
- Vacation schemes and the firms that offer them

Applications and selection — 42
- How make successful applications
- How to succeed at interviews and assessment days
- How to manage job offers

2: Law School

Solicitors' and barristers' timetables — 48

The Graduate Diploma in Law (GDL/CPE) — 52
- How non-law graduates become law students
- Our table of course providers

The Legal Practice Course (LPC) — 54
- The lowdown on the LPC
- Our table of course providers
- LPC provider reviews

The Bar Professional Training Course (BPTC) — 70
- The lowdown on the BPTC
- Our table of course providers
- BPTC provider reviews

How to fund law school — 77
- How to pay those huge course fees... and survive

An A-Z of universities and law schools — 79

3: Solicitors' Practice Areas

Summaries of the main areas of legal practice. Which will suit you best? — 89

www.chambersstudent.co.uk　　　　　　　　　　　　　　　　Becoming a Lawyer

- **Use this book in conjunction with www.chambersandpartners.com to find your perfect traineeship or pupillage**

4: The True Picture

What is the True Picture and how do we do our research? 128

Table of firms 130
Listed by size of firm, number of trainees and location

The True Picture reports 133
Trainees lift the lid on life inside 125 law firms. If you thought all firms were the same then think again

5: Refine Your Search

The application and selection methods of the top firms 515

Our table of salaries and law school sponsorships 521

Picking a firm for its overseas opportunities 529

6: A-Z of Solicitors

The phone numbers, addresses and e-mails you need to make your applications, plus loads of really useful facts and figures on the top law firms. All in simple, easy-to-follow A-Z format 533

7: The Bar

Barcode 671
Unfamiliar terminology explained

A career at the Bar 672
An overview of a career at the Bar and tips for applying

The Inns of Court 678

Practice areas at the Bar 680
Summaries of the main areas of practice at the Bar

Chambers Reports 688
What's it really like to train at some of the country's leading sets? Our reports will help you find the right match

An A-Z of barristers chambers 741

Useful contacts 766

Chambers and Partners publishes a suite of legal guides that you should find helpful in your search for a training contract or pupillage.

- **Chambers UK** is the product of interviews with solicitors, barristers and their clients. It identifies the leading firms, sets and players across the full sweep of legal practice in the UK.

- **Chambers Global** sets out the results of our research into legal jurisdictions worldwide from Australia to Zambia. If you are considering a training contract with an international law firm, it's a must-read resource.

- **Chambers USA** provides a more detailed analysis of the performance of the best firms across all US states.

- **Chambers Asia** covers 23 countries in one of the world's most dynamic legal markets.

- **Chambers Europe** looks at the leading law firms and individuals from Albania to Ukraine.

- **Chambers Latin America** gives country and continent-wide listings.

- **Chambers Associate** is used by American law students and gives an analysis of the top firms in the USA.

These guides can all be read online for free at
www.chambersandpartners.com
and
www.chambers-associate.com

Becoming a Lawyer

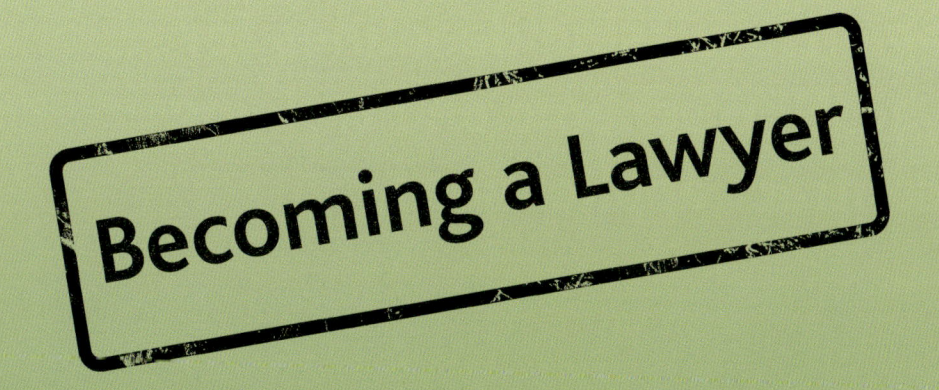

Calendar of events and deadlines	9
What kind of lawyer do you want to be?	15
Useful work experience	34
Applications and selection	42

- **Procrastination is the thief of time:** Plan well ahead to ensure against missing deadlines for vacation scheme and training contract applications.

top tip no. 1

Calendar of events 2009-2010

Law Fairs

October 2009

6	University of Dundee; St Andrew's
13	Robert Gordon University, Aberdeen
15	Northumbria University
22	University of Nottingham
27	University of York
28	City University, London; Liverpool University
29	University of Manchester

November 2009

3	University of Leicester
4	University of Hull; University of Reading; Queen's University Belfast; University of East Anglia
9	University of Leeds
10	University of Leeds; Cardiff University; University of Essex; University of Sussex
11	University of Bristol
12	University of Bristol; University of Birmingham
14	University of Oxford
16	UCL; University of Newcastle
17	UCL
18	SOAS; University of Birmingham
19	University of Southampton
23	University of Durham
24	University of Durham; LSE; University of Warwick
25	Queen Mary London; University of Exeter; University of Sheffield
26	LSE
28	University of Cambridge (Solicitors)

December 2009

1	Kings College, London
2	Kings College, London

January 2010

30	University of Cambridge (Barristers)

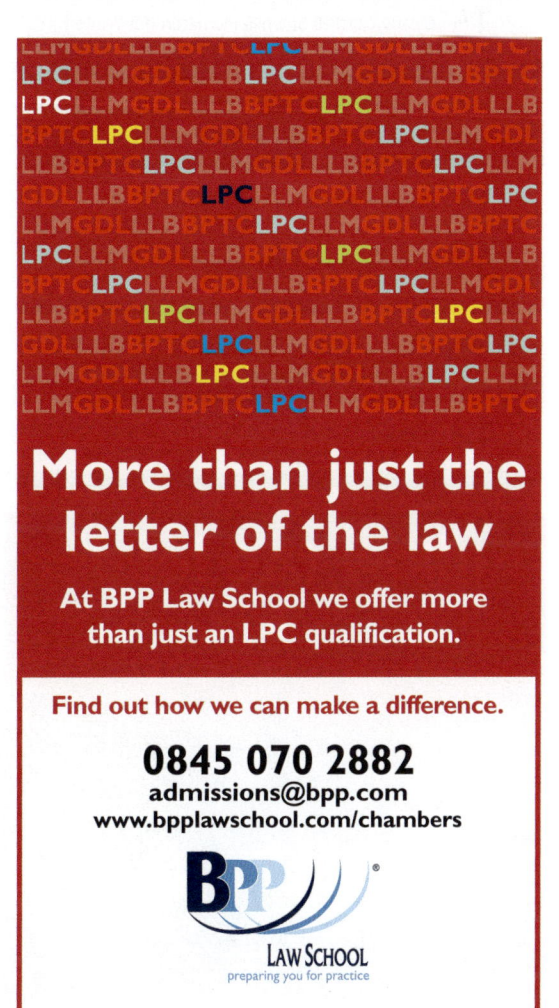

More than just the letter of the law

At BPP Law School we offer more than just an LPC qualification.

Find out how we can make a difference.

0845 070 2882
admissions@bpp.com
www.bpplawschool.com/chambers

BPP LAW SCHOOL
preparing you for practice

Vacation Scheme Deadlines

October 2009

- **16** Slaughter and May (for Winter)
- **31** Allen & Overy (for Winter)
  Jones Day (for Winter – non-law)
  Norton Rose (for Winter)

November 2009

- **1** Stephenson Harwood (for Easter & Xmas)
- **13** Clifford Chance (for Winter)
- **15** Clearly Gottlieb Steen & Hamilton (for Winter)

December 2009

- **18** Slaughter and May (for Easter)
- **31** Latham & Watkins (for Easter)

January 2010

- **12** Skadden

January 2010

- **15** Freshfields, Clifford Chance (for Summer & Spring), Stephenson Harwood
- **17** Allen & Overy
- **22** Slaughter and May
- **28** Cleary Gottlieb Steen & Hamilton
- **29** Reynolds Porter Chamberlain
- **30** Dundas & Wilson   Shoosmiths
  McGrigors
- **31** Addleshaw Goddard   Lewis Silkin
  Ashurst   Lovells
  Baker & McKenzie   Memery Crystal
  Barlow Lyde & Gilbert Mills & Reeve
  Berwin Leighton Paisner Mishcon de Reya
  Clyde & Co   Norton Rose
  CMS Cameron McKenna Olswang
  Dechert   Pinsent Masons
  Dewey & LeBoeuf   SJ Berwin
  Dickinson Dees   Stevens & Bolton
  DLA Piper   Taylor Wessing
  Farrer & Co   TLT Solicitors
  Government Legal Service Travers Smith
  Hammonds   Walker Morris
  Ince & Co   Watson, Farley & Williams
  Jones Day   Weil, Gotshal & Manges
  Kirkland & Ellis   White & Case
  Latham & Watkins   Withers
  Lawrence Graham (LG) Wragge & Co

Follow the leader

What makes BPP Law School the leading provider of the GDL? It's our unique extras that make the difference.

> Access to specialist careers services before, during and after your GDL
> Optional 'GDL Extra' and Company Law programmes
> Flexible study modes and a range of tutorial and lecture formats

Find out how we can make a difference.

0845 070 2882
admissions@bpp.com
www.bpplawschool.com/chambers

BPP LAW SCHOOL
preparing you for practice

Vacation Scheme Deadlines

February 2010

1	O'Melveny & Myers	
8	Nabarro	Boodle Hatfield
9	Muckle	
11	HBJ Gateley Wareing	
12	Speechly Bircham	
14	Holman Fenwick Willan	Cobbetts
15	Manches	
19	Bates Wells & Braithwaite Pannone (for Easter)	
26	Capsticks	Edwards Angell Palmer & Dodge
28	Covington & Burling Halliwells Macfarlanes Michelmores Paul Hastings	Shadbolt Vinson & Elkins Ward Hadaway Wedlake Bell

March 2010

1	Beachcroft Trowers & Hamlins	
31	Bevan Brittan Coffin Mew Foot Anstey Hill Dickinson Lester Aldridge	Penningtons Pricewaterhouse-Coopers Reed Smith Sheridans

April 2010

9	Bond Pearce
30	Howes Percival Laytons

June 2010

25	Pannone

The first rule when choosing a law school. Cross examine it.

	Yes	No
Are you one of the leading law schools in the country?	✓	☐
Do more of the top law firms exclusively send their trainees to you than to anyone else?	✓	☐
Do you provide access to specialist careers support before, during and after each programme?	✓	☐
Do you have flexible hours and lecture formats so I can study in a way that suits me?	✓	☐

With six city centre schools in **Birmingham*, Bristol*, Leeds, London (Holborn and Waterloo)** and **Manchester** why study law anywhere else?

If you've any more questions, please get in touch.

0845 070 2882
admissions@bpp.com
www.bpplawschool.com/chambers

BPP LAW SCHOOL
preparing you for practice

*Subject to SRA validation.

| Undergraduate degrees | Masters degrees | Graduate Diploma in Law | Legal Practice Course | Bar Professional Training Course | Law Summer School | Professional Development Training |

Training Contract Deadlines

January 2010

- **17** Allen & Overy (non-law)
- **31** Bristows (Feb interviews)
     Clifford Chance (non-law)

February 2010

- **18** Baker & McKenzie (non-law)

March 2010

- **31** Wilsons (for 2011 & 2012)

May 2010

- **31** BP Collins (for 2011)

June 2010

- **30** Finers Stephens Innocent
     Freeth Cartwright

July 2010

- **1** Maxwell Winward
     Michelmores
- **30** Edwards Angell Palmer & Dodge
     McDermott Will & Emery
     McGrigors
     Reynolds Porter Chamberlain
     Sidley Austen
     Trethowans
- **31** Addleshaw Goddard
     Allen & Overy (law)
     Anthony Collins
     Ashurst
     Baker & McKenzie (law)
     Berwin Leighton Paisner
     Bevan Brittan
     Bingham McCutchen
     Bircham Dyson Bell
     Bird & Bird
     Bond Pearce
     Boodle Hatfield
     Bristows (Aug int'vw)
     Browne Jacobson
     Burges Salmon
     Charles Russell
     Clarke Willmott
     Cleary Gottlieb
     Clifford Chance
     Clyde & Co
     CMS Cameron McKenna
     Cobbetts
     Coffin Mew
     Collyer Bristow
     Covington & Burling
     Cripps Harries Hall
     Davenport Lyons
     Davies Arnold Cooper
     Dechert
     Denton Wilde Sapte
     Dewey & LeBoeuf
     Dickinson Dees
     DLA Piper
     Dundas & Wilson
     DWF
     Farrer & Co
     Fladgate
     Foot Anstey
     Forbes
     Ford & Warren
     Freshfields
     Government Legal Service
     Halliwells
     Hammonds
     Harbottle & Lewis
     HBJ Gateley Wareing
     Henmans
     Herbert Smith
     Hill Dickinson
     Holman Fenwick
     Howes Percival
     Ince & Co
     Irwin Mitchell
     Jones Day
     K&L Gates
     Kirkland & Ellis
     Latham & Watkins
     Lawrence Graham (LG)
     Lester Aldridge
     Lewis Silkin
     Lovells
     Macfarlanes
     Manches
     Martineau
     Mayer Brown
     Memery Crystal
     Mills & Reeve
     Mishcon de Reya
     Muckle
     Nabarro
     Norton Rose
     Olswang
     O'Melveny & Myers
     Osborne Clarke

BPP opens doors

LLM (Commercial Law)
LLM (Financial Regulation and Compliance)
LLM (International Business Law)
LLM (Professional Legal Practice)

Gaining an internationally recognised masters degree in law (LLM) in your chosen specialist area can seriously enhance your career prospects.

0845 070 2882
admissions@bpp.com
www.bpplawschool.com/chambers

BPP LAW SCHOOL preparing you for practice

Training Contract Deadlines

July 2010

- Pannone
- Paul Hastings
- Penningtons
- Pinsent Masons
- PricewaterhouseCoopers
- Pritchard Englefield
- Reed Smith
- Shadbolt
- Shearman & Sterling
- Sheridans
- Simmons & Simmons
- SJ Berwin
- Skadden
- Speechly Bircham
- Stephenson Harwood
- Taylor Wessing
- Thomas Eggar
- Thomson Snell & Passmore
- Thring Townsend
- TLT Solicitors
- Travers Smith
- Veale Wasbrough Lawyers
- Walker Morris
- Ward Hadaway
- Warner Goodman
- Watson Farley & Williams
- Wedlake Bell
- Weil, Gotshal & Manges
- White & Case
- Wiggin
- Winckworth Sherwood
- Withers
- Wragge & co

August 2010

Date	Firms
1	Beachcroft; Trowers & Hamlins
10	Maclay Murray & Spens
13	Capsticks
18	Higgs & Sons
31	Barlow Lyde & Gilbert; Hewitsons; Laytons; Mundays; Thomas Cooper (for 2012); Vinson & Elkins

September 2010

Date	Firm
30	Stevens & Bolton

The law doesn't rely on luck – neither should your pupillage

With a BPTC (formerly BVC) from BPP Law School you're presenting a stronger case for your future pupillage.

Find out how BPP can make a difference.

0845 070 2882
admissions@bpp.com
www.bpplawschool.com/chambers

BPP LAW SCHOOL
preparing you for practice

- **Start early:** Some kind of legal experience, whether it's involvement with a student law magazine or shadowing your neighbour's lawyer friend, is pretty crucial since you need to convince potential employers that you're serious about the profession, not just following an adolescent fantasy. Always keep your ears open for useful opportunities.

top tip no. 2

What kind of lawyer do you want to be?

Let's start with one of the most basic questions – do you want to be a barrister or a solicitor? Here we give a simple description of each.

Barrister

Ask a solicitor about the key difference between the two sides of the profession and they'll probably tell you it comes down to one thing: ego. At first glance the role of a barrister certainly looks a lot cooler than that of a solicitor. You know the deal – it's all about striding into courtrooms, robes flowing; tense moments waiting for missing witnesses; and razor-sharp cross-examinations. Glamorous? It's downright sexy! The truth, of course, is that there's a great deal more to it than looking good in a wig…

Essentially barristers do three things:

- appear in court to represent others
- give specialised legal advice in person or in writing
- draft court documents

The proportion of time spent on each depends on the type of law the barrister practises. Criminal barristers are in court most of the time, often with only an hour or two's notice of the details of their cases. By contrast, commercial barristers spend most of their time on more academic pursuits in chambers, writing tricky opinions and advising in conference on complicated legal points.

Barristers must display the skill and clarity to make complex or arcane legal arguments accessible to lay clients, juries and the judiciary. Their style of argument must be clear and persuasive, both in court and on paper. It has been some time since barristers have had exclusive rights of audience in the courts, though. Solicitors can train to become accredited advocates in even the higher courts. This encroachment hasn't been an utter disaster for the Bar, although solicitor advocates are handling a lot more of the most straightforward cases. When it comes to more complicated and lengthy matters, barristers are usually still briefed to do the advocacy, not least because this is often the most cost-effective way of managing a case. As a point of interest, solicitor advocates do not wear the wig and gown and are referred to as 'my friend' rather than 'my learned friend'.

Solicitors value barristers' detailed knowledge of the litigation process and their ability to assess and advise on the merits and demerits of a case. A solicitor will pay good money for 'counsel's opinion'. Certainly in the area of commercial law, a barrister must understand the client's perspective and use their legal knowledge to develop solutions that make business or common sense as well as legal sense. If you were hoping a career as a barrister would allow you to rise above the rigours and scraping of modern-day capitalism, think again.

Of the UK's 12,000 or so barristers, over 8,000 are self-employed. This is why you hear the expression 'the independent Bar'. The rest are employed by companies, public bodies or law firms, and they make up 'the employed Bar'. To prevent independence from turning into isolation, barristers, like badgers, work in groups called sets, sharing premises and professional managers, etc. Barristers do not work for their sets, just at their premises, and as 'tenants' they contribute to the upkeep of their chambers. A percentage of their earnings also goes to pay their clerks and administrators. Unlike employed barristers and solicitors, those at the independent Bar get no sickness pay, holiday pay, maternity leave or monthly salary. What they do get is a good accountant.

To enter practice, LLB grads need to complete the Bar Professional Training Course (BPTC) before starting a much sought-after year of 'pupillage'. Hopefully, the set you're with will then take you on as a tenant, though you may have to look elsewhere. Once tenancy is established, you're home free (well, except for the gruelling schedule; high pressure; concerns over how much you'll earn; dedicated wig maintenance…).

Being a barrister is a great job, and the fact that this is no secret means competition is fierce. If your appetite has been whetted you will find much more information in the final section of this book, where we have detailed the recruitment process and laid bare some of the more obscure practices and terminology. We have also tried to give a fair assessment of some of the difficulties that aspiring barristers may encounter. The **Chambers Reports** give invaluable insight into the lives of pupils and junior barristers at some of the best sets. The Bar's professional body is the Bar Council, and it is regulated by the Bar Standards Board.

Solicitor

Most budding lawyers qualify as solicitors: in fact, there are almost ten times more solicitors than barristers in the UK. Their role is to provide legal services directly to lay clients, who could be individuals, companies (private or public) or other bodies. In short, clients come to solicitors for guidance on how to deal with their business or personal proposals and problems. These could be anything from drafting a will to defending a murder charge or buying a multibillion-pound business. The solicitor advises on the steps needed to proceed and then manages the case or the deal for the client until its conclusion. They will bring in a barrister if and when a second opinion or specialist advocacy is needed. The solicitor's role is much more like that of a project manager than the barrister's. There are over 112,000 solicitors in England and Wales with practising certificates issued annually by the Solicitors Regulation Authority (SRA). The majority of them are in 'private practice' in solicitors' firms, though many thousands work in-house for companies, charities or public authorities.

Most readers will be well aware that after an undergraduate degree, law school beckons. Law grads need to take the Legal Practice Course (LPC). Non-law grads must first complete the Graduate Diploma in Law (GDL) before being eligible for the LPC. Next comes the practical training. The most common way of qualifying is by undertaking a two-year training contract with a firm of solicitors, law centre, in-house legal team or public body. Much of the rest of this book deals with the nature of training contracts at different firms and how to procure one. The SRA's website gives all the fine detail you could wish for as to the requirements for training.

However, there are changes afoot. A new scheme should make it possible to qualify as a solicitor without a traditional training contract, instead clocking up relevant work-based learning experiences. A pilot programme started in September 2008 with a small number of firms, full details of which can be found on the SRA's website at www.sra.org.uk/students/work-based-learning.page. The plan is that this second qualification route could dovetail with a new option to take the LPC in two parts, perhaps blending study and work. More on the LPC changes later.

Upon satisfactory completion of their training contract (or work-based learning) and the mandatory Professional Skills Course (PSC), a person can be admitted to the roll of those eligible to practise. They are then fully qualified. There are even enrolment ceremonies for anyone who fancies that graduation experience for the umpteenth time!

Where people often trip up is not being fully aware of when you should apply for a training contract. This will depend on the kind of firm you hope to join. If you are studying for a law degree and you want to work in a commercial firm, the crucial time for research and applications is during your penultimate year at uni. If you are a non-law student intending to proceed straight to a law conversion course before going to a commercial firm we're afraid you'll have to juggle exams and career considerations in your final year. Students wanting to enter high street practice usually don't need to worry about training contract applications quite so early. Unlike commercial firms, which generally offer contracts two years in advance of the start date, smaller firms do so closer to the start date, and possibly after a trial period of work as a paralegal.

Larger commercial firms more often than not cover the cost when it comes to their future trainees' law school fees and other basic expenses. Public sector organisations, eg the Government Legal Service, may also come up with some cash. Students hoping to practise in smaller firms soon learn that financial assistance is far less likely and this can make law school a costly and uncertain endeavour.

Needless to say, your choice of firm will shape the path of your career. A firm's clients, its work and its reputation will determine not only the experience you gain, but probably also your future marketability as a lawyer. At Chambers and Partners, we've made it our business to know who does what, how well they do it and what it might be like working at a particular firm. Our parent publication *Chambers UK* will be an incredibly useful resource for you. Its league tables show which firms command greatest respect from clients and other professionals in different areas of practice right across the country. You can read the entire thing for free at www.chambersandpartners.com and use it to help create a shortlist of firms to apply to.

In the **True Picture** section of this book we've profiled 125 firms in England and Wales. Our goal is to help you understand what kind of firm might suit you and the kind of work you can expect to undertake when you get there. It is the product of many hundreds of interviews with trainees and we think you'll really benefit from making it your regular bedtime reading. You should also read through the **Solicitors' Practice Areas** section to gain an understanding of what's involved in different fields of practice.

It may help you to understand the extent and nature of the solicitors' profession by grouping law firms into the following categories, starting with the biggest.

London: magic circle

David Copperfield, eat your heart out. The membership of this most exclusive of clubs traditionally extends to Allen & Overy, Clifford Chance, Freshfields Bruckhaus Deringer, Linklaters and Slaughter and May. To those for whom bigger is better (bigger deals, bigger money, bigger staff numbers), this is it. Corporate and finance work dominates these firms, as does international big-bucks business. By organising their training on a massive scale, these firms can offer seemingly unlimited office facilities, great perks, overseas postings and excellent formal training sessions. Although these five giants top many lists, not least for revenue and partner profits, consider carefully whether they'd top yours. Training in a magic circle firm is CV gold but not for everyone. One factor to consider is the requirement to work really long hours to keep profits fat and international clients happy. A great camaraderie develops amongst trainees but be prepared to not see your other friends too often…

London: large commercial

The top-ten City of London firms (including the magic circle) offer around 1,000 traineeships between them each year, representing approximately a fifth of all new training contracts registered with the SRA. In terms of day to day trainee experiences, there's not such a huge difference between the magic circle and 'silver circle' firms such as Herbert Smith, CMS Cameron McKenna, Lovells and a few others. Training contracts at these chasing-pack firms are strongly flavoured with corporate and finance practice and, again, international work. The salaries match those paid by the magic circle, which is only fair given that the lawyers work equally hard.

London: American firms

Since the mid-1990s, there has been a steady stream of firms crossing the Atlantic to take their place in the UK market. Currently more than 40 of them offer training contracts to would-be UK solicitors, with new schemes popping up all the time. We'd suggest staying eagle-eyed if you've a thing for stars and stripes. At the risk of over-generalising, these firms are characterised by international work (usually corporate or finance-led), smaller offices, more intimate training programmes and rather long hours. On the other hand they usually give trainees a good amount of responsibility and, famously, many of them pay phenomenally high salaries. Lawyers at the hotshot US firms frequently work opposite magic circle lawyers on deals; indeed many of them were previously magic circle and top-ten firm partners or associates. The arrival of the US firms has had a knock-on effect on City law, not least on City salaries, which soared over the past decade before stalling this year.

London: mid-sized commercial

Just like their bigger cousins, these firms are mostly dedicated to business law and business clients. Generally, they don't require trainees to spend quite so many hours in the office; however, some of the most successful mid-sizers – eg Macfarlanes and Travers Smith – give the big boys a run for their money in terms of profitability. Ostensibly, the size of deals and cases in these firms means trainees can do much more than just administrative tasks. The atmosphere is generally a bit more intimate than at the giants of the City, with the greater likelihood of working for partners directly and, arguably, more scope to stand out within the trainee group.

London: smaller commercial

For those who don't mind taking home a slightly more modest pay cheque in exchange for better hours, these firms are a great choice. After all, money isn't everything (note: those of you subscribing to Gordon Gekko's 'greed is good' credo see above and read no further). Usually these firms will be full-service outfits, although some may have developed on the back of one or two particularly strong practice areas or via a reputation in certain industries. Real estate is commonly a big deal at these firms. Along with commercial work, a good number of these smaller firms offer private client services to wealthier people. At firms like these you usually get great exposure to partners and there's less risk of losing contact with the outside world.

Niche firms

London is awash with firms specialising in areas as diverse as aviation, media, insurance litigation, shipping, family, intellectual property, sport… you name it, there's a firm for it. Niche firms have also sprouted in areas of the country with high demand for a particular service. How about equine law in Newmarket? If you are absolutely certain that you want to specialise in a particular field – especially if you have already worked in a relevant industry – a niche firm is an excellent choice. You need to be able to back up your passion with hard evidence of your commitment, however. Many of these firms also cover other practice areas, but if any try to woo you by talking at length about their other areas of work, ask some searching questions.

Regional firms

Many of you will agree that there is more to life than the Big Smoke. There are some very fine regional firms acting for top-notch clients on cases and deals the City firms would snap up in a heartbeat. There is also some international work going on outside the capital. The race for training contracts in the biggest of these firms is just as competitive as in the City. Some regional firms are even more discerning than their London counterparts in that applicants may have to demonstrate a long-term commitment to living in the area. Understandable, as they hardly want to shell out for training only to see their qualifiers flit off to the capital. Smaller regional firms tend to focus on the needs of regional clients and would therefore suit anyone who wants to become an integral part of their local business community. Salaries are lower outside London, in some cases significantly so, but so is the cost of living. There's a perception that working outside London means a chummier atmosphere and more time for the gym/pub/family of an evening, but do bear in mind that the biggest and most ambitious regional players will expect hours that aren't so dissimilar to firms with an EC postcode.

National and multi-site firms

Multi-site firms are necessarily massive operations, some of them with offices spanning the length and breadth of the country and overseas. To give you just two examples, Eversheds has nine branches in England and Wales plus many overseas; DLA Piper has six in England and many more overseas. These firms attract students who want to do bigger-ticket work outside London, a sometimes unwelcome consequence of which is that they do London levels of work for a lower salary. Some of the multi-site firms allow trainees to stay in one office, whereas others expect them to move offices. Make sure you know the firm's policy or you could end up having a long-distance relationship with friends, family and your significant other while you move to a new town for a few months or are saddled with a punishing commute. The work on offer is mostly commercial, although some private client experience may be available.

General practice/high street

These range from substantial, long-established firms in town centres to sole practitioners working above shops in the suburbs. They act for legally aided clients, individuals funding themselves and local businesses. Staple work includes landlord and tenant problems, conveyancing, personal injury, employment, family, wills and probate, and crime. Given the changes to legal aid funding, these firms now need to take on more privately paying and commercial clients just to stay afloat. Be prepared to earn considerably less than your peers in commercial practice, and don't expect there to be an abundance of amenities or resources in the office. Excessively long hours are unlikely unless you're on a rota for police station duty, in which case you'll be paid extra for that. If you want to grow up fast as a lawyer and see how the law actually affects individuals and the community in which you practise, then this is the kind of firm to go for. Larger firms may take up to ten or so trainees a year; the smallest will recruit on an occasional basis. It is in this part of the profession where salaries are the lowest, often the minimum required or recommended for trainees by the SRA.

As of 1 August 2009:

- Minimum salary Central London = £18,590 pa
- Recommended salary Central London = £19,040 pa
- Minimum salary elsewhere = £16,650 pa
- Recommended salary elsewhere = £16,940 pa

Anyone thinking of entering the legally aided sector should be aware that dramatic changes are affecting the public funding of legal services. Read the section entitled **How legal aid works**.

The recruitment market summarised

You're probably already aware that this is a tough time to try and break into the legal profession. Your prospects of finding a training contract, pupillage, or indeed any other kind of job, were better two years ago. Several factors are at play; they're not all linked in an obvious way, but together they clearly signal changing times.

Factor 1: The economy

The world economy is undergoing a fundamental shift. Many markets that were strong have weakened. To put it in very simplistic terms, financial power is transferring to Asian and Middle Eastern economies, and regions like Brazil and Africa are emerging as more significant players on the world stage, not least because of their reserves of natural resources. The UK legal profession is feeling the effects of this transfer of power, and business law firms find they must adapt and reshape their operations.

The UK's recession resulted from both the shift in world economic forces and a catastrophic failure in the banking system. The latter was undoubtedly the more immediate and hard-hitting cause of a decline in the levels of activity, revenues and profitability of the majority of UK business law firms. The UK economy will recover, of course, but it is impossible to say how fully or how fast. Even our inner Robert Peston cannot predict the UK's likely role in the new world order. In his 2009 report on Fair Access to the Professions, Alan Milburn MP stated that *"some experts believe that... we will need up to seven million new professionals in employment by 2020. At a time when the country is suffering from a deep and painful global recession it is easy to forget that Britain's professions are well placed to take advantage of a huge global growth in middle class employment."* It's certainly true that English law has been a good, exportable commodity, although how those experts managed to predict a figure of seven million is baffling.

Factor 2: Changes in the profession

And what of the law firms that service Joe Bloggs and his family rather than the Masters of the Universe? The recession hit them too. As mortgage lending dried up, conveyancing departments around the country took a beating. At least personal injury lawyers weren't affected in the same way: people are still tripping on paving stones and injuring each other in road traffic accidents. Those PI firms had better watch out though as there are other forces at work, in particular the Legal Services Act.

This Act was introduced in 2007 and allows non-lawyers to own and operate law firms for the first time. Previously, firms of solicitors and barristers' chambers could only be owned by the lawyers themselves. That's all changed. Now, the likes of legal executives, patent attorneys or business managers could potentially have a stake in a law firm partnership. You'll understand the implications of this. If non-lawyers can run law firms, there's nothing to stop any company setting up as a legal service provider. It's what Lord Falconer dubbed 'Tesco Law'. The AA and Halifax are among the organisations that now offer limited legal services. The former handles PI; conveyancing; wills and probate; and inheritance tax issues. It currently outsources its work to a panel of law firms but may eventually employ its own legal staff. That, of course, might mean less work for 'real' firms that handle the same type of work. Or then again, it might not. Tesco Law is still in its infancy, and a 2009 survey of the public found that 69% of those questioned *"would be concerned about the quality of service offered"* by banks and supermarkets offering legal services. The debate continues.

The Legal Services Act also permits outside investment in law firms, and this is one of the next big changes the UK legal sector faces. Again, it's early days but there are indications that a few firms are considering this option. Investors will want a good return on their money and this would influence management decisions in firms. Questions of profitability already affect decision making in most, and it's highly likely that this driver will become more pronounced.

Another driver is the rapid advance of technology. Many processes that once relied solely on human activity can now be undertaken by computers, often more effectively and accurately, usually more cheaply. An increasing number of the functions performed by lawyers are now capable of being performed by legal software packages. As one senior partner of a major national law firm told us, clients will be happy to continue to pay lawyers for their legal expertise but not for processes that can be automated or done by cheaper non-qualified staff. The outsourcing of simpler legal tasks and secretarial functions to countries where wages are lower has already started. As if to prove our point, we were half-way through writing this feature when Eversheds announced that it would be outsourcing secretarial work in a deal with a South African company, Exigent. Result: £2m saved, 95 secretarial jobs lost.

Factor 3: Legal education

Legal education is already an industry, and a booming one at that. The Law Schools section of this book debates the subject in much more detail, but essentially we see it like this. The UK law schools are already teaching the GDL, LPC and BVC (soon to become the BPTC) to more people than can qualify as solicitors and barristers. In their view, the schools are simply meeting a demand from students; they do not see it as their responsibility to limit the number of law school places sold to wannabe lawyers. It is the Solicitors Regulation Authority that approves the number of places available on the LPC nationwide, and the Bar Standards Board that approves the number of BPTC places. Both these organisations are following an agenda to widen access to a profession that has traditionally been the preserve of those from wealthier backgrounds.

With no direct link between the number of law school places and the number of available training positions for solicitors and barristers you have to accept that if you spend your own money on a law school course you do so as a consumer of the course itself; it does not guarantee you a career as a lawyer. Here are the cold, hard facts. Between 1998 and 2008, the number of annual full-time places on the LPC rose by 5,781 (from 6,852 to 10,675). In the same time period, the number of training contracts available annually in England and Wales rose by just 1,477 (from 4,826 to 6,303). If you factor in all the part-time LPC students as well you come to the conclusion that perhaps double the number of people could now be completing the LPC as there are training contracts to go round. While it's true that not all available places are filled, most are. And as if to make matters worse, some law schools are opening additional branches in 2010 and making even more LPC places available. The Bar is no less competitive; indeed it is more so – check out page 676 for details. It gets worse still. In 2009 a number of firms stopped recruiting trainees altogether, so the number of contracts available fell. If you're hunting for a training contract in, say, 2010, you're not only competing with your contemporaries, you're competing with many of the people who failed to get one in 2009 and earlier as well.

"*It's so silly and short-sighted,*" said one managing partner when we spoke to him about firms putting training schemes on hold. "*The firms that have done it will suffer through the nose and I smile when I hear of it.*" Is this some good news, then? If the last recession is anything to go by, when the market recovers firms that stopped recruiting will need to play catch-up and hire additional bodies. So that should mean more training contracts, right? Well, not necessarily. There's now a huge pool of already-qualified lawyers who were made redundant during the downturn. When the market does pick up, it might be cheaper for firms to re-employ them rather than pay a student's way through law school and then spend time training them. We shall have to see how things develop.

We make no apologies for sounding so negative. The simple fact is that significant number of students have always struggled to convert an LPC or BVC into a career, and it is only getting harder. If you are labouring under the illusion that the law firms, the professional regulators and the law schools operate a single system that trains up the right number of students then you are sorely mistaken.

Many students will sail through the process from university to a successful career as a barrister or solicitor; a good number always do. But the fact that the Law Society has embarked on a campaign to caution students to think carefully before parting with hard-earned or borrowed cash for an LPC should speak volumes. The Bar Standards Board meanwhile is attempting to push through an aptitude test for all BPTC hopefuls to weed out those with the least likelihood of forging a career as a barrister. To complicate matters, the Office of Fair Trading has waded in and labelled the aptitude test uncompetitive.

While we're covering all the negatives, there's just one more thing to get you to think about. How much do you really want to be a lawyer?

Now the good news…

It's true that a number of factors have combined to create a 'perfect storm', and it's harder than it's ever been to get a training contract. But it's not by any means impossible. While the corporate and property markets are suffering, litigation, insolvency, IP and employment lawyers are in demand. Perhaps you should thank your lucky stars you're not trying to get into acting or journalism!

By the time we went to press in September 2009, Allen & Overy had already asked some of the people it had deferred to start their training contracts on time after all. In the wider world, commentators were increasingly talking about the 'green shoots' of economic recovery. The signs were certainly looking more hopeful.

Lawyers' pay remains excellent. While some firms have made salary freezes or cuts, in 2009 one US firm became the first in the City to pay its NQs £100,000 a year. Minimum trainee salaries are set by the Solicitors Regulation Authority: they are currently £18,590 in central London and £16,650 elsewhere. However, the *average* starting salary for a trainee in central London is much higher: £32,697 according to the last Law Society report in 2008. The lowest average starting salary is in Wales, where it's £17,171.

Finally, those who do manage to get a training contract will be well placed for the future. Over 82% of qualifiers at our True Picture firms were retained in 2008: the highest NQ retention rate we've ever recorded. In 2009, many firms announced qualification jobs much later, and the retention figure dropped to 74%. That's the lowest we've ever recorded – but still not nearly as bad as some of the dire predictions we were hearing earlier in 2009. See our website for further analysis and retention stats for every firm we've ever covered in the True Picture since 2000.

How legal aid works

Legal aid celebrates its 60th birthday in 2009. It is often referred to as 'the fourth pillar of the welfare state'.

Until 1949 access to justice for people with limited means was dependent on the charity and social conscience of lawyers. Legal Aid changed all this. Initially managed by the Law Society, the scheme has been run by the Legal Services Commission (LSC) since the turn of the millennium.

Who gets legal aid?

From humble beginnings dealing primarily with divorces, legal aid now helps over two million people each year. The scheme has been fundamental to the success of a number of landmark cases with significant social interest, including those resulting from the drug Thalidomide, the Deptford Fire and the Clapham Junction Rail Crash. In the current economic climate the service is more important than ever thanks to a dangerous domino effect. With unemployment at a 14-year high by mid-2009, more people will be forced into debt and this in turn leads to more relationship breakdowns. A rise in repossessions also coincides with a downturn and last year the LSC helped nearly 34,000 people who were in danger of losing their homes. Just over 75% of those helped were able to avoid immediate repossession as a result.

On a day-to-day basis the LSC funds solicitors and other agencies to provide advice to people facing civil and criminal problems and those needing representation in court. Solicitors enter into a contract with the LSC to provide services to clients and are subject to audits to ensure their files are run correctly. The CLS (Community Legal Service) administers funding for civil matters, and to be eligible individuals must satisfy both means and merits tests. The CDS (Criminal Defence Service) administers funding for defendants, who must satisfy an interest of justice test and, if the case is in the magistrates' court, a means test. Means testing will also be introduced for Crown Court cases in Blackfriars, Bradford, Norwich, Preston and Swansea in January 2010 with a phased rollout of the new scheme commencing in April 2010.

Legal aid transformation

The legal aid system has been under review throughout its history, and in the last few years the scrutiny has intensified. The primary driver is the size of the annual spend, which has risen on average by 5% a year for the past 20 years, and now sits at £2bn. This is the highest per capita spend anywhere in the world. The aim of the LSC is to ensure access to justice for the greatest number of people but in practice this is becoming an increasingly problematic. The most significant review in recent years was conducted by Lord Carter of Coles and published in 2006. It outlined ways to make legal aid provision more efficient (you could also interpret that as meaning 'less expensive'). In an attempt to cut spending by almost £200m over three years, changes have been imposed in both the civil and criminal spheres. A system of Best Value Tendering (BVT) was introduced to the criminal sector for a trial period in July 2009, to be implemented across Manchester, Avon and Somerset with a rollout across the rest of England and Wales proposed for 2013. Many in the profession see this scheme as fundamentally flawed and believe it will result in an erosion of quality. Fixed fees have been put in place for legally aided family cases and once again criticism has been rife. It is thought that the plans will hit vulnerable children and families, as the new rates are likely to lead to barristers earning up to 30% less, driving the most experienced out of the sector.

Recent reforms in relation to crime

- Defence services in magistrates' courts and now also Crown Courts are paid for under a newly revised systems of standard and graduated fees.
- Panels of firms work to strict cost and case management rules to provide defence services in Very High-Cost Cases (VHCC).
- All requests for publicly funded police station work must be made through the Defence Solicitor Call Centre (DSCC) and fees are now fixed.
- CDS Direct, a telephone advice service trialed by the LSC during 2007, has now been deployed across England and Wales. Detainees for less serious offences are only eligible to use this service rather than seeing a solicitor in person, unless they are a juvenile or have mental health issues.

Recent reforms in relation to civil/family

- A fixed fee scheme has been introduced for most areas such as housing and debt advice.
- New graduated-fee schemes have been introduced for private law family cases and in-court child care cases.

- The Minister for Legal Aid has affirmed his commitment to harmonise fees for solicitors and barristers carrying out family work.
- BVT for civil services is still under consideration.
- Community Legal Advice Centres (CLAC) are being set up by the LSC and local authorities to provide a one-stop shop for integrated social welfare law provision. Five are currently up and running following a tendering process and the LSC is in various stages of discussion with local authorities about establishing more centres in the future.

The response of the professions

Legal aid practitioners are pretty pissed off about the reforms, the manner of their implementation and the LSC's perceived disregard for the recommendations of consultations. More than 6,000 solicitors have signed up to protest on Downing Street's website, there have been demonstrations outside Parliament, and a campaign called 'What Price Justice?' was launched by the Law Society and supported by a wide range of organisations such as MIND, Shelter and the Refugee Council. So what are people concerned about?

- Competitive tendering is dependent on having sufficient numbers of firms to engender competition, and there just aren't that many in certain areas, like Wales and East Anglia. It could lead to the lowest bidders getting the work, and this won't necessarily mean higher quality.
- Fixed-fee systems will benefit larger firms that can handle a high volume of straightforward cases. They could endanger specialist firms by discouraging them from taking on complex cases. A 'one size fits all' standard service incapable of addressing client needs could emerge. Fixed fees may also see solicitors doing the minimum amount of work for the price.
- Practitioners argue that as the LSC is a monopoly purchaser, the idea of free market forces is redundant and that the government simply wants more for less. They point to evidence from the USA indicating that competitive tendering drives down the quality of representation.

There is also concern that there will be reduced access to justice:

- Many firms have closed down their legal aid criminal departments because they no longer pay their way.
- Opponents fear that consolidation will lead to black spots of meagre or no provision in some areas.
- The 'fewer firms doing more work more economically' argument for BVT doesn't take into account representation of minority clients or vulnerable groups (disabled, children) who are often advised by small firms of specialist or local practitioners. Making practice uneconomical for such lawyers may decrease access to justice for such minorities.
- There is some apprehension that disabled clients will be indirectly discriminated against. As the solicitors of such clients often incur additional expenses, which will not be met in fixed-fee arrangements, there may be less economic incentive to take cases on.
- The Bar Council observes that if legal aid is less accessible there will be an increased number of litigants in person.
- There are fears that CLACs are not sufficiently independent of funding bodies to avoid conflicts of interest, especially in areas such as housing. The fact that CLACs effectively become monopolies in their areas is also perceived as potentially unfair.
- Economic strictures may see firms cutting costs in areas like training, meaning fewer legal aid practitioners in the future.
- The Bar Council and the Law Society fear that top-quality students will be driven away from legal aid work by low remuneration.

The future of the legal aid landscape

Students, trainees, pupils, barristers and solicitors committed to legal aid work have never been in it for the money, but the current state of affairs is giving many ideologically dedicated practitioners and would-be practitioners enormous cause for concern. Uncertainty as to quite how and when legal aid reforms will go forward means a number of firms have held off from offering training contracts in the past couple of years and have taken to recruiting larger numbers of paralegals instead. It seems unlikely that legal aid will die a death any time soon. As one optimistic trainee we spoke to pointed out: *"There are always going to be people who must have legal representation, so there is bound to be some kind of system for providing legal advice."* But, regardless of the exact form ongoing changes take, the trend for greater economic pressure and consolidation/reduction in the number of firms will continue. If you have a burning desire to enter any publicly funded area of practice, none of this will stop you, but we'd advise plenty of thorough research into the practice area, the firms and the current state of reforms.

For more news on this subject check out: www.legalservices.gov.uk; www.whatpricejustice.lawsociety.org.uk and www.barcouncil.org.uk.

Some other career options

There are a number of different organisations and roles to look at other than becoming a solicitor or barrister in private practice. Here are a few of the main ones.

Working in-house for a company

A number of large companies offer training contracts and/or pupillages. In-house lawyers populate the banking, utilities, telecommunications and entertainment industries, to name but a few. There is no easily accessible comprehensive list of organisations offering training, so for further information, aspiring solicitors should contact the Commerce & Industry Group (www.cigroup.org.uk) and aspiring barristers should contact the Bar Council. It's also worth keeping an eye out in the legal press and in *The Times* on Thursdays to see who is recruiting.

We spoke to a newly qualified solicitor who trained in-house with an international bank. Armed with previous financial experience working as a transaction manager, he took the initiative and approached the head of the legal department. Happily for him, the bank was already an accredited training provider and had a solicitor with the time and inclination to act as a training supervisor. The bank was willing to fund him through part-time GDL and LPC courses. It also called on one of the law firms on its legal panel and provided a secondment to make sure he had sufficient contentious training. Our source felt his training was excellent. "*I was given my own work to manage and had a great deal more latitude than in a conventional training contract. I got responsibility earlier and a lot less grunt work to do.*" In-house trainees certainly develop very marketable skills because almost everything they do has a practical application and their sector knowledge is immense.

Cold-calling heads of legal at banks or companies you're interested in is not recommended. Unless the organisation publicises vacancies, usually its trainees will be recruited after having already worked there in some other capacity, and even then they will have needed to exercise discretion when trying to obtain a contract. A softly-softly approach more in line with the tortoise than the hare usually works best.

Most in-house lawyers start out in private practice, switching to the role some time after qualification. They do so because of a general perception that the rewards are good and the hours more manageable than in a law firm. In-house lawyers don't lose touch with private practice; indeed part of the job involves selecting and instructing law firms to provide specialist advice to the company. This part of the job will keep you knee-deep in invites to parties, lunches and sporting events as the different law firms curry favour.

Law Centres

From its roots in North Kensington in 1970, the network of UK Law Centres has grown to around 60 today. Law Centres are members of the not-for-profit sector and registered as charities and companies limited by guarantee. They all have local management committees. Advice and representation is provided without charge to the public, with funding coming from local authorities, the Legal Services Commission and some of the major charities, such as the Big Lottery fund. Many have received additional funding from the newly created Equality and Human Rights Commission. The legal problems handled may vary from one Centre to another, but all who work in the sector can be described as social welfare law specialists. Community care, all types of discrimination, education, employment, housing, immigration, asylum and public law form the caseload. In a recent development, crime has become a specialty for one Law Centre and family advice for another.

Law Centres see themselves as more than just providers of legal advice to the public; their horizons are broader than those of the Citizens Advice Bureau and they tend to take on cases with a wider social impact. A client with a consumer dispute is less likely to be helped than someone who is affected by, say, a local authority's decision on rent arrears. Law Centres identify trends and then use individual cases as a springboard for changing the big picture, perhaps by way of a test case that makes it to the highest courts and the broadsheets. Law Centres are also eager to involve the communities they operate within, providing legal training and education. As a Law Centre employee you might even find yourself at a local comprehensive bringing your legal know-how to young teenagers.

Recent reforms to the provision of legal aid have required Law Centres to become more target-oriented, but there is still a strong political commitment to the sector. Recent highlights include the Streetwise Law Centre based in Bromley that ensures that young people have access to justice; Hammersmith and Fulham Law Centre's successful challenge under the Human Rights Act against the controversial Section 55 of the Asylum and Immigration Act; and the Butterfly Project at Avon & Bristol Law Centre, which thanks to the Big Lottery Fund assists migrant women gain better access to services.

Most Law Centres employ 10-15 lawyers and, if you're attracted to working with colleagues who share your ideals and social conscience, you may want to investigate a career in the sector. Routes to a career are as varied as the work. Newly qualified solicitors with relevant experience in private practice are taken on; so too are those who have worked as paralegals for non-profit agencies and gained supervisor-level status. A career may also begin at a Law Centre itself. Each year the LSC provides funding to support trainee solicitors. Law Centres can apply for 50% of a trainee's salary and in the past many have been successful in gaining this support. Mirroring a training contract in private practice, the trainee will be exposed to different fields of law, learning from specialists in each area. Law Centres often liaise closely with local firms to ensure that trainees gain wide experience.

As a trainee or newly qualified solicitor your salary will roughly match private practice on the high street – £24,000 to £30,000 or more in London. However Law Centres tend lose their competitive edge when seeking to appoint more experienced lawyers. Without wishing to sound trite, those who take up positions generally feel there is more to being enriched than being rich. Law Centres operate along different lines to private practices: there's less hierarchy and more of an equal say for staff at all levels (some even operate as collectives with all staff drawing the same salary). Terms and conditions at work emulate those in local government and, as such, pension and holiday provisions, etc. are good, while flexible and part-time working is common. Law Centres are keen equality and diversity employers and encourage trainees from their local community. You will need to be flexible and willing to accept new challenges. It is an exciting environment and many lawyers have gone on to take up influential roles outside of the movement.

Candidates will only be considered if they respond to an advertisement. Look for these in *The Guardian* (Wednesdays), local newspapers and a monthly publication called *Legal Action* (your university law library should have it) plus on the Law Centres Federation website www.lawcentres.org.uk (updated daily). To enhance your prospects you should be able to demonstrate your interest in social justice. Earn some stripes on committees or with community groups. Working in a local authority while studying a CPE/LPC part-time will also give you a taste of the fields Law Centres plough. While at law school take advantage of any schemes that bring you closer to working for social justice. Some volunteers are accepted by Law Centres to help with administration and (if accredited) translation work. Volunteers usually come via other non-profit agencies so don't expect to just walk into a Law Centre and be accepted. A voluntary role with a Citizens Advice Bureau is easier to get hold of and would prepare you well for the type of clients served by Law Centres.

Government Legal Service

The GLS ostensibly has only one client – the Queen. In practice 'the client' includes all the policymakers and managers within government departments. Lawyers here range from full-time litigators to others who draft new legislation and advise ministers how best to legally put policy into practice. We'd recommend anyone applying to the GLS have a long think about the role of government lawyers, particularly considering how law and politics interact and the impact that they can have on life and society in the UK. If the idea appeals then read our **True Picture** and **Chambers Reports** features on pages 280 and 704. The GLS A-Z is on page 585.

Local government

There are around 4,000 local government solicitors on the roll plus positions for paralegals, legal executives and barristers. There's also a mind-blowing 400+ authorities to choose from in England and Wales. Each acts as a separate employer; some offer training contracts but there's no central list of vacancies and no single recruitment office. Finding out about training contract opportunities is a challenge in itself, as is finding out which councils offer sponsorship for the GDL and/or LPC. A good starting point for research is www.lgcareers.com. Click on 'career descriptions' and then head for 'supporting your community'. Also have a good rummage through the information at Solicitors in Local Government www.slgov.org.uk, where you can find several testimonies from qualified solicitors and trainees. Most authorities advertise vacancies in the Law Society's *Gazette* and *The Lawyer*. You can also try the law and public service job ads in *The Times*, *The Guardian* and *The Independent*, or even approach local authorities directly.

Solicitors in local government advise elected council members and senior officers on a wide variety of topics, incorporating commercial/contracts, conveyancing/property, employment issues, information management, administrative law and governance. Additional work will depend on the type of local authority involved – litigation/prosecution, social care, children, consumer protection, environmental, highways and planning, education and housing to name but a few. Breadth of practice is particularly typical for solicitors in smaller authorities, while those in larger ones usually specialise in a particular area, such as housing, planning, highways, education or social services. Duties include keeping councils on the straight and narrow, making sure they don't spend their money unlawfully and advising councillors on the legal implications of their actions. The typical salary for a local authority solicitor is between £30,000 and £40,000.

Trainees usually follow the same seat system that prevails in private practice, but for local authority trainees there is the added bonus of having rights of audience in civil and criminal courts and tribunals that outstrip those of peers in private practice. Trainees shadow solicitors and gradually build up their own caseload, acting for officers from different departments of the local authority. If you want a sneak preview of what it's really like before you take the plunge then some authorities offer paid summer placements. Others will arrange an informal unpaid attachment during vacations. Contact the head of legal services at a local authority to ask for further information – the more experience you can get the better.

Be prepared to wade through the bureaucratic bog and at times be driven to distraction by the slow machinations of local government. However, the benefits of a great training contract, variety in your day-to-day work, flexible hours and a sense of serving the community commonly outweigh this. The best way to climb the ladder is by hopping from one authority to another. Many local authority chief executives trained as solicitors and we are told the glass ceiling is not so prevalent in local government as it is in City law firms. Training in local government also opens doors to careers in private practice, the Crown Prosecution Service and the GLS.

Crown Prosecution Service

If the idea of billable hours and contract drafting leaves you cold and you've a passion for criminal law, what about working for the Crown Prosecution Service (CPS)? It is the government department responsible for bringing prosecutions against people who have been charged with a criminal offence in England and Wales. The CPS handles all stages of the process, from advising the police on the possibility of prosecution right through to the delivery of advocacy in the courtroom.

The CPS employs over 2,700 lawyers to handle more than 1.2 million cases in the magistrates' and Crown Courts. Its prosecutors review and prosecute criminal cases following investigation by the police. They also advise the police on matters of criminal law and evidence, some working from Criminal Justice Units that operate within police stations to combat the problem of failed prosecutions. Lawyers here advise the police on the appropriate charge for the crime, spending one day in the office preparing cases and the next in the magistrates' court dealing with administrative matters. Lawyers in the Trials Unit handle Crown Court cases, including murder, rape and robbery.

Prosecutors may encounter between 30 and 40 cases each day in the magistrates' courts. In the Crown Court self-employed barristers still conduct many trials but there are increasing opportunities for CPS Crown Advocates. The Director of Public Prosecutions, Keir Starmer QC, is keen to improve and modernise the service offered by the CPS, and an essential part of this is the development of in-house advocacy, such that the CPS will routinely conduct a large proportion of its own cases in all courts. Although prosecutors don't have the same intense client contact as defence lawyers, they do interact with everyone from magistrates, clerks, solicitors and probation and police officers, to civilian and expert witnesses. They also liaise with local communities, racial equality and victim support agencies plus victims and witnesses. For example, where a prosecution is abandoned it is the prosecutor's job to inform the victim of the reasons.

Competition is fierce for training contracts and pupillages, but once you get in, unless something goes wrong, you are guaranteed employment on qualification. "*Commitment to public service, strong communication, sound decision-making skills and advocacy potential*" are just some of the attributes you will need to apply, according to training principal Neil Holdsworth. The service is looking for people who are prepared to devote themselves to its work for at least a few years. Some lawyers give up lucrative careers in the private sector to join the CPS, taking pay cuts in return for a more family-friendly working environment.

Trainees liaise closely with supervisors to determine what they should be working on, sometimes on a daily, often on a weekly basis. All supervisors volunteer for the task, so you can be sure they are willing participants. Although they can state three preferences, trainees must be prepared to work anywhere within the region to which they apply. Expect to be shadowing prosecutors, observing or even helping with pre-charge advice, assisting busy colleagues and interacting with the police on a day-to-day basis. As well as learning the A-Z of criminal litigation within the CPS, there are opportunities in the form of three-to-four month secondments in private practice, the GLS or local government. There have even been opportunities to do placements at organisations such as the BBC. At around the sixteenth month, trainee solicitors have the opportunity to begin a two-week course to become Associate Prosecutors, which gives limited rights of audience in the magistrates' court.

While still a CPS trainee, Sibylle Cheruvier set up the Legal Trainee Network, which aims to connect the trainee solicitors and barristers scattered throughout in the service's different UK offices. Socials, a mentoring and buddy scheme and an online discussion board are just some of the benefits. It's *"a way to link trainees together to share knowledge, experience or good news,"* she told us.

Opportunities for CPS training places are advertised on www.cps.gov.uk. This is also the starting point for vacation placements and work experience. A trainee's salary starts at £18,425 nationally and £19,441 in London (subject to review). Salaries for newly qualified lawyers start at £26,000 nationally and £28,662 in London (again subject to review). The CPS expects all trainees to have completed and passed the LPC or BVC before taking up a post. The traditional LLB to LPC/BVC route is by no means the only route into the CPS. Many trainees juggle work and part-time study; some have entered the service sideways, having left school with few qualifications. CPS caseworkers are the beneficiaries of the service's eagerness to grow talent from within. This being so, perhaps becoming a caseworker is the way forward for future trainees. They assist prosecutors by researching cases and making recommendations on information required and charges to be brought. Beyond these duties, they liaise with advocates, witnesses, police and court staff; provide support to witnesses and victims; and additionally attend court to assist counsel on a regular basis. Impressive organisational skills and an ability to relate to people are essential. Remuneration runs between £18,425 nationally and £19,441 in London (again subject to review). Theoretically you could start anywhere within the CPS and end up as a prosecuting lawyer.

The armed forces

If watching *A Few Good Men* made you want to be a lawyer, have we got news for you. If you are fully qualified with experience at the Bar then your Armed Forces want YOU. The Royal Air Force asks for two years' experience at the Bar, and has a rather unique alternative to the title of partner or QC: after eight years you could be able to call yourself a Wing Commander. The Air Force's legal department is small – only 48 people when we rang them – but the work sounds rather interesting. You're likely to deal with court martials, tribunals and, we're sure, some other pretty challenging stuff. The starting salary is £37,176 and recruitment is by need rather than to an annual deadline.

Much the same can be said of the Army: it requires a year's experience at the Bar, after which time you'll be in line for the shortened officer course at Sandhurst. Usual requirements for both services apply, so you can expect some running and jumping in the mud. The Navy doesn't have such a clear recruitment path, though there are legal opportunities available after you've signed on the dotted line and joined the Senior Service. We'd say if you've got experience at the Bar under your belt and are looking for a change this is an interesting option with a clear career path.

The police

We spoke with the Metropolitan Police force to find out about career opportunities for law grads. You might think police lawyers spend their days rifling through claims related to the abuse of police powers. Though claims of this nature are certainly getting more press of late (take, for instance, the high-profile death of Ian Tomlinson at the G8 summit), they account for only a quarter of the work. The remaining time is divided between things like employment tribunal claims, advisory work (eg child wardship), the maintenance of anti-social behavioural orders and dealing with sexual offenders and the proceeds of crime. Head counsel Edward Solomons recently told *The Lawyer* that there is also a deliberate push to bring more corporate work in-house.

Around 130 lawyers work for the Met, about 44 of them in the organisation's Southbank fortress. The current economy (combined perhaps with the BBC showing *The Wire*) has led to greater interest in careers here. The legal team is divided loosely into three groups: licensing, public order and proceeds of crime; counter-terrorism and safer neighborhoods; employment and corporate governance. Entry-level pay as a law clerk begins at £20,662, increasing to £26,239 as a senior clerk and £38,297 as a junior lawyer. These sums are also subject to a London weighting. The chances of progressing through the ranks to senior lawyer are generally high and we understand that there is a relatively low turnover of staff. Recruitment corresponds to need and doesn't happen annually. You might spot an ad in *The Lawyer* but your best bet is to look for vacancies on www.met.police.uk.

Legal executive

If you haven't found a training contract or are thinking about moving sideways into a legal career, you could consider the Institute of Legal Executives (ILEX) course. Those who complete it become qualified lawyers who are sometimes known as the 'third branch' of the profession. Their day-to-day work is similar to that of a solicitor, although legal executives are more likely to deal with low-value, high-volume cases such as residential conveyancing and personal injury claims. That said, it is possible to climb higher with experience.

Over 80,000 individuals have already qualified with ILEX, and there are currently over 22,000 people studying to be legal executives across England and Wales. No prior legal training is required to enrol on the course, and it is open to those holding GCSEs, A Levels or degrees. This makes it suitable for school leavers, new graduates or those already engaged in a career and looking to branch out. It can be taken on a part-time basis, giving students an opportunity to combine study with practical experience. The ILEX Level 3 Professional Diploma in Law and

Practice is the first stage of the academic training. It usually takes about two years of part-time study. The second stage is ILEX Level 6 Professional Higher Diploma in Law and Practice, which is assessed at honours degree level, again typically taking two years to complete.

On completion, students become associate members of ILEX. To become a fully qualified ILEX Fellow, it is necessary to gain five years of qualifying experience in a legal background (at least two after completing the exams). Timescales for all ILEX courses are flexible according to personal needs and study can be fitted around a job. There is no set time to complete the exams, so people can work at their own pace. The qualifications can be studied at a local accredited centre or via distance learning.

Once qualified, ILEX graduates end up in employment across the full spectrum of legal services from private practice to government departments and the in-house legal teams of major companies. ILEX Fellows can continue studying to become ILEX Advocates, and ILEX Fellows can now become partners in law firms alongside solicitors and can also apply for judicial appointments. Being a legal executive can be a rewarding career in its own right. For those who still want to become a solicitor, ILEX can provide a useful route to qualifying as one, even if it is by no means the quickest. Most people can seek exemption from the GDL (having already covered its core subjects) and move straight on to the LPC. They may also be exempted from the two-year training contract. A full list of institutions offering the ILEX course (including the distance learning option) is available at www.ilex.org.uk.

Paralegal

If you have time to fill before starting your training contract or are yet to decide whether you want to spend time and money on law school, paralegal work can provide a useful introduction to legal practice. There is no single job description: some experienced paralegals may run their own cases; others with little to offer by way of experience may end up doing very dull document management tasks for months on end. Employers view time spent paralegalling favourably as it demonstrates commitment to the profession and enables candidates to gain valuable experience and commercial or sector insight. Some firms and companies – though not all – offer traineeships to the most impressive of their own paralegals, but you should always keep in mind that the job is a valuable position in its own right. It is not a good idea to give the impression that you won't be seen for dust as soon as something better crops up.

The paralegal market is massively competitive, especially since the recession, so those with no legal qualifications or practical experience will find it hard to secure a position. Usually large commercial firms require all paralegal applicants to have completed the LPC and have at least six months prior experience. If you can get a foot in the door, you might find yourself in a number of short-term contracts until one firm decides it wants you on a long-term basis. Some smaller firms insist that prospective trainee solicitors complete a trial period of paralegalling before offering them a contract. Understandably, this does sometimes lead to allegations of exploitation by firms. Should you find yourself in a compromising position the best organisation to contact is the Junior Lawyers Division of the Law Society.

Experienced paralegals with specialist skills can make a very decent living. If you're thinking about becoming a career paralegal you should take a look at the National Association of Licensed Paralegals' website at www.nationalparalegals.com. For information on current vacancies, find out if your law school's careers office has contacts, check the legal press, register with a specialist recruitment agency and trawl law firms' own websites. It's even worth firing off a speculative letter or two as some firms will recruit this way.

Her Majesty's Court Service

Her Majesty's Court Service is the executive agency of the Ministry of Justice responsible for the daily business of the civil, family and criminal courts in England and Wales. Its stated aim is 'to ensure that access [to justice] is provided as quickly as possible and at the lowest cost consistent with open justice and that citizens have greater confidence in, and respect for, the system of justice.' HMCS looks after the management of over 1,200 properties and court buildings, including the modernisation of their physical appearance. It deals with the timetabling of hearings and ensures there are always ushers to manage the process. On a lighter note, the service is even responsible for making courts available as filming locations. Many HMCS jobs are administrative in nature; however, the service recruits Judicial Assistants (JAs) three times a year, with each successful applicant assigned to one of the Court of Appeal's senior judges for a period of between three to 12 months. Duties include legal research, advice and providing assistance in drafting judgements. JAs may also help define the shape and nature of appeals in less well-presented cases. There are usually ten positions available at any one time. Applicants must be qualified lawyers who have or are about to complete pupillage or traineeship; have proved their intellectual ability by achieving a First or 2:1 at degree level; and have the ability to work under pressure as part of a team. Positions are advertised according to need in *The Times* and the Law Society's *Gazette*, as well as on the HMCS website: www.hmcourts-service.gov.uk.

Long-term careers are available for administrative officers, bailiffs and county and Crown Court ushers or clerks. Court clerks do not have a legal advisory role and do not need legal qualifications. Their responsibilities include maintaining the records of a court and administering oaths to witnesses and jurors. Magistrates' clerks do give legal advice to lay magistrates on issues like self-defence, identification of suspects and inferences from the silence of defendants after arrest. All court clerks need to be able to think on their feet and deal confidently with people. Very occasionally they need to exercise the power to order individuals into custody for contempt of court, although the clerks we spoke to indicated that the vast majority of defendants treat them with respect.

A shift in recruitment policy has seen the traditional route (by which those without degrees could train while studying for the Diploma in Magesterial Law) overtaken by the recruitment of LPC and BVC/BPTC graduates as trainee court clerks. As the individual progresses through a structured training programme, the number and complexity of their court duties increase until ultimately they are advising lay magistrates on points of law and procedure. Most courts operate nine or ten sessions a week, and most clerks will be in court for the majority of these. The remaining time is spent exercising powers delegated to them by the magistrates, such as issuing summonses. For more information about careers with the magistrates' courts or any other part of HMCS, visit www.hmcourts-service.gov.uk.

The Law Commission

Many laws are the product of centuries of precedent; others arise from little more than political expediency. Constant reform is needed to ensure that the law is fit for purpose in the modern age, however the government is not always best placed to see where reforms could be made. The Law Commission, an advisory non-departmental public body sponsored by the Ministry of Justice, was set up by Parliament in 1965 to review the laws of England and Wales and propose reform where necessary.

It is not just a case of repealing laws that are clearly archaic; it's equally important not to accidentally remove the legal basis for someone's rights. The Commission employs around 15 researchers every year to help it fulfil its remit, and as a researcher you would analyse many different areas of law, identifying defects in the current system and examining foreign law models to see how they deal with similar problems. You may also help to draft consultation papers, instructions to Parliamentary Counsel and final reports.

The Commission is engaged in about 20 projects at any one time. Among the topics it set out to examine in its most recent reform programme were the extremely complex laws controlling the UK's railway level crossings; the status of the insanity defence; the possible abolition of the common law offence of public nuisance; and treason – an area where the criminal law could be simplified and pruned.

Researchers are normally law graduates and postgraduates, those who have completed the LPC or BVC, or people who have spent time in legal practice but are looking for a change. The job of research assistant involves some fascinating (and less fascinating) subjects and is intellectually challenging. Candidates should have a First or high 2:1, along with a keen interest in current affairs and the workings of the law. The job suits those with an analytical mind and a hatred of waffle. They must also love research because there's a lot of it, be it devising questionnaires and analysing the responses, studying statistics or examining court files. So far, more than two-thirds of the Commission's recommendations have been implemented by the government; for example, wide-ranging reform of homicide law has just been announced following a 2006 report. If you go on to train as a solicitor or barrister you will be streets ahead of your peers in terms of your research skills and knowledge of how statutes work. For further information on 12-month and long-term contracts, check out www.lawcom.gov.uk. The recruitment drive for positions commencing September 2010 is expected to start in December 2009/January 2010.

Legal Services Commission

This government body was created by the Access to Justice Act 1999 and replaced the Legal Aid Board in 2000. It employs nearly 1,700 staff and operates from 15 offices across England and Wales. Its HQ is in London. Helping around two million people every year, it manages the distribution of public funds for both civil legal services and criminal defence services. The work of the LSC is essentially broken down into two departments covering these areas: the Community Legal Service (CLS) and the Criminal Defence Service (CDS).

CLS caseworkers assess the merits of applications for legal funding and means test applicants. They also assess and authorise claims for payment for legal services. Working with legal aid solicitors, Citizens Advice Bureaux, Law Centres, local authority services and other organisations, the CLS ensures people can get information and advice about their legal rights and help with enforcing them. Recent reforms have seen the CLS working with local authorities to create Community Legal Advice Centres in a bid to provide a more integrated service in relation to social welfare law. The organisation's website declares: 'the chance to further our cause of social inclusion is the most compelling reason to work for us.'

The CDS manages the supply of legal advice to those accused of crimes, using local solicitors accredited by the service. It also performs an audit role in relation to authorised providers of criminal legal advice. Part of the CDS's work is the Public Defender Service (PDS). Set up in 2001, its four offices are staffed by solicitors and accredited representatives who are directly employed by the LSC but required to provide independent advice. These offices employ their own lawyers to advise members of the public 24 hours a day, seven days a week, in what the LSC believes to be a more cost-effective and efficient way. A recent independent report said the PDS racked up substantially higher costs than other criminal defence providers during its formative years, but the PDS anticipates that as it grows it will become more cost-effective. The report also referred to a peer review of the PDS, which found that the quality of its work was roughly equivalent to or better than private practice criminal defence firms in most areas.

Jobs at the commission are advertised in local and/or national newspapers, as well as online. A first point of contact is www.legalservices.gov.uk. A few work-experience placements crop up, usually in the CLS, and these tend to last about six weeks.

Patent attorney

The Chartered Institute of Patent Attorneys (CIPA) is the usual place to find these guys and there are currently around 1,700 of them registered in the UK. They work in private firms, large companies and government departments. It is their job to obtain, protect and enforce intellectual property rights for their owners. The website www.cipa.org.uk has a useful careers section. In summary, it takes four or five years to become a UK Chartered Patent Agent and/or a European Patent Attorney. All candidates must have a scientific or technical background (usually a relevant degree such as science or engineering) and the aptitude for learning the relevant law. Attention to detail, good drafting skills and a logical, analytical mind are essential and, increasingly, a knowledge of French or German is seen as key due to the international dimension to the work. The traditional route is to work and study for professional exams simultaneously. It is also an option to take the Certificate or Master's courses in intellectual property. Once qualified, there is the opportunity to obtain a further qualification to become a Patent Attorney Litigator entitled to conduct litigation in the High Court, although all patent attorneys have the right to conduct litigation and to appear as advocate in the specialist Patents County Court. In order to become a European Patent Attorney, candidates must complete another set of examinations.

Trade mark attorney

A trade mark is a form of intellectual property used to distinguish a manufacturer or trader's particular brand from its competitors. It can be anything from a logo, a picture, a name or even a smell (apparently, there's only one instance of this – a Dutch perfume company uses their trademarked 'freshly cut grass smell' to give tennis balls their aroma). There are about 530 fully qualified trade mark attorneys in the UK, all registered with the Institute of Trade Mark Attorneys (ITMA). Most work for large companies or at firms of patent and trade mark attorneys. Their role is to advise clients on all aspects of trade mark registration, protection and exploitation in the UK and Europe, liaising with counterparts in other parts of the world whenever necessary. Good communication and drafting skills are required, but a degree is not a prerequisite to qualification. The minimum educational requirements are five GCSEs (grade A-C) and two A Level passes in approved subjects. The road to qualification involves passing the exams set for ITMA. Candidates with certain degrees, such as law, may be exempt from some foundation papers. It is most common for aspiring practitioners to study while learning on the job as a trainee. With no central admissions procedure, students need to approach firms or in-house trade mark departments directly. www.itma.org.uk has a helpful careers page.

Compliance officer or analyst

Banks and other financial services companies are eager to recruit law and non-law grads into their compliance units, which take on the vital role of advising senior management on how to comply with the applicable laws, regulations and rules that govern the sector. They also ensure that the banks' own corporate procedures and policies are followed. Other functions relate to the handling of complex regulatory and internal investigations and examinations. In essence, through compliance risk management, banks improve their ability to control the risks of emerging issues, thus helping to protect the organisation's reputation. Due to the proliferation of financial regulation, the importance of compliance departments has grown enormously, so that in larger banks they are often equivalent in size to in-house legal teams and offer equally solid career prospects.

The role of compliance officer or analyst requires astute advice, clear guidance, reliable professional judgement and the ability to work in a team. Attention to detail and a determination to see the consistent application of compliance policies and practices are essential. Regular exposure to senior management occurs much earlier for trainees in this area than for trainee solicitors at law firms. A minimum 2:1 degree is standard for successful applicants, and salaries are typically comparable with other graduate trainees in the City. With some compliance teams numbering more than a hundred staff, in the longer term there is plenty of scope for career development. Several banks run a two-year compliance analyst training scheme, over the course of which a trainee will gain a broad base of business knowledge and technical experience. It is not usually necessary to have completed the GDL, LPC or even a law degree before undertaking a graduate scheme, although those with a mind to move across to an in-house legal role later in their career would need to find the time to qualify as a lawyer. Being legally qualified opens up the door to general counsel work and it is not uncommon for a bank's head of legal to also lead the compliance team.

How suitable are you and what do recruiters want?

Now more than ever before, you need to stand out from the crowd if you're looking for a training contract or pupillage. The road to success is smoother for some than others, but a few nips and tucks to your CV and a healthy dose of self-confidence should work wonders.

Hitting a redbrick wall

So you've not got a law degree. So what? From the top sets at the Bar to the little-known solicitors' firms on the high street, non-law graduates are just as able to secure training positions as their LLB peers. In the few cases where employers prefer law grads they will specify this, so unless you hear differently conversion route applicants may proceed with confidence. More and more trainees are telling us that they were advised by friends in the law to do a first degree in a subject they were passionate about and convert to law later on, and indeed many recruiters tell us just how highly they regard staff with language skills and scientific or technical degrees, particularly where their clients' businesses will benefit. Humanities degrees require many of the same research and analytical skills needed by lawyers, and believe it or not, being able to discuss literary criticism with your clients could come in handy, since clients – just like lawyers – are people too.

It's a fact of life that many solicitors' firms and barristers' chambers subscribe to the idea of a pecking order of universities. It's not as widespread as it once was, but there are many firms and sets where the bias is undeniably present and a high number of recruits will have attended Oxford or Cambridge universities. If you feel that your university isn't exactly on the recruiters' hit list then you should make sure you get the best degree possible and work on enriching your CV in other ways.

Your degree result is perhaps the single thing on your CV that has most impact. Net a First and you'll impress all and sundry (at least on paper); walk away with a 2:1 and your path to employment will be made smoother; end up with a 2:2 and you're going to have to perform some fancy footwork to get an offer. In exceptional circumstances the effect of a poor degree result can be softened by a letter from your tutor stipulating the reason why you underachieved. It's rarely relevant that you just missed a 2:1 by a percentage point or two, but if you were a star student who suffered a serious accident or illness as finals loomed, confirmation of this (perhaps also by way of a doctor's letter) might assist. Having spoken to a number of trainees and a couple of pupil barristers who left university with a 2:2, we would never presume to discourage anyone from applying for a training position, but these people all had other very impressive qualities and/or CV-enhancing experiences. If you find yourself at the back of the job queue, think hard about what you can do to overcome that 2:2 – a year or more in a relevant job, a further degree, a commitment to voluntary work perhaps.

Possibly unaware that they could be applying for training contracts and vacation schemes in their second year, many new undergraduates are lulled into a false sense of security concerning their academic performance in the first year. If the only marks you have to show recruiters are thirds or 2:2s, you'll struggle to make headway. As obvious as it may sound, working for good results throughout your degree is crucial. At the very least, doing so will maximise your chances of a great final result.

Get up, stand out

Resist the urge to become an expert on daytime telly. *Jeremy Kyle*, the *Loose Women* and – much as it pains us to say it – Dick van Dyke in the role of Dr Mark Sloan have nothing to offer you. Face it, even *Neighbours* has gone downhill since it decamped to Five. Instead, take advantage of your freedom and the practically unlimited opportunities on offer. Almost every university has a wide range of societies, meeting groups and sports clubs. Pursuing your interests will give an extra dimension to both your university experience and, crucially, your CV.

Some kind of legal experience, whether it's involvement with the student law magazine or shadowing your aunt's neighbour's lawyer friend, is pretty crucial since you need to convince prospective employers that you're serious about the profession. You can acquire experience later on through open days and vacation schemes, but it's never too early to start. Non-legal extra-curriculars can be just as useful to show that you play well with others. It also gives you something to write about when an application form asks 'Discuss a time when you worked with a group to achieve a common goal.' Relevant work experience is vital to almost every successful job application, so keep your eyes open for suitable positions and use them to test your own ideas of what you would like to do. Many universities run law-specific career seminars in association with solicitors' firms or barristers' chambers. Be savvy, go along and find out as much as you can by talking to trainee solicitors and recruiters. A bit of networking never ever goes amiss.

Many graduates adopt a scattergun approach, applying to as many firms as possible and hoping for the best. Simply sending the same covering letter to 50 firms will not make you look good. Recruiters can tell very easily which applicants have a genuine interest in their firm and which have put in minimal effort. It's all about the three Rs: research, research and research. Demonstrating your understanding of what the firm is about, what the work will entail and being able to explain honestly and realistically why you want to do it will be among the most important things to get across. Advice on how to do this can be found in the later section on applications.

Read all about it

If you want to become a commercial lawyer you'll need this thing they call commercial awareness. We're not suggesting you become a mini-Murdoch, rather that you should gain a sense of what's going on in the commercial world. Unless you've been living in a box in a cave on Mars, you'll be aware that the credit crunch and the recession have pummelled the world economies and the UK's legal sector and you should be able to talk reasonably knowledgeably about the main themes. But what other topics should you be aware of? Gain some understanding of the attraction of China, India, Brazil and the Gulf States as international marketplaces, for example, or know something about the convergence of media technologies or the big issues in the energy sector. If you have zero interest in all this stuff, what on earth makes you think commercial law is a suitable career? Why not read the *Financial Times* now and again or make friends with the BBC website's business section? Keep up to date in a way that suits you, and make sure you're not oblivious to the events going on around you at national and international level.

It's also important to understand the role of a lawyer as a service provider. Much like a plumber or an accountant, you will be providing a service to a client and your attitude should reflect this. Lawyers must be able to relate to their clients and know something about their businesses. If the firms you apply to have certain specialisms or target certain industry sectors you'll do yourself a massive favour by finding out a little about those sectors.

Students looking to go into criminal law should be aware of recent legislation and current issues. Future family lawyers should be able to discuss the major cases that have hit the headlines. Needless to say, anyone interested in human rights issues will have a full-time job keeping up to date with all the cases and developments arising out of conflict in Iraq and Afghanistan and anti-terror measures here in the UK. Crime, family and human rights lawyers should also be aware of current issues relating to legal aid provision.

Time out

If you've itchy feet then let them wander – the career can wait. As well as giving you more confidence, navigating your way around a foreign country will develop your organisational and problem-solving skills and it will give you fertile ground for conversation. Recruiters do appreciate that not everyone has the desire or, more importantly, the money to swan off on a gap year. If travel is the last thing on your agenda, don't stress about it or feel you're going to be marked down for being a stay-at-home.

With the advent of new legislation, an employer discriminating against candidates on the grounds of age is officially a thing of the past. Nevertheless, some mature applicants still worry that their years will disadvantage them. Remember (if you still can), with age comes experience and probably an impressive set of transferable skills. You already know how to work, your people/client-handling skills are doubtless better developed and you may even have relevant industry knowledge. We've chatted with successful barristers and solicitors who've done everything from secretarial work, pub management and film production to accountancy, policing and soldiering. But when is old too old? If you're still in your 20s, get over yourself – you're still a kid. If you're in your 30s, ask what it is you can offer a law firm that will make your application stand out. And if you're older still? Never say never. We have run into a small number of 40-something trainees, all of whom were glad to have made the career change. It's not uncommon for them to have taken up a training contract with a firm they already dealt with in some other capacity, perhaps as a client themselves. Given that each year after qualification a certain percentage of the UK's lawyers move firms or even drop out of the profession for good, the argument that employers expect 30 years of service from new recruits simply doesn't hold water. Of greater relevance is the adage concerning old dogs and new tricks, so if your coat is greying, consider carefully how you'd cope with being trained and disciplined like a puppy.

Dealing with disability

Despite the legal profession now being more diverse, for students with mental or physical disabilities things are not straightforward. In the experience of the Group for Solicitors with Disabilities (GSD), many applicants with disabilities have great difficulty in securing work placements and training contracts. The good news is that there are sources of advice and assistance available and the GSD has been actively involved in approaching law firms to set up designated work placement schemes for disabled students. The group also provides a forum in which students and practitioners can meet in order to share experiences and provide one another with guidance and support. Would-be barristers should refer to the Equal Opportunities (Disability) Committee of the Bar Council. GSD's website is www.gsdnet.org.uk.

Show me something different

Gone are the days of firms and chambers populated exclusively by white men smoking fat cigars. Not only has the smoking ban put paid to the Cubans but women and ethnic minorities are now firmly ensconced in the profession. In the course of our research this year more than 125 firms provided us with lists identifying their trainees. In most firms the girls outnumber the boys, something we would expect to see given that more women have gone into the profession than men for well over a decade. The names on most of these lists also reflect a healthy spread of ethnic backgrounds. It is worth mentioning, however, that female and non-white trainees still have too few senior role models and there are always a small number of law firm sex or race discrimination claims going through the employment tribunals. On the subject of sexual orientation, we know scores of gay and lesbian lawyers for whom their lifestyle is entirely a non-career matter. Some firms are definitely more gay-friendly than others, but happily we do not tend to hear complaints from our sources about how their employers and colleagues view their sexuality.

A number of diversity-related organisations have sprung up and you may see evidence of them at your university. Without doubt anything that encourages genuine diversity in the workplace is to be commended, but before signing on the dotted line with any intermediary – especially if you are asked to hand over any money for their services – make sure you know you are dealing with a respected organisation. Ask if they are affiliated with particular law firms and if so, how. The topic of diversity covers more than just gender, sexual orientation, religion and ethnicity. If you think your accent or upbringing or a disability could stand in your way then find out if there is anything these organisations can do for you. Lord knows – or rather the Rt Hon. Alan Milburn knows – addressing the UK's social mobility issues and the dreaded 'glass ceiling' in the legal profession are hot both in the press and on the government agenda.

Likewise, if you know your university gets less attention from law firms than, say, Oxford or Durham, then a diversity-related organisation may well be just what you need to get your foot in the door. One reputable organisation is the City Solicitors' Educational Trust (CSET), which runs summer schools designed to help students not studying at one of the top UK universities, or who might not have excelled in their A levels. More information is available at www.cset.org.uk.

Stranger in a strange land

London attracts professionals from all over the world, so you can skip this bit if you're a Brit intending to work in the capital. If you hold an EU passport or have a pre-existing right to live and work in the UK and you are following the appropriate path to qualification, you should also proceed with optimism. Applicants who tick none of these boxes may find doors are easier to push open if they apply to firms with business interests in the country or region from which they come. Get up to speed on the latest changes in immigration rules, and be aware that a recent employment tribunal finding states that to automatically reject applications from candidates outside the European Economic Area who need a work permit is unlawful. To learn more see: www.ukba.homeoffice.gov.uk/workingintheuk. In all cases, excellent written and spoken English is essential and you will need a convincing reason why you have chosen to commence your career in the UK.

Regional firms and sets are sometimes more comfortable recruiting candidates with a local connection, be this through family or education. Quite simply, they want to know that whoever they take on will be committed to a long-term career with them. The picture across the UK is a variable one: some firms clearly state their preferences for local lads and lasses; others tell us that most of their applicants do have links with the region but that they are happy to consider anyone.

Keep it in perspective

What with studying hard, reading the *FT*, helping out at the CAB, captaining the university rugby and netball teams, debating, acting as student law society president and attending all the careers events that crop up, you'll hardly have time for a pint. Ultimately it's all about finding a good balance. Remember that your years at university are supposed to be fun and that developing your interests and friendships is important because these can last far longer and be more rewarding than any career.

Pro bono and volunteering

Deriving from the Latin *pro bono publico*, meaning 'for the public good,' the idea of providing free legal advice has been ingrained in the legal profession for centuries.

In 1594 the Lord Chief Justice explained to newly qualified barristers that the "*two tongues*" of linen hanging from counsel's shirt collars in court "*signifie that as you should have one tongue for the rich for your fee... so should you also have another tongue as ready without reward to defend the poor and oppressed.*" Traditionally done in a very British, understated way in the UK, the last six or seven years have seen the rise of structured pro bono programmes at law firms and chambers, law schools and universities. One recent development was the launch by Attorney General Baroness Scotland of an international database of pro bono activities, which enables those working on such projects to take a more strategic approach as well as being a valuable tool for attracting new legal resources. Last year pro bono legal advice provided by solicitors was estimated at more than £300m. Set up in 2001, National Pro Bono Week will run from the 9-13 November in 2009.

Why participate?

Involvement in pro bono activities is not just about notching up extra brownie points, although in the current economic climate, when there are more law students than ever competing for far fewer trainee positions, this is no bad thing. Pro bono experience is a clear winner with recruiters, and if you have something to put on your CV it will help take you closer to the front of the queue for training contracts and pupillages. It's not just prospective trainees and pupils who benefit: a scheme launched by website RollOnFriday in partnership with the Law Society, LawWorks and 25 leading international law firms including A&O, Eversheds and Lovells aims to help unemployed solicitors. Participants can continue to practise as lawyers by helping their communities and this should help them in their job search.

But as Kara Irwin, director of the BPP Pro Bono Centre emphasises, it's not all about giving your CV that extra sparkle. "*The key point about pro bono work is that it gives students an understanding of the role of law and the legal profession in society and access to justice issues.*" This is particularly important in a recession when more people need legal assistance, particularly in relation to employment problems.

Many firms now have formal pro bono relationships with community organisations, such as Citizens Advice Bureaux and Law Centres. Arguably the increased scope and visibility of pro bono work is in part due to the greater importance placed on pro bono activities by the influx of US law firms into the UK market. Certainly more home-grown law firms now recognise the business case for doing this kind of work, not least because of the PR benefits of telling the world what caring organisations they are.

Real life

Getting involved couldn't be easier when you're at law school as most now offer students extensive programmes of activity. Cardiff Law School has an Innocence Project, for example, which deals with long-term prisoners who maintain their innocence and have exhausted the initial appeals process. The pro bono unit there has also developed a niche in assistance to elderly and infirm clients, many of whom need to ascertain whether their care is categorised as nursing or social care in order to determine who should foot the bill. The University of Sheffield also has an Innocence Project, as well as providing students with the opportunity to get involved in the Pro Uno centre, which researches social welfare law issues that affect the clients of certain not-for-profit organisations in the South Yorkshire area. The University of Westminster's LPC course has a clinical law elective, during which students work on a pro bono basis for the CAB and submit a project at the end of the elective. And as if you needed a greater incentive than a warm glow in the pit of your belly, there are various national prizes on offer for students who excel in this field, including the Law Society's annual Young Lawyer Pro Bono Award.

At university level, student pro bono opportunities have been more limited, largely because it's too risky for inexperienced undergrads to provide real-life legal advice. This is changing as undergraduates are receiving more support. In October 2007 the Law Society funded the appointment of a full-time project manager for students and law schools. He is Martin Curtis at LawWorks, which is the operating name of the Solicitors Pro Bono Group, a charity that encourages commitment across the profession. Martin's role is to advise universities and law schools on how best to establish pro bono initiatives. You can go to www.studentprobono.net for the most up-to-date information on what each law school is doing.

If you hope to go to the Bar or become a solicitor specialising in any contentious area of law then you should seriously consider becoming a ratified member of The Free Representation Unit (FRU), a charity founded in 1972 to provide legal advice, case preparation and advocacy for people who aren't able to claim legal aid.

If this has gone any way towards whetting your appetite then check out the following selection of organisations. If you do some research you'll find others.

www.probonouk.net

This useful website will identify the organisations working in your area and has a section devoted to students.

LawWorks

A good source of advice and information. It now has a dedicated student officer. www.lawworks.org.uk.

A4ID

Advocates for International Development facilitate free legal assistance to civil society, developing country governments and social organisations to help achieve the UN Millennium Development Goals. Research-based opportunities exist for students. www.a4id.org.

Amicus

Charity providing assistance to US attorneys working on death row cases. Provides training and arranges unpaid internships in the USA for UK postgrads. As only a limited number of scholarships exist, applicants should have a self-funding plan. www.amicus-alj.org. Another similar organisation is Reprieve www.reprieve.org.uk which has focused much of its efforts on advising Guantánamo Bay detainees.

The AIRE Centre

Provides European human rights information and advice. Also offers direct legal advice and assistance on a case-by-case basis to legal practitioners or advisers. Internships are available for students with a good working knowledge of human rights and EU law. European language skills an advantage. www.airecentre.org.

Bar Pro Bono Unit

Established in 1996, the unit matches individuals in need with barristers in private practice. Opportunities are available for students to provide admin support on a part-time basis. www.barprobono.org.uk.

Citizens Advice Bureaux

CAB provides free advice from 3,300 locations. Those with real commitment can take its Adviser Training Programme to gain a widely recognised qualification that may subsequently enable a training contract to be reduced by up to six months. Other less time-consuming work is also available. Debt, benefits, housing, employment, consumer issues, family matters and immigration are the most commonly raised problems. www.citizensadvice.org.uk.

Independent Custody Visiting

Independent custody visitors work in pairs, conducting regular unannounced checks on police stations to monitor the welfare of detainees. Anyone over the age of 18 can apply to become an ICV. www.icva.org.uk.

Law Centres

Law Centres provide free, independent legal services to people who live or work in their catchment areas. Some accept student volunteers to provide administrative support and casework assistance. www.lawcentres.org.uk.

Liberty

Provides advice and representation to groups and individuals in relation to domestic law cases involving the Human Rights Act. Liberty has opportunities for a small number of students to provide general office assistance and help with casework. www.liberty-human-rights.org.uk.

National Appropriate Adult Network

Under-17s and adults considered to be mentally vulnerable must have an appropriate adult with them when interviewed by the police. Organised groups of trained volunteers carry out this important role. www.appropriateadult.org.uk.

Prisoners' Advice Service

Provides free advice and assistance on an individual and confidential basis, taking legal action where appropriate. www.prisonersadvice.org.uk.

Refugee Council

The Refugee Council is the largest refugee agency in the UK. It provides advice on the asylum procedure, support and entitlement. Volunteers can assist in three areas: direct services, office-based and community-based. www.refugeecouncil.org.uk. See also Bail for Immigration Detainees – www.biduk.org.

Victim Support

The Victim Support Witness Service operates in every Crown Court, providing guidance and support to witnesses, victims and their families before, during and after proceedings. www.victimsupport.co.uk.

Youth Justice Board

The YJB oversees the youth justice system. Contact your local board. www.yjb.gov.uk.

Vacation Schemes

In an ever-more competitive market, vacation schemes are an increasingly important piece of weaponry in the battle to get a training contract.

As well as helping you get a foot in the door, vacation schemes are one of the best ways to find out what being a lawyer is actually like, to get a sniff of the truth behind the Denny Crane and Ally McBeal fictions. Also, it'll help you out no end when it comes to your CV since *"vac schemes are definitely one of the best ways to demonstrate a commitment to the profession."* Once you've done one, you'll have a way to back up claims that you knew law was your destiny from birth, your only true love, the thing you always wanted to do 60+ hours a week, etc. We recommend trying several vac schemes so that you can find your groove – are you more suited to national, regional or international firms? Which practice groups do you like best? Who's got the nicest biscuits? Will you actually like being a lawyer?

Below are a few vac scheme FAQs, along with our advice on how to get the best out of time spent with a firm. The quotes all come from people who undertook schemes in 2009.

How do I get on one?

> *"I wouldn't have got a training contract without first doing a vac scheme. Everyone has good academic credentials, but if recruiters have actually seen you, it makes things much easier."*

No secret here: our handy-dandy table over the page tells you what places are available and when to apply. Timing your application is important: certain schemes are frequently targeted at final-year non-law grads or penultimate-year law grads, which can leave other students frustrated. You'll generally find full details of exactly how to make your application on firms' recruitment websites.

As competition for training contracts gets more intense, it's no surprise that competition for vac scheme places is too. It doesn't help that firms are cutting back on their programmes at the moment – making them shorter, accepting fewer people and closing deadlines earlier.

This isn't to say that firms don't value vacation schemes – in fact, they are increasingly relying on them as a recruitment tool. City firm Nabarro, for example, takes *"nearly all"* its trainees from people it saw on its vac scheme. Where firms have cut back it is generally due to the economy. Many don't want to hire as many trainees in 2010, and they also need to trim their recruitment budgets. Expensive summer schemes for students are among the first things to go.

Obvious conclusion: you'll need to put as much effort into vac scheme applications as you do into training contract applications. For some tips on how to do this refer to pages 42-45. The strongest applicants always manage to secure a clutch of offers, and a few become 'serial schemers', perhaps tempted by the money on offer, which can be as much as several hundred pounds a week at City firms. Don't despair if you can't secure a place, however; it doesn't mean you'll never get a training contract. Try and build your CV up in other ways – say with voluntary work or other legal or commercial experience – and then have another stab at vac scheme applications.

Even if you navigate the vacation scheme obstacle course perfectly, don't get complacent. *"After doing well on the vac scheme, one guy didn't prepare enough for the interview and didn't get the job."* You have to ace it at every stage.

What will I get to do?

"It's like an assessment centre that never ends. Well, at least not for a fortnight or so."

Vac schemes differ as much as the firms themselves. In some cases, your time will be structured down to the minute with talks about the firm and the training contract, followed by tasks, then coffee with the partners, then more tasks. Other firms might expect you to muck in on some real work or ask you to shadow someone for a few hours. Talking to people who'd recently been on vac schemes, we found that firms usually fall into one of two categories...

Some firms will:
- Try to razzle-dazzle you
- Set loads of assessment tasks
- Not give you much real work
- Structure the vac schemes tightly
- Put on lots of talks
- Not provide much senior contact
- Have you socialising with trainees

Other firms will:
- Organise fewer social events
- Set you more real work
- Put on lots of talks
- Give you more exposure to senior staff
- Have you socialising with a broader range of people
- Set some assessment tasks

Which type is better? In terms of achieving the end goal of a training contract offer then neither. In terms of finding out what the role of solicitor is really like then it's probably the second type of programme that will score points.

What should I look out for?

When on a vac scheme, become an anthropologist. Observe your environment and its inhabitants; figure out the social structures, the hierarchies, the shared beliefs that bond people (if indeed there are any). Watch how the trainees fit in with all of this. Eavesdrop. You've got to be on your guard though because they know you're there, and some of our sources did end up concluding: *"It can be an artificial exercise – you see what they want you to see."* Anthropologists call this Observer Bias. Your aim is to peer beyond the mask at the living, breathing, sweating entity behind it. Is it really such a 'diverse, approachable environment where employees have a great work-life balance'? How come that trainee's got bags under her eyes? And where's all that yelling coming from? Talk to people and try to find someone who'll candidly tell you their thoughts minus the promotional psychobabble.

Try also to get a feel for how different departments work by reading as much as you can. A starting point would be our practice area features, which start on page 89. It'll help you figure out what sort of work might suit you best and will enable you to ask intelligent questions of your supervisors. Intelligent questions pave the road to success, so lay as many down as possible without becoming annoying.

How will I be assessed?

"It seems like in the good old days you just had to show up and not cock up, but now you've really got to stand out, which is hard to do in a tightly-scripted system."

Vac schemers are often given research to do as a way of evaluating their abilities; expect to be given some specifics to look into before reporting back to solicitors with your findings. You might also be asked to shadow someone, helping them out with their workload. This is an excellent opportunity for you to find more out about the firm while proving yourself at the same time. You might even get to go to client meetings or visit court. Last, but certainly not least, are the mini-assessment tasks, designed to test your ability to present, argue and work as a team. *"Don't be over-assertive, but don't fade into the background either. Remember to ask other people what their opinions are – you have to look like a team player."* Some tasks we heard about: advertising pitches to faux-potential clients, mini-transactions and business scenarios.

How should I act?

"They laid on a great spread with free drinks. I got a little drunk and it was frowned upon. On another vac scheme I received a similar invite and was careful not to reprise my earlier performance, but when I didn't get a training contract that time I was told that I didn't join in enough. They declined me because I seemed to lack enthusiasm! Others bonded with the partners over copious amounts of alcohol – that was the firm's way."

While you're busy watching everyone else, don't forget that they're watching you, watching them, watching you. This recruitment lark is a delicate dance, so attune yourself to the characters around you and follow their lead. More than anything else, people will be trying to see if you 'share the firm's Core Values'. Ultimately, 'professionalism' should be your watchword. This is a job interview, even when you're eating lunch in the canteen. Don't be late for work. Switch off your mobile phone when in the office. Thinking about browsing the BBC website in a slack moment? Why take the risk? If you're given an Outlook account, don't go sending scurrilous e-mails to your mate. Don't ever say an unkind word about anyone to anyone – be it partner, assistant, trainee, support staffer or fellow vac schemer. Even if everyone else is bitching, don't get sucked in. Quite apart from the fact that gossiping is a shabby practice, staying above it all will ensure you'll get a reputation for being (a) professional and (b) a nice person. Both are useful to have.

Drinking. Bankers, lawyers, doctors and even priests all know how effective alcohol can be when it comes to greasing the wheels. But the trick is to drink the right amount – remember the Bishop of Southwark? Don't make a fool of yourself. Even when ensconced in a snazzy club, those mental notepads will still be out. So, gauge the situation, anthropologists: is the firm boozy or abstemious?

And finally...

Now that we've got you all tense by telling you that it's all really serious and Your Future basically hangs on a thread, here are a few final tips: Be yourself, remember your manners, take a handkerchief, smell good, clean under your nails and show enthusiasm.

Vacation Schemes

Firm name	Vacancies	Duration	Remuneration	Deadline
Addleshaw Goddard	90 Easter & summer	1, 2 or 3 weeks	Not known	31 January 2010
Allen & Overy	65 – winter (grads & final year non-law); spring/summer (penult year law)	Not known	£250 p.w.	Winter: 31 Oct 2009 Easter/summer: 17 Jan 2010
Ashurst	Easter (grads & final year non-law); summer (penult year law)	Easter: 2 weeks summer: 3 weeks	£275 p.w.	31 January 2010
Baker & McKenzie	London: 30 international: 3-5	London: 3 weeks Lon/o'seas: 8-12 weeks	£270 p.w.	31 January 2010
Barlow Lyde & Gilbert	Yes, plus open days and drop-in days	Not known	Not known	31 January 2010
Beachcroft	Summer	Not known	Not known	1 March 2010
Berwin Leighton Paisner	Easter (final year law grads); summer (penult year & above)	Easter: 1 week summer: 2 weeks	Not known	31 January 2010
Bevan Brittan	24 across 3 offices	Not known	Not known	31 March 2010
Bird & Bird	20	3 weeks	£275 p.w.	31 January 2010
Bond Pearce	Summer	2 weeks	Not known	9 April 2010
Boodle Hatfield	10	2 weeks	Not known	8 February 2010
Bristows	Yes Easter, summer, winter	Not known	Not known	Not known
Burges Salmon	40 plus open days	2 weeks	£250 p.w.	Not known
Capsticks	summer	2 weeks	Not known	26 February 2010
Cleary Gottlieb Steen & Hamilton	5 at Christmas, 10 at Easter & 20 in summer	Not known	Not known	Christmas: 15th November 2009 Easter/summer: 28 January 2010
Clifford Chance	Easter and summer	2-4 weeks	£270 p.w.	End January 2010
Clyde & Co	20 June - July	2 weeks	Not known	31 January 2010
CMS Cameron McKenna	60 Easter and summer	2 weeks	£250 p.w.	31 January 2010
Cobbetts	Yes	Not known	Not known	14 February 2010
Coffin Mew	Open week in July	1 week	Not known	31 March 2010
Covington & Burling	24	Not known	Not known	28 February 2010
Davenport Lyons	Yes	Not known	£200 p.w.	Not known
Dechert	Easter and summer aimed at penult year law	Easter: 1 week summer: 2 weeks	Not known	31 January 2010
Denton Wilde Sapte	Open days in December and Easter & summer schemes	1 week	Not known	Not known
Dewey & LeBoeuf	20	Easter: 1 week summer: 2 weeks	£400 p.w.	31 January 2010
Dickinson Dees	40 Easter & summer	1 week	£200 p.w.	31 January 2010
DLA Piper	170	2 weeks	Not known	31 January 2010
Dundas & Wilson	Yes	3 weeks	Not known	30 January 2010

Vacation Schemes

Firm name	Vacancies	Duration	Remuneration	Deadline
DWF	50	1 week	Paid	Not known
Edwards Angell Palmer & Dodge	10 + open days	2 weeks	Not known	26 February 2010
Eversheds	Yes	2 weeks	£240 p.w. (London)	31 January 2010
Farrer & Co	30 Easter and summer	2 weeks	£260 p.w.	31 January 2010
Foot Anstey	Yes	Not known	Not known	31 March 2010
Freshfields Bruckhaus Deringer	60	3 weeks	£825 total	15 January 2010 (earlier apps recommended)
Government Legal Service	60	2-3 weeks	£200-250 p.w.	End January 2010
Halliwells	54	2 weeks	£215 p.w.	28 February 2010
Hammonds	25	2 weeks	£230 p.w. (London) £180 p.w. (Regions)	31 January 2010
HBJ Gateley Wareing	Yes	2 weeks	Not known	11 February 2010
Herbert Smith	Winter, spring & summer	2 weeks	Not known	Not known
Hewitsons	Yes	1 week	Not known	Not known
Hill Dickinson	40	1 week	Not known	31 March 2010
Holman Fenwick & Willan	Yes	2 weeks	£250 p.w.	14 February 2010
Howes Percival	Yes	1 week	Not known	30 April 2009
Ince & Co	15	2 weeks	£250 p.w.	31 January 2010
Irwin Mitchell	70	1 week	£100 p.w.	Not known
Jones Day	Christmas: non-law Easter: non-law summer: law	2 weeks	£400 p.w.	Christmas: 31 Oct 2009 Easter/summer: 31 Jan 2010
K&L Gates	Yes + open days	2 weeks	Not known	Not known
Kirkland & Ellis	14	2 weeks	£350 p.w.	31 January 2010
Latham & Watkins	Yes: Easter and summer	2 weeks	£300 p.w.	Easter: 31 December 2009 Summer 31 January 2010
Lawrence Graham	Easter and summer	2 weeks	£250 p.w.	31 January 2010
Laytons	6	1 week	Not known	30 April 2010
Lester Aldridge	8	2 weeks	£125 p.w.	31 March 2010
Lewis Silkin	Yes plus open days	2 weeks	Not known	End January 2010
Linklaters	Christmas (non-law) summer (law) some o/seas	Christmas: 2 weeks summer: 4 weeks	Not known	Not known
Lovells	50	3 weeks	Not known	31 January 2010
Macfarlanes	60	2 weeks	£250 p.w.	28 February 2010
Manches	20	1 week	£200 (under review)	15 February 2010
Mayer Brown	45	Easter: 2 weeks summer: 3 weeks	Not known	Not known
McGrigors	Yes	3 weeks	Not known	30 January 2010
Memery Crystal	Yes: Easter	1 week	Not known	31 January 2010

Vacation Schemes

Firm name	Vacancies	Duration	Remuneration	Deadline
Michelmores	Yes	1 week	Not known	28 February 2010
Mills & Reeve	Yes	2 weeks	Not known	31 January 2010
Mishcon de Reya	15	2 weeks	£250 p.w.	31 January 2010
Muckle	Yes	Not known	Not known	9 February 2010
Nabarro	65	3 weeks	Not known	8 February 2010
Norton Rose	20 at Christmas 40 in summer plus open days	Christmas: 2 weeks summer: 4 weeks	£250 p.w.	31 October 2009 31 January 2010
Olswang	17	2 weeks	£275 p.w.	31 January 2010
O'Melveny & Myers	Yes	2 weeks	Not known	1 February 2010
Osborne Clarke	Yes	2 weeks	Not known	Not known
Pannone	88	1 week	None	Easter: 19 February 2010 Summer: 25 June 2010
Paul Hastings	10	2 weeks	£350 p.w.	28 February 2010
Penningtons Solicitors	Yes plus information days	Not known	Not known	31 March 2010
Pinsent Masons	100	2 weeks	Not known	31 January 2010
PricewaterhouseCoopers Legal	Yes	3 weeks	Not known	31 March 2010
Reed Smith	20	2 weeks	Not known	31 March 2010
Reynolds Porter Chamberlain	24	2 weeks	£275 p.w.	29 January 2010
Shadbolt	6-8	2 weeks	£200 p.w.	28 February 2010
Sheridans	Not known	2 weeks	Not Known	End March 2010
Shoosmiths	Yes	2 weeks	Not known	30 January 2010
Simmons & Simmons	Yes & winter workshops	Not known	Not known	Not known
SJ Berwin	Yes: Easter & summer	Not known	Not known	31 January 2010
Skadden	Yes: Easter & summer	2 weeks	Paid	12 January 2010
Slaughter and May	Yes: Easter, summer & Christmas	1-2 weeks	£300 p.w.	Not known
Speechly Bircham	20	3 weeks	Not known	12 February 2010
Stephenson Harwood	40	1-2 weeks	£260 p.w.	Easter & Xmas: 3 Nov 2009 Summer: 15 Jan 2010
Stevens & Bolton	Yes	1 week	£200 p.w	31 January 2010
Taylor Wessing	30+	2 weeks	£250 p.w.	31 January 2010
Thomas Eggar	Yes	1 week	Travel expenses	Not known
TLT Solicitors	Yes	1 week	Not known	31 January 2010
Travers Smith	Christmas: 15 summer: 45	2 weeks	£250	31 January 2010
Trowers & Hamlins	Yes	2 weeks	Not known	1 March 2010

Vacation Schemes

Firm name	Vacancies	Duration	Remuneration	Deadline
Veale Wasbrough	Yes	1 week	Not known	Not known
Vinson & Elkins	Yes	1-2 weeks	Not known	28 February 2010
Walker Morris	48	1 week	£250 p.w.	31 January 2010
Ward Hadaway	Yes	1 week	Not known	28 February 2010
Watson, Farley & Williams	25	2 weeks	£250 p.w.	31 January 2010
Wedlake Bell	8	3 weeks	£200 p.w.	End February 2010
Weil, Gotshal & Manges	15	Not known	Not known	31 January 2010
White & Case	Easter: 20-25 summer: 40-50	Easter: 1 week summer: 2 weeks	£350 p.w.	31 January 2010
Wilsons Solicitors	Yes	1 week	Not known	Not known
Withers	Yes: Easter and summer (plus Milan for Italian speakers)	2 weeks	Not known	31 January 2010
Wragge & Co	Yes	1-2 weeks	Not known	31 January 2010

How to make successful applications

Preparing applications is both an art and a science. In the current ultra-competitive market, the sooner you develop the right techniques the better.

Here's Cliff Fluet, grad recruitment partner at Lewis Silkin, on the subject of applications: "*I've seen too many copy and paste ones. If you can't be bothered filling in a form properly then your chances of getting a £30k-plus job are severely limited.*" What he says is incontrovertible. In all our conversations with recruiters, they never fail to mention this fundamental error. Don't ever be generic in your applications; tailor them to each firm or set of chambers – recruiters can spot a mail merge from a mile away.

We know it's tempting to send off a generic application to as many firms as you can. It's quicker, and it's tempting to believe the old adage that if you throw enough mud some of it will stick. In truth, we do come across trainees who have succeeded in getting a training contract in this way, but they had made their applications at a time when the competition was less intense than it is now. And even then, we notice that the people who used this method were usually trainees at the less highly regarded firms. The people who had succeeded in their bid to join the most prestigious firms had often targeted fewer organisations and taken more time perfecting their applications.

Note that we are not saying that it's a bad thing to send off piles of applications. As we have repeatedly mentioned, this is a competitive business and even great candidates may have to turn out 15, 20 or more, but the more care you take with each, the sooner it will be before you get an offer.

Do your research

Choosing a firm because it's got a cool name and recruitment literature isn't the best policy; neither is random selection. We spoke to a trainee this year who swore blind that they were only working at Addleshaw Goddard because they didn't get past the letter A in their copy of the *Student Guide*. Luckily, they were pretty happy there. Before you apply, try to work out which firms would best suit you. If you're a 'live to work' type, find an organisation that will give you what you crave. Likewise, if you just have to catch *Hollyoaks* at half six, make sure you seek out firms with shorter hours. If you want to do a certain type of law, apply to the places that specialise in the area. Carefully select your targets – they need to suit your personality and interests, otherwise you'll have a hard time persuading them to hire you, and if you do get hired you might regret it.

- Use the *Student Guide* – it's the best thing we've ever read. The **True Picture**, the **Chambers Reports**, the **Solicitors' Practice Areas** and **Practice Areas at the Bar**, the comparison charts – all good, all useful.
- Only marginally less brilliant, our parent publication *Chambers UK* identifies and ranks all the best firms in over 60 areas of practice. It can be read online, for free, at www.chambersandpartners.com.
- Make use of as many other sources as possible. From legal gossip websites through to *The Lawyer*, *Legal Week* and *The Gazette*: all can be of value.
- Check the firm's requirements. Check your qualifications and abilities. Do they match? The applications and selections table on page 515 should help with this.

Stay organised

- Know the deadlines and diarise the important ones. The calendar at the front of this book should help. Most commercial firms recruit two years in advance, but it might be even earlier. Check. Check again.
- Application forms take far, far longer to complete than you'd expect, especially when they're done well. Two minutes late is too late.
- Some barristers' chambers use the Pupillage Portal, some don't. Make sure you know which is which. Check their websites and call their HR departments. The Bar section of this guide discusses the Pupillage Portal in more detail.
- If you have to handwrite something, practice on a rough version first. If your handwriting is so atrocious that the reader will need a cipher, you're going to have to try especially hard.
- Answer the questions directly – no cutting and pasting or repetition.
- Usually there will be a guide as to how much you can write for each question. It is there to be followed, but if you are well under, don't just waffle, keep thinking.
- Keep copies of everything you send out because before an interview or assessment day you will need to remind yourself of what you wrote.
- Increasingly, firms are making application forms available only to those who perform well enough in online tests, sometimes verbal reasoning, sometimes numerical. There are books and websites with sample tests and hints. Get in some practice ahead of time.

Good form

Here are a few tips on completing application forms and CVs, including some words of wisdom straight from the mouth of Wendy Warburton, HBJ Gateley Wareing's HR manager:

- Avoid chronological gaps in your experience. If you've taken time off, put it down and be prepared to explain why.
- *"Ignore all the fancy stuff and get to the details. Don't waste time with photos or unusual fonts."*
- Bullet points and **bold text** can make things more eye-catching.
- *"Don't just say what you did at uni – mention sports teams, work experience and volunteering. Show that you've not simply gone to uni and gone through the process."*
- A mistake on a CV can be damning. Technology is there to serve us and make things easier. You have spellcheck: use it. Ask a friend to check your CV as well because there are some areas in which us feeble humans still come up trumps.
- *"Don't use glossy terms or jargon. Give concise details, expanding where appropriate – not reams and reams though. We don't want an essay."* A CV should be three pages max, ideally just two.
- Demonstrate your qualities rather than just stating them. Applications should refer to teamwork and problem-solving skills as well as commercial outlook and commitment to becoming a lawyer.
- *"You can use any kind of work to prove you have commercial awareness. Even if it was in a pub you can still talk about being aware of costs, budgeting and the marketing the pub did. People aren't aware of the simple things they could extrapolate on."*

Don't undersell yourself

If you looked at the training contract applications of a handful of different students you'd see that some include more information about their achievements than others. Usually those with less content have omitted to include things because they simply don't appreciate their significance.

- Qualifications, gap year experiences, 17 A*s at A-level, endless vac schemes – these things are obvious essentials.
- Never underplay your work experience or vac schemes and try to speak to lawyers wherever you can; it all helps to show that you understand the reality of practice. Explain to the reader what you learned from your experiences rather than just listing them.
- Write a list of all the jobs you've ever had and consider the list as a whole. It may show that you're a real grafter who has helped pay their way through uni. It won't always be appropriate to list all your part-time employment so you might need to group some jobs into a more general category. Unless the list is extensive then indicate the key aspects of your role in each position, but don't go overboard or recruiters will lose interest.
- If you studied a musical instrument to a high level then say so. It shows you can commit to something and work consistently to achieve it. The same goes for other pastimes or pursuits – eg life-guarding, scuba diving, artistic endeavours.
- Sporting activities are great application form/CV fodder. Again, the commitment factor will come through, and if it's a team sport you play then what better confirmation is there of your being a team player?
- Were you ever selected, or better still elected, to a position of responsibility? To be chosen by your peers as a student representative, for example, suggests that people respect you and have confidence in your abilities. It also shows you are naturally the sort of person who likes to take on a challenge. As to how far back in time you reach for such nuggets, well, this depends on your current situation. If you are still at university, or have very recently graduated, then something from your later school days should still be suitable. If it was some time since you left uni then you need to find some more recent examples. Never forget to mention if you were a (deputy) head boy or girl, the captain of a sports team or held a position of responsibility in a society or club.

Unless otherwise stated, always include a covering letter with your CV. It's a golden opportunity to show off your writing skills, explain your motives, wax lyrical about your qualities and show how suited you are to your target firm or set. A good covering letter will highlight the best aspects of your application. If you have any weaknesses (say a poorer than anticipated degree result), it's a place to mention extenuating circumstances.

And finally...

If all this advice seems totally obvious, that's because it is. You wouldn't think anyone makes elementary mistakes any more, but every year recruiters still find themselves reading applications that look like they've been written by Mr Bean. Poor layout, atrocious grammar, banal comments... all this from university graduates. Just think: by the simple act of not making any stupid errors, you're blowing a significant number of your potential competitors out of the water. Conversely, if you accidentally write down *it's* when you meant *its* or *there* when you mean *their* – even just the one time – then no matter what your other qualities, in the eyes of recruiters you've just lumped yourself in with all the other Beans.

How to succeed at interviews and assessment days

Interviews and assessment days are hard to come by. You'll send out dozens of application forms and get blanked by most firms. Maybe even all of them – it's a tough market. So when you do get an interview, give it your all.

Interviews

The biggest error that can be made while hunting the Lesser Spotted Training Contract is to confuse getting an interview with getting a job. You've worked really hard so far, but it's time to ratchet things up another notch. Turn on the charm, adopt a good posture and be thorough with your homework. It's time for a classic aphorism: 'If you fail to prepare, then you prepare to fail'. As one recruiter acknowledged: "*It's a bit David Brent, but it's true.*"

We know what recruiters want from applicants and what little tricks they have up their sleeves because we asked them. Happily, we can tell you that there are no trick questions – nothing at all about whether Batman could take Spiderman in a fight and none of that 'if a man is your mother's uncle's son, what relation is he to you?' stuff either.*

Before any interview:

Read and think about your application form. Interviewers will pick up on what you wrote and question you on it. A lot of the time, they'll discuss your application form as an icebreaker. It's your chance to speak about things that interest you and to build up rapport. Chat, be expansive, maybe even flash the pearly whites. If you fibbed on your application form, make sure you've got an extensive cover story sketched out to back up your claim or else you'll be found out. Better yet: don't lie or over exaggerate in the first place.

Research the firm. A stock question is 'Why this firm in particular?' Make sure you've got something good, innovative and non-generic to say. Read the **True Picture** reports and find out about the firm's strengths, its history and what is being said about it in the legal press. Ideally you will find a topic or two that can be developed into a reason why you and the firm are a perfect match.

Research the people who are interviewing you, if possible. 'Knowledge is power' and 'know your enemy', as they say. Practice area, precedent-setting cases they've won, previous firms they've worked at, their favourite colour/pet/sport – all of this is gold and law firm websites often contain such details. Don't overdo it though: "*Funny coincidence – I'm really into Bolivian philately circa 1964 as well...*"

Have a finger on the pulse of legal news and current affairs. *The Lawyer*, *Legal Week* and *The Gazette* are all very good, as is Thursday's Law supplement in *The Times*. Be ready to see the connections between law and the real world of politics, society and business. Try to demonstrate that you're commercially aware.

Practice answers, but not too much. It's not that difficult to guess what sort of questions you're going to get; something along the lines of 'Why do you want to be a lawyer?' is a bona fide cert. It is wise to rehearse a little to collect your thoughts, but as great comedians will tell you, you've got to be ready to deviate from the script as the mood takes you. Speaking off the cuff makes you sound more interesting and often a classic question will be slightly altered and you need to be ready to adapt.

Historically, us Brits are modest folk and talking about cash is often judged to be vulgar, but a good number of our sources did say that it was a factor and, as a trainee pointed out to us in an interview this year: "*None of us in law are particularly altruistic.*" Don't be scared about mentioning that the excellent financial rewards are a factor in choosing to be a lawyer. You're among friends. Just make sure you give some other, more wholesome, reasons too.

The default setting is to want to be liked and accepted, but remember that the interview is a crucial opportunity for you to figure out what you like about the firm. You can become the questioner; indeed you should have questions prepared for the end of the interview. There are many things you might ask and it's best to pick something that isn't already covered in the firm's own literature. You could find out what your interviewers like about the firm or ask them about when they trained. You could ask them how the firm has responded to (insert relevant current affair here). Be confident and use this opportunity to build a rapport with your interviewers.

The usual interview tips apply:

- Arrive early. For all the common-sense reasons but also so that you can have a nose around. Have a contact number ready in case some cruel act of divine vengeance makes you late.
- Dress appropriately. Make 'ordinary' your goal.
- Be polite to EVERYONE.
- Shake hands firmly (not so they lose their balance – that's too much) and make eye contact. Smile non-menacingly.
- Speak to everyone on the panel, ensuring you make eye contact with all present.
- Don't fidget or sit awkwardly. Don't allow your body to tense.
- Do practice interviews beforehand and get feedback from whoever tests you. Even family members and friends can be surprisingly good at this if you explain what sort of questions you want them to ask. They may identify an annoying verbal tic. Do what you can to eradicate any annoying erms and umms.
- Listen carefully to questions so you can establish what it is the interviewer seeks. Don't just shoehorn in pre-packaged answers.
- "*Being funny is great if it's born of confidence and directness,*" but don't try to be Russell Brand.

Assessment days

Even though you might have an LPC distinction, a First-class degree, three As at A Level, 29 GCSEs, a gold star from Mrs Haslem's nursery class and many other great qualities besides, some firms still want to see you in action and test you out with their own assessments. In their arsenal, firms have written and negotiation exercises, personality profiling, research tasks and group tasks.

Firms will be keen to see whether you can work as part of a team. Wendy Warburton, HR manager at HBJ Gateley Wareing, says: "*Don't think that you're in competition with everyone. That sounds daft but in a group of five, all five may get training contracts. Don't look at the others as rivals; use them to bounce your skills off. Don't shoot people down, work with them and encourage them.*" Advertising pitches to faux-clients and pretend mini-transactions are two common exercises, but these things are always changing and different firms have different methods (and want to see different traits). One we know of even asks applicants to take part in a debate in front of the entire firm. So, always bear in mind what kind of organisation it is and what type of person they're looking for.

Psychometric tests are as effective as homoeopathy (make of that what you will). Some people swear that they accurately determine an applicant's personality while others denounce them. Although the companies that produce these tests try to keep their secrets safe, the internet is a great place to read up on them. Look into the methodologies of the main ones (start on Wikipedia) and ask careers services for examples. Some firms might post out samples in advance. Two common ones are the Watson Glaser and SHL tests. They're usually comprised of multiple choice, reasoning-based questions based on snippets of information that look for business awareness and intellectual rigour. Some deliberately have too many questions as they're designed to assess your speed under pressure. Make sure you know if you're sitting one of these and, whatever the test, try to plan your time effectively. They may change, of course, but try to quiz people who've done the tests already. Keep in touch with people on your GDL/LPC/BPTC and check out discussion forums on law student websites.

Don't relax too much if there's a social event as these can be just as important when it comes to making a good impression. Some firms have lunches where you sit round with three or four partners and a handful of other applicants and make small talk over the duck à l'orange. Who will your prospective supervisor want to hire? The girl who kept her eyes on the plate for the entire meal and whispered unintelligible answers to every question? The chap who drank too much of the Bourgogne Pinot Noir and spent most of the meal calling him buddy? Or the nice young man who made some pertinent observations on the rise of the Gulf economies and showed an interest in his taxidermy hobby? Similarly, a drink with the firm's trainees is an opportunity to strike up a rapport with them, not to start making comments about how your vac scheme at Norton Rose was so much better.

And finally...

The sad fact is that for very many people it could take a while to succeed. Don't let rejection – now sometimes referred to as a PFO (please f*** off) letter – bring you down as it will only disadvantage you. Treat a failed application like the end of a relationship: convince yourself it wasn't really anyone's fault and that you just weren't really suitable for the firm; ask them why they rejected you and act upon it. Chin up, champ: plenty of fish left in the sea. Badmouthing a firm afterwards is optional (and cathartic) but best done reasonably privately.

* He's your first cousin once removed, we think.

Managing job offers

After all the hard work involved in securing a training contract offer, you'll need to know what to do when you actually land one.

The Solicitors Regulation Authority publishes a 'voluntary code to good practice in the recruitment of trainee solicitors' at www.sra.org.uk/documents/students/training-contract/voluntarycode.pdf.

Read through these guidelines if at any stage you are in doubt as to what you should do. They address the conduct of both recruiters and students. Law firms are not obliged to follow these guidelines, though most will.

On offers, the guidelines say:
- If you're still an undergrad, a training contract offer should not be made before 1 September in your final undergraduate year. If you've impressed a firm during a vacation scheme or period of work experience, it must wait until this date before making you an offer.
- At an interview, you will be told if there is a further stage to the selection process. You should also be told within two weeks of reaching the end of the process whether or not you have been successful.
- Offers should be made in writing. If you receive an offer by phone you don't need to say yes or no: you can ask the firm to send a formal offer in writing for you to consider.

On deadlines, the guidelines say:
- No deadline should expire earlier than four weeks from the date of an offer. If you need more time to mull over an offer, firms are supposed to consider your request 'sympathetically', provided you have a good reason. No definition of 'good reason' is given in the guidelines.
- If a firm is going to pay your law school fees it should set out the terms and conditions of the arrangement in the training contract offer letter. A firm's willingness to provide financial assistance should not affect the time limit for accepting the contract.
- If you feel you need more time, you will have to enter into diplomatic discussions with the law firm, telling them how much longer you need. Make sure you get written confirmation of any extension to the deadline as simply asking for it might not be enough.

You may want to hang on to an offer from one firm while you pursue applications with others. This is okay, but you must bear in mind the following:

- You should not hold more than two (as yet unaccepted or declined) offers at any one time.
- Students are supposed to respond promptly to a firm that's made an offer, either by accepting or rejecting it. The word 'promptly' is not defined in the code.
- Because offers can and will be made with time limits for acceptance, do guard against allowing a deadline to elapse. The stupidity tax you may otherwise pay doesn't bear thinking about.
- Once you have accepted your preferred offer in writing, you must then confirm to everyone else that you are withdrawing your application. This is only fair to busy recruiters and other applicants who may suffer if you clog up a shortlist.

The guidelines are silent on the issue of what happens if a student changes their mind after accepting an offer. It's a rare firm that will be particularly sympathetic to a post-acceptance withdrawal but, on occasions, these things do happen. We can give no general advice on this subject, as each individual case will have its own merits. What we can say is that the smooth running of the whole trainee recruitment market relies on most parties playing by the above 'rules'. So what if a law firm puts pressure on you to accept an offer earlier than the guidelines say they should? Again, there is no simple answer as the SRA's code of conduct is voluntary. If this situation arises you will have to enter into delicate negotiations with the law firm. We also recommend that if the issue causes you problems then you report it to your university or college careers adviser and ask if they can recommend a course of action. This exact situation arose in summer 2009 for students made training contract offers by Bristol firm TLT.

Law School

Solicitors' timetable	48
Barristers' timetable	49
The Graduate Diploma in Law (GDL)	50
The Legal Practice Course (LPC)	54
LPC provider reports	58
The Bar Professional Training Course (BPTC)	70
BPTC provider reports	73
How to fund law school	77

Solicitors' Timetable

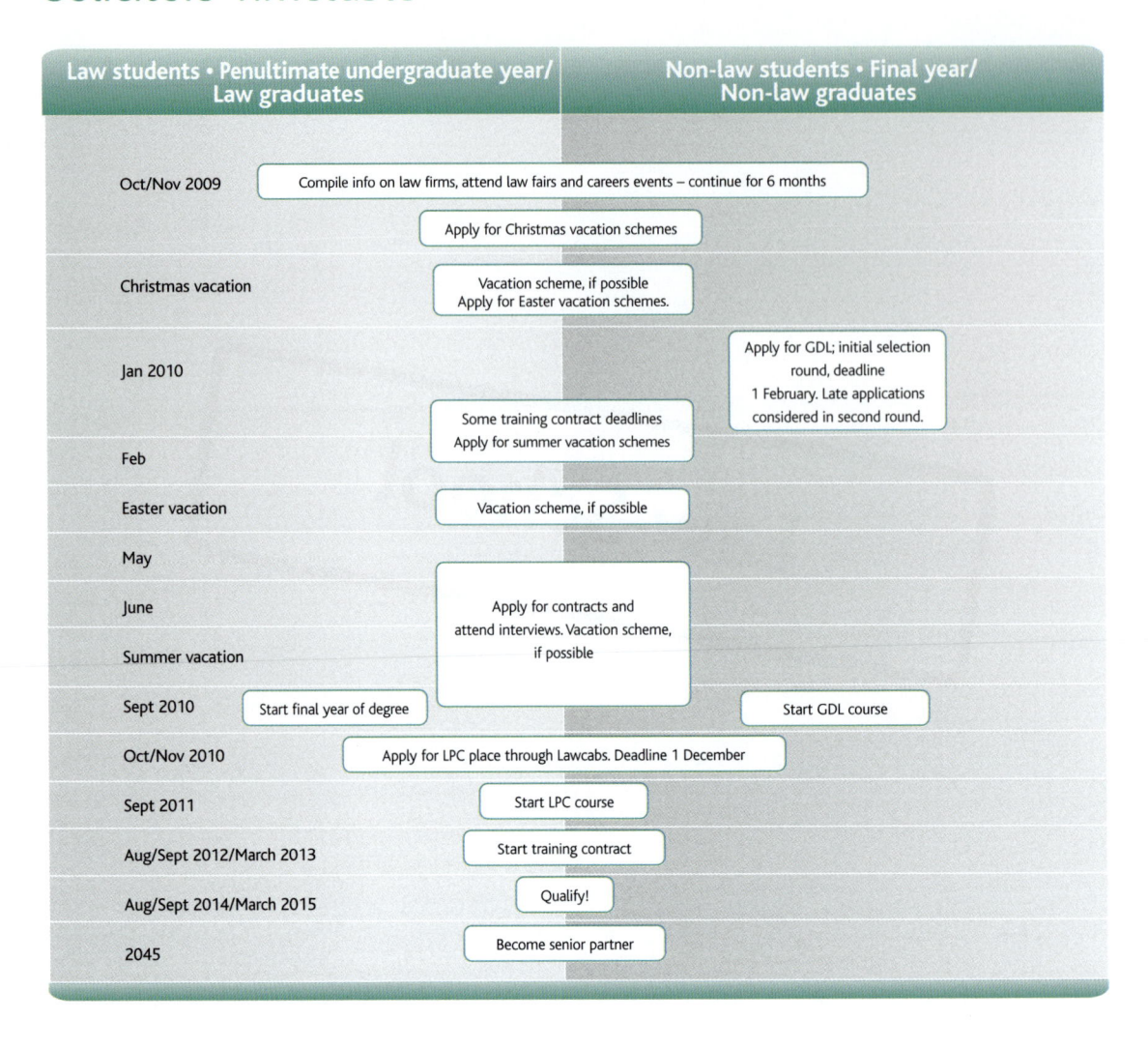

	Law students • Penultimate undergraduate year/ Law graduates	Non-law students • Final year/ Non-law graduates
Oct/Nov 2009	Compile info on law firms, attend law fairs and careers events – continue for 6 months	
	Apply for Christmas vacation schemes	
Christmas vacation	Vacation scheme, if possible. Apply for Easter vacation schemes.	
Jan 2010		Apply for GDL; initial selection round, deadline 1 February. Late applications considered in second round.
	Some training contract deadlines. Apply for summer vacation schemes	
Feb		
Easter vacation	Vacation scheme, if possible	
May		
June	Apply for contracts and attend interviews. Vacation scheme, if possible	
Summer vacation		
Sept 2010	Start final year of degree	Start GDL course
Oct/Nov 2010	Apply for LPC place through Lawcabs. Deadline 1 December	
Sept 2011	Start LPC course	
Aug/Sept 2012/March 2013	Start training contract	
Aug/Sept 2014/March 2015	Qualify!	
2045	Become senior partner	

Notes

1. It is important to check application closing dates for each firm as these will vary.
2. Some firms will only accept applications for vacation schemes from penultimate-year students, whether law or non-law. See A-Z pages for further information.
3. Some firms require very early applications from non-law graduates. See A-Z pages for further information.
4. The timetable refers primarily to those firms that recruit two years in advance. Smaller firms often recruit just one year in advance or for immediate vacancies.
5. This timetable assumes students will progress straight through from university to law school and a training contract. This is not necessarily the most appropriate course of action for all students.

Barristers' Timetable

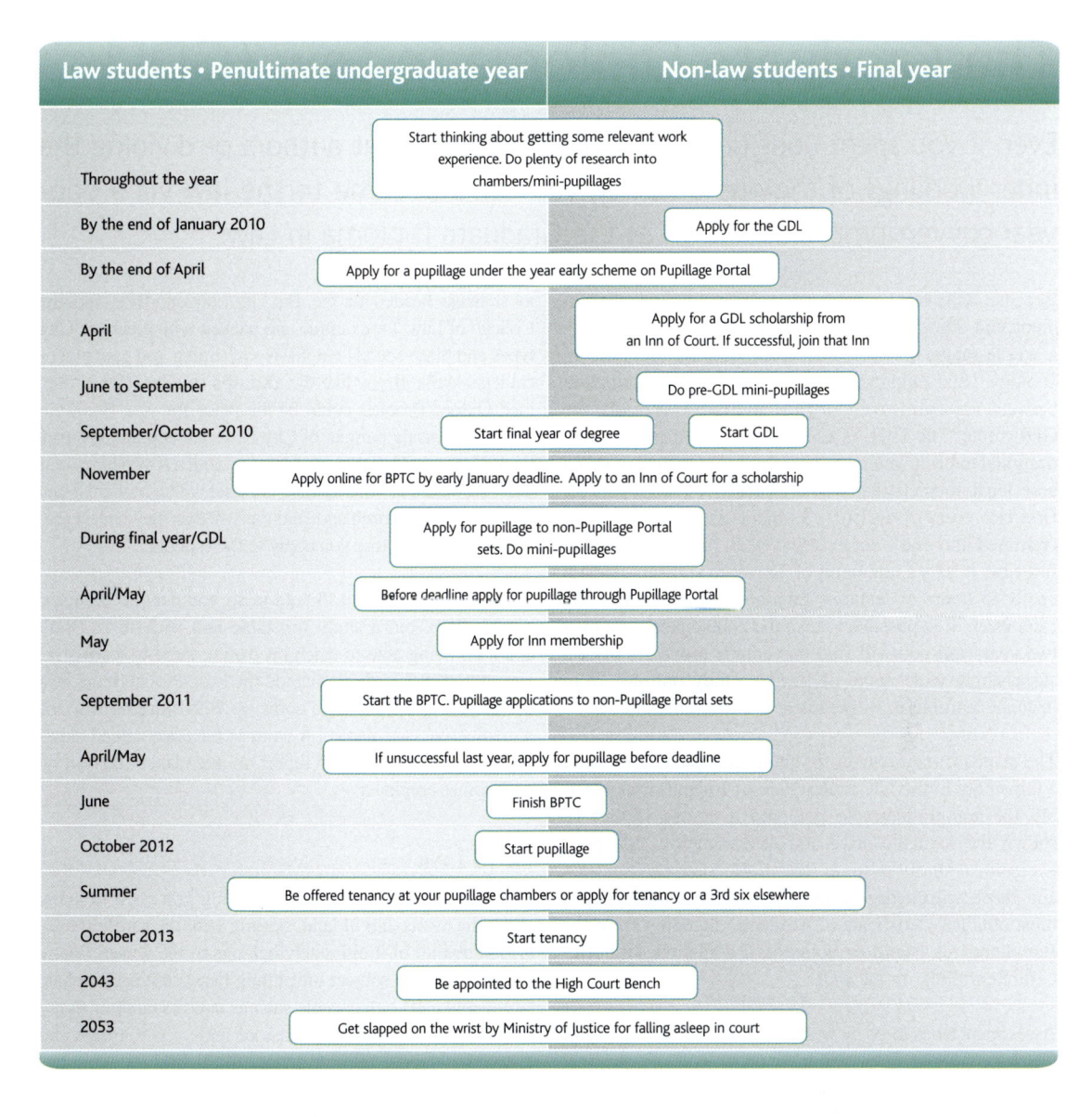

	Law students • Penultimate undergraduate year	Non-law students • Final year
Throughout the year		Start thinking about getting some relevant work experience. Do plenty of research into chambers/mini-pupillages
By the end of January 2010		Apply for the GDL
By the end of April	Apply for a pupillage under the year early scheme on Pupillage Portal	
April		Apply for a GDL scholarship from an Inn of Court. If successful, join that Inn
June to September		Do pre-GDL mini-pupillages
September/October 2010	Start final year of degree	Start GDL
November	Apply online for BPTC by early January deadline. Apply to an Inn of Court for a scholarship	
During final year/GDL	Apply for pupillage to non-Pupillage Portal sets. Do mini-pupillages	
April/May	Before deadline apply for pupillage through Pupillage Portal	
May	Apply for Inn membership	
September 2011	Start the BPTC. Pupillage applications to non-Pupillage Portal sets	
April/May	If unsuccessful last year, apply for pupillage before deadline	
June	Finish BPTC	
October 2012	Start pupillage	
Summer	Be offered tenancy at your pupillage chambers or apply for tenancy or a 3rd six elsewhere	
October 2013	Start tenancy	
2043	Be appointed to the High Court Bench	
2053	Get slapped on the wrist by Ministry of Justice for falling asleep in court	

Note

This timetable assumes students will progress straight through from university to law school and a pupillage. This is not necessarily the most appropriate or achievable course of action for students.

The Graduate Diploma in Law (GDL)

Even if you spent your undergrad years reading great authors or divining the inner workings of the human body, you can still come to the law via a one-year conversion course known as the Graduate Diploma in Law.

Because skills like textual analysis, research, logical argument, and written and oral presentation can be acquired in a whole range of disciplines from English literature to zoology, legal employers tend not to make a distinction between applicants with an LLB and those who take the GDL route. The GDL is essentially a crash law degree, designed to bring you up to the required standard in seven core legal subjects that would typically be taught in the first two years of an LLB. So that's two years of study crammed into one – not exactly a walk in the park. Taken full-time it lasts a minimum of 36 weeks and can demand up to 45 hours of lectures, tutorials and personal study each week. It is possible to take the course part-time over two years and you will find that course providers offer a surprisingly wide range of flexible study options, from distance learning to weekends or evening-only classes.

The standard requirement for admission is a degree from a university in the UK or Republic of Ireland. It is possible for non-graduates to get onto a course if they've shown the requisite drive and determination, and have exceptional ability in some other field. Such candidates – and those with a degree from an overseas university – must obtain a Certificate of Academic Standing from the Bar Standards Board or Solicitors Regulation Authority before enrolling on the GDL.

Assessment tends to be by written exams taken at the end of the academic year. These will make up the bulk of your final grade, so make sure you are adequately prepared. Most GDL providers offer their students the opportunity to take mock exams throughout the year, and while these are generally optional, it's probably a good idea to get as many as you can under your belt. If nothing else, they will give you an indication of your progress and the chance to receive feedback from tutors. Other assessments and essays completed during the year can count for up to 30% of your final grade so do not underestimate their importance. Depending on the institution, there will be more or less emphasis on academic essays, written problem questions or practical preparation for classroom debates. Because the institutions that offer the GDL vary in perceived quality, their approach and the composition of their student bodies, it is well worth doing your research before you apply. City University and Nottingham are renowned for offering more academic courses, thought to be ideally suited to students headed to the Bar. In London, BPP and the College of Law, for example, are packed with plenty of City types and place special emphasis on helping you gain practical legal skills. If you like the idea of a smaller GDL group, then Oxford Brookes could be the place for you. Be aware that an increasing number of City firms are appointing a particular law school as their preferred provider. If you have your heart set on doing your training contract with a particular law firm, do your research and find out whether they have a preferred provider before you apply to the schools.

There's a huge amount to take in so you need to be disciplined. Work out a study timetable and stick to it. Don't count on being able to catch up. You're there to learn a set curriculum, not to think outside the box. Probably the best use of your creativity is to come up with amusing ways of remembering case names. A word to the wise: attend classes! Some law schools will report on attendance if asked by your future employer.

Land law

This module will teach you everything you need to know about the ownership of land, starting with the startling realisation that all of it ultimately belongs to the Queen. Many students find the subject off-putting because it uses archaic jargon and calls on concepts such as overreaching or flying freeholds, which defy any sense of logic. Give it time and everything should fall into place. You'll find the topic has practical implications for everyday life, including tips on how to handle a dispute with your landlord or arrange your first mortgage. The course takes you through the basics of conveyancing and how to acquire interests in land before going through the detail of how those interests operate. The subject is formalistic and particularly statute-heavy. In addition to remembering loads of cases, you will be required to memorise countless statutory provisions on the creation and registration of interests in land. Don't wait to familiarise yourself with the most important sections of the Law of Property Act, start creating flowcharts and checklists early on and you will laugh your way through the exam. As with most topics on the GDL, you will need to gain a good overall understanding of land law to be able to deal with specific matters, so don't bet on revising selected subjects for the exam as there can be important overlap between them.

EU

EU law now affects our lives in many ways. This course should dispel a few misconceptions about the British membership of the European Union – it touches on far more than the way in which EU bureaucrats regulate the shape and size of bananas. You'll learn that the European Court of Justice (ECJ) is effectively the highest court of appeal for all the member states, and that EU law plays a central role in the creation of new rights against discrimination on grounds of age, disability, race, religion or sexual orientation, for example. Students become familiar with the institutional framework, foundations and underlying principles of the European Union before going on to explore certain areas of substantive EU law. Big subjects include the free movement of goods and workers, competition law and the freedom of establishment, as well as the incorporation of the European Convention on Human Rights into our national law. For Euro-philes, this course will provide a fascinating mix of politics, history, economics and comparative jurisprudence, but its case law contains some of the longest and most tongue-twisting names you're likely to see.

Equity and trusts

This course is an introduction to the fundamental principles of equity, an intriguing area of law which calls upon the idea of conscience to remedy injustices brought about by the application of black letter law. It also deals with the concept of trust, which is the legal arrangement whereby one person holds property for the benefit of another. Some assume the subject is the preserve of future Chancery barristers and private client specialists. While this is partially true, equity and trusts form a particularly dynamic area of law, and you'll not only learn about the creation of gifts and trusts in the family context, you'll also see that the concept has many uses in the commercial world, particularly where tax evasion or the tracing of misappropriated funds is concerned. The topic is mostly precedent-based, meaning that you'll have to memorise a huge number of cases. On the bright side, these can be amusing and memorable. You'll hear about adulterous husbands trying to set up secret trusts for their mistresses and illegitimate children or wealthy eccentrics attempting to set up a pension for a beloved pet. Be aware that the concept of equity pervades the GDL course, so what you've learned here will also be relevant to your land law and contract courses.

Contract

You probably already expect this course to be directly relevant to your everyday life. As a practising lawyer, you will apply your knowledge of contract law on a daily basis because it underpins nearly every single legal relationship. You'll start by studying the rules that determine when an agreement becomes legally binding and enforceable and which formalities are required to create a contract. You'll then move on to study what terms are permissible and find out what happens when you omit to read the small print. You'll hear about the doctrine of misrepresentation, mistake and duress, and you'll find out what your remedy is when an art dealer has neglected to tell you the Jackson Pollock you've just bought is actually the product of his son's finger painting. Armed with your knowledge of the Sale of Goods Act, you may be tempted to bring any number of small claims against the high-street retailers whose products fall apart the minute you get them home.

Crime

Studying criminal law will allow you to discover the reality behind the storylines of all those legal dramas you watch. The syllabus will take you through assault, battery, sexual offences, criminal damage, theft, fraud and homicide. Also covered are the liability of accomplices, attempted offences and the defences available to those accused of committing criminal acts. Whether your interest is in policy or the gruesome things that people do to one another, the crime course should provide plenty to engage and surprise. Overall, the subject follows a logical pattern and doesn't hide many difficult philosophical concepts. You will find out early on that you always need to identify the actus reus (the guilty act) and the mens rea (the guilty mind) in order to establish an offence. Follow this structure religiously and you can't go wrong. By the end of the course you'll also be in a better position to explain why killing someone is not necessarily unlawful or why you could be guilty of theft without actually making off with somebody else's property.

Tort

The law of tort is concerned with remedying wrongs committed by one individual against another via the civil rather than the criminal courts. Beyond this very sensible definition hides one of the most intellectually stimulating courses on the GDL. The law of negligence is the big subject and you will devote the best part of the year getting your head around it and applying it to specific situations such as clinical negligence. The course will also cover wrongs ranging from defamation to private nuisance. This is the field which fuels the so-called compensation culture and gives 'ambulance-chasing' lawyers a bad name. You will hear about the fate of victims of gruesome accidents and catastrophic events such as the Hillsborough disaster. You will also come across downright comical stories, including a prolific prankster playing a lavatory joke on a colleague or a case of compensation for scratchy underwear.

Public law

This course includes the study of constitutional law, human rights and administrative law. If you have no interest in politics, you may find the whole subject a little obscure, but ten years on since the passing of the Human Rights Act, and with several constitutional reforms in the works, now is arguably the best of times to study this fascinating subject. The course will normally kick off with an analysis of the UK's constitutional arrangements. This largely academic part covers the doctrines of Parliamentary sovereignty, the Rule of Law, the Royal Prerogative and Responsible Government. Those with politics degrees will hit the ground running. You're likely to enjoy the constitutional bit of the subject if you're a history or philosophy buff. If you do not fit the description, why not Google 'Dicey' and see where that takes you. You'll also be taught about the Human Rights Act with particular emphasis being given to the concepts of freedom of speech, privacy, the right to a fair trial and the nitty-gritty of exactly how much force the police can use when they throw you in the back of their van. After the academic bit is over, much of the rest of the course is devoted to judicial review, the process by which individuals can challenge the decisions of public authorities.

How to apply

In addition to the seven core subjects, certain GDL providers, particularly those with a City slant, offer optional classes designed to ease your passage into the corporate world. These may include additional lectures or seminars on company law, intellectual property and international law. Most also organise mooting competitions and pro bono work. These should give you an early opportunity to try your counselling and advocacy skills and find out if a legal career is really for you, particularly if you're headed for the Bar. A number of providers have degree-awarding powers allowing you to upgrade your qualification to an LLB, either upon successful completion of your GDL and LPC or after a summer course following the GDL. Unlike the GDL, the LLB gives you an internationally recognised accreditation.

Apply online through the Central Applications Board (www.lawcabs.ac.uk). Get your application in as early as possible if you have your heart set on a particular institution, particularly as your referee needs to respond before your application is passed on to your chosen schools. First-round applications for the 2010/11 course can be made between 2 November and 1 February. The institutions will consider these and make offers from 8 March; students must accept a first-round offer by 16 April. Applications made later than 2 February will be considered after 16 April. The later you apply the more flexible you may have to be about where you study. Applications for part-time courses should be made directly to the providers.

The GDL Providers

- University of Birmingham (ft)
- Birmingham City University (ft/pt)
- Bournemouth University (ft/pt)
- BPP Law School, Bristol (ft/pt)
- BPP Law School, Leeds (ft/pt)
- BPP Law School, London (ft/pt)
- BPP Law School, Manchester (ft/pt)
- University of Bradford (ft/pt)
- University of Brighton (pt)
- Bristol Institute of Legal Practice (ft/pt)
- Brunel University (ft)
- University of Central Lancashire (ft/pt)
- The City Law School (ft)
- College of Law, Birmingham (ft/pt)
- College of Law, Bristol (ft/pt)
- College of Law, Chester (ft/pt)
- College of Law, Guildford (ft/pt)
- College of Law, London (ft/pt)
- College of Law, Manchester (ft/pt)
- College of Law, York (ft/pt)
- De Montfort University (ft/pt)
- University of East Anglia (ft)
- University of East London (ft)
- University of Glamorgan (ft/pt)
- University of Hertfordshire (ft/pt)
- University of Huddersfield (ft/pt)
- Kaplan Law School (ft)
- Keele University (ft/pt)
- Kingston University (ft/pt)
- Leeds Metropolitan University (ft/pt)
- University of Lincoln (ft)
- London Metropolitan University (ft/pt)
- London South Bank University (ft/pt)
- Manchester Metropolitan University (ft/pt)
- Middlesex University (ft/pt)
- Northumbria University Law School (ft/pt)
- Nottingham Law School (ft/pt)
- Oxford Brookes University (ft/pt)
- University of Plymouth (ft)
- Sheffield Hallam University (ft/pt)
- Southampton Solent University (ft/pt)
- Staffordshire University (ft/pt)
- Worcester College of Technology at Worcester (pt)
- University of Sunderland
- University of Sussex (ft)
- Swansea University (ft)
- Thames Valley University (ft/pt)
- University of Westminster (ft/pt)
- University of Wolverhampton (ft/pt)

Gender and the law

45% of solicitors on the Roll are women

1922 first woman solicitor Carrie Morrison admitted

63% of law graduates are women

51% of pupils are men

69% of self-employed and **54%** of employed barristers are men

63% of trainees are women

29% the gender pay gap in the law (6% higher than the national average for UK workers)

There is **one** woman Lord of Appeal in Ordinary

11% of equity partners in the Magic Circle are women*

£10,000 the average difference between the salaries of male and female solicitors*

One **fifth** of women solicitors are partners, compared to two fifths of men*

90% of Queen's Counsel are men

Reasons women leave the law
To look after children (27.5%)
To go on maternity leave (18.5%)
Did not enjoy the job (12.8%)
To try something else (10.9%)
Health reasons (7.6%)
Stress (7.6%)

Eleven High Court Justices are women

Three Lord Justice of Appeals are women

All figures from the **Law Society** and **Bar Council** in 2009   *Figures from **Law Society** report of 2007

The Legal Practice Course (LPC)

After a law degree or GDL, prospective solicitors must tackle the LPC. It's a mammoth challenge and rather expensive, so before you fire off an application think carefully about what you want to achieve and how likely you are to succeed.

Most people have tended to view a career in the law as more immune than most to the vagaries of the economy. Sadly, we've seen that the most recent economic slump has been just as problematic for the legal sector as for others. A cursory glance at the legal press reveals just how many solicitors – and their support colleagues – have lost their jobs, and in many cases their livelihoods. Firms from all quarters of the legal profession have deferred the start of their training schemes; new lawyers reaching the end of their training contracts have suffered in relatively large numbers too. To face unemployment as soon as you qualify must be both gutting and financially crippling. These somewhat daunting facts are not made any more palatable when you consider the costs involved in taking the requisite vocational course – the LPC. The situation has reached the stage where the Law Society has undertaken an advertising campaign warning would-be lawyers of the risks of committing to the profession. To be specific, it warns students from starting the LPC without careful thought. Why so? Simply this: every year a certain proportion of LPC students purchase a course that will give them qualifications they will never use. Right now this number is higher than ever.

So should you take the plunge and sign up to the LPC if you haven't yet secured a training contract? First of all, take a good, honest look at your CV and ask whether it really matches up to what firms are asking for. Have a think about what else you could be doing. Are there any other CV-enhancing opportunities open to you? Is there anything you'd like to achieve or places you'd like to visit before knuckling down to a demanding career? Law firm recruiters look out for applicants who've had interesting experiences or come with industry knowledge. These things really will help you to distinguish yourself from the competition.

The Solicitors Regulation Authority (SRA) has not been blind to the impending logjam of wannabe lawyers. In an attempt to improve the odds for aspiring solicitors it has introduced a new course called the LPC3. This course must be run at all 'providers' from 2010/11, although a number of them are already offering their new courses to the 2009/10 intake. The Bar Standards Board (BSB) is the equivalent regulatory body for the Bar and it is facing its own challenges. It too is introducing a new course. While both regulatory bodies have similar goals – namely to ensure that those students who complete the courses are capable and well prepared for practice – the BSB has taken the path of greater uniformity, while the SRA has given the nod to providers to allow them to run increasingly flexible and diverse courses. Only time will tell which approach has the greatest merit.

Counting the pennies

First things first, how much will an LPC set you back? For those who have training contract offers from a generous commercial firm this won't be a major cause for concern as their future employers will foot the bill for course fees and stump up a living allowance. See which firms offer what on page 521. A majority of LPC students aren't so fortunate and need to self-fund both the course fees and their own living costs. There are variations in cost between providers, but none could be described as cheap and some are downright expensive, especially to those who already carry a debt burden from university. In short the price of an LPC ranges from just over £7,000 to more than £12,000. For a comprehensive comparison of course fees look at the **LPC Providers Table** on our website.

One option for future legal aid solicitors is a scheme run by the Legal Services Commission (LSC). The legal aid sector has been struggling for some time and as a result the number of students going into the field has shrunk. The LSC sets aside an annual figure of £3m to help fund students who agree to go into this type of practice for at least two years after qualification. Only around 150 students benefit from the funding annually, but each grant covers 60% of the cost of the LPC so it is certainly worth investigating. The grants are awarded via selected law firms so don't try to apply to the LSC direct. If you want to know which firms are involved, this information is posted on the LSC website. Just as the law firms who fund their future trainees require a say as to which elective subjects students take, so too does the LSC. Beneficiaries of the grant must concentrate on subjects that are pertinent to high-street firms, law centres and local authorities.

Law firm-funded students may make their peers green with envy but they need to realise there is no such thing as a free lunch. With each passing year the conditions imposed on such students become more stringent. Ten years ago few firms cared which LPC provider you chose. Now, more and more have signed up to firm-specific LPCs or require future joiners to attend a specific provider. This has been criticised for creating a two-tier system, limiting choice and stifling diversity, since students headed for the corporate giants won't interact very much with students destined for other kinds of careers. However, law firms like it because it means they get more for their money; future trainees get into the mindset of the firm, learn the firm's internal day-to-day procedures and start to understand the firm's areas of expertise sooner.

Very nitty, very gritty

The LPC is intended to give students a practical insight into the day-to-day requirements of the job of a solicitor and, as such, represents a middle ground between the academic rigours of a law degree or the GDL and life as a trainee solicitor. It doesn't quite teach you BlackBerry etiquette or how to bundle documents for court, but it is chock full of handy tips for the pragmatic solicitor, including: the difference between a balance sheet and a profit and loss account; how much income tax HMRC will take from your first pay cheque; how to determine whether the tenant or the landlord is responsible for fixing a hole in the roof; whether a company can loan money to a director's wife; what documents you do and don't need to disclose to the other side in a dispute; who you can act for and who you can't; and your duties to the court.

Many people find the course somewhat mundane after enjoying the relative freedom of thought and expression of an academic law course, but the LPC does teach skills not previously touched on at university. Students can gain invaluable insight into the practical realities of the job and they learn the benefits of things like keeping well-organised files. The best advice is to approach the course with as much enthusiasm as possible, get your head down and accept that, while there is a degree of rote learning involved, all those classes on board meeting sandwiches and the Civil Procedure Rules will be worth it in the end. The LPC does have its amusing points – when participating in mock advocacy and having to refer obsequiously to the assessor in front of you as 'master', you may feel less like a lawyer and more like an extra from an episode of *Doctor Who*.

A new age

The new LPC3 gives providers a greater degree of flexibility when deciding what should be included in each of the compulsory units that form Stage 1 of the course, and the fact that the providers can now divorce the elective-filled Stage 2 technically means that students have more choice than ever when choosing where and how they wish to study.

Students must continue to take the compulsory units of the course first, and these still consist of Business Law and Practice (BLP), which incorporates Partnerships, Company Law, Tax and Insolvency; Property Law and Practice (PLP) and Litigation. The LPC3 allows providers to adapt the units as they see fit in order to place increased emphasis on the types of practice their students are most likely to encounter in their future careers. For example, those providers catering predominantly for students who will go into high-street practice may include a higher percentage of criminal law on the Litigation course and a pared-down version of the Business Law and Practice. The City-oriented providers may include additional finance or acquisitions elements within their BLP courses. The remainder of Stage 1 comprises Skills units and a Conduct unit.

For Stage 2 of the course students will still choose three elective subjects. There is a vast array of topics on offer across the 29 providers, so make sure you know which electives are available at your preferred providers. For a full list of who offers what, again, refer to the **LPC Providers Table** on our website.

Thanks to the diversity of LPC3 courses on offer it is more important than ever to find an appropriate provider. You don't want to find yourself on a high street-focused LPC if you are yearning for a commercial training contact, or to be stuck learning about derivatives if you see yourself as a high-street solicitor à la Stephen Fry in *Kingdom*.

The timeframe in which the course can be completed has also been tinkered with. For example, BPP is already putting some City-bound LPC students through an accelerated seven-month course, and Thames Valley University is hoping that its part-timers will be able to finish in just 18 months rather than the usual two years. As well as acceleration there is also more leeway for students to take their time over the course. As Stages 1 and 2 are now technically divorced from one another, students could study Stage 1, either on a full or part-time basis, take some time off and then study one elective every year, perhaps with some more breaks in between. The only requirement is that you finish within a five-year period. Having spoken to all the providers it strikes us that most are sceptical about how many students will choose to study in such drawn-out way, and not all are allowing their full-time courses to be split up like this. However there are plenty of providers out there, and with nine in London alone students are sure to find one which structures the course to suit them.

The war

As the legal profession continues to cope with an ailing economy, the biggest LPC providers are waging a war for supremacy in the legal education world. The two frontrunners are BPP Law School and the College of Law (COL), both of which have ambitious plans for expansion over the next two years. Remarkably they have chosen to go head to head with each other in Birmingham and Bristol, despite the fact that they are already competing in Manchester and London. Each has applied to the SRA for validation for more LPC places, and it's happening at a time when students' employment prospects are shrinking. You'd hope the increase in places would drive down the cost of the course. Sadly, we only saw increases this year. A handful of the LPC providers seem excessively preoccupied with the race to sign deals with large law firms to provide either tailor-made electives or entire bespoke courses. As these marriages of convenience between law firms and LPC providers become commonplace it's beginning to look like the individual self-funded student is dropping down the list of priorities at some providers.

Choosing where to study

There are plenty of things to think about when choosing an LPC provider, so arm yourself with as much information as possible. Request prospectuses, attend open days, chat to representatives visiting your university, talk to current students and ascertain your priorities. Obviously if you have a training contract then your employer may well dictate where you should go, however if you have a free choice then here are some issues to take into consideration.

Career path: Even if a future employer doesn't specify where you must study they may still be able to offer advice. If you don't yet have a training contract, look into the range of extra-curricular activities, clubs and societies on offer that may bolster your CV. Also think about the quality of careers advice available at each institution. Will they help to organise placements for you? Will they support you after you have finished the course, and if so for how long?

Electives: If you have the freedom to choose your electives then find out which providers offer the most suitable ones for the type of practice you want to move into, or at least which ones appeal to you the most. Although most providers offer a pretty standard package, some do throw in the odd wildcard such as E-Commerce or Charity Law. For a full list see our website.

Assessment grades and pass rates: Pass rates are published on the SRA's website each autumn and a comparison of the marks achieved by students from different providers is now available on our website. However, be aware that direct comparisons are difficult as each provider examines and marks independently of the others. The SRA visits and inspects each provider and then publishes a report.

When and how: Timetables can vary wildly between providers, with some only requiring attendance for two days a week and others scheduling face-to-face time on four days, either mornings or afternoons. Term dates can also vary substantially, and with the onset of the LPC3 so can the length of the whole course. Think realistically about what timetable structure will fit most easily into your life. Also think about whether or not you will need to work during the course. While all providers are reluctant to acknowledge that students will be able to fit in a part-time job, they have an increasing understanding of the economic realities and some timetables are more accommodating than others. If working during the course is unavoidable you may want to consider studying part-time.

The use of e-learning resources has become an increasingly popular method of delivering the LPC. COL, for example, no longer incorporates lectures into its LPC, so instead of sitting in large theatres with 200-odd other students being taught in real time by real people, you'll assimilate the lecture information via online i-tutorials. These are backed up and built upon in face-to-face, small-group workshops. Meanwhile, the use of online learning is becoming even more pervasive at BPP, which is rolling out an entirely remote learning LPC thus rendering physical attendance entirely unnecessary. Lectures are still available to those that want them, as are face-to-face small-group sessions. Some students thrive on electronic learning methods, and part-time students in particular appreciate being able to fit the work around their already busy lives. However, working from home does require a degree of dedication and self-discipline and so think carefully about what mode of teaching will suit you best before you sign up.

Assessments: The vast majority of providers examine their students using open-book exams and written assessments. A notable minority have stuck with the closed-book approach. Think carefully about what method will suit you best. It is easy to feel drawn to the open-book approach, however the time frames are such that you have very little time to check your books in the exam room and so having a leaning tower of Pisa built of resource materials on your desk is not as advantageous as it might seem.

Facilities: For every provider at which students must search plaintively for a quiet study corner, there is another where they can spread out in blessed peace in their own 'office'. Take the LPC course at a university and you'll belong to a proper law faculty (complete with Klix coffee machine and last week's *Independent*); elsewhere, leather sofas and acres of plate glass might make you think you've strayed into the offices of a City firm. Given the importance of IT to the LPC course, you should consider whether the institution offers endless vistas of the latest flat screens or a few dusty typewriters in a basement.

Atmosphere and direction: A large institution may appeal to students keen to chug anonymously through the system. Conversely, the intimacy of fewer students and easily accessible tutors may tip the scales in favour of a smaller provider. Some places are known to attract Oxbridge types destined to be City high-flyers; others cultivate the talents of those headed for regional practice. Still others purport to offer a mix of students, so the commercially minded can mingle with future high-street practitioners. These distinctions are likely to become increasingly pronounced when the LPC3 gets into full flow, so do consider which flavour of LPC you're after.

Money and location: Fees vary and so do the providers' policies on the inclusion of the cost of textbooks and Law Society membership, etc. Even if you have sponsorship, living expenses still need to be taken into account. The cost of living in London can be an especially nasty shock. Plenty of students find that tight finances restrict their choice of provider. Living with parents will save you a packet of course but if you are striking out on your own (or you haven't lived with The Olds for some time), it's worth considering what you like or don't like about your university or GDL provider and whether you want to prolong your undergraduate experience or escape it. Be aware that certain LPC providers are dominated by graduates of local universities. When weighing up providers in large cities, find out whether the campus is in the city centre or out on a ring road.

Social mix and social life: Studenty cities such as Nottingham and Bristol are always a lot of fun, but the bright lights of the capital may be irresistible. Experience tells us that compared to those in other cities many students in London tend to slink off the moment classes end.

Making applications

The Central Applications Board (www.lawcabs.ac.uk) administers all applications for full-time LPCs and the application form is available from 1 October. Those applications for 2010/11 full-time courses received by 1 December 2009 go into the first round and offers are made from 1 February. Later applications are processed in a second round with offers made from 12 March. Applications received any later than that date are processed as and when received. Later applicants' chances of securing a place at a popular provider are reduced, but be aware that nationwide there are more validated places than enrolled students on both full and part-time courses. Some of the most popular institutions must be placed first on the LawCabs application form. This type of information is in the **LPC Providers Table** on our website. Check also whether your university, GDL provider or future law firm has a useful agreement or relationship with a provider. Applications for part-time courses should be made directly to the providers.

The LPC Providers

Aberystwyth University (ft)
Anglia Ruskin University (ft/pt)
Birmingham City University (ft/pt)
Bournemouth University (ft)
BPP Law School, Birmingham (ft/pt)
BPP Law School, Bristol (ft/pt)
BPP Law School, Leeds (ft/pt)
BPP Law School, London (ft/pt)
BPP Law School, Manchester (ft/pt)
Bristol Institute of Legal Practice at UWE (ft/pt)
Cardiff Law School (ft)
University of Central Lancashire (ft/pt)
The City Law School (ft/pt)
College of Law, Birmingham (ft/pt)
College of Law, Bristol (ft/pt)
College of Law, Chester (ft/pt)
College of Law, Guildford (ft/pt)
College of Law, London (ft/pt)
College of Law, Manchester (ft)
College of Law, York (ft/pt)
De Montfort University (ft/pt)
University of Glamorgan (ft/pt)
University of Hertfordshire (ft/pt)
University of Huddersfield (ft/pt)
Kaplan Law School (ft)
Leeds Metropolitan University (ft/pt)
Liverpool John Moores University (ft/pt)
London Metropolitan University (ft/pt)
Manchester Metropolitan University (ft/pt)
Northumbria University Law School (ft/pt)
Nottingham Law School (ft/pt)
Oxford Institute of Legal Practice (ft/pt)
University of Plymouth (ft)
University of Sheffield (ft/pt)
Staffordshire University (ft/pt)
Swansea University (ft)
Thames Valley University (ft/pt)
University of Westminster (ft/pt)
University of Wolverhampton (ft/pt)

LPC provider reports

There are now so many places to take the LPC, so how do you pick the best one for you?

On our website there is a table detailing all the providers and allowing a comparison of their fees, student numbers, available option subjects and useful tips for applicants. Use it in conjunction with the following provider reports to make your selections. These reports were compiled after speaking to past students and course leaders.

Aberystwyth University
Number of places: 100 full-time

Aber was once ranked the UK's favourite university town for its sense of community and facilities, and it is easy to see why. The university's LPC is taught at a town centre location and students are guaranteed accommodation. The countryside surrounding the university is fantastic as it overlooks the stunning Cardigan Bay. The university aims to provide friendly and personalised teaching, and this can be seen in the importance that it places on face-to-face tuition and an active careers service. The service inserts careers sessions and pro bono work into students' timetables to ensure that their CVs are up to scratch. Aber is waiting until 2010 to start its LPC3, so at the time of going to press the focus of this course and the changes that it will bring were unknown.

Anglia Ruskin University
Number of places: 70 full-time, 40 part-time

Students who plump for Anglia Ruskin will find themselves in a *"small and personal cohort, where they can expect to work hard, but be properly looked after throughout."* The LPC is taught at two different sites depending on whether you're a full-time or part-time student. The part-time course is run in Cambridge; full-timers study in a brand new faculty building in Chelmsford. Approximately two-thirds of the teaching is delivered at small group sessions of no more than 20 students, the remainder at large groups. Anglia is also piloting the provision of business lectures through online streaming from 2010. The university targets those students who are aiming for medium-sized, mixed-practice firms and employers, and it has a mentoring scheme involving local practitioners to help students achieve their goals. There is also a programme of lectures by visiting legal professionals, held in Chelmsford.

Birmingham City University
Number of places: 120 full-time, 40 part-time

Based outside the city centre on the City North campus, BCU has established itself as an LPC provider of choice for Midlands students whose ambitions centre on high-street and smaller regional commercial firms. While the course is set up to cater for all, the choice of electives is such that even the most hardened Gordon Gekko-type could find something to suit. In reality, those Midlands students heading for bigger commercial firms are likely to choose COL or BPP. As is the trend with other providers, BCU is moving towards delivering large-group teaching via online tutorials and this has allowed it to cut the number of hours that students have be on campus. The university has by no means abandoned face-to-face teaching altogether, and large-group lectures still take place, albeit in a shortened format which is supplemented by the online materials. Small-group sessions are taught in groups of 15-18. All in all, students on the full-time course are expected in on three days each week and the part-timers on two evenings each week. The law school at BCU prides itself on its welcoming atmosphere and the accessibility of its staff. Indeed, the lecturer we interviewed had already had three visits from students that day, and this was in the middle of August. The school's supportive ethos is also found in its careers service and students have access to a careers tutor as well as a personal tutor. Many sign up for a highly successful mentoring scheme that pairs students with local solicitors at all levels of the profession. The focus of the programme is on personal contact and support through the application and interview process and it also helps students to build invaluable links with the profession.

Bournemouth University
Number of places: 96 full-time

Former students speak warmly about their time at Bournemouth University, thanks to the small cohort which gives the location *"a real sense of community."* The only detracting comment came from a former student who said: *"If I were to have my time again I think I would prefer a more dedicated legal provider, rather than being somewhere where the proportion of non-law students far outweighs us lawyers.*" The teaching was praised by past students, although some felt it to be quite "*spoon-fed.*" There are a full range of financial incentives for students choosing Bournemouth. These include academic, citizenship, musical and sporting scholarships, and there are also some hardship grants and bursaries available. During the year there are a number of competitions for students to participate in, as well as links with the local legal profession, including the Dorset Magistrates Association. The course is taught within the Business School on the university's Talbot Campus.

BPP

With branches across the country and new locations opening up in Bristol and Birmingham in 2010, BPP is going from strength to strength in spite of the recent doom and gloom in the legal profession. The past year has been a time of considerable change for the company due to investment by US education provider Apollo. BPP hopes that this will have a positive impact on the student experience. For example, BPP aims to learn from some of Apollo's US-based education providers (eg the University of Phoenix), not least with regard to back office functions. Apollo's investment has given BPP access to a wealth of new ideas for its online teaching resources, which will undoubtedly supplement its already established remote-teaching programme. What won't change is the businesslike environment that is characteristic of all BPP's locations. Students describe these as "*slick, shiny and crammed full of hi-tech kit,*" if "*a tad soulless.*" Unfortunately this kind of set-up comes at a premium and BPP is the most expensive of the LPC providers.

BPP has done well to establish itself as one of the leaders among those providers offering firm-specific LPCs, and an increasing number of firms require their future trainees to go there. These include Macfarlanes, Simmons & Simmons, Freshfields, Norton Rose, Slaughter and May, Herbert Smith and Lovells. As this list suggests, the emphasis is very much on commercial and City practice, and it is rare to come across a student at BPP in London who yearns for a career in public legal services or at a high-street firm. The student body at each of the regional branches is noticeably more diverse when it comes to career aspirations.

One comment that we hear time and again is that the course is focused on getting students through their exams, rather than inspiring them. One student summed this up neatly when they said: "*I thought it was a good means to an end. The teaching is exceptional in terms of providing you with everything you need for the exam, but it is not an academic course and you shouldn't expect it to be like that.*"

The LPC3 has introduced several changes to the way the course is taught. Students heading for certain firms will now take an accelerated seven-month long course, which will run from August to February and from March to September to fit in with their firms' March and September training contract start dates. The remaining full-time students will continue to take the course over a full academic year but will be able to opt to timetable classes on two, three or four days a week. Full-time BPP students will not be able to divorce Stage 1 from Stage 2 of the LPC3, and so if you start the course you will have to pay for both stages. Part-time students will be able to divorce the two stages if needed. The other key change to note is that the Business Law & Practice element of the compulsories will be even more City-focused than previously. Furthermore, after a successful pilot in 2008/09, it will now be possible to study the LPC at BPP entirely remotely. In such cases, students from across the UK – and perhaps beyond – will join real-time small-group sessions led online by a tutor sat at their desk at BPP. Online learning is also being rolled out to a greater extent, although it will be up to students how much they want to take advantage of it and face-to-face teaching will not be superseded. The buzzwords at BPP are 'blended learning'.

When it comes to exams, BPP is very much in the minority of providers: it uses closed rather than open-book assessments. Some query whether this accurately reflects practice or is more of a memory test, however it certainly makes students focus on the course from day one.

The careers service is praised by students who attended each of the BPP locations. Said one: "*There are weekly e-mails about jobs and regular workshops on interviews and assessment. People are also encouraged to get involved in the pro bono schemes on offer.*" Careers staff offer students individual appointments to review their CVs and prepare them for the application process with mock interviews. For those who haven't had enough by the end of the course, BPP has run an LLM programme since 2008. The programme can be taken either full-time over the summer or part-time over a longer period.

BPP Law School, Birmingham
Open from 2010

BPP Law School, Bristol
Open from 2010

BPP Law School, Leeds
Numbers of places: 454 full-time equivalents

Past students were full of praise for the facilities at BPP Leeds. One said: "*It is a lovely size and the facilities were a lot better and newer than at my university.*" This branch is ideally located five minutes' walk from the train station, making it accessible to students who need to commute from a distance. The teaching is felt to be strong, with comments from recent graduates suggesting that "*tutors are young and enthusiastic, and generally they haven't been out of practice that long, so they can give you a good idea of what working as a solicitor is going to be like.*" BPP's Leeds centre runs many pro bono activities and boasts the North's only IP Centre of Excellence, through which students can help local businesses and individuals protect their intellectual property rights. While there is "*a good mix of electives for different types of practice,*" students are under no illusion that "*other local providers are aimed more at general practice and smaller types of firms.*"

BPP Law School, London

Number of places: Holborn full-time 1,588, part-time 302; Waterloo full-time 265, part-time 57

BPP is based in two locations in London, and most LPC students will study at the Holborn headquarters, although late applicants are often placed at the Waterloo branch. The facilities are impressive and visitors could be forgiven for thinking that they had walked into the offices of a City firm rather than an education provider. Students rather like studying in BPP's swanky environment, not least because they can see what their money is buying. This must be reassuring because, while all BPP's branches are expensive, the London fees trump them all. This led a few of our sources to suggest some of BPP's practices are a bit tight; for example: "*Free printing runs out pretty quickly and it is 5p a sheet afterwards which I got bit pissed off about.*"

The teaching is praised by students who tell us: "*The tutors are really keen and they want you to do well, not just alright,*" although the course materials are often found to be a touch uninspiring. In the view of one past student, "*a lot of it is really dry so it's amazing that the teachers can stay enthusiastic.*" Another highlighted "*the systematic nature if the course, which felt too much like a conveyor belt at the time.*" There is also no doubting the type of student BPP London attracts and, for some people, "*at times it can seem quite overbearingly corporate*" and "*there are loads of very driven and competitive City types... to the exclusion of others.*" Whatever their career goals, students can get involved with a host of pro bono opportunities including an environmental law clinic and projects enabling students with foreign language skills to provide legal translation services.

BPP Law School, Manchester

Number of places: 378 full-time, 118 part-time

The past year has not been kind to BPP's Manchester operation and it was forced to make staff redundancies. A dip in student applications is no doubt the result of more than one factor, namely the opening of the College of Law (COL) in the city and the economic downturn. Interestingly, it seems that Manchester's other provider (Manchester Metropolitan University) is faring somewhat better than expected in the face of added competition, which is perhaps illustrative of the fact that the 'professional providers' often attract different students to the universities.

The focus of the course is very much on preparing students to work in sizeable commercial firms, even so the range of students is broader here in Manchester than elsewhere and past students report that "*a lot of people were going to smaller regionals as well as bigger firms.*" The recent dip in applications is certainly nothing to do with either the teaching or the facilities, both of which are deemed excellent. In all likelihood, BPP's higher price is the key deciding factor for Manchester-bound LPCers. At least some feel they are getting value for their money: "*Other providers feel more like schools or colleges, but BPP is very nicely done up and has the feel of an office, which is great.*" And as one student pointed out, "*they push you quite hard to get the best grade that you're capable of, but in a really supportive way.*"

Bristol Institute of Legal Practice at UWE

Number of places: 400 full-time and part-time

Unfortunately despite repeated requests we were unable to obtain an interview with a representative at UWE, and as a result we have been unable to ask what they think about the imminent arrival in Bristol of the two behemoths of legal education – BPP and COL. We can only surmise that this will present a significant challenge to UWE, which has until now enjoyed a monopoly in the thriving legal education market in this attractive corner of the UK. September 2009 heralds the commencement of the LPC3 at UWE and it has brought in a new timetable with the options to take classes on two days a week, or four mornings or four afternoons a week. Small-group workshops have also been shortened to two and a half hours. Students will still have the option of attending lectures, but individual tutors will also be able to develop their own alternatives in the form of handouts, podcasts or interactive online lectures, depending on what they think best fulfils the needs of their students. UWE has one of the broadest range of electives and boasts 15 different options, including charity law, media and entertainment, and separate electives for commercial contracts and IP. This undoubtedly goes some way towards explaining why graduates end up at a diverse range of firms.

On the whole students enjoy their experiences here. They tell us "*the course is brilliantly structured*" and that "*the tutors and administrative staff are always willing to help.*

They're not academics sat in ivory towers, they've been out and done it. They can make black and white law seem alive." Students also appreciate the small class sizes and comment that "by the time you end the course you seem to know most people." UWE is one of the providers that allows students to top up their LPC with an LLM.

There is one small problem. Actually, though it's been small until now, it could be rather big from 2010. UWE's campus is "right on the outskirts of Bristol" and numerous past students have told us they would have much preferred to be in the centre of town. While Bristol is chock full of bars, cafés and restaurants, the fact that it's all a drive away from the campus definitely dampens students' social life. The coming competition from COL and BPP must surely force UWE to deal with this elephant in the room.

Cardiff Law School

Number of places: 200 full-time

As one student put it, "Cardiff is absolutely brilliant. It was a pleasure to study there and I felt that it was an excellent gateway into the world of law. I now feel well armed and prepared for my legal future!" Indeed, Cardiff's highly rated course is a fantastic choice for all kinds of Wales-based students thanks to its broad nature. It is suitable for students headed to high-street firms and for future city slickers. At present about half of the student body are graduates from Cardiff Uni, the rest being an assortment of individuals from across the UK, most with some kind of link to the area. Face-to-face teaching is still a priority at Cardiff, although much of the large-group material is now reinforced by resources that are stored on an online blackboard system. Cardiff is equipped with plenty of the hi-tech wizardry. There is a mock courtroom and classrooms incorporate interactive smartboards that can save what is written on them and link to websites to illustrate discussions.

The new LPC3 has allowed the timetable to be streamlined so Cardiff now offers a choice between morning and afternoon sessions. Notable effort is made to help students secure training contracts, and one popular initiative is a placement scheme whereby students spend a short time with a local legal employer. Last year these included the local office of national juggernaut Eversheds, as well as with smaller firms and the legal departments of public sector organisations. Additionally there's a wealth of pro bono opportunities. The Innocence Project, for example, deals with long-term prisoners, and the pro bono unit has also developed a niche in assistance to elderly and infirm clients. Many such people need to ascertain whether their care is categorised as nursing or social care in order to determine who should foot the bill. This latter project is supervised by another major Welsh firm, Hugh James. The social life is thought to be another highlight. Not only do students benefit from being members of a large and flourishing university, they also select "highly active and imaginative" social committees.

City Law School

Number of places: 176 full-time and part-time

City Law School (formerly Inns of Court School of Law) is perhaps better known for training would-be barristers. Over the past eight years it has established itself as one of the capital's top LPC providers, and its reputation is such that its popularity is undiminished by relatively high fees. Indeed, the school is validated to teach 176 full-time students and receives around 1,000 applications each year. The school's premises at the edge of Gray's Inn are more reminiscent of *Rumpole of the Bailey* than the 'shiny City law firm look' of other providers in the capital, and its students do seem to like its "more homely character." This feel is almost perceptible in the teaching, which is usually carried out in groups of eight to ensure that students receive plenty of individual attention. City is not changing its course until the compulsory changeover to LPC3 in 2010, and at the time of going to press the specifics of the course were yet to be formalised. However, with students going on to train at a broad spectrum of firms, including substantial City players, small commercial and high-street firms, and even the Government Legal Service, it is likely that the course will remain broad in its outlook. Pro bono opportunities abound, so students have no excuse for empty CVs. Among the projects on offer are Streetlaw, the Blackfriars Settlement advice clinic and the Liberty letters clinic. For those students with gaps in their CV, there is an option to top up the LPC with an LLM.

College of Law

Number of places: 4,750 full-time, 2,000 part-time across all centres

The College of Law is already everywhere and yet it continues to expand. Not content with two London branches, city centre sites in Birmingham and Manchester, and more suburban locations in Chester, York and Guildford, COL will now offer a Bristol-based LPC from 2010. Although a 'professional provider', COL was given degree-awarding powers in 2006 and so students who complete both the GDL and LPC there will also be able to receive an LLB. Although detractors say this undermines the qualification and that law firms don't particularly care whether an applicant has an LLB or not, it is always nice to add a few letters after your name. Possibly of more relevance is the opportunity for COL LPC students to top up their qualification with an LLM.

Like the other 'professional providers' BPP and Kaplan, COL has been enormously successful in its bid to sign exclusive LPC-provision deals with some of the larger law firms. Students on these firm-specific courses can expect to spend their year in the glass, metal and leather-dominated surroundings of COL's Moorgate branch before they embark on their careers at firms such as Allen & Overy, Clifford Chance, Linklaters, Barlow Lyde & Gilbert and Berwin Leighton Paisner. Unlike BPP, however, COL is well known for the diversity of its student body and it offers a number of very different routes through the LPC course. These include a corporate route, a commercial and private route, and a legal aid route.

COL has been steadily updating its course over the past few years and therefore the introduction of the LPC3 in the 2009/10 academic year will make little difference to how the course is taught. It has led the way in the provision of online teaching, and for the past year it has provided all lecture-format teaching via i-tutorials, which students stream directly from ELITE (an online resource page which carries all the course materials as well as links to online resources such as LexisNexis and Westlaw). I-tutorials are used in conjunction with textbook study and online multiple-choice 'Test & Feedback' exercises as compulsory preparation for small-group workshops. These workshops take up about ten hours a week. The overwhelming consensus is that the online teaching works well: most students like the fact that "*you can do them in your own time*" and find them "*incredibly useful for revision purposes as you can go through them again and keep everything fresh in your mind.*" Even the online 'Test & Feedback' exercises were praised as "*a useful means of self-testing your understanding.*" The workshops themselves are "*functional and effective rather than especially inspiring*" and always involve a great deal of group interaction on whiteboards. Students do find this "*quite repetitive at times*" but "*it does provide* [them] *with a handy set of precedent answers when it comes to the exams,*" which follow an (extremely popular) open-book format.

The careers service is "*forever organising talks and presentations*" and students are able to log into a database containing a list of up-to-date UK-wide training contract and paralegal vacancies. For students hoping to boost their CVs, COL has ample opportunities in the form of mooting and debating competitions and pro bono activities.

College of Law, Birmingham

Feedback from past students is overwhelmingly positive. This branch is located in the Jewellery Quarter of the city, which makes it easy to enjoy Birmingham's lively social life and many amenities. We had a number of reports of students making "*really good and lasting friendships*" on the course. And it would seem that the fun never ends as "*a lot of the graduates go to Birmingham firms and so when we organise trainee nights out we also know the trainees at other firms in the city and can invite them along.*" As the building is still relatively new, everything is "*impressively shiny and up to date.*" Extra-curricular activities include pro bono placements at the Birmingham Employment Rights Advice Line or the Refugee Council, and there is also a French legal exchange with L'Ecole d'Avocats in Lyon.

College of Law, Chester

As one of COL's more rural sites, Chester is not a sensible choice for those who thrive on city buzz. If you're more into the countryside then we'd say it's a fantastic place to study, and its graduates agree. "*I loved Chester,*" gushed one enthusiast, "*it is a beautiful place and it has fantastic shopping.*" For students who can drag themselves away from the shops, there are plenty of relevant extra-curricular activities on offer, including training as a Mackenzie Friend to support victims of domestic violence or participation in a witness support scheme. Many of the students who choose Chester are headed for law firms in the North West.

College of Law, Guildford

"*In many ways Guildford feels more like a smart school than a university or law school. It is set on a beautiful little campus and you feel incredibly well supported by all of the academic staff.*" This feeling is amplified by the range of school sports-style activities that take place on the large lawns in front of the main building. The location is incredibly popular with students who want to avoid London living but still have decent access to the capital. Most Guildford students always rave about the "*fantastic*" social scene, even though some do find it a touch cliquey. Most students will at some stage make a trip to "*a great little pub called The Ship, which is just outside the gates and serves fantastic pizza from a wood oven.*" Teaching staff are said to be "*accessible 24 hours a day if you need them.*" The location attracts individuals with a whole host of legal aspirations. There are a large proportion of City-bound students, clinging onto their final year out of the fast lane, as well as those preparing for careers in the Home Counties.

College of Law, London (Bloomsbury & Moorgate)

COL is one of the cheaper providers in London and easily undercuts its closest rivals, BPP, City or Kaplan. It is also seen as one of the "*obvious choices*" and many students come here without having really thought too much about their options. Few are greatly disappointed by their experience, whether they are stationed at the "*slightly cramped and worn around the edges*" Bloomsbury branch or in the "*extremely smartly built and well kitted-out*" premises opposite Slaughter and May's office at Moorgate.

The Bloomsbury branch operates out of two buildings on Store Street, just off of Tottenham Court Road. The location is popular thanks to its proximity to the night spots of Covent Garden and Soho, and the swanky bars and restaurants of nearby Charlotte Street. Despite an abundance of choice, students commonly end up in the next door College Arms, which frequently tempts them in with student discounts and other irresistible offers. COL has an in-house cyber café, in which students can while away the hours between classes. It has to be said that the layout of this branch is far from perfect, with regular complaints directed at the multiple flights of stairs in the Ridgmount Building and a general shortage of IT resources throughout. Get past niggles regarding the facilities and the teaching is second to none, with students praising the *"thorough preparation"* that they receive for exams. The teachers are also on call to deal with any last-minute panics, thanks to a hotline which is manned by staff in the run-up to exams. Bloomsbury students can choose any one of the commercial, private or legal aid routes.

Moorgate may only be less than two miles from Store Street and yet it is a world apart in terms of facilities. The lobby sets the tone with a broad glass façade and angular leather sofas. Venture further inside and there are wide, shiny lifts to all floors and a library with row upon row of available PCs. Should students grow tired of this monochrome visage, there is a fantastic view onto the green outfields and perfectly maintained wickets of Bunhill Fields. Moorgate students all take corporate route LPCs and most will be heading to the City firms that surround this prime location. Unfortunately this means there's a distinct shortage of student-priced bars in the vicinity and some sources criticised the lack of comfortable social areas within the building. Said one: *"In terms of a professional education environment it's very good. Socially they need to step it up a bit."*

College of Law, Manchester
New in 2009/10

College of Law, York

York is another of COL's campus-based locations, and once again student feedback suggests that the experience is *"not unlike being back at primary school as it is such a lovely set-up and everyone knows your name."* There's a full complement of sports teams and a social committee organises everything from a pantomime to ski trips. A good proportion of the students end up training with local, regional or national firms with offices in the area. Tutors meanwhile earn considerable praise; *"they are extremely friendly and approachable. The majority of them were either ex-solicitors or still* [practise] *part-time, so they can give anecdotal examples to help students learn and remember things in exams."* There's an abundance of extra-curricular activities, including shadowing advocates in court, advising asylum seekers and participation in an Eversheds-run mock Crown Court criminal trial.

De Montfort University
Number of places: 110 full-time, 130 part-time

The 2010/11 academic year will be an exciting one for this Leicestershire provider. Not only will it launch its LPC3, it will also start the year in new £35m energy-efficient premises. Although LPC students will share this facility with the rest of the Faculty of Business and Law, space will certainly not be at a premium and students can expect top-of-the-range facilities, including a dedicated LPC library and common room, mock courtrooms and interview rooms. The new course will bring a few changes to the syllabus as De Montfort has decided to reduce the Business Law & Practice course to bring it more in line with the litigation and property elements of Stage 1. The course leaders feel that this will better reflect the breadth of practice areas that their students go into. De Montfort has taken full advantage of advances in online teaching, and this has helped it compact the timetable to a mere two days a week, with an optional third day if students want to come in for face-to-face lectures rather than watching them online. It is hoped that the pared-down timetable will allow students to spend more time on a broad range of pro bono activities. These include an in-house law clinic for staff and students of the university, as well as Streetlaw, placements with the local council and CAB, and the university project 'Involve', which is De Montfort's student volunteering service. Careers assistance comes in the form of a mentoring scheme, through which students are paired with local practitioners who help to arrange work experience or give guidance on applications.

University of Glamorgan
Number of places: 90 full-time, 40 part-time

Having settled into its new location on the main university campus in Treforest, the law school at Glamorgan has already embraced the LPC3. The full-time course involves both lectures and small-group sessions, which are generally held over four days of the week. Part-time students have a substantially reduced attendance requirement of one day a week. One of the main draws for students is the university's work placement programme, which is possible thanks to alliances with 15 local firms. These range from small high-street players to significant commercial outfits, and the placements are regarded as an excellent way to gain experience. The range of electives on offer is broad, although there is a preponderance of subjects suited to students interested in high-street or public legal services, including Wills and the Elderly Client, and Immigration Law.

University of Hertfordshire

Number of places: 64 part-time, full-time now available

It is all change for the law school at the University of Hertfordshire. In the past this provider has only run the LPC as a part-time course, however from 2010, when it commences the LPC3, Herts will also run a full-time course. The intention is to increase the distance learning element of the course so that students won't have to commit so much time to attendance. Students can engage in a variety of extra-curricular legal activities, including a Streetlaw programme that takes them into schools and women's refuges to give presentations and advice. As with many providers, students can score an LLM in Legal Practice if they commit to a short amount of additional study after completing the LPC. Hertfordshire differs from most in that the additional credit can be gleaned via a work placement that is regulated by the university. It should certainly give students something concrete to talk about in training contract interviews.

University of Huddersfield

Number of places: 40 full-time, 35 part-time

There are now three organisations offering an exempting law degree to students and Huddersfield is one of them. Students who take it are not required to complete a separate LPC, which makes the degree course a canny option for those keen to keep down the substantial cost of qualifying as a solicitor. The course combines the cerebral aspects of a law degree with the more practical know-how of the LPC and this is thought to give students a more realistic idea of what will be expected of them in practice. Huddersfield also offers the LPC as a distinct course. The facilities on the Firth Street campus are excellent and include an impressive IT set-up and mock courtroom. The choice of electives is not especially extensive, however students can choose from seven commercial and non-commercial subjects.

Kaplan Law School

Number of places: 300 full-time

Kaplan has now been up and running in London for two years. Despite its relative youth it has made a big splash and has now signed up an impressive number of firms to exclusive deals. They include Bates Wells & Braithwaite, Bird & Bird, Manches, Mayer Brown, Nabarro, Penningtons and Trowers & Hamlins. The fact that Kaplan has been able to establish itself in such a short period of time is largely thanks to Nottingham Law School's participation in the venture. Essentially Nottingham is responsible for providing the course structure, materials and tutors, while American organisation Kaplan is the money man behind the project. The LPC is taught in a smart new building in central London, which is in every way the rival of COL's Moorgate branch and BPP in Holborn. It has the additional benefit of being within sniffing distance of the gastronomic delights of Borough Market. The course has followed Nottingham's lead in creating "*a close-knit and personal environment*," and it has also adopted Nottingham's multiple pathway approach for the LPC3 and its practice of recording face-to-face lectures. The student body has thus far been mixed, with decent proportions going to high-street and commercial firms, however now that the school has signed up to exclusive relationships with commercial players this may change.

University of Central Lancashire

Number of places: 105 full-time, 45 part-time

Feedback on UCLan is overwhelmingly positive, with students praising the quality of the teaching, the facilities (including a mock courtroom) and the top-of-the-range IT equipment (which includes a virtual firm, inside which all of the materials for the course are held in the appropriate department). Full-time students are expected to attend campus four days a week from 9am until 5pm, and part-timers have a reduced timetable limited to all day on Wednesdays. The course is broad enough to attract students with differing career ambitions thanks to a choice of nine electives, the suitability of which is equally spread between commercial and high-street options. Hardened City types are best advised to plump for another provider, however. At £7,100 for UK students, the course is one of the cheapest, both in the region and nationally.

Leeds Metropolitan University

Number of places: 105 full-time, 45 part-time

Former students speak highly of the LPC at Leeds Met. "*The face-to-face teaching is fantastic and it really helped me to take useful notes throughout the course,*" recalled one. The small-group teaching is delivered to groups of 16 for most subject areas, and smaller groups of eight for some of the skills. Teaching is delivered over four days a week. The main competitor in the region is BPP, but with fees that come in at substantially less than BPP's, and with "*a completely different ethos that is far less focused on commercial practice,*" Leeds Met never struggles to attract sufficient applicants. Students' aspirations span the full range of legal practice, and the law school and the university cater for all of them by providing a good mix of electives. The LPC3 will bring in a new Professional Identity and Career Development programme. This will enhance students' knowledge of the ethical standards expected in the profession and how they may be challenged, as well as providing advice on areas such as networking, market awareness and other practical skills. This

skills. This teaching will be provided via an external speaker programme. Another way in which students' employability is boosted is through a mentoring programme with local practitioners. Students can also top up their LPC with an LLM by completing a dissertation.

Liverpool John Moores University
Number of places: 72 full-time, 72 part-time

The LPC at John Moores is taught in a purpose-built section of the John Foster building in the city centre. Students may have easy access to the city centre during their down time, but they shouldn't expect there to be too much of it as the full-time course is taught over five days per week and on two days per week for part-timers. Most students have links to the area, either because they have studied in the North West or because they have come home to live with family. There is also a substantial minority of Irish students. Eight electives cover both high-street and commercial practice, although there is a distinct lack of any City-type options. Students who enjoy the experience can stay on and upgrade their LPC to an LLM in Legal Practice, although this will take them a complete year, which is much longer than some of the speedier upgrade options available at competitors.

London Metropolitan University
Number of places: 154 full-time and part-time

London Met is one of the better-value LPC options for students and the course tends to attract people who are keen to stay in the capital but want to avoid the monstrous fees charged at some of the other London providers. In the wake of Alan Milburn's report into the continuing exclusivity of the legal profession, the general philosophy at London Met (which is to widen participation as much as possible) seems particularly relevant. It also explains why the student body is more diverse than at most other providers: over half of its students are aged 35 or over. The course is in Aldgate East in a building that has a wealth of snazzy facilities including a mock courtroom, a 175-seat lecture theatre and WiFi throughout. The law library is located in nearby Calcutta House and there is also a part-time evening LPC based at Canary Wharf. Once their LPC is finished, students can top up their qualification to an LLM by studying for an additional year on a part-time basis.

Manchester Metropolitan University
Number of places: 168 full-time, 108 part-time

The legal education market in Manchester has had an interesting year. A new provider has entered the market and an existing one has struggled and made redundancies. From what we can tell, the COL's arrival in Manchester has had less impact on MMU than on BPP. The LPC at MMU has always been focused on preparing students for practice in commercial firms and on the high street, and it is perhaps this breadth of coverage that has kept students coming. Of course, MMU's fees are also substantially cheaper than at the two professional providers in Manchester, and this must be a key factor that students take into consideration. The introduction of the LPC3 has brought an end to face-to-face large-group sessions, and this content is now delivered via online tutorials. The tutors have used the resulting timetable gaps to schedule some whole-group consolidation sessions. As these take place throughout the course, students have the chance to flag up any problems they have with the course materials early on. The course features a virtual law firm – Jordan Maxwell – as well as a vast array of additional careers advice, such as podcasts from partners at local firms discussing topics such as the credit crunch and how it has affected the legal market. There is a dedicated careers adviser and a raft of pro bono activities, such as links with POPs – a charity that helps the partners of prisoners. Students generally have a connection with the North West, whether through family or previous study in the region. There is a fee discount for graduates from MMU, and we've learned that there are typically quite a few Trinidadian students on the course, who come to Manchester to qualify before returning to practise in Trinidad.

Northumbria University Law School
Number of places: 150 full-time, 100 part-time

When it comes to the exempting law degree, Northumbria has always been a leader. Prospective solicitors can do this type of degree at Huddersfield and Westminster now, but Northumbria is still the only place offering the exempting law degree to Bar hopefuls too. Students on Northumbria's four-year LLB (Hons) course for solicitors cover the teaching for the LPC during their undergraduate degree. This makes them ready and qualified to begin training contracts straight after graduation. Many have done exactly this: nearby Ward Hadaway offers a number of jobs to students who have finished this course, as do Dickinson Dees and other leading commercial and high-street players. Graduates of the course recommend the experience. Not only is it money-saving, they say they receive *"a more complete legal education from the off, rather than it being disjointed"* by the usual split between the LLB (or GDL) and the LPC.

Cost and the quality of facilities are two key reasons to consider Northumbria for an LPC alone, say students. In 2007 the entire school moved to impressive purpose-built premises in central Newcastle. The building is stuffed full of swanky features including WiFi throughout, a number of high-spec mock courtrooms, as well as a brand new cafeteria and library. The introduction of the LPC3 a year early has allowed Northumbria to run parallel commercial and general practice routes for the compulsory units and a good range of commercial and high-street electives. One particularly popular elective sees students volunteering at the Student Law Office (SLO) and handing in a portfolio of real work experiences at the end of the course. Students advising SLO clients find themselves drafting court documents, briefing barristers and generally experiencing all aspects of a case, which is fantastic CV candy. One negative we heard from Northumbria students is that the school's administration is *"pretty poor;"* however, apart from this, complaints are scarce and the *"excellent teaching"* is certainly worth publicising.

Nottingham Law School
Number of places: 650 full-time, 100 part-time

Nottingham may have developed a reputation for being a bit of a rough city in years past, but the law school at Nottingham Trent University is second to none. The new LPC3 commenced in September 2009, with the school taking the opportunity to introduce a range of different pathways. The broad-based pathway is likely to remain the most popular, especially for those without training contracts who may not want to narrow their options too early. A corporate pathway serves those who plan to go to firms with strong corporate practices, and if students choose this one they will find that the compulsory criminal litigation element comprises a number of white-collar case studies. The final two choices are the commercial pathway and the public legal services pathway. If students need to change pathways then that will be possible and their choice of pathway will not impact on their choice of electives.

The focus at Nottingham is on employability and the school aims to make every one of its LPC students as attractive as possible to employers. The focus is still very much on face-to-face teaching, although the live lectures are recorded and posted online immediately afterwards so students can use them for revision or simply catch up from home if they were unable to attend. Small-group sessions provide the bulk of the teaching, and group sizes range between 15 and 18 people. In the closed-book exams only primary sources are allowed. While students say this is not the most popular aspect to the course, Nottingham defends its exam format by insisting that it is a closer reflection of practice to be looking at the White Book than at pre-prepared notes. Meanwhile, *"the nightlife is second to none; I had a fantastic time,"* explained one typical source. There are also plenty of law and non-law related extra-curricular activities to get involved with and use as CV boosters. For those students who can't bear to leave, there is an option to upgrade the LPC to an LLM in Legal Practice after completion of a dissertation and a week-long summer school course in June.

Oxford Institute of Legal Practice
Number of places: 150 full-time, 30 part-time

OXILP has decided to hold off on providing the LPC3 until 2010/11, however should all go as planned the revamped course will feature less criminal litigation within the compulsory Part 1 of the course, leaving those students who are set on a career in that area to supplement their knowledge with a new criminal elective. The course will also feature a greater proportion of wills and probate work, which after consulting with the profession OXILP has decided is a lacuna in many LPC graduates' knowledge. Another big change will be the introduction of a commercial and business awareness programme to be run throughout the year via a series of lectures by external speakers. This will encompass practical subjects such as time recording and law firm marketing.

Students choose OXILP for its location and the modest size of its annual intake. One typical past student told us: *"I thought I would enjoy another year in a university environment rather than the more businesslike atmosphere of the London providers."* Students particularly like the fact that *"within the first week the tutors all seem to know your name"* and that *"throughout the course you can have a really personal relationship with them – I credit the fact that I got my training contract to the one-to-one help that I got from one of my teachers."* The LPC programme has recently relocated to Headington Hill Hall (once the home of media mogul Robert Maxwell), which is *"a fantastic building and a great place to work, although it isn't that big so you often have to use other, less smart, Brookes facilities."* This move follows the fact that Oxford University divested from OXILP prior to the 2008/09 course, leaving Oxford Brookes in sole charge. Even so, students are still able to benefit from many of the resources on offer at Oxford University, including its unsurprisingly impressive careers department, which has a comprehensive law firm data bank and a series of talks with big firms throughout the year. Brookes' careers team continues to offer practical advice on applications and interview skills. This dual approach has much to offer, although feedback suggests that careers assistance is something that is there for you to seek out, rather than being offered on a plate. On the whole students feel that *"OXILP is a great choice if you don't yet fancy the stress and expense of London"* and the breadth of the course means you needn't worry about being pigeonholed too early.

University of Plymouth
Number of places: 120 full-time

After three successful years running the LPC (which it took over from Exeter in 2006), Plymouth launched its LPC3 in 2009. It has used the opportunity to modify the structure of the teaching and the content of the course. First, the BLP module is being pared down to be more in line with the other core units (litigation and property). The criminal element within the litigation module has also been reduced, leaving those students who are set on a career as a criminal solicitor to absorb the requisite knowledge through an elective. Both of these changes reflect the aspirations of Plymouth's current students. It is also planned that all students will have a week in practice as part of their Part 1 teaching, with those who already have training contracts spending the week with their future firms. Working the placement into the course will certainly be a popular move for students wishing to boost their CVs. Further changes include offering £2,000 scholarships to up to five high achievers each year (with one place reserved for a student from the Channel Islands). A 10% discount is up for grabs by students who have completed their academic legal training with either Exeter or Plymouth Universities. The LPC earns good feedback from students, who say that it is *"a well-structured course with extremely friendly and approachable teachers and an extremely supportive environment. They seemed to constantly have in mind what it would be like for us in practice and they kept trying to hammer home points that we would find useful in the future."*

University of Sheffield

Number of places: 214 full-time and part-time

In addition to introducing the LPC3 a year ahead of schedule in 2009/10, Sheffield has also decided to run a part-time course from this year. Full-time students attend classes from Monday to Thursday; part-timers come in on Fridays. The university takes a realistic approach to timetabling and offers students the choice of mornings or afternoons. A further development sees the introduction of a master's qualification in legal practice, which is open to anyone who has obtained a distinction or a commendation on LPC and is prepared to take a course in research methods and write a dissertation. As is the way with many providers, an increasing amount of the content that was previously delivered via face-to-face lectures is now accessible to students online and through interactive tests and activities. Feedback from students suggests that this course has more of a university feel than many of its competitors, thanks in part to the fact that it is situated right in the heart of Sheffield's university quarter. For the majority of students who start without a training contract there is plenty of support from the university's careers service, and this remains open to graduates for three years after they leave. One of the best aspects of the careers service is the regular visits from local lawyers who come in to help students prepare for mock interviews. There is plenty of pro bono work on offer for those looking to enhance their CV, including the Innocence Project and the Pro Uno centre, which researches social welfare law issues that affect the clients of certain not-for-profit organisations in the South Yorkshire area.

Staffordshire University

Number of places: 150 full-time and part-time

Staffordshire University consistently achieves good marks from the SRA and offers the LPC course both full and part-time. A decent mix of 11 electives ranges from Corporate Finance & Acquisitions to Private Client, and this makes the course popular among students who need to live at home and study locally for financial reasons, as they need not limit their options for future practice. Those who plump for Staffs find that the facilities at the Stoke-on-Trent campus are excellent and include mock courtrooms, plentiful IT kit and simulated solicitors' offices. The careers department is also far from shabby and runs a practitioner mentoring scheme that connects students with local solicitors and encourages their participation in pro bono initiatives such as the Streetlaw scheme. LPC students can upgrade their diploma to an LLM with further study.

Swansea University

Number of places: 100 full-time

Thanks in part to its proximity to a surfer-friendly beach, Swansea University must occupy one of the most coveted spots in UK education. Once there, it must be hard to drag yourself away, so we weren't surprised to learn that a substantial number of Swansea's LPC students came from its undergraduate degree courses. Students should not expect to have a huge amount of free time on their hands, however, as the course requires an intensive 9am to 5pm commitment, and staff require students to demonstrate *"a professional attitude."* Teaching takes place from Monday through to Thursday and includes a reasonable number of fully interactive large-group sessions. These are then supplemented by small-group sessions and online materials. Fridays are free for students to fill as they wish, and one popular way is to participate in the university's placement scheme, whereby students spend one day a week working for local firms. The university believes that these are more successful than short Christmas or Easter placements as the firms get to know the students. Placements sometimes lead to real jobs, either as a trainee or paralegal. Fees are reasonable and the course is broad enough to cater for many styles of employer, from *"London commercial firms through to the more diminutive players on Welsh high streets."*

Thames Valley University

Number of places: 50 full-time; part-time validation sought for 2010

At the time of going to press this provider was still awaiting validation for its new courses, however if all goes well then the introduction of LPC3 in September 2010 will herald a number of significant changes at Thames Valley

University. The most significant of these will be the introduction of a part-time course, which it is hoped will take students just 18 months to complete. Further anticipated changes include paring down the Business Law & Practice course and beefing up the criminal element of the litigation course. These changes reflect the fact that the student population at Thames Valley is dominated by those who aspire to work at high-street or regional firms, or with the CPS. The course leaders are hopeful that they will be able to condense the teaching into two and a half days per week. Law students have access to the university's careers service, which runs dedicated LPC careers sessions. Past students confirm that the fact that the cohort is so small means that teaching staff are always on hand to help students when necessary, and there are plenty of CV-enriching opportunities, including the Thames Valley Law Clinic and a mentoring scheme.

University of Westminster
Number of places: 120 full-time, 64 part-time

Unless they are required to attend another provider, this central London university could be considered by all students planning to take their LPC in the capital. In addition to its brilliant Oxford Street location and "*inspirational teaching,*" Westminster also makes fantastic financial sense, thanks to very reasonable fees. The starting price can be further reduced by taking advantage of the myriad offers available. These include £500 off the fee for students who passed the LLB with a 2:1 or above or the GDL with a commendation or above, and a further 5% discount if they pay their fees in full by the end of September. Teaching is delivered via a mix of large-group face-to-face and online lectures, with the online component being used to tackle some of the more complicated topics such as taxation. A typical timetable sees students coming in from 10.30am until 4.30pm on Mondays, Tuesdays and Fridays, leaving two days for personal study or, if necessary, part-time work. Note that paid work is not recommended until students start Part 2 of the course, the schedule for which is considered to be somewhat lighter.

The choice of electives on offer is impressive. There are 13 different options, including several unusual courses such as E-commerce and Media & Entertainment law. There is also a Clinical elective, during which students work on a pro bono basis for the CAB and submit a project at the end. Needless to say extended practical experience like this is manna from heaven on a CV. Westminster LPC students have a wealth of dedicated facilities, including a resources room and a careers adviser who scans all of the professional journals looking for vacancies on their behalf. Westminster is also now offering students a four-year exempting law degree, which combines elements of the academic LLB with the practical LPC to produce a cohort of well-prepared would-be solicitors. Initially the course will only be run for 40 students and is likely to be significantly oversubscribed. Those students who are set on law but unsure of whether the Bar or a career as a solicitor is for them should not be put off. If you get half way through the course and decide that it is your destiny to follow in Rumpole's footsteps then it will be possible to transfer to a three-year course and obtain your LLB like everyone else.

University of Wolverhampton
Number of places: 60 full-time, 30 part-time

Wolverhampton has already plunged head first into the LPC3 and as a result the course has been tweaked rather than overhauled. As is the case with other smaller providers, the Business Law & Practice module has been pared down and this has had the effect of shortening the course. Wolverhampton sees itself as primarily targeting students who are headed to high-street practices or smaller regional firms, and the fact that the most popular electives are family and personal injury litigation bears this out. All course materials are stored within a virtual law firm, which is situated in the university's virtual town of New Molton. It is hoped that this approach will help prepare students for the document management systems they will encounter in their future firms. And yet hi-tech Wolverhampton has shied away from providing any of its teaching online so the focus is still very much on face-to-face teaching. Lectures are recorded onto DVDs, but these are only available at a cost after the lectures. Full-time students attend the Wolverhampton Science Park for classes, from Mondays to Thursdays during Part 1, and on a maximum of three days a week for their electives. Part-timers come in two evenings a week. The majority of students are graduates from, or those with familial links with Wolverhampton, and the remainder are people from Birmingham, Cardiff and the surrounding areas.

- **A partner posts online:** "I can honestly say that half of the people who applied to my firm this year have no chance whatsoever of obtaining a training contract. Poor grades, no work experience, no life experience... they have bought an LPC qualification that will never be of use to them in a professional capacity [because] they cannot and will not get a training contract. Legal training is now a business. In my day you applied to law college and got in on merit. Now it is open to anyone with £10,000 and a dream. It is a shame all round. Remember, legal training is a business. Law schools will sell it to you whether or not it will be a good investment for you."

top tip no. 3

The Bar Professional Training Course (BPTC)

The BPTC, which replaces the Bar Vocational Course in 2010, is the one-year practical training course for barristers in England and Wales. It can also be taken part-time over two years. Eight law schools are permitted to teach the course at locations in London, Bristol, Cardiff, Leeds, Manchester, Newcastle and Nottingham.

A cautionary tale

A career at the Bar has many obvious parallels with a career on the stage. Both professions require a certain degree of charisma and an innate talent for performance, as well as the ability to speak clearly and persuasively. Another pertinent fact binds the two together – the limited prospects for most of those aiming to build a career. As one sage law school tutor explained: "*Lots of people are attracted to drama school and pay the fees despite knowing that the chance of them winning an Oscar is remarkably slim. Those signing up for the BPTC are in a similar boat. There is a large group of them vying for very few positions and they must make an intelligent decision about whether or not it is sensible for them to proceed.*" Before making a decision it is imperative to look at the statistics. Figures from the Bar Council show that while 1,749 students passed the BVC during 2007/08 only 561 secured a pupillage. As with the LPC, the BPTC is a qualification that you can buy with reasonably hard graft and a breathtaking amount of money, and yet there is absolutely no guarantee, and not even the likelihood of a job at the end of it.

The Bar Standards Board (BSB) is not unaware of this pretty appalling situation, and in response to a working party chaired by Lord Neuberger it has set about re-branding and tweaking its vocational course and pondered new strategies to try to improve the odds for wannabe barristers. One such strategy, which it was set to launch alongside the newly re-branded BPTC, was an aptitude test for students. At the time of going to press the BSB admitted that it may have to withdraw its plans for the test after the Office of Fair Trading labelled its introduction as anti-competitive. So are we back at square one? Maybe.

Until there is a system that significantly limits the availability of BPTC places students must take full responsibility for their decision to sign up for the course. This means looking at your own CV and comparing it with those of new barristers at the sets that you're aiming for. This can be quite a humbling exercise, especially if you are aiming for the top commercial chambers. As one recent BVC graduate put it: "*You have to be realistic. Think about what area of law interests you before you start. If it is commercial law and you don't have a First from a top university then it is unlikely that you will be successful. If you are drawn to something else, say crime or family, then it will still be a struggle but not such an insurmountable one.*"

What to expect

As with the BVC, during the BPTC the spotlight is on developing the skills needed for advocacy, drafting, opinion writing, conferencing, case analysis and legal research. It is only in the final term that students have some choice, picking two option subjects in areas where they might see themselves specialising. Most teaching is delivered to groups of 12 students, with the rest tackled in classes of six or fewer for practical skills such as advocacy and conferencing. Teaching methods vary slightly between providers, but learning is commonly by way of case studies that track the litigation process. Written-skills classes often involve interactive drafting exercises using multimedia such as electronic whiteboards. Oral skills classes make increasing use of video-recording equipment in role-plays. The skills acquired are then tested in over a dozen assessments in the second and third terms. Written skills are tested through a mix of unseen, seen and take-home tests, while professional actors are drafted into take part in oral assessments. All of these assessments will continue to be set and marked locally by the course providers themselves.

Aside from the (possible) introduction of an aptitude test, which must be passed prior to starting the course, the main changes brought in by the new BPTC are the introduction of standardised assessments for Criminal Litigation and Sentencing; Civil Litigation; Evidence; and Professional Ethics. These centrally set knowledge-based exams will take a multiple-choice format. Despite widespread derision for the multiple-choice format among current students, we do consistently hear that studying for these topics is a tricky and time-consuming part of the course. Another change: the BVC's negotiation skills course is going to be replaced by a module called 'Resolution of Disputes Out of Court'. Snappy name.

Make the best of it

Course directors tell us the BVC/BPTC is a tough course – and some students agree – although the prevailing opinion among those who have recently sat the BVC is that it is a very changeable course. *"When it is full on it is full on,"* explained one recent student, *"but it does tail off a bit at the end, which is a bit frustrating as you wonder whether it could be done a bit quicker and more efficiently."* At least the quieter phases allow students to take advantage of all of the optional, extra-curricular activities that are on offer, including pro bono advocacy opportunities or getting involved with the social life and careers support offered by the Inns. *"You have plenty of opportunities and only yourself to blame if you don't take advantage of them,"* another recent student told us. The best thing is to throw yourself into everything you can with gusto.

How to apply

It costs £40 to make an application for the BPTC, and the process is all done online through BPTC Online. There is no cap on the number of providers you may apply to, but during the first round only your top three choices will look at your application. These providers can see where they have been ranked on your form. The system opens on 2 November 2009 and the deadline for first-round applications is 7 January 2010. First-round offers are made from 2 March until 30 March, with the clearing pool opening on 1 April 2010 and closing to new applicants on 31 August 2010. Late applicants can go straight into the clearing system until that date. The entire system shuts down on 14 September 2010. For more detailed information on the application process see the **BPTC Providers Table** on our website.

The current entry requirements for most courses is a not-particularly-glittering LLB 2:2 or a pass for the GDL; however, a 2:1 is generally seen by most providers as the minimum recommended degree grade when applying for a full-time place due to the overall popularity of the course. A high degree of importance is also placed on your ability to show commitment to the profession, so do your best to gain as much legal experience as possible. Typically this will be through mini-pupillages; volunteering at a relevant organisation such as a CAB or legal advice clinic; and mooting and debating. An applicant's English language skills are also taken into consideration, and yet the most recurrent criticism we hear levelled at the course providers each year is that the standard of spoken English among some overseas students is too low, having a negative effect on the smooth running of certain classes. What we would add here is that not all overseas students on the course intend to try and practise in the UK. Many of them come to earn the qualification before returning to their home jurisdictions to practise.

How to pay for the course

With the course costing nearly £15,000 in London (and not much under £10,000 elsewhere), and not forgetting living expenses, the BPTC is an expensive undertaking. If you decide to go ahead you must do some serious number crunching and work out exactly how you are going to raise the necessary cash. The main funding options are BPTC scholarships from the Inns of Court, career development loans, bank loans and – if you're fortunate – the Bank of Mum & Dad. The Inns and the Bar Council have also negotiated with HSBC's London Barrister Commercial Centre in Fleet Street to offer favourable loan terms for BPTC students (see Bar Council website for details). It's also worth contacting your local education authority just in case it can help. Your chances are slim, but make the call. See page 77 for more funding ideas.

Choosing a provider

You should make your choice of course provider carefully. Read through prospectuses and websites, attend open days, try to speak to current or former students, and have a look through our providers' reports. Here are some topics to think about:

Cost: Some providers and locations are significantly cheaper than others. London is the priciest, but even here there is variation. If you're an international student, look at the differential in price. Part-timers should note whether fees increase in the second year.

Success Rate: Have a look at the comparison table on our website to see what percentage of students pass the course at each institution.

Location: Regional providers are the best option for those looking for pupillage on the circuits, not least because of strong links and networking opportunities with the local Bar. London students benefit from proximity to the Inns of Court and more easy access for pupillage interviews; however, through compulsory dining and advocacy training courses in the Inns, regional students are able to maintain their links with the capital.

Size: Smaller providers pride themselves on offering a more intimate and collegiate environment. Student feedback indicates that this does make a difference, and the friends you make on the BPTC should be a source of support during the search for pupillage and beyond. There's definitely a different feel to those providers that are run as companies (the College of Law and BPP are both plcs), as opposed to those that remain part of a university.

Facilities: Students can tap into a far wider range of support services, sports and social activities by taking the BPTC at a university. Library and IT resources vary from one provider to the next, as does the level of technology used in teaching – some places make it a key feature of the course.

Option subjects: Available option subjects vary. For example, although judicial review and immigration are popular, they are not offered everywhere. The **BPTC Providers Table** on our website sets out what's on offer at each one. This table also compares fees and offers provider-specific application tips.

Pro bono: Opportunities range from minimal to superb across the nine providers.

Extra-curricular English lessons: If you are an international student, find out whether these are included within the course fees. At some providers they are compulsory for anyone whose language ability does not meet a certain standard.

The BPTC Providers

BPP Law School, Leeds (ft/pt)
BPP Law School, London (ft/pt)
Bristol Institute of Legal Practice at UWE (ft/pt)
Cardiff Law School (ft)
The City Law School (ft/pt)
College of Law, Birmingham (ft)
College of Law, London (ft/pt)
Kaplan Law School, London (ft)
Manchester Metropolitan University (ft/pt)
Northumbria University Law School (ft/pt)
Nottingham Law School (ft)

BPTC provider reports

Which of the law schools teaching the new BPTC will be right for you?

BPP Law School, London
Number of places: 264 full-time, 96 part-time

BPP is not a university, nor is it a non-profit organisation; in fact in 2007 it became the first privately owned, publicly traded company in the United Kingdom to be granted the right to award degrees, and more recently it was the subject of investment from specialist US education corporate Apollo. What difference will this make to students? Very little according to BPP, and what changes it will bring should have a positive effect on student experience. The lessons BPP are learning from Apollo are expected to enable it to provide a more personalised and effective back-office function, and the investment also provides BPP with a wealth of new ideas when it comes to online teaching resources. Walk through the doors of its Holborn HQ and it's clear that BPP looks like a proper business. Its swanky steel-and-glass building appears to have more in common with a City law firm than a university campus, and once inside you'll see that no expense has been spared in creating state-of-the-art facilities, including a series of mock courtrooms. BPP is one of the *"obvious choices"* for aspiring barristers, and with the volume of applications it receives it can afford to be pickier than most other providers.

Students can expect a *"positive, if somewhat mixed experience,"* which they feel compares well to competitor institutions. A total of nine options are offered including Judicial Review, Company Law, Property and Chancery. There are more hours of advocacy per week than at any other provider, and each student is required to complete five hours of pro bono activities over the year, not to mention plenty of mooting. The comments we heard about *"mixed"* experiences relate to many parts of the course; for example, students tell us that some of the tutors are *"excellent and thoroughly inspirational, while others really aren't – it's luck of the draw."* Similarly, with regard to timing, students report that they work *"flat out during certain months"* but find themselves swimming in free time at other times. *"This can be galling when you think about how much the course is costing you."* This brings us to the grubby subject of money, which is unfortunately by far the biggest gripe for students. BPP is easily the most costly provider of the BVC/BPTC, and not everyone we spoke to was convinced that it offers enough extras for it to be worth paying the additional price. That said, it's perhaps worth bearing in mind that BPP's BVC was the only one in London to be unconditionally revalidated by the Bar Council for a full six-year term.

BPP Law School, Leeds
Number of places: 48 full-time, 48 part-time

BPP has offered its BVC course to Yorkshire-based students since September 2006. As you would expect, it followed the same successful structure as the London course and past students told us they were *"impressed with the facilities, which are a world away from those that you get at university."* Where the course differs markedly from the one in London is in the fact that it has a much more intimate atmosphere – Leeds is validated for fewer than 50 students on both the full and the part-time courses. As is the case with other regional providers, the location offers students an excellent opportunity to hobnob with members of the local Bar, and BPP helps to facilitate this with the usual round of meet-and-greet sessions. There is involvement on the course from members of the Northern Circuit, which helps the tuition reflect practice. The school offers various extra-curricular activities, including mooting. Although Leeds has its own contest, a team also enters the London-wide competition. Students who choose Leeds pay significantly lower fees than their peers in London, and this has helped to encourage a high volume of applicants. We would therefore recommend putting BPP down as your first choice if you want a shot at coming here. As is the case in London, those who complete the BPTC can undertake additional study in the months after the course finishes to obtain an LLM in Professional Legal Practice.

Bristol Institute of Legal Practice at UWE
Number of places: 120 full-time, 48 part-time

As the LPC course at UWE limbers up for fierce competition from BPP and COL, UWE remains the only place in Bristol where the BPTC can be studied. If you are attracted to a future career on the Western Circuit, or are particularly keen to spend a year in the lovely but hilly city of Bristol, then UWE is the place for you. Teaching is delivered to groups of 12, and fewer for oral skills. When not in the classroom, students have seven-day access to a base room that is equipped with books and IT equipment. There are plenty of pro bono opportunities at UWE, including FRU and two weeks of compulsory work experience as a part of their optional modules. Students also attend inquests, advise juveniles at police stations and carry out prison visits, which is obviously particularly attractive for those who are thinking about a career at the criminal Bar. Inns of Court requirements are met by an introductory weekend, two 'Education Days' in London and a university-based educational dinner. As ever, UWE's location just outside the city is a disappointment to many students, some of whom arrive with the expectation that they'll be studying in the centre of Bristol. However the positives of the course certainly outweigh this one negative, and the money you'll save on the high fees that you would have had to hand over to a London provider will more than cover your bus fares to and from the campus.

Cardiff Law School

Number of places: 72 full-time

Students who opt to study the BPTC at Cardiff University can look forward to a lively university environment that receives consistently glowing reviews from past students. Indeed, the course markets itself as a place where *"the staff know the name of every student and can monitor their progress and help them to achieve their best result."* The strength of its reputation is such that if you are keen to win a place on the Cardiff course you should put it down as your first choice. The law school is located within the university's central campus, just minutes from the city centre, which gives it *"the best of both worlds"* in terms of spacious, purpose-built facilities and easy access to Cardiff's social attractions. Students also have access to all the library and careers service facilities of the wider university. One of the most popular initiatives is run by the law school careers service – a placement scheme gets students either a week-long mini-pupillage with a local chambers or a court marshalling position.

A high proportion of students have either family or other links with the region, and the school also has a notable number of foreign students from Commonwealth countries, many of whom come to Cardiff for a law degrees and then stay on to finish their professional qualification before heading home. Teaching is delivered via a mix of face-to-face lectures (in front of the full cohort of 72) and small-group sessions, which have class sizes of between ten and 14 depending on the subject. Students' attendance is required four days a week, leaving Fridays free, perhaps to travel up to London for a dinner at the Inns of Court. Even though this is undoubtedly an intensive course, the university is realistic and recognises that some students will have to work part-time while they study. We sensed that tutors were quite supportive of this, although as is the case at many providers they urge students not to commit to a job until they have properly gauged its requirements.

The College of Law, London

Number of places: 240 full-time, 48 part-time

This legal education giant has branches across the UK, although it is only validated to provide the BPTC in its London (Bloomsbury) and Birmingham branches. The London HQ is located in the heart of the capital, just off Tottenham Court Road and only a stone's throw from Oxford Street. As the capital's cheapest BPTC provider students may even be able to take advantage of the shopping opportunities this offers. Thanks to the fact that COL has degree-awarding powers, students who complete the GDL and BVC here will automatically gain an LLB, and an LLM is up for grabs by those who extend the academic year to complete three additional modules and an assignment. The main course is taught almost exclusively via small-group workshops, rather than large lectures. The group size ranges from four to 12, depending on the subject being taught. Students must show up four days a week and can choose between morning and afternoon sessions. While this structure is not intended to provide time for a part-time job, COL is switched on to the idea that, especially in London, students may need to work in order to help fund their studies. The timetable is certainly more accommodating than those at other institutions. Teaching follows the litigation process from instruction through to trial and beyond. For the criminal portion of the course this means that advocacy comes up earlier, as students practise making bail applications for their 'clients'; whereas in civil litigation there is initially a greater emphasis on negotiation and other forms of ADR.

The facilities are not as shiny as those at some other providers, but they are *"up to the job."* We hear that an extra floor has been opened up exclusively for Bar students, to help protect them from the hordes of wannabe solicitors on the LPC. There are more than enough extra-curricular activities to get involved with, including standing in as a judge for the LPC mooting competition, training with the Youth Offending Service, participating in the National Negotiation Competition or gaining real-life experience of advocacy at the Tribunal Representation Service, which provides opportunities to appear at a Leasehold Valuation Tribunal. If you are keen on COL then do make sure to put it down as your first choice, and if your grades aren't up to scratch then be mindful of the intensity of the competition.

College of Law, Birmingham

Number of places: 96 full-time

Since the Birmingham branch of COL started offering the Bar course in 2007 it has gone from strength to strength. These days only 60% of those students who put it down as their first choice are offered a place. The structure of the course is identical to that offered by COL London, although a smaller cohort gives the course a more close-knit feel. The premises are located in Birmingham's historic Jewellery Quarter, close to the city centre, and the relatively new building and swanky facilities more than equal those offered in London. A whole two floors of library space are devoted to Bar students. If you are thinking about a pupillage with a Midlands set then it is worth giving serious consideration to COL Brum as the networking opportunities are considered to be *"first rate."* As with London there's scope for extra-curricular experiences thanks to links with groups including the Birmingham Employment Rights Advice Line, Birmingham Employment Advice Clinic and The Refugee Council. The social life is as you would expect from a group of busy, hard-working students, and there is *"a real trench spirit among cohorts when it comes to making pupillage applications and going to interviews. Those friends really stay with you long after you have finished the course."*

City Law School, London
Number of places: 420 full-time, 60 part-time

City Law School (formerly the Inns of Court School of Law) has a long history of educating young barristers, and it is appropriately located in London's legal heartland. The school was once the sole provider of education for the Bar, and it continues to be the biggest provider in the capital. Student feedback suggests that some people feel dwarfed by the size of annual intake, although City does what it can to address this by ensuring that small-group teaching is directed at manageable groups of 12 (or six for advocacy). The school still operates large-group sessions, although it is planning to beef up its use of interactive, online learning and has recently appointed a new member of staff to focus on this area. The aim is to offer students a blend of lectures and online tutorials. City's reputation is well established and extends beyond the UK and across the Commonwealth. As such, the course attracts a large number of foreign students, and as awkward as this might be for City to accept, year on year students tell us that the standard of some of their peers' spoken English is not up to scratch. Those who complain to us say that this does *"diminish* [their] *experience of the course, particularly in the group sessions and when students have oral skills classes together."*

The course is sympathetically timetabled to help students meet other commitments, and in 2009/10 it will allow one free day each week. This could rise to two per week in 2010/11. Students are encouraged to throw themselves into mooting competitions, and the school has links with numerous organisations across the capital. One such link is with FRU, with whom students can complete a Domestic Violence option subject. Other unique options on offer at City include a new Criminal Financial Fraud course. For a full list of options at all course providers take a look at the **BPTC Providers Table** on our website. As the law school is a part of City University, BPTC students have access to all the facilities and services provided for its wider student population.

Manchester Metropolitan University
Number of places: 108 full-time, 48 part-time

Manchester Metropolitan (MMU) is rightly thought of as *"the place to go if you are keen to develop a career with a set on the Northern Circuit."* The law school has an unrivalled reputation for its close links with members of the local Bar and police forces. These make possible a wealth of extra-curricular activities that help to enhance students' CVs. For example, during mock trials students can cross-examine real police officers. The benefit to students is clear, and the officers gain experience of being in a court environment. The law school also participates in the Northern Circuit's programme of advocacy training, so students have the opportunity to play a witness for a qualified barrister to cross-examine. Among the other additional treats are day trips to Strangeways prison, which students usually regard as *"an eye-opening and profoundly useful experience."* The course is taught via a series of small-group workshops, and these are backed up by advocacy demonstrations and interactive online study. There are also a number of large-group lectures covering the civil and criminal litigation knowledge areas. This year the teaching was slightly altered, meaning that students alternate between 'criminal' and 'civil' weeks. MMU reckons this helps them keep track of each subject because they now have the time to fully immerse themselves in each.

The popularity of the course allows the admissions team to be circumspect when offering places and it usually only takes those applicants who have achieved a 2:1 (or 2:2 if someone has a remarkable CV). The course leader recommends that applicants give *"clear, articulate reasons"* for wanting a career at the Bar. While a significant proportion of students have links with the North West, MMU is happy to accept candidates from across the UK and beyond. Whether you are a northerner born and bred, or a southerner desperate to develop your northern soul, if the regional Bar attracts you MMU is a first-rate choice.

Northumbria University Law School, Newcastle
Number of places: 128 full-time, 48 part-time

Students at Northumbria are taught in *"a smart new building"* in the heart of Newcastle. The university moved its law school into the site in 2007, having spent a fortune updating its facilities. These now include WiFi throughout, as well as several mock courtrooms, a new library and a popular student café. The teaching staff includes five practising barristers, which gives students an obvious advantage when it comes to forging contacts with local sets. However you need to appreciate that the Bar in Newcastle is not as well developed as in other cities and there are never going to be enough pupillages in the city for those that want them. CV-enhancing opportunities abound – in particular there are moots, mock trials and volunteering activities with the Student Law Office, which provides free advice to members of the public. In addition to the self-contained BPTC, Northumbria is the sole provider of an exempting law degree for would-be barristers. This course combines the academic study of an LLB with the more practical skills that are taught on the BPTC. Students apply for a place on this 'exempting degree' during the second year of their undergraduate LLB, and then stay on for a further two years. Finally there are two top-up courses available for graduates of Northumbria's Bar course, both of which require only a few months of extra study after the summer term. These are the LLM in Advanced Legal Practice and an MA in Legal Practice & Policy.

Kaplan Law School, London
Number of places: 60 full-time

Kaplan entered the legal education market in 2007 when the school started to offer the LPC. From 2010 it will also offer the BPTC, and its association with the highly successful Nottingham Law School is likely to ensure its popularity among London-bound students. The course taught at Kaplan will be exactly the same as that taught at Nottingham, and course leaders are hopeful that the atmosphere will also be replicated. Indeed to achieve this, James Wakefield, the former director of the BVC at Nottingham, has moved to Kaplan to lead the new course. Teaching will be delivered via a mix of large groups, online resources and small-group sessions for 12 people for subject teaching and six for oral skills. The teaching will follow the life span of a client instruction, with drafting and advocacy training using the same brief. One aspect of Kaplan's course that really helps it to stand out is its strict entrance criteria. As with other providers, the school states that a 2:1 is required (save in exceptional circumstances); however, in addition, students will be interviewed before being offered a place. Such is Kaplan's resolve to remain small and beautifully formed, it has decided to teach only high-calibre students and will not necessarily fill all 60 of its validated places. As the course leader explained: "*I see teaching the Bar course as like coaching sports and so you need to be able to watch [students] perform in order to be able to help them improve. We are looking forward to being able to provide a truly personalised course for a bright and able cohort.*"

Nottingham Law School
Number of places: 125 full-time

This enormously popular course enjoys a fantastic reputation among students, and twice as many first-round, first-choice applications are made than there are places available. The fact that the course is so over subscribed allows Nottingham to be picky and take on only the best applicants. The benefits of this are easy to see when you look at the school's pupillage statistics. On average 50% of enrolling students will have secured a pupillage by the March following the end of the course. The admissions staff "*look for people who have tested their vocation*" and can show that "*they have the potential to succeed there.*"

Nottingham's respected course competes successfully with the London providers and students flock from across the UK to attend. In contrast to some others, the proportion of foreign students is comparatively low here. The course is exactly the same as the Kaplan BPTC (described above) and a similar guiding philosophy is in evidence. Student numbers are kept purposefully low so that each student can receive the requisite amount of personal coaching. Teaching occupies a full four days a week, and the school endeavours to keep Fridays free for students to travel to London for their qualifying sessions. The school helps with these by laying on transport for the journeys. Workshops are taught in groups of 12 or six, depending on the subject, and the teaching follows a number of civil and criminal briefs. The school enjoys strong relationships with the profession, and barristers and judges often present guest lectures. There are also sponsored plea-in-mitigation and mooting competitions, plus a marshalling scheme. As with other providers, Nottingham is offering an LLB to students who successfully complete both its GDL and BPTC. This can then be bumped up to an LLM in Professional Legal Practice if students stay on for a week-long summer school and write a dissertation on a relevant subject.

How to fund law school

Training as a lawyer is an expensive caper. Many of the students who secure training contracts or pupillages before commencing their studies will receive funding to cover their course fees and some living expenses. But what if you're not that lucky?

Taken for granted

We would advise against pinning your hopes on your local education authority (LEA) coming to the rescue with a grant. Still, you may get lucky so it's worth a quick phone call or e-mail to get the lay of the land. You can track down the contact details for your LEA at www.studentsupportdirect.co.uk. There are other possibilities if this proves fruitless: an organisation called the Educational Grants Advisory Service (EGAS) can carry out a charity and trust search on your behalf. Visit its website www.egas-online.org.uk for more helpful information. See also www.support4learning.org.uk. Additionally, the Law Society and the Bar Council have various schemes and bursaries that are worth looking into.

Bank loans

Already got a fat overdraft? No problem. The banks may be a little tighter post credit crunch, but you could still qualify for a special package from a high street lender. Interest rates are relatively low these days and the repayment terms generally favourable, but we'd suggest a thorough reccy to see what different banks are offering. NatWest, Lloyds and HSBC each have graduate loan schemes tailored to the needs of the legal profession, and intending barristers can now take advantage of special terms agreed by the Bar Council and the four Inns of Court with HSBC's Fleet Street-based Commercial Barrister team. Whichever loan you take out, remember that as repayments are delayed interest accrues and the sums involved can be sizeable. It's a huge commitment.

Professional and Career Development Loans

Barclays Bank and The Co-operative Bank provide these on behalf of the government. While you're studying the Learning and Skills Council pays the interest, then it's up to you. Full details can be found at www.direct.gov.uk. You're able to borrow up to £10,000 to fund up to two years of study; however, as the GDL is considered an academic course, not a vocational one, these loans are only available for the LPC and BPTC.

Surf the internet for scholarships
Here are some of the funds we found:

- BPP Law School offers twelve scholarship awards; the noble aim of which is to 'increase the diversity within the legal field and enhance the profession as a whole.'
- City Law School has six awards of £1,500 for students on the GDL. Each of the four Inns of Court nominates one candidate and the university selects the recipients of the other two once the course commences.
- The Law Society Bursary Scheme awards a small number of bursaries each year to candidates who demonstrate their financial hardship is greater than the average student.
- The Law Society Diversity Access Scheme supports talented people who face obstacles to qualification, encompassing social, educational and family circumstances.
- Inderpal Rahal Memorial Trust supports women from an immigrant or refugee background.
- The Kalisher Scholarship works with each of the BPTC providers to ensure that every year one talented but financially disadvantaged student has a free place on the course.
- The Leonard Sainer Foundation provides financial assistance in the form of interest-free loans of £7,500 each, to help fund either the LPC or BPTC in conjunction with Dechert LLP. See www.dechert.com for more information.
- The Student Disability Assistance Fund can award up to £500 for students who are studying on a full-time or nearly full-time basis. See www.bahshe.co.uk.
- Universities and publicly funded colleges have discretionary college access funds available to assist especially hard-up students.

The Inns of Court

Pupil barristers and Bar students can apply for a range of scholarships from the four Inns of Court. Most awards are given to students on the BPTC, but there are funds available for those on the GDL. Indeed, 25% of students studying for the BPTC have managed to secure some funding from the Inns, and many base their choice of Inn on the likelihood of getting a piece of the juicy £4.5m pie paid out each year. Some awards are merit-based; others consider financial hardship. They range from £100 up to about £17,000. During their pupillage year all pupils must be paid no less than £833.33 per month plus reasonable travel expenses. Some sets pay far more and allow students to draw down funds while on the BPTC.

Part-timing and the four-letter word

If the millstone of a decade of loan repayments doesn't appeal then it's time to roll up those sleeves up and get to work. Yes, real work. The difficulty here is that full-time study and earning money are uncomfortable bedfellows. Part-time could be a more realistic and manageable option, particularly as engaging in part-time work while studying for a full-time course is often frowned upon by providers and law firms footing the bill for course fees. Once you've worked out the timetabling requirements on your LPC you can then ascertain what's realistic. Part-time study may be the best way forward, even though it will take you twice as long to complete the course.

For those fresh from undergraduate life, part-timing might seem like an affront. What's more it may force them to mingle with mature students – men and women with wives, husbands, kids, mortgages... those factors that lead to one dirty word: responsibilities. We say get used to it – it will be good practice for when you are a lawyer. Plus, you'll meet some interesting people, perhaps more interesting than you would on the full time course. Studying part-time may also allow you to work in a more rewarding job (handy for the CV) and perform better at college. For LLB grads or students who have completed the GDL, paralegalling might be an option. Indeed, there's a host of jobs on the periphery of the profession, from commercial contracts negotiation and transaction management to social policy or other research. Several of the researchers at Chambers and Partners are or have been part-time law students. Whatever job you do, working while studying brings with it a valuable commodity to be traded on – respect.

If the part-time option really does send you screaming to the hills then it is worth considering an evening or weekend job. Our advice is to be sensible in the number of hours you do. Too much work (like too much play) will cause your studies to suffer.

Capital concerns

Newsflash: The streets of London are not paved with gold and they can eat up your hard-earned cash at an alarming rate. Not good news for your average impoverished student. Rent and living costs in cities like Sheffield, Nottingham and Cardiff are far lower. Don't assume, though, that out of London automatically means within your price range – Guildford, for example, is as pricey as it is pretty. Sit down and add up what you think you'll need for a year of study and then add some more. If you intend to take the GDL and LPC or BPTC in a pricey location the course fees could cost you around £20,000 (GDL/LPC) or £22,500 (GDL/BPTC). Do so at the least expensive schools and these figures could be reduced to around £10,000 and £14,000 respectively. There's plenty to be said for taking in another city too: from grassy campuses to smaller intakes, we heard plenty of praise this year for schools outside London.

> ### Benefits, benefactors, begging...
>
> So bunking up with Ma and Pa during your course isn't a dream come true, yet sometimes needs must. Forget ideas of declaring bankruptcy to evade student debt; consider other creative ways to ease the burden.
>
> - A student card will get you low-cost travel, discount haircuts, cinema tickets and even drinks in some places. If nothing else, it'll make you feel young.
> - Websites such as www.studentbeans.com has discounts and deals for meals, entertainment and more.
> - Law books are pricey so don't get overzealous before term starts. College libraries will have the core texts and you're sure to find former students hawking books. Check out notice boards and online for second-hand tomes.
> - A number of law schools, chambers and solicitors firms run competitions. Do a Google search to find them.
> - Market research focus groups will pay decent money for an hour or two of your time. In terms of more clinical options, consider carefully any decision to become a human guinea pig in a medical trial: you'll need that brain of yours.

Details of what solicitors are now offering their future trainees are given in the **Salaries and Benefits Table** in the **Refine Your Search** section after the **True Picture**. Further information about the funding of pupillages is given in the **Bar** section.

A-Z of Universities & Law Schools

Law School

- **Pace yourself:** The way to climb a mountain is step by step. Completing the GDL, LPC or BPTC is just the same. Keep going at a steady but determined pace and you'll make it to the end.

top tip no. 4

BPP Law School

Admissions: 68-70 Red Lion Street, London, WC1R 4NY
Tel: 0845 070 2882   Fax: 020 7404 1389
Email: admissions@bpp.com   Website: www.bpplawschool.com/chambers

College profile
BPP Law School is a leading provider of professional legal education, located in Leeds, London (Holborn and Waterloo) and Manchester. The school's programmes are flexible, providing more study modes than any other leading provider and several ways of viewing lectures, so you can study in a way convenient for you. The school has the skills and resources to prepare you for the realities of legal practice. This is achieved using both academic and practitioner tutors, first-rate facilities, award-winning pro bono projects and a specialist careers service. This blend of knowledge and experience ensures you receive the knowledge and support needed to secure a training contract or pupillage.

UNDERGRADUATE DEGREES IN LAW (LLBs)
(full-time, part-time and distance learning)
The school's undergraduate programmes, designed in consultation with law firms, are the LLB and LLB (Business Law). If studying full-time you can complete the LLBs in two years, allowing you to begin your legal career early, or the traditional three years – or you can study part-time and take up to six years. Also, because these are new programmes launched after most UCAS applications were completed, if you are going through clearing the school guarantees there will be places available.

GRADUATE DIPLOMA IN LAW (GDL) (full-time, part-time and distance learning)
The school's GDL helps you make the transition from undergraduate study in a subject other than law to legal practice. Taught using a practical, student-focused approach, the GDL provides an invaluable foundation for the LPC or BPTC. At BPP a one-hour tutorial to every one-hour lecture is provided. The GDL features the optional 'GDL Extra' and Company Law programmes, so you can specialise early. Also, by completing two extra modules BPP GDL students can upgrade to an LLB in as little as four months. If you are unsure whether a career in law is for you, the one week law summer school provides an excellent insight into the legal world.

LEGAL PRACTICE COURSE (LPC) (full-time and part-time)
The school's LPC has been designed in close collaboration with leading law firms, many of which exclusively send their trainees to the school. The programme reflects the growing need for lawyers with commercial acumen and uses 'MBA-style' training in business and finance. It's taught by solicitors from various practice backgrounds using a high number of small group sessions and lectures in three different formats. The school offers a wide range of electives, ensuring you can study the area that interests you. Although competition for places is intense, BPP LLB and GDL graduates are guaranteed a place on the LPC.

BAR PROFESSIONAL TRAINING COURSE (BPTC) (full-time and part-time)
The school's BPTC is highly regarded and is designed to prepare you for the Bar. Studying at BPP allows you to concentrate on developing the skills of drafting, legal research, opinion writing, advocacy and negotiation, many of which are refined in groups as small as six. Practising barristers are involved in the programme in a number of ways, including teaching and acting as opponents in negotiation exercises.

MASTERS DEGREES IN LAW (LLMs) (full-time and part-time)
The school's masters degrees (LLMs) are taught by leading academics and practitioners from specialist fields. The school offers the LLM (Commercial Law), LLM (Financial Regulation and Compliance), LLM (International Business Law) and, by completing two extra modules, BPP students can upgrade their LPC or BPTC to an LLM (Professional Legal Practice) in as little as four months. As BPP Law School has been designated a 'Centre of Excellence' in the field of investment regulation and compliance by the Securities and Investment Institute (SII), if you complete the LLM (Financial Regulation and Compliance) you will be eligible for full SII membership and the SII Diploma in Investment Compliance, in addition to your LLM.

Contact
Admissions
To apply:

Full-time LLBs
www.ucas.ac.uk

Full-time GDL/LPC
www.lawcabs.ac.uk

Full and part-time BPTC
www.barprofessionaltraining.org.uk

Part-time LLBs, all LLMs, part-time GDL/LPC and Summer School
www.bpplawschool.com/apply_now

Cardiff Law School

Cardiff Law School, Cardiff University, Museum Avenue, Cardiff CF10 3AX
Tel: (029) 2087 4941/4964 Fax: (029) 2087 4984
Email: law-lpc@cf.ac.uk or law-bvc@cf.ac.uk
Website: www.law.cardiff.ac.uk/cpls

Contact
LPC: Byron Jones
Tel: (029) 2087 4941/6660
Email: law-lpc@cf.ac.uk
BVC: Lucy Burns
Tel: (029) 2087 4964
Email: law-bvc@cf.ac.uk

Other postgraduate law courses:
The Postgraduate Office
Tel: (029) 2087 4351/4353

University profile

Cardiff Law School is one of the most successful law schools in the UK and enjoys an international reputation for its teaching and research. In the most recent assessment of research quality conducted by the Higher Education Funding Council, Cardiff achieved a grade 5 rating, placing it in the top law schools in the country. Cardiff offers opportunities for students to pursue postgraduate study by research leading to the degrees of M.Phil and Ph.D. In addition, taught Masters degrees in the areas of canon, commercial, European legal studies and medical law are offered in full and part-time mode.

Legal practice course and bar vocational course

A part of the Law School, the Centre for Professional Legal Studies is the leading provider of legal training in Wales and is validated to offer both the Legal Practice Course and the Bar Vocational Course. Students are taught by experienced solicitors and barristers who have been specifically recruited for this purpose. The Centre prides itself on its friendly and supportive teaching environment and its strong links with the legal profession. Placements with solicitors' firms or sets of Chambers are available to students pursuing the vocational courses, while students studying the Bar Vocational Course additionally enjoy placements with Circuit and District Judges.

In 2005 Cardiff's Legal Practice Course once again achieved the highest rating following the Law Society's assessment visit. The course has consistently been rated "Excellent" by the Law Society; one of the few providers of this course to hold the top ranking. The Law Society praised the challenging learning environment and stimulating range of activities. To accommodate differing student needs, from September 2010 Cardiff will be offering the LPC part-time* in addition to the existing full-time course. This is an exciting opportunity to expand the the school's high quality legal training. Through both courses the school will continue to provide its excellent learning experience which includes a high degree of hands-on teaching. Please see the Law School website for further details.

Cardiff has delivered a high quality BVC since it was first introduced by the Bar Council in 1997. The Cardiff BVC offers all the advantages of close and regular contact with staff in a generous programme of small group activity and in a convivial staff/student environment. The course is highly regarded and draws on the wealth of practice and teaching experience at Cardiff Law School.

Cardiff also has a Pro Bono Scheme which enables students to experience the law in action, work alongside volunteer legal professionals and develop transferable skills to add to their CVs.

Facilities

The Law School has dedicated accommodation for the vocational courses which houses a practitioner library, fixed and moveable audio visual equipment for recording practitioner skills, interactive teaching equipment and extensive computer facilities. In addition, the main law library contains one of the largest collections of primary and secondary material within the UK. The Law School is housed in its own building at the heart of the campus, itself located in one of the finest civic centres in Britain and only a short walk from the main shopping area. The Law School has its own postgraduate centre, together with a full range of sports and social facilities. Cardiff is a vibrant capital city with excellent cultural, sporting and leisure activities.

*Part-time LPC subject to validation by the SRA

The City Law School

City University London, Northampton Square, London, EC1V 0HB
Website: www.city.ac.uk/law

Contact
GDL
(020) 7040 8301
cpe@city.ac.uk
LPC
(020) 7404 5787
lpc@city.ac.uk
BPTC
(020) 7404 5787
bptc@city.ac.uk
Master Degrees (LLMs)
(020) 7040 8167
www.city.ac.uk/law

College profile

Located in the heart of legal London, The City Law School is one of London's major law schools and offers an impressive range of academic and professional courses. We're the first law school in London to educate students and practitioners at all stages of legal education.

The school's exceptional legal courses are fully accredited by the relevant professional bodies and are developed and delivered by its team of highly respected practitioners and academics. The school takes a personalised approach to your learning experience and aims to develop you into the professional, dynamic, highly motivated, "practice-ready" lawyers of the future.

Graduate Diploma in Law (full-time)

Started in 1976, this internationally renowned course was one of the first Common Professional Examination (CPE) programmes for non-law graduates. The course is designed to provide you with the knowledge and skills traditionally gained from an undergraduate law degree in just one year. The school teaches you the seven core legal subjects through a variety of lectures, tutorials and seminars. At The City Law School you also have the unique opportunity to convert your GDL into a full LLB degree by taking additional units.

Legal Practice Course (full-time)

The school's LPC has consistently achieved the highest possible grading by the Solicitors Regulation Authority (SRA, formerly The Law Society). The course is skills-based and replicates the demands and disciplines of practice through realistic exercises fully preparing you for professional legal life. You are taught in small groups by qualified solicitors on a wide range of specialist subjects. At The City Law School you can add value to your LPC by completing an additional research project to be awarded an LLM in Professional Legal Practice.

Bar Professional Training Course (full or part-time)

The school's BPTC delivers effective training for future barristers and equips them with the key legal skills and networking opportunities to pursue a successful career at the Bar. The core skills of advocacy, opinion writing, drafting, alternative dispute resolution and client conferencing are taught in the context of procedural and evidential knowledge in both criminal and civil practice. Pervading the course are the skills of effective legal research and case management as well as ethical professional conduct. The effective and flexible use of modern technologies on the course is designed to enhance students' learning experience. At The City Law School, you also have the opportunity to gain an LLM in Professional Legal Skills, awarded on successful completion of the BPTC and a supervised dissertation.

Masters Degrees (LLMs) (full or part-time)

The School's LLM courses give you the opportunity to develop your understanding and expertise in a number of distinct areas of law. Its LLM International Commercial Law opens up the world of international commerce and gives you the freedom to choose a specialism or gain a full LLM award in a number of interesting and professionally valuable areas. As the first postgraduate degree course in the UK to be devoted exclusively to criminal litigation, its LLM in Criminal Litigation concentrates on the principles that lie behind the criminal justice system and the need to examine those principles in greater depth in a critical and comparative context. The School's LLMs are offered on a full and part-time basis, allowing you the freedom to fit your study in and around work, family and any other commitments you may have.

The College of Law

Admissions, Braboeuf Manor, Portsmouth Road, Guildford GU3 1HA
Freephone: 0800 328 0153
Email: admissions@lawcol.co.uk
Website: www.college-of-law.co.uk

Contact
Freephone:
0800 328 0153
International:
+44 (0)1483 216500
Email: admissions@lawcol.co.uk
or LLM@lawcol.co.uk
Website:
www.college-of-law.co.uk

College profile

At The College of Law you'll get the best possible start to your legal career. With centres in Birmingham, Bristol, Chester, Guildford, London, Manchester and York, the College is the UK's leading provider of legal education. Its innovative courses are designed and taught by lawyers, with a clear focus on building the practical skills, commercial awareness and independent thinking you'll need to succeed in practice. This is supported by an award-winning pro bono programme, the largest and best careers service in UK legal education and excellent tutor support.

Graduate Diploma in Law (full-time/part-time/S-mode)

Designed to build knowledge and skills that more than match a law degree – with a clear focus on preparing you for life in practice. Academic training is built around real-life examples and case studies, and you'll be given research assignments that directly reflect the way you'll work as a lawyer. Students who pass the College GDL are guaranteed a place on the College LPC, and if you go on to successfully complete your LPC or BPTC at the College, you'll graduate with an LLB law degree without the need to study or pay for additional modules.

Legal Practice Course (full-time/part-time/S-mode*)

The College LPC is rigorous and practical – equipping you with the skills you need to succeed in practice. It has the widest selection of vocational elective subjects available and offers three different LPC routes, allowing you to specialise in your chosen field: corporate, commercial and private and legal aid. The majority of teaching is in small, student-centred groups and the course features extensive use of multi-media learning resources. Students who complete this LPC earn credits towards the College's LLM Masters degrees.
*S-mode subject to validation

Bar Professional Training Course (full-time/part-time)

The College BPTC has been designed to resemble practice as closely as possible. Study follows a logical, realistic process from initial instruction to final appeal, and learning is based around the seven core skills and three knowledge areas stipulated by the Bar Standards Board. Most of your learning will be in small groups, and you'll have plenty of opportunities to put your learning into action through: practitioner evenings, mock trials, court visits, mooting, negotiating and advocacy competitions, and pro bono. Students who complete this BPTC will earn credits towards the College's LLM Masters degrees.

Masters Degrees (supervised online/blended learning)

The College's LLM Masters degrees are truly professional qualifications and reflect cutting-edge approaches to legal practice. They offer a wide choice of flexible, specialist modules to suit your area of interest and enhance your expertise. These can be studied via supervised online modules, or by blended learning modules that combine online and face-to-face teaching. This will lead to an LLM in either Professional Legal Practice or International Legal Practice.

Open days

Find out more about The College of Law and its courses by attending an open day or arranging a centre visit. For further details and to book a place, visit www.college-of-law.co.uk/comeandmeetus.

The College of Law
of England and Wales

Kaplan Law School

Kaplan Law School
Palace House, 3 Cathedral Street, London SE1 9DE
Tel: (020) 7367 6400
Email: admissions@kaplanlawschool.org.uk
Website: www.nottingham-kaplan.org.uk

College profile

Kaplan Law School (KLS) offer Nottingham Law School's market leading courses at their central London campus. KLS have achieved the highest ratings from the Solicitors' Regulatory Authority (SRA), and have also secured a number of exclusive training deals with well established law firms in London reflecting the success of the partnership with Nottingham Law School (NLS) and the quality of training provided.

The school's tutors are all qualified lawyers with a proven record in practice and legal education. They work in close collaboration with both firms and the NLS faculty to ensure the delivery of a consistently excellent student experience.

All students benefit from a proactive and dedicated careers service and many pro bono schemes including a Legal Advice Clinic at the school.

The London campus overlooks the River Thames and has been custom-built with state of the art facilities designed to optimize the student and teaching experience. The South Bank location provides excellent transport links, proximity to the City's legal hub and a vibrant social and cultural community.

GDL: Graduate Diploma in Law (full time)

This one year intensive course is designed for any non-law graduate who intends to become a solicitor or barrister in the UK. The GDL places the academic subjects into a work related context so that students are more prepared for practice. All students who successfully complete the GDL will be guaranteed a place on the KLS LPC. Face to face tuition is a priority and the course is taught through interactive small group sessions and small lecture cohorts. See www.kaplanlawschool.org.uk/gdl for more information.

LPC: Legal Practice Course (full time and part time)

The NLS LPC has long been regarded as the industry leader and is the only LPC to receive the SRA's highest rating every year since its inception. KLS offer the same rigorous, professional standards of course design and delivery, reflected in the same highest rating received from the SRA. The school's teaching model is based around smaller group sizes which helps accelerate student learning and understanding and gives tutors more contact time with each student.

The school offers you a choice of broad-based or specialist pathways through your LPC allowing you to tailor your LPC to a particular area of legal practice. The school also aims to get you ready to practice through its Bridge to Practice programme. See www.kaplanlawschool.org.uk/lpc for more information.

BVC: Bar Vocational Course

The school is delighted to have been validated by the Bar Standards Board (BSB) to deliver in London the NLS Bar Course as from September 2010. The NLS Bar Course is established as one of the best in the country with double the average pupillage rates and the highest student satisfaction rates.

The course was designed by tutors with experience of legal practice and will be delivered with the input of judges, barristers and other practitioners. See www.kaplanlawschool.org.uk/bvc for more information.

Summer School

KLS runs a highly successful two day Summer School to introduce potential GDL, LPC and BVC students to the skills sets necessary to become a transactional lawyer or barrister. See www.kaplanlawschool.org.uk/summerschool for more information.

Scholarships

Kaplan Law School award a number of scholarships each year. See www.kaplanlawschool.org.uk/scholarship for more information.

Contact
Admissions:
admissions@kaplanlawschool.org.uk

GDL and LPC full time:
apply to: Central Applications Board
Contact:
admissions@kaplanlawschool.org.uk

LPC part time:
apply to Kaplan Law School
Contact:
admissions@kaplanlawschool.org.uk

BVC
Apply to BVC online
www.bvconline.co.uk

Nottingham Law School

Nottingham Law School, Belgrave Centre, Nottingham NG1 5LP
Tel: +44 (0)845 845 9090
Email: nls.enquiries@ntu.ac.uk
Website: www.ntu.ac.uk/nls

> **Contact**
> Nottingham Law School
> Belgrave Centre
> Nottingham NG1 5LP
> Tel: +44 (0)845 845 9090
> Email: nls.enquiries@ntu.ac.uk
> Website: www.ntu.ac.uk/nls

Legal Practice Course

Nottingham Law School's highly regarded Legal Practice Course has received the highest possible rating in every Law Society assessment. The LPC is offered by full-time and part-time block study. This course has been designed to be challenging and stimulating for students and responsive to the needs of firms, varying from large commercial to smaller high street practices.

Nottingham Law School will help you make the best possible start to your legal career. 90% of students that completed their LPC with the school in 2008 have obtained a training contract or paralegal work.

From 2009 Nottingham Law School's redesigned LPC programme will allow you to select pathways that lead to a specific type of practice, or maintain a broad based professional legal education if you are not sure yet what type of practice you intend to move to. In addition to the School's broad based LPC, it is planning to offer corporate, commercial and public funding pathways. Nottingham's Legal Practice Course allows you to select your pathway after you get here, rather than having to sign up for a particular route in advance.

Graduate Diploma in Law

The GDL is offered full-time or by distance-learning. Nottingham Law School's GDL is designed for any non-Law graduate who intends to become a solicitor or barrister in the UK. The intensive course effectively covers the seven core subjects of an undergraduate Law degree. It is the stepping stone to the LPC or BPTC, and a legal career thereafter. GDL students who embark on Nottingham Law School's LPC or BPTC will be eligible for a full LLB on successful completion of that professional course. Successful completion of the GDL (full-time) at first attempt guarantees students a place on the School's excellent rated LPC and favourable consideration for the School's BPTC.

Bar Professional Training Course (formerly bar vocational course)

Nottingham Law School has designed its BPTC to develop to a high standard a range of core practical skills, and to equip students to succeed in the fast-changing environment of practice at the Bar. Particular emphasis is placed on the skill of advocacy. Advocacy sessions are conducted in groups of six and the School uses the Guildhall courtrooms for some sessions. The BPTC is taught entirely by qualified practitioners, and utilises the same integrated and interactive teaching methods as all of the School's other professional courses. Essentially, students learn by doing and Nottingham Law School provides an environment in which students are encouraged to realise, through practice and feedback, their full potential.

LLM Professional Practice

Students who complete Nottingham Law School's LPC or BPTC can choose to 'top up' to an LLM. The university will award you 90 credit points towards the 180 credits required for the LLM. You will need to complete both a week long summer school programme in June after you have completed your LPC/BPTC, and a Professional Practice Dissertation (20,000) on a subject relevant to professional practice in the legal services sector. Students who have not completed their professional studies with Nottingham Law School are still eligible to take this qualification, please contact the university in advance as you may need to complete additional modules or provide evidence of learning.

Nottingham Law School has partnered with Kaplan Law School to offer the School's Graduate Diploma in Law (GDL) Legal Practice Course (LPC) and Bar Professional Training Course (BPTC - formerly the BVC) from a central London campus as well as from Nottingham.

NOTTINGHAM LAW SCHOOL
Nottingham Trent University

Northumbria Law School

City Campus East, Newcastle Upon Tyne, NE1 8ST
Tel: 0191 227 4453   Fax: 0191 227 4561
Email: et.admissions@northumbria.ac.uk
Website: www.northumbrialawschool.co.uk

Contact
Law Admissions
Tel: 0191 227 4453
Email: et.admissions@northumbria.ac.uk

College profile

Northumbria is justifiably renowned for the excellence of its range of undergraduate, postgraduate and vocational law programmes. The Law School focuses on law in practice and benefits from a well-rounded mix of academics and practitioners. All staff are committed to ensuring that students learn law and legal practice in a way that equips them for careers as legal professionals in the huge range of different roles that lawyers can occupy in society.

Graduate diploma in law (GDL)- full-time/ distance learning/ e-learning

The GDL provides the academic stage for non-law graduates who intend to practise law. It covers the seven core subjects stipulated by the professional bodies as being the foundations of legal knowledge. Students are also required to choose an eighth optional subject from a wide range available. Successful Northumbria GDL students are guaranteed a place on Northumbria's LPC and are entitled to a £1,000 discount off LPC or BPTC fees (must be studied over consecutive years).

Legal practice course (LPC)- full-time/ part-time

Awarded the highest possible rating of "commendable practice" in all areas of assessment by the Solicitors Regulation Authority (SRA), the Legal Practice Course has recently been revalidated to comply with the new SRA regulations. Students can choose to study a General Practice Stage 1 or a Commercial Practice Stage 1. Each Stage 1 route covers the three compulsory areas of civil and criminal litigation, property law and practice and business law and practice, as well as legal skills and professional conduct and regulatory issues, and allows students to tailor Stage 1 of the Legal Practice Course to their chosen area of practice. Stage 1 is followed by Stage 2, during which three electives are studied, chosen from an extensive range covering both general and commercial practice. Amongst these is the innovative Student Law Office elective, where students undertake live client work.

Bar professional training course* (BPTC) – full-time/part-time

Northumbria Law School is one of only six institutions outside of London to offer the BPTC. In the last monitoring report, the Bar Standards Board wrote Northumbria University "is clearly offering a high quality BVC course in a first class new facility". The Law School is a short walk from Newcastle's legal centre – the Quayside – and many of the staff who teach on the programme are members of local chambers and practice regularly in the local courts. Additionally, local practitioners regularly deliver lectures and run advocacy masterclasses for all students.

LLM – full-time/distance learning

The Law School offers a range of distinctive and innovative Masters programmes which focus on the practical operation of the law. Students studying on the LPC or BPTC at Northumbria are able to study on the LLM programme in Advanced Legal Practice at the same time. Both courses can be completed in 12-18 months.

Facilities

The Law School is part of the award-winning City Campus East, in the heart of Newcastle. Based in a £70 million building, the school is justifiably proud of its facilities, with stunning state-of-the-art lecture theatres, dedicated courtrooms, skills suites, and our outstanding Law Practice Library.

Formerly the Bar Vocational Course

- **Be the best:** While not the be-all and end-all, excellent grades have never been more important. Do yourself a massive favour and resist the temptation to slack off.

top tip no. 5

Solicitors' Practice Areas

Banking and finance	90
Competition/antitrust	92
Construction and projects	94
Corporate	96
Crime	98
Employment	100
Environment	102
Family	104
Intellectual property	106
Litigation/dispute resolution	108
Personal injury and clinical negligence	110
Private client and charities	112
Property/real estate	114
Public interest	116
Restructuring/insolvency	**118**
Shipping	120
Sports, media and entertainment	122
Tax	124
Technology, telecoms and outsourcing	125

Banking and finance

In a nutshell

Banking and finance lawyers may work in any one of the specialist areas described below, but all deal with the borrowing of money or the management of financial liabilities. Their task is to negotiate and document the contractual relationship between lenders and borrowers and ensure that their client's best legal and commercial interests are reflected in the terms of loan agreements. It is a hugely technical, ever-evolving and jargon-heavy area of law.

Straightforward bank lending: a bank lends money to a borrower on documented repayment terms. **Acquisition finance:** a loan made to a corporate borrower or private equity sponsor for the purpose of acquiring another company. This includes **leveraged finance**, where the borrower uses a very large amount of borrowed money to meet the cost of a significant acquisition without committing a lot of its own capital (as typically done in leveraged buyouts (LBOs): read our corporate law section). **Real estate finance:** a loan made to enable a borrower to acquire a property or finance the development of land and commonly secured by way of a mortgage on the acquired property/land. **Project finance:** the financing of long-term infrastructure (eg roads) and public services projects (eg hospitals), where the amounts borrowed to complete the project are paid back with the cash flow generated by the project. **Asset finance:** this enables the purchase and operation of large assets such as ships, aircraft and machinery. The lender normally takes security over the assets in question. **Islamic finance:** Muslim borrowers, lenders and investors must abide by Shari'a law, which prohibits the collection and payment of interest on a loan. Islamic finance specialists ensure that finance deals are structured in a Shari'a-compliant manner. **Debt capital markets:** this generic category covers many types of debt instruments, but generally speaking it deals with a borrower raising capital by selling tradable bonds to investors, who expect the full amount lent to be paid back to them with interest. **Securitisation:** essentially this is where a lender wants to sell its loans to create liquidity. It does so by selling them to a shell company, which then issues bonds to the markets. Bond investors get paid from the interest and principal on the loans owned by the shell company. **Structured finance:** a service offered by many large financial institutions for companies with unique financing needs that traditional loans cannot satisfy. Structured finance generally involves highly complex bespoke financial transactions. **Derivatives:** at its most basic, a derivative is a security used by banks and corporates to hedge risks to which they are exposed from factors outside of their control. They can also be used for speculative purposes by betting on the fluctuation of just about anything from currency exchange rates to the number of sunny days in a particular region. Futures, forwards, options and swaps are the most common types of derivatives. **Financial services regulation:** lawyers in this field ensure that their bank clients operate in compliance with the relevant financial legislation.

What lawyers do

- Meet with clients to establish their specific requirements and the commercial context of a deal.
- Carry out due diligence – an investigation exercise to verify the accuracy of information passed from the borrower to the lender or from the company raising finance to all parties investing in the deal. This can involve on-site meetings with the company's management so lawyers can verify the company's credit profile. If financial instruments, such as bonds, are being offered to investors, the report will take the form of a prospectus, which must comply with the requirements of the EU prospectus and transparency directives.
- Negotiate with the opposite party to agree the terms of the deal and record them accurately in the facility documentation. Lenders' lawyers usually produce initial documents (often a standard form) and borrowers' lawyers try to negotiate more favourable terms for their clients. Lawyers on both sides must know when to compromise and when to hold out.
- Assist with the structuring of complicated or groundbreaking financing models and ensure innovative solutions comply with all relevant laws.
- Gather all parties to complete the transaction, ensuring all agreed terms are reflected in the loan and that all documents have been properly signed and witnessed. Just as in corporate deals, many decisions need to be made at properly convened board meetings and recorded in written resolutions.
- Finalise all post-completion registrations and procedures.

The realities of the job

- City firms act for investment banks on highly complex and often cross-border financings, whereas the work of regional firms generally involves acting for commercial banks on more mainstream domestic finance deals. If you want to be a hotshot in international finance then it's the City for you.
- Lawyers need to appreciate the needs and growth ambitions of their clients in order to deliver pertinent advice and warn of the legal risks involved in the transactions. Deals may involve the movement of money across bor-

ders and through different currencies and financial products. International deals have an additional layer of difficulty: political changes in transitional economies can render a previously sound investment risky.
- Banking clients are ultra-demanding and the hours can be long. On the plus side your clients will be smart and dynamic. It is possible to build up long-term relationships with investment bank clients, even as a junior.
- Working on deals can be exciting. The team and the other side are all working to a common goal, often under significant time and other pressures. Deal closings bring adrenaline highs and a sense of satisfaction.
- You need to become absorbed in the finance world. Start reading the FT or the City pages in your daily newspaper for a taster.

Current issues

- The banking and finance world was in a halcyon period before the financial crisis. Credit was cheap and readily available until the credit crunch brought a sharp correction to the financial marketplace. In 2008/09 many major financial institutions had to write off billions of pounds as a result of their exposure to toxic debt. The collapse of Lehman Brothers brought home the severity of the credit crunch, the vulnerability of the world's best-known financial institutions and the challenges facing governments and regulators to maintain market stability.
- You'll appreciate from the dire reports in the press that these massive financial losses put severe constraints on the banks' ability to lend. The cost of borrowing increased (as reflected in higher interest rates and upfront fees). Banks are now more cautious and have tightened credit controls, even for borrowers with a strong credit profile and established relationships.
- High-end leveraged acquisition financings were hit particularly hard by the dearth of liquidity, with a 65% decline in debt used to finance LBOs and very few new deals being announced.
- 2009 was a turbulent year for debt capital markets. Investors lacked appetite for conventional debt and lost all confidence in highly structured securities, which are believed to have been a catalyst of the crisis.
- It's not all doom and gloom though. As lenders and borrowers tried to manage their excessive debt loads, banking lawyers became busy advising clients on refinancings, recapitalisations and restructurings. Particularly noticeable is the trend for borrowers to buy back their own loans at a significant discount.
- In order to curb the excesses of the banking community, governments are looking at strengthening regulatory controls. This is good news for regulatory lawyers, who can expect clients to ask for more advice on compliance issues and the implication of financial reforms.
- With fewer deals being done, many law firms have had to downsize their banking and finance teams. The big City firms were no exception, but they have fared better than initially expected due to their ability to adapt quickly in tougher market conditions.
- Secondments to banks are available, even for trainees, and subsequent moves in-house are common. In the past year many banks have laid off large numbers of their own legal personnel, which has increased their demand for law firm secondees at all levels of seniority. Some firms say this has put a strain on their own resources.

Read our True Pictures on...

Addleshaw Goddard	Lester Aldridge
Allen & Overy	Lawrence Graham (LG)
Ashurst	Linklaters
Baker & McKenzie	Lovells
Barlow Lyde & Gilbert	Macfarlanes
Beachcroft	Manches
Berwin Leighton Paisner	Martineau
Bevan Brittan	Mayer Brown International
Bingham McCutchen	McDermott Will & Emery UK
Bird & Bird	McGrigors
Bond Pearce	Michelmores
Browne Jacobson	Mills & Reeve
Burges Salmon	Mishcon de Reya
Charles Russell	Morgan Cole
Cleary Gottlieb	Mundays
Clifford Chance	Nabarro
Clyde & Co	Norton Rose
CMS Cameron McKenna	Olswang
Cobbetts	O'Melveny & Myers
Dechert	Osborne Clarke
Denton Wilde Sapte	Pannone
Dewey & LeBoeuf	Paul, Hastings
Dickinson Dees	Pinsent Masons
DLA Piper UK	Reed Smith
DMH Stallard	Shoosmiths
Dundas & Wilson	Sidley Austin
DWF	Simmons & Simmons
Eversheds	SJ Berwin
Farrer & Co	Skadden, Arps
Finers Stephens Innocent	Slaughter and May
Foot Anstey Solicitors	Speechly Bircham
Freeth Cartwright	Stephenson Harwood
Freshfields	Stevens & Bolton
Halliwells	Taylor Wessing
Hammonds	TLT
HBJ Gateley Wareing	Travers Smith
Herbert Smith	Trowers & Hamlins
Hill Dickinson	Veale Wasbrough
Holman Fenwick Willan	Walker Morris
Howes Percival	Ward Hadaway
Ince & Co	Watson, Farley & Williams
Irwin Mitchell	Weil, Gotshal & Manges
Jones Day	White & Case
K&L Gates	Wragge & Co
Latham & Watkins	

Competition/antitrust

In a nutshell

It is the job of the UK and EU regulatory authorities to ensure that markets function effectively on the basis of fair and open competition. The competition rules in the UK and EU are substantially similar, but the UK bodies concentrate on those rules that have their greatest effect domestically, while EU authorities deal with matters affecting multiple member states. The UK regulators are the Office of Fair Trade (OFT) and the Competition Commission; on matters also affecting other EU countries, it is the European Commission. Additionally, there are industry-specific regulatory bodies, such as Ofcom for the media and telecoms industry.

Competition authorities have extensive investigative powers – including the ability to carry out dawn raids – and can impose hefty fines. The OFT has become more proactive and litigation-minded in recent years, and you will certainly have heard about Intel's run-in with the European Commission. The computer chipmaker's record €1.06bn fine levied in May 2009 for anti-competitive practice is the largest ever and it shows that the Commission means business.

What lawyers do

- Negotiate clearance for acquisitions, mergers and joint ventures.
- Advise on the structure of commercial or co-operation agreements to ensure they can withstand a competition challenge.
- Deal with investigations into the conduct of businesses.
- Bring or defend claims in the Competition Appeal Tribunal (CAT).
- Advise on cross-border trade or anti-dumping measures (preventing companies exporting products at a lower price than it normally charges in its home market).
- Regulators investigate companies, bring prosecutions and advise on new laws and regulations.

The realities of the job

- You won't get much independence; even junior lawyers work under the close supervision of partners. In the early days the job involves a great deal of research into particular markets and how the authorities have approached different types of agreements in the past.
- You need to be interested in economics and politics.
- The work demands serious academic brainpower twinned with commercial acumen.
- As a popular area of practice it's hard to break into. Competition-specific studies, say a master's degree, could enhance your prospects.
- Advocacy is a relatively small part of the job, though you could end up appearing in the High Court or CAT.
- In international law firms you will travel abroad and may even work in an overseas office for a while, perhaps in Brussels, which is the hub for European competition work. Fluency in another language can be useful.

Current issues

- There is greater regulatory activity in the UK, EU and USA. The EC's record-breaking €1.06bn fine slapped on computer chipmaker Intel made headlines.
- Following the liquidity crisis and slowing of M&A deal activity, investigations into the abuse of dominance and cartels have become more common than merger control. The OFT successfully used the Enterprise Act to prosecute and imprison three individuals for cartel offences, and in 2009 four British Airways executives faced trial for involvement in a passenger fuel surcharge cartel.
- Competition lawyers are increasingly working with financial regulation, tax, litigation and white-collar crime specialists.
- The remit of the CAT has been widened to allow claims for damages brought by third parties. Private enforcement can be a useful tool for competitor businesses and consumer groups, but thus far has had limited success.
- There are increased opportunities to work for the regulatory authorities; the OFT employs many more investigators than before. Lawyers can switch between private practice and working for the regulators.

Read our True Pictures on...

Addleshaw Goddard	Lovells
Allen & Overy	Macfarlanes
Ashurst	Martineau
Baker & McKenzie	Mayer Brown International
Berwin Leighton Paisner	McDermott Will & Emery UK
Bird & Bird	Nabarro
Bond Pearce	Norton Rose
Burges Salmon	Olswang
Cleary Gottlieb	Osborne Clarke
Clifford Chance	Pinsent Masons
CMS Cameron McKenna	Reed Smith
Denton Wilde Sapte	Shoosmiths
Dickinson Dees	Simmons & Simmons
DLA Piper UK	SJ Berwin
Eversheds	Slaughter and May
Freshfields	TLT
Herbert Smith	Travers Smith
Holman Fenwick Willan	Ward Hadaway
Latham & Watkins	Wragge & Co
Linklaters	

Solicitors' Practice Areas

- **Shameless plug:** The entire contents of our *Chambers UK* directory can be read and fully searched online for free at www.chambersandpartners.com. It is the product of thousands of interviews with lawyers and clients. Searching the rankings and editorial will tell you who is top in which practice areas and what work specific firms have been up to – it makes for perfect interview crib notes.

We also publish *USA*, *Europe*, *Asia*, *Latin America* and *Global* directories, giving you detailed analysis of even the farthest corners of the legal world.

No *Chambers Antarctica* yet, though. Give it time.

top tip no. 6

Construction and projects

In a nutshell

Construction

Construction law can broadly be divided into non-contentious and contentious issues. The first involves lawyers helping clients at the procurement stage, pulling together all the contractual relationships prior to building work; the second sees them resolving disputes when things go wrong. In the past, the relatively high monetary stakes involved and the industry trend for recovering building costs through the courts, made construction a litigation-happy practice. Since the 1990s most new contracts have contained mandatory procedures to be adopted in case of dispute. Adjudication of disputes has become the industry norm and these tend to follow a swift 28-day timetable. Others are resolved through mediation or arbitration; however, some disputes are so complex that the parties do still choose to slug it out in court.

Projects

Specialist construction lawyers work hand in hand with finance and corporate lawyers to enable projects to come to fruition. A few City firms and the largest US practices dominate the biggest international projects, but there's work countrywide. In the UK the Private Finance Initiative (PFI) – an aspect of Public Private Partnerships (PPP) – is an important source of work. It introduces private funding and management into areas that were previously the domain of government. Some law firms consistently act for the project company, usually through a 'special purpose vehicle' (SPV) established to build, own and operate the end result of the project. Often the project company is a joint venture between various 'sponsor' companies. An SPV could also be partially owned by a government body or banks. Other firms consistently represent the organisations that commission projects. Then there are the firms that act purely on the finance side for banks, guarantors, export credit agencies, governments and international funding agencies.

What lawyers do

Construction: procurement

- Negotiate and draft contracts for programmes of building works. Any such programme involves a multitude of parties including landowners, main contractors, subcontractors, engineers and architects.
- Work in conjunction with property lawyers if the client has invested in land as well as undertaking a building project. Together, the lawyers seek and obtain all the necessary planning consents as well as local authority certifications.
- Where the developer does not own the land, liaise with the landowner's solicitors over matters such as stage payments, architects' certificates and other measures of performance.
- Make site visits during development.

Construction: disputes

- Assess the client's position and gather all related paperwork and evidence.
- Extract the important detail from huge volumes of technical documentation.
- Follow the resolution methods set out in the contracts between the parties.
- Where a settlement is impossible, issue, prepare for and attend proceedings with the client, usually instructing a barrister to advocate.

Projects

- Too varied to list. The field has specialists in the areas of funding, construction, real estate, planning, energy, telecoms and all aspects of the public sector, including health, education and housing.

The realities of the job

- Drafting requires attention to detail and careful thought.
- It's essential to keep up to date with industry standards and know contract law and tort inside out.
- People skills are fundamental. Contractors and subcontractors are generally earthy and direct; structural engineers live in a world of complicated technical reports; corporate types and in-house lawyers require smoother handling. You'll deal with them all.
- The construction world is often perceived as a male-dominated environment, but while some clients might see a visit to a lap-dancing club as par for the business entertainment course, there are many successful female construction lawyers, architects and engineers who avoid such activities.
- Most lawyers prefer either contentious or non-contentious work, and some firms like their construction lawyers to handle both, so pick your firm carefully.

- A background in construction or engineering is a major bonus because you'll already have industry contacts and will be able to combine legal know-how with practical advice.
- Projects require lawyers who enjoy the challenge of creating a complex scheme and figuring out all its possibilities and pitfalls. Projects can run for years, involving multidisciplinary legal work spanning finance, regulatory permissions, construction, employment law and much more.

Current issues
- Lawyers are seeing an influx of contentious work across the board.
- Adjudication remains the preferred dispute resolution method.
- House building came to a standstill in many regions.
- The PFI market has experienced a significant slowdown, with few major projects emerging to replace those already completed and others being mothballed as funding becomes harder to find. Projects such as Crossrail and the 2012 Olympics are good news for contractors and lawyers alike.
- The rise in offshore wind and novel renewables projects, as well as the potential for nuclear new-build and gas-storage projects, are vital to energy security and remain a key source of work, credit crunch notwithstanding.
- Thus far the public sector has fared rather better than the private sector. Social housing has become a hot area for firms to try and break into, as private sector development activity and property valuations remain constrained by negative market sentiment and the lack of available finance. The industry is fearful for the period ahead though, especially if present levels of public sector spending are not maintained.
- Despite overseas activity slowing – particularly in Dubai (though on the contentious side things are hotting up as projects fall through) – projects are still being undertaken. Certain countries, such as Qatar and Libya, are seeking increased investment.

Read our True Pictures on...

Addleshaw Goddard	Linklaters
Allen & Overy	Lovells
Anthony Collins Solicitors	Macfarlanes
Ashurst	Martineau
Baker & Mckenzie	Maxwell Winward
Barlow Lyde & Gilbert	Mayer Brown International
Beachcroft	McDermott Will & Emery
Berwin Leighton Paisner	McGrigors
Bevan Brittan	Michelmores
Bird & Bird	Mills & Reeve
Bond Pearce	Morgan Cole
Browne Jacobson	Nabarro
Burges Salmon	Norton Rose
Charles Russell	Olswang
Clifford Chance	Osborne Clarke
Clyde & Co	Pannone
CMS Cameron McKenna	Pinsent Masons
Cobbetts	Reed Smith
Cripps Harries Hall	Reynolds Porter Chamberlain
Denton Wilde Sapte	Shadbolt
Dewey & LeBoeuf	Shoosmiths
Dickinson Dees	Simmons & Simmons
DLA Piper UK	SJ Berwin
DMH Stallard	Skadden, Arps
Dundas & Wilson	Slaughter and May
DWF	Speechly Bircham
Eversheds	Stephenson Harwood
Freeth Cartwright	Taylor Wessing
Freshfield	Thring Townsend
Halliwells	TLT
Hammonds	Trowers & Hamlins
HBJ Gateley Wareing	Veale Wasbrough
Herbert Smith	Vinson & Elkins
Hill Dickinson	Walker Morris
Ince & Co	Ward Hadaway
K&L Gates	Watson, Farley & Williams
Latham & Watkins	Wedlake Bell
Lawrence Graham (LG)	White & Case
Lester Aldridge	Wragge & Co
Lewis Silkin	

Corporate

In a nutshell

Corporate lawyers provide advice to companies on significant transactions affecting their activities, including internal operations, the buying and selling of businesses and business assets, and the arrangement of the finance to carry out these activities. Here are some of the terms you'll encounter.

Mergers and acquisitions (M&A): This is where one company acquires another by way of takeover (acquisition), or where two companies fuse to form a single larger entity (merger). The main reasons for a company to execute an M&A transaction are to grow its business (by acquiring or merging with a competitor) or add a new line of business to its existing activities. M&A can either be public (when it involves companies listed on a stock exchange) or private (when it concerns companies privately owned by individuals). **Equity capital markets:** where a private company raises capital by making its shares available to the public by listing itself on a stock exchange and executing an initial public offering (IPO), as a result of which it becomes a public company (or plc). The London Stock Exchange (LSE) and New York Stock Exchange (NYSE) are the most prestigious exchanges, but companies may list in many other exchanges worldwide. Once listed, the shares can be bought and sold by investors at a price determined by the market. **Private equity funds/houses:** manage multiple investment funds comprising investors who commit capital and mandate the private equity house to invest in numerous businesses on their behalf. **Private equity:** covers a range of transactions in which private equity funds are invested in or used to acquire privately held companies which have potential for growth. Private equity houses typically execute leveraged buyouts, using significant bank loans to complete the purchase of these businesses. A private equity fund's aim is to realise its investment by selling on portfolio companies at a profit or by way of an IPO of their shares on a stock exchange. **Venture capitalists:** groups of wealthy investors who provide capital to start-ups and small companies with perceived long-term growth potential. It typically entails high risk for investors but has the potential for above-average returns. **Corporate restructuring:** involves changes to the structure of a company and the disposal of certain assets, either because the company wants to concentrate on more profitable parts of its business; or because it is facing financial difficulties and needs to free up liquidity.

What lawyers do

- Negotiate and draft agreements – this will be done in conjunction with the client, the business that is being bought or sold, other advisers (eg accountants) and any financiers.
- Carry out due diligence – this is an investigation to verify the accuracy of information passed from the seller to the buyer, or from the company raising capital to the investor. It establishes the financial strength of the company, the outright ownership of all assets; whether there are outstanding debts or other claims against the company; any environmental or other liabilities that could reduce the value of the business in the future. If shares or bonds are being offered to the public, the report will take the form of a prospectus and must comply with statutory regulations.
- Arrange financing – this could come from banks or other types of investors; they will wish to have some kind of security for their investment, eg participation in the shareholding, taking out a mortgage over property or other collateral.
- Gather all parties for the completion of the transaction, ensuring all assets have been properly covered by written documents that are properly signed and witnessed. Company law requires that decisions are made at properly convened board meetings and recorded in written resolutions.
- Finalise post-completion registrations and procedures.

The realities of the job

- Large public companies tend to use the services of large City firms and American firms in London. These firms also claim the lion's share of cross-border deals and compete with smaller City and regional firms for business from privately owned companies.
- The type of clients your firm acts for will determine your experiences. Publicly listed companies, major private equity houses and the investment banks that underwrite deals can be extremely demanding and have a different attitude to risk than, say, rich entrepreneurs, owner-managed businesses (OMBs) and small to medium-sized enterprises (SMEs). To deal with such clients, a robust and confident manner is required and stamina is a must.
- Corporate transactions can be large and complicated, with many different aspects of the company affected in the process. Lawyers need to be conversant in a variety of legal disciplines and know when to refer matters to a specialist in, say, merger control (competition), employment, property or tax.

- Corporate deals involve mountains of paperwork, so you need to be well organised and have good drafting skills. Above all, corporate is a very practical area of law, so commercial acumen and a good understanding of your clients' objectives is a must.
- Corporate work is cyclical and therefore the hours lawyers work can vary depending on the general state of the market and the particular needs of the clients, whose expectations have risen even further since the widespread use of instant modes of communication.
- The most junior member of a deal team normally get stuck with the most boring or unrewarding tasks. The banes of the corporate trainee's life are data room management (putting together and caretaking all the factual information on which a deal relies) and bibling (the creation of files containing copies of all the agreed documents and deal information). More challenging tasks quickly become available to driven junior lawyers.
- You need to become absorbed in the corporate world. Get a taster by reading the FT or City pages in your daily newspaper, and if you don't develop an interest then choose another area of practice pronto.

Current issues

- The recent past has been a challenging time for corporate practices throughout the UK. As a result of the ongoing financial crisis, companies have been finding it more difficult and expensive to borrow money from banks and, in such a volatile market, buyers and sellers are finding it hard to reach agreement on the value of assets. The result has been a massive reduction in deal volume and value, with data providers pointing to a 30% decline in the overall M&A deal activity and a dramatic 95% drop in European IPO deals compared to the boom year of 2007.
- Leveraged buyouts, which are traditionally financed using a large amount of borrowed money, have seen a sharp decline in value and volume. Given the dearth of LBO deals, private equity players have increased their focus on the restructuring of portfolio companies.
- Unsurprisingly, distressed M&A deals have been on the rise, as businesses facing financial difficulties seek alternative strategies to avoid insolvency. Such strategies include the disposal of non-core operations to free up cash or mergers with more financially stable entities.
- Cash-rich investors have their pick of the best assets and often acquire businesses at a significant discount due to lower company valuations. There has been growing interest from emerging markets investors and sovereign wealth funds, particularly from the Middle East, in acquiring assets in the UK and elsewhere.
- Turmoil in the finance sector caused a boom in capital raising, particularly rights issues. Companies use these as an alternative to bank debt to raise further finance by selling new shares to existing shareholders in proportion to their existing shareholdings in the company.
- The downturn has spawned growth in the insolvency sector.
- A sound grounding in corporate finance makes an excellent springboard for working in-house in major companies. Some lawyers move to banks to work as corporate finance execs or analysts. Company secretarial positions suit lawyers with a taste for internal management and compliance issues.

Read our True Pictures on...

Addleshaw Goddard	K&L Gates
Allen & Overy	Latham & Watkins
Ashurst	Lewis Silkin
B P Collins	Lawrence Graham (LG)
Baker & McKenzie	Linklaters
Barlow Lyde & Gilbert	Lovells
Bates Wells & Braithwaite	Macfarlanes
Beachcroft	Manches
Berwin Leighton Paisner	Martineau
Bird & Bird	Mayer Brown International
Bond Pearce	Michelmores
Browne Jacobson	Mills & Reeve
Burges Salmon	Mishcon de Reya
Charles Russell	Morgan Cole
Cleary Gottlieb	Morrison & Foerster MNP
Clifford Chance	Mundays
Clyde & Co	Nabarro
CMS Cameron McKenna	Norton Rose
Cobbetts	Olswang
Coffin Mew	Osborne Clarke
Covington & Burling	Pannone
Cripps Harries Hall	Penningtons Solicitors
Dechert	Pinsent Masons
Denton Wilde Sapte	Reed Smith
Dickinson Dees	Reynolds Porter Chamberlain
DLA Piper UK	Shadbolt
DMH Stallard	Shoosmiths
Dundas & Wilson	Simmons & Simmons
DWF	SJ Berwin
Edwards Angell	Skadden, Arps
Eversheds	Slaughter and May
Farrer & Co	Speechly Bircham
Finers Stephens Innocent	Stephenson Harwood
Foot Anstey Solicitors	Stevens & Bolton
Freeth Cartwright	Taylor Wessing
Freshfields	Thring Townsend
Halliwells	TLT
Hammonds	Travers Smith
Harbottle & Lewis	Trowers & Hamlins
HBJ Gateley Wareing	Veale Wasbrough
Henmans	Walker Morris
Herbert Smith	Ward Hadaway
Hill Dickinson	Watson, Farley & Williams
Holman Fenwick Willan	Weil, Gotshal & Manges
Howes Percival	White & Case
Irwin Mitchell	Wilsons
Jones Day	Wragge & Co

Crime

In a nutshell

Criminal solicitors represent defendants in cases brought before the UK's criminal courts. Lesser offences are commonly dealt with exclusively by solicitors in the magistrates' courts; more serious charges go to the Crown Courts, which are essentially still the domain of barristers, not least because most defendants still prefer this. Everyday crime is the staple for most solicitors – theft, assault, drugs and driving offences. Fraud is the preserve of a more limited number of firms, and the cases require a different approach from, say, crimes of violence. Criminal practice is busy, often frantic, with a hectic schedule of visits to police stations, prisons and magistrates' courts meaning plenty of face-to-face client contact and advocacy.

A summary of the work of the Crown Prosecution Service is given on page 26. Details of the Public Defender Service are on page 29.

The criminal courts of England and Wales

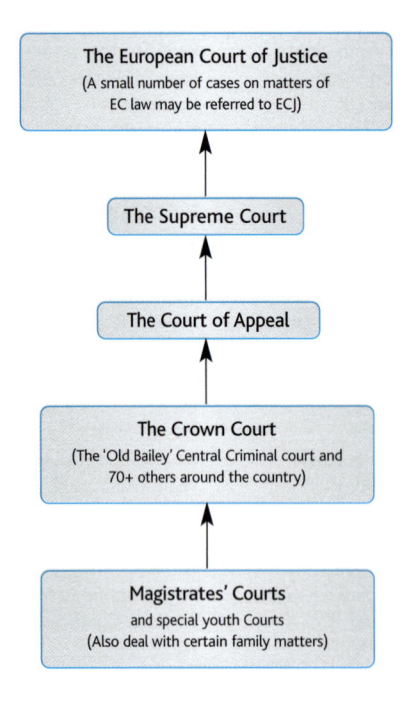

The European Court of Justice
(A small number of cases on matters of EC law may be referred to ECJ)
↑
The Supreme Court
↑
The Court of Appeal
↑
The Crown Court
(The 'Old Bailey' Central Criminal court and 70+ others around the country)
↑
Magistrates' Courts
and special youth Courts
(Also deal with certain family matters)

What lawyers do

- Attend police stations to interview and advise people in police custody.
- Visit prisons to see clients on remand.
- Prepare the client's defence using medical and social workers' reports, liaising with witnesses, probation officers, the CPS and others.
- Attend conferences with counsel (ie barristers).
- Represent defendants at trial or brief barristers to do so.
- Represent clients at sentencing hearings, explaining any mitigating facts.
- Fraud solicitors need a head for business as they deal with a considerable volume of paperwork and financial analysis.

The realities of the job

- Hours are long and can disrupt your personal life. Lawyers who are accredited to work as Duty Solicitors will be on a rota and can be called to a police station at any time of the day or night while on duty.
- Confidence is essential. Without it you're doomed.
- In general crime you'll have a large caseload with a fast turnaround, meaning plenty of advocacy.
- The work is driven by the procedural rules and timetable of the court. Even so, recent figures show that almost a quarter of trials do not proceed on the appointed day, either because defendents or witnesses are absent, or at the request of the CPS.
- Your efforts can mean the difference between a person's liberty or incarceration. You have to be detail conscious and constantly vigilant.
- You'll encounter horrible situations and difficult or distressed people. Murderers, rapists, drug dealers, conmen, football hooligans, paedophiles. If you have the ability to look beyond the labels and see these people as clients who are deserving of your best efforts then you've picked the right job. Some will have drug or alcohol problems, others will be mentally ill, others just children.
- It can be disheartening to see clients repeat the same poor choices, returning to court again and again.
- Public funding of criminal defence means there's a good helping of bureaucracy. It also means you'll never be a millionaire.
- Trainees in fraud find the early years provide minimal advocacy and masses of trawling through warehouses full of documents. Caseloads are smaller but cases can run for years.

Current issues

- Huge changes in legal aid funding are ongoing and many firms that have previously excelled in crime are moving out of the area entirely or no longer accept publicly funded clients. The UK spends more per head on legal aid than any other country, and the government perceives that this spend is increasing at an unsustainable rate. Read page 22 for more detail.
- Ministry of Justice reforms aimed to address legal aid budgeting have been met with disapproval and led to extraordinary consequences. Recently, a defendant escaped confiscation proceedings because she was unable to find an advocate willing to accept the legal aid rates available for her representation.
- A change in police station procedures means the police are cautioning more and charging less in an effort to meet government targets. This obviously has a knock-on effect on the number of available cases.
- The nationwide rollout of the Legal Services Commission's Criminal Defence Service Direct is affecting the amount of work available for solicitors. The CDS now provides telephone advice to those detained at police stations for less serious matters – eg drink driving, non-imprisonable offences, breach of bail and warrants.
- More fraud cases are popping up, and with authorities pushing for criminal charges for competition regulation violations, corporations are facing greater criminal liability. This kind of work tends to go to the firms that have traditionally handled white-collar crime.
- Check out www.clsa.co.uk for other news and discussion on major developments in criminal practice.

Read our True Pictures on...

BTMK Solicitors	Forbes
DLA Piper UK	Herbert Smith
Eversheds	Irwin Mitchell
Finers Stephens Innocent	Pannone
Foot Anstey Solicitors	Simmons & Simmons

Employment

In a nutshell

Employment lawyers guide their clients through the ever-growing area of workplace-related legislation and are intimately involved in the relationship between employers and employees. The divide between employers' and employees' lawyers is often clear-cut, although many firms do act for both types of client. A few are known for their union connections. Always remember that the nature of a firm's clientele determines on which side of the fence its lawyers end up. Usually the job includes both advisory work and litigation, but when choosing a training contract you may wish to check that this is the case, or if the two roles are split.

Disputes are almost always resolved at an Employment Tribunal, or before reaching one. Tribunals are far less formal than a court, so barristers do not wear wigs or robes and modify their performance, while individuals will often be unrepresented. In these situations the tribunal panel usually forgives their inexperience and may expect the employers' representatives to do so too. Appeals are heard at the Employment Appeal Tribunal (EAT). The grievances leading to litigation fall into the following broad categories: redundancy, unlawful dismissal, breach of contract, harassment and discrimination. This latter category can be brought on the grounds of race, religious or philosophical belief, gender, sexual orientation, disability and age.

What lawyers do

Employees' solicitors...

- Advise clients on whether they have suffered unlawful or unfair treatment and establish the amount to be claimed. This will either be capped or, in the case of discrimination, can include additional elements to cover loss of earnings, injury to feelings and aggravated damages.
- Gather evidence and witnesses to support the claim.
- Try to negotiate a payment from the employer or take the matter to tribunal. If there is a breach-of-contract element to the claim, it might be heard in a court rather than a tribunal.
- If the matter does reach tribunal, the solicitor may conduct the advocacy.

Employers' solicitors...

- Defend or settle the sorts of claims described above.
- Negotiate employment contracts or exit packages for senior staff.
- Negotiate with unions to avoid or resolve industrial disputes.
- Formulate HR policies and provide training on how to avoid workplace problems.

Realities of the job

- You quickly develop an understanding of human foibles. By their very nature employment cases are filled with drama.
- Clients may assume your role is to provide emotional support as well as legal advice, so you need to take care to define your role appropriately.
- Acting for employers, you won't always like what you hear, but you still need to protect the clients' interests. Soon enough you will see the advantage of preventative counselling and training programmes for clients.
- Solicitors who want to do their own advocacy thrive here, although barristers are commonly used for high-stakes or complicated hearings and trials.
- The work is driven by the procedural rules and timetable of the tribunals and courts.
- The law is extensive and changes frequently. You'll read more than your fair share of EU directives.

Current issues

- The big story here is litigation and plenty of it. An increase in claims related to discrimination and the breach and enforcement of post-termination restrictions has been blamed on the fall out of the credit crunch. While employers have a greater appetite for litigation to protect business interests, employees facing redundancy are also eager to fight for their rights.
- On the non-contentious side, firms have seen a substantial increase in work relating to redundancy and consultation issues, insolvencies and large-scale restructuring. Businesses such as Lehman Brothers, Zavvi and Woolworths are prominent examples. The huge demand for crisis-response teams is understandable.
- There has also been an increase in TUPE transactions (the transfer of an employee or group of employees to another employer) as businesses merge or are sold, or as a result of outsourcing/insourcing introduced to cut costs.
- There is stiff competition among trainees for employment seats, and it's even greater for NQ jobs. Consider applying to train at a specialist or employment-heavy firm if this is your intended field. Gaining exposure to employment work can be a lottery at some firms.

Read our True Pictures on...

- Addleshaw Goddard
- Allen & Overy
- Anthony Collins Solicitors
- Ashurst
- B P Collins
- Baker & McKenzie
- Barlow Lyde & Gilbert
- Bates Wells & Braithwaite
- Beachcroft
- Berwin Leighton Paisner
- Bevan Brittan
- Bircham Dyson Bell
- Bird & Bird
- Bond Pearce
- Browne Jacobson
- Burges Salmon
- Charles Russell
- Clifford Chance
- Clyde & Co
- CMS Cameron McKenna
- Cobbetts
- Coffin Mew
- Cripps Harries Hall
- Dechert
- Denton Wilde Sapte
- Dickinson Dees
- DLA Piper UK
- DMH Stallard
- Dundas & Wilson
- DWF
- Eversheds
- Farrer & Co
- Finers Stephens Innocent
- Foot Anstey Solicitors
- Ford & Warren
- Freeth Cartwright
- Freshfields
- Halliwells
- Hammonds
- Harbottle & Lewis
- HBJ Gateley Wareing
- Henmans
- Herbert Smith
- Higgs & Sons
- Hill Dickinson
- Howes Percival
- Irwin Mitchell
- Jones Day
- K&L Gates
- Latham & Watkins
- Lester Aldridge
- Lewis Silkin
- Lawrence Graham (LG)
- Linklaters
- Lovells
- Macfarlanes
- Manches
- Martineau
- Mayer Brown International
- McDermott Will & Emery UK
- Michelmores
- Mills & Reeve
- Mishcon de Reya
- Morgan Cole
- Mundays
- Nabarro
- Norton Rose
- Olswang
- Osborne Clarke
- Pannone
- Penningtons Solicitors
- Pinsent Masons
- Reed Smith
- Reynolds Porter Chamberlain
- Shadbolt
- Shoosmiths
- Simmons & Simmons
- SJ Berwin
- Slaughter and May
- Speechly Bircham
- Stephenson Harwood
- Stevens & Bolton
- Taylor Wessing
- Thring Townsend
- TLT
- Travers Smith
- Trethowans
- Trowers & Hamlins
- Veale Wasbrough
- Walker Morris
- Ward Hadaway
- Watson, Farley & Williams
- Wedlake Bell
- White & Case
- Wilsons
- Withers
- Wragge & Co

Environment

In a nutshell

Environment lawyers advise corporate clients on damage limitation and pre-emptive measures, and they defend them from prosecution. In other words, the majority of private practitioners work for, rather than stick it to, big business. Opportunities do exist at organisations like Greenpeace and Friends of the Earth, but these jobs are highly sought after. Another non-commercial option is to work for a local authority, a government department such as the Department for Environment, Food and Rural Affairs (Defra) or a regulatory body like the Environment Agency.

Environment law overlaps with other disciplines such as property, criminal law, corporate or EU law. Environmental issues can be deal breakers, especially in the modern era of corporate social responsibility. However, the small size of most law firms' environment teams means there are relatively few pure environmental specialists around.

Lawyers in private practice

- Advise on the potential environmental consequences of corporate, property and projects transactions.
- Advise on compliance and regulatory issues to help clients operate within regulatory boundaries and avoid investigation or prosecution.
- Defend clients when they get into trouble over water or air pollution, waste disposal, emission levels or health and safety. Such cases can involve criminal or civil actions, judicial reviews and even statutory appeals. They may also be subject to damaging media coverage.

Lawyers with local authorities

- Handle a massive variety of work covering regulatory and planning issues plus waste management and air pollution prosecutions.
- Advise the authority on its own potential liability.

Lawyers working for Defra

- Are responsible for litigation, drafting of subordinate legislation, advisory work and contract drafting on any of Defra's varied mandates.
- Work in a team of over 80 lawyers, including trainees, on GLS-funded schemes. Defra aims to promote sustainable development without compromising the quality of life of future generations.

Lawyers working for the Environment Agency

- Prosecute environmental crimes – this involves gathering evidence, preparing cases and briefing barristers.
- Co-operate with government lawyers on the drafting and implementation of legislation.
- Work in Bristol and eight regional bases and are responsible for protecting and enhancing the environment. They also regulate corporate activities that have the capacity to pollute.

The realities of the job

- In this competitive and demanding field, all-round skills are best complemented by a genuine interest in a specific area. The way in which environmental law spans disciplines requires commercial nous and a good understanding of corporate structures.
- Excellent academics are essential to help wade through, extrapolate from and present research and complex legislation; so too are sound judgement, pragmatism and the ability to come up with inventive solutions.
- A basic grasp of science helps.
- If you want to change environmental laws or crusade for a better planet, then stick to the public or not for profit sectors. The sometimes uncomfortable realities of private practice won't be for you.
- Client contact is key and relationships can endure over many years. Environmental risks are difficult to quantify and clients will rely on your gut instincts and powers of lateral thinking.
- With visits to waste dumps or drying reservoirs, and a workload that can span health and safety matters, corporate transactions and regulatory advice all in one day, this is neither a desk-bound nor a quiet discipline.
- Research constantly advances and legislation is always changing in this field, so you'll spend a lot of time keeping up to date.
- A taste for European law is essential as more and more EU directives prescribe the boundaries of environmental law in the UK.

Current issues

- The EU Emissions and Trading Scheme and the Environmental Liability Directive will affect many businesses as the UK seeks to fulfil the EU's '20/20/20' principle – ie a 20% cut in emissions, a 20% reduction in energy consumption and 20% of energy will come from renewable sources.

- Keep on top of changes in environmental law courtesy of websites like www.endsreport.com. You should enhance your CV and prime yourself by joining organisations such as the Environmental Law Foundation (ELF) and the UK Environmental Law Association (www.ukela.org). Most environmental lawyers are members of UKELA and students are welcome to attend events across the country. The charity ELF (www.elflaw.org) provides a referral service for members of the public, organises lectures in London and produces regular newsletters for members.
- The Environment Agency has been taking a more stringent approach to clamping down on regulatory offences. Where businesses might previously have dealt with them in-house, lawyers are now being instructed to negotiate with EA. The costs involved can run into the millions.
- An increasingly well-informed public also means a increasingly litigious public. A surge in class actions, usually involving pollution, odour or other forms of nuisance, is being witnessed across the board.
- Climate change isn't just for academics any more. It's a whole legal area in itself. Top-flight international firms are encountering this type of work more often, and international issues are coming to the fore. Initiatives like the Equator Principles and Corporate Social Responsibility are now prominent.
- Finally, energy. We all need it and there isn't going to be enough of it. Scores of renewable energy projects (offshore projects are most prevalent in the UK) have led to environmental lawyers working alongside planning and project finance colleagues.

Read our True Pictures on...

Addleshaw Goddard	Hill Dickinson
Allen & Overy	Irwin Mitchell
Ashurst	K&L Gates
B P Collins	Lawrence Graham (LG)
Baker & McKenzie	Linklaters
Barlow Lyde & Gilbert	Lovells
Beachcroft	Macfarlanes
Berwin Leighton Paisner	Manches
Bircham Dyson Bell	Mayer Brown International
Bond Pearce	Mills & Reeve
Browne Jacobson	Nabarro
Burges Salmon	Norton Rose
Clifford Chance	Osborne Clarke
CMS Cameron McKenna	Pannone
Denton Wilde Sapte	Pinsent Masons
Dewey & LeBoeuf	Simmons & Simmons
Dickinson Dees	SJ Berwin
DLA Piper UK	Slaughter and May
DMH Stallard	Stephenson Harwood
Dundas & Wilson	Stevens & Bolton
Eversheds	Taylor Wessing
Freshfields Bruckhaus Deringer	Thring Townsend Lee & Pembertons
Hammonds	Travers Smith
Herbert Smith	Walker Morris
	Wragge & Co

Family

In a nutshell

Lawyers are involved with almost every aspect of family life, from the legal mechanics and complications of marriage and civil partnerships to divorce, disputes between cohabitants, inheritance disputes between family members, prenuptial and cohabitation agreements and all matters relating to children, be these disagreements between parents as to the custody of and access to children or cases involving public authorities intervening to protect the welfare of children. Whether working in a general high street practice with a large caseload of legally aided work, or for a specialist practice dealing with big-money divorces and complex child or international matters, family solicitors are in court a good deal and fully occupied back in the office.

There is effectively a division between child law and matrimonial law, with many practitioners devoting themselves exclusively to one or other. Some plant a foot in each. A few lawyers have developed specialisms in relation to IVF, surrogacy and related issues.

Matrimonial lawyers

- Interview and advise clients on prenuptial agreements, cohabitation arrangements, divorce and the financial implications of divorce. This can involve issues like inheritance and wills, conveyancing, welfare benefits, company law, tax and trusts, pensions and even judicial review.
- Prepare the client's case for divorce and settlement hearings, including organising witnesses and providing summaries of assets/finances, which will require dealing with accountants, financial and pensions advisers.
- Attend conferences with barristers.
- Represent clients in hearings or brief barristers to do so.
- Negotiate settlements and associated financial terms.

Child law lawyers

- In private cases – interview and advise clients on the implications of divorce with regard to child contact and residence. In some instances this will result in court action. Deal with disputes between parents or other family members over the residence of, and contact with, children.
- In public cases – represent local authorities, parents, children's guardians or children themselves on matters such as children's care proceedings or abuse in care claims. Social workers, probation officers, psychologists and medical professionals will also be involved in cases.

The realities of the job

- When it comes to relationships and families, no two sets of circumstances will ever be the same. Advocacy is plentiful.
- You will encounter a real mix of clients, some at a joyful moment in their lives, others facing deeply traumatic times or personal problems. A good family law practitioner combines the sensitivity, trustworthiness and capacity for empathy of a counsellor with the clarity of thought, commercial acumen and communication skills of a lawyer. Your client may treat you as a shoulder to cry on, but you need to retain detachment to achieve the result they need.
- Tough negotiating skills and a strong nerve are vital as your work has immediate and practical consequences. How often your client gets to see their children, what happens to their home, their family or their livelihood are all in your hands. The prospect of telling a client that they've lost a custody battle does much to sharpen the mind.
- A pragmatic and real-world outlook is useful, however you'll also need to spend time keeping abreast of legal developments.
- On publicly funded matters you'll face your share of bureaucracy and it certainly won't make you rich.

Current issues

- London is arguably becoming the divorce capital of Europe, and the most generous jurisdiction in the world for (usually) women in a divorce situation. International instructions regarding divorce are on the rise, as clients with a foot in two or more jurisdictions, not to mention a bundle of cash, seek to get the best outcome.
- Firms admit it is hard to predict what impact the economic downturn will have on divorce cases. The inevitable stresses associated with financial difficulty could force couples apart or keep them together. So far there has not been a significant observable effect on divorce rates. What has been observed is increasing demand for advice on wealth protection and prenuptial agreements.
- Taxation is a major theme as, more than ever, clients seek to reach settlements that are structured to miti-

- gate unnecessary tax or other liabilities. As in many other practice areas, it's worth getting close to a tax specialist.
- These are challenging times for the publicly funded lawyer. Many firms are feeling the squeeze and some are choosing to limit, or even cease, legally aided work. This is the case with both matrimonial finance cases and childcare proceedings, although some firms have stuck with the latter on idealistic grounds. In 2008 the government's implementation of Care Proceedings Reforms (designed to speed up the resolution of cases involving children and avoid court) caused further consternation. For details see www.justice.gov.uk/guidance/careproceedings.htm
- The impact of the tragic Baby P case in the London Borough of Haringey is expected to have a profound effect on public child law. Although there has been no flood of journalists to the family courts, they have been opened up to the press and social workers are also under increased scrutiny.

Read our True Pictures on...

Anthony Collins Solicitors	Irwin Mitchell
B P Collins	Lester Aldridge
Boodle Hatfield	Manches
Burges Salmon	Michelmores
Charles Russell	Mills & Reeve
Coffin Mew	Mishcon de Reya
Cripps Harries Hall	Morgan Cole
Dickinson Dees	Mundays
DWF	Pannone
Farrer & Co	Reynolds Porter Chamberlain
Fisher Meredith	Speechly Bircham
Foot Anstey Solicitors	TLT
Halliwells	Trethowans
Harbottle & Lewis	Ward Hadaway
Henmans	Wilsons
Higgs & Sons	Withers
Hill Dickinson	

Intellectual property

In a nutshell

Lawyers can protect their clients' highly valuable intellectual property assets in several ways. Acquiring a patent provides the proprietor with the exclusive right to work it for a certain period. Acquiring a trade mark provides a limited monopoly to use the mark on certain goods or services, and a registered design provides the exclusive right to use the design. By contrast, copyright exists as soon as material is created, without the need for any registration: it covers things like music, paintings and drawings, works of literature or reference, databases and web pages. Increasingly the work of the IP lawyer is crossing over with other disciplines, not simply IT and life sciences, but also areas such as competition and employment law.

What lawyers do

- Search domestic, European and international registers of patents, trade marks and registered designs to establish ownership of existing rights or the potential to register new rights.
- Take all steps to protect clients' interests by securing patents, trade marks and registered designs; appeal unfavourable decisions; attack decisions that benefit others but harm the lawyer's own client.
- Write letters to require that third parties desist from carrying out infringing activities or risk litigation for damages and an injunction.
- Issue court proceedings and prepare cases for trial, including taking witness statements, examining scientific or technical reports and commissioning experiments and tests. In the world of brand protection, junior lawyers may find themselves conducting consumer surveys and going on covert shopping expeditions.
- Instruct and consult with barristers. Solicitor-advocates can appear in the Patents County Court; the advantages of having a specialist IP barrister for higher court hearings are obvious.
- Draft commercial agreements between owners of IP rights and those who want to use the protected invention, design or artistic work. The most common documents will either transfer ownership or grant a licence for use.
- Work as part of a multidisciplinary team on corporate transactions, verifying ownership of IP rights and drafting documents enabling their transfer.

The realities of the job

- Lawyers must be able to handle everyone from company directors to mad inventors. Clients come from manufacturing, the hi-tech sector, engineering, pharmaceuticals, agrochemicals, universities and scientific institutions, media organisations and the arts.
- A degree in a relevant subject is common among patent lawyers. Brand and trade mark lawyers need a curiosity for all things creative and must keep up with consumer trends. Both need a good sense for commercial strategy.
- Attention to detail, precision and accuracy: you must be meticulous, particularly when drafting, as correct wording is imperative.
- In patent and trade mark filing, everything has a time limit. You will live by deadlines.
- The volume of paperwork involved can be huge on patent matters, though on the plus side you'll visit research labs or factories to learn about production processes, etc.
- The development of pharmaceuticals and inventions is motivated more often by profit than philanthropy. Success or failure in litigation can dramatically affect a company's share price.
- Manufacturing, pharmaceutical and research companies employ patent specialists and there are in-house legal teams at all the large pharmaceutical companies. In the media, major publishers and television companies employ in-house IP lawyers.

Current issues

- The liquidity crisis led to a growing awareness of intellectual property as a valuable asset. Businesses have become more aggressive in protecting their rights and litigation is on the rise. The English Courts' reputation for being patent-unfriendly has been challenged by recent judgments.
- The costs of patent litigation were highlighted by the monstrous £5.2m bill handed to BlackBerry by Allen & Overy in 2008. Renewed calls for more streamlined procedures followed outrage at the expense of this five-day trial.
- In the trade mark arena clients seek strategic advice and want to tackle the growing problem of counterfeit goods. L'Oreal's case about eBay's liability in relation to counterfeit goods sold on their site has been referred to the ECJ by the French Courts and the outcome is eagerly awaited.

- The trend for digitalisation is bringing online copyright issues to prominence, and another eagerly awaited outcome is that of Inter Flora vs Marks & Spencer, in which the latter bought sponsored links from Google for the words Interflora, Inter-Flora and Intraflora. User generated content is also an issue.
- Convergence between different forms of media and technology is giving rise to sensitive issues of data protection.
- European patent attorneys and trade mark agents work as a parallel profession. You can find out more about what they do on page 30. There are early signs of convergence between solicitors and these other professionals. Some law firms provide in-house trade mark and patent-filing services, allowing clients to sidestep patent and trade mark attorneys. Others are working in tandem with them, for example at Marks & Clark and HGF Law.

Read our True Pictures on...

Addleshaw Goddard	Latham & Watkins
Allen & Overy	Lewis Silkin
Ashurst	Linklaters
Baker & McKenzie	Lovells
Beachcroft	Macfarlanes
Berwin Leighton Paisner	Manches
Bird & Bird	Martineau
Bond Pearce	Mayer Brown International
Bristows	McDermott Will & Emery UK
Browne Jacobson	Mills & Reeve
Burges Salmon	Mishcon de Reya
Charles Russell	Morgan Cole
Clifford Chance	Morrison & Foerster MNP
CMS Cameron McKenna	Nabarro
Cobbetts	Norton Rose
Coffin Mew	Olswang
Covington & Burling	Osborne Clarke
Cripps Harries Hall	Pannone
Dechert	Penningtons Solicitors
Denton Wilde Sapte	Pinsent Masons
Dickinson Dees	Reed Smith
DLA Piper UK	Reynolds Porter Chamberlain
DMH Stallard	Shadbolt
DWF	Shoosmiths
Edwards Angell	Simmons & Simmons
Eversheds	SJ Berwin
Farrer & Co	Slaughter and May
Finers Stephens Innocent	Speechly Bircham
Foot Anstey Solicitors	Stevens & Bolton
Freeth Cartwright	Taylor Wessing
Freshfields	Thring Townsend
Halliwells	TLT
Hammonds	Walker Morris
Harbottle & Lewis	Ward Hadaway
Herbert Smith	Wedlake Bell
Hill Dickinson	White & Case
Howes Percival	Wiggin
Irwin Mitchell	Withers
Jones Day	Wragge & Co
K&L Gates	

Litigation/dispute resolution

In a nutshell

Litigation solicitors assist clients in resolving civil disputes. Disputes can concern anything from unpaid bills or unfulfilled contract terms to problems between landlords and tenants, infringement of IP rights, construction-related claims, the liabilities of insurers, shipping cases, defective products, media and entertainment industry wrangles… the list is endless. And that's just in the commercial sphere. The most common types of litigation involving private individuals are discussed at length in our personal injury overview.

If disputes are not settled by negotiation, they will be concluded either by court litigation or an alternative form of dispute resolution, hence the interchangeability of the terms 'litigation' and 'dispute resolution'. The most common of these other methods are arbitration and mediation, the former is often stipulated as the preferred method in commercial contracts, the latter is generally achieved through structured negotiations between the parties, overseen by an independent mediator. These methods can still be problematic: mediation is not necessarily adequate for complex matters and some argue that opponents can use it as a means of 'bleeding' money from each other or as covert interrogation.

Confusingly, there are two divisions of the High Court dealing with major cases – the Chancery Division and the Queen's Bench Division (QBD) – and each hears different types of case. The following diagram depicts the court system in England and Wales, meanwhile in the Bar section of this guide on page 680 we summarise the differences between the QBD and Chancery Division.

What litigators do

- Advise clients on whether they have a valid claim, or whether to settle or fight a claim made against them.
- Gather evidence and witnesses to support the client's position; develop case strategies.
- Issue court proceedings or embark on a process of alternative dispute resolution if correspondence with the defendant does not produce a satisfactory result.
- Represent clients at pre-trial hearings and case management conferences.
- Attend conferences with counsel (ie barristers) and brief them to conduct advocacy in hearings, trials and arbitrations.
- Attend trials, arbitrations and mediations with clients; provide assistance to barristers.

The civil courts of England and Wales

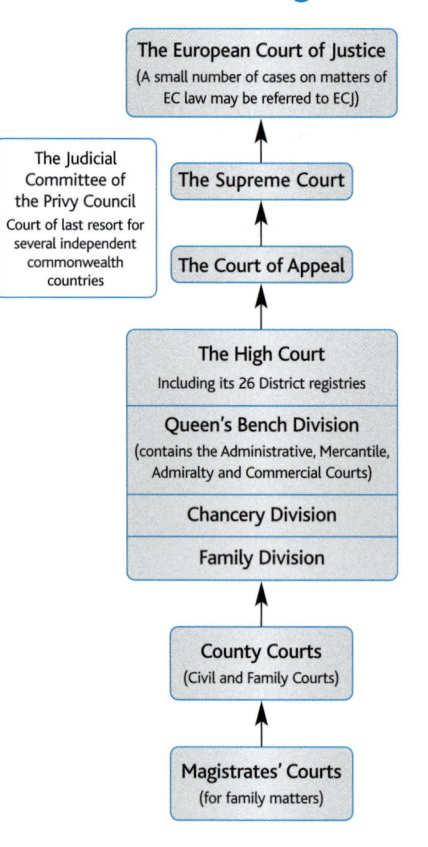

The European Court of Justice
(A small number of cases on matters of EC law may be referred to ECJ)

↑

The Judicial Committee of the Privy Council
Court of last resort for several independent commonwealth countries

The Supreme Court

↑

The Court of Appeal

↑

The High Court
Including its 26 District registries

Queen's Bench Division
(contains the Administrative, Mercantile, Admiralty and Commercial Courts)

Chancery Division

Family Division

↑

County Courts
(Civil and Family Courts)

↑

Magistrates' Courts
(for family matters)

Other Specialist Courts

Employment Tribunals	VAT and Duties Tribunals
Lands Tribunals	General and Special Commissioners (Tax)
Leasehold Valuation Tribunals	Asylum & Immigration Tribunals

Europe

ECJ: Any UK court can refer a point of law for determination if it relates to EU law. The decision will be referred back to the court where the case originated.

European Court of Human Rights: Hears complaints regarding breaches of human rights.

The realities of the job

- Work is driven by procedural rules and the timetable of the courts. Good litigators understand how best to manoeuvre within the system, while also developing winning case strategies.
- The phenomenal amount of paperwork generated means that young litigators spend much of their time sifting through documents, scheduling and copying them in order to provide the court and all other parties with an agreed bundle of evidence.

- Litigators need to express themselves succinctly and precisely.
- Unless the claim value is small, the solicitor's job is more about case preparation than court performance. Solicitor-advocates are gaining ground, and once properly qualified they can appear in the higher courts. Nonetheless, barristers still dominate court advocacy and recently the performance of some solicitor-advocates was criticised by the judiciary.
- Trainee workloads largely depend on the type of firm and the type of clients represented. Big City firms won't give trainees free rein on huge international banking disputes – they might not even go to court during their training contract – but they will be able to offer a small contribution to headline-making cases. Firms handling much smaller claims will often expect trainees to deal with all aspects of a case, from drafting correspondence and interim court applications to meetings with clients and settlement negotiations.
- There are a number of litigation-led law firms that handle cases of all sizes and these present the best opportunities for a litigation-heavy training contract.
- The Solicitors Regulation Authority (SRA) requires all trainee solicitors to gain some contentious experience. People tend to learn early on whether they are suited to this kind of work. Increasingly in big City firms, SRA requirements can be fulfilled by a litigation crash course.
- The competition for litigation jobs at NQ level is fierce. Concentrate on litigation-led firms if you are certain of your leanings.
- Despite a few firms like Herbert Smith and Hammonds starting up in-house advocacy units, the courts remain dominated by barristers, who are felt to have the edge when it comes to the skills and expertise needed to advocate. If you are determined to become both a solicitor and an advocate, certain areas of practice have more scope for advocacy – eg family, crime, employment and lower-value civil litigation.

Current issues

- Historically, London has been a popular forum for international litigation and arbitration. Some suggest this could be affected by an ECJ ruling that arbitration anti-suit injunctions are inconsistent with the Brussels regulation, but the sheer volume of cases (and from places as disparate as Russia and South America) does not appear to be slowing.
- The economic downturn has led to a greater willingness to litigate disputes as the need to recoup losses becomes more important. Insurance litigation in particular has received a boost as more claims are filed and subsequently challenged.
- Significant events, such as the collapse of Lehman Brothers and the Icelandic banks and allegations of fraud involving Bernard Madoff, continue to have wide-ranging consequences. A rise in investigations, and increased regulatory action and litigation, can all be expected.
- Third party litigation funding is emerging. Essentially an organisation that is not involved in a case, say a bank or private equity company, can choose to bank roll the cost of litigation for a share of the winnings.

Read our True Pictures on...

Addleshaw Goddard	Jones Day
Allen & Overy	K&L Gates
Anthony Collins Solicitors	Latham & Watkins
Ashurst	Lester Aldridge
B P Collins	Lewis Silkin
Baker & McKenzie	Lawrence Graham (LG)
Barlow Lyde & Gilbert	Linklaters
Beachcroft	Lovells
Berwin Leighton Paisner	Macfarlanes
Bevan Brittan	Manches
Bingham McCutchen	Martineau
Bird & Bird	Mayer Brown International
Bond Pearce	McDermott Will & Emery
Bristows	Michelmores
Browne Jacobson	Mills & Reeve
Burges Salmon	Mishcon de Reya
Charles Russell	Morgan Cole
Clifford Chance	Mundays
Clyde & Co	Nabarro
CMS Cameron McKenna	Norton Rose
Cobbetts	Olswang
Covington & Burling	Osborne Clarke
Cripps Harries Hall	Pannone
Dechert	Penningtons Solicitors
Denton Wilde Sapte	Pinsent Masons
Dewey & LeBoeuf	Reed Smith
Dickinson Dees	Reynolds Porter Chamberlain
DLA Piper UK	Shadbolt
DMH Stallard	Shoosmiths
DWF	Simmons & Simmons
Edwards Angell	SJ Berwin
Eversheds	Skadden, Arps
Finers Stephens Innocent	Slaughter and May
Foot Anstey Solicitors	Speechly Bircham
Forbes	Stephenson Harwood
Ford & Warren	Stevens & Bolton
Freeth Cartwright	Taylor Wessing
Freshfields	Thring Townsend
Halliwells	TLT
Hammonds	Travers Smith
HBJ Gateley Wareing	Trethowans
Henmans	Veale Wasbrough
Herbert Smith	Walker Morris
Hill Dickinson	Ward Hadaway
Holman Fenwick Willan	White & Case
Howes Percival	Wilsons
Ince & Co	Withers
Irwin Mitchell	Wragge & Co

Personal injury and clinical negligence

In a nutshell

Personal injury and clinical negligence lawyers resolve claims brought by people who have been injured, either as a result of an accident or through flawed medical treatment. Injuries can be as simple as a broken wrist resulting from tripping over a wonky paving stone or as serious as a fatal illness caused by exposure to dangerous materials. Clinical negligence cases could result from a failure to treat or diagnose a patient, or treatment going wrong, be it a botched boob job or a baby born brain damaged.

The claimant lawyer usually acts for one individual, but sometimes a claim may be brought by a group of people – this is a class action or multiparty claim. The defendant lawyer represents the party alleged to be responsible for the illness or injury. In most PI cases the claim against the defendant will be taken over by the defendant's insurance company, which will then be the solicitor's client. Local authorities are common defendants in relation to slips and trips, while employers usually end up on the hook for accidents in the workplace. In a majority of clinical negligence cases the defendant will be the NHS, although private medical practitioners and healthcare organisations are also sued.

Claimant solicitors

- Determine the veracity of their client's claim and establish what they have suffered, including income lost and expenses incurred.
- Examine medical records and piece together all the facts. Commission further medical reports.
- Issue court proceedings if the defendant doesn't make an acceptable offer of compensation.

Defendant solicitors

- Try and avoid liability for their client or resolve a claim for as little as possible.
- Put all aspects of the case to the test. Perhaps the victim of a road traffic accident (RTA) wasn't wearing a seatbelt; perhaps the claimant has been malingering.

Both

- Manage the progress of the case over a period of months, even years, following an established set of procedural rules.
- Attempt to settle the claim before trial or, if a case goes to trial, brief a barrister and shepherd the client through the proceedings.

The realities of the job

- The work is driven by the procedural rules and timetable of the court.
- There is a mountain of paperwork, including witness statements and bundles of evidence.
- You'll spend a lot of time considering medical issues and records. Being squeamish is a no-no.
- Claimant lawyers have close contact with large numbers of clients and need good people skills.
- Defendant lawyers need to build long-term relationships with insurance companies. Clin neg defendant lawyers need to be able to communicate well with medical professionals and health sector managers.
- PI lawyers have large caseloads, especially when dealing with lower-value claims.
- There is some scope for advocacy, although barristers are used for high-stakes or complicated hearings and trials. Solicitors appear at preliminary hearings and case management conferences.

Current issues

- Conditional Fee Agreements (CFAs) – commonly known as no-win, no-fee agreements – continue to be hotly debated and, despite changes to simplify their application, are not always popular with solicitors. The Jackson Review (due in December 2009) is set to address the rules and principles of civil litigation and make recommendations in order to promote access to justice at proportionate cost.
- You may have seen claims management companies – sometimes derided as claims farmers – advertising on the TV. Despite some degree of regulation being introduced, they cause concern to lawyers because they can sometimes adopt unscrupulous tactics. The practice of claims farmers selling cases on to solicitors is under intense scrutiny.
- The limit for compensation in 'fast-track' PI cases has been raised from £15,000 to £25,000, which should have significant costs benefits for insurers.
- Opinion is split as to whether there is a growing compensation culture in Britain. Those who recognise one say CFAs must shoulder much of the blame; those who don't, assert that increased difficulties in securing legal aid have led to a reduction in the num-

ber of claims brought. The credit crunch has seen a greater willingness on the part of claimants to pursue action, however doubtful their claims may sometimes be.
- Clin neg lawyers are concerned about the likely effects of the NHS Redress Act 2006, which gives the power to introduce a scheme allowing lower-value claims to be handled by the NHS without going to court. Obviously this would cut away some of the lawyers' bread-and-butter work, and the proposal incites an important debate about health sector regulation in general.

Read our True Pictures on...

Anthony Collins Solicitors	Halliwells
Barlow Lyde & Gilbert	Henmans
Beachcroft	Hill Dickinson
Bevan Brittan	Irwin Mitchell
Bond Pearce	Michelmores
Browne Jacobson	Mills & Reeve
Capsticks Solicitors	Morgan Cole
Charles Russell	Nabarro
Coffin Mew	Pannone
Cripps Harries Hall	Penningtons Solicitors
DLA Piper UK	Reynolds Porter Chamberlain
DWF	Shoosmiths
Eversheds	Thring Townsend
Foot Anstey Solicitors	Trethowans
Forbes	Veale Wasbrough
Ford & Warren	Ward Hadaway
Freeth Cartwright	

Private client and charities

In a nutshell

You have money. You need to know how best to control it, preserve it and pass it on: enter the private client lawyer. Solicitors advise individuals, families and trusts on wealth management; some offer additional matrimonial and small-scale commercial assistance, others focus exclusively on highly specialised tax and trusts issues, or wills and probate.

Charities lawyers advise on all aspects of not-for-profit organisations' activities. These specialists need exactly the same skills and knowledge as private client lawyers but must also have the same kind of commercial knowledge as corporate lawyers.

Private client lawyers

- Draft wills in consultation with clients and expedite their implementation after death. Probate involves the appointment of an executor and the settling of an estate. Organising a house clearance or even a funeral is not beyond the scope of a lawyer's duties.
- Advise clients on the most tax-efficient and appropriate structure for holding money and assets. Lawyers must ensure their clients understand the foreign law implications of trusts held in offshore jurisdictions.
- Advise overseas clients interested in investing in the UK, and banks whose overseas clients have UK interests.
- Assist clients with the very specific licensing, sales arrangement and tax planning issues related to ownership of heritage chattels (individual items or collections of cultural value or significance).
- Bring or defend litigation in relation to disputed legacies.

Charities lawyers

- Advise charities on registration, reorganisation, regulatory compliance and the implications of new legislation.
- Offer specialist trusts and investment advice.
- Advise on quasi-corporate and mainstream commercial matters; negotiate and draft contracts for sponsorship and the development of trading subsidiaries; manage property issues and handle IP concerns.
- Charities law still conjures up images of sleepy local fundraising efforts or, alternatively, working on a trendy project for wealthy benefactors. The wide middle ground can incorporate working with a local authority, a local library and schools to establish an after-school homework programme, or rewriting the constitution of a 300-year-old church school to admit female pupils. Widespread international trust in British charity law means that you could also establish a study programme in Britain for a US university, or negotiate the formation of a zebra conservation charity in Tanzania.

The realities of the job

- An interest in other people's affairs is going to help. A capacity for empathy coupled with impartiality and absolute discretion are the hallmarks of a good private client lawyer. You'll need to be able to relate to and earn the trust of your many varied clients.
- Despite not being as chaotic as other fields, the technical demands of private client work can be exacting and an academic streak goes a long way.
- An eye for detail and a rigorous approach will help you see through the mire of black letter law (and regular new legislation) so as to spot loopholes and shrewd solutions that will save your clients money.
- The stereotype of the typical 'country gent' client is far from accurate: lottery wins, personal injury payouts, property portfolios, massive City salaries and successful businesses all feed the demand for legal advice.
- If you are wavering between private clients and commercial clients, charities law might offer a good balance.

Current issues

- The private client world is becoming increasingly internationalised. Wealthy people are selecting a wider geographical spread of assets, and London has become a hub for the management of these assets. Many clients come from Russia, the Middle East, the USA, India and France.
- HMRC is clamping down on tax avoidance and the role trusts can play in inheritance tax planning. Major tax changes, such as the abolition of taper relief and a £30,000 annual charge for non-domiciles have led to considerable reorganisation and restructuring of clients' tax and real estate planning.
- After an interminably long wait, the Charities Act 2006 was finalised. The Act addresses fundamental questions about what constitutes a charity and what 'public benefit' means. It also provides for greater regulation in some areas, and greater freedom for charities in others.

- It remains to be seen how the charitable sector will fare in a difficult economic climate; issues such as the collapse of the Icelandic banks and the Bernard Madoff scandal have provoked an increased level of interest in both governance and incorporation matters.
- Firms right across the country bemoan a dearth of young lawyers who can claim to be true private client specialists. It looks like a good time to put your hand up and be counted.

Read our True Pictures on...

Addleshaw Goddard	Howes Percival
Allen & Overy	Irwin Mitchell
Anthony Collins Solicitors	Lester Aldridge
B P Collins	Lawrence Graham (LG)
Baker & McKenzie	Macfarlanes
Bates Wells & Braithwaite	Manches
Berwin Leighton Paisner	Martineau
Bircham Dyson Bell	Michelmores
Boodle Hatfield	Mills & Reeve
Browne Jacobson	Mishcon de Reya
Burges Salmon	Morgan Cole
Charles Russell	Osborne Clarke
Clifford Chance	Pannone
Cobbetts	Penningtons Solicitors
Cripps Harries Hall	Speechly Bircham
Dickinson Dees	Stevens & Bolton
Farrer & Co	Taylor Wessing
Foot Anstey Solicitors	Thring Townsend
Freeth Cartwright	TLT
Halliwells	Trethowans
Harbottle & Lewis	Trowers & Hamlins
HBJ Gateley Wareing	Veale Wasbrough
Henmans	Ward Hadaway
Herbert Smith	Wedlake Bell
Higgs & Sons	Wilsons
Hill Dickinson	Withers

Property/real estate

In a nutshell

Property lawyers, like their corporate law colleagues, are essentially transactional lawyers; the only real difference is that real estate deals require an extra layer of specialist legal and procedural knowledge and there aren't quite so many pesky regulatory authorities. The work centres on buildings and land of all types, and even the most oblique legal concepts have a bricks-and-mortar or human basis to them. It is common for lawyers to develop a specialism within this field, such as residential conveyancing, mortgage lending and property finance, social housing, or the leisure and hotels sector. Most firms have a property department, and the larger the department the more likely the lawyers are to specialise. Note: 'property' and 'real estate' are entirely interchangeable terms.

What lawyers do

- Negotiate sales, purchases and leases of land and buildings, and advise on the structure of deals. Record the terms of an agreement in legal documents.
- Gather and analyse factual information about properties from the owners, surveyors, local authorities and the Land Registry.
- Prepare reports for buyers and anyone lending money.
- Manage the transfer of money and the handover of properties to new owners or occupiers.
- Take the appropriate steps to register new owners and protect the interests of lenders or investors.
- Advise clients on their responsibilities in leasehold relationships, and how to take action if problems arise.
- Help developers get all the necessary permissions to build, alter or change the permitted use of properties.

The realities of the job

- Property lawyers have to multi-task. A single deal could involve many hundreds of properties and your caseload could contain scores of files, all at different stages in the process. You'll have to keep organised.
- Good drafting skills require attention to detail and careful thought. Plus you need to keep up to date with industry trends and standards.
- Some clients get antsy; you have to be able to explain legal problems in lay terms.
- Despite some site visits, this is mainly a desk job with a lot of time spent on the phone to other solicitors, estate agents, civil servants and consultants.
- Most instances of solicitor negligence occur in this area of practice. There is so much that can go wrong.
- Your days will be busy, but generally the hours are sociable and predictable.

Current issues

- Arguably the most obviously cyclical legal area around, property practice will always and has always followed the market. In a down economy there's less demand for properties and new developments, values plummet and conventional bank lending becomes increasingly hard to find. Yes, the recession has hit the property sector hard, but this is nothing new. When the economy picks back up, so will this practice area. Precious little comfort for the scores made redundant lately…
- As commercial and residential work fell by the wayside, more and more firms became eager to get into public sector activity and social housing as these were sources of guaranteed work despite the recession. Firms with existing experience in these sectors largely have the market sewn up however.
- The trends in property finance include a large number of loans being renegotiated, development finance falling off a cliff, increased fire sales, pre-syndication of new debt, the increased viability of Shari'a finance and anxiety that UK Real Estate Investment Trusts (REITs) will breach their financial covenants.
- Property litigation is on the rise as default situations proliferate. The enforcement of, or avoidance of, compliance with contracts for the sale or letting of properties, and general rent recovery and service charge disputes, both commercial and residential, are the main themes.

Read our True Pictures on...

Addleshaw Goddard	K&L Gates
Allen & Overy	Lester Aldridge
Anthony Collins Solicitors	Lewis Silkin
Ashurst	Lawrence Graham (LG)
B P Collins	Linklaters
Bates Wells & Braithwaite	Lovells
Beachcroft	Macfarlanes
Berwin Leighton Paisner	Manches
Bevan Brittan	Martineau
Bird & Bird	Maxwell Winward
Bond Pearce	Mayer Brown International
Boodle Hatfield	McGrigors
Browne Jacobson	Michelmores
Burges Salmon	Mills & Reeve
Charles Russell	Mishcon de Reya
Clifford Chance	Morgan Cole
Clyde & Co	Mundays
CMS Cameron McKenna	Nabarro
Cobbetts	Norton Rose
Coffin Mew	Olswang
Cripps Harries Hall	Osborne Clarke
Dechert	Pannone
Denton Wilde Sapte	Penningtons Solicitors
Dickinson Dees	Pinsent Masons
DLA Piper UK	Reed Smith
DMH Stallard	Shadbolt
Dundas & Wilson	Shoosmiths
DWF	Simmons & Simmons
Eversheds	SJ Berwin
Farrer & Co	Slaughter and May
Finers Stephens Innocent	Speechly Bircham
Fisher Meredith	Stephenson Harwood
Foot Anstey Solicitors	Stevens & Bolton
Freeth Cartwright	Taylor Wessing
Freshfields	Thring Townsend
Halliwells	TLT
Hammonds	Travers Smith
Harbottle & Lewis	Trethowans
HBJ Gateley Wareing	Trowers & Hamlins
Henmans	Veale Wasbrough
Herbert Smith	Walker Morris
Higgs & Sons	Ward Hadaway
Hill Dickinson	Wedlake Bell
Howes Percival	Wilsons
Irwin Mitchell	Wragge & Co
Jones Day	

Public interest

In a nutshell

Human Rights lawyers protest injustice enshrined in law and fight for principle at the point of intersection between a state's powers and individuals' rights. Cases usually relate in some way to the UK's ratification of the European Convention on Human Rights through the Human Rights Act and crop up in criminal and civil contexts, often through the medium of judicial review, a key tool in questioning the decisions of public bodies. Civil contexts include claims regarding the right to education or community care under the Mental Health Act, cases of discrimination at work and even family issues. Criminal contexts could relate to complaints against the police, prisoners' issues, public order convictions following demonstrations, or perhaps extradition on terror charges.

Immigration lawyers deal with both business and personal immigration matters, the former having been embraced by the present government in its quest to manage economic migration. In this more lucrative area, lawyers assist highly skilled migrants to obtain residency or leave to remain in the UK, and help non-nationals to secure visas for travel abroad. They also work with companies that need to bring in employees from overseas. Personal immigration lawyers represent individuals who have fled persecution in their country of origin. They also take on cases for people whose right to stay in the UK is under threat or indeed entirely absent.

Human rights lawyers

- Advise clients on how to appeal a decision made or action taken by a public body, such as the police, a local authority, a court, or a branch of government.
- Collect evidence, take witness statements, prepare cases and instruct barristers.
- Pursue cases through the procedural stages necessary to achieve the desired result. The final port of call for some cases is the European Court of Justice (ECJ), so lawyers need to be fully conversant with UK and European laws.

Business immigration lawyers

- Advise and assist businesses or their employees in relation to work permits and visas. They need to be up to speed on all current schemes, such as those for highly skilled migrants and investors.
- Prepare for, attend and advocate at tribunals or court hearings, where necessary instructing a barrister to do so.

Personal immigration lawyers

- Advise clients on their status and rights within the UK.
- Secure evidence of a client's identity, medical reports and witness statements and prepare cases for court hearings or appeals. Represent clients or instruct a barrister to do so.
- Undertake an immense amount of unremunerated form filling and legal aid paperwork.

The realities of the job

- A commitment to and belief in the values you're fighting for is essential in this relatively low-paid area. Work in the voluntary sector or taking on important cases pro bono can provide the greatest satisfaction.
- Sensitivity and empathy are absolutely essential because you'll often be dealing with highly emotional people, those with mental health issues or those who simply don't appreciate the full extent of their legal predicament.
- Strong analytical skills are required to pick out the legal issues you can change from the socio-economic ones beyond your control.
- In the battle against red tape, bureaucracy and institutional indifference, organisational skills and a vast store of patience are valuable assets.
- Opportunities for advocacy are abundant, which means that knowledge of court and tribunal procedures is a fundamental requirement. Often cases must pass through every possible stage of appeal before referral to judicial review or the ECJ.
- The competition for training contracts is huge. Voluntary work at a law centre or specialist voluntary organisation, or membership of Liberty or Justice, will help.
- Because much of the work is publicly funded, firms do not usually offer attractive trainee salaries or sponsorship through law school.

Current issues

- Issues of asylum (including detention and deportation) and people seeking permission to stay in the UK on human rights' grounds never cease to arouse strong opinions.
- The advent of the Freedom of Information Act, and increased transparency in the public sector in line with Article 6 of the Convention, mean law firms have seen a greater willingness from the public to challenge the decisions of authorities.

- The interface between terrorism and public law, and between public law and the HRA, has become even more acute, as evidenced by the furore surrounding the proposals for 42-day detention of suspects. A recent case concerning the use of secret evidence in control orders drew nine Lords to the bench, evidence of the importance the judiciary places on civil liberties.
- Recent judgments in Beoku-Betts and Chikwamba regarding asylum and Article 8 of the Convention (right to respect for family life) may have far-reaching implications.
- The highly publicised case regarding Gurkhas denied residency represents a significant victory and shows the importance of public opinion in such matters.
- In immigration law there have been many modifications of late, with rules and regulations affecting the highly skilled migrant programme and people applying for leave to remain or settle in the UK. A new points-based immigration system (a source of considerable irritation for the majority of practitioners) means every employer now needs an immigration licence for each employee it wishes to employ. The risk of unlawful employment is high if employers do not keep up with the latest change in provisions. Many people believe that restricting highly skilled migrants from working is farcical, especially in the current climate.

Read our True Pictures on...

Addleshaw Goddard	Irwin Mitchell
Allen & Overy	K&L Gates
Anthony Collins Solicitors	Latham & Watkins
Ashurst	Lester Aldridge
Baker & McKenzie	Lewis Silkin
Barlow Lyde & Gilbert	Lawrence Graham (LG)
Bates Wells & Braithwaite	Linklaters
Beachcroft	Lovells
Berwin Leighton Paisner	Macfarlanes
Bevan Brittan	Manches
Bircham Dyson Bell	Martineau
Bird & Bird	Michelmores
Bond Pearce	Mills & Reeve
Browne Jacobson	Mishcon de Reya
Burges Salmon	Morgan Cole
Capsticks Solicitors	Nabarro
Charles Russell	Norton Rose
Clifford Chance	Olswang
Clyde & Co	Osborne Clarke
CMS Cameron McKenna	Pannone
Cobbetts	Penningtons Solicitors
Cripps Harries Hall	Pinsent Masons
Dechert	Reed Smith
Denton Wilde Sapte	Reynolds Porter Chamberlain
Dickinson Dees	Shoosmiths
DLA Piper UK	Simmons & Simmons
DMH Stallard	SJ Berwin
DWF	Slaughter and May
Edwards Angell	Speechly Bircham
Eversheds	Stephenson Harwood
Farrer & Co	Stevens & Bolton
Fisher Meredith	Taylor Wessing
Foot Anstey Solicitors	TLT
Freshfields	Travers Smith
Halliwells	Trowers & Hamlins
Hammonds	Veale Wasbrough
Harbottle & Lewis	Walker Morris
Herbert Smith	Ward Hadaway
Hill Dickinson	Wragge & Co

Restructuring/insolvency

In a nutshell

Insolvency law governs the position of businesses and individuals who are in financial difficulties and unable to repay their debts as they become due. Such a situation may lead to insolvency proceedings, in which legal action is taken against the insolvent entity and assets may be liquidated to pay off outstanding debts. Before a company or individual gets involved in insolvency proceedings, they will likely be involved in a restructuring or an out-of-court arrangement with creditors to work out alternative repayment schedules. The work of lawyers in the field can therefore be non-contentious (restructuring) or contentious (insolvency litigation), and their role will vary depending on whether they act for debtors or their creditors. What follows are some of the terms you'll come across.

Debtor: an individual or company that owes money. **Creditor:** a person or institution that extends credit to another entity on condition that it is paid back at a later date. **Bankruptcy:** term used in the USA to describe insolvency procedures that apply to companies, but not in the UK, where the term applies to indiviuals only. **Restructuring:** a significant modification made to the debt, operations or structure of a company with its creditors' consent. After a restructuring, debt repayments become more manageable, making insolvency proceedings less likely. **Insolvency proceedings:** generic term that covers a variety of statutory proceedings aimed at rescuing or winding-up an insolvent company.

Insolvency proceedings include the following actions. **Company voluntary arrangement (CVA):** if it is clear that a business could survive if debt repayments were reduced, it can enter a CVA agreement with its creditors. Under this legally binding agreement, a struggling company is allowed to repay some, or all, of its historic debts out of future profits, over an agreed period of time. **Administration:** when in administration, a company is protected from creditors enforcing their debts while an administrator takes over the management of its affairs. If the company is fundamentally sound, the administrator will implement a recovery plan aimed at streamlining the business and maximising profits. If it is apparent that the company has no future then it can be sold or liquidation can commence. **Receivership:** unlike administration, this is initiated by the company's creditors, not the company itself. A receiver is appointed by the court and must look to recover as much money as possible in order to settle the claims made by creditors. Under receivership, the interests of the creditors clearly take precedence over the survival of the company. **Liquidation:** procedure by which the assets of a company are placed under the control of a liquidator. In most cases, a company in liquidation ceases to trade, and the liquidator will sell the company's assets and distribute the proceeds to creditors. There are two forms: voluntary liquidation brought about by the company itself, or compulsory liquidation brought about by court order. **Distressed M&A:** the sale of all or a portion of an insolvent business in an efficient way to preserve going-concern value and avoid the potential for substantial loss of value through a piecemeal liquidation. **Pre-pack sale:** refers to a deal made with an interested buyer to sell the insolvent company's business and assets, negotiated before an administrator is appointed and completed immediately on appointment. Such schemes are becoming increasingly popular and more frequently used in the current economic climate.

What lawyers do

Debtors' lawyers

- Meet with clients to assess the gravity of the situation, highlight the available options and advise on the best course of action to follow.
- In a restructuring, advise the insolvent company on the reorganisation of its balance sheet (such as closing down unprofitable businesses or refinancing its debt) and assist in negotiations with creditors.
- Assist in insolvency filings, and once proceedings have commenced, work closely with the insolvency officeholders (ie those appointed as administrators, receivers or liquidators) and accountants, to achieve the goals set for the insolvent company.
- Provide advice to directors of insolvent companies, explaining their duties to creditors.
- Advise on the sale of assets or mergers and acquisitions of troubled companies.
- Assist clients in insolvency litigation and appeals.
- Provide preventative advice to debtor clients on liability management and ways to avoid insolvency proceedings.

Creditors' lawyers

- Meet with creditor clients to assess the validity of their security over the insolvent company, the strength of their position in the creditors' pool and the best course of action to ensure full recovery.
- Assist in negotiations with debtors and insolvency officeholders.

- Represent clients in insolvency litigation and appeals.
- Assist in the tracing and valuation of debtors' assets.
- Provide training to their clients on how to deal with insolvent companies.

The realities of the job

- Large City firms deal almost exclusively with large-scale corporate restructurings and insolvencies, and the representation of creditor groups in these matters. Smaller regional firms mostly assist on smaller corporate and personal insolvency cases.
- Corporate insolvency as a practice area is extremely varied, as proceedings affect every aspect of the insolvent company. Lawyers therefore need to be conversant in a variety of legal disciplines or know when to refer matters to specialists in employment, banking, property, litigation, corporate, etc.
- When financial difficulties arise in companies, the rapid deployment of a legal team is necessary to provide immediate assistance. This area of law is extremely fast paced, and lawyers are often asked to deliver solutions overnight.
- Insolvency and restructuring involves mountains of paperwork, so lawyers need to be organised and able to prioritise their workload, particularly when dealing with multiple assignments. With so much at stake, attention to detail is paramount when drafting asset sale agreements or documents to be filed at court.
- Restructuring and insolvency situations are understandably tense for both debtors and creditors, and lawyers sometimes need to deal with difficult people, so they must be able to hold their ground and show they are not easily intimidated.
- You will need to immerse yourself in both the financial and corporate worlds. Get started by reading the *FT* or City pages of your daily newspaper.

Current issues

- As the recent financial crisis unfolded, many banks and companies went bust. Market experts predicted that insolvencies in 2009 would rise by 35% compared to 2008. To give you a measure of the epidemic, this means that more than 30,000 UK companies could be declared insolvent in 2009.
- Early signs of decline in the markets were most apparent in the banking sector, particularly with the collapse of structured investment vehicles (SIVs) and other complex financial structures, which led to a serious lack of liquidity in the wholesale markets and resulted in the demise of certain financial institutions, most notably Lehman Brothers in September 2008.
- The turmoil in the financial sector rapidly spread to the real economy due to the shortage of liquidity. The manufacturing, real estate, construction and retail sectors suffered the highest rates of distress. The liquidation of household-name corporates such as Woolworths, MFI and Zavvi brought home the severity of the crisis and the vulnerability of UK businesses.
- Unsurprisingly, the market for insolvency and restructuring legal services is booming. To cope with demand, many law firms are bulking up their capacity and most are running internal training to bring everyone up to speed.

Read our True Pictures on...

Addleshaw Goddard	Lawrence Graham (LG)
Allen & Overy	Linklaters
Ashurst	Lovells
Barlow Lyde & Gilbert	Martineau
Beachcroft	Mayer Brown International
Berwin Leighton Paisner	Michelmores
Bevan Brittan	Mills & Reeve
Bingham McCutchen	Mishcon de Reya
Bond Pearce	Morgan Cole
Browne Jacobson	Nabarro
Burges Salmon	Norton Rose
Charles Russell	Olswang
Clifford Chance	Osborne Clarke
Clyde & Co	Pannone
CMS Cameron McKenna	Pinsent Masons
Cobbetts	Shoosmiths
Coffin Mew	Sidley Austin
Denton Wilde Sapte	Simmons & Simmons
Dickinson Dees	SJ Berwin
DLA Piper UK	Skadden, Arps
Dundas & Wilson	Slaughter and May
DWF	Speechly Bircham
Eversheds	Stephenson Harwood
Foot Anstey Solicitors	Stevens & Bolton
Freeth Cartwright	Taylor Wessing
Freshfields	Thring Townsend
Halliwells	TLT
Hammonds	Travers Smith
HBJ Gateley Wareing	Veale Wasbrough
Herbert Smith	Walker Morris
Howes Percival	Ward Hadaway
Irwin Mitchell	Weil, Gotshal & Manges
Jones Day	White & Case
Latham & Watkins	Wragge & Co

Shipping

In a nutshell

Shipping lawyers deal with the carriage of goods or people by sea, plus any and every matter related to the financing, construction, use, insurance and decommissioning of the ships that carry them (or are arrested, sunk or salvaged while carrying them). Despite being the preserve of specialist firms, or relatively self-contained practice groups within larger firms, the discipline offers varied challenges. The major division is between wet work relating to accidents or misadventure at sea, and dry work involving the land-based, commercial and contractual side. In extension, disputes or litigation relating to contracts means there is also a contentious side to dry work. While some lawyers in the area may be generalists, it is more common to specialise.

Wet lawyers

- Act swiftly and decisively at a moment's notice to protect a client's interests and minimise any loss.
- Travel the world to assess the condition of ships, interview crew or witnesses and prepare cases.
- Take witness statements and advise clients on the merits of and strategy for cases.
- Handle court and arbitration appearances, conferences with barristers and client meetings.

Dry lawyers

- Negotiate and draft contracts for ship finance and shipbuilding, crew employment, sale and purchase agreements, affreightment contracts, and the registration and re-flagging of ships.
- May specialise in niche areas such as yachts or fishing, an area in which regulatory issues feature prominently.
- Handle similar tasks to wet lawyers in relation to contractual disputes but are less likely to jet off around the world at the drop of a hat.

The realities of the job

- Wet work offers the excitement of international assignments and clients, so lawyers need to react coolly to sudden emergencies and travel to far-flung places to offer practical and pragmatic analysis and advice.
- Despite the perils and pleasures of dealing with clients and instructions on the other side of the world, the hours are likely to be steady beyond those international-rescue moments.
- Non-contentious work touches on the intricacies of international trade, so it's as important to keep up with sector knowledge as legal developments.
- Dealing with a mixed clientele from all points on the social compass, you'll need to be just as comfortable extracting a comprehensible statement from a Norwegian merchant seaman as conducting negotiations with major financers.
- Contentious cases are driven by the procedural rules and timetable of the court or arbitration forum to which the matter has been referred. A solid grasp of procedure is as important as a strong foundation in tort and contract law.
- Some shipping lawyers do come from a naval background or are ex-mariners, but you won't be becalmed if the closest comparable experience you've had is steering Tommy Tugboat in the bath, as long as you can show a credible interest in the discipline.
- Though not an all-boys club, parts of the shipping world are still male dominated. Women lawyers and clients are more commonly found on the dry side.
- In the UK, shipping law is centred around London and a few other port cities. Major international centres include Piraeus in Greece, Hong Kong and Singapore. Some trainees even get to work in these locations.

Current issues

- As the industry is inextricably linked to the commodities sector and international trade, the global economic downturn has meant aspects of shipping, such as new builds and finance, are struggling.
- The collapse of freight rates has led to an increase in contentious work, following the unwinding of leverage positions and the reneging of contracts.
- While there is likely to be very little new lending in the short term, there will be more loan restructurings, workouts and loan enforcement work.
- The increased efficiency and daring of pirates, along with the increase in ransom demands, has raised the profile of piracy considerably. The Kenyan port of Mombasa is poised to become the venue for a special piracy tribunal.

Read our True Pictures on...

Allen & Overy	Ince & Co
Barlow Lyde & Gilbert	Linklaters
Berwin Leighton Paisner	Lovells
Clifford Chance	Norton Rose
Clyde & Co	Reed Smith
Denton Wilde Sapte	Simmons & Simmons
DLA Piper UK	Stephenson Harwood
Eversheds	Thomas Cooper
HBJ Gateley Wareing	Watson, Farley & Williams
Hill Dickinson	White & Case
Holman Fenwick Willan	

- **Changing times:** In a less buoyant economy the volume of disputes increases and the number of deals falls. Various contentious areas of law have prospered during the recession – eg IP, shipping, insurance, employment, litigation – and firms concentrating on such countercyclical areas have done well.

top tip no. 7

Sports, media and entertainment law

In a nutshell
Advertising and marketing lawyers offer advice to ensure a client's products or advertisements are compliant with industry standards, plus general advice on anything from contracts between clients, media and suppliers, to employment law, corporate transactions and litigation. Entertainment lawyers assist clients in the film, broadcasting, music, theatre and publishing industries with commercial legal advice or litigation. Strictly speaking, sports lawyers work in an industry sector rather than a specific legal discipline, and firms draw on the expertise of individuals from several practice groups. Reputation management lawyers advise clients on how best to protect their own 'brand', be this through a defamation suit or an objection to invasion of privacy.

Advertising and marketing lawyers
- Ensure advertising campaigns comply with legislation or regulatory codes controlled by the Advertising Standards Agency or Ofcom.
- Advise on comparative advertising, unauthorised references to living persons, potential trade mark or other intellectual property infringements.
- Defend clients against allegations that their work has infringed regulations or the rights of third parties. Bring complaints against competitors' advertising.

TV and film lawyers
- Offer production companies advice on every stage of the creation of programmes and films.
- Assist on the complicated banking and secured lending transactions that ensure financing for a film.
- Help engage performers; negotiate a multitude of ancillary contracts; negotiate distribution and worldwide rights; and manage defamation claims.

Music lawyers
- Advise major recording companies, independent labels and talent (including record producers and songwriters as well as artists).
- Advise on contracts, such as those between labels and bands, or between labels and third parties.
- Offer contentious and non-contentious copyright and trade mark advice relating to music, image rights and merchandising.
- Offer criminal advice when the things get old-school rock 'n' roll.

Theatre and publishing lawyers
- Advise theatre and opera companies, producers, agents and actors on contracts, funding and sponsorship/merchandising.
- Advise publishing companies and newspapers on contractual, licensing, copyright and libel matters.

Sports lawyers
- Assist with contract negotiations, be they between clubs and sportspeople, agents and players, sporting institutions and sponsors, broadcasters and sports governing bodies.
- Handle varied employment law issues.
- Advise on corporate or commercial matters such as takeovers, public offerings, debt restructuring and bankruptcy, or the securing and structuring of credit.
- Enforce IP rights in the lucrative merchandise market and negotiate on matters affecting a sportsperson's image rights.
- Work on regulatory compliance issues within a sport or matters relating to the friction between sports regulations and EU/national law.
- Offer reputation management and criminal advice.

Reputation management
- Claimants' lawyers advise individuals – commonly celebrities, politicians or high-profile businessmen – on the nature of any potential libel action or breach of privacy claim, usually against broadcasters or publishers, before it either settles or goes to court.
- Defendants' lawyers advise broadcasters or other publishers on libel claims brought against them. With the burden of proof on the defendant, the lawyer's must prove that what was published caused no loss to the claimant or was not libellous.
- Help clients stay out of hot water by giving pre-publication advice to authors, editors or production companies.

The realities of the job
- Advertising lawyers must have a good knowledge of advertising regulations, defamation and IP law. The work is real world and fast-paced.
- Clients are creative, lively and demanding. The issues thrown up can be fascinating and must be dealt with creatively.

- Many advertising disputes will be settled via regulatory bodies but some, particularly IP infringements, end in litigation.
- Entertainment lawyers need to be completely immersed in their chosen media and have a good grasp of copyright and contract law.
- Clients look to you for the rigour and discipline they may rarely exercise themselves. This is a sector where who you know makes a big difference, so expect to put in serious face time.
- Sports lawyers need to be proactive, passionate and have bags of commercial nous. They must be able to deal with people involved at all levels of all sports.
- Reputation management lawyers need a comprehensive understanding of libel and privacy laws and a willingness to think laterally.
- Individual claimants can be stressed and upset. People skills, patience and resourcefulness are much needed.
- Solicitors prepare cases but barristers almost always get the glory.

Current issues

- Convergence within the media sector (and with technology and telecoms practices) is continuing apace. Established industries such as book publishing find themselves challenged by online business models and, in broadcasting, the explosion in the use and popularity of online TV has kept lawyers busy.
- The music industry continues to face challenges: illegal downloading and piracy are the biggest concerns. The collapse of Woolworths and its distributor subsidiary Entertainment UK had a damaging impact, and sales of pyschical products are declining rapidly. However, 360° deals that incorporate physical sales with merchandising and live appearances (an area that still performs strongly) are an attempt to redress the balance.
- The UK tax credit for film financing has been firmly established and the weaker pound should boost foreign investment in the UK film and TV production sector. Still, a lot of previously finance-friendly banks have exited the market and the economic conditions will certainly constrain financing.
- In the world of sport, the 2012 Olympics are keeping lawyers busy and the Premier League continues to attract significant media coverage. Sponsorship, advertising and corporate hospitality revenues have all taken a big hit lately.

Read our True Pictures on...

Addleshaw Goddard	Lawrence Graham (LG)
Allen & Overy	Linklaters
Baker & McKenzie	Lovells
Bates Wells & Braithwaite	Macfarlanes
Berwin Leighton Paisner	Manches
Bird & Bird	Mayer Brown International
Bristows	McDermott Will & Emery
Charles Russell	Mishcon de Reya
Clifford Chance	Morgan Cole
CMS Cameron McKenna	Olswang
Covington & Burling	Osborne Clarke
Dechert	Pannone
Denton Wilde Sapte	Pinsent Masons
DLA Piper UK	Reed Smith
Eversheds	Reynolds Porter Chamberlain
Farrer & Co	Sheridans
Finers Stephens Innocent	Slaughter and May
Foot Anstey Solicitors	Speechly Bircham
Freshfields	Taylor Wessing
Halliwells	Teacher Stern
Hammonds	Travers Smith
Harbottle & Lewis	Walker Morris
Herbert Smith	Weil, Gotshal & Manges
Hill Dickinson	Wiggin
K&L Gates	Withers
Lewis Silkin	Wragge & Co

Tax

In a nutshell

Tax lawyers ensure that clients structure their business deals or day-to-day operations such that they take advantage of legal breaks and loopholes in tax legislation. Although predominantly an advisory practice area, on occasion matters can veer into litigation territory.

Tax lawyers in private practice

- Handle tax planning for clients, making sure they understand the tax ramifications of the purchase, ownership and disposal of assets, including advice on structuring corporate portfolios in the most tax-efficient way.
- Offer transactional advice when working with corporate and other lawyers on deals such as M&As, joint ventures or the acquisition of a large property portfolio.
- Deal with investigations or litigation resulting from prosecution by HM Revenue & Customs (HMRC). Litigation is always conducted against or brought by the government.

HMRC lawyers

- Investigate companies and bring prosecutions.
- Advise on how new laws apply to different situations.
- Defend cases brought against the government.

The realities of the job

- This is an intellectually rigorous, rather cloistered area of law and ideally suited to the more academic.
- Corporate tax lawyers are very well paid, treated with reverence by their colleagues and find intellectual stimulation in their work.
- Lawyers must not only have the ability to translate and implement complex tax legislation, but also be able to advise how to structure deals in a legitimate and tax-efficient way to avoid conflict with HMRC.
- If you don't already wear specs, expect to after a couple of years of poring over all that black letter law. The UK has more pages of tax legislation than almost any other country, and there are changes every year.
- In time, extra qualifications, such as the Chartered Tax Adviser exams, will be useful.
- It is not uncommon for lawyers to switch between government jobs and private practice. Some tax barristers were once solicitors.

Current issues

- A fall in transactional work due to the economic downturn has paved the way for other areas such as advisory and litigation to come to the fore. The significant savings to be made as a result of tax lawyers' graft is valued more highly than ever by clients.
- In the wake of recession significant changes to the UK tax regime and the introduction of specific anti-avoidance tax legislation announced by HMRC are likely to keep tax lawyers on their toes.
- Law firms have come into their own in relation to tax advice. Pre-Enron it seemed accountancy firms were taking over. However, companies now prefer to take advice from sources independent from their auditors.

Read our True Pictures on…

Addleshaw Goddard	Lovells
Allen & Overy	Macfarlanes
Ashurst	Mayer Brown International
Berwin Leighton Paisner	McDermott Will & Emery
Bevan Brittan	McGrigors
Browne Jacobson	Mills & Reeve
Burges Salmon	Nabarro
Cleary Gottlieb	Norton Rose
Clifford Chance	Olswang
CMS Cameron McKenna	Osborne Clarke
Dechert	Pinsent Masons
Denton Wilde Sapte	Reynolds Porter Chamberlain
Dickinson Dees	Sidley Austin
DLA Piper UK	Simmons & Simmons
Eversheds	SJ Berwin
Foot Anstey Solicitors	Skadden, Arps
Freeth Cartwright	Slaughter and May
Freshfields	Stephenson Harwood
Hammonds	Stevens & Bolton
HBJ Gateley Wareing	Taylor Wessing
Herbert Smith	Travers Smith
Irwin Mitchell	Walker Morris
Jones Day	Weil, Gotshal & Manges
Latham & Watkins	Wragge & Co
Linklaters	

Technology, telecoms and outsourcing

In a nutshell

The world around us is evolving at breakneck speed: technologies are adapted and hybridised for new usage, new innovations become outdated within just a few years and advances come thick and fast. The legal landscape roamed by the technology lawyer is continually changing and throwing up new legal issues – take Google Street View and the debate over privacy that it sparked. A lawyer working in this area must combine a keen understanding of the latest developments and advances in various technologies with a thorough knowledge of the rapidly changing law that regulates, protects and licenses them. It is their specific industry know-how that distinguishes technology lawyers from other general commercial advisers, athough they will also need a good grounding in general commercial law. For example, if they are to work on a project involving the building of new mobile phone masts, they will need to be familiar with specific laws pertaining to telecoms plus the basic tenets of property, planning and construction law. Or take a minute to imagine the complexities of trading stocks in real time. Some companies (eg Bloomberg, Thompson-Reuters) model all the data that goes into stock pricing, so that others can keep track of the world's markets. A task like this is Herculean, and lawyers are needed to work on the protection, licensing and adaptation of such complex IT systems.

You've heard about outsourcing, but what is it exactly? In essence it's all about getting various processes done cheaper. Why pay someone in the UK to take consumers' calls when you can get someone to do it in Bangalore for a fraction of the price? Not always about sending work abroad, outsourcing may involve getting another more expert business to perform a certain process. The NHS – a good example of a keen outsourcer – offloads some functions to private companies (telecoms maintenance and some of its call centres, for example) because these other companies can get the job done more efficiently. The implementation of BT's NHS National Programme for IT Contracts is the largest civil IT project in the world.

Telecoms and outsourcing go together like spaghetti and Bolognese. Recent advances in telecommunications makes outsourcing even more effective. Inevitably, lawyers are needed to advise on the procurement of systems, organise tenders, create contracts, dispute breaches in contracts and provide advice.

Tracking cars across our road networks, monitoring credit card spend, storing traces of e-mails, phone calls and text messages sent, tallying votes cast and monitoring TV watched or websites visited – it all produces masses of raw data, and data management is now a boom industry. The need to keep data safe has also become very apparent – remember the rumpus caused by HMRC's loss of CDs containing families' Child Benefit details in 2007? Teams of lawyers handle the fallout from such breaches and, more importantly, they advise companies on how to ensure breaches don't happen in the first place.

Lawyers must also understand the business of technology: the ways in which innovations can be yoked to generate money. As forms of media and new technologies converge, clients have come to rely on technology lawyers' skills of innovation and imagination in offering rigorous legal solutions to maximise and protect income and ideas. There are plenty of job opportunities and many of the top 50 firms possess dedicated groups of lawyers. There are also specialists within smaller commercial firms and a number of niche firms.

What lawyers do

- Advise on commercial transactions and draft the requisite documents. There is a heavy emphasis on risk management.
- Assist in the resolution of disputes, commonly by arbitration or other settlement procedures as this is a court-averse sector. Many disputes relate to faulty or unsatisfactory software or hardware.
- Help clients police their IT and web-based reputation and assets. Cyber-squatting, ownership of database information and the Data Protection Act are common topics.
- Give clients mainstream commercial, corporate and finance advice.
- Specialised outsourcing lawyers represent customers and suppliers in the negotiation and drafting of agreements for the provision of IT or other services by a third party.

The realities of the job

- You need to be familiar with the latest regulations and their potential impact on your client's business. Does a website need a disclaimer? What measures should

your client take to protect data about individuals gathered from a website?
- You need a good grasp of the jargon of your chosen industry, firstly to write contracts but also so you can understand your clients' instructions. Read trade journals like *Media Lawyer* and *Wired*, or magazines such as *Computer Weekly* or *New Scientist*.
- The ability to think laterally and creatively is a must, especially when the application of a client's technology or content throws up entirely new issues.
- In this frontier world, gut instinct matters. One in-house lawyer made what looked like a risky move from BT to little-known internet auction site eBay. Six years later he moved to head up Skype's legal team, a perfect example of the convergence of internet and telephone technology.
- High-end private sector outsourcing involves complex, high-value and increasingly multi-jurisdictional work. Mostly, it is the larger law firms that handle such deals. In the public sector, deals involve UK government departments, local authorities and the suppliers of services to those entities.

Current issues

- Digital convergence throws up many legal problems as the business opportunities created by new technologies move beyond the capacity of existing legal or regulatory structures to contract or protect. Copyrighted content being transferred onto handheld devices; film or TV programme downloads from the internet… the list is practically endless.
- Many firms and their clients now believe that technology, media and telecoms are no longer three distinct markets, and structure their departments accordingly.
- Though a downturn in the economy traditionally hits technology spend, the outsourcing model suits recessionary times, particularly as a way to gain cost-effective access to specialist services.
- IT outsourcing began in the late 1980s, followed by business process outsourcings (BPOs) that involve handing responsibility to third-party service providers for functions like human resources,

finance and accounting. Today, the lines between technology outsourcing (TO) and BPOs are blurred. Smart outsourcing – the concept of outsourcing parts of a company, one part at a time, often using different suppliers – is in vogue at present, as is multisourcing (using many different suppliers on shorter term contracts).

Read our True Pictures on…

Addleshaw Goddard	Lovells
Allen & Overy	Manches
Ashurst	Martineau
Baker & McKenzie	Mayer Brown International
Beachcroft	Michelmores
Berwin Leighton Paisner	Mills & Reeve
Bevan Brittan	Morgan Cole
Bird & Bird	Morrison & Foerster
Bond Pearce	Nabarro
Bristows	Norton Rose
Burges Salmon	Olswang
Charles Russell	Osborne Clarke
Clifford Chance	Pannone
Clyde & Co	Pinsent Masons
CMS Cameron McKenna	Reynolds Porter Chamberlain
Dechert	Shadbolt
Denton Wilde Sapte	Shoosmiths
DLA Piper UK	Simmons & Simmons
DMH Stallard	SJ Berwin
Dundas & Wilson	Slaughter and May
DWF	Stephenson Harwood
Eversheds	Stevens & Bolton
Foot Anstey Solicitors	Taylor Wessing
Freshfields	TLT
Halliwells	Travers Smith
Harbottle & Lewis	Veale Wasbrough
Herbert Smith	Ward Hadaway
Jones Day	Wedlake Bell
K&L Gates	White & Case
Latham & Watkins	Wragge & Co
Linklaters	

The True Picture

The True Picture reports on 125 firms in England and Wales, ranging from the international giants to small regional practices. Most handle commercial law, although many also offer private client experience.

The True Picture

Every firm will tell you it is different from all the others because of its friendly culture in which everybody is down-to-earth and where approachable partners operate an open-door policy. If you're feeling bamboozled by brochurespeak we have the antidote...

How we do our research

Every year we spend many months compiling the True Picture reports on law firms in England and Wales, ranging from the international giants to small regional practices. Our purpose is to get to the heart of what you need to know about a prospective employer – what it can really offer you in terms of work and working environment. You'll want to know how many hours a day you'll be chained to your desk, the tasks that will keep you occupied and who you'll be working with. Importantly, you'll want to know about a firm's culture and whether colleagues will turn into party animals or party poopers come Friday night.

Most of our chosen firms handle commercial law, although many also offer private client experience. There are a few general practice firms offering publicly funded advice to their local communities. To take part in the True Picture a firm must provide a complete list of its trainees. After checking the list is complete, we randomly select a sample of individuals for telephone interviews. Our sources are guaranteed anonymity to give them the confidence to speak frankly. The True Picture is not shown to the law firms prior to publication; they see it for the first time when this book is published.

Trainees tell us why they chose their firm and why others might want to. We put on our serious faces and talk about seat allocation, the character and work of different departments, the level of supervision and what happens to people on qualification. And we flirt shamelessly to get the gossip on firm politics, office oddities and after-hours fun. We look for the things trainees agree upon, and if they don't agree we present both sides of the argument.

Your choice of firm will be based on location, size and the practice areas available... then it's a matter of chemistry. Some firms are stuffier, some are more industrious and some are very brand-aware, involving trainees heavily in marketing activities. Some work in modern open-plan offices; others occupy buildings long past their sell-by date. Some focus on international business; others are at the heart of their local business communities. Some concentrate on contentious work, others transactional. The combinations of these variables are endless.

Our findings this year

This is the 'recession edition' of the *Student Guide*, written against a backdrop of redundancies and falling profits. We haven't ignored the economic climate – after all, it's when times are bad that firms reveal their true character – but we're very aware that by the time you, our readers, hopefully begin your training contracts in 2012 and beyond, market conditions might be very different. We've tried to make this a forward-looking guide and we've spent more time than ever speaking to training partners and managing partners about their strategies for the next few years. You'll notice their comments scattered throughout the True Picture features.

This year we found fewer law firms were willing to give us access to their trainees (and frankly some had reactions verging on the paranoid). Consequently, we have covered slightly fewer firms than usual. It's worth reiterating that the purpose of the True Picture is not to put the boot into firms, but nor are we an extension of their marketing departments. Our only agenda is to give you the fairest and most detailed view possible.

Retention rates for the class of 2009 have been the worst for years. Usually, just over 80% of qualifiers stay with the law firms that trained them, but in 2009 total retention at those we covered dropped to 74%. If you intend to use retention rates as a determining factor in your choice of firm, do be wary of the statistics being bandied around. Law firms make their own rules on how to calculate retention rates – you may not be getting a full picture from them. We know of at least one medium-sized outfit that kept on 100% of its trainees in 2008 but made half of them redundant within nine months. We collect our own statistics and include them in each law firm feature. We have collated statistics since 2000 and also publish them on our website.

A word on law firm mergers or closures: thankfully, the latter are rare, but mergers are a regular occurrence in the profession these days. When firms merge, trainees' contracts are honoured, though of course it does mean that new recruits find themselves in a different firm to the one they signed up to.

It's not all bad news and there have been success stories this year. One man's misfortune is another man's gold rush, and while real estate, corporate and finance-focused firms have felt the pinch, insolvency lawyers and litigators have had a busy 2009. We've noticed these departments becoming increasingly popular as savvy trainees aim to maximise their chances of qualification.

Some things never change

- Certain seats are more popular than others. The perfect example is employment law.
- Levels of responsibility vary between departments. In property you might have your own small files. In corporate you will generally work in a very junior capacity as part of a team.
- The experience in litigation depends entirely on the type of cases your firm handles; usually a trainee's responsibility is inversely proportionate to the value and complexity of a case.
- In times of plenty, corporate and finance seats mean long hours, commonly climaxing in all-nighters. The size and complexity of a deal will determine your role, but corporate and finance usually require the most teamwork.
- Most firms offer four six-month seats; some offer six four-month seats and others operate their own unique systems. Trainees switch departments and supervisors for each seat. Most share a room and work with a partner or senior assistant; others sit open-plan, either with the rest of the team or with other trainees. Occasionally trainees have their own room.
- All firms conduct appraisals: a minimum of one at the conclusion of each seat, and usually halfway through as well.
- Client secondments help you learn to understand clients' needs. They can be the highlight of a training contract.
- The Solicitors Regulation Authority requires all trainees to gain experience of both contentious and non-contentious work. Additionally most firms have certain seats they require or prefer trainees to try. Some firms are very prescriptive, others flexible. Remember, a training contract is a time to explore legal practice to see what you're best at and most enjoy. You may surprise yourself.

Jargonbusting

- Agency work – making a court appearance for another firm that can't get to court
- Bundling – compiling bundles of documents for a court case
- Bibling – putting together sets of all the relevant documents for a transaction
- CMC – case management conference
- Counsel – a barrister
- Coco – company-commercial department/work
- Data room duty – supervising visitors to rooms full of important documents, helping them find things and making sure they don't steal them. With electronic data rooms the job becomes more of a desktop exercise
- Dispute resolution – litigation, mediation, arbitration, etc
- Due diligence – the thorough investigation of a target company in a deal
- Equity partner – a partner who receives a contractually agreed share of the firm's annual profits. A part owner of the firm
- Grunt work – administrative (and boring) yet essential tasks including photocopying, bundling, bibling, paginating, scheduling documents, data room duties and proof-reading or checking that documents are intact
- High net worth individuals – rich people
- Infant approvals – court authorisation for a settlement involving a minor
- Limited Liability Partnership (LLP) – a way of structuring a professional partnership such that no partner is liable to any of the firm's creditors above and beyond a certain sum
- NQ – a newly qualified solicitor
- PQE – post-qualification experience
- PSC – a compulsory course taken during the training contract
- Salaried partner – a partner who receives a salary but has no contractual claim on the firm's profits
- Seat – a spell working in a department, usually four or six months
- SRA – Solicitors Regulation Authority
- Training partner – the partner who oversees the training scheme
- Verification – the aspect of a deal in which lawyers ensure stated information is accurate

And finally...

We hope the True Picture will help you decide which firms to target. No matter how hard or how easy securing a training contract is for you, you'll want to end up with the right one.

The True Picture

www.chambersstudent.co.uk

#	Firms by size in the UK	London	S & Thames Valley	South West	Midlands	East	Yorkshire & NE	North West	Wales	Overseas	Trainees	True picture	A-Z solicitors
1	Government Legal Service	●					●				42	280	585
2	Eversheds	●		●	●	●	●	●		●	129	253	576
3	Allen & Overy	●								●	230	137	536
4	DLA Piper	●		●		●	●			●	155	239	572
5	Pinsent Masons	●	●				●	●		●	125	405	631
6	Linklaters	●								●	250	337	607
7	Clifford Chance	●								●	220	203	558
8	Herbert Smith	●								●	199	299	591
9	Freshfields	●								●	200	277	584
10	Addleshaw Goddard	●					●	●			90	133	535
11	Berwin Leighton Paisner	●								●	78	160	543
12	Beachcroft	●	●	●			●	●			62	157	541
13	Lovells	●								●	90	340	608
14	Slaughter and May	●									173	437	644
15	Norton Rose	●								●	105	383	624
16	Hammonds	●			●		●	●			60	287	587
17	Denton Wilde Sapte	●	●							●	70	229	569
18	Ashurst	●								●	106	143	538
19	Mills & Reeve	●			●	●					46	366	619
20	Nabarro	●					●			●	55	379	623
21=	CMS Cameron McKenna	●		●						●	116	211	560
21=	TLT Solicitors	●		●							25	461	653
23	Wragge & Co	●			●					●	53	509	670
24	Shoosmiths	●	●		●			●			29	421	639
25	Hill Dickinson	●						●			32	304	594
26	Halliwells	●					●	●			42	283	586
27	DWF	●					●	●			35	247	574
28	McGrigors	●						●		●	25	361	616
29	Irwin Mitchell	●			●		●	●		●	53	317	598
30	Cobbetts	●			●		●	●			37	215	561
31	Simmons & Simmons	●								●	70	427	641
32	SJ Berwin	●								●	83	431	642
33	Mayer Brown	●								●	55	355	614
34	Osborne Clarke	●	●	●						●	33	392	627
35	Burges Salmon			●							43	191	553
36	Dundas & Wilson	●									18	244	573
37	Baker & McKenzie	●								●	78	247	539
38=	Barlow Lyde & Gilbert	●	●							●	31	151	540
38=	Bond Pearce	●	●	●							25	174	548
40	White & Case	●								●	59	499	665
41	Charles Russell	●	●		●	●					35	197	555
42	Clyde & Co	●	●							●	48	207	559

Notes: Firms are listed in order of size as measured by UK partner and solicitor figures provided to Chambers and Partners.

Firms by size in the UK	London	S & Thames Valley	South West	Midlands	East	Yorkshire & NE	North West	Wales	Overseas	Trainees	True picture	A-Z solicitors
43= Taylor Wessing	●			●					●	44	451	648
43= Speechly Bircham	●								●	25	441	645
45 Dickinson Dees						●			●	30	235	571
46 Olswang	●	●							●	36	387	625
47 Trowers & Hamlins	●		●				●		●	38	471	656
48 Jones Day	●								●	35	320	599
49 Reynolds Porter Chamberlain	●								●	26	413	635
50 Reed Smith	●								●	41	409	634
51 Morgan Cole		●	●					●		27	371	n/a
52 Bird & Bird	●								●	33	171	547
53 HBJ Gateley Wareing	●			●					●	16	293	589
54 Macfarlanes	●									58	343	609
55= Travers Smith	●								●	48	465	654
55= Pannone							●			35	395	628
57 Foot Anstey			●							17	265	580
58 Bevan Brittan	●		●	●						28	163	544
59 Browne Jacobson	●			●						19	185	552
60 Dewey & LeBoeuf	●								●	23	232	570
61 Lawrence Graham	●								●	36	329	606
62 Stephenson Harwood	●								●	29	445	646
63 Walker Morris						●				27	479	659
64 Holman Fenwick Willan	●								●	28	307	595
65 Bircham Dyson Bell	●									14	168	546
66 Freeth Cartwright				●			●			17	273	583
67 Withers	●								●	35	506	669
68 Martineau	●			●						19	349	612
69 Latham & Watkins	●								●	24	326	602
70 Mishcon de Reya	●									22	369	620
71 Farrer & Co	●									20	256	577
72 Cripps Harries Hall	●	●								16	222	565
73 Ward Hadaway						●				20	482	660
74 Lewis Silkin	●	●								10	334	605
75 Manches	●	●								20	346	611
76 Ince & Co	●								●	27	314	597
77 Thring Townsend Lee & Pembertons	●	●								16	458	652
78 K&L Gates	●								●	14	324	600
79 Michelmores	●		●							16	364	618
80 Penningtons Solicitors	●	●								17	401	630
81 Watson, Farley & Williams	●								●	26	489	662
82 Veale Wasbrough			●							15	474	657
83 Capsticks	●			●						11	194	554
84 DMH Stallard	●	●								18	242	n/a

Notes: Firms are listed in order of size as measured by UK partner and solicitor figures provided to Chambers and Partners.

Firms by size in the UK	London	S & Thames Valley	South West	Midlands	East	Yorkshire & NE	North West	Wales	Overseas	Trainees	Pages True picture	Pages A-Z solicitors
85= Sidley Austin	●								●	17	424	640
85= Paul Hastings	●								●	11	398	629
86 Anthony Collins				●						14	140	537
87 Howes Percival			●	●	●					18	311	596
88 Forbes						●	●			11	268	581
89 Dechert	●								●	19	225	568
90= Weil, Gotshal & Manges	●								●	24	495	664
90= Bristows	●									15	183	551
92 Stevens & Bolton		●								8	448	647
93 Wedlake Bell	●									6	492	663
94 Harbottle & Lewis	●									10	290	588
95 Coffin Mew		●								10	218	562
96= Skadden	●								●	12	434	643
96= Bates Wells & Braithwaite	●									9	155	n/a
98 Finers Stephens Innocent	●									6	260	578
99= Lester Aldridge	●	●								11	332	604
99= Wilsons			●							9	504	667
101 Henmans			●							6	296	590
103 McDermott Will & Emery	●								●	6	358	615
104= Fisher Meredith	●									17	262	n/a
104= Cleary Gottlieb Steen & Hamilton	●								●	13	200	557
106 Higgs & Sons				●						8	302	593
107= Boodle Hatfield	●	●								13	177	549
107= Ford & Warren						●				8	271	582
109 Mundays		●								6	376	622
110 Trethowans		●	●							7	468	655
111 Edwards Angell Palmer & Dodge	●								●	15	250	575
112= Covington & Burling	●								●	11	220	564
112= BP Collins		●								6	180	550
114 Maxwell Winward	●									5	352	613
115= Morrison & Foerster	●								●	13	374	n/a
115= Shadbolt	●	●								6	416	636
117 Wiggin	●		●							5	502	666
118 Sheridans	●									2	418	638
119 Teacher Stern	●									6	454	n/a
120= O'Melveny & Myers	●								●	9	390	626
120= Warner Goodman			●							4	486	661
122 Bingham McCutchen	●								●	4	166	545
123 Thomas Cooper	●								●	8	456	649
124 BTMK					●					5	188	n/a
125 Vinson & Elkins	●								●	6	476	658

Notes: Firms are listed in order of size as measured by UK partner and solicitor figures provided to Chambers and Partners.

Addleshaw Goddard LLP

The facts

Location: Manchester, Leeds, London
Number of UK partners/solicitors: 172/485
Total number of trainees: 90
Seats: 4x6 months
Alternative seats: Secondments
Extras: Pro bono – various projects, eg Springfield Legal Advice Centre

Up North this national firm has a king-of-the-hill reputation. In the vast London market it has worked hard and now competes well with top-rung players in many areas of commercial practice.

In the past decade, Addleshaw Goddard has transformed from a strong northern firm to a national big-hitter with a long and enviable list of top-name clients.

Silver circlers

Addleshaw Booth & Co's merger with Theodore Goddard in 2003 ticked all the right boxes: manpower was increased, profits climbed and national firm status was achieved. With this new status came the reinvigoration of two already successful firms. Since then, the stated goal has been "*to be at the forefront of the silver circle.*" Like many other firms of its size, AG's large corporate and real estate practices bring in masses of revenue – almost half of the firm's total of £195.4m in pre-crunch 2007/08. Although these areas have been hit hard by the changing economy (their combined revenue fell by approximately 25% in 2008/09), other areas have prospered. The finance and projects-related practices pulled in £41.4m last year and, naturally, the insolvency practice is also bringing home plenty of bacon. The firm's revenue dipped by 11% to £173m in 2008/09, which was still enough to give it a position in the top 20 UK firms by revenue.

AG has re-evaluated its priorities and trimmed away some of its niches. A family department was cut loose in 2008 and a conveyancing team has also gone. "*It makes sense from a business perspective. They weren't in line with where the firm is going,*" said one trainee, "*so it wasn't unexpected.*" The firm wants to focus on high-value, high-profit-margin areas and target prestigious, dependable blue-chip clients in money-spinning sectors like pharmaceuticals and banking. In 2008/09, it worked for 16 FTSE 100 clients and 13 FTSE 250 clients; impressive when you know it had just 11 FTSE clients back in 2000. It has recently won appointments to four more panels at Barclays (including the much sought-after general legal advice panel), taking its current total to seven. The firm is dominant when it comes to building society M&A work. Financial partner Adam Bennett has been involved in every building society merger since 1999 and AG acts for more than half of all the building societies in the UK, as well as RBS, HSBC and Lloyds TSB.

The firm's London office move to what looks like a big glass castle is emblematic of its aspirations. Internal newsletters often make reference to 'The Milton Gate Effect' and, according to one trainee, there's been a countdown on the firm's intranet showing how much longer there is to wait before all London staff are together under one roof in the swanky new office close to Slaughter and May. Symbolism and sloganeering have significant roles at this firm; for example, much effort has been put into tweaking what is known as 'The AG Way'. However, as one trainee pointed out: "*There's a real danger when you come up with business strategy that when you try to articulate it, it sounds a bit vacuous.*" So please keep in mind when we tell you that AG is instigating a 'From Me to You' mindset, that it has nothing to do with the slapstick genius of the Chuckle Brothers and everything to do with "*improving customer service.*" The firm has not lessened its commitment to TOOT ('Three Offices One Team') now that it is principally targeting 'Bold and Beautiful' clients. Mercifully, trainees can "*pay as much or as little attention as they want*" to these "*slightly cringey*" mottos.

Pulling together

The firm has five main areas, each of which is split into various subgroups. The five areas are: contentious; commercial; corporate; finance and projects; and property. Trainees can expect to take at least two seats from the options in the corporate, real estate, and finance and projects departments. Because of the scale and value of the work, different departments often have to pull together across the whole firm, so in this sense trainees have a great opportunity to see all departments firing on all cylinders, noting the connections between them as the firm gets things done. The corporate department's reputation wins it international instructions such as advising natural gas distributor Gate Terminal on a €745m project financing of an import terminal in the Netherlands. At the same time, "*banking is bucking the trend by growing income despite the market being crap,*" and it has also been getting in on the Gate deal, working for all the lenders ("*there were tonnes*") to seal this complex deal. Another huge matter was the Co-op's £1.57bn takeover of Somerfield. As a general rule, trainees told us they were able to work on a good mix of mega-deals and things that they could dig into and manage themselves.

The real estate department was also on the Somerfield deal (see what we mean about pulling together?). Additionally, it acted for Sainsbury's on the acquisition of a £30m freehold site, for the MoD on the disposal of 700 acres of former barracks near Chatham, and for British Land, preparing certificates of title for the sale of a 50% interest in Meadowhall Shopping Centre. Having done some uncharacteristically "*monotonous*" work, one trainee in London said: "*I hated real estate,*" but apparently "*it's not the same for everyone. Some say there are brilliant seats in real estate.*" Another trainee described real estate as "*a good introductory seat.*" The growing projects group, meanwhile, has picked up a mandate on the largest waste deal in Western Europe – the Manchester Waste PPP, which will build a facility that takes rubbish and turns it into power. Already representing dozens of banks, companies, government departments, borough councils and primary care trusts, in the past year the group has picked up several new clients, not least among them Carillion.

AG is proud to offer a service called 'Control'. Through this litigation-funding product the firm litigates on a reduced-fee agreement and puts after-the-event insurance in place. It also has cases that are funded by a third party. Its aim is to "*take the burden off the claimant's costs, because they merely pay a chunk of the damages to the firm.*" Simply put: "*It's sort of no win, low fee. The clients pay lower fees but, should we win, we recover 150% of our fees. It aligns the clients' interests with the firm's.*" This kind of third-party litigation funding has only just started to establish itself in the UK and AG's lawyers are giving talks around the City on how it all works. Trainees have been involved in cases funded this way and they are also used in the pre-funding assessment of potential claims, a process which required them to gauge the probability of victory. One such matter is the InnovatorOne case in which AG is acting for hundreds of claimants, from hedge fund owners to widows, on claims arising out of failed investment schemes. It is being followed intently for two reasons – because there's £50m at stake and because the case is one of the first to involve this type of funding package.

Out and about

Trainees can opt for a client secondment (eg AstraZeneca, ITV, Diageo, Barclays or Nationwide). The Diageo one sounds particularly impressive because there's the chance to work in Africa. We imagine a *Heart of Darkness*-esque journey through lush tropical jungle to "*sort out the supply chain… chatting to people and finding out their needs in a non-legal, practical way.*" What's more, at Diageo "*there's loads and loads of free booze.*"

It must be said that our sources were very pleased with the quality of their training and felt that the responsibility given to them was pitched just right. They felt stretched but not overwhelmed. Working at any firm that handles high-calibre work will entail some late nights but trainees here were pleased to note that "*going home at 6 or 7pm isn't frowned upon.*" It struck us that the London trainees worked longer hours than the northerners. Some saw this as a badge of honour.

Chambers UK rankings

Advertising & Marketing	Intellectual Property
Agriculture & Rural Affairs	Life Sciences
Asset Finance	Local Government
Aviation	Outsourcing
Banking & Finance	Partnership
Banking Litigation	Pensions
Capital Markets	Planning
Charities	Private Client
Competition/European Law	Private Equity
Construction	Product Liability
Consumer Finance	Projects & Energy
Corporate/M&A	Public Procurement
Defamation/Reputation Management	Real Estate
Dispute Resolution	Real Estate Finance
Education	Real Estate Litigation
Employee Share Schemes	Restructuring/Insolvency
Employment	Retail
Environment	Social Housing
Financial Services Regulation	Sport
Health & Safety	Tax
Healthcare	Telecommunications
Information Technology	
Insurance	

In 2009 the legal sector's most striking leitmotif was that of redundancies. AG let approximately 90 people go from all levels of the firm and inevitably this upset some of our sources. In an attempt to avoid layoffs, the firm also offered sabbaticals, additional holiday in return for a pay cut, reduced hours and internal secondments. At the time of going to press, some fee earners were on a four-day week and salaries had also been frozen, including those of trainees. One interviewee told us: "*The firm tried to consider the business from everyone's point of view and thought carefully.*" Rather than just divesting itself of secretaries and associates, one of the first steps was to remove 10% of the partnership before looking elsewhere for cuts.

All roads lead to London?

AG's position in the financial sphere and its obvious enthusiasm for The Milton Gate Effect led some trainees, especially those in the capital, to claim that London is becoming the focal point for the firm. Our opinion is that it is undeniably trying to increase its presence in the City, but not at the expense of its other two offices (TOOT, remember?). Yes, sometimes the London office will send work north to be dealt with more cheaply, but that is not to say that the northerners aren't pulling their weight. We'd even say they are punching above it. Some of the firm's biggest deals in recent years originated up north, including the Co-operative Group deal, work for 3i and the PFI work done for Greater Manchester Waste. These huge deals impacted on the whole network.

In the north, AG is second to none and consistently hires top-notch trainees with an impressive academic record and personality to match the firm's ambitious streak. In London, where there are bigger fish than AG, trainees tend to be the sort who "*looked at the top 20 and considered the magic circle, but had reservations about working at firms that suck their employees dry in terms of work-life balance.*" In contrast to the north, where the intake appeared to be quite similar and united, trainees in London appear divided into two categories, dubbed by one source as "*alphas*" and "*non-alphas.*" We guess that this is good news for potential applicants, because they can be sure to find other people with similar personalities. The alphas like testosterone-fuelled practices such as banking and corporate, are very ambitious, and when they work long hours they complain (read: brag) about it in well-circulated e-mails. They "*don't see doing a seat up north as a popular step. You work shorter hours in Manchester and generally go home earlier.*" The non-alphas have a more laid-back approach and tend to prefer contentious work and fewer hours (but still put in the late nights when necessary). They like the folk up north, envying the social scene and more relaxed attitudes. It seems that the persona of AG as a whole "*is changing a bit as associates are* [increasingly] *drawn from the magic circle.*"

Book a rest after this holiday

It's possible that these trainees have the highest cholesterol levels in the country. Just before starting their training contracts they go to Romania for three weeks to work alongside locals on a Habitat For Humanity house-building project. All the food served out there is "*dripping in oil – I didn't know what some things were because it was all so fried.*" Trainees absolutely love this team-bonding exercise, as it brings them together as friends as well as colleagues. Perhaps they should be grateful for all that fat lining their stomachs because for some "*it's a week long piss-up. During the days you work hard, then at night obviously you want to go out and have fun.*" To clarify, hard work in this instance can mean "*digging trenches in 30-degree heat.*" Back in the UK, the firm has a good pro bono programme in which trainees can get involved "*as little or as much as they want.*"

Karaoke is a great leveller. Be you public sector or private sector focused, corporate deal junkie or litigator, magic circle, silver circle or crop circle, it doesn't matter. At some point during your training contract at a law firm it's inevitable that you'll get invited to a karaoke night. At AG the favourite genre seems to be power ballad, and preference was expressed for the oeuvres of Jon Bon Jovi and Celine Dion. As well as karaoke nights, AG trainees have played cricket matches against clients, been to bowling alleys and dog tracks and holidayed together in Venice and Marbella. By all accounts if you're an AG type you'll have a lot of fun.

Understandably, 2009 was not the most fun-filled year for those approaching qualification, and it turned out to be a better year than many of our sources had imagined. The scores on the doors were as follows: 36 out of 44 qualifiers were retained, with 12 out of 13 staying in Leeds, 11 out of 14 in Manchester and 13 out of 17 in London. The firm tells us it is mindful of the problems that affected the profession last time a recession resulted in widespread NQ layoffs.

And finally...

This well-oiled, well-managed machine is gearing up for bigger things. Choose it if you are ambitious and interested in mainstream commercial matters.

ALLEN & OVERY

Start at the top
A Career in Law

You might think that some taxis are health hazards, but for cabbies, it's the diseases you're carrying that are the issue. Taxi drivers are required by law to ask all passengers if they have smallpox or the plague.

☐ Law or ☐ Non-law?

Law and business are full of surprises. Whether you are exploring the modern implications of existing laws, or working to find legal solutions to new situations, you'll need to be open-minded, creative and commercial. At Allen & Overy, we are working at the forefront of today's evolving legal landscape, helping to shape and frame the environment in which business, and life itself, is conducted.

Poxy Passengers

You don't need to have studied law to become a lawyer, but business sense, curiosity and a commitment to excellence are essential.

Answer: Law

www.allenovery.com/careeruk
Allen & Overy means Allen & Overy LLP and/or its affiliated undertakings.

WINNER TARGETjobs National Graduate Recruitment Awards 2009 — Sector award: law - solicitors

THE TIMES TOP 100 GRADUATE EMPLOYERS 2009

Allen & Overy LLP

The facts

Location: London
Number of UK partners/solicitors: 207/867
Total number of trainees: 230
Seats: 3 or 6 months long
Alternative seats: Overseas seats, secondments
Extras: Pro bono – Liberty, Battersea Legal Advice Centre; language training

If you're interested in the internal workings of the finance sector then A&O could be your top pick. Trainees here describe the partners and senior associates who teach them as masters of their trade.

Finance-led Allen & Overy is one of the elite firms in the magic circle. Having exported its City know-how and reputation internationally, it is also one of the most successful firms around the world.

A&O: the sequel

Allen & Overy started life in 1930 as a small Holborn firm created by two ambitious lawyers who'd dashed from their old employer with a cab full of files. One was the darkly handsome George Allen, the other Tom Overy, who reportedly had the sort of face that scares small children. A&O's reputation was made six years later as a result of George Allen's role as adviser to King Edward VIII during the abdication crisis of 1936. If these anecdotes have whetted your appetite, we'd recommend you read the firm's riveting biography *Allen & Overy: The Firm 1930-1998* and its sequel – that's right, one book wasn't enough – *A&O at 75*. Fast-forwarding to the present day, A&O now reigns supreme in the world of global finance. Internationalisation has been a defining factor in the firm's success. Rather than going global through foreign mergers, the firm chose to expand under its own steam. It developed an office network across Europe and Asia before setting its sights on the USA and the Middle East. The latest addition to the network is a São Paulo office, and in 2008 the firm announced a formal tie-up with Indian law firm Trilegal. Our sources were well aware of the importance of the overseas offices. "*Most of our revenue comes from abroad,*" they noted, also perceiving a deeper change: "*We're no longer a London firm with overseas outposts – we're a truly integrated global law firm.*"

A&O is a master of finance in all its variations and achieves the highest rankings across all banking product lines in *Chambers UK*. It recently acted for 17 lenders on the £3.6bn financing for the acquisition of Angel Trains by a consortium of investors led by Babcock & Brown European Infrastructure Fund, and advised on the financing of the Saudi Kayan Petrochemical Project, involving the construction of the world's largest integrated petrochemical complex in Saudi Arabia. Islamic finance is a strong suit and the firm routinely advises on Shari'a-compliant debt instruments, such as the first ever mandatory exchangeable sukuk issue by UAE-based National Central Cooling Company (Tabreed). A&O's international capital markets (ICM) division is equally important, and here lawyers focus on large-scale bond and equity-linked offerings, as well as complex structured finance products. These jargon-heavy deals don't need to make sense to you yet, but if they send a shiver of fear rather than excitement down your spine, best to look elsewhere.

The past decade has seen A&O invest heavily in its M&A practice to complement its superior finance practice. Although A&O's corporate team does not match those of, say, Freshfields and Linklaters, the group runs some impressive deals and recently advised Goldman Sachs and JPMorgan Cazenove as joint financial advisers to Friends Provident in connection with its corporate reorganisation and demerger of its majority stake in F&C Asset Management.

Together, finance, ICM and corporate make up three quarters of the firm in London. The remainder encompasses tax, employment, pensions, environment, real estate and, of course, the litigation and restructuring groups, which were among the busiest areas over the past year. In spite of a sluggish market, the firm once again broke the billion-pound global revenue barrier, achieving a fee income of £1.091bn in 2008/09. Profits were hit by the £46m cost of a wide-scale restructuring, which was aimed at preserving long-term profitablity. That programme saw the partner, associate and support staff head count reduced by around 9% (approximately 450 people in total).

Sleepless in the City

Midway through their first seat, trainees attend a presentation given by the various practice groups to help them plan their next moves. The first seat is followed by spells of either three or six months in other departments, overseas offices or on secondment to clients. It's important to emphasise that as the backbone of A&O is its top-tier finance practice, plus corporate and ICM, "*there isn't much room to manoeuvre outside of these seats.*" Indeed, trainees typically spend half of their training contract in these normally fast-paced departments.

A variety of seats fall under the finance umbrella, from leveraged and asset finance to projects, global loans, restructuring and regulatory. All finance trainees learn how to manage the conditions precedent for deals and simple loan documentation, but a finance seat is not just about mundane jobs. Early on trainees also learn how to draft credit facilities, security documentation, waivers and legal opinions. A&O enjoys unparalleled relationships with the banking community, and while acquisition and leveraged finance deals have been sparser of late, the banking groups continue to enjoy a consistent flow of instructions, particularly for restructuring and refinancing deals. Even in a slow market, trainees report that all-nighters remain a common feature of the banking seats.

ICM seat options include general debt and equity securities, derivatives and structured finance (DSF), securitisation and corporate trustee work. Echoing the view of many, one trainee admitted: "*I didn't have a clue about the type of work these groups handled, so I was a little apprehensive at first.*" However, the "*supportive and friendly teams*" try their hardest to involve trainees and there is also access to a fantastic know-how database. The highly technical DSF group received particularly glowing reviews: "*Without exaggeration, A&O has got the best derivatives team in the world – there's nowhere else I'd rather train.*" Chambers Global backs this bold claim.

Depending on when they'd done a corporate seat, some of our sources had experienced an intensely busy six months, while others found the group "*a little lethargic as many of the transactions we worked on got shelved.*" In an active period, a trainee's role normally involves overseeing admin tasks, such as data room preparation, due dili-

Chambers UK rankings

Administrative & Public Law	Media & Entertainment
Asset Finance	Outsourcing
Banking & Finance	Partnership
Banking Litigation	Pensions
Capital Markets	Private Client
Climate Change	Private Equity
Commodities	Projects, Energy & Natural Resources
Competition/European Law	
Construction	Public International Law
Corporate/M&A	Public Procurement
Dispute Resolution	Real Estate
Employee Share Schemes	Real Estate Finance
Employment	Real Estate Litigation
Environment	Restructuring/Insolvency
Financial Services Regulation	Shipping
Fraud: Civil	Social Housing
Information Technology	Tax
Insurance	Telecommunications
Intellectual Property	Transport
Investment Funds	

gence or bibling. "*The teams in corporate are too big for trainees to play a pivotal role in deals, so the work isn't terribly exciting and there's very little client contact.*" The group's reputation for serving up punishing hours also holds true. "*Late finishes are due to the nature of the work: it's common to just sit around waiting for a document to come in from the other side,*" reported a trainee who added: "*There isn't a culture of staying late for the sake of it.*" On the plus side, deals often make headlines and, once successfully completed, trainees are encouraged to take some time off to recuperate.

A world of opportunities

As well as visiting the powerhouse departments, trainees have a 'priority seat', which can be spent in a more specialised area. Unfortunately, there's no longer an option to visit the "*super-friendly*" private client team, since this group recently left A&O to set up independently. Advisory seats such as environment, pensions and competition are particularly popular with trainees who enjoy research and black letter law. Be aware that as these smaller teams aren't core practices trainees are encouraged to only spend three months in them.

The uninitiated may not think of A&O as a major litigation player; however, the firm fields a sizeable department. It was recently reshuffled into specialised subgroups, including arbitration, general commercial, insurance, fraud and an increasingly busy insolvency litigation team. In keeping with A&O's position as a finance-focused firm, most of the contentious work comes from banks and large accountancy firms. An assignment that kept several of our sources busy was the firm's representation of Ernst & Young as the PPP administrators of Metronet, which had overspent by millions of pounds in a failed attempt to maintain and upgrade two thirds of the London Underground network. The luckiest trainees even got to attend hearings. For those who came to A&O to do finance, finance and more finance, there's an opt-out litigation course run by Nottingham Law School.

Most trainees are seconded to an overseas office in their final seat. New York and Hong Kong always attract a lot of interest, and "*good appraisals in previous seats usually form the basis for the decision to send you out there.*" The New York seat is mostly capital markets-related so previous experience is also desirable. Other popular destinations include Singapore, Dubai, Paris and Milan, and even though trainees noticed a slight reduction in the number of overseas secondments of late, they are adamant that "*if you really want to spend time abroad, HR will make it happen.*" Apart from the obvious delights of discovering new cultures, working abroad normally offers the welcome opportunity to be treated as a "*mini-associate rather than a trainee.*" It is also possible to spend a seat on secondment to finance clients or, in a few cases, the human rights organisation Liberty.

Allen & Over-the-moon

Everyone we spoke to was delighted and honoured to have trained at A&O. When pinpointing why they chose it, many mentioned A&O's reputation for being the friendliest in the magic circle. Who knows if that's true: all we can say is that our sources frequently said that "*people here are genuinely supportive.*" Perhaps also reflective of its good-natured ethos is the "*amazing pro bono programme and community involvement.*" Besides its convivial atmosphere, our sources also came to A&O expecting to be trained to the highest possible standard, and for the most part their expectations were met. Training starts as early as the bespoke Allen & Overy LPC at the College of Law, where future joiners' studies are tailored to reflect the nature of the firm's practice. It makes the transition to real-world practice much smoother and allows trainees to cultivate friendships before they officially start at the firm. Once installed in the office, trainee training continues with plenty of on-site and external sessions.

When asked whether the firm looks for particular traits in recruits, most interviewees insisted that "*there's no stereotypical A&O trainee,*" but having observed their counterparts at Linklaters and Clifford Chance on the LPC, some did claim that "*types do emerge – CCs are geeks, Linkies are super-competitive, and here at A&O we're just more relaxed – we're the coolest.*" Why not read our features on the other magic circle firms and make up your own mind. We'd say our interviewees seemed self-assured and lively, and we also got the impression that A&O trainees have more to offer than solid academics. Many of our sources conceded that the firm "*seems to favour well-rounded people who've acquired a range of experiences and soft skills outside of academia.*" Beyond a substantial contingent of Oxbridge bods, people come from a good pool of different universities and each intake includes a respectable range of ethnicities, nationalities and backgrounds.

It goes without saying that working for A&O can be all-consuming, so it's just as well that within their slick, Foster-designed offices in Spitalfields staff have access to all manner of services. There's a health practice, canteen and gym, and in the evenings the stylish sixth-floor café morphs into a subsidised bar. Trainees often congregate on the fabulous roof terrace for a few post-work drinks before moving on to their local, the Water Poet. The trainee committee is normally allocated an entertainment budget, and even though "*it hasn't been increased for about four or five years*" it's still generous enough to cover a big summer ball. Management also puts on regular firm-wide parties and there are plenty of departmental jollies to attend. At A&O, "*you'd be hard pushed not to find an activity that suits your interests.*" There are sports teams galore and even a choir and orchestra.

Staying on top

A&O's grad recruitment motto is that trainees who come here 'start at the top' of the profession. This begs the question: will they all be able to stay there? As a result of its exposure to the banking sector, A&O suffered in the recession, and in addition to the firm-wide restructuring, it downsized its intake of newly qualified lawyers in 2009. The firm employed 99 qualifiers out of a potential 118. Our interviewees imparted a few tips on how to improve your retention prospects in a difficult market. One said: "*It's important to schmooze the partners who will argue your case when qualification decisions are made,*" and another added: "*A&O doesn't suffer mediocrity, so make sure that every piece of work is your best.*" Realising that it may have over-recruited in recent years, the firm has announced its intention to reduce the annual trainee intake from 120 to 105.

And finally...

While none of our sources disputed the widely held belief that A&O is the friendliest magic circle firm, you must never forget that the finance-oriented training here is no easy ride. Be prepared to work really hard.

Anthony Collins Solicitors LLP

The facts

Location: Birmingham

Number of UK partners/solicitors: 23/73

Total number of trainees: 14

Seats: 4x6 months

Alternative seats: None

To fit in here you must share the firm's ethos: ethical awareness and empowering people.

If you want a warm, fuzzy feeling at the end of the working day then this community-minded Birmingham firm could be perfect.

Theme players

Founded in 1973 by the eponymous Mr C, this firm embodies all that many others find impossible. Originally steered by its founder's Christian faith, Anthony Collins' culture is based on ethical awareness and empowering people. *"It's about servicing our clients well and not just making lots of money,"* announced one principled trainee. There is without doubt a shared vision. *"If you are entirely commercial in your thinking and uninterested in the public sector then you will have a bad time here."* Following a restructuring the firm is now organised by *"themes rather than teams"* to maximise working relationships between practice groups and improve client focus. The seven themes are: children and young people; enterprise; entertainment and leisure; faith communities; health and social care; social housing; and transforming communities.

The commercial practice, which encompasses coco, dispute resolution, commercial property, employment and licensing law, has the likes of restaurant chain La Tasca, Aston Villa FC, The Restaurant Group (Frankie & Benny's, Chiquito and Garfunkel's), the Birmingham Hippodrome and Goodyear Dunlop on its books. Commercial law may bring in the big bucks but it's the Transformation team that gains AC considerable attention. Specialising in community regeneration and social housing, this is arguably the heart of the firm. The private client division has a worthy emphasis too. Child-related cases are central to AC's respected family practice, and the firm has an impressive reputation for clinical negligence claims, including birth injury cases and those involving questions of medical ethics, such as the right to life.

Within reach

The procurement, projects and construction team has been combined with the social housing and regeneration team and given the new name 'Reach'. Because the cases here are so huge, trainees tend to *"dip in and out"* of several during a seat. Involvement generally comes through note taking at *"really big meetings,"* plus research and drafting. The firm assisted social landlord Poplar on the regeneration of part of London's Tower Hamlets and advised national social care-provider and social enterprise Turning Point on the construction of five residential support centres. AC represents housing associations up and down the country, lately assisting with a number of mergers. One in particular that took up trainees' time was the Walsall Housing Group's consolidation from eight organisations to three, involving the transfer of over 20,000 homes. Trainee jobs included drafting and carrying out risk assessments of various arrangements. The contentious social housing lawyers encounter some colourful cases, including possession claims due to anti-social behaviour. When pushed for tasty stories our interviewees obliged. As well as the standard marijuana farms and public nudity, there was a rather stinky tale of a man who used a bucket in the bath instead of his toilet. *"There was a mountain of [sh]it,"* a trainee reported, *"and he kept throwing it out of the window."* Fortunately our source didn't witness the mess first-hand but was able to conclude: *"It's shocking what people have to live with."* At simpler possession hearings trainees can conduct their own advocacy.

Charity fare

The commercial property department prompted mixed reviews, probably because it's renowned for throwing trainees in at the deep end and giving them a raft of their own files and meagre supervision. Some trainees sink, others swim. What is not disputed is how much can be learned here. Juggling numerous conveyancing files teaches "*a lot about client care and managing their interests.*" As well as getting to grips with a sizeable caseload, trainees also shadow supervisors on more complex deals, one being the £20m redevelopment of The Baseball Ground in Derby for housing. "*It is definitely a growth seat,*" concluded a source.

Other commercial options include dispute resolution, employment and business law. A stint in commercial litigation involves debt recovery (for the firm and clients), commercial claims, property disputes and, increasingly, insolvency-related advice. Again, trainees are given their own files; "*I was mainly responsible for looking after business tenancy issues,*" said one. The business law team covers a range of subjects – "*everybody has different specialisms*" – not least IP and technology. The arrival of IP specialist Sarah Webb from Wragge & Co has strengthened the department, which represents housing associations, charities and local commercial outfits on a variety of IP, IT and data protection issues. The charity team is ranked top in the Midlands by *Chambers UK* and works for regional and national charities. A number of its clients are religious organisations (eg the Bible Society and Spring Harvest); others such as Livability (a residential care home provider for the disabled) illustrate AC's broader interests.

Second-years are given priority in the seating system, but lately allocation has become somewhat unstuck as the firm caters for its largest number of trainees yet. "*I think it was a bit of a shock for them to have to find places for us all,*" said one. "*It has been fairly common to not get the seats that you request,*" added another. A lesson learned, AC reverted to a 14-strong trainee group for 2009/10.

What price the soul?

While there are no religious artefacts adorning the walls, "*you don't have to look for the Christian feel to know it's there.*" A prayer group meets once a week, and while e-mails invite attendance, there is no pressure to go. Anyway, far from thinking of it as a negative trait, our sources viewed the Christian side of the firm positively, telling us: "*It sets us apart and brings in a lot of work.*" Religious clients feel comfortable as they can guarantee an understanding ear. "*I've been to some meetings,*" mentioned one trainee, "*where clients want to pray at the end. I've never joined in, and that hasn't been a problem.*" It's not just Christian organisations that are attracted: the firm has a growing clientele among the Sikh and Muslim communities.

Chambers UK rankings

Charities	Local Government
Clinical Negligence	Personal Injury
Construction	Private Client
Dispute Resolution	Public Procurement
Employment	Real Estate
Family/Matrimonial	Real Estate Litigation
Licensing	Social Housing

A majority of the partners are practising Christians, but further down the ranks religious affinities become less pronounced and one's beliefs are unlikely to be a barrier to career progression. "*To make partner you have to share a vision, not a religion.*" For the record, most of our sources were simply drawn by the firm's caring reputation, both in the community and among AC staff. "*They are very much about developing you as an individual here,*" was a common view. Said one source: "*As a trainee, I feel extremely valued, and there are a number of forums through which we are consulted.*" This environment, while perfect for many, could be frustrating for anyone with low levels of tolerance or patience. "*The firm wants to be seen as valuing everybody and dictating to no one*" and, as such, moving "*from idea to implementation can take a very long time.*"

Work-life balance is a priority. "*People tend to be out of the door at 5.15pm and you almost have to explain yourself if you're working late.*" Interestingly, some trainees said they'd have liked to have been pushed more and "*given a couple more deadlines.*" We say deadlines are easy to find; commitment to work-life balance that constitutes something more than lip service is rare. Favourable working hours give trainees plenty of time to socialise, and the cocktail bar-cum-Indian restaurant Asha's is their regular Friday night haunt. Big firm events have "*dried up with the recession,*" but there are usually summer and Christmas parties. Each year the trainees are responsible for choosing a charity to support. Last time they opted for local organisation Karis, which helps vulnerable people with practical tasks in the home. Recent charity events include a band night, quizzes and a balloon launch.

And finally...

Trainees assure us that Anthony Collins "*has a real reluctance to let people go, generally.*" Proving this, in 2009 it found NQ jobs for six out of eight qualifiers.

Forget the competition

At Ashurst we work as a team, which means less competition and more communication.

If you've got team spirit call Stephen Trowbridge, Graduate Recruitment & Development Manager, Ashurst LLP, on 020 7638 1111, email gradrec@ashurst.com or visit www.ashurst.com

ABU DHABI BRUSSELS DUBAI FRANKFURT HONG KONG
LONDON MADRID MILAN MUNICH NEW DELHI NEW YORK
PARIS SINGAPORE STOCKHOLM TOKYO WASHINGTON DC

ashurst

Ashurst LLP

The facts

Location: London
Number of UK partners/solicitors: 122/335
Total number of trainees: 106
Seats: 4x6 months
Alternative seats: Overseas seats, secondments
Extras: Pro bono – Islington & Toynbee Hall legal advice centres, Disability Rights Commission, Business in the Community, death row appeals; language training

> The recession hasn't slowed Ashurst's global development plans: it has lately staked a claim in Hong Kong and hired a major finance team in New York.

A. A. Gill once described a table at famous London restaurant The Ivy as 'one of the most sought-after pieces of furniture in London.' We believe City firm Ashurst has plenty in common with the eatery – while it's mighty hard to get in, once through the door you're guaranteed star treatment.

Somewhere over the rainbow

One of the pack of international firms surrounding the magic circle, Ashurst is a renowned high performer. Since its founding in 1822, and subsequent shaping by a genuine Victorian eccentric and two City gents, the firm has nurtured a quality reputation for big deals, good client relationships and good manners. Cast in the standard Square Mile mould, Ashurst is essentially a corporate and finance outfit (these departments net 31% and 25% of revenue respectively) and *Chambers UK* ranks it highly in both areas. Never underestimate the value of Ashurst's litigation and real estate teams though. The excellent banking litigation practice was particularly busy advising in relation to the problems of Northern Rock, Bradford & Bingley, Bear Stearns and Lehman Brothers among others.

Three failed merger bids at the turn of the century convinced Ashurst that an organic approach to growth was best. An injection of vigour in the form of a rainbow-themed rebrand quickly followed. While the new branding was an affirmative move away from what had become a rather stuffy image, Ashurst has not quite shaken off all of its conservatism. According to graduate recruitment partner David Carter, rather than *"a series of whizz-bang announcements,"* Ashurst's approach to its own development is rather measured. *"We simply follow the business and build up our presence in the centres where our clients want us to be."* Senior partner Charlie Geffen vowed in September 2008 that the firm was to place a greater focus on Asia and the Middle East, and just two months later Ashurst staked a claim in Hong Kong by entering into an association with Jackson Woo & Associates. The tie-up complements Ashurst's offices in Singapore and Tokyo.

While Carter admitted that Ashurst *"hasn't attacked these markets as much as competitors,"* the firm does have India covered thanks to a New Delhi liaison office set up in 1994. A 1995 Bombay High Court ruling effectively bars international firms from taking advantage of the subcontinent's blossoming economy. As Ashurst has been the only European firm with a licensed office in this increasingly influential country, it makes no bones about the fact that it'll be standing at the front of the queue when, and if, the Indian profession opens up to outsiders. As for the Middle East, the hire of Dechert's Islamic finance group head Abradat Kalampour bolstered Ashurst's relationships in this important region. It already had two Middle East offices – Abu Dhabi and Dubai – and earlier in 2009 London-based Abradat proved his worth by winning a major instruction to advise on the creation of a £700m offshore sukuk programme for a group of Kuwaiti-backed bankers.

Seeing stars (and stripes)

Ashurst has had a small New York office since 2000, but until recently it largely served as a meeting facility. The recession dealt the firm a lucky hand stateside, and it all came about following the demise of its NY and DC-based ally McKee Nelson. McKee Nelson's heavy reliance on the ailing mortgage-backed securities market (the type of debt conjuring that got us all into such a heroic mess) forced it to lay off around a third of its lawyers. Ashurst nabbed McKee Nelson's 30-lawyer structured finance team, which it's worth pointing out is one of the best in the USA. It is said that the line between genius and madness is fine, perhaps even blurred. When we questioned the firm, we were told "*the opportunity was unusual*" and the decision was "*bold rather than bonkers.*" Lest you think this shift away from Ashurst's self-confessed caution represents a change of philosophy, don't be deceived. We see the US strike as more of a Newton's apple situation: essentially a good opportunity fell into Ashurst's lap, with the arrival of the McKee Nelson team bringing clients of the likes of Goldman Sachs, Morgan Stanley and Merrill Lynch.

Does Ashurst's global groove filter down to trainees? It seems so. "*You can pretty much guarantee an international flavour to your work,*" our sources confirmed. One trainee working on a leveraged finance deal that stretched "*literally across the globe*" learned that organising conference calls was "*quite tough.*" It sounds as if recruits are up to the job though: previously known for its penchant for classic Oxbridge applicants, Ashurst's trainee group now has a distinctly pan-European feel with several people coming from even further afield. Meanwhile, UK-reared trainees commonly speak second (or third) languages. As one noted: "*Ashurst is definitely moving ahead quite rapidly, and the use of languages will become increasingly important.*" Whether through translating foreign documents and making client calls abroad, or by going for full immersion in an overseas seat, there's ample scope to make the training as international as you'd like. The list of foreign offices now taking trainees includes Brussels, Dubai, Singapore, Paris, Milan, Madrid and Tokyo. Such posts are not reserved for linguists, but with 100 or so trainees at the firm competition is certainly fierce. A proven interest in your chosen destination won't go amiss.

Like many of its City peers, Ashurst requires trainees to complete both a corporate and a finance seat. However, compared to some competitors, its training is still pretty broad, despite these mandatory placements. There are other options available in real estate, employment, EU and competition, environment and litigation, as well as regular client secondments to the likes of Citi and IBM. Those lucky enough to score a client secondment found the experience enhanced their knowledge of the role of a legal adviser. "*It helps you understand how the client works and the business rationale that goes behind instructing solicitors.*" Getting "*more responsibility with less supervision*" was another bonus for the more independent-minded.

Chambers UK rankings

Banking & Finance	Intellectual Property
Banking Litigation	Investment Funds
Capital Markets	Life Sciences
Competition/European Law	Local Government
Construction	Pensions
Corporate/M&A	Planning
Dispute Resolution	Private Equity
Employee Share Schemes	Product Liability
Employment	Projects, Energy & Natural Resources
Environment	Real Estate
Financial Services Regulation	Real Estate Finance
	Real Estate Litigation
Fraud: Civil	Restructuring/Insolvency
Information Technology	Tax
Insurance	Telecommunications
	Transport

A traditional first-seat destination, the finance department provides newbies with "*a very good grounding.*" Said one: "*Bearing in mind I had no previous experience in the specifics, everyone in the team was great at explaining things.*" Seats are split between real estate finance, leveraged finance, and securities and structured finance (SSF). Of course, the mega-deals had largely disappeared when we spoke with trainees, but it was clear that Ashurst was still managing to bag some major instructions, one example being online betting company William Hill's £1.2bn refinancing, one of the largest capital raisings of 2009. The team also advised a consortium of sponsors in connection with the acquisition of Gatwick Airport, and worked alongside Linklaters on a £207m rights issue for Greene King to enable it to buy more pubs. On larger deals trainees are generally cast in administrative roles, "*making sure things are signed on time and by the right people,*" as well as taking minutes at meetings and drafting basic documents. While the tasks may not be the most challenging, trainees relish being involved. Even the real estate finance team, which has taken quite a beating, still has top-quality clients including Tesco and Westfield, London's latest retail cathedral.

Responsibility is easier to come by in the SSF seat. "*It's a very steep learning curve,*" remarked one source. "*When I look back over the six months, it's just ridiculous how much I have done.*" The hours in finance go up and down, so each trainee has a horror story or two to share. "*At the end you just feel broken,*" admitted one. At least the team (which is almost 50% female at partner level) "*tries to get you involved as much as possible.*" Regular departmental drinks are occasionally themed; apparently a superhero event featured some "*quite brave*" costumes.

Waxing lyrical about restructuring

Market conditions have led to mixed experiences in the fêted corporate department, and perhaps for this reason some of the most enthusiastic comments were reserved for the busy restructuring and insolvency team. Ashurst has taken various companies through restructurings, including airline Zoom, Land of Leather, MFI, Jessops and MK One. There is still corporate activity among healthy clients – motorway services provider Welcome Break was bought for £500m by investment fund Apia, and Merlin Entertainments (London Eye, Alton Towers and LEGOLAND) bought the London Aquarium. Ashurst oversaw Merlin's £2bn merger with Madame Tussauds in 2008, so the relationship was already established. Once again the strict hierarchy on bigger deals means trainees find themselves *"drafting documents and supporting clients... it's a lot of logistics work."* The team ethos usually makes up for what can sometimes be mundane work: corporate is known for its *"larger-than-life characters"* and *"there is a definite work-hard, play-hard culture."* Trainees state that when a deal is going strong *"you will stay late,"* but equally *"if it's quiet you can leave at six and not get a second glance."* The department has regular Friday evening 'sundowners', for which the managing partner has a tab in a local pub.

The popular energy, transport and infrastructure (ETI) seat has lately been one of the busiest. In December 2008 Ashurst redeployed three corporate partners and three finance associates to support the ETI team, and there have been a number of lateral hires. The work is very international, with much coming from the Middle East and Asia. Trainees tend to *"get a flavour of all the different areas,"* making for a diverse six months. So what can you expect in this seat? Simple answer: loads. Ashurst advised the Petrochemical Industries Company of Kuwait on a £17bn joint venture with multinational Dow Chemical, and was involved in three new petrochemical and refinery projects in Libya. Closer to home ETI clients include Crossrail, various waste management bodies, and participants in the largest Building Schools for the Future (BSF) project to date – a £600m scheme to build/refurbish ten secondary schools in Kent. Once again trainees were complimentary about the team: *"They are a good laugh and really make an effort to get you involved."* On the subject of getting involved, the general downturn in work across the City led Ashurst to engage trainees more in business development activities. This can only be an advantage to all.

The litigation department has particular strengths in life sciences, product liability, competition, banking and fraud. While around 50% of trainees opt for a three-week litigation course instead, those who choose the Full Litigation Monty tend to enjoy getting their hands dirty with legal research. *"I feel like I've gone back to law school, going to the library and picking up various textbooks."* Many trainees were of the view that *"it's very important to spend at least three months in the department because you really get a chance to understand the law."*

Pachyderms and prospects

Like the celebs who frequent The Ivy, Ashurst types just love to glam things up. As well as themed departmental socials, the annual dragon boat race is generally conducted in costume, and the trainee ball took on a 1920s theme last time. We heard a particularly memorable tale about a partner who dressed up as an elephant for Red Nose Day. *"He put a suit on top so he looked professional."* If fancy dress isn't your thing then the firm's obsession with sport could save the day. The football team earns high praise and there are also netball, hockey, rugby, tennis and basketball teams. Essentially, *"whatever you love playing, you can send an e-mail round to see if people fancy getting a team together."*

When asked about their colleagues, one comment from a trainee summed things up: *"At every single law firm you are going to get a certain number of tools, but I think at Ashurst you get a lot less than at others."* Another source told us: *"If I had to make the decision again I would choose Ashurst every time."* A third commented: *"I'm always amazed at how many of the senior people say they have trained here... any firm that trains people and retains them up to partner must be doing something right."* The thing that really stands out for us is how well personal recommendations work for Ashurst's recruiters. Time and again trainees attributed their presence at the firm to wise words from a sibling, other relative or friend – Ashurst is clearly a word-of-mouth kinda place. In 2009 42 of the 53 qualifiers took up NQ positions. Although it followed the lead of others, freezing associate salaries and shrinking NQ pay packets, in contrast to many firms of its size, Ashurst did not have a major redundancy programme or defer new trainees' start dates.

And finally...

Ashurst combines top-quality work with an engaging office environment in which people's personalities have room to move. It has shown an ability to evolve with changes in the legal marketplace without compromising its character.

Your perspective ✕ Our world

Multiplying your potential

"It's exactly how I wanted my career to develop. I'm working in a global, multi-cultural setting, on high quality deals with blue-chip clients, and all within a welcoming and supportive environment. It's about helping me to develop my experience and enabling me to be the best lawyer I can be."

Emily Carlisle, Associate, Corporate

Do you want to multiply your potential?
www.multiplyingyourpotential.co.uk

BAKER & McKENZIE

Baker & McKenzie LLP

The facts

Location: London
Number of UK partners/solicitors: 84/198
Total number of trainees: 78
Seats: 4x6 months
Alternative seats: Overseas seats, secondments
Extras: Pro bono – eg Prisoners Abroad, Save the Children; language training

Founder Russell Baker paid his way through university by entering prize fights, but trainees here find their experiences to be anything but bruising.

Offering access to all the resources of a global firm without the impersonality of some of the City monsters, Baker & McKenzie is a perennial favourite among students of an international disposition. In addition to all the mainstream areas of commercial practice it has some top-notch specialist work.

Packing a punch

There's only one way in which to describe B&M's ascent from a small Chicago firm to global giant in 60 years: relentless. It has around 3,000 lawyers and pulls in an annual revenue in the region of $2bn. Since adding an office in Abu Dhabi, the firm now has a presence in 69 locations. This global spread sealed the deal for one of the trainees we spoke to: *"The internationality of the firm was the main reason I came, as well as the relatively small intake here in London."* Global domination takes the form of relative independence for lawyers in each jurisdiction and B&M *"prides itself on the fact that its partners are almost always local."* The globe-trotting nature of the firm can have its drawbacks at times though, *"like getting called up at 10pm due to accountants in Brazil wanting to access files."*

Opened in 1961, the London office remains the biggest in its network and benefits from having Tim Gee, the global head of B&M's M&A practice, in situ. Many of the highest-value deals are done here; for example, lawyers recently advised Sony Corporation of America on its acquisition of Bertelsmann's £480m 50% stake in the Sony BMG Music Entertainment joint venture. The London-based M&A team is also well regarded among mining, energy and petroleum clients, and it represents major industry players like Rio Tinto and Siemens Energy. Pulling in deals relating to operations around the world, lawyers recently acted for West Siberian Resources on its merger with Alliance Oil, where the combined market capitalisation of the companies amounted to around $2.5bn.

In addition to a sound reputation in the staple areas of corporate and banking, the firm also has specialist practices that draw the eye of many a graduate – for example, employment, intellectual property, IT/commercial, competition/trade and litigation. *"You usually always get your seat preference,"* our sources assured us, though we've noted that the popularity of seats can vary from year to year. This can mean a rush on certain departments; in the past couple of years this has meant *"a big push to get into banking and corporate."* While the latter is a compulsory seat, it's not what everyone we spoke to had come to the firm to do, and one source suggested that *"the firm could have communicated it to us, while they recruited us, that they would increase the trainee numbers in corporate rather than IP, employment or other niche areas – they could have articulated the strategy clearer."*

Just doing it

To be clear then, B&M has a strong desire to develop its corporate and finance practices. One trainee phrased things perfectly when they said: *"If you come to the City, [you must know that] the heart of the City is corporate."* So what's on offer to trainees in corporate? In short, everything from routine matters like due diligence and contributions to the drafting of sale and purchase agreements, to more unusual research into oil and gas deals or convertible bond issues in Eastern Europe. The dominant view was that *"research on regulations can be very dry,"* so it's a good thing that *"corporate is a very sociable and friendly seat with a lot of trainees on those floors."* The seat is additionally viewed as *"very document heavy, especially in capital markets,"* and we could tell that some sources wished *"it wasn't so repetitive and predictable in terms of the type of clients we have in capital markets."* If the work can be formulaic, the pressure can also become intense: *"Having to sometimes cancel your evening plans can be annoying, but it is expected on occasion."* To be fair though, some of the matters did sound pretty cool. Take the acquisition of sportswear company Umbro by Nike, a transaction any football fan would drool over. By contrast, smaller teams within the corporate department – tax for example – *"can be very intellectually challenging."*

The firm's push into banking and finance a few years back was noteworthy because it scooped a team of recognised stars from Norton Rose. The London practice had continued to grow steadily and the firm now represents major clients like HSBC, Citi and EQT (a major Scandinavian bank). Trainees find their work includes *"a lot of project management, co-ordinating, drafting and client e-mail correspondence."*

Niche work if you can get it

The niche areas that had been the reason why several of our sources had chosen B&M are most definitely there for the taking. In IP, trainees have dealt with sexy topics like anti-counterfeiting, an area of work that's *"fast-paced and where lawyers are often engaged with the Southeast Asian offices."* One good example is the firm's representation of L'Oréal before the European Court of Justice in a major trade mark claim that will have wide ramifications for European trade mark owners. Trainees noted *"a balance between the contentious and non-contentious in the seat,"* as well as plenty of corporate support for the M&A team. Lately the team advised Ideal Standard, one of Europe's leading bathroom suppliers, on a major global IP project following its acquisition of a bathroom and kitchen business from American Standard. This matter spanned more than 100 jurisdictions.

We heard high praise for the IT/commercial seat due to supervisors' willingness to allow trainees *"more responsibility than any corporate seat."* We're not just talking about attendance at client meetings. As this seat touches on litigation as well as public procurement and outsourcing matters, *"you can be called in to help seek preliminary injunction for the client as well."* The firm's heavy-hitting commercial disputes team, meanwhile, handles

Chambers UK rankings

Administrative & Public Law	Franchising
Advertising & Marketing	Fraud: Civil
Banking & Finance	Immigration
Banking Litigation	Information Technology
Capital Markets	Intellectual Property
Climate Change	Media & Entertainment
Competition/European Law	Outsourcing
Construction	Pensions
Corporate/M&A	Private Client
Data Protection	Product Liability
Dispute Resolution	Professional Discipline
Employee Share Schemes	Projects, Energy & Natural Resources
Employment	Public International Law
Environment	Public Procurement
Financial Services Regulation	Telecommunications

both traditional litigation and major arbitrations before international tribunals like the ICC. Trainees assist with the preparatory stages on litigations, mediations and arbitrations as well as looking into conflict of laws issues. Expect some time in court but no actual advocacy. Here's another work example for sports fans: B&M litigators represented the British Olympic Association in its successful defence of injunction proceedings brought by disgraced athlete Dwain Chambers. Other clients that have sought the firm's advice include Facebook, Mattel and McLaren.

One of the more interesting and analytical seats looks at competition and trade matters. Here a trainee can expect to be working on contentious antitrust issues and merger control; for example, the firm has represented Hutchison 3G UK before the Competition Appeals Tribunal. In the top-ranked employment department, trainees are exposed to discrimination claims, labour issues, corporate support and general advice to employers on redundancies, disciplinary procedures and a raft of other day-to-day concerns. *"There's a lot of European work, as well as a chance to tackle pro bono matters,"* explained one source. Major clients include British Airways, Prudential and FremantleMedia. The firm also has expertise in employee benefits, so trainees get to *"advise on the remuneration of employees and draft agreements and scheme rules, which require in-depth knowledge of tax schemes and quite a bit of black letter law."* We initially gained the impression that the pensions seat was the boobie prize for trainees but then discovered fans. *"There is a wide range of regulatory and Hansard-related research, as well as a real involvement with the clients."* Some trainees were able to try out pensions litigation and we heard that *"if you demonstrate that you're capable of having responsibility then they give it to you."*

Fly me to Cancun

Those trainees lucky enough to secure an overseas posting generally do it in their fourth seat. Some trainees argued that the three-month stints on offer were *"too short,"* though it should be stressed that it is possible to do a two-year post-qualification assignment to another B&M office. Those who want to second overseas while still a trainee must put forward a business case and can only go to locations that have suitably qualified supervisors. We suspect our business plan for Spring Break in Cancun or Tijuana (B&M has seven offices in Mexico) would not have been approved. IT seats in Sydney and competition seats in Brussels are common, and we heard of people willing to work in some of the more adventurous locations, like Russia and Kazakhstan. Even though some offices may have a distinct and very different culture to London, secondees still felt included. Said one: *"They gave me a great apartment in an astounding location and made me feel at home."* The firm provides lunchtime language courses for trainees who are keen to try one of the Spanish or French-speaking locations and want to brush up rusty skills. Back in the UK trainees can take client secondments (eg UBS, Standard Chartered and Lloyd's of London) and Judicial Assistant roles at the Court of Appeal.

From Bakers with love

The trainee group is usually diverse. Many newbies come from elsewhere in Europe or even Africa and Asia. Most speak second or third languages and are well travelled. Trainees say: *"There doesn't seem to be as much of an Oxbridge bias compared to the magic circle firms."* In terms of personalities, *"they go for a range, from really academic to the party-goers; most are intelligent and fairly normal."* Future intakes are likely to know each other well before starting at the firm as their LPC training will be done together. Over the past year the firm upped the amount of soft skills tuition for its existing trainees, covering topics such as presentations, drafting and communication.

Social events aren't in short supply. We heard about Halloween parties, karaoke, outdoor theatre, cocktail nights, ice skating, go-karting, tenpin bowling and that perennial favourite – Friday night drinks. The Evangelist at Blackfriars is a favourite haunt among trainees. The last Christmas party was held at the Natural History Museum, where the trainees performed an amusing skit that contained some biting satire on the nature of the professional worker and the meaning of life. A highlight for many is the annual Baker Cup football tournament (for boys and girls), which pits teams from different European offices against each other. We're told that the Madrid office, the home team, won in 2008 (coinciding with Spain's victory in Euro 2008), but London may have a better chance of securing victory in 2009. The firm pays for most of the expenses and the trip is seen as *"a real bonding ritual."*

The London office has beautiful views of the river, St Paul's Cathedral and the London Eye, but *"the aesthetics are dated,"* commented one critic, and others agreed. Don't they say it's what's on the inside that counts? Well, inside the B&M client conference rooms you'll find some interesting artwork including miscellaneous pictures of shoes, briefcases and *"a man examining a horse."* The office atmosphere was praised for the approachability of staff and partners, and our sources spoke well of the canteen, which is large, subsidised and perfect for breakfast, lunch and dinner. The firm has recently begun a green initiative, though several sources thought extra effort could still be made to use less electricity and recycle more. In 2009 31 of the 40 qualifiers stayed on with the firm, with just two of the 2009 new trainees deferring their training contracts until 2010. Elsewhere in the office there were 90 redundancies, about half of them lawyers. One trainee appreciated the openness of the management during the process, telling us: *"Before the information went public we did get to know about it."*

And finally...

Our thanks to the source who pinpointed the top three reasons for choosing Baker & McKenzie: quality training, a big international element to the work and a pretty flat hierarchy in the office. Sounds spot on to us.

BARLOW LYDE & GILBERT

www.blg.co.uk

WINNER
Litigation Team
of the Year

WINNER
Litigation Team
of the Year

WINNER
Dispute Resolution
Team of the Year

WINNER
Best Law Firm in
the London market

WINNER
Best Law Firm in
the London market

BEST RECRUIT
Medium City Fi...
(2004)

For more information please contact Caroline Walsh, Head of Graduate Recruitment and Trainee Development

Barlow Lyde & Gilbert LLP
Beaufort House
15 St Botolph Street
London EC3A 7NJ

Telephone 020 7643 8065
Facsimile 020 7643 8500

grad.recruit@blg.co.uk

Barlow Lyde & Gilbert LLP

The facts

Locations: London, Oxford, Manchester
Number of UK partners/solicitors: 78/202
Total number of trainees: 31
Seats: 4x6 months
Alternative seats: Overseas seats, secondments
Extras: Pro bono – LawWorks; language training

You want to litigate? You can do so to your heart's content at this City mid-sizer. You'll even get the chance to run your own cases in some seats.

For insurance litigation in the City, it doesn't get better than this. BLG handles many of the biggest and best cases and still finds time to cultivate a full-service practice.

The sky's not the limit

BLG was opened by Stephen Barlow in 1880 and its first client was insurer Cuthbert Heath, who famously sent this cable to his San Francisco agent following the 1906 earthquake: "Pay all our policyholders in full irrespective of the terms of their policies." Stirring stuff. Insurance was then, and remains today, the beating heart of BLG. The firm has over 200 lawyers dedicated to insurance and reinsurance across offices in London, Hong Kong, Shanghai and Singapore, and it acts for all the big insurers in matters ranging from clinical negligence to financial disputes with banks. Trainees told us: *"You will not escape insurance research or insurance law as a trainee at Barlows; even the corporate department works for insurers."* Corporate makes up just 20% of the business at BLG, and you'll do well to appreciate that litigation rules the roost. Though there are numerous non-contentious opportunities, trainees euphemistically said: *"It would be 'interesting' if you wanted to come here and do corporate."*

Bucking a trend by expanding in a down economy, the firm opened two new offices in 2009: Manchester and São Paulo, Brazil. Much like the resurrection of its Oxford office (which lay largely dormant for some time), Manchester has been set up to provide clients with an alternative to London-based legal services. *"It's important for us to give clients an option of being able to give work to other offices where they can be charged less,"* explained a source. The São Paulo launch is aimed at better serving the needs of an increasing number of aviation insurance clients with interests in Latin America. BLG's niche aerospace practice is ranked by *Chambers UK* as best in the UK, alongside Clyde & Co. More on that later. In addition to these new outposts, BLG has moved to *"more of a business model as opposed to legal model"* in appointing a CEO in the UK and a COO for its Asian ventures in Hong Kong, Shanghai and Singapore.

You're really spoiling us

"The jewel of the firm" that was the professional liability and commercial litigation (PLCL) department has been split into two parts – professional financial disputes (PFD) and commercial lit (CL). Despite this, trainees told us there was a significant amount of crossover and that you are likely to get exposure to both divisions' work. PFD covers *"a plethora of professions in the City,"* with the firm representing accountants, surveyors and fellow solicitors on claims brought against them. The department seems to be as highly regarded internally as it is externally, and trainees say: *"You have to be on top of your game"* here, despite the fact you may be stuck with *"the grunt work – bundling and all of that"* on larger cases. Other tasks will include *"research on finite parts of fine arguments,"* note-taking at meetings and writing reports for clients. The advantages of assisting with multimillion-pound cases include extensive court attendance and exposure to barristers. *"It was great to get an insight into the discussions that go on parallel to a case,"* recalled one source. On lower-value claims, perhaps relating to solici-

tors' negligence, trainees have more scope to run files. *"It's brilliant training because you learn what mistakes other solicitors make."* In terms of big-stakes matters, lawyers are representing Clifford Chance in a professional negligence claim brought by a Jersey-registered property company, and the firm featured in *The Lawyer*'s top ten litigation list of 2009 for its work on the $94m accountancy case of Stone & Rolls Ltd v Moore Stephens.

On the commercial litigation side the firm is representing the Italian maker of Ferrero Rocher (the world's largest purchaser of hazelnuts), which is defending complex fraud claims brought by the Bank of Tokyo-Mitsubishi UFJ and KBC Bank NV. Arising from a failed structured loan facility for the importation of hazelnuts, the claim could be worth €30m. Working on cases such as this, or a £50m claim regarding an exploded power station in South Africa, trainees play a crucial role. Among their duties are *"being the communication point for the team and ensuring everyone knows what is going on,"* as well as *"analysing data, drafting pleadings and briefing witnesses and counsel."* Smaller cases are there for the taking too, for example debt recovery matters.

Who let the dogs out?

When discussing a seat in the aerospace team, one trainee explained: *"It's more industry-focused than practice area-focused."* The firm can handle *"everything under the umbrella of aviation,"* from small claims relating to damaged cargo to massive commercial litigation over craft leasing disputes. Current cases include acting for BAE Systems in connection with the loss of a Nimrod XV230 over Afghanistan in 2006 and acting for insurers for INFRAERO (Brazilian Airports) in relation to the TAM A320 crash at Congonhas Airport – Brazil's worst ever aviation disaster. The same point about focus could be made for the marine, energy and trade group. This is a *"very technical"* department that mostly works on insurance disputes. *"From cases to do with sinking ships spilling oil, to ruptured oil pipelines, to ships crashing into each other or having nowhere to moor,"* this is a terrific opportunity to sink your teeth into some intricate international work.

Reinsurance is a technically complex area, so our thanks go to the trainee who helpfully explained what it's all about. *"There are two types of work: the dispute element of bringing a claim, or any other element of policy coverage, and then there's advice on policy coverage."* On the contentious side, trainees' tasks include research, compiling memos and attendance notes. Case management is also the order of the day. Product liability is a big issue for this department, a good representative case being the advice given to Munich Re and QBE International Insurance in relation to the £30m Seroquel drug litigation

Chambers UK rankings

Aviation	Insurance
Banking Litigation	Personal Injury
Clinical Negligence	Police Law
Commodities	Product Liability
Construction	Professional Discipline
Corporate/M&A	Professional Negligence
Dispute Resolution	Real Estate Litigation
Employment	Restructuring/Insolvency
Environment	Shipping
Financial Services Regulation	Transport
	Travel

in the USA. Seroquel was prescribed for bipolar conditions and a class action has been filed by patients who have developed diabetes since being given the medication. On the non-contentious side, trainees' research is often used for client updates. Said one source: *"At the minute I'm doing research into the implications of a new EU directive."* In this department, *"every day is different; you never really know what kind of work you'll be doing."* The superlative client roster runs the gamut from big boys Deutsche Bank, Swiss Re and Lloyd's of London to little-known internationals Israel Phoenix Assurance and La Boliviana Ciacruz de Seguros y Reaseguros.

Closer to home the casualty department represents local authorities, hospitals and the police. Incorporating clinical negligence and other insurance issues, cases range *"from a £15k claim related to a police dog biting someone evading arrest, to a police employee claiming in excess of £250k for breach of duty of care."* BLG was famously appointed as solicitors to the coroner in the Jean Charles de Menezes inquest. Standard litigation tasks abound (witness interviews, liaising with barristers, research notes), and there is also the opportunity to go on secondment to a local authority, where a trainee's day-to-day work ranges *"from investigating slips-and-trips to people nicking iron from school buildings and the related insurance issues."* When it comes to personal injury, one interviewee admitted: *"It may seem an anathema to have a department like that in a firm like this,"* but added: *"PI is classic litigation, and litigation is our bread and butter."* This being BLG, nothing is done by halves, and last year it represented the Catlin Group in the €42m settlement of Schoss v The Road Accident Fund (understood to be the largest known personal injury settlement to date).

Don't scoff at the Hoff

What about that 20%? Yes, a fifth of BLG's business is non-contentious. In the down economy, however, trainees say the deals have been *"sporadic."* For the most part trainees have been *"ticking over,"* assisting with public-to-private deals, drafting joint venture agreements and reviewing companies' articles and memoranda. Having expanded in 2008 (one new partner, two consultants and three associates) and landed new clients such as Deutsche Bank and Britannia Pharmaceuticals, the team saw its head leave the firm earlier in 2009. Indeed partner exits have not been uncommon at BLG over the years: it has lately lost some insurance lawyers and unfortunately could not hold onto one of the City's top litigators, Clare Canning, who aced the defence of Ernst & Young in a £2.6bn negligence claim by Equitable Life. Debate the issue with legal pundits and some will question whether BLG's partnership has always agreed on exactly where the firm should be going.

Among our interviewees, commercial technology was the most popular of the non-contentious seats. Coming within the remit of this seat are competition issues, data protection, outsourcing and IP. Trainees advise clients on the potential sharing of information and how to meet outsourcing needs; they draft contracts and prepare monthly legal updates. Recent work has included advising Tesco on the procurement of complex IT hardware, software and support in order to provide an in-store money transfer service to Poland. Lawyers also advised Ernst & Young on the outsourcing of all of the print functions of its UK offices to Xerox.

Trainees can turn their hand to non-contentious work when on secondment to the Hong Kong office. From a fully serviced apartment (complete with swimming pool) a trainee can walk the ten minutes to the office. Predominantly advising *"multinational companies doing business out of Hong Kong,"* in this seat they also deal with the Securities and Futures Commission (HK's FSA) when providing regulatory advice on setting up funds. There's plenty of litigation available here, too, and BLG has lately been handling *"one of the largest litigation cases Hong Kong has ever seen."* One trainee was especially excited at having sat in a court with Lord Hoffmann presiding. We're not surprised – The Hoff sounds like one heck of a judge.

A seat in Singapore focuses on aerospace-cum-insurance work, and there are also some client secondments. The other departments in which trainees can sit are employment and pensions, tax, marine, and energy and trade.

How Barlow can you go?

Socialising is a key aspect of life at BLG. *"As soon as you're through the door, you're one of the team and are included in everything. You're invited and expected to attend all client and firm-wide events… and the fact is, we enjoy doing it."* Entertaining clients is vital at a firm working in the insurance sector, both for the purposes of keeping existing clients happy and attracting new ones. This lot get up to all sorts, from *"drinks at the firm to bowling, golf, tennis, cookery classes, wine tasting – there was even a Wii event, which was a bit of an odd one."* It is expected that trainees *"work hard during the day and are happy to do things in the evening as well."* In short, with insurance clients *"there's more of an old-school client-lawyer relationship."*

It's not all schmoozing clients: there's plenty of opportunity for socialising with colleagues. The materialisation of the 5.30pm Friday drinks trolley is cause enough for celebration, and the Christmas and summer parties are usually quite lavish events. Each summer brings softball in Hyde Park and there's a whole range of sports teams to join. For the trainees, *"extra-curricular"* activities usually see them crammed into the nearby Slug and Lettuce or in Aldgate's best-kept secret, Fernando's. The free pizza with drinks almost prompted the *Student Guide* team to traipse over to the far eastern edge of the City.

The vac scheme, not abnormally, also provides scope for socialising and its curry night is a cracker. *"The free-flowing wine can result in some great bits of gossip the next day,"* though of course *"getting obscenely drunk is a no-no…"* BLG's vac scheme is notable for its key role in recruitment. About 70-80% of trainees are recruited from the scheme each year, and our interviewees suggested that *"you've got a damned good chance of being offered a job if you do the vac scheme."* Not only that, serial vac schemers told us BLG's programme had a lot more to offer than others they'd attended. *"Before the vac scheme Barlows was one of my last picks… but the work was interesting, they gave you a focus and a structure to it;" "some other firms just plonked you in an office from 9am til 6pm."* The qualities that recruiters look for are fairly obvious – *"an interest in litigation is a pretty big thing"* and you have to have *"the ability to really work within a team."* The firm does not show an Oxbridge bias; it recruits from, and sponsors, student events at a wide range of universities.

And what happens when the training is over? Over the past decade between 60-something and 80-something percent of qualifiers have stayed on with the firm each year. In 2009 some 15 out of 20 people took up jobs.

And finally…

If litigation is your bag and you're sociable and chatty to boot, BLG is an excellent choice in the City. Make sure you do your utmost to nab a place on the vac scheme and polish up those Wii skills.

- **Challenge your preconceptions:** Great training isn't the preserve of the magic circle – don't apply to these firms just because you're a high flyer and you feel it's expected of you. Conversely, don't ignore the most prestigious firms because you don't think you have a chance. Perhaps you have the exact combination of skills and experience they are looking for.

top tip no. 8

Bates Wells & Braithwaite LLP

The facts

Location: London
Number of UK partners/solicitors: 25/49
Total number of trainees: 9
Seats: 2x6 + 3x4 months
Alternative seats: None
Extras: Pro bono – Blackfriars Legal Advice Centre

This liberal-minded firm stands out from the City crowd. One partner has a following among gangsta rappers like Busta Rhymes, 50 Cent and Snoop Dogg.

"*I wanted a medium-sized firm that wasn't a corporate horror,*" a Bates Wells trainee told us. They chose well. Known for its charitable clientele, this firm can rightly tout itself as a conscionable alternative to the major outfits.

Suds law

"*Wherever you go in the building you get the impression that this firm has a conscience,*" said one source. And yet trainees caution anyone expecting a utopia for tree-huggers and do-gooders: "*The ethos here is great, but don't get carried away as this is still a business.*" However, the firm is home to prominent Lib Dem Lord Phillips of Sudbury, who has been instrumental in the creation of UK charities legislation. Furthermore, it really encourages staff to undertake pro bono work and allows them time out from regular duties to deal with it. The charitable focus permeates most departments, including employment, immigration and dispute resolution. Trainees become immersed in a range of (usually) domestic matters for top-rung charitable clients like the British Red Cross, Shelter, CRUK, Oxfam and NSPCC, as well as a host of lesser-known names within the sector and in the commercial world more generally. While this may not be a 'corporate horror', you won't find the corporate lawyers here are any less commercial than their peers elsewhere. "*Bates Wells may help charities, but it is no charity itself.*" Nuff said.

Come fly with me

Perhaps the most important piece of advice for a potential trainee is this: choose your flight path wisely. The available seat options are in charity, employment, litigation, immigration, corporate/commercial and property, and trainees complete two seats in their first year and three in their second. Given that the charities department is the largest, trainees can expect to visit it at least once. Not that a seat here is a chore: on the contrary, the team sits right at the top of the *Chambers UK* rankings and, as a trainee, "*you really feel at the heart of everything.*" The work spans constitutional and governance issues, applications to the Charities Commission and wide-ranging trusts advice. Our sources agreed that this is where you'll work the hardest as it gets the largest volume of work by far. Trainees appreciated the fact that there are plenty of things that are "*quite standalone and can be done with little supervision,*" despite the high level of client contact involved.

In 2008 BWB represented 278 of the top 300 charities in the UK – a hundred more than its closest competitor. One example of its work is the help it gave to ActionAid International on the second stage of its international restructuring across more than 15 countries. Huge effort is directed at educational charities, like the Independent Schools Council, the Camphill charities and the Teachers Support Network. Interestingly, only one of our interviewees had come to BWB to fulfil a burning desire to work for charitable clients, but as one perceptive source pointed out: "*Charity law is never really studied in university.*" In recognition of this, newbies are given a full introduction to the subject.

The media and entertainment department also impresses. Along with the sports department it devotes about 35% of its time to charity clients. The theatre lawyers in particular are known for their advice to the likes of the Royal Shakespeare Company (lately concerning rights agreements relating to

David Tennant's time on stage) and the Edinburgh Fringe, the disabled-led Graeae Theatre Company and the English National Opera. In saying this, however, working in these specialist fields is more likely after qualification.

Notorious B.W.B.

The firm is a solid performer in lower mid-market corporate deals so don't go expecting too many big-name clients. The firm utilises its existing strengths in the education, media and entertainment sectors, as well as sports and fashion. Lawyers recently acted on the sale of luxury handbag company Lunan Group to Synova Capital, as well as the sale of the publisher of *Birdwatch* magazine to Warners Group Publications. The department benefits from the firm's connection with Parlex, a network of European law firms created in 1971.

The immigration team handles a host of different personal and business-related problems. A seat in this smaller team means working with Phillip Trott, a partner with increasing street cred and a following among gangsta rappers like Busta Rhymes, 50 Cent and Snoop Dogg. The trainees we spoke to had "*not had the pleasure of meeting Mr Dogg or Mr Rhymes,*" but thought it was quite cool for the firm to be associated with such entertainment luminaries. The department has also sought US visas for World Championship boxers. One source found immigration work to be "*faster-paced and a bit more human, as each client has a distinct history.*"

The dispute resolution department has two limbs, one dealing with public and administrative work, the other with commercial disputes. First-years are thrown into commercial litigation. Said one source: "*The first-year partner was fantastic and really got me involved in cases – it was a good introduction to working in a law firm.*" Second-years, meanwhile, can sink their teeth into meatier administrative law and regulatory matters affecting charities and public authorities. For example, lawyers have been defending a group of Isle of Wight councillors over allegations of unethical behaviour regarding a planning application made by one of their number. Public law geeks will also be attracted to the holy grail of judicial review work. A media and defamation group poached from Addleshaw Goddard resides in this department and is known for its work for *The Times* and the Advertising Standards Authority.

The employment team is a magnet for some trainees. Working on unfair dismissals, discrimination and sexual harassment cases, they divide their time between charitable and non-charitable clients. Nearly 80% of the team's efforts are devoted to contentious matters, so expect to clock up some tribunal or arbitration time. Recent highlights include a whistle-blowing case for International Contraceptive & SRH Marketing, plus advice to Diabetes UK on a religious discrimination claim where the employer was sued for having a Buddha statue in the office.

Chambers UK rankings

Administrative & Public Law	Media & Entertainment
Advertising & Marketing	Partnership
Charities	Real Estate
Corporate/M&A	Real Estate Litigation
Employment	Sports Law
Immigration	

And the winner is...

Someone fresh out of uni is less likely to impress recruiters than someone with a bit of life and work behind them. Said one source: "*The firm wants individuals who can bring experience and help shape the firm.*" We also sensed a lack of a strong hierarchy, something that one trainee noted at the monthly fee earners' lunch. Another agreed, telling us: "*You may talk about one or two partners from time to time, but there's little in the way of difficult personalities.*" The firm is described as "*very enterprising*" and sometimes brings in motivational speakers. Trainees have to be enterprising too. They assist at seminars for clients, although not everyone enjoys the "*more menial*" aspects of this, "*like handing out name badges.*" The only other moan we heard came from those who wished office hours were more flexible. That said, "*it's very rare to have someone stay after 6pm on a Friday night.*" BWB's office is just across the road from St Paul's Cathedral in a building shared with "*a horde of friendly Scandinavian bankers.*" Every trainee sits with a partner, which means that help is never far away. In terms of feedback from partners, trainees said: "*We have half-seat and end-of-seat appraisals with our supervisors, but sometimes it can be difficult to gauge your progress on a day-to-day basis.*"

New starters have an NQ mentor to help them tackle the initial period and future trainees get to tag along to some social events, so they're likely to recognise a few people on day one. For that after-work ale or vino, trainees drop in to the nearby Wine Tun. The Christmas party is usually a swish affair; last time it was held at The Hilton on Park Lane, appropriately the same venue as the BAFTAs.

And finally...

Bates Wells is a cracker of a firm and offers relatively unusual experiences in the City. In 2009 all four qualifiers accepted jobs, going into the charity, employment and public and regulatory teams. There were no redundancies or deferrals.

Beachcroft LLP

The facts

Location: Bristol, Leeds, London, Manchester, Birmingham, Winchester, Newcastle
Number of UK partners/solicitors: 139/c.450
Total number of trainees: 62
Seats: 4x6 months
Alternative seats: Secondments
Extras: Pro bono – The Prince's Trust

This steady-as-she-goes firm is one of our top picks of the year. If its practice focus appeals then we'd recommend you apply.

Now with offices in every corner of the country, Beachcroft is a full-service firm with particular expertise in healthcare and insurance.

Dublin' up

Beachcroft employs around 1,500 people, making it one of the UK's largest firms. Unlike others of its size, it has steered relatively clear of the corporate sphere, preferring to focus on insurance and public sector work. This approach has made Beachcroft a solid prospect in the current economy, which has seemingly played directly to its strengths. *Chambers UK* rankings reflect Beachcroft's dominance in its chosen fields: it wins a glut of Band 1 rankings across the UK for public law, healthcare, PI and insurance. In addition to these considerable strengths, the firm has a full complement of other practices. It would be worth examining the *Chambers UK* website to gain a deeper understanding of which of Beachcroft's many offices do well in what practice areas. As an example, for corporate finance it scores a Band 2 ranking in London, Band 3 in Bristol and Band 4 in the North West.

This has never been a highfalutin', boastful organisation, and the trainees we spoke to all exuded a quiet confidence. "*Traditionally, the firm has been very litigation-heavy and that side of the business is carrying it through,*" said one, while another suggested that "*the real headline ought to be about how well Beachcroft has handled the recession – better than any other firm I know of. We must be one of the only firms not to have let people go.*" This year, as in years past, trainees were surprised that "*despite having good clients, doing great work, being friendly and commercially aware and offering a good work-life balance, we suffer from a lack of profile.*" We think this softly spoken and pragmatic firm will come to the notice of many more students this year.

Indeed, this past year has seen it quietly and successfully forging ahead. New offices have been opened in Newcastle and Dublin. The former was started with the acquisition of Eversheds' clin neg team in Newcastle. One of the new recruits was David Weatherburn, a man who had won Eversheds a position on the NHS Litigation Authority panel and was reportedly pulling in £4m a year for the firm. He has now brought that work over to Beachcroft, further bolstering its position as one of the country's leading health practices. Meanwhile, an English firm opening an office in Ireland was sure to raise some eyebrows. Others have tried and failed to break into that market in the past, but senior partner Simon Hodson was upbeat when we met him, believing that the targeted practice areas – health and insurance, of course – will prove lucrative for Beachcroft.

In the know

A specialist claims-handling service called B2 has also been launched, "*driven by one of our major insurer clients who wanted us to take on more volume work.*" Trainees "*don't really get involved*" with it, but it does demonstrate both the firm's flexibility in meeting the needs of its clients and its willingness to make adaptations in a changing legal market. We also find it interesting that four Beachcroft lawyers have established themselves in some very prominent positions within the profession. Former managing partner Bob Heslett is currently serving as the

Law Society's president; senior legal executive Judith Gordon-Nichols is now the president of the Institute of Legal Executives; former senior partner David Hunt is investigating how the profession should be regulated; and strategic litigation partner Andrew Parker is advising Lord Justice Jackson's review of litigation costs. Although it's hard to measure the effects of all these things, it does send a good message about the respectability and position of the firm within the legal establishment. And it also indicates that the firm is fully aware of the likely direction the profession will take following regulatory changes brought about by the Legal Services Act.

When we heard about the new offices, we expected to find a big chunk bitten out of the firm's wallet because new branches don't come cheap. While Beachcroft's profits did dip slightly, its revenue rose by 6% to £121m in 2008/09. Considering the economic conditions, the firm has done rather well, and the only major changes it had to make involved transferring people from real estate to contentious teams and putting some associates in the real estate department on a four-day week.

Under good management

The locations that accept trainees are Bristol, Leeds, Manchester and the two offices in London. The firm has other offices in Winchester (insurance and health) and Birmingham (construction and injury risk), but neither takes trainees at present. As for the offices that do take trainees, work-wise "*there are slight differences between them,*" for example "*there is no projects department in London.*" The real differences (such as they are) seem to be found in the culture and social life. In short, the trainees in the regions felt that they socialised more than the Londoners. This, they say, is caused mainly by London's vastness – "*a lot of people live quite far away, on the edges of the city, which makes it more difficult.*"

Technically there are no compulsory seats at Beachcroft, but the sheer volume of insurance work means that "*a seat in that department is a given.*" The injury risk department deals with all kinds of mishaps. There's your common-or-garden slips and trips; work-related illnesses like industrial deafness; stress; and more complex cases such as asbestos poisoning. The benefit of doing this seat is that "*you definitely get a lot of exposure. You get to see things from start to finish and settle a few cases on your own.*" Clients served by the firm include Zurich, Allianz, Aviva and Fortis. The other major part of Beachcroft's insurance practice is professional indemnity. The firm is advising law firms and their insurers in the coal health claims investigation in which a large number of firms have been accused of regulatory breaches over their handling of claims seeking compensation for miners. Clinical risk is another hefty area. "*Without a doubt we're the foremost provider for the NHS and I think that's well estab-

Chambers UK rankings

Administrative & Public Law	Insurance
Banking & Finance	Intellectual Property
Clinical Negligence	Licensing
Construction	Local Government
Corporate/M&A	Personal Injury
Debt Recovery	Product Liability
Dispute Resolution	Professional Discipline
Education	Professional Negligence
Employment	Projects, Energy & Natural Resources
Environment	
Franchising	Public Procurement
Health & Safety	Real Estate
Healthcare	Real Estate Litigation
Information Technology	Restructuring/Insolvency
	Retail

lished. It's certainly something Beachcroft hangs its hat on.*" The firm is instructed by the NHS on cases that few other firms can handle, often involving weighty clinical issues like consent to treatment, confidentiality, access to medical records and mental health law.

That Beachcroft is willing to focus on practices that offer relatively slender profit margins may contribute to its character: when margins are tight, management must be effective. It's a well-organised firm. Just as an example, if you look at its website you'll see a section that describes the management structure, telling you exactly what each person is responsible for in this very "*open and inclusive*" firm. This inclusiveness extends to its recruitment policies: it accepts applicants from law and non-law backgrounds, 23-year-olds who've come straight through university and people who have had previous careers. Our interviewees talked of highly effective, rigorously organised training schedules and easy internal communications. As they go along, they submit work they've done to an e-portfolio – a system designed to monitor progress and help deliver improved feedback at monthly reviews. One trainee, deep in the flow of issuing compliments, said: "*I can honestly say, hand on heart, that they are completely focused on investing in the trainees.*"

Balancing act

So far we've only really discussed Beachcroft's insurance and public sector work, which does the firm a bit of an injustice. According to trainees, it strikes "*a good balance between public and private sector.*" Worthy of note is the *Chambers UK* top-ranked construction team, which has been involved in a big case regarding an airport in Bulgaria. "*This is a huge matter,*" but trainees managed to get "*a good level of involvement*" in various aspects of the deal, which could be "*very stimulating at times, a little mundane at others.*" The speciality of the department is work for public bodies – schools, hospitals and so on – in disputes over PFI projects.

Thanks to its presence in the public sector, the firm's real estate department hasn't quietened down too much. Recent instructions have come from the Home Office's real estate department, the Tribunals Service and Her Majesty's Court Service. In the private sector it has attracted work from the Westfield Shopping Centre (300 lettings) and acted for a national hotel company on the sale and leaseback of a five-star hotel and spa. In this department, *"when you start it is the usual form-filling, but as you go on you get to negotiate leases and sales"* and trainees confirm a high amount of client contact.

In the financial services department, even though *"the downturn is affecting it,"* there is *"a steady flow of work coming through… enough to occupy us."* Trainees say it is *"all incredibly complicated,"* but because it's *"quite a small department there's a 'heads down, get things done' work ethic. You get a fair amount of autonomy – you know what you've gotta do, and you go out and do it."* Trainees have been involved with the drafting of share agreements and muck in on *"anything the client needs a hand with."* Over in commercial services, they become involved with *"a tech and commerce group that specialises in telecoms and communications."* This team handles a lot of IP work for clients including the Welsh Assembly, for which it helped facilitate a broadband aggregation programme. Reflecting the general desire to bring them on as quickly as possible, trainees can attend face-to-face client meetings and assist with the drafting of parts of the main contracts.

Always keen to improve trainees' commercial awareness, the firm is increasing the number of secondments available from 2011. As well as client secondments to companies like Unilever, these will include short stints in the firm's HR and accounting departments.

Life's a beach

Bristol is the firm's HQ, and in 2008 it moved into new purpose-built offices in the city. The Bristolians used to be split across two offices and this change has *"made the office feel more inclusive and coherent."* Specifically, trainees told us that *"people are a lot happier with the everyday working conditions; it's really had a good, positive impact and makes us feel more like a team."* Up in Leeds and Manchester there's a move to get the two offices working more in tandem. *"They call it the northern initiative, where they're trying to treat it as one northern office. It is working well,"* a source explained. *"The different locations have their own outlooks on things, but everyone's getting to know each other well."* In London, most of the contentious work is done at the smaller Eastcheap office – *"construction, professional risk, general property and commercial risk. It's all insurance-related in one way or another."* A larger office on Fetter Lane houses the PI, real estate, employment, tax, corporate and public law departments. Trainees noted how *"there does seem to be an aversion to working in the Eastcheap office;"* it's a less sociable place and some say *"it is seen as a bit of a misfit, a completely different firm."* Others insist these criticisms are baseless… unless you end up working for *"one of the individuals who are kinda feared."* Yes, Beachcroft has a couple of *"anomalous partners, people you just don't want to go near."* We were told that some trainees specify with whom they don't want to work on their seat preference forms. That said, it's worth bearing in mind that these are the exceptions, that all the supervisors are trained and that trainees who have battled their way through with 'difficult partners' have emerged at the end of the seat with their skills thoroughly enhanced. Tough love.

The work-life balance at Beachcroft is excellent, a fact that pleased our contacts no end; indeed, many cited it as one of the firm's best qualities. People usually go home between 5.30pm and 6pm. *"After that, partners will ask you why you're still in the office – you work to live, not live to work."* One trainee said that *"although the social life is good, in all honesty most things we organise ourselves."* Trainees do get the opportunity to attend networking events and seminars for clients, which although not exactly socialising, as such, does give them a good idea of the non-fee earning aspects of being a solicitor. In a similar vein, the firm has an active charity committee. As for parties proper, Beachcroft tends to throw good Christmas parties and trainees are encouraged to take vac schemers out for high-budget nights of food and drinks. Other fun events mentioned by trainees were a Three Peaks challenge, quizzes to raise money for The Prince's Trust, barbecues, a party on board the *'SS Great Britain'* in Bristol and the AGM in Birmingham, where there was *"a massive great meal and loads of entertainment."* The firm also gives corporate membership of Bristol Zoo to every trainee.

And finally...

Beachcroft has adapted well to its clients' needs and the changing economy. Reflecting this, the firm retained 29 out of 38 qualifiers in 2009 and made no redundancies or trainee deferrals.

Berwin Leighton Paisner LLP

The facts

Location: London
Number of UK partners/solicitors: 182/439
Total number of trainees: 78
Seats: 4x6 months
Alternative seats: Brussels, secondments
Extras: Pro bono – Sonali Gardens Legal Advice Centre

BLP's ability to lure successful partners away from other firms is a clear indictment of its confident business strategy and growing reputation. Students would be well advised to follow the lead of these senior lawyers.

The product of mergers between Berwin & Co, Leighton & Co and Paisner & Co, Berwin Leighton Paisner is now far more than the sum of its original parts.

Respect my authoritah!

"I chose BLP mainly because at the time I was applying everyone seemed to be talking about it. There was a really big buzz about the firm." So said one of this year's trainees, succinctly summing up the recent history of this top-20 outfit. The plan since 2000 has been to become the most 'respected' firm in the City. If money equals respect, it's been an unqualified success. In nine years, turnover grew from £58.7m to £186m.

BLP was traditionally known for its excellent performance across the spectrum in real estate. It still scoops *Chambers UK* Band 1 rankings in that area but, more recently, lateral hires – many from magic circle firms – have strengthened its other commercial practices. *Chambers UK* also recognises BLP's work in mid-market corporate finance, particularly in respect to AIM-listed companies. The firm gains further top-tier rankings in construction and licensing, and its growing prominence in a variety of fields is perfectly demonstrated by the fact that since 2007 it has risen from Band 5 to Band 2 in *Chambers UK*'s employment table, and from Band 4 to Band 2 in the IT rankings.

Managing partner Neville Eisenberg has masterminded this success story. He's a popular figure among employees, and in 2009 was re-elected unopposed for a fourth term. We made our calls just after the redundancies of 85 staff (including 30 lawyers), so naturally morale had taken a hit, but our contacts spoke in confident tones about the firm's future, reminding us that *"it hasn't based its business model on investment banks."* Even mid-recession, BLP made up five partners in its giant real estate department and opened offices in Moscow and Abu Dhabi to add to existing ones in Brussels, Paris and Singapore. We spoke to Mr Eisenberg, who admitted: *"We're feeling the effects of the economy in the same way as everyone else, but for a firm like ours, which has been developing rapidly, the current market offers lots of opportunities to expand further by bringing in new people and acquiring market share from other firms."* He identified corporate and finance as key growth areas and this, combined with a self-proclaimed emphasis on quality, does lead us to wonder if those redundancies might have been a clearout of dead wood as much as anything else. Trainees also pointed to the tax department as one to watch. *"It has quadrupled in size in the past couple of years. Clearly they want to make it another pillar of the firm."*

Every little helps

Trainees are expected to complete a real estate seat, a corporate seat and a litigation seat, plus one other of their choice. There was praise for HR, who trainees say *"genuinely do want to accommodate peoples' preferences as well as put bums on seats."* But with 80 trainees to sort out at each rotation, it was acknowledged that not everyone gets exactly what they want. People do get their first choice at some point, however.

In practice it's sometimes possible to avoid doing one (or on rare occasions even two) of the compulsory seats, though don't arrive expecting to be able to. Given the firm's superb real estate reputation, we were surprised to discover that the department divided opinion among trainees, with a number of them keen to "*dodge*" it. Some who had completed the seat found the work "*menial*" and said "*they should hire more paralegals.*" Others described it as "*a breath of fresh air*" and suggested that it would be "*incredible as a first seat because you run your own files and learn how to juggle things.*" There's no doubt you'll be working for some big names here, both partners and clients. BLP has done exceptionally well at luring industry stars from firms like Clifford Chance, Herbert Smith and Pinsent Masons, and these hires have added further credibility to a practice that was already performing marvellously. Not least among the firm's big clients is Tesco. The retailer and the firm have a relationship that goes back 30 years, and it's probably no surprise that BLP's rise has coincided with the supermarket chain's increasing market dominance. In the past year lawyers advised Tesco on the acquisition of 16 stores from the Co-op and nine from Woolworths, and on the sale and leaseback of a further 13 stores and a distribution centre worth £605m. At a time when the property market was in a slump, the department still managed to pick up new clients including National Grid, Thames Water, The Football Association and Cambridge University. Perhaps if 'core' real estate doesn't appeal, a seat in real estate finance might be a better option. "*It's completely finance. We work closely with the real estate department but they draft most of the property-related documents themselves.*"

Among the investment clients on BLP's books are Land Securities, Hammerson, Hermes, Canary Wharf Group, Great Portland Estates and Qatari Diar Real Estate Investment Company, which the firm helped to acquire an option to buy the Chelsea Barracks site for a proposed development that got Prince Charles hot under the collar. Students who start at the firm in 2012 will doubtless hear much talk about the Olympics. The firm has done a great deal of work for the 2012 Olympic Delivery Authority, particularly in the vast, top-ranked planning department.

The corporate department is split into work groups. There's core corporate, "*which is a mix of IPO and M&A,*" then there's private equity and investment management. We're told "*there is a lot of crossover*" between the three, however. As at April 2009, BLP represented a total of 41 AIM-listed clients; only five other firms do better. In one recent £100m deal, it acted for retail entrepreneur Linda Bennett on the sale of her high street fashion chain LK Bennett to Phoenix Equity Partners and Sirius Equity. Corporate is a department that will always attract a certain type. "*I would say they are workaholics there!*" said one trainee. Nevertheless, all our sources were happy with the responsibility they were given. Said one: "*I drafted a large part of the back end of the key document in a transaction, and on a couple of occasions my supervisor left me on my own in client meetings.*" Supervision at the firm is described as "*reactionary.*" That is to say, "*it's very much whatever's required by the*

Chambers UK rankings

Asset Finance	Local Government
Banking & Finance	Media & Entertainment
Banking Litigation	Outsourcing
Capital Markets	Parliamentary & Public Affairs
Charities	
Commodities	Pensions
Competition/European Law	Planning
Construction	Private Client
Consumer Finance	Private Equity
Corporate/M&A	Projects, Energy & Natural Resources
Dispute Resolution	
Employment	Public Procurement
Environment	Real Estate
Financial Services Regulation	Real Estate Finance
Franchising	Real Estate Litigation
Information Technology	Restructuring/Insolvency
Insurance	Retail
Intellectual Property	Shipping
Investment Funds	Tax
Licensing	Telecommunications
	Transport

individual. If you need your hand holding, that's available, but people are also willing to step back if you want." Appraisals are scheduled every three months and taken seriously – "*HR chases people relentlessly.*"

A good bet

Also falling under the corporate banner are the insolvency and BTS groups. "*That's Business Technology Services – essentially it's commercial contracts.*" This team has a highly regarded licensing practice, particularly for betting and gaming, with clients including Betclick, Betfred, Electronic Arts, Gala Coral and even the Seminole Tribe of Florida, which has been involved in casinos and gambling since the 1970s. The seat involves "*drafting, little bits of research, going through contracts to see what the issues are and advising clients.*" The growing tax team is an increasingly popular destination: "*The work is research-based so you really have to use your brain.*"

In its drive to beef up corporate, BLP has been hiring more transactionally oriented trainees, and perhaps this is why the contentious training requirement of the SRA didn't weigh particularly heavily on the minds of all our sources. "*A few people do the two-week course* [instead]*, but I would encourage anyone to do a litigation seat,*" said one who was more disposed to contentious work. Commercial lit, insurance, real estate, construction, IP and banking litigation are among the contentious seats on offer. This last team acted for the Central Bank of Nigeria on an application to discharge a third party debt order which challenged the ownership of £35m in a UK account owned by the bank. We do wonder if they received that particular instruction via a badly spelt e-mail. The litigation teams "*aren't the biggest, so everyone is expected to get involved: there's less of the classic trainee work of paginating and bundling.*" That sounds like excellent news, and furthermore we understand that a few trainees even manage to do some advocacy. Among the other seat options are slots in Brussels and secondments to clients.

Your future's immense

Trainees here have strong personalities ("*vivacious would be a good word*") but "*if you are an arrogant, cocky type there will be an immediate response to you.*" Many of our contacts had seriously considered magic circle firms when applying but baulked at the idea of a work-work-work lifestyle. "*I think a common feeling here is that we don't like working late,*" said one. "*No one minds doing it on occasion, but we would generally begrudge staying beyond 8pm all the time.*" Trainees can generally expect 9am to 7pm to be the standard hours, although we were amused to hear from one who told us: "*Sometimes I forget to go home because my office is so wonderful.*" The firm's premises are located on London Bridge and many rooms have spectacular river views.

Does the disinclination to work late mean that this is a trainee group of limited ambition? Not a bit of it. In fact, an unusually large proportion of them already have an eye on partnership. At most firms the people we speak to haven't thought that far ahead, but for many here the chance to make partner quickly was "*a big selling point.*" The precedents are there for all to see. "[Managing partner] *Neville was a senior associate who won a big client and kept corporate finance afloat in the last recession, and he was rewarded instantly for it.*" Trainees say that "*if you're doing well you'll know your partnership prospects sooner than at other firms,*" and that "*leadership*" is one of the main things BLP looks for when recruiting. Use that information with caution – we're picturing an assessment day of 25 people all trying to be leaders and it's not pretty.

By the left...

BLP is one of the firms that pioneered the LPC+ at the College of Law. The course gained good reviews from our interviewees and, since the entire intake does it together, everyone in a group of new starters already knows each other when they arrive at the firm. As if the LPC isn't enough of a bonding experience, BLP also runs a three-week induction to the firm, which includes "*know-how, team-building exercises and personal development stuff like networking and presentation skills.*" The induction includes a two-day residential course at Sandhurst. Yes, the military academy. Yes, trainees do the assault course.

You'll find plenty of BLP lawyers having a drink or two in either The Monument or The Fine Line on a Friday evening, and there's an active sporting side to the firm. Trainees suggest that perhaps because "*we all went out together every night during law school,*" by the time they arrive at BLP they don't feel the need to hang out as a group so much. Despite the fact that "*it's not a huge party scene,*" trainees remain the "*social epicentre*" of the firm. "*The associates enjoy the trainee gossip, and it's very much frowned upon if you haven't got any gossip to give!*" Naturally we probed and got a good story about partners, associates and trainees in a French nightclub's swimming pool during a charity cycle ride from London to Paris. Our source insisted: "*It was all good clean fun really! But for me it really highlighted the lack of hierarchy we have here.*" From what we can tell the trainee magazine (ominously entitled *Disclosure*) is closer to *Heat* than *The Economist* in tone. "*Basically it's all about what's going on with the trainee intake,*" said one contact innocently. Some light-hearted ribbing is a feature of life here, so keep quiet if your significant other has an embarrassing nickname for you – the trainee now universally known as 'Chicky-pig' found that one out to his cost.

The buzz that has surrounded BLP hasn't died away, and when talking to trainees we got a real feeling of potentiality; a sense that despite all the firm's recent success more is still to come. It's not just us, though. "*I heard one of our lateral hires say the other day that BLP reminds him of how Clifford Chance was years ago, just before it took off,*" said one trainee, "*slightly perturbed*" at that thought. Maintaining a mid-sized firm culture in the face of huge growth is difficult and, said some, "*what makes BLP a great firm is that it does feel quite friendly. It would disappoint me if we expanded a lot and fast. It might just become a bit anonymous.*" Neville Eisenberg denies the new foreign offices herald aspirations of world domination. "*We are not going to be planting lots of flags. We have our preferred law firms in 65 countries and we invest heavily in deepening those relationships, which broadly gives us global coverage.*" Trainees too felt confident that the culture would be maintained. "*In the last five years a lot of laterals have come to us from the magic circle or American firms, but they are all people who buy into the BLP way of life.*" In the past few years the firm has clocked up consistently good retention stats and in 2009, 30 out of 40 qualifiers accepted NQ positions.

And finally...

More than "*the traditional bod who's brilliant technically,*" BLP is also looking for "*someone who's a salesman.*" Show confidence in your interview because "*they want to see a bit of spark.*"

Bevan Brittan LLP

The facts

Location: Bristol, Birmingham, London
Number of partners/solicitors: 48/150
Total number of trainees: 28
Seats: 4x6 months
Alternative seats: Secondments
Extras: Pro bono – ProHelp

Positive trainee feedback reflects the rising mood within Bevan Brittan. One to consider in Bristol, London or Birmingham.

This firm is a public sector powerhouse. Its key markets are communities and local government, health and education, and major corporates.

Free at last

Five years ago Bevan Brittan emerged from an unrewarding marriage with a West Country firm now known as Ashfords. Attracted by the money to be made in the ballooning private sector, it seemed to try to redefine itself as a player in the corporate market. Some commentators doubted it could make the transition from the public to the private, and to an extent they were right. Over the course of four years, profits started to ebb away and at one point revenue per lawyer was the lowest in the top 100. Speaking about the partnership in 2008 a trainee told us: "*They don't seem to have the conviction to actually do what they want to do.*" Now, following some downsizing, management reshuffling and soul-searching, BB appears leaner and more focused on a clear and workable strategy for the future.

The transformation started in May 2008 when, accompanying a statement declaring that 'a number of practice areas are underperforming, certain markets declined and investments in certain areas have not proved as profitable as hoped', the firm made redundancies. Rather than heralding an irrevocable decline, this knock seems to have provided the jolt the firm needed. Management was changed. Andrew Manning, a non-lawyer with a background in the firm's finances, was voted in as new chief executive, the board was reshuffled and a partner lock-in was put in place to stabilise the upper echelons. The new management took stock of the firm's position and plotted a course of consolidation based on the organic growth of core areas. To our mind, it was at that point that the firm struck a good balance between ambition and its traditional strengths. Today, the firm has a 60/40 split between public and private sector work. Trainees commented favourably on management's decisions, saying: "*A lot has changed in the last twelve months. It's not been like one big change though – it's been lots of little changes contributing to the whole picture.*" On the new CEO, one said: "*Andrew is more of a presence. He updates us and is there more. Also, being from a business background is a really good thing. He's got something about him.*"

Lost and found

The recession lobbed a massive spanner into the works of many firms but BB's performance has been astonishing. As others watched their profits fall precipitously, BB's increased in 2008/09, buoyed by continued public sector spending. As a result, partner profits rose by 6.2%. Arguably the recession has helped the firm find itself. As corporate markets tanked and banking departments up and down the country collected cobwebs, the temptation to push the firm increasingly towards private sector business became far easier to resist.

BB isn't the only firm targeting the public sector; indeed more and more commercial firms have been looking hungrily in this direction over the past year. In the face of added competition, will the firm be able to maintain its market share? Admittedly, it has lost a few good clients – but it has gained new ones too. BB has been representing North Bristol NHS Trust on a project to build a £374m hospital, is working to claw back millions from Icelandic banks on behalf of local authorities, has struck a deal with

Kent County Council's legal team to handle complex clinical and medical negligence cases, and has been retained by the Solicitors Regulatory Authority (SRA). The trainees we spoke to were confident that BB would be able to hold onto its market share and assessed the situation thus: "*Larger firms were hit harder because they are less agile and able to respond. They might think the public sector is a great place to look for new work, but firms stuck in the private sector just do not have the expertise to get into the public sector. They can't adapt fast enough to get into that market.*" We'd add that BB's own experience proves just how hard it can be to target a new market, even when the economy is booming.

Trainees were glad they had chosen the firm and described it as "*very welcoming.*" More than anything, they were pleased about the quality and volume of work they received; "*we've had some quite challenging things and there's been no getting pushed over onto the photocopier, as the old cliché goes.*" They struck us as rather philosophical types, very aware of the firm's progress and intentions, and as interested in its internal machinations as they were in the work that occupied them, like street lighting and waste management projects (described as "*really cool*" and "*a lot of fun*"). One point worth mentioning is that trainees tend to assist more public sector clients than private sector ones as this helps to keep bills more affordable for such clients.

A few basics: trainees are recruited into all three BB offices, the largest number of them being based in Bristol. Having picked an office they tend to stay there. Bristol was deemed the most sociable thanks to its size, and trainees reckon it's also the one with most private sector clients and work. Apart from a few minor exceptions (like getting contentious construction and IP work in Bristol but "*not so much*" in London), the same types of work are available in all offices. Most trainees pass through four of the following seats: projects, construction, litigation, regulatory law, employment, property, commercial healthcare and clinical negligence/personal injury. Other seats are available in the commercial/corporate teams. London trainees seem to have the longest days (finishing at 7 or 7.30pm in some seats), but overall most people spoke of finishing work around 6pm.

Top of the pile for rubbish deals

The firm achieves numerous excellent *Chambers UK* rankings and offers a multitude of legal services to both the public and private sectors. Large projects, for example, is an area in which BB is a titan. Its lawyers can take a client from the initial tender process through to the planning and construction stages, and then deal with any long-lasting issues or disputes arising out of a project. Trainees in this department get involved with the procurement of services for local authorities, then help them to imple-

Chambers UK rankings

Administrative & Public Law	Planning
Clinical Negligence	Professional Discipline
Construction	Projects, Energy & Natural Resources
Dispute Resolution	
Education	Public Procurement
Employment	Real Estate
Healthcare	Real Estate Litigation
Information Technology	Restructuring/Insolvency
Local Government	Social Housing
Personal Injury	

ment the delivery of these services – anything from waste management and rubbish collection through to state-of-the-art hospitals and schools. The projects team is a master of integration with the rest of the firm and trainees quickly learn that it's all about being able to see the bigger picture. Partner Susie Smith was singled out for praise, specifically for her good supervision and vast experience advising governments, both in the UK and abroad. "*One of the great things that distinguishes the firm is its unique individuals,*" gushed one trainee. Another fee earner was described as "*one of the foremost experts in street lighting*" and "*truly inspirational.*"

Trainees get front-line experience in contentious seats, be this making small applications or note-taking and strategising in courtrooms. "*Compared to my friends elsewhere, we get a lot more detailed stuff here. When I was doing litigation I went to court loads of times and went in front of masters. I was once warned before going to see a master that he had made a girl cry a week earlier, but I was used to it and handled him fine.*" On the one hand the firm has represented the likes of Motorola and Sony Ericsson on commercial disputes; on the other it has established itself as a leader in the field of clinical negligence, where it recently appeared in the House of Lords test case of Savage v South Essex Partnership NHS Foundation Trust. This centred on the suicide of a detained mental patient and the trust's obligations to them. Some work is "*by its nature very political,*" and a seat in the health department can give trainees a taste of both sides of the fence, sometimes representing individuals in their appeals for access to treatment and sometimes defending NHS decisions to withhold drugs. These cases are emotional, which only adds to their appeal for those who want more "*person-based*" work. Matters of life or death are par for the course. Said one source: "*The reason a lot of people are interested in medical law is that there are a lot of ethical issues and very topical human rights stuff. The firm is also well known for its clinical negligence… the claims of the day to day, defending hospitals.*" They say the work is "*incredibly technical: in prac-*

tice it is incredibly complex and you've got to take the time to understand the lexicon. When you read an expert's report, you don't know what every other word means. I was involved in defending a hospital from a brain-damaged baby claim. Often things are not clear, so they go to court, hypothesising about what could have happened."

BB's appointment by the SRA led it to the much-publicised case of Raleys Solicitors and its dealings with miners' compensation claims. The lucky trainee in that seat got "*really involved with the case and the 20-day hearing.*" As well as seeing Arthur Scargill perform as witness, there was court preparation aplenty, including looking after the disclosure bundles, and many discussions with a partner about case strategy. In another big professional negligence matter, a BB partner acted as prosecutor for the SRA in a case where a solicitor represented a client who sold feudal titles. Described as one of the most complex matters ever heard by the tribunal, the case established a new ethical precedent about when solicitors should cease to act for clients.

Last year BB mustered only a 50% NQ retention rate. In 2009 it found jobs for ten out of 14 qualifiers. A good result for the times, but there were quibbles over the messiness of the process, and the NQ job farrago was taken as proof of Bristol's controlling influence over the firm. Bristol offered nine jobs for six qualifiers; London had no vacancies at all. The firm says that is simply due to the larger size and greater range of practices in the West Country office. Apparently BB "*is addressing the problem of Bristol seeming like the centre of the universe.*" Those who criticised the firm's handling of the NQ jobs were aggrieved enough to grumble that "*if you question the authority of the firm or the status quo, it might come back to bite you*" and that "*toeing the line is the route to success.*" This could be a time to break out the old adage 'there's no smoke without fire,' but maybe also to say that such comments probably wouldn't be levelled at firms that hired duller trainees. We found BB trainees to be more independent-minded and questioning than most.

No sausages

The occasional kvetch notwithstanding, trainees said the atmosphere in the firm was excellent. They happily spoke about a "*young and vibrant*" atmosphere bereft of "*stuffed-shirt types.*" Instead, "*there are some real characters,*" and partners don't mind being mocked by the trainees in a Christmas party sketch. They say the trainee group has "*no real geeks, but everyone's quite intellectual and wants to have a good time.*" A Friday night drinks tradition is observed in all offices and there are away-days to bring trainees together. Recent trips have taken them to Cheddar Gorge and a stately home. A 'toothbrush weekend' involved trainees turning up at an airport before being whisked off to a secret holiday destination on the company tab. At times, the trainees' role extends beyond what they'd normally expect: "*They try to get you to do marketing, which is half and half good and bad. Half was writing letters and sending them out looking for work. The other half was researching into clients and contacting them. Partners go to an authority and try to get some work out of them based on your research.*"

"*If you want to stand out, apply here. If you want to be a sausage, go to a sausage factory,*" declared one interviewee. We sense that some people apply to BB because they want a mid-sized, friendly firm where "*you're not just a cog in the machine.*" Others apply because of its specialist work, perhaps wanting to practise law for the public good. The future might see a different type of applicant: people who normally turn to the more finance-driven firms might be put off by poor retention rates and dwindling profits. They may even start to question the value of a life spent shovelling more fuel into a wretched, broken, capitalist machine. BB can lure people in to experience the current relative stability of the public sector pound, and yet it also offers the chance to move into more corporate areas should these pick up.

Overall, what emerged from BB this year was a more transparent, better functioning and more clear-headed firm than we've commented on before. Trainees sensed it has become "*more pragmatic*" and agreed that "*general communication with staff has improved.*" Perhaps the most impressive thing is the calibre of BB's training. Our sources said they "*never get crappy grunt work*" and were evidently integral to the deals and cases on which they work. They spoke highly of their supervisors' ability to train them, and not only were most keen to stay on at the firm, but they also noted that "*people can get into partnership at a fairly early age.*" The final thoughts of one source were thus: "*I just think that BB goes under the radar sometimes because it doesn't do the big corporate stuff or have offices abroad, but you do get a hell of a good experience here.*"

And finally...

Some commentators judged that 2008/09 would be make or break for Bevan Brittan. We think it's the year the firm began to really understand itself.

Bingham McCutchen (London) LLP

The facts
Location: London
Number of UK partners/solicitors: 13/21 + 2 US-qualified
Total number of trainees: 4
Seats: 4x6 months
Alternative seats: Hong Kong (occasional)
Extras: Pro bono – LawWorks

"*I can say hand on heart that Bingham's key aspect is it's a non-hierarchical meritocracy, not a culture where 'you can't do that because you are only 2 PQE.*"

Natasha Harrison
Grad Recruitment Partner

"*We didn't do much trendy M&A, but all of a sudden it's trendy restructuring!*" We detect a firm that's become very busy in the downturn...

Bada Bing!

Bingham McCutchen certainly has good reason to feel pleased with itself. Massive in the USA, it arrived in London over 35 years ago but never felt the need to go full-service. Instead it chose to remain a petite operation concentrating on restructuring, banking litigation and financial regulation, earning *Chambers UK* rankings for each area. As recession bit, it quickly became apparent that this decision would pay off in spades.

For trainees, the focus on such specific areas means a top-notch but highly specialised training, so be sure when you apply to Bingham that this is exactly what you're looking for. No one arrives here by accident. "*Lots of second-year law students will just shoot off generic applications to as many places as they can; that will get you nowhere at Bingham.*" There are just four seats available to trainees – corporate, finance, litigation and the financial restructuring group (FRG). Trainees generally don't get a choice as to the order in which they take these seats, but this doesn't matter as "*the office is so small, by the time you get to your fourth seat you already know everyone there, so it's not a problem for qualification.*" When business needs have permitted, trainees have also been able to jet off for a seat in Bingham's Hong Kong office.

Seen and heard

In such a small office the responsibility a trainee can take on is really magnified. "*You are expected to be almost an associate almost from day one. Seriously, I was closing deals in my first couple of weeks,*" said one source. FRG is the largest team (though still only about 20 lawyers). "*It has become incredibly busy and will continue to be for some time,*" explained a source. Indeed, it even found it necessary to pull people over from corporate to cope with the workload. Bingham (London) has been doing work involving many of the biggest credit crunch casualties; "*I was reading things in the paper and the next day we'd be on it,*" said a trainee. For example, it advised holders of bonds issued by three ailing Icelandic banks, as well as numerous creditors of both Lehman Brothers and Northern Rock. This seat is "*very quick-fire; you have to be on the ball all the time.*" Though "*high-pressure,*" it's nonetheless "*fun*" and offers "*huge*" responsibility with bags of client contact, drafting, research and "*really making sure you are on top of the deals.*" Finance, too, is described as "*a tough seat. It's great, but they drop you in at the deep end.*" Again, "*you are definitely allowed to be visible in front of clients.*" Proving that trainees must be heard as well as seen, our sources sometimes found themselves speaking to clients at quite a high level. "*These are very intelligent people,*" one explained, "*and investors aren't always easy to deal with.*"

The majority of work in litigation is also finance-related. One case that occupied much of the team's time for several years, and was close to trial at the time of our interviews with trainees, involved a large Polish conglomerate called Elektrim. One of Poland's earliest blue-chip companies, Elektrim expanded and diversified rapidly and, in short, became rather tangled up and overburdened with debt. In the process of fending off bankruptcy, the group became embroiled in proceedings in multiple jurisdictions. Bingham acted for a representative bondholder that was pursuing Elektrim for damages valued at approximately €700m. The litigation team always has a number of smaller cases also going on, and lawyers are frequently called upon to give pre-litigation advice. "*I got to research advisory pieces and write notes and memos for clients,*" said one trainee. "*More normal trainee stuff*" (we take that to mean bundling and document management) is lined up alongside "*drafting at a level that you might never get in a magic circle firm.*" Our sources had additionally gained experience of interviewing prospective clients and taking witness statements.

Finally, corporate is a more typically mainstream seat. Here the trainee will be exposed to private and public mergers and acquisitions. The client base is still mainly financial – hedge funds, investment funds and other capital providers. Recently, Bingham acted for SISU Capital Partners (a private equity fund) in its role in a recommended takeover offer for Coventry City FC; Glam Media on the acquisition of online media business Monetise; and Swiss fund manager Gottex on an investment into a wind farm project.

Jay Z and the London Massiv

Just watch the clips of Bingham chairman Jay Zimmerman on the firm's website and you'll appreciate that this is a slick and media-savvy organisation. We reckon this influence even trickles right down to the trainees. Jay Z's control is limited in the London office, however. Around 90% of the office's work is sourced from the UK and "*the most American thing here is the bagels in breakfast meetings. Actually even that's changed: we asked for croissants instead.*" Over here, the main man is James Roome. "*James has been in charge for a while and has stamped his personality on the office,*" say trainees. Adhering to a "*hands-on*" management style, "*he personally approves everyone who joins us.*"

And by the way, that includes trainees. "*It was the only interview I had with a managing partner at any firm, but he was one of the people I felt most comfortable with,*" a source recalled. We asked for tips as to how to impress. "*James likes someone who's prepared to think about things rather than just follow precedent.* [Grad recruitment partner] *Natasha* [Harrison] *also wants to see people who know what they are talking about,*" theorised trainees. Prior experience in finance isn't necessary, but a genuine interest is, so at the very least you should be spending some quality time with the *FT*. The fact that Bingham has deliberately kept the training scheme small

Chambers UK rankings

Banking Litigation   Restructuring/Insolvency
Financial Services Regulation

ensures a high level of personal contact between trainees and partners. "*People are very willing to give you time and involve you as much as they can.*" The fact that "*they help but won't spoon-feed you*" suggests a maturity of approach is prized in recruits.

With NQ salaries hitting a cool £100,000 in 2009 (*"I am spending it already!"*), to our knowledge no firm pays more than Bingham in London. The firm is certainly not chucking cash around like an over-enthusiastic game show host for no reason though. One trainee came clean: "*There is not as much focus on work-life balance as they would like to pretend.*" Associate billing targets are reputedly the highest in the City, 50 to 55-hour weeks aren't unusual and trainees will inevitably have to make use of complimentary night taxis home, though we're told weekends are largely respected. This seems mainly to be a feature of FRG, because "*those transactions can move very quickly indeed.*" It's not something that our interviewees resented, especially as everyone puts in a fair shift and "*there's no wishy-washy swanning off by partners.*" Perhaps because of this the social side isn't overdone. "*When we are not working we are sleeping,*" said one contact, only half-jokingly. Nonetheless, trainees "*make full use*" of a social budget, associate drinks are semi-regular, and in addition to summer and Christmas parties, the firm occasionally organises quiz nights, etc.

Bingham was rightly proud that since its training programme started in 2006, it had managed to keep every single qualifier. In 2009 it finally lost this record, with only one of the two qualifiers staying.

And finally...

In this demanding training the rewards – financial and otherwise – are high. If you have a serious interest in finance or restructuring, and aren't afraid of hard graft, Bingham looks a very sound bet. Top tip: crawl over this firm's website.

Bircham Dyson Bell

The facts

Location: London, Cardiff, Edinburgh

Number of UK partners/solicitors: 50/72

Total number of trainees: 17

Seats: 4x6 months

Alternative seats: Secondments

Extras: Language training

Combine some unique work with a comfortable mid-sized setting, take away much of the stress found in EC-postcode firms and you're left with the perfect recipe for commercial/private client training.

Westminster's Bircham Dyson Bell doubled revenue in five years as it pursued a £50m annual turnover by 2011 and a place in the top 50. The downturn put the brakes on its ambitions, but it's still hugely attractive to trainees.

Saved by the Bell

Birchams is known for parliamentary, public affairs and planning work (PPP). Despite its desire to be *"seen as a commercial law firm rather than just for our specialities,"* the truth remains that *"PPP is quite a pull and probably half the trainees come for that."* We understand why Birchams wants students to appreciate its business as a whole, as this long-established firm offers the gamut of services from private client to corporate. It represents major charities such as War on Want, English Heritage and the Breast Cancer Campaign, plus public utilities like Thames Water, numerous schools and colleges, and corporate big shots like Esso and ExxonMobil. Clients often engage several departments: Transport for London, for example, uses the PPP and employment departments. The structure of the four-seat training contract is *"transparent and easy to understand,"* and seats are available in real estate, corporate, commercial, employment, litigation, private client, charities and, of course, PPP. None are compulsory and all are punctuated by regular feedback and appraisals. Trainees with a hankering for in-house experience can second to Esso, and it's usually a popular choice despite its Sussex location.

Lately the busiest area has been the growing employment department, which caters for top clients including Royal Mail Group, Moorfields NHS Trust, accountancy firm Baker Tilly and Virgin Trains. The hefty real estate group benefits from the input of a large, experienced planning team and a leasehold enfranchisement team that specialises in assisting tenants on the grand London estates. Property litigation has, at times, gone as far as the House of Lords. Linking in with the work of other departments, the real estate lawyers have recently represented the Docklands Light Railway on five major projects including London City Airport and the proposed Dagenham Dock Extensions. The corporate team runs AIM/smaller-sized deals but was hit by the recession and, trainees say, *"reduced to a skeleton crew from its heyday."*

Probate and Prejudice

It used to be a truth universally acknowledged that a single man in possession of a good fortune must be in want of an offshore trust to keep the taxman's mitts off his hoard. Thanks to the Finance Act 2008, things are changing and new rules relating to offshore trusts and non-UK domiciles brought tonnes of instructions to the private client team as clients sought advice on over £3bn worth of assets. All of this was in addition to a regular flow of instructions for wills, probate assistance and the restructuring of people's (often fabulous) wealth. For some trainees the department is a major draw; others seem put off by its *"old-schoolness... a couple of partners have been around since the early days and are quite protective of their clients. What comes out is the need for things to be done just so."*

A formidable charities department keeps clients on the straight and narrow amid myriad regulatory changes. If that sounds dry then consider the implications of some of these regulations. For example, when the Equality Act (Sexual

Orientation) Regulations 2007 came into force, two Catholic charities had difficulty accepting new obligations to non-heterosexual couples. This case became the first to be appealed at the Charity Tribunal. Other activities include advice on fund-raising, building relations between charities, establishing new charities or making constitutional changes to existing ones. Trainees described the seat as *"a big pull"* and enjoyed their research-heavy assignments.

Chambers UK rankings

Administrative & Public Law	Local Government
Agriculture & Rural Affairs	Parliamentary & Public Affairs
Charities	Planning
Education	Police Law
Employment	Private Client
	Public Procurement
Environment	Transport

Alive, alive-o

Deep in our vaults lies a worn copy of the first ever *Chambers UK* directory. After blowing off the cobwebs and prising open the vintage tome, we found that Birchams' reputation for parliamentary agency services long predates our records. This is one of very few firms that employs parliamentary agents licensed to draft, promote and oppose bills and other forms of legislation, so it's unsurprising that Birchams attracts people interested in such matters. In the *"colourful, varied"* PPP seat, trainees become immersed in the manifold issues surrounding major transportation projects such as Crossrail and the Nottingham Express Transit. There are field trips, days spent poring over blueprints or liaising with affected businesses and drafting petitions against schemes or helping clients through public inquiries. *"Your supervisor takes you to meetings so you get to see how they deal with things."* Praise was heaped on this *"brilliant seat"* where *"ideas are bounced around the team."*

At Birchams you can watch the domino effect of legislation. The nuances of government at work become apparent, with new bills making for more petitioning and appealing, inquiring and planning. The work offers insight into seemingly insignificant and quotidian matters of governance that, when examined closely, reveal themselves to be far-reaching. Take the Dee Estuary Cockle Fishery Order 2008. Without this fairly innocuous-sounding piece of legislation, the fishery would have to open to all, the result of which would probably be a rerun of three years ago when it was fished out in two days, causing massive environmental damage, the obliteration of the cockle stock and police costs of over £250,000.

Interviewing trainees on their mobiles proved difficult as nearby Scotland Yard's surveillance equipment interfered with the signal. Although working here won't mean you're privy to everything that goes on at The Yard, as the Metropolitan Police is a client you'll gain some insight. Lawyers handle many issues for the force, from allegations made against officers to the supply of IT systems. One case involved Mark Saunders, the barrister shot in his Chelsea flat after opening fire in the direction of police outside.

A pretty happy crew

The responsibility granted to trainees depends on the business needs of each department. One day they could be sat in the House of Lords taking notes, the next filing mountains of paper. These are the type of people with the maturity to say: *"Frankly, whether something is interesting is entirely subjective and completely off the point."* Should trainees need advice or a chat about seat options, *"you can sit down with training partners, HR or your supervisor, and you're never left wondering whether you've done something right."* We're repeatedly told that the firm is not stuffy. In truth, the private client team does sound a little stuffy but we make no criticism, and besides, the atmosphere might suit some to a tee. We'd say that the following sentiments reflected trainees' views. *"This is an open firm that's responsive to people from all backgrounds. It isn't looking for textbook applicants and isn't a kind of factory processing assembly line trainees."* That many of the current group had previous careers probably contributed to their suitability, given that Birchams looks for people who are *"commercially aware team players, lateral thinkers and communicators with a professional outlook."* Discussing the firm's ambitions, one trainee said: *"In terms of direction, we're pretty settled. I don't see us diversifying a huge amount before growing again."*

There is life beyond the walls of the smart, teal-coloured office. The day tends to finish by 7pm and rather than forming a marauding horde after work, trainees meet in the firm's subsidised canteen for lunch. Every year a rowing regatta sees departmental crews race on the Thames at Putney. Pub quizzes are well attended, as are internal networking events hosted in the reception area. A couple of trainees said they'd like more client-networking opportunities.

And finally...

Qualifiers make formal applications for jobs before being interviewed. In 2009 just four out of ten were successful. This, along with some redundancies, *"revealed a slightly more ruthless character and a temporarily tense atmosphere in the office."* Our sense is that this mood will pass.

ACCESS ALL AREAS

BIRD & BIRD

We believe in letting our graduates have the freedom they need to make the most of their careers. The fact that every single qualifying trainee has been offered a position this year proves that our unique approach is the right one. Our trainees take on responsibility from day one and enjoy varied and challenging work for industry-shaping clients. If you become a trainee with us, you will be given the chance to excel.

www.twobirds.com/graduates

BIRD & BIRD

where do you want to be?

Bird & Bird LLP

The facts

Locations: London
Number of UK partners/solicitors: 70/158
Total number of trainees: 33
Seats: 4x6 months
Alternative seats: Overseas seats, secondments
Extras: Language training

TwoBirds' appetite for international growth seems insatiable. This clever operator is attracted to equally clever applicants.

Nothing flighty about this lot. One of the best in Europe for niche areas such as IP, sport and aviation, TwoBirds is nonetheless a full-service firm with plenty of mainstream commercial work.

Flying high

Okay, so it's hard to stay away from the avian metaphors. We'll try, but the fact of the matter is there's so much to crow about! Already well established internationally, the firm successfully continued its merger spree in 2008, both away (Helsinki's Fennica Attorneys Ltd) and at home (with Lane & Partners). Bird & Bird now has 21 offices across Europe and Asia and over 1,000 staff. Its expansion across Europe has paid dividends: income rose by an impressive 30% in 2008/09.

The firm is best known for its work in trendy, niche-y sectors for trendy, niche-y clients. Yahoo! and Jack Daniels are among the ones we can name. For IP, it can lay claim to being the best in Europe, let alone London. It also ranks highly in *Chambers UK* for IT, data protection, life sciences, telecoms and media. Its list of clients from the world of sport speaks for itself: the Football Association, the Premier League, Wembley Stadium, the Rugby Football Union, the Rugby Football League, the Lawn Tennis Association, the International Cricket Council, the International Tennis Federation, the British Darts Organisation, the World Professional Billiards & Snooker Association, Puma, UK Sport, Sport England... The story doesn't end here, however; there's plenty to say about Bird & Bird's corporate department and its proficiency in dispute resolution. As one interviewee put it: *"Considering the work we do and the clients we have, we're top of the game a lot of the time."* Though it would be hard to describe these departments as powerhouses of the firm, they do sit comfortably in London's mid-market. For corporate finance, *Chambers UK* ranks it with the likes of Nabarro, Clyde & Co and K&L Gates, while for dispute resolution it sits alongside BLP, Dechert, RPC and Travers Smith.

vIP status

Trainees acknowledge that the IP department is Bird & Bird's *"big selling point."* It's no wonder. Regarded as being in a league of its own in the London market, the department is bursting at the seams with *"stellar people."* They recently acted for Yahoo! in a ground-breaking trade mark infringement case concerning keywords and sponsored search results (the offending words 'Mr Spicy' filled our immature hearts with glee). In patent litigation, lawyers represented Nokia in defence of various claims made against it. Sources told us there's a *"50-50 split"* of those who come to Bird & Bird expressly for IP and those who don't, and that *"the trainees in IP know they want to qualify there before they even start work."* The department has plenty to keep people busy, with key client Nokia being at the forefront. The role of a first-year trainee is usually more organisational: *"There were a lot of tables of who's got what documents to sort out. It was great to get an overview of what everyone does and how it fits into the bigger picture."* For second-years with greater experience the work becomes more significant: *"I was writing correspondence to the other side, speaking to barristers, attending meetings and going to trial every day."*

This is not a department you "*fall into,*" and more often than not it demands some prior science experience, particularly for 'hard' IP matters. That's patent and industrial designs by the way; 'soft' IP is the trade mark and copyright side of things, and this requires less specialist knowledge. Of the four qualifiers who took up positions in the group in September 2009, only one had a non-scientific background. To this end, some trainees with less of an eye on the IP prize felt the group is "*not very accessible*" and "*like a different world.*" Others agreed, saying: "*They're not integrated in the same way as other departments. They're in a separate building and have their own parties and retreats.*" The suggestion was that "*it's a shame because there could be more opportunities for cross-departmental work.*" Those within the department were aware of this predicament. "*I know it could feel separate as there's not a huge overlap of work, but hopefully because we're aware of it we'll make that effort to change it.*" Perhaps, but this same point has cropped up in our trainee interviews for years.

The IT crowd

For those not mesmerised by IP, the commercial department has a wealth of options as it spans technology, telecoms, data protection, outsourcing, IT and sport. Interviewees cooed: "*It's just great for a trainee as there's lots of diverse work you can get involved in.*" The department is highly regarded internally, with sources describing it as one where "*everyone's really approachable and there's great relationships between partners and associates.*" There's scope for trainees to "*get involved in negotiations*" on all sort of issues, including the hot topic of outsourcing, and they often find themselves working at the heart of small teams. BT is a key client, and much of the department is working on the implementation of BT's £2.6bn NHS National Programme for IT contracts, currently the largest civil IT project in the world. Client secondments are also an excellent way to get a leg up – we were told by one trainee that upon returning to the firm's Fetter Lane HQ his colleague "*was given what I thought was a quite senior role working on subcontracts.*"

Dispute resolution and corporate stand out as departments where a trainee can gain exposure to interesting work without being left out in the cold. In dispute resolution, one trainee told us that the firm was often happy to "*take a hit on fees,*" seeking cases that were "*designed for someone like me to see how it all works.*" The firm's higher-value cases have lately included defending eBay subsidiary PayPal in High Court proceedings and advising Yahoo! on defamation, media and IT disputes. Of course at junior level "*the nature of dispute resolution is a lot of photocopying, bundling, paginating and research,*" but alongside these "*more menial*" tasks trainees were thrilled to be given tasks that make them feel included. "*They really listened to my opinion. I would look into an issue and then we'd discuss and analyse it, sometimes for over an hour.*"

Chambers UK rankings

Asset Finance	Immigration
Aviation	Information Technology
Banking & Finance	Intellectual Property
Competition/European Law	Life Sciences
Construction	Media & Entertainment
Corporate/M&A	Outsourcing
Data Protection	Private Equity
Dispute Resolution	Product Liability
Employee Share Schemes	Public Procurement
Employment	Real Estate
Fraud: Civil	Sports Law
	Telecommunications
	Travel

Of the relatively small corporate department, trainees said: "*The deals here usually aren't massive or exciting-sounding*" and they admitted it could feel "*slightly ancillary*" to other departments. However, "*the flipside is that if you're doing a giant merger at the magic circle you'll never be let near it.*" At Bird & Bird "*there's a good focus on proper chargeable client work for trainees.*" Pan-European deals are common, and the firm recently advised Hellman & Friedman Capital Partners on aspects of its $2.4bn acquisition of Getty Images across the UK, France, Germany, Ireland, Italy, Portugal and Spain.

The firm excels in sport and aviation. The Lane & Partners merger has boosted the profile of the latter practice considerably. Trainees said the department had been "*transformed*" and that "*you really feel like you're learning from people with great experience.*" Working on a mix of "*aircraft leasing and finance, alongside regulatory, advisory and dispute-related work,*" clients range from commercial airlines easyJet and Flybe to Airbus Military. The team advised this last company in relation to the much anticipated €100m-per-unit A400M aircraft. The sports team (technically part of the commercial department) has only one dedicated place for a trainee every six months and is consequently much sought after. Our sources stressed that "*people applying here have to realise there's only one seat,*" and that "*you have to make your interest clear and shout loudly to get it.*" The firm recently handled a series of the largest sponsorship deals in rugby history, working with Six Nations Rugby, the British Lions, the European Rugby Cup and the Rugby Football Union.

There's good news if you're interested in overseas seats. "*Because there's not a massive number of trainees you can engineer them as you want.*" They can be for three or six months, and trainees have most recently spent time in Madrid, Stockholm and two of the German offices. Where Bird & Bird differs from many other international firms is that these are "*local offices with local lawyers rather than English outposts of an English firm.*" This means proficiency in the local language is vital (luckily, the firm does provide language training for those sliding backwards to monoglotony).

Birds of a feather...

Bird & Bird trainees come from good universities. "*Some have come straight from uni to a training contract; there are people with PhDs and lots of others who've spent a couple of years in industry.*" The obvious positive of this is that "*you have something additional to offer if you've done something other than law.*" One trainee recently made headlines in the legal press by qualifying at the age of 50.

Personality-wise, trainees admit there are key similarities. "*The sort of people who work here are outgoing and confident*" and "*there are some amusing personalities. You've got to roll with the chat... if you were too bookish you'd struggle.*" One trainee even went as far as to say that everyone has "*their own weirdness... a slight oddity about them.*" We pressed, but couldn't quite get to the bottom of that one. "*Standing up and being heard*" is key to being successful here, whether it's on the subject of seat allocation or hours. "*People do respect it if you say, 'It's 5.30pm on Friday and can I finish this on Monday?' Establishing your presence gets you respect.*" Bird & Bird trainees are not night owls, and very few had experienced early mornings in the office. Those who had worked long hours recognised that "*it's the exception rather than the norm,*" and said they'd sometimes been rewarded for exceptional effort with the next day off or a rather nice celebratory supper.

Lunchtimes at the firm's restaurant (The Bird Table) and impromptu drinks at The Swan and The Castle form the basis of trainee social life. In a recent charitable venture, they completed the NatWest Tower vertical run, "*obviously up the stairs, not scaling the building Spider Man-style!*" An annual football tournament with all the other European Bird offices was held in Stockholm in 2009.

Firm-wide, the culture is based on "*collaborative effort,*" and a senior source told us that maintaining the Bird & Bird ethos across offices had been the key to international expansion. "*It's quite rare to get the culture flowing through the whole network. The fact we're unified as a firm is something I find particularly attractive.*" In London, trainees told us: "*You really feel like a team, no one's competing with each other.*" One especially happy trainee was thrilled to find out that the firm's assertion that "*you can speak to anyone about anything*" was true. "*The head of commercial asked me to do some work on a contract written many years ago, and I'd never seen anything like it before. So he sat down with me for half an hour to draw diagrams and explain it to me – they really do have time for people here.*" Formal training is also abundant, and on this topic we do have one very important insider tip: "*Make sure you go to training at 15 Fetter Lane rather than the old building, as the sarnies are so much nicer.*"

And finally...

If you want IP, there's no better place. For bags of other commercial practice areas it is also a good pick. All 16 trainees qualifying in 2009 stayed with the firm, five of them going into IP jobs.

Bond Pearce LLP

The facts

Location: Bristol, Southampton, Plymouth, London, Aberdeen

Number of UK partners/solicitors: 80/200

Total number of trainees: 25

Seats: 4x6 months

Alternative seats: Secondments

Litigation, insurance, energy, wind, regeneration, public sector... Bond Pearce has its fingers in some very 'now' pies.

This firm is a stalwart of the legal profession in the South and South West. It has an impressive client base, a measured work-life balance and some interesting niches.

Playing FTSE

With companies like Marks and Sparks, Hilton UK, AIG and AXA on speed dial, Bond Pearce knows how to please household-name clients across its various departments. It certainly has an impressive track record in areas as diverse as real estate, energy, education, retail and insurance, and it has managed to build a list of 12 FTSE 100/250 clients. "*The breadth of the client base is what drew me here and it's a shame more graduates don't know about it,*" announced one source. Their sentiments were echoed by another who said: "*I wanted a regional firm with great clients and that's what's come through in my training contract.*" The firm is clearly interested in further enhancing its reputation and growing revenue. In 2008 managing partner Victor Tettmar was quoted in *The Lawyer* as saying that he wanted Bond Pearce's £48m annual turnover to more than double to £100m by 2012. Alas, the economy tanked and the firm was only able to add £1m to its annual income in 2008/09.

Three years ago Bond Pearce took the painful step of restructuring part of its business by reducing the size of its personal injury division. In 2008 it closed its office in Exeter and relocated staff to either Bristol or a single Devon base located in Plymouth, so reducing Exeter to a 'touchdown' facility for clients and making notable costs savings. Management must have seen the writing on the wall: just as it pulled back from Exeter it opened a new base in London and one in North Sea Oil Central, aka sunny Aberdeen.

Winds of change

Trainees are recruited to Bristol, Southampton and Plymouth. At the time we conducted our interviews these offices had 12, eight and six trainees respectively, although the firm tells us that this score reflected the trainees' preferences when they first applied to the firm and that the figures could easily be reversed. On the assumption that most applicants would have a preference for a specific geographical location, it's a useful exercise to look at what each office can offer.

Bristol is the largest in terms of lawyer numbers and it has the "*swishest*" premises. Activity here is evenly balanced between transactional and litigation matters, and the office has a number of specialist areas like financial services, employment and IP. Southampton, on the other hand, is best known for its commercial property team, while also impressing trainees with the "*genuine commercial nous*" of seniors in departments like corporate, professional indemnity, employment and commercial litigation. The Plymouth office ("*fantastic sea views on a daily basis*") has a nice line in personal injury ("*high-volume work, lots of ringing up clients and case management*") and also offers a range of other seats, including planning and environment, property finance and corporate. This office is a hub for lawyers handling an increasing amount of wind farm work, something for which Bond Pearce is developing a great reputation. The smaller London office first cut its teeth on professional indemnity and insurance work. It now also handles regulatory matters like food hygiene law and assists the Aberdeen and Bristol offices on oil and gas matters.

We've presented the firm on an office-by-office basis thus far as trainees do generally stay in their home office unless there's a clear reason to try another. This said, our interviewees were careful to point out that the firm was "*essentially organised around departments not offices, and there's real integration between departments.*"

Regeneration generation

Those in the mood for solid transactional experience should look directly to Bond Pearce's real estate department. Although in the wake of the financial crisis, many of the firm's redundancies were from this department, it has been able to rely on instructions from an established institutional clientele and major corporate and occupier clients like The Crown Estate, Associated British Ports and Gala Coral. We've also learned that the firm thought creatively and found work for under-utilised fee earners by switching them to busier areas like mortgage recovery and renewable energy projects. Further to this, Dreams plc and Hargreaves Property Investments became new clients and Bond Pearce was awarded a panel appointment by HSBC. Of real estate, one source recalled that "*the department was more than happy to let me have a go at running my own files*" and client contact was abundant. Some people admitted to being pleasantly surprised by a seat here, one telling us: "*People say I'm mad for liking property but it becomes more interesting the more you do it.*" The work on offer extends from wind farm issues and planning law to portfolio management for retail landlords. Although the commercial property team is largest in Southampton, the Bristol office perhaps offers more variety. For example, Bristol focuses its efforts on regeneration matters, public sector transactions and the energy sector, and it also has significant corporate occupier clients like the BBC. For good measure, we'll add that Bond Pearce's real estate litigation unit topped the *Chambers UK* rankings for the South West and has had a busy year responding to the rise of tenant insolvencies in the region.

Oily matters

Nearly half of the firm's activities are contentious, and in no litigation area is Bond Pearce more prominent right now than professional indemnity, where the firm represents insurers like QBE, Aon, and Bar Mutual. Lawyers recently acted for the defendant in a case reported as one of the top court battles of 2009 – AXA Insurance v Composite Legal Expenses – where AXA brought claims against firms of solicitors for breach of contract and negligence relating to an after-the-event expenses scheme. Trainees here enjoy the challenge of balancing the interests of the insured and the insurer client and spoke of how the seat gave them a good overview of the litigation process. "*It's quite an interesting and specialised area, not typical of what you might do at law school.*" One source who'd spent time in the group told us: "*It's a really nice team with quality work. It feels like a good place to be at the moment.*" Also available are seats in construction and commercial disputes, where an increasing number of cases come from the oil and gas sector. When we spoke to him about the effects of the economy, partner James Robins was reassuringly confident that "*the growth of the litigation departments will go a long way to mitigating the problems in property and corporate.*" The firm must certainly be encouraged by the success it has so far had in aligning itself with the energy sector. For example, lawyers recently resolved a multimillion-pound dispute on behalf of an upstream oil and gas company regarding the breach of a 'time of the essence' clause on its drilling operations.

Of course trainees can't get much of a grip on massive cases, so it's good to hear that they have access to plenty of trainee-sized matters. The commercial litigation team also deals with small cases, including debt matters, so allowing trainees to get "*a feel for the client's business as you deal with them on a one-to-one basis.*" Our sources had good things to say about employment seats too. As in most firms, the employment team has had a busy time working on a raft of unfair dismissal and redundancy matters. For example, it took instructions from insurance giant AIG in relation to unfair dismissal and discrimination claims made against its customers in the education and not-for-profit sectors. Part-time tribunal judge Simon Richardson, who oversees operations in the Southampton office, heads a team that is equally well regarded for its transactional and advisory work. After time in an employment seat, one source concluded: "*You realise how technical human resources is.*"

Chambers UK rankings

Banking & Finance	Licensing
Competition/European Law	Local Government
Construction	Pensions
Corporate/M&A	Personal Injury
Debt Recovery	Planning
Dispute Resolution	Product Liability
Education	Professional Negligence
Employment	Projects, Energy & Natural Resources
Environment	Real Estate
Health & Safety	Real Estate Litigation
Information Technology	Restructuring/Insolvency
Intellectual Property	Retail

Other seats are available in banking and insolvency, corporate finance, environmental law, restructuring and tax. The restructuring placement was described as *"really interesting and dynamic with quite a lot of parallels with property practice. There's a real hard-nosed commercial edge to it."* In addition to all the aforementioned seats, secondment opportunities are considered both a good way to learn about client relationships and a chance to step into a client's shoes. Of late there have been places available at Network Rail and DIY-specialist B&Q, where trainees can opt for either employment or commercial/IP experience. Depending on business need, one trainee may also be able to spend six months in Bond Pearce's Aberdeen office focusing on oil and gas clients. Scottish-bound trainees are given a flight allowance and a flat just five minutes away from the Georgian office building. We hear also that the firm is investigating similar opportunities in the London office. Trainees find seat allocation reasonably satisfactory; *"although there is willingness to listen, we would appreciate having more input in the seat rotation process."*

Team Bonding

We asked our sources why they chose Bond Pearce and one theme emerged loud and clear – a shared desire to avoid a manic London lifestyle. *"The firm made me feel at ease and gave me a great opportunity to have quality work and stay out of the City,"* said one typical interviewee. Others raved about *"the regional law firm lifestyle,"* truly believing that it helps shape them as lawyers. For one, it was a blessing that *"you can express yourself with the people here."* Interestingly, not all our sources had grown up or studied locally to the office in which they worked. We also know that some trainees get their jobs after making a good impression while paralegalling with the firm.

First-years are eased into things with the help of a buddy who can discuss things like seat choices, and each office has a partner to keep an eye on the trainee group. These support systems exist in addition to the usual trainee-supervisor relationship. All up, the safety net looks quite sturdy and there's additionally a forum for trainees to air their views. By all accounts newbies soon learn that *"there's not really a 'getting ahead' competitive streak"* in most people and that communication is pretty good. In 2009, the firm retained 14 of its 15 qualifiers and allowed another one to defer the start of their qualification job for a year. We heard praise for the way in which the job allocation process was handled. *"The timetable they promised us was stuck to, which was a great relief at a tough time."* So are there any tips to succeeding here? Yes, say trainees. *"Think about what value you can add to your role, be commercially minded and not just bookish. Add value to your role by doing extra things."* Simple.

The social scene at each office seems to reflect the personality of its city. Bristol staff get into sporty things like softball, football, cricket, netball, touch rugby and the odd game of rounders. A trainee who'd relocated to Bristol from Exeter spoke of being won over by the social life – *"There's more going on here, whether it be bars and restaurants or tennis and dancing."* We should also give a mention to CSR activities such as the redecoration of a local youth centre. In Southampton things sound quite chilled out, with staff enjoying beer festivals and dinners as well as Friday night drinks in a bar called Jo Daflo that was once a church. Plymouth trainees told us about an enjoyable evening at a Junior Lawyers Division ball, complete with after-party cocktails. Some of our sources suggested that the entire trainee group would benefit from more opportunities to meet up and socialise – *"It would be great to see the other trainees more."* One or two also thought that although *"there are a few characters who are good to have a drink with,"* routine social events were not attended by enough partners or, more importantly, their credit cards.

And finally...

From Scotland to the South Coast, Bond Pearce's experienced and respected lawyers are leaving trainees feeling very satisfied. And, as a bonus, people are apparently *"much less pretentious than at some other big firms."* Nice.

Boodle Hatfield

The facts

Location: London, Oxford

Number of UK partners/solicitors: 28/28

Total number of trainees: 13

Seats: 4x6 months

Alternative seats: None

This is a modest firm with an impressive 300-year history, some key clients in the real estate sector and a stack of wealthy individuals knocking at its door for advice.

Could there be a more 'London' location than Boodle Hatfield's corner of New Bond Street and Oxford Street?

Packing a property punch

Old-timer Boodle Hatfield knows a thing or two about looking after the assets of wealthy private clients. It's been doing it successfully since the days when men wore curly white wigs even if they weren't judges or barristers. Remarkably, some of the families and estates that turned to the firm at its beginning are still doing so today. More recently the engine room has been the firm's property department, which currently accounts for around 40% of its earnings. But with the recession hitting the property sector like a tonne of bricks, how has old Boodle fared? Some redundancies have been made (mostly from the property department), but there is no need to run for the hills. This firm has been in business for almost three centuries and must have coped with more than its fair share of economic booms and busts.

A number of Boodle's clients boast gladiatorial levels of endurance too – the most notable being the vast Grosvenor Estate, owned by the Duke of Westminster and a client since the 18th century. With £3bn worth of property in London alone, Grosvenor is the largest urban landowner in Britain and controls swathes of wealthy Mayfair and Belgravia, as well as large rural estates across the UK and Spain. With Boodle's help, Grosvenor has evolved over the years and recently completed the massive Liverpool One development, comprising 30 individually designed buildings with more than 160 retailers. The project finished in time for Liverpool's year as Europe's Capital of Culture. But if you're beginning to view Boodle as one-(rich)man's band, you should also be aware that it represents other major landed estates, including the Bedford Estate, which controls much of highbrow Bloomsbury. These long-standing relationships with substantial old-money clients must feel rather reassuring right now.

Boodle doesn't just line its pockets with old money; newer property clients include Marriott Hotels, the IBM Pension Fund and Nationwide Building Society. Partner Andrew Wilmot-Smith won Nationwide as a client in 2007, and since then the firm has advised the society on a £25m loan facility for the purchase of an investment property in London's High Holborn. Whether for new or old clients, Boodle is most definitely familiar with multi-million-pound properties.

When posh comes to shove

Lately, the more resilient tax and financial planning area has been in sharp focus at Boodle. Additional private client specialists joined the team in 2008, one bringing an impressive roster of international clients. In terms of lawyer numbers, the team now competes with the property department; the consensus among the trainees is that Boodle's *"general direction is to push private client work, as it is recession-proof."* The firm acts for large agricultural and urban estates, families with assets held in offshore trusts and wealthy businessmen. Some clients are from overseas, others UK nationals. The common denominator is money.

A stint in both property and private client is par for the course. Some trainees even do two property seats. Previously, they'd know from the start which four seats they would tackle. Now, "*incoming trainees give their seat preferences as time goes on, and HR lets them know where they are going a month before they start their new seat.*" It is an attempt to stop trainees "*swapping things around,*" and because Boodle is a relatively small firm, "*it can't just conjure up new seats like in the magic circle,*" meaning that requests for change cannot always be accommodated. Having said this, "*I don't think anyone here wanted to be in the City*" was a common refrain among our sources, who were looking for better levels of responsibility, a broader approach to practice and more humane hours. Dealing with so many wealthy individuals does seem to affect the firm's culture, however. Trainees agree that to fit in at Boodle you need to be "*on the ball but unobtrusive,*" and although the firm "*comes across as posher than it actually is*" there is an understanding that "*everyone here is presentable and can talk well.*"

Chambers UK rankings

Agriculture & Rural Affairs   Real Estate
Family/Matrimonial   Real Estate Litigation
Private Client

Oodles of Boodle

The property department offers four seats – residential, commercial, development and construction. Each has its own flavour, but all trainees agree that even if property is your first seat "*you do get quite thrown into it.*" Partners are quoted as saying: "*Here are your 20 (or so) files, now get on with it.*" Trainees also mentioned having "*a huge amount of client contact,*" particularly when compared with private client seats, where those who instruct the firm "*can be very particular and want to speak to their lawyer.*" There's no need to feel anxious about rapid immersion into the world of property – trainees assure us that "*there are always people on the side to help if you get stuck,*" and the department's training provision gains high praise. "*There is some kind of lunchtime seminar at least once a week.*" Hardly surprising when you consider that getting to grips with property law goes hand in hand with getting to grips with Boodle Hatfield. Grosvenor files make up a large proportion of the work, "*perhaps 60%*" for some trainees, particularly in the development seat. This need not mean a lack of variety. Trainees are kept busy with a good mix of lease renewals, licences, meetings with surveyors, loan restructurings and property sales and purchases. They find their seats ideal for learning about the breadth and scope of property practice.

Private client trainees learn how to manage the assets of some rather wealthy folk, sometimes after they are dead. The team has its own particular character – "*fairly academic*" and "*very gentle and softly spoken.*" They attribute this primarily to the clients they deal with, or in the case of the dead ones their executors and trustees. The pace is "*noticeably slower*" than in the corporate and property departments, which were described as more "*gung-ho.*" Trainees in the non-contentious private client seat do a lot of research, often into complex offshore tax and trust issues. Most admitted it was hard to get their heads around things at first but relished being able to immerse themselves in the "*nitty-gritty.*" One talked of investigating the VAT implications of importing a piece of artwork into the UK, commenting that "*although we were looking at tax it was nice to know there was something real at the end of it all.*" Over in the contentious side of the department the 'something real' is usually a feuding family. Watching "*family members having a dig at each other*" must be educational, to say the least. One interesting case "*involved a carer who in the space of six months had been left 90% of the individual's assets.*" The remaining family were not best pleased.

Oxford Street or dreaming spires?

Fifty miles from the main London office is a smaller branch in the city of Oxford dedicated to private client work. The firm positively encourages trainees to go there for a seat and communication between the two private client teams is frequent, with "*someone from Oxford down in London almost every day.*"

Opportunities for contentious work spread far beyond the offering in private client. Boodle's litigation seats also cover matrimonial and commercial disputes, the former being extremely popular even though the team very rarely takes on newly qualified solicitors. Many of the commercial disputes involve landlord and tenant issues and, once again, trainees spoke of "*running smaller files yourself*" where "*the client's first contact is with you.*" The good news is that "*court visits are pretty regular here for trainees*" and a number of our sources had appeared at small hearings before masters and district judges.

The small but popular corporate team has been viewed as a support to the larger departments, but there is feeling that its importance is starting to grow as the group brings in more of its own work. Recent new client wins include Nordic Fashions and troubled Icelandic bank Kaupthing. Several trainees deemed this their favourite seat and highlighted its smaller size (just two partners, two solicitors and two trainees) as a plus, meaning they "*learned a lot more quickly*" and were soon drafting "*all sorts of different documents – asset purchase agreements, shareholder agreements, debentures, etc…*"

Brave new world?

With all this talk of landed estates and feuding families, you could think you'd time-travelled back to the 1800s. Boodle's long history is certainly a source of great pride, but trainees insist that it doesn't define the place. "*On the floor where all the clients come in there are portraits, old books about the firm and marble busts,*" yet the offices are described as modern with "*lots of glass*" and an open-plan layout. It's a far cry from the dark rabbit warren of the firm's previous Davies Street lodgings. We wonder if Boodle is trying to follow in the footsteps of a firm such as Withers; shaking off history's shackles to emerge, glass walls glistening, into the 21st century. The trainees don't think the firm is quite there yet. "*It is fair to say that there are older partners who know how they like to have things done,*" remarked one, but as a counterbalance there are many younger ones, and notably plenty of female partners (a whopping 50%) who "*bring new ideas and energy.*"

The sticking point mentioned most often was the lack of electronic resources. Trainees complained that there was no general access to important legal resources, such as LexisNexis and Westlaw, and remarked on how "*most fee earners don't even know how to do electronic searches.*" They sensed that improvements were in the pipeline, and by the time we went to press the firm had indeed subscribed to LexisNexis.

The social scene prompted no complaints. After a hard day in the office Boodle employees can sometimes be found across the road at the "*hot and sweaty*" Bonds bar or The Duke, a quieter pub nearby. Numerous departmental drinks were also mentioned and the firm hosts Christmas and summer parties every year. There is a real advantage to working so centrally: "*You can get anywhere and do anything after work.*" Boodle has a popular football team and a netball squad may or may not have materialised in 2009. For the less energetic there are yoga classes and a book club.

And finally...

Trainees are clearly fond of Boodle Hatfield and they cite manageable hours and a friendly working environment as major pluses. It should come as no surprise that they all wanted to stay on. In 2009, four out of six did so.

B P Collins

The facts

Location: Gerrards Cross

Number of UK partners/solicitors: 19/27

Total number of trainees: 6

Seats: 4x5 + 1x4 months

Alternative seats: Occasional secondments

This established Bucks firm's range of clients and practice groups make it a smart choice for students hoping for quality training just outside the capital.

This Gerrards Cross firm has no shortage of wealthy private clients. Being close to the meeting point of the M40 and the M25, just beyond the outer fringe of the capital, it's also in a rather good spot for commercial business.

Collins, B P Collins

Established in 1966 above a butcher's shop, B P Collins has come far in its first 43 years. Its commercial clients include Pinewood Studios (where the Bond franchise is shot), Brentford Football Club, food manufacturer Sacla and various other Thames Valley and Buckinghamshire companies, charities and educational establishments. Work also comes from overseas; for example, air cargo company Transafrik turned to the firm for help in setting up UK operations. Though the majority of work flows in from the local area, trainees tipped us off about instructions that would make even City lawyers envious. On further investigation we learned that the likes of Baker & McKenzie and Orrick (both international law firms) refer clients to the firm, and that on some deals the opposing solicitors are major City names. Rather than expanding into the City, BPC's plan is to grow locally to exploit even more of the riches on its doorstep while also continuing to draw in work from the capital using attractive pricing.

Trainees complete four five-month seats and finish off with a further four months in their preferred department. The system looks to have been a winner in 2009 – all three qualifiers took up NQ positions. Seat rotation works well too: trainees discuss their preferences in a monthly meeting with new training partner Matt Brandis, who is pretty informative on the different options. To clarify, seats are available are in coco, employment, litigation, property, family and private client. It is also occasionally possible for trainees to go on secondment to a client for a few months.

Small is beautiful

Gerrards Cross is less than 30 minutes by train from London's Marylebone Station. A new visitor could be forgiven for thinking they'd got off at the wrong stop as its village-y appearance is deceiving. BPC has two offices in the town – Stirling House and Collins House – both of which are close to the station. Said one source: *"I get my own office, which is quite nice!"* Stirling House contains the litigation, employment, coco and private client departments and is the larger of the two.

The litigation practice, which services both businesses and individuals, has grown by more than 30% in the past year. Trainees enjoy their time in this department because they get their own caseload. *"It was very challenging dealing with solicitors on the other side, but it was a good type of pressure,"* recalled one. As well as meeting barristers and *"tagging along to county courts,"* they can also make small applications themselves. Although daunting at first, rookies normally get into the swing of advocacy fairly quickly. Their role on bigger cases is naturally more restricted. Last year the team assisted Jawad Fashion Group, a large Middle Eastern retailer with outlets in Saudi Arabia, Bahrain and the UAE, on its withdrawal from a multimillion-pound franchise agreement.

The coco seat is popular, not least because trainees believe the department has real potential. *"We've got some really experienced partners here and coco is probably going to expand as they get more quality work."* Lawyers have lately acted on a number of commercial matters for multinational clients like wireless technology developer QUALCOMM and the Avisen Group. Indeed a source tells us *"there are a lot of American clients in company commercial."* Overall the trainee experience here is rewarding, and trainees put this down to the size of the BPC coco team and the deals on which it works. *"We have much more client contact and a lot more legal work here,"* said one; *"we absolutely get more client exposure and real responsibility."*

Although litigation and coco seats bring their own drafting challenges, nothing compares with employment, where you can expect to be knee high in drafting on both contentious and non-contentious assignments. Trainees *"get good feedback from the supervisor"* and they like the *"young and sociable feeling"* of the department. It has recently defended claims of race discrimination and unfair dismissal brought by a former employee of an engineering client and continues to act for the national epilepsy medical charity NSE on various issues.

What a waste!

The property and family teams work across the road in Collins House, the former representing clients like Clydesdale Bank, nightwear specialist Bonsoir of London and Grundon Group, which is the UK's largest privately owned waste management business. More on waste later. Trainees generally work on commercial property deals, although given its location BPC gets some juicy high-value residential instructions and the area even has some celebrity residents. As you might expect, the slump in the residential market did cause problems for the firm, resulting in nine redundancies, mostly among conveyancing and support staff. Other staff were working reduced hours for a while. Our sources appreciated that the firm had kept them informed of these developments. More happily, the *"dynamite"* property litigation team has been busy, recently representing the National House Building Council in claims worth around £500,000 made by the residents of several prestigious flats in north London. And another related group – the environment team – has been developing a special interest in the waste management sector. It recently advised client Greenstar on the acquisition of Bedfordshire firm Dunstable Waste Group. Proving that it has more than a passing interest in the environment, BPC also has expertise in renewable energy, having had a relationship for 20 years with one of the pioneers – the Summerleaze Group.

In the family department, trainees become involved with everything from 'without notice' applications in front of judges to roundtable meetings with clients and barristers. In relation to children, the team works more on private matters like custody cases, rather than public matters involving child welfare. In relation to divorce, some of

Chambers UK rankings

Charities	Environment
Corporate/M&A	Family/Matrimonial
	Private Client
Dispute Resolution	Real Estate
Employment	Real Estate Litigation

the clients have substantial assets at stake; for example, in the case of the wife of a senior executive of a multinational business, the assets were worth over £6m. No matter how wealthy, some clients can be fragile and demanding; *"it is always difficult as they're going through the hardest time of their lives. You really develop sympathy for them."*

Big Bucks

Gerrards Cross is *"renowned for being a very affluent part of Buckinghamshire."* For most of the trainees, geography was a factor in choosing the firm. Some live in London and reverse-commute every day; others were born and bred in the area. In terms of temperament, one trainee advises that *"if you're competitive and obviously out to get to the top you should probably stick to London."* And what of the social life? The office atmosphere is described as genial and trainees tell us that *"though you sometimes have late nights you can also sometimes go home early if your work is done."* We hear the trainees like a good night out in the capital, but that's not to say the local area is without its attractions. Staff frequent The Ethorpe pub, as well as trying their luck at the race track in Windsor. One recent highlight was a murder mystery dinner dance in Wycombe. The biggest difficulty in organising events is the fact that so many staff drive to work, though this clearly doesn't stop the diehards. Said one: *"This place used to have a bad social reputation, but now we do quarterly dinners and hang out with each other at our own places too."* Cricket, netball and rounders fulfil sporting desires.

And finally...

One source summed up B P Collins as *"very much a regional firm, not really City,"* and we sense that this is precisely why people choose it. Trainees insist that they get much more client contact and that their jobs are *"more than just paper pushing posing as legal work."*

TOGETHER

If you're one of the handful of graduates who join Bristows each year, you'll be exposed to top tier work right from the start. You'll also be surrounded by some of the most respected lawyers in their fields. This is a firm where you'll learn fast and be stretched, but you'll also get plenty of support and encouragement along the way. There's no over-hiring of trainees, either. We're particularly proud of the fact that so many of the lawyers who trained with us have gone on to become partners.

If we sound like the kind of firm for you and to find out more, please visit www.bristows.com/trainingcontracts

BRISTOWS

Bristows

The facts

Location: London
Number of partners/solicitors: 28/55
Total number of trainees: 15
Seats: Seats of 3 to 6 months
Alternative seats: Client secondments
Extras: Pro bono – LawWorks; language classes

> *"The question we often get asked is: 'If I don't have a science background will I be disadvantaged?'"* In short, the answer is no.

Bristows puts the intellectual into intellectual property. It has many scientists-turned-lawyers and a formidable reputation across a range of IP fields.

IP-so facto

Founded in 1837, Bristows has a sensational client list. Canon, T-Mobile, French Connection, British Airways, Samsung, MTV, Honda and a huge number of pharmaceutical and life science companies all rely on Bristows to protect their IP assets. It's a rock-solid foundation for the firm, but in 2007 five partners and six associates left to start an IP boutique. While this must have been a blow, one source suggested it had *"a positive effect in the long run... it made everyone buck up a bit and try harder."* Since then, the firm has hired three new IP partners and four more in commercial disputes to widen its appeal to clients.

With the profession going through the wringer, now wouldn't seem like a good time to tinker with a winning formula, but Bristows feels confident. There has been no redundancy programme, salaries have not been frozen and new intakes have not been deferred. Our interviewees were forthright about plans for the future. Rather than an IP boutique, they speak of Bristows as *"a general firm with a very good IP practice"* and *"aware that it can't just be good at one thing."* They didn't envisage expansion going too far: *"We're never going to become a firm that does everything,"* said one gratefully.

Trainee seats last three or six months; it's an arrangement people really like. They usually spend six months in either corporate or property, or three months in each. With seats in IP litigation, trade marks and commercial IP also available, *"you could essentially do a year of IP"* if you were lucky. Although no longer in *Chambers UK's* top tier for IP and life sciences, Bristows is still one of the best in these areas and represents the likes of Nomura, Bayer and Wyeth in some of the pharmaceutical industry's most complex cases. It is currently protecting Novartis' patent on wonderdrug Cyclosporin, an immune response suppressant that makes transplant surgery possible. Following the IP departures, Bristows hit back by hiring 11 new associates and set about winning new clients. One of the most lucrative of these has been the Business Software Alliance, a US-based not-for-profit organisation supported by major suppliers like Microsoft and Apple. Note that the majority of the firm's work has an international dimension, and Bristows often acts as a nexus for globe-spanning matters.

Preparing for a trial in IP litigation *"isn't the most exciting work,"* as it involves acres of photocopying, but at least you'll attend client meetings. Other tasks include research notes and letters to opposing counsel. On long-running matters, trainees sometimes find they are given *"discrete tasks without appreciating their greater impact"* because *"there's not always the luxury of time to get up to speed on the entire matter."*

The BBC, Freeview, Diageo, Odeon Cinemas and L'Oreal all use Bristows' branding practice for trade mark portfolio management. New client UK TV recently sought help with rebranding and protecting the Dave channel, and chocolate-loving lawyers had a feast over a confectionery markings dispute between Cadbury and Nestlé. This smaller group offers individual responsibility, client contact and interesting field trips. *"One case involved going* out and buying different types of drinks," explained a source. For those with less of an appetite for contentious work there's commercial IP, which has *"less bundling,"* more drafting and is *"more akin to the work of a qualified solicitor."* While *"at some firms secondments are like gold dust,"* at Bristows *"virtually everyone"* gets one, often at an entertainment or pharmaceutical client.

Chambers UK rankings

Advertising & Marketing	Intellectual Property
Data Protection	Life Sciences
Dispute Resolution	Media & Entertainment
Information Technology	Partnership

Science reliance?

Bristows' commercial litigation group has gone from one of its smallest to its second-largest, and is now ranked in Band 2 in *Chambers UK*'s London mid-market table. GE and Kodak have Bristows batting for them on mainstream disputes, and it is assisting Chrysler with a prolonged action over the collapse of Castor Holdings, known as the 'Canadian Enron' and possibly the largest Ponzi scheme litigation before Bernie Madoff's misadventures came to light. The corporate team works for The Greyhound Board of Great Britain, Associated British Foods, French IT firm Sogeti and *"spinout companies – where universities develop technology and want to commercialise it."* The popular EU/competition seat is actually run in conjunction with the firm's regulatory group, which means *"you get to do a bit of both."*

Aside from rare applications before High Court masters (*"the opportunities are there but you'd have to push yourself forward"*), advocacy must wait; otherwise the quality of work progresses steadily throughout the contract. Supervisors are typically partners, and trainees get work from across departments. PSC training is delivered externally, but there are *"lots of internal know-how meetings,"* plus French and German lessons.

With so many BScs and even PhDs among trainees, is there an especially academic environment? *"While there are always jokes about people getting excited by technical things, it's not like everyone walks around the corridors discussing biochemistry and the latest pharmaceutical developments." "The question we often get,"* expounded one trainee, anticipating our next move like a chess grandmaster, *"is, 'If I don't have a science background will I be disadvantaged?'"* In short, no. The proportion of trainees coming from non-science degrees is now far higher – deliberately so, the firm says – and *"partners have told us to not just think about IP, IP, IP."* Naturally Bristows is *"still looking for a hard core of scientists,"* and science grads rightly continue to view it as a logical choice.

Lincoln's out

Bristows' new office was built by soap tycoon Lord Leverhulme in the 1920s. Compared to its previous digs in four buildings at Lincoln's Inn, Unilever House might as well be something out of science fiction. With departments close to each other, shared kitchens and a common area called The Hub (table football and Playstation included), *"you always bump into people from other departments."* All up, *"the move has been fantastic for getting to know each other."* Bristows' character emphasises gentility and courtesy. *"It's traditional in that we don't have dress-down Fridays or things like that;"* indeed, *"you'll get pulled up if you're dressed inappropriately – one guy got told not to wear a jumper."* But *"after 18 months you'll know 90% of the firm, including support staff."* Said one source: *"I don't think anyone who's particularly arrogant or pretentious would work well here. They'd have it knocked out of them pretty quickly."* Bristows' nature shows in the open and helpful relationships between lawyers. There's a sense that *"partners aren't trying to squeeze as much money as they can out of you,"* and trainees have no difficulty asking for assistance. *"You can't help but overhear their conversations with their wives or children,"* reminisced one fondly, *"so you do get to know the partners. It's sad moving seats."* Trainees have associate mentors as well as supervisors, formal end-of-seat appraisals and monthly training diary meetings that are *"taken very seriously."*

Except during the run-up to a trial or the close of a transaction, *"you can effectively manage your own time,"* which typically means leaving between 6pm and 7pm. The social life is *"quieter than in a big firm,"* possibly because *"trainees here tend to be older, a little more settled."* There are drinks in The Hub on the first Friday of every month, pub quizzes and an annual black-tie ball. Trainees put on a performance at the last big party – entirely fitting given that the venue was under Shakespeare's Globe Theatre.

And finally...

Bristows is undeniably one of the top choices for IP, but its appetite for success in other fields should ensure the training contract is not excessively specialised. NQ retention rates have always been good and in 2009, four of the six qualifiers stayed.

Browne Jacobson LLP

The facts
Locations: Birmingham, Nottingham, London
Number of UK partners/solicitors: 68/120
Total number of trainees: 19
Seats: 4x6 months
Alternative seats: None
Extras: Pro bono – CAB, Pro Help, Criminal Injuries Compensation Scheme

Browne Jacobson successfully spans the East and West Midlands' legal markets. There's plenty on offer here, especially if it involves litigation, insurance or the public sector.

Having quadrupled in size since 1999, the ambitions of this Midlands-based, full-service firm are more than evident. Its training offers a heavy dose of litigation and much more besides.

The have and have Notts

From humble roots in nineteenth-century Nottingham, Browne Jacobson has become a force to be reckoned with in the legal markets of both the East and West Midlands. Trainees say: "*It's quite comfortably and firmly at the top in Nottingham,*" and "*Birmingham is expanding and doing very well.*" A small London office, meanwhile, primarily focuses on professional indemnity matters. Our interviewees labelled BJ as "*a very positive firm to be a part of*" and eagerly pointed to differences in culture between their own employer and its major Midlands rivals. "*There are firms with bigger names, but we have more of a local presence. Also, at firms like Eversheds it's more structured, more of a straight down the line business with a very serious attitude. Here we're a bit more relaxed,*" they claimed.

This approach obviously pays dividends as the majority of our interviewees recalled having very favourable initial contact with the firm; "*easily my favourite firm, not a difficult decision,*" was one typical comment. For the trainees we spoke to, these initial positive impressions gained substance as they progressed through their contracts. "*They take the training element very seriously here,*" said one, others mentioning a thorough two-week induction to the firm at the start of the contract. "*We had some really nice initiatives for bonding, and the training was good and informative.*"

NHS direct

BJ is a world of many possibilities when it comes to seats. "*There's so much you can do here that it's hard to fit it all in.*" One source viewed it like this: "*You get paid as well as Eversheds and Wragge and yet you don't have to do their hardcore corporate departments.*" The firm is organised into the following areas: business and professional risk (BPR); business services; insurance and public risk (IPR); and property. This translates into a wealth of seat options: employment, professional indemnity, commercial litigation, and construction and property risk sit within BPR; commercial, commercial health, corporate and private client sit within business services; environment, health, social care and education, personal injury and technical claims within IPR; and property is split into development, retail and public authority seats. There is a definite litigation bias, which itself is skewed towards insurance (sources told us around 40% of the firm's litigation activity was insurance-related).

In IPR, the overwhelming majority of work involves acting directly for insurers, with some liaison with the insured parties (including local authorities, health trusts and commercial enterprises). Within this department, trainees "*start with a broad focus, for example motor claims and personal injury,*" and later have the opportunity to narrow it. "*The attitude is this – experience everything, and if you want to focus on something, you can.*" With lower value claims trainees are likely to be "*the first port of call for clients,*" and the rest of the time it's a matter of reviewing files, drafting defences and being responsible for all the necessary litigation documents. "At any one time you can have a caseload of ten to 20 files," and there is "an awful lot of court experience, which is mainly sitting behind counsel." Our sources seemed to understand the enormous value in working on smaller cases (such as claimants suing local councils for tripping over potholes). "People seem to turn their noses up about lower-value stuff at other firms, but I know for a fact I got a more hands-on experience." Chambers UK ranks the department alongside Beachcroft and Berrymans Lace Mawer as one of the best in the Midlands.

Professional indemnity is another popular IPR seat. It involves the representation of insurance companies and their insured parties – solicitors, surveyors and, increasingly, financial advisers. Big-name clients include Aviva, AXA and Hiscox. Again, there's no scrimping on client contact, as trainees find "a lot of the work involves client reporting and obtaining instructions." These cases arise when professional advisers are accused of providing negligent services, and if the 2009 economy follows the pattern of the last major recession then there will be a glut of professional negligence claims as banks and mortgage companies try to recover losses sustained in the downturn. With a little experience behind them, trainees in this seat can really fly as they learn about "[developing] the correct tactics, the related risks, the amount at stake and how to proceed." In this way, trainees come to believe that "it matters what we think – our opinions are important."

Medical negligence is another key area. BJ represents the NHS Litigation Authority and obtains direct instructions from NHS trusts and primary care trusts across the Midlands and beyond. The quality of the firm's reputation in this field means that on bigger claims, as a trainee, "you won't necessarily be known to clients, but you will get a lot of work." Again, on smaller claims "you can be given the reins." Birth and catastrophic injury cases are a speciality, often valued at several million pounds. For a trainee such cases mean "a lot of research, contacting experts, organising conferences [with barristers] and attending trials." Sources confided that it could be tough at times, not to mention emotionally demanding. However, we were told: "Often it really is the case that the birth would have gone that way anyway, and there was nothing the doctors could have done." There are also ample opportunities for drafting court documents and reports for clients. Recalling their seat, one trainee said: "I was run off my feet constantly."

Danger: high voltage

The IP department bridges the gap between contentious and non-contentious practice and is arguably the most up-

Chambers UK rankings

Administrative & Public Law	Intellectual Property
Banking & Finance	Personal Injury
Clinical Negligence	Planning
Construction	Private Client
Corporate/M&A	Professional Negligence
Dispute Resolution	Real Estate
Education	Real Estate Litigation
Employment	Restructuring/Insolvency
Environment	Social Housing
Healthcare	Tax

and-coming department in the firm. The recruitment of additional non-contentious IP lawyers, and new litigation partner Mark Daniels from Wragge (fresh from the landmark Nokia v InterDigital litigation), demonstrates "a genuine commitment to IP." For now, the commercial team is home to the non-contentious IP lawyers, who work alongside specialists in general commercial contracts and procurement, serving public and private sector clients. Trainees spoke of "a real variety of work" in this department, including trade mark searches and supporting fee earners in the negotiation and drafting of agreements. The firm has an exciting roster of clients seeking IP advice, including the manufacturers of luxury perfumes, fast food restaurants and television companies. Among the big names are Siemens and Goodyear.

Corporate may have been through a quieter than usual phase but trainees were still able to help with M&A deals, sales of small businesses and company secretarial duties. Said one: "I was given as much responsibility as they could give me," including handling small sales with minimal supervision. Less exciting but essential "trainee tasks" include "organising data rooms and managing due diligence reports." A particularly perceptive trainee impressed us with their interpretation of a corporate seat as "almost a rite of passage. You see the marketing side of the firm more, and I think it's important to realise how you win and keep clients." With this in mind, the firm was pleased to win an appointment to the panel of a major UK retailer this year (which we unfortunately can't name). What we can divulge is the department's work for Lloyd's Development Capital over the past year. This has included electrifying acquisitions of VSG, Omega Red Group Limited (companies providing electronic security and lightning protection respectively), and the £75m sale of plastic packing manufacturer Brittons to HSBC Private Equity. With high-profile deals such as these, it will come as no surprise that our parent guide Chambers UK ranks BJ in the top tier for corporate M&A in the East Midlands.

The Euthymics

No, this isn't a misspelling of the band that made stars of Annie Lennox and that bloke who did a film with All Saints. *"Euthymic"* was the descriptor used by a trainee to sum up BJ's culture. It means 'somewhere in between euphoria and depression' on the mental health scale and we think what they were trying to say is that BJ is a pretty pleasant and unstressed place to work. Our interviewees identified some differences between the three locations and suggested that *"Nottingham will probably always be the main office."* Its after-hours culture is centred on the nearby Royal Children pub. Not everyone is down with 'The Kids', however. *"The toilets stink! The Castle is where we go in summer and much nicer,"* came a rebellious voice. Interviewees put the comparative lack of pub culture in Brum down to the fact people commute in from places like Wolverhampton and Shrewsbury, rather than living in the city centre (as many do in Nottingham). The firm is keen to encourage the links between its offices and quite a few trainees will spend six months in a different office to the one in which they started. That does include London, and the office in the capital also has its own intake – presently just the one recruit per seat rotation. Our sources suggested that *"inter-office cohesion"* could be improved, though in all fairness one did add that within their own office *"there's no one I'd walk past and think, 'I don't know who you are.'"*

Don't expect a rigid hierarchy at BJ. We heard of a trainee who had the one-time managing partner hotdesking next to him, and apparently he wasn't averse to fetching the trainee a brew every now and then. Likewise, people at all levels of the firm enjoy getting together in the pub, and a lot of work goes into the major annual parties. We learned that some partners put in months of training for an intra-firm ballroom dancing competition. *"People are certainly not afraid to have a laugh, and that's important,"* one trainee summed up. We reckon a sense of humour is essential for newbies in the Nottingham office. *"It's a rabbit warren, and even after two years I can't really profess to know my way around it,"* chuckled one interviewee. Brum's office is a much more straightforward affair right next to Victoria Square. The London branch has recently moved from the Aldwych to *"very new and nice"* offices on Gracechurch Street, not far from The Bank of England.

Aside from the usual great academics and enthusiasm for a career in the law, the main quality to be found in a Browne Jacobean (or should that be Jacobite?) seems to be a *"down-to-earth and outgoing"* personality. Evidence of links to the area are important, though it could be as tenuous as having attended the University of Warwick and wanting to settle in Brum. Trainees insist: *"There's a really good mix of people who have paralegalled at the firm, some with second careers, some coming straight through at 22."* It is worth noting that while the majority will have at least a 2:1 at degree level, the firm told us it will *"consider all applications and any circumstances surrounding the degree."*

In an uneasy year for the profession that has required most firms to make some tough decisions, it was all the more impressive that our BJ interviewees, whether being kept on after qualification or not, didn't have a bad word to say about the firm. One told us: *"Any negatives are down to what's going on with the economy, and that's not the firm's fault."* Approximately 20 redundancies were made in an initial round, and at the time of publication a second round was underway. Still, the firm found jobs for six of its 12 qualifiers in 2009, placing them in all departments bar property.

And finally...

Our interviewees may have frequently sized their workplace up against Wragge and Eversheds, but BJ doesn't need other firms to define it. It is a Midlands giant in its own right.

BTMK Solicitors

The facts

Location: Southend on Sea, Chelmsford

Number of UK partners/solicitors: 11/14

Total number of trainees: 5

Seats: Flexible

Alternative seats: None

Do you want to be trained within an inch of your life? If so, take a look at one of Essex's finest firms.

BTMK's recruitment webpage states that the firm looks for 'high-calibre individuals who have a business mind and a social conscience'.

Court you

Asked what brought them to the profession, one trainee told us it was "*solving people's problems.*" Another said they "*really wanted to give something back to the community.*" These simple statements help you understand the ethos of BTMK, a full-service firm based in Southend and Chelmsford. As with other firms offering both publicly and privately funded services, it is pushing hard to extend its commercial practice while still deriving approximately 50% of its income from legal aid work. Its crime department picks up a *Chambers UK* top ranking, but it is the growing commercial department that is a strong focus at the moment.

The broad range of seats available to the firm's handful of trainees requires different skills. They can complete seats in crime, civil litigation, family, commercial, employment and personal injury, fitting four seats into a hectic first year and two into a steadier second year. Trainees state their preferences before each seat and they say the firm is "*very accommodating,*" even if ultimately "*business need is the primary concern.*" All seats are located in the firm's larger Southend office.

Would you be surprised to learn that many trainee solicitors never see the inside of a courtroom, spending their entire two years in glass offices poring over contracts? We don't make any criticism – horses for courses and all that – but if you do want to get within earshot of a gavel during your training contract then BTMK can sort it out for you. "*Everyone does advocacy at some point; it's really important and doing it is the best way to learn,*" said a source. And learn you will: BTMK goes to great lengths to develop recruits' skills, and trainees say there is "*always a good support network.*"

Back to school

Believe it or not, family seat trainees have homework every fortnight. "*It takes a long time to do it, but it's well worth it. At the end the partner gives up an hour of her time to go through it with you.*" Maybe it is this thorough approach to teaching that makes the seat so popular, or it could be the "*really great work*" or the other people in the department, who trainees say are "*in a different league.*" Cases range from child care to divorces, and you learn to "*deal with emotions and irrational behaviour.*" The golden rule is to stay detached; "*you're there to advise and, though it can be hard, you can't get emotionally involved.*"

"*Crime was brilliant, really good,*" declared one source, presumably speaking about legal practice rather than the social phenomenon. BTMK represents defendants in everything from small-scale knock-about crimes to very high-cost cases involving major drug cartels. Reflecting this, trainees are exposed to murder, drugs, theft, fraud and all manner of assault cases, leading them to be "*in court practically every week.*" They are involved right from the first meeting with a client at a police station to the eventual trial and sentencing, tackling all stages in between including visiting prisons to take witness statements and analysing evidence from forensics and CCTV. In the ongoing war against legal aid cuts, BTMK plays its part, recently doing what it could to combat a 'best value tendering' scheme proposed by the LSC.

The employment department has a good relationship with the Citizens Advice Bureau, and the firm also gives free 20-minute advice sessions to people who are concerned about how to get their cases funded. They also advise on the tribunal process, helping by giving people the tools to fight their own cases. Accordingly, one trainee reckoned that around 50% of their junior caseload was funded by legal aid. Employment is a very engaging area of practice, and because it's *"about people, not the delivery of 500 cans of beans or something,"* trainees find it especially interesting. They feel the same about the *"very wide and interesting"* civil litigation seat which entails plenty of court attendance and client contact. BTMK takes on bigger cases than you might expect for its locations. We heard about one trainee's valiant defence of a client who was being pursued for a tonne of money gleaned through an alleged insurance fraud. On a Friday, after familiarising themselves with all the paperwork, assembling a defence and working *"all hands to the pump,"* the trainee found themselves at the High Court in London facing *"a very big City firm."* As our hero waited for the barrister to arrive, *"the other lawyers approached me – two fee earners and counsel – to try to persuade me to settle out of court."* Our hero stood their ground, won an extension for the client and was able to prepare a defence for the following Monday. In this *"team-oriented practice"* trainees get early-stage responsibility and their own files, commonly in relation to personal injury and the defence of housing repossessions.

Because local business owners come looking for generalists who can handle a broad spectrum of issues, the *"fast-paced"* commercial department covers every type of work from corporate and M&A transactions to commercial property and commercial litigation. *"You might be drafting a licence to assign* [a property] *one morning then working on something totally different like design rights, planning permission or drafting a new lease the next day."*

The Ceremony of The Pen

Last year we reported that BTMK wasn't very sporty. This year, we must eat our words. A team assembled by the trainees completed a 60-mile charity cycle from London to Southend, raising £2,500. Our sources had fond memories of their adventure – people tumbling into ditches, a partner's chain getting stuck at the bottom of a particularly toilsome hill, resulting in a two-mile push… Enthused by the success and the *"absolutely fantastic atmosphere"* of the event, they have already planned future trips. Other sporting pursuits include running, football and golf.

Chambers UK rankings

Crime

Trainees go out for drinks and meals together, and three of them are currently on the committee of the newly formed South Essex Junior Lawyers Division, membership of which is *"a good way of socialising with other lawyers in the region."* Back at the firm, *"there's a really good social aspect too – everyone joins in with everything."* Last year there was a charity quiz night with questions devised by the trainees. Apparently the crime team bent the rules to steal victory.

The impression we get is of a firm that works and plays well together, despite operating from two separate towns. *"I know it must sound cheesy,"* said one source, *"but I can't avoid saying that there's a real family ethic here: everyone looks after each other."* Such comments can sound disingenuous or saccharine, but in the case of BTMK they really didn't. Every year there's something called The Ceremony of The Pen, a much-anticipated and long-standing rite of passage at the keenly anticipated summer barbecue. It is so called because qualifying trainees are presented with a fancy pen in recognition of their impending change of status to qualified solicitor. BTMK doesn't normally keep all its qualifiers, and it was much the same story in 2009 when only one of the two took an NQ job, going into the firm's employment department.

Eager to keep up appearances locally, BTMK organises plenty of networking opportunities at which trainees *"meet clients in an informal setting and chat whilst getting the firm name out there."* Clearly it must be working as *"there's a lot of repeat work from satisfied clients, some of which we've had for years."*

And finally…

Trainees were unanimous in their praise of a firm that *"is a brilliant place to work because you get great training and plenty of advocacy."*

sardines

salmon

Quality is clearly defined in everything we do. Whether it's the journey to work, the calibre of our clients or the opportunities we offer our graduates. But we don't like to brag, so we'll leave that up to someone else:

"The firm has managed to win work that other national rivals would kill for… with client wins such as EMI Group, Reuters and Coca Cola HBC, Burges Salmon has quietly built the elite firm outside London" LAWYER AWARDS.

"Work on deals of all sizes and complexity is praised as 'impeccable' by a client base that appreciates the firm's blend of technical excellence and commercial nous" LEGAL 500.

For further information, please contact our trainee solicitor recruitment team on 0117 902 7797.

BURGES SALMON

WINNER AWARDS 2006
WINNER AWARDS 2007
WINNER AWARDS 2008
WINNER AWARDS 2009

www.burges-salmon.com

Burges Salmon LLP

The facts
Location: Bristol
Number of UK partners/solicitors: 69/233
Total number of trainees: 43
Seats: 6x4 months
Alternative seats: Secondments
Extras: Pro bono – Barton Hill Settlement, Bristol Enterprise Development Fund, Bristol Uni Law Clinic, CAB, Environmental Law Foundation; language classes

"The economic upturn will come, we'll have a new office and we have a new managing partner. We are going from strength to strength and for those of us that stay there is an awful lot to look forward to."

This Salmon is a fish in mid-leap. Its stated goal remains unchanged – to be the premier firm outside London – but it's going through an exciting period.

Big fish, small pond

Burges Salmon has always been a big name in the Bristol pond, but its ambitions stretch beyond that and in the past ten years we've watched with interest as the firm with the famous pink notepaper picked up top-quality client after top-quality client. National and international names like BNP Paribas, Coca-Cola, Corus, the Foreign and Commonwealth Office, FirstGroup, Lloyds TSB, the MoD, Nationwide, Orange and The Crown Estate all now instruct the firm, and over 70% of its work comes from outside the South West.

BS markets itself as London-quality outside London. *"There is a lot of consultant-speak, but it has a legitimate aspect to it. The firm is quickly becoming a large national-slash-City player,"* said one trainee. It's quite an achievement when you consider that BS has always turned its back on opening offices elsewhere in the country, sticking resolutely to its one-site philosophy. But in the main, it's worked: the core practice areas of corporate, commercial, banking and property scoop 'Best in the South West' rankings in *Chambers UK*, while a number of more niche departments have a national reputation. For instance, Burges Salmon sits in *Chambers UK*'s top tier for rail transport matters alongside City big boys Freshfields, Linklaters and Norton Rose and national giant Eversheds. It scoops other nationwide rankings for environment and PFI/PPP projects, among others.

But in the words of Dylan, the times they are a-changing, and BS recently stepped things up a gear. Between 2007 and 2008 partner numbers increased by eight, and overall the number of staff went from 550 to 670 – both big jumps compared to slow but steady prior growth. *"A lot of relatively young partners"* are increasingly influential, and a new managing partner gained possession of the big leather chair in May 2009. What's more, an office move scheduled for 2010 edges ever nearer. The trainees are especially looking forward to this, since it will have two things that the current building lacks: a canteen and air conditioning. *"There's lot of symbolism in the new office,"* said one contact. *"It will be a building that a firm of this nature deserves."* Ah, but does air-con mean the firm will stop giving out free ice creams on hot days?

Within the training scheme the seat structure is very regimented. Trainees take six seats of four months each. The first four seats consist of property (compulsory) and a range of either/or options – one seat in either commercial or corporate; one in either commercial disputes and construction (CDC) or agriculture, property litigation and environment (APLE); and one in employment, pensions and incentives (EPI) or tax and trusts. The fifth seat is a free choice, with the final one normally taken in the department a trainee is due to qualify into. Client secondments are available with Nationwide, Airbus and Mitie.

Into each life some grain must fall

Property, the only compulsory seat, remains a major part of the firm's business. It's a tough field to be in at the moment because of the economy, but trainees hadn't noticed work dry up too much: *"My list of things to do never ended!"* chuckled one. This may be because only around 11% of the firm's clients are actually from the property sector: its manufacturing, energy and infrastructure customers still need real estate work done, even in this climate. A trainee backed this up: "*Some of the biggest clients are rail-related, so they are okay as far as I know. Then there's insolvency issues – we have a cross-firm team with a property element. Also, the nuclear and wind farm clients are keeping people pretty busy.*" Therefore, at the moment a trainee's busy-ness in this department depends on what sort of work their supervisor does. Nonetheless, it's praised for being "*definitely the seat which provides the most responsibility day-to-day,*" as trainees are given control of smaller files. A popular alternative to a straight property seat is a trip to the planning team, which often deals with lengthy matters as "*quite a lot of wind farm applications get rejected first time round and then there's a big planning inquiry.*"

How to choose between the corporate and the commercial teams? The former has the "*glamour*" of blue-chip companies and multimillion-pound deals – actually 71 deals were completed in 2008, with a combined value of over £800m. These included FTSE 100 marketing company WPP Group's £13.5m acquisition of 75% of Heath Wallace's share capital, and the merger of Centaur Grain and Grainfarmers to establish Openfield (a seminal deal within the grain industry, apparently). The commercial team has the benefit of a pick-n-mix selection of work, including some IP, IT and competition law, and some top public sector clients like the MoD and the Metropolitan Police. Within the team, IP lawyers police the Harrods brand on the high street and on the internet, and represent Coca-Cola, the Discovery Channel and Virgin Mobile on trade mark issues. The competition lawyers advise the London Waste and Recycling Board and the Carbon Trust on compliance with state aid issues, and are involved with some interesting (though sadly confidential) price-fixing and bid-rigging cases. We can, however, tell you about advice given to Cardiff Bus during an investigation by the Office of Fair Trade to discover if it engaged in predatory conduct intended to eliminate a competitor. Despite the difference in focus, in essence the corporate and commercial departments offer similar experiences to trainees. Both will involve big deals, quite a lot of legal research, drafting letters, board minutes and resolutions and the obligatory bibling.

The APLE department concentrates on agriculture, property litigation and environmental law, with trainees choosing which of these they want to take the biggest bite out of. An agricultural caseload involves issues such as "*farming partnership disputes, compensation for animal slaughter and boundary disputes.*" Responsibility levels vary from one day to the next. Said one trainee: "*I dictated an attendance note – boring, mindless; it happens, I know. But afterwards I made a suggestion that ultimately*

Chambers UK rankings

Agriculture & Rural Affairs	Investment Funds
Banking & Finance	Outsourcing
Charities	Pensions
Competition/European Law	Pensions Litigation
Construction	Planning
Corporate/M&A	Private Client
Debt Recovery	Private Equity
Dispute Resolution	Projects, Energy & Natural Resources
Employment	Public Procurement
Environment	Real Estate
Family/Matrimonial	Real Estate Litigation
Health & Safety	Restructuring/Insolvency
Information Technology	Tax
Intellectual Property	Transport

was used as a realistic way to get our client more time. So I wasn't just the guy who dictated the note, I was actually involved in the discussions and the strategy. Everybody is listened to as part of the team." Property litigation also has a strong agricultural flavour. "*Lots of our clients are quite small farmers,*" so landlord and tenant disputes are common. Work in the environment team can involve research on anything from hazardous waste disposal to hydroelectric power to the train driver's eternal curse – leaves on the line. Trainees in both APLE and CDC get the chance to go to court on occasion.

The level of formal training differs between departments. "*Property made it very easy: there were some organised sessions and a lever arch file of precedents.*" By contrast, training in somewhere like tax and trusts is much more ad-hoc. What all trainees get at the start of their contract is a two-and-a-half-week blitz of information: everything from "*learning about the IT systems to going on a mail round with the legal support team. We even see where they store the fluorescent light bulbs in the basement!*" Never let it be said that Burges Salmon doesn't show trainees every nook and cranny of its business.

Salmon vs. Puma

It's the question mankind has been asking since the dawn of time: who would win in a fight between a salmon and a puma? The big cat in question is Burges Salmon's perennial rival in Bristol, Osborne Clarke, which – with its feline logo and history of technology work – has sometimes been seen as a more trendy option compared to the supposedly conservative BS. Trainees point to a "*friendly and open*" atmosphere as evidence that BS is by no means a stuffy firm. They do acknowledge its more conservative reputation, but say that this is "*paying dividends in the current climate. Some firms over-expanded in the good years.*"

Which brings us to the economy. Burges Salmon hasn't fully escaped the downturn, with 18 lawyers losing their jobs in spring 2009, salary freezes for support staff and future trainees being offered £5,000 to defer the start of their contracts for a year. A second round of redundancies was announced in August 2009, with 31 more jobs under threat. Even the new office was briefly in doubt, as the developers went into administration. Fortunately it's all going ahead and the firm recently showed vac schemers (in goggles, hard hats and hi-vis vests) around the building site. The office move in 2010 will be a time for good housekeeping and upgrades to facilities. The internal systems would be first on the list for several of our sources. Said one: "*Our IT systems could use a bit of a prod in the right direction. They were developed largely in-house, and I think a deep breath and a step back could go a long way to making things more efficient.*" The firm assures us this will happen.

The second-years we spoke to were understandably "*less sure than a year ago*" that they would be retained on qualification. In a frank Q&A session for trainees, held after the redundancies were announced, "*the firm said for the first time, 'Cards on the table: in reality we are probably not going to be able to keep all of you.'*" That said: "*They are still looking long-term, and if they can take one or two more than they have capacity for, they will.*" All our contacts remained quietly confident they would be kept on, although maybe not in their first-choice department. "*Some of the second-years have gone very quiet about where they want to qualify,*" said a first-year with a wry smile, expecting litigation jobs to be oversubscribed. In the final reckoning, 19 out of 21 trainees stayed with the firm, 14 in their first-choice team. The various litigation teams found space for nine of those NQs; corporate, property and banking all took just one apiece.

In the navy/Go west

In an increasingly competitive market, how can you appeal to Burges Salmon? The best academic results won't be enough. "*No one here just has a first from Oxford,*" said one trainee. Among the current intake is "*an ex-investment banker, someone who managed his own business, a former semi-pro boxer who is also a doctor of chemistry, people who have done a lot of extra-curricular pro bono things at uni, and an Olympic gold medallist.*" A first from Oxford would help, of course, although actually many BS trainees come from good universities outside of the traditional Oxbridge/redbrick mould. Plenty also have a link to the South West, even if it's just having done UWE's LPC. Another common thread is an unwillingness to face the grind of the big city – a fact not lost on the firm, which markets itself to trainees as offering more of a work-life balance than is possible in London (though don't take that to mean a nine-to-five working day is standard). The best advice we can give comes straight from a trainee: "*The main thing I would say is that a two-dimensional application is going to get the standard response of 'we had an unusually high level of applicants this year.' A three-dimensional application shows you have an understanding of what it takes to be a solicitor at a large firm. That will get the invite, and will get the job.*"

BS is an exceedingly sporty firm and athletes won't find themselves short of activities: footballers, cricketers and netball, basketball, softball, hockey and rugby players are all catered for. For the non-sportsmen and women (there are some), an active social committee arranges everything from discounted concert tickets to bus trips to London. The trainee group goes out fairly regularly, with The Famous Royal Navy Volunteer, one of a cluster of salty sea dog pubs in the Old City, currently a popular venue. Another, the Llandoger Trow, was the inspiration for the Admiral Benbow pub in *Treasure Island*.

This firm's future looks bright. Despite its successes in the field, BS has never been overly reliant on transactional work. Litigation is busy, the pensions team is busy, employment is busy. The firm's specialist sectors (rail infrastructure, energy, etc,) are well placed to minimise the effect of the downturn, and clients from these areas also need lawyers' corporate, property and banking skills, so while the volume of traditional deals is obviously down, work should still come to these departments. One trainee compared Burges Salmon to "*a phoenix rising from the ashes,*" saying: "*The economic upturn will come, we'll have a new office and we have a new managing partner. We are going from strength to strength and for those of us that stay there is an awful lot to look forward to.*"

And finally...

Burges Salmon has swum vigorously upstream to build an excellent name for itself, and it's a real national player now. Is this a genuine alternative to the best London firms? Absolutely.

Capsticks Solicitors LLP

The facts

Location: London, Birmingham
Number of partners/solicitors: 34/68
Total number of trainees: 11
Seats: 6x4 months
Alternative seats: Secondments
Extras: Pro bono – Putney Law Centre

> "*Students tend to think that they should have a background in medicine. That's not necessary, but they need a genuine interest in the field.*"
>
> Majid Hassan, Partner

Moving recently to new premises in Wimbledon and a new office in Birmingham, this specialist law firm is the picture of health.

Number-one seed

Created less than 30 years ago from an in-house legal team at the NHS, Capsticks has grown into a leading authority on healthcare law. Aware of its top-dog status, *Chambers UK* awards it the highest possible marks for clinical negligence and health and social care matters. The client list speaks volumes: in addition to many independent healthcare organisations, Capsticks advises over half of the 267 NHS acute trusts in England and over a third of the 152 primary care trusts (PCTs). Among its newest clients are East Midlands Strategic Health Authority, Haringey PCT and Great Ormond Street Hospital NHS Trust.

What does the future hold for this healthcare expert? First on the agenda is a move from a "*stiflingly hot*" Putney gaff to newer offices in Wimbledon. Our research was conducted when trainees were still in Putney, but most were excited about the change of scene, albeit that they're going even further south west of Central London. Whatever the location, everyone is clear that "*the main aim is to remain the key healthcare advisers in the country.*" This view of the firm can only have been helped by an expansion last year into Birmingham. Other law firms may have felt the pinch during the recession, but trainees here seemed relatively unworried: "*Because of the nature of our clients we don't really have a problem.*"

Our sources had all completed a vac scheme at the firm, and it had convinced them that Capsticks was "*a place where we knew we'd get a good quality of training.*" The contract requires all to take six seats of four months, chosen from clinical negligence, commercial, dispute resolution, employment and property. With just five departments available, it's clear that people are in for a repeat seat or two. Fortunately "*after four months you can get a real feel for a department.*"

Hospital visits

The outstanding clinical department handles advisory and negligence instructions. Trainees commonly choose to visit twice as they enjoy "*the nitty-gritty of handling cases, writing instructions and reviewing medical records.*" Carefully supervised, they can expect good exposure to clients on matters ranging from brain damage and orthopaedic problems to negligence in midwifery. For some people it is the human dimension that makes the work so worthwhile. "*People have had their lives turned upside down and there's always something different about each case that we can help out with.*" The tragic case of Baby P in Haringey is a good example. Lawyers advised the NHS on the criminal processes involved, dealt with a number of requests under the Freedom of Information Act and ensured appropriate disclosure of information to professional regulators. In a key consent-to-treatment case an HIV-infected patient with strong religious beliefs refused a caesarean and anti-retroviral drugs prior to going into labour. Capsticks obtained a court order for Croydon's Mayday Healthcare NHS Trust just in time to ensure adequate treatment. Expect some heavy reading in this seat; you'll "*develop familiarity with medical documents and get used to reading doctors' handwriting.*" Despite the heavy workload, one trainee advised sticking with health law. "*Getting to grips with the work was hard at first... I was working long hours and I didn't get a broad range of things to work on. I enjoyed it much more second time around though.*"

The dispute resolution team, which also handles regulatory issues, earned unqualified praise. "*This is definitely where I want to qualify when I'm done,*" declared one interviewee. Working on all the contentious matters that don't fall under the ambit of clinical negligence, the department is something of a catch-all. As well as claims that are specific to NHS trusts, lawyers handle more general commercial claims and property disputes. Trainees sometimes get to investigate misconduct inquiries, ranging from simple drug use to defamation claims. Part-time secondments to hospital and PCT clients are occasionally available. "*The clients are really lovely and it's wonderful to get their perspective on things,*" concluded a source, though another noted that it can take a while to find your bearings in a large NHS organisation.

The health of the nation

The real estate department brings a change of pace. The NHS is the largest landowner in the country, so Capsticks' property folk are kept on their toes. Even during the property slump the department has been active on PPP instructions for the construction of new clinics under the NHS LIFT initiative. And in order to reconfigure learning disability services, it has recently effected extensive stock transfers to registered social landlords in Kent, East Sussex and South-West London. Supervision was given a thumbs-up. Said one source: "*My supervisor always made me feel I could go to him if I had questions.*"

Life in the employment department is "*dynamic, due to the ever-changing law, and exciting, given the tribunal opportunities.*" The NHS is a massive employer, probably the biggest in Europe, so trainees don't have much time to catch their breath. "*It's fast-paced as the tribunal deadlines come around very quickly,*" stressed one source. These days the staple diet of unfair dismissal claims is supplemented by a tide of equal pay cases affecting over 40 trusts. The firm also has expertise in doctors' disciplinary issues, including assisting healthcare organisations in managing and handling investigations. Take the case against Dr Mezey, who was subject to an internal inquiry when one of her patients absconded and killed a member of the public. The department has additionally provided advice on the issue of the EU's Working Time Directive and junior doctors' hours. On occasion trainees run their own seminars (in London or Birmingham), giving them the opportunity to hone their client skills.

Chambers UK rankings

Administrative & Public Law
Clinical Negligence
Healthcare & Social Care
Professional Discipline

The commercial department has a broad remit and its projects lawyers, in particular, work on some huge matters. Capsticks' input was vital in implementing Healthcare for London, which was one of the largest ever reconfigurations of NHS services. Many clients are London-based, but the firm also works for authorities from north Norfolk to the South Coast.

You're hired!

We were very flattered to hear that "*one of the most appealing things is working with Chambers-ranked people... I get a real buzz from that.*" As you'd imagine, an aspiring trainee must be able to demonstrate an interest in the health sector. Good grades are important, too, as the academic challenges can be considerable. "*Even on the vac scheme,*" said one source, "*I got a few bits of research that really involved engaging my brain.*" A bright, willing personality and adaptability are equally prized.

"*Things are a bit more relaxed at Capsticks and less hierarchical,*" said trainees. On the downside, "*mundane things like seating arrangements can be fought over,*" and "*although there are very few people in the firm who are difficult to work with, when you do get someone like that it's hard to get help sometimes.*" That said, people sensed that HR are willing to assist as much as they can, and we also hear that secretarial and library support is good. Capsticks' social life accentuates the importance of work-life balance. In addition to rugby sevens, cricket matches and after-work drinks, staff get involved in charity fundraisers. At one gala event, first-years raised over £750 for a neuro-disability organisation. They competed with second-years in an *Apprentice*-style face-off with partner Peter Edwards standing in as the curmudgeonly Suralun. In 2009 all four qualifiers stayed with the firm.

And finally...

Healthcare clients and healthcare cases are what you'll get here. If that's the medicine you want to self-prescribe then we can think of no better place to train.

- **A total of 6,303 training contracts were offered in 2008, of which...**

   47.8% were based in London,

   13.7% in the South East and East,

   11.5% in the North West,

   10.8% in the Midlands,

   9.8% in Yorkshire and the North East,

   3.5% in the South West...

   and 2.9% in Wales.

Source: The Law Society's annual statistical report 2008

top tip no. 9

Charles Russell LLP

The facts
Location: London, Guildford, Cheltenham, Oxford, Cambridge
Number of UK partners/solicitors: 96/189
Total number of trainees: 35
Seats: 4x6 months
Alternative Seats: Overseas seats, secondments
Extras: Pro bono – LawWorks, Bethnal Green Legal Advice Centre, Surrey Law Centre, RCJ Advice Centre

This London headquartered firm can take trainees through the A-Z of legal practice. Its larger regional offices are among the strongest in their respective locations.

In business for over a hundred years, Charles Russell has more than maintained its ancestral strengths while remodelling itself as a commercial player.

Holla, 'We want pre-nup!'

Charles Russell has five UK and two overseas offices. The London HQ is oldest and largest, the Cheltenham and Guildford offices are well established, and Oxford and Cambridge are recent additions. The firm has also opened in Geneva and Bahrain. London understandably offers the widest range of services; Guildford and Cheltenham are broad in their coverage; Oxford focuses on corporate finance and IP; in Cambridge the practice is dominated by an employment and pensions group.

Charles Russell's longest-running practice groups are family law and private client. As one observant source noted, the family department is *"one of the biggest in the country and considered among the magic circle of family law practices."* Given London's developing reputation as the big-money divorce capital of the world, the team is sought after by those with plenty at stake. One such high-end client was Lady Ann Judge (former wife of Tory politician and businessman Sir Paul Judge); indeed, the firm has represented numerous spouses in faltering relationships where assets are substantial and/or based overseas. Inevitably some cases involve emotional disagreements over the custody of children. Far from having a negative impact, the economic downturn looks likely to bring in more work, and the two cleverly located overseas offices have done well as sources of new wealthy clients. The team achieved a revenue increase of more than a fifth in 2007/08. Three new family partners were made up in 2008, and senior figure Grant Howell took over as joint general editor of *Butterworths Family Law Service*. The seat can be quite demanding, say trainees. *"There's a lot of finance and asset-based work, so it helps if you're numerate."* Lucky trainees may even see the odd *"high-profile celebrity pre-nup."*

The family department has a fraternal twin – the private client department. Over in that seat, trainees say: *"There's a great deal of independence and you don't have to wait around to have work allotted to you."* Clients are frequently loaded, and many have overseas assets and/or foreign nationality. Drafting wills and researching tax and trust issues are all staples for trainees, and the client exposure includes *"perks like dinners and lunches every now and then."* Again, the team is one of the largest and strongest in the UK, and it too saw partner promotions last year.

Charles in charge

These traditional practices contribute about a third of the firm's income, with the larger remainder accruing from commercial clients. By way of example, the firm has attracted a slew of big-name banks onto its books (Barclays, Credit Suisse and HSBC Private Bank) and also represents a number of business start-ups. The firm's mid-market corporate achievements are impressive, with AIM a dominant feature. Client JPMorgan Cazenove, for example, was involved in the financing of two African mining deals last year, taking a Zambian emerald miner and a South African coal and uranium mining company through market fund-raisings. We pick these examples because the firm has found a rich seam in the international mining sector. Other corporate clients include ITV

Productions, easyJet, Gulf Air, the Government of the Falkland Islands and the deliciously named Buff Snacks. Work comes in from Russia, the Middle East, Africa and the Indian subcontinent as well as the UK.

Some of our sources had come to Charles Russell with the preconception that it is exclusively traditionalist and were "*surprised to see how prominent the commercial departments were.*" Said one: "*Corporate is one of the friendliest teams here, and a trainee can expect to get involved in anything and everything that's happening.*" Commercial litigation is another drawcard and Charles Russell has a good reputation for matters ranging from real estate disputes to reputation management. Client Ardentia is a subcontractor to BT in the roll-out of the biggest health sector IT project in the world, the NHS's National Care Records Service. When Ardentia and BT's relationship became problematic, Charles Russell litigators swung into action to settle the matter so the relationship could continue. Another case involved LighterLife, a supplier of food packs to dieters. The company got into a spat with HM Revenue & Customs about the appropriate level of VAT to be charged for its services. While trainees are unlikely to perform much, if any, active advocacy on behalf of clients, they do become very involved in case preparation and can sit in on hearings. Most of their work centres on the pre-trial aspects of litigation, such as research, drafting witness statements, letters, disclosure and discovery of evidence and the time-consuming preparation of court bundles.

The firm is well regarded in IP, sports law and media matters. The IP team covers both 'soft' issues like trade marks and copyright and 'hard' patent litigation. Clients include Dunlop Slazenger, wagamama, Weymouth & Portland National Sailing Academy, Tourism Malaysia and the owner of the Spandau Ballet trade mark. Let's hope the band's 2009 comeback results in plenty of instructions. Understandably, there's a growing popularity for sports law among trainees; who can blame them when the firm is key external counsel to the FA, assisting it on dispute resolution and regulatory work? Just as alluring is a healthy roster of music, film and publishing clients. With production companies such as Goldcrest Films (*Chariots of Fire*, *Ghandi*) and HandMade Films (*Lock Stock, Withnail & I, Life of Brian*) plus Virgin Radio, the Royal Philharmonic Orchestra and the London Philharmonic and Symphony Orchestras using the firm, there's never a dull day in this department.

Russell sprouts

Of the trainee group of 2008/09, 27 trainees were London-based, with eight in Guildford and four in Cheltenham. The firm also had a trainee in Cambridge. London trainees can work in almost any of the departments (private client, family, employment, litigation, coco

Chambers UK rankings

Agriculture & Rural Affairs	Media & Entertainment
Banking & Finance	Outsourcing
Capital Markets	Personal Injury
Charities	Private Client
Clinical Negligence	Professional Discipline
Construction	Professional Negligence
Corporate/M&A	Projects, Energy & Natural Resources
Defamation/Reputation Management	Public Procurement
Dispute Resolution	Real Estate
Education	Real Estate Litigation
Employment	Restructuring/Insolvency
Family/Matrimonial	Sports Law
Intellectual Property	Telecommunications

and property, plus more specialist areas like banking, corporate tax and media). Guildford trainees choose between the same main seats, plus property litigation and insolvency. A narrower range of seats in Cheltenham offers private client, property, coco and litigation. Secondments are organised with clients such as Honda and retail giant Arcadia, and a lucky few can spend six months in Bahrain, where "*the weather is good and accommodation and a car are provided.*" We also hear that some trainees have wangled business trips to the Bahamas and Geneva.

As a rough guide, London is the place to go for the more specialist commercial work (eg sports and media law). There is also more of the international work in the capital, though this is not to say that other offices are entirely devoid of offshore action. The most popular London seats are litigation and employment, the latter being competitive because there is generally only one seat in London and another in Cambridge. Given the high proportion of commercial seats, trainees recommended we reiterate that applicants should not assume they can linger overly long on the private client side of the firm, even if that is their intended qualification destination.

Fleet foxes

In 2009 London staff decamped to a modern building at Fleet Place, just a stone's throw from the Old Bailey. Most of our sources were delighted at the new feeling of openness the move had brought, even if some warned that it was "*quite hard to have a messy desk as everything's visible.*" A few regretted that "*it's hard to have privacy here sometimes as everyone can hear your conversations.*" We guess that also rules out a sneaky mid-morning peek at Facebook. Happily, everything looks much smarter than in the old office, and the lifts work properly. Another benefit of the new abode is a canteen with options ranging from salads to three-course meals. Sadly, no such facility exists in Guildford or Cheltenham, though each office is close to the centre of town. The Cotswolds are a lovely part of the UK, relatively wealthy and fashionable among A-listers; the Cheltenham office occupies a large Regency period house in one of the smartest parts of the town. Just metres from chi-chi shopping opportunities and extensive ornamental gardens, the location matches the firm's up-scale position in the county's pecking order of professional service providers.

It was the pace of life and reasonable work ethic in Guildford that appealed to at least one of our sources. The office occupies a modern block with a view of the River Wey and plenty of green space around. The local pub is The Keystone, and curries with colleagues are a nice way to spend an evening. Less than an hour by train to London, visits to the firm's HQ for training days are easy. We sense that the smaller trainee groups in Guildford and Cheltenham promote closer relationships between first and second-years than in London.

The firm continues a tradition of asking unusual questions of training contract applicants, and it was recently revealed to us that the questions themselves might come from trainees incentivised by champagne. Past applicants have been asked 'what kind of animal would you be?' and 'what was the best invention?' After lengthy debate among *Student Guide* researchers we selected the fox and the sombrero. Actually our sources suggest that there's a great deal of diversity among answers from students, perhaps reflecting the range of characters and types that are attracted to the firm. Of those who make the grade, "*many have travelled and people come from a number of different universities in the UK.*" One person described the typical recruit as "*quite confident, self assured... and sporty;*" another saw their peers as sociable "*all-rounders.*"

The economic crisis curbed social splurges: last year the Cheltenham office was deprived of a Christmas party while the London office was reduced to watching partners duelling with a Wii at a games-themed event. Plans for the 2009 summer ball were shelved. Sources found this all "*sad but understandable, as people are losing their jobs in this economy.*" Not all was misery though, as the entire firm was invited to the annual 'sports dinner' in London. One trainee was hesitant to call it "*a laid-back piss-up,*" so we'll just go ahead and do it for them.

Fee culpa

London trainees had an unfortunate introduction to their legal careers last year, after the firm mistakenly told them they would be starting on £35,000 rather than the actual £32,500 filling their pay packets. The trainees were informed of the change by letter on their first day at the firm, and the lack of an open apology or a chance to air concerns left an "*unfavourable impression among London trainees.*" New starters from Cheltenham were also expected to arrange their own accommodation for the weeks spent on the initial induction in the capital, and again our sources thought this was something the firm should have dealt with differently. In saying this, however, the rest of their experiences have clearly been very positive: we heard minimal complaints about the demands of the workload and plenty of assurances that "*there's lots of support if you need it.*" Trainees generally find mid and end-of-seat appraisals both helpful and efficiently run, though one source did say: "*One of my reviews was late and of little benefit to me. More feedback would have been helpful.*" Most trainees can expect to sit next to a partner, which can be "*daunting at first but you get used to it.*" As for formal training sessions, these are deemed "*helpful, particularly the substantive ones. The more admin-based ones tend to drag on a bit, given that guidance is given via e-manuals on all of that stuff anyway.*"

The economic crisis caused some 50 redundancies and certain solicitors moved to work a four-day week or took unpaid leave. Our sources felt Charles Russell had been fair in its approach, even if one thought there was "*little communication from up top and messages were sometimes poorly timed, like on a Friday afternoon, for example.*" In the 2009 NQ recruitment round, 13 of the 19 qualifiers stayed on with the firm, going into several different departments. Meanwhile, six of the 2009 intake of new trainees were deferred for a year and they received a £6,000 payment.

One trainee summed Charles Russell up perfectly as "*a hybrid of a traditional law firm and one that is fairly dynamic in areas like media, sports, telecoms and international transactions.*" With unanimous agreement on the firm's friendliness and the approachability of seniors, there was little surprise among trainees that Charles Russell nudged in at number 92 in the *Sunday Times'* '100 Best Companies to Work For' survey in 2009.

And finally...

Like a tried-and-tested Delia recipe, Charles Russell is a modern classic. For those looking to avoid the corporate giants of City law, this firm offers the chance to sink your teeth into family and private client matters as well as commercial practice.

Cleary Gottlieb Steen & Hamilton LLP

The facts

Locations: London
Number of UK partners/solicitors: 16/44
Total number of trainees: 13
Seats: 4x6 months
Alternative seats: Overseas seats
Extras: Pro bono – FRU

Over in the States, Cleary has a reputation as the "*quirky*" BigLaw firm. Over here, it's the City's best-kept secret.

Make no mistake: this big-league international firm is looking for the best of the best. A non-departmentalised approach, combined with financial prudence, means that in these tough times Cleary's still been hitting it out of the park.

Cleary blue skies

Cleary is a transatlantic success story. Right from its earliest days in 1946 New York, international aspirations were at the top of the agenda. Paris opened in 1949, and Cleary has since racked up 12 offices around the globe, only two of them in the USA. Its achievements in Europe can be traced back to the Marshall Plan, when founding partner George Ball worked closely with chief architect of the European Community Jean Monnet on the implementation of the USA's post-WWII aid package. Cleary has an impressive track record for recognising emerging markets and developing trends, and exploiting the consequences of political and economic change. If you want to know more about the wider Cleary picture, it might be worth taking a look at the firm's profile on our new sibling website www.chambers-associate.com. Aimed at American law students, this site gives plenty of detail on Cleary's US operations.

The London office (opened in 1971) puts a premium on capital markets, finance and M&A, with more specialist areas including competition, tax and a growing IP practice. Cleary is non-departmentalised, which essentially means that over the course of two years the work that trainees do depends largely on business needs (and to some extent where their interests lie). They change seats and supervisors every six months, but this doesn't necessarily mean they will specialise in a particular area for the duration of the seat. Cleary is looking to shape generalists, not specialists. The advantages of the approach are several: working on deals from start to finish, getting real experience of "*what life will be like as an associate,*" and not being "*tied to what you did as a trainee*" on qualification. The downside is that if you're looking at niche areas "*like aviation finance or something – you should look elsewhere.*" The strategy certainly pays dividends for the firm. As one interviewee told us: "*When it's cold we make coal, when it's hot we make ice – we perform well when the market changes and the non-departmentalised structure is how the firm is able to make itself strong.*" The firm claims never to have made a redundancy, and an interviewee told us: "*We can pick things up quickly, change up and do different types of work – it means we're not redundant in any sense of the word.*"

High stakes

Litigation is not a major focus here, though the up-and-coming arbitration department is now taking trainees. On the whole, trainees find that three of their four seats are "*a mix of capital markets, finance and M&A.*" Discrete areas such as tax and competition are nonetheless available (indeed Cleary has a world-beating competition group) and so "*if you're really keen on something you should make it clear.*" Trainees with an interest in employment, for example, were able to take on this type of work in conjunction with another seat.

The capital markets deals on which Cleary works are indicative of its international nature. The firm was counsel to EDP Renováveis in its €1.6bn IPO, the largest European IPO in 2008, and represented Lucky Cement, Pakistan's largest producer, in its global offering of 60m equity shares. More recognisable clients include Banc of America Securities, Barclays Capital, HSBC and Morgan Stanley. The firm represented this group as underwriters in an offering of $3bn guaranteed notes by BP Capital Markets. For a trainee, the work in a capital markets seat is *"fairly broad – from debt and equity to structured finance and derivatives."*

In relation to M&A, trainees experience everything from small African deals (*"a nice size so someone junior can have an important role"*) to massive Russian and South American ones. Clients include industrial and manufacturing giants as well as private equity groups, and the work is almost always cross-border and frequently complex. *"Whirlwind overseas trips"* are not uncommon. The firm was counsel to ArcelorMittal on its $810m acquisition of London Mining Brasil from LondonMining plc, and on its simultaneous $40.5m acquisition of an 80% stake in Adriana Resources' planned port facility. Cleary lawyers also represented US private equity group TPG on its acquisition of 50% of pharmaceutical distributor SIA International for $800m. That deal was the largest-ever private equity investment in Russia.

The finance work is no less impressive, and as further evidence of its foothold in Russia Cleary helped raise a syndicated loan for United Company RUSAL. A total of $4.5bn was raised for the '25% plus one share' stake in MMC Norilsk Nickel. Such big-ticket deals will routinely be done in conjunction with major investment banks and the likes of Clifford Chance or Linklaters on the other side, so while you may not understand the nitty gritty just yet, you should appreciate that the stakes are high.

As well as foreign business trips, overseas secondments are possible. Not that many people go – perhaps getting used to the pace and requirements of the London office is challenge enough – but there are slots available in Paris, Brussels, Moscow, Hong Kong and New York. On qualification, some people choose to go and live and work outside the UK; others study for the New York Bar.

The chosen few

Our interviewees admit that Cleary isn't incredibly well known among UK students (though we hear the London office gets many applications from overseas, where the firm's profile is higher). For this reason we can't help thinking it's one of the best-kept secrets in the City. The intake is usually limited to six people a year – a vast difference from magic circle firms encountered on the other side of deals – so you can see why some people argue that

Chambers UK rankings

Banking & Finance	Corporate/M&A
Capital Markets	Private Equity
Competition/European Law	Tax

Cleary is the connoisseur's choice. This is definitely a place for high-flyers, and we were dazzled by the accomplishments of the trainees we encountered. Trainee and lawyer recruitment is run not by an HR team but by lawyers who volunteer for the task. Insiders told us: *"Academic excellence is the key thing we're looking for"* and some of the applicants have CVs as long as your arm. Naturally, *"a lot of these guys are used to competing,"* but if you're one of those types who enjoys a challenge, just be careful on the vac scheme. Backstabbers and those with an over-competitive nature don't go down well. Cleary recognises that *"it's tough being a junior in a law firm"* and *"really frowns upon giving people an unnecessarily hard time. An obnoxious attitude would be picked up on very quickly – say an applicant who kisses arse to the partners but who's markedly less attentive to associates and trainees. Similarly, associates who don't work well with juniors don't make it very far."*

With the odds stacked against you and a mouth-watering starting salary of £40,000 (rising to £92,000 on qualification), gaining a place at Cleary is like winning the lottery. Not that much is left to chance; *"here, people know what they want in terms of their career"* and it is *"not a place where people will have drifted in."* This is a place where you will have to work hard... and long. *"Trying to protect your calendar"* at Christmas is difficult, and being called back to the office on a Friday night or working seven days a week for a solid month are part and parcel of being one of the chosen few. Nevertheless, when it's quieter, Cleary lawyers find time for a few jars in the nearby Corney and Barrow, and the business-casual dress code makes for a more relaxed atmosphere. *"It's hard to believe it,"* said one interviewee, *"but despite our nerdy CVs Cleary manages to be quite a human place to work."* In 2009 all six qualifiers stayed on at the firm, and who can blame them?

And finally...

Cleary is a lifestyle choice, and the lifestyle we're talking about involves hard graft and stiff challenges. Chances are you already know if you're up to the task.

- **Training partners talk work-life balance:** "[City law] can be very demanding and involve a lot of late hours – although for people who thoroughly enjoy their jobs, seeing things through to fruition can be very stimulating. It's a mistake to look at things in terms of work and life – as if your job isn't a part of your life. [People who think like that] might find embarking on this type of career quite tricky."

"Lawyers can get a little dramatic: 'Woe is me, I work so hard'. No graduate job is a nine to five anymore – not teacher, not doctor, none of them."

top tip no. 10

Clifford Chance LLP

The facts
Location: London
Number of UK partners/solicitors: 220/545
Total number of trainees: 220
Seats: 4x6 months
Alternative seats: Overseas seats, secondments
Extras: Pro bono – various law centres, death row appeals; language training

> Working here can be very demanding and involve a lot of late hours. For people who thoroughly enjoy their jobs though, seeing things through to fruition can be very stimulating.

Clifford Chance does things on a massive scale: it has a far-reaching international network, a substantial global workforce and generates huge revenues.

The big daddy

Clifford Chance is arguably the law firm most familiar to people outside the profession. Never one to follow the well-trodden path, it strives to be the first at everything. This first-mover status was notably achieved when it embarked on an aggressive campaign of international expansion. Following mergers with New York firm Rogers & Wells and Frankfurt's Pünder, Volhard, Weber & Axster in 1999, CC has grown exponentially and today fields over 3,500 lawyers across 27 offices located everywhere from São Paulo to Shanghai. CC's latest ambition has been to penetrate the Indian market by tightening links with alliance firm AZB & Partners. In a booming market, CC's reach certainly proved to be an advantage, and over the past decade it beat all others in revenue terms.

That reign ended abruptly in 2009 when as a result of the financial meltdown, and perhaps hindered by its size, CC reported a 5% dip in turnover and that profits per equity partner had fallen by 37% to £733,000. Worldwide revenues for 2008/09 were still a massive £1.262bn, which should give you an idea of the scale of the firm. The disappointing financials followed a difficult year in which CC made numerous redundancies (including 80 London lawyers) and carried out a partnership reshaping, expected to shrink the partner count by 15% by April 2010 (equating to around 90 partners).

It's not all gloom and doom. CC has more than enough stamina to withstand a global economic crisis and remains one of the City's most powerful players. The firm is often benchmarked against Allen & Overy as one of the two finance-driven members of the magic circle, although CC arguably operates on a larger scale. It covers the waterfront of finance and capital markets product lines, from securities and acquisition finance to asset, project and Islamic finance. The firm's capacity to lead and deliver on cross-border transactions was evidenced by its recent advice to Permira on the $3.7bn financing for the acquisition of NDS Group, and again when representing InBev on the financing for its $52bn acquisition of Anheuser-Busch. In common with other City firms, CC is currently responding to a shift towards more financial restructuring work, and because it fields a leading restructuring team it is mandated on particularly large and complex matters, including the recent $27.5bn debt restructuring for LyondellBasell, one of the largest chemical groups in the world. While finance and capital markets aficionados are clearly well catered for, it needs to be said that CC is more than a finance firm. Its corporate department achieves the top ranking for high-end cross-border M&A in *Chambers UK* and CC is also thought to have Europe's top private equity practice. Recent M&A mandates include Chinalco's £9.1bn acquisition of 12% of Rio Tinto, the largest international investment yet by a Chinese entity. A full-service firm then, CC also covers competition, tax, insolvency, real estate, construction, employee benefits, environmental law, etc... Uncharacteristically for a top City firm, it also has a highly respected public law team.

Money trains

If on paper CC is multifaceted, there's no denying the prevalence of the finance, capital markets and corporate groups, so don't expect to pick and choose your seats from among the niche practices. Time must be served in the finance department, whether in a general banking seat or a more specialised project or asset finance one. Our sources rather liked breathing the air at the pinnacle of the banking profession – "*CC acts for the world's largest banks and the sums of money involved made my head spin,*" commented one. Deals often exceed the billion-pound mark. In asset finance, for example, lawyers advised Network Rail in £13bn negotiations with the Department for Transport on the terms of an Access Option for those parts of the organisation's track network that will be used by Crossrail. In transactions of this scale trainees are rarely involved in the nitty-gritty of drafting and negotiations and are usually limited to the ground-work of managing loan documentation or collating conditions precedent. Our sources agreed that this "*relatively low level of responsibility is perfectly adequate for first or second-seaters, but can leave you wanting more challenging assignments as you become more senior.*" Sensibly, most of our sources had expected the very long hours finance is renowned for; "*you work flat out towards closings, but there are also prolonged periods of inactivity.*"

Capital markets seats can be hardcore too. Having heard of the firm's top reputation in this field, most trainees commence this seat bright-eyed and bushy-tailed before then falling in one of two categories. There are those who "*love it – love the adrenalin, the pressure and the satisfaction of seeing the results of your work almost instantly.*" There are others who find it "*repetitive, because to be honest there isn't a lot of scope to move away from bond offerings.*" The corporate department is another usual stop on the training route. And, again, the hours can be "*quite punishing, with early starts, late finishes and regular all-nighters.*" Thankfully trainees are adequately compensated for their sacrifice by being given "*full responsibility for discrete parts of very interesting deals,*" ranging from public M&A to private equity and corporate restructurings. It'll often involve a hefty chunk of due diligence or data room management, but better assignments are available too, so you might end up drafting board minutes or reviewing overseas counsel's legal opinions.

Always up for a fight

Research assignments, reviewing disclosure, drafting witness statements or instructions to counsel are all on the agenda in the dispute resolution division and trainees' feedback on the seat is pretty good. The group deals with everything from insurance matters to defamation, IP disputes and fraud investigations, and has absorbed the smaller international arbitration team. The arbitration group is hugely popular among trainees, so our sources advised that although the team prefers third and fourth-seaters, you shouldn't wait until the last minute to make an impression on the partners there. "*Let them know you're keen from the start of the training contract.*" More transactionally minded trainees tend to shun the litigation seat in favour of a short course or a placement at Liberty or Law for All, where they advise on housing, benefits and employment queries on a pro bono basis. While most trainees agreed that "*you barely notice the hierarchy at Clifford Chance,*" those who spent time in litigation and arbitration found the atmosphere a little more formal and the partners a little less accessible in comparison with other departments. Clearly though, the positives of working in these groups must outweigh the negatives, as both are consistently oversubscribed for NQ jobs.

Rising in the east, setting in the west

Beyond the mainstream departments, there's a raft of smaller teams and client secondment opportunities, particularly with the finance team's clients, including Barclays, UBS, Airbus and EADS. The chance to experience an overseas seat is also a major draw, and many trainees mentioned that this was a crucial factor in their decision to join CC. In reality, however, some found that overseas opportunities weren't all they had hoped for and that languages skills commonly dictate the allocations made. "*Better keep quiet about that German A-Level you did years ago if you don't want to end up in Frankfurt,*"

Chambers UK rankings

Administrative & Public Law	Investment Funds
Asset Finance	Media & Entertainment
Banking & Finance	Outsourcing
Banking Litigation	Parliamentary & Public Affairs
Capital Markets	
Climate Change	Pensions
Commodities	Planning
Competition/European Law	Private Client
Construction	Private Equity
Corporate/M&A	Product Liability
Data Protection	Professional Negligence
Defamation/Reputation Management	Projects, Energy & Natural Resources
Dispute Resolution	
Employee Share Schemes	Public International Law
Employment	Real Estate
Environment	Real Estate Finance
Financial Services Regulation	Real Estate Litigation
	Restructuring/Insolvency
Fraud: Civil	Retail
Immigration	Social Housing
Information Technology	Tax
Insurance	Telecommunications
Intellectual Property	Transport

one advised. With six places to fill in that office and fewer volunteers, trainees with a smattering of the language can often feel pressured to spend time there. On the plus side, "*it's give and take – graciously accepting a seat you don't really fancy more or less guarantees you'll get one of your first choices later on.*"

In previous years trainees have mentioned "*arbitrariness*" in the allocation of domestic and international seats, suggesting that the system lacked transparency. Apparently things haven't improved much on that front, as trainees report that "*some people always get what they want and others don't, but it's impossible to tell what factors are taken into account.*" The more charitable trainees appreciate the difficult task HR have on their hands: "*Placing 250 trainees is bound to be tricky; I think HR do an admirable job,*" said one. To avoid disappointment, it's a good idea to "*make your seat ambitions known early on,*" or do a spot of behind-the-scenes networking with the relevant partners. "*Things can get quite political and you just have to play the game; you can't afford to be complacent.*"

Swimming in luxury

When we asked our contacts what made them bin their training contract offers from other firms and accept the one from CC, we got the usual mentions of "*great international reputation, fantastic clients and amazing deals.*" Delving a bit deeper, ambitious trainees revealed they simply "*wanted to train with the best*" and didn't even bother applying anywhere else. We also asked whether the firm favoured particular educational backgrounds and our sources all insisted that CC makes a point of recruiting talented newcomers from a wide array of universities. By our reckoning, the firm boasts an impressively diverse trainee group: our interviewees studied everywhere from Oxbridge to Bristol, Leeds and Manchester as well as at many foreign universities. A solid academic record isn't the be-all and end-all though, and we're told that one of the essential qualities the firm looks for is the ability and desire to work really hard. "*Confidence, resilience and being able to maintain a positive demeanour under stress*" will also help you survive in this environment.

We got the impression that the social scene isn't too full on, as people recognise the importance of preserving friends and interests outside of the workplace. For those who fancy it, there's ample scope to socialise with colleagues, whether it's over impromptu post-work drinks at the in-house Budgie Bar or at a bigger event organised by the trainee liaison committee. Last year, the firm stumped up for a well-attended James Bond-themed ball. Sporty types are also well catered for. They can join the cricket, football, rugby, netball, softball, golf or sailing teams, and to satisfy their competitive nature there are even tournaments organised against other CC offices.

Opinion was divided on the firm's Canary Wharf location. Some of our sources hated the fact that "*it's far away from everything and can be a commuting nightmare,*" while others thought "*the place has great buzz about it and it puts you in the mood for doing business as soon as you step off the DLR.*" The ladies also mentioned the "*great shopping opportunities*" the area has to offer. One thing everyone agrees on is that CC's building is simply "*amazing.*" Often likened to a "*mini city,*" it offers an impressive range of amenities, including a health practice with dentist, hairdresser, dry cleaner, gym complete with swimming pool and, for those long nights, a 24-hour catering service.

It's freezing up here...

Whether it's because of the work they receive or their luxurious surroundings, trainees are left feeling spoiled, which explains why most hope to stay on qualification. Unsurprisingly, the economy took its toll in 2009 and, like other magic circle players, CC achieved a lower than usual retention rate of 102 out of 135 people. Fewer positions were available in the finance, capital markets and corporate departments, and even though the dispute resolution group created a few more positions, it wasn't enough to accommodate everyone. In light of this, trainees emphasised the importance of taking a coherent seat combination and also advised: "*You have to take matters in your own hands and have a quiet word with the hiring partner. You can't expect people to fight your corner if you haven't made any effort to network.*"

The firm also froze associates' salaries at 2008 levels, and our sources were not best pleased when NQ salaries fell from £66,000 to £59,000. That said, they were prepared to earn less because they wanted to continue to be part of the CC adventure. Said one: "*The firm remains a legal powerhouse and is still looking at expanding – these are difficult but exciting times to be joining Clifford Chance.*" Some of the 2009 starters had to wait until 2010, by our estimate possibly as many as 40 or so.

And finally...

If you are academically successful, passionate about working on big international deals for prominent clients and happy to join such a massive operation, then what are you waiting for?

Commercial awareness

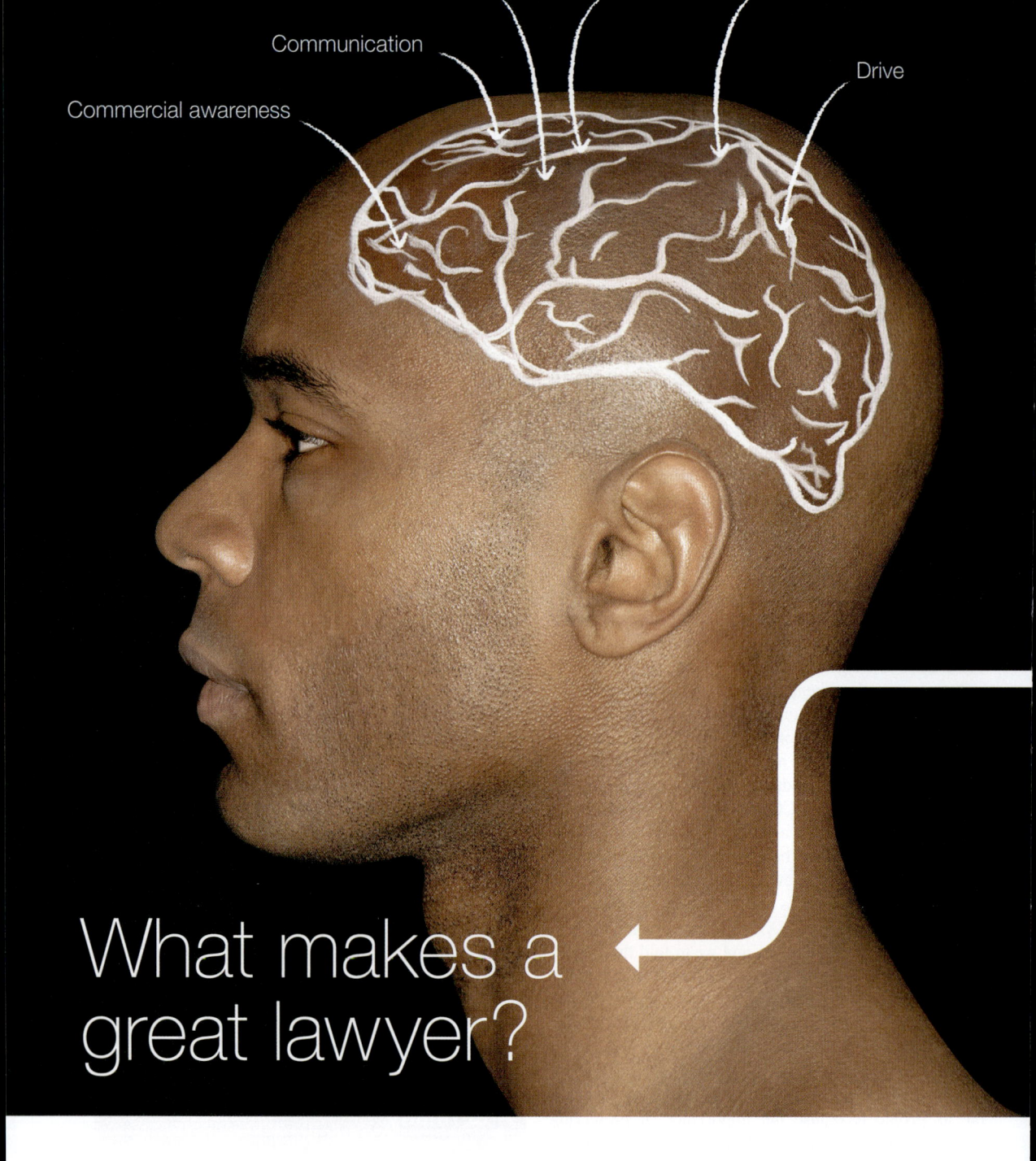

Communication

Drive

What makes a great lawyer?

At **Clyde & Co**, we believe that a variety of different qualities combine to make a really great lawyer. So if you've got what it takes, we'll provide the rest: first-class training and top-level exposure at an internationally renowned firm.

In terms of a career choice, we think it's a **no-brainer**.

Email us at: theanswers@clydeco.com
Apply at: www.clydeco.com/graduate

CLYDE&CO

Clyde & Co LLP

The facts
Location: London, Guildford
Number of UK partners/solicitors: 90/180
Total number of trainees: 48
Seats: 4x6 months
Alternative seats: Overseas seats
Extras: Pro bono – LawWorks, RCJ CAB, Surrey Law Centre, Lambeth Legal Advice Centre

> "*Someone who likes the variety of international work will love it. I've had a chance to work on matters in the USA, Guatemala, Mexico and Kenya in my time here.*"

Stints in Dubai, Piraeus, Abu Dhabi and Guildford are all possibilities for a trainee at this international firm with a penchant for the contentious.

On course

With a watertight reputation for shipping, aviation and insurance, Clydes is a top option for those looking to train at a global firm that focuses on something other than big banking and corporate deals. It has some 21 offices across four continents, and these earn it top rankings not only in *Chambers UK* but also in *Chambers Global* and *Chambers Asia*. It is particularly well established in the increasingly lucrative Middle Eastern market and recently represented the government of Yemen in a multibillion-dollar arbitration with an ExxonMobil/Hunt Oil joint venture company relating to the country's national resources and wealth.

Trainees are in no doubt that they are at a firm that's making waves, saying: "*Clydes is looking to expand and it is exciting to be a part of that.*" The global financial mess hasn't thwarted the firm's ambitions to spread across the world. For example, Clydes now has a precence in Riyadh in Saudi Arabia after forming an alliance with the Islamic finance specialist firm Abdulaziz Al Bosaily, and it has recently broken into the Indian legal market after forging ties with Indianfirm ALMT Legal. Clydes borrowed £45m to assist its international expansion programme (it has also opened two US offices in New York and San Francisco in recent years) and this investment seems to be paying off. In June 2009, it reported a turnover of £185m, up nearly 18% on the previous year. The firm also promoted a record number of associates to partner in 2009 – ten in total. Unsurprisingly then, our sources thought the firm was "*very well managed.*" Said one: "*Clyde's performance in the last few months speaks for itself. There have been few redundancies.*"

Although traditionally a firm that has prided itself on its contentious achievements, Clydes has made a push to build up its transactional side, particularly in relation to its core client sectors of shipping and aviation, where it does a considerable amount of financing work. In relation to corporate matters it sits solidly in London's mid-market alongside the likes of Bird & Bird, Nabarro and fellow shipping expert Stephenson Harwood. Like these other firms it often acts for AIM-listed clients.

All at sea

No department is compulsory in Clydes' four-seat training contract, and trainees tell us they are pleased with the flexibility shown by the firm in allocating assignments. It sounds as if there has been an improvement of late; according to one source the system has "*become more transparent and less of a lottery. Our graduate recruitment team is now really taking our preferences into account.*"

Before you imagine flitting from one top-choice seat to another, you must consider the firm's leanings as these govern the availability of seats. Shipping is the area with which Clydes is traditionally associated, and for good reason. It acts for shipowners, shipyards, ship financiers, ports, P&I clubs, traders, charterers, salvors and insurers on both contentious and non-contentious matters. For each of the past five years Clydes has been the top or joint top in the tables showing which firms have been involved in the highest number of reported cases in Lloyd's Shipping and Insurance law reports. Some of these cases run for years: the team is still acting on the insurance fallout from the grounding of the 'MSC Napoli' (the ship that ran aground off the coast of Devon back in 2007). It also worked on the arrangements for the release of the Thai-owned vessel 'Laemthong Glory' and its full cargo of sugar after it was seized by Somalian pirates, and on the 'Hyundai Fortune' case, which may prove to be the largest ever cargo loss as a result of a single maritime casualty.

Trainees with a nascent interest in the high seas but no background in marine law can rest easy, as Clydes provides a rigorous induction to the shipping team. You can find more details about this area of law on page 120, but all you need to know for the moment is that the department is split into 'wet' work (tort-based, involving collisions, salvage, piracy and so on) and 'dry' work (contract-based, involving, well, contractual matters). The shipping seat is praised for being "*varied and very busy*" with plenty of unusual research to do. Trainees spoke of helping to defend applications for interim injunctions and drafting correspondence and court submissions at various stages during the litigation process. The firm recently overturned a $100m freezing order in the High Court, and some trainees had dealt with newsworthy piracy and ship hijacking cases off the coast of Africa. The shipping finance team advises on a variety of sale and purchase transactions, new build projects and leasing arrangements. The superyacht market is also big business. This is a department where the firm's global reach is at its most obvious. Said one source: "*Someone who likes the variety of international work will love it, I've had a chance to work on matters in the USA, Guatemala, Mexico and Kenya in my time here.*"

The sky's the limit

More comfortable in the air than at sea? Clydes' top-flight aviation department can't be beat and it's even been luring in partners from rival firm Stephenson Harwood. The bread and butter of the group is the buying and selling of aircraft, and dealing with regulatory matters and investigations. For example, the team recently acted for a major airline in connection with the Aviation Commission's investigation into alleged cartel behaviour for air cargo surcharges. It also acted on a World Bank-funded project, advising on civil aviation policy for Ghana. Though long hours come as standard here, and they were "*plunged in at the deep end,*" trainees told us they enjoyed the fast-paced action and the strong rapport they built with the partners. The department was also thought to be "*less old-school*" than the more traditional shipping department.

The aviation litigation team takes on some fascinating cases, so nervous flyers may want to look away now. In one matter, the team advised on issues arising out of the crash of a Spanair flight in Madrid, which resulted in the death of all 172 passengers. Anyone looking at this seat must be comfortable with the idea of working on major air disasters such as this as "*Clydes is a world leader in it.*"

The third jewel in the firm's crown is its insurance and reinsurance practice. Clydes represents many of the key players in the industry, including ACE European Group, AXA and Hiscox. We were told that not only was the research quite interesting in this seat, but that the team itself was an easy one to get along with. In addition to dealing with marine and aviation matters, the insurance group works in all sorts of sectors, from healthcare to engineering to energy. Political risk insurance, for example, covers CEND – confiscation, expropriation, nationalisation and deprivation – and basically involves providing insurance to foreign investors in unstable countries where the laws may be slightly arbitrary or where there is political unrest. Recently the group was instructed by the insurers of a construction company that was repairing a bridge in the Czech Republic when it collapsed onto the track and was subsequently hit by an express train. Closer to home it advised on matters relating to flood damage to the British Motor Industry Heritage Centre in Warwickshire and defended claims made by farmers against the owner of the Purbright laboratory following an outbreak of foot and mouth in the vicinity in 2007. The insurance team is on a roll right now and recently scooped a team of three partners plus some associates from rival Barlow Lyde & Gilbert.

We're only here for the beer

Seats are also available in the firm's other departments, which include commercial dispute resolution; corporate and commercial; banking; construction; energy, trade and commodities; non-marine transport and logistics; EC/competition; employment; and real estate. The firm is winning some sweet transactional instructions, proving there's more to Clydes than litigation. Earlier in 2009 it advised the shareholders of brewer Cobra after it incurred debts of around £100m and was forced into pre-packaged administration. The company is now owned jointly by its founder Lord Bilimoria and large Canadian brewer Molson Coors.

Clydes' international reach allows trainees to sample life elsewhere in the world, though potential applicants should keep in mind that secondment opportunities are currently restricted to Dubai, Abu Dhabi, Piraeus and occasionally Hong Kong. Some were disappointed that they could not present a persuasive business case for six months in the Rio de Janeiro office; realistically the best chance of time in the sun is a posting to Dubai, which has the highest number of places available. The contentious lawyers here deal mostly with cases before the Dubai courts, while much of the corporate work for trainees involves setting up UAE companies. As is so often the case with overseas placements, our sources say that the responsibility on offer is higher than in London. "*In Dubai it's so busy; you get really good-quality work,*" confirmed one source, though another noted that "*the Dubai office is more political as the associates are under pressure to climb the career ladder.*" Our sources also reported being pleasantly surprised by the social opportunities available, telling us: "*The UAE-based lawyers got us involved with the culture of the region.*" Trainees in the Abu Dhabi and Greece offices may have to keep in mind the hermetic qualities of the seat: "*You can feel a little isolated from the other trainees,*" but the work is certainly engaging. In Greece, for example, "*you get to see the clients, who can sometimes be quite temperamental!*"

If an international seat is a definite possibility, a seat in Clydes' second UK office in Guildford is a certainty. Even though it's made expressly clear before the start of the training contract that six months in Surrey is pretty much non-negotiable, this is a perennial thorn in the side of many trainees, who describe it as "*a sore point.*" Despite the fact that travel expenses are reimbursed, the biggest complaint we received concerned how the commute affected trainees' work-life balance – some have to spend up to four hours a day travelling between their homes in London and the office in Guildford. "*They really should just recruit local trainees, it's quite a long trek,*" was a common theme. One trainee also warned that "*if there's a department you want to qualify into, don't do the equivalent in Guildford as it may affect your chances to qualify into that seat in London.*" Guildford is not without its charms, however, and it has some excellent work to boot. It scores *Chambers UK* rankings for corporate finance, employment, dispute resolution, IT and real estate in its region.

Corn law

In London, Clydes works out of two buildings, one on Eastcheap, the other just around the corner in the Corn Exchange. The latter is more focused on general commercial work, and trainees say it has a different ethos to that of the Eastcheap building. "*It's mandatory for guys to wear a tie in the Corn Exchange and it's more integrated as an office.*" Trainees can take advantage of a subsidised canteen and a well-laden fruit and snacks trolley that rattles along the corridors. They also spoke highly of the social scene: firm drinks are held frequently at two local hostelries – Auberge and The Ship. "*I quite like that there's no formulaic social scene going on,*" said one source; "*it's more casual here and you tend to socialise with your department more in the second year.*" A trainee social budget is available and has lately been used for things like bowling and karaoke. As for how late they have to work, well, for such a busy and successful firm you might be surprised to learn that the regime is "*not as stiff as other City law firms and we have generally good working hours.*" This, dear reader, is the advantage of working at a litigation-heavy law firm. One downside at Clydes is that many partners have quite an independent streak and this sets the tone in some teams. "*At times they could have made more structured plans for trainees to get access to work. Different partners deal with different things differently and I think it would have been good to balance things out. Sometimes in London they are more reluctant to let go of their work.*"

Very few trainees who find their way to Clydes are shot directly out of the university cannon. Many come from previous careers. "*Diversity is the standard here,*" and as befits a truly international firm, newbies come from a wide variety of backgrounds. At least two had a previous shipping connection and several were schooled abroad. Some of our sources were pleasantly surprised to discover how approachable people were at their initial interview: "*They weren't role-playing good cop, bad cop as firms usually do – I think they're all good cops here!*"

When it came to the qualification process in 2009, some second-years felt they had difficulty getting concrete information; few, however, could complain about the retention rate. By the time everything was finalised some 22 out of 25 qualifiers learned that they were being kept on.

Chambers UK rankings

Asset Finance	Insurance
Aviation	Product Liability
Capital Markets	Professional Negligence
Commodities	Projects, Energy & Natural
Construction	Resources
Corporate/M&A	Public International Law
Dispute Resolution	Real Estate
Employment	Restructuring/Insolvency
Fraud: Civil	Retail
Immigration	Shipping
Information Technology	Transport

And finally...

Clydes' traditional strength in litigation and the scope of its international interests have served it well in a tough economic climate, but it will doubtless want to continue its drive to bolster its transactional practices.

Talking point.

Intelligent conversations can win you friends in the highest places. For us, it was number 30, St. Mary Axe. You'll know it as the Gherkin. We advised property giant IVG when they wanted to acquire it. They talked to us, because we listened. Now we want new trainee solicitors to help us build more great relationships. So, let's talk. **Visit cmstalklaw.com**

Let's talk law

CMS

CMS Cameron McKenna LLP

The facts
Location: London
Number of UK partners/solicitors: 138/276
Total number of trainees: 116
Seats: 4x6 months
Alternative seats: Overseas seats, secondments
Extras: Pro bono – Islington Law Centre, ProHelp Bristol, Advocates for International Development, LawWorks; language training

One of the 'nice guys' of the City, this firm has great appeal for students looking beyond the magic circle but still wanting a heavyweight international training.

Top-ten City player CMS Cameron McKenna offers big deals with a friendly air and foreign travel with a distinctly Eastern European flavour.

CMS: BFG

The preconception that has followed Camerons around for years doesn't always sit well with its lawyers. *"They hate the fact they're called the friendly firm,"* said one of its trainees. *"They want to be seen as cutting-edge."* Yet it still rings true. In March 2009 Camerons was one of only ten law firms on the *Sunday Times'* list of the '100 Best Companies to Work For'. We're not saying this is a carefree firm where recruits have an easy ride. Far from it. *"We're clearly not in the magic circle,"* admitted a trainee, *"but I don't think there's any sense that magic circle people are better than us. Rather, they're more expensive. They have more gravitas, but we see ourselves as the best in the business."* Managing partner Duncan Weston is *"driving and pushing the firm forward,"* giving our interviewees the sense that *"our star is in the ascendant."* Camerons set itself the ambitious target of achieving an annual revenue of £250m by 2009, and it was well on its way to meeting this until the economic crisis took hold. It eventually fell just short of its goal, managing a total revenue of £240m: still a reasonable result.

Camerons was not unique in taking a hit from the poor economy, but what marked it out from many firms was a willingness to *"bend over backwards"* to avoid redundancies. Its most conventional move, perhaps, was to defer trainees' start dates by 12 months, offering a generous, no-strings payment of £7,500 into the bargain. Some 12 partners volunteered for de-equitisation, and instead of laying off lawyers in its quiet real estate group, the firm retrained and rehoused them elsewhere. It followed Norton Rose in offering staff a four-day week at 85% of pay, and a sabbatical option was also put on the table. Unfortunately, these measures weren't sufficient to prevent the redundancies of 27 fee earners and 46 other staff in the first half of 2009. Nonetheless, trainees appreciated the firm's efforts, telling us at the time: *"It is doing its best to keep as many people as it can and that's certainly something I'd look for if I were starting out."* *"These are tough times,"* acknowledged one, *"but we'll come out smelling of roses."*

Let's talk about seats

During their four seats, trainees must visit either corporate or banking and spend one seat in a litigation department and one on secondment. The fourth can theoretically be in any of the firm's other practice groups. Corporate and banking are, in the words of one trainee, *"essentially what the firm is about."* The former's 250 transactions in 2008 put it sixth in the Mergermarket European volume league table, and *Chambers UK* ranks Camerons in London's top band for mid-market corporate deals and Band 4 for high-end deals. Lawyers acted for Talisman Energy in the $480m sale of Dutch subsidiary Goal Petroleum to Total, and helped Nuffield Hospitals with its acquisition of the Cannons Group, which required the sale of nine hospitals for £140m. Interviewees' experiences of the *"very Darwinian"* corporate seat ranged from having *"a hell of a lot of work"* to being *"completely dead."* The idea is that trainees solicit work from around the group if they have time on their hands or want more responsibility. Proof-reading?

"Yes, it does happen, but not so much that you get sick of it," and because recruits "never really do copying and scanning" they're "not just standing there doing mundane tasks all day." Past highlights for the banking team include representing HBOS as it funded the £95m acquisition of UK ticketing agency See Group, and advising Lloyds TSB and Allied Irish Banks on the management buyout of home and gardens emporium Robert Dyas. The deal was expected to safeguard the future of 1,200 jobs and 99 stores across the UK.

Another of the firm's biggest departments is energy, and it's a consistently popular choice among trainees. The group was experiencing a lull when we interviewed though, and recruits were researching and writing articles for client publications. The team is prominent in the oil and gas sector, recently advising BP and the Abu Dhabi National Energy Company on acquiring interests in North Sea oil fields. It has been pushing to expand its capabilities in renewables and energy/emissions trading, and to this end it recently merged with the firm's highly rated environment group, where "you've got to keep up to date as this green revolution is producing a constant flow of new regulations." Camerons also has a nice line in nuclear decommissioning and is retained by the Atomic Weapons Establishment. Working closely with the energy lawyers is a team of projects lawyers. Accomplished transport experts advised the Indian Ministry of Railways on the redevelopment of New Delhi Railway Station and London Underground on the long-running Victoria Line upgrade.

Rounding off the 'EPC' division is a construction group. This team works on both contentious and non-contentious matters for clients such as EDF Energy, Imperial College London, the National Maritime Museum and Great Ormond Street Hospital. Trainees were full of praise for its "absolutely brilliant" lawyers: "They're stand-up guys – great on the social scene but really get their heads down when they work." Early starts are the norm, and "if you start at 7am you might be the last one in." Sticking with contentious practice, commercial litigation is "hugely popular from a trainee point of view." If your timing is lucky, you get plenty of chances "to attend court as well as do background research." The team's reputation is still riding high from representing Ferrari in the 2007 F1 'Spygate' scandal, but some of its more recent matters are equally worthy of attention. Its action on behalf of H. Clarkson & Co, the world's largest shipbroker, in claims relating to allegations of bribery and conspiracy has been named one of The Lawyer's top ten court cases of 2009, and Camerons' litigators are defending trendy London eatery Cipriani in a dispute over naming brought by the Cipriani Hotel in Venice. We suggest you check out Chambers UK for details of just how well the firm does across its full range of practices.

Chambers UK rankings

Advertising & Marketing	Life Sciences
Banking & Finance	Outsourcing
Banking Litigation	Pensions
Capital Markets	Pensions Litigation
Competition/European Law	Planning
Construction	Private Equity
Corporate/M&A	Professional Negligence
Dispute Resolution	Projects, Energy & Natural Resources
Employee Share Schemes	Public Procurement
Employment	Real Estate
Environment	Real Estate Finance
Financial Services Regulation	Real Estate Litigation
Immigration	Restructuring/Insolvency
Information Technology	Tax
Insurance	Telecommunications
Intellectual Property	Transport

Here no evil, CEE no evil

Trainees' second seats are usually spent outside Camerons' main Mitre House office near the Barbican Centre. They can visit one of the firm's clients or another CMS Cameron McKenna office, either in the UK or the Central and Eastern Europe region. Presentations tell trainees what kind of work to expect in each – for example, Moscow offers corporate, banking and real estate. Trainees fill out a form, ticking as many options as they fancy, and we hear that with so many people to be accommodated you'll be doing HR and yourself a favour by selecting more than one. "There were people in our intake who only ticked one box. I don't think any of them got what they wanted." Some sources saw allocation as "a bit of a mystery," but others seemed to understand that it is based on interviews and feedback from supervisors. Consistently popular destinations include Budapest, where "you work with hugely intelligent people" and are "expected to be as intelligent as them," and Moscow, which is "a bit more laid-back" and lets trainees see matters "right from due diligence all the way through to until post-completion." Anyone going abroad gets 10-20 hours of language lessons before they leave and continued lessons on arrival. One source hypothesised that trainees are "almost guaranteed" a seat abroad given the number of people in each intake who typically want to stay in the UK.

Six months in a domestic office is hardly drawing the short straw. Bristol's strong insurance practice is "popular with people who want to get out of London and save some money... and with people in relationships." A source confided that the energy work in Aberdeen sometimes requires trainees go out on the rigs. "Stunning countryside, skiing in the Cairngorms and trips to Balmoral" are just some of the distractions on offer in

Scotland. "*I now have a penchant for deep-fried haggis,*" admitted a recruit. Client secondments also elicited rave reviews. Among those typically on offer are recently bailed-out AIG ("*even more popular now as you get the inside gossip*"), Exxon, National Australia Bank, Goldman Sachs and the Wellcome Trust, which was praised for its "*fantastic*" atmosphere and the chance to "*do something worthwhile*" for a charity.

Making the grade

"*One of the problems*" of formal training, confessed an interviewee, "*is there's so much of it, it can get in the way of you doing any work. I had three hours of it this morning* [a Thursday]. *None yesterday, but two hours on Tuesday and tomorrow we've got another hour.*" There's no official mentoring scheme but our interviewees couldn't see the need for one given other avenues of help. Even library staff are "*always happy to point you in the right direction.*" Additionally, each intake elects two trainee representatives ('Treps') to attend monthly meetings with the graduate recruitment team and training partner "*to voice any concerns people have anonymously.*" Mid and end-of-seat appraisals are "*honest*" and "*generally useful,*" although they were the subject of one of the few criticisms we heard. Trainees are given an appraisal grade from one to six, but "*scores don't seem to be applied across the board in a standard way.*" More than one recruit complained it was "*not fair if you get someone who never gives out fives or sixes, even though you slogged away, while someone else gets a six for just as much.*"

It was an especially pertinent "*bugbear*" for trainees when we interviewed them in the run-up to qualification. Those finishing in September 2009 were expecting worse-than-average job prospects, partly because of very high March 2009 retention, when jobs were offered to 26 of 29 qualifiers. In our summer interviews with them trainees told us: "*We're pretty sure that because of that we'll be thrown to the lions. It was all looking very healthy, but then after Christmas things dropped off.*" The firm's honesty and willingness to talk about the issue with trainees was appreciated. "*One of the things I like about Camerons is they're straight down the line about this kind of thing,*" said a trainee. "*They're not going to screw me over,*" added another. As it turned out, 22 of the 30 September qualifiers were kept on, making for a total of 48 out of 59 in 2009. Most were permanent NQ jobs, some were paralegal roles and some were initially arranged as secondments to clients. As for the deferral of new starters, those who delayed their arrival by a year were offered a £7,500 payment.

Nice guys finish this report

Trainees are given a budget for socialising. Last year the money went towards pub quizzes, a comedy night, a boat cruise and a roller disco ("*in fancy dress with neon colours, the lot*"). Camerons organises a few blowouts, including a trainee ball, and there are ample sporting opportunities. Just before our interviews a team of lawyers and trainees had returned from a seven-a-side tournament in Valencia, where they'd beaten PwC in the final. The annual CMS World Cup brings together players from CMS offices across the international network, so although you can't do a seat in Zagreb, you can tackle its lawyers on the football pitch. Individual departments – litigation is notoriously sociable – host Christmas lunches, away days and after-work drinks, but most trainee socialising is spur of the moment. Of course impromptu need not mean unpredictable. "*If anyone wants to meet anybody from Camerons, including partners, I suggest they go to the Hand & Shears on a Friday night,*" chuckled one trainee. This tiny and often crammed boozer is a hit with those who believe a proper pub should serve a proper pint of ale. To keep a promise to one of our sources we'd like to mention Arthur, the "*proper old-school landlord,*" who will hopefully now offer that trainee a free pint.

When it comes to the kind of candidate Camerons is looking for, we end as we began. Friendliness is one of the few constants we could discern in an otherwise varied group of trainees. "*On the whole,*" said one, "*I think the way Camerons tries to recruit is to look at personality.*" We should also reiterate that with its extensive European presence the firm offers much to multilingual candidates, and anyone interested in the EPC seats should certainly apply. Ultimately, most people will probably simply be attracted by the firm's reputation as a nice place to practise City law. Trainees had many stories of partners asking after them when they were ill and teams creating a "*familial atmosphere*" by putting up pictures from social events in the shared kitchen spaces. These things clearly matter at Camerons.

And finally...

FYI: Trainees wanted readers to know that, contrary to suspicions, the recruitment team "*deliberately doesn't ask us to give feedback*" on vac schemers. It does however solicit impressions of those they meet at law fairs. You know what to do...

cobbetts | graduate recruitment

FUTURE PROOF

At Cobbetts LLP, we're developing the next generation of legal talent.

Our partners and solicitors have the expertise to turn our trainees into confident and capable newly qualified solicitors. Future proof your future and let them release your potential.

With over 87 partners and 650 staff, we are a leading full service law firm with offices in Birmingham, Leeds, London and Manchester. No hard sell, no exaggerated promises.

Apply on-line for training contracts and easter and summer vacation placements. Visit www.cobbettsgraduate.com for more information, plus blogs, videos and trainee profiles.

YOUR FUTURE STARTS HERE...

Cobbetts LLP

The facts

Location: Manchester, Birmingham, Leeds, London

Number of UK partners/solicitors: 90/254

Total number of trainees: 37

Seats: 5 x approx. 5 months

Alternative seats: Occasional secondments

It's been as tough a year for Cobbetts as any other firm but we found trainees in good spirits nonetheless.

Property-heavy Cobbetts spent much of the past decade fanning out from its Manchester HQ through a series of mergers. It went west to Leeds in 2002 and south to Birmingham in 2004.

Merger market

Having grown quickly and convincingly to join the UK top 50, the firm then needed to streamline a partnership that had become cluttered by mergers and donned a more corporate hat. It got shot of its family department, opened up a small corporate-focused London office in 2007 and fattened up its corporate department elsewhere. As if to ring in the changes, it moved into fresh offices in all locations, each one branded to look alike. Things were looking up again. The shake-up boosted the firm's financials to a degree, and our overall impression last year was of a firm reinvigorated by change. Then of course, the recession's emaciated fist came knocking at the door, a swathe of redundancies had to be made (largely in the property and corporate departments) and the transactional departments slowed to a four-day week.

Cobbetts' current strategy is that *"there will be no fundamental change of direction,"* meaning that the long-standing focus on property and the organic growth of the corporate department is set to continue. Despite slipping in some of the *Chambers UK* rankings in the past couple of years, the firm told us it *"has had a clear strategy that it will continue to pursue... we think that because many competitors are London focused there is a space in the market for a firm that can focus on the regions but also have a national presence at the same time."* Arguably, the firm has been wrong-footed. The recent boom years filled the firm's coffers so an increasingly corporate stance made great business sense. But having pushed in this direction, Cobbetts was caught by the change in the economy. When property and corporate were no longer cash cows, the parts of the firm doing brisker business became commercial and banking litigation and social housing. The strategy seems now to be one of paring down and consolidating; holding on and waiting for the recession to ease. In a valiant effort to save jobs and to retailor the firm *"people were redeployed internally, migrating property and banking people into banking litigation."* Cobbetts has also hired new talent (some at senior level and from the likes of Pinsent Masons), including into its busier employment and social housing departments.

Kendall Mint

This year's interviews with trainees were rather schizophrenic. Some told us the firm was coping admirably, tackling a tough situation with steely pragmatism and giving them a great training with plenty of challenges. They said redundancies had chopped away the fat, making for ample work, even in the recession-swept departments of property and corporate. Others said the firm had taken a hammering and that there was insufficient work to keep them busy. It's hard to know who to believe when positive and negative comments came from all offices, from trainees who'd been offered jobs and those who hadn't. The mid-ground of the debate was best summed up by the trainee who said they *"loved it when it was busy."* On a more certain note, trainees unanimously offered praise for Cobbetts' style of working. They were won over by how friendly the firm was, many describing near epiphanies brought on by the working environment, sleek offices and the good nature of staff. Despite cutbacks, the irrepressible folk at Cobbetts told us morale had "*bounced back.*"

Cobbetts training has just switched to a five-seat rotation. This innovation was introduced to the trainees by way of "*something we found in a photocopier.*" First it looked like it was going to be rolled out in a fortnight, then it was scrapped at the behest of some partners, then it was scheduled for a September 2009 start. There have also been changes in HR: "*…people coming and going. Someone left and wasn't replaced for six months at one point.*" Fortunately, trainees say new grad recruitment adviser Paul Kendall has already begun to improve communications and sort things out, for example by getting the appraisal system running smoothly again.

Going for gold

"*There's a similar choice of seats in Birmingham, Leeds and Manchester,*" trainees told us. Around half of the group works in Manchester, with the remainder spread between Leeds and Birmingham. The smaller London office does not accept trainees at present. Worth knowing, too, is the fact that because "*property envelops everything and provides useful foundation knowledge*" most trainees will do a property-related seat.

Although trainees acknowledged that the corporate and property departments had quietened, it hasn't all been doom and gloom. The firm has demonstrated its ability to grab a decent share of what work is going around, even in the constricted world of banking. It acted for Swinton Group on a revised working capital and acquisition finance facility for £175m from Lloyds TSB, making Swinton the UK's biggest insurance retailer. It also worked for the Bank of Scotland on funding for the acquisition of the Grafton Shopping Centre in Altrincham. Over in the related field of corporate finance there was more work to be done for Swinton when it acquired Equity Insurance Brokers for £50m, and the firm also acted in public markets advising Royal Bank of Canada and Strand Partners on Central African Gold's £15.6m fund-raising for gold projects in Africa. Impressively, Cobbetts is up there with the big boys when it comes to advising AIM-listed companies. The overwhelming impression of the corporate seat from trainees was that when there was work, there was decent responsibility. Alas the sporadic nature of new instructions has left some trainees "*twiddling their thumbs*" or doing low-quality tasks.

Following the slowdown in commercial and residential property development, Cobbetts had to make redundancies across its network. And yet even in these parched times the firm has been involved in some decent deals. The firm continues to be instructed by Orange in relation to its network of communications masts and, also in telecoms, lawyers have drafted legal precedents for Freedom4 (formerly Pipex) in connection with the roll-out of its electronic communications portfolio. Important client Whitbread used Cobbetts in all aspects of a £78m swap of 41 pub restaurants for 21 hotels owned by Mitchells & Butlers.

When the private sector dries up, law firms look to the public purse. Cobbetts was already an experienced name in the field of social housing and it has chosen to further boost its capacity here by hiring extra staff and partners. It has acted for Salford City Council on a huge overhaul of its housing strategy entailing the transfer of stock to new landlords. It has also scored work from Warrington Borough Council, which is developing a large mixed-use scheme with an eight-screen cinema, 97-bed hotel, office, leisure and retail space, residential apartments and 'an enhanced public realm' (which we think means a fancy pedestrianised area).

Pizza the action

A trainee in the "*quite exciting*" litigation department reminded us about the old adage of 'when in doubt, sue.' This motto has clearly been adopted by enough of Cobbetts' clients to make the litigation department the busiest. The experience and training was considered to be good, and trainees spoke of working some of the longest hours here. Our sources had been kept busy on "*winding-up petitions and bankruptcies,*" meaning that they'd been able to attend court to obtain charging orders and other rulings. Some had also assisted on injunctions and mediations. Notable cases from the past year include advising the Secretary of State for Business Enterprise and Regulatory Reform on the winding up of an unregulated debt management company. This case involved some serious allegations and a five-day trial.

The firm's strong property focus means that trainees can take a contentious construction law seat. They spoke of a "*good, sociable team*" and detailed what had kept them busy, for example establishing culpability for delays and

Chambers UK rankings

Banking & Finance	Intellectual Property
Banking Litigation	Licensing
Charities	Pensions
Construction	Planning
Corporate/M&A	Private Client
Debt Recovery	Real Estate
Dispute Resolution	Real Estate Litigation
Employment	Restructuring/Insolvency
	Social Housing

missed deadlines on building projects. To gain a better understanding of matters, trainees sometimes go on site (sporting snazzy Cobbetts-branded hard hats). A seat in non-contentious construction is "*very contract-heavy*" and largely involves wading through documents in order to "*make sure that the chain of contracts links up.*" One trainee spoke of the satisfaction gained from "*walking past a building that you have prepared the collateral warranties for.*"

If the recession has been like a cloud over some departments then the increased workload experienced by the banking litigation, employment and insolvency teams is the silver lining. The firm recruited from HSBC to boost its banking litigation team in order to deal with the volume of new cases, and trainees said there was "*plenty of work to get on with*" as banks take stock of the debts on their books. One trainee had gone into the seat feeling apprehensive about the idea of a busy six months spent foreclosing on mortgages and recovering properties, but they felt welcomed by the team and fulfilled by the work, especially mortgage fraud cases where "*there's a lot of research and investigating – it became quite sophisticated and involved the Serious Fraud Office.*"

The insolvency seat is a good place to develop drafting skills and observe transactions involving distressed businesses. One source summed it up as "*lots of sales and purchases, debentures, guarantees, and management and trading agreements to work on.*" The scope of the cases varies considerably, so sometimes trainees will make a small contribution to bigger matters and at other times they will handle their own files. Proving that financial problems can hit anyone, one trainee worked on the case of an insolvent Premiership footballer.

In the employment department clients range from pizza manufacturer Dr Oetker to home shopping group Shop Direct and local authorities in Blackpool, Stockport and Blackburn. Trainees gain good insight into contentious cases, with multimillion-pound equal-pay claims, TUPE class actions and discrimination tribunals all covered. One trainee told us that they reached the point where they were "*running files on my own like an NQ.*" In other practice news, the firm is starting to assemble an energy team, and trainees have hinted at "*a big push in renewables.*"

Future tense

Our sources heaped praise on those supervisors who made efforts to ensure they were up to date on matters and happily pointed out that there was always someone they could go to with questions. Nevertheless, they did find some supervisors more attentive than others. Trainees asserted that claims of a good work-life balance were well founded at Cobbetts. Save for the litigation department, where sometimes people are there until 8 or 9pm, "*in all other departments there's no reason you can't be out the office by 5.30 or 6pm.*" Manageable hours mean plenty of time for extra-curricular activities and we hear that "*the amount the firm spends on activities is amazing.*" Drifting briefly into hyperbole, someone described the Cobbetts Young Professionals group as "*the future.*" The networking group is certainly popular and well invested in. Strictly speaking, involvement isn't compulsory but "*if you weren't involved people would wonder why.*" The Junior Lawyers Division of the Law Society offers yet more activities, and then there are charity events and impromptu meet-ups between trainees. In general the firm has a pretty lively social calendar.

Right now, Cobbetts' long-term direction is a "*slightly mystifying*" subject to some trainees. There was wildly disparate feedback on how busy the firm is; that said, looking at deals it has been involved with in the past year, Cobbetts is clearly still getting good instructions, especially in the silver lining areas of litigation, insolvency and employment. In terms of retention, the firm has done reasonably well: out of 25 qualifying trainees, 17 got jobs in 2009. Much to the horror of some of of our sources, the firm cut the NQ salary from £38,000 to £30,000 to keep more people on. A few sources worried what signal this would send to the market about where Cobbetts sat in the pantheon of large regional law firms. For those without jobs, the firm took the praiseworthy steps of offering advice sessions and talking to clients to scout out possible vacancies. The 2009 intake of trainees were given the option to defer, and in light of some of the comments we heard this year, some deferrals were clearly necessary, especially given the relatively high number of new NQs that will now be soaking up simpler instructions and tasks.

It's possible to see something of Voltaire's Candide in Cobbetts' personality. As much as we enjoyed speaking to the trainees, who largely seemed very happy with their choice of firm, we were left with concerns over just how hard the recession had affected the firm's financial performance. Cobbetts has a relatively narrow profit margin compared to many rivals and in 2008/09 revenue plunged by 16%. Logic says this will have hurt profits badly, which is surely a real concern. Do look into this further, as we were unable to before going to press.

And finally...

This is one firm that is hoping the bear market will metamorphose into a bull again soon. If so, Cobbetts should be ready for things to take off.

Coffin Mew LLP

The facts

Location: Southampton, Fareham, Portsmouth, Gosport
Number of UK partners/solicitors: 27/48
Total number of trainees: 10
Seats: 6x4 months
Alternative seats: Occasional secondments

At Coffin Mew you are looked after, consulted and feel involved in its success, but you shouldn't assume that this is a soft-touch firm or a soft-touch training contract.

Coffin Mew trainees benefit from exposure to a careful balance of commercial and private client work. Embedded in the local community, this firm is a South Coast oasis from City law.

Padgi Nation

Let's get things straight: "*If you're the kind of person that is not interested in the City but does want commercial work, this is a good place to be.*" Especially if you're also hankering after the very different world of private client practice. One commercially minded source said: "*The reason I came here was the mix of work. There are high-value clients from London and smaller regional clients, which means you can get more involved.*" As a trainee in the family seat told us: "*It's real people, it's real problems and it's real life.*" How fitting then that the firm has a social housing department nationally recognised by *Chambers UK* and an excellent team working in the niche area of brain injury cases.

In the six-seat training contract your first three seats are selected for you, thereafter there is more choice. "*Six weeks after starting we identify the top three seats we'd like to do and why, and one we don't want to do and why.*" The firm makes no bones about the fact that trainees are often most closely scrutinised in a seat they didn't fancy. And why not? It's surely a good way to gauge character. Whether you spend multiple seats in the same department or try out something different every time, the training contract is made to suit you. As one satisfied interviewee put it: "*You can carve out your own path with the support of the firm, and that's not an opportunity you get everywhere.*" Training partner Malcolm Padgett has an uncanny eye for such tailoring. He receives substantial praise year after year, and current trainees assure us this is justified. "*Malcolm is one of the characters that embodies the firm. He's very friendly and great fun, but there's still a level of professionalism and commercial-mindedness. He's such a good advert for the firm when it's looking to bring trainees in.*"

The family business

So, what's available for the six seats? Our interviewees undertook a real range – corporate; commercial property; commercial services; commercial litigation; family; insolvency; personal injury; contentious and non-contentious social housing; employment and private client. At the time of our interviews, employment was proving popular. Acting for both employers and employees, sources were glad to "*see both sides of the story*" and praised the fact there was "*a lot more scope to get involved in lower-value employee work.*" Trainees experience both contentious and non-contentious work in this seat. Said one: "*I went to employment tribunals and sat behind counsel, but also drafted contracts, policy documents and handbooks.*" Trainees also found themselves playing an assisting role in some of the bigger cases. Clients come from the public and private sectors, and matters include discrimination and workplace bullying. The variety of work and opportunity for advocacy make commercial litigation an enjoyable posting. The department acts for some of the region's major businesses on cases relating to everything from property disputes and breaches of contract to defamation, partnership bust-ups and debt collection.

The impressive personal injury team acts *"solely for claimants"* and specialises in brain injury claims – often worth in excess of £1m – and clinical negligence, for which there is often legal aid funding. Praised for being *"well-structured,"* this seat sees the trainee undertaking duties relating to costs, assisting with legal aid applications and attending court hearings and conferences with counsel.

Moving away from litigation, transactional work abounds in the commercial property seat. Trainees learn to draft and exchange and complete contracts, often working for developers on residential properties. One such example is a major mixed-use development in Greenwich worth £10m. Closer to home, the firm advises the University of Portsmouth on property matters and is currently working on the refinancing of a marina on the Isle of Wight with Nordic banking giant Handelsbanken.

From dealing with global banks to the intricacies of family law, we can't emphasise enough the varied opportunities at Coffin Mew. One family law devotee advises: *"You've got to be a people person to be able to do it,"* informing us that *"you develop a completely different set of skills than you would in a more commercial practice area."* Dealing predominantly with divorces, the family and childcare department also handles child protection cases. A trainee can expect court attendance and client meetings alongside petition drafting and other more desk-bound duties. Just as 'up close and personal' is the private client seat. A trainee raved: *"You get so much client contact – even in the first week they'll let you loose on the clients."* In this department, trainees are given files to run and typically will handle the affairs of clients who are unable to manage themselves due to frailty or illness. One interviewee told us: *"I'm the first point of contact for clients calling in and I deal with small queries about wills or powers of attorney."* These two departments act for a mixed clientele that includes both wealthy people (some from overseas) and those with more modest incomes. Given the firm's location, it's no surprise that it represents many armed forces personnel.

The cat's mew

Coffin Mew is split over four sites in Southampton, Portsmouth (North Harbour), Fareham and Gosport. It's typical to take seats in two or three different offices (Gosport doesn't host trainees) and secondments are also available so a car is pretty essential unless you're prepared to put yourself at the mercy of public transport. Despite the multi-site set up sometimes *"proving a bit awkward on the travelling side,"* trainees are not too concerned by their intimate knowledge of the M27. Insisting the firm *"identifies as one,"* they praise the effort made to *"keep the offices together."* This is done through social events and cross-referrals of work. Apparently *"no one hoards their work here."*

Chambers UK rankings

Clinical Negligence	Personal Injury
Corporate/M&A	Real Estate
Employment	Real Estate Litigation
Family/Matrimonial	Restructuring/Insolvency
Intellectual Property	Social Housing

A far cry from the corporate machines of London, Coffin Mew is proud of its community roots. This is a distinctively South Coast firm, with most of its trainees either having existing ties to the area or a passion that prompted them to relocate. As one told us: *"I'm local and have always known about Coffins."* Parents and elders commonly *"only had very good things to say about the firm."* Trainees singled out its association with The Honeypot Charity, which is big in Hampshire, as an example of engaging with the community. A recent charity breakfast for Red Nose Day saw a bunch of trainees cooking up a storm and wheeling fresh butties around the offices to raise money. Not that it's all about do-gooding: *"This morning I had an e-mail about a netball tournament,"* chuckled one. *"Most of us haven't played since school, but I replied to say I'd have a go and practically everyone else did too saying, 'Let's do it!'"* Fancy dress parties at Christmas, networking events and the varied calendar of the local branch of the Junior Lawyers Division keep this affable bunch entertained.

This is a firm where you are looked after, consulted and feel involved in its success. What this breeds is a happy, positive group of trainees, but you shouldn't assume that this is a soft-touch firm or a soft-touch training contract. In an uncertain economy Coffin Mew says its recent decision to move to a more corporate-style structure led by a CEO shows *"the firm's willingness to address strategic planning for the future in a professional manner."* In 2009 it kept on four of its seven qualifiers, but in response to the downturn was forced to make some redundancies and defer a handful of incoming trainees.

And finally…

Coffin Mew is one of the Solent's most established law firms. It has a real family feel and an excellent tailored training contract. Whether you're local and want to stay in the area or looking to relocate down South, this is a good bet.

Covington & Burling LLP

the facts

Location: London
Number of UK partners/solicitors: 17/29 + 5 US-qualified
Total number of trainees: 11
Seats: 4x6 months
Alternative seats: Secondments
Extras: Language training

> "*Covington is moving increasingly Eastward. We are looking long-term at India... London will play a key role in linking the firm to its Far Eastern operations.*"
>
> Grant Castle, Training Principal

Covington & Burling is a regulatory law specialist with rapidly growing transactional and litigation capabilities in London.

Kings from the Hill

Part of the Washington, DC Establishment, Covington was founded in 1919 and has always stayed close to the heart of US government. One of its first associates went on to become a Secretary of State, and senior partner Eric Holder became the first African-American US Attorney General. Last year was the 20th anniversary of the firm's arrival in London. In the past two decades it has built a reputation in the regulatory field that belies its small size. *Chambers UK* ranks Covington among the best for life sciences, data protection and product liability advice. Not content to leave it there though, the London office has "*changed fundamentally to become a full-service firm... our regulatory and industry knowledge can help us provide better services and add value when looking at big-ticket litigation and corporate work,*" argued training principal and life sciences partner Grant Castle, explaining the firm's recent push to expand other practices.

The plan, in short, is to grow. With a Beijing office already established, and sidelong glances being cast at India, "*London will play a key role in linking Covington to its Far Eastern operations.*" A firm-wide '2012 Strategy' plans for the UK office "*to grow, not aggressively – Covington never does anything particularly aggressively – but in a clear and obvious way.*" It aims to have 80 lawyers within four years and "*the training programme is an important element of that growth process.*" As such, Covington has upped its annual intake from four trainees to six. Trainees all spend six months in litigation and six in corporate, reflecting the priority the firm now places on these practices.

Oil, drugs, booze and hogs

AstraZeneca, Merck, Novartis, Genentech, Pfizer, Wyeth, Johnson & Johnson, GE Healthcare: all the great and good of the pharmaceutical, biotech and medical device industries have Covington on speed dial. As well as the core food and drug regulatory work carried out by the firm, trainees can get involved in transactional and IP work for its clients. Advice on labelling, due diligence on M&A matters, High Court patent disputes and incorporating subsidiaries are among the things recruits might see. "*My supervisor will give me a brief on what the client wants, I'll go away and do the research,*" said one. "*On the more commercial side it's reviewing agreements to make sure obligations are being complied with.*" Closely tied in with life sciences is product liability. Lawyers have advised animal health company Merial on government investigations and litigation brought by the National Farmers' Union following the foot-and-mouth outbreak of July 2007.

The IP/IT team does a similarly broad, if different range of regulatory, litigation and transactional work. It helps long-standing clients like the Business Software Alliance and Microsoft navigate EU policy initiatives, and lobbies government on behalf of the tech sector, so trainees will often be "*keeping track of legislation and seeing what the European Parliament is up to.*" The team is especially noted for its internet enforcement work and has been training cybercrime units in Nigeria, Russia, Egypt and the EU. The data protection team, headed by trainee favourite Dan Cooper, fixed a feather in its cap last year with its appointment to assist Privacy International in filing an amicus brief for the case of Marper v the United Kingdom, which ruled that the government's retention of fingerprints and DNA samples of unconvicted persons was illegal. Those who'd done this seat told us *"responsibility builds pretty quickly,"* with Cooper regularly asking for trainees' input and taking them to client meetings.

Corporate, now the biggest single team in the London office, is increasingly central to Covington's business. The group advises an array of clients; certainly a lot from the life sciences and IP teams' address books, but also the British Horseracing Authority, Baltic Oil Terminals and fashion labels like Giorgio Armani. A trainee's experience really *"depends on who you sit with,"* but it typically boils down to research, writing memos and drafting board minutes and prospectuses. The litigation team does a lot of work for Covington's established food and drug clients, also regularly acting for names like ExxonMobil, Bacardi, Harley Davidson and National Geographic. On the arbitration side, high-value insurance coverage issues crop up, and one source had spent time *"writing very in-depth memos – really getting into the cases, with word-by-word analysis of what we thought on a particular issue. It taught me a lot."*

Trainees can also go on secondment to a number of clients, including pharmaceutical companies, where they *"basically deal with every single matter that comes in."* There are plans to make secondments more available as the trainee intake increases. There is not yet a formal programme of overseas seats, although bespoke three-month stints in Brussels and the USA have taken place in the past.

Leave it to the prose

Most weeks, a few hours of training given by practice groups, either in London or in the States via video conference, keep trainees up to date with current legal issues or explain the US perspective. Covington cultivates an academic, studious environment that prizes abstract legal ponderings and *"immense attention to detail."* For example, *"quality writing is seen as hugely important."* *"My first piece of work came back to me with more red ink than white paper,"* admitted one slightly embarrassed source. Corrections generally address *"the general concept of how to write"* rather than being *"pernickety"* for the sake of it. There are *"some very smart people here,"* our sources said, suggesting a sort of professorial vibe among lawyers. *"The partners' offices look like studies, with pictures on the walls, hearth rugs and coffee machines. One even has a cuckoo clock!"* Most sources rejected any implication that the firm was *"dusty and academic."* Much seems to pivot on whether you're on the regulatory or the corporate side, as one helpful trainee outlined: *"Regulatory law is academic – it's interpretation of statutes – and much of the end product is written. In corporate you have e-mails and calls left, right and centre, and your advice is given as much orally as in writing."*

Chambers UK rankings

Data Protection	Life Sciences
Dispute Resolution	Private Equity
Insurance	Product Liability

A fine balance

There's a common assumption that US firms own their staff 24/7, but while *"there are times when you have to work late,"* it doesn't happen consistently at Covington. Obviously *"it's a balancing act: if you want input on big deals you have to expect to work for it,"* but *"office hours are 9am to 6pm and if you leave at 6pm no one will look at you funny."* Interviewees appreciated the *"grown-up attitude,"* whereby *"if you need to work from home one morning because the plumber's coming, you can."* Another, more positive aspect to life at an American firm is the greater emphasis placed on pro bono work. Trainees can take a lead role on pro bono cases, even going to court or on overseas trips. Last year an NQ was sent to Beijing to assist the International Paralympic Committee with anti-doping efforts.

The typical Covington personality is pretty modest; *"none of us here are big boasters or schmoozy people."* While the life sciences practice regularly ensures a number of applicants with science backgrounds, a degree in a particular subject (or from a certain institution) is unlikely to affect anyone's chances of securing an interview. *"If you want to work with academic types from Yale and Harvard you can find that,"* shrugged one interviewee. *"However, a lot of people like myself haven't been to elite Ivy League or Oxbridge universities and have a more commercial outlook."*

Socialising entails a fortnightly Thursday drinks trolley and various annual events. The Fourth of July barbecue and Thanksgiving lunch are balanced out by more British St George's and St Patrick's Day jollies. There is *"a sporty atmosphere,"* with softball, netball and rugby available. Although Covington lawyers are *"not ultra-competitive,"* the softball team plays successfully against other firms.

And finally...

Covington previously had a 100% positive track record for NQ retention and training principal Grant Castle assured us: *"We're not going to be letting anyone go who reaches our standards."* Two of four qualifiers were offered jobs in 2009.

Cripps Harries Hall LLP

The facts

Locations: Tunbridge Wells, London

Number of UK partners/solicitors: 39/64

Total number of trainees: 16

Seats: 4x6 months

Alternative seats: None

Trainees choose this firm for its small and collegiate nature, with many also expressing the desire to avoid London but still experience quality work.

Working from four large Georgian houses in the heart of Royal Tunbridge Wells, this commercial/private client hybrid offers a comprehensive training.

Contract and tortilla

Tucked away in genteel Tunbridge Wells, Cripps Harries Hall's roots lie in private client practice. It doesn't merely advise on tax compliance and the administration of trusts and estates, it also litigates disputes for a wealthy clientele. How wealthy are we talking? Ultra-wealthy, according to Cripps – some are household names, others are resident in tax havens. Private client law is by no means the whole story however; Cripps has a meaty commercial operation positively dripping with juicy business. The real estate team, especially, advises major names like Crossrail, Wagamama and accountants PwC, as well as a variety of top institutional landowners such as Land Securities and British Land. The firm is ranked top in the South for real estate by *Chambers UK*, and with good reason. Recent highlights include the sale of the Pantiles (Tunbridge Wells' historic centre), including over 50 shops, residential premises and the title of Lord of the Manor. Lawyers also recently assisted SJ Berwin's corporate finance team, handling the property aspects of British Land's £116m sale of Peacocks Shopping Centre in Woking. Why would SJB's own property lawyers not do this? Probably because Cripps' lawyers can give the same level of service more cheaply. In a similar vein, City firm Lovells has subcontracted work to Cripps for years, most notably for leading client PruPIM. This arrangement is charmingly called The Mexican Wave.

Cripps has experience in all aspects of real estate: it has scores of house builder clients and a fair few social housing organisations. It was recently appointed by Genesis Housing to assist in the sale of several hundred homes on a large regeneration site in Stratford, East London. When the flow of work from house builders dried up, the firm was at least able to take comfort from its social housing and public sector clientele. Cripps represents a variety of local authorities and is on the government's 'Catalyst' property and estates legal panel. And those big institutional clients have still been active too. Cripps' appointment to the Crossrail legal team shows that it is up there with the big boys and, as one trainee pointed out: "*You get the impression that they're geared up for high-quality work.*" Trainees say Cripps is staying true to its ten-year plan; "*the aim is to keep growing, maintain a high standard of work and get bigger clients.*" Simple.

Stairmasters

Trainees generally visit six departments, and these are decided before the training contract begins. It sounds rigid, but it's not really. "*I wanted to try one department and they restructured the contract for my preference,*" said a source. Nor are the seats of a prescribed length; they can sometimes be extended to gain extra time in a department. At least one seat in the property department (which includes real estate, farms and estates, development, residential conveyancing, planning and property dispute resolution) is guaranteed; indeed it's likely that you'll do two. The other options are construction, commercial dispute resolution, corporate, employment, family and private client. Unfortunately, as the departments are split across several buildings "*it can be a little annoying if you have to shoot off across the road and up flights of stairs.*"

The corporate team has a French flavour thanks to dual-qualified partner Olivier Morel. He was instrumental in the disposal of Oddbins, when he advised French wine retailer Nicolas. Cripps also acted on the purchase of Eggar Chemicals for Safic-Alcan, a European leader in speciality chemicals. To cope with the downturn in deals, four associates in the team agreed to cut their hours and pay.

Willing hands

"In the course of four months you are giving cradle-to-grave litigation and transactional services to the clients," one source said of a seat in private client. There's good variety and client exposure here, and trainees are *"not given jobs so small that they don't affect the larger case."* Said one: *"The seat taught me a lot about drafting documents and my skills improved a great deal."* Another added: *"My supervisor was very good in taking me to client meetings and getting me involved in follow-up work."* Recently the contentious lawyers acted for the children of a prominent businessman who were challenging the validity of a will and lifetime gifts relating to an estate worth £4m. Meanwhile tax advisory lawyers were involved in an multimillion-pound inheritance tax case relating to a collection of paintings by Sickert that was due to be exhibited at the Ashmolean Museum in Oxford to satisfy the wishes of the deceased. Despite having many ultra-wealthy clients, Cripps doesn't turn its nose up at more ordinary folk. Said one trainee: *"I drafted wills worth £300 and £15m on the same day."*

Our sources liked the construction team, which has lately seen an increase in disputes and insolvency-related advice. Lawyers settled a £4m dispute brought by a hotel chain against a national contractor following acoustic work at one of its nightclubs. Trainees have also been able to take part in a marshalling scheme that is more usually undertaken by Bar students and pupil barristers. *"For five days we go up to London to see the inside workings of the Technology and Construction Court."* Meanwhile, the main dispute resolution team was praised for its quality of supervision. *"They always talk you through things when you're struggling"* and *"really treat you as a member of the team, quickly getting you involved in the commercial aspects."* The department advised a magazine publisher on copyright and trade mark issues regarding one of its motoring publications, and a logistics company in a dispute with a vehicle manufacturer. That dispute included a successful international arbitration with connected proceedings in both Italy and the Netherlands. Property litigation is *"kept as a second-year seat as it's a lot of hard work."*

When the Cripps are down

Our sources had generally chosen Cripps for its *"smaller, more collegiate style."* Many grew up locally and wanted to avoid London, but at the same time were also looking for a quality of training and work that is usually associated with larger cities. More particularly they wanted to sample a range of commercial and private client areas. From the sounds of it their expectations were exceeded, and several people spoke warmly of the enthusiasm and experience of partners. Said one: *"The firm treats us as individuals, and part of why I like this is that I'm always comfortable with the challenges proposed."* In 2009 Cripps retained only four out of seven qualifiers, its lowest score in years. The bottom line is that despite profits holding up in 2008/09, *"a lot of property and corporate work has gone."* Trainees say Cripps allocated the available jobs fairly and *"the HR team gave people help to look for other work."* Unfortunately, *"when we came in we were at the end of a very buoyant market and now it's a different feeling."* That everyone here remained so positive about Cripps despite its lowest retention since 2004 is a testament to the character of the firm and the type of positive-minded recruit it takes on.

One minor complaint concerned the comparatively low salary – £21,500 for a first-year, £23,500 for a second-year and then £37,000 on qualification. In Tunbridge Wells, *"the general cost of living is quite high"* and this can make the early years harder than expected, often requiring newbies to live with family. At least it doesn't put a dampener on the firm's social life. As well as the usual Friday night pint, the odd charity quiz and the occasional trip to the town's one and only club, Da Vinci's, trainees have recently enjoyed a Wild West barn dance. They were also involved in a photo-op when a helicopter from the Kent Air Ambulance collected a cheque for £10,000 from the firm. Cripps fields a higher class of sports team than the average employer: cricket, rugby, croquet and even polo can all be expected.

Chambers UK rankings

Agriculture & Rural Affairs	Licensing
Charities	Local Government
Construction	Partnership
Corporate/M&A	Personal Injury
Debt Recovery	Planning
Dispute Resolution	Private Client
Employment	Real Estate
Family/Matrimonial	Real Estate Litigation
Intellectual Property	Social Housing

And finally…

Cripps' near-London location allows it to win great instructions while working in relaxed surroundings. If Kent is where you want to be, this firm comes very highly recommended.

- **Name names:** During assessment day group exercises, use people's names when you address them – recruiters love to see this. Name badges are usually given out so you shouldn't have to worry about remembering people.

top tip no. 11

Dechert LLP

The facts

Locations: London
Number of UK partners/solicitors: 35/52
Total number of trainees: 19
Seats: 6x4 months
Alternative seats: Overseas seats, secondments
Extras: Pro bono – North Kensington Law Centre

Want to discover whether you're a Mississippi lawyer or a Loch Ness lawyer? There's a man at Dechert who can tell you...

Philadelphia-born Dechert is a highly successful international firm whose London focus is squarely on financial services and corporate. A place for those who "*keep their head down and their feet on the ground,*" its small intake and six-seat system can make for a rewarding contract for the right person.

FRE-dom

From a base of 11 US offices, Dechert cements its international reach with two branches in Asia (Hong Kong and Beijing) and six in Europe (Paris, Brussels, Luxembourg, Munich, Moscow and London). The activities of the London office reflect the aims behind a well-planned merger back in 2000. This is when Dechert formally hitched itself to one of our capital's well-known mid-sizers – Titmuss Sainer. Though still very British in many repects, the American influence is tangible in the officeas "*quite a few American associates are seconded over here, and American partners too.*" For the most part trainees felt London did maintain a certain amount of independence; "*we've got our own clients – it's not like we're dictated to from over the pond.*" Long-standing English partners also help to "*retain that small-firm English feel*" and trainees assured us that "*with only around 150 fee earners in the office you know everybody by name.*"

If you're considering Dechert, it is crucial to be aware of where its focus lies. The London office has a clear emphasis on financial services (FS) and corporate. "*FS and corporate are the bigger departments, and the work they do in FS is similar to the top firms,*" confirmed a source. Dechert London has consistently moved towards more finance-oriented practice since 2000, and the clearest evidence of this was the subsuming of Titmuss Sainer's highly regarded property department into a new combined finance and real estate group (FRE). A second-year explained: "*There's a clear message from the chairman* [Burt Winokur] *in the States that FRE, corporate and FS are the three core areas he's pushing for and wants to be bigger.*" But how could you possibly know if financial services law is for you? As our interviewees rightly pointed out, "*you won't learn anything about it at university.*"

Mississippi vs Loch Ness

One trainee was particularly candid. "*Coming into financial services, I didn't know anything about it, and so I guess I only felt one thing – terror!*" You'd be forgiven for feeling the same as it's a complicated area. In essence, "*financial services clients are investment managers of* [things like] *large hedge funds, and so the firm deals first and foremost with* [fund] *launches and then ongoing issues, which at the moment seem to be to do with liquidity and restructurings.*" On the regulatory side, Dechert continues to provide advice for asset managers and investment funds regulated by the Financial Services Authority here in the UK and the Securities and Exchange Commission in the USA. If you're already feeling a little lost, don't worry, you're not alone. The consensus among our interviewees when asked if they'd been clued up when they started was "*absolutely not. No one knows what it is when they first join.*" The firm is obviously aware of this and makes provision accordingly, with excellent and thorough training. "*You get pre-reading before you start, lots* of breakfast training meetings and more interactive tasks for the first two to three weeks." Trainees say the significant thing to learn is the vocabulary as financial services has "*a completely different language.*" We turned to Dechert's London director of training Bernard George for a few tips on how a student might recognise their inner financial services lawyer. Showing Confucian wisdom he told us: "*Here it is necessary to make a distinction between Mississippi lawyers and Loch Ness lawyers.*" Huh? "*The Mississippi is wide but shallow: a litigator is the best example as you cover a wide range of interests but as such cannot become a technical expert in any. Loch Ness is narrow but extremely deep: in FS and in tax you can mark out your area of expertise and become extraordinarily technically proficient. It depends on which of these distinctions appeals to you more.*"

Day-to-day working in the FS department is largely dictated to by the economic climate. In a buoyant economy the group's work is dominated by hedge fund launches, which for the trainee means "*a lot of drafting, creation of prospectuses and proof-reading.*" It is document-heavy and the hours are long. Said one source: "*It was more consistently hours-intensive than any other department, with a few weeks of finishing between 1 and 2am every night.*" In a down economy the department "*hasn't slowed down, but has had a change of focus.*" A recent occupant of a seat here said: "*It was definitely a very different type of work I was doing.*" This trainee was dealing with "*a lot of work connected to hedge fund restructuring and liquidation of assets.*" The trainees all appreciated just how busy this department can get, with one even suggesting that "*it's the only department I could say has always been running at full capacity.*" With 150 lawyers dedicated to it across the Dechert network, FS is certainly its largest and most profitable department so preparing yourself for its considerable challenge comes recommended.

Dechert's other prime department, corporate, has felt the chill in the air. In busy times though it is just as hours-intensive as FS. "*During the peak of one deal I went to 100 hours in a week,*" revealed one source. After the completion, trainees, paralegals and "*everyone who had worked on it*" were "*invited to Amsterdam for a post-completion dinner.*" Pro bono work has bubbled up during the recent quieter period and supervisors also took the initiative to "*run a mock share purchase exercise whereby the partners act as your clients,*" enabling trainees to "*get a better understanding of higher-level work than you normally would.*" In M&A, Dechert's international capacity is evident in its instruction by investor Campos Verdes on its acquisition of Argentine agricultural business El Tejar SAACEI, valued at $613.2m, across multiple Latin American jurisdictions. Closer to home, the firm also acted for Deloitte, as administrators of Woolworths, on the disposal of more than 100 stores.

Chambers UK rankings

Capital Markets	Intellectual Property
Corporate/M&A	Investment Funds
Defamation/Reputation Management	Planning
	Real Estate
Dispute Resolution	Real Estate Litigation
Employment	Retail
Financial Services Regulation	Tax

Great salary = great responsibility

In the corporate and financial services departments, newly qualified solicitors get £5,000 more tacked onto their starting salary. This encourages trainees to qualify into these priority departments and makes up for what can be hellish working hours at times. On the whole Dechert fares extremely well in terms of remuneration – its £38,000 trainee starting salary is in line with the major City firms and on qualification Decherteers are paid more than their counterparts in the magic circle. On the subject of NQs, retention was pretty low in 2009, with just three out of ten staying on. Firm-wide quite a few Dechert support staff and lawyers were laid off in the past year, though not a vast number came from the London office. Three of the 2009 trainee intake deferred their start dates for a year in exchange for the princely sum of £10,000. Chairman Burt Winokur is bullish about the future nonetheless. He suggested in an interview with *The Lawyer* that structural changes in the legal market bring significant opportunities as well as risks. "*They favour the nimble, the brave, the people who have courage and who embrace change,*" he declared with a Churchillian flourish. Despite redundancies, many in the profession believe that Dechert will come through the recession strongly.

What you do in the FRE group depends very much on your supervisor's work speciality. On the real estate side there is scope for trainees to take on their own smaller lease files and gain plenty of direct client contact. That said, there is a definite sense among trainees that a major function of the real estate group is to provide support to the larger FS and corporate departments. "*A lot of what we deal with is property aspects of corporate deals.*" On the finance side of the FRE group some trainees found themselves working on a large "*mezzanine finance facility being put in place across various jurisdictions.*" This "*document-intensive*" deal provided a great opportunity to liaise with foreign lawyers. More generally, the department is described as older and "*more family-oriented*" compared to the buzzy, sociable atmosphere in FS and corporate.

Looking at the non-contentious elements of the training contract, we see that the litigation department has been involved in some interesting international arbitration in Latin America, particularly in the representation of the Republic of Ecuador. In 2008 Dechert helped the country defend claims commenced by Perenco Ecuador Limited, Burlington Resources and Occidental. Closer to home, litigators represented Argos in two sets of proceedings brought by Currys for malicious falsehood and trade mark infringement arising out of Currys' 2008 comparative advertising campaign. Trainees described activity in this seat as *"the usual litigation-type tasks of drafting letters and taking witness statements plus a lot of involvement in disclosure."* Again, interviewees pointed to the fact that much work comes via FS or corporate. Other trainee-friendly departments include IP, tax and employment. There are also client secondments and a seat in Brussels (largely revolving around competition law and EU reporting assignments for US clients).

Dechert the halls

So what makes a Dechert lawyer? Trainees were hard pushed to answer this one, so here's what we found – a proliferation of law (as opposed to non-law) degrees and scarcity of those who had taken gap years. *"Everybody has a 2:1 from a decent university,"* though we found no discernible Oxbridge bias. Personality-wise, Dechert trainees come across as more low-key than at some of the brasher US firms in London (or the big City giants). They told us: *"Being overbearing or overconfident doesn't come off well here,"* and they also claimed to be *"working too hard"* for mid-week socialising. *"Put it this way,"* one trainee volunteered, *"I don't think wearing pink socks or garish ties would be a good idea."*

There is a decent little sporting scene at the firm. Teams convene for hockey, cricket and football, and there's a newly formed mixed netball team. Socially, Dechert *"always has something in the calendar to look forward to,"* which trainees say *"makes it okay when you do have to work the long hours."* A 'pub of the month' event sees management put money behind the bar, and there's generally a spot of Friday night drinking somewhere in the Blackfriars area. The Christmas party stands out in particular. The formal black-tie affair has been held at Lincoln's Inn and the Tate Modern in past years.

And finally...

Dechert provides an excellent training for those with their eye on financial services clients and a temperament that's more down-to-earth than it is head-in-the-clouds. Pronunciation tip: think deck-urt, not de-shirt.

DentonWildeSapte...

Find out more and apply at
friendly-firm.com

> Wherever we are in the world, we're down to earth.

Graduate Opportunities

The world might not know your name. Yet. But we will. All of us, from partner to trainee. Perhaps more importantly, you'll know theirs, whatever their level. That may not sound like a lot. But think about it. It's symptomatic of our lack of hierarchy.

It's demonstrative of a culture built on trust. It's about being in it together. And believe us, you won't find an environment like that in every major City law firm — whether that city is London, Moscow, Paris, or Dubai, for example.

Denton Wilde Sapte is committed to providing equal opportunities in employment

Denton Wilde Sapte

The facts

Locations: London, Milton Keynes
Number of UK partners/solicitors: 133/330
Total number of trainees: 70
Seats: 4x6 months
Alternative seats: Overseas seats, secondments
Extras: Pro bono – PopLaw advice clinic; language training

A long-standing interest in Africa puts DWS ahead of the game in relation to this set of emerging markets.

With a marked emphasis on banking, real estate and energy matters, this silver circle firm has bags of international opportunities for the adventurous and is a discerning choice for those City-minded folk for whom work-life balance is an important consideration.

Wilde world

Having recovered from some setbacks in the early noughties, Dentons is a firm on the up. Its impressive global imprint incorporates offices in London, Milton Keynes, Paris, Istanbul, Almaty (Kazakhstan), Moscow, Tashkent (Uzbekistan), Cairo, Doha, Dubai and Muscat, with associate offices in St Petersburg, Ashgabat (Turkmenistan), Amman, Kuwait and Riyadh. We certainly mustn't leave out all-important established links with nine African law firms in countries including South Africa, Botswana and Ghana. Phew! And we're not done yet. Merger talks with a major US firm seems to be gaining momentum, and although we have nothing concrete to report, we can't help but feel that something's brewing.

The firm identifies its core areas as financial institutions; real estate and retail; energy, transport and infrastructure; and technology, media and telecoms (TMT). The TMT department has lived through some interesting times (back in 2004 pretty much the entire team decamped to DLA Piper) and as one trainee pointed out: *"You need to be aware where our strengths are – the TMT department was massive but is now considerably smaller."* Another said: *"Look at what we do – it is quite specific and if you don't like banking, property and energy this is not the place to come."* Our interviews confirmed that banking, real estate and energy are indeed the big boys at Dentons, and as a trainee you can expect at least two of your four seats to be within these three core departments.

Try something new today

Banking is split into distinct areas such as general banking, asset finance, trade finance and financial markets. Trainees reiterated: *"We are a banking-oriented firm and it's important to know this when you apply."* In general banking our interviewees were pleased they were able to *"see and understand a transaction from start to finish."* For a trainee, document management is the name of the game and *"there are lots of bibles to compile."* Trade finance, the *"upfront financing for people who want to make products out of raw materials,"* requires superlative organisational skills in dealing with parties in countries as diverse as Nigeria and Vietnam, while asset finance might see you delivering a plane to an overseas client. An advantage of the latter is the fast turnaround of transactions, whereas in the former the hours can be punishing. All that said, as we'll come back to later, *"everyone tries to get you home as soon as they can here."* In an area that has been hit hard by the credit crisis, it seems Dentons' banking department has two things to be thankful for: first, *"we never developed a securitisation practice so didn't have one to lose,"* and second, an awful lot of work is generated overseas. Recent deals include a $370m term loan facilities between Bank Muscat S.A.O.G and a host of international financial institutions including The Bank of Tokyo-Mitsubishi UFJ, Deutsche Bank and JPMorgan. In another deal lawyers worked on a loan facility of up to $275m between JSC KazTransOil and BTMU (Europe), ING and French bank Natixis.

Real estate is another practice area that has been hit hard, and it's another chief focus of the firm. We certainly found that fewer trainees were being taken into the department in 2009; nonetheless, those who spent time there were involved in a wide variety of things. "*I worked on a lot of large matters, but I was also given small files to run myself,*" said one. Smaller files might include the conveyancing of a residential property or the remortgage of a restaurant. You find yourself "*very client involved from the first day,*" we were told. Another example of classic trainee fare was "*a large pro bono matter concerning rights of way.*" In a down economy, Dentons has the considerable fortune of having key retailer Sainsbury's as a client. Work with the supermarket giant includes a well-publicised £1.2bn joint venture with British Land to invest in and redevelop 36 superstores across the UK.

This firm has an enviable position in the energy sector and acted for all of the 'Big Seven' (EDF Energy, RWE npower, British Energy, ScottishPower, Scottish and Southern Energy, Centrica and E.ON) in 2008. It has a healthy spread of domestic and international work – an example of the former is advising the government on its multibillion-pound power procurement contracts and ancillary power services. Overseas work includes advising on a $6.8bn power and water project in Saudi Arabia and advising Botswana Power Corporation as the host nation power utility in relation to the proposed $5bn 2500 MW Mmamabula power project, touted as the key power scheme on the African continent. Our sources praised the nature of the work in this department, which seems to presently take in a fair bit of marketing; "*every day I'm doing something different – last week I did a proposal for pipeline work in Kazakhstan and this week I'm writing an article for a British magazine.*" Secondments to Shell also focus on energy matters, specifically in "*downstream supply and distribution.*" Trainees say that time in-house is "*drastically different to private practice.*"

Working for peanuts

Client secondments abound, with the likes of Total, Shell, Thames Water, Goldman Sachs and Citi all taking trainees. When it comes to getting out of the office, the real story is the overseas seats. Abu Dhabi, Dubai, Muscat, Moscow, Istanbul and a split London/Paris seat are all up for grabs. The Dubai placement is especially popular and it has plenty of interesting work to get involved in. For one source it was "*a lot of local law advice on setting up companies in Dubai, advising on joint venture agreements and due diligence on the purchase of companies.*" Add to that "*an apartment with a pool and gym*" and "*dinners at partners' houses*" and this corporate-focused seat is not a bad bet. Likewise, a banking seat in Muscat has its advantages; the accommodation includes "*an en suite bedroom, a porter downstairs, the beach just down the road and a car provided...*" and don't

Chambers UK rankings

Administrative & Public Law	Intellectual Property
Asset Finance	Local Government
Aviation	Outsourcing
Banking & Finance	Pensions
Banking Litigation	Planning
Capital Markets	Projects, Energy & Natural Resources
Climate Change	Public Procurement
Commodities	Real Estate
Competition/European Law	Real Estate Finance
Construction	Real Estate Litigation
Corporate/M&A	Restructuring/Insolvency
Data Protection	Retail
Dispute Resolution	Shipping
Employment	Social Housing
Environment	Sports Law
Information Technology	Tax
	Telecommunications
	Transport

even get us started on the Intercontinental Hotel gym membership! Overseas secondments aren't restricted to trainees, and there's also the possibility to qualify abroad, as a few did last year.

The TMT department, though more streamlined than before the exodus of 2004, is still strong, and here trainees can gain some great experience in drafting and contracts. A recent coup was landing ITN Source as a new client. Source needed advice on its joint venture with Diagonal View to package content and syndicate it to a range of commercial partners including MySpace, YouTube and MSN. Dentons' restructuring and insolvency group is worth a mention too. It includes *Chambers UK* top-tier lawyer Mark Andrews – who is regarded by clients and many peers as the best in the City – and "*generally always goes for fourth-seaters.*" We hear that recently a staggering 26 people applied for a handful of seats in this department. One lucky trainee told us of working on restructurings or insolvencies for "*a large investment bank, a large retailer, a large pay TV channel and a large peanut company.*"

Contentious training requirements can be met during a seat in the dispute resolution department. Here the lawyers cover all kinds of commercial spats from property dilapidation claims and energy disputes to more standard debt collection cases. Trainees usually find there is "*a lot of law compared to other seats,*" and a lucky one or two told us how beneficial they found it to "*be involved in cases from direction to trial,*" though "*the downside was there was a lot of disclosure to be done.*" One trainee colourfully laid out the particulars of debt collection:

"You have to instruct a tracing agent to track people down, do over-the-phone negotiation to reach a settlement, and still we may have to advise the bank to write off debts of hundreds of thousands of pounds because the accused simply has no assets." Hello, credit crunch! A "heavy focus on rare oil and gas disputes in Africa" underpins the department's international interests.

Marching to the beat of its own drum

Whether it's overseas seats, offices or clients, Dentons is a place where you will get significant exposure to cross-border work. Its trainees agree that the international flavour of the firm is a definite attraction. Said one: "I've always wanted to work for a firm with that international aspect." There are, however, other standout reasons why trainees pick this firm over others within the silver circle.

Eager to avoid the negative connotation of the term "relaxed" in reference to a City law firm, our interviewees nonetheless could not help using this seemingly incongruous adjective. Trainees agree that "there's a really positive work-life balance;" "it's just a really nice firm, everyone's friendly and inclusive;" "although it's got a lot of prestige it's just not an uppity place at all." CEO Howard Morris is so obviously held in high regard. "When it snowed really heavily, every day he came by and asked how everyone was, telling us to make sure we got home okay. He's just really lovely." This is a firm for those who expressly don't want to work in the magic circle and "wouldn't want to be just a number." The people we spoke to gratefully extolled the virtues of a firm that "doesn't want to take away your life in your twenties." Though there will be late hours in banking seats, trainees say: "It's quite a story if someone stays really late or overnight… it shows it's not that regular." A senior source confirmed: "There are tough times in which you should expect to work hard and long, but it is nice sometimes that you can leave at 6pm and be passed out at Embankment by midnight!"

The social life of Dentons trainees is by no means confined to, or even centred on, drunken antics. Our interviewees admitted that they were "not crazy drinkers," and instead could reel off a more varied list of pursuits. A trainee social committee organises things like a trip to the Comedy Store, tapas evenings and bowling. There's also a trainee Christmas party alongside the usual departmental festive shindigs, a firm-wide summer party and various client events and quizzes throughout the year. The sports on offer include football, rugby, cricket, netball, softball and, somewhat unusually, dragon boat racing. When asked what that entailed we were reliably told: "Basically charging up and down a river… and there's probably a drum involved."

Each and every one of our interviewees wanted to stay at the firm, but acknowledged that due to the economy "it doesn't look great." Of the 45 people who qualified in 2009, only 27 were able to take up jobs at the firm. It's worth stating here that the widely reported 36% drop in partner profits (from £470k to £300k) was not that unusual for firms of this type, and in this extraordinary year there was a costly redundancy process (£3.5m; 76 UK job losses). Additionally, future trainees were offered a staggering £10,000 to defer for a year (£7k if not undertaking any voluntary projects). On the plus side, the firm has also responded to a need to do business "on the ground" in the Middle East and Africa, and there has been a new office opening in Singapore. The fact that Dentons has gone back to the Asian market (which it had abandoned prematurely during its troubled times) and has actually seen a rise in annual turnover is certainly encouraging.

Perhaps this is how the management at Ohio-headquartered Squire Sanders have been looking at Dentons. The two firms have some remarkable similarities: their practice areas are in sync (particularly in banking), they have similar profitability and both have roots going back many years. The only stark difference is in office locations. Squire Sanders brings a hefty US, Asian and Latin American presence to the table, whereas Dentons has Europe, CIS and the Middle East covered and, to an extent, Africa too. These last two regions are going to be increasingly important and Dentons is in a good position in each. Moscow is the only overlap. What we'd be looking at here – should it go ahead – is a transatlantic tie-up that leaves only Australasia untouched. Joining forces would put them at close to 1,500 lawyers worldwide and well placed to rival other international giants such as DLA Piper. So, from a business perspective, this merger looks pretty tasty. What remains to be seen is what effect it would have on the established Dentons culture. Stay tuned and check out our report on Squire Sanders at www.chambers-associate.com.

And finally...

Denton Wilde Sapte is a firm that knows how to look after its own. It also has some great clients and an enviable and exciting international reach. This could be the perfect choice for those who like their City 'lite'.

Dewey & LeBoeuf

The facts
Location: London
Number of UK partners/solicitors: 49/130
Total number of trainees: 23
Seats: 4x6 months
Alternative seats: Overseas seats
Extras: Pro bono – Liberty Advice Line, East London Small Business Centre, The Medical Foundation, LawWorks; language classes

Expect Dewey to continue benefiting from its extensive operations in the CIS, the Middle East and Africa. It is work from those regions that is keeping the London office buzzing with activity, particularly in energy and projects.

If you count its age from the merger that created it, Dewey & LeBoeuf has just reached its 'terrible twos', however global revenues of over $1bn and an established London practice prove it's anything but a legal toddler.

Dewey & LeBoeuf, hanging tough

In the fast-paced world of commercial law, a merger that happened in October 2007 is already old news, even if it was one of the biggest combinations in history. Two New York firms with global outreach, Dewey Ballantine and LeBoeuf, Lamb, Greene & McRae, after failing to find love elsewhere (Dewey seemed certain to merge with California finance giant Orrick for a while), ended up in a fitting *pas de deux*. They were of similar size and profitability, and their respective strengths and international networks seemed to dovetail nicely. Now more than 1,400 lawyers operate in a massive worldwide network that includes offices as far flung as Almaty and Johannesburg.

Dewey LeBoeuf's creation drew a lot of attention, and since then its every move has been closely scrutinised. Eyebrows were raised shortly after the merger when it was announced that some of the smaller US offices were to close, but that streamlining had always been part of the agreement and the firm already is back to its expansionist ways. Dubai and Doha offices were opened in 2008, and 2009 has seen it open in Madrid... with another office in Abu Dhabi set to arrive as soon as the licence is approved. The legal press took notice when Dewey underwent a redundancy consultation, but in the end the 15 lawyers laid off in London remains a far lower number than those let go from some of its competitors. Trainees admitted the process hadn't been easy ("*Show me a firm where morale is fantastic right now and I'll show you a liar*"), but most were confident the firm had handled everything "*to the best of its abilities.*" A small number of incoming 2009 trainees were deferred, and offered a no-strings £12,000 payment. Going forward, we expect Dewey to continue benefiting hugely from its extensive operations in the CIS and the emerging markets in the Middle East and Africa. Indeed, it is work from those regions that is keeping the London office buzzing with activity, particularly in energy and projects. Following a "*bedding-in period,*" our interviewees think the firm is "*starting to see the shoots of the merger.*" While they accept "*you'd be stupid to carry on with blind expansion*" in this economic climate, "*when things pick up, we're back to plan A.*"

Know what we MENA?

Dewey has two-dozen offices on four continents. It's a big family, so we were keen to know the role played by the London lawyers from their digs in Mincing Lane, a looming Gothic pile that served as Cruella De Vil's lair in the live-action *101 Dalmatians* – a fact we're sure its patient trainees never tire of hearing. It's "*not just a satellite doing New York's work,*" interviewees averred; it sources most of its own instructions. There is a sizeable American presence in the office and wider strategic decisions are still made in New York, but London is an important centre for the firm's European and other overseas work. Indeed, "*there's always some cross-border element*" with jurisdictions like Russia, Dubai or South Africa, and trainees report that international work dominates their time. "*I don't know that I've done anything that's been 100% domestic,*" bragged a source.

One of the gifts LeBoeuf Lamb brought to the merger table was a strong international energy practice that acts for some of the world's biggest names. Its global reach greatly expanded by Dewey Ballantine's input, the team is ranked by *Chambers UK* among the best in the UK for energy and natural resources matters, international infrastructure, and energy projects. It counts BP, ExxonMobil and Shell among its clients. Notable instructions include the €2.5bn acquisition of Russian electricity company TGC-10 by Finnish Fortum Oyj; Veolia Water's investment into various Saudi Arabian projects; and $1bn of financing for the US-based regasification component of a $5bn project by Angola LNG involving deep water pipelines and transatlantic shipping. Closely related to project finance, trainees told us they have heavy involvement in drafting while in the energy seat, as well as more mundane-but-vital tasks like collecting conditions precedent documents. There's "*quite a lot of responsibility at first and a lot of paper flying around, so you need to be good at keeping a cool head.*"

LeBoeuf Lamb's other major legacy practice is insurance, and the merged firm has retained extremely close links with Lloyd's. Specifically it is the insurer's US general counsel. There is a dedicated seat covering insurance regulatory issues, but work for insurance clients seeps into other areas of practice too. "*You kind of touch on insurance in so many things,*" confirmed a source, and this is especially true of litigation and M&A matters. In the insurance seat itself trainees should expect to draft articles of association and instruct foreign counsel much of the time. In terms of the contentious work in this area, a lot of what goes on is confidential, but we can tell you the firm advised insurers following the collapse and subsequent nationalisation of Northern Rock.

M&A and fund formation expertise was one of Dewey Ballantine's contributions, and this type of work was a breath of fresh air for some of our more transaction-minded sources. "*After the merger there were Dewey clients coming in and much more on offer in terms of straightforward corporate work. Before that it was all insurance or oil and gas.*" Still, it's good to have some energy sector clients on which to fall back in difficult times. One recruit told us that when the profession as a whole was suffering from a downturn in corporate instructions and it became "*difficult to find work to become involved in and see things progress past even tentative stages,*" the group "*concentrated on petrochemical deals.*" In 2008, as well as helping the Central European Distribution Corporation snap up the Parliament Vodka Group and 40% of the Russian Alcohol Group, the M&A team also advised ArcelorMittal on buying two Russia-based coal mines for $650m. Joining forces with the Moscow office, the London team also advised Italian utility Eni on a £2.9bn sale of assets to Gazprom in 2009. This emphasis on Russia/CIS countries and emerging markets is also found in the capital markets team which, between its debt and

Chambers UK rankings

Capital Markets	Environment
Climate Change	Insurance
Dispute Resolution	Projects, Energy & Natural Resources

equity practices, has handled the first listing of a Hungarian company on the London Stock Exchange, the first Eurobond issue in Egyptian pounds, the largest privatisation IPO in Central Europe to date and the largest ever IPO on AIM. Dewey's focus on the Middle East and North Africa (MENA) region sees the group work closely with the firm's offices in Dubai, Doha and Riyadh, and eyeing Abu Dhabi hungrily for further expansion in 2009. The team "*very much sees things like due diligence as a trainee task,*" but recruits also get the chance to write the first drafts of board minutes and reviews, albeit "*heavily supervised.*" Apparently, "*if you're enthusiastic, it's greeted likewise.*"

Ghana be okay

As well as acting for major companies, the dispute resolution and international arbitration team advises foreign governments. It has been representing Ghana in a dispute over a cocoa processing joint venture and works for the government of Indonesia as it seeks to terminate a $6bn mining concession concerning the Batu Hijau gold and tin mine on the island of Sumbawa. Interviewees who'd done a litigation seat indicated that "*responsibility was pretty much piled on,*" with trainees able to run minor aspects of cases themselves and attend court. Sources also indicated that while the volume of Dewey's instructions isn't high, matters tend to be long-running. Said one: "*You're going to be involved in cases that go on for eternity – if you want to work on your own files maybe it's not the right firm.*" Trainees can take on greater responsibility through pro bono matters however, and these are "*a really good way to get involved and get over any nerves about meeting clients.*" Other available seats include real estate, tax, employment, construction and competition, as well as overseas seats in Moscow, Dubai and Paris. All three foreign seats are offered at each rotation and recruits estimated that generally "*every person who's wanted an international secondment has got one.*" More generally, the first UK seat is chosen for you, but after that, "*if you want something badly enough and are prepared to be proactive... they'll try to accommodate you.*"

The state of the economy makes typical work hours difficult to estimate. For example, in previous years "*litigation was notoriously a ghost town by 7.30 pm; now the majority could still be there by nine, ten or 11pm.*" What remains consistent is a lack of "*face time.*" Despite a target of 1,800 hours a year for anyone seeking a discretionary bonus, there's "*no hours culture... I would happi-*

ly leave at 6pm if work was finished, rather than feel pressured to stick around reading the BBC website." Recruits might sometimes need to stay until the wee hours, "*but never alone – you're never the lonely trainee.*"

Study LeBuddies

Dewey provides people with experience quickly, but this is no sink-or-swim environment. The quality of the work is "*unquestionable when held up to any scrutiny*" and "*the graduate recruitment bumpf about higher responsibility is true.*" Importantly, "*it gives you the feeling they're setting you up to be a qualified lawyer.*" Helping you out when you start will be your 'LeBuddy'. A trainee from the year above is LeBuddied to a new joiner and is there to answer any awkward questions. It's "*not as formal as a mentoring system,*" which Dewey doesn't really do, but that suited our interviewees down to the ground. An official mentor is "*just a person whose name you forget and never end up using,*" and anyway recruits have no trouble getting informal help from partners when they need it. "*The kind of people we take as trainees aren't those who have a problem coming forward if they need anything,*" suggested a source. Appraisals are officially every three months, though "*if there's anything that needs to be discussed, it is done so beforehand.*"

While Dewey favours informal and ad hoc mentoring, it's big on formal training. In fact trainees say it's "*absolutely first-class.*" Under the umbrella of the recently revamped 'Dewey & LeBoeuf University' there are regular sessions throughout the year. A mix of substantive law and "*tips and tricks,*" everything is "*pitched at a level everyone can understand.*" From trainee survival sessions to "*quite intensive programmes organised by each department*" (corporate is particularly enthusiastic but the last 18 months have seen a general upswing across the board), it's all mandatory unless you're working on a client matter.

Real people

Overseas seats aside, trainees may travel abroad for closings or to deliver documents, sometimes alone. Recruits found that while language experience is by no means a prerequisite for any of this, it can make things easier (especially in Paris). Indeed, Dewey has traditionally taken on quite a few multilingual trainees, as well as candidates with varied backgrounds and previous experience of other careers. "*It seemed like they were trying to find people from the most diverse backgrounds,*" cooed an appreciative recruit. However, as the firm's profile has risen following the merger and the expansion of its training scheme, trainees suggest there's a growing number of people coming off the "*younger, fresh-out-of-law school treadmill.*" What has resulted is a mix of "*people straight out of university, without a single language and very young, and people who've had two careers and done everything under the sun.*" Candidates are advised to make sure they consider their application carefully and emphasise experience. Just as important, trainees say, is personality. "*If you're not a person they can sit in a room with 14 hours per day on a horrible deal, that's it.*" No pressure then.

Luckily, the preference for personable candidates is borne out in the firm's healthy trainee social life. Big blowouts are normally limited to the summer party and "*quite a lavish event*" at Christmas, but there are "*none of those contrived bonding activities where you feel like you're being lumped together because you have to get along.*" Instead, trainees are "*very good about getting together themselves.*" There's no designated break room or cafeteria in the office, so the regular Friday night haunt is the Bertorelli's across the street. It's not perfect ("*You get to look at the office while drinking. Joy!*") but it's a tradition. "*There's rarely anyone there you don't know. When there is, it's like, 'Gosh! Real people!'*"

Recently, a new system of submitting CVs and covering letters followed by an interview to apply for available NQ jobs replaced an older, "*much more informal process.*" The firm found space for 11 of the 12 qualifiers of 2009. It awarded them initial six-month contracts, with the intention of making them permanent later on.

And finally...

With the merger still fresh in people's minds and a new firm identity being sculpted, trainees are confident this is a great time to be at Dewey & LeBoeuf: "*We get to be a part of defining that culture.*"

Dickinson Dees LLP

The facts

Location: Newcastle, Stockton-on-Tees, York, London

Number of UK partners/solicitors: 72/194

Total number of trainees: 30

Seats: 4x6 months

Alternative seats: Brussels, secondments

"Long-term, our objective remains the same: to be the leading independent law firm outside London."

Jonathan Blair, Managing Partner

Giant. Heavyweight. Powerhouse. Over the years we've employed all these clichés to describe Dickinson Dees. They remain true.

Northern Light

Dickie Dees is a 200-year-old Newcastle institution, and *"you'll see its adverts all over the city."* But it's not just venerability and blanket advertising that give it such a great reputation. Rankings in 27 sections of *Chambers UK* prove that it's one of the country's strongest regional outfits. It's hard to pick out star performers with so many areas to choose from, but the firm has a national reputation for charities, local government, education, PFI/PPP and rail transport work, and many of its other departments are top-ranked in the North East. Its client list is enviable. Abbey, Arriva, Barclays, the Co-operative Bank, EDF Energy, Nike, Nissan, RBS and Siemens are just a handful of the big names – there are many, many more. Having almost outgrown Newcastle, Dickie Dees sought new markets to exploit. Anyone arriving at York station in the past couple of years will have seen its distinctive black and white branding on the platforms. The firm moved into a landmark location in York – the old Terry's chocolate factory near the College of Law. There's another office in Stockton-on-Tees, which is more *"provincial"* in setting. Though this smaller office only employs about 50 people, don't be fooled – *"the clients are still big."* York and Tees Valley each have their own client base and also regularly cross-refer work to and from Newcastle. Each also now recruits its own trainees. At the time of our investigations, York had six and Tees Valley four.

In the four-seat rotation, stints in coco, property and litigation are compulsory. If that sounds restrictive, it's not. Within each of those departments there is a huge choice; in fact in Newcastle there are 38 seat options for trainees, including agriculture, banking and finance, competition, commercial disputes, construction, corporate finance, corporate recovery, education, employment, energy, IP, insurance litigation, private client and various property options. York now offers property, litigation, corporate, charities, corporate recovery and employment, and Tees Valley offers the same except with family in place of charities. Additionally, six-week secondments are available to Brussels, and a number of the firm's clients also welcome trainees. Chemical giant Huntsman invites trainees to its offices in Basel, Switzerland and there's a potentially fascinating opportunity at Northern Rock. All this choice doesn't stop some areas from being consistently oversubscribed. Even though it now takes two trainees at a time, *"if you want employment you'd better be asking for it from day one."* To make the seat allocation system more transparent, the firm now asks trainees to put forward three preferences before each change.

Academy awards

Of late the commercial dispute resolution team has advised a Premier League footballer during a dispute with his former agent; a national construction company in relation to the OFT's investigation into alleged bid rigging in the industry; several local authorities after challenges to procurement processes were made by disappointed tenderers; and a high-street bank regarding a complex claim in relation to mortgage fraud. Trainees here experienced a mix of working on small to medium-sized claims. *"A couple I ran myself, and a couple I was in a supporting role,"* revealed one source who sensed they gained *"real exposure to big litigation."* The insurance lit seat is something

235

of an oddity. "*Because it's personal injury, a lot of trainees who come to a commercial firm like this don't think they want to do it, but it provides a really good basis for any contentious work,*" said one convert. There's plenty of client contact and ample practice at drafting witness statements and court documents. "*The best thing is we act for the insurance companies. They call us in after all the early stages have already been completed so almost every case goes to court. I went seven or eight times; you don't get to do that in other teams.*"

The sizeable property department is top-ranked in the North East by *Chambers UK*. It recently acted for the AA on transactions regarding its portfolio of service centres, and for Nike on the reorganisation of its UK real estate. As at other firms, many trainees' property seats coincided with "*a quiet 12 months*" in that department. Nevertheless, "*partners tried to get us involved.*" One trainee particularly enjoyed working on a large transaction in which councils were selling their stock of "*thousands of properties*" to housing associations.

The much sought-after employment seats offer a blend of contentious and non-contentious training, so "*you get the best of both worlds.*" Our contacts had seen plenty of deals relating to local authority schools transferring into independent academies. The team has also been defending a number of NHS trusts on thousands of equal pay claims, and advised Northern Electric and Yorkshire Electricity on industrial action by unions. Even before it became a boom area, corporate recovery was another popular choice. "*One of the partners is famous in the firm for being quite a character. He does an introduction to insolvency once a year and his enthusiasm is really appealing.*"

On track

As you might imagine, private client involves plenty of client contact, and in Dickie Dees' case this means anyone from "*landed gentry to new-money businessmen.*" Our interviewees had advised on trust structures for people wanting to keep their personal wealth safe if their business was to go under, and drafted simple wills. Commercially oriented trainees found this a "*different*" seat but nonetheless "*a very useful experience that has really helped me hone my client skills.*" Dickie Dees actually fills two offices in Newcastle, and the private client and property departments are based in the modern Trinity Gardens building near the river. Trainees find it a more heads-down environment compared to the chatty atmosphere in the nearby St Anne's building. Some suggested that the Trinity Gardens people managed to get home earlier because of this, although it seems more plausible that its departments simply have more predictable hours. Despite being a regional firm, this is not a soft option and late nights will be required occasionally. "*I had the ultimate trainee nightmare week in my first seat,*" said one

Chambers UK rankings

Agriculture & Rural Affairs	Intellectual Property
Banking & Finance	Local Government
Charities	Pensions
Competition/European Law	Planning
Construction	Private Client
Corporate/M&A	Projects, Energy & Natural Resources
Debt Recovery	Real Estate
Dispute Resolution	Real Estate Litigation
Education	Restructuring/Insolvency
Employment	Social Housing
Environment	Tax
Family/Matrimonial	Transport

source. Fortunately it didn't become a permanent feature, and trainees say 9am to between 6.30 and 7pm is normal.

The corporate department's rail team "*historically had two large transport clients in the North East*" and has now built a nationwide reputation. "*Since the rail network was privatised, the firm has got involved in the franchises.*" And since the bid process comes round every seven or eight years, and bids then go on for around a year and a half, there is plenty of this type of work. The team advised Govia on its bid for the South Central rail franchise, which commenced in 2009. Trainee tasks on such matters range from "*drafting very small side letters which change small features of the agreement, to researching larger points of law.*" Said one trainee: "*I also negotiated three separate maintenance agreements on my own.*" The seat was especially praised for its great supervisor ("*easy to talk to but the respect was never lost*") and, judging from the positive comments we received regarding most other seats, the overall quality of supervision certainly seems to be something Dickie Dees can be proud of. There is the right balance between oversight and letting people off the leash. Said one interviewee: "*You won't be force-fed or nannied. Actually, if you don't demand good work they might think you're not interested.*"

London calling?

Passing unmentioned in our initial overview of Dickie Dees is an office in London. It doesn't take trainees and until recently was simply an unmanned outpost for when lawyers needed to be in the capital (the firm acts for half a dozen London boroughs). Times change. "*They won't admit it but they have people working there almost full-time now,*" whispered one source. Actually, when questioned, managing partner Jonathan Blair happily admitted that this office now has a full-time partner and that by 2012 we will see the firm making a push in London's corporate and banking/finance arenas. "*But you should definitely not take that as an indication of us switching our allegiance from the Northern market,*" he added. Trainees concurred. "*The heart of the firm will always be in the North. We don't have any ambitions to jump into Birmingham or Bristol and be the new Eversheds,*" said one. "*Give it another hundred years maybe!*"

Expect in the medium term a continued focus on expanding the York office. It's not a city known as a buzzing legal hub, but the firm's investment here was carefully thought-out. "*When we were contemplating our next move* [in 2006], *we looked at Leeds,*" says Blair, "*and the reality is it's a city which is overpopulated with lawyers. But if you look at the marketplace east of the Pennines, there are actually more plcs in North Yorkshire than in our immediate North East region, and they have a degree of reluctance to use the Leeds market. Just because the competition is diving into Leeds doesn't mean we should.*" As well as all those plcs, North Yorks has numerous wealthy private clients, not to mention plenty of farm-based industry.

As for the short term, there will be a pause to ride out the recession. Its mix of big national and loyal regional clients, and its reputation for high-quality work, give Dickie Dees a fairly secure platform and trainees feel it has coped better than other local firms. That said, it hasn't been unaffected by the downturn. A volume business division, D3 Legal, was sold off after profitability slumped, and support staff and fee earner redundancies occurred earlier in 2009, the bulk of departures being from the property department. Trainees say this was generally "*handled quite well,*" though some questioned why in the "*very partner-heavy*" corporate department it was junior lawyers and NQs facing redundancy. The response we got from Dickie Dees is that there was depth of experience among the corporate partners that it couldn't afford to lose. In fact, the firm as a whole is quite top-heavy, and some of our contacts had the impression that a number of younger partners were champing at the bit to have their day in the sun.

In previous years we've heard moans about salary from trainees. To be fair, Dickie Dees actually pays at the top end for Newcastle, but some of our sources felt this still wasn't enough. "*They claim they are the biggest and the best – prove it,*" said one. "*They tout themselves as equivalent to Walker Morris in Leeds, so they should pay the same as them at least.*" About half of our contacts felt this way; the remainder thought they received a fair wage, especially in the present fragile economy. We made our calls in April 2009, so getting a job was more important than salary for most. In the end, the firm held on to 15 out of 17 qualifiers – ten of 12 in Newcastle, three of three in York and two of two in the Tees Valley. A couple of those who were retained actually went off on long-term secondments to clients.

Dee-linquents

Among the cohorts we spoke to, Durham, Northumbria and Cambridge Universities were the three biggest suppliers of trainees, with some 11 other institutions also represented, from Sunderland and Teesside in the North East to Bristol in the South West. About two thirds of the group are law graduates, and many have a local connection through family or university. Several trainees said that "*there is definitely a big focus on hiring people who are quite outgoing and able to communicate.*" We did get the distinct impression that a handful of the current batch, fairly or unfairly, are perceived by some of their more gregarious peers to be lacking in confidence. "*If you want to be a brain box sat at the back, well, there probably is a place for you, but I'm not sure if it's really what the firm wants going forward,*" said one forthright source. Others (mainly the girls) were more charitable: "*There are a small percentage who are a bit quieter but the firm clearly sees something in them.*" When we asked, the firm confirmed this. Theorised trainees: "*Maybe they are the intellectual heavyweights of the future.*"

There's an active social life at this firm. In Newcastle, the Pitcher & Piano remains the venue of choice, despite its recently raised prices. "*It's just so close. I'm sure there are people who just sleep at the office after a night out in the Pitcher. In fact I know there's one NQ who slept in one of our toilets.*" Trainees from York and Tees Valley will often travel to Newcastle to join in the fun, or alternatively the Newcastle and Tees Valley groups will head down to York to sample its numerous pubs – The Woodman in Bishopthorpe is a popular Friday lunch venue. There's also a long-standing tradition of a trainee weekend jaunt to Brussels to visit the secondee in the Belgian capital.

Historically, Dickie Dees has had a well-developed sporting scene. The netball team is strong, but the current footballers shamefully admit: "*It's embarrassing that a firm of 700 people can't string together 11 half-decent players.*" A five-a-side team did uphold firm pride at the York College of Law sports day, narrowly losing to Leeds Uni Law Soc in the final of a cup tournament. And the annual staff v partners cricket match is always keenly anticipated: "*You get to throw a really hard ball at the partners and see if they like it up 'em.*" Mostly, "*they don't.*"

And finally...

The quality of work and training on offer makes Dickie Dees deeply attractive to anyone wanting to practise in the North East. For that reason it receives plenty of attention from students, so get on the vac scheme if you can.

SQUEEZE MORE INTO TWO YEARS
WE OFFER YOU ONE OF THE SHARPEST TRAINING CONTRACTS AROUND

Everything matters and every day counts when you're a trainee at DLA Piper. We squeeze huge amounts of experience, responsibility and personal development into your 24 months with us. That means you get to know more about the law, our firm and about yourself.

Working with one of the world's leading practices also means more opportunities: the chance to try the things you want to try, work on secondments abroad or with clients, and get involved with headline making matters.

Enjoy every last bit of your training contract and develop the all round skills that all top lawyers need. Visit our website for more details: www.dlapiper.com

EVERYTHING MATTERS

DLA PIPER

DLA Piper is a global legal services organisation, the members of which are separate and distinct legal entities. For further information please refer to www.dlapiper.com/structure.

DLA Piper (UK) LLP

The facts

Locations: Birmingham, Leeds, Liverpool, London, Manchester, Sheffield, Scotland
Number of UK partners/solicitors: 294/603
Total number of trainees: 155 (in England)
Seats: 4x6 months
Alternative seats: Secondments, overseas seats
Extras: Pro bono – various advice clinics across the offices

DLA Piper has an impressively diversified legal offering. It's all part of the grand plan to be able to cater to all clients in all corners of the world.

Global juggernaut DLA Piper is unabashed in its quest for a leading role on the legal stage, and it has a newly knighted CEO to boot. Join the Order of DLA and plug into an international network that's a world apart from tilting at windmills.

From Dubai to LA

In 1996 Sheffield firm Dibb Lupton Broomhead merged with fellow Yorkshire firm Alsop Wilkinson, and DLA was born. This was the first of several ground-breaking moves that today leaves the firm with more than 3,500 lawyers in 66 offices in 28 countries. One trainee joked that if there were a market for legal services in outer space "*this would be the firm to tap it.*" DLA Piper's rise is quite a story. The most pivotal move was the Brits' integration with US firms Piper Rudnick and Gray Cary Ware & Freidenrich in January 2005 – the single largest transatlantic merger in recent history.

Or was it? Rumours abound that it was not a real merger as the UK and US outfits are still not on the same books. This accounting variance has led commentators to suggest that DLA Piper's monster success story has more smoke and mirrors than substance. Interviewees confessed that this was "*a hot topic,*" but put their cards on the table by saying: "*An accounting difference is no difference really.*" Each of our interviewees had been in contact with foreign colleagues, whether in Spain, Dubai or, as one trainee chuckled, "*East Brunswick, New Jersey!*" Certainly the assertion that "*clients use us because they know if an issue arises in another country we can handle it*" holds water.

So why the big debate over the definition of a merger? Trainees were quick to identify why DLA Piper is often victim to sniping in the legal community. "*This firm is keen to move ahead, and that's why it comes in for a bit of flak. It sticks its neck out in a conservative profession where people like the established order.*" Acknowledging DLA Piper's partiality for publicity and branding, our source continued: "*We're shouting quite loudly about what we're doing.*" While some people cringe at the firm's unapologetic trumpet blowing, the trainees we spoke to were very matter-of-fact about it: "*If we have good lawyers and provide good services there's no reason not to let people know about it.*" Joint CEO Sir Nigel Knowles, the man credited with the firm's fairytale rise from Sheffield to infinity and beyond, was knighted in early 2009. He has attracted controversy in the profession for, among other things, his disregard of traditional methods and the 'cult of personality' built up around him in the earlier years.

We say forget the merger/not merger issue. It has little practical impact, and certainly not on the training available. And what a training it is! Our interviewees were full of praise for the firm, not least because "*supervisors take their time to explain what you have to do and where you fit in.*" Apparently "*for the first few weeks it's relentless training: online, physical meetings, legal updates, group updates, department drinks, anything to get you quickly embroiled in a particular seat.*" Best of all, "*people around you really want you to succeed and are really behind you, which is a great feeling.*"

TV and football

DLA Piper has an impressively diversified legal offering, all part of the grand scheme to be able to cater to all clients in all corners of the world. It's great for trainees, who can, for example, steer themselves towards niche departments such as safety, health and environment as well as the more mainstream litigation or corporate divisions. The litigation division is split into groups – financial and general commercial litigation – and a trainee can benefit hugely from exposure to the broad range of cases handled. A Birmingham trainee summed up the scope of work thus: *"A higher-value case could be in relation to a leak in an oil depot in which we're instructed to recover the losses of the owner. At the other end of the spectrum we'd be defending a bank against a claimant seeking £1,000 mistakenly transferred to his account."* Small-value banking claims are often handed to trainees to run, while larger cases involve *"massive disclosure exercises"* for which trainees *"gather evidence and review documents."*

Recent major cases include the successful defence of HSBC Private Bank in a $400m claim brought by former customers and acting for EDS in defence of claims amounting to £700m brought by BSkyB for breach of contract, negligence and deceit. In the UK, the bulk of the highest-value cases are run from the London office, although the Leeds office in particular has an impressive reputation for banking litigation, having advised one of the main UK clearing banks on matters related to bank charges – this issue prompted massive public interest and was worth over £100bn to the banking sector. In other news, the Liverpool office represented Wigan Athletic AFC on its successful Court of Appeal bid concerning charges levied by the Greater Manchester Police for match day policing. Further litigation subdivisions include aviation and property litigation, the former dealing with cases ranging from lost baggage and flight delays to multimillion-pound disputes between airports and airlines.

The corporate and finance departments are also common places for a trainee to spend six months. *"Hit hard"* by redundancies, these departments (together with real estate) certainly felt the slump in deal activity. Of corporate, some trainees reported *"an uneasy atmosphere which made it hard to settle in,"* but noted as early as summer 2009 how *"things have started to pick up again."* When work was available, trainees were quick to praise their level of involvement. *"I'd be drafting board minutes, ancillary documents for transactions, deeds of indemnity, stock transfer forms, and in one disclosure exercise there was a lot of client contact."* Large deals include the London office's advice to Kraft Foods on the sale of its salted snacks business in the Nordic and Baltic regions. The client was able to take advantage of DLA Piper's international network across the 12 jurisdictions involved.

Chambers UK rankings

Administrative & Public Law	Intellectual Property
Advertising & Marketing	Investment Funds
Asset Finance	Local Government
Aviation	Media & Entertainment
Banking & Finance	Outsourcing
Banking Litigation	Parliamentary & Public Affairs
Capital Markets	Pensions
Commodities	Personal Injury
Competition/European Law	Planning
Construction	Private Equity
Corporate/M&A	Product Liability
Data Protection	Projects, Energy & Natural Resources
Dispute Resolution	Public Procurement
Employment	Real Estate
Environment	Real Estate Finance
Financial Services Regulation	Real Estate Litigation
Franchising	Restructuring/Insolvency
Fraud: Criminal	Retail
Health & Safety	Shipping
Information Technology	Sports Law
Insurance	Tax
	Telecommunications
	Transport

Sheffield lawyers advised the management of metals manufacturer Frith Rixson in a £945m buyout, the largest ever in Yorkshire and the Humber. Staying in the north, 2008 also saw the sale by ITV of its 50% stake in Liverpoolfc.tv. The deal was run by lawyers in Liverpool and Manchester. In typically adaptable style, trainees found themselves more involved in business development in the quiet times, with one in Manchester admitting: *"It wasn't a side I'd thought about before."*

Fashion icons

To stay in sync with the economy, the firm increased the number of trainees taking a restructuring seat over the past year. One source even commented on the irony of *"having dealt with the same companies, first in finance, then in restructuring after seeing them go under."* Across the offices, restructuring is a smaller department than litigation and corporate/finance, and it presents the opportunity for *"more responsibility"* alongside *"a feeling that you are a valued part of the team."* Tasks range from *"winding-up petitions and producing bankruptcy orders to advising insolvency practitioners and shutting companies down."* The Zavvi administration dominated the seat in late 2008/early 2009; there were *"leases on 120 different properties throughout the country that had to be surrendered or reassigned."* The upside of the *"very pressurised"* atmosphere is the high-profile nature of the work. A London trainee told us about working on the administration of Mosaic Fashion, the Icelandic-backed group which owned Karen Millen, Warehouse and Oasis, and seeing what had just been discussed in a meeting "*pop up on the BBC website ten minutes later!*"

The firm offers secondments to a number of FTSE-listed clients, among them retailers and banks. During 2009 it suspended its international secondment programme for trainees. We were assured, however, that this would be back up and running in time. For details of which of the international offices trainees have previously been able to visit, refer to page 560. In the UK, the seats with the most international flavour are projects and construction; the former has lately seen trainees preparing documents for power plants in South Africa. Birmingham is the centre of DLA's construction practice, which has a healthy involvement in projects related to the 2012 Olympics and London's Shard of Glass building, set to be the tallest mixed-use structure in Europe.

Growing pains?

Far from the "*bulldog that fought its way out of Yorkshire in the 1990s,*" DLA Piper is now one of the biggest firms in the world. When discussing its scale and ambitions, trainees mostly agreed with the person who said: "*As long as expansion is sustainable and not for its own sake, I'm happy with it.*" Whereas in years past the mention of Sir Nigel elicited passionate responses, this year's trainees were more measured. They extolled the virtues of a CEO who "*you feel you can talk to,*" but didn't get carried away. Said one: "*People here are bright enough not to be persuaded by marketing speak when it's not appropriate.*" Perhaps as the firm's rapacious appetite for expansion subsides and having witnessed colleagues being made redundant, trainees are able to think more critically. A Leeds source pondered: "*I'd have thought the firm will look to stabilise now as it can't really grow much more.*" A Manchester interviewee went further, saying: "*It can be a bit big for its boots – sometimes you feel nothing seems good enough and think, 'Can't you recognise that we're doing really well already?'*" Trainees worry that too much of a thirst for world domination "*may put people off,*" especially as the firm becomes "*less work hard, play hard and more just work hard.*" In the regions, trainees questioned whether it was fair to sell students the idea that "*you're not expected to work the hours and have the lifestyle of a London lawyer.*" In the opinion of a number of these sources, "*it's not necessarily true, and the pay gap* [with London] *is significant.*"

Despite these limited misgivings, our interviewees were keen to express what "*an inspiring, dynamic place*" DLA Piper is to work. Supportive, too, they add. "*Everyone is willing to help you*" and "*you can speak to anyone, no matter how high up they are.*" They believe applicants need to be "*outgoing,*" "*enthusiastic,*" "*confident*" and able to show commitment to the geographical area if they want to work in a regional office. While some acknowledge that DLA Piper has a mild redbrick bias, our sources also wanted to tell students: "*Don't be afraid to apply here. People don't need to fit a unique mould to work here – and don't feel it's overly competitive, because it isn't.*" A Birmingham interviewee told us: "*There's a real range of characters – in my intake there's a bit of a gentleman farmer and a guy from an inner-city comprehensive.*" What the trainees do have in common is an impressive work ethic. They say that before applying "*people should consider whether they want an easy life or to come and do some real work. If you want real experience and to be chucked in at the deep end then DLA is the place to come.*"

Play together, stay together

Trainees from across the UK (and increasingly the world) meet at a two-week induction at the beginning of their contracts. Contact is then maintained through regular training and social events. Our sources said the firm was "*nicely aligned in national terms.*" January sees trainees braving the Scottish winter to attend celebrations for Burns Night in conjunction with the Edinburgh and Glasgow offices. A curry night in Birmingham is always popular. Liverpool trainees, famous for their sense of fun, host a Grand National day out in April. Independently, Birmingham has its very own rock stars in the shape of The Sued (the lead singer is called Sue); London organises rugby sevens in Richmond Park – "*always nice on a sunny day.*" Manchester has lost The Pitcher & Piano from the ground floor of its office building but nonetheless makes the most of its central location, and in Sheffield trainees enjoy a few laughs at Bar Ha!Ha! and ice hockey at the Sheffield Arena.

In 2009, 54 of the 86 qualifiers stayed on, many going into the litigation, regulatory, restructuring and employment teams. The firm also helped source jobs with clients for some of the others. Just six of the 2009 intake of new trainees were deferred until 2010 in return for a no-strings £5,000 payment. In a bad news year for many businesses, the firm made at least 124 UK redundancies. Following this it took flak from the legal press and online posters, as many people were let go on statutory minimum terms. As a major global business, however, DLA Piper needs to bear in mind the health of the whole firm whenever it makes local decisions, so do consider this factor when you size up your options.

And finally...

DLA's ambition is to be all things to all clients – everywhere. Such magisterial aims are tempered by a commitment to detailed, personalised training and interesting work.

DMH Stallard LLP

The facts

Location: Brighton, Crawley, London
Number of UK partners/solicitors: 52/46
Total number of trainees: 18
Seats: 4x6 months
Alternative seats: Secondments

Some reassuring words for those attracted to DMH: trainees say they feel highly valued and reckon the firm "*definitely lives up to its spiel.*"

DMH Stallard's mission is to become a top 50 firm. It is already one of the big players in the Southern Home Counties and the plan is now to build up in London.

The story so far...

The product of a three-way merger between Sussex firms, Brighton-headquartered Donne Mileham & Haddock set off, slowly at first, on a revolutionary road. One of the biggest milestones was the opening of a large office in Crawley. Surrounded by the so-called Gatwick Diamond business region, Crawley has attracted several law firms keen to exploit the growing technology and transportation business in this area. Re-branded as DMH, the firm resolved to capture more business from the capital. A merger with London corporate firm Stallards in 2005 boosted its fortunes, and in 2008 it merged with another small London firm called Coutts & Co.

Meanwhile, a shift inland from the South Coast to Crawley was gathering pace, leaving Brighton as more a spiritual home than a headquarters. If any of the offices leads then it's Crawley. For now at least. Actually, Gatwick is DMH's preferred name for its Crawley base (see the likely explanation later). Since moving to flasher premises in London last year, the emphasis on the capital has been growing, and management speaks openly about wanting London to match Gatwick in size.

So what's the firm up to in its three offices? Smallest first, so that means Brighton. This branch now focuses on private clients and, just like the town itself, is pretty laid-back, probably because lifestyle concerns matter as much as anything else to staff. Said one source: "*It's great as I can walk to work, but the offices are shabby compared to London and Gatwick. They're very light and airy, but also very quiet, not as chatty.*" In the view of another: "*Brighton is now more of a limb than a fully fledged branch.*" Twenty miles up the A23 is Crawley, where most of the firm's commercial departments operate and where you'll find most trainees. Crawley is a great business centre but dire on most other measures, not least architecturally. "*Crawley as a place is not conducive to socialising and most lawyers tend to live elsewhere,*" reported one source. Actually we couldn't find anyone who would sing Crawley's praises, apart from one fan of a bar called JaJa, the self-proclaimed best cocktail establishment in town.

And so to the well-appointed London office, which has "*good views of St Paul's Cathedral and even to Wembley Stadium on a good day.*" Corporate is king here, although other commercial teams are pushing forward. Trainees suggest the merger between Stallard and DMH initially revealed inconsistencies in working practices, but that the firm is now more consistent between branches. The only issue that still jars among trainees is a salary that feels more regional than capital. Be aware also that trainees must be prepared to move between offices for seats, the most likely switches being between London and Crawley.

DMH and Goliath

One consequence of the size of DMH's property practice is that seats here are compulsory. Major clients include

EDF Energy and retail Goliath Tesco. Property gets *"very busy and gives good experience of drafting, amending and negotiating leases."* All our sources had enjoyed the work, one quipping: *"Loved the seat, great clients and some great transactional work."* Having secured planning permission for the new £88m Brighton and Hove Albion Community Stadium, DMH is now helping the club get the place built on time and on budget. Public sector projects are also a speciality – take the regeneration of Shoreham and Newhaven Ports, for example. The South East England Development Agency is another client.

DMH is no corporate minnow. A strong aviation focus sees lawyers working for businesses orbiting Gatwick airport. For example, a major North American aviation simulator operator sought advice on the expansion of its UK operations. Public sector clients also come through for the team; the London Borough of Croydon, for example, took advice when it entered into a major street lighting contract. *"You don't have your own files in corporate – you work on other people's matters, though this means heaps of client contact and drafting practice."* Trainees encounter deals that are commonly worth several million pounds. In the banking team, too, deals generally lie in the £5m region – not earth-shatteringly large, though most of our sources preferred it that way. *"I haven't had to work weekends,"* said one gratefully; *"compared to City firms the hours are fantastic."*

There are popular seats in litigation, IP, employment and a specialist planning law practice. Litigation trainees have ample client contact, court exposure and satisfaction while helping to pull cases together. The firm handles plenty of property and construction disputes: it recently represented Norwich Union against a subcontractor on a multimillion-pound contract and successfully defended the University of Sussex from a subcontractor's claim. The volume of cases in litigation has risen noticeably, in part due to the client-winning qualities of the London office, but the big news in 2009 was DMH's appointment to the government's prestigious Lit-Cat legal panel.

The employment lawyers usually act for bosses, so trainees help prepare for tribunal hearings on matters ranging from whistle-blowing to discrimination. They learn to draft compromise agreements for departing executives and how major redundancy programmes work. There's even a spot of business immigration law. *"You get responsibility but you also feel well-supported,"* said a source. Another core practice is IP, and for at least one source this was the firm's key attraction. While there has been change at the senior end of the team, the client base is reassuringly solid and includes BAA, ICI, Alcatel-Lucent and shoe retailer Office. Through dealing with smaller claims in the personal injury team, trainees learn numerous skills. *"You get a large number of varied files and there's a huge amount of client contact and court experience."* Work has included a claim against a tour operator for an accident in Greece and the liability of a restaurant owner after his employee stabbed a customer and fled the country. Maybe not the best place for a first date…

Chambers UK rankings

Banking & Finance	Environment
Construction	Information Technology
Corporate/M&A	Intellectual Property
Debt Recovery	Local Government
Dispute Resolution	Planning
Employment	Real Estate
	Real Estate Litigation

Open for business

Who is DMH recruiting? *"People with really good academics and an outgoing personality,"* someone suggested, while another said: *"Trainees tend to be open and confident, and they range in age; many here are on their second career."* Of the open-plan offices and the firm's culture we hear that *"you have easy routes to gaining help and you can listen in to phone calls."* Moreover, *"the firm publishes quite a bit of financial info; for example, pay scales are all on the intranet which indicates an open culture."* As one source put it: *"The firm makes you feel a part of things."* This is not to say there aren't departmental variations: *"Some are friendlier than others where, instead, you just have to put your head down and charge through so much work."*

The trainees have a good network due to their relatively small numbers and the regular rotation around the offices. Put simply: *"Trainees connect the firm."* The AGM in Brighton performs this function too as the meeting is always followed by a lively dinner and dancing. At the last AGM, questions were raised about the effects of the economic crisis and resulting redundancies. Management were *"grilled but their answers were reasonable."* Trainees say management *"haven't wanted to keep us in the dark about these things, but they do like to respect the privacy of those who have been let go."* In 2009 trainees did rather well, with eight of the nine qualifiers gaining jobs.

And finally…

Having decided to honour the original start dates of all 2009 trainees, DMH is holding back from recruiting 2012 starters for now. Keep an eye on its website and be ready to apply when the scheme reopens.

Dundas & Wilson

The facts

Location: London, Edinburgh, Glasgow

Number of UK partners/solicitors: 85/212

Total number of trainees: 18 (in England)

Seats: 4x6 months

Alternative seats: Occasional secondments

> *"We're appealing to people who want to grow in a smaller environment."*
>
> Donald Shaw, Managing Partner

Scottish heavyweight Dundas & Wilson made the move to London in 2002 and hasn't looked back.

North Star

Dundas & Wilson is the cream of the Scottish crop and has a whole host of nationally recognised clients on its books – RBS, Bank of Scotland, Barclays, Standard Life, EDF, E.ON and ASDA. Consistently ranked by *Chambers UK* in almost all areas of corporate and commercial practice north of the border, it is a force to be reckoned with. Major instructions include representation of Clyde Blowers (energy, mining, transportation and engineering) in its $1bn purchase of four separate businesses from American Fortune 500 company Textron. Lawyers also advised Lloyds Pharmacy on its £70m acquisition of the Munro Pharmacy Group, one of the largest independents in the UK. Since 2002, meteoric growth has seen the London office become the firm's second largest, overtaking Glasgow in terms of lawyer numbers. Our sources insisted that the London base had outgrown any accusations of it simply being an offshoot office. *"The reputation in Scotland is obviously very good, but certainly the mentality is that we are a national firm,"* said one source.

Corporate and property are currently the largest departments in London. Although undoubtedly a rising star in the capital, D&W's London corporate team (ranked by *Chambers UK* in the lower mid-market alongside the likes of Beachcroft, RPC, Salans and Trowers & Hamlins) still has a hefty roster of Highland clients such as Scottish and Southern Energy, Bank of Scotland and RBS. The team advised Bank of Scotland Integrated Finance on the debt and equity financed acquisition of Quartix, which produces vehicle-tracking systems; it also aided a subsidiary of Scottish and Southern Energy, Southern Electric Contracting, on its acquisition of building services company Hills E&M. While we do get the feeling that the London office is yet to really shine in its own right, the corporate team has been involved in some significant standalone deals. Notably, it acted for Royal London, the UK's largest mutual life and pension company, on its purchase of Fundsdirect Group, and assisted meat and fish wholesaler Seafood Holding on its £7m acquisition of Southbank Fresh Fish and Kingfisher.

In other practice areas, *Chambers UK* team rankings are finally starting to emerge, in all likelihood because of *"internal promotions and lots of lateral hires* [from other City firms]." Until now the number of team rankings belied the office's size and it had to content itself with individual lawyer rankings. The ugly duckling is looking more and more like a swan.

Look out for cow pat

Trainees largely have free rein over their seat choices, but due to the rapid growth of some teams and the unstable economy slowing the pace in others, they *"don't always quite know what's going to be available at each seat change."* Luckily they *"always get plenty of time to decide."* Corporate and property seats are the most common. The other options are commercial litigation, corporate recovery, EU/competition, environment, banking, employment and IP/IT. Opportunities for client secondments (eg BAA) *"are not set in stone, but happen as and when."* Trainees are assigned mentors in each seat (usually a relatively junior assistant) and because *"they remember being a trainee you feel you can go to them with stupid questions."* Work is passed down via mentors, and in the open-plan office "*everyone is approachable,*" so it's easy enough to pick up wisdom from a nearby partner. In fact, the office layout is so much a part of the D&W culture that one trainee warned: "*If you don't like open-plan then this isn't the best place for you.*" This advice must have escaped the attention of a recently arrived partner, who apparently insisted on having his own office as a condition of joining.

Corporate trainees see a mixture of drafting ("*more generic documents like resignation letters and some of the simpler clauses*") and document management. "*You also attend completions and make sure all the documents are there and signed and then taken away after.*" While none of the tasks are particularly cerebral, they do help you to understand the processes involved, as well as providing valuable client contact. The corporate team is applauded for being "*very friendly*" with some good assistants acting as mentors. "*Mine was especially great... he was very patient, knew his stuff and was happy to help and teach me,*" said one source. Among the property seats is an option covering planning, development and environmental law and then options in real estate funds, real estate finance and real estate management. Trainees can expect decent responsibility across the board in this department, often running their own small transactions. Environment-related work is picking up pace rapidly at D&W, and clients include the Environment Agency, National Grid, British Energy and South East Water. Work here is "*heavily research-based,*" but there are plenty of opportunities to accompany supervisors on site visits to "*attach CPO notices to various points on the land.*" Start practising your cow pat and angry bull avoidance techniques.

Tartan ties

D&W's London office was not known for its contentious clout, preferring to concentrate on transactional and advisory work. Until recently that is. The litigation department has undergone explosive growth over the past couple of years. "*It was half the size it is now when I was there, and a couple of months before that it was very different again,*" noted one source who'd visited. Turnover rose by a colossal 350% in 2008. Fronted by Martin Thomas, previously head of property litigation at Herbert Smith, the team divides its time between contentious property work and general commercial disputes. Trainees don't deny that there is a "*fair amount of bundling*" to get through, but there is also a chance to get their teeth into some "*meatier*" stuff. Advocacy is not unheard of and trainees are regularly involved in drafting letters and witness statements.

Despite the 300-odd miles and differing laws separating London from its bonny parents in Edinburgh and Glasgow, there is "*constant contact*" between the three offices, making it "*feel like one firm.*" The summer ball sees all D&W employees travel up to Edinburgh to dance the night away "*at a nice country estate outside the city,*" and new recruits come together in the Scottish capital for induction and training in the areas of law that are the same on both sides of the border. Hard work is part and parcel of a D&W training contract, but sources report that "*there is a good atmosphere around the office*" and recruits are "*a good mix. It's not the bog-standard straight-out-of-law-school.*" "*Grades count,*" explained one source, "*but they also look at what else you've done and where you are now.*" Some of the 2009 new starters were deferred for six months and received a payment of £2,500. The situation is to be reviewed again in spring 2010. As for existing staff, 16 people lost their jobs in London in 2009 and of the seven 2009 qualifying trainees, just two were awarded NQ jobs, with a further two London positions being filled by Scottish qualifiers.

If they are not doing a charity fun-run or playing in one of the sports teams, on Friday night your typical D&W recruit can be found in local wine bar Daly's, which is a magnet for lawyers. We'd like to also tell you about the annual trainee sketch show at Christmas but unfortunately our sources encouraged us to "*just move on from that!*"

Chambers UK rankings

Administrative & Public Law	Investment Funds
Banking & Finance	Local Government
Competition/European Law	Media & Entertainment
Construction	Outsourcing
Corporate/M&A	Parliamentary & Public Affairs
Dispute Resolution	
Education	Partnership
Employee Share Schemes	Pensions
Employment	Planning
Environment	Professional Negligence
Financial Services Regulation	Projects, Energy & Natural Resources
Franchising	Public Procurement
Health & Safety	Real Estate
Healthcare	Real Estate Litigation
Immigration	Restructuring/Insolvency
Information Technology	Sports Law
Intellectual Property	Tax
	Transport

And finally...

D&W London offers solid commercial training for those who would happily sidestep the cut and thrust of an HQ experience. No longer a pioneering office, London's job is now to grow in influence to allow D&W to acquire a national reputation.

- **In 2007 the total number of ethnic minority solicitors in England and Wales passed 10,000 for the first time** and as of 2008 the number of solicitors declaring membership of a minority group was 11,249 – out of a total of 112,433 with practising certificates.

top tip no. 12

DWF LLP

The facts

Location: Liverpool, Manchester, Leeds, Preston, London

Number of UK partners/solicitors: 126/230

Total number of trainees: 35

Seats: 4x4 + 1x8 months

Alternative seats: Secondments

DWF has the North covered and is now targeting London. It has consistently broadened its practice profile, which means plenty of choice for trainees.

DWF's chief exec Andrew Leaitherland wanted to turn this Lancashire-born insurance specialist into a top-30 firm by 2010. It's certainly there or thereabouts.

The grand plan

The firm that would eventually become DWF was founded in 1977 by Guy Wallis and James Davies (who still serves as senior partner). It grew quickly on a diet of mergers. The first came in 1989 with Dodds Ashcroft and a year later it joined forces with Mancunian firm Foysters. It was only relatively recently that Mr Davies, Mr Wallis and Mr Foyster's names were dropped from the firm's name and replaced by their three initials. The most recent merger – with fellow northerner Ricksons – was inked on New Year's Day 2007 and added offices in Preston and Leeds. The punky young upstart has become a major player in the north of England: it now has around 800 staff and its annual turnover has passed the £60m mark. In 2008, the firm debuted in London with a team of insurance lawyers setting up shop on King William Street and, with a celebratory flourish, it has recently moved into new premises in Liverpool.

The escalating figures have been accompanied by a broadening of the firm's expertise. Although its core practice in insurance remains the largest area (and a de facto compulsory seat), DWF has zealously poached partners and teams to enhance its other areas. In 2007 it snatched up a *Chambers* top-ranked private client and family team from Cobbetts and days later lured a couple of people over from DLA Piper's real estate team. More real estate lawyers followed from Hammonds, nudging Leeds towards full-service capability, and 2008 and 2009 have seen a steady trickle of hires from well-respected firms.

These include personal injury supremo Graham Dickinson, who has arrived in the London office, and Peter Allen from Macfarlanes and Stephen Houston from Addleshaw Goddard, who both joined Manchester's corporate team.

The firm's steady climb to prominence clearly caught the eye of many trainees. "*I was interested because DWF is a pretty big force in the North West and I knew it was broadening its horizons. I wanted to get in there while it's on the way up,*" said one. Year on year, the firm has posted ever-larger turnover, a trend that has continued through the present recession. Although profit margins were damaged, the firm managed a fantastic NQ retention rate in 2009, with all 16 qualifiers staying on. "*The idea is to keep everyone and redeploy them as and when things pick up. What's the point of spending so much money on trainees to not keep them?*" The only real concession that had to be made was a pay freeze. Aware of the bigger picture, a typical source suggested that although it's "*a little unfair* [to freeze salary when turnover has increased], *I'm sure it'll be rectified when the economy sets itself right. The main thing was having a job on qualification. Now that's sorted I'm very happy.*"

Lancashire hot shots

'Very happy' was indeed the general consensus. DWF is moving smoothly, seemingly unperturbed by economic conditions, and confidence is high among trainees, who are sure that they've hitched themselves to a good firm. In truth, the only complaint we heard was that *"you don't get much say in what seats you get and they don't give you much notice."* Indeed several trainees were angry when told they had to switch offices in a matter of days. The firm says it has to be like this for the sake of flexibility: fair enough, but having heard complaints on this issue for some years, we say that there must be room for some improvement. Trainees complete four seats of four months each and then a final eight-month posting to really polish their skills in the area they intend to qualify into.

Manchester and Liverpool, the largest offices, have the most trainees but there will always be four or five in Preston and Leeds as well. London does not take any at the moment, although this will change in the future as the office continues to expand. For the most part, trainees stay in the office to which they are recruited, but sometimes, due to oft-cursed *"business needs"* they relocate. The offices are all open-plan with the exception of Preston, which maintains separate rooms for its partners. In terms of atmosphere, trainees hinted at something of a paradox. While being *"very friendly – more so than Manchester,"* Preston is also *"much tougher and a little more old-school."* Here, the (usually almost invisible) hierarchy is more apparent, with partners' expectations being higher and praise being comparatively hard-won.

No fault Sherlock

Insurance is a big deal at DWF – it accounts for around 45% of the firm's manpower and revenue. If fact, we had to interrupt the trainee who started reeling off all the different types of insurance work available (*"there's a growing fraud team, workplace injury, road traffic accidents, catastrophic injuries, property recovery, injuries in childbirth, commercial insurance claims, asbestos-related claims..."*) because we didn't know when the list would end.

Luckily claims don't dry up in a recession so there's still been *"an awful lot"* of work in this area and trainees can get first-rate experience. For personal injury, *Chambers UK* describes DWF as a touchstone of excellence. Why? A multimillion-pound recovery for RSA Insurance Group goes some way to explain it, but as well as that DWF has set precedents in numerous PI cases and enjoys a steady stream of property recovery work. The PI department has a turnover approaching the £6m mark, earned usually (but not always) by acting on behalf of defendants. It is presently working on some confidential cases that could have a direct influence on current legislation. Asked what happens in property recovery, one trainee enlightened us: *"Basically what we get is a situation where, say, a car crashes through your front wall or a plumber makes a mistake and floods your whole house. The insurer tries to recover what it can from whoever's fault it was."* DWF's role in this is to represent the insurer, investigating the

Chambers UK rankings

Asset Finance	Information Technology
Banking & Finance	Insurance
Banking Litigation	Intellectual Property
Construction	Partnership
Corporate/M&A	Personal Injury
Debt Recovery	Police Law
Dispute Resolution	Real Estate
Employment	Real Estate Litigation
Family/Matrimonial	Restructuring/Insolvency
Health & Safety	

costs and litigating if necessary. Trainees were able to handle matters worth up to £100k and felt that the work *"really gets you used to the litigation process."* If you fancy yourself as a bit of a sleuth, there are *"really interesting"* insurance fraud cases available on which trainees *"try to crack fraud rings by investigating staged accidents."* Another factor behind DWF's top-tier status is its range of clients, who read like a list of daytime TV advertisers – Admiral, Norwich Union, Capita, Lloyd's, Fortis, Royal SunAlliance and Brit Insurance.

Real estate is the second-biggest practice at the firm and, despite the obvious slowdown in the field, DWF has managed to add some new names to the client list, including Instore (Poundstretcher) and Vertex Data Systems. Over on the finance side, it is now on Abbey's legal panel and works for Lloyds TSB, Alliance & Leicester and a whole slew of others. A recent instruction from Fylde and Blackpool Borough Council adds that body to a growing roster of public sector clients including Liverpool and Manchester city councils. As non-contentious real estate work has petered out, real estate litigation has seesawed upwards. Lawyers have successfully advised developers in matters such as rectifying rent review clauses and defending them from injunctions brought by tenants. It recently fought against a major supermarket over the development agreement for a new store. Trainees reported that they had prepared and served notices on tenants and also mucked in on some construction litigation.

Schadenfreude durch technik

The level of personal insolvency work at DWF has increased by 30% since the economy went tits up. DWF has been kept busy with instructions from insolvency practitioners at accountancy firms Grant Thornton and KPMG. As for corporate insolvency, one trainee with tongue firmly in cheek told us: *"I really enjoyed it – there was a kind of schadenfreude seeing others going bust."* On a more serious note, they continued: *"I assisted the partner with investigations into whether a company had been run into the ground, and whether the board had failed to take any remedial action. We were trying to find out if they did it on purpose to get out of paying people."*

Leeds sounded like a good place to do this seat because at the time of our interviews trainees benefited from "*pretty much one-to-one tuition working through files with the partner.*" In Leeds, the insolvency work is mainly corporate, whereas in Liverpool it's more for individuals.

Commercial litigation "*keeps you on your toes*" and trainees find themselves hopping from work for privately funded clients to those with legal expenses insurance, from disputes over the workmanship of a wristwatch to shareholder tiffs. This means they gain experience of working as part of a team on big claims as well as being able to run their own smaller files. As is generally the case at DWF, there are few formal training sessions in this seat but "*slowly, by increasing the level of involvement, you get more knowledge.*" Clients include Allianz Cornhill and Iceland (the shop not the country) and, in the education sector, expertise built up from work with Liverpool's John Moores University has led to instructions from Manchester College.

Musical differences

One trainee described DWF as "*quite quirky. I say quirky – it's as quirky as a law firm can be. We're not in media here.*" The oddities begin with the initial interviews where one question was reported to ask what song you would have as your personal soundtrack. Perhaps The Clash's *I Fought The Law* might not be the best answer here. The partner profiles on the firm's website prove that the quirks don't wear off as people progress. They feature a photograph of each partner accompanied by some choice items that reflect their hobbies. Senior partner Jim Davies appears dressed for fishing and we learn that he likes Liverpool FC, rare roast beef, the occasional par on the golf course and clients, but not tedious meetings or BlackBerrys…

The quirky, fun-loving attitude is flaunted in the firm's promo materials. One ad we saw a while back featured DWF lawyers 'avin' it large with glosticks and whistles, hands aloft during an evening spectacular. When quizzed further on the matter, trainees were unable to confirm or deny whether partners wore yellow smiley face t-shirts beneath their suits. "*They might have gone clubbing back in the day at the Hacienda. Who knows?*" What we do know is that the photo wasn't staged. "*It was like a proper rave – very surreal to see partners throwing shapes.*"

DWF trainees "*always get through the whole tab*" when money is put behind a bar at a social gathering and, despite some cutbacks, the firm is still happy to pay for tickets to balls and other social events. There are ladies-only networking nights and the firm holds season tickets for Liverpool, Everton and the mighty Preston North End. It also sponsors a box at Manchester's MEN Arena. Trainees were keen to debunk a myth that the firm once spent only £5 a head on the Christmas party, saying that "*it was more like £25*" and gleefully reminisced that they managed to go to several parties, not just the one for their own office.

And finally…

A 100% retention rate, high-calibre hires, expanding offices and quirky, fun-loving lawyers – what's not to like about this ambitious young firm?

Edwards Angell Palmer & Dodge LLP

The facts

Locations: London

Number of UK partners/solicitors: 20/28

Total number of trainees: 15

Seats: 4x6 months

Alternative seats: Client secondments, overseas seats

Extras: Pro bono – RCJ CAB; Fair Trials International

> EAPD lacks a strong hierarchy in its small London office, giving it a distinctly close-knit feel.

In 2008 UK insurance stalwart Kendall Freeman merged with US insurance stalwart Edwards Angell Palmer & Dodge. Is it a match made in heaven?

Angells & Freemans

With 11 offices across nine states, EAPD is well established in the land of the bald eagle. Its arrival over here is part of an international drive that has been in progress since 2005. The Kendall Freeman merger was the most significant move, but the firm has also opened up in Hong Kong and signed a co-operation agreement with a firm in Bermuda to help establish an insurance and reinsurance practice on the island. Bermuda is seen as strategically important in this industry and it's hoped the operation will refer work to the UK and US offices. It would be reasonable to presume that international expansion isn't over yet (indeed, the managing partner has said as much) and further Asian offices would seem the most likely next development.

Interviewees said that a good cultural fit was a requirement before any merger took place, and this appears to have been achieved. In fact, little appears to have changed from the last days of Kendall Freeman. "*No American lawyers have come over; we've basically stayed the same apart from the* [addition of some] *IP lawyers.*" Even with this boost in numbers, one trainee told us: "*Despite the fact it's a huge beast with the US* [operation] *behind it, it's still small compared to most London firms.*" As in Sam Malone's famous Boston watering hole Cheers, "*within the office everybody knows your name.*"

The merger has been "*good news for trainees.*" Said one: "*There are more opportunities for secondments abroad, there was a New York retreat and I doubt we'd have an IP department without the merger.*" Unsurprisingly, insurance remains the heart of the business, a fact trainees said should not put off prospective applicants. They reckon it "*adds an extra intellectual dimension which is just that little bit more challenging.*"

Insuring success

We can't overstate the focus on contentious matters, and "*it's pretty much certain you'll do a seat in commercial litigation and insurance litigation.*" In addition, there's public international law (PIL); corporate; insurance insolvency; employment; IP; secondments to Harrods, Shell and the FSA; and some foreign seats (as of 2009, IP in New York was on offer, with Hong Kong on the cards).

Insurance litigation is "*traditionally the heart of the firm.*" A large department, it tackles disputes related to asbestos liability, energy, personal accidents, professional indemnity, directors' and officers' liability and significant reinsurance issues. The firm represented Dow Chemicals' captive insurer Dorinco Reinsurance in three arbitrations totalling in excess of $300m covering property damage and business interruption losses as a result of Hurricanes Katrina and Rita. For trainees, these large and intricate cases generally mean "*there's not that much free rein.*" Typical tasks include document management, "*reviewing and analysing reinsurance contracts,*" and "*looking through disclosure information.*" Nevertheless, "*you certainly feel like you're part of the team.*" In some ways an extension of the insurance department, corporate has seen a welcome boom as a result of the merger. Recent disposals and acquisitions have been focused on insurance companies. Those with an ear to the ground suggested a private equity group could be on the horizon, which would further bolster the firm's non-contentious offering, for both clients and trainees.

"*Generally a lot of people's favourite department*" was the accolade bestowed on a commercial litigation team whose work has been dominated by the Buncefield oil depot litigation in recent years. The firm represented Hertfordshire Oil Storage Limited – the joint venture company formed by Total and Chevron – against claims related to the 2005 explosion at the depot. On cases such as these, trainees stay busy with "*preparation, disclosure, pre-trial review, lots of correspondence, meetings with the clients and barristers,*" and if that wasn't enough, "*pretty much attending every day of trial.*" Defamation and reputation management is another important source of instructions. One of EAPD's most famous clients is Sheikh Khalid Bin Mahfouz, whom it has represented since a newspaper published allegations connecting him to the funding and supporting of terrorism. Trainees working in this team praised the international aspect of the work and liked the fact that they liaised with foreign lawyers.

A very rare opportunity

Overlapping with commercial litigation is PIL, where lawyers trace and then attempt to recover the assets of "*corrupt former public officials.*" Without doubt an exciting area, you can find yourself playing detective in the fight against corruption in conjunction with domestic and foreign governments. "*I was tracing records and looking for bank details, trying to find out where stolen assets were stashed,*" said one investigative trainee who also told us about "*dealing with the relevant institutions in asset recovery and liaising with Swiss lawyers, trying to get the Swiss authorities to open up bank accounts.*" This is a prestigious department in a rare and highly specialist area. *Chambers UK* puts EAPD alongside Clifford Chance, Freshfields, Latham & Watkins, A&O and Herbert Smith as the only firms up to task. It's a small team within commercial litigation though, so while you may have a far better chance of sampling this work than a trainee at one of the big firms, don't get your hopes up for a qualification job in the team.

One department that does look poised for growth is IP. This is the new kid on the block at this firm and the team only came into being in 2008 after 16 lawyers were pinched from Field Fisher Waterhouse. In an effort to get the UK operation to "*more closely mirror the practice focus in the US,*" the department has benefited from some high-profile Stateside clients, including MasterCard, Elizabeth Arden and American Greetings Corporation. Work for the latter has involved numerous customs seizures with respect to its Strawberry Shortcake and Care Bears trade marks. Spare a moment for all those impounded fake Tenderhearts…

Chambers UK rankings

Corporate/M&A	Insurance
Dispute Resolution	Intellectual Property
Fraud: Civil	Public International Law

Dodge City

Tenderhearted may be too saccharine a description for the culture at EAPD – but we don't often hear of a City firm with a staff appreciation day, let alone one that sees the senior partner delivering cake around the office. As one trainee laughed: "*I can't see anyone at Slaughters doing that!*" Trainees noted that EAPD lacks a strong hierarchy and has a distinctly close-knit feel. "*The floors are so small that you see everyone every day.*" By the same token the firm is genuinely interested in trainee feedback and we were told of management meetings in which trainees had "*put forward ideas which resulted in changes. We wanted more clarification on what to expect from a seat, and now there's a list of ideal tasks and experiences for a trainee in each department.*"

While the interior of One Fetter Lane could do with "*freshening up,*" the location "*slightly out of the City means you're not surrounded by countless numbers of suits.*" If there's a downside, it's perhaps that "*we've established it's not a very good location for pubs.*" Still, no one's afraid to venture a little further afield, and "*karaoke is a big favourite.*" Our contacts ranged from those who happily admitted to blasting out a bit of Westlife to those who mumbled with embarrassment – "*I try to avoid it.*" On the whole the firm knows how to enjoy itself, global economy notwithstanding. The last Christmas party was held in-house with "*meeting rooms turned into festive grottos, a cocktail bar, Wii consoles, vodka luge and, of course, karaoke!*" Trainees were impressed and some told us: "*It was all the better for being in-house – rather than stuffy black tie it was a relaxed atmosphere.*" A historical problem for trainees at Kendall Freeman was less-than-impressive NQ retention rates. This was almost entirely "*a size issue*" – the firm simply wasn't big enough to take everyone it trained. However, in September 2009 six of eight qualifiers took jobs with EAPD: a significant improvement on past years. "*It seems things will get better as the firm grows,*" said hopeful trainees.

And finally...

Don't go thinking the 2008 merger has warped the charms of Kendall Freeman: this remains a small, friendly outfit with a keen focus on litigation.

Eversheds Graduate Opportunities

WANTED:
RARE TALENTS

The best lawyers are multi-faceted; they combine wit with wisdom and drive with diplomacy. They're competitive but controlled; single-minded yet team oriented.

They're Rare Talents and we're searching for the next generation of them – the Eversheds lawyers and partners of the future. Our training will enhance their existing skills and teach them many new ones. If you've an inkling that you're a Rare Talent – that you're not single-faceted – then satisfy your curiosity at **www.eversheds.com/graduaterecruitment**

EVERSHEDS

Eversheds LLP

The facts

Location: Birmingham, Cambridge, Cardiff, Ipswich, Leeds, London, Manchester, Newcastle, Nottingham
Number of UK partners/solicitors: 309/828
Total number of trainees: 129
Seats: 4x6 months
Alternative seats: Overseas seats, secondments
Extras: Pro bono – Mary Ward Centre and others; language training

This ambitious firm's website invites us to 'find out where the legal profession is heading'.

Eversheds dubs itself 'an international law firm for the 21st century'. It's an apt description.

Shedloads of Chambers rankings

In its 21 years of life Eversheds has grown furiously. Starting from offices in Norwich, Manchester, Sheffield and Birmingham, the UK network expanded to include Ipswich, Newcastle, Derby, Nottingham, Cardiff, Leeds, Bristol, London and Cambridge, although some of these no longer exist. Following a merger at the age of seven, Eversheds gained its first international office (Brussels) and has not looked back. There are now offices in 29 countries and at home the firm scores masses of *Chambers UK* rankings across multiple practices.

The international strategy is very important and Eversheds earns a healthy clutch of rankings for its overseas work. As one trainee noted: *"If you look at the flow of investment and the flow of trade, everything is global,"* so Eversheds is zealously following the money by setting up shop in strategic hubs around the world. It has opened an incredible nine overseas offices since January 2008 in locations including Mauritius (an important gateway for foreign investment into the expanding Indian market and Africa), Hong Kong, Saudi Arabia, Singapore and Scotland. It also has its eye on India. Rather than setting up on its own, Eversheds prefers to associate with well-established firms in the target market, then allowing them to trade in their old colours for the Eversheds brand. By growing this way it maintains local ties, taking work from that area as well as facilitating international deals. One sharp trainee pointed out that this allows the firm to get in early with big corporations from emerging markets. *"In theory, the strategy is good,"* said another, *"but we shouldn't lose sight of the firm's primary market in the UK."*

Hours to cherish

The gist of the domestic strategy is this: Eversheds wants to broaden its capability in order to increase its share of high-value work. It doesn't want to focus on big-ticket instructions at the expense of lower-value matters; it's more a case of giving clients what they want by offering a wide selection of services at different price bands. The unusually useful buzz-phrase 'Networked Law' alludes to the fact that work can be passed from one office to another according to capacity and speciality. Different offices have different strengths so it is worth identifying what they are – look at the *Chambers UK* rankings for each office.

Eversheds can do what trainees describe as *"London-style work in the regions,"* cutting costs by paying regional lawyers less and spending less on office overheads. Illustrating this point, London trainees start on a £35,000 salary, whereas it's £24,500 in the regions. The downside, say some in the regions, is that they end up with London-style work and hours when they might have chosen their location precisely to avoid this. One source told us: "[The hours can be] *bad, but that's the nature of what you're getting yourself into."* Eversheds' regional trainees confirm that they often find themselves working longer hours than their peers at nearby firms. For example, one Leeds source reported frequent 3am finishes. Clearly Eversheds is now looking for regional trainees with a really ambitious streak, the sort who would say: *"You want that opportunity to step into the breach now and then. The hard work makes it more of an occasion, lends it more significance."*

Every day's a school day

Despite the recession, property and corporate remain Eversheds' core areas. Trainees are encouraged to do seats in each, but as they break down into smaller subteams there's a good number of choices available. The departments take on both private and public sector work, some quite substantial. Matters like Crossrail or the Building Schools for the Future programme engage numerous departments firm-wide, some tasks requiring partner time only, others suitable for trainees. Most recruits enjoy the "*buzz*" of big deals and they're not simply left with the document management aspects. "*In my second week I was in a completion meeting where a UK business was being bought by a foreign investor and we were trying to stall to get the best exchange rate,*" enthused a keen source. "*There were so many interested parties, so many things to sort out at the last moment. It becomes so real and you appreciate things from the client's perspective.*" Wow! Meanwhile, property supervisors "*encourage you to do stuff on your own.*" One trainee "*handled work on behalf of developers, reviewing leases and researching the viability of their different options.*" The quality of tuition was generally praised. "*I think that Eversheds has given me a good training... my supervisors have been fantastic,*" admitted a source who'd displayed a critical streak during their interview.

Across the country trainees take four seats of six months. Business need is a primary concern when it comes to seating arrangements, so don't expect to get every one of your top picks. Right now the growth areas are pensions, employment and litigation, so more seats are available in these departments. Thanks to Eversheds' sprawling size, there are also many other options. Under the umbrella of 'commercial', for example, come niches like IP and outsourcing; there are also IT, tax and local authority teams. Leeds, Birmingham and Cardiff additionally handle some volume claims work. Hotly contested seats are up for grabs in Paris and Shanghai.

Public sector work has been a sturdy crutch for the firm through the recession – and profitable too. Lawyers advised the Greater Manchester Waste Disposal Authority on a £4bn PFI forecasted to reduce landfill use in the North West by 75%. Always one to get stuck into emerging sectors, Eversheds was appointed as an international adviser to Liverpool John Moores University as it sets up joint ventures for overseas campuses and courses. When this deal was struck, partner Glynne Stanfield pointed out that education is the UK's third biggest export. Eversheds' catchily named branch in Hungary – Sandor Szegedi Szent-Ivany Komaromi Eversheds – landed a £9.3bn deal that typifies the firm's current aspirations. Closed by Hungarian Prime Minister Ferenc Gyurscany and Russian PM/self-styled action man Vladimir Putin, it involves building a pipeline that will bring gas from the Caspian Sea region to Europe. Eversheds' role was to advise the Hungarian Development Bank. Development agencies being something of a speciality, the firm has been selected for the panels of the London Development Authority and Transport for London. These should supply good income streams as London's transport systems undergo transformation.

Following on from its success with electronics giant Tyco and multinational conglomerate DuPont, the firm has won some sizeable new clients like Boeing and Nestlé. For such major instructors (the Tyco one being the prototype), Eversheds will sometimes organise billing differently using a Global Account Managing System, through which it is scored on a variety of measures to determine the legal spend. This innovative approach allows massive clients more control over their vast budgets. Another client won thanks in part to the pioneering use of GAMS was FMC Technologies.

Looking after number one

Speaking to conference delegates in May 2009, Eversheds' senior partner Cornelius Medvei outlined the firm's hopes for the future. "*We had to change the culture if we were to succeed and remain ahead of the curve,*" he said while discussing the relationship between workspace and atmosphere. Eversheds is generally becoming (in the words of new Chief Executive Bryan Hughes) "*more businesslike*" as it pursues "*top-quality, pure-City, high-value work.*" In the words of some trainees, it is becoming "*more*

Chambers UK rankings

Administrative & Public Law	Licensing
Aviation	Local Government
Banking & Finance	Media & Entertainment
Banking Litigation	Outsourcing
Capital Markets	Parliamentary & Public Affairs
Climate Change	Partnership
Competition/European Law	Pensions
Construction	Pensions Litigation
Consumer Finance	Personal Injury
Corporate/M&A	Planning
Data Protection	Private Equity
Debt Recovery	Product Liability
Defamation/Reputation Management	Professional Discipline
	Professional Negligence
Dispute Resolution	Projects, Energy & Natural Resources
Education	
Employee Share Schemes	Public International Law
Employment	Public Procurement
Environment	Real Estate
Financial Services Regulation	Real Estate Finance
Franchising	Real Estate Litigation
Fraud: Criminal	Restructuring/Insolvency
Health & Safety	Retail
Healthcare	Shipping
Information Technology	Social Housing
Insurance	Tax
Intellectual Property	Telecommunications
Investment Funds	Transport

ruthless" and "*not the same firm I started at two years ago.*" They tell us the trade off for "*getting better work*" is that the firm is going from "*personal and personable to a more corporate atmosphere*" and that billable hours are becoming ever more important. If it was ever a slightly cuddlier version of its national firm competitors, it isn't now. This forward-thinking, rapidly developing firm has profits at heart and bigger instructions in its crosshairs.

The London office is becoming ever more important as it strives to increase its presence in the private equity and financial services markets. In order to crack these über-competitive fields, top-flight lawyers are required. Because, as one trainee put it, "*none of us are particularly altruistic in commercial law,*" Eversheds must maintain high profitability to attract top talent. In May 2009 it was announced that it had seen profits drop by 27% – unsurprising given the recession and the inevitable expense of expanding internationally. With that in mind, Eversheds began 'Project August', a programme of cost cutting, office closure and redundancy.

The legal press reported that in 2008/09 some 618 staff (20% of the UK workforce) left the firm. Eversheds tells us that in the last financial year, "*16% of the workforce*" left "*as a result of redundancy, natural attrition or retirement.*" That figure doesn't include a fourth round of redundancies that was announced just as we were going to press. The trainees we spoke to displayed a sense of perspective on the subject. One told us: "*It brings home that you are part of a business, not just here to serve the greater good. The number-one fact is that we're a business.*" And from another we heard: "*It's one of the necessities of today. You have to make decisions based on figures, otherwise you'll be making them with your heart.*" The hardest hit departments were property and corporate. We got hold of Eversheds' new managing partner Lee Ranson to talk about this. "*We went early with the redundancies and made tough decisions based on the idea that the recession would be severe and quite long lasting,*" he said, adding that by making cuts early, redundant staff would have a better chance of finding work elsewhere. Project August's first blush brought with it the closure of the Norwich office. Some staff relocated to Cambridge; others walked away. Inevitably, trainees were upset by the move, one complaining that they were not kept well informed: "*The people who should have taken responsibility didn't... it's a cultural thing.*" Although speculation abounds – usually along the lines of "*looking at the wider strategy, I think some regional offices will be cut*" – we have it on good authority (thanks, Mr Ranson!) that there are no more closures in the pipeline, despite various teams (banking, clin neg) leaving the Newcastle office.

Then again, outsourcing is becoming attractive enough to make lawyers up and down the country reach for their calculators to see what they could save. This process allows firms to have simpler work completed more cheaply in other countries. In May 2009, hot on the heels of the closure of Norwich, a pilot scheme was introduced in the Cambridge office that allowed the firm to remove ten secretaries from the payroll by outsourcing work to South Africa. Just before we went to press, the firm announced that it would be sending significant amounts of secretarial work to South Africa. Like it or not, this type of scheme will become a part of the UK legal profession in the future.

Fantastinificent trainees

Although it was technically possible to move before, most trainees stayed put in their 'home' office. From now on they will be expected to rotate between offices according to business need and seat availability. Some people we interviewed were "*ecstatic*" about this proposal; others less than pleased. Certain firms already run this type of nomadic scheme, and it allows trainees to test the atmosphere of different locations and stand a better chance of qualifying into another office. We asked Mr Ranson about this and he confirmed that Eversheds would still consider candidates who didn't want to move around, but that "*if they were up against a more flexible candidate, they wouldn't score as highly.*" It's hard to describe a typical Eversheds trainee, particularly as the profile of the ideal candidate is changing. According to its recruitment campaign, Eversheds wants eight specific models of individual. These include The Winnomat, The Prioricator, The Proactiloper and The Logithiser. Ne'er a blemish blighting their precise appearances, these characters are the physical manifestations of Eversheds' bold dream for the future. Check them out on the firm's website. Relaxafarians need not apply.

The firm has never been one to squander vast sums on social events but trainees did tell us about trips to the theatre, meals out and Friday drinks. The impression we got was that the Cardiff trainees were the most fun-loving and that morale was especially high in that city (they were all offered NQ jobs, which must have helped). The Cambridge office reportedly had the poorest social scene, partly because of the number of commuters among the staff. The London cohort typically see less of each other than those in the other big cities, but generally trainees at all branches were pretty happy with their social lives and maintained that "*people are really friendly at ground level.*" In 2009 55 of the 78 qualifiers were retained.

And finally...

Finger on the global pulse, Eversheds is recalibrating itself to maximise profits and evolve into an international heavyweight. The transition may be tough but it makes this firm a hot prospect for the ambitious applicant.

Farrer & Co

The facts

Location: London
Number of UK partners/solicitors: 69/74
Total number of trainees: 20
Seats: 6x4 months
Alternative seats: Occasional secondments
Extras: Language training

Interesting cases, interesting clients and interesting colleagues. Receiving a training contract offer from Farrer is like winning a Golden Ticket.

At more than 300 years old, Farrer certainly has its fair share of fascinating tales and well-developed client relationships. If you value the past this is a great firm, but don't expect to be living anywhere other than in the present.

Travelling through time

According to the comprehensive timeline on its website, Farrer has been open for business since at least 1701. The first member of the Farrer family – Mr Oliver Farrer – became sole partner in 1769. The following year his brother James joined him in practice, and from then on until 1999, one and usually several Farrers have been partners. Unbelievably there are still members of the family at the firm today. The firm is justifiably proud of its history. And so it should be, when it includes such tasty morsels as an 18th century divorce involving an attempted duel in Hyde Park, and representation of literary legend Charles Dickens.

When it comes to interesting cases, things are no different today. Farrer recently helped England win its bid to stage the 2015 Rugby World Cup. In the words of Chief Operating Officer Ben Bennett: "*If you want work with lots of zeros at the end then go elsewhere, but if you want interesting work, interesting clients and the company of interesting people then Farrer is the place for you.*" The most recent financials aren't half bad either, with turnover topping £40m – a 9% increase on 2008. The firm also managed to retain all ten of its qualifiers in 2009.

Farrer has called 66 Lincoln's Inn Fields home since 1790. The building was originally designed by Sir Christopher Wren, and trainees love it, as do the tourists who regularly gather to snap its elegant frontage. Its location in a square "*away from the frenetic corporate environment*" and "*at the epicentre of legal life*" appeals to many. Gushed one trainee: "*We have one of the oldest legal systems in the world and here I am right in the middle of it.*" In 2009 the offices underwent a refurb that was "*a little overdue.*" Far from the standard law firm refit – modern art and glass walls – this was merely a neatening up to "*make it a little more contemporary.*" An open-plan layout, "*so conducive to modern working life,*" has been designed to create more space, but the meeting rooms remain largely unchanged, ensuring their delicate stucco ceilings and chandeliers can continue to wow clients for years to come.

If all this talk of antiquity has you grabbing your iPhone to call the fuddy-duddy police, now would be a good time to note that there is so much more to Farrer than a top-notch pedigree and the workplace equivalent of a stately home. Just take a look at its clientele – alongside traditional clients (members of the royal family, for example) it represents entrepreneurs ("*Russian oligarchs and Swiss bankers*") as well as newspapers including *The Sun*, *The Sunday Times*, *News of the World* and *The Daily Mail*. Trainees assure us that Farrer's "*outward reputation is far more conservative and traditional than what you actually find once you're here,*" and many ached for the firm to topple its old-fashioned, staid image. And yet, at the same time, trainees love Farrer's eccentricities and don't "*ever want to lose the general ethos of the firm.*"

Taste the rainbow

A glance at the rankings in *Chambers UK* should tell you one thing about this firm – it is very good at lots of things, both commercial and private client-oriented. To complement this, a six-seat training scheme allows newbies to sample a good spread of legal practice. It is *"brilliant to have such a broad experience,"* say trainees. *"Four months is plenty of time to know whether you like a seat, and plenty of time to know whether you hate it!"* The practice areas on offer are divided into four streams: private client (domestic and international) and charities; commercial (which includes corporate, employment and IP/commercial seats); property (commercial, residential and estates, and private); and litigation, where trainees have a choice of the recently merged media and disputes seat or family law. A trainee's fifth seat is viewed as a *"wild card,"* allowing them an additional go in one of the streams, which is useful *"in case you missed out on your favourite the first time round."* For their final seat they return to their hoped-for qualification department.

Seat allocation works well. Trainees have regular meetings with the graduate recruitment manager and training partner, both of whom *"try their damnedest to ensure everyone is satisfied."* The HR manager meets with them part way through each seat to *"check up on us and see how we are doing."* The training partner meets them at the end of each seat to find out what they did and didn't like. Apparently he takes his job *"incredibly seriously."*

Farrer recruits some highly intelligent folk. *"Across the board people are over-achievers, although generally modest about it."* Everyone we spoke to also seemed to display a special 'fit' with the firm. *"This place grabs you and you immediately know it is where you really want to be,"* said one. Another agreed that *"when you first come to Farrer you know quite early on if it fits you or not."* This is not to say everyone is the same; indeed our sources gave the impression that recruiters *"try to take a balance of trainees who will have different interests and characteristics that will fit them into different teams."*

An oil and a will that ended well

When you ask trainees about private client seats, it's obvious that they appreciate the *"breadth of clients"* serviced by the department. Whether your interest lies in art and heritage property or the juxtaposition of English law with foreign law, there's something to engage. In 2009 a deal was completed whereby the Duke of Sutherland transferred ownership of Titian's painting of Diana and Actaeon to the National Galleries in London and Edinburgh for £50m. In another case the firm obtained a court order to make a will for an elderly recluse living in the USA after he lost the capacity to deal with his own affairs. Due to inherit a Cornish estate, had he died without making a will, a cousin would have landed the estate rather than the individual's immediate family. For a newbie it can be an eye-opener to see how they could one day *"become a client's trusted adviser,"* not just their lawyer. Some trainees in the 'domestic' seat even *"arranged and attended clients' funerals."* Those in the 'international' seat, meanwhile, had a lot of *"nit-picky trust and tax issues"* to get their heads around, but generally enjoyed the *"intellectual workout."*

Chambers UK rankings

Agriculture & Rural Affairs	Financial Services Regulation
Charities	Intellectual Property
Corporate/M&A	Media & Entertainment
Defamation/Reputation Management	Partnership
Education	Private Client
Employment	Professional Discipline
Family/Matrimonial	Real Estate
	Sports Law

Tales of quirky cases are many. One particularly interesting example was a contested trust case where the assets were held in England but *"problems had come about because of the way Shari'a law conflicts with our national law, and the courts had no idea how a particular inheritance should be divided up – they all said something different."* The excitement for one trainee involved *"one tiny thing that needed to be sorted before going to trial."* The trainee rushed to get paperwork signed by a partner and then literally ran through the Gothic corridors of the High Court to put the papers in the barrister's hand two minutes after the hearing should have begun. *"The barrister very coolly sauntered into the courtroom and got us the judgement we were looking for."*

Farrer's charities team is one of the best. A recent case involved a major multi-jurisdictional merger that transformed Help the Aged and four national Age Concern organisations into four new charities – Age UK, Age Scotland, Age Northern Ireland and Age Cymru. Farrer also acts for nearly all of the national museums in England, as well as a growing number of clients in the higher education sector. Trainees talked of the *"broad umbrella of work"* covered in this seat – property, employment and trusts issues, for example, as well as a large amount of corporate advice. The scope of the team's activities usually comes as a pleasant surprise.

Healthy progression

Commercial services may not be what Farrer is best known for but that isn't to say they're unimportant to the firm; indeed, trainees say it is an *"up-and-coming"* part of the business. They complimented the commercial teams for their commitment to "*teaching and training*" and said: "*It was incredible how accommodating they were.*" For example: "*A partner arranged one-on-one tutorials for me. It's been great to have a sense that they want to invest in you.*" Farrer works closely with private banks such as Coutts, and the sort of people who use these banks often have business interests to manage. At times, trainees end up carrying out complex research, and for one this was ideal. "*I loved spending four hours or so poring over a problem and coming away at the end of the day really feeling as though I had got my head around it.*" Among the clients are a Qatari sovereign wealth fund, the Ping Pong restaurant chain (currently expanding operations in Dubai, Brazil, the USA and Thailand), the family trustees of the multimillion-pound James Villa businesses and M.C.C. (which sought advice on the latest Lord's debenture issue). The deals might be classified as lower midmarket, but usually this makes them very accessible to trainees still learning the ropes.

The busy employment team represents both employees and employers. "*We were negotiating for lots of bankers who are being made redundant,*" revealed one source. There can be a huge level of responsibility in this seat and plenty of attendance at client meetings and tribunals. "*After the initial meeting I would be the one the client called, and by the end it would be me advising them,*" reported one source, while another chuckled about a time when negotiating a compromise agreement. "*The other side had provided a qualified lawyer and she was quite annoyed that she was negotiating with a trainee!*"

The contentious family and media seats are popular, albeit for very different reasons. As in the private client seat, family department trainees are "*constantly on the phone to clients, almost being a counsellor and helping them through hideous times, while also trying to practise the law.*" As well as divorces, cases can involve prenuptial agreements, child abductions and residency issues. It is "*big money*" that binds all the cases together; some even involve well-known personalities, in which case it is sometimes necessary to bring the media team on board.

We get the impression you're either made for the media team or you're not. High-profile cases and a cracker of a client list ensure the team a place in the spotlight. Remember the notorious Max Mosley case in 2008? Farrer represented the newspaper on that. The firm rightly garners a lot of praise in this field, but several trainees warned that it can be "*hard to get exposure to brain work*" in this seat and much of the time can be taken up with bundling, photocopying and paginating. Having said this, Farrer's stable of regional newspaper clients means there are smaller claims on which trainees can get their hands inky. As well as representing newspapers and magazines,

trainees say that "*it's really exciting to go up against a national paper and stop them from publishing something.*" Some sources spoke of "*sitting in on interviews with big-name journalists on a regular basis*" and others mentioned "*great perks*" such as media parties. "*A bunch went to the British press awards,*" revealed a gleeful source. Recent hot cases include the defence of newspapers from claimants like Kylie's old squeeze Olivier Martinez, Mohammed George (Gus in *EastEnders*), Sienna Miller and Ashley Cole.

High times and hangovers

"*We are eccentric and proud of it,*" announced one interviewee. Naturally we wanted to know more. Excellent wines and traditional ales at client events, rumours of a secret royal vault somewhere beneath the building – the firm certainly delivers on character, and don't let's get started on some of the more interesting partners! Yes, some are quite posh, but don't make the mistake of assuming that this is a firm of blue bloods. Once you get beyond the client areas it is more high brow than high society, and what connects people is talent, charm and subtle ambition, not old school ties.

Farrer's very healthy social scene includes Christmas and summer parties, a much-anticipated trainee revue being a popular element of the former. An annual pub quiz is packed out, and we hear that at one departmental jolly a partner proved that am dram was not the preserve of the younger generation: "*He got down on his knees while singing karaoke to the Rolling Stones,*" chortled a source. Informal socialising is also a big part of the culture, and there's a regular Friday gathering at The White Horse, a tiny old pub off the beaten track. It's not all about supping with colleagues, as the members of the firm's sports teams will vouch. An annual cricket weekend is held at a client's estate, and the girls sometimes get together for netball. "*Sports make up a lot of the social scene,*" said one source, while another described how they often left the office to the sounds of "*someone practising an instrument in a meeting room*" or the dulcet tones of the office choir.

And finally...

While Farrer trainees loved telling us about the firm's quirks, the staunchest praise was reserved for the calibre of work and the broad spread of practice areas available to them at a time when they most wanted to experience the colour and variety of the law.

- **Philately will get you everywhere:** Extracurricular activities prove you are more than just a mean lean legal machine. There's no point in just listing your personal qualities in an application, you need to demonstrate them by way of example.

top tip no. 13

Finers Stephens Innocent

The facts

Location: London

Number of UK partners/solicitors: 39/28

Total number of trainees: 6

Seats: 4x6 months

Alternative seats: None

"We are trying to grow organically and bolting on good teams from other firms. Employment has been stunningly busy and litigation is going great guns."

Sara Wax, Head of Training

This appealing West End firm was created through a 1999 merger between property specialists Finers and media outfit Stephens Innocent.

Star quality

A rebranding and a refurbishment have ensured that FSI's West End offices now match its vibrant marketing package. Trainees described themed meeting rooms (the 'woods' room is not only wallpapered to look like a forest but also contains numerous wooden bowls hand-carved by partner Robert Craig), bright colours and a *"phenomenal reception."* A glass atrium stretches upwards for three floors allowing *"funky sculptures to hang down and change colour with a light installation."* So does FSI live up to this innovative and individual image?

The firm's focus on character is evident even in trainee interviews, when applicants are required to make a short presentation. *"The point of it,"* said one trainee, *"is to show that you are more than just a lawyer. Do you have a passion for something? And can you present that passion and perhaps pass it on to someone else?"* The topics chosen by current trainees ranged from classical Indian dance to international piracy. FSI is clearly keen on trainees who can conduct themselves well in a professional environment from the off. *"Most have worked in other backgrounds and this is genuinely quite important here,"* commented one. Previous employment experiences include PR, the media and 25 years in the Royal Military Police. Even those who come straight from academia have plenty of life experience, such as time spent with a human rights lawyer in Belize. Mostly people seem drawn to FSI because they *"had absolutely no intention of being just a number"* in a City firm. The numerous celebrity clients (Lewis Hamilton, Salman Rushdie and The Killers, for example) of course create their own magnetic pull.

If it is the glamorous IP/media department that brings you to FSI then be aware that a seat here is not guaranteed. All trainees take a commercial property seat, as this is the firm's largest department, and most also do a corporate seat and one in commercial litigation. However, while IP/media is assumed to be the *"oh-my-god seat,"* and its supervisor Mark Stephens is viewed as some sort of magician, trainees did agree that *"work-wise it really is no different to any other department."* When we heard some of the things that trainees were getting involved in elsewhere we had to agree. And who is Mark Stephens? From now on, note the identity of legal talking heads appearing on radio and TV news shows. As often as not it'll be Mr S.

It is written

Trainees may observe celebrity divorces in the family seat (*"sometimes they come in and I am a bit star struck"*) as well as abduction cases where a parent has taken a child abroad. Recently there was a sexual abuse matter. The private client team works closely with the family team as after a divorce *"it is likely the individual will desire a will."* One trainee had drafted the wills of some *"very famous"* writers. Trainees in other contentious seats assist partners, instruct counsel and attend court. Said one: *"I went to court ten times in my commercial litigation seat. Quite impressive really."* Apart from pro bono cases, they're unlikely to conduct any advocacy of their own, primarily because the firm works on *"such valuable things it would be seen as reasonably negligent!"* In the IP/media seat, clients range from major international businesses to creative individuals and entrepreneurs – broadcasters and newspapers, publishers and distributors, dotcoms, schools, universities, museums and galleries, artists, designers, photographic agencies, telecoms companies and, of course, celebrities. Many come from overseas; more specifically, trainees talked of *"representing US newspapers in defamation claims."* One project the team has involved itself with is an ethical fashion initiative. The firm hosted an event to increase awareness of brand and rights management in response to a marked increase in concern for ethically sourced products. This has resulted in FSI drafting ethical terms and conditions for businesses.

"Phenomenal" levels of responsibility can be found across the board, trainees say. *"The label 'trainee' doesn't mean much here"* and *"when you are up against bigger firms you realise you are working at the level of a junior assistant."* In addition to their regular departmental work, every trainee is put in charge of a few debt collection cases as soon as they start their contract; *"some have gone all the way to witness statements, which is good experience."* Even for the most independent and intelligent trainee, things can all get a bit much on occasion, with one source admitting that you can feel quite low when you are in *"a state of confusion at your desk."* That same trainee also told us that their high point is *"every time I overcome a hurdle I don't think I can handle. You will be pushed here so there are mini victories all the way through the training contract."* FSI's size means trainees work in small teams, sometimes with a partner alone, meaning that discussing work and absorbing new information is easier. All six qualifiers stayed with the firm in 2009 to continue this close style of working.

FSI: London

The property department is particularly known for its work in the retail sector, where clients include such high-street classics as Monsoon, Quiksilver and Calvin Klein. Recently FSI was forced to reduce the 25-lawyer team by a fifth (and the rest went to a 4-day week), but while the retail and leisure sectors may be quieter, advice to further and higher education institutions has gone from strength to strength. FSI is also the first port of call for a number of issues relating to the 2012 Olympics and Crossrail. The team advised over 100 businesses in the Olympic zone on their relocation, the largest compulsory purchase order in Europe to date. Trainees tell us: *"In property, the supervision structure is good, whereas in other departments it needs to be bolstered a bit."* Two property partners hold weekly training sessions that are compulsory for first-years, *"starting from the basics and then debating issues."* Other departments run firm-wide lunchtime sessions and trainees try to attend as many as they can.

The corporate department has a well-established AIM practice, which despite the market's battering continues to find deals. It advised on nine AIM admissions, ten secondary placings and three reverse takeovers last year, and trainees got a taste of most of what was on offer by *"going from deal to deal."* One worked with a client that was acquiring a company with subsidiaries in several different European jurisdictions. This involved *"understanding how each country works, lots of file and project management and a number of late nights."* But from what we already know about FSI trainees, it shouldn't be a surprise to hear that late working was sometimes a high point. *"It's great after an all-nighter completing a deal to sit there at three in the morning drinking champagne when all you should want to do is go to bed!"* This 'when the going gets tough' approach is evident on a larger scale at FSI. Those property redundancies aside, the firm has actually taken steps to enhance various practice groups during the recession through a series of strategic partner hires in litigation, business crime, construction, professional regulation and employment.

Trainees do find time to let their hair down. *"There are often e-mails going round,"* usually directing people to The Mason's Arms on Great Portland Street, where there's *"guaranteed to be someone on any Thursday or Friday."* Even when partners are present, the *"informal culture"* means *"nobody thinks it's odd if you're swaying a little bit."* The firm is also *"crazy about the theatre"* and people make the most of their West End location. A social committee organises events – a popular annual quiz and recently a wine-and-Wii party in the office atrium. At karaoke nights *"people are a bit shy at first but once they get some alcohol down them you can't get them off the floor."* Competitions to find the best partner/secretary combo add to the entertainment. Last year's summer party was held on Westminster Pier and took a *Pirates of the Caribbean* theme. Such events are important to the firm, but socialising isn't compulsory. As one source neatly put it: *"If you recruit people with personalities then they tend to have busy lives."*

Chambers UK rankings

Capital Markets	Fraud: Criminal
Corporate/M&A	Intellectual Property
Defamation/Reputation Management	Media & Entertainment
Dispute Resolution	Partnership
Employment	Real Estate

And finally...

Our sources stress that this is "*an extraordinary training contract so long as you're not timid and are willing to get off your arse and do stuff.*"

Fisher Meredith LLP

The facts

Location: London

Number of UK partners/solicitors: 17/43

Total number of trainees: 17

Seats: 4x6 months

Alternative seats: Secondments

Excellent academics and a huge heart are prerequisites for one of the most rewarding training contracts around.

Kennington-based Fisher Meredith advises private and legally aided clients and has a Rolls-Royce reputation for rights-based work. Economic exigency has forced a period of transition, but the firm's ethos remains unchanged.

Standing moral ground

It's 1975, flares are in fashion, disco is all the rage, NASA has sent a spacecraft to Mars, the Cold War is still simmering and on a dusty inner-city street in Stockwell, South London, Fisher Meredith is founded. Undoubtedly a product of the hand-holding, tree-hugging, free-love and liberty-for-all era that blossomed in the late 60s, Fisher Meredith began by focusing its energies on representing the downtrodden and disadvantaged of its local community. It was not long before the firm established itself as a force to be reckoned with when it came to prominent cases of public interest, working on the Deptford Fire case, acting for some of the accused in the Damilola Taylor case, and representing one of the suspects charged with involvement in the failed London bombing in July 2005.

Today FM is housed in modern offices in Kennington and recognised by trainees as *"very professional."* These words are echoed by managing partner Stephen Hewitt, who told us: *"We are a progressive and professional management team. The perception is that we are going places."* Those who already have an interest in legal aid will be aware of the immense challenges the sector faces, but with its gold-standard reputation, FM is less exposed than many firms. Said one trainee: *"If any firm is going to survive we will."* Even so, the severe cuts to legal aid funding imposed by the Carter Reforms have left their mark. The firm closed its criminal legal aid practice in 2008 and is pushing hard to increase the proportion of more profitable private work. Currently privately funded clients – these include individuals, charities such as Shelter, the retail stores John Lewis and Peter Jones, the National Association of Head Teachers and the Royal Embassy of Saudi Arabia – make up around 30% of work, but the firm hopes to increase this to 50% *"quite soon."*

If alarm bells are ringing for those of you who dreamed of following in the footsteps of Atticus Finch, fear not. Hewitt assures us that *"our values remain much the same. I've worn the T-shirt for over 20 years and there is a very solid commitment to access to justice here."* The reality of the situation is that without diversification into the private sector FM would be unable to continue serving its legally aided clients. *"People have got to understand that if we are going to continue doing legal aid it has to be cross-subsidised by private work."* Trainees were equally optimistic (and realistic) about the firm's future: *"It's not airy fairy and it's not a charity. It is a business,"* they reminded us. *"You can't run a business at a loss."* Sources were confident, however, that *"it is more of a direction thing and not necessarily a lack of commitment to the cause. The fact that private work is being talked up does not mean that public work is being talked down."*

Another brick in the wall

With its broad spread of expertise – family and children's law, immigration, mental health, community care, education, actions against the police and housing law – it is no wonder trainees told us that *"every seat is really quite interesting."* None are compulsory, and apart from the first seat recruits are free to shape their training to suit their interests. *"It is quite common to do two seats in the area you are particularly keen on, which is great because you get more experience."*

Stints in the children's or public services law (PSL) departments are common for newbies. The former provides exposure to a *"really good mix of public and private work."* Private work involves contact disputes between parents whereas the public work is primarily care proceedings and domestic violence cases involving children. *"It is a good place for a first seat,"* agree trainees. *"While it can be quite issue-complex, it isn't very law-heavy. You are only working with one or two acts and things have their processes."* The opportunities to go to court are numerous: as well as *"supporting the client and explaining things to them"* there is ample opportunity for advocacy. *"If you are enthusiastic about it you can do quite a lot."* One trainee described an application for a non-molestation order on a domestic violence case.

The young and growing (it took all three of last year's qualifiers) PSL department covers a broad spread of issues, and trainees relish the opportunity to *"carve out their own area. Any action against a public body is included."* As well as representing NGOs, charities and organisations such as the Howard League for Penal Reform, Bail for Immigration Detainees and the British Family Public Association, the team acts for individuals who have come in off the street or have been referred from organisations such as the Refugee Council and The Helen Bamber Foundation. One source described working with the *Chambers UK* top-ranked education team, focusing on children that have been illegally excluded from school, many of whom have special educational needs. *"The school is supposed to give the child and parents notice before an exclusion and go through an appeals procedure, but often they are just told to go home and then never go back. I have done about 25-30 cases and there have been quite a lot that haven't been in school for a long time. It makes you think more about the ramifications. There is all this talk of less social mobility, and it's not surprising when so many people are just not in school."* It is worth noting that the broad nature of the PSL department means that a trainee's experience *"depends a lot on what supervisor you have."* But apart from complaints of the occasional *"supervisor that withholds too much work and doesn't give the proper autonomy"* there were few grumbles when it came to levels of responsibility.

Fish(er) for a home

A seat in housing law is *"more structured"* than most and essentially divided into two halves. The first three months are spent on homelessness cases and the second on pos-

Chambers UK rankings

Administrative & Public Law	Family/Matrimonial
Civil Liberties	Immigration
Debt Recovery	Police Law
Education	Social Housing

sessions. Homelessness work is *"very fast-moving"* and trainees here see some of the most vulnerable clients, a few of whom *"can be pretty difficult and have multiple problems."* But this can make the job all the more rewarding as *"you are doing things that have a massive impact on people's lives."* Several sources located their high points as *"getting individuals or homeless families into accommodation."* Possessions work is *"quite varied depending on what agencies and organisations your supervisor has a relationship with,"* but cases tend to involve individuals referred from drug support agencies or those involved in anti-social behaviour who have been given an eviction order.

About 95% of the cases currently handled by the *"relatively small"* immigration team are legally aided, but *"they are trying to expand [the] private client [element]"* through more instructions for work permits and cases arising from the Highly Skilled Migrant Programme (now known as a Tier 1 Visa). The team has some *"extremely interesting work,"* say trainees, who are *"mostly involved in asylum cases, particularly unaccompanied minors,"* as well as *"quite a lot of human rights applications."* Referrals come from places like domestic violence support group The Gaia Centre and The Refugee Council. One particularly interesting case, which illustrates FM's determination and tenacity, was that of M v UK. M was, as a minor, trafficked for sexual exploitation, firstly within Uganda and then in the UK. M's appeal was refused by the Asylum and Immigration Tribunal and thereafter the High Court, despite her account being accepted. It is now the first human trafficking-related claim from the UK to be brought to the European Court of Human Rights. FM is arguing that M's removal to Uganda will breach several Articles of the European Convention on Human Rights, including risk of re-trafficking, risk of gender-based harm, suicide risk and unlawful interferences with her private life and physical and moral integrity.

Sense and sensibility

The team of *"exceptional lawyers"* handling police and prison law is, according to trainees, *"one of the best in the firm."* *Chambers UK* agrees, awarding Fisher Meredith top-band status for police law alongside firms such as Hickman Rose and Bindmans. It is here that trainees are really able to flex their anti-establishment muscles. *"It is really fundamental work. The police have so much power* in the community, but who keeps them accountable? It's the police policing themselves. We play a really vital role in regulating them," explained one proud source. Loads of work has come out of the G20 protests, the climate camp and the DNA retention policy, proving that FM still stands at the vanguard of contemporary, socially important legal issues. The prison law side of the team throws up cases such as the right for a prisoner to not be handcuffed while receiving chemotherapy or the disabled prisoner who was unable to access all the areas of the prison. One trainee described a client who rang up, "saying that his willy would fall off if we didn't take his case on, blaming it on the prison he had been in. But that's not something that's going to shock anybody here." Suffice to say, our sources did not hold back when describing some of the clients they came across on a daily basis. There are too many tales to relate here but the words "there are an awful lot of nutters" should give you some idea. On the flipside, there was not one trainee who did not stress the importance of "contextualising things. You rarely meet a client where you cannot recognise why they are so unpleasant. When you look behind it all it is a mentally ill person."

Being able to deal effectively with even the most difficult clients is a huge part of what makes a successful trainee. Actually, the list of required skills is exhaustive: patience; an open mind; efficiency; confidence; a good sense of humour and being able to switch off were just a few of the attributes our interviewees thought invaluable. Managing client expectations is a really important skill too as "sometimes they expect more than is possible. If they plead guilty and they get an amount of years custody it can be hard explaining to them that it's a good result." At times even getting to a legal point is a challenge as "often they just want to come in and tell their story." Alongside the impressive academics and strong work ethic expected at all top law firms, previous experience in the field of rights-based law, as well as a deep-seated desire to improve the lives of individuals, are common traits at FM. "No one comes with a cold CV," as a quick glance at the trainee profiles on the firm's website confirms. However, this is something that may change with the added emphasis on private work. Stephen Hewitt stressed that recruits "must not be completely starry-eyed about helping people. They need their feet on the floor and good commercial acumen." There is a definite focus on efficiency and "a lot of pressure on chargeable hours," our sources revealed; indeed several felt that there was at times "a bit too much stick and not enough carrot." A number of the incoming recruits are on their second careers, with previous occupations including advertising, research chemistry and journalism.

Bear in mind that despite the enormous talent individuals must possess, they receive a notably lower salary than their City contemporaries – £20,000 for first-years, £21,000 for second-years and £30,000 for NQs. Our sources were impressively sanguine when questioned about the weight of their pay packets. Said one source: "What we earn isn't awful. I still go out for dinner and everything, but I don't have the extravagant lifestyle that a lot of other lawyers do." Another added: "It depends on where your motivations lie. I wouldn't have wanted to work in a corporate environment."

Smelling of roses

The rolling hills and fluffy clouds depicted on FM's website are a far cry from the turbulence affecting the UK legal aid system. "The future of legal aid isn't particularly secure," admitted trainees, "but firms like Fisher Meredith are constantly thinking up new ways to keep it going." The decision to crank up private work has caused some disquiet among the ranks, and people recognise the potential for a divide between those who work primarily on publicly funded matters and those operating in the private sphere. "The private lawyers ask why we continue to do unprofitable work and those who are undertaking principally legal aid ask why we are representing x or doing y." Trainees stressed that it is important for any lawyers parachuted in from City firms, drawn by FM's stellar reputation and the work-life balance, to "buy into the ethos." A couple of Fridays down at stalwart locals, The Dog House or The White Hart, should help grease the social wheels. There is also the annual surprise summer outing, Christmas party and quarterly drinks and pizza in the boardroom.

Undoubtedly this firm has had to make some difficult decisions recently, but all the signs are pointing up. Plans for a central London office are in the pipeline and Stephen Hewitt hopes to expand the current £6.5m turnover to £10m within three years. "The future is rosy," he says. While its radical roots may have been forced slightly further underground, there is a firm-wide recognition that it is FM's legal aid pedigree that got it to where it is today. A healthy dose of realism, savvy management and dogged determination will ensure this firm lives to fight many more battles.

And finally...

Fisher Meredith trainees were among the most contemplative, articulate, mature and genuinely interesting that we spoke to this year. Four out of eight were retained on qualification in 2009.

Foot Anstey Solicitors

The facts

Location: Exeter, Plymouth, Taunton, Truro
Number of UK partners/solicitors: 41/160
Total number of trainees: 17
Seats: 6x4 months
Alternative seats: Secondments
Extras: Pro bono – CAB, Age Concern legal clinics, the Competition Pro Bono Group

"The new five-year strategy is to focus on organic growth in the South West, securing good national clients, particularly through the media sector and our corporate and employment teams."
John Westwell, Managing Partner

The largest law firm in Devon, Cornwall and Somerset and resolutely South West in character, Foot Anstey makes no bones about its commercial ambitions. It is an increasingly competitive, well-oiled machine with plenty to offer trainees.

The game is afoot

"*Foot Anstey is about being the biggest and best in a defined area.*" Unlike its competitors, it has stuck to the South West and operates from offices in Exeter, Plymouth, Taunton and Truro. We're not suggesting it's a stick-in-the-mud. Interviewees told us they had witnessed major changes in the firm's direction and attitude. Said one: "*It's a lot more commercially focused than it used to be, and I imagine it will continue to go that way.*" Others agreed: "*There used to be a wide range of private client practices but the firm has shifted to become more commercial.*" For this reason, interviewees were eager to point out that "*if you're looking for a high street practice that's very legal aid-based this won't be the place for you.*" Some considered this unfortunate, as "*it's much less of a multifaceted firm than when I applied,*" but generally trainees' interests were in line with the firm's, or they could see opportunities in the shift. For example, one told us: "*A positive of the commercial side of things is more high net worth divorce clients.*"

The new emphasis on commercial work sees the firm "*raising its game and raising its profile.*" Trainees enthused: "*We've got some pretty good clients in commercial disputes and we're acting in million-pound cases which you'd never expect in the South West.*" Someone whose focus was originally on Bristol said: "*I was under the impression* [Bristol firms] *would have more prestige, but this is one of the firms down here that's in the same league – or will be soon.*" One trainee in particular saw the region as a growth area and the firm as "*an expanding outfit with a real ambition.*" We agree that Foot Anstey is "*one to watch*" and are aware of examples of impressive recent work, including acting for Lloyds TSB Corporate Markets in its purchase of a 95,000 sq ft retail park, and assisting with multimillion-pound private equity acquisitions.

A nice cup of coco

Coco ("*corporate commercial to those not down with the kids*") has seen a drop-off due to the downturn in the economy. Even so, the firm boasts increased capability and draws work from within and beyond the region. A joint venture between two big players in the blended feed market was an undeniably South Western affair, while the firm also advises clients such as Wrigley Company (based in Plymouth) and Odeon Cinemas, an undeniably national business. Trainees tell us the majority of clients are established local businessmen looking to "*expand their portfolios,*" often in "*shops, hotels and pubs.*" As you might guess, the region's tourism industry is of key significance to the firm. Trainee tasks are what you might expect in a typical corporate department – "*taking minutes, drafting ancillary documents and due diligence.*" The good news: there's none of the horror hours experienced by trainees in big cities – "*the latest I'd ever stay was only 7.30 – 8pm.*"

Linking into coco is commercial property. Again, a seat here will see "*lots of local businessmen*" as clients, and a focus on the trappings of tourism. "*I worked on a caravan site bought out by developers for a high-value holiday homes project,*" recalled a source. Other interests include wind farms and retail and manufacturing premises. The attraction in this department is responsibility: "*You run your files from instruction to completion, looking at all the deeds and contracts – anything you'd need to buy or sell a property.*"

Take one for the team

A wealth of contentious opportunities span commercial and financial disputes, through property and construction litigation. Trainees were thrilled with the "*amazing variety of work from disputes concerning trusts, boundaries, prescriptive rights, contracts, agriculture, debt recovery…*" A trainee's role involves "*communicating with clients and the other side, attending court hearings, putting together bundles, research, witness statements and filing and serving documents.*" The more specialised property litigation seat has "*a more intense focus on technical knowledge.*" The firm represents tenants and landlords in "*possession claims and service charge and dilapidations disputes.*" Its technical nature leads first-year trainees to "*shadow their supervisor rather than getting heavily involved.*" Professional negligence is another key area and here recent cases include a complex three-way reinsurance dispute and securing £1m compensation for a married couple in an action involving compulsory purchase orders and breach of duty. There is unlikely to be much scope for advocacy, though it does sometimes materialise for lucky trainees.

Advocacy is a realistic prospect in the family seat. Broadly split into divorce and child law (both public and private), for some private client practice can be overwhelming: "*It was difficult dealing with bereaved people. I even had to take a deathbed will – far too personal for me.*" Others raved about it. In public child law in particular, "*when you're representing parents it's very satisfying on a personal level what you can achieve for them, seeing them progress hugely from having their children removed to getting them back.*" The drafting of orders, witness statements, letters to the other side and "*simple wills*" sits alongside "*a lot of court work.*" Divorce trainees help with "*preparing petitions and negotiating financial settlements*" for wealthy individuals, sometimes dealing with up to £5m in assets. Given that a question mark hovers above the financial viability of legal aid practice at all firms, our sources wondered if Foot Anstey's commercial shift would affect the availability of this type of service, and possibly even family law in general at the firm.

Sometimes business needs trump trainees' wishes when it comes to seats. For example, a hectic time in the conveyancing team saw a bunch of trainees (as well as other staff) called upon to step in. Some had reservations: "*It's a bit of a sorry situation to use trainees to plug the gaps.*" Others were pragmatic: "*Every now and then the firm calls on you to take one for the team, which is unfortunate, but everyone has to do it and it is taken into account.*"

Chambers UK rankings

Agriculture & Rural Affairs
Banking & Finance
Banking Litigation
Charities
Clinical Negligence
Corporate/M&A
Crime
Debt Recovery
Defamation/Reputation Management
Dispute Resolution
Employment
Family/Matrimonial
Information Technology
Intellectual Property
Licensing
Personal Injury
Planning
Private Client
Real Estate
Real Estate Litigation
Tax

Stand on your own two feet

Moving around offices is something the firm encourages, particularly as some teams are larger or stronger in certain locations. Few people have a problem with this. Said one: "*I saunter up and down the A38 listening to audio books.*" While the Truro office might seem a bit of an odd one out due to its more recent Foot Anstey status (it was added in 2007 and was previously a separate firm called Hancock Caffin), the others feature the trade mark blue and orange colour scheme and the same furnishings. Taunton is the smallest office, and we understand that Plymouth has taken over from Exeter as "*the nicest office.*" The "*prestigious flagship office*" in Plymouth ("*on Sutton Harbour with views right out to sea*") has "*freshly ground coffee*" and "*a stunning roof garden.*"

The firm has sought to instil a competitive edge in trainees. A new seat allocation system left our interviewees with "*mixed feelings;*" "*you have to officially apply for your seat and go through five stages of selection, including sending your CV and presenting to the relevant supervisor/partner.*" Though they felt "*it was a lot more onerous,*" our contacts saw the thinking behind the new system. "*There's a sense of getting the best out of trainees and preparing us for future development,*" said one. Another added: "*This is where the firm is moving to. It wants more ambitious and competitive individuals.*" Less readily justified by trainees was the firm's "*very strict*" chargeable hours requirement. Again, "*installing the competitive aspect,*" the firm (like many others) produces a weekly spreadsheet "*with everyone's time recorded on it. You should be recording five hours a day as a trainee, in* which case you'd be in green. Any less than four and a half though and you'd be in the red." Alongside a redundancy programme that some deemed "*over-enthusiastic*" in relation to property, there are some clues as to why the nickname "*Foot Nasty*" has emerged of late. We should say that none of our sources were overly bothered by it.

Torquay or not Torquay?

The trainees we spoke to were anything but nasty. Being spread across offices does make socialising difficult, but there are still plenty of informal outings and sports teams, not to mention the annual Christmas party. Usually held at a hotel in Torquay, we heard rumours the location might be shifted this year. With "*discounted hotel rooms for yourself and your partner, a proper three-course meal with coffee and great music,*" it's a very popular and no-expense spared type event. Far from being one of your stiff, corporate affairs, "*it's a party for everyone to let their hair down and have fun. There's no need for networking and you're encouraged to thoroughly enjoy yourself.*"

We think we can identify a new breed coming through the firm, and understood well why one trainee wondered if "*they might find it hard to become close on a social level as they're very ambitious, driven types.*" Not necessarily, thought others. "*We knew it would be more competitive and that we'd be looking to scrap for business and need to be flexible to business needs,*" said a first-year. We reckon the writing has been on the wall for ages – fresh Foot Anstey recruits should be "*dynamic, get-up-and-go people*" and "*commercial awareness is much more important than has ever been the case before.*" To use trainees' words to put it plainly, "*the filtering system on CVs is a lot stricter*" and "*the premier law firm in the South West has to have the premier trainees.*" A connection to the South West may be a little less important, but a commitment to the area is a must. With "*the coast, the moors and beautiful villages,*" and importantly, "*the time to enjoy them,*" enthusiasm for the region shouldn't be too hard to muster. Six of nine qualifiers stayed with the firm in 2009.

And finally...

"*If you want a South West firm with a South West lifestyle but you're still as ambitious as if you lived in Bristol or London, this is the place for you.*"
We can't put it any better.

Forbes

The facts

Location: Blackburn, Preston, Accrington, Chorley, Manchester, Leeds
Number of UK partners/solicitors: 35/53
Total number of trainees: 11
Seats: 4x6 months
Alternative seats: None

With a strong regional reputation, strategic organic growth and the increasing scale of its work, Forbes shows that it has no need for flashy sloganeering and posturing.

Last year we described Forbes as unpretentious, and since there really is no better word to sum up this straight-talking, down-to-earth firm, we'll use it again.

Cracking cheese, Gromit

Although Forbes' feet are firmly positioned on the North Western high street, it has started looking to the high-rise offices of the region's cities for new sources of revenue. It now complements its private client services with a scaled-up capacity to serve businesses. The 'Corporate Law Firm of the Year 2008' award from *North West Business Insider* magazine and loyalty from clients such as Blackburn Rovers, Europrint and Lloyds TSB demonstrate how firmly entrenched Forbes has become in the region's commercial landscape. Reflecting this shift, Forbes has slowly but surely moved from the towns into the cities. Having built a fine reputation in Blackburn, Preston, Chorley and Accrington, the last seven years of steady organic growth have led to offices in the metropolises of Leeds and Manchester.

Forbes has a veritable cheeseboard of practices. Commercial and residential property, commercial litigation, crime, employment law, personal injury, clinical negligence, wills and probate make up the dependable Edams and Cheddars you come to expect of a substantial high street firm, but then it also has more exotic varieties – the sort you might usually have to look for at the deli counter. Its versions of a Wensleydale with cranberries, or a deep, mature Comté, are sports law, white-collar crime and defendant insurance work. Trainees say the cheeseboard-like selection of departments is very appealing, especially for those who want a little taste of many things.

Sports clients commonly require assistance in several areas, so Forbes' sports department is comprised of lawyers from several different practices – business law, commercial property, employment, licensing and commercial litigation. If you ever eat a pie at Blackburn Rovers and, overawed by the delicate balance of potato to meat, feel moved to thank someone, Forbes deserves a portion of that gratitude: it renewed the club's contract with caterers Northcote. If your allegiances lie with the mighty Preston North End, you too might want to doff your enamel badge-encrusted hat in the direction of the folk at Forbes – they worked on the licensing for the new stand. These and other accomplishments for Burnley FC led to the firm being shortlisted for an award for professional services to football at the North West Football Awards.

The defendant insurance practice has been a major growth area and the firm now works for major clients like Zurich Municipal, Co-operative Financial Services, AIG, Royal SunAlliance and The Travelers Companies, as well as over 50 local authorities. On one matter the lawyers worked in conjunction with Forbes' fraud team and uncovered a large criminal network that had made 52 separate claims against numerous organisations and insurers. Another case involved an environmental claim made by over 500 people and worth over £1m. Originally a practice established in Blackburn, the "*lovely little office in a five-storey block*" in Leeds now also focuses on this type of work, as does the office just off Manchester's Deansgate. Apart from these two commercially focused locations, each of Forbes' other offices has family law and crime departments, but it is Preston and Blackburn that offer the full sweep of services.

The range of legal issues faced by public bodies is reflected in the work done by Forbes. Assistance to over 90 public bodies has ranged from employment matters to ASBOs and allegations of failure to take children into care. In the last year Forbes has been involved in leasing land for the construction of a new fire station, injunctions against uncooperative council tenants and compliance with gas-servicing regulations.

Eager for advocacy

Trainees take seats in most departments (a notable exception is social housing) and there are no compulsories, so long as you take at least one contentious and one non-contentious assignment. People usually get what they ask for, especially in the third and fourth seats. Naturally trainees develop preferences for certain areas of law and tend to stick to similar seats, some going for mainly commercial roles, others choosing to do property-related seats and some opting for a mix. Our sources seemed happy with the level of responsibility granted. As people move through the training contract, they often find their newly acquired skills transfer well from one seat to another, enabling them to tackle larger files and more complex work as time goes on. Advocacy is a distinct possibility too, and it is described as "*an exhilarating experience.*" Several people told us they were "*eager to do more.*"

All in all, Forbes' seating system wins a good deal of praise from trainees for its winning combination of flexibility and transparency. Though four six-month seats is the norm, this is not set in stone and if they are sure of what they want to specialise in trainees can request an extended third seat instead of a fourth in a new department. Overall, trainees receive a high level of attention and feel well supported and secure in the knowledge that "*there is always someone to ask if you have a question.*" They have mentors at each office, chosen from among the partners and solicitors in their department. Trainees often have their own offices, but this does vary from seat to seat. Clearly Forbes likes structure: our sources spoke of always knowing what's expected of them and when they've got to do things by. When starting a seat, trainees know they need to work through a checklist of achievements so they always keep a record of their activities in their diaries. Progress is checked at about six weeks into each seat, and again roughly six weeks before the end when they get to chat to the powers that be about the next department they'd like to visit.

Chambers UK rankings
Crime Personal Injury
Dispute Resolution

Evening all

Forbes started off as a crime firm and crime remains a core area; indeed, it has one of the biggest departments in the North West. When the Legal Services Commission ran a preferred supplier pilot scheme, Forbes was one of only 25 firms (out of over 4,000 countrywide) to be selected to participate. It also deals with privately paying clients and is very well known in the community. Some clients (usually small-scale drug offenders) are endearingly referred to by trainees as "*regulars.*" Crime trainees can also get a taste of Forbes' more complicated cases, including murders, sex trafficking, large-scale drugs importation and white-collar crimes/fraud. This sort of work may not be for everyone – trainees described some situations as "*nerve-wracking.*" Forbes has managed to break into the more elite group of firms working on more serious crimes such as high-profile murders, 'supergrass' cases and serious frauds. Some involve large networks of criminals, for example a national conspiracy to defraud relating to waste disposal agreements. Some cases have an international dimension: the firm has investigated the fraudulent movement of over €90m across Europe and Africa, and even sent a solicitor to Johannesburg on a complex conspiracy case involving people-smuggling from India to the UK.

If trips to the copshop to meet clients are your bag, then a two-part Police Station Accreditation course will become important. During Part A, candidates visit the cells under the supervision of a trained solicitor to write up reports, first detailing what their supervisor does and then, once they've got an idea of what to expect, going through the steps themselves. Once Part A is satisfactorily completed, they start to visit the police station on their own, taking statements, compiling reports and giving advice. The final stage is a role play where the candidate has to react to scenarios played to them from a tape, giving the correct response to the situations that unfold. If you're not particularly keen on nipping out to visit detainees at some ungodly hour, you'll be relieved to know that this is not always required. "*Generally, I don't end up talking to someone in a cell at three in the morning, because normally people are drunk at that time!*"

The hole truth

If you ever have the misfortune to trip in one of the 4,000 holes in Blackburn that The Beatles warned us all about, Forbes would be a good firm to turn to. Its *Chambers UK*-ranked personal injury department believes it will fare well despite the threat of new entrants into the market through the so-called 'Tesco law' regulatory changes. These will allow the likes of supermarkets and insurers to provide legal services direct to the public. As one Forbes source put it: "*Claims factories and ambulance chasers aren't always the best and people still want the solicitor they know by reputation.*"

The popular family law seat handles divorces, domestic violence and the removal of children into care so, unsurprisingly, emotions can run pretty high at times. "*Forbes sometimes acts for the parents to prevent kids being taken away. I worked on something like that. The local authority wanted to take the kids, but we were successful in stopping them. It's satisfying when clients keep their kids and you hear they've turned their lives around, but sometimes it can be frustrating when you advise clients to do something and they don't... alcohol problems, drugs problems, they don't stop.*" In divorce cases "*you have to tailor things to the client. Sometimes they just want someone to listen to them, and I found that quite rewarding. And sometimes it's quite heart-wrenching too when they're fighting over children.*" Forbes' divorce practice caters for all and has handled some big cases, such as when lawyers won over £200k for the wife of a man with £1.2m worth of property.

Who wants to be a millionaire?

The working day is usually 9am to 5pm, though preparation for and travel to court appearances can extend this. Quite a few people start at Forbes as paralegals and move up through the ranks, and because it's not uncommon for paralegals to be studying for a degree (or for trainees to be juggling the LPC whilst completing their contract), these people must be hard workers indeed. People who rise up from the paralegal ranks are treated the same as those trainees recruited as graduates, but most of them choose to take their first seat in the department in which they worked as a paralegal. One paralegal-turned-trainee told us (after a sigh and a meditative pause) that they would be "*very upset*" if they didn't get a qualification job because this was a firm they wanted to stay at for their whole career. One of the firm's vital principles is that if someone shows talent and has the desire to work hard and progress, Forbes will support and invest in them.

Although most traineeships go to people born and bred in Lancashire, this is by no means a policy decision. Forbes also employs people who've come from outside of the Rose counties, even from daahn saarf. On the whole they're a sociable bunch here. Staff frequently go out for post-work drinks, take lunch together or hit the town at weekends. Social events are a mixture of firm-organised jollies and more impromptu meet-ups organised among friends. The main event has got to be the annual party at Blackburn Rovers' Ewood Park. "*There's a free bar – I think everyone enjoys that – and a DJ, so everyone has a dance and a chat.*" On a more professional note, the trainees are invited to network with local businesses at regular dinner and drinks events.

None of the trainees mentioned anything lacking in the offices, but the sweet-toothed might want to note that "*there are always lots of cakes at Rutherford House* [in Blackburn]." Apparently it's all to do with a commitment to charity fund-raising, and several times a year employees bake and raffle goodies. The more health-conscious among them also participate in sponsored runs. Another activity that brings people together is the drinking of cocktails at work during charity fund-raisers. When this is going on, there's a sign put out in the reception area to let people know that the beverages aren't alcoholic. There are other little perks too – if you go six months without any absences you get a bonus, and there are discounts at local restaurants, shops and hairdressers. This might also be the only firm in the country to give you a chance of becoming a millionaire on your birthday, thanks to free lottery scratchcards.

And finally...

All seven 2009 qualifiers were able to stay on in roles at Forbes. This is a firm with huge breadth and a well-tested training scheme, so if its work is up your street then get that application form filled in.

Ford & Warren

The facts

Location: Leeds

Number of UK partners/solicitors: 20/36

Total number of trainees: 8

Seats: 4x6 months

Alternative seats: None

> F&W is a straightforward and sensible place that shows, and values, loyalty.

This proud Leeds outfit is confident in its understated approach. It has built its business through firm Yorkshire handshakes and word of mouth.

No nonsense

If mottos weren't anathema, a good one for F&W would be 'Quality Graft at a Fair Price'. Its reputation is ingrained locally among owner-managed businesses and small to medium-sized enterprises, and it also attracts national clients like pub chain Greene King and the vast transport company First Group. It recently became a member of Primerus, a network of North American firms, in an attempt to gain more international work. As one trainee put it, the firm represents *"everyone from national and international corporations right through to Mrs Smith from the end of the street."* In addition to solid real estate and commercial practices, it has strong niche areas like sport and transport law and caters for private clients.

Founded back in the day (1816 to be precise), the firm has expanded into ever-larger premises without ever straying from its hometown. Today the Ford & Warren name illuminates the Westgate Point building, an open-plan red-brick edifice surrounded by the buzz of Leeds traffic. The firm hasn't merged in almost two centuries and we don't expect any radical change of direction now. The most newsworthy change of the past few years came in 2007 when the managing partner announced an increasing focus on the transport and insurance sectors. The firm immediately secured a position in *Chambers UK*'s insurance rankings, and its sterling work at the forefront of road transport law cemented a *Chambers* top-tier ranking there too. The firm is neither complacent or stagnating. *"There are strong plans for growth,"* trainees said; *"and the idea is to build for the future."* F&W did not lay any- one off during the frenzied period of law firm rationalisations following the sudden plunge in the country's economic fortunes. Instead it made cutbacks on luxuries (like biscuits and parties).

Trainees here take four seats of six months, often spending their final one in the area they want to qualify into, which means that some people get to spend a whole year in their preferred area. The way one source viewed each of their seats was as *"20 full weeks for you to learn as much as you can."* We think this no-nonsense approach is typical at F&W.

Driving forward

Who'd have thought that transport law could be exciting? Partner Gary Hodgson has proved it can, having involved the firm in *"a major tachograph conspiracy investigation,"* acted for Preston Bus Company in a public inquiry into a *"bus war"* with arch rivals Stagecoach and stepped in to become hero of the hour when a transport-related gross negligence manslaughter prosecution was lodged. In addition to these high-octane matters, the transport team acts in health and safety proceedings, handles stacks of regulatory issues and has worked on public inquiries into the reliability and quality of service rendered by large transport companies. While there's no specific transport law seat for trainees, interested parties may be able to cadge work from one of the partners, and most trainees will encounter transport clients in other departments anyway. For instance First Group, National Express, Scot Rail, Arriva trains and First Great Western all instruct the employment team. Trainees in this seat enjoyed the busy atmosphere and client contact, saying that the level of responsibility was set at just the right level to stretch them. Other clients of the department include NHS trusts, Leeds City Council and Punch Taverns.

In litigation trainees work on contentious matters for businesses and individuals. It's a very popular seat at the moment, partly because there are always plenty of juicy lawsuits in a recession, and also because *"you get so much out of it."* Indeed the only downside seems to be the volume of court bundling that needs to be done. Trainees work on matters with IP and fraud elements to them and speculated that these areas will continue to grow in importance to the firm. Brian Clough always considered himself a practical man and we'd venture that he probably would have considered F&W a kindred spirit. The litigation team advised his family in relation to *The Damned United*, a film based on his time at the helm of Leeds United FC. In another piece of sports litigation, the firm acted for sprinter Dwain Chambers, who after testing positive for steroids in 2003 was banned from athletics for two years. When UK Athletics then tried to prevent him from challenging for a place in Team GB for the World Indoor Games, F&W managed to get the ruling overturned and Chambers went on to win a silver medal in the men's 60m sprint in Valencia. Other work has involved contract disputes for leading footballers, teams and their agents. Over in finance litigation trainees can expect piles of work in connection with lease agreements for vehicles (eg hire cars, diggers) and get the opportunity to polish their drafting skills and learn about breaches of contract and consumer credit regulations. As for advocacy experience, well this shouldn't be in short supply!

F&W is *"among the handful of firms that do insurance and fraud work,"* which trainees tell us is *"a really interesting area of law where you can get a few files to do in your own name."* It's all about making sure that insurance claims are kosher – *"sometimes someone might say that they've had their car nicked, but then you see it being sold on eBay."* Trainees revelled in the chance to investigate cases like this, and they liked that fact that there was also some claimant work to allow them to see both sides of the coin.

Pubs, pub chains and restaurants often take advantage of F&W's expertise in property and licensing law. The licensing seat is *"pretty contentious"* and involves ensuring that premises adhere to regulations, such as those for late-night opening or the performance of live music. This work occasionally involves liaising with the police to tackle drugs problems in pubs. Property practice was described as *"good to know about"* and is an excellent department for client contact on matters pertaining to everything from the redevelopment of city centres right down to the small sales and leases.

Chambers UK rankings

Debt Recovery	Licensing
Dispute Resolution	Personal Injury
Employment	
Insurance	Transport

Seek and ye shall find

It's the little vignettes of office life that best illustrate F&W's ethos. For example, the firm believes that *"it's better and cheaper to retain clients than win new ones,"* and *"that idea applies to the staff"* as well. Rather than churning through employees, trainees report that *"it's not the sort of place where people come for a couple of years and then leave."* F&W doesn't go courting applicants with freebies at law fairs, instead it relies on them to seek out the firm for themselves and then carefully selects those who it thinks are likely to stay long term. One trainee theorised that this helps the firm get well-suited candidates: people who really want to be there. Also of significance is the firm's tidy-desk policy. Everyone adheres to it because it's a firm where *"people take pride in doing things in an organised way with no corners cut."* Join up these seemingly unrelated dots and you get a good picture of the firm's culture – a straightforward and sensible place that shows, and values, loyalty.

Some of the chaps have formed a band called Red Light Revival. *"They're... umm... I wouldn't like to pigeonhole them,"* said one trainee. They can't be too bad as their gigs are always packed with the firm's employees. When not rocking out, the trainees like to go to bars Baby Jupiter and Indie Joze. Although it isn't in the firm's character to host expensive fancy networking events each week, trainees have been involved in a few, most notably the one involving the release of Dwain Chambers' new book. They got stuck into organising the event and were invited along on the night to help out and chat with clients.

Trainees comment favourably on the level of support they get (the managing partner takes a personal interest, meeting with them to discuss their progress), the advice given (every day they meet with their supervisor for 15 minutes to discuss their work) and the training. They feel well prepared for NQ life and in 2009 all four NQs found positions at the firm.

And finally...

One person summed up Ford & Warren as *"loyal and fair."* All things considered, we have to agree.

Freeth Cartwright LLP

The facts

Location: Nottingham, Leicester, Derby, Birmingham

Number of UK partners/solicitors: 78/84

Total number of trainees: 17

Seats: 4x6 months

Alternative seats: Secondments

Extras: Pro bono – Nottingham Law Centre

One of the big names in law in the East Midlands, Freeth has previously shown itself to be an adaptable firm with a strong sense of identity. These days such qualities are vital.

Freeth Cartwright has worked hard to spread its name around. It has offices across the East Midlands and newer branches in Manchester and Birmingham.

Freeth'll fix it

Freeth made its name in civil litigation, particularly in relation to multi-party claims. It worked on major cases concerning products such as the infant MMR vaccine and the Trilucent and 3M breast implants. Over the past decade, however, it has set its eyes firmly on the commercial prize and has gained *Chambers UK* rankings left, right and centre. It currently performs at the highest level in its region for corporate finance, dispute resolution, real estate and social housing. There are still a couple of gems remaining from the firm's pre-commercial days, namely a stellar product liability practice (one of the top four in country) and a top-notch claimant clinical negligence team. The product liability lawyers, led by highly experienced Paul Balen, have represented clients in relation to Salmonella poisoning from Cadbury's chocolate and handled cases of gambling addiction following use of medication for Parkinson's disease. Another problematic medication has been antipsychotic drug Zyprexa, which is alleged to cause diabetes. The clin neg team has helped numerous individuals claim millions of pounds in compensation, including one child with a severe birth injury for whom it achieved a payout with an equivalent conventional award value of £7m. Trainees hoping for seats in these claimant departments should be aware that "*you have to express a real desire to get a seat, and even if you do it's not a guaranteed outcome.*"

Previously the firm operated an East Midlands contract with most trainees based in the Nottingham HQ. The two newest offices in Birmingham and Manchester have now opened their doors to recruits. While "*each office has its own atmosphere, they do interact quite well,*" say trainees, who are expected to "*muck in right away.*" As the firm's largest office, Nottingham has the advantage of full secretarial support – apparently as a trainee "*you don't have to do filing in Nottingham at all.*" In the smaller offices recruits "*have to help out more in the admin tasks.*"

Freethstyle

There's no compulsion for trainees to work in any of the smaller Freeth offices, although business needs may lead to some Nottingham trainees making the commute to either Derby or Leicester for a seat or two. Second-years get priority in the allocation process, and with the property department making up around a third of total revenue and spread across four of the offices, it's unlikely trainees will avoid time in one of its teams – commercial, finance, planning and construction. Property seats give "*a broad perspective of the business*" and trainees clearly enjoy the good level of responsibility available. "*I got lots of client contact and was running files on my own,*" reported one.

Commercial real estate development has traditionally been a strong area for Freeth. Of late, this type of work "*has dried up*" a bit; nevertheless, the firm has had a number of major of projects on the go. On home turf, it is advising Bildurn Properties on a prestigious £10m mixed-use development in the heart of Nottingham's Lace Market; further afield, it has advised Liberty Property Trust on sales of sites for residential development in Kent. Diversification into the areas of healthcare, the public sector, education and regeneration has paid off, with Freeth securing two standout transactions for Blueprint, which aims to regenerate major urban areas in the East Midlands. One project is a £21m Digital Media Centre in Leicester and the other an extension for Nottingham Science Park. Over in the highly praised construction team lawyers helped Balfour Beatty secure a £302m contract for the Olympic Aquatic Centre.

The corporate team is present in all offices and its lawyers move around as work requires. The group has gained a reputation for providing a highly personalised service, despite its impressive size. Trainees say the corporate finance group has "*a team-focused environment.*" In fact, a pleasant culture can be found across the firm and partners are deemed to be relaxed and approachable, so much so that "*you can just go and knock on the managing partner's door.*" If you require empirical facts to support all this, then Freeth's selection as one of a handful of law firms in this year's *Sunday Times*' '100 Best Companies to Work For' list should do the job.

The care home sector has been the source of some of Freeth's biggest corporate transactions lately: for example, it represented Orchard Care Homes in a £175m management buy-out. In more traditional deals, the team represents a number of blue-chip and AIM companies, notably Experien, the FTSE 100 global credit information organisation behind most of the world's credit cards. A recent transaction was the merger of international company Belle (which specialises in compaction, cement and concrete equipment) with French-based Altrad group. Due diligence makes up a significant part of a trainee's workload, but the supportive atmosphere in the team means they should never feel left out of the action. "*I was scanning stuff late at night with my sleeves rolled up and everyone else from the partner down was doing the same thing alongside me,*" said one source. With deal flow down, hours have not been as intense in this department as in previous years and trainees were pleased to report that 8.30am – 6pm was an average day. Just as importantly, they told us they had a "*sufficient workload*" to keep them busy.

Contentious experience can be gained in Freeth's highly respected commercial litigation team, where trainees receive assignments "*from any number of people,*" ensuring an excellent variety that can include IP litigation, professional negligence, employment and insolvency. Recruits can expect to draft witness statements, prepare client bulletins and staff employment handbooks and generally be "*kept up to speed on a number of cases.*" Clients include Brit Insurance, Carlsberg, Centre Parcs and American Express. There's even a private client seat offering "*a bit of everything,*" including some interesting contested probate. Trainees get plenty of exposure to clients so "*people skills*" develop quickly here.

A breath of Freeth air

The recession hit Freeth just as it did other firms. It posted a 36% drop in profitability in 2009 and was forced to make

Chambers UK rankings

Banking & Finance	Private Client
Clinical Negligence	Product Liability
Construction	Projects, Energy & Natural Resources
Corporate/M&A	
Dispute Resolution	Real Estate
Employment	Real Estate Litigation
Intellectual Property	Restructuring/Insolvency
Licensing	Social Housing
Personal Injury	Tax

around 68 members of staff redundant. After retaining all seven of last year's qualifiers, we were sorry to hear that three of these were victims of the cuts. Our sources were measured in their response. "*I can understand why they did it but it would have been better if they had been given more warning,*" said one. Renowned for being a chatty bunch, the recent turbulence may have had some bearing on the slight lack of sparkle we got from recruits this year. However, they did assure us that Freeth looks for "*outgoing people*" who are "*strong-minded*" but also "*quite relaxed and not overly serious.*" Having a Midlands connection is reasonably important as "*they are concerned people will flock back to the big cities.*" Applicants who come from further afield are by no means ruled out if they exhibit a strong commitment to the Midlands. "*We all have different backgrounds; we're a real mixed bunch,*" a source assured us.

Get your Freeth on

"*Partners say to us that social events are important to the firm as we all have to work together, so we might as well get along.*" If those sentiments sound lukewarm, rest assured that the social scene is actually pretty active, with regular nights out bowling, go-karting or at the dog track, a touch rugby team, cricket matches against clients and events to which future trainees are invited. The Castle is the favourite pub in Nottingham and in another establishment called Chambers (good name), trainees have been known to belt out 'I Will Survive' on the karaoke machine. Those not based in Nottingham aren't left out: the firm "*gives you extra time to get to social events.*" There is also a committee responsible for organising events with future trainees to help integrate early.

And finally...

Talk of expansion into London may have dulled to a whisper for now, but Freeth still managed to offer three of its five qualifiers jobs in 2009 and did not defer new trainees.

- **Smile!** As an astute trainee points out: "Don't forget to show you're human." Let your CV do the talking when it comes to academic credentials. In an interview most recruiters just want to know what you would be like to work with.

top tip no. 14

FRESHFIELDS BRUCKHAUS DERINGER

A collapsed building society, an Australian thoroughbred, 5,000 blood tests and an unmissable 2012 deadline.

EXPERIENCE LIFE AT FRESHFIELDS

We offer our trainees a breadth of training, opportunity and experience that few firms can match – so it's not surprising that many of our lawyers have amazing stories to tell.

This is due to the nature of our firm – truly international with over 2,600 lawyers in 27 key business centres around the world – and to the flexibility of our training programme. You can choose up to eight different seats, spend time in one of our overseas offices or go on secondment to one of our clients (and sometimes do both).

It's no wonder the people who work with us have such an eclectic range of experiences to look back on over their careers.

And as you'll be working with and learning from some of the most talented business lawyers in the world, you'll gain the experience and knowledge you need to become not just a world-class lawyer but a trusted business advisor too.

Find out more at:
www.freshfields.com/uktrainees

FRESHFIELDS BRUCKHAUS DERINGER LLP

provider — London 2012 Olympic Games
provider — London 2012 Paralympic Games

Freshfields Bruckhaus Deringer LLP

The facts

Location: London
Number of UK partners/solicitors: 158/546
Total number of trainees: 200
Seats: 3 or 6 months long
Alternative seats: Overseas seats, secondments
Extras: Pro bono – RCJ CAB, Tower Hamlets Law Centre, Liberty, FRU, US death row appeals; language training

A respected part of the magic circle, Freshfields is the official law firm for the 2012 London Olympics.

Freshfields has grown to become one of the world's finest corporate law firms. This powerhouse employs over 2,400 lawyers across 27 offices worldwide.

Timeless appeal

Freshfields is an ancient firm, and certainly the oldest member of the magic circle. Way back in 1743 it famously advised the Bank of England, and what do you know, the Bank is still a client today. Its long and illustrious history is the perfect basis for Freshfields' reputation as a traditionalist, but rather than dismissing the label we found our sources took pride in this aspect of the firm's character, which they also described as "*collegial, genteel and conservative.*" There's nothing too conservative about the way in which successive management teams have pushed the firm forwards to become the slick global organisation it is today. They responded to the deregulation of the UK's financial services market in the 80s, picking up the considerable cross-border transactional work made possible by investment banks. The 90s was a decade of international expansion for the firm as it launched new offices throughout Europe, Asia, the USA and the Middle East. Along the way, it secured mergers with two major German law firms, Deringer Tessin Herrman & Sedemund and Bruckhaus Westrick Heller Loeber, inheriting a mouthful of a name in the process.

Then, in 2006, Freshfields underwent a bold restructuring. It slimmed down certain niche practice groups, offered early retirement to older partners and launched a programme of de-equitisation within the partnership. This phase of consolidation saw the firm retrench around its corporate practice and shift its centre of gravity even further towards M&A. The strategy has evidently paid dividends. Despite the slow corporate market, turnover was up 9% in 2008/09, bringing global revenues to £1.287bn.

These record-breaking financials are not the work of the corporate department alone, and credit must be given to the excellent performance of Freshfields' litigation and restructuring departments, among others.

Short your position or buy long

Freshfields' training involves a recommended initial six-month seat, generally spent in either corporate, finance or dispute resolution, followed by spells of either three or six months in other departments, overseas offices or on client secondment. Our sources were delighted with the flexibility this system affords, telling us: "*You can try a greater range of practices, extend your stay if you like the work, or move on to something else if you don't.*" Three-month seats also allow more trainees to sample the delights of oversubscribed specialist areas such as arbitration, restructuring or competition. The only drawback is that "*it'll normally take about three months to properly settle into a team, and you'll have to leave just as you're getting into the swing of things.*" That issue comes into focus more sharply when trainees spend too little time in a department into which they hope to qualify. Our sources therefore advised that it would be unwise to "*lose yourself in too many niche seats; it's probably a good idea to devise a coherent seating plan and keep your eyes on the qualification prize.*"

No seats are compulsory but because "*Freshfields is very much a corporate law firm*" the chances of dodging the corporate department are scant. If this were your intention then Freshfields wouldn't be right for you anyway.

Now we're motoring

Freshfields' European corporate finance operation has no equal and our colleagues at *Chambers UK* and *Chambers Europe* have ranked its M&A practice in the top tier since for ever. When a megadeal is up for grabs it will frequently land in Freshfields' lap; for example, the team notably won the European mandate on the industry-saving strategic alliance between Chrysler and Fiat. Other highlights include acting for healthcare company Roche on its £26.7bn acquisition of Genentech in January 2009, and Best Buy Co. on its acquisition of 50% of The Carphone Warehouse Group for £1.1bn. Freshfields also handled the biggest Chinese M&A of 2009, representing power company GCL-Poly Energy in its $3.4bn purchase of a solar-cell parts manufacturer.

On transactions of this scale trainees are rarely trusted with significant responsibilities. Whether in a general M&A seat or one more focused on private equity, *"there's no escaping dogsbody work."* More testing tasks do become available to those with the aptitude for them. *"You have to be proactive and seek out more work, you can't sit back waiting for it to come your way."* Hungrier trainees get to *"draft share purchase agreements, prospectuses, articles of association or board minutes."* There is one caveat: *"The quality of your workload very much depends on whether your supervisor is interested in your progression."* Said one regretful trainee, echoing the view of some others: *"Mine didn't seem bothered."*

The hours in corporate are pretty tough whenever the markets are busy, and for Freshfields they're rarely quiet. Towards the close of major deals things get very intense for trainees, who are often asked to spend nights in the office or give up weekends. On the plus side, pulling an all-nighter is a good way to endear yourself to senior figures. *"It earned me some respect,"* one trainee enthused, while another reported: *"I got to know my colleagues a lot better. A sort of fellowship develops among those who put in very long hours."* Such sacrifices usually don't go unnoticed by partners, who encourage trainees to take time off in lieu or to knock off early when things are quiet.

Freshfields' decision to streamline its finance departments led to claims that it had put all its eggs in the corporate basket and no longer valued finance work. In reality, it remains an important focus and trainees are strongly encouraged to spend time here, either with the structured and asset finance subgroup or with the banking and restructuring team. While lacking the visibility of the likes of A&O or Clifford Chance, Freshfields' finance department is best described as specialised. It eschews commoditised transactions for cutting-edge deals. Given the unprecedented market conditions, trainees this year noticed a dramatic fall in leveraged deals, but reported that the team has remained busy restructuring existing deals and giving advice to stretched corporates. Of all the subgroups, asset finance is thought to provide the most rewarding work at trainee level. While some of our sources found it *"precedent-based and repetitive,"* they acknowledged that the discipline lends itself to lower-value deals, which they can handle solo. In other areas, deals are often too complex or technical for trainees to provide significant input, so they're normally left collating conditions precedent and managing simple loan documentation.

In fighting form

Litigation is a recommended destination. Freshfields offers a two-week opt-out course for transactional types who perhaps don't realise that it has one of the top-rated teams in the City for high-value litigation. At the other end of the spectrum are trainees who have come hoping to qualify into this impressive group. Those people certainly aren't disappointed by the quality of instructions coming through the door, lately ranging from white-collar crime investigations to credit crunch disputes. A good example of the City nature of the caseload, earlier in 2009 Freshfields went head to head with Clifford Chance in a dispute between the London Stock Exchange and rival exchange Plus, which is doing its best to usurp AIM.

Our sources felt the litigators had made a real effort to involve them. *"My supervisor was very thoughtful and copied me in on all the correspondence. It makes the menial tasks more bearable when you know the context,"* one explained. Besides inescapable mundane jobs, trainees also receive better assignments, including drafting witness statements and instructions to counsel or attending client strategy meetings and court hearings.

Chambers UK rankings

Administrative & Public Law	Investment Funds
Asset Finance	Media & Entertainment
Banking & Finance	Outsourcing
Banking Litigation	Pensions
Capital Markets	Private Equity
Competition/European Law	Product Liability
Construction	Professional Negligence
Corporate/M&A	Projects, Energy & Natural Resources
Dispute Resolution	Public International Law
Employee Share Schemes	Public Procurement
Employment	Real Estate
Environment	Real Estate Finance
Financial Services Regulation	Restructuring/Insolvency
	Retail
Fraud: Civil	Sports Law
Information Technology	Tax
Insurance	Telecommunications
Intellectual Property	Transport

Those crying out for independence and advocacy experience can ask to take full responsibility on a pro bono case.

Freshfields also boasts a world-beating arbitration group. The Paris office is the hub, and those who are serious about specialising in the field "*would sell an arm and a leg*" for a secondment to the French capital. Staying in London isn't bad either as plenty of arbitration is conducted under English law. The quality of instructions is "*second to none*" and recently included representing Dutch and US companies in ICSID proceedings arising under bilateral investment treaties with Georgia following state intervention in its energy and chemicals sectors. Because this department is heavily oversubscribed for seats and NQ jobs, making your mark is crucial. "*The politics of this department can be quite tricky to figure out,*" a source advised, while another said more bluntly: "*Your prospects depend entirely on working with the right partners – there are a few rainmakers who decide arbitrarily who gets the work. If you can't get access to them, you've got no future in this group.*"

All out?

Trainees really are spoilt for choice; once done with their 'recommended' seats in corporate, finance and litigation, they can apply to spend time in a swathe of smaller departments like IP, competition, employment, environment, real estate and tax. Although they'll usually have to wait until their very last seat, trainees can also spend time abroad. Securing a placement in New York or Hong Kong will require you to fend off extremely stiff competition, but there are plenty of other destinations to explore. Another option is a client secondment, which trainees can use to perfect their knowledge of a particular industry. It's also a good way to test the waters for an in-house career.

"*Work hard, play hard*" was a cliché oft-used by our sources. Freshfields attracts sporting talent in spades, and among the intakes of trainees we spoke to there was a member of the Olympic sailing team and somebody who'd swum the English Channel. Everyone is encouraged to use the on-site gym or join one of the sports teams, which are too numerous to list. We must mention the cricket team, which recently beat the grass-stained pants off the Cyprus national team. Socially speaking, at the beginning of the training contract, "*there is a lot more demand for everyone to go out together, then people settle down in smaller groups.*" For those who just can't get enough of their peers, Freshfields puts on firm-wide events including summer and winter balls, and there are also team-specific jollies. Things have been a little quieter on the party front lately, particularly for trainees. The litigation team decided its budget couldn't stretch to inviting them to this year's summer bonding session. Shame.

Blueblood, sweat and tears

Oxbridge graduates make up more than a third of each intake. "*I see no oddity here, it's simply where the best graduates are from,*" a source reasoned. The 'blues and blondes' stereotype of yore still also holds some truth. "*Let's just say there is a significant body of public and grammar school boys and girls.*" This said, the recruitment committee engages with many more universities and also seeks high-achievers from around the world, making each intake much more diverse. Trainees perceive little change in the firm's other requirements: "*Freshfields looks for enthusiastic and ultra-conscientious people who are willing to crack on with the work.*" Apparently, the firm's also got a soft spot for "*more adventurous people who've shown initiative in the past, be it in travelling, doing charity work or learning new languages.*"

Once enrolled, you'll soon find "*you need a thick skin to work here.*" A number of interviewees picked up on the "*very hierarchical nature of Freshfields,*" and warned: "*Don't expect partners to know your name. You must know your place and learn not take things personally.*" Trainees must conduct a delicate balancing act: they need to be proactive and push for more challenging work, while bearing in mind that "*management isn't keen on excessively outspoken trainees.*" From what we can tell, those who strike the right balance get the best out of their two years and don't let minor gripes colour their judgement of what is overall "*an absolutely amazing experience.*"

Qualification prospects have traditionally been excellent, but the firm saw its NQ retention drop from a superb 95% in 2008 to a merely good 80% in 2009, as 80 of the 100 qualifiers got jobs. A number of our contacts had questions about the qualification process. One said: "*We were assured the official selection procedure would be followed religiously, but at the end of the day those who had schmoozed the right partners jumped straight to the front of the queue.*" Whether fair play or foul, this is a lesson for prospective trainees: to succeed you'll have to stand out from the crowd, so don't hesitate to make contacts and treat your training contract like a perpetual job interview.

Freshfields deserves kudos for not having implemented a redundancy programme among staff, although you'll probably be aware that it cut the pay of NQ lawyers and froze salaries for associates. The firm also asked a number of trainees from future intakes to delay their arrival for six months, offering them £5,000 payment.

And finally...

Training at Freshfields usually marks the beginning of a great career in law. If you wish to become one of the chosen few, be aware that the firm will demand considerably more effort than you perhaps imagine.

Government Legal Service (GLS)

The facts

Location: London, Manchester
Number of UK lawyers: c.2,000
Total number of trainees: 42 (sols)
Seats: 4x6 months
Alternative seats: None
Extras: GLS Pro Bono Network; language training

"There is definitely a new breed of civil servant now. We are more touchy-feely. We're not just going to sit in an ivory tower and type out our very well considered legal advice to send to you."

The Government Legal Service. What is it and what does it do? In this report we try to throw some light on an oft-misunderstood organisation with a totally unique training contract.

Hidden depths

The GLS is the UK's largest employer of lawyers – around 2,000 of them – yet it has only one client. Every autumn, the Queen puts on her best crown and saunters down to the House of Lords to announce Her Government's policies for that year. It's then the lawyers' job to best advise on how legally to put policy into practice, plus how to interpret changes in European law, how to comply with treaties the government might become party to and a million other problems besides. They also handle contentious issues as and when they arise... which is basically all the time.

If helping big business make more and more money isn't really why you went into the law, you should seriously consider the GLS. "*At heart I am a public servant... I am interested in tax accumulation rather than tax avoidance,*" said a cheery trainee in Her Majesty's Revenue & Customs (HMRC). "*What we do is hugely significant. You can't tell your friends at the time, but later it will be on the front page of the paper and you can say 'I did that! That was me!'*" Take urban regeneration, for example. East London's redevelopment in time for the Olympic Games simply wouldn't happen without the massed ranks of the GLS. Or there's the plight of the Gurkhas. It took a national treasure to spearhead their campaign but, once St Joanna of Lumley had shimmered alluringly from the stage, who was on hand to sort out the fine details? Government is "*like the iceberg. The tip is the MPs; the huge unseen mass is made up of the civil servants who spot the problems and spend years trying to solve them.*"

A couple of years ago the GLS made its application process more onerous in an attempt to ensure higher-calibre applicants. Suffice it to say that if you haven't got a genuine commitment to public service you're unlikely to make much headway. A tip for the assessment day, should you get that far: "*You need to be able to listen to other people's viewpoints.*" The assessment tasks reflect what the job can be like. "*Quite often there's no correct answer, just the answer that allows most groups of people to achieve some of what they want to achieve. It's about getting the best fit for a number of departments.*"

Trainees work for specific departments. Applicants indicate their preferred two, although there is no guarantee of receiving an offer from either. It hardly matters because to avoid "*stagnancy*" GLS lawyers tend to switch to a new area every few years. Depending on their individual budgets and needs, different departments take trainees each year. It's safe to assume that there will always be vacancies in the Treasury Solicitor's department (TSol), which with over 450 lawyers is the largest of them all. The Home Office recruits every other year and is always popular. At the time of our calls, there were also trainees in HMRC, the Ministry of Justice and the departments for Transport (DfT); Environment, Food and Rural Affairs (Defra); Communities and Local Government (CLG); and Business, Innovation and Skills (BIS). In 2009, the Serious Organised Crime Agency (SOCA) and the Serious Fraud Office (SFO) accepted applications for the first time. The Ministry of Defence only takes trainees on secondment. A full list of recruiting departments is available on the GLS website.

This feature focuses on solicitors, but the GLS also trains pupil barristers. If you're not sure which path to take you can tick the 'either' box on your application form. Why not take a look at our GLS pupillage feature on page 704.

Bona contention

"If you are an adrenalin junkie TSol is the place to go." It *"prides itself on being the law firm for the government"* and *"does have kind of a corporate feel to it. Sometimes it almost feels like you are in private practice."* TSol is also the department that sees the most litigation, often handling cases for other ministries. For example, it frequently handles personal injury claims for the MoD, not to mention claims by Iraqi civilians in relation to alleged human rights abuses.

TSol trainees usually spend their first year in contentious seats and their second year in advisory ones. Immigration, a team that is always *"crying out for trainees,"* is one of the former. *"It's quite high-pressured. You are expected to get up to speed with the relevant legislation very quickly. I started ten cases on my first day and was expected to handle them from beginning to end."* Our source had liaised with immigration teams at embassies all over the world. By contrast, planning litigation is *"very academic and there's not a lot of procedure involved."* Cases range from the *"little old lady down the road who wants a greenhouse"* (GLS trainees talked repeatedly about little old ladies) to the Stansted Airport expansion plans, which one trainee found *"terrifying – I just had visions of putting one foot wrong and a billion-dollar deal collapsing because of it."* Again, trainees get their own caseload: *"You pick counsel and draft instructions. For every case that comes in you have to prepare advice, look at the law and see if it's winnable."*

The bona vacantia team works slightly off the beaten track looking into *"ownerless goods."* These arise when someone dies intestate without close relatives or when a company is dissolved. The team has *"the thankless task of trying to liquidate those assets."* It's thankless because *"there's no big cases to show off."* At least it makes money for the Treasury – something not everyone is pleased about. *"You have people calling up getting quite unpleasant, saying, 'The government doesn't deserve this money. I don't have a claim to it but I was the deceased's neighbour and visited every him week and I deserve something.'"* Not to mention *"the shady Del-Boyish types who call up and try to do a deal."* Bona vacantia is *"not sexy"* but *"you learn a lot."*

Shoes, sandwiches and strippers

HMRC isn't popular with Joe Public; *"we're seen as the bad tax man,"* acknowledged one source. Actually we came across some very happy trainees who enjoyed *"meeting people from every sector of society, from big CEOs to little old ladies."* One was keen to point out that tax is *"not all about maths and accountancy. I'm the least mathematical person I know."* What trainees do is far more fascinating (apologies to maths geeks). In the VAT and excise litigation seat, many cases rest on interpretation. You could be researching, as one trainee did, whether Subway sandwiches count as hot or cold food, or *"what makes a child's shoe a child's shoe for VAT purposes."* Apparently it's defining the teenage sizes that poses a problem. One trainee even got to pass judgement on the age-old Jaffa Cake conundrum – *"cake or biscuit?"* We wonder which lawyer had to research whether lap-dancing club Spearmint Rhino was liable for VAT or not.

Advisory work is the bread and butter of a government lawyer. Communities and Local Government (CLG), for example, handles almost no litigation and its trainees go to TSol to gain contentious experience. This department is all about *"how people live together."* For example, S106 agreements *"give planning permission to housing developers if they promise to build a community facility like a playground or something as well."* Trainees have to make sure the drafting is watertight as surprise, surprise, *"agreements are often drafted quite weakly by the developer."* Plus there are always *"weird bits and pieces"* like Tree Preservation Orders to deal with. *"You can apply for a tree to be protected if it's due to be cut down. The first decision is made at local level. We get involved if there's an appeal from a little old lady."* She gets everywhere, doesn't she?

CLG's regeneration seat deals with large compulsory purchase projects to allow urban redevelopment. The eco-towns scheme, the Thames Gateway development and the Olympic village are just three examples. Simple plans can become incredibly complex. *"What happens when someone wants to compulsorily purchase a burial ground?"* A seemingly straightforward idea suddenly needs involvement from Defra, the Ministry of Justice, the Department of Health, *"maybe Transport if you want to drive a road though it, Culture, Media and Sport because there might be heritage issues..."* Meanwhile, landlord and tenant problems are a major aspect of the housing seat. *"We've got difficulties at the moment with tenants of people who are behind on their mortgage."* What's their legal status and how can they be protected? That sums up the work of the GLS: answering the vital questions that most people don't think about.

These are just a few of the departments and a few of the seats. We couldn't possibly cover the entire scope of the GLS, and it (almost) goes without saying that deeper research will bring enormous dividends.

Partly political

Some kind of interest in current affairs is a given, but many of our contacts were not hugely party-political, happily admitting: "*I don't know who to vote for because they're all the same.*" For them, neutrality is easy, but what about those who have deeply held left or right wing views? "*I thought a lot about that when I applied,*" said one such trainee. "*A lot of our work is fairly harmless, but sometimes you are asked to do things that you don't think are politically right. That's the only thing I've found uncomfortable, but that's what you sign up for. If you really can't cope with that, you shouldn't be applying.*" Another agreed: "*In some ways it does curtail what you can do in the outside world.*" Any activities where you would pass political comment on government policies – protest marches for instance – are a no-no. All our sources, wherever they put their X, said: "*It was something we were prepared to give up.*"

How else is working in the civil service different from practising at a normal law firm? Well, TSol aside, "*some people might find the pace a bit slow.*" Said a lawyer in CLG: "*There are no real time pressures. The nice thing about the work is that you can spend time to make sure you get the answer right.*" Another quirk is that "*everything we do comes from policy, and that can be chaotic. If the minister changes, something that was a burning issue might suddenly be dropped.*" Slow-paced, beholden to ministers – sounds like the typical cliché of the bowler-hatted civil service of old. Not really, say our contacts. Large parts of the organisation have moved to open-plan offices, some of our contacts hot-desked and overall a more "*holistic*" attitude now prevails. While "*remnants of the older school*" remain, "*there is definitely a new breed of civil servant now. We are more touchy-feely. We're not just going to sit in an ivory tower and type out our very well considered legal advice to send to you. The ability to communicate with absolutely anyone is very important.*"

Ministry of Fun

There's no point ignoring the cold, hard fact that GLS lawyers don't get paid as much as their counterparts in the City. And there's no point pretending that GLS trainees wouldn't mind being paid a bit more. But for all of them the bonuses outweigh the drawbacks. There is "*an element of idealism, the idea that we are doing something a little bit more selfless,*" of course. But there are more practical benefits too. The hours much shorter, for one. Midnight working? "*You wouldn't find that here, there'd be a revolution!*" Instead, 9.30am to 5.30pm is standard, although occasionally slightly longer hours are required. When those hours are given is very flexible. Lots of people, including trainees, work from home two or three days a week. "*One of my colleagues lives in France; others live in Oxford or Brighton.*" This naturally suits people with children, and it might be of interest to note that a high proportion of GLS trainees are over the age of 30.

Then there's the pension – "*always worthy of a mention*" – and there's "*probably more job security*" than in private practice. Although the GLS is ultimately subject to the same economic forces as any other organisation, it's more sheltered than most and this year kept almost all of its qualifiers, as usual. Finally, "*I think we probably have the better work here,*" chimed a confident interviewee. "*These trainees in the City appear to spend two years photocopying, get to meet a client once and seem really chuffed by that.*" Of course, we know that's not quite the true picture, but there's probably a grain of truth in it.

The social scene "*might take a little looking for*" but it's there. A cross-departmental network keeps trainees in touch and has organised wine tasting, bowling, quiz nights and ice-skating among other things. The Union of Government Lawyers, Youngish (UGLY) also organises activities and is open to trainees. The annual sports day in Chiswick doesn't sound hugely sporty to us: "*It's a nice day out of the office, smoking, drinking and having a great time.*" A lecture series has also been organised, with high-profile speakers including the Attorney General of the Falkland Islands.

And finally...

If you've an interest in public law this would be a fantastic choice. None of our contacts expressed the slightest dissatisfaction, happy in the knowledge that "*the work we are doing affects the whole nation.*"

Halliwells LLP

The facts

Location: Manchester, Liverpool, London, Sheffield

Number of partners/solicitors: 145/220

Total number of trainees: 79

Seats: 5x5 months

Alternative seats: Secondments

> Halliwells really does pay attention to its trainees. In July, we heard them complain about the appraisal system. By August, HR had changed it after listening to their feedback.

Halliwells trainees like our use of the word 'swashbuckling' in relation to their firm. It's an apt way to describe its assault on the UK top 30; an ascension characterised by confidence, mergers and a driven, can-do attitude.

The grand plan

Trainees believe that *"most law firms are quite conservative, but we're not and we don't make apologies for it."* The recession only dented Halliwells' revenue by around 5% and although there were some 45 redundancies, a heady atmosphere and optimistic outlook remain at this prominent NW firm. Established 41 years ago, the ambitious Mancunian went on to open another three offices in Sheffield, London and Liverpool. Seemingly happy with its geographical spread, it then wanted to enhance its range of practices and hired voraciously from firms like DLA Piper, DWF, Nabarro, Cobbetts, Clyde & Co, Charles Russell and Hill Dickinson. Its main practice areas are property and corporate, but it also has a wide range of other work and achieves *Chambers UK* Band 1 rankings in a variety of contentious areas, all of which should provide a dependable revenue stream. In 2008/09, the contentious side of the business grew from around £30.5m to £34m.

Trainees usually complete five seats in the office to which they are recruited, but if they express a strong desire to move elsewhere, their wishes can usually be accommodated. The offices take on a mixture of national work and instructions from its local markets. The Liverpool office, for example, has the honour of representing the new Museum of Liverpool and Everton FC, while the Manchester office assists Manchester United. All offices concentrate on the same core areas of corporate and property, with the Manchester office having by far the most diverse range of seats for trainees. If you're looking for a specific practice or niche area, it is worth checking which offices do what before applying. If you intend to try for a secondment (common ones include Man United, Cable & Wireless, AIG, Ladbrokes and InBev, the world's biggest brewer), it's worth knowing that the London office offers *"a comparatively high proportion."* Recalling the time they spent with working in a client's office, one trainee said: *"It was one of the best things I've done. It was interesting to see things from the client's perspective, and that's something Halliwells is keen to encourage."*

Climbing spiders, collapsing hedges

The pace in the corporate department slowed in 2008/09. One source told us the sad tale of a trainee who, over a whole summer, clocked up just three hours of billable work because his boss was hoarding everything. *"In a way it's swings and roundabouts"* said one source; *"when everyone's massively busy there's less time for feedback, but when there isn't as much to do you get your work run through more thoroughly."* The more we asked about it, the clearer it seemed that it's been a classic feast-or-famine scenario. Some trainees had been rushed off their feet for periods and stayed late to finalise deals in *"the most pressurised department in the firm."* For others the corporate experience had been a disappointment. The volume of deals may be down, but the situation is far from disastrous. The group lately worked on the acquisition of London Southend Airport for £21m, as well as several deals that broke the £50m mark. Clients include JJBSports, 20:20 Mobile and institutional investors like Infinity Asset Management and Zeus Private Equity. An upbeat trainee in London reported that "*there's a surprisingly large amount of work,*" adding that the team in the capital takes on more AIM instructions than its northern counterparts.

One trainee told us they'd arrived in their property seat worrying that there would be nothing to keep them busy. "*I don't like not having anything to do, especially since they've taken Facebook and Hotmail away.*" They ended up finishing at 7pm every day and "*not getting much time to surf through Wikipedia.*" Instead they were attending meetings, managing their own small files and assisting on larger projects. As well as working on the Museum of Liverpool project, the firm has lately advised on the development of an 800 MW power station and represented Liverpool City Council in a complex agreement with National Rail and other bodies regarding the development of Lime Street Gateway. One of the most unusual examples of Halliwells' legal brawn involved getting clearance for a gigantic mechanical spider to climb up a building in Liverpool city centre as part of the Capital of Culture celebrations. On the contentious side, property lit trainees have "*very good experience with lots of drafting and a few court attendances.*" For one there was some satisfaction to be gained from "*issuing my own bills.*"

Most commercial law firms have responded to the recession by ramping up their insolvency and corporate recovery practices. Halliwells is no exception. "*One partner billed 700 hours in a month. He was often working until two in the morning and receiving calls from about 6am.*" Halliwells has experience in hedge fund litigation, "*and a lot of hedge funds are collapsing, so the practice has gone mental.*" It is all good news for the balance sheet and, needless to say, trainees here have been working longer hours too.

Plenty to fight over

The dispute resolution team (commercial litigation, construction, insurance litigation and regulatory matters) was described as "*very welcoming, very sociable and very good at what it does.*" Trainees see large cases as well as handling their own files, and the good news is that there are plenty of cases right now, particularly in relation to professional negligence claims. Another trend is the increased use of conditional and risk-sharing fee arrangements. One trainee had the good fortune to help with a long-running advertising dispute and got a lot of client contact, not least through taking witness statements. Insurance litigation is a common discipline for northern law firms and Halliwells has a slice of this lucrative pie. Trainees have involvement in matters ranging from workplace slips and trips and road accidents through to the enormous explosion at the Buncefield oil storage depot. The insurance lit department "*has been making lots of*

Chambers UK rankings

Banking & Finance	Information Technology
Banking Litigation	Intellectual Property
Capital Markets	Licensing
Clinical Negligence	Partnership
Construction	Pensions
Corporate/M&A	Personal Injury
Debt Recovery	Planning
Dispute Resolution	Police Law
Employment	Private Client
Family/Matrimonial	Real Estate
Health & Safety	Real Estate Litigation
Healthcare	Restructuring/Insolvency

progress" in the Sheffield office; indeed the office there is becoming overcrowded. One Sheffield source spoke enthusiastically about what they'd learned in the insurance lit seat, despite some initial reservations.

The construction department has been involved with the Liverpool Life museum development and instructions from a national hotel chain. It has recently helped Bank of Scotland in respect to a large development in Salford Quays, and advised Everton FC in connection with a proposed new stadium at Kirkby. Trainees appreciated the chance to complement their usual desk work ("*very technical drafting*" and contract negotiations) with site visits.

Hardmen?

Approximately two-thirds of all staff work in Manchester – roughly 700 people – making it the largest law firm in the city. Halliwells has a new, state-of-the art, eight-storey, Norman Foster-designed building, rather appropriately in Hardman Square in the Spinningfields district. You might think that all this sounds a tad expensive, and you'd be right. It may even have cost people their jobs. Just as last year, some trainees said: "*The feeling is that if it wasn't for the expensive building, not as many people would be let go.*" Though in financial terms it may look like "*a giant millstone around the firm's neck,*" the office is extremely well appointed and the only one in the network to have its own canteen. In Liverpool some people nip across the road and use Hill Dickinson's.

The British press love building people up and then watching them tumble; there's no story that sells like a fall from grace. Halliwells' quick, ballsy growth meant its progress had been reported on for years. It became a prime candidate for some knocking and, sure enough, when redundancies were announced the legal press had a field day. The first casualties were eight people in London's corporate department. The fever spread and jobs were axed from corporate and real estate departments across the network. Despite the redundancies and the sense that the firm was "*being used as a whipping boy,*" trainees say Halliwells sees the glass as half full and that "*there isn't a tendency to wallow in bad press.*"

We found the vibe in the London office was less positive this year. One source revealed how "*each office has its own identity, especially London because London is London, if you know what I mean.*" Before the recession, Halliwells had been growing rapidly and had given the London office "*a more critical role.*" London's energies were directed more at financial institutions so, unsurprisingly, it had the wind knocked out of its sails when the economy went pear shaped. Redundancies "*slimmed the office down; it was a bit lopsided before in terms of fee earner-to-partner ratios.*" Back in Manchester, one source viewed London as "*a satellite office*" that took a harsh blow, "*perhaps due to a lack of support from Manchester. Being completely honest, I don't think they took enough steps to develop it.*" Although trainees are "*quietly confident*" that the London office will ride out the storm, "*the firm has had its fingers burned so there's not the same brash positivity or claims it can achieve anything.*" The way trainees see it, it's a "*watch-this-space*" kinda place.

Halliwells evidently wants to recruit people with more than just a good academic record. Trainees describe themselves as "*extremely assertive,*" and see this as an essential quality at a firm where you have to "*show you've got something about you... show some get up and go.*" In short, recruits need to demonstrate that when the time comes they'll be able to bring in their own business. They tend to relish responsibility and welcome the steep learning curve that sees them working like NQs from early on. They say the firm "*does push you quite hard,*" but think "*it is good to be pushed because it makes you work more efficiently.*" One factor that leads to them experiencing high levels of exposure is the structure of the firm, namely its "*flat, pared-down hierarchy, where there aren't too many assistants.*" "*It's like a short isosceles triangle,*" one source ventured; "*that middle ground between the long, flat base and the point at the top is very short so you get the ultimate exposure to partners.*"

Party animals

Combined with their fun-loving attitude, the sheer number of employees at "*the mothership*" in Hardman Square means that Halliwellsians are a force to be reckoned with on a Friday night in Manchester. And on weeknights too. When we asked if the office fizzed with the sound of dissolving Alka Seltzers in the morning, we were told that "*people have gone past that – you get used to it. As well as being really clever and hard-working, people are incredibly sociable and outgoing.*" At a party held in the office, a trainee was surprised by the amount of wine set out, only to find yet more booze stockpiled in a fridge. The folks in Sheffield and Liverpool reported similar tales. Down in London, although things were a bit more restrained, there was still time for "*loads of fun,*" including monthly trainee outings, plenty of networking events and parties on the office's balcony overlooking the NatWest Tower and another Foster creation – the Gherkin. The trainees are brought together for an enjoyable fortnight in Manchester to take the PSC course and have a jolly good knees-up in between classes. Each office organises outings and parties, all of which sound good, but the best anecdote we heard came from the Manchester office. Staff had gone to Boggart Hole Clough to give it a bit of a tidy and, instead of chopping trees down with the axes provided, one trainee "*tore them down with his bare hands.*" Rargh!

A corporate responsibility day and the trip to Boggart Hole Clough demonstrate a dedication to pro bono work. Siobhan Howard-Palmer, a trainee in the Sheffield office, has been commended by the Law Society's Junior Lawyers Division for her efforts and this has "*rubbed off on the rest of the firm and we now get involved in various Young Enterprise schemes.*" Trainees go into schools to chat about careers and business, or help students with YE business projects. On one occasion, a Halliwellsian appeared on TV with "*a gang of lads from a primary school, all saying they aspire to become traders when they are older.*" Whatever happened to astronaut and fireman fantasies?

When hiring, great academics aren't enough: Halliwells looks for hard workers with personality; people who are a good craic and show loyalty. The firm is introducing bi-annual intakes to give people "*a better chance to get to know trainees, and so there's less of a squabble for jobs.*" This may be due in part to the consternation caused by this year's NQ job process (it "*wasn't as transparent as it could have been*"). Eventually, the firm found 24 jobs for its 34 2009 qualifiers. They qualified at an interesting time as the last rumblings coming out of the firm before we went to press pointed to the possibility of Halliwells entering into a merger deal with another firm. You should keep an ear out for news on this topic. Better still, check our website version of this report for news.

And finally...

While this has not been a vintage Halliwells year and management has had to display some fancy footwork, the firm's verve will be its saving, just as it has been its making.

Be involved

Paris. One of six challenging seats. International transactional work and great use of my French law qualification. Total involvement – every day.

JENNA RIDLEY | LAWYER | MANCHESTER

0800 163 498
hammonds.com/trainees
Hammonds LLP is an equal opportunities employer

Hammonds

Hammonds LLP

The facts

Location: Leeds, London, Manchester, Birmingham

Number of UK partners/solicitors: 146/329

Total number of trainees: 60

Seats: 6x4 months

Alternative seats: Secondments, overseas seats

Year on year, trainees at this international firm tell us how valuable they find their training contracts.

After a 20-year rollercoaster ride, multi-site firm Hammonds is now looking calmer and more confident than it has in a while.

Party's over

In the 1990s, Hammonds grew extravagantly. From humble origins in Bradford it swaggered confidently into Leeds, Manchester, Birmingham and London. Ambition not sated, more expansion followed across Europe and Asia. The legal profession watched it ascend the list of the UK's most profitable firms with wide eyes; from a blip on the radar, it grew into a giant, an unmissable partygoer in the age of Cool Britannia. But, as any hardened partygoer knows, excesses take their toll.

The discovery of a multimillion-pound overdraft was the equivalent of the record skipping and the lights coming on. When in 2004 and 2005 profits tumbled for two consecutive years, Hammonds was yanked back down to earth and left with a crushing hangover. Horrified by the mess they had been dancing in, a fair few partners decided to get their coats and leave. The same pundits who had marvelled at its growth began to criticise Hammonds' mismanagement. Action had to be taken. The management was restructured, costs were cut and, although it would be an exaggeration to say that it has completed its turnaround, since 2005 the firm's position has vastly improved. In the past three years Hammonds' profits per equity partner had returned to a much healthier level and revenue steadied. The past year has been tough for all the national firms, Hammonds included. It had a 5% fall in revenue and 25% dip in profits, but it's hard to say that these are other than a consequence of poor economic conditions. Summing up its position now, a trainee said: "*Hammonds is a very big and successful national firm, but it's not magic circle and it doesn't have pretensions to* become one. It's quite honest in what it can do and what it wants to achieve. Clients trust us and give us work because of it."

This trust was evident when, even as its reputation took a battering, Hammonds managed to retain major clients and added some new ones too, including Royal Mail and Tesco. Although depressed market conditions haven't radically altered the firm's focus, trainees report "*a big push in litigation and commercial, and a plan to expand the competition practice.*"

Stay put and network

Hammonds' six-seat training scheme has compulsory corporate, litigation and property assignments and a wealth of options to choose from thereafter. Management has recently removed the need for trainees to rotate between offices in favour of location-specific contracts, but it is still possible to qualify into a different office from the one you trained in, possibly even overseas. This ability to take advantage of the sizeable network continues as you rise up the ranks – we heard about partners who have left London and migrated north for a better work-life balance. As is usually the case with national networks, the London office hours tend to be a little longer (albeit largely still reasonable, finishing at around 6.30 or 7pm) and the social scene more dispersed than in the regional offices.

When asked to name the busy departments, trainees mentioned employment, IP, asset-based lending (a London practice), the burgeoning insolvency group and a growing pensions department. The firm additionally has notable expertise in projects, particularly for alternative energy matters. Though the nature of the work in projects means that the volume ebbs and flows, trainees reported having a high level of responsibility on some big projects and certainly seemed to enjoy the variety of tasks on offer. On one PFI matter, a trainee was struck by the cross-disciplinary nature of the work. It called for knowledge of employment law, financial arrangements, property law and even quite obscure research into barium testing to be brought together. Essentially it's a seat that requires the ability to think on one's feet while working to tight deadlines. In the words of one trainee, it's suitable for *"someone who is very, very organised, quick-witted and able to learn lots of things fast."*

Chambers UK rankings

Advertising & Marketing	Pensions
Banking & Finance	Pensions Litigation
Banking Litigation	Planning
Capital Markets	Private Equity
Construction	Projects, Energy & Natural Resources
Corporate/M&A	
Dispute Resolution	Real Estate
Employment	Real Estate Litigation
Environment	Restructuring/Insolvency
Health & Safety	Sports Law
Intellectual Property	Tax

Trainees were similarly enthusiastic about the competition seat, saying it was a good springboard to getting posted to Brussels. Hammonds has argued both for and against corporate mergers at the competition authorities, and in one case a trainee reported heavy involvement with a state aid matter where a computer manufacturer lobbied that the assistance given to a competitor was unfair. *"It was interesting to work on stuff for which there is no precedent. For example, we got to draft things submitted to the European Commission – trainees had a lot of input in that."*

Train lines and white lines

Hammonds' *"outgoing"* property lawyers have not been as *"horribly busy"* as in the past, but trainees were still able to speak about major work being done for local authorities, including the redevelopment of Rochdale's town centre and Plymouth Grove in Manchester, which will involve the construction of social and private housing and a shopping centre. Down south, Hammonds has advised London Underground on the property aspects of its King's Cross Northern Ticket Hall project, part of a £900m scheme to link the underground with St Pancras railway station by 2012. Other clients include the South East England Development agency and Aviva Investors.

The corporate division (*"full of blokes, more testosterone-fuelled"*) may not be as active since the economy took a pounding, and there were redundancies, but Hammonds certainly has a talent for mid-market and AIM deals. In conjunction with colleagues in the firm's Hong Kong and Beijing offices, lawyers have been assisting Chinese companies with admissions to AIM. Among them are private equity business Yangtze China Investment and Chinese media group Cosmedia Group Holdings. In addition to the core practice groups common to most commercial law firms, Hammonds has some attractive specialist areas. Its team of sports lawyers has lost a few partners recently but still does high-quality work for big clients – everything from litigation to contract negotiation and financing. You may think the team is chock-full of vainglorious cash hunters, but Chelsea FC is a big club nonetheless and not one to settle for second-rate lawyers. When it was revealed that one of its players, Adrian Mutu (a law graduate who should have known better), had a fondness for cocaine, Hammonds helped Chelsea to rescind his contract, sue him for a record-breaking £13.8m and offload him onto Juventus. The firm also acts as main legal adviser to Aston Villa and handles work for UEFA, the International Tennis Federation and Formula One Management. Working on big, complex deals like the purchase of Manchester City FC is *"excellent, even if you're not that fussed about sport."* Trainees report supervision that is *"up there with the best in the firm"* and tell us that they enjoyed meeting players, agents and associations for the purposes of taking statements. To examine Hammonds' multifarious practice strengths in more detail, check out the rankings on the *Chambers UK* website.

Trainees were pleased with the wide range of seats available and told us they could usually get the ones they wanted. For some, foreign seats were a major attraction when choosing the firm and Hammonds tries hard to accommodate those with a travel bug. Although some foreign secondments are oversubscribed (especially Hong Kong and Brussels), trainees can usually get an overseas placement, especially if they speak the local language. From the accommodation offered (the Hong Kong apartment is *"outstanding, like living in a hotel,"* while the Parisian one is *"gorgeous, feels like I'm in Versailles"*) to the responsibility in the office, we found all to be extremely satisfied by their overseas experiences. Foreign seats tend to be more general in scope than UK-based seats, so trainees often find themselves working with several departments simultaneously. The offices are not without their specialities however, so if you fancy improving your chances of winning the place, some relevant experience would certainly help. Brussels, deep in the EU's regulatory heartland, specialises in competition, public procurement and state aid work, while the Paris branch offers a broad range of commercial work. Hong Kong leans towards corporate and litigation, especially for AIM-listed companies. The impression we got is that the hours are more 'continental' in Europe (ie start later, finish later) and longer in HK, where you are contracted to do 44 hours instead of the UK's 40, and are also expected to come in on Saturday mornings. In the UK there are secondment opportunities to clients including INEOS.

Every dog has its day

Right from the word go the "*gut reaction*" of many trainees was that Hammonds was a friendly firm. "*Some interviews have a master-and-servant dynamic, but the Hammonds one was very enjoyable. I found the people to be personable and down to earth.*" Before starting their contracts, trainees complete a two-week training course in Oxford, of which they "*couldn't speak highly enough.*" "*The firm went above and beyond what it had to do,*" said one, "*my peers from law school didn't get anything like it.*" The newbies stay in the (rather nice) halls of St Catherine's College, dining together and socialising between the seminars and training sessions designed to prepare them for their training contracts. As well as leaving with a solid understanding of the firm's IT systems, trainees told us they managed to get their Professional Skills Course out of the way, were "*taught how to wear appropriately sized heels for our body shape*" and left feeling united as a cohort.

That unity is important to Hammonds, which sees itself as 'one firm' despite its several locations. When we asked trainees about this slightly clichéd claim, they maintained that the network was well integrated and that work passed smoothly between offices. Indeed, throughout the interviews we were struck by the uniformity of the culture and type of trainee the firm hires. It wasn't a bad kind of uniformity either. The offices all sounded like they benefited from a good level of friendly banter, and the trainees we spoke to struck us as being straight-talking, sociable, bright and pragmatic. The majority of our sources were in their twenties; a few were older with other careers behind them. For some, the firm's chequered past was actually a draw: "*To be honest, I think its underdog status was an attraction. Everyone likes an underdog. It's exciting to be somewhere you feel is going to pull it together.*" Summing up their time at the firm, another interviewee reflected that "*ultimately, if someone had told me when I was 21 that I'd be doing this and still enjoying it, I'd have been very happy. I hope that I can stay at this firm for the rest of my life; you can't get much better than enjoying being in work.*" That's certainly an option: trainees remarked upon the fact that there's "*a lot of opportunity to move forward in Hammonds,*" with some solicitors making partner at quite an early stage in their careers. In 2009 some 26 out of the 40 qualifiers stayed on – we wonder if one is a managing partner of the future.

When the firm had to make redundancies, it did so candidly. As one trainee put it: "*Hammonds handled a difficult situation very well.*" Having taken past criticisms on the chin, the firm now strives to be ahead of the pack when it comes to tackling difficult decisions. Faced with a purse-tightening recession, the firm announced that it was going to pay a very handsome £7,000 (£5,000 in the regions) to those trainees willing to defer the start of their training contracts. All credit to the firm, it also set up several paid client secondments to keep some of them busy. Even before the recession kicked in, the firm took an innovative approach towards secondments, not only offering them during the training contract, but before as well. We heard about one trainee who had done a five-month placement with an advertising company, auditing its internal systems.

Hammonds' trainees "*socialise a lot – including with the NQs and some partners.*" Events range from bowling and meals out to networking events including the World Corporate Games which saw Hammonds pit its sporting abilities against other firms in events like go-karting, badminton, football, netball and golf.

And finally...

Hammonds had a lot of trouble in the past, but beneath the bad press is a good law firm. In conversation, trainees are emphatic about the great working atmosphere, responsibility and support they have found here.

Harbottle & Lewis LLP

The facts

Location: London

Number of UK partners/solicitors: 28/52

Total number of trainees: 10

Seats: 4x6 months

Alternative seats: Secondments

> The law is not a world of glamour and celebrity air-kisses, but it needn't all be about boilerplate loan documents and late nights either.

Harbottles' speciality is entertainment law, so you'll get to represent celebs and the businesses that employ them.

Star stories

Instead of bamboozling your flatmates with details of some financier's innovative mezzanine loan transaction you'll be able to wow them with information regarding a hot band's new recording contract, regale them with gossip about the royal family or, ratcheting the conversation up even higher, give them the lowdown on Roy Keane's PR activities (as long as it's all in the public domain, of course).

Harbottle & Lewis came into being when way back in 1955 Laurence Harbottle and Brian Lewis decided to set up a law practice to serve the theatre world. That the firm still exists in its current form just proves that dreams can come true. Harbottles still does exactly what it was originally intended to do – provide a specialist service to the entertainment industry. It has, of course, diversified over the past 55 years, but then so has the world of media and entertainment. The firm has *"managed pretty well,"* through the recession. Although *"it has not been completely immune,"* Harbottles is one of the few firms that has not had to make redundancies or defer any of its trainees.

Our sources declared that the training scheme has become more organised and is vastly improved as a result. If you can win a place here you'll work through four six-month seats with the option of a client secondment along the way. All trainees have to do property, litigation and a commercial seat, this last obligation being fulfilled by time with the corporate; MIPIES (media, IP, interactive entertainment and sport) or film, theatre and TV departments or on a client secondment. Cross-selling is the name of the game at Harbottles, so you can expect plenty of nipping between floors in most seats. To keep everyone on the straight and narrow, as well as the appraisals at the start and end of a seat, meetings with supervisors take place every two months.

No seat struck fear in peoples' hearts, but it was clear that it was MIPIES (pronounced 'my pies') and film, theatre and TV that attracted people most. In these departments, trainees oscillate between different media; juggling film cases alongside music, often observing the relationship between the two. They may find themselves licensing music for a video game, then looking at IP issues and perhaps even helping get clearance to buy replica firearms for filming action scenes. The firm's reputation in theatre is second to none and it has worked on shows like *Billy Elliot*, *Spring Awakening* and *Strictly Gershwin*, assisting with everything from licensing to employment regulations specific to showbiz. The firm has a strong presence in the computer games industry (a market worth around $40bn) and was involved in giving legal advice to Rockstar Games, producers of *Grand Theft Auto IV*, which sold a record-breaking 3.6m copies on its first day. Though the names are household and cool, the work isn't always glam. Trainees spoke enthusiastically about their roles, but leavened their comments by mentioning that they do their fair share of unexciting tasks.

Romans, royalty and virgins

Although it probably won't be the primary reason for their application to the firm, the corporate seat gives trainees a thorough grounding in the 'behind the scenes' aspects of the entertainment world and they often "*enjoy it more than they thought they would.*" There is a fair amount of transactional activity in the sector – "*lots of M&A, investments and start-ups of film companies and the like*" – and trainees remarked on how commercially minded they had to become. Most of the lawyers in the corporate department didn't train at Harbottles; instead "*many came from the magic circle for a more relaxed environment.*" The Mama Group deal is a good example of the type of work done here. It involved the sale of several music venues across London and required close working between the corporate, property and employment teams. On big deals such as this trainees end up doing administrative chores and photocopying, but we definitely got the impression that they really liked being trusted to meet the clients. "*I was more involved than I would've been at a larger firm,*" claimed one. The working day runs longer in this department, but trainees still enthused about the responsibility available and the energised atmosphere.

A stint in the litigation department was described as "*a baptism of fire.*" You have to be quick-witted and able to work to tight deadlines. Trainees were relieved to find that they still managed to leave the office by 6.30pm though. As well as the type of commercial litigation you can expect at any firm – breach of contract, unsatisfactory performance, etc – Harbottles gets instructed on high-profile privacy issues. Defamation advice has been given to clients as disparate as Roman Abramovich, Anne Robinson, Chelsy Davy, David and Victoria Beckham, Her Madge the Queen (remember that BBC documentary where she supposedly stormed out?) and Kate Moss. It's an evolving area of law where, although the principal of privacy is established, its application can be highly debatable – take the Max Mosley case for instance. Technological developments pose new questions too. Should a blog be treated like a casual conversation in the street when it can be read by so many? And how can a false statement be retracted once it's spreading through the electronic ether?

A secondment to Virgin Atlantic (coming with the bonus of some free flights!) is up for grabs and was the recipient of a lot of praise. The role is based in Crawley (near Gatwick) and it's a corker. Trainees "*get so much responsibility. You're part of a four or five-person team and people come in with contract problems that get you going right off the bat. You have a lot more licence to do the job.*" Trainees here encounter general commercial agreements, IT contracts, trade mark issues and much more. One of the best aspects of the job is the ability to "*just [concentrate on] law – no billing, none of the extra stuff that comes with being a solicitor – you can be more commercial and work with the business.*" There are other ad hoc secondments on offer too.

Chambers UK rankings

Advertising & Marketing	Franchising
Aviation	Immigration
Charities	Information Technology
Corporate/M&A	Intellectual Property
Defamation/Reputation Management	Media & Entertainment
	Private Client
Employment	Real Estate
Family/Matrimonial	Sports Law

Reach for the stars

One thing to remember is that, as with any media-related job, there are a lot of people gunning for a Harbottles training contract. To stand a chance you've got to be able to distinguish yourself from the crowd. Your mental arithmetic and ability to recite cases won't suffice. Nor will wearing that old Iron Maiden t-shirt to the interview. Only a third of the current trainees have a degree in law, whereas many have already worked in the media in some shape or form. Without doubt applicants need to intelligently demonstrate a real, burning desire to work for media and entertainment clients if they are going to be in with a chance. One good piece of advice is to take electives in media law and IP during the LPC. Our contacts firmly believed that if they weren't offered an NQ job at Harbottles, the training they'd received would stand them in good stead for a position elsewhere in media. In the event, three of the four 2009 qualifiers stayed with the firm.

The cornerstone of the firm's social life is arguably the free lunch. "*You get a starter, main course, bread rolls, cheese and crackers – everything from brie to Babybels. You save a fortune not having to buy lunch.*" Thrift aside, "*the lunch is a really good idea – it's a good way of meeting people as this isn't a place where partners eat in a separate dining room.*" Socialising isn't forced upon trainees by some Committee for the Advancement of Fun, so they tend to organise things on an impromptu basis and, in a place where "*you're bound to meet people with similar tastes,*" this happens a lot. Helpfully the firm is based just off Oxford Street in the heart of Theatreland.

And finally...

In essence this is a classic West End media practice. It is focused, successful and people here are pretty happy with their lot.

- **Public good?** Nearly 95% of trainees were with private practice firms in 2007/08, but have you thought about doing your training contract in-house at a company or with a public body like the Government Legal Service, the Crown Prosecution Service or a local authority? Check out our feature on alternative career options on page 24.

top tip no. 15

HBJ Gateley Wareing

The facts

Location: Birmingham, Leicester, Nottingham, London, Scotland
Number of UK partners/solicitors: 102/122
Total number of trainees: 16 (English)
Seats: 4x6 months
Alternative seats: None

Interesting fact: Edinburgh partner Alistair Duff is not only responsible for the naming of Greenland's Mt HBJ, he is also joint world record holder for the Mount Everest Marathon.

This rollicking band of sleeves-rolled-up lawyers has roots that go deep into Brummie soil. Once the champion of owner-managed businesses in the Midlands, the firm has lately been busting moves in Scotland, London and the Middle East.

From the Highlands to Dubai

Née Gateley Wareing, the HBJ part of this firm's name was added after a union with Scots firm Henderson Boyd Jackson. The first major Anglo-Scottish merger in legal history, it gave the Midlanders a presence in Edinburgh and Glasgow, and the newly amalgamated firm was catapulted into the UK top 60. Although this was an unexpected match made by mutual client RBS, it has been a rather successful one. Since 2006 HBJGW has shown expansionist urges and looks determined to make a name for itself down in the Big Smoke.

The Scottish side of the firm had a strong shipping practice, which was probably a motivating factor behind the choice to enter the London market via a merger with shipping firm Shaw & Croft, and to then build other practices around this nucleus. Unfortunately, things didn't go entirely smoothly and several Shaw partners jumped ship after the deal. This may have been a major factor in prompting a second London union, this time with transport specialist Holmes Hardingham in 2008. The firm's recent move into larger City offices can be read as a statement of intent: space has been boosted by 50% and while we're sure the 50 staff are enjoying the extra room, it won't necessarily be for long. The firm intends to add 25 more people as it grows its corporate and restructuring practices.

As for Dubai, the firm's surprise new outpost in 2007, we expect a similar focus. Upon its opening, the office's proud new leader Paul Taylor announced plans "*to rapidly build a high-profile construction practice in Dubai, and the future strategy will be to use that visibility as a platform to extend into the firm's other core areas, including shipping and transport, corporate and commercial property.*" Last year, we reported on how the firm was forcing its way into a construction market that some commentators said was already overcrowded. Back then, the firm was engaged in the representation of a client that was constructing a multimillion-pound jet fuel pipeline, and defending a large real estate developer. Now that the shockwaves of the credit crunch have reached the region, the Dubai economy is suffering and some law firms have been forced to downsize rapidly. We'll wait to see how HBJGW fares.

The firm's Midlands core has been strengthened of late by the addition of Simon Pigden from Pinsent Masons. Trainees noted that Pigden has had a Pied Piper effect on the commercial team, reporting that more lawyers have joined the firm, doubling the size of the department. Another focus area is pensions, which has seen the addition of two new partners and some new clients. In 2008/09, full-firm profits fell 24.3%, but this is comparable to similar firms and the expense of developing new offices probably goes some way towards explaining it. Revenue climbed a comforting 6.2% in the same period.

The big three

In the UK the two largest departments are property and corporate, which according to an insider *"generate around 50% of our cash."* Trainees take four seats of six months, with compulsory stints in property, corporate and litigation seats to give them a thorough grounding in what the firm considers to be the basics. The arrangement is a relatively new one so trainees had plenty to say about the fact that they now only had one totally free choice. Some presumed that *"in light of the current climate the firm needs to be able to control what trainees do."* Others were slightly aggrieved at not being able to spend more time working in their preferred area of law or suggested that while the compulsory seat system certainly had its merits, it would be better if it was incorporated into a six by four-month seat system. For what it's worth, our opinion is that the system suits the firm: HBJGW does not have an excess of overspecialised departments and the current arrangement can provide a solid frame onto which more specialist knowledge can be attached as and when necessary. Seats can be taken in the large Birmingham office, Leicester, Nottingham and now London.

Variety can be built into the seats. In property, for example, you can try commercial deals, property finance, residential development and property litigation. *"You can pick and choose between them. If you ask for a certain type of work, they'll accommodate you."* As you'll be aware, segments of the property market have stalled lately, so HBJGW's decision to build up a residential development unit targeting social housing was a shrewd one. *"They're hitting and exceeding targets,"* said one trainee, and according to the firm this group doubled its client base and tripled its turnover in 2008. In social housing there are *"extra levels of complexity and certain considerations to take on board that you don't have in other areas."* Clients include housing associations like the Riverside Housing group, Caldmore Housing Association and Maidenhead and District Housing Association, as well as developers like Bovis Homes and Larkfleet Homes which are contracted to build social housing using National Affordable Housing Programme grants. Trainees have been involved in bulk purchases of housing plots, taken minutes at meetings between local authorities and clients, and *"drafted a lot of documents."* The firm represents many of the country's top house builders and counts HSBC, Lloyds, RBS and BT amongst a long list of occupier clients. Current projects include Wolverhampton City Council's £350m redevelopment of Wolverhampton Railway Station.

The classic ethos of 'work hard, play hard' definitely applies in this firm, and working closest to this credo is the other main department – corporate – where lawyers *"definitely put in longer hours but also party a lot harder than anyone else."* It's got a distinctly different atmosphere to the more relaxed property department, where trainees often work on their own. Here people *"very much have their specific role in transactions… it's more teamy."* The *"buzz"* in the group comes from the people, who *"thrive on being busy and enjoy their work."* Typical deals include a £36m buyout of a technology company by a private equity funder, Yorkshire Bank's investment in the management buyout of engineering specialists BWB Consulting and advice to private equity funder Gresham and the borrower in the £82.5m acquisition of East Midlands-based workwear company Johnson Clothing. In the banking seat, refinancing has been the goal of many companies, although not as many deals have been completed as usual since the credit crunch. Clients include Bank of Scotland, Alliance & Leicester and the Co-operative Bank.

Completing our round-up of the compulsory seats, we arrive at the litigation department. Encompassing commercial dispute resolution, employment, construction claims and corporate recovery, the group has been pretty busy. Simply put, when the economy takes a beating, businesses need to recover what they're owed to survive, hence *"construction disputes have gone through the roof."* Many of these disputes are ironed out at adjudications, which trainees can sometimes attend. One proudly told us that they had interviewed a client and drafted a witness statement that contributed to the success of a case and a big saving for the much-relieved client. In this department all sorts of matters crop up, so it's not just a case of hitting similar-looking nails with the same old metaphorical hammer day in day out. Sometimes it is breaches of warranty, sometimes negligence claims, and occasionally a good old-fashioned fraud matter rears its ugly head. Again, there's enough breadth in employment cases to keep a trainee occupied: unfair dismissal, employment issues relating to insolvency, the consequences of selling a business and broad-themed strategy advice are all undertaken for clients like The Football League, Deloitte and BT.

Chambers UK rankings

Agriculture & Rural Affairs	Pensions
Banking & Finance	Personal Injury
Commodities	Private Client
Construction	Real Estate
Corporate/M&A	Restructuring/Insolvency
Debt Recovery	Shipping
Dispute Resolution	Social Housing
Employment	Tax
Family/Matrimonial	Transport

By George!

Initially a support group, the firm's pensions team has really developed, doubling its size and establishing a new clientele. Trainees found the seat "*really enjoyable and quite technical with a lot of research.*" Some felt invigorated to be part of a newly formed group instead of a large well-established one. Insolvency, the enfant terrible of bust economies, is booming business at HBJGW and the team recently nabbed a partner from Brummie Goliath Wragge & Co. One source told us they'd been to two hearings, once to assist a barrister and once to do some advocacy of their own. "*I was arguing for the repossession order to become effective. The guy had gone bankrupt and had a certain amount of time to sell his house. I made my submissions and then there were questions.*" It was clearly a real high point for our source. In England, the shipping and transport practice is limited to the London office. It covers yacht law, yacht finance and shipping, both wet and dry. Thanks to the London mergers and the established Scottish practice group, the transport department is top-ranked in *Chambers UK*.

Trainees make their way through the seats knowing that there's a good support structure behind them. The training principal and dedicated partners who act as trainee reps (one in each office) are there when they have any questions and to act as a point of liaison between trainees and management. The only real complaint we heard related to the slightly Orwellian approach to e-mails. These are checked and deleted if not deemed pertinent to work and personal e-mail access is blocked. We were also informed by our sources that the firm asked trainees to notify HR if we contacted them for interviews, which kind of defeats the object of the True Picture as a source of anonymous feedback.

Ain't no mountain high enough

HBJGW employees are practical, forthright, karaoke-loving, and big fans of *The Godfather*. They love networking events (especially those with booze and sport), they find it easy to get on with clients and they're intent on delivering commercial solutions rather than getting bogged down in point-scoring and legal esotericism. A look through their online profiles provides a good insight into their characters and is indicative of the firm's gregarious streak. Instead of the usual potted career history and largely superfluous waffle concerning their practice areas, they are quick and to the point, telling you what you need to know. This includes their favourite films, books, sports and who they would like to have with them on a desert island. "*We're not typical law geeks. Other firms have got geeks in them, but we're not a geeky firm,*" insisted one trainee. Interesting fact: Edinburgh partner Alistair Duff is not only responsible for the naming of Greenland's Mt HBJ, he is also joint world record holder for the Mount Everest Marathon. Respec.

The firm prides itself in its ability to network and socialise. In the words of one of our interviewees: "*Other firms aren't as up for going out on the lash.*" Trainees are "*well supported by the marketing department who pay for us to be part of various organisations.*" These include the Birmingham Trainee Solicitors Society (BTSS) and the Birmingham Futures group, both of which organise balls, excursions, networking events and sports competitions. We heard from trainees who had been to festivals and art galleries, as well as attending seminars and motivational events, and we learned that the firm was planning an art exhibition of its own. The discussion we had about people's artistic talents segued into one about their singing abilities. This was a real leitmotif in our interviews: many of the events organised by the firm involved a good old sing-song, and we heard that at the Xmas party onlookers were wowed when they heard a trainee duet with a partner on 'Guess That's Why They Call it the Blues'. You might want to brush up on your knowledge of Neil Diamond before an interview with the firm – senior partner Michael Ward's favourite song is 'Sweet Caroline'. Or you could perhaps engage him with a conversation about football. Rather fittingly, he is the "*leading striker*" on the Midlands offices' football team. Other organised events include ice-skating, a family day and a pub quiz.

Historically, the firm has had a very decent record of NQ retention in its English offices, and in 2009 five of the nine English qualifiers stayed on.

And finally...

The unpretentious, hard-working nature of this firm has endured as it has grown. Definitely one for those who reckon they can take a bull by its horns.

Henmans LLP

The facts

Location: Oxford
Number of UK partners/solicitors: 23/41
Total number of trainees: 6
Seats: 4x6 months
Alternative seats: None
Extras: Pro bono – Oxford CAB

There's a great range of private client and commercial experiences awaiting trainees at Henmans. In 2009 all three of its qualifiers were retained and no new starters were deferred.

This Oxford firm is regionally rooted and nationally minded. If you're thinking Thames Valley, you might want to think Henmans.

Playing ball

Private client services still make up a significant part of Henmans' business – just over 20% in fact – and with 17 fee earners, its private client team is the largest in the county and ranked top by *Chambers UK* for the Thames Valley. Actually Henmans scoops quite a few impressive rankings in the guide, reflecting its expertise across a range of legal services for individuals. This is not to say the firm has no commercial muscle: Henmans has made headway in this respect, but it's fair to say that its private client arm is longer established and better developed.

By hiring former City firm accountant Matthew Keegan from Allen & Overy as head of finance in 2008, Henmans signalled its intention to ratchet up its financial performance. Trainees mentioned *"more of an emphasis on billing"* and suggested *"targets are becoming increasingly more important."* They saw this as a positive step. As one put it: *"Henmans was a small regional firm, jogging along nicely. Now they want to bring it into the 21st century."* Part of this involves improving external relationships through marketing. Trainees are encouraged to get involved *"as much as they want to be,"* which means rubbing shoulders with clients and sending out regular legal updates. Client events include drinks parties, trips to Wimbledon and ping-pong tournaments. Why does the firm love hitting balls so much? Simple. Henmans was founded by tennis ace Tim's great-grandfather in 1890.

Although most trainees already have links to Oxford or the surrounding area before coming to Henmans this is not a prerequisite. An interview process that includes a problem-solving exercise, verbal reasoning test and presentation makes it clear that Henmans is looking for *"life skills and personality"* as much as academics and geographical suitability. A number of the current trainees are now on their second careers and, despite a variety of ages, *"most have a similar outlook. We are very focused on what we want to get out of the training contract, and we are very committed to Henmans."*

Henmans' trainees say the firm prides itself on winning *"top-notch work equivalent to that of London firms."* So how accurate is the claim? Certainly the firm manages to lure former City solicitors searching for a quieter life, and they bring experience of London lawyering with them. There's a convincing argument that in Henmans' most successful practice groups, service standards cannot be beaten in the capital. Certainly the cost of services represents better value for money.

Out on the field

Trainee seats are available in personal injury, clinical negligence, private client (incorporating charities), property and dispute resolution. A newly created corporate seat completes the offering. Henmans determines the first two seats, and apparently *"it can be rather daunting when you get your letter in September and your first one turns out to be something you deliberately avoided on the LPC."* Given that a training contract is essentially the only time for trying multiple areas of practice, being thrown into unfamiliar territory is no bad thing. One source even told us: *"The seats were not what I would have chosen, but turned out to be my favourites."*

Expect "*far more negotiation in your second year,*" and with only three trainees per year choosing between six seats "*you are likely to get what you want.*" Our interviewees had high praise for the new training partner: "*He is extremely approachable and really wants to make sure we are happy.*" However, when it came to the subject of supervision their responses were mixed, primarily because "*there is no set formula and it can be extremely varied between departments.*" Trainees felt that the "*supervisory role should be made more uniform, with positives being taken from those who have got it right.*" Getting it right generally equated to supervisors being "*hands on*" and seats being "*quite structured*" with "*regular feedback,*" while still allowing for responsibility and "*a free rein*" when sufficient experience has been gained. An elusive mix, you might think, but the "*big, friendly and non-hierarchical*" private client team scored top marks on all measures. This, plus "*interesting, out-of-the-ordinary work*" and excellent charity sector clients (eg Cancer Research UK, the RSPCA and the British Heart Foundation) means the private client seat is perennially popular. Most trainees complete a seat here, and as well as working with wealthy individuals and national charities there is often the opportunity to run a few smaller, less valuable files solo. Client contact is plentiful, as are site visits (often involving mud and Wellington boots). When not visiting country estates, trainees are thrown "*interesting research problems.*" Again, their reactions to such tasks were mixed: one claimed to "*mostly just try and hide under the desk when trust laws were mentioned,*" while others "*enjoyed being stretched academically.*" Exposure to Henmans' top-ranked charities practice means "*a lot of estate administration.*"

Also common is a seat in the personal injury department, either in personal injury proper (both claimant and defendant work) or clinical negligence. Henmans defends a number of large insurers and businesses, and also pursues claims on behalf of individuals who've been injured in workplace or other accidents. One case concerned a City trainee solicitor who was injured abroad and suffered whiplash. Henmans secured her a massive seven-figure sum "*for damage to her career prospects.*" With the spectrum of cases covering fatal accidents, brain injuries, medical negligence, industrial disease and sports injuries, trainees had no complaints about lack of variety. Some clinical negligence cases can last for years, "*perhaps five to ten because of the problems quantifying damages.*" When individuals die as a result of negligence, cases move quicker but are "*very delicate because you are dealing with people recently bereaved.*"

The corporate seat is worth a mention as this is an area of growth. Turnover in its employment subgroup was up by 10% last year, and since the arrival of a lawyer from Isis Innovation – a subsidiary of Oxford University – bringing knowledge of intellectual property and technology transfers, the corporate team too is taking the hi-tech road. Trainees have been able to influence the way this new seat works, and supervisors allow them to interview clients on their own and run small files. "*I loved it. I was acting like a proper solicitor,*" said one.

Home comforts

While trainees were all smiles about their work, positivity wavered on the subject of socialising. Said one bluntly: "*I'm not too in love with the social scene at Henmans.*" This isn't to say people aren't friendly; indeed "*there is a real community feel within each department*" and a Friday night pub group has emerged. The point seems to be that "*there are a lot of people of a similar age with smallish children who want to get home to their families.*" Many trainees are just not at that point in their lives. For family types, flexitime is a real boon. Core hours are between 9.30am and 4.30pm; beyond this, staff can adjust their schedules to better suit their home lives. Henmans was even named one of Britain's most family-friendly employers by the Jobs4Mums website. A massive 45% of the partnership is female, well above average.

With so many staff already established in the Oxford area, a quieter social scene doesn't affect the majority. One trainee did admit, however: "*If I'd moved to Oxford to work at Henmans I think I'd be quite lonely.*" Arguably Henmans' business park location is a drawback, but the fact is Oxford doesn't have enough centrally located office space. Christmas and summer parties are "*quite relaxed*" and "*good for firm bonding.*" The other highlight is a tennis tournament at which everyone is encouraged to play. Until a couple of years ago, the finals were held at Tim Henman's dad's house.

Chambers UK rankings

Agriculture & Rural Affairs	Family/Matrimonial
Charities	Personal Injury
Clinical Negligence	Private Client
Corporate/M&A	Professional Negligence
Dispute Resolution	Real Estate
Employment	Real Estate Litigation

And finally...

This compact, high-quality firm is a champion among private client firms and has the capability to climb the rankings in the commercial sphere.

Legal Career *or* Life Investment

Do you want your legal training to turn you into a good lawyer or an exceptional talent?

----

www.herbertsmithgraduates.com

Herbert Smith LLP is an international practice with a commitment to excellence and diversity. Its distinctive "twin engine" capability in corporate and contentious matters is complemented by leading practices in finance, real estate, competition and employment.

Invest in yourself

Herbert Smith

Herbert Smith in association with Gleiss Lutz and Stibbe

Herbert Smith LLP

The facts

Location: London
Number of UK partners/solicitors: 167/585
Total number of trainees: 199
Seats: 4x6 months
Alternative seats: Secondments, overseas seats
Extras: Pro bono – FRU, RCJ CAB, Whitechapel Legal Advice Centre; language training

"Instead of going headfirst and not thinking of their employees, Herbert Smith does things steadily and slowly."

Already king of the hill for litigation, international superstar Herbert Smith now goes head to head with the big corporate and finance giants.

It's a kind of magic

Herbert Smith's push into non-contentious areas has been a resounding success. Massive corporate deals such as EDF's £12.5bn takeover of British Energy and Tata Motors' $2.3bn acquisition of Jaguar and Land Rover from Ford speak for themselves. As for litigation, trainees say the firm's strength and scope in this area is unrivalled in the City. *"None of the magic circle, let alone anyone else, have the litigation opportunities you get here."* The firm had a key role in the Buncefield oil depot explosion litigation and represented BSkyB in a substantial deceit, negligent representation and breach of contract case against EDS. In the legal sector, CMS Cameron McKenna sought Herbies' counsel in defence of proceedings brought against it by accountancy firm Kidsons. The firm's prestigious advocacy unit adds an extra string to an already impressive litigation bow, and our interviewees contended that *"the contentious focus really is unique, especially as corporate isn't presently the be-all and end-all."*

Over the past decade Herbies has expanded internationally and now has 13 offices across Europe, the Middle East and Asia, established alliances with German firm Gleiss Lutz and Benelux firm Stibbe, and a newer tie-up with Saudi Arabian firm GPA. It is also keeping a keen eye on emerging markets, notably operating a dedicated India practice.

We asked trainees whether the firm has aspirations to be a part of the magic circle. To be honest, whether the firm possessed the magic circle moniker didn't really bother our contacts one way or the other. *"Practically it makes no difference: we get paid the same, do the same work, and everyone seems happier here,"* they explained. *"We don't care what we're called; it's about the firm and its culture rather than these archaic distinctions."* Others were quick to assert the benefits of avoiding this most exclusive of legal memberships. *"Here they don't want work to be your life. They don't want to encourage sleeping pods or have TV screens and bars to keep you in the office."*

One of our interviewees did put forward another theory: *"They're not risk takers. Herbert Smith will see where other firms go and then try it themselves. If you follow, you can't be a leader."* Not that they were disheartened by this. *"Standing back I see that maybe this is why I don't come across cut-throat people here. Instead of going headfirst and not thinking of their employees, Herbert Smith does things steadily and slowly."* A measured approach has been a clever approach. The firm was able to announce a 5% increase in turnover to £444m for the 2008/09 financial year. Profits dropped a little in the same year to just below the million-pound-per-equity-partner level.

Raising the bar

Herbies' trainees commonly tell us: *"I wasn't sure if I wanted to go to the Bar or to a law firm."* For the contentious-minded this firm is an obvious City choice. Trainees can choose between a huge range of contentious work, from insurance and construction seats to international arbitration and banking disputes. Across the different groups trainees perform many similar tasks – *"trawling through documents and evidence;"* going along to meetings and interviews to take attendance notes; researching points of law; "*liaising with counsel and making sure documents are in order.*" Sources admitted that "*there are times when the dull work gets on top of you,*" but what's crucial here is the caveat that "*you do know what you're doing is important.*" A litigation seat can be crushingly document-heavy for trainees, and the bigger the case the less high-level involvement they are able to have. At Herbert Smith this problem is addressed by partners keeping newbies appraised of the ins and outs of headline-making cases, such as their work acting for directors in the firing line during investigations conducted by the Department for Business Innovation and Skills.

There are occasions when trainees can break free of document management and get to grips with substantive tasks. In specialised groups handling defamation, insolvency and fraud cases, for example, there is "*a lot more involvement and a higher degree of expectation.*" Insurance seats can involve handling lower-value claims solo. One source recalled: "*I worked on two professional negligence cases, more or less on my own, and went to trial on my own with the barrister.*" The real estate litigation seat is "*a steep learning curve*" as, again, trainees have their own cases. As one first-year discovered: "*If you do that seat straight away nothing can scare you.*" In international arbitration you just might get the chance to travel abroad to interview witnesses and the firm encourages trainees to "*tackle business development at an early stage, entertaining clients and maximising client contact to build those skills from the outset.*" The advocacy unit is unfortunately not quite as Hollywood as it sounds (though perhaps we've just been watching too many US courtroom dramas). Still, it's a unique experience for a trainee solicitor, "*akin to having a pupillage experience in that we get instructed internally from different litigation groups.*" Those in 'The Unit' confirm that "*you get an awful lot more responsibility,*" with tasks including "*research and drafting opinions and parts of skeleton arguments.*" In short they are exposed to anything related to "*the mechanics of advocacy.*" You can't qualify here, though as an associate you might be lucky enough to be seconded to the unit.

Off to a flying start

While the prestige of the litigation departments will be well known to readers who've done their research, the high quality of the corporate practice may cause a few raised eyebrows among those who assume Herbies is still the bruiser it was a decade ago. As well as the aforementioned EDF and Tata Motors deals, Herbies advised US oilfield services giant Halliburton on a £1.8bn battle for British company Expro, and a consortium including Credit Suisse, JPMorgan and Morgan Stanley in RioTinto's defence of a hostile $147bn offer from BHP Billiton. These were big-ticket matters, and trainees con-

Chambers UK rankings

Administrative & Public Law	Media & Entertainment
Banking & Finance	Outsourcing
Banking Litigation	Partnership
Capital Markets	Pensions
Competition/European Law	Pensions Litigation
Construction	Planning
Corporate/M&A	Private Client
Data Protection	Private Equity
Dispute Resolution	Product Liability
Employee Share Schemes	Professional Discipline
Employment	Professional Negligence
Environment	Projects, Energy & Natural Resources
Financial Services Regulation	Public International Law
	Public Procurement
Fraud: Civil	Real Estate
Health & Safety	Real Estate Finance
Information Technology	Real Estate Litigation
Insurance	Restructuring/Insolvency
Intellectual Property	Retail
Investment Funds	Sports Law
Life Sciences	Tax
Local Government	Telecommunications
	Transport

ceded that the Tata affair was "*the kind of deal where everyone in the firm was involved.*" For some trainees this meant "*working around the clock for three months in the data room, doing due diligence, reviewing documents and producing weekly reports.*" This is where the toughest hours will be, and we were part-impressed, part-horrified by the tale of a trainee who, burnt out by their experiences, was "*physically sick and sent home after not being able to hear what people were saying.*" We understand this story is more than an urban myth, so even though things may have been quieter of late it is important to acknowledge that "*when there's a deal going through you'll often be working until midnight to 2am.*" The more deals that go through the more often this happens. As in litigation (which is the only compulsory seat apart from corporate), trainees do feel very much in the loop: "*The big picture was there even if I was doing tedious due diligence.*" Said one source: "*They really will get out the marker pen and whiteboard to explain it to you. They're passionate about what they do and are happy to take time out for trainees who show a genuine interest.*" When there aren't deals on the table, trainees were impressed with the firm's eagerness to find other tasks for them to do – helping prepare a company for its AGM, for instance.

In real estate "*you get a lot of contact with clients*" and "*as a trainee you can have small properties to deal with.*" Here, "*you hit the ground running and have to get on with it.*" Smaller matters, such as lease renewals and the management of commercial units, are complemented by assistance on giant deals such as BAA's planned forced disposal of Gatwick Airport (comprising over 100 registered titles and over 400 leases). The real estate group acted as support for Herbies' increasingly important finance department in BAA's previous £12.2bn refinancing of Heathrow, Gatwick and Stansted – the largest ever refinancing of its type. Real estate and finance seats are no longer compulsory, but the quality of work continues to attract trainees.

Overseas seats and client secondments (to companies including BSkyB, Coca-Cola and insurance company Marsh) are strongly encouraged by the firm and "*if you want to do one it is competitive.*" The message, according to one source, is this: "*If you've had good appraisals you'll be fine.*" Another agreed, saying: "*It's rare for people to miss out if they want to go abroad.*" Opportunities abound from Paris and Moscow (which is "*a bit more John Grisham than you get in the City*") to Dubai and Tokyo. With contentious and non-contentious opportunities available, the system is working well. A fourth-seater told us: "*The support network of an international firm really hits home when you call London and they are really there for you.*"

A spoonful of Sugar

'I don't like liars, I don't like cheats. I don't like bullshitters, I don't like schmoozers, I don't like arse-lickers.' Who else could have said this but hard-nosed businessman-slash-loveable TV grump Sir Alan Sugar? Sorry, that should now be Lord Sugar of Clapton in the London Borough of Hackney. A client of the firm, in 2009 he enlisted the expertise of fearsome litigation partner Alan Watts to grill the final five *Apprentice* candidates. Mr Watts took particular exception to the 'arrogant' Debra, and from our interviews we can understand why. Two anecdotes in particular stood out for us. The first concerned a conversation between two flatmates, one a trainee from Herbert Smith, one training at a magic circle firm (we won't say which). Our hero, the Herbies trainee, was a little upset that a partner had neglected to thank him for a piece of work he had done that day. The magic circle trainee was shocked, saying: "*They would never say, and have never said, thank you to me.*" That surprised our contact: "*I didn't even know that could happen. I'm so used to people being civil and nice.*" The second is that of a trainee struggling with seat choices and the mentor who called from an overseas partners' conference to advise. "*We were on the phone for 20 minutes. He went out of his way to help me and he really didn't have to.*"

Trainees believe that culture at Herbert Smith is one of collaboration, and although a hierarchy exists, it's perfectly feasible for trainees to strike up friendships with associates, supervisors and support staff. There's a distinct absence of "*backstabbing or bulldozing:*" like S'ralun, Herbies has little time for the liars, cheats, bullshitters, schmoozers and arse-lickers of the world. From what we could tell, straight talking is highly valued, and we enjoyed speaking with some lively interviewees who provided us with many amusing quotes, a few of them sadly unprintable as they were way beyond cheeky. Herbert Smith trainees are a confident, expressive and diverse bunch. The firm recruits internationally, and has Russian, Indian, African and Australian trainees to name but a few of its foreign-born hires. University-wise, "*people might think conservative, Oxford, white middle-class law firm,*" but as one interviewee said: "*If that was the case, I wouldn't be here.*"

At such a large firm it can be "*hard to get to know a lot of people as well as you'd perhaps like to.*" Our contacts recognised the blessing of not being compelled to partake in firm socialising. One summed it up well by saying: "*Not all my friends are lawyers. I like the other trainees and we do socialise, but there's no pressure to do so.*" Of course, there's still the biennial trainee ball (last time "*a black-tie do at Kensington Roof Gardens*"), curry nights, summer and Christmas parties and a whole host of sporting teams to join.

The trainee retention rate dropped in 2009 and, rightly or wrongly, one theory that circulated was that Herbies was getting rid of the "*larger-than-life personalities.*" Though this is hard to believe, we did see the sense in one trainee's comment that "*being a bit of a joker could backfire. Yes, the partners are characters, but as a trainee you're expected to stay in your shell a bit more.*" Some 48 of the 68 qualifiers were retained this year, with these people spreading themselves across all departments. Like the other big City firms, Herbert Smith pulled the NQ salary down to £60,000 from £64,000 in 2009. The final bad news stories are that Herbies had to make 84 staff redundant this year and deferred 17 new trainees. At least they got a £7,000 no-strings payment.

And finally...

An excellent academic record and confident, effective communication skills are required here. You must also be prepared to work long hours, though you just might have a bit of fun while doing so...

Higgs & Sons

The facts

Locations: Brierley Hill, Stourbridge, Kingswinford

Number of UK partners/solicitors: 30/29

Total number of trainees: 8

Seats: 4x4 + 1x8 months

Alternative seats: None

> "*The future's bright, the future's Higgs! We have weathered the storm and are doing well. We've always been committed to a broad range of disciplines.*"
>
> Catherine Junor, Partner

Forged from the Black Country's heavy industries, family outfit Higgs is still firmly anchored in the local community.

Bedrock

When Joseph Higgs founded his firm in 1875 the Black Country was one of the most heavily industrialised areas in Britain. Booming coal mines, iron foundries and steel mills led to a proliferation of manufacturing businesses. Higgs was there to guide them through whatever legal strife they encountered. More than 130 years on and heavy industry has all but disappeared, but Higgs remains and continues to advise regional businesses and entrepreneurs. Over the years it has grown into one of the largest firms in the West Midlands and now competes with some of Birmingham's commercial players. Recent significant hires include a private client partner from Martineau and a former Wragge & Co partner who is just one of a number of recent additions to Higgs' dispute resolution team. Partner Julia Lowe, also from Wragge, joined the department as head in 2007 in order to spearhead its growing focus on commercial cases. Higgs' clientele now extends beyond its traditional Black Country stomping ground: on its books are Edgbaston-based Claimar Care Group, one of the UK's foremost suppliers of home nursing, Dutch engineering company Eriks and Giles Insurance Brokers.

Higgs may be "*pushing forward*" (two words we heard numerous times during our research), but this doesn't mean it has forgotten where it came from. Both the senior and managing partners trained at Higgs. In fact over 50% of the current equity partners started their legal careers with the firm. "*From my point of view,*" said one source, "*it makes it feel like a family. Partners have grown up here and there is real pride in the firm and how it has grown.*" Ambitious trainees recognise that it "*makes you feel there is room for progression.*" With four out of five qualifiers being kept on in 2009 it seems that this is true.

As for the idea of moving to Birmingham to capture more second-city business – well, on this subject Higgs' true Black Country character emerges. Round Higgs' way people refuse to be seen as Brummies and they speak with a distinctive accent. Trainees agree it would be "*completely wrong to move. Our roots are in the Black Country and that is important.*" Most (though not all) Higgs trainees haven't come from too far away. Academic credentials are important but not the be all and end all as the firm is keen for its recruits to be "*down-to-earth and approachable*" all-rounders. Such credentials are important in a firm that is "*big enough for good work and a broad practice, but small enough that everyone knows your name.*"

Awesome foursome

The training scheme is split into four seats lasting four months, followed by a fifth seat lasting eight months. Some sources found the quick changeovers frustrating and told us: "*By the end of the four months you know what you are doing and are just becoming useful and then you move again.*" Others saw "*the beauty*" of the system; "*once you know where you want to qualify you get to spend a year there and will hopefully be able to hit the ground running.*"

Bringing in 25% of the firm's income, private client is still Higgs' biggest department and its highest ranked practice group in *Chambers UK*. Spread across all three offices and spearheaded by the illustrious Robert Leek, trainees described the department as "*a microcosm of the firm as a whole.*" The clientele is an interesting mix of people coming in off the street for simple wills and high net worth individuals and their families. No stranger to big money, the team has recently administered a number of estates worth in the region of £10m and is currently advising the executors of an estate that is likely to exceed £40m. As well as getting their hands dirty on these complex trust cases, trainees also draft wills, run their own probates, spend time with clients, both on the phone and in person, sometimes even making home or hospital visits. While many liked the work, one knew the seat wasn't for them – "*I'm not good with death.*"

The separate family seat gained high praise, with trainees here given the opportunity to have their own clients. These cases were generally divorces by consent, where all financial arrangements are agreed. "*It was a definite high point for me,*" said one source. "*It was great to be given that responsibility and be able to see how far I've come.*" Trainees also assist more complex cases, covering ancillary finance, cohabitation and childrens' matters.

Body-building

Having made a strategic decision to invest in it, Higgs' dispute resolution department has grown from three to eight fee earners and experienced a 63% growth in income between 2007 and 2008. In the current climate the team has been very busy and kept "*trainees involved in all aspects*" of the available work. This has included contentious probate, debt recovery, insolvency, and commercial and property disputes. The employment department is another busy one. It represents individuals and employers, assisting the latter with restructuring and redundancy on a regular basis. Major commercial clients include the brewer Marston's, London & Cambridge Properties and Warwickshire County Cricket Club.

The crime team has just one partner and one associate, nevertheless it has grown its fee income by almost 40% lately. A seat here means "*a lot of chargeable work. A lot of responsibility.*" The role involves preparing defences, research and thinking about questions to ask clients in interview. As a rule there's a lot of "*learning by osmosis.*" "*I wasn't running any of my own files, but I was taken to every initial meeting and was heavily involved in assisting with the files.*"

Higgs is keen to provide trainees with a hands-on training. "*The further you go into the training contract the more responsibility you get,*" said one. Another continued: "*Higgs is very willing to give us good work so we have the opportunity to learn.*" Alongside all this responsibility

Chambers UK rankings

| Employment | Private Client |
| Family/Matrimonial | Real Estate |

"*there is always someone there that can help*" and trainees always share an office with their supervisor. "*Most of your work comes from them but gets fed from all over the department,*" ensuring a broad but balanced workload. When they start, trainees are assigned a partner-mentor for "*general support about the firm or anything regarding work.*"

Location location location?

Higgs operates in Stourbridge, Brierley Hill and the more high-streety Kingswinford. Consolidating the offices has been on the cards for years apparently and the firm has finally found somewhere that fits the bill. Occupants of both the Stourbridge and Brierley Hill offices will move to brand new waterfront premises in Brierley Hill at the beginning of 2010. This is great news for the firm's social life as trainees agree that the waterfront offers an excellent selection of bars and restaurants, and having most people under one roof means it will be even easier to go out together.

Christmas and summer parties are a chance for the whole firm to get together, and incoming trainees are invited along. "*The sea of anonymous faces*" sounds pretty daunting, but sources assured us that there is no pressure to be on best behaviour. Trainees are heavily involved in events run by the Birmingham Trainee Solicitors' Society too. Every year the Higgs employees champion a charity and make fundraisers a priority. There have been quizzes, dress-down days, a football tournament and barbecue, and the famous Higgs Olympics involving classic summer fête races. Trainees have full responsibility for organising events, giving them the opportunity to hone their networking skills. If you do manage to make good contacts, partners positively encourage you to develop them. "*It's an exciting time to be at Higgs,*" agreed trainees. "*We are focused on developing and expanding.*"

And finally...

With a reputation for good career progression, Higgs is a firm that expects long-term commitment. If its practice areas appeal and you can find your Black Country groove then this sounds like a great choice.

Hill Dickinson LLP

The facts

Location: Liverpool, Manchester, Chester, London

Number of partners/solicitors: 160/217

Total number of trainees: 32

Seats: 4x6 months

Alternative seats: Overseas seats, secondments

> Admittedly this firm's reunification was not quite as significant as the fall of the Berlin Wall, but it did mark a turning point in its fortunes.

Hill Dickinson's story stretches way back to Shropshire in the year 1808, when Beethoven was still pounding away on the piano and the importation of slaves into America was banned by that young nation's Congress.

The Mersey beau

In 1813, sole practitioner Edward Morrall upped sticks and relocated to Liverpool to enter into partnership with Richard Radcliffe and seek his fortune. At that time Liverpool was one of the most important cities in the world – a bustling port that saw 40% of the world's trade pass through its docks. It's hardly surprising that the men's firm developed a focus on shipping. The titular Mr Hill came along in 1865, followed nine years later by a certain Mr Dickinson, and by 1879 the firm bore their names. Hill Dickinson prospered (it was even instructed to work on the legal matters concerning the 'Titanic') and eventually opened branches in Manchester, Chester and London.

When, in 1989, the northern partners opted to diversify their activities beyond shipping it became apparent that the southerners no longer shared the same vision. The two halves of the firm separated, with the Londoners taking the name Hill Taylor Dickinson. In 2002, Hill Dickinson (the northern bit) expanded its property and commercial capacity by merging with Manchester firm Gorna and Co. and then with Liverpool property specialists Bullivant Jones in 2004. Finally, after 17 years apart, Hill Taylor Dickinson remarried its old northern beau.

Though united as one firm, the legacy of the split is evident insofar as the activities of the firm are more diverse up north, whereas the work in London "*is all related to shipping in one way or another.*" Despite the turbulent economy, the trainees we spoke to were confident about Hill Dicks' prospects and, referring to a new Singapore office, pointed out that "*it speaks volumes that we're opening new offices rather than sacking folk.*" On the domestic front, the corporate department may have been "*very quiet*" but the insolvency lawyers have formed a distinct team of their own and are very busy. Meanwhile, the northern-based health law department enjoys a very good position in the market.

Liverpool, with around 700 employees, is the largest office in the network. London and Manchester both have around 200 people each, and there's a small office in Chester plus outposts in Piraeus (Greece) and now Singapore. The purpose-built Liverpool office is the newest. "*It's fantastic,*" said one contented trainee; "*the canteen overlooks the Mersey, it's spectacular. I once watched a parade of ships go sailing past.*" Trainees speculated that an overhaul might be in the pipeline for the Manchester offices, adding that it's not ideal for staff to be in two buildings across the road from one another. As for the London office, trainees showed a palpable envy for their Liverpudlian colleagues – "*Don't expect to be impressed when you come in because the decor is pretty shoddy and stuck in the 70s a bit.*" They charitably added that if saving money on the building prevented staff from being cut, the scruffiness was okay.

Near, far, wherever you are

The training scheme and recruitment is run on an office-by-office basis, although trainees are encouraged to move between different locations for their four seats. Changes have been made to the review system so now, as well as being appraised by their supervisors, trainees appraise themselves at the end of each seat and give feedback on the quality of the seat and supervisor. To keep the offices integrated and trainees in contact with one another, there are monthly meetings (using swanky video conferencing equipment). During these meetings trainees give presentations on the seats they are in to help their peers decide if a particular department is going to be right for them. Every two months the trainees in the northern offices get together in person for these meetings, which helps breed familiarity. By contrast, we got the impression that the London trainees were rather separate and likely to only rarely meet up with the northerners after the initial induction sessions. HR says it is working on this.

You don't have to have a passion for shipping to work at Hill Dicks, but it might help you down south. London trainees are almost certainly going to experience maritime-related seats because this is the main thrust of their office. Making the point, one source revealed: "*There are model ships and pictures of ships everywhere.*" Maritime law is also the primary focus of Hill Dicks' Piraeus and Singapore offices, and trainees can request a posting to either. The firm has recently completed a merger that should pep up its London office. In July 2009 the lawyers and staff of the successful commodities law firm Middleton Potts came on board. You may never have thought much about international commodities trading but it's big, big business. Whether the price of commodities (coal, crops, precious metals, etc) rises or falls there is always work for lawyers as these fluctuations place strains on the contractual relationships between buyers, suppliers and transporters. In this area of law, commercial expertise and good-old-fashioned experience is often as important as legal knowledge. In one recent case a client sold cargo to the government of Iraq, which then failed to pay the full purchase price, alleging quality defects. Proceedings were brought in the English courts and multiple parties were joined to the action. Other cases have resulted from a strike by Argentine farmers that paralysed the transportation of agricultural products from the country's hinterland to its ports. All in all, the merger could well be a genius move for both the ex-Middleton lawyers and Hill Dicks.

Flotsam and jetsam

Some northern trainees get to take maritime seats, but it was mainly the Londoners who spoke in detail about this type of work. They reported a good level of responsibility and had encountered both 'wet' and 'dry' work. Dry matters include, among other things, contract disputes for commercial vessels and financing for the purchase of yachts. Many disputes relate to the standard of vessels delivered. As one source explained: "*It is unreasonable to expect that everything will be bang on in accordance with the contract straight away, and whoever drafts the contract puts in provisions for stuff that isn't up to spec. It can be as simple as the vessel being the wrong colour, through to it not being able to go at the right speed.*" Such cases often require extensive research, especially into complicated regulations regarding things like the storage of fuel on vessels. Bear in mind that because it is "*very, very unusual to have vessel, yard, owner and territory in the same country,*" even before litigation begins a trainee can become embroiled in questions over where it should take place.

Yacht cases meander into different areas of law since you might have to set up a company through which the yacht is owned, seek expert opinions in particular geographical locations and then liaise closely with various ship registries around the world, dealing with all the enquiries before a yacht's nationality can be altered so that it can be chartered in different parts of the world. Trainees tell us they frequently get the opportunity to use their language skills.

Wet shipping practice relates to collisions, salvage operations and injuries. Some wet lawyers are ex-mariners; indeed, one of the trainees was previously a marine engineer with experience of commodities claims. These people have an edge as they understand the experts brought in to report on collisions, salvage and arrests of vessels. They have the sea in their blood you might say. Environmental issues and piracy are both headline-grabbers these days. One trainee saw how an oil spill case became quite political. "*A lot of damage was done to the coral, and businesses that thrive off the natural beauty of the area were affected. We had to wade through a lot of legislation to find out who pays for what.*"

Chambers UK rankings

Banking & Finance	Healthcare
Clinical Negligence	Insurance
Commodities	Intellectual Property
Construction	Pensions
Corporate/M&A	Personal Injury
Debt Recovery	Private Client
Dispute Resolution	Professional Negligence
Employment	Real Estate
Environment	Real Estate Litigation
Family/Matrimonial	Shipping
Fraud: Criminal	Sports Law
Health & Safety	Transport
	Travel

All varieties of litigation

Up north, the sheer number of other practices available means Hill Dicks can justifiably claim to provide an all-round training ranging from insurance litigation to private client advice. If anything, the northern offices would suit those who have a penchant for litigation, be this clinical negligence cases, commercial disputes, personal injury or professional negligence cases among lawyers and other advisers.

The firm's largest department is insurance litigation. In the main the lawyers represent insurers and defend everything from repetitive strain injury claims and deaths (both at sea and on land), through to construction disputes and product liability cases. Sometimes cases are tainted with fraud (people staging accidents or faking injuries), so there is a dedicated team to deal with that. As well as taking on a high volume of lower value claims, the insurance litigation division caters for retail sector clients such as Laura Ashley and Somerfield, for whom it primarily deals with more complex matters. The clinical negligence department can be an eye-opener. "*One part of the department is devoted to the NHS Litigation Authority, and although you don't often get your own cases to manage because the sums involved are so large, you do get a lot to do and are exposed to plenty of trial preparation.*"

The past five years have seen the firm assiduously scale up its commercial departments through mergers and lateral hires. The coco division (which includes employment, commercial property, corporate finance and pensions) accounts for just under 20% of the firm's income. Clients include the NHS, Barclays, Tesco and RBS Structured Debt Solutions, which the firm assisted with the management buyout of property and construction consultancy Cunliffes last year. Property has been an important area for Hill Dicks and most northern trainees do a seat here. Clients of this department include public sector organisations such as Liverpool Council for Voluntary Services, Liverpool City Council and private sector names like UPS and Chester Zoo.

Mersey sound

Some of our sources were keen to compliment the firm's ability to adapt to change. "*They have started to bring in a wider managerial team to implement changes needed for a larger firm. For instance they brought someone in who has produced a booklet to raise awareness of the different practices.*" Others praised it for "*not having spread itself too thin*" and working hard at retaining major clients. The training scheme sounds well organised, too, and trainees assure us "*there is a good support structure in place.*" Often it's the little touches that make a big difference. Every new starter is matched with a mentor from the year above to help settle them in, "*someone who has done the seat you're starting in... It's a fairly informal scheme that allows you to voice any concerns outside of the more formal structure.*" There's really no reason for problems to fester as each trainee shares a room with their supervisor. "*When you first start it can be scary sitting in an office with them... you know they're listening to you on the phone, but it's good really. They're there to ask questions and you can listen to them on the phone and absorb things.*" One of the most encouraging things we heard was this: "*The firm tries very hard to develop the junior lawyers and they trust junior fee earners. The discipline* [in the firm] *is quite commercially oriented... Partners are sound.*"

Run to the Hills

Trainees enjoy a good work-life balance, generally starting at 9am and finishing at around 6pm. There are ad hoc social activities and organised jollies such as Christmas parties and sailing events. Our sources were enthusiastic about the networking they'd been involved with, for example "*football games against clients and everyone going for beers after.*" We also understand the people play a lot of cricket here. Charitable fund-raisers are popular, including a Six Peaks Challenge (three peaks aren't enough?), a poker night and a Scalextric party with "*a monster track spanning two meeting rooms.*" "*Morale is pretty good,*" said one source. "*There's a good holiday system – you can buy or sell five days – and you get your birthday off too. Also, if you go a year without absence you get about £250.*"

It's easy to see why people want to stay on qualification. In 2009 most opportunities were in contentious departments such as com lit and insurance, although some qualifiers did find homes in the energy, health and marine departments. The final score for the year was 11 jobs for 15 qualifiers, not at all bad given the economy. As for the firm's performance as a whole, in 2009 it reported that revenue for the past year had risen by 12%, with partner profits down a modest 5.8%. There were only a few redundancies in 2009 and no trainee deferrals.

And finally...

Maritime law is "*a major pull*" for southern trainees, who reckon it "*definitely adds to the character of the firm.*" Up north it is litigation that really drives things, so make sure your appetite for contentious experience is substantial.

Holman Fenwick Willan LLP

The facts

Location: London
Number of UK partners/solicitors: 71/97
Total number of trainees: 28
Seats: 4x6 months
Alternative Seats: Overseas seats, secondments
Extras: Language training

"We have taken advantage of the downturn by snapping up transactional lawyers: most have come from associate level into corporate projects and finance."
Ottilie Sefton, Training Partner

International firm Holman Fenwick Willan has 11 offices and a terrific reputation in all matters maritime. With secondment opportunities in major shipping jurisdictions, the world is most definitely your oyster as a trainee here.

Holman's flustered? Hardly.

One hundred and twenty-five years working on all things shipping and insurance-related hasn't diminished this firm's lust for life on the high seas. Established in 1884, HFW offers us one of the good-news stories of the year: it has sailed through the treacherous economy, posted a 27% increase in revenue and made no redundancies. An increase in litigation and insurance instructions has put wind in the firm's sails. As to who's responsible for these instructions, well we're talking about some of the biggest charterers, insurers, banks and shipowners around. Trainees put HFW's good fortune down to it being a *"forward-thinking"* firm that has *"covered its bases without being everywhere."* It has offices in Paris, Hong Kong, Singapore, Piraeus, Rouen, Shanghai, Dubai, Melbourne and Brussels. Back in the UK the firm organises itself into the following departments: shipping; trade and energy; insurance; commercial; and corporate projects & finance.

Most of our sources had deliberately sought a training contract that could give them an international perspective. As one put it: *"I came here so I could get a global view of the law."* One issue that exemplifies this is the growing problem of piracy, which now seems to dominate news headlines on a frequent basis. HFW's clients are directly affected by such maritime security threats, and as such the firm has been pushing governments to implement tougher regulations. Lawyers here were involved in some 23 piracy cases in the second half of 2008 alone. Piracy always sounds like an exciting area to be working in – and Johnny Depp has made it rather cool – but the unfortunate reality is that shipping is becoming a dangerous business again, despite the fact that navigation and technical ship safety is better than ever. If they succumb to pirates, shipowners and charterers can now face ransom figures of millions of pounds.

Marine psychology

Wet shipping lawyers deal with things like collisions, oil spills and… did we mention piracy? Claims for contaminated cargo also crop up, and in such cases it's necessary to establish where fault lies, for example did the crew fail to ventilate the cargo? Wet shipping *"appeals to people with more of a maritime background,"* said one source, noting that a few of the lawyers at HFW (including one of the current trainees) are qualified mariners. But what if you don't know a charter party from a P&I club, or worse still have no idea about the music played at either? Thankfully there's a thorough training programme for newbies, involving seminars and webinars aimed to bring them up to speed on nautical know-how. In time, trainees run small internal seminars of their own, which can be *"nerve-wracking."*

On the dry side of shipping practice, trainees can end up on major cases. It's *"good to be a part of what the firm is known for,"* said one source, who also commented on the sneaky nature of the job. *"You sometimes get to come up* with some hare-brained reason to get out of a contract; it's quite creative contractually!" Actions against shipyards by ship-owners are increasingly common, as are maritime insolvencies.

Pieces of crate!

Shipping litigation seats are pretty exciting. "*It's amazing working for the leading partners in the field,*" said one source, while another explained that much of their enjoyment came from "*looking at the facts* [of a case] *and condensing them into a claim and presenting it to the partners.*" Court attendance is another rewarding element of the job, albeit that trainees have little chance to advocate. Most matters are too valuable for this, and they can also take a long time to settle or go to trial. For example, HFW lawyers are still working for the owners and insurers of the 'MSC Napoli' in a long-running saga that began in 2007 when the vessel was abandoned in gale-force winds off the coast of Cornwall. Among the challenges posed by the event were environmental damage to wildlife near Branscombe and a concerted bid by scavengers to loot the cargo that reached the shore. Mercifully a shipment of cider brandy was saved as it was tightly packed next to a consignment of bibles written in Zulu. Now that's what we call divine intervention. The 'Ice Prince' on the other hand, washed up more than 2,000 tonnes of timber in Dorset and HFW was able to negotiate contracts to clean up the subsequent oil spill within a day.

The finance teams might be a less swashbuckling alternative to the litigation teams, but they are an important part of the firm and take three trainees at each seat rotation. Trainees can work with specialists in areas such as new build financing and aviation finance, working for the likes of Commerzbank and Tsako Energy Navigation. And while drafting loan documents and securities "*isn't anything to get too excited about,*" trainees do have plenty of client contact in this seat, whether it is liaising with buyers or through de-flagging and re-flagging ships at various national registries. Trust us when we say you will be dealing with ship magnates and captains of industry here. "*The very first transaction I had involved drafting corporate minutes for a guy with very deep pockets,*" recalled one source. Apparently at the beginning of 2009 the ship finance market was slow due to a shortage of liquidity. "*It was quite ugly for a while,*" said one frank interviewee. Thankfully the situation has already eased following a bottoming out of asset prices, and new build and ship recycling work is flowing in again.

Another department that has become rather important to the firm is trade and energy. This team now takes five trainees at a time (up from two) and it accounts for 20% of HFW's revenue. The lawyers deal with everything from soft commodities like sugar and cotton to hard commodities like gas, bullion and uranium. A typical day can involve anything from major grain contract disagreements in Eastern Europe to the arbitration of mining disputes. Trainees say that in this seat there's a great deal of overlap with shipping law, and certainly the firm advises numerous independent and national oil companies on their shipping concerns. The scale and international nature of the work seemed to really appeal to our sources. "*I didn't have a UK client the whole time I was there,*" said one. Major energy contracts can be quite complicated at times and you'll certainly learn about what goes on in the market, be it in the north of the UK or somewhere like Angola or Nigeria. This is a seat where you can expect a lot of responsibility. "*I was acting like an NQ rather than a trainee,*" confirmed one interviewee.

Chambers UK rankings

Asset Finance	Fraud: Civil
Commodities	Insurance
Competition/European Law	Shipping
Corporate/M&A	Transport
Dispute Resolution	Travel

The other seat options form a smorgasbord of international, contentious and transactional opportunities. They include commercial property; competition; corporate projects and finance (including IT/IP and outsourcing) and a transportation-based seat called logistics ("*lots of fun*"). The possibility of client secondments also exists. Our sources had noted a growth in transactional areas of practice, with corporate and finance transactions occupying more fee-earning time. Said one: "*My first impression of the firm was that it was very strong in maritime law but also clear that it wanted to grow in non-contentious areas like corporate and commercial.*" One real highlight was the firm's representation of Soya Mills, a Greek commodities company that listed on AIM and was valued at around €50m.

Even though no single seat is compulsory, given HFW's strength in litigation you should expect at least two, and possibly three, contentious seats. The first seat is always chosen by the firm, and after that trainees' preferences are taken into account. The smart trainee will investigate their options early, paying particular attention to the secondment opportunities. "*It's quite an integrated firm and for trainees there's every opportunity to go abroad if you want to.*" At present the locations on offer are Paris, Dubai, Piraeus, Melbourne and Hong Kong. Beware though, getting an overseas posting can be very last-minute so make sure you're able to pack your bags with just a couple of weeks' notice, if necessary. Everything else is dealt with by the firm, including a convenient pad not far from the office. HFW has invested heavily in the Far East, particularly in Shanghai and Hong Kong, where the economy has remained strong. Asian business is vital, and lawyers recently worked on a highly publicised European Commission case involving Chinese exporters accused of selling products at especially low prices to European customers – a practice commonly referred to as dumping. A lead figure in this matter was partner Anthony Woolwich, who was recently poached from Lawrence Graham for his expertise in competition and EU law.

Come aboard. We're expecting you.

That reference to seventies' TV smash *The Love Boat* shows our age. But is HFW showing its age? "*We still have the ships in glass cases,*" chuckled one trainee before deciding that they "*wouldn't describe it as an old place any more. Since we've moved, it's a place where you can really enjoy yourself and progress.*" The move they referred to was long overdue. In 2008 the entire London staff decamped from shabby premises above a City newsagent to more commodious digs at Friary Court near Fenchurch Street Station and Lloyd's Registry. "*The new offices are very smart indeed, but the only problem is that we are growing really quickly and we may need to move again soon!*" Trainees agree that since the move there is "*a more unified brand and the firm feels more progressive.*" On the subject of working practices, trainees say that the hours are reasonable, even if on occasion client needs are prioritised over a work-life balance. In general however, the firm's litigation focus does make a trainee's working week more predictable than it might be at a more transaction-led firm.

HFW tends to recruit students who've have had a bit of work experience. Many speak another language and we noted that this year's trainee group included a few continental Europeans. Personality-wise, our sources thought the ideal type was "*a bit more outgoing as there are plenty of personalities throughout the firm.*" We came across some tough-minded and independent trainees who don't just face challenges, they embrace them. Even while still paralegals or vac schemers, our sources had taken on responsibility – "*attending closing meetings and drafting documents. We're definitely not just photocopying here.*" Supervisors were praised across the board for giving appraisals that are "*open and professionally managed, and the HR department gives you feedback from people you've worked with.*" Partners are always willing to talk as well, "*whether it be in the office or in the pub.*" This being said, it was felt that "*official communication from top-down could be better.*" As an example, one trainee suggested the introduction of partner/trainee lunches – "*something like an informal get-together would be good as a trainee's perspective is sometimes not heard over the associates' or partners'.*"

No grind

With such a strong maritime practice, we would have expected at least one of HFW's many social functions to be on a boat, particularly given its impeccable reputation in the superyacht market. Instead, most of the firm's downtime is spent on dry land, with sporting events popular for client entertaining. We're talking about things such as the Ashes, the Lions tour, golf days and a "*quite heated*" football tournament. More serene affairs include summer barbecues, park soirées and a Christmas bash at the Grosvenor Hotel. For Friday night drinks, the trainees' habit is a conveniently located pub called The Habit. The office has a subsidised café with swish coffee machines "*that grind the coffee for you*" and an outside seating area. Although your initial social circle will revolve around the other trainees, in time it "*gradually evolves to include people from your departments.*" If you're in the know, you'll realise that "*the shipping teams are best known for their parties.*"

And finally...

"*I hope to retire here,*" said one source, clearly thinking about the long haul. What better recommendation can we give? In 2009, 11 of the 12 qualifiers stayed course with the firm.

- **In English, please?** Capital whats? Wet and dry shipping? Restructuring? Our Practice Area pages explain the mysteries of all the main fields of law, describe what lawyers actually do within them and tell you which firms covered in the True Picture section are the best regarded for such work.

top tip no. 16

Howes Percival LLP

The facts

Locations: Leicester, Northampton, Norwich, Milton Keynes

Number of UK partners/solicitors: 28/65

Total number of trainees: 18

Seats: 4x6 months

Alternative seats: None

> Don't come to HP expecting too much of a sleepy regional lifestyle. The firm expects trainees to put the hours in – and pays them accordingly.

Howes Percival offers broad commercial experience in the East Midlands and Norfolk and prides itself on being able to compete with bigger firms.

Howes things?

Its distance from the City hasn't stopped this all-round commercial firm from competing with the country's bigger legal guns. It remains an attractive prospect for major clients like Welcomebreak, Nampak ('packaging solutions, not just packaging products'), Shanks, Alliance & Leicester, communications company THA Group and tyre people ATS Euromaster International, and trainees confidently talk about how well the firm is respected in its regions. More than this, they say that as trainees they get "*quality training with good exposure to clients and plenty of responsibility.*"

The firm has offices in Leicester, Northampton and Norwich. Each one offers seats to trainees in coco, commercial property and employment. Leicester and Norwich both have litigation as well, while Northampton has a private client seat instead. In 2008, a fourth office in Milton Keynes was raided by City giant Denton Wilde Sapte, which also has a branch in MK. Six of HP's partners and 24 other fee earners upped sticks and left, leaving HP MK without much of a commercial operation. At the time, Jit Singh, the managing partner of the Leicester office, told *The Lawyer* that the firm's aim was to "*increase overall turnover within 12 months, despite the inevitable reduction in fee income from our Milton Keynes office.*" HP MK is now solely focused on volume residential conveyancing work and is no longer a major destination for trainees. Four of the 2008 new starters joined Denton Wilde Sapte along with three second years who were working in MK.

It is common for East Midlands trainees to switch between Leicester and Northampton over the course of their training contract. Norwich trainees stay in one place for the duration – it's a long trip over the Fens to the East Midlands, after all. We get the strong impression that each office gives trainees a very different experience. Leicester has the most corporate mindset, Northampton is a bit more relaxed, while Norwich, 120-odd miles away from the others, has its own clients and operates quite independently.

Don't be shy

A study in "*very slick chrome, leather and glass,*" the Leicester office is known for its clout in corporate and commercial work and has a variety of clients from across the Midlands and beyond. For example, it acted for the Bank of Scotland, drafting, negotiating and advising on a senior debt funding facility for the creation of freehold sites in a neighbourhood scheme in Somerset. It also acted for HSBC Bank Canada in obtaining security in excess of C$10m from a UK company. The corporate unit advised the directors of the Fleet Auction Group – a car auction business which sells old fleet cars and commercial vehicles into the motor trade – on a multimillion-pound joint venture with a Kuwaiti investor. It's worth noting that HP has a number of good contacts in the automotive industry. The Leicester corporate team also works for Kia Motors and Renault Trucks, while its Northampton counterpart has Silverstone Circuits, The British Racing Drivers' Club and easyCar (UK) among its clientele. Trainees also noted the team's involvement in the packaging industry, dealing with clients like Benson Box and Nampak. Benson Box used it during its acquisition of a collapsed rival, Cameron Linn. We're told that the corporate department is quite "*brash, with more of a London feel to it*" than the rest of the firm. Trainees were proud of the strong client base and also said that the seat was well structured for a trainee to be able to get a constant supply of work. Supervisors here were generally praised as easy to deal with, however we did get consistent complaints about work hours and the general treatment of trainees from some other partners: "*It was too intense: the people who work in that department are stress-heavy,*" said one, while another complained of having "*had a few panic attacks working on one due diligence matter.*" Make no mistake, this may be a regional firm but "*they do put you on the front line and you can't be shy – you're expected to put the hours in.*"

Late nights can also be expected in the highly praised employment department. Having expanded steadily in previous years, it continues to act in various contentious and non-contentious matters with a large amount of respondent tribunal work and complex discrimination litigation. With a "*good, wide range of work where a trainee can be heavily involved from day one,*" the assiduous recruit can expect anything from drafting witness statements for a tribunal claim to dealing with major layoffs to getting involved with marketing. Trainees found the senior members of the group "*inspiring for the hours they put in.*"

Trainees spoke well of Leicester's commercial property team, where one can amass "*a lot of responsibility – sometimes you have 25 files on the go.*" Clients include the Alumasc Group which deals in building and engineering products, European transport and logistics company Christian Salvesen and shoe retailer Brantano (UK). One deal involved the disposal of 160 dwellings to a registered social landlord, including a land sale agreement and a separate development agreement with a total value of £18m. High-value insolvency is also a speciality of the firm and there are teams dealing with this kind of work in both Leicester and Northampton.

From the East Midlands to East Anglia

Trainees see Northampton, the firm's hometown, as "*the sleepier side of HP.*" It suits trainees looking for a more regional type of lifestyle. The office is correspondingly less corporate-looking than the swish Leicester building, and it has a proper boardroom with a massive table and an enormous chandelier hanging above it. Gerald Couldrake, the man who calls the shots in Northampton, is apparently pretty laid back and he seems to set the tone of the place. The other USP is a private client team which trainees enjoy for its wealth, probate and tax work. Partners in the property department were found to be very approachable: "*You can ask lots of questions here and it's*

Chambers UK rankings

Agriculture & Rural Affairs	Employment
Banking & Finance	Intellectual Property
	Private Client
Corporate/M&A	Real Estate
Dispute Resolution	Restructuring/Insolvency

not frowned upon." Employment, too, gives "*really good training. It's run like clockwork!*" Unlike in Leicester, employment work in Northampton is about 80% non-contentious, so preparing seminars and advice on redundancy and unfair dismissal is par for the course for trainees.

Somewhat divorced from the Midlands offices, and even recruiting its trainees separately, Norwich is almost a firm apart. If you end up here, you probably lived in or near Norwich to begin with and have a hankering for general commercial work. This office is ranked in the second tier in *Chambers UK* for private client in East Anglia and it specialises in estate planning and taxation. The clients are often land-owning families and the office contains considerable agricultural expertise. Family disputes can be particularly difficult in the agricultural sector because farms tend to be passed down from generation to generation leading to complications for those who have married into the clan. The largest department is litigation, which recently acted for the government, seeking recovery of about £100m of fraudulently claimed VAT. Litigators also represented private parties in a £1m-plus claim involving allegations of commercial fraud. In property matters, the firm receives multiple instructions from Norwich Cathedral every year. Trainees enjoy the friendly atmosphere of an office in which each department "*really makes an effort to involve you in its social life.*" Recently they participated in a treasure hunt around the city.

As for the Leicester/Northampton trainees, they also often have local connections but the group is still varied enough to keep things interesting. "*They do take in quite a diverse bunch here but in general,*" said trainees, "*you have to be polished and quite outgoing as well as compliant.*" Compliant? It seems that many of our sources didn't take too well to the gruffer approach taken by some of the firm's partners. "*The management style here is quite bullish and it's hard to see how it's going to change as it's still a bit of a boy's club,*" theorised one, noting that very few of the firm's partners are female. We did our own research and, according to the firm's website, in July 2009 four of 23 partners were women. Looking at these stats, we have to say that HP scores pretty averagely on this measure.

For some reason we found the morale of the HP trainees we spoke to this year generally quite low. In 2009, just four of the nine qualifiers stayed on at the firm (two of seven in the East Midlands and two of two in Norwich), and no doubt this was a big contributing factor. The departures from the Milton Keynes office have also clearly had an effect: "*It's made the firm seem smaller; it doesn't feel as corporate as it used to,*" say trainees. And of course, the firm's remaining departments are under increased pressure to perform in a tough economic climate. The lack of a social scene was also a recurring gripe among the East Midlands trainees. "*I expected drinks every Friday or payday but that culture isn't here – there's no real play-hard attitude.*" Although they had fun at the AGM at Sandringham (where they got to meet the Norwich trainees), the burden of organising social events at other times falls to the trainees themselves. A few renegades in Leicester have taken things into their own hands by organising road trips to Birmingham. Finishing on a more positive note, we're pleased to report that trainees are delighted with what is a "*spectacular salary*" compared to most firms in their region. East Midlands second-years earn £26,500, rising to £39,000 on qualification, "*which goes a long way in Leicester.*"

And finally...

It's been a tough old year for Howes Percival but the firm shows real grit and remains a big player in Leicester, Northampton and Norwich. A vac scheme would be a good way of giving it some closer examination.

Ince & Co

The facts

Location: London
Number of UK partners/solicitors: 55/70
Total number of trainees: 27
Seats: Notionally 4x6 months
Alternative seats: Ad hoc overseas seats
Extras: Language training

"Ince likes people with a bit of a spark about them. At some of these City firms trainees are a bit meh; they can be chatty and charming but have nothing about them. Here some are clearly mad."

You're a ship owner. Your tanker's had a collision and its cargo is spilling into the ocean at an alarming rate. Who ya gonna call?

Classically trained

From the bombastic tone of its telephone hold music (we got Wagner's *Ride of the Valkyries*), to the upbeat tone of trainees, Ince radiates confidence at the moment. And well it might. Its long-standing focus on litigation, with sector specialisms in shipping and insurance, means that it doesn't now face the same problems as most City firms with their large transactional departments. In fact Ince doesn't even have departments. Rather, it encourages its lawyers to develop broad practices based roughly around seven core areas of which shipping and insurance/reinsurance are its two strongest. In these two areas it has *Chambers UK* top-tier rankings. The other five are aviation, commercial disputes, energy, international trade and business, and finance. So, while partners might specialise in one of these areas, they will probably also turn their hand to others from time to time.

It isn't any different for trainees. Unlike most other firms you'll read about in this book, there is no rotation through departments here. They do sit with a supervisor for six months at a time, but because there are no departments trainees are not tied to any one kind of work, nor do they have to abandon a case when their six months are up. Instead, they are expected to build up relationships with partners in order to secure assignments. *"It's a bit like being self-employed; you treat the partners like your clients."*

And what's the best way to win a nice bit of business? There are several different methods. You might go on a *"walkaround,"* poking your head around doors. Naturally, this *"can be quite nerve-wracking when you start, but people know the system and are pretty welcoming."* If you don't fancy this method, *"capacity e-mails"* regularly get sent out to trainees with the offer of work and *"fastest finger first"* gets the job. Answering these e-mails is rather-like reaching into a lucky dip: *"You never quite know whether it will be a one-off piece of research that will take a few hours or a huge case that will last a year or more."* Alternatively, if you happen to be a member of one of Ince's sports teams, or perhaps its choir, you might find that *"partners approach you there and ask if you are free."* Most use all these methods in their early days at the firm, and as they progress they develop relationships with a small group of partners whose working styles match their own.

In past years many of our contacts have observed that this way of doing things means that often the only person who knows exactly what a trainee is doing is the trainee. To counter this the firm has introduced a traffic light system: trainees can put themselves on red, amber or green depending on how busy they are. *"Some partners do use that frequently. Some partners don't at all."* Our contacts had spent most of their time on amber, only switching to red if they were staffed on a long-running case. Traffic lights notwithstanding, *"it's not a firm where you are mollycoddled. You are very much in charge of your own timeframe."* Trainees here need to learn to turn down work: partners have no problem with this – *"after all,"* said one interviewee, *"they wouldn't be very impressed if you said you'd do it and then handed in a sub-standard piece of work because you didn't have the time."* Help, say trainees, is always on hand for those who ask for it.

There's no face-time requirement, so trainees typically vanish for the day between 7pm and 8pm.

Quick! To the Incemobile!

You know that bit in *Titanic*? Not the naked Kate Winslet bit, but the bit at the end where she's clinging to a plank and Leo sinks below the thunders of the upper deep? It wouldn't happen like that today. For one thing, there'd be search and rescue helicopters zooming all over the place, and on one of them there would be a cadre of Ince lawyers all narrowing their eyes and working out who to blame. The firm has a big red 'International Emergency Response' button on its website so when disaster strikes, someone can be on the scene in super-fast time. When the 'Hebei Spirit' spilt 11,000 tonnes of crude oil off the coast of Korea, leading to a $330m clean-up bill, Ince was on hand to establish pollution compensation arrangements, negotiate the release of the vessel, defend the crew against criminal charges and advance indemnity claims against the owners of a crane barge. When the 'MSC Joanna' collided with the 'W D Fairway' outside a Chinese port, it led to proceedings in China and the United States and became the most expensive collision case in the world with claims exceeding $325m. Ince was involved. And after the 'Cosco Busan' collided with one of the towers of San Francisco Bay Bridge causing a 100-foot gash in the ship's hull, guess who acted for the ship owners and their P&I club?

There's no guarantee that you'll be staffed on a sexy collision case (an example of what is known as 'wet' shipping). Equally important is 'dry' shipping – cases where there's been no emergency. Instead these relate to contractual disputes, ship mortgages, charter parties and the like. But wet or dry, it's a fascinating area of law. "*Just within shipping the work can be so varied. None of my cases have been really alike,*" said one trainee. The practice area offers "*a nice mix of legal strategy and the technical side, talking with experts – really top people in their field.*" If this sounds complicated to you then you're not wrong, but trainees insist that "*if you haven't encountered shipping before, you mustn't be put off. It doesn't matter at all as long as you are on the ball.*" At the beginning of the training contract, new arrivals are given a two-week crash course in some of Ince's core areas. "*It's a good attempt and appreciated, even if it can be boring,*" confessed one source. Learning by doing is better: "*I have a clause to redraft and disclosure to do on a shipping case today, and it probably won't be checked,*" said an interviewee.

Insur-Ince

Okay, so you know that bit in *Titanic*? Not the naked Kate Winslet bit, but the bit at the end where she's old and drops her pendant over the side to let it sink far beneath the abysmal sea? Wouldn't happen like that today. Just think of

Chambers UK rankings

Asset Finance	Insurance
Aviation	Professional Negligence
Commodities	Projects, Energy & Natural Resources
Dispute Resolution	Shipping

the insurance complications. Ince lawyers certainly do. It's not the Heart of the Ocean, but the firm successfully represented underwriters in litigation concerning a late 19th century clock egg. It was claimed that the clock had depreciated in value after it was allegedly damaged during transit from a Fabergé exhibition in the USA. As with shipping, insurance is an incredibly varied and complex area. Two major events of 2005 – Hurricane Katrina and the Buncefield oil depot explosion – are still producing work four years on, and less high-profile cases, like a fire at a meat factory in Northern Ireland, are always coming in.

"*A lot of people make the mistake of thinking we're just shipping and insurance but we're not. Primarily if you work here you're a litigator,*" said trainees. Ince does indeed have a strong commercial disputes practice. For instance, the firm acted for Cambridge City FC in High Court proceedings regarding alleged fraudulent misrepresentation and bribery on the sale of the club's premises, and for the Romanian State Privatisation and Asset Recovery Agency in various pieces of international litigation, so it's not just limited to clients from its core areas. With so much litigation going on, court time is a given and trainees will often sit behind a barrister during hearings. Because the amounts involved are huge "*even most of the qualified solicitors don't do much advocacy. The judges have high expectations and everybody uses counsel.*" Another given is time spent bundling papers for court. "*We have a paralegal department that I can pass most of it to,*" said one trainee, but "*on one big trial I had to run the bundles myself until I knew them better than the solicitors.*"

We mentioned last year that Ince was developing a transactional practice and the recession hasn't changed its plans. The business and finance group (BFG) is becoming more visible within the firm and trainees are increasingly being encouraged to get involved. As we've repeatedly mentioned, Ince doesn't do departments, but the BFG, "*because of its nature is slightly self-contained.*" While the firm's trainees are naturally more litigation-minded, they do value the non-contentious work that's available and view the numerous training sessions provided by the BFG as useful.

Best of British

This firm tends to attract an interesting trainee group. Many come from abroad or have language skills (travel to one of the firm's international offices is a definite possibility), but many don't. Some have Master's degrees in shipping law, many don't. About half are highly academic; about half are incredibly practical. One or two have, shall we say, industry connections. We rather liked the view of one trainee who pronounced that the firm "*likes people with a bit of a spark about them. At some of these City firms trainees are a bit meh; they can be chatty and charming but have nothing about them. Here some are clearly mad. Shall we use the word eccentric? Ince attracts its fair share of characters – shipping and insurance always will.*" Universal traits: they all have "*adaptability,*" "*common sense,*" a "*gutsy and ballsy*" nature, they are "*confident and resilient and will hit the ground running.*" And "*because it's litigation you have to be able to get on with people.*" This is a "*quite British*" firm that values "*frank upfront-ness. You don't have to worry about treading on people's toes.*" Ince is also good at helping trainees make contacts that will serve them well later in their careers. "*Yesterday we took a group of under-35s from the reinsurance industry round the Royal Courts of Justice and had a talk from a judge.*"

A budget is provided for two trainee social events a year, firm drinks occur monthly, there are plenty of sports groups (sailing is big) and of course the choir, but our contacts said "*organised fun*" was not the Ince way. "*Twelve is a nice number for a year group*" though, and the current crop of second-years is notoriously tight-knit, eating lunch together in the breakout room every day.

Down by the docks

Ince is changing. Not hugely, but it is. The firm moved to attractive new offices on St Katharine's Dock a couple of years ago and trainees noted that it is still expanding, even now. Most suggested that "*as we continue to grow there is a feeling that we will probably departmentalise to an extent. They worry about it becoming unmanageable.*" Some thought this would be a good idea: "*Something like international trade is so specialised; certain partners might like to have a small team of people with a little more focus.*" Others expressed mild concern, saying: "*Hopefully they will just firm up the business strands. The worry is that you might have to pick a department to qualify into. If you have people who can do so much it seems a waste of resources to force them down one furrow.*" The firm commented that there are no plans to create departments but that "*invisible lines*" may form.

Talking of qualification, the firm looks to be in a good place right now as revenue grew by a remarkable 23.5% in 2008/09, but our contacts still weren't counting their chickens. "*On the surface of things we are incredibly busy,*" they said. "*The only problem is that the litigation will stop because there will come a point when people don't have the money to sue each other any more. We'll get a lot of work in the next six months but then I expect things to quieten down considerably.*" It must be a good sign that the firm isn't getting carried away. While one cynic expressed the opinion that "*they say qualification is always down to your abilities rather than business needs – that's guff of course,*" most felt rather more "*invested in*" than that, and Ince does have a very impressive retention record. Not only does it boast in its recruitment literature that more than two thirds of its partners trained with the firm, but it kept 100% of trainees on in both 2007 and 2008. In 2009 it didn't quite repeat this feat as 11 out of 12 qualifiers remained with the firm.

And finally...

We'll quote the trainee who said: "*I feel prepared for what it will be like when I qualify as a solicitor.*" If that's not the mark of a damned fine training contract, we don't know what is.

Irwin Mitchell

The facts

Location: Birmingham, Glasgow, Leeds, London, Manchester, Newcastle, Sheffield
Number of partners/solicitors: 135/210
Total number of trainees: 53
Seats: 3x4 + 1x12 months
Alternative seats: None

> IM's rich heritage in PI is hugely important, but it now sees commercial law as an equally essential part of its future.

Irwin Mitchell distinguishes itself through its public law, personal injury, Court of Protection and clinical negligence work. It also has a mature commercial practice.

Choose your own adventure

IM's recent past is characterised by lateral hires, mergers and office expansions. Its latest move was to nab a squad of lawyers from South West and Midlands firm BPE to bolster its commercial presence in Birmingham. To help head off the looming threat of Tesco Law following deregulation in the legal services sector, the firm entered into a couple of strategic mergers, building its commoditised legal services capacity by incorporating Alexander Harris in 2006 and Gold's Solicitors in 2007. IM's headquarters in Sheffield now houses over 1,000 staff, many of them working on low-value cases; its other offices are in Manchester, Newcastle, Leeds, London Birmingham, Glasgow, Madrid and, rather unusually, Málaga. Currently, all UK offices undertake both PI and commercial work, except the Newcastle office, which is limited to PI. The Spanish offices mainly cater for expats looking to buy property, claim compensation for an injury, set up a business in Spain or seek family law advice. Sadly trainees aren't posted to España, so no chance of working on a tan.

The structure of the training contract has undergone major changes and the trainees we spoke to were the last of the old guard, able to take seats across the full range of departments, from personal injury to corporate. From 2009 trainees will choose between either a PI stream or a business stream. In the former they will also see clinical negligence, public law and Court of Protection matters; in the latter the choices will vary from office to office but usually include things like corporate, employment, property, insurance and business crime. Trainees will no longer move between offices, instead staying in the same place for two years. The new seat system is a little unusual too – three four-month seats are followed by a year-long stint in one department (hopefully the one into which the trainee will qualify).

The new system has its pros and cons. For some, the flexibility and breadth of the old training contract had major appeal. If still unsure of their end goal, a trainee could experiment with PI and business law, and they could also road-test different offices. Reflecting on the new system, some people were unsure if it would have appealed to them when they were applying. On the other hand, the new system does mean that *"for people who know what they want to do and what they don't want to do, it'll be better."* The competition for specific seats should be less intense and, unlike in the past, trainees ought not to spend a year in an area that has minimal appeal. As the firm's HR team told us, the new system will *"allow trainees to get experience in related areas of law, making them more specialised on qualification, and it allows us to plan the training contract around business needs, bringing in the right number of people through each stream."* This should *"help to keep more people on in the areas they want to work in."* We were told that, irrespective of stream, all trainees will be paid the same and that *"one stream will not be seen as more important than the other."* PI NQs will be paid £31,000, while their business stream/private client counterparts will pull in between £31,000 and £36,000. Another change is the institution of an additional training course – *"a sort of generic training programme to train them in the basics of delegation, managing people, time management, networking and cross-selling that will keep bringing the trainees together as one group."*

Thinking about PI?

Irwin Mitchell is to personal injury and clin neg what Simon Cowell is to Saturday night telly – a giant. In the past it has been associated with major cases such as the 'Marchioness' riverboat disaster and vCJD. Of course some people dismiss PI law as ambulance chasing, or conjure up images of Lionel Hutz and cheap daytime TV ads, but it can actually be a pretty interesting field. *"When you look up leading cases on Lawtel, you'll see a whole lot of Irwin Mitchell lawyers' names."* We're not talking about office stapler injuries either – IM trainees are thrown into big cases that are high on emotion, often short on time and packed with arguments of both a technical and legal nature. It's more likely for trainees to be helping on *"£8m claims, not £3,000 claims."* The related fields of clinical negligence and product liability can be even more emotive. The firm hit the headlines for representing Ann Marie Rogers in her landmark fight against Swindon Primary Care Trust for access to the breast cancer drug Herceptin. It also represented over 250 claimants against pharmaceutical company Merck regarding the alleged side effects of its drug Vioxx. Trainees have to be able to combine legal nous with tact, sympathy and people skills: *"One of the main skills is being able to deal with emotionally fragile people. Part of the process is to get them some counselling too. Clients give you disclosure and whilst they're not comfortable initially, you earn their trust and more comes out about their problems, meaning that the cases have to be flexible, ready to change when new information surfaces."*

In the neurotrauma seat, many clients have sustained catastrophic injuries, often from car accidents. Wear a seat belt, folks. Trainees enjoy a high level of involvement, seeing cases at various stages from the initial appraisals and meetings with experts through to trial and the ongoing monitoring of clients' conditions. Although *"liability isn't usually an issue because generally you know where the culpability lies, the costs of care might get debated in court."* A mass of information is presented to determine the costs of the client's care, and trainees have responsibility for preparing notes, conducting research and keeping clients informed. Though there are similarities between the subsets, each group in PI requires specific knowledge. For example, the industrial disease seat requires an understanding of asbestos poisoning. In this seat, trainees deal with mesothelioma sufferers with only a year or two left to live. Their illness may have emerged 30 or 40 years after their exposure to asbestos, and in cases such as these the onus is on trainees to wade through medical and insurance documents to establish who could be liable.

Summing up the clin neg seat, one source explained how IM lawyers *"argue with the NHS Litigation Authority, who defend their doctors' actions, saying that it was not them who caused a given injury."* This sort of litigation requires research that is carefully tailored to each individual case. One day it might mean looking into liver diseases or a failure to diagnose cancer, the next it could be a badly mended leg bone. Cases come in thick and fast and trainees enjoy learning how to juggle several at once. The public law seat covers wide-ranging topics from securing life-enhancing drugs for the terminally ill and making cases for keeping people on life support, to provisions for prisoners. Again, trainees are often the initial point of contact for clients and can manage some cases themselves, only turning to their supervisor for technical assistance. The role involves drafting letters to drugs companies, liaising with the families, assisting barristers and taking witness statements. At times, it can be a real challenge, especially when bad news must be given to a family. At other times the feel-good factor is amazing. Said one source: *"When we were successful it was one of the best parts of my job – telling the family was great."*

"One of the things that impressed me was that Irwin Mitchell doesn't just offer compensation, we offer so much more, like if a client suffers from brain injury we can offer assistance in education issues and help organise finances." The remit of the Court of Protection department is to deal with clients' ongoing support. When someone has been injured to the extent that they are unable to manage their own affairs, someone else has to take responsibility. Trainees get involved in making decisions about clients' access to their money, balancing their rights as individuals against the long-term management and proper use of any compensation award.

Given that much of the work is done under conditional-fee arrangements (ie 'no win, no fee') and because of the specific protocols that have to be followed, IM has instituted a so-called 'costs' seat for those in the PI stream. In this non-billing team, trainees learn about how cost disputes unfold, and how to manage costs and run files in the

Chambers UK rankings

Administrative & Public Law	Health & Safety
Banking & Finance	Intellectual Property
Civil Liberties	Personal Injury
Clinical Negligence	Police Law
Corporate/M&A	Private Client
Debt Recovery	Product Liability
Dispute Resolution	Professional Discipline
Employment	Real Estate
Environment	Real Estate Litigation
Family/Matrimonial	Restructuring/Insolvency
Fraud: Criminal	Tax
	Travel

most appropriate manner. Although some of those we spoke to thought that four months studying this topic was unnecessary, HR assured us that these skills were "*absolutely crucial; they are real fundamentals from a PI point of view and are absolutely vital.*"

Dead set on business?

IM's rich heritage in PI is hugely important, but it now sees commercial law as an equally essential part of its future. To this end, new partners have been coaxed into the firm and mergers have brought new clients. None of this has escaped the attention of trainees, who say that "*the difference is palpable; the new blood is really committed to driving business forward.*" We sensed the firm's commercial capabilities are in a state of flux at present, so it's worth checking with the firm which offices host certain departments. In general, however, a quick look at the firm's *Chambers UK* rankings will reveal just how broad the commercial side is, and it should also explain why we can't cover every practice area here. For anyone who equates business law with late hours, it's worth knowing that most people work 9am – 6.30pm and only occasionally stay longer.

The employment team has been busy advising clients with respect to new legislation and on matters emerging as a result of corporate acquisitions and restructurings. On the contentious side, there is no shortage of tribunals to attend. The business crime group is growing well in the current climate too and has been added to the Legal Services Commission's Specialist Fraud Panel. Despite the occasional monotony ("*you'll get boxes and boxes of paper served to you and you have to look for one piece of paper buried somewhere amongst it all*"), it is a very enjoyable seat in a department that "*varies immensely.*" Trainees aren't restricted to sorting through paperwork: they effectively get to know the background of the cases through taking witness statements, attending court with barristers and making prison visits. Other contentious options include commercial dispute resolution and IP. The property department has some "*fairly big clients,*" including names from finance, local government and education. Said one source: "*We act for high-street retailers and do a fair amount of land development, due diligence and sorting out acquisition agreements.*" There's also some residential work for a few choice clients, but the vast majority of cases are commercial. In addition to their regular fee earning, trainees help set up networking events and attend breakfast seminars and presentations to clients.

Un-macho

It's hard to describe a unified culture at IM because of the size differences between offices. What's more, "*the culture differs from department to department and people from corporate don't meet people from PI often.*" All the trainees we spoke to were cheery and rather down to earth, and one commented that IM was "*not a macho firm... there are more girls than guys.*" All the offices have social events, newsletters and favourite watering holes, and netball, rounders, football and cricket are played in most locations. To grease the wheels a little, the firm gives trainees a small social budget, but we did hear a few grumbles to the effect that IM is "*historically stingy.*" For example, when Leeds trainees went to visit their Sheffield counterparts, the firm wouldn't pay for their accommodation, whereas they did for the London crowd.

IM is certainly no slouch when it comes to pro bono; it spends over 5,000 hours a year on such matters, including the representation of victims of the 2006 London bombings. The main force behind this is Michael Napier, who was made an honorary QC in recognition of his pro bono work and is the Attorney General's envoy for pro bono. The firm operates a free public clinic in association with Citizen's Advice and is also involved in the Pro Uno scheme with Sheffield University Law School and Sheffield Volunteering. The aim is to provide a legal research facility for non-profit organisations in South Yorkshire.

Trainees were enthusiastic about the atmosphere in the office, saying that it wasn't like the firms some of their friends were at. "*You hear about some trainees being made to fetch the coffees the whole time, but here, the partners might fetch you one.*" Irrespective of department, trainees seemed happy with their responsibilities, observing that the firm's ethos is "*that as a trainee you are new to the firm and the job, and you are here to train.*" Like most firms, trainees have reviews in the middle and at the end of each seat. We also heard gossip of "*a secret rating system that trainees officially know nothing about, and if you're rated well then they'll find a place for you* [on qualification]." Fortunately the 2009 qualifiers must have ticked the right boxes since 21 out of 23 stayed on. The two that left didn't do so because there weren't enough jobs – in fact, six additional NQ positions were advertised externally.

And finally...

This is an unpretentious and hard-working place. The new scheme should be free from many of the problems of the old one, so whether you're business-minded or looking for the personal touch, it could be a good prospect.

Jones Day

The facts

Locations: London
Number of UK partners/solicitors: 47/199
Total number of trainees: 35
Seats: None
Alternative seats: None
Extras: Pro bono – Waterloo Pro Bono Clinic, LawWorks, FRU

Jones Day's training contract will suit our more confident readers as there's a real element of making your own luck here.

A training contract at the London office of this full-service international player is a unique proposition. The blurring of departmental boundaries allows trainees exposure to almost everything that's going on at the firm.

Jonesing for some independence?

Once a very independent-minded firm called Gouldens, which was known for its convivial after-hours culture, today Jones Day's London office is part of a fully fledged international beast with 2,400 lawyers in 32 offices around the world and stellar practice groups in most of them. To give just one example, the firm's IP practice (clients include Amazon.com, Halliburton Energy and Nokia) is ranked by *Chambers Global* in its top tier worldwide. Likewise, the global competition practice is placed alongside Linklaters and ahead of Clifford Chance, scoring juicy instructions from Apple on its iTunes business and Procter & Gamble on scores of matters. The London office's strongest suit is in corporate finance, but it has full-service capability and plays an important role in the firm's wider plans, particularly in Europe. Our sources told us: *"Most things we get involved in are international in some respect."*

While some may lament the demise of the Gouldens Way, most of our contacts had nothing but enthusiasm for the product of the 2005 merger between the Brits and the Cleveland-born legal Goliath. Current trainees had chosen the firm in order to work *"somewhere not magic circle but able to compete on that level,"* and the smaller intake (around 15-20 per year) was a key draw. Said one: *"You feel like you're making a difference, rather than just being the guy at the bottom of the food chain."* Sound good so far? Well, here's what will swing it for you, one way or the other – Jones Day does not operate a seat system. There are no rotations, there are no set departments, there are no rules. Okay, we're getting carried away. Of course there are rules, though one of the trainees confirms that *"this is a firm where, to a certain extent, anything goes."* As a Jones Day trainee, you are expected to *"go out and find your own work."* On your first day you are given your own (spacious) office with a piece of work on the desk and a floor plan of the building. It's then up to you to command and conquer.

Asking for it

Our interviewees lavished praise on the Jones Day system, saying: *"There are so many things about this training contract that you won't get anywhere else."* Including: *"the independence to carve your own path;" "flexibility;" "control;" "the sense of there not being much of a hierarchy"* and *"a more personalised experience."* In practical terms it means trainees can run very different types of work concurrently and *"always have things in departments you enjoy going on in the background."* They are able to see all matters through to completion and are able to *"pick and choose"* who they work for. Trainees were particularly proud of having their own office, with one stating: *"I was a bit apprehensive about getting lonely, but the fact is you sit with your door open and you can hear other people. We have a lot of banter and are always calling out to each other."*

There is certainly scope to tailor your own contract. One entrepreneurial spirit *"spent the first year getting experience of everything and then specialised in the second year."*

However, others admitted the system is not always plain sailing. *"With a lot of the work you end up doing it's luck of the draw; whether you happen to knock on the right door when something big comes in."* Trainees are not left out in the cold: *"You've got recourse to training supervisors and partners who you can discuss things with – there is a lot of supervision but it's there for you, rather than enforced on you."* A particularly frank trainee conceded that *"you have to be forceful to a pretty extreme extent to get feedback,"* but went on to praise the quality of feedback that eventually materialises. The firm takes appraisal meetings seriously, and deadlines are *"rigorously met."* At the same time, a new work-based learning scheme has been introduced which provides *"a much more structured approach to training."* Each trainee is also assigned a trainee-level mentor and partner-level mentor, so they should feel well supported. The trick to keeping on the straight and narrow, we hear, is to simply ask for guidance.

Madoff and madder

So how does the system work in practice? Simple: you steer yourself towards the types of cases and clients you most enjoy. Said a second-year: *"I've done a bit of employment, IP, property, tax, pensions, environmental."* More generally, our sources told us that, *"even if you haven't done substantive work in an area, you will usually have had exposure to it as the boundaries between departments are less firm here."* On the whole, trainees usually focus on three main areas: litigation, corporate and finance.

Banking litigation is a real strength at Jones Day. Its client list includes Standard Bank, JPMorgan and RBS, and it picked up quite a high-profile case in 2008 – advising Bear Stearns in a dispute with a Crédit Agricole subsidiary over the completion of a $600m CDO transaction. A CDO or collateralised debt obligation is a type of asset-backed synthetic security that no longer has quite the same credibility since the credit crunch. Trainees also found themselves embroiled in big fraud cases that involved *"sitting in on meetings with clients and witnesses, note-taking, court attendance"* and *"a lot of long hours."* The department has lately been enlisted to advise on matters arising out of the Bernard Madoff fraud. Other litigation has included the defence of cartel allegations against a major pharmaceutical company and representing XL Airways, which left 90,000 stranded passengers across 50 global destinations when it fell into administration in September 2008. Brilliant fact: some of these stranded passengers were flown home to the UK from Sharm-el-Sheikh by Iron Maiden frontman, rock legend and *bona fide* commercial airline pilot Bruce Dickinson. On smaller personal injury or personal debt claims trainees can be *"involved in everything, from witness statements and expert evidence to day-to-day contact with the client."*

Chambers UK rankings

Banking Litigation	Outsourcing
Capital Markets	Pensions
Corporate/M&A	Private Equity
Dispute Resolution	Real Estate
Employment	Real Estate Finance
Fraud: Civil	Restructuring/Insolvency
Intellectual Property	Tax

XL deals... and hours

This 'front of house' approach to trainees also applies on corporate deals, where *"you can be the major fee earner on a matter."* Trainees looking for corporate work can get involved in everything from listings to straightforward acquisitions or restructurings. One trainee indicated the range of deals available: *"There was an absolutely mammoth acquisition of immense complexity involving 11 jurisdictions, but at the same time an M&A in which we sold the company for just £1."* Our sense is that these straightforward, *"typically English"* transactions are becoming less prevalent as international deals take centre stage. Recent work includes Nomura International's $213m acquisition of a majority interest in SaudiPak Commercial Bank and Goldman Sachs International's acquisition of Russian Alcohol Group. While the hours are certainly demanding when working on corporate matters, the hard work does foster a collegiate atmosphere. *"Once, I worked a week and weekend, finishing between 1am and 3am, as the other side hadn't hired lawyers or done any work,"* said one trainee. *"It was hell, but at the end the client gave fantastic feedback to everyone, including the managing partner, about us being the best lawyers he'd ever had. Coming after a time when you've felt like crying, or killing yourself, it's so incredibly satisfying."*

It's much the same story on finance deals, where standard fare is now *"drafting loan amendment and restatement agreements,"* with an increasing emphasis on business restructuring and refinancing. XL Leisure, owner of the aforementioned XL Airways, enlisted the firm to advise on debts in excess of £200m in relation to restructuring negotiations with its primary creditors.

One thousand and one nights out

It may all sound peachy, but we've long believed you have to be the right kind of person to train happily here. While this year our interviewees were largely unwilling to be labelled as 'bolshy', one trainee joked: *"If we're bolshy, it's in a charming, charismatic way."* Sources were unflinching in their support of the Jones Day system. *"The general thrust is to be outwardly and upwardly mobile in terms* of speaking to people" and "*if you need supervision and comfort in terms of having someone there for you, sometimes that isn't there – you need to get things done yourself.*" In short, "*the emphasis is on you to prove yourself and make yourself stand out.*" The superlative confidence of Jones Day trainees comes across in the following statement: "*I may not know how to do something, but I'll ask to do it, and within a couple of weeks I will know.*"

If you blanch at any of the above, Jones Day isn't for you. If you're still unsure, however, the vacation scheme is an excellent way to make your mind up. Vac schemers are expected to approach associates and partners for work, and are given real tasks. Recalling their own scheme, a second-year told us: "*You're actually made to feel quite important and over a two-week period are exposed to many different levels of people.*"

The social side can be a blast. A "*somewhat dingy*" pub called The Harrow is packed out with Jones Dayers on a Friday, and there are always sporting opportunities available. The biggest event in the Jones Day social calendar is a little eccentricity left over from the Gouldens era – the Christmas pantomime. It seems few at the firm can resist a bit of thespian tomfoolery; "*everybody absolutely loves it!*" First-year trainees tread the boards to perform a show written and directed by second-years. Designed as a "*bonding activity*" for trainees, partners "*take a lot of stick*" as they are caricatured by their juniors. "*It's become a kudos thing – if they don't get into the panto, partners get upset, thinking they're not popular or funny enough!*" Last year's *Aladdin*-inspired production was held at the Bloomsbury Ballrooms and was oft-cited as the highlight of the year for the trainees involved. Another great event is the trainee trip to Washington, DC. Jones Day newbies from all over the world gather for a week, and we hear it can get "*pretty messy.*" There are plenty of training sessions and formal meet-and-greets, but people are also encouraged to let their hair down. London has a "*reputation for being the party office,*" and apparently New York, LA, Brussels and Milan are well aware of how to cut a rug too. One trainee told us: "*When you're in Washington you really feel like you've arrived... it's a good start before you crack on.*"

And cracking on is certainly something the firm is eager to do, global recession notwithstanding. Run on a "*no-debt basis,*" Jones Day is "*less dependent on the finance world*" and has not had to make redundancies in London. "*Rather than getting rid of people, they've reallocated them – for instance from M&A to restructuring,*" and with new offices recently opened in Dubai and Mexico, JD isn't holding back on plans to grow. Said one source: "*Our managing partner has said the intention is to expand, especially the London office.*" In 2009, 11 of the 19 qualifiers stayed on to do their bit.

And finally...

The non-rotational system may sink the wrong type of person, but if you're independent and confident it's going to provide one hell of a rewarding swim.

- **Be spontaneous:** Remember that it's important not to sound over rehearsed at interview. Sufficient practice can make perfect, but rote recitation of answers will bore both you and the panel.

top tip no. 17

K&L Gates

The facts

Location: London
Number of UK partners/solicitors: 59/64 + 3 US-qualified
Total number of trainees: 16
Seats: 4x6 months
Alternative seats: Occasional secondments
Extras: Pro bono – LawWorks, Battersea Legal Advice Centre; language training

US firm with Asian offices plus US firm with European offices equals international superfirm? K&L Gates certainly hopes so.

K&L Gates is a full-service US firm with a mid-sized office in London and an increasingly international outlook.

(K&L + NGJ) + PG&E = K&LG

Many of our interviewees admitted that they had not heard too much about K&L Gates before applying there. That's understandable because it has only been around in its present incarnation since 2007 when two giant American firms hooked up. The first was Preston Gates & Ellis (the 'Gates' in question is Bill's dad). It was a West Coast firm with a foothold in Asia. The second was Kirkpatrick & Lockhart, an East Coast firm with eyes on European expansion. To this end, it had already gobbled up sleepy London mid-sizer Nicholson Graham & Jones in 2005.

The superfirm that is K&L Gates has effectively been created by squishing firms together like wads of Blu-Tack. Extra bits continue to be added, and frankly this appealed to several of our interviewees. *"It was evident it was on the up because of the mergers,"* said one, referring to the strategy of aggressive expansion that has included takeovers and office openings in Texas, Chicago, Charlotte, Singapore, Frankfurt and Dubai in recent years. During 2008, K&L Gates' global revenue grew by 27%, reflecting the growth in its empire. *"Work flows from other offices,"* say trainees, and the merger has breathed a new lease of life into the London office, bringing US clients to its established teams.

The biggest departments in London are corporate and real estate. All trainees are likely to visit both, and most *"get these seats out of the way in the first year."* The process of seat allocation runs pretty well and the firm's approach is *"very accommodating."* Trainees can also experience banking and finance, dispute resolution, IP, employment, projects, construction, tax and pensions.

Quality time

On the K&L Gates joyride, the real estate department can be *"a bit of a baptism of fire."* Armed with *"a heck of a lot of your own files,"* a trainee in this department will deal with anything from licences to assign leasehold property and rent reviews to sales of freeholds. They work for several institutional investors, like pension funds, and deal largely with routine property management for these clients. *"Having files teaches you to be responsible and take ownership of your own work."* The firm has met with some success in the public sector; for example, new partner Neil Logan Green secured the mandate to act on Rushmoor Borough Council's £70m regeneration of Aldershot town centre. The department became quieter at the beginning of 2009, though most sources agreed that they were still kept fairly busy.

The corporate department is the best bet for international work, despite being categorised as a largely mid-market M&A kinda place. On its books are some well-known names (Continental tyres; Arena Leisure, which is the UK's largest horseracing operator), some less familiar names (Teledyne Technologies, which makes electronic components and communications products) and some of the most notable corporations of the decade (Halliburton; KBR, both deeply involved with the war in Iraq). On the upside there is a great deal of client contact. On the downside, extensive processes like verification can be "*tedious.*" Nevertheless, trainees found that even the more mundane tasks serve to increase their understanding of the deals and, more particularly, the listing process for public companies. The team has been doing a great deal of AIM work, though one trainee confessed to liking M&A more as there's "*hard-hitting negotiations for the client and more exposure to the deal.*" Late nights can happen here, though usually only when major deals push through to completion.

Another department with an international clientele is dispute resolution. "*You can really get into the underlying law in this seat, and there's a great cut and thrust to it.*" The team often works on high-value international arbitrations. Cricket fans will be pleased to hear that the firm represented the West Indies Cricket Board in relation to last year's Stanford Series in which the 'Stanford Superstars' were pitted against England in a 20/20 international. No allegations of cheating or dodgy umpiring decisions here: it was a contractual dispute between the principal sponsor, Digicel, and Stanford LLC. The firm also regularly represents hedge funds in disputes against banks in its specialised banking litigation team.

K&L Gates has 33 offices around the world, the latest additions being Singapore and Dubai (its first Middle Eastern outpost). Trainees looking to rack up frequent flyer miles by capitalising on the firm's international reach may be disappointed: although previous trainees have been sent on secondment to clients like Orange and Warner Music, they haven't yet had overseas seats. This has been a major disappointment for some, and all we can say right now is that foreign seats may arise in the future. To compensate, there's an annual trip to Washington, DC for new starters. Joining their peers from around the world, they are inducted into the firm by way of talks and meet-and-greets at which they are wined and dined at the firm's expense. "*It was exciting as we met trainees from Berlin, Hong Kong and Shanghai, and you felt like you were part of something global,*" recalled one source. More generally, trainees told us that the wider network clearly influences the London office's personality and day-to-day work, through not to the extent that it has destroyed its more intimate and British nature. "*The work is varied due to its internationality,*" say trainees, "*but the deal structures in the London office are small enough for you to spend quality time with a supervising partner.*" Praise was also heaped on the firm's management of trainees: "*It's a small intake and the supervisors tend to be able to deal with people – there's good man-management here.*" Though the firm has had to make deferrals and redundancies in the UK (including six associates), trainees were still confident that it is "*keen to retain as much trainee talent as it can.*" The firm had not finalised its September 2009 NQ retention by the time we went to press in the middle of that month. Check the website version of this report for the figures.

Chambers UK rankings

Capital Markets	Licensing
Construction	Parliamentary & Public Affairs
Corporate/M&A	Real Estate
Dispute Resolution	Real Estate Finance
Employment	Real Estate Litigation
Environment	Sports Law
Information Technology	Telecommunications
Intellectual Property	Travel

I love my brick!

Future trainees will arrive at the doors of shiny new offices currently being constructed on the site of Allen & Overy's old home next to St Paul's Cathedral. "*Probably just as well,*" said one source; "*our current offices are a bit dated.*" Fortunately, everyone seemed pleased with the atmosphere inside, though with the firm growing at warp speed technology can sometimes lag behind. "*You get an embarrassing BlackBerry; it's a dinosaur... a brick!*" That said, the type of person who comes to K&L Gates probably isn't too concerned with looking like the coolest trainee in the City. The firm looks for "*well-rounded individuals, both academically and socially,*" and "*someone who has the ability to not take themselves too seriously.*" Said one source: "*We all gel as a group and bring something slightly different to the firm.*" A relatively relaxed atmosphere in the office means that the usual stereotype of US firms demanding long hours doesn't apply. As one interviewee saw it: "*Trainees are willing to share the burden, and I've only had about four late nights here in my two years.*"

The firm's social scene is in good shape. Organised fun has included leisurely lunches in the summer and a day out with strawberries and champagne on the London Eye. There was also a "*scaled down*" but "*still fun*" Christmas party in the office's main conference rooms. Recent intakes of trainees have ventured beyond the traditional watering hole (The Vintry) into other more stylish bars such as Dizzy's, Revolution and Abacus: "*Birthdays are always quite special, with most of us going out for a drink or a meal.*"

And finally...

Despite its big US merger, we get the feeling that in this office there's enough that remains unchanged from its days as a quintessentially English firm. For now at least.

Latham & Watkins LLP

The facts

Locations: London
Number of UK partners/solicitors: 47/100
Total number of trainees: 24
Seats: 4x6 months
Alternative seats: Overseas seats
Extras: Pro Bono – Redress Trust

Latham NQs earn a massive £96,970 and as one source readily admitted of the trainee group, *"people are lying if they say it's not something they considered even a little bit."*

Widely perceived as a bellwether for the US legal profession, Latham & Watkins built phenomenal global success on ballooning private equity/leveraged buyout work, but received a sharp shock as those markets collapsed.

Barnstorming and beguiling

Latham & Watkins is big. No. Huge. Founded in 1934 in Depression-era Los Angeles, in recession-era 2009 it has 28 offices worldwide staffed by over 2,000 lawyers. This global giant is praised to the heavens by virtually every directory Chambers and Partners publishes. Its strategy over the past decade has centred on private equity, leveraged buyouts and other high-value transactional practices, and it has enjoyed stellar success. Global revenue in 2003 was $1bn, and only five years later it became the first firm to break the $2bn barrier.

California is still home to the majority of Latham's US attorneys and its influence is also regularly cited as the key to understanding the firm's relentlessly laid-back, democratic and egalitarian culture. As one associate told our sister publication *Chambers Client Report* in late 2008: "*In hiring, there's a huge emphasis on asking, 'Is this person culturally qualified to be here?'*" Maintaining this easy-going persona while soaring high on the legal thermals of the past two decades has made Latham the BigLaw pin-up of the nineties/naughties boom. It is barnstorming and beguiling in equal measure.

The first thermal was globalisation: Latham subscribed vigorously to the growing belief that firms working across as many markets as possible would have the greatest allure for clients in an ever-shrinking world. Between 1990 and 2008, it opened in numerous of international locations (ten in Europe, four in Asia and – most recently – three at once in the Middle East). Gaining a reputation in legal markets across the globe for providing local law at the highest standard, Latham promulgated a 'one firm' ethos: the idea that, though founded in Los Angeles, it has no headquarters. Thus, there are no 'dominant' or 'satellite' offices – each is as important as the other.

The second thermal was hot practice areas: as private equity and leveraged buyout work ballooned, with big-ticket, billion-dollar financial and corporate M&A deals proliferating, Latham's transactional groups went into overdrive. The firm acted for major financial institutions, hedge funds and private equity firms like Bank of America, Bear Stearns, Citi, Credit Suisse, Deutsche Bank, Goldman Sachs, Merrill Lynch, JPMorgan, Morgan Stanley and many, many more.

Ploughing furrow-ward

In London, the US firms are still "*a corner of the legal market many people don't imagine is even there.*" Latham & Watkins has positioned itself well here in the UK, so even with the difficult market conditions this could be the year for it to break though into the recruitment mainstream. The London office was opened in 1996, beginning as a finance boutique and growing to around 150 lawyers offering a full commercial service. Rather than merely taking on the UK aspects of deals sourced in the USA, the London lawyers provide a hub for the firm's European and Middle Eastern work (the latter being a major thrust right now). "*Other than major policy decisions,*" said interviewees, "*we plough our own furrow.*" Latham aims to further strengthen its UK arm, and ultimately any plans for London's future may hinge around its training programme. It began in 2006 with just two trainees, but the intake in 2009 was 15 strong and Latham intends to consistently recruit around 14 per year from now on. The expansion is the culmination of several years of planning and shows a determination to grow the office headcount organically.

Of course, that determination will be challenged in the current market. Like any firm with prominent transactional practices, Latham was exposed to the liquidity crisis and has definitely felt the pinch. Its worldwide profitability took a big hit and revenue dipped by a few percentage points. What resulted was a whole bunch of layoffs. Some 440 employees went worldwide: that's 12% of the associates and 10% of the paralegals and support staff, albeit with a market-topping severance package in the USA. The London office has also been hit by the recession. Only 15 of those laid off were in the UK, but the office's revenue dropped 12.8% and it had to make money-saving cutbacks. All this said, the bullish trainees we spoke to were convinced that the firm was "*bouncing back.*" Given the quality of the London client list (Diageo, Nike, Deutsche Bank and ABN AMRO, among others), you can understand their confidence.

Shopping spree

In the four-seat training scheme, as well as a mandatory contentious seat, trainees do stints in the finance and corporate departments. It's far from restrictive as the wide array of subgroups within each department gives trainees a varied contract. Finance seats encompass banking, restructuring, structured finance or project finance, while corporate includes general M&A and capital markets, but also tax and outsourcing/IT. Contentious options include commercial dispute resolution, employment, IP and competition. Referring to the amount of choice on offer, one trainee said: "*It's like saying you're only allowed to shop in London.*"

Given the general slowdown in finance instructions, we found trainees in the banking and structured finance subgroups were "*essentially doing a lot of restructuring work.*" The teams (especially the banking group) still handle some impressive deals, such as advising on the €8bn financing for Italian power company Enel to bring its stake in Spanish utility company Endesa up to 92%, and representing Morgan Stanley in supplying First Reserve Corporation with $1.25bn in secured facilities to acquire a Canada-based helicopter supplier. Lately, it's been the project finance group that's really been carrying the flag and picking up huge instructions. For example, lawyers represented Qatar Gas Transport and Nakilat on a $6.8bn debt programme to pay for a fleet of LNG vessels – the largest ship financing ever conducted – and acted for Ras Girtas Power Company in a $3.25bn debt financing for the development of the largest cogeneration plant in Qatar.

Chambers UK rankings

Banking & Finance	Intellectual Property
Banking Litigation	Investment Funds
Capital Markets	Outsourcing
Competition/European Law	Private Equity
Corporate/M&A	Projects, Energy & Natural Resources
Dispute Resolution	Public International Law
Employment	Restructuring/Insolvency
Information Technology	Tax

Finance may have been the initial focus of the London office, but these days "*the corporate department is probably the biggest.*" Corporate/M&A seats encompass "*a mixture of private equity, sovereign wealth funds, traditional transactions and anything else.*" Our sources reported involvement with "*important*" due diligence on major transactions and also told us: "*There's room in smaller transactions to almost be the wingman of a senior or junior associate.*" Because of the cross-border nature of the deals, trainees are constantly making international calls to seek opinions on non-English law documents. Meanwhile, frequent attendance at meetings means that clients "*stop seeming like such frightening, distant figures.*" Lately clients have included antivirus software king Symantec (in its $695m purchase of web security provider MessageLabs) as well as Deutsche Bank, Fortis Bank, the sovereign wealth fund Qatar Investment Authority and Yahoo!. Also under the corporate umbrella is a crack outsourcing/IT team that is top-ranked by *Chambers UK*. Attracting names like EMI Music and HBOS, it recently acted for BSkyB in its agreement with IBM to deliver new telephony, internet and cable TV services through digital terrestrial television.

Report drafting and the inevitable court bundling are a feature of trainee life in the litigation department, but it's good to hear that "*if they've got a court hearing they'll tend to try to get you down there if you've been involved.*" Commercial litigation gives recruits a chance to "*dig into the law,*" researching and producing their own memos. IP seats usually bring the opportunity to go along to the patent court at the Royal Courts of Justice. The public international law (PIL) team gets some of the firm's most glamorous instructions. It represents the governments of Ukraine, Malaysia, Croatia, Azerbaijan and Barbados before the English courts, The Hague, the ICSID, and the UN Commission on the Limits of the Continental Shelf. If you are interested in PIL then be aware that this is one of the few firms where you can become involved in this kind of work.

Several sources were keen to let us know that Latham is flexible about creating new overseas opportunities, recently facilitating a trainee's request to work in another of its European offices.

Gentle giants

The firm's flexibility and "*willingness to rethink existing policies*" drew praise from our interviewees. "*I think they make a big point about people being individuals and not having formalities around you,*" said one. "*Often there's no 'Latham Way' of doing document production or engaging with clients.*" We heard a lot about the firm's flexibility on the training scheme, but can it last, given the rapid expansion of the trainee intake? Time will tell. While sources admitted there are still some junior associates who aren't sure how to use trainees, it is clear that the scheme is becoming an established part of the fee-earning structure of the office. Trainees perceive a willingness on the part of the firm to listen to them; they believe Latham "*wants us to be involved in the process of making the training programme a success and feeding back any concerns or comments we have.*" Quarterly meetings with the trainee committee are "*a two-way process*" and one or two of our sources spoke about "*not having to go through all the political crap of greasing up the recruitment person or trainee co-ordinator.*" More importantly, the meetings are effective at bringing about improvements. "*When you come to a seat you don't always know who the important people are, all the subsets, how to book holidays, when monthly meetings are,*" explained a source. "*Once we raised that point they produced a beginner's guide to each department and week-long inductions.*"

Sources were confident "*you can go to anyone, no matter how senior*" to ask a question, and there was a lot of talk about the "*non-hierarchical*" atmosphere in the office. To an extent, trainees believe this openness is part of a "*laid-back American cultural thing,*" but Latham doesn't fit every US stereotype. For example, while late nights can and do occur, the "*myth*" of trainees "*chained to BlackBerrys at the weekend*" is "*a total fallacy.*" "*I don't think we're working longer hours than people at magic circle firms,*" protested one interviewee, and while there is a "*loose target*" of 1,200 billable hours per year, it's "*purely for departments to make sure trainees are being utilised.*" One stereotype that does fit, however, is a big salary. Latham NQs earn a massive £96,970 (only Bingham pays more in London) and as one source readily admitted of the trainee group, "*people are lying if they say it's not something they considered even a little bit.*" Trainees speculate that Latham's lack of a hard-charging ethos could be because "*it's not a New York firm – it's based out of LA and that certainly comes through.*" The atmosphere can and does differ by department: corporate and finance, for example, "*exude more of a Latham personality than litigation, which is more conservative and London-like.*"

Don't underestimate the importance recruiters place on personality. One source insisted that "*the thing that binds the trainee group together is our friendliness.*" Another added (slightly more bluntly): "*I've never met anyone at Latham who's a complete dick.*" Vac schemers beware: trainees will be asked for their impressions of you, but don't try buttering them up – they see themselves as "*a very perceptive bunch.*" In general, the firm wants to find trainees with strong academic backgrounds, and there's an important new element to the interview process in the shape of a half-hour chat in which applicants are able to demonstrate their commercial awareness.

The firm's "*collegiality*" comes across in a healthy social life. Latham arranges a few annual parties, and our interviewees had enjoyed a trip to the USA to join American summer associates for a few days of entertainment and bonding. Latham is not "*your typical law firm extension of Oxbridge, where you live your whole life through the firm;*" informal, ad hoc socialising is more common. Someone organised a ski trip last year, and teams will often go out for Friday drinks. For those with gentler tastes and sweeter teeth, "*some of the people in litigation have started up Cake Fridays.*" "*I think it's excellent,*" beamed a happy Battenberg aficionado.

And finally...

Having been relatively slow off the mark in setting up a training scheme, Latham seems to have bought into the idea wholeheartedly. Experience suggests it will do a fine job. A healthy seven of 2009's nine qualifiers took up jobs with the firm.

Lawrence Graham LLP (LG)

The facts

Location: London
Number of UK partners/solicitors: 73/105
Total number of trainees: 36
Seats: 4x6 months
Alternative seats: Occasional overseas seats and secondments

From stylish offices overlooking the Thames, this firm has one eye on the City and the other on international business.

This London firm remains strong in its traditional stomping ground of real estate and is pushing hard in corporate, particularly in relation to mid-market deals and overseas business from India and China.

Jai Ho!

Having rebranded itself as LG two years ago, the firm's new motto is 'Lawyers: Just different.' Nuff said? Not quite, according to some trainees who consider the similarity with that of a certain South Korean electronics giant to be both a) too close for comfort and b) a well-worn inside joke. We say, forget the branding: looking at the firm's business is a much more productive exercise. Once a snoozy property-led firm occupying a shabby building on The Strand near the Royal Courts of Justice, LG's makeover highlighted its changing direction. Its international expansion is worth a mention straight away. Having run a Monaco office for high-end private clients for a while, LG launched in Dubai in 2008 to deal with both wealthy individuals and construction work. Clearly it understands the importance of following the money (albeit at a leisurely pace), as it opened in Moscow in 2009. Many Russian clients come from the energy sector. Furthermore, the firm has developed ties to the dynamic markets of China and India, particularly with blue-chip companies like Patni Computer Systems and Xcite Energy. What better evidence could we have of the firm's achievements overseas than trainee reports of "*international work from India in corporate and dealings with Azerbaijan in litigation.*" As for overseas seats, there's nothing formal, although a couple of trainees have previously visited the Dubai office.

The firm tells us it is trying to be "*a little more nimble on [its] feet*" these days. The corporate department, which had doubled in size in three years, took the biggest hit in the recession, despite its growing international business. The property department was also hit but seems to have been helped along by a number of institutional clients as well as public sector and social housing organisations. And besides, it's not as if LG has all its eggs in these two baskets: groups such as tax and dispute resolution (especially in relation to the banking sector) have benefited from earlier investment.

AIM High

All LG trainees must take seats in dispute resolution, corporate and the large real estate department. They have several other options for their fourth seat, like private client, insolvency, employment, competition and IP. Some bemoaned the fact that they had three compulsory seats and believed two would be enough. Some also thought the allotment of seats was a bit arbitrary and didn't take everyone's preferences into account: "*I got my second choice which was weird as another trainee got* [my first choice] *without even having stated a preference.*" Seat selection grumbles aside, few questioned the quality of training they received and one source spoke positively about the challenges involved in some deals: "*It was a bit stressful at times… there were a lot of moving parts!*"

One jewel in the firm's crown is its AIM practice, and this is reflected in a solid *Chambers UK* ranking. With 56 clients in the sector, LG advises more AIM-listed companies than any other firm in the country. It assisted oil services business Thalassa Energy on its admission to AIM and Landsbanki Securities in connection with Aqua Resources Fund's admission to trading on the London Stock Exchange. Investment in an India practice group (based in London) is now reaping rewards in the form of regular deals, such as the placing and admission to AIM of Indus Gas. This deal was the eighth AIM listing of an Indian-focused company by LG. Indus is by no means the only energy business for which LG acts. It helped another Indian-focused company, Hardy Oil and Gas, with its move from AIM to the London Stock Exchange, as well as Clipper Windpower, a developer of international wind energy projects, on a series of deals raising over $200m. The AIM market has suffered in the recession and so the international component of the corporate department is increasingly vital. LG must be pleased that it has a foothold in one of the most hotly tipped parts of the world economy.

Trainees described the corporate seat as "*quite team-focused and fast-moving,*" a few adding that "*the hours can be a bit longer too.*" Undoubtedly some people's experiences suffered in the quiet market. "*It was a steep learning curve,*" said one, "*I had a decent amount of responsibility, though I noticed some trainees weren't as busy and a couple of times I was caught twiddling my thumbs.*" For others the main disappointment was that they'd originally been told the firm's emphasis was on property and they then learned that corporate was being pushed more aggressively. Generally we sensed that people thought "*the partners are great,*" even if "*the shape of the corporate department is weird as there are more partners than assistants.*"

Social healing

Real estate has long been LG's bread and butter, and this department remains an attractive option for trainees. The seat offers more independence than most: "*You're in charge of files and hence there was more of an appeal for me,*" said one. Split between two floors, the department acts for major clients like Zurich Assurance and Sainsbury's. It recently advised development and investment company Helical Bar on the financing of its Morgan Estate in Cardiff. It also helped the Universities Superannuation Scheme purchase a £605m 50% share in an investment property joint venture with Tesco. The market slump could have hit LG even harder than it did, but a solid chunk of the team is focused on social housing and public sector clients. One source praised the atmosphere here, telling us: "*Property is the friendliest place to work – everyone from the partners to support staff are great.*"

Real estate litigation was a favourite for some. Again, trainees are able to manage their own files, and lately people have experienced quite deep immersion into insolvency scenarios. Instructions coming into this team have certainly softened the impact of the property slump. For example, lawyers advised Whitbread Group on its tenant liability arising out of the sale of over 300 pubs as a result of the owner's insolvency.

Chambers UK rankings

Advertising & Marketing	Local Government
Capital Markets	Media & Entertainment
Charities	Pensions
Construction	Planning
Corporate/M&A	Private Client
Dispute Resolution	Public Procurement
Employment	Real Estate
Environment	Real Estate Finance
Fraud: Civil	Real Estate Litigation
Insurance	Restructuring/Insolvency
Investment Funds	Social Housing

Lifestyles of the rich and the famous

Just because corporate and real estate rule the roost doesn't mean that trainees see little else. A variety of other commercial departments are available, for example LG has been building up its banking litigation team and recruited three new partners. Across the board LG gets some pretty interesting litigation instructions; for example it recently helped InBev successfully challenge excise duty assessments at the VAT and Duties Tribunal. Lawyers have also been representing Glenn Nobes, a former consultant to the owner of the largest onshore oil and gas field in Azerbaijan, in a £35m claim against the purchaser of the company following its forced sale by an international bank. The firm deals with interesting matters like civil fraud, and one of its juiciest cases was for the government of Brazil and the City of São Paulo. The case alleged fraud on the part of the former mayor of the city and rested on a claim that vast sums were embezzled from public works contracts through elaborate structures involving offshore havens. The seat can certainly be a buzz for trainees: "*I got quite a lot of involvement and it was good from the point of view of getting an interesting perspective on things.*"

In the private client realm, LG represents some of the super-rich and a number of old and illustrious families, including those of the Earl of Derby and the Dowager Marchioness of Bath. Lawyers also advise the trustees of the estate of Diana, Princess of Wales. Trainees were impressed with the firm's standing in this field (it is ranked in Band 2 in *Chambers UK*) and considered this a department with pulling power. "*You deal with enormously rich people and so you need to be a smooth operator to handle them,*" advised one source.

LG is renowned for its reinsurance work, which trainees find to be "*very complicated and involving quite a bit of court time, bundling and witness statements.*" The construction team is highly successful, too, and works for major clients like LaSalle Investment Management, National Farmers Union Mutual Assurance and Canada Life. Not everyone loves the work here; some find it involves "*a lot of admin and chasing people up.*" The "*very technical seat*" in the pensions team, meanwhile, involves "*nice clients*" and requires trainees to "*really use their brains.*" Employment – a boom area right now – is hugely popular. And finally, LG also earns a very creditable *Chambers UK* ranking in advertising law, an area in which it recently advised a leading US direct sales company in relation to its UK business and plans to launch in Germany.

Biblical proportions

A curious aspect of the firm's office building overlooking the Thames at More London is that it manages to flood once a year. Or at least it has for the past two, and the firm has only been in situ for two years. Most sources were quick to lay blame for the flood and subsequent power outage on adjoining buildings, though we daren't say if they were casting a knowing eye at either neighbour Norton Rose or Boris Johnson, whose London Assembly occupies City Hall next door. Trainees love the offices and describe them as "*brilliant, light, airy and very commodious.*" A river's width away from the hustle and bustle of the City proper, there are "*splendid views in the summertime*" and the regular, free entertainment laid on at The Scoop just in front of the building is a bonus. Jamie Oliver's old haunt, Borough Market, is a top spot for lunch if you want to avoid the tourist hordes.

The people we spoke to included Brits and non-Brits and most had come from Oxbridge or leading redbrick universities. It came as no surprise to learn that "*you have to be sociable with good people skills; they don't just want you to be at your desk squirrelling away.*" To perfect natural-born talents, "*the firm runs courses on how to talk to clients... You don't have to be excitable, but you do have to enjoy talking to people and working in teams.*" In summary, one source described LG trainees as "*certainly not jocks, not really nerds either... kinda average.*"

When we asked how LG could improve the training experience, we heard two reasonably clear messages – one call for more inter-departmental understanding and another for greater clarity over how trainees should manage their own careers. "*It's not very clear as to when you should voice your opinion,*" worried one source. This was not news to us – the firm has previously explained its view that trainees need to take responsibility for managing their own working relationships and career progression. Not everyone thought this an easy task and there was some level of discussion about how strongly "*a trainee should be able to emphasise what seat they want to be in when they have an appraisal.*"

Some of the partners, particularly in corporate, seem to expect trainees to "*just knuckle down and get work done*" but are nevertheless quite a genial bunch save for "*one partner who is quite mean.*" Speaking of the firm as a whole, interviewees insisted: "*This is not a stuffy environment: people are professional but very friendly as well.*" One source stressed how "*you can approach anyone with a question. Sometimes you have to be tactical, though I've never had anyone tell me to come back later.*"

Neither the transactional or contentious real estate groups offered NQ positions in 2009. As in past years, trainees spoke with disappointment about the "*pretty opaque process*" involved in landing an NQ position. "*There's no official list* [of jobs] *and we need to learn the lie of the land for ourselves.*" Worryingly, "*some information doesn't get to the whole group.*" The final score was 12 jobs for 21 qualifiers. In 2009 the firm held off recruiting new starters for 2011 and deferred ten of the trainees due to arrive in 2009 and ten due in 2010, paying them each £5,000 to delay. LG also made 46 redundancies, 15 of them lawyers. One source echoed the views of others when they said: "*The firm has managed redundancies quite well, we were all notified and the partners were clearly choked about it. We have had to cut back on certain things and we now manage the resources we have more concertedly.*" All of this ties in with the 11% drop in revenue for 2008/09, and the consequent 35% drop in partner profits.

In addition to sporting opportunities (netball, football, rugby, cricket), social events include quiz nights, summer balls and lively Christmas parties featuring "*drunkenness and bad dancing.*" At last year's there was a bit of a ruckus, though we're assured it involved no lawyers. Networking opportunities crop up regularly and "*the firm is keen for you to get involved in client events. Some people even got to attend the Lloyds Rugby Football Sevens Tournament in Richmond.*"

And finally...

It's difficult to say precisely where this firm's ambitions lie right now. As one cryptic source stated: "*The game plan is quite secretive.*" Nevertheless, "*there's still plenty of ambition here, though the recession has made it clear that no law firm is invincible.*"

Lester Aldridge LLP

The facts

Location: Bournemouth, Southampton, London

Number of UK partners/solicitors: 39/27

Total number of trainees: 11

Seats: 4x6 months

Alternative seats: Occasional secondments

> "*I hate to sound complacent, but I don't think the recession has affected us as much as others... we are looking to grow all areas and have a particular desire to increase our presence in London,*"
>
> Michael Giddins, Managing Partner

Headquartered a stone's throw away from Bournemouth beach, dominant South Coast firm Lester Aldridge has a spread of offices and broad expertise.

The ninjas of LA

The first half of this past decade was characterised by a flurry of activity for this southern firm. A Southampton office was opened in 2001, and in 2004 two more joined the clan, one in Milton Keynes and another in London following a merger with property specialists from Park Nelson. This brought the total to five as Lester Aldridge also has a base just outside Bournemouth in Hurn. But turbulent times were to come. While it bedded in well in the capital, in MK it didn't settle down so comfortably and the office was soon closed. A restructuring followed, which in turn led to about a dozen redundancies. The most recent development has been the "*rejigging*" of the Hurn office. The fast-track debt recovery and residential conveyancing and remortgaging lawyers based there have been relocated to the Bournemouth HQ, centring all the legal activities in the three larger offices. Hurn is now "*the hub of the admin and support services.*"

With all this reshuffling behind it, Lester Aldridge is keen to press on, and trainees are confident that the firm "*is riding out the recession*" and will concentrate on "*developing all three offices,*" with a particular focus on London. Managing partner Michael Giddins agrees: "*I hate to sound complacent, but I don't think the recession has affected us as much as others. The fat was cut out three years ago when we had our restructuring exercise. We are now looking to grow all areas of our practice and have a particular desire to increase our presence in London.*"

All three of the main offices take trainees, and while the bulk of the seats are to be found in Bournemouth, recruits must be prepared for a slightly nomadic existence. "*The mechanics of moving are easy*" though. One source described the support staff as being "*just like ninjas. They pop up from nowhere and move your computer and everything.*" As long as you go in with an open mind it isn't too much of a culture shock. "*Just treat it like starting a new job,*" interviewees advised. Wherever they find themselves located, the similarities in decor and the e-mails that fly back and forth leave trainees in no doubt that they are in an LA office, but they did detect some cultural differences. "*It really depends on whether you are open-plan or in offices,*" explained one. Interestingly, thoughts on the various merits and pitfalls of the two layouts differed. Some felt that the open-plan Bournemouth office not only allowed trainees "*to see how other solicitors work*" but ensured "*more of a bond,*" with the "*interaction amongst the teams greasing the social wheels.*" These people dreaded getting "*stuck in a room alone on a research task.*" Others felt that the Bournemouth office was "*less relaxed and a lot quieter*" due to people being "*careful about how loud they are talking;*" they championed the individual office set-up of Southampton, where "*it is not an issue for me to shout through the* [glass] *wall to my boss who sits in the next office.*" A seat in London sometimes leaves trainees "*feeling a bit out on a limb*" as there is often only one trainee there at a time. Nevertheless, its small size ensures a laid-back atmosphere and the whole office "*lunches out together regularly.*"

Dodge the dormice

A glance down the firm's rankings in *Chambers UK* shows that LA is an impressive all-rounder. It gains a top-tier spot for debt recovery in the South, and performs well in its region for dispute resolution, employment, family, charities law, partnership law, construction and planning. It's unlikely you will avoid a stint in property. This is no bad thing as recruits are thrown in from the off and "*given absolutely loads to do*" – lease renewals, agreement drafting and post-completion formalities. The London property team, which is effectively a niche retail sector practice, has clients such as 3UK and Big Yellow, while on the South Coast, Abbey and Marine Developments instruct the department. Trainees are given "*client contact from day one*" and often are left to manage their own files under supervision. Time with the planning and environment group can throw up some "*odd, interesting research topics,*" such as the "*protection of dormouse homes in the demolition of derelict buildings on waste land.*"

LA is renowned for its respect for work-life balance – most people leave the office between 5.30pm and 6pm – but the fast-paced debt recovery team reportedly "*work a lot, lot longer.*" Among the clients are waste management companies, local authorities, building suppliers, utilities and publishers. Trainees get files from the off, "*and there is not much time to ask your supervisor for help.*" "*I had my most responsibility here,*" noted one source. There are plenty of hearings to prepare for and attend, and trainees get used to "*dealing with incoming calls from debtors every few minutes.*" Dispute resolution provides alternative contentious experience, and the range of work – professional negligence, health and safety, IP disputes, director disputes and insolvency – means it is likely you will find something to tickle your fancy. A growing international capability, enhanced by the firm's membership of the MSI global alliance, has resulted in work from jurisdictions ranging from America to South Korea. When it comes to advocacy, trainees agree that "*generally if you want to go and gain experience at the local courts and do hearings then they are all for it.*"

Adopt the lifestyle

Away from the commercial side of the practice, trainees can gain experience in the family and private client teams. The *Chambers UK*-ranked family team, headed up by the indomitable Jane Porter, carries out the usual high net worth ancillary relief and contact cases. Associate Natalie Gamble adds an unusual element with her fertility advice for clients after donor conception and surrogacy. "*Given the fact that the surrogate is often already pregnant there is quite a strict time pressure,*" one trainee pointed out. This is in stark contrast to work in the respected tax, trust and wills team where "*matters progress very slowly over months or even years.*"

In a firm that takes pains to promote a pleasant atmosphere, it came as no surprise to hear that trainees advised future recruits to "*show you are human*" during the application process. "*No one is expecting you to be a law-making machine. Everyone has a family outside work and you hear about it.*" That said, no one is avoiding hard work and trainees have a chargeable hours target, albeit a "*very low*" one. All our sources agreed that "*the hours are brilliant,*" and while "*on paper the salary may look terrible*" (£17,250 for a non-London first seater, £33,000-34,000 for an NQ) trainees were in no doubt that the trade-off was worth it. When we heard about some of the things LA lawyers get up to out of the office we were quickly convinced too: parties at partners' houses complete with barbecues, bucking broncos and barn dancing; cycle rides in the New Forest; sponsored walks up Ben Nevis; sailing in Bournemouth Bay; and eating and drinking at various establishments. The Cricketers is a Southampton favourite while Bournemouth staff frequent Downes Wine Bar. The Christmas party and the AGM are the only occasions when the whole firm gets together. Trainees commented that they would appreciate a few more firm-wide shindigs, but that was as far as any grumbles went. In 2009 six out of eight qualifiers stayed on.

Chambers UK rankings

Banking Litigation	Family/Matrimonial
Charities	Healthcare
Consumer Finance	Partnership
Debt Recovery	Planning
Dispute Resolution	Real Estate
Employment	Real Estate Litigation

And finally...

"*I don't really think there is anyone that wouldn't fit in, to be honest,*" said one trainee. We agree – unless, of course, you have a particular aversion to sun, sea, sand and quality legal work.

Lewis Silkin LLP

The facts

Location: London, Oxford

Number of UK partners/solicitors: 51/86

Total number of trainees: 10

Seats: 6x4 months

Alternative seats: Secondments

This open-minded and respectful firm was a worthy and highly placed entrant to the *Sunday Times'* list of the Best Companies to Work For in 2009.

Peoplescape, Mediascape, Landscape. Will you want to make a Great Escape from this characterful firm or settle in for the rest of your career?

Less quirky, more modern worky

The Lewis Silkin trainees we spoke to were keen to hammer a stake through the heart of the idea that this is an "*oddball, quirky, lefty place.*" Though it was historically closely linked to the Labour Party, has cool clients, dressed-down lawyers and modern attitudes, they vigorously assert that LS's defining trait is not its attention to Core Values, its youthful Podcasting managing partner or meticulously planned social life (a *Eurovision* party had trainees practising for months) but rather the work on offer. When pressed on cultural matters, our sources usually drew us back to the subject of work, maintaining that the firm's philosophy was that it ought to be as enjoyable as play.

First, name checks for key individuals who have shaped the firm. Mr Lewis Silkin, post-WWII minister for planning, housing, New Towns and the like. His legacy is a renowned social housing and regeneration practice. In the 1970s Roger Alexander developed a focus on the advertising industry. LS is now top-ranked for advertising and marketing law and represents a stable of top agencies. Human dynamo John Fraser, former senior partner and government minister responsible for consumer protection legislation in the 1970s: he developed some of the firm's most productive client relationships, including Mohammed Al Fayed and several housing associations. Michael Burd and James Davies, two of the UK's hottest employment lawyers and co-heads of the firm's largest department. The firm is top-ranked for employment. Finally, current managing partner Ian Jeffrey, a Silkinite man and boy, and generator of considerable goodwill among staff.

These lawyers, and those who've worked with them over the years, have allowed LS to develop a reputation for being a both a breeding ground for experts and a pretty cool place to work. The firm touts itself as 'a rather more human law firm' and to this end its employees "*try hard not to be stuffy or pompous,*" preferring instead a straight-talking, plain English approach to ensure that when clients come to the Chancery Lane HQ they feel at ease. In the past five years, profitability has grown year on year: between 2005 and 2008 it soared 104% to £330,000 per partner, largely thanks to media and employment work. Recent high-profile cases have included the representation of Mohammed Al Fayed in the inquest into the death of Diana, Princess of Wales and his son Dodi, and the advertising dispute between O2 and Hutchison 3G.

We fit

Lewis Silkin is "*certainly not a chalk-striped suit place,*" but don't let the loafers and unbuttoned collars deceive you. For all that trainees were friendly, polite and straightforward with us, they sounded ambitious. While diverse of character, they were united by a good deal of confidence. Judging from some of their previous career experiences, there isn't really a predominant type. Here you'll find ex-violinists and music producers alongside people who've worked as paralegals and those for whom LS represents a first career step. "*There's a Lewis Silkin person, not a Lewis Silkin type. It's not very cookie cutter,*" said recruitment partner Cliff Fluet. Trainees agreed that the firm "*definitely prefers individuals with personality. It doesn't want people who will sit meekly.*"

The structure of the training contract has changed to a six by four-month rotation allowing trainees to try their hand at each of the five departments (Peoplescape, Mediascape, Landscape, Corporate and Dispute Resolution) and then "*repeat the one that they particularly liked.*" Although trainees sit with a partner and "*to some degree learn by osmosis,*" they must be "*a resource for the whole department,*" actively seeking out work from whoever is at full capacity. One told us: "*After two months in media, brands and technology I'd worked for everyone.*" The system leads to "*plenty of challenging work. Initially you're borderline terrified, but when you get something checked and its mostly right, you feel like you've achieved.*" Even those close to the start of the contract reported high levels of responsibility and client contact.

The available seats include commercial litigation, commercial property, media brands and technology, employment, corporate, property, housing and construction. So long as partners are satisfied that it will be enriching for the trainee, they sometimes accede to clients' requests for secondees. Our sources couldn't speak highly enough of these in-house experiences… "*absolutely brilliant; it was the best kind of client contact you could imagine, very, very rewarding.*" The firm also has a small Oxford office that concentrates on employment law.

Decency and dancing

Various clients use LS as a one-stop shop, and as such trainees can get a good handle on them. In one seat they'll help with a client's trade mark litigation, later they'll work on its employment problems. What this means is that no single department has all the cool clients and each has a reasonably similar feel. The firm's culture is greatly influenced by its clients, a number of whom come from media or brand-related industries. We're talking about the likes of ad agencies Saatchi & Saatchi and Abbott Mead Vickers, games company Electronic Arts, Marks & Spencer, Abercrombie & Fitch, PizzaExpress, BNP Paribas, ABN AMRO and mining giant Rio Tinto.

As much as they loved their work, our sources were pleased that LS honours its promise of work-life balance. Generally, trainees leave the office between 6.30 and 7pm, and partners are more likely to be disturbed than impressed if they see someone consistently staying late. "*The first question is 'are they overworked?' and the second 'why are they here?' The point being that the firm believes that if people have their life in perspective, they'll be better lawyers.*"

At a time when firms are being forced into layoffs, it is important to consider the manner in which they swing the axe. When LS was faced with the need to cut staff from its property (Landscape) and corporate teams, it said goodbye to as few as possible, offering the remainder a say over the next step. Staff unanimously voted to take a 10% pay cut in return for 10% more holidays, thus saving further jobs. Some people in quieter departments also took sabbaticals or moved to busier ones. Needless to say the employment department (Peoplescape) has been mad busy during the downturn. The reputation it has gained through work on big City discrimination cases (including representing top law firms), plus the reasonableness of its fees, has paid dividends.

When you read phrases like 'Core Values' or 'Mediascape', do you cringe? Some people here give 'bandwidth' rather than paying attention, and we ended up in a discussion about the level of 'disconnect' between departments. Yet again, trainees steered us away from style and back to substance. Said one: "*We are working with experts in their fields. At bigger firms you might be photocopying a lot, no one would know your name and it'd all be about the chargeable hours – I know where I'd rather be.*"

Trainees socialise together both in and out of work. There are free meals in the canteen every Thursday and "*there is plenty of banter in the corridors.*" A flat hierarchy means trainees can speak to most partners as they would to one another. Departmentally hosted parties are among the most important social events and, as well as the *Eurovision* event, these have included a *Strictly Come Dancing* challenge and a loved-up Valentine's party.

The NQ job application process sometimes includes tests, sometimes just interviews, and sometimes both. Despite up and down results in past years, our sources felt they were given every opportunity to stay on. The firm advertises jobs externally but allows internal applicants a good head start. In 2009 five of the six stayed on.

Chambers UK rankings

Advertising & Marketing	Intellectual Property
Construction	Media & Entertainment
Corporate/M&A	Partnership
Defamation/Reputation Management	Real Estate
Dispute Resolution	Real Estate Litigation
Employment	Social Housing
Immigration	Sports Law

And finally…

Choose Lewis Silkin for its media, employment or social housing practices, or for its all-round commercial training.

- **Training contract been deferred?** It's not the end of the world if you've time to kill. Here's how three people filled a gap between law school and starting their training:

"I did a year at the International Bar Association doing human rights work. The internship was a great experience."

"I worked as a substitute teacher until Christmas and then went to Vegas on holiday. I got offered a part in a Vegas show, and then I played poker for four or five months and worked on a film over the summer. I guess it might not work out the same way for everybody..."

"I work for Chambers and Partners as a researcher. It's turned out to be very interesting interviewing top lawyers and their clients. I never imagined I'd learn quite so much about the profession and I think it will help me a lot when I start my training."

Whatever you do, try and make it rewarding and ideally of benefit to your future career.

top tip no. 18

Linklaters

The facts

Location: London
Number of UK partners/solicitors: 200/620
Total number of trainees: 250
Seats: 4x6 months
Alternative seats: Overseas seats, secondments
Extras: Pro bono – Hackney Legal Connections, Mary Ward Legal Advice Centre, FRU, RCJ CAB, Disability Law Service, A4ID and others; language training

Linklaters is about as ambitious as a firm can be. Consider applying if you're prepared to put career centre stage. You'll quickly learn that both the effort required and the rewards available are huge.

"*What we want is global domination. Don't quote me on that,*" says a trainee. Oh, please! Links' quest for supremacy is the worst-kept secret ever.

Innovation nation

The perpetual innovator of the magic circle, Linklaters is unafraid to try new things, and it's that which has made it so ludicrously successful. It was one of the first firms to embrace international expansion and now has 26 offices in 19 countries. While already a world leader for corporate matters, it has worked its socks off over the past five years and *Chambers Global* now also ranks it in the top tier worldwide for banking and finance matters. Of direct relevance to students, Linklaters was a pioneer of the firm-specific LPC.

Frequently topping the M&A deal tables, Links recently acted on the non-US aspects of the $50bn Merrill Lynch/Bank of America merger, represented Rio Tinto on its defence of a hostile takeover move by BHP Billiton, and is lining up opposite Freshfields on a potential $41bn merger between mining giants Anglo American and Xstrata. It was also behind the acquisition of a 58% stake in Royal Bank of Scotland by Her Majesty's Treasury (a £20bn matter), and is advising PwC in its role as administrator of Lehman Brothers. Turnover was up ever so slightly in 2009, to £1.298bn, enough to make it the largest firm in the UK by revenue. Trainees certainly feel the firm is on the right track. "*I just think Links places a huge emphasis on getting their business model correct,*" said one. "*We won't take work from just anywhere. The focus has been on reducing the number of clients and just working for the best ones.*" Or, to put it in a catchphrase oft-used during our interviews: "*Premium work for premium clients.*" Despite all this, Linklaters has made redundancies – around 100 fee earners in total. More on that later.

Soliloquise this

Linklaters now requires all of its future trainees to study its own tailored LPC at the College of Law. Many of our interviewees were part of "*the guinea pig year*" and we're pleased to pass on an entirely positive judgement on the arrangement. The two recurring comments were that having 70 familiar faces around you on your first day in the office makes it "*a little less like starting school,*" and that Links' way of doing things is already ingrained even before you join the firm. Trainees complete four seats of six months. Mid-way through the first one, they meet with HR to sort out what their next three will be. There's nothing compulsory, but obviously there are some big departments with many places to fill. It's likely that at least three of your seats will be some combination of corporate, banking, capital markets, derivatives, structured finance, asset finance, litigation, real estate and projects, which together bring in 80% of the firm's revenue. The fourth can be in one of an array of specialist areas: there's tax, pensions, employment and more. There is also a 'seat change' option that you can pursue if you change your mind about the third or fourth seats.

Seat allocation was the one area where we heard a number of complaints. "*I don't give this feedback with relish, but give it I must: everyone in my intake has said the seat allocation process has been dealt with poorly,*" said one trainee. "*It creates a great deal of resentment. Some people have managed to do purely advisory seats, when there are people who would sell their grandmothers to get one. We are repeatedly told that we need to be flexible and that's all very well, but there is a tendency to think that we are just numbers and have to be fitted in somewhere.*" Others alleged:

"*You need a partner backing you to get the seat you want,*" and one went so far as to admit: "*I asked a corporate partner to pull strings for me.*" In all honesty, a number of other trainees expressed "*a certain amount of sympathy for HR because some people are very demanding.*" The best advice we can give is to "*be very focused, have a fixed idea of what you want to do and clearly justify why you should be given that.*" But this is not a kooky niche firm and if you come in thinking you will definitely get to see a kooky niche seat you may be sorely disappointed.

Oops there goes another rubber tree plant

The corporate department is the one on which Links' reputation was built, and "*you realise pretty quickly the magnitude of some of the deals going on.*" It's true that there's "*an enormous amount*" of dull, low-level work to do. "*I did vast quantities of document management and production, and a lot of proof-reading,*" sighed one contact. But "*everyone accepts that's what is needed*" and some found the bright side. "*Due diligence is different every time,*" said an upbeat contact. "*On a pharmaceutical deal I spent my week on Wikipedia looking up different drugs. Looking at a different business, say an auto company, makes it a completely different deal.*" It would be wrong to say corporate is all grunt work, especially for third and fourth-seat trainees. There are opportunities for drafting and client contact as well. "*Listening in on conference calls and going to meetings is one of the most beneficial things you can do, even if you don't participate, because you get to see how negotiations work.*" We're also told the quality of supervision in the department is generally high, with the "*amazing*" Rob Cleaver and the "*outstanding*" Owen Clay singled out for praise. "*If you had a problem he would drop everything for you,*" trainees said of the latter. "*He's the kind of partner who would make you want to qualify there because he cares about his trainees as people rather than numbers.*" We heard a number of heart-warming stories about kindly partners right across the firm, and only one about a trainee being shouted at, so we can only conclude that Linklaters has got its workplace values in pretty good order.

The 'finance' seats can offer completely different experiences. For example, banking is "*very commercially orientated. You're not asking, 'What does the law say about this?' What the parties say, goes.*" By contrast, derivatives is "*a very complex field of law, just hugely technical.*" It's an exciting seat for trainees because deals go through quickly. "*You see lots of closings and lots of technical work in between.*" There's ample training to get newbies up to speed and "*trainees with a strong background in economics can almost be doing the work of an associate.*"

Many see corporate and finance seats as "*a rite of passage*" before they find a department with less "*relentless*" hours – although you won't find less than 9am to 7pm in many Links teams. There will be plenty of "*periods of working until five in the morning every night,*" a fact our contacts accepted sto-

Chambers UK rankings

Asset Finance	Life Sciences
Banking & Finance	Media & Entertainment
Banking Litigation	Outsourcing
Capital Markets	Partnership
Climate Change	Pensions
Commodities	Pensions Litigation
Competition/European Law	Planning
Construction	Private Equity
Corporate/M&A	Professional Negligence
Data Protection	Projects, Energy & Natural Resources
Dispute Resolution	
Employee Share Schemes	Public Procurement
Employment	Real Estate
Environment	Real Estate Finance
Financial Services Regulation	Real Estate Litigation
	Restructuring/Insolvency
Fraud: Civil	Retail
Information Technology	Shipping
Insurance	Tax
Intellectual Property	Telecommunications
Investment Funds	Transport

ically. At the same time, trainees will sometimes get days off in lieu and aren't expected in at the crack of dawn after a deal has gone through. "*It's all about taking the rough with the smooth.*" And when that deal finally closes, there's the "*euphoria*" and the satisfaction of "*knowing that the part you played, however small, has made a difference.*"

Czech returned, no cash

Litigation is popular. "*It's a busy place to be*" and, while Links is not as well known for contentious matters as transactional ones, "*if you want to be a litigator in a City firm this is as good a place as any other.*" The recent hire of star partner Christa Band from Herbert Smith goes a long way towards confirming that. In fact, said trainees, Links is better for litigation in some ways, because "*you're doing a broad contentious seat: you're not pigeonholed into one area of litigation. You get to work with lots of different teams, and if you hear of something interesting going on you can ask to have a go at it. And that's good for qualification as well.*" Our interviewees were very positive about their experiences in litigation. "*I'd get a point of law to look at and would sit with the books and the case files and build up an impression of similar cases, then have a meeting with counsel about it. It really felt like I was achieving something.*" Links defended RBS in the bank charges litigation and has represented BP in claims related to the Buncefield explosion. It also has a substantial international arbitration practice, which is currently acting for the Czech Republic. A Luxembourg investor that put cash into the Czech television industry is claiming a multimillion-dollar award for losses and damages allegedly incurred as a result of the wrongful destruction of its investment following actions and inactions of the Czech Media Council.

Though some trainees will get to go to court, the best chance of advocacy comes to those who involve themselves with pro bono work. All trainees are allowed one day for pro bono each year, although some manage more than this. There is the option for litigators to spend every other Wednesday afternoon for six months at the Disability Law Service and some trainees get to spend a full seat on a pro bono secondment.

With tons of foreign placements to choose from, there's no danger of missing out on six months abroad. We heard similar grumbles about secondment allocation as we did about seat allocation ("*we all submit applications and then it's decided: how is not always clear*") but, once overseas, trainees have little to complain about. "*It's true you get a lot more responsibility on secondment,*" said one; "*I've run signing meetings and get very regular client contact – they'll ring me directly all the time.*" For some locations (Paris, for example) you'll need strong language skills; for others (say, those in Asia) it isn't necessary. Check out a full list of overseas seats on page 560.

Brave new world?

You'll have seen in the legal press that the firm made a swathe of redundancies in early 2009. "*Around 100*" London lawyers, including a number of partners, left in a programme dubbed 'Linklaters New World' ("*we've been told not to call it that any more*"). That equates to around 17% of the firm's fee-earning workforce, one of the largest culls in the City. We've already noted that its financials held up relatively well this year, so why so many layoffs? And, when a number of other firms have bent over backwards to avoid making redundancies, doesn't this just prove that ultimately Links cares more about profits than people? "*I think that there are probably a few people made redundant who were absolutely beasted in terms of hours who will share those sentiments exactly,*" said one source. Some "*thought it a little bit odd*" that the firm could afford to renovate the canteen (and install a wood-burning pizza oven) and offer plenty of NQ jobs at much the same time as the cull.

But several others "*couldn't in all honesty say Links didn't do the right thing. There was a certain amount of dead wood that had been hired during boom times.*" And when the boom turned to bust, "*even with Lehmans, which kept the firm flat-out busy, there wasn't enough work to go around.*" All agreed: "*Better to do it in one brutal cut,*" and said further redundancies were unlikely. Most also thought morale had bounced back. But when comments range from "*I think it was handled fairly well*" to "*it wasn't handled particularly well*" and from "*as a trainee I felt like a guilty spectator*" to "*I felt quite removed from it all,*" perhaps it's impossible to give one definitive answer.

Sometimes the hare beats the tortoise

"*I didn't want to end up at a firm full of classic City wide-boys,*" said one trainee, echoing the thoughts of many. In Linklaters they made the right choice. Nor is this an "*old-boys club;*" it's a "*meritocracy*" and it recruits "*a real mixed bag.*" Of the current trainee intake, 33% are minority ethnic – we're open to correction here, but we don't think there's a large firm in the City that equals this. Links doesn't mind travelling a long way to find the best and even runs an Indian vac scheme. You'll also find plenty of Aussies. Among the homegrown contingent, Oxbridge is still a major supplier of trainees, although we did encounter a few from other top UK universities.

These are all high achievers and "*healthy competition*" among trainees is only to be expected. Several warned: "*You do have to play the game a bit.*" Some denied this altogether – but then, it's noticeable that there was a distinct split between trainees who had got the seats they wanted and those who hadn't. Our suspicion is that if you aren't among the ones setting the pace in this training contract marathon, there's a danger you'll find yourself boxed in at the back of the pack. One or two interviewees noted that perceptions about which trainees are the best can quickly arise among partners and associates.

"*We work ferociously hard but we also socialise incredibly. We're the type who will finish work at 2am, then go out on the town, and be back in the next morning at nine.*" Feisty words! But trainees all agree that the social scene is "*great.*" There are weekly drinks trolleys, monthly departmental get-togethers, twice-yearly balls, annual departmental retreats (to which trainees may or may not be invited), booze-ups with the vac schemers, "*a team for every sport you can think of*" and more besides. We also suspect there's truth to the statement that there is "*a very strong sense of humour running through the firm.*"

Let's have a Jerry Springer-style final thought. In an unusual year, what are we to make of Linklaters? Our conclusion is that the firm is in a strong position going forward. It runs an excellent training programme and "*on a day-to-day basis*" our trainee contacts felt well looked after. But ultimately, this isn't cuddly Cameron McKenna or nice Norton Rose. It's Linklaters The Ambitious and "*there is an element of cut-throat.*" And you know what? By and large, the class of 2009 didn't have a problem with that. Retention was reasonable despite the depressed economic conditions: 109 out of 141 qualifiers stayed on.

And finally...

Are you as personally ambitious as this firm? If you're applying here, we hope so.

Lovells LLP

The facts
Location: London
Number of UK partners/solicitors: 144/428
Total Number of Trainees: 90
Seats: 4x6 months
Alternative seats: Overseas seats, secondments
Extras: Pro bono – All Party Parliamentary Group on Extraordinary Renditions, CABs, Royal British Legion war pensions tribunals and others; language training

This classic City player has much to offer aspiring solicitors, but don't make the mistake of assuming you can leap from one niche practice area to another. Corporate and finance are the main drivers here.

Top-ten player Lovells has been attracting high-flying graduates for decades. To some this is the magic circle firm that never was.

More than meets the eye

After several under-performing years marked by partner defections and relatively disappointing financial results, Lovells was finally registering more healthy profits when the global financial crisis reared its ugly head. However, this top-ten UK player enjoyed a reasonably strong past year, posting an 11% rise in global revenue (£531m) for 2008/09. The firm's international offices – located everywhere from Alicante to Zagreb – are more than paying their way. Lovells' Asian outposts have performed particularly well, so it is betting big bucks on the region. In early 2009 the firm launched a Hanoi office in Vietnam and announced a formal tie-up with Indian law firm Phoenix Legal later in the year. Meanwhile, the continental European offices are also pulling their weight, contributing 43% of that revenue.

Back in the UK, Lovells' litigation, finance and corporate teams continue to grab the limelight. In a slow market, the corporate group has fared better than expected, closing several transactions valued in excess of £1bn. Admittedly, few transactions have come close to the highlight deals of 2007, when Lovells advised SABMiller on its joint venture with Molson Coors, a deal valued at approximately £6.6bn. There have been a number of major transactions though. Lovells' finance folks still crop up on deals such as British Energy's £12.65bn acquisition by EDF, and over in litigation, lawyers have cleaned up on some major cases arising directly out of the financial meltdown. A particularly high-profile instruction came from the government of Iceland, which the firm now advises on disputes relating to the banking crisis. There is also plenty of work following the collapses of Northern Rock and Lehman Brothers.

Corporate, finance, litigation, fine. But don't write Lovells off just yet if your aspirations are less mainstream. As remarked upon by several of our sources, *"outsiders probably don't suspect the enormous variety of work that Lovells can handle. Certain practice groups tend to fly under the radar."* Some trainees speculated that these departments' lack of visibility could be the result of the firm's relatively low-key marketing drive. They certainly haven't escaped the notice of our colleagues at *Chambers UK*, however, who rank Lovells' pensions, product liability, professional negligence and insurance practices among the best in the UK.

All aboard for training

The corporate department is one of the mandatory stops along the training contract route. The group is subdivided into several specialist teams, including private equity, commercial, energy, corporate insurance and public companies. Given the size of the groups and the sheer complexity of the transactions it pulls in, trainees here normally find themselves at the bottom of a long chain of command, doing mundane jobs such as verification, due diligence or data room management. There were very few complaints though, as our contacts appreciated that input at the lowest level forms a critical part of the bigger picture. Said one source: *"There is only so much a trainee can do on such big deals – it remains great learning experience."* There is usually scant opportunity to knock off early here and an 8pm finish is deemed reasonable when activity levels are healthy.

As with corporate, those who took a finance seat reported a dip in activity, particularly on the capital markets front. In banking, trainees can try out acquisition, project or asset finance, and there is also plenty of restructuring work. *"The group is a bit thin at junior level, so depending on how forthcoming you are you can end up with jobs normally given to associates,"* a source reported. Others echoed the view that this seat offers the chance to develop faster and shoulder more responsibilities. *"I did my fair share of tedious tasks, but I also got to run smaller matters by myself,"* said one interviewee.

Litigation: in the blood

Litigation is another compulsory destination. The practice is grouped into teams as follows: investment banking and funds litigation; corporate and commercial banking litigation; product liability; pensions litigation; insurance and reinsurance; international arbitration; professional indemnity litigation; civil fraud; and contentious projects, engineering and construction. Absolutely no shortage of specialisms there! Banking disputes are Lovells' forte, and the group has experienced a real boom following the credit crunch. It acted on the collapse and restructuring of a number of structured investment vehicles (SIVs), the most high-profile being the Cheyne and Sigma vehicles.

Product liability litigation is another strong suit. Sizeable cross-border cases are the bread and butter of this practice, which is routinely involved in defending major global product liability issues across a range of product sectors, including pharmaceuticals, blood factor concentrates (eg HIV and hep C contamination) and tobacco. Trainees sitting in the arbitration group seldom assist on purely domestic matters. One reported: *"To give you an idea of the international dimension of the practice, I worked on a Singapore-based arbitration, I then assisted on a dispute between two French and Chinese companies and moved on to work on an investment dispute in Africa."*

A trainee's role in the litigation group very much depends on the sub-team they are assigned to. Those who sat with the banking litigation group readily conceded that disputes were often too big for them to make a meaningful contribution and they were left proof-reading and bundling for six months. A niche litigation seat normally delivers more challenging work. In real estate litigation, for example, trainees handle their own small files, collect evidence and interview witnesses. If you're looking for advocacy experience then Lovells has *"an amazing pro bono programme"* and encourages trainees to take on cases to practise their oral skills.

Getting away from it all

Real estate seats are renowned for offering rewarding work. *"The discipline lends itself to smaller matters that trainees can manage on their own, such as leases and*

Chambers UK rankings

Administrative & Public Law	Intellectual Property
Advertising & Marketing	Investment Funds
Asset Finance	Life Sciences
Banking & Finance	Media & Entertainment
Banking Litigation	Outsourcing
Capital Markets	Parliamentary & Public Affairs
Climate Change	
Commodities	Pensions
Competition/European Law	Pensions Litigation
Construction	Planning
Consumer Finance	Product Liability
Corporate/M&A	Professional Negligence
Data Protection	Projects, Energy & Natural Resources
Dispute Resolution	
Employee Share Schemes	Public Procurement
Employment	Real Estate
Environment	Real Estate Finance
Financial Services Regulation	Real Estate Litigation
	Restructuring/Insolvency
Fraud: Civil	Retail
Information Technology	Tax
Insurance	Telecommunications
	Transport

licences," said sources, but here they'll also assist on big-ticket deals such as the £2bn King's Cross regeneration project. This department has very recently been restructured into more obvious groups and is now targeting clients more by sector, for example development, corporate occupiers, institutional investors and public sector. The IP group is a hot favourite, and several of our sources indicated they were hoping to qualify into the department, which offers patent litigation as well as non-contentious advisory work. Recently the team represented toy manufacturer Mattel during its dispute with the Indian brothers who created Scrabulous. As keen players of the online game, we hate Lovells a little for getting it removed from Facebook. Other groups that trainees can visit include employment, pensions, tax, competition and TMT.

There is always a healthy level of competition for international secondments to exotic places like Singapore, Tokyo and Dubai, though placements in Russia or Germany don't attract the same level of interest. Even a swine flu scare in the firm's Hong Kong office couldn't dampen trainees' enthusiasm. *"I'm Hong Kong-bound and I just can't wait to be there,"* one enthused. All is taken care of for expat trainees, from travel arrangements to accommodation, and they can also expect a salary top-up. Keen to see what life on the other side is like? How about a client secondment? *"Spending time with a client is a great way to become more commercially aware,"* one trainee rightly pointed out. Placements are available at clients such as John Lewis, SABMiller, Lloyds TSB, Standard Chartered Bank, Prudential and Save the Children.

There is a fantastically broad array of practices to explore at Lovells, but beware – getting more than one specialist seat or international placement isn't easy. Trainees can state a preferred seat and "*HR will do their utmost to give you that, but there's no guarantee.*" The secret to getting what you want, we are told, is to "*not simply tell HR where you want to go, but make the extra effort to explain why you'd be a good fit and introduce yourself to the team you're hoping to join.*"

Paul Daniels eat your heart out

If the quality of work isn't enough to convince you to join, then Lovells' famously convivial atmosphere might seal the deal. Interviewees confirmed that it resembles a "*big happy family, with only the odd relative you'd want to stay away from.*" For the most part our interviewees felt management takes a genuine interest in their individual progression rather than treating them as "*just another bunch of interchangeable trainees.*" So what does it take to become part of the family? Education-wise, Oxbridge bods are very well represented, and while our sources thought they perceived some change in the firm's recruitment drive, the statistics tell a different story. The vast majority of our sources studied at Oxford or Cambridge, leading us to suspect the firm hasn't expanded its horizons much further than the redbricks. Whatever the truth, interviewees say what Lovells looks for (in addition to "*people at the top of their game intellectually*") is real dedication to the profession. "*I think the times of indecisive trainees who start their training contract without being 100% sure they want to be lawyers are well and truly over,*" said one. We agree. You'll also need to show confidence, autonomy and social skills. "*You basically have to be someone who can be trusted with clients, and that includes doing the small talk as well as the legal talk.*"

Working at a top-ten firm is no walk in the park, but at Lovells at least you'll have the privilege of working hard in the magnificent surroundings of Atlantic House. The premises offer all manner of services: canteen, health care practice, subsidised Starbucks, gym. There are even functional sleeping pods for those pulling an all-nighter. There's plenty to do outside the office too. Sports teams include cricket, rugby and football for the lads and netball and softball for the ladies. This year's most memorable charitable initiative was 'Legally Ballroom', a *Strictly Come Dancing*-inspired contest, which was well attended. Youtube it.

There are parties galore, including barbecues at partners' houses, team-bonding weekends and Christmas jollies. The annual summer party always draws in a nice crowd, not least because it promises some daring antics by senior partner John Young. Last year he donned a silver catsuit and delivered his yearly speech suspended from the ceiling. During this year's masquerade ball, he jumped out of a giant Rubik's cube wearing a kilt and proceeded to entertain the audience with Derren Brown-esque tricks. Cynics might say it's the closest the firm's ever going to get to breaking into the magic circle.

Tough love

Unfortunately, due to the economic downturn, the social calendar has had to take a back seat. The once-generous budget for trainee festivities has been slashed and other cost-cutting measures implemented. "*They've cut down on free lunches at meeting, and we were quite upset when they took away the free crisps,*" trainees moaned. It is well understood that these cuts are inescapable in the current climate. Said one interviewee: "*It's perfectly normal, and we're happy to party less if it allows the firm to keep on more people.*"

If only… Sadly, the NQ attrition rate was higher in 2009, with 54 people out of 77 taking qualification jobs. There were fewer slots than usual available in the corporate and finance departments, very few openings in the niche practice groups, and even though the firm took on more NQs in litigation, that still wasn't enough to accommodate everyone. As in past years it would be unwise to come here assuming you can qualify into one of Lovells' smaller groups: "*Those without an interest in the firm's mainstream areas of corporate and finance just set themselves up for disappointment.*" While the majority of our sources agreed that HR and partners had been transparent in their dealings and managed trainees' expectations reasonably well, they couldn't help thinking that having given them a top-quality training, it was a mistake for the firm to waste so much talent. "*It's pretty short-sighted on their part, I'd have thought that a firm of this calibre could come up with a more innovative approach,*" one source reflected.

Like many firms, Lovells deferred many new starters in autumn 2009 and spring and autumn 2010. These people received a no-strings-attached £5,000 pay-off for a year's deferral and half that if they stayed away for six months. As for other members of staff, 79 redundancies were made in London, only a minority of them lawyers.

And finally…

If you fancy your chances at Lovells, remember that to even get a look in you're going need a bullet-proof academic record. Once enrolled onto the training scheme, give careful consideration to the seats you apply for.

Macfarlanes LLP

The facts

Location: London
Number of UK partners/solicitors: 75/145
Total number of trainees: 58
Seats: 4x6 months
Alternative seats: Secondments
Extras: Pro Bono – Cambridge House, LawWorks, Bar Pro Bono Unit; language training

Macfarlanes' defining traits are timeless, as is its appeal to students looking for a bespoke City training. Apply here if you consider yourself to be a top candidate (or you would do, were it not for your innate sense of modesty).

If Macfarlanes did buzzwords, 'quality' would most certainly be one. Not into any of "*that snazzy marketing stuff,*" this classic City firm prides itself on "*understated excellence.*"

Evolution, not revolution

With just one office and 300 lawyers, Macfarlanes embodies the phrase: the best things come in small packages. Not one to succumb to fads and trends, it has shunned mergers, global expansion and "*vulgar marketing gimmicks*" to simply concentrate on providing a quality, cost-efficient service to its clients. A quick glance down its *Chambers UK* rankings reveals that it has done just that, gaining top-notch positions in an array of practice areas, as well as a top ranking in *Chambers Global* for its private client work. An intricate network of 'best friend' firms across the globe allows Macfarlanes involvement in more than its fair share of international work, and it regularly competes with magic circle firms on deals. Major clients include Goldman Sachs, 3i, RBS, Kellogg's, Trainline, Umbro, Reebok, Paramount (the owners of Chez Gerard, Bertorelli, Caffe Uno and Livebait restaurants) and DC Thompson (publishers of *The Beano*). Macfarlanes may have a decidedly unfashionable approach to growth and a reputation for conservatism, but there is no arguing with the impressive figures. Macfarlanes is one of the most profitable firms in the City and helping to fill the coffers are juicy deals such as ITV's £25m sale of its interest in Friends Reunited.

While not keen on revolution, Macfarlanes is by no means stagnating in its own success. Previously nesting in "*rather shabby*" offices, the firm has found new premises to house its litigation department and client meeting rooms, and it has finally given its old buildings a lick and a spit. Trainees happily report that "*wherever you sit now you get nice offices.*" The computers too have been upgraded. And while the firm was forced to make redundancies at the beginning of the year, it opened its doors to rare lateral hires at senior level, starting with regulatory partner David Berman from Dresdner Kleinwort bank to boost its investment funds and financial services group. It sounds as if that's plenty of change for one year and, in true Macfarlanes style, trainees do not see any major reshuffles on the horizon. Confident in the firm's unwavering belief in the Darwinian theory of law firm evolution, they say: "*We are going to try and continue in the same way but get better.*"

Gunning for good work

Trainees work their way through a four-seat system. Corporate and property are compulsory but after that trainees are free to choose, generally ending up in private client, litigation, debt finance or investment funds and financial services. Those who don't want to spend a full six months honing their contentious skills can opt for a short litigation course at BPP instead. Trainees who do spend a seat with the litigation team can expect "*quite a lot of court work*" as well as a broad variety of tasks including drafting letters, witness statements and particulars of claim for clients such as B&Q, Red Bull Racing and Music Sales Limited. There is also a secondment available to 3i, if requested, but Macfarlanes is not the place to come if you're looking for overseas seats. The firm's graduate website announces that "*training at Macfarlanes is not for the faint-hearted,*" and our sources agreed: "*It's certainly not an easy ride. They really expect you to be good,*" said one. "*You get stuck in straight away, from minute one, day one,*" added another. And because of the firm's size, "*it's very difficult to hide. If you're crap you do get found out double quick.*" But having said this, "*Macfarlanes isn't a shouty firm.*" "*If you are stuck, or have been given a task that is too difficult, you aren't going to get into trouble. Partners are always on hand to answer questions.*" There is also an extensive programme of educational seminars to help trainees get to grips with the work.

Corporate instructions are Macfarlanes' bread and butter, accounting for 55% of turnover. The department runs like clockwork. There is a monitoring meeting every Thursday at 8.30am sharp, when all the team members get together to "*talk about business development and work capacity.*" Macfarlanes is renowned for its small deal teams, so as a trainee "*you are very much seen as part of the team and are expected to pull your weight and really contribute.*" The deals that have been keeping the department busy include advising Alcoa (a Pittsburgh-based producer of aluminium that operates in 44 countries) on its joint venture arrangements with Chinalco (a major state-controlled Chinese mining enterprise) and their joint $14bn purchase of a 12% stake in the multinational mining and resources group Rio Tinto. This deal also illustrates quite how international Macfarlanes' work is.

An increase in activity within the sports sector has been a feature of the team this year. It has been involved in several deals involving premiership football clubs, including instructions from Stan Kroenke, a significant investor in Arsenal FC, in relation to both his private holding and his acquisition of a 50% stake in the online business of the club. While trainees won't be calling any shots in the corporate department, they are "*one of the few people that have an overview of the whole deal. You get to witness the top-level negotiations with the partner and then you are involved in the lower levels too. You have a fly-on-the-wall perspective from all angles.*" As well as pure M&A, private equity is a big part of Macfarlanes' work and trainees get exposure to "*some quite interesting discreet tasks*" as well as the standard due diligence and bibling that "*you just have to suck up.*" Although deal flow is at a low ebb ("*smaller peaks and bigger troughs*") there are still late nights to be had. Said one trainee: "*In a one-week period I did three 4ams in a row... this is also when the work is most interesting!*" Another added reassuringly: "*There is a good sense of camaraderie when you are working late.*" The hours at Macfarlanes are generally not unbearable these days, with most teams working an average day of 8.30am to 7pm.

Chambers UK rankings

Advertising & Marketing	Franchising
Agriculture & Rural Affairs	Intellectual Property
Banking & Finance	Investment Funds
Charities	Pensions
Competition/European Law	Planning
Construction	Private Client
Corporate/M&A	Private Equity
Dispute Resolution	Real Estate
Employment	Real Estate Finance
Environment	Real Estate Litigation
Financial Services Regulation	Sports Law
	Tax

Standard bearers

Time in the property department gives trainees "*a seriously good level of responsibility*" and "*around 20 or 30 files that you are running straight away.*" For one source, "*the structured supervision meant that I didn't feel out of my depth at any point. The hardest thing was getting used to my phone ringing all the time!*" Smaller leases, purchases and sales, plus management issues for clients with large property portfolios all keep trainees busy on a day-to-day basis. "*Property is very paper-heavy so there are always things to do, but out of every department it has the potential to produce tasks that are quite mind-numbing,*" said one source, clearly not a fan of the work. But they did go on to admit that "*deed scheduling can be quite a nice thing to do on a Friday afternoon when you don't want to have to think about anything else.*" The team recently steered Arora International Hotels through a number of transactions, including a £100m hotel development at Heathrow's Terminal 5 and the acquisition of the Renaissance Gatwick Hotel.

Macfarlanes' private client practice is the firm's not-so-secret recession weapon. Over the past 20 years other City firms culled their private client teams in favour of more profitable practice areas (that are now suffering in the downturn). Macfarlanes has continued to nurture a stellar reputation in this field. While it only makes up an eighth of total turnover, its strategic importance must not be underestimated. As trainees pointed out: "*Having a private client practice that is at the top of the tree means that a lot of our clients are important people in important businesses. If we look after their personal wealth well they are likely to trust us with their business. It's a great way to guarantee cross-exposure between departments.*"

While there are families the firm has worked with for generations, trainees who'd taken the private client seat were pleased to report that "*it was definitely not the old-school client base that I imagined it would be.*" "*There is always the odd celebrity*" and clients come from all over the world – Americans, New Zealanders, Indians, Russians and Kazakhs. Responsibility is not always free-flowing, but trainees frequently accompany their supervisors on client meetings where they are expected to take conclusive notes in order to then be able to write letters containing "*pages and pages of complex tax advice.*" In such instances, practice makes perfect: "*A lot got scribbled out by my supervisor at first, but I improved and improved and was covering quite advanced issues by the end,*" said one source. Some of the partners here are "*as eccentric as you might imagine*" and most are "*immensely clever,*" but our sources were more inspired than intimidated. "*Working with extremely clever people all the time makes you constantly try and raise your game.*" The lawyers who completed a purchase and sale of a Mayfair town house for around £30m for American private clients were certainly on form. The transaction was done and dusted in just four hours.

Flavour of the old school

"*Market perception is one thing and what goes on inside is another,*" stated one source emphatically when questioning turned to Macfarlanes' culture. So in an attempt to get a firmer and more creative grip on what Macfarlanes is really like we asked trainees to liken the firm to an item of clothing. Responses ranged from a black cocktail dress ("*it's quite a classy elegant firm*") to a fedora hat and a "*nicely-tailored jacket. Navy blue, because Macfarlanes is quite classic, slightly conservative, smart, and hits the right note when you're trying to impress people.*" Make of this what you will. What trainees did agree on was "*however much the powers that be deny it, there is a Macfarlanes type.*" Said one: "*The people who are interested in the firm are from a middle-class background, but the partners do also recruit people that reflect themselves – probably unwittingly though.*" Another continued: "*We have all followed the same sort of path and I don't think there is anyone here who hasn't done their fair share of wandering the world.*" Beyond well-educated and reasonably well-heeled, what more is there to say about the Macfarlanes clan? Polite, interested, well-mannered and quietly confident complete the package. "*People here aren't bolshy or flash. We aren't City-boy 'Alright Geezers'.*"

A three-line whip is never needed for parties – this lot like to have fun. A group of Macfarlanes lawyers, from trainees right up to partners, can always be found at The Castle pub next door. A lavish summer ball is held every four years, the most recent one was in 2008. You name it, they had it: a big marquee, a fairground with Ferris wheel and bumper cars, a huge sit-down dinner, a free bar, a Caribbean band, acrobats, girls on stilts wearing carnival costumes, a marching band and even soul sensation Beverley Knight. Entertainment also comes at unexpected moments – a partner was serenaded by a bagpipe parade from outside his office when he retired.

And finally…

Macfarlanes instils a real sense of loyalty in its trainees. The firm's consistently high NQ retention rate wasn't badly affected in 2009 when 21 out of 25 qualifiers took up jobs.

Manches LLP

The facts

Location: London, Oxford, Reading
Number of UK partners/solicitors: 57/70
Total number of trainees: 20
Seats: 4x6 months
Alternative seats: Occasional secondments

A traditional firm with some surprising clients, both wealthy individuals and interesting businesses.

Manches lawyers are known as the crème de la crème of family law, and the firm has also cultured an excellent commercial practice.

Keeping it in the family

Sidney Manches founded this firm in 1936 with his wife, and it has been a family affair ever since. Today, Sidney's daughter Jane Simpson holds the position of chair(woman) and is founder and head of the family law department. Her brother Louis is managing partner of the London office and head of the firm's property department, and a third generation Manches is an associate in the litigation department. Fittingly, it is in family law that Manches particularly excels. As one of London's small handful of Rolls-Royce family practices, it earns a top ranking in *Chambers UK* each year. It is this department that has helped the firm post better-than-expected financial results this past year, with revenue only falling by £300,000 (to £34.1m) and profits dropping just 8% despite the property slump.

The team has a reputation for acting in some of the country's leading divorce cases and prides itself on not only securing substantial assets for its clients, but also securing their privacy. Partner Helen Ward made legal history when she represented Beverley Charman in her divorce from insurance tycoon John in 2007, winning her a record £48m. This (and then the failing economy) brought a windfall of big-money divorces to the door, many of them quite high-profile. The family team grew in response, adding eight new associates in September 2008, half of whom had completed their training contracts at Manches. Guy Ritchie subsequently chose Manches to guide him through his split from Madonna, and the team secured him a whopping £50m, perhaps the largest ever payout to a man. Bernie Ecclestone signed up for representation in his split from wife Slavica, who could take up to £1.08bn from the marriage; in the process he ditched Manches' closest rival firm, Withers. Lest you think the work is all about grabbing or withholding as much money as possible, no matter what, we should tell you that Manches has been integral to the development of alternative dispute resolution in cases where clients are keen to negotiate proceedings outside of the high-pressure, high-visibility court arena.

Almost all trainees spend time in the family department, usually in their first year. While this is without doubt "*the jewel in the crown,*" a faultless reputation and sensitive cases mean that "*in terms of responsibility it is a much more regulated area,*" with some trainees feeling that they were "*really just paper-pushing.*" There are exceptions to the rule, however, when clients are keen to keep costs down. A couple of trainees talked of working on Children Act matters in contact disputes: "*I went to hearings, interviewed lots of witnesses and prepared statements,*" said one. But although it's clear that "*you are very much the lowest part of the team,*" as one trainee sanguinely put it, "*you learn an awful lot because there is such a creative buzz around you. And doing a mindless task leaves your mind and ears open.*"

Mixing it up

Time in Louis Manches' domain is usually a given for first-year trainees: there are seats in commercial property, property litigation and construction (London only). A popular construction secondment to London

Underground is also open to trainees in both the London and Oxford offices. Manches receives substantial instructions from London Underground, including advising on construction aspects arising from the Thameslink 2000 upgrade at Blackfriars and the redevelopment of Cannon Street station. A trainee who moved to the property department after a stint in family was pleased to find work that was *"very hands-on and gave me the confidence boost I needed."* Smaller files are handed to trainees to run themselves, and these are interspersed with large deals *"where you do isolated pieces of work and never hear about them again."* Manches represents a number of retailers, banks, developers and investors, including All Saints, Moss Bros, Gap, Kew, Swarovski, Kookai, WHSmith, Barclays Bank, Bank of Ireland and Laing O'Rourke. The team undoubtedly took a hit in the recession, but with so many established clients and big personality Louis Manches at the helm, it is likely to continue bringing in a significant portion of the firm's income.

The corporate, employment and tech/IP departments have recently been brought together under a general commercial umbrella *"in order to build on the synergies that already exist."* This does not mean the separate seats have lost any of their individuality though. Quite understandably, those experiencing the corporate department during a recession see *"far fewer AIM listings and a lot more financing and sales deals, as well as restructuring."* What goes with this is a greater sense of crossover with lawyers in other parts of the firm. Insolvency cases often come from the tech/IP team, for example; referrals also come from the family department when separating couples divide their assets and *"groups of companies need to be looked at, dissected and valued."* When the individuals are non-UK domiciled, cases such as these often have international elements.

The loss of media lawyer Richard Dickinson and his team from the London office to US firm Arnold & Porter caused a level of restructuring in the tech/IP team, but the arrival of John Doherty from Lovells suggests an increase in the emphasis placed on trade mark disputes. Recent representative work of this type has involved MasterCard, Shell UK and retailer All Saints in relation to their UK and worldwide trade mark portfolios. We hear that one trainee was lucky enough to go on secondment to All Saints for one day each week. Woolworths was another secondment opportunity until… well, we all know what happened there. Tech/IP is a popular seat because *"you never know what is going to come through the door each day."* Trainees carry out a mixture of *"drafting and legal research,"* and one mentioned that at times they were *"the main point of contact for the client; people would entrust things to me."*

Chambers UK rankings

Banking & Finance	Intellectual Property
Corporate/M&A	Media & Entertainment
Dispute Resolution	Private Client
Education	Real Estate
Employment	Real Estate Litigation
Environment	Retail
Family/Matrimonial	Social Housing
Information Technology	

The commercial litigation team has also taken a hit recently with the loss of department head Clive Zietman and partner Andrew Shaw to Stewarts Law (which also took a family partner). The departure is a blow for the firm, which built a litigation practice off the back of Zietman's willingness to sue major banks when other firms steered clear. In response, Manches has combined its remaining litigation expertise in technology, property and commercial cases, and hopes to make new hires. It has started with a former Clyde & Co partner.

Bright lights and big boats

All those we spoke to agreed that Manches was a friendly firm, but despite the recent reshuffle in the commercial departments there was still the feeling that areas of the firm were too separate. The family department in particular was described as *"self-regulating"* and *"quite self-contained."* A consequence of this dispersed nature is that *"departments are very much run according to their heads."* As a trainee, therefore, it is important to *"find out how the head works and respond accordingly."* While some senior partners are keen to hear about what you got up to at the weekend or on the infamous trainee/associate ski-trip, there are others who are less approachable. Louis Manches was held up as one of the more sociable partners, with *"a proper open-door policy."*

The annual Manches Cup sailing regatta is renowned as a time *"when the hair really comes down."* Trainees, associates, partners and *"a few special clients"* all enjoy two days of racing and two nights of partying. The opposition? Other law firms. Sadly, in 2009, as a response to the economic climate, everyone was asked to pay for their own tickets to the jolly. The 2008 firm-wide Christmas party also fell foul of the recession, and departments celebrated separately in local restaurants instead. Of course, such measures are primarily a sign of the times and Manches is by no means alone in such cost cutting.

This doesn't mean there is a lack of informal fun: after all, the firm's West End location means you are never far away from a pint or a fancy cocktail. *"There always seems* to be someone going for a drink," commented one source. "Whenever you join a department they normally try to get everybody together for welcome drinks, and when you leave someone will usually offer to take you out for lunch." Netball and football teams are there for those so inclined, and the summer is a time for softball in one of the capital's vast parks. Involvement in sports teams "breaks down a lot of barriers" and "is a good way of getting people mixing on all levels." We should big up Manches' location a little more. Sited on the Aldwych, just off The Strand, it is practically on top of the Royal Courts of Justice and close to Lincoln's Inn Fields and the River Thames for summer strolls. Also a feature of the neighbourhood are thousands of tourists and LSE students.

The Oxford office takes two to three trainees each year and, apart from the initial firm induction, interaction between Oxford and London is nigh on non-existent at trainee level. "*Our offices are really separate. You wouldn't know the others existed,*" said one source. Oxford trainees can expect to commute into London at times for client meetings or trials. One trainee mentioned making regular trips down to the Royal Courts of Justice for a "*big malicious falsehood claim.*" The Reading office, meanwhile, is a trainee-free zone. Established in 2008, it has a particular focus on the technology and life sciences sectors. Oxford trainees can choose between corporate, litigation, property, employment and tech/IP seats, with family also occasionally thrown in if requested. Oxford's IP team is particularly well respected for its work in publishing: academic and educational publishing is the team's forte. It advises Oxford University Press and the Tolkien Estate, which filed proceedings against New Line Cinema in Los Angeles for unpaid royalties amounting to an estimated $150m regarding the three *Lord of the Rings* films. The case was settled favourably shortly before the trial date in October 2009. Non-contentious work for the Tolkien Estate includes the granting of worldwide e-book rights to Harper Collins and the publication of two previously unpublished poems. Trainees generally felt that the impressive reputation of a number of the Oxford lawyers meant that they got a higher quality of work than would be expected of a regional office.

Trainees were loath to say that Manches sought a particular type of person for its training contract, but they did mention that "*everyone has got to be ready with a smile, sharply dressed and bright-eyed.*" With such exacting standards in the family department, where "*everything has to be absolutely on the point,*" one trainee predicted that Manches is the perfect place for an "*outgoing perfectionist.*" Those who feel they fit the bill should form an orderly queue and prepare to impress with finesse. Eight out of ten qualifiers stayed on in 2009.

And finally...

If you're seeking guaranteed exposure to top-notch family cases Manches is a must, but be prepared to learn by osmosis at first. Cutting your teeth is easier in the property and commercial departments.

Martineau

The facts

Location: Birmingham, London

Number of partners/solicitors: 48/100

Total number of trainees: 19

Seats: 6x4 months

Alternative seats: None

The firm has a burgeoning energy department, a strong and well-known private client practice and an education clientele that sends instructions to several departments.

In Birmingham, just as in England's other largest provincial cities, the big national law firms dominate. As one of Brum's leading independents, Martineau has over 170 years of experience and wisdom behind it.

Standing the test of time

Martineau has just one other office, a smaller base down in London. Despite not being part of a vast network, its local presence, ties to the second city and quality of work make it worthy of being called a Birmingham institution. Of course the term institution can convey a sense of stuffiness; of cracking paintwork and anachronism reminiscent of ex-champions now hobbled by age. However, with its move in 2005 to a smart, modern office and a re-branding in 2008 that coincided with a 48% increase in partner profits, Martineau demonstrated that it was by no means going to fade out and let other Johnny-come-lateleys take over. Today, it is still one of the largest and most competitive firms in the West Midlands, strong across a wide range of commercial areas and a specialist in niche hotspots. It even walked off with last year's Birmingham Law Society 'Firm of the Year' gong.

Martineau has a six-by-four month seating system that enables trainees to sample a cross-section of departments. These can be "*startlingly different.*" They say the system is a winner as they often opt to take a second turn in a department, which means they can spend eight months in the area in which they hope to qualify. Martineau trainees usually have to do a seat in corporate and property, but because these groups don various guises, this isn't as prescriptive as it first appears. In fact none of the trainees we spoke to even seemed aware of this obligation.

Around the world

Led by its commercial groups, Martineau has been busying itself assisting clients such as Lloyds TSB, Bank of Ireland, Alliance & Leicester and Fortis. Some of the work has involved the restructuring of debt; one case saw the firm arrange £42m of customer debt for a bank and reorganise its security arrangements. Before the recession, the corporate department had a barnstorming year of deals deals deals (over £95m worth were funded using venture capital and private equity, including £30m worth of environmental infrastructure deals). Things have quietened, of course, but the firm keeps its eyes and ears open for good instructions. As well as winning work from businesses in the UK, Martineau enjoys a good standing in the Multilaw international lawyers network (managing partner William Barker is its chairman). Multilaw, which spans 44 countries and comprises over 5,000 lawyers, allows firms to send work to one another, sharing their expertise. The biggest deal in the firm's history originated from Multilaw and it is looking to increase the amount of instructions it wins from overseas, particularly from North America.

As well as being there to seal deals, Martineau lawyers also help to form new funds, restructure or merge them. Economic conditions have led to a great deal of this type of activity lately. One major asset to Martineau in the current climate is its wealth of public sector clients because, unlike many private companies, these guys are still building. Universities such as Staffordshire and Teesside have been keeping the firm's construction department busy. As one trainee said: "*Construction contracts can be bloody complex!*" That doesn't stop the construction seat from being popular. Here, as in most others, trainees said they enjoyed a good level of responsibility and were able to act as the client's first point of contact in some instances.

Niche work if you can get it

As for more specialist work, the firm has a burgeoning energy department, a strong and well-known private client practice and its education clients bring instructions to several departments. That Martineau's large education department includes lawyers from a raft of other practice areas including employment, finance, property and litigation is indicative of its scope. On behalf of almost 100 clients, it deals with all manner of issues affecting universities and higher education institutions, from wayward lecturers and students to whether universities can clamp cars parked on their land.

The firm has a successful and admired private client practice and, spinning off from its rural/agricultural group, there's a small equine team dedicated to the legal issues behind all things horsey. Martineau's private client group is not just a minor side project that the firm sometimes dips into; it's a major area. The impression we got was that the trainees were surprised when they enjoyed this seat because it's notorious for being deadly boring and unnecessarily complicated to study during the LPC. In reality it sounds like a different gig entirely. Trainees were enthusiastic about the client contact and sounded a little bit like detectives – investigating dead people's estates, following the paper trail and tying up all the loose ends, or organising clients' estates so that they can pass on the wealth. It's a seat where attention to detail is paramount, but if you are interested in piecing together peoples' histories and helping to arbitrate when wills are disputed, then it can be a very rewarding experience.

The energy practice has represented clients like British Energy, National Grid and Thames Water, and it's trying to expand into the renewables market and pick up carbon trading-related work. So far it has assisted with devising an alternative to the Kyoto Treaty, ready for when it expires in 2012, advised people involved in setting up wind farms and is advising on preparations for new nuclear plants in Cumbria. Trainees in the energy seat get involved in drafting commercial contracts for energy provision and write material for the firm's blogs and website. They report enthusiastically on how the firm is pushing for further involvement in energy trading markets. The appointment of new senior partner Andrew Whitehead (who is an energy lawyer) is perhaps an indicator of the level of importance Martineau places on this industry sector.

Chambers UK rankings

Agriculture & Rural Affairs	Employment
Banking & Finance	Information Technology
Charities	Intellectual Property
Construction	Pensions
Corporate/M&A	Private Client
Debt Recovery	Private Equity
Dispute Resolution	Real Estate
Education	Real Estate Litigation
	Restructuring/Insolvency

Moving from environmental climate change and back to the economic climate, the firm has two major growth areas to help it weather the storm – its debt recovery department and the IP/technology group. The firm describes the debt recovery department as flourishing, which considering that it has big-name clients like Lloyds TSB, npower and British Energy is unlikely to be an exaggeration. It also represents the Solicitors Regulation Authority, so it must be doing something right. Perhaps they should adopt a new tagline: Martineau – The Lawyers who Represent the People who Regulate Lawyers. The conventional wisdom states that IP fares well when the economic chips are down so it's a good area of business for the firm to be pushing. One happy trainee got to work on trade mark infringement cases for retailers and patent cases for small hi-tech companies, seeing some from start to finish. In this role you can expect to draft instructions to counsel, attend conferences and generally get a good amount of responsibility and client contact.

Open planet

Most of the Martineau trainees we spoke to had genuinely enjoyed every seat of their contracts, were glad they came to the firm, pleased with the work-life balance, happy with their training and impressed with the type of work they were given. Some people who had planned to move on after their training contract became convinced it was where they wanted to stay long term. Trainees' gripes mostly focused on the salary, which has hardly risen in three years and, according to one source, may deter future talent from coming to the firm because it is "*not sufficiently competitive.*"

Trainees for whom the lights of Birmingham aren't bright enough can apply for a seat in Martineau's London office. An added perk is that the lucky visitor gets to stay rent free in a flat just near Tower Bridge. Although the office is a lot smaller than the Birmingham HQ (just a dozen people) and lacks its reputation ("*When you tell people in London you work at Martineau, they ask, 'Isn't that a high-street firm?'*"), the experience of working there is both fantastic and faster paced. The problem of reputation is being addressed by the firm: it is talking of expanding the London office through 'bolt-on' mini-mergers with smaller firms or departments.

Some sociologists like to examine links between physical environment and behaviour – the effects of landscape or architecture upon culture, social structures and so forth. They could profit from a visit to the *"bright and airy"* Martineau office, maybe using it as a case study. When we asked about the culture of the firm and the social life, one source cited the open-plan office as a major influence: *"People are busy with lots of work, but within the constraints of that it's a very friendly place."* Another trainee agreed: *"The open-plan layout helps because there's always a friendly face, someone to talk to or ask questions. It's not distracting – when you've got your head down, people respect that you have work to do, but when you look up and give a little smile, you can get into a chat."* Even naturally private people are won over, finding that it can help them get better work: *"I prefer to work in my own room and I was worried about working in a communal area, but it's actually been good. I do definitely prefer the open-plan style. I can pick up work easier and I ended up going to a mediation because I'd asked someone nearby for some work."* Thanks to a (presumably influential) partner's interest in Feng Shui, each floor contains an artificial waterfall which, although nice, must surely be bad news for anyone with a weak bladder.

The word 'open' tripped off trainees' tongues on almost every subject. When it comes to appraisals, held twice during each seat (one after six weeks, one at the end), we hear that *"all the supers explain exactly why they've written what they have. It's all very open."* At times, Martineau began to sound like the setting for a beatnik novel. One trainee recalled how a supervisor had asked if there were any areas he could improve on and, because the partner listened to the response and *"actually gave a rat's ass,"* the trainee was impressed.

Join the family

Once you've gone through the appraisals and completed your seats, it's time for the real deal – qualifying into a department. Martineau prefers to release information about jobs early to alleviate some of the tension for waiting trainees. This isn't the case for all firms and one Martineau source told the tale of friends at a large national firm in Brum who were becoming increasingly worried because no jobs had yet been announced. By comparison, they felt Martineau was doing the best it could. *"They try to be as open as possible – they release the jobs that are definitely available then more come out gradually."* Although there is always going to be a risk of not getting a job in a more niche area, the firm tries *"to make a real effort to be fair to trainees and bring them in as part of the family right off the bat."* Martineau certainly made sacrifices to look after its own in 2009. There were under ten redundancies among staff, which was doubtless a contributing factor to the 24% fall in partner profits. Overall, the firm's revenue fell by 9% in 2008/09 and of the ten qualifiers, six were given jobs.

Martineau trainees *"tend not to be wallflowers or shrinking violets,"* so it is hardly surprising that they're social animals keen to get involved in events organised by the firm or among themselves. These range from the ubiquitous (Friday drinks, the Christmas party) through to the sporting and charitable. Fridays are *"usually pretty riotous. You get to the pub at about 5.30pm and there are always the same three or four people still going at one in the morning... everyone's welcome."* Trainees really do believe that the sense of togetherness at Martineau is made possible by the sociable nature of the place. The firm is eager to nurture this and does so in several ways: it pays for trainees' membership of the Birmingham Trainee Solicitors Society (BTSS), all trainees are assigned a role on Martineau's internal social committee, and they are encouraged to get involved in the football and netball teams which are said to *"punch above their weight."* Whether the BTSS aims at nurturing networking skills or whether it's more about just blowing off some steam and having fun is open to debate as many of the images connected with it feature pint-holding people looking tired and emotional.

And finally...

We reckon this intelligent and engaging firm, which remains as independent as ever, is just the ticket for Brum-bound students looking for an employer with a more contained and manageable business model than the big nationals.

Maxwell Winward LLP

The facts

Location: London

Number of UK partners/solicitors: 19/25

Total number of trainees: 5

Seats: 4x6 months

Alternative seats: None

> "A fair amount of our work is international, with a large proportion of it coming from construction disputes in the Middle East."

You want hard-hitting construction and property work without feeling like a cog in a machine. For this firm that's not an unreasonable demand.

Maxwell's smart

The name Maxwell Winward is relatively new to the UK legal market. The firm is the product of a merger between real estate-heavy Maxwell Batley and construction specialist Winward Fearon. These are testing times for property lawyers and Maxwell Winward has, like so many other firms, felt the pinch. Roughly 10% of all staff were made redundant in 2009, most from the transactional real estate team. Fortunately, this firm is smart: it hasn't focused all its attention on transactional matters and also has a hefty contentious workload to keep things ticking over. The other key point to make is that it has a loyal client base of major real estate businesses like Hermes, British Land, the BT Pension Scheme, Thames Water and the Duchy of Lancaster. The construction arm of the firm has never been busier, we hear. Among its clients are major names like Barratt Homes and Fitzpatrick Contractors.

Even though the merger was only effected in 2007, this is now a unified entity with little to distinguish between the two sides of the firm. Perhaps the last vestige of separation is "*a noticeable split in the client-sharing between the two parts;*" however, management has recently taken steps to promote client-sharing prospects. There is certainly much to share. "*A fair amount of our work is international, with a large proportion of it coming from construction disputes in the Middle East.*" The firm has also lately acted for a major Scandinavian pension fund on property matters. This being said, we mustn't overstate the international component as real estate matters are by their nature usually domestic.

Winward and leeward

There are four departments: construction, corporate/projects, real estate and dispute resolution. An employment team is embedded within the corporate/projects department. Trainees will either visit all four departments for six months each or repeat the seat they most enjoyed for their last placement. While some rate this second option, others recommended that it's "*better to do one of each to make an informed decision when you finish.*"

Some of those we spoke to had chosen Maxwell Winward for its outstanding reputation as a construction law expert and they were not disappointed. A trainee in this department experiences both contentious and non-contentious work and our sources spoke of involvement with major disputes where "*the quality of the work is really challenging.*" To give a recent example, lawyers represented a claimant subcontractor in a spat concerning the refurbishment of the Blackwall Tunnel. In the non-contentious arena, trainees can expect to be occupied with everything from research and document management to negotiating warranties over the phone and preparing building contracts. "*You have very high responsibility here,*" said someone who also appreciated the on-the-job training available. "*We conduct seminars for external clients and also attend talks at the Society of Construction Law.*"

In corporate finance the team has some novel work in the small to mid-sized deal range. Aurelian Oil & Gas (which operates in Central Europe) sought advice when it farmed out 40% of one of its Polish concessions to a private equity-funded upstream oil and gas company, and lawyers advised on the disposal of a majority shareholding in AxiCom Group, a leading pan-European technology PR agency. Meanwhile, OpenGate Capital came calling when it needed help with its acquisition of a major shareholding in the Models 1 agency. Trainee tasks include the staples of drafting commercial contracts and board minutes, as well as registering charges and issuing shares. "*Each partner has their own style, but they generally take an interest in giving you good work rather than just making you do photocopying.*" Sit with the employment subgroup and you'll draft client newsletters and compromise agreements for departing senior executives; trainees also learn about disciplinary actions and tribunal claims. It looks as if the firm is investing more resources in this area. It recently hired Julian Cox, the former head of employment at troubled firm Hextalls.

Stamp duties

The real estate seat involves some of the tedium of conveyancing, like post-completion form-filling for land registration and dealings with the HM Revenue & Customs. Somewhat more of a challenge are drafting exercises and lease negotiations. One source was brutally honest about the experience and told us: "*It's not the most exciting time to be in this business.*" On the other hand, another source felt that "*while some menial tasks were involved, I didn't feel like I was being used as a temp or something.*" In more normal economic conditions, "*there's quite a bit of responsibility in terms of managing files, and although you get constant supervision, you do feel like you are making a real contribution.*" The firm has still had good deals coming through: it lately acted on a number of prime lettings for clients, among them significant developments for Hermes in the City of London. If you know the capital at all you'll be aware of the massive regeneration of the King's Cross railway lands by Argent. When completed, the scheme will include acres of office, retail, leisure and community space plus 1,900 homes (40% of which will be affordable housing). Maxwell Winward has been helping Argent to structure the project and the corporate entities involved. A key role in such a vast scheme is a major feather in the firm's cap.

The disputes team deals with scores of property cases and "*time flies*" in this seat. Trainees find their days "*very exciting, as you're on the front line.*" Said one: "*Clients expect the best... they're far more emotional as they have an impetus for results.*" On the cards for trainees are client meetings, drafting instructions to counsel and dealing with costs assessments. One source warned: "*Disclosure exercises can be a bit lame and involve weekends on occasion.*" There is a difference in culture between the real estate and disputes teams: "*The real estate culture is very relaxed but for-

Chambers UK rankings	
Construction	Real Estate

mal, whereas disputes is more informal and dynamic.*" The firm additionally acts in commercial disputes, some quite eccentric. Take the vexatious philatelist who sued the firm's client for diminishing the value of his collection by awarding him third place in a stamp collecting competition.

Keeping it personal

This is a small firm with a very personal recruitment process. After a preliminary CV-based chat with charming partner Lisa Calderwood, there's a more formal pre-prepared discussion with other partners. Topics might range from renewable energy or globalisation to fair trade issues. In all of this an individual's personality has scope to shine. Everything takes place at the firm's relatively new home on Ludgate Hill, between St Paul's Cathedral and Fleet Street. "*The building is modern but very tastefully done, 1930s art deco and unique in the area.*" Too small to warrant its own canteen, the office is in a location where it's "*easy to get cheap food, and it is an interesting part of town.*"

With around 100 staff members, it's not hard to get to know everyone, particularly as trainees find the senior lawyers "*very approachable and friendly.*" At firm jollies, "*people turn up because they want to socialise with each other and not because they have to.*" There is one small criticism: "*It would be nice if all the lawyers were up on the website and not just the partners. It would make us feel more included.*" Trainees seem to mix well though and a social committee makes a good effort in organising activities like bowling, ice skating and trips to open-air cinema events in the grand setting of Somerset House, just a short stroll down The Strand. The Christmas party is "*a good chance to catch up with people in the workplace who you don't usually get to talk to.*"

And finally...

This firm deserves to be chosen specifically for its construction and real estate expertise and its more intimate atmosphere. In 2009, three out of four qualifiers were retained.

MAYER•BROWN

1*

*The day that you will count as a vital part of our firm.

When you are a trainee solicitor at Mayer Brown, you are more than just a number. We focus on giving you the one-on-one attention, support and opportunities you need to succeed in the legal world.

For more information on trainee solicitor and work experience opportunities at Mayer Brown visit mayerbrown.com/london

Alternatively, get in touch with Isabella Crocker, Graduate Recruitment Manager in London

T +44 20 3130 8524   E graduaterecruitment@mayerbrown.com

Mayer Brown is a global legal services organisation comprising legal practices that are separate entities ("Mayer Brown Practices"). The Mayer Brown Practices are: Mayer Brown LLP, a limited liability partnership established in the United States; Mayer Brown International LLP, a limited liability partnership incorporated in England and Wales; and JSM, a Hong Kong partnership, and its associated entities in Asia. The Mayer Brown Practices are known as Mayer Brown JSM in Asia.

Mayer Brown International LLP

The facts

Location: London
Number of UK partners/solicitors: 110/206
Total number of trainees: 55
Seats: 4x6 months
Alternative seats: Overseas seats, secondments
Extras: Pro bono – several legal advice clinics; language training

The firm is looking to recruit students with an appetite for hardcore City experience, primarily in its corporate and finance divisions.

With its 1,800 lawyers and vast global network, Mayer Brown is quite the international full-service heavyweight. You may just need the grit and determination of Rocky Marciano to duck and weave in this increasingly mercantile firm.

Golden Brown?

In London this firm was once an old-school City establishment called Rowe & Maw. Back in 2002, through one of the most transformative transatlantic mergers, Mayer Brown London became an altogether different contender. The combination of oh-so-British R&M with a group of sophisticated finance lawyers from one of Chicago's most successful firms changed the Brits' prospects noticeably. Not only did they gain access to new international clients and instructions, but the merger was a catalyst for growth, and in 2008 MB took another significant leap forward when it merged with leading Asian firm Johnson Stokes & Masters (JSM). The economy has curtailed aggressive expansion for the moment, and the firm has had to endure bad press following redundancies across its international network. However, the opinion among London trainees is that MB's thirst for "*world domination*" remains unquenched.

Multi-jurisdictional is the name of the game now and the firm is getting bigger and better deals than it would have done pre-merger. For example, London corporate lawyers worked closely with former JSM offices on disposals for Akzo Nobel and EMI Group. Meanwhile, London litigators have been representing Electronic Arts in an ongoing worldwide dispute with Emporio Armani over the initials EA, and outsourcing specialists have helped run the £5bn transfer of the management and operation of IBM's global telecoms network to AT&T. Across the departments, MB is a far bigger fish than it used to be in the global legal pond. Going forward, the structure of the training contract will look to incorporate a compulsory seat in corporate or finance, and a secondment to a client or overseas office (both of which trainees say can be hugely rewarding). All trainees need to take a contentious seat as well. While there is ample opportunity to gain an all-round training, we did find that experiences in the different parts of the firm are far from consistent and not all trainees have found all seats rewarding. We sense there are two contributing factors underlying our findings: the way in which the London office culture has developed in recent years and the scale of the cases and deals on which many trainees spend their time. More on each later.

Highs and lows

The finance division has experienced a boom, and the firm believes that this department in particular has responded well to market turbulence. Trainees say this remains an incredibly busy department with "*intense*," "*challenging*" and "*daunting*" experiences in store for those who visit. While some massive restructuring deals require that trainees "*do mainly admin work*," this department makes an effort to cater to their needs. "*When I was just doing admin, partners did intervene. In finance they do want to train you up*," assured one source. Another was pleased to have "*worked on three main projects over the six months*" and enjoyed "*becoming integral to the team*." The idea that in this department you "*sink or swim*" is mitigated by a lively social environment, though this does have its drawbacks. "*You're great friends with everyone, but the reason for this is that the long hours can mean you lose your friends outside work.*" Trainees point to the culture of casual arrival times as an obvious cause of late working. And when we say late, yes we are talking about "*prodding and poking each other to stay awake.*" It's worth pointing out that deals often span jurisdictions and involve working with MB teams overseas, hence the need to factor in other time zones. Leading clients include Bank of America, BNP Paribas, RBS, Macquarie, Allied Irish Banks, Nationwide and Wachovia. While the team can turn its hand to a variety of finance deals, there has been a shift towards asset-based lending since the credit crunch and, in a recent development, three leveraged finance partners have been hired in.

Corporate has been quieter. Still, warmth of feeling for this department was apparent – "*some of the people are fantastic.*" Where finance can sometimes be "*a bit cliquey or political,*" trainees here are largely impressed with the atmosphere. For many years under the influence of "*big daddy*" Paul Maher (who was an extraordinarily powerful, if not universally popular, member of the worldwide management committee), it now faces a new future following his somewhat public departure to start up the London office of Florida-headquartered Greenberg Traurig. Maher was instrumental to the success of the merger; however, not everyone appreciated his style. The corporate department now moves forward with a client list that is fat with well-known names from industry, particularly in relation to chemicals, manufacturing and steel, meaning that MB is not as reliant as some firms on banks or private equity funders.

Generally taken after a corporate or finance seat, client secondments are clearly important to the firm and also provide excellent opportunities for trainees. Destinations vary year on year but tend to include distinguished clients. Naturally some are more popular than others. MB now also offers international seats in Brussels, Hong Kong, São Paulo, Chicago and New York. In many ways the programme is at a fledgling stage, though trainees told us: "*The firm is getting a lot better at it.*" Other seats back at home include IP, employment competition, real estate, tax, insolvency and pensions.

We've left our discussion of litigation seats until last as this is where we found it hardest to find glowing reports. A number of our interviewees described feeling "*like I've gone a bit backwards*" after time spent in commercial dispute resolution and construction litigation. On the one hand, tasks revolve around "*photocopying, scanning, proof-reading, bundling and indexing,*" with blessed relief sometimes available in the shape of "*very focused legal research.*" Luckier trainees do get exposure to running small cases on their own, though the majority view on the work is that "*it's such high-level stuff there's not much trainees can do other than sort out files.*" It appears to be a classic equation of big cases plus big clients equals minimal scope for trainee inclusion. In short, MB's capacity to run large, complicated, international cases, combined with what trainees see as seniors' unwillingness to delegate more responsible tasks, leaves trainees with what feels like the profession's equivalent of a shovel and a mountain of horse manure.

Trainees also felt that in commercial dispute resolution their seniors could be very introverted, leading to a less than collegial environment where "*often no one will even make eye contact with you.*" We were told this may be the department's 'academic' atmosphere being misconstrued, but it is fair to say that quite a few trainees remarked that they felt uncomfortable in this seat. By contrast, the property litigation and insurance and reinsurance seats leave a far better impression. Until recently away from the main office and occupying its own nest on the 31st floor of the Gherkin, the latter is rather popular and trainee reports suggest the team atmosphere is "*a lot more intimate.*" Product liability is a major area of activity for this team, and one where cases can cover almost any subject matter. Take a couple of oil cases, for example – one relating to petroleum and another the sunflower variety. Professional negligence and auditors' claims also form a core part of the group's work. Sensitivities prevent us from publishing case examples, but in comprehensive MB style, bar about six letters, the team really does represent the A to Z of the world's insurers and reinsurers.

It is interesting to note that in the past two years the majority of the established CDR partners (five of them) left to seek their fortunes elsewhere, and the senior end is now populated by lateral hires for whom the recent past will have been as much about settling into a new firm as anything else. In theory there is every reason to assume

Chambers UK rankings

Advertising & Marketing	Insurance
Banking & Finance	Intellectual Property
Banking Litigation	Investment Funds
Capital Markets	Media & Entertainment
Competition/European Law	Outsourcing
Construction	Pensions
Corporate/M&A	Product Liability
Defamation/Reputation Management	Professional Negligence
	Projects, Energy & Natural Resources
Dispute Resolution	Real Estate
Employee Share Schemes	Real Estate Finance
Employment	Real Estate Litigation
Environment	Restructuring/Insolvency
Information Technology	Tax
	Telecommunications

the trainee experience in the main CDR department can improve. Certainly the department is getting some excellent instructions.

Don't hate the Mayer, hate the game

Our sources were explicit: "*This is a very ambitious firm with a very clear idea about where it wants to go.*" A swanky new office at 201 Bishopsgate is a powerful emblem. "*Looking like a Habitat showroom,*" the new building is spacious and has a much-needed canteen. In "*better proximity to firms with which MB wants to identify*" (such as A&O, Latham & Watkins, Ashurst and Herbert Smith), the new position in the financial heartland is "*indicative of the way the leadership wants to go.*" To this end, we can understand why some second-year trainees spoke of their unease with how the office's ethos has shifted since they were recruited. The push to "*be at the top*" has, in some instances, led trainees to feel "*they've lost sight of the people element.*"

Trainees hypothesised that MB was "*in a transitional phase.*" What we think we have here is a firm that has transitioned quite well work-wise and quite poorly culturally. Comments like "*the firm has become bedevilled with politics and micromanagement*" and "*if it is not right from the top it will be bad all the way down*" go some way to explaining some of the things we heard from trainees. As for whether this is an American v British issue, we don't think it is that straightforward. Some interviewees implied that in parts of the firm there was an undercurrent of "*we don't necessarily like the idea of being run out of the US;*" other sources feel the problems should not be laid at the door of the Americans. For example, finance is praised for being "*more the American way... more innovative.*"

Coherence is not something MB trainees recognise: "*Each department is like a totally different firm,*" from the hours to the dress code to appraisals. They also say that "*it's difficult to be judged by different people who judge so differently.*" The good news is that trainees believe 201 Bishopsgate should help to change this. Said one: "*Now everyone is mixing more in the new building I'm hoping the culture will move forward.*"

In the absence of a singular culture, we must do what we can to illustrate the different elements of the environment. First: be aware that trainees' pay and hours are similar to those in the magic circle. The cases and clients are of an excellent standard, and the JSM merger added real clout to the firm's international credentials. There is even one significant respect in which MB outshines many other City firms – it has shown itself to be open-minded when it comes to recruitment, and this is a topic on which our interviewees agreed the firm could not be faulted. Recruits include mature second-careerers ("*we have a beautician, a DJ, an actor*"), international graduates and those fresh out of UK universities. Significantly, our interviewees came from a broad range of universities. One fourth-seater told us: "*I liked that they didn't just recruit people from redbricks or with amazing grades. Some of the bigger firms would have turned me down on that basis.*" It was suggested that "*MB takes a cross-section of people so they can relate to different clients.*" Business development, it seems, is an important area for trainees, and so you should be willing to get involved in marketing and client wooing.

After speaking at length with trainees, we were left concluding that you must be prepared to get political at MB, to put in the grunt work and to settle into a system that can be conversely hierarchical or maverick. Confusing? Not to some of those we spoke to: "*There's an eagerness among many people here – they're proactive and strive to be positive even in difficult times.*" Determination is the key to success, and at MB the happy trainees are those who are strong-minded and "*able to adapt*" because they possess an unwavering "*dedication to getting things done.*" Right now, we'd recommend you avoid the firm if thin-skinned.

The Light (Bar) at the end of the tunnel

MB was unable to avoid redundancies and other cost-cutting measures. A first round saw 11 people exit, with round two putting 55 in the firing line and associates' pay frozen. The firm was able to find 21 jobs for 31 qualifiers in 2009 and seven of the September starters were deferred until 2010 in exchange for a £7,500 no-strings payment.

Just down the road from the office is Shoreditch's trendy Light Bar. It is "*high-end and overpriced*" and you can mingle with the young and fashionable. Trainee and vac scheme events are on the more studenty side, with curries on Brick Lane, whereas firm-wide events such as the Christmas party are more sedate.

And finally...

While Mayer Brown is an international giant that could become champion among transatlantic law firms it has some work to do on its general commercial litigation training.

McDermott Will & Emery UK LLP

The facts

Location: London
Number of UK partners/solicitors: 30/33
Total number of trainees: 6
Seats: 4x6 months
Alternative seats: None
Extras: Pro bono – Amnesty International

A relatively petite operation, MWE London is a perfect place to test the theory that small is beautiful when it comes to training contracts.

US-born McDermott, Will & Emery has an interesting set of strengths in its UK branch, which remains an important piece of the firm's global jigsaw.

Unique mixture

Founded in Chicago in 1934 as a tax practice, and now with 17 offices across the USA, Europe and Asia, this well-rounded commercial outfit's London office attracts graduates looking for a City firm with good work and a compact feel. "*We try and make sure people can have the quality without disappearing into 1,200 or so staff,*" explained training principal Prajakt Samant. The 11-year-old office is staffed by around 70 lawyers, and trainees enjoy the benefits of a smaller intake: "*You always get the seat that you want as there's so few of us.*" The training contract is entirely UK-based, but trainees say London is "*not just a satellite office – it's really important to the global practice.*"

Not everyone entirely agrees. The office has just one partner on the management committee and some commentators suggest that chairman Harvey Freishtat has prioritised US business above the international network during his tenure. True, his two newly elected successors (in post from January 2010) have made positive noises about renewed international commitment, but many perceive them as US-focused McDermott traditionalists. This said, MWE London does stand tall on merit in the global network. Around 75% of its work is self-generated, with the office strongest in employment, IP, structured finance and tax. There's also a well-hedged corporate team. What's more, the branch has held its own through ebbs and flows, with prominent partner departures balanced by arrivals in recent years. In 2008 the pattern continued: four partners and two senior lawyers departed from the important tax and structured finance practices, but litigation and competition teams grew. The latest hires are private client specialists.

Absolutly fabulous

MWE's range of strengths make it a good option for those hungry to explore a broad palette of commercial law. The employment department is regarded highly for its litigation nous, particularly in high-value discrimination cases. For example, it has been defending F&C Asset Management in a protracted multimillion-pound City sex discrimination claim brought by Gillian Switalski. New clients include healthcare products manufacturer Covidien and Islamic investment bank Gulf Finance House, while UEFA has sought help on things like restrictions on the transfer of young players and the appropriate assessment of damages for a player's unilateral breach of contract.

The IP practice grew by a third in 2008 and is now led by ex-Taylor Wessing partner Gary Moss. It's a strenuous seat where you can expect "*a flood of work*" in patent prosecution and other contentious aspects of IP, not to mention transactional issues. The owner of the Absolut trade mark recently turned to MWE when it had a problem with TIML Radio's launch of a new station, Absolute Radio. In another case the firm scored a whopping $267.5m triumph for client Visto Corp in an alleged patent infringement and validity claim by Research In Motion, which makes the BlackBerry.

The tax team may have lost some partners this year, but is still a major MWE asset, primarily handling tax-led consultancy work and transactions. Not only has the level of instructions from existing clients like Société Générale gently increased, but the firm has also signed up new finance clients like Citadel, Goldman Sachs and Nomura UK. A major highlight of the past year was representing Italian designer sunglasses specialist Luxottica in the consolidation of its Sunglass Hut companies in the UK and Republic of Ireland.

Flying the coup

MWE's dispute resolution team also had an excellent year, particularly in the oil and gas sector, where a stand-out instruction saw the firm advising Nippon on its recession-hit North Sea drilling programme. Getting involved in major international disputes in a seat based very much on "*black letter research with a lot of case management*" clearly appealed to our sources. "*There are no menial tasks here,*" they explained; "*we have the opportunity to get our hands dirty.*" The firm's US clientele generates plenty of cases for MWE London, be it disputes in the UK or further afield. Working with colleagues out of Washington, DC, the team advised the government of Equatorial Guinea in the prosecution of former British Army officer Simon Mann, a mercenary who was imprisoned for his role in a failed coup in 2004. There has also been an increase in instructions from the pharmaceutical, telecoms and financial sectors. A sought-after competition seat brings cross-office experience: London, Brussels and DC work closely, offering trainees exposure to everything from cartels and hedge funds to sports deals. Be warned: pedantry is a prerequisite – "*it's a very precise area of law with complex cases where you have to pick out minute rationes.*"

The five-partner *Chambers UK*-ranked structured finance team is ideal for those keen for capital markets experience. The arrival of new partners balances two more recent departures and the firm has plumped up its client list with The Bank of New York Mellon, Lux Kapitalmarkt and Lyxor Asset Management. Work of late includes various restructurings on behalf of BNP Paribas, UniCredit and Fortis Bank, as well as regulatory advice for staple client Société Générale on an exchange-traded note programme. After helping out with some of the "*biggest deals in the area,*" trainees suggested that the seat is more admin-heavy than some others. That said, the banking and corporate seats offer much more client contact on international matters and were consequently popular among our sources. One recalled: "*I was the first point of contact for clients, which was an invaluable experience.*"

Now we are ten

The fact that MWE is an American firm is a major draw for some recruits; many were particularly sold on potentially working in the USA post-qualification. For others, the firm's small size in London sealed the deal. Said one trainee: "*There's a strong sense of collegiality here as there's only seven of us, and most lateral hires are from the UK so there's no hard-core Wall Street mentality.*" "*A very flat hierarchy*" makes trainees feel a part of things, but at times an excess of pdfing and bundling duties can lead to the niggling feeling that "*trainees are not the firm's primary focus.*" However, sources recognised that "*it does put a lot of effort into our development*" and highlighted "*on-the-spot feedback*" and various informative internal seminars.

Many trainees come with previous legal experience (eg paralegalling) and recruiters do seem to regard this as advantageous. Training principal Prajakt Samant suggested the firm is after "*independent, strong-willed people,*" a statement given weight by the ambition and determination we detected among our sources. Certainly, an entrepreneurial outlook and the stamina to work late hours are required. "*Once you've been in a seat for a couple of months they trust you with timekeeping and you'll also find that some late hours into the evening and the odd weekend are expected.*"

Four new starters delayed their September 2009 arrivals until the following March and were paid £5,000 to do so. The recession also forced MWE London to make three legal and nine non-legal staff redundant so it's not surprising that social events have slipped down the list of priorities, leaving the scene somewhat subdued of late. Unfortunately the annual trainee induction programme in the USA – a lively week in DC with US counterparts – was also cut, and the last Christmas dinner (to which future trainees were invited) was low-key. Celebrations at the Globe Theatre to mark the firm's tenth London birthday were also reportedly modest. More broadly, sources told us: "*The social side could be a lot better here, not just within the trainee group but also among the whole firm.*" One suggested: "*It might help to have more communal areas where you can bump into people.*" Speaking of the office building, trainees say it's a little "*shabby.*"

Chambers UK rankings

Capital Markets	Intellectual Property
Competition/European Law	Projects, Energy & Natural Resources
Dispute Resolution	Sports Law
Employment	Tax

And finally...

MWE is looking for independent, strong-willed, entrepreneurial types. In 2009, all three qualifiers stayed on, going into the banking, structured finance and corporate teams.

SPRINGBOARD OR STRAITJACKET?

Your training contract will set the foundations for your career. At McGrigors we do not put a lot of effort into turning you into a good trainee. We put our effort into turning you into a great lawyer for life.

To find out more about a training contract that's springboard not straitjacket, visit www.mcgrigorsornot.co.uk

M
McGrigors

DRIVEN BY BUSINESS. *Powered by people*   www.mcgrigorsornot.co.uk

McGrigors LLP

The facts

Location: London, Manchester, Scotland
Number of UK partners/solicitors: 84/269
Total number of trainees: 25 (in England)
Seats: 4x6 months
Alternative seats: Scotland, Falklands, secondments
Extras: Pro bono – LawWorks

A timely merger with London litigation boutique Reid Minty should help McGrigors further its ambitions in the capital.

With further national expansion still in its sights, this 200-year-old Scots firm has a London office with an interesting tale behind it, a good future in front of it and a star tax litigation team lighting the way.

Out of kilter

Scottish giant McGrigors landed in London in 2002 when it merged with the old legal arm of Big Four accountancy firm KPMG. This was a time of change in the accountancy profession: a corporate scandal at Texan energy company Enron brought down global firm Arthur Andersen, and the other big players got jumpy about the fact that they'd effectively set up in-house law firms. There was a sense that clients would shy away from the concept of multidisciplinary professional practice. This left KLegal in need of a new champion and McGrigors came to its rescue. The influence of KPMG is now largely historical and the McGrigors brand and the McGrigors plan have taken over.

One part of the plan is further expansion. In 2007 a Manchester office was added to a list of McGrigors addresses that already included Edinburgh, Glasgow, Aberdeen, Belfast and, of course, London. "*Before, it was suggested we were a Scottish-based firm, but we are actually a national player now,*" insisted our sources. Another part of the plan is to market the firm through a rebrand featuring a snazzy technicolour logo and new website. Trainees welcomed the change as they thought the previous imagery, although professional, was "*a little confusing.*" They also see the new branding as "*fresher*" and more likely to articulate McGrigors' core values (as suggested by a survey of clients) of pragmatism, innovation, excellence, ambition and approachability. We take these things with a pinch of salt – any number of law firms bandy such words around – but we do rather like the sound of the new firm motto as it makes us think of a flashy car advert. 'Driven By Business. Powered By People.' Vroom…

A Minty task

Trainees can sample a variety of seats, such as employment law, construction, a range of corporate options and the prestigious tax litigation team. Every trainee must spend at least six months in a corporate seat, be this straight corporate, banking, IP or with a team focusing on energy matters. The other must-do is six months in a contentious seat like dispute resolution, employment, tax litigation or construction.

The tax litigation group is a jewel in the London office's crown and it consistently earns a top-band ranking in *Chambers UK*. McGrigors has been representing a group of over 100 of the country's largest pension funds seeking nearly £1.5bn in tax credit reclaims from HMRC, with litigation proceeding innovatively in both the High Court and the tax tribunals. It has also advised a well-known professional footballer who was at risk of prosecution in connection with undeclared payments received on his transfer to a new club. "*The tax team wins awards year after year and the emphasis is on getting it perfect every time,*" said one trainee who felt the seat had the most supervision compared with the other contentious options. "*The tax team always beats its tar-*

gets, always outperforms," concluded another. Trainees here can expect anything from compound interest claims to fraud investigations.

There was enthusiastic praise for the general commercial litigation seat, where lawyers have lately dealt with everything from scores of debt recovery cases to a major Wembley Stadium dispute. Lucky trainees may get to do some of their own advocacy, but we heard good reports on the trainees' lot even from those who'd missed out on a moment of glory in court. Earlier in 2009 the firm merged with London litigation boutique Reid Minty, taking on all of its operations minus a personal injury department. This move boosted McGrigors' white-collar crime capacity (perfect in an economy where increased emphasis is placed on regulation and scrutiny) and introduced a unique seat for trainees looking for a challenge. Speaking with trainees we got the impression that McGrigors wants to expand its litigation capacity generally, and that white-collar crime and fraud will become a core area, possibly incorporating criminal practice too. The employment team has also gone from strength to strength: trainees can expect to prepare witness statements for unfair dismissal claims, sometimes touching on sex, race and disability discrimination. One trainee who'd had a ball in the seat told us: "*I would love to go back to that team as it gave so much responsibility and client exposure.*" They particularly liked how "*everybody discusses cases with each other in the open-plan office.*" As an added bonus, the employment trainee also learns about the ever-changing field of immigration law.

Construction seats mean exposure to clients like retail giant Morrisons. There's also the unusual-sounding Qatar Dairy Company, which has sought advice on disputes regarding professional appointments for the construction of a large industrial-sized diary farm in the Middle East. Sportier trainees might get excited about the firm's representation of the architects of the Olympic Aquatics Centre. As for real estate seats, well, sadly here trainees felt there had been "*a noticeable reduction in work in London, though the Scottish offices anomalously have remained as busy as ever.*"

Wind and waves

McGrigors takes advantage of its Aberdeen office, right in the petroleum centre of Europe. Its corporate expertise in the energy and petroleum market is undoubted: in 2008 its capital markets team advised on two of the biggest AIM IPOs of the year – Valiant Petroleum and OPG Power Ventures. The flotation of Valiant raised £50m of new funds. The team also recently advised Belfast Gas Transmission Financing on a pipeline network in Northern Ireland. Although a lot of the firm's energy projects work is with petroleum, it maintains a healthy level of activity in relation to wind farms, biofuels and national grid work.

Chambers UK rankings

Administrative & Public Law	Licensing
Banking & Finance	Local Government
Competition/European Law	Parliamentary & Public Affairs
Construction	
Corporate/M&A	Pensions
Dispute Resolution	Planning
Employee Share Schemes	Projects, Energy & Natural Resources
Employment	
Environment	Real Estate
Health & Safety	Real Estate Litigation
Information Technology	Retail
Intellectual Property	Tax

McGrigors has a keen interest in the education sector, too, having recently assisted a leading Spanish education group on its first UK acquisition – an independent school in England (along with an associated schools' accessories and property lettings business).

Trainees say the corporate team is among the most popular. Its banking subgroup has major clients such as RBS, Bank of Scotland, HSBC, Lloyds TSB, Barclays and Co-operative Bank. It's a sign of the times that trainees have lately seen more insolvency and restructuring instructions than lending deals. If nautical nonsense be something you wish, as our old mate SpongeBob would say, you'll be pleased to learn that the firm has a growing ship finance practice, acting for lenders. In the IP seat, trainees encounter client O2 on a host of matters. There may also be the option of a secondment with O2, where trainees can expect to gain an understanding of employment, procurement, contracts, small claims and IP law as well as an in-depth knowledge of the client's business needs.

You and McGrigors

London trainees are encouraged to take a seat in one of the firm's Scottish offices, and it's clear that they have a better chance of a place north of the border than their Scottish counterparts do in securing an English placement. There's help with moving expenses and accommodation. Soul-searching aesthetes can make a bid for a seat in the Falkland Islands. It brings a mix of company work, family law and other private client matters, drugs importation cases and fisheries-related advice. Life in Port Stanley is relaxed as "*the island works at its own speed,*" and the pubs are pretty welcoming, including The Trough, where you bring your own alcohol. Given that there's only one flight out of the Falklands every week, and the seat involves six full months in the South Atlantic (the closest point in South America is 500 km away), the posting is more attractive to those who have few commitments in the UK. As a bonus, two weeks of travelling time in South America is granted after the seat is finished.

McGrigors recently started accepting trainees into its Manchester office for seats, although it is usually a Scottish recruit who gets to go. According to a source, *"the Manchester office has gone from strength to strength since its inception and is thriving with lots of lateral hires."* Previously some trainees had the opportunity to work at KPMG for six months, but this option was withdrawn in 2009 for financial reasons. Trainees are sometimes able to tag along on business trips, be it for a negotiation in Prague or a tour of a confectionery factory (Willy Wonka style, we hope).

All our sources were quick to point out the benefits of working in a smaller office. *"Partners jumped up to greet me when I first got here,"* recalled one source. Another felt the firm would be ideal for *"people who like their work but don't want it to define them… it's a bit more free-thinking than the magic circle firms."* When it comes to late working, McGrigors has been quite upfront in its recruitment material. At times trainees do have to burn the midnight oil, and this aspect was a low point for a number of our sources. That said, they were reflective about the importance of such challenges. As for other gripes, a couple of people felt that *"expectations aren't well communicated to trainees,"* although most described the review procedure as *"very efficient."* Formal training gets a thumbs-up, particularly departmentally organised sessions.

The firm recruits from a good range of universities and around half the London intake had law degrees in 2008/09. Of themselves, trainees say they are *"very normal and not too eccentric."* Sadly, in 2009 just five out of 15 English qualifiers found out they'd be able to continue their careers at the firm, the lucky few going into contentious teams and the Manchester office.

The London office in Old Bailey sits in the shadow of the statue of Lady Justice. Also within her gaze is the trainees' regular venue for after-work drinks – All Bar One. We had consistently good reports about the atmosphere in the office, usually along the lines of: *"We have a small-firm character where you can get to know a lot of people."* The partners are deemed to be quite sociable, although people had noticed a reduction in the number of social activities, something they felt was *"understandable given the current climate."* Some people play cricket on a weekly basis in the summer, and there was a fun, superheroes-themed charity event recently. The firm makes a point of celebrating St Patrick's and St George's days and there's always a big Burns Night bash up in Scotland. The Edinburgh office was particularly noted for its Café McGrigors – a monthly get-together in the office. Back in London we should point out that the staff canteen offers a free dinner to those working after 8pm.

And finally...

Despite this being a shocking year for NQ retention, trainees repeatedly told us McGrigors' training and office atmosphere had lived up to their expectations. To say a firm is down to earth is a terrible cliché, but it does seem to fit here.

Michelmores LLP

The facts

Location: Exeter, Sidmouth, London
Number of UK partners/solicitors: 41/80
Total number of trainees: 16
Seats: 4x6 months
Alternative seats: Secondments

"Some fairly significant growth is still planned. London is going to feature quite strongly. We are the only firm down here with a proper London office."

Training Partner, Tim Richards

Now with a London office that is rapidly gaining muscle, South West dynamo Michelmores is developing into a firm with real clout.

Growing in a glass house

Senior partner Will Michelmore's great-grandfather founded this firm in 1887, and in 2005, after more than a century nestled on Exeter's ancient Cathedral Green, it upped sticks to a purpose-built, glass office in a business park outside the city. A London office was launched the same year and the two bases complement each other perfectly. The London pad attracts new clients and sends work to Exeter, while the South West HQ benefits from a W1 postcode on its letterhead. Busy Michelmores has achieved an average growth of 20% over the past five years through lateral hires and organic expansion. One significant acquisition for the London office was commercial litigator Peter Sigler, previously a partner at Nabarro. Meanwhile, the Exeter office undertook two raids on local rival Foot Anstey, nabbing an insolvency team in August 2008 and childcare abuse, surrogacy and adoption specialist Vanessa Priddis and two associates soon after.

In order to cope with the firm's increasing size there has been an inevitable *"formalising of systems and processes,"* and Malcolm Dickenson was elected as Michelmores' first managing partner. Training partner Tim Richards explained: *"We'd got to a stage in our growth when a full-time management concentrating solely on strategy needed to be in place."* The training contract too has been evolving as the firm grows. Traditionally recruits worked their way through a strict four-seat system that required one stint in each of the main departments – property, litigation, corporate/commercial and private client – with the option of spending six months in London. Now, increasing numbers of individual teams can support a trainee of their own, resulting in a *"less formulaic"* system that allows trainees to spend six months working solely on more specific sectors like projects, insolvency, government property or IP/IT. Tim Richards stressed that *"while trainees might be in a specialist team, we encourage them to take work outside it in order to maintain a broad training."* 2009 also saw Michelmores welcome its first full-time London trainee, but more about that later. Interviewees say all this growth and new formality have not changed the firm's essential character. It is keen to maintain *"a sense of its family-run roots. It doesn't want to destroy itself by growing too quickly. Lateral recruitment is quite selective. They are not just looking for someone who is good, but for people who will fit the Michelmores mould."*

Public property

Commercial property is the biggest group, and with a team dedicated exclusively to public sector matters, acting for more than 20 government departments and agencies, Michelmores' is healthier than most, for now at least. Proof of the department's vigour and confidence for the future is illustrated by the positions that were found for two qualifying trainees and the promotion of new partner Joe Gribble, who joined the London office in 2006 from Freshfields. The Exeter practice advised HM Courts Service on its new Business Court in London. Other clients include Summerfield Developments, Midas Homes and Barratt Homes, for which Michelmores acted on the acquisition of a site in Yeovil with planning permission for 700 dwellings. Despite the size of many of the transactions, trainees are given "*an active role.*" Said one: "*I was able to make contributions, give my opinion and offer advice.*"

Some recruits get slightly anxious at the prospect of a seat in the projects team. "*You don't study it at university so I wasn't even really sure what it was,*" one explained. Most quickly appreciate that the experience gained here, under the watchful eye of Carol McCormack, is "*exceptional for the South West.*" Many of the deals are "*massive and involve lots of other areas of the firm,*" so a trainee's role is primarily organisational, "*managing all the documents and keeping track of what has and hasn't been agreed.*" A lot of time is spent travelling to London ("*always first class*") to attend client meetings and negotiations.

No paws for the wicked

Michelmores' commercial litigation department is top-ranked in the South West and, supported by the small but impressive London team, is handling an increasingly international workload. The department covers the full range of commercial disputes, including those relating to computers/IT, shareholders, contractual claims, warranties and IP. The London office nabbed partner Charles Metherell from Bevan Brittan in February 2009 to head up a dedicated 'interventions' practice that trainees believe is "*going to be an area of growth.*" Interventions lawyers deal with the aftermath of SRA actions against law firms found guilty of misconduct. "*We go in and take the files and distribute them at the client's request,*" explained one source. While there is "*not a lot of legal nitty-gritty, you are working a lot on your people skills and writing to or phoning the clients.*" Technology, media and communications work continues to be a growth area and the team counts The Met Office, Flybe, HM Courts Service, Opal Health, Devon County Council and the world's largest online gaming company Miniclip among its clients, offering advice on both contentious and non-contentious IP and IT. "*It was a complex seat,*" reported one source, "*but I had great support and the work I was given matched my ability.*"

The private client department is "*less formal*" than the rest of the firm (Will Michelmore occasionally brings his dog in and "*if you ask nicely you can take it for a walk*") but the work available is some of the best in the South West. "*I felt the whole time I was working on very important matters and was an important part of the team,*" beamed one source. Renowned for its sensitive approach, the group continues to attract new clients including a family that owns and runs a multimillion-pound company and three landed estates of some significance.

A breath of fresh air

Those interested in swapping the green fields of Devon for the bustling streets of London (the office is just a short walk from Covent Garden) can expect bags of responsi-

Chambers UK rankings

Agriculture & Rural Affairs	Employment
Banking & Finance	Family/Matrimonial
Clinical Negligence	Information Technology
Construction	Planning
Corporate/M&A	Private Client
Dispute Resolution	Real Estate
	Restructuring/Insolvency

bility and invites to sparkling marketing events. Henley Regatta, a ball at the Globe Theatre and breakfast functions were just a few mentioned. Exeter-based trainees loved the opportunity "*to have a London experience without having to spend my whole training contract there.*" Those keen to spend two years in the capital need to be "*quite flexible,*" as the size of the office necessitates "*doing the work that needs to be done rather than being officially assigned to a team.*" This does mean that "*the breadth of experience is great and you get to work with the top people, rather than being just a number.*" With London at the centre of Michelmores' expansion plans it is certainly an exciting time to be there.

When it comes to recruitment, Michelmores trainees say: "*It's not just about your grades – they really want you to stand out and not be ashamed of your personality.*" Due to the firm's long history with the institution, the majority of trainees are graduates of Exeter University. However, the firm has begun to spread its net wider and is actively targeting in London, Birmingham and Bristol.

The social life is "*what you make of it.*" As most people drive to work, after-work boozing is difficult, but Michelmores does have the requisite Christmas and summer events as well as staff drinks every couple of months in its café. While an out-of-town location may not be good for hanging out in pubs, there were few complaints when it came to the office's setting. The views from the aptly named Woodwater House are "*beautiful… there are hills right into the distance.*" If you have a particularly vivid imagination, "*when the weather is really lovely and you don't want to be in the office, the windows are so big that you can almost imagine you're out there.*"

And finally…

Michelmores trainees may not be "*sheep that come in to be cannon fodder,*" but this is an ambitious firm that expects commitment and hard work. It also has a habit of employing its qualifiers: in 2009 all six were kept on.

Mills & Reeve LLP

The facts

Location: Birmingham, Cambridge, Norwich, London, Leeds, Manchester
Number of partners/solicitors: 92/354
Total number of trainees: 46
Seats: 6x4 months
Alternative seats: Occasional secondments
Extras: Pro bono – Free Legal Advice Group, ProHelp

Although it has shown itself to be a fast-growing firm, Mills & Reeve has followed a careful expansion plan. Train here and you'll discover a wealth of practice areas.

For many years the biggest player in East Anglia, Mills & Reeve has shed the 'regional firm' label like an old skin. Nurtured by healthy profits, it has emerged as a national player with a diverse range of practices in six offices.

Nationalisation

Not merely a commercial all-rounder, M&R distinguishes itself with a clutch of specialist practices in the areas of education, healthcare, private client and indemnity and reinsurance. It enjoys prominence in public sector markets and new public sector clients are still being added. Despite the recession, the firm saw profits rise by 8% and turnover increase to £66.6m. At the same time, trainees have noticed that "*it is now focused on targeting more private sector work.*" But before we discuss the firm's work in detail, we should fill you in on the story of the past ten years to give you an idea of the speed of change here and where the firm might be headed.

Decades of work in the East Anglian market gave M&R a great start: its first office opened in Norwich as early as 1880, and by the tail end of the 1990s it had earned a reputation for quality both here and in Cambridge. A sea change occurred in 1998 when it branched out to Birmingham to exploit the growing legal market in the Midlands, initially concentrating on the health sector. Now a full-service branch, the Brum office continues to grow in size and influence. Emboldened by its success here, M&R set up shop in London in 2000 and for a while seemed happy to steadily build its service offering to attract more clients. Another growth spurt marked 2008. When Addleshaw Goddard excised its family law practice, M&R pounced, grabbing the drifting department and seizing the opportunity to plant its flag in Leeds and Manchester. These offices now have insurance practices too. Although managing partner Guy Hinchley kept his cards pretty close to his chest when we spoke to him, we sensed that more service lines (private tax and trusts were hinted at) will be added to these newer branches and, based on recent history, it wouldn't be uncharacteristic of the firm if there were more developments in the pipeline.

Other offices may see growth, including London. Every five or six years, the firm develops a new strategy, the most recent being described by Hinchley as "*an evolution of the previous one*" based on further development of the six key practices of health; higher and further education; regeneration projects; real estate; indemnity and reinsurance; and private client. We see it like this: many firms grew swiftly in the late nineties and early noughties only to be sucker-punched by the recession. Instead of hiring hordes of finance lawyers, M&R plotted its own course in private client, education and healthcare matters, and by taking the road less travelled M&R has a hardy perennial set of practices that should help it infiltrate its newer geographical markets. It is also worth noting that its clients look to the firm not only for specialist advice but also seek a range of more general commercial services. BUPA, for instance, uses M&R for corporate deals up to £10m in value.

Surgeon Mills

The firm's healthcare practice covers the gamut of issues from claims of negligence and employment disputes through to financial concerns, property management and governance issues. Recent work has included adapting current policies to realign them with new legislation, advising on executive-level terminations of contract, insurance liability cases and high-value construction projects. Some of the cases undertaken result in the setting of precedents; others pertain to long-running debates about healthcare provision in the UK. For example, the firm successfully represented Stoke-on-Trent PCT at the High Court in a case concerning the long-term care of a patient who had been injured at work. Their insurers insisted the NHS should pay for their care, but M&R pursued the argument that the insurers were liable. If successful, the firm could save the NHS hundreds of millions of pounds. Cases like this draw on the expertise of lawyers from many different disciplines and, as such, the healthcare seat affords trainees exposure to the way in which problems are handled holistically.

One offshoot of the healthcare practice is the regulatory team. Here keen trainees assist clients like the General Dental Council on cases of negligence or malpractice: *"If a patient or trust complains about a dentist, we investigate and see if it has any merit. We take interviews to gather facts and see if the dentist is fit to practise."* Although some of the cases *"are enough to put you off going to the dentist ever again"* as *"they sometimes take out the wrong tooth,"* trainees enjoy the responsibility, the opportunity to sleuth and the chance to attend the panel hearings at which strike-off decisions are made.

And so to education work. There are over 140 lawyers in the university business group which, like the healthcare group, provides a full service to education sector clients nationwide (including locals at Cambridge University). Recent work has touched upon research contracts, tax disputes and a lot of property and construction deals, especially relating to student accommodation.

Buddy, can you spare a dime?

A six by four-month seat rotation allows trainees to roam the practice groups and office network. After the first seat they get a say about what they do, and our sources were largely satisfied with how their allocations had worked out, especially in the second year. Ideally, a trainee will take two seats in the department into which they qualify, giving them eight months of crucial experience where it matters most. As well as having a seat supervisor (partner or associate), trainees each have a principal and a buddy. *"The principal does as little or as much as you want; you can discuss the job with them, discuss the partners, any problems – mine was very helpful and gave good advice."* The buddy *"shows you where the pub is"* – vital in a firm where people like to go for a couple of drinks on a Friday. The consensus was that the training contract is well organised and

Chambers UK rankings

Agriculture & Rural Affairs	Intellectual Property
Banking & Finance	Licensing
Charities	Local Government
Clinical Negligence	Pensions
Construction	Planning
Corporate/M&A	Private Client
Dispute Resolution	Professional Discipline
Education	Professional Negligence
Employment	Projects, Energy & Natural Resources
Environment	
Family/Matrimonial	Public Procurement
Healthcare	Real Estate
Information Technology	Real Estate Litigation
Insurance	Restructuring/Insolvency
	Tax

strikes a good balance between responsibility and supervision. *"If you want a well-rounded training with lots of areas of law, then this is definitely one of those firms. About 90% of the partners know who you are and take an interest in you and encourage you, which is really important."*

Although it isn't compulsory to do so, trainees can work in different locations. They are given some assistance if they opt to move elsewhere (the firm points them in the direction of some estate agents) and the *"general attitude is that you won't be out of pocket if you choose to move office."* Our sources explained that making a move can be stressful because they're only given one day off to find a flat in the new city, and the fact that they may only get two weeks' notice of a relocation definitely rankles. Still, no one said anything about kipping in doss houses, claiming sanctuary in a church or occupying a park bench, so perhaps it's enough.

A large part of choosing an office boils down to the departments available. Luckily we encountered some trainees with an encyclopaedic knowledge of the options. *"Birmingham has a lot of public sector and healthcare, which is the largest area. It does insurance, private client, construction, real estate, education, employment, corporate and commercial. Planning and environment and real estate disputes are the only things you can't do in Birmingham."* Cambridge does all of the above *"except regulatory and insurance,"* and Norwich is the wrong place to go for healthcare, planning or construction, but is the only place that does real estate disputes. As for the northern offices in Manchester and Leeds, they just offer family law and insurance work at present. Down in the capital it's mainly insurance and health regulatory. Other trainees volunteered further information – *"Cambridge has more biotech,"* while *"Norwich is more commercially based"* and *"smaller, not as broad."* Still, as we said earlier, new service lines are being added, so it will be well worth checking with the firm if you get an interview.

Krypton factor

Interesting fact: the "*three-floor, purpose-built, open-plan and glass-fronted*" office in Norwich is sited on top of the ruins of an ancient burial ground. Thankfully there are no reports of paranormal activity. Although the other offices can't boast a 13th century monastic crypt in their basements, we received no complaints, except from the trainee who said that the Cambridge office is looking "*slightly tired, even though it still has everything you need.*" As for the social life, the impression we got was that the trainees in East Anglia were far more wholesome and outdoorsy. They balanced a fondness for cheesy chips at the pub during their lunch break with tennis, cricket, netball and football. As for the Brum trainees, well they prefer to drink and hit the town. The Londoners go for pints on a Friday, but because the office is quite small with fewer trainees and the City is so large, people tend to have their own things going on.

To get the whole firm together there is a Charity Challenge and a Christmas party. Last year the challenge saw enthusiastic trainees conquer a snow-covered Helvellyn (a treacherous mountain in the Lake District much beloved of Wordsworth and Wainwright) before completing a 30 km cycle and chilling row across Ullswater. This year they had a choice of a 75-mile bike ride or a 25-mile hike in the Peak District. Office parties "*vary year to year – the summer party is either for the whole firm or just an office party, and the Christmas one is either sub-teams or the whole office.*" The trainees put a good deal of effort into these socials, and last Christmas they produced a film that made "*a light-hearted jab at the M&R Visions & Values presentation. The partners took it in good spirit.*" All this while the boys were dressed as girls in what is apparently the "*classic Christmas party way.*"

When leafing through recruitment brochures you'll often find bold claims about a good work-life balance and law firms' respectfulness of trainees as 'real people with real lives'. Sadly they don't always deliver. Of course, every trainee is going to end up swigging a late-night espresso at some point, but at M&R it won't happen regularly. Trainees say they work to standard office hours, and the firm's sixth appearance in the *Sunday Times'* 'Best Companies to Work For' survey in six years is proof that it does deliver on its promise of a life outside the office.

Because a good lawyer has to combine the ability to push a pen with the ability to engage with clients, M&R encourages trainees to attend networking events. "*They vary from team to team because different types of clients need different things, from breakfast seminars to art exhibitions. Recently we went to see some modern art at Kettle's Yard* [a gallery in Cambridge]. *I wasn't impressed with the art. It was… a talking point.*" Still, "*the canapés were good.*" For one trainee, networking events were one of the most enjoyable aspects of the training and were the deciding factor in choosing Birmingham over Cambridge. "*Cambridge is a nice place to live but there's not the same emphasis on marketing and half the battle in winning clients is having interpersonal skills.*"

Waiting NQ

The likelihood of being kept on as an NQ was a major source of stress across the profession this year and M&R trainees were not exempt. "*People have been quite bothered about it; in the past there was good retention but the economic realities are that some departments aren't that busy and we understand that the firm hasn't been able to find jobs for all of us.*" To deal with the recession, the firm prudently tightened its belt, freezing pay, reducing the NQ salary by £1,000 and paying the new intake of trainees a bit less. As a result, it remained profitable and avoided a major redundancy programme. Trainee retention was reasonably good too, despite our sources' initial concerns: for the 22 qualifiers, 14 permanent contracts were found across a range of practice areas, and the firm additionally offered fixed-term contracts to four others which could turn permanent depending on market conditions. Consequently just four qualifiers were let go.

And finally…

M&R is ideal for those seeking an ambitious firm. If you're East Anglia-bound then it's a natural choice. In the capital, Birmingham and up north, where the competition is hotter, a vote for M&R will be based more on the type of work available and the feel of the firm.

Mishcon de Reya

The facts

Location: London
Number of UK partners/solicitors: 53/92
Total number of trainees: 22
Seats: 4x6 months
Alternative seats: None
Extras: Pro bono – Pink Law Legal Advice Centre

> "*Mishcon likes personality, so don't do that thing of trying to be what you think a lawyer ought to be. You are allowed to have personality – what's more, they will like it.*"

'Mishcon de Reya: thirteen letters to strike fear into any man's heart...' That may be so, but this is far more than just a divorce firm.

Mishcon da playa

The above quote from *The Times*' 'Slummy Mummy' column is just one example of Mishcon's extensive press coverage, which extends from the sublime (*Sunday Times* '100 Best Companies to Work For' survey) to the ridiculous (*The Daily Star*'s coverage of the imminent bankruptcy of Grant 'Anthea Turner's bloke' Bovey). Trainees admit that "*all publicity is good publicity to some extent,*" but add that the problem with representing the likes of Heather Mills and Princess Diana in headline-making divorces is that "*people think of us as a divorce firm when it's only about 10% of what we do. So many of our clients have nothing to do with the celebrity world. Acting for celebrities isn't really what it's all about.*" Indeed not.

Founded in a rented room in Brixton in 1937, Victor Mishcon & Co became Mishcon de Reya after a 1988 merger. Lord Mishcon was an inimitable figure who came into the office every day until his death in 2006. He also had four wives; a fact we only mention to justify using the above header. "*You can't replace someone like that,*" say trainees, "*but the ethos is still there. To say we're a big family is cheesy, but you want the best for the firm. People here are dedicated to it.*"

Mishcon de Reyality

Mishcon works in four key areas: family, property, corporate and litigation. The latter accounts for nearly half the firm's turnover. Trainees confirm that clients "*come to us because a letter from Mishcon scares people enough that proceedings may not even ensue.*" However, "*there's something for everyone,*" and aside from the main four departments there are opportunities in "*spin-offs*" like art law, contentious private client and immigration. "*I don't think there's any department that wouldn't give work to a trainee if they asked for it,*" said one source, although the time you can spend in very niche departments might be limited.

The fraud group is a particularly popular destination. Contributing almost half of the litigation department's revenue, there's exciting work to be had that might make you feel more like a detective than a lawyer. On the cards are obtaining restraining orders, tracing wrongly transferred bank funds and travelling the country in the middle of the night to "*execute search orders on different commercial and residential sites.*" The firm represents companies and individuals, and has acted for HM Treasury Solicitors in connection with the forgery of a £1m will. It's also represented a high-ranking bank official defending serious civil and criminal fraud allegations. For trainees there's "*a huge amount of client contact*" and the opportunity to take on smaller matters that will often "*start and finish within the span of a seat, so you are really able to own them.*" Trainees can also get to grips with insolvency, financial dispute resolution and media/PR issues.

In property litigation trainees "*get into the nitty-gritty of running of files*" and "*at the same time get exposed to large cases.*" The wider property group has a great reputation among trainees, who said: "*They're so well organised in taking care of you.*" Though the department has been hit by redundancies, it remains one of the largest in the firm and occupies the entire first floor of Mishcon's West End art deco home. Property trainees have ten to 15 matters on the go at any one time, encompassing "*leases, sales and purchases, licences for alteration and some involvement in the negotiation process.*" The trainee's role as a co-ordinator on bigger deals is vital and one source enthused: "*Getting involved in an £18m transaction across 15 sites was nerve-wracking, but equally exciting.*"

Much of the trainee experience in corporate is about "*listening and learning*" as "*you have to wait until you're higher up to get more responsibility.*" Listings on AIM formed the bulk of the work pre-crunch, when it was "*quite normal for a trainee to be verifying applications – which can be all you do for two months.*" Interviewees who visited the department more recently described a variety of work including "*setting up shelf companies, company filings, funds work, company takeovers, big asset sales and share sales.*" Within the corporate department an employment team acts for both employers and employees, handling contentious and non-contentious work. These range from high-profile tribunals that "*are being reported on daily in The Times*" to drafting compromise agreements, employment contracts and handbooks.

And what of the renowned family team? It has "*lots of work linked to immigration and private client,*" giving trainees the chance to get to know other departments. Head Sandra Davis is reputed to be a formidable character and "*a lot is expected of you.*" Client contact is extensive and essentially the most important thing to get right here. The ability of Mishcon lawyers to impress and charm clients is what leads to instructions on high-profile divorces such as those of Thierry Henry and Matt Lucas (the first gay separation to reach the courts).

Your Mishcon, should you choose to accept it...

At this firm, stuffed alligators hang from the ceiling, partners have super-villain laughs and trained chimps do all the due diligence. Actually, that's all lies, but what's certainly true is that Mishcon is "*not your average law firm.*" Say trainees: "*We're an eclectic mix of people – charismatic, tenacious and flexible.*" This firm unabashedly "*employs characters who can use their personalities to win over clients,*" and larger-than-life managing partner Kevin Gold will regularly stick his head round doors and cheerfully enquire: "*How much are you billing then, sunshine?*" Trainees agreed: "*We're not very stiff upper lip. There's no expectation that you'll say the right thing.*" One added some interview advice: "*Mishcon likes personality, so don't do that thing of trying to be what you think a lawyer ought to be. You are allowed to have personality – what's more, they will like it.*" Another declared: "*I couldn't go to another firm and be the way I am.*"

Chambers UK rankings

Banking Litigation	Immigration
Corporate/M&A	Intellectual Property
Defamation/Reputation Management	Licensing
Dispute Resolution	Private Client
Employment	Real Estate
Family/Matrimonial	Real Estate Litigation
Fraud: Civil	Restructuring/Insolvency

We encountered plenty of second careerers and unconventional trainees. The reason for this is simple: Mishcon "*sells something more than just legal advice*" and the focus is squarely on having "*a business head as much as a law head.*" A senior member of the firm says: "*We are looking for that bit of entrepreneurial flair – but it's not The Apprentice.*" Lawyers here must have the ability to laugh at themselves and to wow clients with their charisma and devil-may-care wit. The client-lawyer relationship maintains that old-school closeness you rarely find in more corporate firms. Whether getting "*banned for all eternity*" due to bad (trouser-related) behaviour at posh restaurant Nobu or simply taking the wind out of opponents' sails, this firm has got that indefinable *je ne sais quoi*. But still no stuffed alligators. Step it up, Mishcon.

Mish-cellany

In 2009 the firm made 17 redundancies and deferred training contracts "*in line with the market,*" offering £5,000 as compensation. Whereas before the recession it had been bolstering the numbers (the 2008 trainee intake was the largest ever), pondering an image change and considering new offices, these plans have all been put on hold. But not for long. Prospective trainees shouldn't fret. "*There will be fewer places but we will be recruiting, and we will never cut back on the summer scheme.*" In line with Mishcon's freethinking ways, "*if we see someone outstanding we're not such a regimented firm that we can't take them.*" In 2009 the firm found places for six of ten qualifiers. A significant number of those jobs were six-month contracts, but most were "*confident*" that they would be extended.

And finally...

We agree with the trainee who said "*we're different from the rest of them,*" but don't go thinking that this is a choice for the oddballs. Mishcon's success is no joke.

Morgan Cole

The facts

Locations: Bristol, Cardiff, Oxford, Reading, Swansea

Number of UK partners/solicitors: 56/187

Total number of trainees: 27

Seats: 4x6 months

Alternative seats: None

> *"Here, if you're good it will be acknowledged. You will be noticed. We can give you a very good training – even if we don't have a gym and all those other things."*
>
> Guy Constant, Training Partner

With a new insurance-led office growing in Bristol, this Anglo-Welsh full-service firm has the M4 corridor sewn up.

St George and the dragon

In 1998 Morgan Bruce of Wales merged with the Thames Valley firm Cole & Cole. After a faltering start, including the closure of insurance-based offices in London and Croydon, the union now appears to be a good one. In a year that has seen many firms' profits tumble, Morgan Cole hasn't fared too badly, all things considered. In 2009 profits did dip by 10%, but revenue increased by 4% to £33.5m. Our sources readily admitted that corporate work had *"slowed right down,"* but Morgan Cole never had all its eggs in the corporate basket anyway. Its large public sector practices (such as health and social care), its weighty insurance business and good clients such as Thames Valley Police and various UK universities have kept it buoyant. Its growth in the insurance sector was particularly noticeable in its new Bristol office, which it acquired in January 2009 through a merger with boutique CIP Solicitors. Added together, these strands of Morgan Cole's business made a great safety net in a recession economy. The firm made just three fee earners and nine support staff redundant and has not deferred any intakes of trainees.

Each year the trainee intake is split into two groups – one for the Thames Valley and one for Wales. Though they may move around within their chosen geographical region, as one interviewee put it succinctly: *"Welsh trainees stay in Wales, English trainees stay in England."* For TV trainees this means splitting their two years between an office at Apex Plaza in Reading (*"a big shiny building that has that real in-the-thick-of-it feel"*) and an Oxford office out on the ring road near Botley. Welsh trainees divide their time between centrally located offices at Bradley Court in Cardiff and the far more Welsh-sounding Ilys Tawe in Swansea. The Bristol office does not yet take trainees, though training partner Guy Constant tells us: *"It is definitely something we are looking at."*

An energetic bunch

Are we talking about a Welsh firm and an English firm that happen to share the same name? Not at all, says a Thames Valley second-year: *"It can sound like they're one firm and we're another, but it's not like that. The way the practice areas are split up means you're working in teams and are in contact with your Welsh colleagues quite a bit on a day-to-day basis."* Seats in corporate, commercial property, banking, commercial (including IP), dispute management and employment are available in both the Thames Valley and Wales. Insurance is only available in Reading, private client only in Oxford, and the well-regarded health and social care team only takes trainees in Wales.

Our interviewees described commercial property as *"a good all-rounder"* seat and a *"common non-contentious one that the firm feels is important to experience."* This definitely came across, as every trainee we interviewed had spent six months here, and a happy six months at that. *"You're given good client contact, taken to all the meetings, are able to run some of your own files and get involved in some marketing too."* Trainees are called upon to tackle *"the bulk of the more procedural things"* such as local authority searches and dealings with the Land

Registry, but supervisors go the extra mile to involve them at every stage. One source said: *"Towards the end I was drawing up contracts and negotiating terms with the other side."* There's a real range of clients in this department – *"everything from Joe Bloggs leasing out his commercial property on the high street, to the NHS working on huge developments."* Significant instructions also come from the energy sector: in the Thames Valley, the firm acted for Severn Power on the purchase of a brown field site for the development of a new gas-fired power station worth £50m. Across the Severn Bridge, lawyers acted for Welsh Power in its acquisition of land at Fleetwood in Lancashire for the construction of a £600m station near Blackpool.

Trainees in the corporate department were under no illusions about the effects of the recession, but they at least saw some personal benefit to everyone being less busy, namely that *"the more senior fee earners could spend more time with us."* Our sources said they had picked up valuable drafting experience in this seat, as well as getting involved in *"setting up shelf companies, post-completion work and doing research for partners when they're going out to get new work."* The firm has won a place on the panels of Lloyds and the Co-operative Bank this year, rounding off an already impressive list of lender clients.

The greatest wealth is health

Employment is a popular seat that bridges the gap between contentious and non-contentious practice. Morgan Cole is well respected in this area and counts the Independent Financial Ombudsman and Thames Valley Police as clients in its English offices. In Wales it advises posh skincare retailer Crabtree & Evelyn and shoe and clothing retailers Russell & Bromley and Diesel. The range of work is varied, from discrimination tribunals and TUPE advice to transactional support and training for clients. Trainees appreciated working on *"really juicy cases"* (things like *"people gossiping about each other in offices"*) and certainly got good contentious experience. *"You get a brilliant level of contact with clients and a lot of drafting work. You're involved in setting out a defence and then going back to the client with it."* Significantly, the Welsh offices are heavily involved in issues surrounding equal pay in the public sector. It's an extremely high-profile area of employment law at the moment.

The connection to the public sector is arguably strongest in the Welsh offices. Clients on home turf include the Welsh Assembly Government and Newport City Council, and the health and social care practice advises national institutions such as the Department of Health and the Human Tissue Authority (which the firm has assisted since its establishment in 2004). *Chambers UK* gives Morgan Cole a Band 2 UK-wide ranking in this area,

Chambers UK rankings

Banking & Finance	Insurance
Construction	Intellectual Property
Corporate/M&A	Licensing
Debt Recovery	Media & Entertainment
Dispute Resolution	Pensions
Education	Personal Injury
Employment	Private Client
Family/Matrimonial	Professional Discipline
Health & Safety	Real Estate
Healthcare	Real Estate Litigation
Immigration	Restructuring/Insolvency
Information Technology	Social Housing

alongside Eversheds and Browne Jacobson. This is a highly coveted seat and only available in Wales, so you should make your preference for it very clear early on.

Tasty cases

In the realm of commercial dispute management, ties to public sector clients are less obvious. *"Here it's a bit more wide-ranging client-wise, with lots of private companies."* Trainees were impressed with the *"huge range of different things"* available in this department. *"You could be advising clients, taking new instructions, instructing counsel, drafting court proceedings, attending mediations and going to court… you are involved at every possible stage."* There's always a fair amount of disclosure and *"mundane document work"* on larger cases, but nonetheless our sources felt they were *"really able to contribute quite a lot."* The disputes can touch on anything from defamation or breach of contract to negligence on varying scales. *"Some of the really small matters were not that far from the small claims court, and there was also much bigger Chancery Division litigation that had been going on for some time,"* recalled one trainee. Clients include The National Trust and PricewaterhouseCoopers in the Thames Valley and the Royal Mint and NFU Mutual Corporate in Wales. French chef Raymond Blanc is a notable client in the Thames Valley, and in the past year Morgan Cole successfully brought a cybersquatting case against a Bahamian company that had registered an unauthorised domain name piggy-backing on Blanc's name and success.

The insurance litigation department is able to boast potentially more exciting cases than defending a chef's good name. In its representation of Thames Valley Police, *"we'd defend claims brought against them by criminal suspects. An example might be someone suing for property damage after a drug raid."* Work for local councils also ensures trainees see a wealth of different types of cases. Because *"councils can't be seen to be settling left, right and centre,"* trainees *"go to court a lot and really get to grips with the process."* A typical case might include someone suing after a door had shut on their finger. We reckon you'll quickly form views on the 'compensation culture' debate after a few weeks in the seat.

Howzat?

So, not two firms under one name, but surely one office must come out on top? Not so, say trainees. *"Nowhere can lay claim to being the firm's HQ. Each office is so well established where they are that you couldn't have a head one. It's a level playing field."* One interviewee insisted that *"it's obviously one of the most prominent firms in Wales, and while Bristol is relatively new it is growing. Reading and Oxford are already established and secure."* Geographical distance does of course prevent staff from becoming an all-singing, all-dancing completely cohesive unit, but it's *"not like people don't like each other."* Far from it; we heard about trainee-organised walking holidays in Wales and various nights out in Bristol, which seems to be acknowledged as the perfect half-way point between Wales and the Thames Valley.

All trainees get together for the first two weeks of their training contracts. While staying in an Oxford college, incoming trainees are *"able to strike up relationships"* with both fellow new starters and the second-year trainees (who are there for the compulsory PSC training). There are also firm-wide away days once or twice a year: *"You get together in your teams, there are a few seminars and a dinner and socialising after that."* Socially, Reading and Cardiff seem to have the best scene. Reading is full of the joys of a *"young professionals' scene,"* whereas Oxford is *"a bit more family-oriented."* Cardiff scores points for being in the centre of the city with *"lots of pubs to hit up"* and *"all the rugby, of course!"* Swansea is more low-key. A wide array of sporting teams can be found across the offices and we particularly liked the sound of the cricket team in Oxford. It gets to tour around the city of dreaming spires and plays its home fixtures at Wadham College. Nice.

The Constant partner

Being confident and amiable will hold you in good stead for getting a training contract here. It was definitely a quality shared by our contented interviewees. Said one: *"We're all open, chatty, bubbly characters. There's no one in the firm I don't like!"* Another told us an anecdote that we feel sums up the firm's affable culture: *"I knew I wanted to apply to Morgan Cole when at a law fair the recruiter at their stand gave me a bag to carry all my brochures in. She wasn't selling anything, she was just being decent."* Yet another trainee said: *"Even though it does big commercial transactions it seems to have a pretty down-to-earth feeling."* The firm has a keen eye for candidates with previous work experience, and we found a fair share of second careerers had shuffled in with those straight out of university and people who had paralegalled at the firm. Trainees felt Morgan Cole also *"looks for people who can get on with the human side of the law – there is an emphasis on people who are practical and unstuffy with clients."* Is it important to have a connection with Wales or the Thames Valley? Said one source: *"I don't think you need to have links with the area, though I suspect if you haven't got a reason for wanting to come to this part of the country it will count against you."* Very little was working against the qualifiers of 2009 though; six of eight of them were kept on when they finished their contracts.

If Morgan Cole is sounding like it's up your street, we'd recommend that you apply for its vacation scheme. Consisting of a week spent in two departments, it received glowing reviews from trainees. The assessment days were also recommended and trainees suggested that the presence of *"six or so important partners"* means *"you can really tell the firm cares about who they hire as trainees. They're willing to put a great amount of effort into who they choose."* Another clue as to the importance of trainees within Morgan Cole is the mentoring scheme. *"Each of the mentors – who stay with you during the two years – are pretty influential partners within the firm."* When we spoke to him, training partner Guy Constant (who has put a lot into this role over many years) set out the benefits of coming to Morgan Cole quite succinctly: *"Here you'll have a good breadth of training, and if you're good it will be acknowledged. You will be noticed. We can give you a very good training – even if we don't have a gym and all those other things."*

And finally...

If you don't want a City-style experience but you do want decent commercial work plus the opportunity to get into more niche areas such as private client or public sector law, Morgan Cole should be high on your list.

Morrison & Foerster (UK) LLP

The facts

Location: London
Number of UK partner/solicitors: 19/17 + 5 US-qualified
Total number of trainees: 6
Seats: 4x6 months
Alternative seats: Overseas seats, secondments
Extras: Pro bono – legal advice for Action Against Hunger, Choices 4 All and others; language training

> MoFo is eager to expand in London and the training scheme is a big part of its plans for growth.

San Francisco. City of fogs, cable cars and a big ol' bridge. It's also the spiritual home of the firm with the irreverent nickname – MoFo.

Garage band guy

Morrison & Foerster's Californian origins set it apart from most US firms in London, many of which are dyed-in-the-wool New Yorkers. Americans will often assert that there are cultural differences between firms founded on the East Coast and the West, and if the stereotypes are to be believed, West Coast firms are supposedly a little more chilled out than their New York peers. Maybe that's so, but you don't become a firm with 1,000-plus lawyers and 16 offices worldwide without some serious graft. We suggest you look at our new sister guide www.chambers-associate.com to get an impression of what junior associates think in the USA. At the end of our research for that publication, we concluded that MoFo is a little bit like that guy who left your garage band for a corporate job: he's still cool, but you know he's always hard at work.

'Hard at work' is certainly the *mot juste* for the London office. It first opened back in 1980 and has grown substantially in the past five years to reach 57 lawyers, all but four of them UK-qualified. While the firm is full-service in the USA, here its practice profile can be likened to a three-legged stool resting on a trio of transactional practice groups: the technology transactions group (TTG); the corporate group; and the financial transactions group (FTG). Orbiting these primary groups are smaller teams of tax, employment, litigation and privacy lawyers. Recent analysis of the work in the London office showed that around 80% of matters are locally sourced, with the remainder coming via MoFo lawyers in North America and Asia. That percentage is expected to drop due to increased traction between the London and Asian offices.

The client base is loaded with technology and life sciences businesses, and this is reflected in the deals conducted in London. *Chambers UK* rankings also illustrate this: the firm is in Band 1 for its work in life sciences; Band 2 for IT; Band 2 for lower middle-market corporate/M&A; and Band 3 for data protection and private equity/venture capital investments.

It's not all about the rankings, of course; there are real clients and noteworthy deals to talk about. Amsterdam Molecular Therapeutics has been a MoFo client for a number of years, including when the firm advised the company on a €22m fundraising led by ABN AMRO. MoFo's work with AMT is a good example of both the pan-European nature of its London practice and its long-term relationships within the life sciences sector. The firm also advised vaccine company Acambis on a £276m recommended takeover offer by pharma giant sanofi-aventis. This transaction was one of the largest European pharmaceutical deals announced in 2008. While the firm is happy to hear from applicants with degrees in all subjects, it doesn't take a genius to work out that much of its work in London would be well suited to science graduates.

Popcorn not included

MoFo plans to grow its office in London even further and the training scheme is a big part of that. The programme started in 2006 and London managing partner Trevor James has indicated that going forward the firm expects to take three trainees per year. Most will take seats in TTG and corporate, plus a contentious seat in either litigation or employment law. The fourth seat will be either tax or FTG, or a return visit to one of the earlier seats.

TTG is currently advising Odeon Cinemas on the roll-out of digital cinema in Europe, including its procurement of technology from suppliers, negotiation of agreements with film studios and the negotiation of 3D-specific deployment arrangements for future releases, which all sounds very exciting even if we don't quite know what it means. Other major clients include HMRC and Royal SunAlliance. In this group the workload fluctuates. *"If there is a new sourcing agreement being drafted, it is busy and they involve the trainee more, but for the long-term contracts it's the associate doing renegotiations and the bulk of the work."*

The employment team is headed by one partner, and its size is conducive to substantial trainee involvement. *"I drafted statements and attended meetings with clients; it's a smaller team and that's nice because you have the opportunity to be involved in every matter,"* said one source. The capital markets department brings *"quite a bit of responsibility, but only to a certain level because people need the background to do the really cutting-edge stuff… it's a steep learning curve."* Corporate is a busy department offering a lot of client contact. Said one interviewee: *"I did a big transaction for a publicly owned company and they sent me to the client, where I was left to my own devices. I learned a lot and by the end I had a sense of achievement."* Work in the tax department is unsurprisingly *"quite intellectual with a lot of research."*

Ties not necessary

Salaries are firmly in the mid-Atlantic range, so trainees start on £37,500 and receive £42,500 in their second year. The current NQ salary is £67,000 – above the magic circle but far lower than the jaw-dropping pay packets available at certain US firms in London. There is potential for trainees to travel overseas, and although it seems unlikely that the US offices will be included in the future, MoFo has recently added a seat in Tokyo, where its office is substantial and transactionally-oriented. A Hong Kong exchange programme could also commence in the near future.

An associate's billing target is 1,600 hours per year (in keeping with most London firms). This figure is halved for trainees, and working hours also seem pretty reasonable. A number of the deals do involve working across time zones, and some of the projects can be pretty big, but weekend working and excessively late evenings don't appear to be a frequent occurrence, at least not in

Chambers UK rankings

Corporate/M&A	Life Sciences
Data Protection	Outsourcing
Information Technology	Private Equity

the current market. The firm is looking for trainees with good grades at A Level and a 2:1 or higher at degree level. Managing partner Trevor James says MoFo would consider equally applicants from any geographic location or university as long as they can *"handle extreme pressure, because with corporate transactions it's the clients that dictate the pace."* A two-week vac scheme runs twice a year and accepts six students each time. The firm hires largely from within this scheme, so it's obvious what you need to do.

MoFo occupies a single floor in the CityPoint tower near Moorgate. The management likes to regard the office as a collaborative working environment, and one trainee confirmed that *"everybody is laidback – people don't even necessarily wear ties. The partners are not stuffy and we have contact with the managing partner."* The small size of the office has made it easier to maintain a flatter hierarchy and good lines of communication. As in the US side of the operation, emphasis is placed on pro bono activities in the London office, and issues such as diversity are taken seriously. A recent group of trainees led a MoFo-sponsored fund-raising auction for Action for Hunger, which garnered contributions from members of the firm as well as surrounding businesses.

Friday evenings mean wine and cheese in the office – a brilliant time for trainees to *"meet everybody from the firm's secretaries to its partners."* The favourite local bar is The Cuban, conveniently also located in the CityPoint complex. A netball squad is starting to emerge while the football team, amusingly named Real MoFo, is well-established. The trainee players send out regular Friday match reports.

And finally…

The ability to fit into a personal, relatively small office is a must at MoFo. In 2009, two of the four qualifiers stayed on. One went into the corporate department; the other into litigation.

Mundays LLP

The facts

Location: Cobham
Number of UK partner/solicitors: 27/26
Total number of trainees: 6
Seats: 4x6 months
Alternative seats: None

This is Mundays' first appearance in the True Picture. Its haul of *Chambers UK* rankings is impressive and we spoke to some very satisfied trainees.

Nestled in the town of Cobham in Surrey, Mundays' proximity to the capital makes it a haven for ex-City lawyers.

Frisky in franchise

Established in 1960 by Mr Fred Munday (his picture still hangs in the office), this firm began life as a multi-site high street private client practice serving the numerous wealthy folk of Surrey. It was Munday Sr's son Peter (recently retired) who developed the firm into the commercial outfit it is today. After consolidating into one office in Cobham it merged with local niche property practice Browns in 2007 and has since gone from strength to strength. The property department is now the firm's largest, accounting for just under 50% of total turnover, and last year it worked on a number of residential and commercial development deals valued in excess of £10m. The team is packed full of ex-City lawyers searching for a less hectic Surrey life. Head of commercial property is Miles Unwin, previously a partner at Eversheds, while George Georgiou, formerly of international firm K&L Gates, leads an impressive retail team that advises the likes of Budgens and Boots. In fact refugees from some of the top firms in the capital pepper Mundays' workforce. One of the more recent hires was into the dispute resolution team – Joseph Kean, another partner from Eversheds. Such hires, and the high-profile clients that accompany them, make Mundays one of a small cluster of firms that sit just outside the capital and offer City quality services sans Square Mile price tag.

As well as regional rankings for practices such as corporate finance, dispute resolution, real estate, employment and family law, Mundays scoops a *Chambers UK* national ranking for its franchising work. This team is led by "*down-to-earth*" and "*passionate*" Nicola Broadhurst. Household names such as Holland & Barrett, Prontaprint, Kall Kwik and Clarks Shoes all consult her team and it often carries out work with an international flavour. It recently advised leather care and repair specialists The Furniture Clinic on its expansion into South Africa, and Holland & Barrett sought advice on its international roll out of franchised operations. Another client, Nut Tree, used the firm when it wanted to expand into the Middle East.

Hands on, hours off

Mundays' trainees generally work their way through four seats, but most agreed that this rule is "*not set in stone.*" Recruits can put forward a case for spending longer or shorter periods in certain departments, depending on their specific goals and subject to the general understanding that business needs dictate eventual decisions. "*I wanted to spend a full year in corporate, but because of the market I couldn't,*" explained one. Speaking of the market, the firm had to make a total of 16 staff redundancies across the firm and temporarily put the corporate team on reduced hours.

By all accounts, the levels of responsibility given to trainees are great, and consequently we heard the words "*hands on*" a record number of times. "*You are offered responsibility as soon as you get here,*" said one source; "*I went to a client meeting on my first day.*" Supervisors "*expect you to learn quickly and will give you the autonomy to work on your own files. You get good quality drafting experience as well as a chance to manage your own caseload.*" It sounds as if "*there are plenty of occasions where the learning curve is *very steep and there will be things you haven't dealt with before.*" Far from putting trainees off, this seems to be exactly what they're looking for.

Mundays has strict academic requirements: AAB at A Level and a 2:1 degree result. Despite their excellent credentials, we sensed that several of our sources had actively avoided the big City firms, preferring instead to find an employer that gave them better work-life balance. The average day runs from 8.30am to 5.30pm and "*people generally take a full lunch break.*" That's not to say Mundays offers an easy ride: working for fee earners who have honed their skills in the hothouse of the City requires concerted effort – "*they do expect trainees to pull their weight.*" Emphasising this point, trainees have their own billing and marketing targets, albeit that these are "*artificially low*" and "*not strictly adhered to.*" Of course Mundays is not a City firm so "*you are never going to find a billion-pound deal,*" but "*the advantage of that is you see things from conception to closure.*"

A seat in the large commercial property team involves a varied workload and "*quite a lot of client contact.*" Trainees see a combination of "*proper hands-on, thrown-in-the-deep end*" lease work and smaller tasks designed to assist the supervising partner on much bigger deals. Across the firm supervisors were praised as being "*generally approachable,*" but the commercial property department earned particularly positive commendations. "*The partner there has a lot of experience and has a check list that's essentially like a curriculum so she can satisfy herself she has given you the right training.*"

Waxing lyrical, talking gospel

Mundays' corporate and commercial teams are managed separately but trainees typically spend six months taking work from both. As one source explained: "*I'm more into commercial so the first thing I did was say I want commercial work and they gave it to me. It's that simple. They let you know if there's something you can do and if you do it well they will give you more.*" The sort of matters you'll see here range from "*a heck of a lot of franchise deals*" with Nicola Broadhurst, to IP/IT development agreements with managing partner Val Toom.

Retail giant Boots is a major client and it kept the corporate team busy with its acquisition of over 100 pharmacies last year. The team also advised Tayto Golden Wonder, the third largest crisps and snacks business in the UK, on its multi-million-pound purchase of Red Mill Snack Foods. On more "*meaty agreements*" such as these, trainee tasks primarily consist of managing the due diligence. This tends to involve "*asking lots of questions of the companies we are buying and reviewing the documentation.*" While they admit it is "*very time-consuming*" and rather daunting at first, they soon learn how to be "*firmer and more matter of fact when it comes to getting the seller to tell us anything that might

Chambers UK rankings

Banking & Finance	Family/Matrimonial
Corporate/M&A	Franchising
Dispute Resolution	Partnership
Employment	Real Estate

cause problems in the future." Trainees know their limits; "*we can't wax lyrical and talk gospel about tax,*" but as they gain more experience there is the opportunity to draft various documents for lower-value transactions.

Happy Mundays

Contentious experience can be found in the family and dispute resolution departments. Higher value family cases often have an international element, and on such matters our sources enjoyed the "*quite forensic*" task of going through bank statements and investigating trusts that need to be shared between parties. Meanwhile, smaller cases gave them a chance to meet and interview clients and go to court alone. Family seat trainees are all but guaranteed advocacy experience by way of applications for injunctions. They also attend court with barristers to "*take copious notes.*" Time in the dispute resolution department exposes trainees to "*some really meaty matters*" for clients such as Talkback Thames Productions, shirt people TM Lewin and PhotoMe. Trainees often run debt collection files solo, which involves "*client communication, sending out letters and issuing proceedings if necessary.*"

And so to the social scene. Sadly, "*because everyone drives there isn't really an after-work drinks culture,*" meaning there is less interaction between the ranks than trainees hoped for. "*The young ones do tend to organise nights out once or twice a month,*" alternating between Wimbledon and Guildford. These generally involve the classic combo of "*drinks and then a crappy club.*" There are three firm-wide events throughout the year: Christmas and summer parties and a lively quiz. These are "*always fun.*" The lack of a raging social life is the trade-off trainees make for the idyllic location of café-filled Cobham, where "*people smile even if it's raining.*"

And finally...

Trainees summarised Mundays' key attraction quite succinctly. "*You have City standards in terms of the support but you are outside London and aren't expected to be here every night until midnight.*" In 2009 one of the two qualifiers took up a job at the firm.

- **Vacation vacation vacation:** If you have your heart set on a firm, get on its vacation scheme; they're an increasingly important a way to show an outfit you're serious about them.

top tip no. 19

Nabarro LLP

The facts

Location: London, Sheffield
Number of UK partners/solicitors: 134/287
Total number of trainees: 55
Seats: 6x4 months
Alternative seats: Brussels, secondments
Extras: Pro bono – LawWorks

New starters find this a very welcoming firm. Its vacation scheme is the primary route to a training contract.

Nabarro has done much to shake off its old property firm image and embrace a fresh persona. So long Nabarro Nathanson, bienvenu Nabarro!

Brand clarity

In 2007, tired of being portrayed as a dependable and decent sort of place, this firm underwent a swift transformation. It abbreviated its name to simply 'Nabarro', changed its logo and introduced the 'clarity matters' strap line – a promise that the firm would never baffle clients with legalese. To illustrate the point, management even commissioned comedy duo John Bird and John Fortune to make a YouTube ad promoting the firm's ethos. Search for the 'Ungobbledegooked' clips if you want to watch. Cynical types would call this a clever publicity stunt but our sources insist that there is substance behind the campaign. *"It's amazing what a rebrand can achieve. It really modernised the image of the firm – it is now a name that my peers recognise."* Everyone has been asked to adhere to the new clarity policy, as trainees reveal: *"The ability to communicate intelligibly with clients forms part of the training and we're appraised on that too."* The people we spoke to also perceived deeper change: *"The firm has set itself new aims; it is expanding into new areas and getting better work."*

Market onlookers will readily acknowledge that Nabarro has been successful at diversifying its practice, yet real estate has always been and still remains the jewel in the firm's crown. With over 150 qualified lawyers in the department, there is no debating the prominence of this practice group. Its work is characterised by high-value and headline-grabbing transactions such as Land Securities' sale of a 50% stake in a major retail block on London's Oxford Street for £105m. The team also acts for the London Development Agency on the handover of land in the Stratford area to the Olympic Development Authority and arrangements for the land after the 2012 Games.

While real estate remains Nabarro's backbone, the firm has been keen to enhance its market share in other disciplines, particularly corporate. As a result, trainees are required to spend at least four months in each of the two departments. There is also a compulsory stint in one of the litigation teams, which have been busier than ever in the wake of the credit crisis. Showing resilience in a slow market, Nabarro indulged in a shopping spree, recently completing a series of lateral hires to bulk up the real estate finance, investment funds, dispute resolution, competition and IT practice groups. Diversity of practice means plenty of choice for trainees, as does the six-seat system, which *"is a major draw for those who come here with an open mind about what type of lawyer they want to become."*

What property crisis?

The property market was severely affected by the financial crisis and casual onlookers could be forgiven for thinking that Nabarro must have suffered massively as a result of its exposure to the industry. However, due to the size, quality and institutional nature of its client base, the firm has fared better than expected. Big institutional clients such as Land Securities, Hammerson, British Land and Liberty have remained active throughout the downturn, providing Nabarro lawyers with a stream of work. Several of our sources confirmed the buoyancy of the practice, saying: *"It's as manic as it's ever been."*

Trainees here normally handle their own small files, ranging from drafting licences to lease renewals and negotiations. "*The level of responsibility and client contact can be daunting at first, but it's not an opportunity you often get as a trainee and you should embrace it,*" one source advised. In addition to managing their own caseload, trainees assist on large-scale disposals and acquisitions, property developments and lettings, by putting sale packs together, bibling or conducting searches and registrations.

A seat in the property litigation department is a rite of passage for those who are serious about specialising in real estate. Those who'd spent time here felt "*it was a privilege to work alongside some of the most talented lawyers in the UK,*" but they also warned that "*it's the most demanding seat in the house.*" We heard that in order to cope with the sheer volume of cases, the group now takes on four trainees at any one time and that the problem of partners dumping obscenely dull or onerous tasks on trainees is being addressed. Nevertheless, it remains a challenging four months. The mandatory contentious seat may alternatively be spent in the commercial litigation team. While this group covers a wide range of other sectors, it is particularly sought after for financial regulatory disputes and has seen an upswing in this type of claim. Other contentious seat options include clinical negligence or construction litigation. Trainees who choose the latter may get the opportunity to spend a week with construction barristers at Keating Chambers.

Arrested development

We mentioned previously that corporate is an area Nabarro was keen to grow into. It has already gone some distance towards establishing itself as a credible alternative to top City firms, particularly in the field of AIM admissions. It also started to enjoy a healthy flow of mid-sized M&A mandates before the economy was hit. These included acting for long-standing client Vega Group on its recommended £69m takeover by Italian defence giant Finmeccanica. Another highlight was representing Premier Recruitment International in its £45m offer for competitor Imprint plc. Corporate seats can be taken in the public companies team, the private companies/private equity team or the indirect investment team, so there is a real variety of work for trainees to sample. Within these seats, the trainee's role often consists of "*making sure all the documentation for a deal is in order, organising communication between the parties and generally ensuring that closings go smoothly.*" Because of the nature and size of the transactions, these seats have been known for longer hours. This year's adverse market conditions have largely stopped this and, to be perfectly candid, the corporate department's plans have suffered a setback. Against this backdrop, some of the trainees who served time in the department told us they'd experienced a quiet four months

Chambers UK rankings

Banking & Finance	Local Government
Capital Markets	Pensions
Clinical Negligence	Pensions Litigation
Competition/European Law	Personal Injury
Construction	Planning
Corporate/M&A	Private Equity
Dispute Resolution	Professional Discipline
Education	Projects, Energy & Natural Resources
Employee Share Schemes	Public Procurement
Employment	Real Estate
Environment	Real Estate Finance
Health & Safety	Real Estate Litigation
Information Technology	Restructuring/Insolvency
Intellectual Property	Retail
Investment Funds	Tax

and we also heard about corporate lawyers being reallocated to busier departments.

In lieu of a corporate seat, some trainees spend time in Nabarro's banking department. Unsurprisingly, given the firm's set-up, it handles a significant amount of property-related work. Traditionally leaning towards the representation of borrowers, the department has enhanced its reputation with lenders. The group notably advised BayernLB on a string of high-profile financings of Crown Estate lettings and landmark buildings such as the former Reuters HQ on Fleet Street. Our sources perceived a shift in the nature of the work coming through the door: "*It is less transactional than before, but facility reviews and restructurings have picked up significantly.*" Trainees enjoy a good level of responsibility here, and it is not unusual for them to be involved at all stages of the drafting, negotiation and closing of major matters.

In London, further seats are available in pensions, employment, construction, IT and tax. Various client secondments are on offer, lately including RAB Capital, the University of Oxford and Mercedes-Benz.

At the coalface

For historic reasons, the Sheffield office offers a slightly different range of seats, including posts in the environment and health claims teams. The latter harks back to the office's previous incarnation as the in-house legal team of the old nationalised mining industry, British Coal. For many years Nabarro has been one of the market-leading firms in the defence of group litigation. It represents the Department for Business, Innovation and Skills (BIS) on miners' vibration white finger and respiratory disease actions involving claims in excess of £7bn and 700,000 claimants. More recently a new action has kicked off: a knee injury litigation scheme for BIS involves around 200,000 claimants going for their share of £4bn. Given the sheer volume of cases, trainees who try this seat are normally entrusted with their own files and can expect plenty of client contact and court time.

Nabarro's sole international seat is in its Brussels office. This compact team is the first port of call for all other departments on competition law. The seat is mostly research-based, requiring trainees to delve into EU legislation to produce memoranda on merger control, abuse of dominant position or state aid issues. One of the trainees' most important tasks is to update the firm's newsletter, designed to keep lawyers up to date with recent changes in this ever-evolving field. While the office only welcomes one trainee at a time, there is no need to feel lonely as new arrivals are put in touch with other English law firm trainees via e-mail.

The main preconception about the firm that our sources were keen to dispel was the idea that it's all about real estate. Without contesting the importance of the property groups, trainees were adamant that Nabarro offers a comprehensive and first-rate training contract. The six-seat training scheme allows them to sample quite different practice groups and to repeat a seat before deciding which team to join on qualification. Throughout the process there is constant dialogue with the "*very accommodating and supportive*" HR department, which strives to assign trainees to their first-choice seat. Our sources also commended the quality of the continuing legal education provided to them. "*They give us training on a plate; it is nicely spread out and covers everything we need, from legal know-how to IT and soft skills.*"

Nabarro's Got Talent, have you?

The social scene is very civilised. "*An e-mail goes out on Friday evenings for those who fancy a drink and it's usually well attended,*" but there is no pressure to show up as "*everyone acknowledges that work must be balanced with life and friends outside work.*" Nabarro's London office is located in the Bloomsbury area; "*we have Covent Garden on our doorstep so we're spoilt for choice in terms of restaurants and bars.*" Trainees are also invited to join Nabarro's sports teams, with the boys taking part in the London Legal Football League and the girls preferring netball or hockey.

Among the bigger firm-wide events, our favourite has to be the 'Nabarro's Got Talent' charity show, where everyone from trainees to partners was encouraged to perform. The winning number by 'Stu & Dumpling' saw a tax partner and senior corporate associate dressed in funny outfits gesticulating to disco beats. "*It was hilarious – definitely more about entertainment than talent!*" a trainee revealed. This initiative reflects the inclusive and warm culture of the firm and illustrates some of the attributes required to succeed here. In short, "*you have to be approachable, self-assured and sociable.*"

Nabarro trainees are in the main "*bright people who are enthusiastic but not excessively ambitious.*" Apparently, the firm is no Oxbridge extension; "*it is not elitist – it recruits high achievers from a wide variety of universities.*" What is more important, we are told, is that trainees demonstrate an ability to get on well with clients, and the firm is certainly keen to get them into the networking habit from an early stage. At 'Contact Nabarro' evenings, trainees and junior lawyers invite along potential new clients and work contacts for a spot of mingling and fun. Self-starters and those who love responsibility are in a good position to succeed here, even if metaphors mix in the process. So remember: "*If you're willing to step up to the mark, then the world is your oyster.*"

Scheming your way in

When asked for tips on landing a training contract, our sources confirmed in unison: "*Get onto the vacation scheme!*" Almost all Nabarro recruits come off the scheme, "*probably even more so now, as it's a really good opportunity for the firm to get to know you and vice versa.*" Our interviewees shared fond memories of their time on the scheme; "*everyone was so friendly and caring, by the end I was completely sold on the firm.*" The summer slot has just been revamped and it gives candidates plenty of time to impress. "*Don't sit back and observe – act like a fully-fledged trainee, seek out work and try to meet as many people as you can,*" a source advised. The scheme also comes with a jam-packed social calendar of drinks, bowling and karaoke. Get that Elvis impersonation down pat and who knows…

Save for a blip in 2006, Nabarro has an excellent track record of retaining qualifiers. Naturally, no law firm is recession-proof, and like many of its rivals Nabarro resorted to a redundancy programme in 2009, albeit a relatively modest one. As far as trainees are concerned, however, 2009 was a good year – the firm held on to 24 of its 29 qualifiers (a hefty number of them going into litigation) and did not defer future intakes.

And finally...

Nabarro shouldn't disappoint anyone looking for a fulfilling career at a very pleasant and progressive mid-sizer. If you developed a powerful allergy to property law during your studies then Nabarro might not be the best choice as so much of its work bolts onto real estate.

NORTON ROSE

Putting you in the picture

Can you see yourself as part of Norton Rose Group? Do you want to be part of the bigger picture? Before you decide anything, you need to do your research.

Our clients are among the world's top corporate bodies and financial institutions and our job is to provide them with world-class legal advice. We are looking for people who we can train to do that.

We need individuals who show ambition and determination and who want an international career. We already have over 2000 people worldwide, including more than 1000 lawyers. The work is hard, but it's fascinating. It's the toughest intellectual challenge you could hope for.

If you can picture yourself as part of that mix, we'd like to hear from you.

Norton Rose Group is a leading international legal practice, offering a full business law service from offices across Europe, the Middle East and Asia. We are strong in corporate finance; financial institutions; energy and infrastructure; transport; and technology. The Group comprises Norton Rose LLP and its affiliates.

To find out more, go to our website for graduates or contact our graduate recruitment team on +44 (0)20 7444 2113.

www.nortonrose.com/graduates

Norton Rose LLP

The facts

Location: London
Number of UK partners/solicitors: 137/343
Total number of trainees: 105
Seats: 6x4 months
Alternative seats: Overseas seats, secondments
Extras: Pro bono – FRU, Tower Hamlets and Tooting Law Centres; language training

This firm bent over backwards to protect staff during the worst ravages of the economic downturn. Its actions were very much in character and distinguished it from many other leading City players.

In what can only be described as challenging times for the City, Norton Rose stands out for composed handling of the economic downturn.

There's oil/diamonds in them thar hills

Norton Rose has not played the waiting game or put its big plans on hold: in 2009 it pursued international expansion, launched new offices in Abu Dhabi and Tokyo, and posted a 6% increase in revenue (to £341m) while avoiding redundancies, suggesting that its strategic positioning is paying dividends. Part of the strategy is to target five key sectors, which the firm refers to as its 'headlights': corporate finance; financial institutions; energy and infrastructure; technology; and transport. Focusing on emerging and transition markets is also at the core of the strategy. For example, NR recognised the enormous growth potential of the Middle East earlier than most, and today, while many competitors are scrambling over the remaining piece of this lucrative market, it fields no fewer than 70 lawyers dotted across four outposts in the region. There are also plans to increase the firm's involvement in India and Africa, and in June 2009 management announced a major merger with successful Australian law firm Deacons to take effect at the beginning of 2010. It signals good things to come in the growth markets of the Asia-Pacific region.

While the firm has many respected practice groups, its most resounding successes originate from the finance and corporate divisions. Our colleagues at *Chambers UK* rate its asset finance group as a market leader across the aviation, rail and shipping sectors. The practice is characterised by complex high-value transactions, often with cross-border input. Recent noteworthy mandates include acting for European Export Credit Agencies and lenders Calyon and Dekabank on a $1.4bn loan facility for AerCap to finance 15 Airbus A330s. In corporate finance, lawyers have carved a particularly profitable niche in the field of AIM floats. The practice now operates at the top of this market, with transactions being of significant value and increasingly international. The firm's involvement in the AIM IPO of Petro Matad, the first Mongolian oil and gas company to join AIM, evidences these trends. But there is more than AIM to Norton Rose's corporate offering. In recent months, in spite of a slow market, the firm acted on a number of high-quality M&A deals across its chosen sectors, including advising Archangel Diamond Corporation, a subsidiary of De Beers, on a joint venture with LUKOIL for the exploration and development of one of the world's largest known diamond deposits.

'Putting trainees in the picture'

Such is the promise made to prospective trainees in recent graduate recruitment literature, but what do current trainees make of it? Well, our sources certainly agreed that the firm does a lot to help them find a team to fit into long-term, and that there is *"scope for trainees to influence the way their training contract is shaped."* First, there is the six-seat system, which means that trainees can sample several practice areas before settling on one. For those who make up their mind early on, there is also the possibility to repeat a seat in order to gain a greater understanding of a particular practice area. While the seat allocation system may seem *"a little perplexing at first"* – each trainee having to list seats in order of preference from 1 to 24 and hope for the best – we're told there are very few mishaps, as *"HR really go out of their way to give you your first choice."*

Unsurprisingly, given the importance of the finance and corporate practices, trainees are required to take at least one seat in each department. While a wide variety of seats fall within the finance area, the chances of a four-month stint in the leading asset finance group are pretty high. Aviation finance is what keeps trainees busy here, with a few shipping and rail deals thrown into the mix. On a typical day, trainees manage mountains of paperwork, amend documentation or collate conditions precedent. There were a few moans about the tedious and repetitive nature of the work – "*it felt like doing the same deal over and over again*" – but people appreciated being part of "*such a friendly and supportive team,*" and the lucky ones even get to travel to take delivery of aircraft. General banking, projects and real estate finance are other possible seats, as is Islamic finance (at which the firm excels).

Corporate seats, whether in the M&A, AIM or private equity group, are renowned for offering more responsibility. Trainees who sat in the department before the financial crisis took its toll had the opportunity to assist on big-ticket AIM floats and takeovers, including Carlsberg's £10.2bn joint venture with Heineken for the takeover of Scottish & Newcastle. Those who more recently served time in the department reported that, due to the slower economy, fewer deals were coming through the door and the department was much quieter. "*I spent most of my seat doing research or dealing with less-than-exciting post-completion tasks,*" a trainee reported. On the plus side, those trainees did not have to endure the very long hours corporate work is known to serve up.

Litigation is a perennial favourite for those who prefer to work with black letter law and "*use their intellect rather than execute mundane tasks.*" The seat is research-oriented and allows trainees to "*build on skills gained at law school and pick up new practical ones.*" In the wake of the credit crisis, there is no shortage of work in the litigation division, which comprises three subgroups: finance and corporate litigation, transport and construction. The group has experienced a significant increase in loan-related disputes and is assisting a large number of financial institutions on the close-out of derivatives trades. Trainees who don't like litigation can opt out of this seat and take a two-week course instead. This option is apparently popular among those who came to the firm with their heart set on finance. The availability of the course also reflects the fact that NR trainees "*have a say in their career path – it is up to us to decide whether or not we're interested in litigation.*" The other London departments open for trainee visits are competition and EC; tax; property, planning and environment; incentives and pensions; and media and technology.

Friends in high places

A big plus with this training contract is that it guarantees time overseas. "*They're not overselling the international seat opportunities,*" trainees report; "*time abroad is a dead cert for those who want it.*" With 23 offices around the world there is plenty to choose from and it is not unusual for trainees to go abroad twice or even three times. Athens, Paris, Frankfurt, Rome, Hong Kong and Beijing are just some of the locations on offer. One of the most popular destinations is Singapore, where trainees can get a taste of life as a fully-fledged associate. "*It is well known that trainees who go there are expected to perform as qualified lawyers from day one.*" The Middle Eastern offices also attract a fair share of trainees. The Dubai and Abu Dhabi branches are relatively recent additions to the firm's international network, and those who spent some time there were absolutely ecstatic: "*I had a fantastic time! Because the teams are smaller, trainees get a lot more responsibilities and client exposure than in London. It's also fascinating to see how the firm penetrates new markets.*" Norton Rose has a very good-looking clientele in the region, and it notably benefits from strong ties with a number of sovereign wealth funds, so there are heaps of top-end deals for trainees to dig into.

Those with no taste for adventure can stay in London for the duration of their training contract, or they can opt for one of many client secondment options. The firm has ties with most of the leading investment banks and also places trainees with the likes of AIG, ExxonMobil and Nestlé.

The people we spoke to painted a very positive picture of life pre-qualification. Before joining, many had heard that NR was "*a great place to train,*" and they were keen to confirm that this reputation is well deserved. On the subject of formal training, everyone we spoke to agreed that

Chambers UK rankings

Administrative & Public Law	Information Technology
Asset Finance	Insurance
Aviation	Investment Funds
Banking & Finance	Life Sciences
Banking Litigation	Outsourcing
Capital Markets	Pensions
Climate Change	Private Equity
Commodities	Professional Negligence
Competition/European Law	Projects, Energy & Natural Resources
Construction	Public Procurement
Corporate/M&A	Real Estate
Dispute Resolution	Real Estate Finance
Employee Share Schemes	Restructuring/Insolvency
Employment	Shipping
Environment	Tax
Financial Services Regulation	Telecommunications
	Transport
Fraud: Civil	Travel

the various sessions, talks and presentations organised by the firm are a great complement to the practical skills gained on the job. As far as appraisals are concerned, they told us that "*the system in place is excellent in theory.*" It provides for mid and end-of-seat feedback sessions with a supervisor, but in practice these do not always materialise. This is a relatively minor gripe though, and overall our sources seemed genuinely content with the scheme.

Two years ago the firm relocated its entire staff from "*dingy*" offices sprinkled around the City to a sleek new one in the More London Riverside development, adjacent to City Hall. Those who remembered Norton Rose's former digs commented on the vast improvement the move has had on morale. "*It's brought everyone together – now this is a great place to work in every sense of the term.*" The signature Norman Foster building "*does not offer a great deal of privacy, but who cares when you get such magnificent views over London,*" a trainee enthused. There's also much to enjoy in the neighbourhood.

Want to join the scrum?

The trainees' favourite watering hole is The Bridge on Tooley Street. They fondly refer to it as "*our pub*" or as "*an extension of the firm itself – we take over the place on Friday evenings.*" Among the big social events organised by the firm are the annual trainee party, the traditional Christmas party and a family fun day, to which everyone can bring along children and other halves. Said one source: "*It's a great way to remind everyone that Norton Rose encourages life outside of work.*" The firm is said to nurture something of an obsession with sports, particularly rugby – "*many partners are former public school boys after all!*" Other sports are well catered for, so "*there's a softball team, a netball team, a cricket team... you name it, we have it.*" Thankfully there is "*absolutely no pressure on the less athletic to participate.*" For them, the offices offer a music room where staff can enjoy subsidised lessons, or they can join the firm's choir. If their schedule still allows it, trainees can sign up for a language class.

We were told the firm does not recruit exclusively from top universities; it simply looks for "*switched-on and practically minded people who show a lot of potential and enthusiasm.*" However, those seduced by the firm's friendly ethos should not forget that, as a top City law firm, NR can afford to be choosy. A strong academic record should therefore be the starting point for those wishing to apply. From talking to a range of trainees, it is also apparent that they truly enjoy each other's company. "*There is no question that in my intake people are normal, down to earth and genuinely kind. I think the firm is good at recruiting like-minded trainees who will get on well. I wouldn't bother applying if you're the aggressive and overly driven type.*" For those who display the right qualities and temperament, there is still the not-so-small hurdle of the recruitment day to overcome. This will normally involve a case study, a group exercise designed for applicants to show their commercial awareness, and then comes the formal interview with two partners. The good news for those who impress throughout the day is that they may receive an offer within an hour of leaving the building.

Coming up smelling of Roses

The weakening economy did not spare Norton Rose. Like most transactional firms, its deals have been sparser than in previous years. It did achieve something of a PR coup, however: the various measures it implemented to cope with the economic downturn received widespread approval from staff, trainees and future joiners. The firm managed to avoid redundancies by implementing a 'Flex scheme', under which it could ask staff to work a three or four-day week on 85% of base salary for a year, or take a sabbatical of four to 12 weeks on 30% of base salary. Our interviewees concurred: "*Better to have a four-day-a-week job than no job at all.*" The scheme is also thought to have allowed the firm to offer NQ positions to the majority of the 2007 intake: 47 out of 55 2009 qualifiers stayed on. And the cherry on the cake: "*Most also got their first choice of qualification department.*" A particularly insightful (or maybe well-indoctrinated) trainee pointed out that the firm came to regret laying off younger lawyers during the last recession. "*When the markets recover, the firm will need junior lawyers just as much as senior ones, so they're keen to take a long-term view this time around.*" Going forward, our sources were confident that the firm's response to staffing levels in 2009 will allow it to continue to attract candidates of a high calibre. We suspect they're right.

Because of SRA regulations, trainees were not eligible for the Flex scheme, but the firm has made "*clever use of client and international secondments to keep them busy.*" As for future joiners, it resorted to a deferral plan for trainees due to start in September 2009 or January 2010. Those who accepted were eligible for a payment of up to £10,000 if they could come up with a bright idea for how to spend the money to develop new skills.

And finally...

Students looking for a fulfilling career in the City but wanting to eschew its ruthless environment fall easily for Norton Rose. At the peak of the pre-crash boom we questioned whether the firm was too nice for the City. Right now its more measured nature looks to be serving it well.

- **'Prestige' means nothing:** Don't apply to a firm just because some random survey says it is the 'best'. It may not be the best place for you. Choose a firm for the work, for the people, for the international opportunities or even just for the money. Don't choose it for the 'prestige' because when you're sitting in a room at four in the morning, knee deep in documents, surrounded by people you have absolutely nothing in common with, prestige means sod all.

top tip no. 20

Olswang

The facts

Location: London, Reading
Number of UK partners/solicitors: 85/174
Total number of trainees: 36
Seats: 4x6 months
Alternative seats: Overseas seats, secondments
Extras: Pro bono – LawWorks; language training

One of the most glamorous names in the legal profession, Olswang attracts almost as many applicants as *The X Factor*. No longer labelled the cool kid of the City, it has matured into a solid commercial all-rounder.

Long known for its media expertise, Olswang has significantly grown its corporate and property departments since the turn of the millennium.

Olswang that ends well?

"*I wanted clients I could relate to, like the BBC and Microsoft – not your run-of-the-mill investment banks.*" This was how one of our interviewees explained why he chose Olswang. He won't have been disappointed, but on arrival he may have been surprised to find that alongside trendy media clients like eBay, Guardian Media, ITV, Time Warner and Hustler Hollywood (UK) you'll see plenty of those 'run of the mill' finance names – Anglo Irish Bank, Investec Bank, Monument Asset Management, Star Investment Trust and Prestbury Investment Holdings to name but a few. This is because the 'Swang is far more than a media boutique; it's a place to get a rounded, not a specialist, training. In London's corporate finance market, the *Chambers UK* rankings put it alongside firms like Baker & McKenzie, Denton Wilde Sapte, LG and Pinsent Masons. So, though it is still heavy with media clients, if you're thinking of applying here then you need to realise just how much emphasis is placed on corporate business. In 2007, the firm ran a huge marketing campaign to play up this part of its activities: "*There was even a big advert which took up a whole escalator in London Bridge tube station.*"

Are we done talking about corporate yet? Well, no. Several of our interviewees confessed that, despite all the marketing, they had still been surprised at the firm's practice profile. "*We're not quite as media as people think,*" said one. Another added: "*I thought there would be more media seats than there actually are. The firm is quite clear about it, but people choose not to see it.*" We repeat, don't be one of those people: select the firm for what it is, not what it is perceived to be. It's compulsory to do a seat in corporate – whether that be private equity, mainstream M&A or tax – although we did hear a whisper that "*some people get out of it if they show zero interest.*" Remember, you didn't hear that from us! Media seats are unsurprisingly the most popular and competition for them is fierce.

Current managing partner Mark Devereux ("*one of the nicest guys in the world*") founded the firm in 1981, along with Simon Olswang. Since then, the firm has broadened its horizons, opening outposts in Brussels (a competition seat is available here for trainees) and Berlin to add to its UK offices in London and Reading. The Berlin office has gone from strength to strength since its launch in 2007. Having added a posse of Linklaters lawyers, it most recently scooped a team of 11 from Freshfields in Germany. Olswang also had American connections courtesy of a 'best friend' relationship with Florida-headquartered Greenberg Traurig until recently, when the US firm set up its own office in London. Olswang asserted that the separation was of little consequence: the link only provided 2% of its annual revenue and the two firms still work together on some matters.

In other news, 11 staff were made redundant in early 2009 as a result of the recession. The firm also decided to stagger its annual intake of 24 trainees, allowing 12 to join in August 2009 and deferring the remaining 12 until March 2010. If necessary, this arrangement will also apply to 2010/11 starters. Most trainees work in London, but each year a small number are recruited to Olswang's second office in Reading, which handles employment, real estate and corporate matters.

The big bang

We'll get to the sexy stuff later, we promise, but let's talk more about corporate. As you might expect, media clients permeate this department anyway, and in fact the firm is counting on its established relationships with media, technology and telecoms clients to see it through the recession. For instance, it advised RDF Media Group, an independent television production company, on a management buyout; it acted in the £53.2m acquisition of Virgin Radio by Times of India Group; and Australian client Photon Group came to the firm for its largest UK deal, the acquisition of Naked Communications (which rather disappointingly turns out to be a multi-jurisdictional communications planning agency). Sports enthusiasts may take interest in the acquisition of the Outside Broadcasts division of BBC Resources, which aids coverage of events including Wimbledon, the Olympics and the football World Cup.

Despite all this, the department has seen less work coming in lately, and most of the firm's redundancies came from here and real estate, a trend noted by the trainees themselves. "*People are a bit nervous here as the market is the worst it's been in ten years.*" Still, trainees who were previously resistant to the idea of a corporate seat found themselves won over by this hard-working team: "*You might think that corporate can be a bit dry after having done the LPC, but when you deal with real companies and real people it becomes much more enjoyable.*" Trainees noticed the distinct lack of client interaction in this seat compared to others but did mention a number of important skills they had picked up.

The finance seat is an admin-heavy experience and trainees spoke of being involved in documenting debt transactions and drafting board minutes. Some sources complained about a lack of support staff to help with less glamorous tasks, saying: "*Bundling takes about 30 to 40% of the time, and we really shouldn't have to sort out bills when on a major transaction.*" Trainees said they felt comfortable in putting such issues to seniors and were confident that management would listen to their concerns. We were also told that Olswang does not have a late night culture and, though long hours are sometimes necessary, "*you get praise for what you do well, so doing late nights is easier in that atmosphere.*" Free taxis are laid on for those who do have to stay late. At this point we should comment on matters that pre-date the current trainees. Way back when, during the dotcom boom, Olswang lawyers had to work their stylish socks off to keep up with the demand for their services.

Chambers UK rankings

Administrative & Public Law	Information Technology
Advertising & Marketing	Intellectual Property
Banking & Finance	Licensing
Capital Markets	Life Sciences
Competition/European Law	Media & Entertainment
Construction	Outsourcing
Corporate/M&A	Planning
Data Protection	Private Equity
Defamation/Reputation Management	Real Estate
	Real Estate Finance
	Real Estate Litigation
Dispute Resolution	Restructuring/Insolvency
Employee Share Schemes	Retail
Employment	Sports Law
	Tax
	Telecommunications

In property – an important department to the firm – trainees can run their own files, mainly landlord and tenant and conveyancing matters. The group drew praise for the amount of trust it placed in trainees, and it certainly has a good roster of clients, including Timberland (the shoe people not the man himself) and Legal & General. Liked for its relaxed atmosphere, an adept property litigation team acted for UBS Global Asset Management against Tesco in a lease renewal matter regarding a large city centre store. Another explosive dispute arose out of the major blast and ensuing inferno at the Buncefield oil depot. The firm's client, RO Developments, sought damages from Buncefield's owners and operators when the sale of its property fell through after it was damaged in the explosion.

Thriller

And now, the moment you've all been waiting for... drumroll, curtain up, ta-dah! Yes, it's Olswang's much-vaunted – and much-praised – commercial group. Much as we played up the corporate department, it's easy to see why students start to drool when they read about this area, which includes seats in IP, competition/regulatory and media, communications and telecoms (MCT). John Malkovich, Cate Blanchett, Ricky Gervais and Jeremy Clarkson are some of the famous names that have used the 'Swang in the past. And there are plenty of film, TV and theatre projects in which the lawyers have been involved. The list of hits (and misses, to be fair) is impressive – Olswang advised Celador Films on *Slumdog Millionaire*, Left Bank Pictures on *The Damned United*, Pathé Pictures on *The Duchess*, Littlestar Services on the stage version of *Mamma Mia!*, Cameron Mackintosh on *I'd Do Anything* and Momentum Pictures on *Lesbian Vampire Killers*. RandomHouse, Yell Group and Guardian News and Media are some of the clients from the publishing sector. "*I'm allowed to do it all as a trainee, whether* it be film, sport, music or whatever," said one contact excitedly. Additionally, a few trainees manage to get secondments to media clients.

In the world of broadcasting, the firm is getting to grips with new developments in television online. You may have read about Project Kangaroo – BBC Worldwide's joint venture with Channel 4 and ITV to create one huge video-on-demand service incorporating BBC iPlayer and the commercial channels' own services. Olswang advised BBC Worldwide on this project, which was later scrapped after the Competition Commission stepped in. Shame.

Trainees don't entirely miss out the showbiz lifestyle. "*I nearly got to meet David Baddiel, but I had Keira Knightley and some directors as well,*" said one, unwittingly winning our *Student Guide* award for Cheeky Brag of the Year. We heard also that having Channel 4 as a client has its advantages: "*At an industry event we learnt how to moonwalk!*" Of course, rubbing shoulders with slebs is definitely the exception, not the rule. Tasks like working on cast, crew and directors' agreements, composing acknowledgment letters and helping to run film finance deals are more common. On smaller TV deals, trainees might even do some of the negotiating. Trainees have "*a feeling*" that this team is tilting more in favour of tech work, particularly outsourcing. They got twice as many outsourcing instructions in 2008 than in 2007, and won a number of new clients, including Orange and NASDAQ OMX. Royal Mail and the organisers of the 2012 Olympic Games have also used the team for outsourcing projects.

The IP seat drew rave reviews. Trade mark and copyright work is the mainstay of this team, which advises many high-street fashion retailers including River Island and Hugo Boss. Check out the firm's blog at fashionistaatlaw.blogspot.com.

O goodness

In Olswang's grad recruitment brochure (hardback – posh) there's a lot of talk about its unstuffy nature and lack of hierarchy, complete with little anecdotes from trainees about how they can wear no ties and 'uncorporate shoes'. Our own conversations with trainees support these ideas: interviewees described the atmosphere as "*liberal, relaxed and less straight-laced than other firms.*" We prodded a bit more and were told that not only do trainees "*get on really well with the secretarial staff,*" but also that there's "*no need to behave around partners.*" Perhaps this is the reason why Olswang regularly features in the *Sunday Times'* list of '100 Best Companies to Work For'. Interestingly, secretaries are also listed along with the partners and other fee earners on the firm's website, which is a nice touch. As for the trainees themselves, they are "*not shy or retiring,*" yet despite having a successful rapper among their number, don't make any claims to be "*cool.*" They do, however, have an understanding of just how competitive it is to gain a training place at the 'Swang, so be under no illusion as to the ease of impressing the recruiters.

Olswang doesn't have its head in the clouds so those expecting "*a lot of blue-sky legal thinking*" might be disappointed. Instead why not look at its commendable feet-on-the-ground corporate social responsibility programme? "*We've got heaps of initiatives to make this firm a little more altruistic and sustainable,*" trainees told us. For instance, "*5% of our time has to be spent on pro bono work.*" Surprisingly few UK firms have set such a clear pro bono policy. Olswang does its bit for the environment too, with one green initiative being "*O-cycle, where you can advertise items you may want to get rid of on the firm's website.*" So far such items have included a DVD player, a TV, gig tickets and plant seeds.

Sited on High Holborn, not too far from BPP Law School or the delights of Covent Garden, the exterior of Olswang's office looks as trendy as folk assume it ought to be. The firm's busy social calendar typically includes theatre trips, regular trainee lunches, themed drinks on the roof on the last Friday of the month and, in a dangerous flirtation with copyright infringement, a mock talent show called "*The O Factor.*" Some MCT team members entered the competition as Village People and the tax team produced an Abba tribute. The winner of the show was an Amy Winehouse impersonator.

And finally...

If you're interested in media law but want to couple it with a more mainstream corporate experience, Olswang is ideal. In 2009, 17 out of 24 people stayed with the firm on qualification.

O'Melveny & Myers LLP

The facts

Location: London

Number of partners/solicitors: 10/25

Total number of trainees: 9

Seats: 4x6 months

Alternative seats: Overseas seats, secondments

Over here from California, OMM wants its London office to be a springboard into European business. For now it's big deals, big cases and a small trainee intake.

Are you looking for international work in a small office? OMM's relatively new training programme offers a close-knit workplace and guarantees a seat overseas.

Building and rebuilding

Founded in 1885 in what was then a desolate Los Angeles landscape, OMM has emerged as an international firm with 14 offices – five in the Sunshine State, two more in New York and Washington, five in Asia (Shanghai, Beijing, Hong Kong, Singapore and Tokyo), plus London and Brussels. It employs approximately 1,000 lawyers worldwide, although only a small number of them are based in the UK. Unlike the broad full-service profile of its West Coast offices, OMM's London branch focuses on transactional work in three areas: corporate, finance and funds. The corporate practice has a particular emphasis on private equity deals, which ties in nicely with its funds practice; indeed all three groups work closely. Supporting the core groups are lawyers specialising in real estate, employment, tax and related litigation.

Some of the work here is pretty complicated for a newbie. The *Chambers UK*-ranked funds department advised Actis, a leading emerging markets private equity investor, on its closure of a £2.9bn fund called Actis Emerging Markets 3 (AEM3). The complex AEM3 was one of the largest such funds closed in 2008 and it involved co-investment by a series of English, Scottish and Guernsey-based corporate vehicles. Other notable deals include prominent Dutch mid-market private equity house Egeria's close of its third fund. Investment fund clients also send litigation to the firm. Apollo is a good example. One of its portfolio companies, Norwegian Cruise Lines, became embroiled in a major Commercial Court case arising out of two shipbuilding contracts for new cruise vessels worth approximately €2bn. Another set of high-value actions involves Vivendi Universal following its investment in PTC, which is Eastern Europe's largest mobile phone operator. Brought by T-Mobile and worth approximately €2.7bn, this is one of the world's largest telecoms disputes.

Two years ago when we first visited OMM London we found a work in progress. After opening in 2003 the office grew rapidly, doubling in size during 2005. By 2007 it had six partners and 35 other qualified lawyers. It now has ten partners and only 25 other qualified lawyers. Media reports in April 2008 noted the exit of one fifth of the office's partners and what was described as a generation of senior associates. That included the departure of office co-head Chris Ashworth, whose arrival was highly acclaimed when he joined in 2005 after a stint as Ashurst's corporate head. Other partners have been recruited, including David Watson from Watson Farley & Williams (who joined to head up the litigation practice) and dual-qualified acquisition finance lawyer Sherri Snelson from Fried Frank, but the disastrous economy since 2008 has certainly not helped OMM achieve its goals in the capital.

The plan to grow London remains a priority – in the short term by strengthening already established areas such as investment funds, and in the long term by expanding its fledgling litigation department. At present, all the London lawyers are UK-qualified and, from what our sources say, there seems to be no overwhelming US culture in the office.

Hard day's night

The three-year-old training scheme is one way of growing the UK operation, and the current aim is to recruit up to four trainees per year. The majority of the work they encounter is UK-generated but not necessarily UK-based. Many transactions are conducted either in tandem with other OMM offices in the USA or Asia, or with firms in a developing network of European contacts. There are no compulsory seats for trainees, but due to the office's narrow focus, they usually sit with the funds and corporate teams. Since the addition of a litigation team in 2008, recruits are now able to fulfil their contentious training obligation in-house, having previously been seconded to Charles Russell for three months. A fourth seat is usually taken overseas.

Given the small annual intake, trainees are guaranteed a six-month placement abroad, if they want it and are progressing well in their training contract. In Singapore they work on finance and restructuring matters; in Brussels it's competition and in Hong Kong they are welcomed by an international arbitration group. As well as some pretty fancy accommodation, in Singapore and Hong Kong trainees are given a private office, which is a big draw considering one associate told us that in London they share a workspace with a supervisor and *"don't always get windows, so sometimes depending on where you're sitting you can't tell whether it's day or night."*

Back on home soil it's clear that lawyers in the three main practice groups work together closely on transactions and that the practices are well integrated. Even though the deals are complicated, trainees say they have constant access to the partners running them and are given good responsibility. Paralegal assistance means there's not as much grunt work as you might find at a larger firm, but the workload is a mixed bag for trainees, depending on the department and market conditions. The funds seat is *"great for gaining experience, entails loads of client contact and offers lots of responsibility early on,"* while the corporate seat can bring *"the most client contact and high-level work because the deals are more intense and take a shorter amount of time."* Some late nights and the odd weekend are par for the course, but there are no chargeable hours targets to be met by trainees.

Balancing act

New starters immediately complete the compulsory PSC and are provided with additional informative sessions on subjects ranging from an introduction to the City, to how to balance work and social life. Formal training is then delivered through weekly sessions for junior associates and trainees, and there are further firm-wide presentations. In time, trainees are expected to assist with the presentation of at least one training session, and are invited to do more, which encourages them to master certain topics

Chambers UK rankings

Investment Funds

and sharpen their public speaking skills. Beyond this, training is on the job. There are mid and end-of-seat appraisals in each department, with the former being designed to pass on general advice and the latter being a more structured meeting with the trainee's supervisor and training partner. Our sources found the system helpful and fair, and when there have been disagreements trainees were able to discuss them with an associate or partner.

The firm is looking for recruits with a reasonably mature outlook and good grades, whether or not in the form of an LLB – the current trainee group includes graduates of marine biology and American history. As for who would do well to apply here, it's obvious that an appetite for complicated transactions is essential. The office is small and therefore newbies are expected to interact with lawyers at all levels, including partners. Accordingly, you must not only impress with the quality of your work – you should also be able to fit in with the existing fee earners and support staff.

The office location in the smart Paternoster Square development next to St Paul's Cathedral puts OMM within range of any number of City bars and restaurants, and it's a quick hop over the river via the Millennium Bridge to many of the South Bank's arts venues. Every month a committee organises a social event for all staff, and there are football and netball games during the summer. Come winter some employees jet off for a popular ski trip, which takes them to a new resort for three or four days every year. Due to OMM's small intake, trainee-only outings are relatively sporadic, but Friday evening drinks at the local Paternoster Chop House are a great way to get to know the other staff. There's no need to worry about paying for a round: salaries are pitched at slightly above those of the big City firms, and despite firm-wide redundancies at the outset of 2009, London trainees have since received a pay rise. NQs are paid pretty handsomely too, and in 2009 one of the three qualifiers was offered a job.

And finally...

The scope of activities will broaden in time, but for now finance and private equity are the real drivers. First-hand exposure is the best way to see if this kind of work appeals so why not try out for OMM's two-week vac scheme.

Osborne Clarke

The facts

Location: Bristol, London, Reading

Number of UK partners/solicitors: 110/198

Total number of trainees: 33

Seats: 4x6 months

Alternative seats: Secondments

Full-service with a digi-business twist, OC has a strong track record with technology clients. Trainees can choose from Bristol, Reading or London options.

Osborne Clarke is an interesting beast. It has three UK offices, in Bristol, Reading and London, and each brings something a little different to the party.

The Osborne identity

In Bristol, OC is an old-established full-service outfit – in fact it was founded as far back as 1748. Trainees boldly declare the firm to be "*the main player in the South West,*" and *Chambers UK* ranks it as a regional leader in construction, corporate finance, dispute resolution, employment, insolvency, IT, IP, pensions, real estate and tax. You might compare it to Bristol's other big player, Burges Salmon, with which it shares many of those top-tier rankings.

In London on the other hand, trainees place the firm "*just below the silver circle.*" It has built up a strong corporate reputation working for AIM-listed companies (29 in total, putting it 13th in the AIM client league table), so you might liken it to any number of mid-tier City firms – Field Fisher Waterhouse, for instance. To give an example, OC has recently advised Nighthawk Energy on its £14m secondary placing, independent television production company Boomerang Plus on its £15m AIM IPO and clinical research organisation Premier Research on its £60m public-to-private move. Another client is the hedge fund RAB Capital, to which the firm has regularly sent trainees on secondment.

In Reading, the firm acts for many of the Thames Valley's technology companies. These relationships hark back to the late 1990s, when OC was one of the firms knee-deep in the internet and technology boom. It got burned when the dotcom bubble burst and has since re-diversified but kept its specialist partners and techie clientele. The client names are very impressive – Microsoft, Vodafone, Dell, Xerox, BSkyB and Facebook all use the firm. In a number of respects then there is a sense of similarity with the trendy, media-focused Olswang, which also operates in London and Reading. To be clear though, technology work isn't limited to the Reading office: a London partner is one of the country's leading computer games lawyers and advises Nintendo on the ongoing development of the online functionality of the Wii console. Nor does the Reading office solely do technology-related work: its corporate and banking teams are definitely top end in the Thames Valley.

In truth, OC is like none of the other firms we've mentioned. It has a more national outlook than the one-site Burges Salmon, it's possibly less media-focused than Olswang, and it's definitely less London-centric than FFW. Foreign offices in Cologne, Munich and Silicon Valley add an extra dimension, so let's just say that OC is unique and that the key to understanding it is to realise that its 'one firm, three UK offices' mantra isn't just marketing speak.

Quoting from the firm's most recent five-year plan, managing partner Simon Beswick tells us that by 2015 OC aims to be "*a leader in its chosen sectors: digital business, natural resources, financial institutions and real estate.*" The foreign offices exist because "*many of the firm's clients are demanding pan-European or international coverage. One wanted something done in two countries in two days. We have to meet those new needs.*" The German offices are particulary important and account for about 17% of OC's overall revenue.

Should I stay or should I go?

In the past, trainees were hired to "*the firm, not the office*" and many were happy to flit between the three locations over the course of their training contract. As numbers have grown this has become a logistical problem, so as of September 2009 trainees are assigned to a specific office, although they will still have the opportunity to request seats in the others. All three locations offer corporate, commercial litigation, banking and property seats. In addition, in Reading there are general commercial and employment seats; in London you can do general commercial, employment and insolvency, while Bristol has the widest selection – here, additional options in private client, tax, incentives, pensions and construction are all available.

In the four-seat system you should assume that corporate and property are mandatory. While we're told "*there is some room for discretion,*" we didn't actually speak to anyone who hadn't done both. Each location now has its own head of training, and the current trainees declared themselves a lot happier with seat allocation than in the past. "*The process has become more transparent, so thumbs up to grad recruitment for that.*"

Talking to trainees about the corporate department, there was an obvious split between those who had completed a seat there before the credit crunch ("*busy*") and those who had been there after the recession hit ("*quiet*"). When it was busy, trainees occupied themselves with "*verification exercises on AIM floats, company search reports, drafting corporate resolutions and minutes, running data rooms and taking instructions from clients.*" When the market went quiet, we're pleased to report "*there was a positive effort to make sure trainees were not twiddling their thumbs.*" Said one contact: "*My supervisors gave me every bit of work they possibly could,*" and even in the slow times trainees had done "*an incredible amount of drafting.*" Supervision was praised firm-wide, by the way.

Commercial property seats offer a standard real estate experience in which trainees handle their own small files. ASDA, Barclays and Carphone Warehouse are among the department's biggest clients. Quite a number of trainees get to spend six months in the more niche planning group. Although it counts as a property seat and many instructions are shared with the commercial property team, "*there isn't really much crossover*" with the type of work done by 'mainstream' property trainees. "*My role was more that of assisting on planning applications and negotiating highways agreements with local authorities,*" confirmed one source. There's also plenty of research and time spent on the phone to councils. "*You speak to all manner of people. Some of them can be incredibly rude and difficult… it's a really great experience,*" an enthusiastic source told us.

Chambers UK rankings

Advertising & Marketing	Intellectual Property
Agriculture & Rural Affairs	Investment Funds
Banking & Finance	Media & Entertainment
Banking Litigation	Outsourcing
Capital Markets	Partnership
Charities	Pensions
Competition/European Law	Planning
Construction	Private Client
Corporate/M&A	Private Equity
Data Protection	Projects, Energy & Natural Resources
Dispute Resolution	Public Procurement
Employee Share Schemes	Real Estate
Employment	Real Estate Litigation
Environment	Restructuring/Insolvency
Financial Services Regulation	Retail
	Sports Law
Health & Safety	Tax
Healthcare	Telecommunications
Information Technology	Transport

Its-a-me, Vorderman!

Commercial litigation offers a mixed bag of work. Said one trainee: "*I had an absolutely massive arbitration but, equally, I had cases for more local clients.*" Last year Bristol litigators represented Energy Standard Group in a $200m dispute involving power assets in Ukraine, and assisted Yahoo! on a number of contentious matters. The Reading litigation team was only set up in 2005 but its clients include Bank of Ireland and Hyundai. The Londoners, meanwhile, picked up several instructions from India and Russia last year and are clearly hoping for more work from these emerging markets. And what of our sources' experiences? Said one: "*The disclosure bundle will probably end up with the trainee,*" but "*I took the first shot at drafting a lot of the interesting documents – witness statements and the like.*" Another enjoyed running smaller files: "*It's good litigation experience. I mean, it's not the big money-spinning cases, but you are using the Civil Procedure Rules every day and learning all the tactics.*"

A "*sexy*" IP litigation seat involves managing small trade mark portfolios and "*quite a lot of know-how and compiling updates about what's going on in IP law.*" The team's highest-profile recent case was defending Marks & Spencer against a High Court trade mark infringement claim brought by Interflora after M&S bought the Interflora Google adword. However, our eye was drawn by the fact that OC acts for Nintendo to negotiate licences that secure content rights for its computer games and leisure applications – including digitised books from HarperCollins and food recipes from Carol Vorderman. We hope Carol's culinary skills are as good as her maths. Employment seats also offer a hefty dose of contentious experience. "*I went to two employment tribunals and worked on a lot of redundancy and discrimination matters,*" said one trainee. There's also non-contentious work to get involved with: OC is advising the Japanese conglomerate Nomura on the employment aspects of its takeover of Lehman Brothers' European operations.

London calling?

We do sense cultural differences between the firm's three locations. Some interviewees told us that "*no one thinks of any one office as the HQ,*" but others disagreed. "*Of course we have a head office! It's Bristol – you've got to give respect to where the firm started.*" OC Bristol still has the most lawyers, a full building to itself and a high profile in the South West, which is perhaps why some trainees see it as dominant. By contrast, in London the firm occupies two floors in a building shared with DLA Piper, so some sources suggest that perhaps it has a less distinct identity there. The Thames Valley office is the smallest with only around 60 people. "*It's lovely – everyone knows each other. People like visiting us because we'll always notice if someone is new and say hi.*"

These minor differences aside, a higher "*OC mentality*" transcends the geographical divide. While each location has its own client base, cross-referring work is common and regular videoconferences and shared know-how sessions keep Bristol, London and Reading trainees in constant contact. The firm is completely open-plan, "*so they don't have this hierarchical closed-door nature. You can march up to whoever you like.*" Working hours of about 9am to 6.30 or 7pm are also roughly the same in every office.

Trainees all agreed that "*Osborne Clarke feels like it has a sense of purpose – it's quite forward-thinking and modern.*" The firm is good at keeping everyone in the loop and our contacts could tell us a fair amount about its strategy for the next few years. The plan seems to be for "*fewer clients but bigger ones with better quality work, rather than small-scale work and lots of clients.*" To this end it is currently "*doing a lot on the business development front*" to increase its visibility and take on more big M&A deals. "*If you look at those deal activity tables, it does seem that OC has been punching above its weight,*" pondered one trainee. And, should you be wondering whether the London office might become increasingly dominant because of this: "*The firm will always have a Bristol and London presence. Bristol is the stable, solid part; and London will flex as the market requires.*"

Not unaffected by the recession, OC posted a 12% drop in its annual revenues in July 2009, and eight fee earners and one member of support staff were made redundant in January. A total of ten people from the 2009 and 2010 intakes volunteered to defer for either six or twelve months, and were offered £3,000 and £6,000 respectively. An additional £2,000 was offered for 'personal development' purposes. As at many firms this year, trainee retention was lower than usual, with 12 out of 21 staying with the firm on qualification. Of those that didn't stay, one went in-house to one of OC's clients; two more had decided not to pursue a career in law and so didn't apply for NQ positions.

Girl power

"*I think it's important to say that OC is looking for people with different backgrounds,*" said a second careerer. The firm does indeed take on a high proportion of older trainees, as well as a few from elsewhere in the EU. A calm disposition is important. "*There is nobody who is too stressed out or too manic, or even too academic,*" we were told. Most – though not all – will have attended a redbrick university, however. Among the 41 trainees of 2008/09, about 75% were female, nudging the firm towards the extreme end of a general trend in the profession. The September 2009 intake is apparently more male-dominated.

Bristol was generally regarded as offering the best social life. The office canteen is a place for trainees to hang out and have "*secret squirrel conversations.*" We're told "*the people in the kitchen give good banter – and they'll offer you a great fry-up when you're hungover.*" Bristol itself is "*a great city for just nipping out for a drink*" and "*The Cornubia gets a lots of OC custom,*" as does Severnshed, The Apple cider bar and cheesy club Lizard Lounge. London has had a quieter scene in the past but trainees have noticed "*a real pick-up recently,*" especially on Thursday and Friday nights. The Spectator near St Paul's "*gets more love*" than old favourite The Lord Raglan nowadays. While in Bristol socialising is trainee-centric, "*you probably have more of a mix of levels of seniority drinking together in London.*" The entire firm comes together for the "*awesome*" summer party, which last year was 80s-themed and held in the Madejski Stadium hotel. On the sporting front football, rugby, touch rugby ("*girls included!*") and dragon boat racing are available.

And finally...

Those looking to work in Bristol or Reading should obviously have OC on their radar. Don't discount it if you're considering City law because, according to its trainees, this firm is a hidden gem in the capital.

Pannone LLP

The facts

Location: Manchester, Hale

Number of UK partners/solicitors: 111/107

Total number of trainees: 35

Seats: 4x6 months

Alternative seats: Occasional secondments

Consistently the best-performing law firm in the *Sunday Times'* annual '100 Best Companies to Work For' survey.

This self-styled 'complete law firm' balances commercial capabilities with an esteemed private client practice.

Secret formula?

There are many things that are too good to be true: money that grows on trees; a four-day weekend; chocolate that keeps you skinny – so you could be forgiven for thinking that Pannone, with its impressive list of clients spread evenly across private client and commercial, and its consistent position as the top-ranked law firm in the *Sunday Times'* '100 Best Companies to Work For' list, was another. But try as we might to unearth some grizzly truths, our investigative digging kept striking gold. We asked training partner Andrea Cohen what Pannone's secret was. Her response? *"I don't know if there is one. We treat people the way we want to be treated. If people are happy then they will put their all in."*

Pannone's roots lie in its personal injury and clinical negligence practices, both of which are consistently ranked top in the North West by *Chambers UK*. Rodger Pannone, descendent of the original founder, is now a consultant at the firm. During his time in practice Rodger worked on the Opren and thalidomide cases, the Manchester air crash and the Piper Alpha and Lockerbie disasters, which gives some insight into the calibre of work this firm is involved with. But it is not just clinical negligence and PI that draw trainees to the firm; it is the rare breadth of practice areas that they find particularly appealing. *"Here you are literally doing the whole book,"* said one source. *"It's a very good place for trainees to come because there aren't many firms of around this size that cover such a broad range, and it's all interesting stuff,"* added another.

Other seat options on offer are family, private client, commercial property, commercial litigation, corporate, employment, construction, insolvency and regulatory (previously known as business crime). Trainees generally stick to either a commercial or a private client stream, but *"there are always the odd few who aren't sure so they mix it up and they love it."* With no compulsory seats it's a perfect system for those who want to pick 'n' mix, but it is generally understood that trainees will have spent a full year in their qualifying seat by the time the two years are up.

Heart on your sleeve stuff

While it isn't compulsory to spend time in PI before going to the smaller clinical negligence team, it is certainly preferred. *"One assists the other and an understanding of the medical jargon helps as it is quite a niche little area."* Half a dozen trainees sit in PI at any one time and each is assigned a partner whose specialisms range from catastrophic head injuries, industrial diseases and death in custody to sports injuries, child abuse issues and holiday accidents. 'Slip-and-trip' is a major part of the day-to-day work of the department, but a large support team means that trainees are *"never on the run-of-the-mill stuff."* They are freed up instead to cut their teeth on the more complex, higher-value cases – over the past year several claims have settled at more than £1m. Trainee roles include taking witness statements, instructing barristers and expert witnesses, drafting schedules and attending client meetings. Those who spend a second seat in PI can expect a couple of their own files to run. Be aware that some of our sources found the work too emotionally draining. "*I don't want to learn to switch off from this,*" lamented one. Thankfully others thoroughly enjoyed the challenge of dealing with clients on a regular basis, particularly the more awkward ones, including "*those with greater expectations than they should have.*" Whether trainees loved PI or felt it wasn't quite for them, most agreed it is "*a fantastic experience*" in terms of "*getting a good grounding in litigation and client contact.*"

Pannone's clinical negligence practice is the largest in the North West. Work is a "*real mixed bag*" with the common denominator being huge settlements that range from tens of thousands to millions of pounds. Trainees "*need to develop medical knowledge quite quickly,*" and there are regular talks from a variety of experts as well as departmental training to aid understanding of "*where the medical principles lie and how it correlates with the law.*" Our sources found that the hardest part of their job was "*informing clients that there isn't always someone who can be blamed for their misfortune. Trainees are involved a lot with new clients, so you learn how to manage them and explain why their case can't go forward. These are skills that can be transferred to any area of law.*"

The private client team carries out standard wills and probate work, but is also in possession of an "*evolving*" Court of Protection team "*for clients who are mentally unable to look after their own affairs.*" The caseload has increased by around 40% over the past year, and the vast majority of clients are referred from the clinical negligence team. "*We run these people's lives. Most have received quite large compensation payouts and we look after all their money. What they need us to do for them depends on the severity of their brain injury. We will order their food for them or arrange to buy property if necessary,*" explained one source. Offices in "*the more well-off areas*" of Alderley Edge (where all the footballers live) and Hale also offer wills, probate and family advice to private clients.

Commercial trimmings

On the commercial side of the firm there are a multitude of seats available. The flourishing commercial litigation department is one of the most popular and it houses IP/IT, property, banking and debt litigation. "*Every day in commercial litigation you come across something new.*" The team is increasingly focused on high-value disputes, but at present still works on cases "*from £15m to £20m at the top end, right down to being in the small claims court for a few hundred pounds.*" Some of the bigger clients are Kellogg's, Chevron, The Co-operative Bank and property company Derwent Holdings. In what is a "*fast-paced*" environment, some trainees loved the adrenalin rush that comes with court deadlines. "*Something might land on your desk at 2pm and it has to be in court at half past four. You just drop everything and do it.*" Others found it "*too

Chambers UK rankings

Banking & Finance	Fraud: Criminal
Clinical Negligence	Information Technology
Construction	Intellectual Property
Corporate/M&A	Local Government
Debt Recovery	Partnership
Defamation/Reputation Management	Personal Injury
	Private Client
Dispute Resolution	Real Estate
Employment	Real Estate Litigation
Environment	Restructuring/Insolvency
Family/Matrimonial	Travel

intense.*" As with most contentious seats the majority of trainees' time is spent researching and preparing court documents and bundles, but there is also client contact, not to mention enough time in court for one source to state: "*If you don't like court work then just don't bother with this seat.*"

Pannone's corporate group has been on the ascent. It is pushing to expand from its traditional public sector clientele and now counts private equity house Infinity Asset Management and mobile marketing company 2ergo Group as clients. The employment team is also becoming increasingly busy, providing both contentious and non-contentious advice to The Bank of England, National Grid, TetraPak, Reebok and Umbro. Trainees here "*absolutely loved the great variety of work, the great autonomy and the access to clients.*" The regulatory team exposes trainees to "*a lot of big fraud cases*" as well as smaller issues such as the implications of trading standards on unsafe products. While there is "*a lot of mundane schedule checking,*" and this type of work wasn't necessarily something our sources had ever thought about doing, most were pleased to discover that "*it is actually quite an interesting area of law.*" Civil fraud matters involve asset location and tracing, and freezing and search orders; meanwhile there is an increasing caseload of internal corporate investigations, such as one involving allegations of fraud by senior company officers at a FTSE 50 utilities company. Evidencing the success of the team, partners have joined from heavyweight commercial firms Pinsent Masons and DLA Piper.

Red lolly, yellow lolly

Pannone chose corporate lawyer Steven Grant to be the firm's new managing partner in 2008, and we were interested to know whether this was a statement of commercial intent after private client partner Joy Kingsley's 14-year tenure. Kingsley is now senior partner and presides over a partnership that is quite an even mix of men and women (it's just over 40% female, which is very high for the profession). "*It hasn't changed anything with regards to the way we run things,*" says Andrea Cohen of the switch in management, and trainees agreed. "*I think Pannone will always keep the split [between commercial and private client]. It's good to have a spread. Both sides of the firm look after each other when one isn't doing so well.*" The few changes that have been made were in order to cope with the firm's increasing size: one example being the creation of new associate and senior associate positions. "*We now have so many people we can't make them all partner or equity partner. We want to recognise contribution without necessarily making people partner.*"

The recruitment process has also become more formalised. "*It's so massively competitive now, they are getting candidates of a high calibre from all over the country,*" said trainees. Paralegals no longer get preferential treatment in the process and Andrea Cohen confirmed trainee suspicions that "*only an exceptional [external] candidate*" would get an interview without having done a Pannone vacation scheme. "*We want people who treat everybody properly and will work well with people. You can only really tell that from a vac scheme.*" But despite this "*more businesslike approach*" to management and recruitment, trainees assured us that the famed 'cuddly' culture has not disappeared. "*It's not like working in a law firm, which is the highest praise I can give it really,*" said one. In a nice touch, two of the trainees we spoke to were actually handed ice cream while they were on the phone to us. "*We normally have cakes when we hit target, but it's so hot today we have gone for ice lollies instead,*" they explained. Other perks include additional days off for good performance, going home early on your birthday and vouchers for meals.

A family affair

Housed in three adjoining buildings in Deansgate, Pannone is a Manchester outfit through and through. "*The firm relies heavily on being solely North West-based,*" said sources. "*We have strong local roots compared to much of the competition, and that appeals to businesses in the area.*" Pannone also supports a number of local charities and always has employees sponsored to compete in the Manchester Run. The firm is keen for its trainees to show a similar level of commitment to the region, and the majority have either grown up or studied not far away. Southerners need not be disheartened: we spoke to a couple of trainees who had spent their formative years south of the Watford Gap and they were welcomed with open arms. "*It's not just a cliché about northerners being friendly. It's absolutely true!*" beamed one enamoured source. The firm assures us that "*if their application is as good as the others and they can show they have done their research,*" nobody is ruled out.

Pannone takes full advantage of its city centre location when it comes to firm socialising. There are monthly drinks held at various venues around Manchester, "*and the partners put some money behind the bar.*" Trainees regularly organise their own lunches and nights out as well. Beyond the pub, interviewees talked of paintballing, greyhound racing, comedy nights and occasional trips further afield to places like Devon and Brussels, subsidised by the firm. "*People here are generally pretty sound,*" said one trainee. "*It's like a family,*" added another. The latter statement is truer than you might think. Apparently around one in six Pannone employees are related in some way. "*We have got trainees and solicitors who are children of partners,*" says Andrea Cohen. "*We would far rather go on personal recommendation. Obviously they have to be up to standard, but there is no reason why we shouldn't look after family.*"

This past year has shown that not even a successful business like this one can escape the worst the economy can throw at it. Pannone has been through two rounds of redundancies. During late 2008 and 2009, a total of 60 jobs were lost, including a small number of salaried partners. Of 19 qualifiers, 13 were kept on: nine on permanent contracts, four on fixed-term ones with a view to them becoming permanent.

And finally...

If Pannone had a circus trick it would be juggling. Somehow this firm has managed to keep all its balls in the air, proving year on year that healthy financials and happy workers can go hand in hand.

Paul, Hastings, Janofsky & Walker LLP

The facts

Location: London
Number of UK partners/solicitors: 20/47
Total number of trainees: 11
Seats: 4x6 months
Alternative seats: Secondments
Extras: Pro bono – LawWorks, Addaction

"About 75% of our work is domestically generated. We have been successful at taking US clients and making them UK clients."

Justin Hamer, Training Principal

The London office of global US firm Paul Hastings has been singled out for growth. A training contract here means hard work for excellent rewards.

There's something about Seth

Paul Hastings is half the age of many of its BigLaw American peers, but a broad practice spread and tactical expansion means it now rivals the best of them, and has fared better than many in the downturn. Founded in LA in 1951 it was almost a quarter of a century before it made its first step beyond the City of Angels. Today it has 18 offices worldwide and over 1,000 lawyers. The London office debuted in 1997, and in 2006 chairman Seth Zachary singled it out for growth (the idea being to make it the firm's second-largest office behind New York). A year later the firm welcomed its first trainees.

Despite the downturn, the firm has remained committed to its aims, securing a flurry of lateral hires, many from reputable US cousins such as O'Melveny & Myers and Kirkland & Ellis. In March 2008, the commitment to London was reinforced by the relocation of the firm's global real estate head to the City. Perhaps the most symbolic development, and certainly the biggest coup to date, was the acquisition of seven partners and their teams (including trainees) from struggling Cadwalader, Wickersham & Taft in January 2009. As one trainee put it: *"Paul Hastings is looking at the recession as an opportunity to bring talented people to the firm and to the London office. We see the opportunity rather than the risk."*

The new Cadwalader team includes specialists in restructuring and insolvency, litigation, structured finance, investment funds and real estate finance. If you take a look at Paul Hastings' European rankings it would seem that the Cadwalader acquisition is a move to help the London office achieve what its siblings across the Channel already have.

Settling down and settling in

We couldn't help but wonder how well the two trainees groups had gelled. Our sources agreed that the incorporation of Cads' trainees had gone very smoothly. *"When Paul Hastings was looking to expand, it certainly did its due diligence to ensure a good fit,"* said one. There were lots of integration events and the firm has *"really tried to mix the trainees in the departments."* Trainees complete four seats of six months, and the Cadwalader additions mean there is even more choice than before. Said one source: *"By the end we are going to be so well rounded and there is more chance of finding something you really like."* Trainees can choose from real estate, corporate, finance, project finance, tax, litigation and employment, and there are new seats in real estate finance, restructuring and capital markets, as well as a secondment to Credit Suisse. There are no mandatory seats. *"There used to be an unwritten rule that everyone had to do a corporate seat but now it just has to be corporate-based."*

The London office has finally begun to flourish in its own right rather than relying solely on deals coming from across the Atlantic. Currently around 80% of its work is sourced from the UK and Europe. Trainees feel that *"there is a greater autonomy at Paul Hastings London than at other US firms in the City."* Having said this, the firm certainly has the feel of being run as *"a global oper-*

ation." Trainees regularly work on international deals that spread across a number of jurisdictions. Said one interviewee: *"In my corporate seat I did a deal with the Atlanta office as well as some due diligence for a Chinese company."* One major deal was for new client Reliance Globalcom, a subsidiary of India's largest integrated telecom service provider Reliance Communications, on its acquisition of a rival out of administration. The deal involved 50 lawyers from the London, Paris, Frankfurt, Milan, New York and Washington offices.

Footloose and fancy freeway

Trainees in the corporate department say deal teams tend to be quite small, meaning they *"get flung into it"* from the off *"and have no option but to get involved." "The team just lets you draft,"* said one source; *"on one deal I basically drafted all the documents. I started them all from scratch."* The department's culture is quite hardcore, *"but the nature of the work makes it that way. If things have to be done then they have to be done."* And judging by what we heard from our sources, Paul Hastings' corporate team is busy. *"I am literally working the whole time,"* gasped one. *"If I get out at 8pm it's a good day, but I am often here later."*

The finance department has particular strengths in aviation and regularly represents Engine Lease Finance Corporation, the world's leading independent spare engine financing and leasing company. There was a significant deal for Deutsche Capital Management on the acquisition of four B777 freighter aircraft totalling $860m. The popular project finance team work on numerous infrastructure and energy projects in South East and Eastern Europe. As well as advising the government of the Republic of Croatia on the refinancing of the Zagreb-Macelj motorway, the team represented the government of the Republic of Srpska (Bosnia and Herzegovina) on the design, construction, financing, operation and maintenance of five motorways. This transaction is the first of its type in the Republic of Srpska, illustrating that the team is at the forefront of Eastern Europe infrastructure. This reputation is likely to bring in a much-needed cash flow for the firm while deal flow from other parts of the globe is at a low ebb. The team has also represented Bulgarian company Bulgaraz Holding on a number of gas pipeline projects with billion-euro price tags. Trainees were pleased to inform us that *"pretty much everything my supervisors are doing I am doing,"* including joining them on business trips to meet clients and get documents signed. *"I got the afternoon free to wander round Zagreb, which was pretty cool,"* recalled one. If getting overseas is a priority then make this known early on as there could be a chance to take a seat in the firm's Hong Kong office.

Chambers UK rankings

Asset Finance	Capital Markets

Paul Hastings treats its trainees like associates and expects them to behave accordingly. *"It's a two-way street,"* agreed our sources. *"The partners put a lot of trust in you, but you need to put the hours in and work hard."* And put the hours in they do; indeed, several trainees highlighted this as a downside. *"Sometimes the hours are quite long or you have to work at the weekend and cancel plans."* Trainees are even given a billable-hours target – *"It is 1,000 hours in your first year, which is quite reasonable, and then 1,500 in your second year to get you more used to the associate target, which is 1,800 hours."* But it is *"more of a guide rather than a set structure. If you are doing a lot of research, which isn't billable, they don't seem to hold it against you."*

Tough love

The word that one interviewee felt best described Paul Hastings trainees was *"resilient." "There isn't much room for weakness here,"* they told us; *"if you're not good enough you'll get found out quite quickly."* Our sources also suggested that you have to take responsibility for your own progression. *"To get on well in this firm you need to be highly motivated and not expect people to be overly worried about you."* Furthermore, *"the partners tell you how it is. At the end of the day, you are there to learn and they are there to teach you. While they might be quite blunt, I think it's probably necessary."*

While there were a few integration events when the Cadwalader teams joined, the social scene seems to have settled back down to monthly drinks for associates and trainees, as well as annual Christmas and summer parties. The words of one source sum things up perfectly: *"It is not necessarily a bad thing that we don't all go to the pub together. It means you know where the boundaries lie. It is part of the professional atmosphere of the firm."*

And finally...

While Paul Hastings' trainees must be prepared to work hard, the starting salary of £40,000 (rising to a tasty £80,000 on qualification) sweetens the deal. In 2009 three of the five qualifiers stayed with the firm.

- **Have faith:** Failing to get a training contract at the end of university is not the end of the world, even though you feel bad because many of your friends have one. Get some paralegal or other useful experience and a firm will be more likely to take you seriously.

top tip no. 21

Penningtons Solicitors LLP

The facts

Location: Basingstoke, Godalming, London

Number of UK partners/solicitors: 52/64

Total number of trainees: 17

Seats: 4x6 months

Alternative seats: None

Whether in London or the southern Home Counties, trainees will see interesting and sometimes quite unusual work.

Two-hundred-year-old Penningtons maintains a 'one firm ethos' by sharing its clients between three South of England offices. It offers trainees a healthy work-life balance and a diet of quality commercial and private client experiences.

Survivor!

Penningtons is a survivor. It has proved time and again that it can adapt to change and rise to a challenge. In 1993 an IRA bomb attack damaged the firm's London office, putting it into temporary accommodation for two years. A partner exodus shortly afterwards saw it lose its Bournemouth office. Less resilient firms would have crumbled, or at least sought a merger, but this tough old organisation kept going. Today, it remains a respected top-100 outfit with offices in London, Godalming and Basingstoke, having lost its Newbury office to South East rival Thomas Eggar following a strategic review in 2007. At that time management decided to reorganise the firm into three main categories: business services, commercial property and private individuals. *"We are trying to share a pool of clients, rather than have three discrete offices,"* said trainees of the rationale for the *"makeover."* A new chief exec has lately set the goal of doubling revenue and profits by 2012, which is probably a smart move given that the firm is not at present one of the most profitable among the top 100. Penningtons' cracking reputation in some quite unrelated areas of law, such as clinical negligence and electoral law along with North American and Indian practice groups, all tell us that Penningtons has a wider range of clients than your typical South East firm.

When applying here, choose your office wisely because opportunities for moving between the three have traditionally been limited. Although trainees say there *"may be scope to move around in the future,"* it wasn't something that was particularly important to them. We found the Hampshire and Surrey trainees to be mostly locals who had joined the firm in order to work locally. Our London sources had usually selected Penningtons for its size and ability to offer *"a decent training in the City."* The three locations all offer seats in the firm's main practice groups (property, dispute resolution, corporate and private client), although some of the more niche areas aren't available firm-wide. Trainees take four seats of six months each, often repeating one if they really like it.

...all I got was this lousy T-shirt

Given Penningtons' devotion to the one-firm philosophy, instead of doing a tour of the offices we'll visit each of its three main practice groups, starting with the one servicing private individuals. Some of our sources had specifically chosen the firm for its expertise in this sector and were happy to find their experiences lived up to expectation. They reported *"lots of meetings with clients"* and the opportunity to deal with their own files. In the London office, where there was praise for *"really enthusiastic"* partner Mark Eaton, the team works mainly for pension providers and wealthy families. Basingstoke is the only office in which contentious private client work is offered. Admittedly trainees have few opportunities to try advocacy until after qualification, but there are enough negotiations to whet their appetites. Non-contentious tasks, such as the drafting of wills, are much more common.

Also coming under the 'private' umbrella is the clinical negligence team, which works out of Basingstoke and Goldalming, and is ranked by *Chambers UK* as one of the best in the South of England. In one case, the team acted for a woman suffering from nervous shock after the death of her daughter from meningitis. She claimed on the basis of the failure of doctors to suspect and investigate the illness, and the consequent shock of being called back to hospital to find her daughter on life support. The firm achieved a settlement shortly before trial. In another case, the lawyers won £2.75m in damages in a claim brought against a former GP after a delay in diagnosing what turned out to be tuberculous meningitis. The disease left the claimant disabled. Trainees found clin neg to be a demanding but rewarding seat consisting of managing smaller cases and attending conferences with barristers.

Godalming has a top-notch specialist travel litigation unit handling cases involving accidents and injuries abroad, claims against tour operators and the intriguingly vague 'claims for loss of enjoyment of holiday'. Trainees can expect to see "*quite meaty cases, often involving issues of jurisdiction.*" One became known as the Dirty Dancing case. Penningtons' client, while on a package holiday booked through Thompson, was cajoled onto a stage to recreate the famous lift scene between Johnny and Baby. The woman he was paired with was rather large and, well, you can imagine how badly things went. Given that all that the best performers of the night would have won was a T-shirt, the client's severe foot injuries were definitely too high a price to pay for his reluctant participation.

Smooth regulator

The second major practice group is named 'commercial property', but there are "*several teams within the wider department*" covering work relating to banking and finance; construction; projects and infrastructure; property investors; property tax; retailers and tenants; and social housing. A seat here is a "*very beneficial*" placement "*because it is very transactional and gives you a good grounding in landlord and tenant matters.*" Through necessity trainees start out with post-completion tasks like Land Registry and stamp duty forms, although these can relate to deals for all sorts of clients, including those from France and the Middle East. In Basingstoke, trainees can expect social housing transactions to be mixed in with commercial property work. Major clients include Sentinel Housing, Sovereign Housing and Family Mosaic Housing, all of which have continued to be active during the economic downturn. Having said this, the flow of property work did generally become weaker following the credit crunch and the firm was forced to make some redundancies from its commercial property group. Overall, the firm let a total of 23 staff go in 2009, and by speaking with trainees we learned that the redundancy process had been "*transparent*" and that Penningtons

Chambers UK rankings

Clinical Negligence	Personal Injury
Corporate/M&A	Private Client
Dispute Resolution	Professional Discipline
Employment	Real Estate
Immigration	Real Estate Litigation
Intellectual Property	Social Housing
Parliamentary & Public Affairs	Travel

had tried to minimise the impact of the poor economy by moving some lawyers between departments. As for future trainees, a small number deferred the start of their contracts for a year in exchange for a £5,000 payment. Unfortunately, in 2009 just six of the 11 qualifiers could be accommodated when they finished their training.

The last of the three divisions, 'business services' covers corporate, commercial, employment and dispute resolution. The commercial team has a couple of massive clients, plus some that will be more familiar to those who are local to its county offices. The Dubai government-owned Jumeirah hotel group selected Penningtons as its IP/IT legal adviser in 2008. It has properties and developments in the UK, North America, the Middle East and Asia, it's most recent project being the Jumeirah HanTang Xintiandi hotel in Shanghai. Lawyers also advise Farnborough International, the organiser of the air show of the same name, on IP issues such as website redevelopment and privacy. In Basingstoke, trainees felt that this seat put them "*not so much on the front line, as clients prefer to deal with more senior people,*" however they were not left twiddling their thumbs and had plenty to keep them busy. By contrast a shortage of associates in the Godalming office meant trainees were very much the first point of contact after partners. One source described their experience as "*a huge learning curve and very stressful as you're helping investors with start-ups.*" The dispute resolution team handles standard commercial matters (contractual and shareholder disputes and the like) and also has a number of specialist subgroups.

In London a placement in business immigration is always interesting. Though very small (it has just one partner), the team is rated highly by *Chambers UK* and counts famous actresses and foreign royals among its private clients. Penningtons' successful representation of *Big Brother 6* contestant Makosi Musambasi in an asylum claim led to further instructions from Zimbabweans fleeing Robert Mugabe's regime. The lawyers also advise businesses such as Foster + Partners Architects and Bank of India on the UK's ever-changing business immigration rules. Another niche practice in London relates to professional regulation. The seat is "*very busy... we do a lot of work for the Solicitors Regulatory Authority and also matters relating to pharmacist's rules.*" You can imagine the stories – solicitors up to no good with clients' money, pharmacists committing dispensing errors. The team recently represented regular client the Royal College of Veterinary Surgeons in two appeals against disciplinary rulings involving the mis-certification of horses for export. Other clients include the Chartered Institute of Management Accountants and the General Osteopathic Council.

Really lucky trainees in the capital may also get to work on electoral law issues. Penningtons is one of only four firms ranked by *Chambers UK* in this field. It has acted for the Conservative Party for almost a century, although it remains to be seen if the recent loss of partner Sue Dixon will affect this relationship. Of late the firm has represented a candidate who alleged corrupt practices relating to postal voting in the Slough Borough Council election.

Penn pals

For those not intimately acquainted with Surrey and Hampshire, Godalming is a prosperous town in London's stockbroker belt – a fact that may shed some light on the success of Penningtons' private client practice. The firm has recently made an office move in Godalming. Previously split between two buildings, staff now enjoy spacious, open-plan accommodation on Brighton Road. Basingstoke is unfortunately "*not as picturesque*" due to the fact that 1960s developers had their wicked way with what was once an inoffensive market town. On the upside, the commute to London is pretty easy. Perhaps in an attempt to inspire genius amongst its inhabitants, Penningtons' Basingstoke building is called da Vinci House. It wasn't lauded for its location, but the office was praised for its decor: "*They redid the lobby recently, which is very good now.*" Although "*very close to lot of bars and clubs,*" Basingstoke trainees still prefer to take the 40-minute up train to London to socialise with their peers in the capital, where The Livery, Apt or The Red Herring are all popular destinations. Completing the trio of offices, the London base, which is spread across two floors of a building not far from St Paul's Cathedral, "*is good for getting to know everyone – though it should be noted that the fifth floor is quieter than the sixth.*"

During our interviews, trainees tended to highlight the gentler manner in which the firm works. "*Anyone looking for a hard-hitting or aggressive way of dealing with clients may not like it here,*" concluded one. The current intake was slanted in favour of women who had read law at university – in fact just two of the eleven 2008 starters were male and only one had done a non-law degree. Previous intakes have been more balanced in this regard, so we've no reason to suppose that this is anything other than an anomaly. As for other common traits, one London source divulged: "*We're quite thrifty – sometimes we bring in our lunch and sit out in the sun.*" That's not thrifty, that's nice! Doing its bit to help diversify the profession, Penningtons is one of 13 member firms of the City Solicitors' Educational Trust which funds a summer school project to encourage students from non-Russell Group universities to aim for a coveted City training contract.

Trainees rarely graft past 7.30pm and we're told "*the work-life balance is really good, although everyone seems to want to work hard.*" Sports and social committees in each office organise events for staff, including a fun sports day in Godalming. The firm had its first firm-wide Christmas party in some while last year. It was held in the presence of a Warhol exhibition at London's South Bank Centre, so we'd love to imagine a Studio 54-style romp. Then again, maybe not...

And finally...

With its commercial/private client mix, Penningtons may look snugly regional, and in many ways it is. But don't forget those star departments that could give a training contract here real spice.

Open for business

Pinsent Masons is a law firm with no barriers – no barriers in the way we work and no barriers to what you can achieve in your career.

- Top 15 UK Law Firm & Top 100 Global Law Firm
- A supportive, collaborative, and open culture
- Cutting-edge work delivering business solutions
- Open access to partners and experienced lawyers
- Opportunities and responsibility open to all

Doors will continually open at Pinsent Masons. Find out more and apply for a summer vacation placement or training contract at
www.pinsentmasons.com/graduate

Pinsent Masons

London · Birmingham · Bristol · Leeds · Manchester · Edinburgh · Glasgow · Beijing · Dubai · Hong Kong · Shanghai

WINNER LC AWARDS 2009 BEST TRAINER NATIONAL/LARGE REGIONAL FIRM | TOP LEGAL EMPLOYERS UNITED KINGDOM 2009 AWARDED BY crf.com | 2008 Excellence Awards WINNER | Stonewall DIVERSITY CHAMPION | INVESTOR IN PEOPLE | NATIONAL COUNCIL FOR WORK EXPERIENCE AWARDS FINALIST 2008/09

Pinsent Masons LLP is an equal opportunities employer

Pinsent Masons

The facts
Locations: Birmingham, Bristol, Leeds, London, Manchester, Scotland
Number of UK partners/solicitors: 288/653
Total number of trainees: 125
Seats: 4x6 months
Alternative seats: Overseas seats, secondments,
Extras: Pro bono – various, including a business advice clinic; language training

The firm's *"open and clear channels"* for communication no doubt facilitate the palpable sense of loyalty here.

Five years on from a successful merger, respected national player Pinsent Masons is a flourishing full-service firm with an ambition to become more international and an emphasis on substance over style.

A cultured pearl

Back in 2004, when the merger was conceived, some pundits were sceptical, saying: 'Quite why the two management teams are determined to push through a deal that has surprised and underwhelmed many rivals in equal measure, is [not] clear.' Seen as a high-risk strategy back then, the union has paid off. Pinsents had a well-rounded commercial service offering across the UK, while the Masons side of the business brought particular strengths in construction, technology and outsourcing. The combined firm now has Dubai, Hong Kong, Shanghai and Beijing offices alongside bases in seven UK cities. Until recently we'd have said its foothold in Europe was limited to a 'best friends' network and that most other parts of the globe were untouched. When we spoke to trainees in May 2009 they said: *"This is an ambitious firm and it has plans to increase its presence and significance within the UK and internationally."* They also said of corporate and finance: *"Judging by the growth in those departments,"* they are set to become ever more key to the business. *"It's evident where the firm wants to go."*

Right on cue, a month after our interviews Pinsents announced a major alliance with international firm Salans, which has around 700 lawyers in 21 offices sweeping through Europe and Central Asia and into the Far East, Middle East and New York. Salans operates both in established financial centres and emerging or fast-growing markets. If you're interested in Pinsent Masons then do go online and read our 2009 edition report on Salans too as it will give you a better understanding of the potential of this major new association between law firms.

Pinsent Masons organises itself by way of 12 practice themes: property; dispute resolution; corporate; insurance and reinsurance; outsourcing, technology and commercial (OTC); pensions; projects and international construction (PIC); domestic construction and engineering; tax; banking/finance and employment. Over the course of four seats, a trainee can follow a distinct path; equally there's scope for a very broad training. The world of Pinsent Masons is their oyster, and with well-run systems for training, appraisal and support, you can bet some real pearls are created.

PIC and mix

With a multitude of seats available to trainees in the UK offices, the HR teams have their work cut out for them. Fortunately they're up to the task. In fact, they even publish a centralised list of the seats trainees ask for and what they get. This tends to prevent *"underhand, clandestine conversations that will secure you your preferred seat."* Our interviewees appreciated the transparency: *"It's to their credit that they do it. They want us to see they are approaching allocation in as fair and equitable a way as they can."* At the time of our calls London was home to most trainees (50 in all). Then came Birmingham (29), Leeds (26), Manchester (13) and Scotland (six). Four more had split their time between two offices, including the tiny Bristol outpost. One trainee stressed the importance of being open-minded as *"there's such a wide range of departments and what you do within them varies enormously."* However, in an attempt to save a hectare or two of rainforest, let's focus on what we consider to be the most prominent.

First, corporate. Pinsent Masons is among the top firms in the country for AIM clients and deals, and there's also fund-raising, private equity, financial services regulation and M&A. Recent highlights include advising Wal-Mart on the sale of Gazeley Limited Group (the property development arm of ASDA) and acting for Angel Trains during its £3.6bn sale by RBS. Lawyers also advised Regal Petroleum, the AIM-listed oil and gas group, on its $165m placing. One trainee who had focused on private equity summarised: *"The main aspect is project management. You're in the centre of it all, and while senior people are negotiating documents you are producing the due diligence report and discussing it with the client."* For trainees in other areas there is more *"collating information to feed into drafts, preparing ancillary documents, plus general support and research."* In a regulatory seat, you might get the opportunity to take on your own files. We spoke to a trainee whose delight was palpable: *"Today's the joyous day when I send the entire pack off to the FSA. It's a very exciting time as this has been my baby!"*

While plans to further advance the firm's corporate capabilities continue, the impressive construction practice is already at the top of its game and billion-pound deals abound. The firm represents consortium Viridor Laing in the ground-breaking Manchester Waste PFI project, worth £4bn; it's advising Thames Water on the procurement of its £5bn five-year asset management programme and is acting for Balfour Beatty Civil Engineering and Skanska on the widening of a 100 km stretch of the M5. These gargantuan matters are handled out of the construction and engineering and PIC departments. Within these seats *"the trainee's role is often more menial,"* but *"you do get heavily involved in small, specific parts of the deal."* Seats in these departments provide an opportunity to *"make contacts around the firm,"* as trainees frequently assist with client updates and communications between offices. Much of the international work has focused on the Middle East and Eastern Europe lately, although the team has advised the government of Cyprus on two major PPP projects – the conversion of Larnaka Port to a cruise terminal (including the redevelopment of its marina) and the design, build, financing and operation of a 31 km road between Pafos and Polis.

In terms of contentious construction and engineering matters, a good example comes from the firm's Bristol office, where lawyers represented Norwegian energy contractor Aker in relation to contract disputes over the construction and delivery of two North Sea drilling rigs. Additionally, some trainees had undertaken trial preparation for *"a dispute over the breaking properties of glass."* In more general commercial litigation, topics have included professional negligence, legal partnerships, competition law, land disputes, overseas agency and distribution rights, product safety and public procurement. Pinsent Masons has a host of strong litigators and advised two oil joint venture companies in recent high-profile actions pertaining to the Buncefield depot explosion. The firm also has a strong international arbitration practice working on matters as far afield as Spain, Qatar and Japan.

The OTC department offers *"a spread of work, all connected by technology. There's an IP practice with a contentious side; there's the general commercial side; IT and outsourcing…"* The team makes an effort to ensure trainees see a mix of work, *"and if you express a particular interest they'll do their best to accommodate you."* Outsourcing is a major strength, and the firm is ranked alongside all five magic circle members in *Chambers UK*. Historically strong in representing public sector interests, lawyers have been advising the Statistics Board on the £150m outsourcing of services supporting the 2011 census. They've also been acting for the Metropolitan Police Service on a project to transform its HR services. Trainees appreciated the *"client-facing opportunities"* in this seat, *"attending meetings and taking notes which are then distributed to clients."* Other tasks include *"managing data rooms, IP searches and making presentations to partners via video conference."*

Further seats are available in property, pensions, banking and finance, insurance and restructuring, and various

Chambers UK rankings

Banking & Finance	Media & Entertainment
Capital Markets	Outsourcing
Competition/European Law	Pensions
Construction	Pensions Litigation
Corporate/M&A	Planning
Data Protection	Private Equity
Dispute Resolution	Professional Negligence
Education	Projects, Energy & Natural Resources
Employee Share Schemes	Public Procurement
Employment	Real Estate
Environment	Real Estate Litigation
Health & Safety	Restructuring/Insolvency
Healthcare	Retail
Information Technology	Social Housing
Insurance	Tax
Intellectual Property	Telecommunications
Local Government	Transport

client secondments are on offer, as is a seat in Dubai. Foreign opportunities could soon extend to the Asian offices, so watch this space.

All for one and one for all

Centralisation is a vital theme of the highly systematised management of both the training scheme and the firm as a whole. As trainees put it: "*It's all about one Pinsent Masons.*" They said the firm's approach is to "*break down the office mentality to get to a firm mentality*" and spoke of "*a lot of sharing of work and good communication and interaction between offices.*" As such, "*when you go into each department you're part of the national department.*" It is also possible that as a trainee you will move between offices (though this is not mandatory). The qualification process was entirely centralised for 2009, so we asked trainees how they felt about this. "*It might be that when the job list comes out the position I want might be in Leeds, which would be great as I already know a load of people there,*" a Manchester source said. While we sensed a commitment to the firm rather than a location from most, we understand that London-based trainees were generally less willing to consider a move elsewhere on qualification. When everything was finalised a much lower than usual 35 of 63 qualifiers ended up with jobs in 2009. "*Literally the day after it was announced where jobs were going to be available,*" the firm opened an anonymous forum for people to submit questions to managing partner David Ryan.

The firm's "*open and clear channels*" for communication no doubt facilitate the palpable sense of loyalty. Sources said: "*We're told everything – there's no attempt to exclude trainees.*" On National Trainee Day, first and second-years from across the firm gather in one location (Arsenal's Emirates Stadium last time round). We'd like to imagine a modern-day Feast of Fools in which trainees are treated like kings and can order partners around like slaves. In fact the day simply brings a talk from the firm's management followed by a booze-up. At the last one David Ryan addressed "*all of us in a room where we were invited to ask the most awkward questions we could think of. It was really good because they spoke to us about retention rates. They were open, honest and positive without giving false hope.*" A London trainee enthused that "*it felt really personal, although there were 100 of us in the room.*" Trainees were reassured that "*the firm is doing what it can to keep people, and is moving people around and seconding corporate lawyers to other departments.*" Several sources concluded that "*the firm really values its people.*"

The recession has hurt the firm. While the outsourcing, projects, and technology and commercial practice groups did well, the 2008/09 period was poorer for much of the corporate and property divisions and profitability plummeted by a third, even though revenues held up. Having staved off job cuts for as long as possible, in June 2009 Ryan wrote to all staff outlining a a seven-point plan for coping with the downturn. He proposed more staff deployment between offices, more client secondments, flexi-working, sabbaticals, a pay freeze (amounting to a reduction at NQ level), various other cost-cutting measures and a pretty minimal number of redundancies.

Star(fish) performers

A Pinsent Masons lawyer is measured and well ordered with distaste for all things bombastic or self-promoting. From trainees to the managing partner, "*there's no element of showing off.*" A fourth-seater had the following advice for newbies: "*Come in, work hard and do your best – don't try to impress people with just talk.*" Another added: "*Don't feel you have to have done lots of impressive things – what they look for is someone who will work hard and be conscientious.*" Nevertheless, it's at the top universities that the firm looks hardest for its recruits. Switched-on types do well here, and one trainee extolled the virtues of being "*commercially aware and client-focused. There's no point living in a legal bubble where you can't translate things into something a client could use.*" Team players are valued and trainees told us: "*It's important to be flexible – if you are for them, they will be for you.*"

A healthy social budget for all departments means regular departmental drinks, and then there are office-wide summer and Christmas parties. The latter event is generally fancy dress themed in Birmingham and Manchester (those cheeky Mancs nicked the idea from the Birmingham lot), whereas London opts for black tie. Across offices, trainees "*genuinely get along,*" not only meeting for Friday drinks but often jetting off on holiday together. "*We went to Prague in January and are going to Dublin in two weeks!*" a source said excitedly. This is a great place for sports too: "*there's football, hockey, netball, softball, cricket – anything you want.*" Another key extra-curricular activity comes out of the firm's CSR program, Starfish. Lawyers at all levels of the firm work with children in local communities. "*It's certainly a major draw, and it's clear how much they care about their local environment.*"

And finally...

We get a picture of a solid firm inhabited by sensible, team-driven lawyers. Pinsent Masons would be a smart choice anywhere in the country. Keep an eye on the Salans story...

- **Shameless Plug:** To explore the individual strengths of American law firms in more detail, search www.chambersandpartners.com/usa. The *Student Guide*'s new American sibling www.chambers-associate.com should also give you some good insight into these firms.

top tip no. 22

Reed Smith LLP

The facts
- **Location:** London
- **Number of UK partners/solicitors:** 104/140
- **Total number of trainees:** 41
- **Seats:** 4x6 months
- **Alternative seats:** Overseas seats, secondments
- **Extras:** Pro bono – A4ID, Liberty, Fairbridge; language training

A brand new office that shoots up like a glass arrow from the London skyline says that this US-headquartered firm has serious plans for London.

US firm Reed Smith has grown and grown over the past decade. It has 1,600 lawyers in 23 offices across seven countries, but the word now on trainees' lips is "*consolidate.*"

Partner poaching

In 2001 a 14-office Pittsburgh-based law firm decided it was time to take its first international steps. It set its sights on the UK and secured a merger with London and Midlands outfit Warner Cranston. In 2007, after several more US mergers and office openings in Paris (now gone) and Munich, Reed Smith joined forces in London with the internationally minded mid-market City firm Richards Butler. The marriage gave Reed Smith more than 250 extra lawyers, making the London office the largest in a global network that now also includes Abu Dhabi, Beijing, Brussels, Greece and Hong Kong. Richards Butler was a full-service firm known best for its specialist practices in media finance and shipping. These niches weren't the primary incentive for Reed Smith; it was mostly keen to bolster its European corporate and finance capabilities. Reed Smith now has aspirations to become a realistic alternative to the magic circle firms in London.

Following the merger, Reed Smith has been hiring left, right and centre in London, with Freshfields, DLA Piper, Akin Gump and Herbert Smith all donating partners. At the same time, the firm has re-evaluated its UK coverage and at the start of 2009 it shed its 25-lawyer Warner Cranston legacy office in Birmingham to focus on "*bigger things.*" Training principal Terry Green told us plainly: "*While things are difficult to predict at present, we are continuing to hire laterals in busy areas. We are going to get bigger.*" Reed Smith certainly has ambitious designs for its London office, and while current market conditions mean that growth in real estate and corporate are on the backburner, the firm has built a new investment funds team, having raided fellow London mid-sizer Nabarro in October 2008 and grabbed a further partner from the UK office of US firm Gibson Dunn.

A pitta here and a party there

In theory trainees can choose all four of their seats and they also have the possibility of taking an overseas seat or client secondment (at the BBC, Rank, Barclays Asset Finance and Koch, for example). "*Occasionally people do both, but you certainly can't do two of the same.*" With international placements available in Dubai, Abu Dhabi, Hong Kong and Greece – and the possibility of San Francisco in the future – it is no wonder trainees agree that "*this is definitely a place to come for opportunities abroad.*" While the Hong Kong seat is perennially popular, the others are generally a dead cert for anyone who asks. Amazingly, "*a lot of people express an interest but at the end of the day those who actually go for it are small in number. By the time it comes to making the final decision they decide they will miss their girl or boyfriend or whatever.*" In case you're someone who may need convincing, everyone we spoke to who'd been abroad gave glowing reports. The teams overseas are generally smaller so responsibility is easier to come by, and trainees are well catered for outside work. Those who venture to Greece are put up in "*a beautiful flat with three bedrooms and a huge balcony overlooking the sea, the harbour and the mountains.*" One trainee we interviewed "*had friends out almost every weekend." The office in Abu Dhabi has three Jacuzzis and an outdoor pool on the roof, and Hong Kong trainees are given a large studio flat *"five minutes' walk from everything."* With a daily maid service thrown in, you can *"forget about doing your laundry or cooking... It's nothing but working and partying for six months."*

Back home, most trainees spend time in the office's two biggest departments – corporate and dispute resolution. Because of each department's size, even though trainees are assigned a supervisor, they are encouraged to seek work from other lawyers. This prompted our interviewees to single out these departments as good for first seats *"because there are a lot of trainees, and because we all float about, you end up helping each other."* The reality of representing heavyweight clients such as AXA Insurance, the BBC, PwC, RBS and Tate & Lyle on multimillion-pound matters is that responsibility is hard to come by. One trainee described a $600m case that required 300 bundles of documents for court. *"They all need to be looked after so a trainee is going to be doing that more often than dealing with correspondence."* Having said this, trainees get their hands on *"very interesting ad hoc tasks;"* for example *"there was one insurance dispute where I was asked to draft a list of questions for the witnesses. It forced me to analyse the case and think about the issues, which I think means I was quite heavily involved."* Another told us: *"The work is anything from general admin to hands-on, practical, oh-my-goodness, got to get this to the court right now stuff!"*

Sink or swim

A stint in the corporate department brings company secretarial duties, which are *"really good for giving you an understanding of the workings of companies,"* even if they can become repetitive. London's corporate finance team is ranked in *Chambers UK's* mid-market table, and the global network of offices means there's a strong international aspect to its work. Lawyers frequently represent huge corporations such as McDonald's and L'Oréal in transatlantic matters. The firm also advised Microsoft on the acquisition of Multi Media Mapping last year, and Tate & Lyle used the firm for its £78m acquisition of 80% of food additive manufacturer GC Hahn & Co. Several trainees were able to combine general corporate work with time in the impressive life sciences group. *"It was essentially transactional work involving life sciences companies and patent due diligence."* Ranked in *Chambers UK*, the team is one of the foremost players in non-contentious commercial matters. It represented Swedish speciality pharmaceutical company Meda AB on its acquisition of Valeant Pharmaceuticals' Western Europe, Eastern Europe and Middle East businesses for $392m. Competition is another popular seat in the corporate department and it has *"a constant flow of very inter-*

Chambers UK rankings

Asset Finance	Insurance
Banking Litigation	Intellectual Property
Commodities	Life Sciences
Competition/European Law	Media & Entertainment
Construction	Pensions
Corporate/M&A	Product Liability
Defamation/Reputation Management	Professional Negligence
	Real Estate
Dispute Resolution	Real Estate Finance
Employment	Real Estate Litigation
Fraud: Civil	Shipping

esting work." Clients include such household names as Apple and Channel 4.

The respected media team, ranked in *Chambers UK* for broadcasting and digital content, film and TV finance and production and non-contentious music, has recently been brought under the general corporate umbrella too, prompting some trainees to voice concern over the *"generalist future"* of Reed Smith. *"I get a sense that the niche practices are getting smaller and the bigger areas are getting bigger,"* said one. The firm's official response to this is that *"the intention is to get bigger in the right profitable markets for us."* Nevertheless, time in the media seat brings *"great responsibility on some juicy stuff."* The client list sparkles with names such as the UK Film Council, Tiger Aspect and Sony BMG. The team recently advised Universal Pictures in connection with all production work for the record-breaking film *Mamma Mia!* Reed Smith's Greek office even assisted with on-location issues. Ever the pragmatists, trainees reminded us that while *"there is a whole buzz around* [film work]*, at the end of the day you are still in your office doing legal work."*

The old Richards Butler shipping department is split into dry and wet teams. Wet shipping is all about *"crashing and sinking ships,"* whereas dry shipping involves contract disputes and sale and purchase agreements. The dry shipping team has a reputation for being quite old-fashioned and hierarchical, at one time even gaining the nickname The Morgue. *"It was when we were in the old building and still open-plan and it was always deadly quiet."* The wet shipping team is much smaller with a more familial atmosphere; it provides trainees with loads of client contact. *"A lot of the work is quite tangible. I could actually imagine the ships colliding,"* said one source. The energy, trade and commodities team is *"inextricably linked"* to the shipping department and is ranked top in *Chambers UK*. Unfortunately all the work is rather confidential so we can't go into detail. What we can say is that trainees enjoy extremely high levels of responsibility. Said one: *"I was basically working as an associate"* in *"a* very intense environment where everyone is expected to reach a certain level because it is one of the best departments in the world. It's kind of sink or swim."

U.S. and them

So Reed Smith's ascent to the top of the legal profession has been dazzling, but let's return for a moment to that word we mentioned right at the start: 'consolidate'. Why was it that our sources were so eager for the firm to pause for breath? Had they experienced quite enough change for the time being? There was definitely a sense of unease among those we spoke to. "*I don't feel there is much direction,*" announced one plainly. Another stated more benignly: "*There might be a bit of confusion with regards to the future. It's not a question of a lack of information, it's just that we are in a transition stage.*" A third interviewee summed up by saying: "*The firm should stop trying to get so big and look at what it has rather than what it wants in the future. The partners and managing partners need to remember that the people who aren't in charge need to feel valued too, rather than just concentrating on making the firm into a big corporate monster.*"

For some trainees, the root of any discontent does lie in a perceived lack of communication. While our sources were keen to inform us that the culture of the London office is not American ("*I don't really get the feeling that I am in a US firm in terms of aggression and motivation. We get paid less but our experience is a wholly more pleasurable experience than at other US firms. We don't get pummelled*"), trainees couldn't deny "*the policy of the firm is dictated by America.*" One source spelled things out in no uncertain terms: "*There are partners from the London office on the senior management panel but ultimately the power does lie in the USA. With things like redundancies and trainee jobs, for example, the USA makes those decisions and then it is left to the London office to carry things out.*" Essentially, trainees would like "*more information to come down the chain*" and for it to be "*conveyed with a personal touch by practice group leaders in London, rather than via a three-line e-mail from America.*" Terry Green admitted that perhaps sometimes the announcements "*do come over a bit cold*" but assured us that they are never meant to. As for where the decisions are made, he said: "*People are looking globally with regards to decisions, so things can't be done locally.*"

One of the most significant decisions for trainees is the deferral of all September 2009 and March 2010 new starters. The firm is by no means shy of taking tough decisions.

Spot the different

Despite the worries voiced by trainees it certainly seems that Reed Smith is keen to make an impression in London town. It has recently moved to the top floors of the new Broadgate Tower near Liverpool Street. The third tallest building in the City, this crystal palace shoots up like a glass arrow from the London skyline. "*It's so thin you get scared it might blow over when the wind picks up,*" worried one source, while another said: "*It looks like the kind of office you would see on TV.*" Most agreed that the new premises are "*phenomenal,*" and with the canteen on the top floor there is plenty of scope to waste hours ogling at the "*fantastic views of London.*"

"*The firm is looking for something a bit different,*" say trainees. "*Someone a bit more balanced than just focusing on academics.*" Having said this "*unless you have a 2:1 from a good university there is no point in even applying.*" The trainees we spoke to were still a mix of Richards Butler and Reed Smith hires. Despite the fact that RB was known for recruiting slightly more laid-back types, and Reed Smith for those who are more academic, integration doesn't seem to be a problem. Amongst themselves, trainees organise regular drinks after work and there are departmental outings every month or so. The firm is still getting to grips with its new Spitalfields surroundings, so people are enjoying sampling the numerous local establishments. The Light Bar next door to the office has taken an early lead as the favourite. The firm is big on extra-curricular activities and "*sport and pro bono is heavily part of what we do here.*" There's a successful football team, plus cricket, softball and netball squads. The new canteen has a whole wall dedicated to "*seeing us differently,*" so there are photos of people doing various things away from the office.

And finally...

Things have been changing fast for this firm over the last few years and trainees are certainly feeling it. Happily, 21 of the 29 qualifiers were retained in 2009. Will they come to see Reed Smith achieving its aim of becoming a realistic magic circle alternative?

Reynolds
Porter
Chamberlain LLP

presents...

DECISION IMPOSSIBLE

rpc

THE TALE OF TWO TRAINEES' JOURNEY INTO THE WORLD OF LAW

The recruitment process, a seductive world of beautiful brochures, snazzy exhibition platforms and high-spec websites... you read them all and still don't know which firm is right for you.

However, if you're looking to train with a London law firm where you're in touch with what's happening right from the word go; where you can get hands-on experience of important, high profile issues; where you know your contribution is valued – you've found just what you're looking for.

email us at **training@rpc.co.uk**
or visit **www.rpc.co.uk/training**
or call **020 3060 6000**
to request a brochure.

Reynolds Porter Chamberlain LLP

The facts

Location: London

Number of UK partners/solicitors: 65/180

Total number of trainees: 26

Seats: 4x6 months

Alternative seats: Secondments

RPC is on a roll right now. We came across some of the happiest trainees here and would recommend it wholeheartedly.

London mid-sizer Reynolds Porter Chamberlain is a king in insurance-based litigation. In a quest for balance in our boom-and-bust business world, the firm is also pursuing transactional work to even out its practice profile.

Insurance is sexy

Really, it is – just watch Faye Dunaway and Steve McQueen in *The Thomas Crown Affair*. RPC trainees are certainly convinced. Speaking of their insurance litigation experiences, one told us: "*What I'm working on every day is being reported in the news.*" They are also fully aware that in a down economy, advice to the insurance sector is a lucrative area to be in. Trainees admitted they "*hadn't studied insurance before coming to RPC, other than a bit on a discrete topic during the LPC,*" and that "*maybe people at law school don't understand what the hell insurance is.*" A significant number of our interviewees told us that in their ignorance they had assumed they "*wouldn't fancy it.*" Happily most are proved wrong.

Essentially, almost anything can be insured, from damage to buildings caused by a natural disaster or terrorism to Mariah Carey's legs (worth $1bn, believe it or not). A trainee expressed this idea succinctly when they told us: "*The label 'insurance' doesn't necessarily describe what the work really is. What you're getting here are the real big-ticket cases,*" even if "*the client relationship is different as the instructions come direct from the insurer.*" To give you a bit of insurance market background, soft conditions in 2007 were swept away by credit crunch issues in 2008. The number of cases has increased exponentially as insurers became less inclined to part with their money when claims were made. Insurance lawyers are certainly aware of RPC's appeal: Eversheds' insurance chief David Webster jumped ship to join the firm recently along with colleague Paul Castellani. It has also attracted a new head of restructuring and insolvency from Edwards Angell Palmer & Dodge and a corporate partner from Dechert. With increasing demand for lawyers' services, RPC's all-equity partnership (which, take note ladies, is 25% female) is hoping the volume of work coming in will intensify, allowing its own modest profitability to receive a boost.

Litigate to accumulate

When it comes to insurance at RPC the message is crystal-clear: you will be exposed to big-money litigation in a dizzying array of sectors. Alas, many of the cases are confidential so we can't disclose all we'd want to. We can cite a few recent examples though, including advising insurers on a £250m claim over Wembley Stadium and defending transport and energy company Alstom over a £48m claim filed by an African power company. The firm also continues to act for insurers on matters relating to 9/11 and Hurricane Katrina. "*On the face of it insurance sounds boring, but it's been the most interesting for me purely because you are dealing with such high-profile cases.*" About 65% of RPC's business is litigation, with 70% of it being insurance cases. If you're coming to RPC you will litigate, and you will take at least two insurance-heavy seats. Of the trainees we spoke to, the three most common seats were property and casualty risk, international risk, and reinsurance and professional risks.

Within property and casualty risk, the medical group is popular because of the "*vast amounts of client contact.*" Instructed by clinics, hospitals, out-of-hours GP services, health check and screening services, care homes and hospices, the lawyers defend claims made by and on behalf of patients. Increasingly claims also include complaints to professional regulatory bodies, and sometimes even criminal allegations or references to the Human Rights Act. Trainees sense that they are "*at the heart of the department*" and that there is the real opportunity to practice "*people-based*" law while developing crucial case management skills. Though attendance at coroner's inquests left one trainee feeling "*queasy,*" the seat is generally seen as exciting: cases turn around quickly and the advocacy opportunities are prized.

The professional risk team is described as "*a stalwart department.*" It started as a lawyers' liability practice and now has what trainees refer to as an "*influential client base.*" Who are they acting for? Legal and accountancy firms, both major and minor, plus construction, finance and insurance professionals whenever they get into hot water over their performance for clients. We heard about one plucky trainee who travelled to the USA on a multi-jurisdictional case, as well as attending depositions in London. Across the board, trainees seem to have had plenty of advocacy opportunities – "*being tested in front of a master at the Royal Courts of Justice was daunting but great experience*" for one interviewee, while another praised the firm for being "*great at letting people have a go.*" Nevertheless, much of a trainee's time is spent "*reading into cases and doing research, drafting instructions to experts and witness statements, and concentrating on trial bundling.*" Known as a "*document-heavy*" department, trainees have to expect some late nights of prep for hearings, but at least this "*can be fun as you're in a big group of people all trying to hit a deadline*" and "*you're always thanked if you have to stay late.*"

Staying late is sometimes to be expected in the international risk and reinsurance department. One source was more than aware that an "*influx of claims*" had meant "*long hours*" for them while in that seat. At least "*it was such interesting work so I didn't mind too much;*" another trainee "*loved it so much I didn't want to leave.*" Perhaps the most complex of the insurance areas RPC works in, this department has been dominated by claims relating to financial institutions and officers' and directors' liability following the subprime collapse. Key clients include Marsh, Munich Re and Zurich. Additional lawyers have joined from rival firms, including two who had previously worked at RPC and decided it was time to return. Trainees take responsibility for lower-value case files, compile monthly client bulletins and experience a significant amount of client contact. Other areas covered by the department are product liability and energy. The firm has developed a real niche in onshore oil and gas disasters, and this is proving a lucrative area; some cases have involved pipeline explosions and the like in South America, so trainees with languages skills have been able to use them. One trainee "*worked mainly on a really big £42m claim about a power station.*" Another found themselves "*liaising with insurers and speaking to the insured clients*" on product liability cases. These often relate to faulty products in the food, cosmetics, pharmaceutical, chemical, energy, IT and automotive sectors, and the firm is making ready for any potential wave of class actions following legislative changes. Recently the firm gave product recall advice concerning tainted whisky. In construction, another insurance-heavy seat, trainees valued "*one-on-one*" partner contact and exposure to trials and mediations.

Chambers UK rankings

Advertising & Marketing	Information Technology
Clinical Negligence	Insurance
Construction	Intellectual Property
Corporate/M&A	Media & Entertainment
Defamation/Reputation Management	Partnership
	Personal Injury
Dispute Resolution	Product Liability
Education	Professional Discipline
Employment	Professional Negligence
Family/Matrimonial	Tax

Harry Potter and Chambers' secrets

In past years the firm was responsible for assuring that stolen *Harry Potter* manuscripts were not reproduced before the book hit the shops. Publisher Bloomsbury was so impressed by the lawyer who handled these matters that it hired her as its general counsel. Key client Associated Newspapers (*Daily Mail, Mail on Sunday, Metro, Evening Standard*) has kept the firm busy with defamation and privacy cases, locking horns with a range of public figures from a queen among WAGs to the future King of England. Mirroring Bloomsbury's experience, Associated was so impressed with former team leader Liz Hartley that it gave her a permanent in-house job recently. Within the firm it's no secret that "*despite the media practice being way up there, it is not really what RPC is about,*" so applicants must be realistic about their chances of working in the team. Last year, interested parties had to provide written submissions as to why they should spend six months there. The message is clear: "*If you want straight media, go somewhere that specialises in it.*"

There are several non-contentious seat options, among them corporate, real estate and client secondments to the likes of Carillion and Sportsworld. "*I don't think I had the greatest experience in corporate due to today's market,*" said one regretful source, perhaps speaking for more of the UK's trainees than they imagined. They were nonetheless pleased with the level of client contact, and told us: "*If there is a deal on, the trainees are integral and become the main point of contact for documents.*" According to another source, the open-plan nature of the office is ideal – "*I was with two partners and a lawyer, and learned so much from them in how they spoke to clients.*" A third revealed how the firm has lately staffed the quieter corporate department more leanly, opting instead to "*put trainees where the work is.*" The real estate seat did not appear to be suffering from reduced workload: "*You're in at the deep end with about ten to 15 files to run. It's really hard!*" This seat allows people to take on real responsibility, with client contact again abundant "*from day one.*" One source concluded: "*I came out six months later much better at dealing with people than I was previously.*" Corporate and real estate clients include Bob Geldof's media company Ten Alps, HMV Group, Daily Mail Group, The Ultimate Fighting Championship and ICI. Lately there has been a substantial increase in the number of infrastructure projects coming to the real estate team, many relating to gas pipelines and the importation of liquefied natural gas.

RPC is keen to address the issue of the smallness of its slice of the transactional pie. A partner told us: "*While everyone is suing each other right now and litigation is very busy, in a buoyant economy non-contentious is very important.*" The firm has bulked up its real estate and projects team, installing a new head of department and additional partners and solicitors. It has also made strategic lateral hires from the FSA to bolster its regulatory department. Corporate stalwart Jonathan Watmough was recently made managing partner, and the firm has appointed former BDO Stoy Hayward and Deloitte marketing manager Richard Emanuel as chief operating officer. The number and types of lawyers and business professionals RPC has brought in over the past couple of years is solid proof that it "*wants to have more of a 50-50 balance in order to be safe in any economy.*"

Baa-ram-ewe

Much as Babe the talking pig recognised the nobility of the humble sheep, so too does RPC: in a quirk that is characteristic of the firm, three life-sized imitation sheep "*wander the halls.*" In the run-up to Christmas, a large model reindeer "*stalks the premises*" before returning to the North Pole. In the same vein, departments display props that illustrate the nature of their work – a toy ambulance and the classic game Operation! in the medical team; "*trendy gadgets*" in the IP team. Speaking of the firm's light-hearted side, one trainee chuckled: "*Yes, we have the impressive big glass building, but we don't take it all too seriously.*" A case in point is RPC's idiosyncratic comic strip-style recruitment brochure. "*Stylistically, we're trying to go away from a glossy, business-like feel and be more humorous and entertaining. We may be lawyers, but we've got a sense of humour too!*"

The firm appreciates good universities, but this is not a place brimming with Oxbridge grads. "*There are people from King's, Birmingham, Durham, Leeds, UEA – all quite spread out, really.*" Trainees told us: "*If you're a very academic, grades-focused person this is not necessarily the firm for you,*" and a fair few did non-law degrees or had gap years before settling into law. Something they have in common is an "*outgoing and lively*" temperament and the ability to "*strike up a conversation with anyone.*" We can vouch for the fact that RPC trainees are "*very good at expressing themselves and introducing themselves.*" One insisted: "*Enthusiasm will get you everywhere,*" and emphasised the importance of being open to trying new things and meeting new people.

A sociable, inclusive atmosphere has evolved at RPC: an accomplished choir sings at Christmas, and at summer parties the managing partner delights in fancy dress. Chatting to partners about how their football team did at the weekend is easy. There are many ways to connect socially with colleagues. There's a fine dining option in the staff restaurant and any number of chain eateries in the vicinity of the firm's St Katharine's Dock base. The trainees' favoured watering hole is Prohibition, at the foot of the office building. An excited source declared the scene "*all very Ally McBeal.*"

Trainees clearly enjoy each other's company; first-years in particular were keen to tell us that "*every day at 12.30 an e-mail goes round about what to do for lunch.*" Said one: "*It was great to come to London, knowing nobody, and have 14 ready-made friends.*" Others enthused about how "*genuine*" partners are, and with the firm making offers to 100% of NQs for the past two years it's little surprise that we encountered such a contented and cohesive bunch. This year the firm kept on 16 of 18 qualifiers. In fact, the only complaint concerned the office lifts – "*They're the worst! Every time you get in you're guaranteed an electric shock.*" We have now learned tips for avoiding a jolt should we need to scale the heights of Tower Bridge House. Simply go for an elbow on the control panel and wear rubber soles.

And finally...

One trainee's belief in the firm was unshakable: "*We'll never be magic circle and don't want to be, but we will be the best of the middle tier.*"

Shadbolt LLP

The facts

Location: London, Reigate
Number of UK partners/solicitors: 21/19
Total number of trainees: 6
Seats: 4x6 months
Alternative seats: Overseas seats, secondments
Extras: Pro bono – LawWorks, various initiatives in Tanzania

> Shadbolt will never be a one-stop shop for every type of law. *"The strategy going forward is to provide everything that a construction client might need."*

Shadbolt came into existence almost by accident but is now one of construction law's major players.

The firm that Dick built

In 1991, Dick Shadbolt, a partner in the firm that became CMS Cameron McKenna, decided he had tired of City working. He set up a little practice of his own in the Surrey countryside aiming for a quieter life. The business gained momentum, and his small, specialist construction practice grew into the Shadbolt we know today. *Chambers UK* recognises it as one of the country's premier construction outfits, and so do big names in the field, including Amey, Balfour Beatty, Costain and Galliford Try. The firm has one office in Reigate, another in London, and it works in tandem with associated firms in Romania and Tanzania.

Although construction law remains at its core, Shadbolt has diversified to the point where it has a number of other respected teams. With this in mind, we asked trainees if this should still be regarded as a niche firm. In typical lawyerly fashion, they replied: "*It depends how you define niche. The big national service we provide is in projects and construction, so in that respect, then yes we are. But if you want to do corporate, commercial or property seats then you can do them and you will still get a really good training.*" We were surprised to learn that none of our contacts had chosen Shadbolt for its construction prowess. They did however stress that, since seats in projects and dispute resolution are not only compulsory but also likely to be construction-heavy, students with zero interest in the construction industry might want to think twice about applying. Shadbolt will never be a "*one-stop shop*" for every type of law, instead "*the strategy going forward is to provide everything that a construction client might need.*"

Since the credit crunch, what many construction clients have needed is less time with lawyers. The downturn in the building sector hasn't passed unnoticed at Shadbolt, and there have been redundancies at the firm. Other than describing it as "*a sore point,*" trainees were reluctant to go into details. The firm said it was a small number but refused to clarify exactly how many were let go. Unfortunately, in 2009 none of the three qualifiers managed to secure jobs with Shadbolt. At the same time, three new starters deferred, and were given £2,000 or £4,000 to do so for either six months or a year.

Back to school

Broadly speaking, there are two parts to the dispute resolution department: the construction litigation specialists and the lawyers who concentrate on more mainstream commercial matters. Trainees sometimes referred to the two as the 'international' and 'domestic' teams respectively, so when most spoke of doing an international dispute resolution seat, we knew they meant contentious construction. In many of these cases, the emphasis is on avoiding expensive litigation by opting for arbitration. In one matter, Shadbolt represented Kier, the contractor appointed by Tube Lines to construct accommodation for train crew in Stratford, East London. The two parties disagreed over the extent of their design responsibilities and whether Kier was entitled to be compensated for £3m additional costs. The case went to an adjudicator, who found in found in Kier's favour. Many of the disputes handled at Shadbolt are huge, long-running beasts. Not all though: some are as simple as "*a house-building project where the main contractor has walked out."* The firm takes on low-value work like this for major industry players in the hope of getting repeat instructions on a larger scale. It's a perfect arrangement for trainees as smaller matters provide research assignments as well as opportunities to draft pleadings, run to court and attend mediations. Larger cases naturally require them to concentrate on more administrative tasks due to the often large volumes of evidence and technical papers.

PFI/projects is an increasingly important part of Shadbolt's non-contentious business, and it's one that has not been as badly affected as some other areas within the construction world. The government's Building Schools for the Future (BSF) investment programme has remained a major source of work for the industry and Shadbolt. For example, it advised Costain and Ferrovial Agroman on their £40m joint venture to build three new primary schools in Bradford. Trainees praised the projects seat for offering *"real hands-on responsibility"* and a great working environment. *"I was given one document in a deal and told to run with it and negotiate in a certain timeline,"* said one source. Those unfamiliar with this area of law shouldn't panic: *"It's very much based on contract and tort, but with certain nuances."* The firm runs a core skills programme to introduce trainees to the world of construction projects. Described as *"a really good beginners guide,"* the only complaint was that it came a little too late in the year to be useful to everyone.

On safari

So what of the non-construction seats? Spend time in the coco team and you'll encounter a mix of IT, IP, employment, insolvency and corporate matters, working mainly for plcs in the South East. *"The work is a little more regional, but you will get right into the thick of things."* And if you fancy *"a slightly weird taste of top-flight corporate law,"* how about a secondment to Shadbolt's associate office in Tanzania? Krista Bates-van Winkelhof, formerly of Linklaters, is one of the firm's representatives out there. *"She's Tanzania's top corporate lawyer. It doesn't sound like a tremendous accolade, but it's actually a huge deal."* Look her up on the *Chambers Global* website. Out in Dar es Salaam a trainee will work their way through company secretarial tasks and get to grips with Tanzanian bureaucracy, which is *"muddled, slow, and perhaps a little corrupt – not that I saw any of that personally."* There are several advantages to six months in this *"beautiful, politically stable country where the people are really friendly."* Said one source: *"I went on safari and popped over to Zanzibar at the weekends."* The client placement to WS Atkins might not be as exotic but we're assured it's very good.

Chambers UK rankings

Construction	Information Technology
Corporate/M&A	Intellectual Property
Dispute Resolution	Projects, Energy & Natural Resources
Employment	Real Estate

Town and country

Seat allocation is *"quite an informal process"* and *"essentially you just lobby."* Our contacts felt okay with this casual way of doing things – with one caveat. *"You will probably get the seats you want, but maybe not your choice of location."* Business needs dictate whether trainees work in London or Reigate, and most spend time in both. There's no getting away from the fact that Reigate is *"a sleepy provincial town with not very good rail links and not much going on at night."* Reflecting its provincial setting, the Reigate office is quieter than the one in the capital, which is open-plan and largely staffed by younger lawyers. The hours in both are *"fantastic,"* with anything past 6.30pm the exception rather than the rule. While the social life isn't exactly banging, a group of people go out pubbing fairly regularly. Located just a few feet from the office, Mustard is usually the bar of choice for London nights out. The firm is *"reasonably sporty,"* and when we interviewed trainees the first cricket match of the season was looming.

Shadbolt *"doesn't necessarily want someone with straight As, a first and a distinction on the LPC."* More important are commercial awareness and the ability to get on with people. *"Being a construction firm, we deal with down-to-earth clients: they aren't like corporate-minded City workers. You need to be able to take your client for a drink and get on with them, not just give advice on the phone."* If you're picturing laddy, all night booze-ups with burly builders and wondering if this is really the firm for you, be aware that Shadbolt's managing partner and chair are women, and the projects team in particular is quite female-dominated. While *"you can't be too shy and retiring,"* this is by no means a rufty-tufty boy's club.

And finally...

Arrive knowing that Shadbolt is a construction-led firm and you'll be able to enjoy training under top practitioners in the field.

Sheridans

The facts

Location: London
Number of UK partners/solicitors: 24/13
Total number of trainees: 2
Seats: 4x6 months
Alternative seats: None

> If there was a chance that Kylie Minogue or Dizzee Rascal would be popping into our offices, we'd be early for work every day.

You may not think Andrea Bocelli, The Rolling Stones and Valentino Rossi have much in common, but they all choose Sheridans to service their legal needs. This West End law firm, founded in the 1950s, is small in size but big on expertise.

The next big thing

Sheridans offers a broad range of services to clients in the creative industries. To clarify, that's litigation, employment, corporate and commercial, property and IP advice. The firm tells us that even during the recession it's been business as usual and that its clientele need it just as much now as they did before the economy lost its balance. Primarily composed of players from the worlds of music, film, TV or sport, Sheridans' clients demand one fundamental thing – that the lawyers can keep up with developments in their business sectors and advise on the next big thing. For example, broadcasters have been hit by reduced advertising revenues, so now there's more legal advice required in relation to advertiser-funded programming or 'product placement'. Consider also the speed with which technology is changing and converging across gaming, music, film, internet and mobile telecommunications. To be an expert in this sector you need much more than an ability to ace entertainment questions in your local pub quiz.

Having built strong entertainment, litigation and film groups, Sheridans has lately focused on expanding on its corporate/commercial capacity and added a sports law capability centred on new hire Morris Bentata from Bird & Bird. His experience includes commercial and regulatory matters relating to the exploitation and acquisition of sports media and marketing rights.

Feeling Dizzee

The seating plan is quite structured though its inherent flexibility should satisfy trainees who are curious about other departments. "*I wish I could stay a trainee for a couple more years so I could sample a little of everything,*" a source told us. Let's take the tour. Apologies: there's no T-shirt at the end.

As the biggest department, every trainee will spend time in the entertainment group, comprising music, theatre and sports. It is the nucleus of the firm and brings in the lion's share of client instructions, some from large organisations. We're talking about major record labels like EMI, music festival organisers like Womad International and artist management agencies like Empire. Russell Roberts heads the music group and he is partly responsible for the firm's impressive roster of 'talent' clients – Welsh warbler Katherine Jenkins, Kate Bush and rebel artist Damien Hirst among others. Managing partner Howard Jones also has impressive contacts and advises such legends as Sir Paul McCartney, Lord Lloyd-Webber, guitar hero Jimmy Page and lovable Robbie Williams. "*You run into famous celebrities like renowned cricket stars and talent show wannabes,*" said one source about the benefits of being in a media firm. Frankly, if there was any chance of people like Kylie or Dizzee Rascal popping in to our offices we'd be early for work every day. Do any mere mortals use the firm, we wondered? Apparently the corporate and property teams do indeed represent a limited number of clients who have no connection to the creative industries. These two teams also take trainees.

The entertainment department provides trainees with "*an incredibly interesting seat*" and one told us they'd been able to stay there for "*ten months in total,*" which is just one advantage of choosing a firm as small as this. The seat provides plenty of commercial experience and newbies quickly get to the point where they are drafting contracts for an up-and-coming songstress or protecting the copyright of an industry heavy hitter. Although trainees don't run their own files, they are in constant contact with clients and shoulder a good deal of responsibility.

Ready for your close-up?

The smaller film and television department has accrued new clients like HBO, American Movie Classics and the super-indie DCD Media. It already counts the BBC, Channel 4 and National Geographic as clients, so you can see how established it is. The department advises on matters relating to production finance as well as distribution and broadcasting. It also has a steady flow of international work, much coming from the USA and the Middle East. It recently advised the Abu Dhabi government media investment organisation twofour54. One trainee had a hands-on role on the oversight of a film production that involved "*insurance, actors and a whole lot of fun.*" When prodded for further details our source told us nothing more than the fact that the actors were Swedish and some of the work did involve a content-check of the movie to look for IP infringements. We can divulge the names of some of the films on which Sheridans lawyers have advised – the Oscar and Bafta-winning documentary *Man on Wire* about Philippe Petit, *Mamma Mia!* and new occult movie *Chemical Wedding*, produced and directed by Iron Maiden front man Bruce Dickinson. For more Bruce trivia see our feature on Jones Day.

Trainees can also spend time in the expanding and tech-savvy computer software and games department, where trade mark registrations, loan agreements and sports games are all in a day's work. And finally, they can also sample litigation and employment seats, both of which take them to courts and tribunals. Best of all, perhaps, are solo applications before High Court masters. There's a massive amount of client exposure in contentious work and this was a real bonus for one source. "*I can't say I would be doing more than pushing paper in the bigger firms.*"

Lex factor

If this feature inspires you to apply to Sheridans then be aware that you must compete with many others for the one training place offered annually. The successful candidate will need to enjoy all the attention they'll get, but it's good to know that "*everyone listens to what you have to say, it's the benefit of being at a small firm.*" One disadvantage is that there won't always be a job available on qualification. Unfortunately this was the case in 2009.

So what's in store if your application results in an interview with Sheridans? You'll face a three-member panel of partners and there will be written exercises. A past winner in this game told us the process is not as intimidating as it sounds because "*the partners are all amiable*" and the written exercises are simply aimed at testing a basic knowledge of contract law. If you do get to this stage, be sure to check out your surroundings: the office is decorated with vintage music posters and other 'meeja'-inspired artwork. You should also check out the firm's website for more clues as to Sheridans' ideal recruit. Essentially you need to have a demonstrable interest in IP or media law and you should know that the firm prefers law graduates (though exceptional candidates from other disciplines won't be ruled out).

Once in the club, people generally find Sheridans to be a relaxed and genial kind of place. Late hours are rare and often arise for something engaging like a content check on a new movie (popcorn provided, we hope). Socially, "*everyone here knows each other and is very like-minded and accommodating.*" The social life engages the firm as a whole rather than just the junior fee earners. "*The usual suspects go for a beer on Friday, and they have their pick of the pubs in the West End.*" Major organised events have included a Christmas party in an art gallery near Buckingham Palace and a summer party at the Casino at The Empire. When we rang the firm it was hoping to help raise more than £100,000 in an annual charity football match for Nordoff-Robbins Music Therapy. The six-a-side competition was set to involve 16 music industry teams.

Chambers UK rankings

Media & Entertainment

And finally...

Though narrow in its client focus there's no reason to worry about being short-changed on your legal apprenticeship. Keep an autograph book for the more eventful days!

- **Average trainee starting salary: £23,865*** You're best off if you're a male trainee starting in central London, as the average for them was £33,146 in 2008. It's less lovely news for lasses in the land of leeks: females at Welsh firms pull in an average of £17,017 during their first year.

* The Law Society's Annual Statistical Report 2008

top tip no. 23

Shoosmiths

The facts

Location: Birmingham, Basingstoke, Northampton, Milton Keynes, Nottingham, Reading, Fareham, London, Manchester
Number of UK partners/solicitors: 115/265
Total number of trainees: 29
Seats: 4x6 months
Alternative seats: Secondments

Shoosmiths' network is spread like a spider's web across the country. While some of its lawyers are pushing for bigger business, others are happy to handle the little problems in life.

Originally established in Northampton in 1845 by William Shoosmith, this firm is now a national player with a commercial division and a volume business handling residential conveyancing and PI.

Shooting upwards

'Old-fashioned manners, telling it straight and absolutely no stuffiness. Welcome to Shoosmiths.' That's the tagline on the firm's website: clearly, it's an organisation very sure of its own identity. Despite still holding on to high-volume business (comprising PI, residential conveyancing and lender services), Shoosmiths describes itself as 'unashamedly commercial'. Reflecting this, it has been steadily climbing up the table of the UK's largest firms, increasing turnover, moving into new premises and expanding its range of services. It now has nine offices across the country, has picked up a nice long list of *Chambers UK* rankings in a diverse range of practice areas, and caters for what one trainee described as "*very reputable clients – really good in fact. Some clients are beyond my original expectations.*" They include names like Volkswagen, Thomas Cook, the NEC, Santander and HSBC. Commenting on the firm's future, its new CEO Claire Rowe has said that she intends to ringfence consumer litigation, PI, clin neg, private client and the property conveyancing parts of the business to establish a clear demarcation between the volume and commercial parts of the firm.

Rounding off this synopsis are some cold, hard stats. In 2009, revenue dropped to £99m, down just 4% on the previous year, while profits per equity partner were down 54%, a pretty substantial profit collapse by anyone's standards. Chairman of the firm Andrew Tubbs has suggested that the opening of a new Manchester office and the firm's recent redundancy programme were contributing factors. In early 2009, 25 lawyers and 44 support staff were let go. Only time will tell whether that dip in profitability is purely a consequence of the global economic crisis or whether it points to a deeper malaise within the firm. For the record, our money is on the former.

Encouragingly, one thing that Shoosmiths has proved good at is knowing when to jump on and off a bandwagon. Ex-CEO Paul Stothard's comment about bulk work ("*If the legal element of that work is squeezed then we'll walk away*") is illustrative of the firm's ethos of flexibility. As the recession kicked in, it saw opportunity in crisis: even as it was forced to make redundancies (mainly in the Property Direct conveyancing team), it opened in Manchester, paving the way for future growth with lender services and dispute resolution teams. Theoretically, it could be possible for trainees to do seats there from next year.

The offices in Basingstoke, Northampton and Solent (in Fareham near Southampton) are situated on business parks, while branches in Reading, Birmingham, Milton Keynes, Nottingham, London and Manchester are in the centre of town. At the time of our calls, the firm's 31 trainees were split very evenly between six of these offices. Whether for business needs or to get a specific seat, trainees may have to make the occasional move between offices. Those in Nottingham must go elsewhere for commercial litigation, for example. The Northampton and MK offices meanwhile are treated as one for the purposes of training.

Waine's world

"*Nice guy*" Waine Mannix is the eponymous head of Waine's World – Northampton's booming finance litigation and recovery (aka lender services) department. The recession means that there are loads of people unable to keep up with their repayments and so Waine's World, which is involved with reclaiming debt and managing consumer finance, is flat out. The newly opened Manchester office's sole purpose is lender services, and one trainee commented that the firm was probably expanding this area to offset the slowdown in others. Emperor Mannix has proudly announced: "*Our lender services team continues to go from strength to strength and is well on the way to achieving year-on-year growth of 25%.*" In this department the role of a trainee covers "*everything from professional negligence claims to repossessions. You get to go to court a lot, acting on behalf of the banks and putting forward their case.*" Other seats in Northampton include private client; health and safety; PI; insurance litigation and asset finance.

Despite being 20 miles apart, "*Milton Keynes and Northampton are almost classed as one office*" and trainees will often commute between the two. The atmosphere in MK is considered to be slightly more staid than Northampton due to the partners being slightly older and the fact that "*most people drive to Milton Keynes because they don't want to live there.*" It's one of two offices that offers an IP seat, which trainees enjoy for its "*hands-on experience and client contact.*" Chasing down counterfeit goods is a big part of the job. "*A member of public might write into our client alerting them to a crappy item. Then we go after the counterfeiters, following the trail through wholesalers and corresponding with quite a lot of parties.*" Fittingly for a firm with this name, "*we act for a lot of shoe companies.*" MK also has commercial property, properly litigation, commercial litigation, corporate, commercial, pensions and employment teams.

Touring the regions

When Shoosmiths opened in Birmingham in 2003, it put all its efforts into one practice area and then expanded. Starting off with just property, trainees can now do construction, planning, corporate, commercial, commercial litigation ("*there was a lot of small claims work that I could do myself*"), property litigation, lender services, PI and employment. Phew! It's also built a banking finance team around hires from Midlands competitors and nabbed a top-notch social housing team from Cobbetts. Another big piece of Brum news is that the National Exhibition Centre ditched Pinsent Masons to be advised by Shoosmiths instead. Quite a coup for a firm that is keen to promote its name in the city. The Nottingham staff occupy flash new digs on Waterfront Plaza, and this branch has coco, employment, property litigation and commercial property seats on offer for trainees. This latter team is arguably its strongest, and its clients include Alliance Boots, Gala Coral, Nottingham City Council, WHSmith, IKEA, Games Workshop, Nottingham City Transport, British Waterways, HMV and Thomas Cook.

Chambers UK rankings

Banking & Finance	Licensing
Banking Litigation	Pensions
Clinical Negligence	Personal Injury
Consumer Finance	Planning
Corporate/M&A	Product Liability
Debt Recovery	Public Procurement
Dispute Resolution	Real Estate
Employment	Real Estate Litigation
Health & Safety	Restructuring/Insolvency
Information Technology	Retail
Intellectual Property	Social Housing

The Solent office is based in Fareham and is still expanding. It has seats in corporate, commercial property, commercial litigation, commercial and employment. The pick of the departments on the South Coast is corporate. Among its recent deals, the group advised aerospace company Cobham on its £13.6m acquisition of MMI Research and acted for RBS on a £30m buyout of Rathbone Trust International led by Dunedin Capital Partners.

Two Thames Valley offices, in Reading and Basingstoke, complete the picture. In Reading, employment is a popular seat, despite being quite technically demanding. Property litigation is also "*so complex. You're really arguing about legal points.*" Thames Water is a huge client, "*and we have some really big ones from the world of retail too. It's quite exciting and the clients are quite demanding.*" Reading is the other office with an IP seat. Shoosmiths doesn't actively recruit trainees into Basingstoke. If a paralegal based here manages to progress to a training contract, they will do employment and PI seats, but will need to also work in Reading.

Walk a mile in their Shoos

Okay, let's address the elephant in the room. Even the most rudimentary of internet searches will turn up stuff about Shoosmiths' refusal to pay incoming 2009 trainees to defer their contracts for a year. The legal press and message board posters laced up their hobnails and gave the firm a right old kicking over this issue, decrying Shoosmiths' management as miserly and constructing a story that linked this decision and the ensuing brouhaha to Paul Stothard's subsequent resignation from the role of CEO. Insinuations were made about how attractive or otherwise Shoosmiths would be to future applicants. When a couple of the deferees stuck up for the firm, things intensified, with critics rather harshly panning their response as a nefarious marketing ploy to cover up the firm's (supposedly) grievous error. Having talked to Shoosmiths about the subject we'd say such criticisms aren't entirely fair. The firm was put in a position where it had to cut costs and make people redundant. In that situation, it would have sent out a confused message to give money to future joiners who hadn't yet started working at the firm, while simultaneously laying off staff of long standing. In the words of a partner: *"Any amount would have been the wrong amount."* Ultimately, eight new starters deferred, two voluntarily and six compulsorily.

When we asked the trainees about the matter, it's fair to say that some unequivocally took Shoosmiths' side. Others didn't feel that it had dealt with the *"sticky situation"* particularly well, saying that *"the firm's argument isn't enough."* Pressing them further on the issue, these latter sources considered the whole issue symptomatic of a lack of communication within the firm that in their minds extended to seat allocation and NQ job offers. Some were left *"disillusioned and unsure about the future."* One trainee believed that poor communication has soured relationships to the extent that *"even if the people offered jobs stay, they will have been annoyed enough not to stay long."* Clarifying the general position, another said: *"Most people are quite happy, and I feel that I have got good training. The office environment is good but recent HR issues have been bad."* In all, nine of the 15 qualifiers of 2009 stayed with the firm.

Not Shoopid

Despite uncertainty over jobs and the recent bad press, *"things remain quite pleasant"* at Shoosmiths. And why shouldn't they? Trainees are adamant that the old chestnut of *"a great work-life balance"* actually applies (they finish at 5.30pm) and that *"people are really nice."* They talked at length about getting great exposure and responsibility, telling us: *"They find out what you're capable of and give you suitable work. I've never felt out of my depth but never been treated like I'm stupid."* Shoosmiths also deserves a slap on the back and a hearty cheer for setting an example to other firms in how to achieve a good gender balance. Across all of its offices, just over 50% of trainees and 30% of the partnership is female – that second figure is very good indeed compared with UK law firms in general. The firm's new CEO Claire Rowe is, as the name suggests, also a woman. She came to the firm as a trainee and worked her way up. Pretty inspirational, no?

Broadly speaking, most of the current trainees came to Shoosmiths for the nice environment and reasonable hours. They weren't ambitious ladder climbers (*"I wouldn't describe anyone as ruthless or hardnosed"*) and although tempted by a broad selection of seats that includes rarer practice areas like procurement and competition, they weren't lured to the firm by its expertise in any specific area. We'd recommend that applicants research thoroughly what different practice groups are available in their preferred geographical location, because a few of our sources felt that the offices are *"definitely quite separate."* While some trainees stressed that it was easy to pick up the phone to colleagues elsewhere in the country, some insisted that branches *"operate as distinct entities in terms of how they contact each other and in terms of socialising, and you seldom get a situation where they transfer clients between offices."* This next point is not something we've heard much about from Shoopeople in past years, but perhaps it's the reality of a harsher economy. In the words of one source: *"It's all motivated by money and targets, meaning people are reluctant to move work between offices. I'm not sure that it benefits the firm to have the offices in competition with each other."*

And so we come to the social side of the firm. A trainee who had visited the business park offices summarised the situation like this: *"You consider Solent, Basingstoke, Northampton... as far as I can see, the social life is non-existent."* It's true that an out-of-town location and the prospect of a long commute home is not conducive to a fun-filled Friday night, and we got the impression that the Birmingham and Nottingham offices have the most youthful atmosphere and the best social life. Shoosmiths has sports teams for football, cricket and netball, and after gathering up feedback on social activities we can tell you that these have included events like a wine tasting, cinema, theatre trips and Christmas parties. There are also *"random things like a cakeola"* – that's a tombola with cakes – *"and in MK there was a Battle of the Businesses dragon boat race."* The firm also encourages trainees to get involved with trainee solicitor societies and subsidises the cost of buying tickets to balls. Trainees in Birmingham, Reading and MK can get involved with the New Fridays initiative, a young professionals networking scheme started at Shoosmiths. At one of the last Christmas parties there was a talent competition. *"It was won by one of the partners in property litigation. He was Neil Diamond and he was very good. The outfit helped because it was proper stagey and sparkly."*

And finally...

Some communication issues aside, trainees like Shoosmiths for its good work and relaxed nature.

Sidley Austin LLP

The facts

Locations: London
Number of UK partners/solicitors: 37/60
Total number of trainees: 17
Seats: 4x6 months
Alternative seats: Brussels
Extras: Pro bono – LawWorks

As focus shifts from securitisation, expect a *"redefined, re-profiled"* office. On the agenda: legacy and debt finance, restructuring, regulatory advice and derivatives.

The tenth largest firm in the world by revenue, Sidley is on the frontline when it comes to credit crunch fallout work, and we don't see it running up the white flag any time soon.

Long live securitisation

Sidley Austin has moved far beyond its Chicago roots. It now has 16 offices worldwide and over 1,800 lawyers. The London office has been around since 1974 and is at the forefront of specialised finance work, the mainstay of which has been securitisation, that ever so thorny area of finance that is so closely associated with the credit crunch. Trainees say that the downturn has led to a shake-up at the firm and *"that regular source of income has been taken away."* They admit: *"If we were to say all we do is securitisation we'd have no work."* Consequently Sidley has needed to diversify its London practice and our sources were well versed as to exactly how. *"We're expanding litigation, corporate, IP, insurance, tax;" "we've added a funds practice, regulatory's grown and capital markets and corporate are billing crazy hours."* They were keen to discourage people from *"misconceiving Sidley as just a finance boutique."*

However, as one pragmatic source told us: *"Securitisation isn't dead: it will return in a much simpler form and we'll have the capability to deal with that."* And we don't doubt that Sidley's roster of impressive finance clients – the key ones being AIG, Citi, JPMorgan, Deutsche Bank, Lloyds TSB and UBS – will continue to use the firm where required. As focus shifts away from securitisation, Sidley's finance gurus see four main 'pillars' of activity emerging to create a *"redefined, re-profiled"* Sidley London. On the agenda: legacy and debt finance, restructuring, regulatory advice and derivatives. As for questions of culpability in the face of economic meltdown, trainees were adamant: *"It's so easy to push blame around. At the time these securitisation transactions won awards for being innovative, and now everyone's saying, 'You caused this.' I don't think you can blame law firms, especially not an individual law firm. The government should have been able to foresee this. If anyone's to blame, it's Gordon Brown."*

BFGs in IFG

The international finance group (IFG) makes up almost half of the London office and incorporates structured finance, derivatives, regulatory and real estate seats. As the area hardest hit, there are presently fewer seats in structured finance. More of the moment is the restructuring of flawed loans, and the chance to see firsthand the practical implications of the credit crunch. *"We were taught to see the perspective from the other side, and you really do feel sorry for the high-street mortgagees in trouble,"* said one source, conceding: *"It's a bit sad to be involved in that kind of work."* Though we heard about *"no radical plans to reduce IFG to a quarter,"* trainees knew that *"we do have to focus on getting different types of work."* As compliance issues come to the fore in the financial sector, regulatory advice is a significant growth area for IFG and an *"exciting challenge"* for trainees. They need to keep abreast of the changes that materialise *"every single week,"* and believe that this will become one of the core IFG seats from now on, certain others already having become less likely destinations on the training contract route.

Don't go thinking of IFG as a wasteland, though. One trainee told us: "*When I was there I had by far my longest hours, even though it was comparatively quiet. People who were in it before me just never left the office. Ever.*" We're talking "*an average leaving time of 10.30pm,*" and, on occasion, "*staying for 36 hours at a time.*" Not a seat for the faint-hearted, then! Still, the firm isn't beastly about it. "*They're not monsters at all, it's just the nature of the work and clients who want their work product yesterday.*"

No sprouts beyond Brussels

Other seats are available in 'corporate and securities' (which incorporates employment, hedge funds and competition); insolvency; insurance and financial services; IP; capital markets; and tax. The corporate department has handled some major deals: acting for Discover Financial Services (owner of the Goldfish card) in the sale of its UK business to Barclays (worth £2bn) and acting for GE Capital Bank on its disposal of a corporate payment card business to American Express. "*Strong relationships with global financial institutions*" are key in the corporate department, as is the firm's global reach, which is crucial for attracting the biggest and best clients. At present there is a competition seat available in Brussels, though the firm told us this "*fulfilled a particular need*" and that "*it is not an objective of ours to have trainees sit in international offices.*"

Tax is only available as a split seat, even though trainees "*really wish it was six months.*" They find themselves wrestling with endless cross-border tax issues, hardly surprising considering the international nature of Sidley's work. As one source put it: "*Basically, my brain hurt.*" A seat in the small IP department ("*essentially a one-man band*") is influenced by Sidley's US strength in life sciences. GlaxoSmithKline and other pharma companies make up the core of the client base. For the contentious-minded, a finance-heavy litigation seat is available in a team that was strengthened "*in preparation for the credit crunch*" with the hire of barrister and solicitor advocate Dorothy Cory-Wright. Die-hard transactionalists can opt out of a litigation seat and sacrifice a few Saturdays for a Kaplan Law School litigation course. Summing up the available experiences, trainees told us: "*You get work that is easily of the same quality as the magic circle, with the same clients. At the same time, you're one of eight or ten trainees* [per intake] *and if you work hard and do a good job, it gets recognised.*"

Chambers UK rankings

Capital Markets	Real Estate Finance
Financial Services Regulation	Restructuring/Insolvency
Investment Funds	Tax

A lot at steak

What makes a Sidley lawyer? We found a mix of the ultra-keen ("*one first-year was just so happy to get a BlackBerry, saying, 'Now I'm like a legal doctor, on call 24/7!'*") and the more sedate ("*If I decide I don't want to lose my life to a law firm, I still trained at a really prestigious firm and can go anywhere with it*"). Dedication is a prerequisite for recruits, so you'll hopefully agree with the idea that "*having to sacrifice your social life in favour of work pays off in the end when you get a good outcome for your clients.*" Sidley specialises in "*high-pressure work,*" and it is looking for "*people who can deal with that.*" Often the firm takes older people with master's degrees or other careers behind them, and the current set of trainees is "*hugely diverse,*" with Chinese, Russians and Americans among them. The spirit of redefinition seems to have filtered down to trainees, who said: "*We are trying to educate ourselves on how to bring in business, as we can't sit around hoping clients will come... which they have done in the past.*" In 2009, some seven of the ten qualifiers took jobs with the firm, with only three going into IFG. Four of the 2009 intake of trainees deferred their start dates for a payment of £7,000, and earlier in the year the firm had to make around 30 lawyers and support staff redundant.

It's not all work and no play; the Christmas party at Claridge's is a lavish affair and for a regular week's end drink there's always the new Davy's Wine Bar near the firm's Woolgate Exchange office. Foodies are going to love Sidley's in-house chefs – "*If the French guy does steak, you're gonna stay* [late]*!*" one trainee joked.

And finally...

The firm that brought Barack and Michelle together remains a finance heavyweight, though it has shown the wherewithal to adapt where necessary.

- **Think ahead:** You can read a legal or business article the day before you go for interview and think you've got a feel for the topic, but it's probably just the latest update in an ongoing story. If you have been reading the same publication for two or three months beforehand, you will be much more sound on the way stories have developed.

top tip no. 24

Simmons & Simmons

The facts

Location: London
Number of UK partners/solicitors: 117/223
Total number of trainees: 70
Seats: 4x6 months
Alternative seats: Overseas seats, secondments
Extras: Pro bono – Battersea Legal Advice Centre, Oxfam; language training

> Simmons is a finance-based practice and you must have a genuine interest in this type of business if you're to come here.

Founded in 1896 by twin brothers Percy and Edward Simmons, this firm's history is characterised by international expansion and a quest to find its true calling.

Regroup and consolidate

Now a full-service global business, Simmons employs over 2,000 people in some 20 offices across the financial centres of Europe, the Middle East and Asia. In its current incarnation, it is best known as a leading finance-focused City firm and a pioneer in the highly technical fields of structured finance and investment management. As the financial markets deteriorated the firm was hit hard and redundancies inevitably followed, particularly in the suddenly very quiet capital markets group. The uncertain times led Simmons to embark on a phase of consolidation and last year saw it reduce its global network by pulling out of certain jurisdictions and downsizing in others. It opted to demerge from its Portuguese arm and reshaped its Russian and Chinese offices by sending senior partners back to London and shedding a number of associates. For now, the focus remains on four core client sectors – financial institutions, energy and infrastructure, life sciences and technology – and the firm is keen to pitch a more diverse skill set to this clientele.

Growing the corporate practice has been high on the firm's agenda in recent years and, while it is not yet on a par with the finance practice, the corporate team has taken lead roles in several well-publicised M&A deals and AIM floats. Recent successes include advising Lebedev Holdings on its acquisition of a majority shareholding in the *Evening Standard* newspaper from the *Daily Mail*. Simmons also advised HMV Group on a joint venture with MAMA Group, the UK's second largest multiple live music venue operator, and on the associated fund-raising.

Then there is the litigation department, which regularly advises on large-scale cross-border commercial and financial disputes. The IP litigation team, considered to be one of the best in the City, acted on behalf of Virgin Media in its dispute with Gemstar-TV Guide International concerning three patents relating to the use of on-screen TV guides for selecting channels and recording programmes. Other specialist practices deserve a mention, particularly the information, communications and technology (ICT) group and the financial services regulatory and life sciences teams, each of which is ranked highly by *Chambers UK*.

Make no mistake: finance remains the big earner here and there is still ample activity in this division. The compact banking group is currently engaged in a number of restructurings and advisory matters, and the award-winning funds practice continues to attract plenty of instructions, particularly from the hedge funds industry. When we spoke with Simmons' managing partner Mark Dawson he emphasised this aspect of the firm's business. *"We advise some of the key players, who have emerged stronger, and we have plenty of confidence in growth going forward. What puts us in an interesting position is our relationships with a large number of hedge funds and investment banks, so we advise on both sides of the equation."*

How many divisions?

Diversity of practice means that trainees can experience a wide variety of work. Seats must be taken in the finance, corporate/projects and litigation departments, where there is always plenty of room for trainees. Overall, seat allocation is a straightforward process. *"Because three out of four seats are compulsory, the choice is largely out of our hands... and more often than not people get their first choice for the fourth seat."* That seat can be spent on a client or international secondment, or in one of the firm's smaller departments.

A seat in the financial services division can involve working in any one of the banking, asset finance, capital markets or funds sub-teams. Unsurprisingly, the funds group is hugely popular. It is home to the City's leading hedge fund practitioners, and besides that *"it's well known that you get loads more responsibilities in this team."* The deals are big and, consequently, trainees cannot be given free rein, but they'll normally have *"a first stab at drafting parts of a prospectus, which is the fun part of the job."* While the volume of transactional work and new fund launches has dropped off, the *"restructuring and regulatory sides of the practice are booming."* The capital markets seat usually offers trainees the opportunity to work on the complex structured products at which the firm has excelled, such as CDOs, CPPIs and swaps. Due to the decline in transactions of this type, our sources revealed that the group has quietened significantly, but they insist it should not be written off just yet. *"There is still a healthy level of activity and the conventional deal flow has been replaced by other streams of work, including restructurings and risk management advice."*

Depending on the timing of their stint in the corporate department, certain trainees experienced a very busy six months, while those who arrived after the crash naturally found it slow-moving. Still, several got the chance to assist on an M&A deal or an AIM float, but found that *"the transactions are usually too big for trainees to have a meaningful role and client contact often seems like a long way away."* Trainees readily concede that they're expected to do *"a lot of mundane jobs like bundling and bibling."* A common gripe among our interviewees was the lack of secretarial and paralegal support, which inevitably means that some of the menial jobs will fall to them.

In years gone by, those who came here to do finance above all did not eagerly anticipate their litigation seat. Things are changing, and many of our interviewees now considered this to be their best seat. The vast array of work on offer includes commercial and financial litigation (including white-collar crime) plus arbitration. Additionally there are specialist teams working in employment, professional negligence and IP. The seat naturally involves a lot of research and document management, but several lucky trainees got the chance to attend High Court, Court of Appeal and even House of Lords hearings. The return to popularity of the litigation, employment and IP seats (after a few years of finance mania) is symptomatic of the fact that, with fewer NQ positions available in the firm's mainstream practice areas, trainees are transferring their hopes for qualification onto these busier countercyclical departments.

ICT team members *"are keen to get trainees involved in the deals; they trust you to take ownership of your work and get on with things."* Trainees here also get plenty of direct contact with the clients. These include Virgin Media, which Simmons advised on the £100m outsourcing of the operations and maintenance of its voice network to BT. The group also represents Transport for London in relation to its use of congestion charging technology. Over in the real estate department trainees can experience a higher level of responsibility. *"It can be daunting as a first seat because you need to be hands-on from day one and end up running several of your own matters,"* sources explained. This will typically involve negotiating sale, licence and lease agreements or assisting on much larger projects such as Network Rail's proposed £1bn redevelopment of the 14-acre Euston Station site in North London.

Secondment front

The list of potential locations for a six-month spell abroad includes Tokyo, Hong Kong, Amsterdam, Paris, Milan, Dubai, Abu Dhabi, Moscow and Lisbon, while UK-based client secondments are readily available, usually to investment banks such as JPMorgan,

Chambers UK rankings

Administrative & Public Law	Information Technology
Asset Finance	Insurance
Banking & Finance	Intellectual Property
Banking Litigation	Investment Funds
Capital Markets	Life Sciences
Commodities	Outsourcing
Competition/European Law	Pensions
Construction	Product Liability
Corporate/M&A	Professional Negligence
Data Protection	Projects, Energy & Natural Resources
Dispute Resolution	Real Estate
Employee Share Schemes	Real Estate Finance
Employment	Real Estate Litigation
Environment	Restructuring/Insolvency
Financial Services Regulation	Retail
	Tax
	Telecommunications
Fraud: Civil	Transport

Deutsche Bank or Credit Suisse. But beware, the "*international placement opportunities are not all they're touted to be,*" said disappointed trainees. Perhaps as a result of the firm's international retrenchment, "*the European secondments have massively subsided*" and there is "*even stiffer competition*" for the much-coveted Hong Kong seat. That is not to say that the firm is putting an end to its international secondment programme. The Middle Eastern offices are going great guns and there is a sense among trainees that Simmons is making a big play in this region. "*A secondment in Dubai or Abu Dhabi is relatively easy to get and hugely enjoyable,*" we're told.

A number of our interviewees found the appraisal system a little too subjective: informal mid-seat feedback is normally followed by a formal assessment at the end of the six months, but this is not always the case. "*The amount of feedback you get largely depends on your supervisor – some are more forthcoming than others.*" Where ongoing professional education is concerned, however, trainees have no complaints as seat-specific and firm-wide training sessions are of an exceptional standard. "*I really can't fault the quality of my training contract,*" said one.

When they are not hard at work, trainees can take a minute to appreciate their surroundings. Simmons is based in the ultra-modern CityPoint building near Moorgate. "*The offices are fantastic – they're spacious with plenty of natural light,*" and lovers of fine art will not fail to be impressed by Simmons' collection, which is an "*eclectic mix*" of drawings, paintings, sculptures and photographs by young artists and well-known names including Tracey Emin, David Hockney and Damien Hirst. The subsidised canteen received mixed reviews. "*It can be a bit hit and miss in the evenings,*" but the surrounding area has plenty of restaurants and bars. At first the whole intake flocks to the nearby Corney & Barrow wine bar for a post-work drink, interviewees tell us, but as time goes on, they tend to venture beyond Moorgate to enjoy the more exciting nightlife around Old Street. Although Simmons puts on a big summer party for its staff every other year, social activities tend to be intra-departmental rather than firm-wide. Team jollies range from tea and cakes on Fridays to various sporting events, including much-anticipated ski-trips.

Be prepared and stay calm

For quite a few years now the firm has channelled most qualifying trainees towards its corporate and finance departments. Due to the impact of the credit crisis on those departments' needs, fewer qualification jobs were offered in 2009 and out of 49 people, just 30 found positions, again most going into corporate and finance teams. To alleviate the oversupply of trainees Simmons deferred much of its 2009 intake for 12 months. These individuals were offered the chance to enrol on an MBA programme specifically designed by the firm in conjunction with BPP Law School; 28 people took up the offer and were provided with a £15,000 grant to cover their expenses. In our interviews trainees said that management had tried its best to take both a long-term view and to come up with ways in which trainees and qualifiers could be helped. Nonetheless, frustration was clearly running high after the announcement of qualification prospects had to be delayed for many weeks. In fairness Simmons was not alone in delaying decisions.

Simmons' training contract recruitment process is no easy ride. In addition to showing excellent academic credentials, applicants need to jump through several tricky hoops before meeting the partners for a formal interview. One such hoop is an infamous 'document test'. A tip from those who've made it is "*not to be overwhelmed by the size of the document – 30 pages of fine-print financial jargon – skim through it and be ready to answer questions about the way it's structured.*"

Despite the catastrophic turn of events in the world of global finance, Simmons remains a finance-heavy firm and it should come as no surprise that you must have a genuine interest in this world if you're to come here. "*You can get through the training contract without being a complete finance buff, but it would be a risk to come hoping to qualify into, say, the employment or IP department.*" Current trainees are convinced that, given the quality of the firm's client list (which includes "*most of the major investment banks*") and the quality of its lawyers, Simmons will come out on top when things return to normal.

And finally...

Simmons & Simmons has a reputation as a friendly City firm. While trainees tell us this is deserved, they also warn that "*this should not misguide you – you're here to work really hard.*"

Visionary

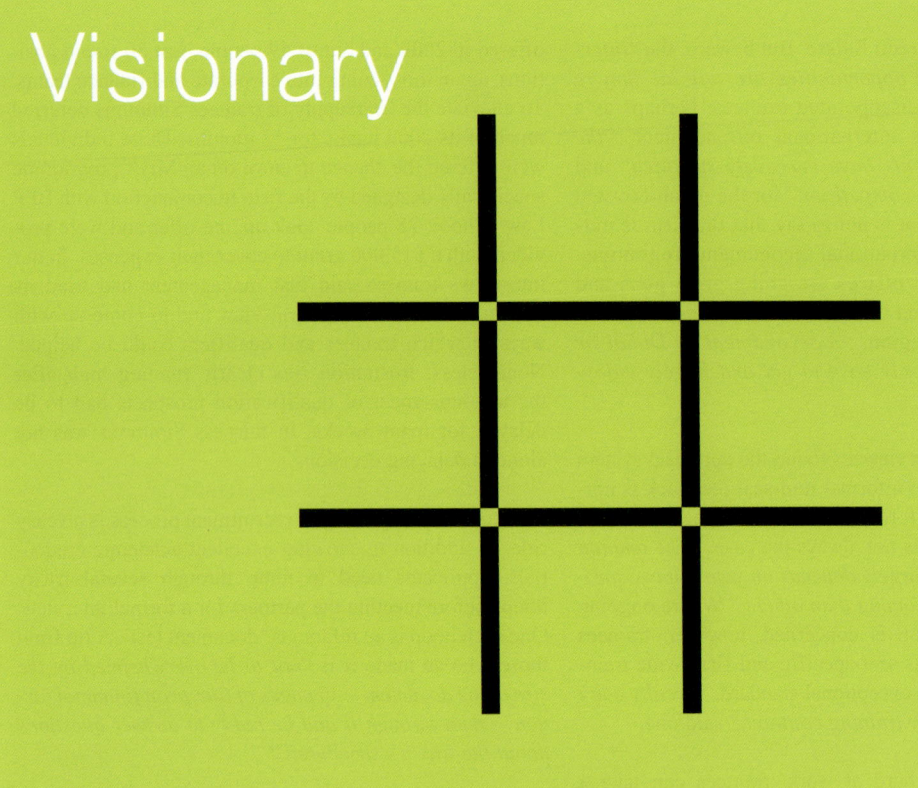

Move only three blocks to get three perfect squares

Interested in a career in law?

For open days, Easter/summer vacation schemes and training contracts please apply on-line at
www.sjberwin.com

For enquiries contact:
E graduate.recruitment@sjberwin.com
T Graduate Recruitment Helpdesk 020 7111 2268

www.sjberwin.com

sj berwin

Berlin   Brussels   Dubai   Frankfurt   Hong Kong   London   Madrid   Milan   Munich   Paris   Turin

SJ Berwin LLP is a limited liability partnership registered in England no OC313176. 18290/P07

SJ Berwin LLP

The facts

Location: London
Number of UK partners/solicitors: 101/236
Total number of trainees: 83
Seats: 4x6 months
Alternative seats: Overseas seats, secondments
Extras: Pro bono – Toynbee Hall Law Centre; language training

This client-focused, high-energy City firm is perennially popular with students looking for quality City work, particularly in relation to corporate deals.

Established in 1982, corporate-focused SJ Berwin is now firmly ensconced in London's silver circle.

I ❤ my client

To understand what makes SJ Berwin tick, you need to understand the man who started it all. Here's his potted history. Stanley Berwin, a charismatic City lawyer, was the founding partner of Berwin & Co (now Berwin Leighton Paisner). He left to go in-house with Rothschild, but when he returned four years later expecting to reclaim his position as senior partner, the firm said thanks but no thanks. Unperturbed, Stanley founded SJ Berwin. It was a no-nonsense, fast-paced, full-bore, work-you-hard-and-pay-you-well kind of place – definitely a child of the Thatcher years. In a short space of time this young upstart forced its way into the UK's top 25 firms.

Stanley died in 1988 so why devote a paragraph to the man? Quite simply, it's because his influence is still felt 21 years on. The restaurant in the firm's stunning riverside offices is named after him, and we're told that a sentimental 'what Stanley would have wanted' speech is a feature at Christmas. You see Stanley's time working for Rothschild had given him an insight into what clients wanted from their lawyers, and this client focus is the driving force behind the firm to this day. Current trainees may only "*hear his name mentioned from time to time,*" but when they come out with quotes like: "*I think the clients like that we identify their commercial interests and focus on those rather than chewing over the niggling details of a tiny clause,*" they might be channelling the spirit of the man himself. All law firms want to provide good client service, of course, but at SJB it's practically a fetish.

To say that this full-service firm is rather stronger on the transactional side than in litigation is accurate in terms of numbers of lawyers involved, though not necessarily calibre of work product. One of the first firms in the City to embrace private equity and fund formation work, it now faces stiff competition from Clifford Chance and Kirkland & Ellis (which stole some of SJB's top partners a while back), but *Chambers UK* still ranks it as one of the leaders in this field. Real estate remains a core area of practice, as do banking/finance and standard corporate M&A. SJB isn't afraid to try out new areas or cut old ones as necessary, as evidenced by the departure of a *Chambers* top-ranked film finance team in early 2009, deemed a non-core asset by management.

Alphabetti private equity

At least two out of a trainee's four seats must be spent in the firm's corporate group. It's divided into four teams, imaginatively named A, B, C and D. The A team is the "*deal seat*" – M&A and flotations. It's recently acted for Qantas during merger discussions with British Airways and advised a bidder on a potential acquisition of Northern Rock. "*Trainees are responsible for the project management side of things*" so expect to be liaising frequently with other departments in the firm and dealing with ancillary documents.

Team B is where the main private equity buyouts take place. It's "*hard work but an increasingly popular seat*" for a combination of reasons. One: "*We have great clients and our reputation is second to none.*" Two: "*It's pretty high-level work with superb training at regular Friday meetings.*" Three: "*Private equity is a relatively new thing so it's like* you're involved in creating the law and trying new things out." There's also a simple fourth reason – the team has remained busy during the economic downturn. SJB currently sends more bodies to Team B as "*they are trying to divert us to where the work is.*" Trainees keep busy working on "*public-to-private deals and a lot of refinancing,*" but the representation of the management of Pret A Manger in the sandwich chain's £325m buyout by Bridgepoint Capital should give you an idea of the kind of matter that's typical. Team C is all about fund formation, be it private equity or hedge funds. It's "*quite technical,*" though again "*you get to work with a lot of different departments.*" Team D does "*a little of everything,*" handling smaller deals, buyouts and funds than you'll find in the other three.

Tax seats are much in demand. "*It's a bit like Marmite,*" we heard, and more people love it than hate it right now. Several savvy interviewees said they chose tax "*predominantly because it backs up a corporate seat. It is a very good grounding for corporate practice and I was told that if you have tax it's a big bonus for qualification into corporate.*" Tax naturally appeals to those who like research. There are scores of specialist topics to investigate and "*a real sense of community in the team. Everyone drew on everyone else's trainees.*" Real estate is ever popular. "*They really do allow trainees to go with their own matters. You get more responsibility than in any other department and you are pretty much allowed to negotiate deals on the client's behalf.*" The firm's first ever client, British Land, is still a major source of instructions, last year seeking help on the £400m sale of the Norman Foster-designed Willis Building in London, the sale of six regional Debenhams stores for £85m and a £1.2bn joint venture with Sainsbury's to develop 39 new superstores. The lawyers also represent The Crown Estate; Marks & Spencer; AXA; Christ Church, Oxford and the Secretary of State for Health.

Pirates of the Czech Republic

If the thought of six months of contentious work leaves you cold it's not a problem as around 50% of trainees opt to complete a short litigation course instead of a full seat. For those who do want to try dispute resolution, SJB has plenty of options. The 30-strong com-lit group receives some interesting instructions, such as the defence of Viktor Kožený aka 'The Pirate of Prague' in a multimillion-dollar fraud case and a $1bn arbitration involving allegations of contractual breaches, deceit and breaches of fiduciary duties in the Russian construction industry. Our contacts had seen plenty of finance litigation because "*a lot of the clients come though other departments.*" Even for those who prefer transactional work, the seat can be helpful. Said one: "*You see things from the other side. If you've done nothing but corporate, at the beginning of a deal you might not consider the issues you should be considering.*" Lit trainees get to sit in on witness interviews and take statements though, sadly, they can't escape the drudge of court bundling. Speaking of court, "*I went along and basically sat in on a hearing from beginning to end. I also got to sit in on a mediation which was really interesting,*" said one trainee. IP and property litigation are also offered, and EU/competition is a mix of contentious and non-contentious experiences. A final twist to the SJB seating plan is the opportunity to visit one of the firm's European offices or clients.

Just what the doctor ordered

SJB has a reputation for aggression, in case you didn't know. It was something our trainees were aware of, and wanted to address. "*Obviously I've seen the comments on the Legal Week website,*" said one, "*and I think that really concerns partners.*" But is it true? Opinions were mixed. Said one first-year: "*Maybe it was like that a few years ago, but I don't feel it at all.*" In the words of a second-year: "*I think it stems from the corporate department. In a business sense we are out there negotiating hard but the people are not aggressive. There is no ordering about or shouting in the corridors. You just want to retain your clients and provide the best service you can.*" What was that we were saying about a client fetish? We won't pretend it's a big love-in: a greater emphasis on courtesy was the wish of one trainee. "*The last man I sat with treated me very well and was everything I could wish for in a supervisor, but there are partners you could work with who will walk past and they won't say hello.*" Another interviewee countered this bluntly: "*Look, if you take any thousand people and line them up, not all of them are going to be nice.*" The general consensus from our contacts was that: "*This outside perception is a little bit unfounded.*"

The other reputation SJB has is for working its people extremely hard. "*A lot of it is down to the client demanding long hours – we sort of like to produce a silver serv-

Chambers UK rankings

Banking & Finance	Information Technology
Banking Litigation	Intellectual Property
Capital Markets	Investment Funds
Competition/European Law	Life Sciences
Construction	Outsourcing
Corporate/M&A	Planning
Dispute Resolution	Private Equity
Employment	Real Estate
Environment	Real Estate Finance
Financial Services Regulation	Real Estate Litigation
	Restructuring/Insolvency
	Retail
Fraud: Civil	Tax

ice." Client fetish, anyone? At the time of our interviews, mid-downturn, working hours were actually at manageable levels for most, but the simple fact is that working hard is "*not something trainees really resent.*" "*There have been a couple of times where I have worked until 9.30pm because I have wanted to, because I was doing some interesting research and was on a roll,*" confessed one. "*You do work hard but at the end of the day they will all take you for a drink, and you'll get a pat on the back and a well done,*" said another. The firm is skilled at making staff feel valued. "*On Fridays at 5pm we head up for drinks and a little barbecue on the roof terrace, and no one's in a hurry to leave. You feel like you are looked after.*" Other perks include daily free lunches, nice Christmas presents and an in-house doctor who visits three times a week. "*Naturally, the press sneered at that as well, saying it's so you can spend more time at work,*" sighed one trainee. "*But for someone of my age who's just moved to London it's really useful.*"

Best friends forever?

Now in its late 20s, does this energetic firm show signs of settling down? No way! "*SJB still considers itself quite young. You still get that energy and enthusiasm from everywhere. We win all these awards but with each one, it's like, 'Yeah! This is great, we've won another award!'*" Looking to expand internationally, the firm left Europe for the first time in 2009, opening offices in Hong Kong and Dubai. "*The offices we've opened are based on what our current clients need,*" and the firm is "*definitely looking at other jurisdictions.*" One initiative sees several trainees a year hired from top Indian law schools. SJB has a 'best friends' relationship with US firms Goodwin Procter and Paul Weiss, and although merger rumours a few years ago were "*totally fabricated*" it must be said that its mid-sized nature and Euro-network would make it an attractive proposition for Americans in search of a partner.

Without doubt, "*confidence is imperative*" for trainees here. It doesn't matter if you've led a charmed life or worked your way up from the gutter, "*you have to be ambitious and must want to work in an ambitious environment.*" Said one source: "*Come appraisal time they will tell you that you are doing well, but they will also tell you what you need to do if you want to become an excellent lawyer.*" With that in mind, SJB's formal training was praised highly by our contacts. What's a bit different is that "*in real estate and corporate we also have training tailored to the client you are working for. We get taught about the history of, say British Land, and their expectations and quirks, what they like to see in their leases, who you are in contact with.*" Ahem. Client fetish, anyone?

Apart from SJB's gorgeous roof terrace overlooking the Thames, the other chief drinking destination is The Banker. There are "*regular Friday attendees*" among the trainees, along with "*people who will just come to the Christmas party,*" so whether you're a social butterfly or not, there's a place for you here. Said one source of the poorer employment prospects of 2009: "*Obviously there have been redundancies across the City but I think SJB has done well, and I think the [people let go here] feel they were treated with respect and understood the reasons.*" For the record, around 50 lawyers and staff fell victim to a redundancy programme in 2009, while some 34 out of 46 qualifiers stayed with the firm.

And finally...

Almost certainly the City's hungriest firm, SJ Berwin will suit confident, talented people who thrive on the excitement of being part of an organisation still shaping its own destiny.

Skadden, Arps, Slate, Meagher & Flom (UK)

The facts

Location: London
Number of UK partners/solicitors: 17/57 + 35 US-qualified
Total number of trainees: 12
Seats: 4x6 months
Alternative seats: Overseas seats
Extras: Pro bono – LawWorks

"If, when they say we work harder here, people are implying that we're put in a position of greater responsibility and take on higher-quality work, then I wholeheartedly agree."

Skadden employs over 2,000 lawyers in 24 locations around the world. After only five years in London, its training scheme is already highly coveted by students.

Bedtime reading

Avid readers of the financial press won't need any introduction to Skadden, Arps, Slate, Meagher & Flom, but for those less familiar with the business world, it's a Wall Street juggernaut that has put its stamp on some of the most prestigious corporate deals in recent history and been a permanent fixture at the top of the US M&A league tables. Having just celebrated its 60th birthday, it is one of the world's largest law firms, and if you're interested in the fine detail of its unyielding ascension, we recommend you read the book *Skadden: Power, Money and the Rise of a Legal Empire*. In London, it's now snapping at the heels of the magic circle in its chosen areas of practice. Initially set up to take advantage of the US-UK cross-border corporate deal flow, the office has grown organically to service the entire European M&A market, while also developing an indigenous clientele and establishing itself as a big hitter in sectors including capital markets, restructuring, banking and arbitration.

To give you a measure of the M&A work coming in, the UK team recently advised on the $52bn acquisition of Anheuser-Busch by InBev; on the $5.6bn acquisition of APP Pharmaceuticals by Fresenius (owner of the world's largest provider of dialysis); and on News Corporation's $3.6bn take-private of NDS Group. Mega-deals also characterise the firm's capital markets practice, which advised on New World Resources' €1.4bn IPO – the biggest IPO in London in 2008. Like other firms in the City, Skadden has felt the effects of the downturn in capital markets work; however, it has been able to stay reasonably active advising on rescue rights offerings and private placings.

The London office has grown opportunistically, reacting to new market openings almost instantaneously. This business model seems particularly suited to the current economic climate, as lawyers have been trained to adapt to changing conditions and can turn their hands to different types of work. Of late, the firm has seen an upswing in restructuring work and notably advised Nomura on the acquisition of the assets of Lehman Europe, Asia and India. We understand that the volume of work from Russia has subsided somewhat, but the country remains an important source of instructions for the London team, as are other markets in Eastern Europe.

Flom the beginning

In their first year, trainees are required to take seats in the litigation and corporate departments. Despite its corporate focus, litigation is an important department at Skadden London. In addition to a busy commercial litigation group, the firm fields a strong international arbitration team, which *Chambers UK* ranks alongside dispute warlords Herbert Smith. Trainees in this department have a principally research-based role and are also trusted to prepare instructions to counsel and draft case statements. *"The seat is never monotonous,"* said one; *"you routinely liaise with colleagues and clients around the world. You'll be working on a Hong Kong-based arbitration one day and a London-based dispute the next."* Our sources reported a surge in construction and telecoms-related disputes.

In the corporate department, *"ready or not, you're quickly thrown in at the deep end without a life jacket."* Said one trainee: *"I was asked to produce a substantial piece* of work for a FTSE client on my second day in the office." A running theme with our interviewees was the significant level of responsibility they were given from an early stage. Skadden trainees are not wasted on month-long due diligence exercises: "*I came here knowing I would have a meaningful role in high-quality international deals and I've not been disappointed,*" said one. Another elaborated: "*Taking ownership of your work is the least partners expect of you. Don't expect people to hold your hand all the time as you'll be put in situations where there is no one to look to for advice.*" It's common for trainees here to conduct negotiations or drafting sessions on their own, rubbing shoulders with partners and senior associates from other firms across the deal table. Trainees work on public company, private equity and capital markets deals and there is every chance of a second seat here at a later stage.

In the second year, seats in tax, banking, restructuring or an overseas placement are offered. Overseas seats can usually be taken in Moscow or Hong Kong, but we heard that last year, due to the Russian deal flow drying up, Moscow had been put on hold. During a six-month Hong Kong secondment trainees see a mixture of corporate, capital markets and banking work, and with the recent launch of the Asian international arbitration and litigation practice, it's now possible for them to get some contentious experience there.

Nature of the beast

US firms are commonly perceived as ruthless, dog-eat-dog workplaces, where people soon give up any hope of life outside the office. Supporting that cliché is a story that in the 1960s, Skadden NY associates used to give a 'Beast of Burden award' to their hardest-working colleague, in honour of a partner who is said to have literally worked himself to death. But, 40 years later, things have moved on and our sources were keen to challenge some preconceptions.

The annual New York retreat provides an opportunity for new joiners to appreciate the true measure of Skadden. "*New arrivals from offices worldwide congregate for this event, so you get hit by the scale of the firm. When you get back to the London office you have some context. It has a very different feel: it's a leaner outfit, so things are more personal this side of the Atlantic.*" London fields both American and English-qualified lawyers, and while there has been talk in the past of the US lawyers being a little cliquey, our sources insisted that no such divide exists.

Another preconceived idea about US firms in London is that their trainees can look forward to impressive rewards, and while our sources insisted that money was never their key motivation, they recognised that "*no one would sniff*

Chambers UK rankings

Banking & Finance	Private Equity
Capital Markets	Projects, Energy & Natural Resources
Corporate/M&A	Restructuring/Insolvency
Dispute Resolution	Tax

at our salary on qualification." NQ lawyers at Skadden get £94,000 per year, before bonuses. Such pay comes with strings attached, and there's no point denying that hard work and utmost dedication are key to succeeding here. However, our sources vehemently denied that work hours are much worse than at other City firms. "*It's a myth; work comes in waves so certain periods will be hectic and others much quieter. We're not chained to our desks for weeks on end,*" they assured us. "*If, by working harder, people imply that we're put in a position of greater responsibility and take on higher-quality work, then I wholeheartedly agree,*" added one.

When they're not busy closing multimillion-dollar corporate deals, trainees can unwind at one of the firm's social events. At this year's annual retreat, members of staff and their other halves were treated to a weekend of luxury at a spa resort in Hertfordshire. Skadden also invites staff on annual ski trips and, true to its roots, normally puts on a little Independence Day party. If you trek over to Canary Wharf you'll usually find a few trainees enjoying a quiet Friday evening drink.

In case we haven't made it clear enough, it bears repeating that the training contract at Skadden is designed for those who relish a challenge and thrive under pressure. It is "*not for passive progressers.*" There is no hiding place here and relatively little pastoral care, so know what you're getting into: true independence and masses of self-assurance are essential attributes. The qualification prospects are good – excellent even – with the firm holding on to all three of its 2009 qualifiers.

And finally...

Considering the quality of work and rewards it offers, Skadden is no longer a leftfield choice for the brightest students. If you think you've got what it takes, brace yourself for extremely stiff competition.

- **A training partner on social mobility:** "Being well connected is an amazing advantage in life, and some people need a leg up. My parents knew a partner at a City firm and sometimes that's all you need."

If you think you might need a leg up, check out the summer school run by the City Solicitors' Educational Trust, which seeks 'to unlock the potential in students in higher education who might not have excelled in their A Levels or are not studying at one of the top UK universities.' The website you need is www.cset.org.uk.

top tip no. 25

Slaughter and May

The facts

Location: London
Number of UK partners/solicitors: 116/410
Total number of trainees: 173
Seats: 4x6 months
Alternative seats: Overseas seats
Extras: Pro bono – RCJ CAB, FRU, Islington and Battersea Law Centres, LawWorks; language training

"The impression I get is that people think Slaughters is stuck up. That's totally wrong."

Q: How many Slaughter and May partners does it take to change a light bulb?
A: *Change?!*

Who's laughing now?

Independent-minded Slaughters has never been one to tamper with a winning formula. Its determination to do things its own way rather than follow trends might be interpreted as arrogant or conservative, but one of our interviewees had a more thoughtful interpretation: *"It makes decisions carefully because it doesn't want to go back on them."* During the boom times, Slaughters' magic circle stablemates opened offices across the globe, joining (and topping) the lists of the world's highest-grossing firms. Slaughters faced derision for not following suit, but as managing partner Chris Saul told us: *"If we went truly global, we would give up the kind of partnership we have and that is very precious to us."* The relatively small, all-equity partnership *"has grown up together,"* keeping its values solid and its profits high.

Our interviewees backed Saul to the hilt. *"The best way to do business is to cut out all the rubbish – not by taking over smaller firms, sticking your name above the door and not training them up to the same standard you expect."* Indeed, nowadays Slaughters' conservatism looks like a real strength: a lean operation leaves it flexible and so far it has avoided the massive layoffs humbling its competitors. Aside from having to freeze salaries, the firm has found itself quite well insulated. *"I think it's pretty much business as usual,"* shrugged one trainee. We heard the corporate groups aren't as busy as they once were, but *"litigation and finance are really busy"* and *"credit crunch-related work has occupied huge teams of people."*

Big business

So what counts as business as usual? Generally, taking the lead on some of the country's biggest and most complex instructions. A quick glance at *Chambers UK* will show you all the areas in which Slaughters comes top or is highly ranked. In reality, *"probably 75 to 80% of our work is corporate or finance,"* estimated a trainee. The firm received several instructions in 2008 that would have made headlines had adverse market conditions not intervened – namely, BA's proposed mergers with Qantas and Iberia, and the attempted buyout of Rio Tinto Ltd (valued at AUS$44.8bn) and Rio Tinto plc (£63.79bn) by BHP Billiton, the world's biggest mining company. That would have been one of the largest hostile takeovers of all time, but the firm just had to content itself with helping Italian energy company Eni secure a 57% stake in Belgian company Distrigas. Banks get a look in too, with the likes of Banco Santander and Commonwealth Bank of Australia instructing. Other top clients include General Electric, Unilever, Diageo and Marks & Spencer. The UK government has become a bigger client than ever. The firm advised the Treasury on the recapitalisations of Lloyds TSB, HBOS and RBS (involving £37bn investment between them) and BERR (now BIS) regarding the recommended offer by EDF to acquire British Energy Group. It was reported in March 2009 that since the start of the credit crunch Slaughters had totted up £22m in billable work for Whitehall.

The dispute resolution team has also been busy. *The Lawyer* identified two of its cases as worthy of being labelled a top-ten court battle of 2009 – the judicial review actions brought against Northern Rock and the bank charges test case by the OFT against eight major current account providers, in which Slaughters is representing Nationwide. Lawyers also acted for Toys 'R' Us in relation to an accounting fraud by an employee, and handled matters for Porsche and Royal Mail.

Such impressive clients and deals aren't unusual for the magic circle. What is more unique is a generalist approach that means "*all groups do a huge variety of work,*" even if some focus more heavily than others on certain areas. Big instructors always have a main contact at the firm to whom they go first for a wide range of matters, which means apart from a few partners, lawyers rarely specialise in one area alone and might even be "*doing something for the first time even eight or nine years into their career.*" It's "*very good for the vast majority of people,*" although interviewees accepted it might not suit those with very particular interests: "*If someone wants to be a derivatives lawyer, of course a different system would be better, as then they can go and do derivatives work for as long as they can master the boredom.*"

All trainees spend six months in corporate, with virtually all adding another six there or in financing. The remaining seats can be chosen from a collection of "*specialist*" options. Bar one or two grumbles, "*most people broadly get what they ask for.*"

NPB? OMG!

"*Slaughters likes to say it doesn't ever do anything standard,*" and that's most evident in its flagship corporate groups. First off, there are four main groups, each named for the initials of the partner that heads them. So there's NPB for Nigel Boardman and SJC for Stephen Cooke. Confusingly, the name of the group changes when its partner head moves on: one recruit told us the group they were in "*has been called three different things in the last five years.*" All of them cover a wide range of corporate-commercial matters but have entirely separate client lists. There is "*a tiny bit of rivalry*" between them, and we heard a lot of boasting that NPB was "*the corporate powerhouse with big-name lawyers*" and "*the best-run group in Slaughters,*" where "*you turn up and there's a file with everything you need to know.*"

Which group you join is down to the luck of the draw but fairly "*menial*" admin tasks are always going to be part of your time in corporate. However, "*the positives far outweigh that. You're really seeing the firm operate at the highest level*" and good-quality tasks always seem to pop up. Typical responsibilities include the analysis of contractual relationships, drafting board minutes and small documents, arranging client meetings and plenty of academic research points. In financing, Slaughters' other major practice area, "*there's a bigger spread of work and more responsibility.*" That translates into "*a lot of drafting and a lot of document production.*" Research tasks are common, like comparing precedents in corporations' bond programme guarantees. "*What I've said in research notes has shaped the way our deals have been handled,*" bragged one trainee.

Chambers UK rankings

Administrative & Public Law	Life Sciences
Asset Finance	Media & Entertainment
Banking & Finance	Outsourcing
Banking Litigation	Partnership
Capital Markets	Pensions
Competition/European Law	Pensions Litigation
Construction	Private Equity
Corporate/M&A	Professional Negligence
Dispute Resolution	Projects, Energy & Natural Resources
Employee Share Schemes	
Employment	Real Estate
Environment	Restructuring/Insolvency
Financial Services Regulation	Retail
Fraud: Civil	Sports Law
Information Technology	Tax
Insurance	Telecommunications
Intellectual Property	
Investment Funds	

Contrary to the broad corporate experience, "*in litigation you can be pigeonholed into one thing for a few months.*" Competition is "*one team, half in the UK, half in Belgium,*" and either your first or second three months in the seat can be spent in Brussels. The regular work in here is "*academic-y research, producing notes on fine points of law, drafting... that sort of thing.*" Of course there's also "*a fair share of admin tasks that aren't glamorous but have to be done.*" Other seats include IP, real estate, financial regulation and employment.

A Slaughters training contract can be quite an intense experience. "*People have to be prepared to be independent here,*" we heard, and because "*there's not always time for people to explain exactly what they want*" you have to "*anticipate what they might ask you next.*" Your experience of a seat can very much depend on the partner with whom you're sitting. Some will give you all your work themselves, while others will display a more hands-off attitude. Some are "*quite eccentric*" and "*some are real stars – you need to be careful around them.*" "*There are characters among them,*" explained a trainee knowingly. While this means you should make sure you've attempted to solve a problem before you take it to a partner, the firm's strong sense of hierarchy means they'll rarely be the first person you ask for help.

Don't judge a brochure by its cover

Pre-eminence generates assumptions. One of the most long-standing is the idea that Slaughters is a bad firm to choose if you want to go overseas. Its current recruitment brochure tackles this preconception, showing no fewer than five double-page spreads of trainees in exotic locales, gazing intrepidly into the middle distance. Some interviewees acknowledged that "*the pictures in the brochure aren't perhaps as warranted as they'd like them to be.*" So what's the truth of the matter? Around 17 to 20 people (mostly fourth seaters) go overseas at each rotation and Slaughters can send them to 'best friend' firms beyond the reach of most competitors – Scandinavia and New Zealand, for example. Wherever they go, recruits get rent-free accommodation and a salary top-up. That also holds true for postings to Slaughters' own international offices in Brussels (part of a competition seat), Paris (mostly finance) and Hong Kong (commercial). All in all, "*it's an injustice to think you can't go away on secondment here.*"

Another assumption common to the magic circle is one of round-the-clock working. It's just not true, say Slaughters trainees. "*It's certainly true that if you come here you'll be working pretty long hours,*" they conceded, "*but not all the time. As a trainee it's considered late past 6pm or 7pm,*" and if there's no work it's acknowledged that "*there's nothing to be gained by staying late.*" Part of the reason for this is Slaughters' lack of billing targets (although recruits do have diary monitors). We can well believe "*it's great not to have to worry about doing X number of hours,*" but where's the motivation if no one's standing behind you with a stopwatch? "*If you're a trainee and there's a big transaction going on,*" one clarified, "*the last thing you want to do is go home at 5.30pm and miss a crucial part of it.*"

Violet tendencies

There is (yet another) enduring perception that to get into Slaughter and May you have to have been born to the same purple that bathes its gorgeous website. Referring to everyone administratively by their initials is "*like something you'd expect to see on a cricket scoreboard or a dormitory,*" but this is Bunhill Row, not Brideshead. "*The impression I get is that people think Slaughters is stuck up,*" worried one interviewee. "*That's totally wrong.*" Granted, people can be direct, and "*it's certainly a 'no bullshit' culture,*" with "*very little rubbish business jargon – if you can say it in two words, say it in two words,*" but "*arrogance is massively frowned upon.*"

It's true there's a heavy Oxbridge contingent among those who make it through the famously no-nonsense application process ("*there's no psychometric test... or testing your ability to shout at one another*"). However, "*the overriding thing is meritocracy*" and Slaughters does select from a wide range of backgrounds. One interviewee who'd attended a state school and gone on to a less prestigious university said: "*I thought those kinds of things would put the firm off hiring me but they didn't appear to be an issue.*" Ultimately, it wants "*straight-A students who are diverse and different.*" It's difficult to find many unifying characteristics, although we heard a few suggestions. "*There is a kind of seriousness in a lot of people,*" said one recruit. "*That doesn't mean you can't have a joke or that people go around scowling all day, but people want to achieve and produce excellent work.*" Still, there's a mix of personalities: "*You get the quiet ones, the loud ones, the ones who say inappropriate things, the ones who're always smiling. It's the same as any schoolyard, except none of them dress badly.*" And yet it would be a mistake to assume that every applicant is right for the firm. Leaving aside superb grades, the ideal Slaughters trainee is someone with plenty of self-confidence and little need for hand holding.

With so many trainees arriving each year, "*people tend to socialise within their intake.*" "*The budget for trainee stuff got slashed a couple of years ago,*" but there are summer parties and departmental Christmas dos to look forward to, as well as regular pints at the Artillery Arms – unfortunately abbreviated to "*the AA.*" Those of a sporting bent will find subsidised netball, hockey, tennis, squash, volleyball and football societies. Partners are "*obsessed*" with cricket and matches are "*very keenly contested.*" If not at the crease, you'll quite likely run into fellow trainees at the "*very cheap and good*" staff restaurant, where steak is cooked to order for £4.50.

In any given qualification year there is an expectation that most who want a job will find one waiting for them. It's a strong testament to Slaughters' overall health that retention was predicted to be high even in a recession year, although sources acknowledged it might be "*tempting fate*" to say so and admitted they might have less control than usual over exactly which department they qualified into. "*People aren't as nervous as they are at other firms,*" said second-years when we rang them; "*it's pretty good for morale.*" In the end, 72 of the 79 qualifiers were retained in 2009 – 91%, which is about average for Slaughters. It's even more impressive when you find out that four of the seven who didn't stay were moving on because they wanted to leave either London or the law.

And finally...

The reasons to apply here are obvious and mostly boil down to quality and reputation. Trainees tell us that "*any ambitious and talented person should consider working at Slaughter and May.*" We'd add that you have to be pretty confident to boot.

Got that Speechlys something?

Here at Speechly Bircham, we're as interested in your personal qualities as we are in your qualifications. We're looking for graduates who share our passion for the law and who relish the idea of building relationships with colleagues and clients alike. In return we're offering an environment where you'll be encouraged to make your own mark and you'll be rewarded for the difference you make.

Think you've got that Speechlys something? Find out more at speechlys.com/trainingcontracts

Speechly Bircham

Speechly Bircham LLP

The facts

Location: London

Number of UK partners/solicitors: 87/138

Total number of trainees: 25

Seats: 4x6 months

Alternative seats: Secondments

"We don't try and do the glossy magazines and entice people in by looking cool and sexy: we're a great firm, we've got great clients and we'll give you an excellent training."

Speechly Bircham has its foot on the accelerator and shows no signs of braking. A June 2009 merger with Campbell Hooper has strengthened and expanded many of the firm's practices.

A safe bet

In a period of change that has seen a move to LLP status, swanky, environmentally sound offices and now a substantial merger, we have no qualms with trainees' assertions that *"this is a firm that has ambitions."* Many spoke of the management's plans for expansion that would see it *"pushing into the top 50 firms with 250 fee earners"* and were darned impressed that, with the merger, *"the firm has condensed this three-year plan into three months!"* Not that the union with West End fixture Campbell Hooper wasn't well thought out. Our sources could see the firm's thinking: *"When you look at Campbell Hooper and all the things they did well, we do them well too."* This applies especially to construction and property, although CH also brings interesting niche groups focusing on charities law and computer games and gambling. From what we heard, the merger has gone down well on the ground (*"it all happened very smoothly"*), with Campbell Hooperites fitting in nicely. *"We've been sharing work and all get on very well."* No doubt this has been helped by *"lots of drinks."*

The new, bigger, better Speechlys has impressed trainees, who are pleased to now find *"people are more aware of the firm."* Speechlys' large private client practice is particularly well regarded and concentrates on tax, trusts (contentious and otherwise) and family issues. The firm is also strong in property, construction, corporate and employment. IP is an up-and-comer, and Speechlys is one of the few firms in the City at which a trainee can take an immigration seat.

Technicolor training contract

Seat allocation is a smooth process, and we hear that *"you get at least two of your choices over the four seats."* Said one source: *"I've never known any trainees to be sold out on what they really want to do."* Private client is a really popular choice – the department was described by one source as *"world class"* and, indeed, it picks up a *Chambers Global* ranking because of its specialist teams offering advice covering a range of jurisdictions worldwide. Interviewees told us that as *"one of the best"* departments, *"the work is quite exciting."* Here, as elsewhere in the firm, being a first-seater is no reason not to have responsibility. *"Within the first half an hour on my first day I was asked to draft a will,"* said one interviewee. Trainees relish the client contact here as much as the responsibility: *"You always meet the clients and often have daily contact with them."* The work is wide-ranging, from wills and trusts to divorce, children's claims and prenuptial and civil partnership matters. Non-contentious tasks include the drafting and preparation of wills, writing articles and answering clients' questions. When it comes to contentious work, you might just be lucky enough to get involved in a *"major international case worth hundreds of millions of pounds."* If so, you'll be *"liaising with foreign lawyers and counsel, preparing and drafting affidavits and dealing with a vast number of other documents."* Unfortunately we can't tell you too much about the cases, but we can tell you Lord Lloyd-Webber is a valued client alongside scores of high-profile figures from the worlds of entertainment, politics and business.

In a private client seat there may well be the opportunity to make applications before a district judge, and in the burgeoning dispute resolution practice some trainees get *"more advocacy than you can shake a stick at."* Alongside this is *"bread-and-butter trainee work"* such as bundling, preparing for trial and cost estimates. One recent high-profile matter involved MFI's 2008 administration and our sources said they were *"seeing a lot of credit crunch litigation."* Several of our sources handled their own lower-value cases: *"They'll entrust these to you as a trainee and invest a lot of time in you."*

Other contentious opportunities are available in the construction and employment practices, both of which have seen some exciting cases this year. The former was instructed by contractor PC Harrington in a dispute regarding Wembley Stadium. Trainees took witness statements and tackled *"a lot of document management."* The merger has extended an already impressive client list: Kier Construction and the Shaw Group are among the new names now on the firm's books. In employment, a headline-making whistle-blower case put Speechly on the side of an individual against their megabucks financial employer. Settled before trial, it was nonetheless a highlight for trainees who were involved in the preparation of the case.

Handbags at dawn

Speechly's corporate department has not escaped the malaise affecting law firms up and down the country. That said, the firm has certainly made an effort to keep trainees busy and, crucially, learning as much as possible despite the economic climate. *"I've taken on a company secretarial position and so I'm attending meetings and taking minutes,"* said one. Everyone agreed that *"getting that kind of interaction with clients and seeing how they're running their businesses is invaluable."* The funds practice was touted as an exciting growth area, and one where trainees say *"you can be quite creative."*

The property market is not exactly booming either, but one contact did tell us that in this seat *"although it was quieter than it would have been, in actual fact I had six billable hours a day so I was always occupied."* The things keeping trainees busy are *"document management, drafting leases, requesting searches and site visits,"* and in one case *"attending a planning tribunal."* RBS is a significant client and the team has acted for the bank in the sale and leaseback of 62 major operational properties to TeleReal and The Prudential. In other matters, the firm has had dealings with a major private client concerning a 90-acre Marylebone estate and been involved with multi-million-pound acquisitions in the West End and aspects of the retail regeneration of Marylebone High Street.

Like the firm itself, the IP department has experienced considerable change and growth. It is not without glamour – none other than Elle 'the Body' Macpherson turns to Speechlys for advice about trade marks and brand management. She used the firm during the expansion of her underwear brand (including the opening of a retail outlet in the UK) and returned again for advice relating to her appearance agreements for Montblanc, Tiffany and Revlon. Representing high-street luxury retailer LK Bennett, the team has been pitted against Hermès and Gucci in a literal handbag fight in connection with their respective Birkin and Kelly designs. Trainees say the department has *"so much in so many areas,"* including *"copyright, trade marks, patent litigation, franchising, licensing of image rights and data protection."* Summing up the thoughts of the majority, one IP seater told us: *"There isn't a typical day – the department tries very hard to get the trainees involved in all types of work. The partners like you to have a good grounding."*

The immigration team (a recent acquisition from Harbottle & Lewis) is fully fledged, *"not just tacked on to the employment department."* By all accounts it has a *"great client base from retailers, airlines, record companies and financial institutions to private clients."* The law in this area changes fast and the work trainees get is *"not run-of-the-mill stuff."* Rounding off this exhausting list of seat options are secondments to clients. These involve *"a steep learning curve,"* so are generally viewed as a really worthwhile experience.

Pushing the boat out

We rather like the no-nonsense approach this firm takes to recruitment. *"We don't try and do the glossy magazines and entice people in by looking cool and sexy: we're a great firm, we've got great clients and we'll give you an excellent training."* Speechlys prides itself on its *"traditional values"* and as a result, trainees said, *"you'll get to know the firm and the firm will get to know you."* The trainee group is mixed in age. They come generally from redbrick universities, though our sources said the firm was *"not overly"* obsessed with the prestige element. We

Chambers UK rankings

Agriculture & Rural Affairs	Immigration
Banking Litigation	Intellectual Property
Charities	Investment Funds
Construction	Media & Entertainment
Corporate/M&A	Pensions
Data Protection	Private Client
Employment	Real Estate
Family/Matrimonial	Real Estate Litigation
Financial Services Regulation	Restructuring/Insolvency

were also told: "*You won't go far if you have an aggressive City banker style*" and that "*we're a relaxed bunch who just want to have a decent career rather than bite each other's heads off.*" A "*positive ethos*" is apparent at the firm and it has certainly rubbed off on trainees, whose morale was palpably high this year. "*I will do whatever I can to stay,*" said one typical recruit; "*I really do love working here.*"

The "*state-of-the-art*" New Fetter Lane office got glowing reviews, not least because it is part of "*one of the greenest developments in the City.*" Apparently "*everything is recycled*" and "*the lights are motion-activated,*" which sometimes leads to the slightly odd scenario where a single worker bee can be seen toiling under a single light. Though some staff initially had reservations about open-plan working, our contacts certainly agreed that "*the positives outweigh the negatives,*" particularly because "*you learn so much from hearing people with more experience talking around you.*" The location is a hit. "*As we're on the very edge of the City, it's slightly less suity than the area around Bank.*" Having a close-knit workforce is really important to the firm, and "*from the secretaries and the post room to the most senior of partners, you can sit and talk to anyone.*" A book club draws "*a real mix of characters*" and gives the literary-minded a chance to discuss their thoughts over a free lunch. Speechly isn't a firm to skimp on the big socials.

The "*stunning locations*" of previous Christmas parties include the Great Hall at Lincoln's Inn and the Banqueting House on Whitehall. The vacation scheme also has its fair share of enjoyable events; last year's included "*speedboating on the Thames,*" cocktail making and a table football tournament. The vac scheme is a great way to get to know the firm: three weeks means "*you get to know a lot of people*" and our sources were impressed that "*you get taken to meetings and given good work.*" In fact, several people told us that by the end of their vac scheme they'd been sad to leave. Tearful goodbyes were not in store for the majority of the 2009 qualifiers, however: eight out of 12 people stayed on.

And finally...

Speechly's friendly, collegial culture shouldn't change one bit with the arrival of the folk from Campbell Hooper. Last year we gave both firms a good review and so hopefully two plus two will now equal five.

Journeys in Business.
Careers in law.

How would you like to cut your teeth guiding a major Singapore property and development company through a £300 million reverse takeover bid? Or working on the launch of a renewable energy fund on London's Alternative Investment Market? Or advising a middle-eastern airline startup on its fleet financing requirements under Shari'a law?

A lot of firms talk about early responsibility. We can point to just what that means – day-to-day, working closely with international clients across a full spectrum of sectors and services. Solving their real-life business problems out in the real commercial world is what we do. And from day one, it's what you'll be doing too.

- 14 training contracts starting 2012
- Vacation Schemes: Winter, Easter and Summer
- Open Days: January, February and March

For further information and details on how to apply, please visit our website.

London - Guangzhou - Hong Kong - Paris - Piraeus - Shanghai - Singapore

shlegal.com/graduate

sh
STEPHENSON HARWOOD

Stephenson Harwood

The facts
Location: London
Number of UK partners/solicitors: 77/98
Total number of trainees: 29
Seats: 4x6 months
Alternative seats: Overseas seats, secondments
Extras: Language training

Positive feedback from trainees, oodles of different practices to sample, and a strong name in litigation – what's not to like about one of the City's most established mid-sizers?

Historical links to Asia combined with greatly improved management on home turf puts Stephenson Harwood right back in the running as a perfect mid-sized pick for City-bound applicants.

The Yes We Can man

No one at SH is shy when it comes to discussing problems past. A *"disaster merger"* combined with an exodus of personnel a few years back left the firm feeling vulnerable. Step forward, Sunil Gadhia. The poster-boy for a firm reinvigorated, Gadhia trained at the firm, rising through the ranks of commercial litigation to become CEO in 2004. Trainees expressed pride in their wunderkind: *"He single-handedly turned it all around"* and *"everyone at SH openly credits him with the transformation."* Across the board interviewees told us how *"he always takes the time to speak to vac schemers and new trainees."* New recruits on a residential course in Hertfordshire were delighted that *"he came along in the evening for dinner"* and *"spent all evening with us, leaving at midnight."* Seriously, from some people we sensed almost Obama-like love for the man. After five years as CEO, Gadhia has now reverted to fee earning.

What we're talking about with SH is not a transformation per se, but a working symbiosis between the old and the new. A wonderfully eloquent trainee used the partnership to illustrate the point. *"We broadly have two categories: old-school partners and the newer breed. Whereas the old school are more inclined to maintain client relationships by wining and dining, the newer breed are more into glossy marketing and will go out and tender for work. It's a good structure as there are obvious merits to both."*

One thing you need to appreciate about this firm is its international scope. Where some firms look to the East and despair at the idea of missing the boat, SH can feel confident in the longevity of its international network. This includes offices in Guangzhou, Shanghai, Hong Kong and Singapore (currently, overseas seats are available in the latter two, but more on that later) plus European offices in Paris and the Greek shipping port of Piraeus. The international dimension is certainly a draw for trainees, one of whom told us: *"My main criteria was an international firm so I have the chance to go international when I'm qualified."* Another *"was looking at international firms as I wanted to use my languages."* Recent international work includes the biggest ever IPO in sub-Saharan Africa and the first-ever Shari'a-compliant insurance outsourcing deal. Also worth noting is the firm's association with HSBC. A strong connection with the Hong Kong and Shanghai Banking Corporation goes back to 1875 and founding partner William Harwood. Trainees credited big-name clients such as this in explaining why *"people know who we are."* They are no doubt influenced by this when admitting: *"This place really inspires a level of loyalty – you want to make sure you don't let the standard drop."*

Shipmates

Much has been made of SH's shipping credentials. This very publication has been awash with maritime metaphors in previous years. The fact is, despite the spread of practices at SH, shipping remains an important aspect of its business. Trainees admitted: *"We have a broad client base* but shipping does pervade most departments." With Maersk, the world's largest ship owner, and Daewoo, the world's second largest shipbuilder, this is not surprising. However, trainees and SH partners alike were keen to point out that "*there is not the emphasis there was historically*" on shipping and that it is "*now one of the smallest mainstream departments.*" For the record, the mainstream areas open to trainees are: shipping and commercial litigation, corporate, finance and real estate. There are further options in more niche departments, and more niche subgroups within the bigger departments – for example property, IP and construction within commercial litigation, and aviation and shipping options within the finance group. All trainees are expected to take a seat in corporate or finance and are required to take a seat in commercial or shipping litigation.

Of the 'ship lit' seat, trainees say "*you either love it or you don't.*" With cases typically relating to contractual disputes, the department is dominated by long-running matters. "*I was involved in one massive case that had been going on for six to eight years and looks set to continue,*" explained one source. Generally tasks include research and court bundling, but trainees also reported substantial court exposure after filing claims, observing hearings and even spending time in the House of Lords. Described as "*testosterone heavy,*" the ship lit department is undoubtedly the bastion of the old-school ethic at the firm. An "*established social culture*" makes the department "*good fun,*" if "*a little aggressive.*" Trainees found the London finance seat also dominated by shipping work: "*There are six trainees in finance and probably five of them will be doing shipping work.*" Specialists in ship and aircraft financing, SH has lately seen a decline in the aircraft sector, whereas "*the shipping deals have just kept going.*" An interesting question is just how long this will continue to be the case as lately some major ports have looked like container ship car parks following the drop-off in world trade. Until now at least, in this somewhat pressured seat trainees have been "*getting to do a lot*" and "*feel involved.*"

Premier League litigators

While trainees acknowledge "*it would be good to have a reasonable interest in ships and oil,*" there's plenty for landlubbers to get stuck into. Real estate stands out, not least because of the matchless popularity of the team. Unanimously seen as "*comfortably the friendliest department in the firm,*" there was effusive praise for the lawyers and secretaries ("*they're great, I love them!*"). In this seat, trainees can work on big acquisitions, handle their own files and deal with the other side directly. A real joy for some, the seat has "*less micro-management than in others.*" A significant number of trainees had the chance to work on a £400m acquisition for Kuwaiti investment vehicle St Martin's Property Group. The building in question was

Chambers UK rankings

Asset Finance	Information Technology
Aviation	Investment Funds
Banking Litigation	Pensions
Capital Markets	Planning
Commodities	Private Equity
Construction	Professional Negligence
Corporate/M&A	Real Estate
Dispute Resolution	Real Estate Finance
Education	Real Estate Litigation
Employment	Restructuring/Insolvency
Environment	Shipping
Financial Services Regulation	Tax
Fraud: Civil	Transport

the iconic Norman Foster-designed Willis Building opposite the Lloyd's Building. At the time it was the "*biggest property transaction in the City of London.*" Employment law was also popular among our interviewees. There is only one seat for a trainee in the small team but it offers a "*demanding and fulfilling experience.*" Market conditions meant a lot of compromise agreements and redundancies for trainees in 2009, with bags of research thrown in for good measure as "*every two to three days there are cases which change the way things are done.*" Of course, in a down economy real estate gets hit, and given the small size of employment department, 2009 qualifiers were realistic about their chances of being offered a job. One was especially candid in telling us they didn't expect to see anything available in the non-contentious areas, but that "*if you want to do litigation you're guaranteed a job.*" In the end, 15 of the 18 qualifiers found jobs in 2009, eight of them going into litigation.

Having hired an extra 15 lawyers last year (more than the number of staff laid off in the London office due to the recession), the litigation team is SH's "*single biggest group in London.*" A senior partner told us: "*As long as I can remember we've been on high-profile cases. Currently, some of our cases would no doubt be recognised as in the top ten litigation cases for this year.*" There's a good flow of finance sector disputes coming through from major banks, and new clients include the Republic of Bolivia and the Venezuelan national oil company, PDVSA. Reflecting the standing of the practice group, cases are also referred by magic circle firms, US firms and the Bar. One of the cases consuming SH lawyers at the moment involves points of Russian, Swiss, Liberian and Maltese law. The firm is defending two Russian men who it is claimed committed fraud on the companies they ran by entering into a series of unlawful and uncommercial shipping and banking transactions. These two defendants claim they were bribed into doing so by a third individual who is also a defendant. Suffice to say it is a complicated case with intrigue and drama. Amongst trainees though, enthusiasm for litigation seats was variable. Our senior source pondered on this lukewarm reception. "*If you're not on one of those big cases perhaps you don't get the same buzz and, conversely, if you are on a big case there may be 25-plus lawyers and you're only getting a snapshot.*" The fact remains though that litigation is a key part of the firm and SH has a "*premier league team.*" If you want to qualify into litigation the message is clear that SH is "*a great place*" to do so.

The new silk road

The foreign secondment opportunities definitely do not disappoint. In any given year between four and six trainees will have the opportunity to take either a largely corporate-based seat in Hong Kong or a largely finance-based seat in Singapore. Francophiles, watch this space – we were also alerted to an upcoming Paris seat, again likely to focus on non-contentious areas. In Hong Kong, trainees admitted that market conditions meant they hadn't been overrun with work lately, but they did lavish praise on the extramural benefits, including travel. The deal includes a small, ideally located apartment and it sounds as if socially the place can't be matched. Trainees visiting Singapore enjoy a rather more imperial existence in a large three-bedroomed apartment that gives them use of the country's largest swimming pool. Speaking of the lifestyle, one lucky trainee admitted that "*getting used to it can be kind of dangerous.*" Finance work including AIM listings and asset finance for ships and aircraft have kept trainees busy in Singapore. "*There are only 20 staff so if there's work going you're expected to get stuck in.*" In areas of the business that were quieter (such as capital markets) trainees found they became more involved in business development and credited this experience with "*broadening horizons.*"

The growth of the Singapore branch is certainly something to watch, according to our sources, one adding that "*three new partners arrived when I was there.*" Attracting these partners from magic circle firms such as Freshfields, the Singapore office is definitely going places and "*they may need more trainees to go there in future.*" A new publication – The New Silk Road – has been produced to highlight opportunities in Asia for clients. All in all, Asia is deemed to be a "*very important*" market to the firm. "*If the Indian market was to be deregulated sooner rather than later that would be great,*" declared one source, clearly aware that SH has "*people on the ground putting plans in place for when it does happen.*" SH's ambitions don't stop with Asia either: other global relationships are key, such as an association with the Al-Saraf & Al-Ruwayeh law firm in Kuwait and Bahrain. For a firm where "*more than half of revenue comes from overseas clients,*" a strong international network is clearly of paramount importance.

Baroque steady

SH's central London location facing St Paul's Cathedral is crucial in appealing to foreign clients who "*see the location as very prestigious.*" It likewise had our interviewees cooing with delight. A lucky few have views "*straight onto the steps*" of Sir Christopher Wren's masterpiece, leading to one source telling us: "*Even if I've had a bad day it always cheers me up.*" The only down side is that at lunchtimes "*tourists are often in the way and you're always in someone's lens.*" The social scene has suffered lately and "*it is noticeable that they're not doing as much as they did.*" Interestingly, this didn't seem to bother everyone. Said one trainee: "*It's not university anymore.*"

It's normal for new trainees to have taken at least one gap year; some have even had a previous career. Interviewees found it hard to distinguish a firm culture, suggesting that "*there's no coherent way to describe Stephenson Harwood as the departments are so radically different.*" Each of our interviewees had established that they "*didn't want to work for a magic circle firm*" but nonetheless wanted quality work. One aptly summarised this as a desire for "*a mid-sized firm with blue-chip plans.*" At SH they had gained exposure to FTSE 100 clients, albeit in relation to mid-market level deals, so avoiding the assumed stereotypical magic circle experience. The belief is that "*the risk at a larger place is you'll be used as a glorified photocopier.*" With a more limited number of trainees taken on each year our interviewees were convinced of the fact that at SH "*you get a good-quality training experience. You're going to enter the profession knowing something.*"

And finally...

Exposure to good clients, sexy overseas seats and a 'Yes We Can' ethos mean there's a lot more to learning the ropes at SH than, well, learning the ropes.

Stevens & Bolton LLP

The facts

Location: Guildford

Number of UK partners/solicitors: 30/52

Total number of trainees: 8

Seats: 6x4 months

Alternative seats: None

The firm says: "*Being outside London with ex-City lawyers and providing cheaper services is very much part of our strategy.*"

Stevens & Bolton prides itself on having attracted FTSE 100 clients and a truckload of ex-City lawyers to the Greenbelt. We put its claims of London-quality training to the test…

Down by the riverbank

Situated just beyond the M25 in Guildford, Stevens & Bolton boasts the tagline, "*EC quality work with a GU price mark.*" But it wasn't always like this. Not so very long ago this was a high-street firm operating a private client, family and residential property practice from five small offices. That was until the early 1980s when management decided the future lay with commercial work. Consolidation into a single Guildford office quickly followed, and Stevens & Bolton began its not-so-secret mission to bring the Square Mile to Surrey. Having never merged, the firm prides itself on "*organic growth,*" albeit with a healthy dose of fertiliser from some of the top firms in the capital – "*they love their ex-City lawyers.*" Just a few to have been lured to the halcyon streets of Guildford are ex-Simmons & Simmons corporate honcho Ken Woffenden and employment expert Stephanie Dale, formerly of Denton Wilde Sapte. More recent additions include leading tax and trusts specialist Stuart Skeffington from private client powerhouse Withers, and associates Charlotte Tillet and Victoria Pope from Herbert Smith and Burges Salmon respectively to boost the firm's burgeoning IP/IT capabilities. A quick glance at the firm's recruitment pages shows there is no sign of a slowdown. "*The rate of expansion is pretty huge,*" say trainees. Today company/commercial work makes up around a third of S&B's £15.7m revenue, and the firm is one of the most profitable in the South East region outside London. Partners here take home an average of £250,000 per year.

"*Setting up a London office has been mooted once or twice but the management just isn't keen,*" our sources revealed. Determined to stay in Guildford, but having grown out of its "*rabbit warren-like*" premises on the banks of the River Wey, Stevens & Bolton took on the almost impossible task of finding a suitable premises in an already crowded town. The search finally came to an end this year, and when we spoke to them staff were soon to make the exciting move all the way… next door. The new office, which recieved an S&B-style refurb, is "*a lot bigger*" with "*terraced gardens going down to the river.*" Trainees were pretty excited about the prospect of "*having everyone under one roof.*"

All change, please

The S&B training contract has also undergone a bit of an overhaul recently and recruits now complete six seats of four months rather than four six-month seats. While some sources did voice concern about the length of each new seat ("*Four months is a short time to get settled in, especially if it's your first seat. You will have to hit the floor running*"), most responses were positive. It gives trainees "*more choice and an option to go into seats they might not usually have gone into,*" and because "*there are seven main departments, it means everyone can do almost everything and there will be no bickering about missing out.*" There is also the possibility of going back to do a second stint in the department you hope to qualify in. As for the identity of the seven departments, they are coco;

real estate; employment; pensions and immigration; tax and trusts; dispute resolution and family.

The corporate group, ranked top in its region by *Chambers UK,* is the firm's engine room. Large national companies form the bulk of the client roster, a number of which feature in the FTSE 100. Recently the team has been particularly noticeable for its work with international companies interested in investing in the UK, and new client wins include Australian software company MYOB and Spanish manufacturer Azkoyen. The S&B team recently advised on the sale of MYOB's UK and Ireland accountancy software division to a Dutch company for £3.5m. Trainees in the combined corporate/commercial seat can expect slightly longer hours compared to the rest of the firm, but sources claim that *"you don't really notice it because everyone is busy and there is such a buzz."* They also report that they are always kept in the loop with the goings-on in the department. *"There is a meeting every week and you are kept really up to speed and involved to quite a good level."* Tasks include research, attending meetings and drafting board minutes and resolutions plus Companies House documentation. Of course there is the *"dreggy stuff"* like bibling, photocopying and due diligence, but trainees see it as *"almost a rite of passage"* and understand that despite it being *"very time-consuming and not really that interesting, you have to know how to do it to see how it fits into the rest of the deal."*

The Uggly face of modern Britain

The growing dispute resolution team is one of the most popular departments among trainees. Its turnover has leapt sharply and it has growing capabilities in IP, representing clients such as auction house Christie's and media companies Future plc and A&E Television Networks. Trainees gain exposure to *"a vast array of work"* and are able to get *"quite involved"* on everything from debt recovery and injunctions to trade mark applications and defence. What's more, trainees *"usually get a chance"* to do some of their own advocacy.

Another popular seat is to be found in the *"really busy"* employment team where trainees are *"pushed pretty hard and learn a lot in a short space of time."* As well as representing internationally recognised companies such as amazon.co.uk and KIA Motors, the team has been instructed by an increasing number of senior executives. A property seat, on the other hand, is recognised by some as *"the short straw,"* and they are pleased when they *"manage to dodge it."* The more pragmatic trainees, however, appreciate that *"even if you don't want to qualify there it gives you really good skills for later on"* as you quickly *"get your own files and lots of responsibility."* The work is mostly commercial property but recruits are given the opportunity to dip into some property litigation and construction work. A big department, trainees informed us that *"it's good for making contacts. Wherever else you are in the firm you will probably have to liaise with property lawyers so it makes it easier if you already know them."* By the time they reach qualification there's little excuse not to know most people at the firm, and in 2009 three of the four qualifiers stayed on.

Stevens & Bolton manages to occupy a happy halfway house where there is *"a professional environment and the standards are high, but everyone is very friendly."* Even its location enviably straddles two different worlds: nestled in the *"quintessential English countryside"* of Surrey but close enough to London to allow a reverse commute that is just *"40 minutes door to door from Clapham."* The London/Surrey split does hamper evening socialising, which some trainees found *"a little bit frustrating."* Staff more than make up for it by taking advantage of their hour and a quarter lunch breaks *"pretty much every day,"* picnicking in Guildford Castle's grounds in the summer or heading to one of the town's numerous cafés and restaurants. And when we heard about what happens to Guildford after the sun sets we decided that missing out on the nightlife perhaps wasn't such a bad thing. *"Guildford is full of pashmina and Ugg boot-clad yummy mummies during the day and then takes on a different face at night. It can be pretty chavvy and there are only two clubs, neither of them that nice."* You'll be pleased to hear then that S&B's black-tie Christmas party *"with all the trimmings"* is held in *"a country hotel in the Ascot area."*

Chambers UK rankings

Banking & Finance	Intellectual Property
Corporate/M&A	Partnership
Debt Recovery	Pensions
Dispute Resolution	Private Client
Employment	Real Estate
Environment	Restructuring/Insolvency
Immigration	Tax
Information Technology	

And finally...

New premises, quality work, top-notch partners and a regime that won't demand *"every hour god sends"* – it's no surprise trainees have hardly a bad word to say.

- **Don't believe everything you read.** Some legal websites love nothing better than to blow a tiny story out of all proportion and then have a good sneer at those involved. Equally, some firms will try to spin news to make themselves look good. Take it all with a pinch of salt and don't be afraid to ask firms the tough questions so you can form your own opinions. How they respond to you will probably tell you a lot about their culture.

top tip no. 26

Taylor Wessing LLP

The facts

Location: London, Cambridge
Number of UK partners/solicitors: 103/165
Total number of trainees: 44
Seats: 4x6 months
Alternative seats: Secondments
Extras: Pro bono – LawWorks, Blackfriars Settlement; language training

This full-service firm has a top-notch IP practice and is transitioning from a European player into a global business.

Taylor Wessing is well known for IP work, but with an excellent range of other practices on offer there's plenty of other things to get your teeth into at this City mid-sizer.

Tinker Taylor

Although once regarded as predominantly an IP firm, many trainees come here with no interest in this area of law, instead being drawn to the full-service nature of the firm. That practice profile is evidenced by a long list of *Chambers UK* rankings, including a top-tier placing for mid-market corporate finance. TW is typically rather modest about its achievements, and our interviewees confessed that *"many people have never heard of Taylor Wessing, whereas they will have heard of similar mid-sized firms."* You could also be forgiven for not knowing about TW's extensive international network. Having started out as an Anglo-German venture, it now has 14 offices across Europe, the Middle East and Asia. *"We're branded as a European firm, and are looking to push the international aspect outside Europe,"* say trainees. *"We want to get the brand out into the market more effectively and integrate the foreign offices further... we've got good lawyers here and are full-service enough to compete with any top-level firm. And we should be proud of it."* A big marketing drive looks imminent. A recent move to New Street Square (a major development in London where 'thecitymeetsthewestend') certainly represented a step in the right direction. Trainees say: *"You can see how impressed clients are. It really does compete with magic circle firms in terms of the impact of the office."*

The election of a new managing partner has provided an additional shake-up. Tim Eyles swooped in to replace Kiwi Michael Frawley in early 2009 and immediately abolished dress-down Fridays. Is this a death knoll for a more relaxed TW? *"There are signs the firm could change. The new managing partner is a more serious character, more business-driven."* But trainees aren't complaining. *"It's exactly what the firm needs in this kind of market."*

Bespoke Tayloring

One thing that doesn't look set to change is the range of seat options for trainees. The majority of our interviewees admitted that they *"didn't know exactly what I wanted to do,"* and were pleased that at TW *"you can explore a wide range of areas during your training contract."* A corporate seat is mandatory, but other than that it's a case of weaving a path through IP, employment, commercial disputes, real estate, construction and engineering, private client, IT, telecoms, competition, finance, financial institutions, corporate recovery, tax, pensions and projects. There are no international seats but *"if you were really keen you could negotiate"* and perhaps score yourself three months in a foreign office. The feeling we got was that most trainees here aren't *"sitting around dreaming of Frankfurt."*

Even though trainees don't usually go abroad, the London office does receive significant instructions from overseas. The corporate department recently took its first instruction from new client Times Infotainment Media (part of The Times Group, which is the largest media services conglomerate in India) as it acquired Virgin Radio Holdings for £53.2m. Lawyers also advised the senior executives of European management consultancy Lindorff Group on the €1.12bn secondary buyout of the company. Corporate seats are varied at TW, and you can sit within teams focusing on any of the following: corporate finance transactions (including IPOs and other stock exchange-related work), mergers and acquisitions, private capital, corporate tax, financial services and funds, EU law and general company law issues. It has to be said that "*things haven't exactly been buoyant*" of late. However (and this is typical of TW's approach to training), you are nonetheless made to "*feel part of the team*" and "*valued as a trainee.*" Corporate seat trainees take responsibility for the proper organisation of the documents involved in transactions, and they also "*draft ancillary documents, deal with the other side directly and attend one-on-one client meetings.*" In time they have the opportunity to run smaller deals themselves, also branching into the area of general corporate governance and "*advising a company's board at their AGM.*"

Chambers UK rankings

Advertising & Marketing	Insurance
Agriculture & Rural Affairs	Intellectual Property
Banking & Finance	Life Sciences
Banking Litigation	Media & Entertainment
Capital Markets	Outsourcing
Construction	Pensions
Corporate/M&A	Pensions Litigation
Defamation/Reputation Management	Planning
	Private Client
Dispute Resolution	Private Equity
Employment	Product Liability
Environment	Real Estate
Financial Services Regulation	Real Estate Finance
	Real Estate Litigation
Franchising	Restructuring/Insolvency
Fraud: Civil	Tax
Information Technology	Telecommunications

The real estate department has previously contributed around 13% of the firm's annual turnover. It is heavily involved in investment matters, working for institutional clients such as Canada Life, private entrepreneurs, charities and overseas investors. As an example of the latter, it recently advised HSBC's Specialist Investments arm on its €100m investment in the creation of 40 self-storage units across eight cities in Germany. Closer to home it has also advised Canada Life on transactions totalling more than £380m, including the purchase of Santander House on Ludgate Hill. TW is also highly regarded in the hotels and leisure sector and clients here include British Airways, Kew Green Hotels, Malmaison and Hotel du Vin. Very swanky. Recently trainees have worked on the redevelopment of High Wycombe Town Centre, worth £200m and containing more than a million square feet of retail space. The seat is known for the high level of client contact for trainees, who concentrate largely on leases and refinancing. Said one source: "*It makes you so much more confident.*" A well-organised mind is important when you're collating all the information necessary for a deal to go through, and the chance to run your own files has real appeal.

Into the groove

Half transactional, half litigation and advisory work, the construction and IP departments bridge the gap between contentious and non-contentious practice. The former has a "*very popular seat*" and was praised by trainees who felt "*visible*" within the team. On contentious construction cases they have a largely administrative role: one trainee described a 70-volume bundle of documentation as their "*baby.*" On the non-contentious side, trainees experience "*a mix of drafting, consultancy agreements, client meetings, e-mails and phone calls.*" Conceding that much of what they were doing amounted to "*lower-level work,*" they also insisted that "*it is still real work.*" The 'real world' aspect is definitely an important element of the job and those who were able to make the occasional site visit told us: "*It's good to actually see something built and achieved.*"

"*Incredibly competitive*" to get into, the IP seat brings plenty of opportunities for advisory work; for example, assisting Unilever on its anti-counterfeiting activity within the UK. The contentious-minded can also have a ball on some headline-making cases. Said one interviewee: "*Associated Newspapers is a client and the Daily Mail is always getting itself into trouble, so that's quite fun.*" One such incident involved Madonna, who made a £5m claim against the *Mail on Sunday* alleging infringement of copyright and breach of privacy in relation to her wedding. IP has close links with the firm's highly regarded media group and sees trainees "*liaising with counsel, taking witness statements*" and, "*as it's an academic area, conducting lots of research.*" The firm also represents Burberry in its war against chav counterfeiters everywhere, with particular attention paid to defending the trade-marked Burberry check.

Life sciences is a significant niche department (and the main reason behind the existence of an office in Cambridge, which doesn't take trainees). Understandably, a seat in the patent litigation team is likely to require a scientific background. The firm has been involved in a host of high-profile cases of late: the case of Actavis v Novartis related to a drug that lowers cholesterol and was described by the judge as 'a significant development in United Kingdom patent law'. Another TW case, Monsanto v Cargill, was one of the first GM crop-related patent disputes in Europe.

For the hardcore litigators, TW's commercial disputes seat doesn't disappoint and we found one trainee's story particularly enlightening. "*On the case I'm working on, which is multimillion-pound and against a top-ten firm, they don't have a trainee on the other side, or not that we'd know of.* [I've] *never seen them in court, never seen their name on e-mails. I've written two e-mails and two letters with my name on them. We took a vac schemer to the hearing. Of all the experiences I've had, this has been the most revealing as to the level of involvement we get and what firms use trainees for.*" Smaller claims give trainees the opportunity for "*something to run with,*" and some had been lucky enough to travel to Spain or Monaco to take witness statements. Across the seats, trainees were united in their conviction that not only are their efforts valued by the firm, but that the work itself is of a high level and worthy of "*a lawyer rather than an administrator.*" A particularly effusive fourth-seater said: "*My work product has become Taylor Wessing's work product; they clearly trust me to deliver and so keep on giving me work to get out to clients.*"

Let me paint you a picture...

"*Everyone's got different stories to tell,*" one source said of the trainee group. By this, they didn't mean raucous tales of debauchery, but that there's no typical TW recruit. There's "*quite a large age range – from early twenties to mid thirties. Lots have had other careers or years out, some a master's degree...*" The firm is said to "*embrace loads of different types of personalities,*" from "*very quiet, intellectual people to the more chatty types.*" From a range of good universities, including Oxbridge, London, Bristol and Leeds, our interviewees appreciated the fact "*we're not all clones of each other.*" That's not to say they don't have things in common: "*There's no backstabbing types here,*" and arrogance is a turn-off. "*You come in at the bottom and gain respect, which won't happen if you walk in shouting about how great you are.*"

The firm's culture may be undergoing some changes since the election of new managing partner Eyles – his motto, we hear, is: 'the clients, then the firm, then you'. Nonetheless, trainees told us: "*We like to think of Taylor Wessing as not being one of those firms that beasts you unnecessarily.*" They also said it was the type of place to "*do things with a smile on its face.*" Apparently, "*there's one partner with a very annoying laugh,*" and the fact that "*he's always doing it*" has to be a good sign. Trainees confessed to being impressed with their seniors, irritating chortle or no. "*A lot of them have come from magic circle firms. Nothing's changed in their work: they just don't need to put on this whole act of bravado and attitude. And they have better working hours and more of a life here.*"

We must thank our sources for their succinct synopsis of the nearby pubs. "*We've not found fit to move much beyond The Corney and Barrow, though The White Swan's up there, and The Cartoonist gets an honourable mention.*" The new office provides a glorious setting for firm-wide events, and numerous departmental Christmas outings show that the firm's "*not shy of throwing some money behind the bar when the occasion demands.*"

TW's pro bono work was recently recognised at *The Lawyer* magazine's annual awards: it came second for its not-for-profit efforts (behind seven-partner City firm Oury Clark, should you be wondering). Trainees are able to get involved with Blackfriars Settlement in Southwark on Wednesday evenings. "*Normally more logical than legal,*" this walk-in centre gives all kinds of advice and can lead to follow-up work. The firm also sponsors The National Portrait Gallery's Photographic Portrait Prize, no doubt a great marketing tool and representative of a love of art that permeates the new offices. "*There's loads of artwork: portraits, landscapes, abstract stuff...*" Perhaps the best work of art is the City itself, as viewed from the "*incredible*" tenth floor of TW's office. The new digs are clearly a source of joy for trainees, whose only reservations were at "*getting really fat constantly eating lasagne and fish and chips*" at the "*excellent*" cafeteria overlooking the London Eye.

Unfortunately, a forbidding economic climate led to quite poor retention in 2009 – only 15 of the 24 qualifiers stayed on. A small number of the new trainees due to start in 2009 and 2010 were deferred by a year in exchange for a condition-free payment of £7,500. The firm's turnover did not suffer in 2008/09 but profitability did fall by around a third.

And finally...

A new age is dawning at TW and we'll be interested to see if the firm develops a more aggressive attitude. For now, we recommend it as a solid and pleasant mid-market choice.

Teacher Stern LLP

The facts

Location: London

Number of UK partners/solicitors: 18/18

Total number of trainees: 6

Seats: 4x6 months

Alternative seats: None

Teacher Stern provides a fluid training contract and is keen to produce well-rounded lawyers.

A snazzy rebrand in 2008 revealed a new image for Teacher Stern.

A year of change

Founded in the 1960s and based in Bedford Row in London's legal heartland, to the casual observer TS would appear to be a modest firm. A sneaky peak behind the office's Georgian façade reveals, among other things, ground-breaking education litigation, a legacy of defending film stars and shamed footballers, and a stalwart property practice. Last year, determined to improve itself, the firm abbreviated its name, became an LLP, smartened up its office and created a new website – all topped off with a champagne party at the Royal Academy. We want to "*focus on media, sports and defamation law to become a real force in the market,*" said one of last year's interviewees.

What a difference a year can make. Having already stepped down as managing partner, well-known media and sports lawyer Graham Shear and fellow partner Joby Davies were snapped up by Berwin Leighton Paisner in late 2009. Shear's prominence within TS extended beyond his management role: his client list could fill the Hollywood Walk of Fame, in fact a few of them do have a star on the famous boulevard. As well as celebrities, Shear represents dozens of premiership footballers and a number of clubs and agents. Having handled various cases for Ashley Cole and the contentious transfer of Carlos Tevez from West Ham to Man U, Shear became the lawyer the stars wanted onside.

We asked trainees what we should make of the departures and got some stern responses. "*I don't think people are crying. I don't think the firm is particularly nervous. I think there is life beyond Graham,*" said one. Another continued: "*The clients that he's got, that is the stuff that gets the headlines, but it certainly isn't the only aspect of what we do... It's going to be odd at first but I don't see it causing lasting damage.*" Our sources were optimistic for the future: "*It may give us a chance to put emphasis on stuff that hasn't gained due recognition.*" Training partner Russell Raphael echoed these thoughts. While admitting that Shear "*opened a lot of doors,*" he stressed that "*[his practice] was never a core area for us.*" There has now been "*a shift in emphasis*" and TS has "*taken the opportunity to refocus and make lateral hires. We have used it as an opportunity to build up other teams,*" with a particular concentration on contentious IP/IT work.

Feel the fear and do it anyway

Trainees take four seats, spending time in each of the main departments – property, corporate-commercial and commercial litigation. Their final seat is taken in their intended qualification department. This may sound restrictive but we're assured that each of the departments can show trainees plenty of variety. Recruits are able to express a preference as to who their seat supervisor is but because "*you usually end up working for whoever needs you*" if you are unsuccessful in nabbing your favourite partner as a mentor it isn't the end of the world. "*Certainly the lack of specialisation is something I would stress,*" commented one source. "*Here, being a rounded lawyer is really important. They give you room to develop in your own way. They don't want to crowd you, they want to let you grow.*" Trainees have two appraisals each seat, one after three months and one after six. The appraisals are not only a chance for recruits to find out how they are progressing but also to have some input into their trainee experience. One source talked of requesting involvement in a couple of things they *"liked the sound of"* in their corporate mid-seat appraisal and was pleased to report that *"it went down fine and people tried their best to accomodate that."* High responsibility levels were mentioned over and over again as a real high point. *"A lot of firms will keep you away from the action, but here you do have to get right involved and be willing to take that on at an early stage and not be afraid of it."*

With over 20 fee earners, the property department is the largest, and you'll be given a lorry load of files on your first day here. *"It was a bit daunting. The clients want things done very quickly and you have to keep updating them. They are very focused and sharp on picking you up on things,"* explained a source. Once trainees get to grips with the work, they generally appreciate the *"buzzy atmosphere"* and the chance to *"just get on with it."* The majority of clients are wealthy individuals, developers, entrepreneurial investors, landlords and retailers. They value their confidentiality so we can't name names, but we can tell you that the value of the largest portfolios exceeds £1bn and lately lawyers have helped on the purchase of an £80m shopping centre in London's Victoria and a £15m nursing home portfolio. Trainees spoke of day trips to expensive houses, site visits and auctions, as well as organising numerous sales, mortgages and repossessions. *"It was good to do that seat first as it set me up well,"* said one.

Jumpin' Jack Flash

The coco lawyers feed off the property department for the majority of their work, but they are developing a standalone practice. The group does all the usual things from M&A to AIM listings and even has a small capital markets team. Trainees reported working on everything from property finance deals to IP advice for online gaming clients and a price comparison website. One recent transaction was the sale of communications service provider V Networks to Carphone Warehouse. As the deals don't get anywhere near the billion-pound mark, trainees can have substantial involvement. *"You're not asked to do one discrete task – you're encouraged to understand what's going on."* Their responsibilities include research, drafting board minutes and attending completion meetings. Despite being officially assigned a supervisor, because the team is quite small *"you work for pretty much everybody. If there is work you want there is really nothing to stop you."*

Litigation teams specialise in commercial and property litigation, arbitration and mediation. Because the client list is largely comprised of wealthy individuals, owner-managed businesses and AIM-listed companies, trainees don't have to go through *"an apprenticeship of photo-copying."* They draft defences and witness statements, as well as *"actually going to court and presenting things. It was absolutely terrifying but winning gives a real sense of achievement."* There may also be a sense of achievement to be gained from running your own debt recovery files. One lucky trainee is assigned to the *"incredible"* Jack Rabinowicz, who excels in the field of medical and educational negligence and *"takes you to every single meeting he's got."*

TS has a strong Jewish tradition that dates back to its founders. A notable proportion of staff are practising Jews, and if you are too then you'll likely feel very much at home. Plenty of clients and staff, including a majority of trainees, are not Jewish however, and a couple of years ago the firm underwent a secularisation of its office policies, including its holiday system.

While most people we spoke to were happy with their training, there was a suggestion that some individuals might feel they are left to their own devices too often. The words *"fearless," "flexible"* and *"adaptable"* cropped up a number of times during our interviews, so make of that what you will. We couldn't help but feel that TS trainees were slightly jumpy this year and less talkative than usual. Of course, they've not only had the recession to deal with but there's been a big change at the top of management. Caginess aside, recruits were more than happy to sing the praises of the healthy work-life balance – 9.30am to 6pm is an average day – and the firm's location means *"you are within walking distance of about 20 pubs."* Bedford Row is stuffed with lawyers due to its proximity to the Inns of Court and the Royal Courts, and it additionally has a strong literary tradition with Charles Dickens living just around the corner in Doughty Street in the early part of his writing career. One source did comment that *"maybe the social committee needs a kick up the arse,"* but another favoured the *"ad hoc arrangements"* model over *"enforced fun."*

Chambers UK rankings

Sports Law

And finally...

Two of the three qualifiers stayed with the firm in 2009. A good result in a difficult year, especially given the firm's major interest in the real estate market.

Thomas Cooper

The facts

Location: London
Number of UK partners/solicitors: 17/10
Total number of trainees: 8
Seats: 4x6 months
Alternative seats: Overseas seats

> "*Fairly soon after you start, you might be interviewing witnesses almost anywhere. Trainees need to grips with the job without someone senior looking after them all the time.*"
>
> Tim Goode, Managing Partner

One of the oldest names in shipping, Thomas Cooper has doubled in size in recent years and is making waves in its chosen markets.

The prize is right

First a brief history lesson before embarking on the HMS Here and Now. This firm was founded in London in 1825 by the eponymous Mr Thomas Cooper, an Admiralty lawyer by trade. He worked in an arcane area of practice called Prize, an important element of Royal Naval income consisting of the divvying up between the Crown and the crew of the value of ships and cargoes captured from enemy fleets. Following the end of the Napoloenic war in 1815 there was an abundance of Prize cases and subsequently a healthy income for Cooper. Things continued in much the same way until the firm was sold to private client, banking and commercial firm Stibbard Gibson in around 1870, creating Thomas Cooper & Stibbard. By the early 1970s the shipping side of the practice was once again dominant. A banking practice is now all that remains of the Stibbard legacy and in 2007 the firm's name reverted back to that of its original founder.

TC challenges the generally held belief that overseas offices are an expensive luxury inaccessible to small firms. Managing partner Tim Goode explained that while London is undoubtedly the engine room, "*all the* [foreign] *offices work for the London-based marine insurers who cover at least 80% of the world's tonnage.*" They also get additional work directly from local shipowners and commodities traders. So where are they? A Singapore office handles Admiralty matters (casualties, collisions and salvage) and is also taking on insurance and commodities work. Athens originally serviced Greek banking clients but today works in marine law. Madrid advises Spanish and South American clients, and there are two solicitors in Vancouver offering English and Canadian advice. A Paris office was acquired from Reed Smith in 2007 and primarily focuses on French marine law and commodities.

It's a colourful life

Chambers UK pegs TC as an expert not only in shipping but also in commodities work. Commodities are products such as sugar, oil or copper that have no qualitative differentiation. This area of law, "*basically, is sale of goods disputes,*" generally "*quality or delivery disputes.*" Because the terms of trade for over 50% of commodities come from trade associations arranged in 19th century London and governed by English law, "*when these disputes arise both the sellers and buyers will instruct lawyers in London.*"

All the trainees we spoke to had an interest in the shipping industry before joining TC. They talked about the breadth of law involved, the international aspects to the work and an abundance of interesting cases. Having looked at some of the cases we can see what they mean. At times it felt as though we were dipping into a swashbuckling adventure novel. Take the story of the 'Alondra Rainbow', hijacked by pirates off the coast of Indonesia. TC assisted in the crew's rescue and the recovery of the cargo of aluminium ingots. While the crew washed up on the coast of Thailand after two weeks adrift in the Indian Ocean, recovering the ship took more work as the pirates had repainted and renamed it. The Indian Navy eventually effected a high seas capture and shots were fired. The pirates were sentenced to seven years hard labour, marking a rare move by a national court to assume jurisdiction over a crime committed in international waters.

Learn the ropes and it's plain sailing

The London office is split into three departments: shipping, commercial litigation and banking/finance. Trainees spend time in each, usually sharing an office with their supervisor. There's officially a six-month rotation, but trainees often only spend three months in the smaller finance seat, before *"falling back into one of the other seats, depending on what you want or where you're needed."* In the large shipping team, partners specialise, be it in collisions, salvage, marine insurance or contract disputes. *"Your experience is very much dependent on your supervisor,"* trainees say, but *"there is no short straw."* In broad terms, shipping is split into dry and wet work (for more information see page 120) and most time is spent in dry teams, working primarily on contract matters – *"anything from a fuel dispute as to whether cargo was delivered on time."* *"It takes a bit of time to build up a relationship with the partners"* and *"some are really controlling while others are more informal,"* but once you know the ropes the quality of work quickly improves. *"I've had some cases where I've been given all the materials,"* reported one proud interviewee.

TC represents a number of ship operators and P&I clubs in defence of fatality and personal injury claims. Trainees in commercial litigation see huge cases such as that of the tragic 'al-Salam Boccaccio 98', reported to have involved one of the largest losses of life at sea. A good example of a smaller case is a claim brought by the dependents of a dockyard worker following his electrocution. The banking and finance department works on many things, including the sale and purchase of ships, restructuring of loans, property matters, and even wills and probate.

Nautical but nice

Stints in Athens are *"positively encouraged."* In this relatively small office *"everybody works to capacity, so you need to be much more proactive."* Increased responsibility means *"client contact every other minute,"* and we hear that *"generally a Greek client wants things done yesterday. That's the way it has always been."* Out of the office, trainees hang their hammocks in an apartment in a friendly residential area just five minutes' walk from work. Back in London there's a nautical theme to the decor of the office, which is situated just behind the Tower of London. Trainees described *"paintings of bays and crashing waves"* and various *"artefacts from shipping days gone by."* We're talking bells, clocks and one of the old benches from Lloyd's Registry of Shipping.

Shipping is still a heavily male-dominated industry and this is reflected in the higher echelons of the firm. One trainee told us she got *"a lot of e-mails addressed to Mister."* While a number of the partners are described as *"quite old-school Oxbridge types,"* interviewees assured us that you *"don't get the feeling that you can't speak to anyone."* And a bit of old-school chivalry certainly doesn't go amiss in the pub after work, where partners *"are very insistent on buying drinks."* *"Sometimes you get home at 9pm and realise you are hammered and haven't spent a penny,"* chuckled one trainee. Other firm jollies include a black-tie Christmas party and a summer boat party on the Thames.

Other than having a strong liver (*"shipping people are all very nice and drink too much"*), our sources couldn't see a common thread between them. Tim Goode explained that TC wants people who will gel with the existing team; *"since we are not a very large firm that's actually quite a significant factor."* It's clear that recruits must have initiative. *"If you need to be spoon-fed this isn't the place for you,"* trainees agreed; *"you often have to think outside the box."* And with some partners keeping offices that *"look like a tornado has struck,"* it helps to be organised as *"at times you end up being a bit like a secretary."* The only real grumbles related to the amount of bundling, photocopying and document delivering required of trainees, ranging from *"a couple of hours at least once a week"* to *"at least half a day of copying at least three times a week."* Some saw it as *"wasting valuable time on stupid jobs,"* while others saw the silver lining. *"It's quite useful to know how to put a bundle together. And sometimes when you have done one academic thing after another it can be quite a nice break."*

Chambers UK rankings

Commodities	Shipping

And finally...

Thomas Cooper suits self-starters who can demonstrate an interest in all matters maritime. In 2009 three of the four qualifiers stayed with the firm, all in the shipping department.

Thring Townsend Lee & Pembertons

The facts

Location: Swindon, Bath, Bristol, London
Number of UK partners/solicitors: 58/65
Total number of trainees: 16
Seats: 4x6 months
Alternative seats: Secondments

A 'lifestyle' firm in the best sense of the word.

Thring Townsend has undergone substantial growth over the past decade, but the firm retains its 'people first' culture.

The M4 corridor and beyond

The TTLP story began at the turn of the millennium when Swindon firm Thring & Long and Bath outfit Townsends joined forces. Five years later Laytons' Bristol office was added to the mix. A sweeping SW empire is one thing, but an SW1 postcode is quite another and in 2007 the firm got exactly this thanks to a merger with 200-year-old Westminster private client specialist Lee & Pemberton, pushing the firm up another level. Most recently, TTLP merged with niche private client practice Wood, Awdry & Ford, adding offices in Marlborough, Chippenham and Cirencester as well as access to a cartload of wealthy Wiltshire and Cotswold folks.

The worsening economic climate saw all three Wood, Awdry & Ford offices close at the beginning of 2009 and the relocation of 25 people to Swindon in an effort to save around £1m in overheads. Managing partner Thomas Sheppard has described the move as "*people over property… we have tried to prioritise protecting jobs rather than offices.*" The decision illustrates that despite the firm's growth – TTLP broke into the top 100 UK firms in 2008 and has an annual turnover exceeding £20m – and its increasingly commercial direction, staff welfare is still a priority. "*It's one big happy family here,*" beamed a satisfied trainee. "*There is definitely no whispering behind closed doors.*" All the senior partners "*were really open and honest about what was going on, so people didn't panic.*" There are quarterly meetings specifically for trainees and associates to learn about "*profits, budgets and why the partnership make certain decisions.*" Understandably these have proved particularly popular lately.

While "*the firm's movement is down a commercial route*" and trainees are confident that TTLP wants to expand, they say: "*It doesn't want to be a law firm that just does everything. We will still have our specialist areas in personal injury, private client and agriculture.*" Trainees can do seats in all of these, although business needs play a part in what's available from year to year. A client secondment at Future Publishing is also on offer. Merging with a London practice was "*not about conquering the capital but about providing a convenient location for our clients,*" said our sources. When we spoke to graduate recruitment partner Brian Jacomb, he agreed: "*We are always going to be a balanced practice with agriculture spanning both [commercial and private client] sides of the business.*" The South West is still where the firm's heart lies; indeed, according to one interviewee, "*I'd say it was embedded in the community.*" Apparently, even the London office has "*got the South West way of doing things.*"

All four office locations host trainees. The majority split their time between the three in the South West, but the London office recruited two trainees of its own last year. "*In some respects we are slightly out of the loop in London,*" admitted a source in the capital, "*but less so as trainees because we are encouraged to go to Swindon a lot for meetings and training to ensure integration.*" The firm's view on training in the capital is that "*there is no hard and fast policy on where trainees spend their time. We have asked those who are currently in the South West offices if they want to spend time in London, and one London trainee is heading to Swindon for a seat next year.*" There are rooms full of hot desks for people to come and go, so moving between offices is very much part of the firm culture and trainees quickly get used to whizzing up and down the M4.

No wasted energy

TTLP's commercial property team is spread across all of its offices and is one of the largest in the south of England, so consequently trainees are likely to spend time here. The team handles almost every aspect of real estate and trainees get access to "*really wide-ranging work,*" often acting as the main contact on smaller files. Major clients include Hamptons Estate Agents and EDF Energy. A new relationship has been struck up with Cyclamax, a business that specialises in turning waste into energy. Thring Townsend represented the company in its acquisition of 300,000 square feet of units to be used in waste energy processing. There is also a growing construction department and the firm has a *Chambers UK*-ranked property litigation team that again is one of the largest in the region.

The lawyers in the company commercial department "*get their heads down and work some of the longest hours but do know how to have a giggle.*" Trainees split their time between writing terms and conditions for businesses and helping with transactions. The team acts for a number of banks, assisting them with corporate due diligence, and was appointed to HSBC's commercial panel for the South West last year. As yet there are not many junior staff in the London office, so trainees "*do a lot of the lower-level work.*" Said one: "*I was working quite long hours going through all the due diligence.*"

Family-friendly

The Swindon-based personal injury department is top-ranked by *Chambers UK* in its region and specialises in complex high-value catastrophic injury and industrial disease claims. The industrial disease group is particularly recognised for its work on mesothelioma claims, a form of lung cancer that is almost always caused by exposure to asbestos. It can be quite emotional work as "*many of the clients do not have long left to live and want to provide for their families. They put a lot of trust and faith in you.*" Ultimately the work is rewarding and the team regularly secures millions of pounds of compensation for its clients.

Members of the family department "*go out of their way*" for trainees. The "*close team*" provides them with a lot of client contact (just like in PI this can be "*quite emotional*") and the seat is known for its regular court visits for divorce and ancillary relief claims. TTLP no longer handles legal aid cases, preferring to concentrate on private payers, an increasing number of whom have either been resident abroad or own assets abroad. The merger with Lee & Pembertons strengthened the agricultural practice, bringing the family team new challenges in the form of farming divorces, as well as making it the largest 'standalone' agriculture practice in the country. Clients range from the owners of landed estates and large farms to the Country Landowner's Association and the NFU and its members.

Chambers UK rankings

Agriculture & Rural Affairs	Intellectual Property
Construction	Personal Injury
Corporate/M&A	Private Client
Dispute Resolution	Real Estate
Employment	Real Estate Litigation
Environment	Restructuring/Insolvency

Café culture

The Swindon office is open plan while the older Bath office is a mixture of open plan and individual rooms. Both have popular cafés that provide free breakfast to those who arrive before 8.30am. On Fridays staff can tuck into a "*full works*" fry-up. The Bristol office moved in September 2009 to "*brand new, open-plan premises right in the centre of the city. We have the two top floors with a balcony.*" The all-important café was not forgotten. The London office is sadly sans eatery but its location right next to Trafalgar Square means "*you can access everything.*"

TTLP is a 'lifestyle' firm in the best sense of the word. Not only is it applauded for its excellent work-life balance, but our interviewees were adamant that it will draw anyone in to its warm culture. Said one: "*If you want to just come in and work and then go home, you aren't going to fit in here.*" Trainees regularly meet up for lunch and go out together after work, and there are also numerous marketing events for them to become "*heavily involved in.*" Regular firm-wide events include London theatre trips and an annual Christmas party. "*Always a really swanky do,*" the Christmas bash is an employee-only event (including incoming trainees) but "*for most of the things we arrange, you can bring your family along too.*"

And finally...

It is no wonder that at such a "*friendly, approachable and non-stuffy*" firm the general consensus among trainees was: "*I think everyone plans on being here long-term.*" What a good thing then that five out of six qualifiers were offered jobs in 2009.

Exception is the rule

TLT

Grow

TLT Solicitors is part of a new wave of law firms. We're a top-100 firm, with some 650 people across London, Bristol and Piraeus, Greece. An award-winning commercial firm, we're built around the needs of our clients. We're progressive in our thinking and in the eyes of the Financial Times, one of Europe's most innovative law firms.

As a full-service law firm, we concentrate on providing industry-focused, multi-discipline integrated solutions. Our leading strengths are in the financial services and leisure sectors, and we have outstanding experience in retail, technology and media, and the built environment. Our core legal specialisms are real estate, banking and finance, commercial, corporate, employment, dispute resolution and litigation.

Our trainees are genuinely ambitious, talented and technically impressive. We look for people who stand out. People with vision. People who embrace team working and share our passion for outstanding client service. And while academic achievement is important, personal qualities and legal work experience count for a lot here.

Join us on a week's vacation placement and you'll pick up a phenomenal amount, especially when you consider the amount of Partner contact you'll enjoy. But it's more than that. We've built assessments into the week, which means you won't have to make a separate training contract application or attend an assessment day.

We're one of just ten top-100 law firms to offer a full flexible benefits plan. This gives you the opportunity to design your benefits package to meet your lifestyle needs, picking and choosing from a selection of rewards and benefits. You'll also be encouraged to get involved in community support work, pro bono legal advice, fundraising activities and environmental initiatives.

If you want to grow and flourish with a firm that's going places,
visit **www.TLTcareers.com/trainee**

TLT LLP

The facts

Location: Bristol, London
Number of UK partners/solicitors: 64/350
Total number of trainees: 25
Seats: 4x6 months
Alternative seats: Secondments
Extras: Pro bono – Competition law advice scheme

Of the leading Bristol firms, this one has shown the greatest ambition over the past decade.

This ambitious mid-market firm has a desire to break into the UK top 50. Turnover has almost tripled since 2002 and head count has risen more than three-fold to nearly 700.

No limits

TLT's story is an impressive one. Through the strong leadership of three-times managing partner David Pester, and a series of mergers, the Bristol firm has come from relative obscurity to a position where it is challenging the historical dominance of Burges Salmon and Osborne Clarke. Things really started moving in 2000, when two firms, Trumps and Lawrence Tuckett, came together. Renamed TLT, the merged firm then seized the opportunity to play corporate in the City by acquiring banking and financial services law firm Lawrence Jones in 2005. Still hungry for a new challenge, it then acquired shipping law experts Constant & Constant. By now you'll get what we mean when we say ambitious! At some stage however, the firm will have to start promoting more partners from within its ranks as, compared to the number of lateral partner hires, there have been precious few TLTers who've managed to climb the greasy pole.

Thanks to its excellent financial services litigation and banking departments, and the patronage of major clients like Barclays, Lloyds TSB and Bank of India, TLT has been able to grow certain aspects of its business, even in a rubbish year like 2009. Its bid to reach the top 50 might yet be achievable, despite profits for 2008/09 dipping by around a quarter and revenue falling by 5% to £39m. What you have to bear in mind is that the majority of firms have suffered in the past year. TLT is pursuing its goal by concentrating on clear target markets: over 65% of its revenue comes from financial services, leisure, retail, technology and media and the built environment sectors, and over 35% is from the financial services sector alone.

Full TLT

TLT's core seats are to be found in its banking and financial services litigation, property and corporate divisions. Others crop up in teams like employment, insolvency, general commercial litigation, construction, pensions, planning and social housing. In addition the firm also has one seat in its Bristol family team, which looks after the financial affairs of wealthy divorce clients. There are also seats in its London office (accommodation and travel expenses paid on top) and a possibility of secondments to clients like Somerfield and Orange. The process of allocating seats is said to be a fair and open one, with fourth-seaters getting first pick. Trainees also find their mentors can be a useful source of advice regarding seat selection.

The banking and financial services litigation team is by far the most active and expanding group at present. As well as a staple list of British banks it also has a hefty Indian clientele that includes the Bank of India, Punjab National Bank, State Bank of India and ICICI. Lawyers assist on matters ranging from pure banking recovery litigation and mortgage fraud, to a special focus on professional negligence, particularly among surveyors. For example, they recently dealt with a £7m negligent overvaluation claim against a national firm of surveyors. And, because of their numbers, mortgage fraud claims alone could have kept the team busy this past year, seeking freezing injunctions to recover assets and appointing receivers in insolvency situations. Some claims have been worth in the vicinity of £35m. More complex recoveries and distressed debt situations are also flooding in and, overall, it sounds as if TLT is a place where the big banks have made themselves comfortable for the time being. Most trainees run their own files and this is clearly a seat for those with litigation in both heart and mind. Our sources were fully aware of the advantages of spending time in such a rapidly expanding team. Not only do they "*have a real chance to impress clients*" but the prospects for a job on qualification are good. The only disadvantage is that "*you can expect long hours.*"

Chambers UK rankings

Banking & Finance	Licensing
Banking Litigation	Partnership
Competition/European Law	Pensions
Corporate/M&A	Planning
Debt Recovery	Private Client
Dispute Resolution	Projects, Energy & Natural Resources
Employment	
Family/Matrimonial	Real Estate
Franchising	Real Estate Litigation
Information Technology	Restructuring/Insolvency
Intellectual Property	Social Housing

Corporate Kumbaya

The "*supportive*" property department offers a mix of private and public sector work. Representing names like Somerfield, Aardman Animations, British Waterways Board, the Environment Agency, Imperial Tobacco and Ladbrokes, trainees learn how to run lease renewals or grant various licences over property. The firm assisted Somerfield on the property aspects of its sale to the Co-operative Group for a whopping £1.7bn. Recently, lawyers also beat Stephenson Harwood to the finish line in a bid to advise on the major redevelopment of the UK's largest fresh produce market in Covent Garden. Though by its own admission the department is not what it was before the economy took a dive, the fact that it has public sector clients has helped greatly. For example, it assisted with the disposal of publicly owned properties in the West Midlands, Coventry and Teesside at a total of £10m recently. A rise in renewable energy deals has also helped its cause, and it recently represented Ecotricity on various projects and bids around the UK to build sustainable structures. Trainees get their own files in this department and most were surprised they were still busy, even during the downturn. "*I got a good idea of what goes on in a property department,*" said one, "*and the clients were all easy to deal with.*" Some trainees were also able to sample planning law, becoming heavily involved in enforcement work and S.106 planning-gain deals. Given the high degree of independence in the seat, job satisfaction can run high, particularly towards the end of a large matter that a trainee has seen through from start to finish.

Having increased its turnover by 36% in 2007/08, TLT's corporate department developed an insatiable appetite for more clients and more deals. In addition to its regular financial services clients, the growth in London was reflected by the appearance of new FTSE-listed companies. TLT now represents 34 such companies between its two offices, and it has many well-known names on its books, including Mitsubishi, Orange, 3i, Avon Rubber, the Metropolitan Police, Caterpillar Group, Punch Taverns, Proton Cars, MUJI and Merlin Entertainments Group, which owns Alton Towers, LEGOLAND, Madame Tussauds and the London Eye among other attractions. Bristol corporate lawyers ran the henhouse on the £40m acquisition of one of the largest producers and distributors of eggs in the UK. They also acted for TUI Travel, a new client, on its acquisition of two sports tour operators specialising in cricket, rugby and football. Trainees can get into the thick of things in corporate seats, and several raved about the quality of work and continual feedback. "*The challenges were a lot more complex than anything I'd come across before,*" said one. Corporate also seems to be a very sociable department – the team went on a camping trip to Wales last summer. At this point we should warn the property lawyers that their corporate colleagues are making property team life seem "*dull*" by comparison.

The insolvency team is a popular destination these days. One source liked "*the balance of contentious and non-contentious work. You're not necessarily dealing with primary sources of law all the time – there's more of a commercial basis* [to the work]. *You're coming up with novel situations and ideas, and there's a strong research element to the job.*" One of the team's highlights of 2008 was helping community transport and recycling charity ECT Group sell some major assets to get rid of substantial debts that built up as a result of some poor investments made during the booming economy. For a purely contentious six months, trainees can try commercial litigation, where they encounter "*quite a lot of foreign clients*" as "*there are close relationships with foreign sources of work.*" An ideal juncture to mention that TLT has membership of two international alliances – the European Law Firm network (ELF) and the International Practice Group (IPG).

Ship shape and Bristol fountain

London handles much the same work as Bristol and we heard some positive feedback about the banking seat ("*fantastic, there's good opportunities to network and you get commandeered by different departments*") and the litigation seat, which offers "*a variety of matters, including some debt recoveries worth £10,000-plus that I could run myself.*" One source was clearly impressed by litigation in the capital: "*It gave really good experience and I got involved with some larger cases including a £10m dispute. I saw settlements on some matters and I went along to a mediation, which was cool.*" London also has a shipping practice thanks to the addition of lawyers from Constant & Constant. As yet there is no shipping seat for trainees but that's not to say there won't be. Incidentally the Constant & Constant merger also added an international office in Piraeus in Greece, though again, there's no suggestion that trainees can visit at this stage. Until now London seats have always been filled by Bristol-based trainees, often leading to them missing out on end-of-the-week fun as they travel back home for the weekend. In the future the firm may recruit specifically for London, which should ensure that trainees can swing by for departmental drinks without worrying about catching the last train west.

Speaking of TLT's high-rise Bristol base, one trainee explained: "*It's lovely on the inside and it has a fantastic reception and meeting area. The outside is open to interpretation and my interpretation is that they could do better!*" The office is open-plan and more airy than the one in the capital, where people have become accustomed to working in individual offices. "*It meant the culture in London was a bit closed,*" we heard; "*I always felt one step removed, which was especially frustrating as I know how good it was to listen in to partners there.*" The good news is that the London branch is moving at the end of 2009 and may well go open plan.

The question of what makes an ideal TLT recruit apparently crops up regularly over trainee drinks. The perfect pick is quite likely to have some connection to Bristol or the South West, whether it is through education or family. Many of the people we spoke to had applied to other Bristol outfits like Osborne Clarke, Burges Salmon and Bevan Brittan, but chose TLT for its growing potential. Said one: "*TLT was on the up and it made it feel like you could be part of something that was steadily improving.*" Trainees also highlighted a sense of vibrancy at the firm compared to these other places, telling us: "*There will never be a silent one if you sit us all at a table; we're an energetic bunch!*" The current group ranges in age from 23 to 36, so the firm is obviously not looking for people who have followed a particular path. Above all, trainees appreciate the professional way of life in Bristol which, although not slow, is certainly more measured and arguably more sustainable than the hyperspeed working and long hours of the City. Perhaps this is why one source found that "*the interview at TLT was definitely the most enjoyable and the people were the most enthusiastic.*" Who knows, maybe management is sitting on a secret fountain of youth because trainees say: "*In general you get this feeling of a young firm.*" Whatever the explanation, it was good to hear trainees say: "*I got the sense that TLT was somewhere I could have a career and be happy.*"

Full house!

In truth it could be the reasonable length of the average working day that keeps people perky. "*It's very rare to get home late,*" said one source. "*I like to get out by 6pm.*" The firm has an active social life and softball, netball and cricket are available for those who need to run off any excess energy. On a weekly basis you'll always find people going for a drink at nearby Toto's, which is "*especially lovely during the summer.*" Impromptu trainee nights out are also on the cards, and there's "*usually a good turnout once every month when we go on to various other bars.*" The hard core tend to end up at the Lizard Lounge to "*dance to cheesy music and let their hair down.*" Other key events for trainees include the Junior Lawyers Division ball and an annual dinner hosted by the managing partners, last time at posh Hotel Du Vin. TLT usually has a big summer party for all staff after its AGM, "*but there wasn't one this year due to the recession and the redundancies.*" On this subject we'd say TLT hasn't fared any worse than other Bristol firms: it laid off 15 members of staff earlier in 2009, having previously culled 11 people in May 2008, mainly in its licensed trade team after a regulatory-induced boom in that kind of work subsided. In 2009, all six qualifiers were able to stay on with the firm – an excellent result.

In late summer 2009 news broke that TLT had asked successful training contract applicants to confirm their decision in advance of the SRA-recommended September deadline adhered to by most firms. It gave successful candidates a week to decide instead of the usual four. Some commentators decried this as 'underhand' and said TLT was 'taking advantage of students' desperation.' TLT said it simply wanted to secure the best possible candidates, didn't want to wait, and that candidates who felt they couldn't make their decision within the week could get an extension of the deadline. We doubt the issue will harm the firm.

And finally...

The people at TLT are described as friendly and hard-working and we reckon this sums up the business as a whole. It's a simple but effective recipe for success.

The adventure you're looking for, the guidance you need

It starts the moment you do – work of the highest quality with the support and guidance of some of the best people in the business. At Travers Smith, we are big enough to offer the most exciting opportunities but small enough for each individual to count. Choose a more inspiring path.

Please visit **www.traverssmith.com** or contact Germaine VanGeyzel, Graduate Recruitment Manager: **graduate.recruitment@traverssmith.com** Travers Smith LLP, 10 Snow Hill, London, EC1A 2AL, 020 7295 3000

TRAVERS SMITH

Travers Smith LLP

The facts
Location: London
Number of UK partners/solicitors: 64/154
Total number of trainees: 48
Seats: 4x6 months
Alternative seats: Paris, occasional secondments
Extras: Pro bono – Paddington Law Centre, City Law School Advice Centre, Caribbean death row appeals; language training

> *"What makes us special is we have a combination of features all under one roof: financial success; collegiate; career opportunities; retention; opportunity to work with talented people; big clients."*
> Tom Purton, Training Partner

City institution Travers Smith is in no hurry to change a winning formula that has seen it through more than two centuries.

London stalwart

One of London's oldest law firms, over the years Travers has nurtured a solid reputation for quality and professionalism without compromising on size and culture. This firm is undoubtedly comfortable in its own skin and is known for its independent streak and conservative nature. *"We have a core set of values,"* agree trainees. *"World domination is not the aim. We are not a massively ambitious firm, we just want to consolidate what we have and continue to provide a quality service."* Tom Purton, head of Travers' commercial group and graduate recruitment partner, stated plainly: *"We know what we're good at... when you look at other firms that have lost their way or got into difficulty, it's because they have tried to diversify or expand too quickly and have lost the focus on what it was that made them successful in the first place."*

What has made Travers successful is its corporate practice, so while the firm will never be one of the global behemoths, its deals regularly sport multimillion-pound price tags. Examples include the representation of British oil and gas company Burren Energy through its purchase by Italian energy giant Eni for £1.7bn and international private equity outfit Bridgepoint Capital in its £350m acquisition of everyone's favourite sandwich chain Pret A Manger. Other significant clients include the Bank of Scotland and JPMorgan, as well as companies such as easyGroup, Trainline, SeaFrance, Virgin Media, the AA, American Express and Gourmet Burger Kitchen. Such quality instructions, combined with the more intimate environment provided by the firm, mean that Travers appeals to top students who want to avoid the magic circle. *"I wanted a firm with a good reputation and somewhere that was friendly,"* said one trainee.

At the feet of the masters

Travers now asks all its future trainees to take the LPC at BPP to ensure that when newbies start at the firm there is a level of consistency to what they have already covered. On arrival, trainees are introduced to a four-seat model with compulsory visits to the core corporate department (corporate finance or private equity), either banking or real estate and either employment or litigation. A final wildcard selection gives choice between seats in financial services, corporate recovery, tax, pensions, competition law and commercial (covering general commercial and IP/IT). There are also regular secondments to 3i and RBS. The relatively small intake may make it easier to keep trainees happy with the way seats are allocated; they generally get to experience their first-choice departments. The other important thing to note is that Travers' trainees share a room with a partner and an associate. The system is credited with promoting easy communication between the different levels of seniority and is acknowledged to be a great way for trainees to learn as they see how lawyers work and what they work on at different stages of their careers.

The corporate team accounts for around 40% of the firm's £81m turnover and gains a top ranking for both mid-market and AIM-related work in *Chambers UK*. The economic downturn meant that there were eight redundancies here, but the firm feels that the department is *"in the right shape now."* Trainees love the *"adrenalin-filled atmos-*

phere" with plenty of joshing. As one recalled of their time in the seat: "*When people did need to work hard then we would just get our heads down. There was a good balance.*" Despite the market slowdown Travers completed over 100 transactions in 2008. The well-known private equity practice advised Barclays Private Equity Fund on the sale of luxury shoe retailer Kurt Geiger for around £95m, Bridgepoint in its £360m acquisition of Fat Face, and 3i on the public-to-private takeover of software and services company Civica for around £237m. The team also advised Marwyn Value Investors in connection with its listing on the Specialist Fund Market (SFM), a branch of the LSE. This was the first fund to move from the AIM to the SFM, and only the second to become listed on the SFM. Trainees are able to learn by looking over the shoulder of the masters on these big deals. While there is always a certain amount of grunt work to be done, because the partners are "*constantly aware of what you are doing, you are able to progress quite quickly.*" One trainee was sent to a client board meeting on their own in their second week in the seat. "*It was a huge confidence boost to not feel mollycoddled.*" And trainees regularly negotiate deals with solicitors on the other side who are three or four years qualified.

French speakers can opt to spend their corporate seat in Travers' small Paris office. Trainees are set up in a "*nice big flat*" just a few minutes walk from the Champs Élysées and a few more from work. For those concerned about being out of sight, out of mind, fear not. Trainees who bag a place in Paris spend one month in the London corporate department before they go. Additionally, trainees often work one-on-one with the sole Paris partner, who regularly travels back to the London office.

The banking seat provides a different perspective on similar deals to those in corporate, and trainees spend much of their time "*making sure all the nuts and bolts are sorted out,*" as well as drafting facility and loan agreements. A stint in the real estate department gives trainees the chance to handle some of their own files while assisting on larger deals. "*I really enjoyed juggling lots of different things,*" commented one interviewee. Travers acted for commercial property company Criterion Capital on the construction of a hotel in the Trocadero in Central London, and French company Fimalac Group on the development of its 15-storey headquarters in Canary Wharf.

Fraudsters and footballers

When it comes to the contentious experience all trainees must acquire, there is the option of ditching a full seat for a short course at the College of Law. Most trainees choose to do the full seat, however, either with the employment department or the commercial litigation department. In the latter trainees can get a taste of "*almost any type of corporate litigation you can think of.*" Travers' banking

Chambers UK rankings

Banking & Finance	Fraud: Civil
Banking Litigation	Information Technology
Capital Markets	Investment Funds
Competition/European Law	Media & Entertainment
Corporate/M&A	Outsourcing
Dispute Resolution	Pensions
Employee Share Schemes	Planning
Employment	Private Equity
Environment	Real Estate
Financial Services Regulation	Real Estate Finance
Franchising	Restructuring/Insolvency
	Retail
	Tax

litigation branch is an ascendant force in the sector, defined by its successful defence of Rabobank's $220m counterclaim against NatWest in 2008. But if you like your litigation with a glint of glamour, there are sometimes quite dazzling cases. Take the tale of Carlos Tevez. Travers acted for West Ham during the Argentine player's protracted transfer to Manchester United. One trainee was lucky enough to interview "*a load of West Ham players as well as the West Ham manager.*" Another talked of attending meetings with an investment manager who had allegedly defrauded his clients of around £400m. "*It was all quite bizarre. He kept producing all these documents that he maintained were real, but they looked as though they had been produced on his laptop.*" Much of the employment work our sources had encountered consisted of redundancy and restructuring programmes. Not too surprising given the economy. They also spoke about race and age discrimination cases. Employment clients include TV channel Five, Virgin Active, Royal Automobile Club, AIG Group and construction group Kier.

Equally "*sexy work*" can be found in two seats in the commercial department. Examples include work with Musto, a specialist technical sportswear brand, on a long-term endorsement agreement with the reigning three-day eventing world champion and minor royal Zara Phillips, and advising the Force India Formula One Team on a deal with McLaren Mercedes for the supply of engine parts. While there were no free trips to the Grand Prix, one source talked of meeting a client in his suite at Claridges. But sexiness isn't everything, is it? Three more seats provided our interviewees with a chance to indulge their more cerebral side. Tax, pensions and financial services involve acres of black letter law. Most trainees found they could become "*thoroughly absorbed*" by single points once they got into these fields and "*really enjoy the problem-solving aspect.*" The social side of these smaller departments is less pronounced, we hear. "*There is liter-*

ally no sound because everyone is thinking so hard," joked one source. Certainly the quality of work is very high and among the clients are the likes of HBOS, Barclays and Clarks Shoes.

To the Bishop's Finger!

Work of the calibre to be found at Travers often demands long hours, but trainees insist "*weekends are sacred.*" A number of our sources had stayed in the office as late – or should that be early? – as 4 or 5am but agreed that "*in terms of what I signed up for, it hasn't been that bad.*" After a hard day there is almost always someone to be found at the local pub, The Bishop's Finger ('The BF' to those in the know) just around the corner from the office in West Smithfield near to the ancient Bart's Hospital. "*It's really great that you can work hard with someone and then socialise with them afterwards,*" said one source. And if you're up for more than a couple of pints then there's always the nearest karaoke bar. If you don't have the voice of an angel, stick with the corporate department who are renowned for "*just roaring down the microphone.*" When it comes to formal social events Travers doesn't disappoint. It puts on a fine black-tie Christmas party, with a champagne reception and sit-down dinner, a casino, dancing and a free bar. Summer parties tend to be departmental affairs.

Travers has a reputation for recruiting from a small pool of universities, not least among them Oxford and Cambridge. At the time of writing, half of trainees hailed from these hallowed halls. Training partner Tom Purton insists there is no bias: "*We just take those people who are the best, and those two universities are providing some very good candidates.*" While aware of the stats about trainees' universities of origin, our sources did not have a problem with the situation, instead feeling that the most important attribute of a Travers trainee is their ability to "*engage with others without an arrogance or conceitedness, while having a very strong intellectual footing. There is no room for the Brain of Britain who is no good with clients.*" They tell us that everyone here "*is comfortable enough in their own abil-ity to not have to assert themselves at every opportunity.*" There's a certain brand of confidence you find at Travers. To our minds it comes from the sense of collegiality within the firm. These people have largely similar backgrounds and they understand the rules of interaction. It's a place where people can feel they fit. So long as they do actually fit.

While at trainee level there are now equal numbers of guys and girls, women make up just 12% of the partnership, and only one of the eight female partners can be found in the core corporate department. When pressed on the imbalance, Tom Purton responded: "*More women than men decide to leave as they become more senior assistants,*" citing the most common reason as a desire to become a full-time mother. He did note, however, that over the next five years "*there are quite a few women coming through who I am sure will make it.*" However, of the 17 people promoted to partner over the last three years, just one has been female (the most recent round, in May 2009, saw four men and no women made up). Putting the demographics aside, Travers' NQ retention rate has sat above 80% for the past four years, and in 2009 13 out of 18 qualifiers stayed on.

The overwhelming opinion among our sources was that Travers provides a great training experience, and with around 75% of the current partners having trained here themselves, the firm must be doing something right all the way up the hierarchy. Again, the high number of 'lifers' suggests that Travers is good at recruiting Travers types.

And finally...

Travers has a definite sense of self and works hard to maintain it. If you're lucky enough to fit its mould then you will be taken under its wing with enthusiasm.

Trethowans LLP

The facts

Location: Southampton, Salisbury

Number of UK partners/solicitors: 22/28

Total number of trainees: 7

Seats: 4x6 months

Alternative seats: None

New managing partner Simon Rhodes says the three year plan *"is to be a dominant legal provider in the South. We're going to have to get one or two more offices in order to be a serious threat."*

Having grown up with private clients, the last decade has seen this South of England firm successfully assert itself in the commercial sphere.

It's all bespoke

Trethowans was founded in Salisbury in 1866 by Mr George Nodder and quickly established itself with the wealthy folk of Wiltshire. Almost 150 years later, it has a second office in nearby Southampton (acquired through a small merger in 1996) and now boasts solid commercial capabilities for big-name clients such as Ladbrokes, Nando's, Pizza Hut and Bacardi. Trethowans' turnover has increased by around £1m a year for the past three years, with some 25 lawyers joining since 2003. The firm has plans to expand further and become "*dominant*" in the Southern legal market.

Until a year ago the Salisbury lawyers operated out of the city centre, but a move to a purpose-built, open-plan office on a business park has added to Trethowans' more modern, commercial image. "*The facilities at the Salisbury office are fantastic now,*" trainees agreed. The glass building is laid out over two floors and has a spiral staircase with "*a big skylight at the top so we get loads of natural light.*" Each floor has a communal area with "*a mixture of comfy armchairs and tables to eat around.*" The office has its own parking, and a minibus runs into town once a week so employees can do their banking and shopping. There are no plans yet to move out of the firm's listed Georgian building in Southampton, but it recently had a "*lick of paint*" and a refurb. Its close proximity to the city centre means there are "*a bunch of places nearby where you can pick up sandwiches,*" as well as plenty of bars. Trainees generally feel that "*the Southampton office comes across as slightly more sociable.*"

When it comes to choosing seats trainees have it pretty good: "*The firm tries to find out what you want to do and, as far as possible, tries to match it,*" particularly if you already have a fair idea of where you'd like to qualify. "*I've had my first seat choice every time, and I'm not the only one to have that,*" said a satisfied source. Seats are currently available in corporate/commercial, commercial litigation, commercial and residential property, employment, personal injury and clinical negligence, family, and private client: something for everyone really. Trainees generally tend to take either a private client or a commercial route, with their seats spread across both offices. Given that there's just a 40-minute drive separating the two, this doesn't seem to cause problems.

Serving the people

Trainees in the private law seats rave about the client contact available to them and particularly enjoy the feeling that "*you really are helping someone.*" They also feel there is "*a general progression of responsibility.*" The family team has recently seen a significant growth in income, with an increasing number of instructions coming from individuals with assets worth over £1m. Trainees spend a lot of time "*going to hearings and supporting the client through the whole process,*" which is more often than not a child dispute or a divorce.

The proximity of the specialist Duke of Cornwall Spinal Injuries Unit at Salisbury District Hospital ensures that trainees in the personal injury seat work on head and spinal cases. One such matter, concerning a man who fell off a ladder at work, reached the national press; another involved a sorry chap who was injured while sitting on the toilet when a car careered into his house. Trethowans' eight-strong clinical negligence team ranks in the top band of *Chambers UK's* Southern section. It has lately settled a number of cerebral palsy cases, plus claims involving delayed diagnoses of cancers, and an alleged negligently performed cardiac surgery and cardiology follow-up that caused brain damage.

Some interesting stories crop up in the general private client seat too, which should allay the fears of those who worry it is simply wills and codicils. One case involved the death of a lady with no next of kin. It was left to Trethowans to sort out her house, which looked like "*she had been accumulating stuff for 20 years and hadn't thrown anything away. There were cases of sherry and Tupperware all over the place.*" A bed apparently had jewellery underneath its mattress, but "*there was about four feet of clothing piled on top of it.*" As for the "*something supposedly hidden under the floorboards... we have no idea where it could be.*"

Waugh stories

If that all sounds too personal, don't forget that Trethowans has some tempting commercial opportunities. The commercial property seat involves "*a lot of lease work, and buying and selling commercial premises.*" Agricultural and rural property is important too. The team advises landowners and tenants who collectively farm in excess of 35,000 acres of land in the UK. In the last year lawyers worked on bank funding for the £5.5m purchase of Brympton D'Evercy near Yeovil, which Auberon Waugh once described as the most beautiful house in England. A residential conveyancing seat is usually offered to those with private client interests due to the frequency of crossover cases.

The employment team has recently seen three lawyers arrive from Devon-based Foot Anstey. What we're looking at here is a combination of "*clients wanting day-to-day help, while others have big projects on the go.*" Generally "*there is a lot more responsibility, because the client quickly becomes aware that they can always get in touch with you but not always your supervisor.*" Trainees prepare for hearings at the Employment Appeal Tribunal, where they also gain experience of liaising with barristers. In the corporate seat work comes "*from all the associates and partners in the department.*" This not only ensures a varied caseload but "*means you have to be more independent in getting your own work; it isn't just plonked on your desk.*"

Team Trethowans

Trainees are given an annual social budget to spend as they wish on four separate events. Previous outings have included bowling and the dog track – "*the budget covered pizza, entrance to the races and a few bets.*" Similar departments often get together for drinks, meaning there is some cross-office socialising, but big firm-wide events are rare because getting everyone together is "*quite unwieldy.*" Informal Friday night socialising goes on, but it's on the sports field that Trethowans really gets enthusiastic. Everyone is encouraged to get involved, regardless of talent. The firm sponsors a cricket pitch in the New Forest and hosts games against other law firms and local businesses, usually followed by a barbecue. As well as touch rugby, five-a-side football and netball, there are also things like swimathons and abseiling to raise funds for local charities. The "*enthusiastic, get-involved attitude here*" extends to marketing: as the firm pushes for further growth new trainees quickly become aware of what head of commercial property and former managing partner Miles Brown calls 'Team Trethowans'. "*We are always looking for ways to make the firm that bit more appealing,*" said one interviewee. "*It's important to get the word out there, and everyone is happy to do that.*"

While trainees' voices are valued outside the firm, they also feel they are listened to in the office. When one mentioned that they wanted "*communication lines to be improved*" it was not long before this happened. E-mails inform trainees of changes at the firm and copies of many board-meeting minutes are made available: "*obviously not everything, but definitely enough to give us a good idea of what is going on.*" What can they expect in the short to medium term? Well we have it on good authority that Trethowans will look to enter into mergers once the economy picks up. Thus far the firm has not been badly hit by the downturn and has made only a few staff redundancies.

Chambers UK rankings

Agriculture & Rural Affairs	Employment
Clinical Negligence	Family/Matrimonial
	Licensing
Debt Recovery	Personal Injury
Dispute Resolution	Real Estate

And finally...

Most of Trethowans' trainees have a prior connection to the region in which the firm works, and this helps promote good NQ retention. It held onto the sole 2009 trainee who had qualified by the time we went to press.

trowers & hamlins

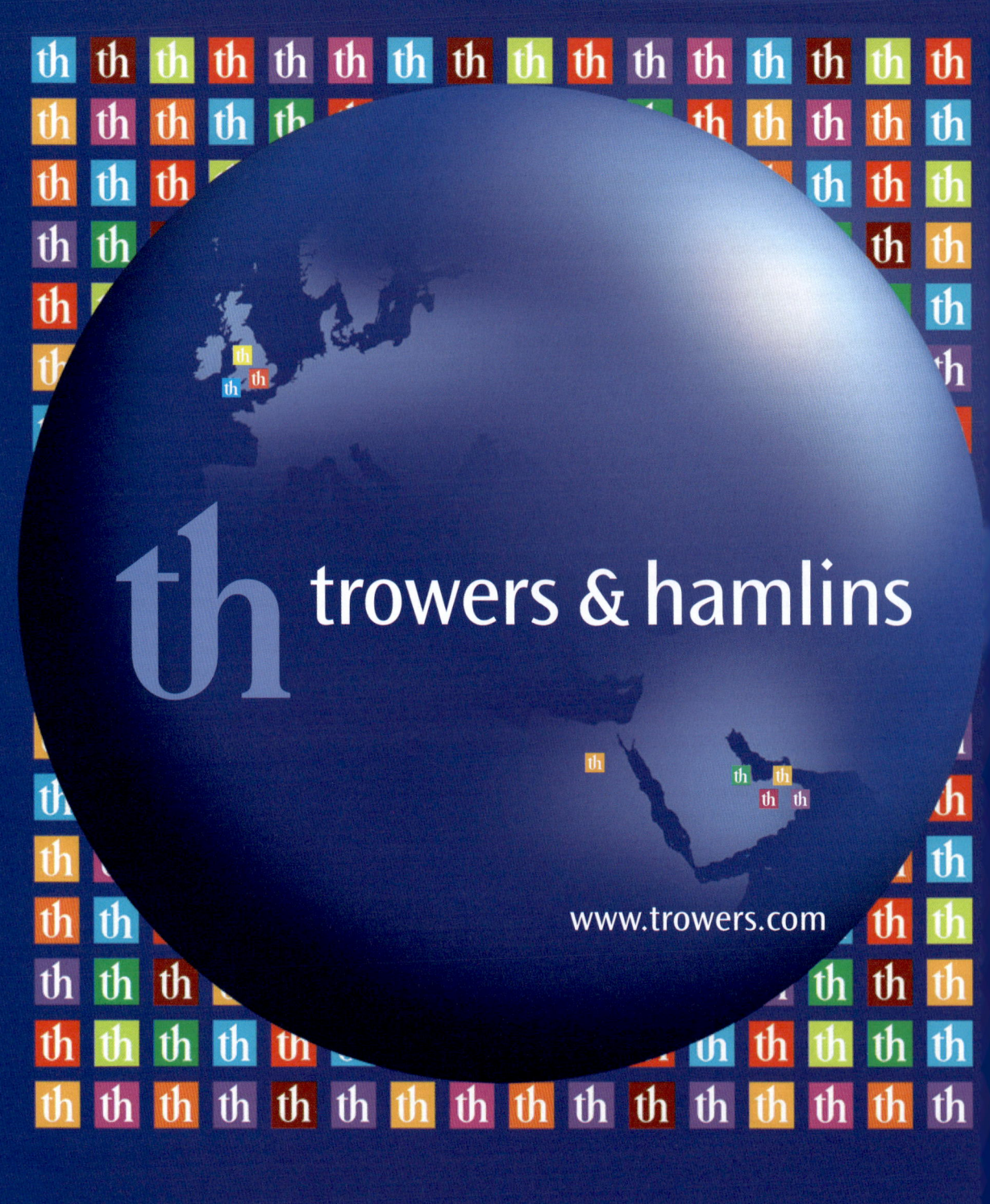

www.trowers.com

For further information about our graduate process please contact the graduate recruitment team on tel +44 (0)20 7423 8312 or hking@trowers.com

Trowers & Hamlins is an equal opportunities employer

INVESTOR IN PEOP[LE]

Trowers & Hamlins LLP

The facts

Location: London, Manchester, Exeter
Number of UK partners/solicitors: 98/154
Total number of trainees: 38
Seats: 4x6 months
Alternative seats: Overseas seats
Extras: Pro bono – ProHelp

Year on year this firm becomes an ever-hotter prospect. Right now its public sector expertise and its long established Middle East interests make it a scorcher.

With its involvement in social housing and Middle East business, graduates can expect an unorthodox ride with this mid-sized, property-heavy firm.

An affordable home is where the heart is

More than 230 years old, Trowers first established itself outside London in 1973 when its Manchester office was opened. Over the last 30 years further expansion has resulted in offices in Exeter, Oman, Dubai, Abu Dhabi, Bahrain, Cairo and Saudi Arabia. We'll talk about the Middle East in detail after an analysis of domestic business.

We wouldn't be on point if we discussed Trowers without reference to its property law capabilities. In fact, so important is the property practice to the firm, a first-year can expect at least one of their seats to be property-related. Astute readers will understand that 2009 has been a terrible year in the property industry, and yet fortunately for Trowers its expertise has less to do with the devastated private real estate market and more to do with deals for clients in the public sphere. Social housing, local government and public sector work generally is massively important for the firm. If these kinds of clients go down, we'll meet you all at the border with our shotguns. Actually, the first formal insolvency of a housing association did take place last year and, surprise surprise, Trowers was there to guide the organisation through the special statutory provisions governing the situation.

One reflective source asserted that "*there are no competitors in social housing and the majority of our clients in the UK seem to be public sector clients.*" While other firms working within the social housing movement might be a bit miffed at that statement, none would deny that Trowers is the out-and-out heavyweight champ. Over the years its top partners have advised government on crucial policy issues, they have written the sector's precedent agreements and leases, and they've pulled together a client list to die for. On Trowers' books are scores of registered social landlords, among them Peabody Trust which has an absolutely vast portfolio of London homes. Numerous London and provincial councils also turn to the firm for advice. It recently assisted Family Mosaic Housing on the regeneration and development of the Stonegrove Estate in Barnet, London. The aim was to demolish and rebuild housing to form a sustainable community. Another good example is the firm's representation of the London Borough of Brent in a project to develop 400 units of new accommodation, including provision for adults with learning disabilities.

ExCeL-ent deals

For anyone who feels strongly about the availability of affordable housing and social assistance for vulnerable people, working for social housing clients can be hugely satisfying. Trainees certainly appreciate the client exposure they get in this practice area: "*Usually the trainee is a point of contact and deals with the correspondence between client and firm.*" Most trainees handle up to 25 files for which they have sole responsibility. These include "*a lot of social landlord matters where you have the standard proofreading, deeds, planning agreements and straightforward conveyancing.*" Knowing how well you're doing is generally easy as "*you get a good mix of on-the-spot feedback and more comprehensive feedback at the end of your seat.*"

On larger development projects, good old-fashioned land law problems often need resolving, and trainees can learn about EU regulations, procurement practices and even charities law. The firm's public sector work extends beyond housing too: take for example Greenwich Council's £20m project for the redevelopment of a former district hospital site and procurement of landmark community and leisure facilities as part of the Heart of East Greenwich scheme. Our sources also spoke with admiration for the allied construction and projects team, where they are inducted into the world of collateral warranties and construction contracts.

Trainees wanting contentious work need look no further than the litigation department. In saying that, the commercial litigation team is probably the hardest to get into given the relative paucity of seats (in London only) and heightened interest recently. Nonetheless, evidence suggests the litigation group is picking up speed and becoming a more important part of the business, though at this stage there is little to suggest that it will move beyond London. In litigation, "*the continuous hours on some nights can be stressful.*" While not customary, one trainee found themselves in the office on a Saturday. As you might expect, there's an abundance of property-related litigation at the firm.

Unlike so many firms in the City, the corporate department is not the be all and end all here. Trowers is ranked well in *Chambers UK's* lower mid-market table for corporate and stands out for the deals that flow in from its overseas offices. For example, when Abu Dhabi National Exhibitions Company made a cash offer to the owner of the G20's chosen venue, ExCeL London, Trowers was brought in to work on the deal. If you've a flea-ridden cat or dog, you might be interested to know that the firm advised Bob Martin (UK) on the acquisition of the pet and animal healthcare business of Seven Seas.

Lawyers of Arabia

Trowers has five offices in the Middle East (Abu Dhabi, Dubai, Muscat, Bahrain and Cairo, remember?). It also has associations with Saudi Arabian law firm Feras Al Shawaf in Riyadh and Syrian firm Sultans Law, and given the growing level of investment in Libya, it is hinting at a venture in the Tripoli market too. Trainee secondments are presently offered to the UAE, Bahrain and Oman offices only. "*Everyone who shows interest in going will get to go,*" said one trainee, though some may be seconded to Manchester or Exeter, meaning that if you're desperate to avoid either of the two smaller UK locations, you may want to "*press very hard for a Middle East secondment early in the process.*"

Overseas seats place trainees in "*a much smaller environment where you know everyone else and feel more relaxed as a result of that.*" Those who go to Abu Dhabi value the amount of client exposure that is possible on smaller files, and they also assist on larger pieces of work. Trowers acted as the UAE and Fujairah law advisers to JBIC and others in relation to the $2.5bn financing of a combined cycle gas-fired power generation and seawater desalination plant in Fujairah, which is one of the seven emirates that make up the UAE. In Dubai, trainees can work with the construction team and the finance and projects team, often being roped in by the corporate team as well. The office takes up two floors of a building just a stone's throw away from the Burj Dubai Shopping Mall, where you can invest in some serious bling at the gold souk. The Muscat office drew praise for feeling "*more spacious than London,*" and here trainees experience a variety of corporate files. Although there is less of a connection with other expatriates in Oman, it's easy to take advantage of the scuba diving, hiking and horse riding opportunities close by. While abroad, trainees learn that parties and socials are usually restricted to hotels, given the region's views on the consumption of alcohol, but those we interviewed fully accepted the cultural differences from the UK. Apparently Le Royal Méridien, with its great views of the Arabian Gulf, is their favourite watering hole in Abu Dhabi. The firm normally provides generous benefits to those in the Middle East, including a car, an apartment, an allowance and flights worth up to £600.

Trowers has the kind of reputation in the Middle East that only comes from decades-long involvement in the region; it truly is a top law firm there, and some of the firm's most valuable work emanates from these hard-working offices. The inevitable extra responsibility experienced by trainees in these smaller offices can be a huge confidence boost, and returning to London allows them to appreciate the ways in which the Middle East business benefits lawyers in the UK. "*The largest amount of integration is in corporate,*" as evidenced by the ExCeL deal. At times, however, "*the other teams tend to feel a little disconnected from the other offices,*" and this comment also applies to Manchester and Exeter to an extent. We did hear mutterings that the video links to London meetings and training seminars didn't allow people to feel adequately included.

Chambers UK rankings

Administrative & Public Law	Employment
Agriculture & Rural Affairs	Healthcare
Banking & Finance	Local Government
Charities	Projects, Energy & Natural Resources
Construction	Public Procurement
Corporate/M&A	Real Estate
	Real Estate Litigation
Education	Social Housing

On the flipside, in the smaller UK offices trainees tend to be "*treated like a fee earner with lots of responsibility; you gain insight into the life of a real lawyer.*"

Some sources expressed frustration at the seat allocation process, claiming "*people don't often get their first choices of department or secondment.*" At the same time, another made the point that "*many people don't know what they want after law school and are pleasantly surprised when they start work.*" It suggests that Trowers' practices can engage even those trainees with minimal prior experience of or interest in its core work.

Showers for Trowers, but not a downpour

In 2008 the firm made seven redundancies in the Middle East and a couple of handfuls across its UK offices. Our sources did not seem overly worried by this, generally feeling confident that Trowers' vast public sector and Middle Eastern clientele would see it through the downturn. They were for the most part also happy with the transparency with which the partners were dealing with difficult decisions. "*They're doing the best in the circumstances,*" opined one. Another pointed out that "*a partner made it a point to come and see us individually to ask if there were any concerns. That was thoughtful of them.*" In any event, the firm's finances don't suggest any cause for concern: profitability levels are rather impressive for a firm of Trowers' size. Total revenue was £89.5m in 2008/09, a 15% rise on the previous year, while profits per equity partner only dipped slightly to £509,000.

Commonly quite a few of Trowers' new recruits are well travelled, and their ages range from early twenties right into the thirties. Among the current group we heard about people who've worked for NGOs, charities and a publishing house. "*It's clear from the group we have,*" one source concluded, "*that they think a lot about people before they hire... they don't order in bulk.*" The work ethos is demanding but not excessive, trainees say. "*Everybody works bloody hard but not quite as under the cosh in the same way as other firms. People are genuinely accessible here and you can get help when you need.*" In part it's the firm's size that breeds this level of intimacy, but one can't help wondering if the significant numbers of lawyers dedicated to social housing provision in the UK also impacts on Trowers' culture. A good example of the firm's attitude is its involvement with the organisation East Potential, which assists young people in East London and Essex. Trowers has welcomed several of them into its London HQ for work experience and some 17 people have secured proper jobs with the firm as a result. In 2006 it introduced a trainee legal secretarial programme, which provides 12 months of training and experience for participants. The other offices all pursue green and/or charitable initiatives to some degree or another. All our trainee sources indicated a desire to stay with the firm on qualification and in 2009 a very healthy 17 out of 21 were able to do so.

Social activities among trainees have included tenpin bowling, paintball and a mammoth *Guitar Hero* session. One trainee revealed that the Exeter office hosted a conker competition with a hotly contested prize up for grabs. Christmas is usually celebrated on a smaller scale by individual teams, rather than the whole firm en masse, although there is a summer ball, held last time at the elegant Dorchester Hotel in London. "*The girls made more of an effort when it came to their dresses, whereas the guys just turned up in their work suits.*" For shame. We're in no doubt that a good time was had by all, and yet we sense that this is not a full-time party-hard firm. "*Somebody who likes drinking every night won't enjoy it here very much,*" warns one source. In London, the office canteen is ripe with social opportunities and offers free breakfasts before 8.30am (dangling carrot anyone?) and free dinners between 8pm and 9pm, just like the biggest City firms. The canteen itself didn't draw wide praise for its aesthetics or underground location, with one trainee even going so far as to christen it The Dungeon. Its subsidised potato and pasta-based dishes are a staple for the typical trainee.

And finally...

If you're an Arabic speaker, Trowers is going to be of particular interest. Indeed, any graduate with a hankering for travel to the Middle East or keen to work in social housing should find this approachable firm a very good fit.

Veale Wasbrough

The facts

Location: Bristol
Number of UK partners/solicitors: 31/73
Total number of trainees: 15
Seats: 4x6 months
Alternative seats: None
Extras: Pro bono – BRAVE Enterprise Agency

Specialist work in areas such as education and charities help make this amiable firm popular with staff and clients.

Revered most for its strengths in the education sector, Bristolian Veale Wasbrough is an attractive option for someone looking for commercial training in the South West.

The Veale deal

At the time of our interviews VW already had more than 250 staff and a turnover in the region of £17m per year, but one source told us: "*I was searching for a firm that was looking to expand, even in times of challenge.*" Within weeks of our calls it emerged that VW was in merger negotiations with an ancient firm in the heart of Legal London called Vizards Tweedie. We won't jump the gun and say too much about VT, even though it has a fabulous history and once employed Charles Dickens as a clerk. Of more relevance to VW's management is the fact that Vizards can give it a useful foothold in the capital and add experience and new clients in the public, charities and real estate sectors. Having recently elected insolvency specialist Simon Heald as managing partner, this is a new era for VW following a solid decade during which turnover doubled. As well as looking at breaking into London, it has recently brought in new partners for its education and charities practices in Bristol. "*The firm is filled with ambition,*" announced one trainee, "*and judged against its competitors it stands up well.*"

By choosing VW, trainees opt for a firm with a mixed public/private sector clientele. Most notably it targets clients in education, charities, healthcare and government. It has all the usual commercial practices – corporate, real estate, employment, dispute resolution – and stands out for its expertise in projects, construction, education issues, charities law and personal injury. There are no compulsory seats for trainees, although most spend time with at least one of the education teams.

Education doesn't stop after graduation. All students proceed to the University of Life, but for VW trainees it continues in a more tangible way through the firm's *Chambers UK*-topping education work. "*I like the relationship you can build up with clients,*" said one source. "*You get to deal with intelligent and thoughtful people.*" Independent schools remain central to the practice group (over 700 are on its books) and there are three different teams, so a trainee can sample education/pastoral, education/employment or education/charities. The pastoral team focuses on relationships between institutions and parents, often looking at topical subjects such as the refunding of fees following swine flu closures. One source "*enjoyed it as you just never knew what was going to happen, and we got quoted in the press quite often.*"

Trainees relish the challenges of the education/employment seat, even helping out with marketing initiatives. One had looked at "*a lot of teachers' contracts, lots of compromise agreements and some discrimination. I also did immigration work.*" The third team deals with the charities aspect of the education sector. "*Independent schools are regulated by the Charities Commission and are also companies, so you do both corporate work and charity law. You really get insight into the area.*" VW takes on some international matters, for example assisting the government of Moldova on the establishment of a national children's social care services inspectorate, as part of a wider plan to establish a national child protection system.

Fees simple

The property department has a core of public sector clients and 12 central government agencies on its books. It represents lenders like HSBC, Clydesdale and Allied Irish Banks and has a hefty caseload from healthcare and education clients. Given the size of the department, *"you are likely to run into a property seat."* In the construction team, eco-friendly types will be pleased that VW advised the Environment Agency on the construction of its new HQ, a building that aims to be self-sustaining. It also advised Airbus UK on the £85m building and engineering contract for a factory for its A350. *"Construction,"* say trainees, *"is renowned for being a great team."* The impressive projects practice handles major schemes such as the MoD's £690m PFI build of a new communications centre and accommodation for 2,200 military and civilian staff in Wiltshire. Taking a supporting role, trainees must be organised. Said one: *"I enjoyed the complexity of it. The contract had lots of schedules and I did a lot of post-completion work."* The projects team also deals with major oil industry players like Esso and Total.

Commercial litigation is *"one of the busiest parts of the firm at the moment,"* and as other practices have slowed lawyers have transferred over. VW is one of 40 firms on the Treasury Solicitor's Lit-Cat panel, allowing it to represent government departments and bodies. The debt recovery team has flourished. Most recently, it has been retained by major public schools to induce payments from slack parents. By contrast, of their corporate seat one trainee said regretfully: *"It's a pity we weren't too busy."* They had at least gained some experience of sales and acquisitions and drafting shareholder agreements.

The substantial PI department focuses mainly on claimants. Branded as 'Augustines', it is presented to clients as a separate business; *"we even answer the phone differently and have different stationery."* Over £8m of damages was recovered for clients during 2008, often as a result of instructions via the National Accident Helpline and Injury Lawyers 4U. Augustines additionally acts for defendants such as the Royal College of Nursing. Trainees are exposed to everything from unfortunate accidents caused by aggressive farm animals to latex allergies. Working on their own files is a welcome challenge: *"To have that level of responsibility straight after university is character building."*

The nature of VW clientele has kept it relatively stable during the economic maelstrom, yet management still had to cut 17 staff. *"We were told from the start about the restructuring,"* explained one trainee; *"there were moves from real estate and conveyancing to commercial and property litigation. The projects team also offered to work part-time."* Most trainees approved of the way the firm handled layoffs and cutbacks, though they were disappointed that only three of the five 2009 qualifiers got jobs. Said one: *There's been a definite change in atmosphere. The focus was on people before but now it is on numbers and costs."*

Chambers UK rankings

Banking & Finance	Employment
Charities	Information Technology
Construction	Partnership
Corporate/M&A	Private Client
Debt Recovery	Real Estate
Dispute Resolution	Real Estate Litigation
Education	Restructuring/Insolvency

Bath time

Not every trainee comes from the South West, but they all have an obvious affection for Bristol and are exceptionally loyal to their firm, which they say is *"generally known as the friendliest in Bristol."* So who is VW looking to recruit? *"Someone who is a hard worker and can talk to clients;" "they like proactive people who can work in a team and show independent thought."* All newbies can nominate someone to be their mentor, and there's no need to rush the process. *"I haven't chosen one yet,"* a second-year announced, *"but I've always had someone I can talk to."* And this is one of VW's best qualities – people look out for each other. For example, *"there's a good community of people who drive each other to work from Wales every day."*

As the office is spitting distance from the bars and eateries of Bristol's Waterfront there's plenty going on socially. The open spaces of The Downs are ideal for playing cricket and softball against clients and other professionals, and trainees lunch together and are heavily involved in Junior Lawyers Division events. A generous social budget has led to days out to the Tamworth Snow Dome and Bath's Roman sites, and each year there's a summer barbecue and Christmas ball, last time at Bath's elegant pump rooms. We like stories about partners paying for drinks, and VW trainees didn't disappoint. *"Whenever we've had something to celebrate the partners have kept their cards behind the bar until the very last person has left."*

And finally...

Decent hours, decent colleagues and interesting areas of work. What's not to like about Veale Wasbrough? Keep your eyes peeled for merger news.

Vinson & Elkins LLP

The facts
Location: London
Number of UK partners/solicitors: 5/15 + 6 US-qualified
Total number of trainees: 6
Seats: No formalised rotation
Alternative seats: Overseas secondments
Extras: Pro Bono – LawWorks; language classes

Partner Alex Msimang says: *"There's been a lot of navel-gazing over the last couple of years, and everyone realises we're still underweight outside the USA."* Expect to see some 'Easternisation' as V&E grows its operations.

Vinson & Elkins is big on energy in more ways than one. Don't let the Texan drawl fool you: there's nothing languid about this Southern gentleman.

Energetic

On a reconnaissance mission, standing in a reception area with bright sunshine streaming in through the windows and cacti nestled in adobe-coloured pots, we could have been in V&E's Texan birthplace. Up on the 33rd floor of the CityPoint tower, that wasn't Houston spread out below us but the City of London. Founded in 1917, V&E made its name in the emerging oil industry. More than 90 years and 13 worldwide offices later, V&E is now synonymous with the energy sector. Opened in 1971, V&E London has a hand in massive deals from Africa to Russia. Lawyers steered HgCapital's acquisition of a majority interest in the €275m Havsnäs onshore wind farm – Sweden's largest – and Aguaytia Energy sought representation from the international dispute resolution group in a major arbitration against the government of Peru. In the $650m financing of an Indian oil terminal, V&E acted for an international group of banks. *"Not everything boils down to energy,"* and there are instructions where the energy aspect is *"a very small component of the deal from a legal perspective."* It is perhaps more important to understand that everything has a strong international element. Said one source: *"I can't remember the last time I've worked on anything purely local."*

V&E's focus on energy clients has protected it to an extent. *"We don't seem to be suffering massively by what's going on in the markets,"* said a confident trainee, and partner Alex Msimang confirmed that V&E's core clientele has been *"less affected by the lack of liquidity in the credit market."* Transactions continue to roll in as larger corporates buy up smaller companies' assets, and litigation gets busy when oil prices fluctuate. Indeed, several sources speculated that V&E's contentious practice is a target for growth. London is expected to be at the centre of any plans for (albeit cautious) expansion. *"There's been a lot of navel-gazing over the last couple of years,"* explained Msimang, *"and everyone realises we're still underweight outside the USA."* Expect to see some 'Easternisation' as V&E grows its operations.

Non-rotation vocation

V&E's training comprises four six-month stints with partners or senior associates. Although cycling through the different departments and groups gives a sense of shape to the contract, these aren't seats as such. Recruits can indicate where they would prefer to sit, and while they get plenty of work from their supervisor, they're simultaneously staffed on matters from more than one field. Although encouraged to seek out work that interests them, careful monitoring means trainees aren't left twiddling their thumbs. The arrangement is popular. *"Maybe in a six-month seat you'd get a more dedicated approach,"* however *"you're able to work with more people and get wider exposure."* It's a win-win situation. *"You can follow a deal all the way through, and if you don't like a certain area, you don't have to stick with it for six months."* Partners take *"a realistic and practical approach to workloads"* and *"it's easy to approach people if you're swamped."*

With relatively few lawyers in the office, a trainee's share of responsibility can be exceptional. Indeed, *"it can sometimes be difficult to have the time to learn the fundamentals as you're thrust in at a higher level."* Trainees find themselves "*very quickly mocking up first drafts of contracts,*" say on a big wind farm or other projects from the renewables sector. "*It's nice to know we have some sensitivity to environmental issues and aren't just a mean American oil firm!*" In fact, in most departments there are drafting opportunities for trainees. Corporate deals also demand "*a lot of due diligence,*" but "*working in a pair with someone, you get a much better understanding of every single part of the deal.*"

V&E is "*careful*" to ensure trainees gain the mandatory amount of contentious experience, even if it's not in one six-month block. One source said in praise of a litigation supervisor: "*He keeps a very close eye on us and seeks us out – we don't have to go to him.*" Although measures might be taken to give a trainee a primary focus on litigation if they've not done any by their third seat, it is rarely an afterthought. Litigation assignments tend to come with "*a lot of client contact.*"

Snow drifts and sand dunes

With places available every six months, trainees can spend time abroad. "*There's no science to it,*" one told us; "*you just express interest and if they can accommodate you, they will.*" Currently Moscow and Dubai are available, with Hong Kong and Tokyo on the cards. Indeed, one of this year's qualifying trainees was given a job in the Hong Kong office. Moscow primarily focuses on energy and M&A and trainees are expected to be proactive, so you need to "*think on your feet.*" "*It's interesting seeing how business is done in Russia,*" said one. "*They're hard people to negotiate with sometimes, and everyone smokes in meetings.*" Russian lessons make things easier and there's a salary top-up and a centrally located flat available. Apparently it's "*romantic to see Moscow in the snow.*" Dubai seats offer similar responsibility and independence. The office targets energy work, M&A, construction and Islamic finance. The Sunday-to-Thursday working week "*takes getting used to*" but makes for quiet Sundays when Western offices are off-duty. Trainees may also experience foreign business trips if they're needed or partners feel they'd benefit.

V&E are family

While "*very conscious of being part of the bigger firm*" and positive about the US-produced training DVDs, international teleconferences and beefy salaries, trainees feel the firm is "*not as much American as it is English in London.*" They say it lacks an "*eat-what-you-kill*" culture and that the enduring myth of unending hours is unrepresentative. "*When it's busy they expect you to be available, if not, it's no big deal if you go for a longer lunch break or whatever.*" Some cultural debt is owed to the Land of the Free though. "*I think there's a difference between American and Texan,*" posited one source. There are "*people

Chambers UK rankings

Projects, Energy & Natural Resources

throwing in y'alls and goddamns,*" but one trainee saw a more genteel side to visiting US partners: "*They always assume I'm 'Mrs'– it makes me feel older but it's very respectful.*" V&E has real "*lone-star pride*" and celebrates Texas Independence Day at the Texas Embassy Cantina with tequila and plenty of cowboy boots on show. Other socials include a christmas party at Claridge's and ski trip to Courmayeur in 2009.

A more easygoing Southwest culture at the firm allows "*a clear means of communication between partners and trainees.*" New joiners are assigned an associate mentor who will take them for lunches and act as "*a really good sounding board.*" In general, the quality of feedback from lawyers is high, even outside the biannual appraisals. "*At this stage I'm far less interested in compliments – although it's nice to get them – and more interested in areas to improve,*" reasoned one recruit. Another possible reason behind the firm's openness with trainees is its plan to solidify and expand what is still a small-scale training contract. "*They're laying the foundations to take on more trainees and not have it be completely disastrous.*"

Sources rejected "*the myth that US firms only like Oxbridge graduates,*" believing that personality counts more. "*From your CV they can see the kind of grades you can get and your background, but they want to know if you're a genuine, easygoing person who'd fit with how we work.*" Part of this is "*not panicking when asked to do something you've no clue about,*" but it's also about being able to "*have a beer with someone and have more than law to talk about.*" Often this means experience in another career or a demonstrable interest in areas relevant to V&E's business. Said one source: "*If I had a friend applying I'd urge them to do the vac scheme and really take the bull by the horns.*" The firm puts a lot of weight on its vac scheme, so this is good advice.

And finally...

An informal qualification process has worked well thus far. Both 2008 qualifiers stayed, but in 2009 the expanded intake and economic downturn meant that only two of four were retained.

- **It's never too late:** Good news for mature applicants. They are more than welcome in most firms: plenty of our interviewees didn't commence their training contracts until they were in their thirties and in 2009 a Bird & Bird trainee qualified at the age of 50.

   More mature applicants need to approach applications slightly differently. For them it is all about showing a recruiter the value in their previous career experiences.

top tip no. 27

Walker Morris

The facts

Location: Leeds
Number of UK partners/solicitors: 51/120
Total number of trainees: 27
Seats: 6x4 months
Alternative seats: Secondments

"We are the only independent name in Leeds. That independence is so important. There's so much freedom to develop the practice, it's very un-bureaucratic."
Neil Lupton, Training Partner

You have a passion for all things Leeds and want to build your career in the land of the Chippendale (chair that is, not dancer). Enter stage left Walker Morris, a commercial success story that's bursting with regional pride.

The proof is in the (Yorkshire) pudding

Walker Morris is the only independent firm among the Big Six in Leeds, the others being regional offices of sprawling national players. Trainees could barely contain their enthusiasm for Walker Morris' Leeds-only strategy, saying: *"It's so crucial to be one-site; there's so much interdepartmental work"* and *"everybody knows your name, from the concierge to the senior partners."* At Walker Morris, *"you do feel like you're part of the team,"* and the philosophy of the *"tight unit"* that is the partnership trickles down through the ranks.

The firm has flourished in the face of competition from the nationals, not only retaining but also continuing to win big-name clients. In 2008 it announced several welcome additions to its client roster, from financial powerhouses Alliance & Leicester, RBS and Sweden's Handelsbanken, to rather more sumptuous brands like Diptyque (parfumeur Parisien depuis 1961) and Godiva Chocolate. Trainees suggested the firm *"punches way above its weight,"* believing the reason for this is clear – *"everyone works bloody hard!"* As a reward, the partners earn extremely well and the firm has an aura of solidity.

The varied opportunities at Walker Morris made the firm a *"no-brainer"* for our sources. Practically every commercial area of practice is offered here, from debt recovery and construction law to employment and tax. What's more, there isn't really an area in which the firm doesn't impress: it's one of those successful all-rounders.

High-street humbug

The six-seat system is a key asset as it broadens trainees' legal horizons during their first year and then gives them the opportunity in the second to knuckle down in an area they wish to pursue long-term. Second-years were adamant that the lack of early choice was *"a good thing,"* as it kept them open-minded. One interviewee professed to having *"hated litigation with a passion"* at law school only to subsequently find that *"it was wonderful in practice."* Another interesting aspect of the seat system is the commendably democratic process of divvying out the slots. Second-years are encouraged to sort things out among themselves, and a higher power will only step in following a stalemate.

The firm has historically singled out corporate, litigation and property as its three core areas of practice. To this end, trainees are generally expected to take a seat in each. The commercial property department remains core: in the past year, Walker Morris has acted for luxury clothing chain LK Bennett in the acquisition of 15 properties, including a flagship store on London's Regent Street. Starbucks, another key high street client, instructed the firm on 20 acquisitions and ten concessions in 2008. Illustrating the variety within the department's clientele, lawyers have been acting for Liverpool City Council in relation to the Reds' lease of its Stanley Park Stadium. Trainees can expect responsibility, client contact and exposure to *"lots of smaller files you could take on and do on your own."* Trainees acknowledged that *"learning-wise it's a great seat*" as it introduces many of the procedural aspects of "*how to be a solicitor*" while allowing newbies a chance to "*see something through from beginning to end.*" The "*incredibly busy*" property litigation team has lately represented Caterpillar, HBOS, Barratt Homes and Debenhams. A case that amused us was the successful representation of Manchester's Trafford Centre following the Ebenezer Scrooge-inspired action taken by Boots the chemist, which declined to contribute to the cost of Christmas decorations.

Chambers UK rankings

Banking & Finance	Local Government
Banking Litigation	Pensions
Construction	Planning
Corporate/M&A	Real Estate
Debt Recovery	Real Estate Litigation
Dispute Resolution	Restructuring/Insolvency
Employment	Retail
Environment	Sports Law
Intellectual Property	Tax
Licensing	

Say hello, wave goodbye

Commercial dispute resolution assignments perhaps suffer a little from the nature of litigation itself when it comes to first-seaters. "*Looking back, I was really quite useless,*" one candid trainee told us; "*you're only able to do time-consuming menial tasks and everything is checked.*" With some experience behind you, though, CDR can involve handling your own smaller files ("*disputes below £15,000*"). Our sources had touched on debt recovery, medical negligence and construction disputes, and the current economy has provided stacks of bank litigation. Trainees told us: "*Every case is so different to the next,*" and praised the significant levels of court attendance in this seat.

An IP seat, though difficult to get, can provide some of the best exposure to high-profile cases. This department has an international feel to the caseload, with the firm keen to promote recent notable wins. A High Court victory regarding the Hotel Cipriani trade mark attracted media interest, with the partner travelling to Venice and the trainee "*just missing out on getting to go too.*" The firm scored a major victory in a trade mark infringement case on behalf of Chinese electronics manufacturer aigo (sponsor of Lewis Hamilton). The first time a Chinese manufacturer has won such a case in the UK, this matter is illustrative of a growing relationship with the most populous country on Earth. Through the employment of Chinese lawyers, the creation of a China Trade practice group and even a version of the firm's website in Mandarin, Walker Morris is carving a name for itself in this complex but lucrative market. The IP team found themselves working with Hong Kong lawyers on behalf of Jemella (owner of the frizz-busting ghd hair straighteners) against a major counterfeiter. Goods were seized and then dutifully snapped in half by the trainee assigned to the case.

Soccer stories

On the transactional side, in a quieter corporate department, interviewees found their seats involved the "*twiddling of thumbs from time to time,*" significant dealings with Companies House at others and plenty of document bibling, which is "*every trainee's nightmare but you've got to do it.*" Each of those who had sat in corporate regretted that their time was so affected by wider economic conditions, but they said that when deals had materialised they got to "*deal with all the big guys at the really big banks.*" In 2008 corporate deals included advising HBOS on acquisition and development funding for Development Securities plc worth £65m and advising a syndicate of banks on the refinancing of a major portfolio of shopping centres (aggregate value of £450m). In the finance seat, credit crunch-related work has meant late nights. A source told us of a particular experience quite at odds with Boots' miserly attitude (above). "*I was working until 1am for a few nights before Christmas. It was tough but good at the same time as we were working urgently to refinance a plc, and if we hadn't done it, thousands of people could have lost their jobs.*" If you find yourself in a tight spot, it sounds like this is a firm you'd want on your side.

This port in a storm reputation and the current economy has led to the insolvency department going into overdrive. The team has long been ranked by *Chambers UK* in the top band for restructuring and insolvency in Yorkshire. Historically, the firm has enjoyed celebrated status in the niche area of football administrations, with the infamous Leeds United spectacle of a few years back giving way to work with Luton Town FC, Bournemouth AFC and Rotherham United. The firm is now able to capitalise on strong relationships with major banking clients to exploit opportunities within a down economy. The team has two insolvency subgroups, broadly commercial insolvency and insolvency litigation. Second-year trainees had zeroed in on these, expressing excitement that "*everything you see on the news affects what you do in the office that day.*" Trainees presently focus on high street administration sales, and budding Alex Fergusons get the chance to juggle players' contracts and transfers on behalf of club administrators. You may even find yourself on *Sky Sports News*! Recognising that in this department you can expect "*very, very late nights,*" trainees nonetheless said: "*Once you get going, the late nights are not so bad. They are such a great bunch and so the team spirit buoys you along.*"

I predict a riot

According to our sources, Walker Morris is well known by the people of Leeds and inextricably connected to the city itself. A Yorkshire-bred trainee summed up the Leeds psyche better than we ever could – "*It means to be very proud of anything from Leeds. An example: everyone loves the Kaiser Chiefs, whether they're into that kind of music or not.*" The city retains a high proportion of its university students (over half of the 20 due to qualify in 2009 were undergraduates at Leeds or Leeds Metropolitan universities), and several of our sources were unabashed about saying: "*I didn't want to go to London, but I wanted to work for a firm with similar quality of work.*" It is this Leeds factor, alongside the big-name clients, a turnover of £44.2m in 2009, and an impressively broad commercial practice that ensure the firm is "*a good retreat for those who want to be successful without selling themselves to a London firm.*"

While the office building may be looking a little "*dated*" following a Leeds property boom, the location "*slap bang in the city centre*" can't be bested. In typically straight-talking Yorkshire fashion, one interviewee pointedly quipped: "*No, we haven't bought an enormous building that we paid so much for that now we're making our staff redundant.*" Of course, in tough times social budgets have been scaled down and, as trainees quite rightly pointed out, "*many of our clients are banks, so we have to be sensitive.*" Still, these people are a sociable bunch and the phrase "*work hard, play hard*" did come up rather a lot. Being centrally located, staff have their pick of Leeds' night spots, with Bar Work the place "*for a quick one,*" and Indie Joze or Restaurant Bar & Grill (or RBG for those in the know) also favourites. Trainees sadly informed us that "*lots of places are going bust,*" in particular girly favourite Room, previously frequented for cocktails. The vac scheme social is a big event: last time it involved a pool competition at the Elbow Rooms with nibbles and drinks laid on thick. After an event such as this there are "*always stories to tell,*" but the fact it takes place on a Wednesday can prove tough. "*You can style it out on a Friday, but it's less easy to do that on a Thursday!*" At other times of the year, social events are either firm-wide or organised by department – perhaps dog racing in Manchester, a dreaded karaoke gig or sushi making at Harvey Nichols. Wine and cheese tasting nights proved educational for one trainee in particular. They told us: "*My knowledge of wine was divided into red or white!*" We shouldn't dwell on the boozy side of things too much though; "*a few of us don't drink, so they are careful about arranging things everybody will enjoy.*"

One thing certainly enjoyed by all is the office band. We know, we know, firm bands are not uncommon, but, as one trainee told us: "*They're really very cool!*" Composed of the firm's "*big partners,*" the unimaginatively titled Walker Morris Band can play many a tune, from "*current indie rock music*" to "*a more swing kind of thing.*" Check out the firm's website for a photograph of the musos posing at Leeds Idol, an event that raised £25,000 for Mencap in 2008. Imposing 6ft 6in training partner Neil Lupton is on lead guitar. A trainee enthused: "*Seeing people who are very serious about work really let it go in their band just goes to show how approachable they are.*" Said another of partners: "*However senior they are, they always know how to chill out after work.*"

And finally...

This stable, hard-working and successful law firm seeks bright people with the confidence and determination to push themselves during the training contract. In 2009, 14 of the 20 qualifers took NQ jobs at the firm.

Ward Hadaway

The facts

Location: Newcastle, Leeds

Number of UK partners/solicitors: 59/79

Total number of trainees: 20

Seats: 4x6 months

Alternative seats: None

"The North East and Yorkshire are our prime hunting grounds" but Ward Hadaway picks up plenty of national public sector work.

Despite a tough year, this firm exudes confidence. Not content with dominating the North East market, Ward Hadaway is looking to broaden its geographic horizons while maintaining a top-notch service.

Top of the Tyne

In previous years we've painted Ward Hadaway as the new kid on the Newcastle block: young, energetic and ambitious, experiencing growth spurt after impressive growth spurt and keen to make noise. Born in 1988 after the fortuitous meeting of Hadaway & Hadaway and Septimus G. Ward & Rose, Ward Hadaway is no longer a boisterous teen; it has settled into its twenties and no longer needs to prove itself at every turn. And why should it? With a plethora of *Chambers UK* rankings, enough partners poached from local rival Eversheds to fill a small bus, and a brand new office in Leeds, it has slotted comfortably into the top of the North East market, alongside grand-daddy Dickinson Dees.

It's no secret that the recession dealt the firm a blow, and with all the money it has pumped into its expanding business recently it should come as no surprise that partner profits fell 53% in 2008/09 (revenue dipped by a much lower 6.5% to £26.5m). The corporate and property departments were particularly hard hit. There were a number of redundancies and a four-day week was implemented for a trial period over the summer. Plans to open a Manchester office to complement the Newcastle HQ and newer Leeds branch have been shelved until 2010. Despite this, the trainees we spoke to had confidence in the firm's resilience. While it is clear Ward Hadaway has been forced into a period of stabilisation, *"there is still a lot more to come,"* trainees say; *"it's a 'you haven't seen nothing yet' kind of thing."* Managing partner Jamie Martin spoke to us about the extent of Ward Hadaway's ambitions. *"I very much hope we do extend south, but it will be long after I am retired, I expect. I think for the current generation of equity partners, continuing investment in Leeds and moving into Manchester when the time is right is achievable. What the next generation do is up to them. I will be watching with interest from my bath chair."*

Although the firm represents a growing number of national, household-name clients – Sage, ASDA and Orange are three of the largest – the majority of Ward Hadaway's clientele hail from the North and North East. Trainees feel this is unlikely to change, even as the firm grows. *"It still likes the fact it's a regional firm, and so do the clients,"* said one. Mr Martin confirmed this exact point: *"We are fundamentally a regional law firm and the North East, and Yorkshire and Humberside are going to be our prime hunting grounds."*

The NHS is a major instructor: Ward Hadaway is one of just 11 firms nationwide selected to be on the NHS Litigation Authority legal panel, defending the service against clinical negligence actions. It also advises the NHSLA on equal pay schemes and has a number of primary care trusts and other NHS trusts on its books, spreading from the North East and Cumbria down to Leicestershire.

A real speciAldi

The training scheme operates a four-seat system with stints available in most departments. One source joked:

"*If you want gossip, ask trainees because we have infiltrated every department!*" There are no compulsory seats and recruits generally spend a year in their intended qualification department. A few trainees did mention that "*sometimes you don't find out about your seat until the last minute. It doesn't sound like much but you are on edge until you know;*" however most agreed they had "*done pretty well*" with their allocations. In most seats trainees work primarily with either a partner or an associate supervisor but also get work from a number of other fee earners in their department. Responsibility "*develops as you go through the seat.*" It can be "*pretty crap for the first few months*" apparently, with some partners being "*very protective over their files,*" but then, "*if you show you are capable and eager, they are a lot more willing to give you responsibility. It's a case of proving yourself.*"

Time in the large property group has been strongly encouraged in previous years, but with the recession keeping the market in the doldrums, this was not the case in 2008/09. The firm does have a great reputation for property work though, so it's definitely worth mentioning the kind of cases the team handles. For their part, trainees who'd spent time in the property department since the downturn recognised there was "*a bit of a black cloud over things,*" but still had "*a positive experience,*" enjoying the opportunity to manage their own files as well as assisting partners on larger transactions. The department is split into three main units, dealing with development, commercial property and public sector/regeneration matters. The development team advises residential developers Barratt, Persimmon, Keepmoat and Gladedale, while on the commercial side one of the most important clients is Aldi, whose aggressive expansion plans will see it invest £1.5bn over the next five years to increase the number of stores nationwide from 400 to 1,500. Now that's what we call a fantastic client! Public sector clients include Durham County Council, a consortium of 18 South Yorkshire NHS trusts, and the five Tees Valley local authorities. The hire of partner Philip O'Laughlin from Addleshaw Goddard to the Leeds office has significantly boosted the firm's already strong property litigation offering.

Lightsabers at the ready

The corporate and commercial teams call the firm's Keele Row office their home, and in previous years this building has jokingly been referred to as the Dark Side because of its reputation for long hours. We asked this year's interviewees about the nickname. Said one: "*It's the Dark Side mainly because* [the other office] *Sandgate blocks out the sun. It's more of a physical dark side rather than anything more sinister!*" Having said this, the hours in corporate finance are reportedly "*much longer than other departments.*" One trainee talked of doing two overnight completions in a row, admitting that "*it gets to three or four in the morning and tempers start to fray.*" "*You do get quite a buzz out of doing the transactions,*" added another. The team acts for a combination of large corporations, private equity houses and smaller owner-managed businesses. During the course of the past year the team advised NorthStar Equity on 30 investments into a range of companies based in the North East.

Public sector projects and IP/IT are two of the most popular commercial seats. The public sector team is divided into two projects subsets, one dealing with the Building Schools for the Future programme and the other handling different types of PFI project. Clients include NHS trusts and county and city councils, and Ward Hadaway's portfolio of past schemes is now valued at over £2bn. "*Much of the stuff you do involves running through the project agreement, checking definitions and making sure the document flows,*" trainees reported. Apparently, when it comes to a deal completion there can be hundreds of different documents to keep track of.

The IP/IT seat is where our sources found the most responsibility, thanks to a programme called Gleam set up to help young entrepreneurs. Trainees manage start-up files for university graduates. "*I'm their main contact,*" said one. "*They want a range of advice: terms and conditions and IP mainly. It is probably the best opportunity to get your own files and clients.*" We couldn't agree more. The team also has a key role in the development of several new IP initiatives in the North East, including acting for Newcastle Science City, which is a nationally funded scheme to develop new businesses in the bioscience and healthcare sectors.

If contentious issues are more your bag then a seat in healthcare is a must. "*It's proper litigation,*" announced one source. "*It covers all the stages of any litigation that anyone would want to practise,*" gushed another. The work primarily involves defending various NHS trusts in clinical negligence, employer's liability and personal injury claims. Smaller PI files, "*where someone slips over on a latex glove or has been provided with a faulty Zimmer frame,*" allow trainees to have full responsibility, while larger, more complex clinical negligence files

Chambers UK rankings

Agriculture & Rural Affairs	Healthcare
Banking & Finance	Information Technology
Clinical Negligence	Intellectual Property
Construction	Planning
Corporate/M&A	Private Client
Debt Recovery	Professional Discipline
Dispute Resolution	Real Estate
Employment	Real Estate Litigation
Family/Matrimonial	Restructuring/Insolvency

require them to take more of a supporting role. Either way, "*you learn something new every day,*" even if it's only how many horrible ways medical treatment can go wrong. "*I never want children after being in that seat and hearing about 40-hour labours and third-degree tears,*" one source cringed.

Under Harm Hayre

An employment team is top-ranked by *Chambers UK* for work in the North East, and it is particularly recognised for its work in the public sector. The team handles well over 3,000 equal pay claims a year for a variety of NHS trusts spread across the country. Ward Hadaway's new Leeds office has swiftly grown a significant employment presence too, headed up by Harmajinder Hayre, previously a partner at both Hammonds and Beachcroft. "*There were only three in employment when I started, now there are far more,*" said one trainee of the office's growth in this sector. Hayre brings ten years of experience and particular knowledge of the retail, financial services and transport sectors. Corroborating this are new appointments to the UK-wide three-firm legal panel for ASDA and an appointment to Orange's national legal panel.

Trainees experience a broad mix of work, but it is in the contentious arena that they are able to really dirty their hands. As well as getting involved in larger and more complex cases, trainees can handle a number of their own smaller cases, such as unfair or constructive dismissals. "*I got to draft everything,*" recalled one source. "*The response, the witness statements and the instructions to counsel.*" There is also "*a great deal of tribunal work,*" and in addition to assisting counsel with the negotiations they can even try a spot of advocacy at case management conferences. Trainees explained that while the outcome of each CMC "*depends on its own facts, they usually involve an appointment with a district judge to make sure the directions* [on a case] *are being followed, that things are ticking along and to raise any issues.*" Ward Hadaway is quite keen to give trainees court experience, "*otherwise how are you going to do it when you are qualified?*"

Take the heat

On Ward Hadaway's home page, a picture of a plate of red chilli peppers is accompanied by the caption 'Helping you to overcome the strongest of challenges.' It hints at the firm's sense of humour and suggests a lack of stuffiness.

Trainees are proud of what they see as the firm's "*modern outlook*" and its "*novel approach.*" "*I've never seen it as a 'peering over your glasses', stuffy environment really,*" concluded one. Most trainees have pre-existing links with the area but this is not to say southerners won't have a chance if they apply for a training contract. "*As long as you can understand a Geordie accent you will fit in,*" say our interviewees. Just like the firm, trainees are "*self-assured, confident and hard-working.*" The word "*competitive*" was also bandied around by several sources. "*Some people keep their cards very close to their chest about what they are doing,*" but we were assured that while "*you have got to try and promote your own cause there is no cloak and dagger atmosphere.*"

Ward Hadaway's offices sit proudly on Newcastle's Quayside and have views of the River Tyne, the majestic Gateshead Millennium Bridge and the imposing BALTIC Centre. The area is overflowing with restaurants and bars, making it ideal for going out for lunch. In the evenings, trainees can generally be found in the Pitcher and Piano across the road as it's such a convenient staging post on the long walk up the steep bank back into town. Apparently, they're such regulars they now get a 20% discount. Trainees report that before the recession there was "*a fairly decent scheme of social events,*" but sadly there were no Christmas or summer parties to report on this year. Our sources were confident that things would pick up again. "*The recognition that these things are good for the morale of the firm is there.*" One partner is so convinced by this that he took his whole department orienteering in the Lake District this year and put it on his own credit card. Well done him.

Following on from full NQ retention in 2008, Ward Hadaway was able to offer jobs to six of its nine qualifiers in 2009.

And finally...

Ward Hadaway is committed to the idea of being a regional outfit and expects the same level of loyalty from its trainees.

- **A managing partner speaks:**
  It may have been all doom and gloom lately but take heart!

  "When the upturn does happen I think there will be strong demand for new people, particularly at the junior end of the market. I don't think your readers should be unduly pessimistic."

top tip no. 28

Warner Goodman LLP

The facts

Location: Southampton, Fareham, Portsmouth

Number of UK partners/solicitors: 13/22

Total number of trainees: 4

Seats: Flexible, minimum of 3

Alternative seats: Management, marketing

Trainees take between three and five seats, depending on when and whether they want to move. Our sources described the system as *"very flexible."*

Warner Goodman's practice ranges from family law and personal injury to commercial, employment and financial services. Its clients are private individuals, local businesses and larger enterprises. What's more, it could be the only law firm where you might hear one of the bosses strumming a guitar between client meetings.

Can't keep a Goodman down

The history of this *"familial and homely"* firm stretches back to 1852, since when it has cultivated a strong local reputation and grown to fill three offices in Southampton, Portsmouth and Fareham. Lately, the firm has made strides in its business law offering, launching a separately branded division called WG Commercial in 2007 to handle commercial litigation, employment, commercial property and coco instructions. The majority of the commercial work is done in Southampton, although there is also a smaller group in Portsmouth. Since only the family department appears in all three branches, trainees are likely to have to move around for their seats, but the branches are all fairly close to each other so this need not be off-putting.

Most larger firms have a similar structure to their training contracts – either six seats of four months or four of six months – and usually all the trainees switch at the same time. At Warner Goodman things are a little different. Trainees take between three and five seats, depending on when and whether they want to move. Our sources described the system as *"very flexible"* and explained that in addition to seats in fee-earning teams, it is presently also possible to complete a three-month seat in marketing or management. In the marketing seat they learn how to promote the firm and develop the Warner Goodman brand through networking and advertising. In the management seat they get to spend time with the board and managing partner, exploring Warner Goodman's finances and getting to grips with how law firms are run. *"They want trainees to be part of the firm from the outset. A lot of the directors* [for this, read partners] *trained at the firm and you get the impression that they want people to be prepared to go on to greater things."* Trainees were grateful for the flexibility in the system and happy with the guidance given to them by the training principal and HR staff. They also feel that there is a good support network from department heads down, including the supervisors from whom they get their work. The training principal won special praise for his seat recommendations and ideas on how trainees can improve their individual skill sets.

Don't drop the dead donkey

Warner Goodman has recently invested in *"really good and up-to-date"* IT systems that making work easier to manage. Improvements were certainly noted by the trainees who'd taken residential conveyancing seats. Although the housing market crash inevitably took its toll on the conveyancing group, trainees told us as early as mid-2009 that the flow of instructions was *"picking up substantially,"* in part due to *"a lot of local contacts who give us a steady supply of work."* Because trainees are expected to be able to run files on their own, and because of the amount of client contact, conveyancing is considered to be *"a good department to start in."*

Despite its ramped-up commercial side, the firm hasn't neglected its high-street origins. Trainees reported that teams such as personal injury and family had been growing at the same rate as the commercial ones. The PI department in Southampton was described as *"doing fabulously well"* and trainees spoke about the *"really varied work"* given to them by the whole team. Some of it is *"straightforward, like traffic accidents, which are usually cases of quantifying and settling claims."* Others cases are more complex and require a good deal of research in related fields, like the one that involved a donkey. Exactly how the donkey became embroiled in the case we were never told, but our imaginations were kept busy for a while. Trainees are often given responsibility for taking witness statements, researching and interpreting the law, gathering expert evidence (from donkey psychologists perhaps?) and advising clients.

In the family seat our sources encountered custody and divorce cases where, *"even if you have rational clients, they are so emotionally involved that when you interview them, you have got to strike a balance between advising them and being a shoulder to cry on."* In this *"very human department"* trainees can even do some advocacy. Despite the inevitable apprehension that builds up when given an opportunity to make a palpable difference to the outcome of a case, trainees got *"a real buzz out of it"* and were pleased that, unlike some of their friends in larger firms nearby, they found themselves on the front line in real-life situations. Family law requires a balance of tact, professionalism and people skills: *"People often come to divorce cases with good intentions about keeping things amicable, but can falter. It's our job to maintain the clients' focus on the matters in hand, keeping them informed and giving them well-rounded advice."* In the family department, you can expect to work with clients from a diverse cross-section of society, *"some with very considerable assets; others not so much."*

Trainees can also try advocacy in the debt collection department. It can be fast-paced because the *"papers come in a few hours before the hearing, giving you a short amount of time to find out what on earth is happening before going to court."* Once at court, it is often a matter of meeting the debtor to discuss the issue with them before taking the case before a judge who decides their fate. Usually these cases are *"relatively stress-free"* because *"there's little that can go wrong."* Sometimes trainees are really kept on their toes. Recalling one incident, a source told us: *"The other side had a barrister representing them and they ambushed us, trying to bury us in lots of documents in an attempt to buy time, whilst filing applications at the last minute. They did everything they could to postpone the hearing and in the end the judge had to adjourn to wait for the applications to go through."*

Chambers UK rankings

Employment

Commercial litigation can be fun. One trainee excitedly told us about the tactical jousting that occurred when they went to London for a mediation with a respected City firm. After several hours of strategising and discussion, the issue was settled favourably for WG's client. With the commercial side growing, trainees see that the firm is attracting bigger clients and a steadily increasing workload. The employment department offers exposure to employers in many different sectors as well as employees. Trainees were very satisfied by their experiences in this team.

Warner lovers

HR meets regularly with trainees to discuss their progress and department heads get involved too. Across the firm *"people always really encourage your strengths – if you're good at something, they'll help you do more."* If a trainee is happy to crank things up a notch, the level of responsibility will be tailored accordingly. *"Some trainees prefer not to run their own matters, but equally if you're looking for the added responsibility, they try to give you as much as you can do where appropriate."*

Smaller regional firms like Warner Goodman enable trainees to *"feel well linked to the local community,"* and marketing events give them the chance to mingle with fellow professionals, some even organising seminars for local businesses to advise on topics like employment law. Trainees were pleased to tell us that when they go out together to have fun as a firm, there are *"no barriers about who socialises with who,"* which adds to the feeling of *"not being just another number."* Our sources also had plenty to say about the firm's location, mentioning good weather, water sports and lunches on the coast. In 2009, two of the four qualifiers stayed on, going into the residential conveyancing and commercial litigation departments.

And finally...

There are several firms in this part of the country that bang the recruitment drum more loudly than Warner Goodman. In our view this smaller firm seems to be doing an equally good job with its training scheme.

Watson, Farley & Williams

Challenging.
Matt Leigh, Assistant

Distinctive.　Integrated.　Opportunities.　Real.

"We've just closed a deal with a funding structure involving seven jurisdictions, throwing up a number of challenging political and tax elements."

Vacation Placements
31st January 2010
Training Contracts
31st July 2010 (to start 2012)

www.wfw.com/trainees

Watson, Farley & Williams

The facts

Location: London
Number of UK partners/solicitors: 44/69
Total number of trainees: 26
Seats: 6x4 months
Alternative seats: Overseas seats, secondments
Extras: Pro bono – Toynbee Hall Legal Advice Centre, competition & regulatory pro bono scheme; language training

Three of 2009's NQs have gone to practice abroad: one in Paris, one in Singapore and one in Bangkok.

Despite its relatively small size in London, Watson, Farley & Williams has an extensive international network that stems from its shipping and asset finance expertise.

The rose and rise of WFW

WFW was set up in 1982 by three Norton Rose partners – although it almost never existed at all. When Alastair Farley suggested to his two colleagues the possibility of breaking away, he did so in such a roundabout and ambiguous manner that they almost missed his point altogether. Fortunately, they got the message in the end and set up a firm based on shipping and aviation finance. Those strengths endure to this day, and *Chambers UK* ranks WFW in the top tier for shipping finance in London (and in the second tier on a global scale), and in very respectable positions for other types of finance work. The firm also has a range of other practices, including litigation, property, employment and competition law. Trainees can do seats in all of these, but it's fair to say the departments are smaller and less well recognised in the market. The exception is a growing projects and energy team: all our contacts clearly recognised this as the area WFW is most keen to develop in the next few years.

Because of its shipping finance background, WFW is prominent on the international scene and has ten overseas offices. What's more, every trainee is guaranteed the opportunity to go abroad, which is obviously something to consider if you're desperate for more sunshine than you'll get in Blighty.

Defying the downturn, WFW announced a turnover of £73.5m in 2009: a 25% increase on the previous year. Managing partner Michael Greville isn't getting carried away, describing the firm as "*stable.*" He pointed out to us that "*utilisation is down*" and that the turnover increase reflects the growth of the firm (there was a 17% rise in the number of fee earners between 2008 and 2009), as well as the amount of non-sterling income that it has. The international network, which stretches across Western Europe to Asia and also includes a New York base, has played an important part in keeping WFW's head above water during the recent economic storms: "*London always supported the overseas offices; recently I get the feeling it's flipped,*" a trainee remarked. Mr Greville says: "*We have got some very profitable businesses, some more profitable than London – but London is no laggard.*" It remains the HQ and is still the largest in the network (it has just under half the firm's fee earners), but the other offices are certainly on the rise. Note that when WFW offered NQ positions in 2009, three were in overseas offices. Note also that it managed to give jobs to 11 out of its 12 qualifiers in a year when retention rates fell dramatically across the country.

Messing around with boats

In addition to the overseas seat, back on home soil there are five more to complete. The merits and drawbacks of the six-seat system can be (and have been) endlessly debated – while there's greater exposure to different departments, a number of our interviewees expressed regret at having to leave a team just as they were starting to get into the swing of things. Fortunately, it's not uncommon for trainees to go back for another seat in the area they are due to qualify in.

As "*the most important area,*" all trainees will see the ship finance department at some point. "*It's asset finance with a twist*" and not something that most people will have studied at uni or law school. We're happy to say that the team is "*very supportive*" when it comes to helping trainees understand the quirks of shipping. "*They are absolutely great at teaching you. They know new trainees don't know much about the area and are very good at making it simple.*" Besides, it's not too alien when you get the hang of it. "*I could see the direct link with the finance elective on the LPC.*" Trainees are generally responsible for collating all of the documents required to complete a deal. It's not an incredibly glamorous job, "*but it's balanced out by lots of client contact. We get really involved with advising them.*" Here's a nice little story from one trainee to illustrate the point: "*I went to a closing meeting on my own. At the end the solicitor on the other side complimented me and asked how many years qualified I was. She was really surprised when I said I wasn't! She said that at her firm, a trainee wouldn't get to do something like that.*"

At the time of our calls in May 2009, the number of deals taking place had diminished as banks were reluctant to lend, and the department was relying on transactions supported by export credit agencies (ECAs). For example advising Fortis and Calyon on financings with Finnvera, the Finnish ECA; and Citibank with China Exim, Korea Exim and KEIC. Most major banks have used the firm for ship financing at one point or another, among them BNP Paribas, Credit Suisse, Deutsche Bank, Fortis Bank and Royal Bank of Scotland.

Wind up

A wide-ranging corporate department has a number of different seat options, and trainees must do at least one of them. WFW is in the top 20 in the City for the number of AIM clients on its books, so it has a team dedicated to them. Another team focuses on oil and gas work, and another on hotels and the leisure industry. The hot area at the moment, however, is the 'corporate projects' seat, which is all about renewable energy. All of our contacts talked about its increasing importance to the firm. Quotes from multiple trainees along the lines of: "*The rest of the world is realising that oil won't last forever*" and "*wind energy will become ever more important to the UK*" are probably a good indicator of what's being said in meetings within WFW at the moment. A major wind farm in the Thames Estuary called the London Array is under construction and set to be completed by 2012. Shell pulled out as the major backer of the £2bn project, but WFW is acting for DONG Energy (Denmark's biggest energy company), which has stepped in to buy Shell's stake. For trainees, this is often a research-heavy seat. "*I had a cou-

Chambers UK rankings

Asset Finance	Employment
Commodities	Projects, Energy & Natural Resources
Corporate/M&A	Shipping

ple of data rooms to keep an eye on, but for me there were less billable matters. I learnt a lot about how renewable energy works in this country and all the government incentives that are available.*"

We said that the corporate department was wide-ranging: the same is true of litigation. "*There's a focus on commercial litigation but we have various other high-value cases which may or may not be purely commercial,*" said one trainee. "*I had some contractual disputes, and referrals from the shipping team obviously.*" Britannia Bulk became the first major shipping group to go under in the economic downturn, and the firm acted for Nordea Bank and Lloyds on issues arising from the insolvency. For another litigation trainee though, "*the shipping element was minimal. I worked on about six different matters, including a very large international arbitration that took up the majority of my time. I was third in the chain after the partner and senior assistant.*" WFW is acting for the government of Pakistan in proceedings brought in the English High Court for the enforcement of an ICC arbitration award. A dispute had arisen out of a $345m agreement to construct and lease housing for 45,000 Pakistani Hajj pilgrims in Mecca. Yet another worked on finance disputes and property litigation: "*My partner give me some work with a firm in trouble with the FSA, and a claim over how much was owed from dilapidations.*" Trainees seemed generally happy with the level of responsibility on offer – "*having a bash at first drafts, looking after the clients during arbitrations*" – although we got the impression that high-level strategy meetings in litigation are out of bounds.

Four of WFW's ten foreign offices have secondments available to trainees. Paris is finance-oriented, Bangkok leans heavily towards litigation and arbitration, while Piraeus and Singapore are all about the shipping work – trainees have to do a ship finance seat in the UK before they can go to Piraeus, and the firm says it's "*preferable*" for Singapore and Paris too. "*You get a lot more exposure in the overseas seats,*" said trainees. "*You really act like an assistant sometimes.*" There's a massive contingent of UK law firm trainees in Singapore, so there's a ready-made group to go out with. By contrast, Allen & Overy is the only other firm to offer a placement in Bangkok, so instead trainees get involved with the local expat community. Bangkok is a sweet deal: "*You get a superb apartment and membership of a five-star hotel's gym and leisure complex*" and there's huge scope for travel and having fun at the weekends. The Paris and Piraeus secondments are often popular with those who want to be a bit closer to home, and French or Greek language classes are provided for anyone going on a Eurotrip.

All comers welcome

Of the current WFW trainees, there's an even mix of law and non-law grads, and an equally level spread of "*people who are clearly more intellectual and people who seem to be a little more practical in their thinking.*" Plenty had taken at least one year out somewhere down the line, often to go travelling, and the overseas seat and international business had clearly been the firm's biggest selling points for most. We also noticed that our interviewees were a savvy bunch, clearly conscious that a training contract "*is a two-year job interview. We're very aware of what is expected of us – that's differed from a number of previous year groups. It's knowing how to play the game, isn't it? There were people in the past who didn't know how to do that.*" We asked for further clarification and were told by several people: "*Your overall attitude is very important.*" Said one trainee: "*What's expected is that you should be keen, show an interest, be enthusiastic even in the face of the most mundane tasks, and when you get good work – which you will – that's when you can seize the chance to progress.*" Consequently, there are "*no prima donnas*" among the current trainees and everyone is happy to get their hands dirty.

"*Some of my friends say their firm is friendlier than mine,*" mused one trainee. "*When I ask them what they mean by that, it just turns out that they go out drinking a lot more.*" Our contacts certainly didn't have a problem with warmth of the office environment. Partners are "*approachable,*" which is fortunate because a "*very low assistant per partner ratio*" means they need to be. However, trainees did conceded that there is "*not so much of a going-out culture*" as at some other firms. They understood why though: "*Lots of people have children and I wouldn't judge people if they want to spend their free time with their families.*" The trainees will have the odd drink on a Friday evening and go out en masse every few months. "*More often the lads will have a night out – sometimes it's just good to be all boys together.*" There's no gender divide in the canteen as everyone sits together for lunch cooked by WFW's "*brilliant*" French chef, Philippe. Ditto the mixed cricket team: "*All comers welcome, girls or boys, whether spectators or participants. There's a cracking little sports ground down in Dulwich. We leave at 4.30pm and have a slap-up meal afterwards.*" Half past four isn't the standard check-out time, of course, and "*magic circle hours*" do happen occasionally, but this is a firm where a work-life balance is possible and hours seem to "*average out*" at about 9.30am to 7pm.

The two biggest social events of the year are the fee earners' dinner and the firm's birthday party (rather quaintly, this is celebrated every year). It's here that the vision for the future is set out. "*Our managing partner gave a speech stressing that we are doing okay, and said we have some natural hedges against recession, like a variety of clients and a high concentration of work abroad.*" For the next few years, however, it seems that WFW will "*consolidate rather than spread itself too thin.*"

And finally...

As one of the smaller UK firms with significant overseas business, WFW stands apart from the big City names. We believe it can offer a different style of training experience, and we're impressed – yet again – by the level of satisfaction among our sources.

Wedlake Bell

The facts

Location: London

Number of UK partners/solicitors: 39/42

Total number of trainees: 6

Seats: 4x6 months

Alternative seats: Secondments

Quality UK and international work, all from "*a bright and characterful office, a stone's throw from Chancery Lane.*" What more could a trainee ask for?

Wedlake Bell's recruitment website may appear Joan Miró-inspired, however there's nothing too surreal about this London mid-sizer.

Oldest swinger in town?

After two centuries in the business, WB proves that old does not have to mean old-fashioned. Illustrating this is the firm's close relationship with drinks giant Diageo, which is surely as good an example of modern corporate Britain as you will find. WB assists on all its IP and franchising matters and even has a regular trainee secondment to the company's central London HQ. Or what about classic British fashion brand Jaeger, which instructed the firm on its new flagship store in the Westfield mega-mall?

Appointing a non-legal CEO and acting for alcohol, luxury car and fashion brands at the age of 228 suggests WB is undergoing a delayed mid-life crisis, but the past year is actually best described as a period of reflection and consolidation. It still harbours a desire to rise to the ranks of the top 100, and we see no reason why it shouldn't. Trainees noted a growing interest in India – partner Kim Lalli heads a group that is securing an increasing amount of work from the subcontinent – and this could be a catalyst for further groups to target overseas business. Quality UK and international work, all from "*a bright and characterful office, a stone's throw from Chancery Lane.*" What more could a trainee ask for?

Ashes to ashes

Expect at least one seat in a property-related department, whether it be commercial/residential property, property litigation or construction. Trainees get to work with major clients and always end up with a portfolio of their own matters. "*I liked the responsibility. Sometimes you'd be involved in the negotiation process with enormous public companies,*" recalled one. Business dipped noticeably when the recession hit, however by the time we spoke to trainees in summer 2009 some sensed things were picking up again. Recession or no, WB has managed to land new clients like Warner Estate Holdings and airline businesses Air France Services and KLM Ground Services. Of late it has handled major instructions relating to leisure centres, hotels, student accommodation and prime retail space. There's even a group entirely devoted to hotel and leisure matters, and in 2008 a sports business group emerged and property lawyers ended up advising on the redevelopment of The Oval Cricket Ground. Lucky trainees can keep score from the firm's corporate box.

In residential property, trainees handle high-end conveyancing for established private clients. Meanwhile, construction law sharpens skills in the dark arts of contract law. "*The seat was academically challenging, had a high volume of work and was excellent training.*" Trainees here manage a helpline for the National Specialist Contractor's Council and are frequently asked for advice on non-payment or other breach of contract matters. The real estate litigation unit often represents commercial landlords in possession proceedings and naturally has been busy of late. Our sources were empathetic towards evicted tenants, but noted the importance of their representation. "*It's quite satisfying that you know you've done the best for your client.*"

The corporate team, which had previously suffered senior-level departures, has been negotiating the turbulent waters of the recession with new head Hilary Platt at the helm. Typical work includes asset finance and small to mid-sized M&A/AIM deals. One top matter involved a £40m loan facility for the acquisition of two care homes. Individual supervisors earn great feedback. Said one source: *"When he was training me, I had* [my supervisor's] *full attention."* Expect research into black letter law, as well as *"soul-destroying"* verification notes and Companies House filings. It's important to have *"good attention to detail and a flexible personality to deal with fluctuations in workload."*

High-street monies

Commercial litigation experience is paired with the contentious aspects of the IP and IT departments. Engaging with clients like BMW, Tesco and i-CD Publishing means that *"walking down the high street you have more of an idea of what goes on behind the scenes."* And online too: lawyers recently achieved a favourable settlement for Teletext, which sought to prevent Directline Holidays from using its trade marks on Google's AdWords. Complementing the commercial/IP seat is a six-month secondment to Diageo – *"a brilliant experience"* centred on commercial contracts, franchising agreements, international licensing and a fantastic staff bar. In the business recoveries team trainees assist on debt cases and conduct insolvency-related investigations. They encounter major clients and learn to appreciate the international flavour of their businesses. Time management skills come to the fore as *"you must push things yourself and get on with them."* Alas, some people find aspects of the work less than exciting, namely ennui-inducing tasks like disclosure and bundling.

In what seat could you expect to act for an ancient association set up by Letters Patent? WB's private client team, obviously! This group has experience in contentious trusts matters, as well as tax and probate advice for the wealthy. So established is the team that one trainee divulged that they'd been told about it halfway around the world! On the client list you'll find lords, ladies, successful entrepreneurs, City bankers and the CEOs of major companies. Dealing with such clients can be challenging and the firm is skilled in allocating the right trainee for the task, as *"you wouldn't want someone too hip looking after private clients."* This department works closely with WB's Guernsey office. Though no secondment is available to trainees, island life is an option after qualification.

Other seats include the *"responsibility-heavy"* employment team, where a significant amount of instructions are multi-jurisdictional or relate to outsourcing for corporate catering and hospitality providers like KLM's passenger lounge services. The seat brings responsibility as well as a significant litigation component. A pensions seat, meanwhile, will suit the more academically inclined. Whichever seats you choose – and trainees say they mostly get what they want – you'll share your space with one other fee earner. Random fact: the air-conditioning is systematically perfect and *"never dries out your contact lenses."*

Chambers UK rankings

Construction	Intellectual Property
Employment	Private Client
Information Technology	Real Estate

Saved by the Bell

Trainees describe WB as optimistic, sociable and meritocratic. They appreciate people's honesty and frankness, saying: *"No one really blows smoke up your arse, they just give their opinion."* Most come to WB for its mid-size attractions, keen to get to know everyone and eager for quality work. Everyone advises students to try the vac scheme; indeed one source confessed to having *"fallen in love with the firm"* on theirs. Many trainees arrive after previous career experience or extensive travel; a few come straight from university. In a sense, the intake is just like the firm as a whole: a balance between experience and youth, tradition and an edge.

WB made 19 redundancies in 2008/09 and deferred its five incoming trainees of 2009 (giving them £5,000 to do so). Qualification was an anxious business this time round as the firm delayed announcing the available positions until two weeks before the end of the training contract. *"In the past the strategy has been to grow the firm from the roots up,"* said one source of the value WB normally places on its qualifiers. Sadly, only three of the six people were able to stay on in 2009. At all times management kept lines of communication open and it was heart-warming to hear one source say: *"Whatever happens, I will stay in contact with the firm."*

A social committee organises film nights, bowling, black-tie dinners and family picnics, and every couple of months there are 'drop-in drinks' in a local pub. Top tip: get there early as the partners' cards only flex so far! Trainees are considered a vital part of the social scene and are even invited to wine and dine clients on occasion. Back in the office, they are *"the source of gossip and know what's going around!"*

And finally...

This firm expects trainees to *"prove their worth," "share their knowledge"* and *"know their clients."* We reckon WB's clients aren't the only ones worth knowing; it sounds like partners and staff rub along nicely too.

After 15 years helping UK law students find the right firm, the Student Guide has expanded across the pond...

CHAMBERS ASSOCIATE

www.chambers-associate.com

The free legal careers guide to top US law firms

"Our lawyers have commented on the high level of professionalism and integrity Chambers has achieved in this new publication."

Gibson Dunn & Crutcher LLP

To learn more about the guide please email the Assistant Editors, EmilyL@chambersandpartners.com or GrantC@chambersandpartners.com

Weil, Gotshal & Manges LLP

The facts
Location: London
Number of partners/solicitors: 24/59 + 5 US-qualified
Total number of trainees: 24
Seats: 4x6 months
Alternative seats: Overseas seats
Extras: LawWorks, Bar Pro Bono Unit, Battersea Law Centre

"The magic circle look at us and say 'Oh, Weil Gotshal, they're a US firm.' It's almost as if it's a badge of shame. I like to think the people we've got could have walked into the magic circle but chose to come here."

Weil, Gotshal & Manges asks trainees to do something that scares them. With a global reputation for restructuring/insolvency and a muscular London corporate practice, there should be enough challenge for anyone.

Weil-y as a fox

New York titan Weil Gotshal has a world-beating reputation for bankruptcy and restructuring work. To illustrate its pre-eminence, the *Wall Street Journal* pointed out that of the four major partners from four different firms handling the majority of work on the restructurings of American auto manufacturers GM and Chrysler, all were either current or former Weil attorneys. The firm's pedigree has served it extremely well, and while others' 2008/09 revenues tumbled with the markets, Weil's actually increased slightly from $1.18bn to $1.23bn, with profits per equity partner rising by 7.5%. In London (the firm's second-largest office), profits increased by a whopping 22%.

Despite the firm's heavyweight reputation in bankruptcy, in the UK it is known for something else: since the London office was founded in 1996 to service New York private equity house Hicks Muse Tate & Furst (now HM Capital), its raison d'être has been private equity. Among the clients are funds like Lion Capital and Fidelity Equity Partners, and *Chambers UK* ranks Weil in the second-highest band, with only Clifford Chance in the tier above it. Chambers also places four of its partners among the best in the field. One of the four, Mark Soundy, warned us that the economic downturn would probably see business slow in 2009, but stressed that Weil had a well-crafted business plan for London. We wondered if the firm might try and build up its small but strong UK restructuring group. Although its *Chambers UK* ranking dipped slightly following the 2007 departure of team head Chris Mallon for Skadden, the 2008 hire of Tony Horspool from Cadwalader provided a healthy boost. While the bankruptcy practice will no doubt continue to prosper, Weil's immediate plan is to create a more balanced transactional practice. The hire of public M&A star Peter King from Shearman & Sterling is a major step in that direction, and Soundy pledged that "*in the longer term I think you will see this firm with a strong private equity focus and a growing public M&A focus, all combining into cross-border M&A.*" Weil is also eyeing up the Persian Gulf for further expansion – in 2009 it opened a Dubai office – and India is another possible target. We're told to expect any growth to be deliberate and cautious: "*We're not going to be the Mumbai, Shanghai, Dubai, Goodbye type of firm,*" Soundy assured us.

Food for thought

This past year wasn't the best time for corporate finance (as one trainee put it: "*private equity has fallen off a cliff*"); however, in tough times what work there is goes to those firms with the best reputation. Weil's is one of the best in the UK. Benefiting from client Lion Capital's market-defying activity in 2008, the firm secured a role on Lion's acquisition of frozen seafood honcho FoodVest, as well as its investment into Russia's largest producer of vodka. For the firm's other clients there has been "*much more portfolio and managerial advice than mega-deals,*" and private equity seats – compulsory for trainees – have been somewhat quieter than usual. Trainees can expect to take on "*complicated drafting*" and will get virtually all of their tasks from a close group of partners and associates.

Weil's UK corporate lawyers draw most of their instructions from home-grown client relationships. The bankruptcy and financial restructuring (BFR) team, meanwhile, will often take on the UK or European aspects of large-scale US bankruptcies: for example, the group helped defunct bank Lehman Brothers with the non-US aspects of its Chapter 11 proceedings. Significant European matters come through to the team too: in November 2008 Premier Foods (producers of Mr Kipling, OXO and Angel Delight) gave Weil the lead role restructuring its £1.7bn debt, and the team is acting for Kaupthing Bank following the collapse of the Icelandic financial services industry. Understandably, BFR has become a very competitive seat as its profile has risen and "*people want the exposure.*"

Finance is the other compulsory seat for trainees: here, our interviewees had been given "*really good drafting opportunities*" and attended frequent meetings with clients, something which "*gives meaning to what you're doing.*" The capital markets team is being kept occupied with instructions from clients like BSkyB and Gate Gourmet; here trainees are able to participate in conference calls and negotiations, again giving them good insight into how deals run.

Although around half of Weil's trainees usually take a litigation course to meet official requirements for contentious training, some of our sources hinted that the London litigation team doesn't deserve its reputation as merely a corporate support group. Tax, on the other hand, unashamedly does ("*I don't think anyone would begrudge that being said,*") and in addition to giving trainees a better grasp of how corporate deal are structured, a seat there can offer a more academic experience. Also available for trainees are stints in employment, property and IP/IT. There's a mix of internally and externally delivered PSC courses, and departments like insolvency and corporate run "*very frequent*" training sessions.

Biting the Big Apple

Weil trainees consistently compare the firm to the magic circle rather than other American firms in London, perhaps because these firms are often across the table on deals. It allows them to make direct comparisons between their own experiences and those of their peers in these much larger firms. "*Because you're the only trainee on a deal you're not fighting for work with three or four others, so you get all the good work a trainee could do,*" asserted one. "*Compare that with a magic circle firm where you have really good work but tens of trainees to help with everything,*" posed

Chambers UK rankings

Banking & Finance	Private Equity
Capital Markets	Restructuring/Insolvency
Corporate/M&A	
Media & Entertainment	Tax

another. "*Here, if you're on a big deal you'll be expected to do as much as possible.*" Our interviewees raved about being stretched in this way. "*Supervisors are keen to protect you from rubbish,*" and very often trainees will be "*up against associates at other firms.*"

Bearing in mind the firm chooses your first seat for you, and you have to do stints in both corporate and finance, "*after your third seat you only really get one true option.*" New starters are strongly advised to "*make particular preferences very well known before they join the firm.*" Weil "*definitely tries to please everybody as much as it can,*" but some departments are small and disappointment isn't uncommon. Cogently arguing your case for doing a certain seat helps, and "*if you've got the backing of someone within the department that's obviously fantastic.*" The issue came to a head this past year over the allocation of overseas seats, which are popular enough to be consistently oversubscribed. Trainees can go to New York, California's Silicon Valley or, provided their French is good enough, Paris. Reflecting the Big Apple's popularity, it is now taking two secondees every six months (seven applied for it in the most recent round). Weil provides free accommodation within walking distance of its headquarters on one corner of Central Park. With the USA lacking the equivalent of a traineeship, "*you're treated like a first-year associate,*" which means having to quickly learn how to use unfamiliar resources and working on your own matters. Overall the experience goes down a storm and trainees really enjoy hanging out with their American counterparts.

Scare tactics

Weil proudly claims the quality of its recruiting has come on in leaps and bounds, and last year's almost perfect NQ retention rate was a testament to its ability to find good matches, even if in 2009 there was only space for 11 of its 13 qualifiers. Weil takes a forthright approach to finding the right kind of trainees: its hard-hitting recruitment material shows rough-edged images of darkened rooms and blazing lamps, while looming words like 'Intense' and 'Challenging' make for arresting viewing. The intention is to weed out those who are "*put off by that*" and thus "*clearly not meant to be here.*" Even an interviewee who thought it was all "*a bit cheesy*" grudgingly acknowledged that the campaign has been "*incredibly successful.*" Accurate, too. "*Our slogan, 'Do something that scares you', is quite apt,*" whispered another source, adding: "*It* can be scary at times!" Long hours are on the cards, with trainees often staying until 10pm or 11pm. BlackBerrys for everyone mean "*you're on call all the time.*" Other firms' more conventional and genial marketing wouldn't fly at Weil. "*That would be ridiculous. It's not a warm and fuzzy firm and nor should it be,*" insisted one trainee. "*If you're advising serious private equity clients you don't want to be known as the firm cuddling the opposition. You don't want to back down from a fight.*"

That isn't to say the environment is a harsh one. There is a degree of competition among trainees, but "*not in a particularly bad way,*" and an optional and confidential mentoring scheme is typical of the generally supportive atmosphere: "*You're certainly not spoon-fed here, but you're not expected to know what you're doing all the time.*" Our interviewees noticed a growing emphasis on Oxbridge candidates, but still insisted that educational background is far less important than an interest in the kind of corporate-based work on which the firm thrives. As for character type, our sources said: "*You'll have to be willing to get along with the whole office to make it here.*" They believe Weil trainees are "*not cookie-cutter types,*" but we'd comfortably hazard the generalisation that they're all pretty assertive individuals. Confidence is essential: the small teams mean "*you don't want to screw up as it'll be very visible,*" and the firm "*wants people up for a challenge who want to push themselves a bit more, not hide in the corners. It's definitely not a place for the shy, retiring type.*"

Whisky missed

Such hard-charging ideas fit most people's preconceptions of what an American firm must be like; however, Weil London's character really doesn't owe too much to its parent across the Pond. Aside from occasional firm-wide e-mails and an annual "*corporate boot camp*" in New York, where "*you get to go see the mothership and meet US colleagues,*" it doesn't feel particularly American. "*It's not what I expected from a US law firm,*" confessed one trainee, "*I expected red braces and cigar-chomping.*" London is indebted to its star-spangled origins for a few things. Reflecting US trends, the office places a high priority on diversity, with female lawyers the primary beneficiaries. Last year there was a diversity week with a timetable of "*client events aimed at women,*" such as a flower-arranging course ("*it's not so clichéd as that*") and wine tasting. The permanent Women@Weil affinity group regularly brings in guests (such as the editor of *Grazia*) to give talks for lawyers of both sexes. In another nod to American sensibilities, "*pro bono is a huge deal.*" All lawyers are encouraged to do 50 hours per year (you get a little award if you succeed), and non-chargeable work for organisations like Oxfam and the NSPCC is viewed "*no differently to fee-paying work,*" except trainees are given more scope to run matters themselves.

If lawyers want to socialise during the day they head to the firm's on-site restaurant, which has big sofas and a TV usually tuned to Sky Sports... "*or if it's the associates from upstairs, EastEnders or Coronation Street.*" Ad hoc nights out and organised trainee events are rare. "*I think everyone has a life outside work and is keen to head back to it,*" explained an interviewee. Office-wide social events bring out Weil's best. As well as a bi-annual retreat there's a Thanksgiving lunch in November, a yearly summer social and a "*proper black-tie*" Christmas bash that gets a good turnout and often continues long past the venue hire finishes. Last year some kept the party going at Royal-watching hotspot Whisky Mist. Assuming law firm budgeting someday returns to past levels, fans of the high life will love it when American summer schemers come over to visit, bringing a huge entertainment budget with them: in past years this has meant "*magnums of top champagne in nightclubs.*" And yet, proving that the best things in life are free, some of the biggest laughs are to be had at the annual charity quiz night, which last time involved a costumed karaoke round and plenty of liquid refreshment. There aren't many other places you'll be likely to see a partner wearing a coconut bikini.

And finally...

A training contract at Weil is never going to be an easy two years, but if you're interested in corporate deals and you've masses of determination and stamina – and you'll know very quickly if you do – it can be one of the most rewarding available.

A CAREER IN LAW

- **TALK TO WHITE & CASE**
  - GUARANTEED OVERSEAS SEAT
  - A TAILORED CAREER PATH
  - HIGH TRAINEE RETENTION RATES
  - IMMEDIATE RESPONSIBILITY
  - CUTTING EDGE WORK
  - GREAT CHOICE GREAT CAREER GREAT LIFE ☺

- **DON'T TALK TO WHITE & CASE**
  - FIND A JOB SOMEWHERE ELSE

Make the right choice
www.whitecasetrainee.com

WHITE & CASE

White & Case LLP

The facts
Location: London
Number of UK partners/solicitors: 67/210 + c.50 US-qualified
Total number of trainees: 59
Seats: 4x6 months
Alternative seats: Overseas seats
Extras: Pro bono – eg A4ID, Bar Pro Bono Unit, RCJ CAB, Lawyers without Borders, LawWorks; language training

> *"We are crying out for lawyers who go for a secondment, come back and want to go overseas again. One thing you won't find is here is any restriction on working abroad."*
>
> Philip Stopford, Training Principal

Though born in America, over here White & Case has much in common with the true Brits of the magic circle. It's certainly one of the most internationally minded US firms.

Transatlantic trailblazers

In 1927, Charles Lindbergh made his famous transatlantic flight from New York to Paris in the Spirit of St Louis. When he touched down, among the crowd of 150,000 cheering spectators that greeted him would have been employees of White & Case, asking "What took you so long?" The firm had made the same journey as Lindbergh the year before, opening an office in the French capital in 1926. This arguably gives it a strong claim to be the first American firm to have recognised the benefits of globalisation. Today, with 2,300-odd lawyers in over 20 countries, it's one of the world's biggest legal beasts.

W&C is an old-timer in Britain too. It was one of the first US firms in the UK, arriving on the scene in 1971. Its training programme, which is also well established, went through a major growth spurt relatively recently (16 trainees in 2002; 55 by 2008). The London office is at its best whenever cash is splashed: it secures *Chambers UK* rankings for asset finance, Islamic finance, corporate finance, project finance and real estate finance, not to mention capital markets, investment funds and banking. Massive deals are commonplace, and many have cross-border elements. "*In my current seat at least 50% of the matters I have worked on have been international,*" said one trainee of project finance. "*In my corporate seat, all of them were.*" In one such transaction, the corporate team advised Angel Trains (a provider of railway rolling stock in the UK and Europe) during its £3.6bn sale by RBS to a consortium of investors. In another, it advised the Chinese insurance group Ping An on its acquisition of a 50% shareholding in Fortis Investment Management in a $3.36bn deal.

Despite recording gross worldwide revenue in excess of $1.4bn in 2008, the market conditions at the end of that year led to redundancies across the firm. The London office was heavily hit, with 18 employees losing their jobs in November 2008 and around 95 more going in April 2009 – a not insignificant proportion of the UK workforce. Unsurprisingly, we hear a large number of these layoffs came in the finance-related teams, and partner defections (and rumours of defections) to other City firms further added to the perception that all might not be well within that department. It was surprising to discover, then, that the trainees we spoke to were upbeat about their qualification prospects, even after the corporate team announced that there would be no positions available. When we questioned training principal Philip Stopford about this, he told us that this was because the firm "*has kept the trainee programme small relative to the size of the office. We are significantly lighter than the normal UK law firms in this respect and that is reflected in the fact that despite what we have gone through, we have kept our retention up. We want to keep the office as a whole, not only the right size, but also the right shape.*" A cynic might add "at the right cost." Still, that's not something trainees will be complaining about, and sure enough, 25 out of 28 qualifiers were kept on in 2009.

Given its importance to the firm, it shouldn't come as a surprise that a seat in one of the finance teams is compulsory; indeed "*it would be quite strange if you came to the firm and didn't want to do one of them.*" The finance practice is split into two: the energy, infrastructure, projects and asset finance group (EIPAF), and banking and capital markets. Six months in one of W&C's foreign offices is also a near-certainty: most trainees go abroad in their fourth and final seat. In an unusual twist to the allocation process, trainees can not only request which seat they do, but also which supervisor they do it with.

Inside the engine room

EIPAF is a "*powerhouse*" of a department with megadeals aplenty. It had a role in the largest ever energy project financing, the $21.3bn Qatargas series of a few years ago. More recently, it acted for a Malaysian company financing a $4.5bn aluminium smelter. Other clients include Air Asia X, China Development Bank, Carillion and Barclays. A trainee in the projects subdivision of EIPAF had worked on a Building Schools for the Future PFI deal: "*I got stuck in on the constitutional documents. My supervisor kept tripping over all the conditions precedent trolleys in my offices.*" Another "*was on the phone quite a bit to BNP Paribas – that was really good.*" Similarly, asset finance offers "*lots of client contact,*" but when push comes to shove the sheer size of the deals means EIPAF "*is the kind of department where you don't get huge amounts of responsibility as a trainee.*" Said one: "*There is a lot of document management, proof-reading, checking and double-checking. Ultimately the trainees are the ones co-ordinating that.*" We also heard whispers from some that EIPAF is "*made up of so many different sectors and is very male-dominated, so it can get quite aggressively competitive and there can be tension.*" In fairness, we were told that "*some of the trainees are quite sheltered*" from that aspect of the department and indeed, other interviewees declared themselves ignorant of any internal politics, saying: "*It has a really nice feel; it's quite casual but everyone is very committed.*"

W&C sees itself as equivalent to the magic circle and expects a similar level of commitment. EIPAF has the most "*brutal rep*" among trainees in this respect. "*Yes, I have done all-nighters, coming in on Thursday morning and going home on Friday evening,*" said one interviewee. "*It's tough, but it gets the adrenalin pumping.*" For another, 10pm finishes were standard for "*a couple of nights every week. I was leaving at around 8pm otherwise.*" Weekend work and cancelled holidays can also be a regular occurrence. Still, at least there's no face-time culture: apparently "*you'd be mocked for staying if there was nothing to do.*" W&C trainees can also console themselves with the fact that though they might be working as hard as their magic circle counterparts, they are being paid substantially more: at last check a first-seater was pulling in £41,000 and an NQ £72,000.

Chambers UK rankings

Asset Finance	Employment
Banking & Finance	Financial Services Regulation
Banking Litigation	Information Technology
Capital Markets	Intellectual Property
Commodities	Investment Funds
Construction	Projects, Energy & Natural Resources
Corporate/M&A	
Data Protection	Restructuring/Insolvency
Dispute Resolution	Telecommunications
Employee Share Schemes	Transport

Let's talk about the litigation group because, although it plays second fiddle to corporate, trainees were keen to talk up its increasing importance. "*Slowly, slowly, it is growing and getting some of the biggest cases,*" they said. We hear the department is now regularly taking two qualifiers on from every six-month intake. W&C also won a couple of 'litigation team of the year' gongs in 2008 (from *The Lawyer* magazine and at the British Legal Awards) and has been instructed on some high-profile matters. It successfully fought the extradition of former Morgan Crucible CEO Ian Norris to America on price-fixing charges and is representing SRM Global Fund, a Monaco-based hedge fund, which was the largest shareholder in Northern Rock. Trainees praised the real "*brain work*" available: "*real law points where you come out with your head hurting.*" A "*mini-department*" within litigation is international arbitration. "*I have just been on an arbitration for a large Turkish conglomerate against a Russian bank. It sums up everything we do – it's multi-jurisdictional, long-running and quite glamorous,*" a trainee told us, adding with fingers crossed: "*There is going to be a full-on trial back in the British Virgin Islands and they will need a trainee to go out there.*"

Bear necessities

Another major department, construction, "*has quite a chilled attitude – it's full of Aussies.*" They handle both contentious and non-contentious matters and are currently working for a number of companies, including E.ON, on the construction and financing aspects of a €7.4bn gas pipeline project linking Russia to the EU via the Baltic Sea. "*In huge matters there's limited opportunities for a trainee but I have also worked on a lot of much smaller deals and one-off pieces of work where you can take the full lead,*" said an interviewee. There's drafting and research experience to be had on transactional matters, helping out with pleadings on litigation cases, and the department is also "*keen to get trainees writing articles.*" The remaining UK-based seats are corporate, real estate, IP and employment.

The firm's presence in every corner of the globe, from Abu Dhabi to Warsaw, doesn't just give W&C trainees something to brag about in the pub. A guarantee of an international seat allows them the chance to go to some of these exotic locations. New York, Hong Kong, Paris and Singapore are perennially popular (and you can read more about their charms and what they offer to lawyers on our website), but we were naturally interested in some of the more obscure secondments that W&C has to offer. It's the only firm to send a trainee to Johannesburg, for example. Or what about six months in Almaty, the largest city in Kazakhstan? "*A certain class of person applies for Almaty,*" we hear. "*They are the suicidal people who want to head out in the middle of nowhere. The same goes for Riyadh,*" said a bemused trainee (who had chosen a safe bet in Asia). Others were more understanding of wanderlust. "*The people who choose Almaty are those who are even more interested in international travel than the rest of us,*" said one. "*Or, as it's a capital markets seat, if you're really interested in that it would be good.*" Whatever stamp ends up on the passport, an overseas seat is a great chance to take on more responsibility than you might get at home. "*You're not really a trainee out there,*" said one satisfied source. Although most go abroad towards the end of the training contract, travel could come at any time. One lucky soul arrived for work on his first day at the firm, only to be told to go home and pack his Gucci shades – a couple of hours later he was flying to Milan. Others have been sent on business trips to France and India.

Trainees can also experience higher levels of responsibility by getting involved in pro bono work. American firms are perhaps slightly ahead of their British peers when it comes to not-for-profit work, and a number of W&C trainees were keen to tell us about some of the cases they had seen. "*There are lots of opportunities, especially in the main litigation department, and you can basically run the matter yourself as a trainee.*" One of our contacts had worked on IP matters for the organisers of the Homeless World Cup; another had done a spot of matchmaking with a twist: "*Basically brown bears are dying out in Austria. There are only two left and both of them are male. We're working on the campaign to get a few females in.*" The firm sends lawyers to the Citizen's Advice Bureau at the Royal Courts of Justice and is also involved with non-legal corporate social responsibility: for instance, "*one of the girls reads with local schoolchildren at lunchtimes.*"

Passport stamp collecting

So who does W&C want to recruit? "*The firm doesn't have a type,*" trainees insisted; "*we are a really diverse group.*" We can believe it. There's "*a fair sprinkling*" of traditional Oxbridge recruits but, as befits W&C's international nature, the Smiths, Joneses and Browns on the trainee roster are matched by surnames from every continent. The firm is clearly looking for people who won't be fazed by moving to another country at a later stage of their careers. Indeed, Philip Stopford admits that the firm is "*crying out for lawyers who go out for a secondment, come back and want to go overseas again. One thing you won't find is here is any restriction on working abroad.*"

When the going gets tough, "*trainees have each other's backs.*" Said one third-seater: "*Our intake is incredibly close – we talk about everything and even go on holiday together.*" The social scene is lively. "*We have slightly less drinks these days. In my first year it was non-stop. But it's still good – almost every Friday we have a trainee session.*" The Rocket and the Corney and Barrow are the bars of choice, and curry on Brick Lane is "*always popular.*" Bowling and various sporting events also came up in conversation. Christmas and summer parties take place every year: the last one was held at Billingsgate Vaults and had a 1920s theme.

And finally...

'International' is the watchword here. Pick W&C if you want to push yourself hard, live abroad for at least six months and immerse yourself in the world of global finance.

Wiggin LLP

The facts

Location: Cheltenham, London
Number of UK partners/solicitors: 16/22
Total number of trainees: 5
Seats: 4x6 months
Alternative seats: Secondments

"We're a very unusual firm," says training partner Simon Baggs. We couldn't agree more.

Wiggin: an unconventional law firm in an unlikely location.

Wiggin out

Wiggin's website reflects its position as the go-to firm for all things media. Fuchsia and lime livery, randomly ticking counters, a bikini-clad woman and a corporate video that declares the firm to be 'BANG ON!' adorn a homepage that looks more like that of an ad agency than a law firm. But then Wiggin has always been a bit cool. It was set up in the 1970s by two City escapees looking for a little less ritual and a lot more fun and quickly established a base of media clients. And what a base! From the world of sport: Manchester United, Middlesbrough and West Bromwich Albion football clubs, The International Cricket Council and numerous racecourses. From broadcasting: ITV, Channel 4, Channel 5, Virgin Media, Al Jazeera and HBO. From music: the BPI, Universal, Napster, The Feeling and New Order. From publishing: Random House, Trinity Mirror and Oxford University Press. And from film: Twentieth Century Fox, Warner Bros, Paramount, Columbia, Miramax, Film Four, BBC Films, Pathé and loads of independents.

Naturally, this attracts a certain type of trainee. If you're seriously interested in training in media law, Wiggin guarantees you'll get exactly that. It's a true boutique, *"not a big London firm with a media department that you'll never actually get to see."* Seats are available in film, broadcast media, corporate and litigation. The employment team has recently taken its first trainee, and there are also secondments to the BPI and Universal Pictures. Property is the only department that is entirely non-media in outlook, and business needs occasionally require a reluctant trainee to spend a seat there. Trainees can express their preferences but don't really get much choice in what seats they do.

Take a break... or not

Wiggin's contentious practice is divided into two teams. One team, covering music litigation, is heavily involved with the big issue of the day – illegal downloads. As you can imagine, *"it's a fairly mammoth task"* chasing down those responsible. Our sources agree that this is an *"in at the deep end"* seat where the work can be *"super-complicated."* As well as *"quite complex bits of research with no precedent,"* trainees also contact clients, draft witness statements, and spend a lot of time on disclosure for cases. A big trade mark dispute saw them go out onto the street to ask members of the public how they would interpret a particular logo.

The other team is largely concerned with the publishing industry. In the past year, it has defended *Grazia* in relation to a privacy claim by Victoria Beckham, and publishing house H Bauer in a defamation claim relating to a 'real life' story published in *Take A Break*. The biggest recent case, however, was gambling-related. Wiggin represented 23 defendants in proceedings brought by William Hill, Ladbrokes and Betfred, alleging breach of competition law in the establishment of a new service, TurfTV, to provide pictures to bookmakers. It involved the review of over one million documents, and you can guess who became intimately acquainted with quite a lot of them. During the trial at the High Court in London, trainees had two months of *"long, hard days: 8am to 2am, seven days a week."* Media law may be fun, but don't be fooled into thinking it's an easy ride. Apparently Wiggin trainees are the ones who always miss the local Junior Lawyers Division events because they're too busy working.

My mate Dave

Broadcast is *"very niche"* but *"essentially it's a commercial seat."* The work the team does for UKTV is typical. It advised the broadcaster on carriage agreements (*"they can be a logistical nightmare now that there's on-demand and all these other delivery mechanisms"*), Ofcom licensing and regulatory issues, the acquisition of new digital terrestrial capacity and the rebranding of all its channels – UK Gold to Dave, for instance. One of Wiggin's partners is in charge of *"gambling and pornography"* (great job title) and has been negotiating the launch of a gambling channel for Virgin Media. The porn aspect is more *FHM* than *Asian Babes*, we're told. In this seat it's *"slightly harder to get hands-on experience because it is so niche,"* but trainees have attended conferences with clients and can do things like drafting terms and conditions. *"That's really good because you can get stuck into them and do them from start to finish."*

The film team handles both film finance and film production issues. Film finance is exactly as the name suggests: it's all about drumming up funding for movies, including the recently released *Dorian Gray* and political comedy *In The Loop*. On the film production side, trainees draft lots of contracts, mainly cast, crew and location agreements. *"The high-level cast agreements for the big stars are done by the partners, but underneath that there are less complex negotiations for the head of editing, the head of costume and so on."* Getting third-party consent is another trainee task: if in a period film you want to use, say, a retro tin of Colman's Mustard, clearance from the owner of the trade mark must be gained.

Spa afield

"The training contract is very good, the exposure to clients is very good. You will be given excellent work provided you ask for it. You get fantastic hands-on media experience. The down side is that you have to move to Cheltenham." The firm has a London office that trainees will visit reasonably often, but the Cotswold spa town is where they are based. Wiggin doesn't recruit heavily from the local area and many of our interviewees had relocated from big cities. They didn't regret it, but said that applicants should consider carefully whether they are *"prepared for a quieter life"* outside office hours. *"For all that people say that Cheltenham's got some nice bars and clubs, it isn't London."* It seemed to us that the most content Wiggsters were the ones who had chosen the firm not just because of its media expertise, but because they *"quite liked the idea of being based out here."*

There's a lot of people queuing up for a shot at a Wiggin training contract and the application process is a tough one because the firm has been *"burnt"* in the past by

Chambers UK rankings

Defamation/Reputation Management	Licensing
	Media & Entertainment
Intellectual Property	Sports Law

"trainees who thought the two years would be an easy ride because it was in Cheltenham." The job interview lasts two days, and the best advice we can give comes from a trainee: *"If they ask you to research something, make sure you do it very, very well."* We're not guaranteeing the process will be the same next time, but in the past, applicants have had to mark up contracts, write notes of advice, give a client pitch to the board of Man United (or partners pretending, anyway) and hold their own in *"a big debate in front of the entire firm."* Shrinking violets and bookish types are most certainly not what Wiggin is looking for. Previous experience in the media will serve you well, although it's not essential. We had a tip-off that partners appreciate those who show a little initiative in their applications, but we'd advise you to interpret this advice with care: as media lawyers, these guys will have seen more gimmicks than most.

The recession has made Wiggin *"grow up"* a little bit. *"In this economy, it's not the firm it used to be. The wackiness is slowly subsiding. It's a young firm built on the idea of vibrancy, but what they have realised is it all costs money."* The Nintendo Wii in the London reception has been packed away; the champagne drinks trolley has gone. Heck, some of the first-years had never even seen anyone racing space-hoppers round the office. Although the firm held off making them for as long as possible, a handful of redundancies had dampened the mood, and trainees weren't confident about their prospects of retention. Training partner Simon Baggs was far more upbeat, however, and in fact three out of five qualifiers were kept on in 2009: two on permanent contracts, the third seconded to a client in the hope that Wiggin would be able to offer them a job in a year's time.

And finally...

If you're seriously interested in media law and don't mind the idea of leaving the capital, this is the ideal firm. It's put on a more serious face for the recession, but we're sure Wiggin will eventually revert to unconventional type.

Wilsons

The facts

Location: Salisbury, London

Number of partners/solicitors: 31/35

Total number of trainees: 9

Seats: 4x6 months

Alternative seats: Occasional secondments

> "*People either apply to Wilsons because it is more in the country yet still a large firm, or because they want to stay in the area but don't want a high-street firm.*"

Wilsons has called Salisbury home for almost three centuries, but it was not until the 1970s that its influence spread beyond Wiltshire's chalky Downs.

The City in the countryside

It was the addition of lawyer Anthony Edwards from London private client supremo Farrer & Co that really got the proverbial ball rolling. And during the 1990s, when so many top firms were turning their backs on private client work to concentrate on more lucrative (but arguably less reliable) commercial practice, Wilsons mopped up the luscious leftovers – most notably a team from McKenna & Co (now CMS Cameron McKenna). This decision served it well. Its annual turnover has doubled over the past six years to hit £13m. As well as a private client team that is ranked in the top band of *Chambers UK* for the South West, Wilsons boasts excellent capabilities in charity work (its specialist legacy team is the largest of its kind outside London) and agricultural and rural affairs. Over the past year the employment team has been really busy too, spending much of its time advising clients on restructuring and redundancy programmes.

While locating Wilsons' skills is easy, the words "*there isn't really a firm culture*" caused our hearts to sink a little. This was attributed to the lawyers' dispersal over four proximate offices in Salisbury as well as a new London base in Lincoln's Inn Fields that is thus far dedicated to charities law. Each of the Salisbury offices is within walking distance of the others and a stone's throw from the stunning cathedral and city centre, however "*the holy grail for the firm is finding somewhere where it can put everyone in the same office in the centre of Salisbury.*" Following neighbouring firm Trethowans to a business park is out of the question apparently.

The old idea of dogs looking like their owners can (almost) be applied to lawyers and their offices. The private client and probate teams work in individual offices rather than the open-plan format found in the other buildings. Trainees felt this more traditional layout better suited the "*wealthier, older*" clients who come in to see a particular solicitor, while the "*drab*" interior was in tune with the probate lawyers "*who are dealing with death all day and so have to be a bit more solemn.*" Conversely, in the employment building where the law is constantly changing and the work is faster paced and "*in the here and now,*" trainees talked of fancy spotlights, colourful chairs and a chill-out room containing a Playstation. Not that anyone could remember anyone using it except for "*perhaps the kids of some poor divorcee at half term.*"

Rich relations and raggedy aunts

Seat allocation has gone slightly awry due to the turbulence in the economy, but nobody had any grave complaints. Most found that if they spoke to HR about specific desires they could often be accommodated. It should be noted that a stint in the property department is usually compulsory, and with the firm announcing itself as a "*specialist law firm focusing on wealthy individuals and their legal needs,*" it should be no surprise that time with the private client team is encouraged.

Private client is split into two groups: offshore/new wealth and landed estates/old money. Trainees get a taste of both. Sources described being "*dropped in at the deep end*" and receiving "*a very good quality of work,*" such as drafting complex trust documents as well as "*conducting minor client interviews towards the end of the seat.*" Reassuringly, "*partners understand there is a lot to learn and take their time to explain things.*" The offshore/new wealth branch of the team has grown in significance over the years and it has a substantial client base in the Channel Islands, Hong Kong and, increasingly, Singapore. Some 10% of the firm's turnover currently comes from the team's overseas work, which spans more than 45 jurisdictions worldwide.

The probate seat is often seen as private client's raggedy aunt, but even those who didn't think it was for them at first "*ended up really enjoying it.*" Over 40% of the probates handled are valued at over £5m, and with more than 250 trusts to manage the department is consistently busy. Cases have a much longer timeframe than in other departments, with "*no real deadlines because nine out of ten times the client is, well, dead.*" Those we spoke to enjoyed seeing smaller files from start to finish; regular trainee tasks include drafting wills and inheritance tax forms as well as meeting with clients to legalise probate papers.

Charitable purposes

The probate lawyers work closely with the highly regarded charities department, which is pre-eminent in legacy and contentious probate matters. After losing its previous head Alison McKenna in February 2008 to the newly formed Charity Tribunal, Wilsons bagged a top-class London lawyer called Moira Protani who formerly headed up Berwin Leighton Paisner's charity team. It didn't stop there; the team has doubled in size (to 15 lawyers) in just a year, and with the opening of a new London office in March 2009 it's clear that Wilsons is keen to stamp its authority in this sector. With so many of its clients situated in and around the capital – Cancer Research UK in central London, the RSPCA near Horsham and Guide Dogs for the Blind near Reading – people see the new office as a "*natural progression.*"

Wilsons' charities practice covers governance issues and disputes, so a trainee's time is split between research, setting up and managing charities and assisting with cases going through the courts. One source witnessed a "*fascinating*" will dispute at a time when a colleague was on maternity leave. The responsibility for "*instructing the QC and briefing witnesses as well as arranging transcribers*" was passed to the trainee. A mainstream litigation seat offers a popular month's secondment to barristers' chambers, where trainees shadow counsel and "*begin to build relationships and learn the skills you need to become a litigator.*" The range of disputes they see is wide and the "*fast pace and tactics of it all*" make litigation an absorbing assignment. As for other commercial areas, well, we sensed that these were not a priority for many of

Chambers UK rankings

Agriculture & Rural Affairs	Employment
Charities	Family/Matrimonial
Corporate/M&A	Private Client
Dispute Resolution	Real Estate

the trainees we spoke to. Nevertheless, stints in the employment and company/commercial seats are available and quality clients include upmarket estate agency Savills, a global pharmaceutical company and new client Dental Patient Advisory Service, the UK's third largest dental plan company.

Love The Slug

"*People either apply to Wilsons because it is more in the country yet still a large firm, or because they want to stay in the area but don't want a high-street firm.*" Our sources agreed that "*you wouldn't come to Salisbury for the social life,*" but despite this they found plenty to keep them busy. Trainees "*often go out for dinner together*" or for drinks in The Slug and Lettuce "*because it's situated between all the offices.*" Seniors often come along but tend to leave early to get home to their families. Weekends are for classic country living or perhaps partying in the capital. The firm's Christmas and summer festivities are always well attended, even if grand plans to hold the 2008 Christmas ball at the Aviation Museum (in 2007 it was the National Motor Museum) were quickly readjusted for financial reasons. Staff instead made the most of a buffet and disco in Salisbury. Regular quiz nights are popular too, and Wilsons is home to an active cricket team as well as netball and rounders teams that surface intermittently.

Unfortunately none of the four 2009 qualifying trainees were retained, but this is more of a reflection on the market conditions than the firm's normal practice. Nor does it reflect the value the firm places on its trainees: lately it introduced a new mentoring scheme and designed an intranet page and handbook specifically for them.

And finally...

The new London office signifies growth, so don't let Wilsons' age and 'genteel' practice areas fool you. This is an ambitious firm with big plans for the future.

Withers LLP

The facts

Location: London
Number of UK partners/solicitors: 56/100 +11 non-UK-qualified
Total number of trainees: 35
Seats: 4x6 months
Alternative seats: Overseas seats, secondments
Extras: Pro bono – CAB at the Principal Registry, Own-It IP advice service; language training

Withers' ethos is that "*it's about building a relationship with a person throughout their life and delivering for them at every stage.*"

Bespoke fashion houses, Russian oligarchs and flashy entrepreneurs: just a few of the clients you'll come across at this private client giant. Training here means high-stakes work.

Virgin territory

"*Like a fresh pint of ale: old-school and making a comeback.*" That's how one trainee described Withers, and we're inclined to agree. Founded in 1896, the firm quickly made its name acting for the blue-blooded gentry of London and the Home Counties. While it is still home to a solid backbone of green-wellied domestic clients, Withers has spent the past decade nurturing a sparkling reputation for managing the affairs of overseas clients, entrepreneurs and even the occasional celebrity. "*Look at the strategy,*" insisted one interviewee; "*we go where the money is.*" This has resulted in a global network of offices in the European and American goldmines of private wealth – London, Milan, Geneva, New York, New Haven and Greenwich, Connecticut. In 2008 a new office opened in Hong Kong and in March 2009 Withers set up shop in the British Virgin Islands, one of the world's leading offshore centres. It is estimated that more than 40% of all offshore companies are registered there. As our sources were keen to point out: "*The global offices put Withers in an absolutely unique position. We are the biggest private client firm in the world.*"

In 2007 Anthony Indaimo was appointed as the firm's new chairman. He's the first corporate lawyer to hold the position, marking Withers' decision to move into a more commercial sphere, but with almost 50% of the firm's work generated from private clients we wondered how realistic this was. "*I'd say the other departments are starting to grow legs of their own,*" remarked one trainee. "*The private wealth department is the largest on the whole, but the other departments don't rely on it for referrals and offshoots.*" This may be true, but it's probably worth saying that compared to the likes of the magic circle (or even the London mid-market) Withers is not viewed as a big hitter in the corporate game. It prefers its commercial clients to be quirky and cool, acting for The Arts Council, UK bag designer Lulu Guinness, Italian fashion house MaxMara, Renault Formula 1, and Sienna and Savannah Miller's fashion label, Twenty8Twelve. At the end of 2008 the firm's commercial lawyers helped fashion designer Matthew Williamson negotiate a licensing agreement with H&M in relation to a series of pieces for the retailer, including his first menswear line.

Most of the trainees we spoke to were drawn by Withers' emphasis on the individual. "*I would much rather be dealing with people and their personal and business needs. It brings up a whole spectrum of really interesting work.*" Withers' ethos is that "*it's about building a relationship with a person throughout their life and delivering for them at every stage.*" One trainee told us: "*There is one client I am working for in probate who was divorced three times and came to Withers for at least two of those. We drafted his prenups and oversaw his properties. And now that he is dead we are working on his will.*" The corporate department is essentially an extension of this service. "*Often the clients use several different departments within the firm,*" say trainees. "*We start off by acting for them as wealth planners and then they want to set up a company so we run that for them as well."*

Where there's a will, there's Withers

Trainees have a largely free choice of seats, but time in the huge wealth planning department is a given. It *"stretches from the really traditional domestic stuff like landed estates, wills and domestic trusts, to the more corporate-y,"* so it is likely that something there will take your fancy. With almost a quarter of the *Sunday Times'* Rich List on its books Withers has no shortage of high-profile, big-money work. Much of it is quite technical and there is *"a real emphasis on making sure everyone is up to scratch,"* so a lot of training is provided. *"Almost every lunchtime there's a department having a training session. At times it can be overwhelming."* One source admitted that they *"didn't expect to be reading up quite as ferociously"* and advised prospective applicants to do their homework.

The *Chambers UK* and *Chambers Global* top-ranked private client group is split into three subsections: FAB (family and business planning); FITT (funds, investments, tax and trusts); and international wealth planning. The FAB team is the home of the firm's more traditional clients. *"There are a lot of landed estates and families that have been with us for generations."* It comes as no surprise to discover therefore that *"the department is very thorough. Nothing goes out unless it has been checked by at least two partners."* There is ample scope for client contact and trainees can expect to draft wills and lasting power of attorney for them. *"Essentially there are two things to FAB,"* explained one source. *"We try to avoid inheritance tax, and ensure that assets are passed down in the right way."* Work in the international wealth planning team involves *"a lot of research into tax treatments"* while also juggling between several jurisdictions. Withers acts for members of a Latin American family in connection with the creation of private trust company structures to hold assets required for the long-term benefit of the family, and an African-based family on the structuring of their assets, believed to be worth in the region of £2bn.

The FITT team is *"essentially wealth planning with a corporate slant."* A seat here offers *"a real mix – from working for business entrepreneurs to working for listed companies. You can go from a multimillion-pound deal one moment to taking board minutes for a small business the next."* Trainee work includes drafting share purchase agreements or reviewing documents for people who are setting up their own companies, entering into partnerships or setting up investment funds. The firm's corporate department acts for many of the same clients: directors and entrepreneurs who have set up their own businesses. But while *"it is almost accurate to say that 80% of the work in corporate originates from the private client team,"* the department is now attracting work in its own right.

Chambers UK rankings

Agriculture & Rural Affairs	Family/Matrimonial
Banking Litigation	Fraud: Civil
Charities	Intellectual Property
Defamation/Reputation Management	Private Client
Employment	Professional Negligence

Last year we reported that Withers was making a concerted effort to avoid recruiting trainees who were solely interested in the often-oversubscribed family and private client departments. It appears to have been successful as a number of trainees are choosing to go down the commercial route and taking seats in the corporate, commercial litigation, commercial property or charity teams. Withers acts for a number of well-known charities including The British Red Cross, Macmillan Cancer Research, Concern Worldwide and the Imperial War Museum.

Break ups and break downs

Those who still dream of spending time in the glossy, self-contained family department (*"it has the top floor all to itself and gets all the light"*) should expect long hours, lots of bundling, hours spent making attendance notes and plenty of time in court. *"Our reputation is immense and we do huge cases, so you are not going to be running your own files in any sense. But you do get exposure to some amazing things."* Withers worked on the Miller, Charman and Crossley divorces, and this year represented Marco Pierre White's ex-wife Mati in her divorce from the celebrity chef. As one trainee succinctly put it: *"It's not your run-of-the-mill one house, one car, two bank accounts and pensions. The assets can be immense and all over the place."* Trainees were quick to remind us that *"it is emotional work"* and we hear that it is sometimes left to trainees to comfort wives *"who often break down under harsh cross-examination."*

Contentious experience can also be found in the employment department, which has more than doubled in size since 2006. The team acts for employees and employers but is particularly recognised for its work for senior executives. Trainees often get to speak directly with the clients in order to obtain information for drafting compromise agreements and preparing for hearings. Clients on the employer side include small companies and charities. Other contentious seats include property litigation and a spot in the *"really hectic and frantic"* contentious trusts team.

Property seats (rural, commercial and residential) provide trainees with some real independence. *"I was pretty much running the show in terms of my files,"* one source recalled. *"I learned so much from the hands-on work and* began to see how it could be applied to bigger deals." One such deal was the sale of an estate comprising 2,500 acres of farmland, 29 cottages and four commercial leases – the largest country estate sale of 2008. Trainees regularly make site visits and we couldn't help but laugh when we heard about one who visited a £6.5m estate and thought they were in the master bedroom, when in fact they were in the boot room. "*There was just a bed there in case the master wanted to sit down while undoing his boots!*"

More Kings Road than Camden

There's an overseas corporate seat in Withers' Milan office, but start brushing up on your Italian as it's only offered to fluent speakers. The firm specifically recruits with this in mind and tries to ensure that there at least two people who have mastered the language in each intake. As a result Withers claims to have the largest number of Italian speakers in the City.

These trainees are a civilised bunch and describe themselves as "*classic Kensington as opposed to wild City slickers.*" Said one: "*Let's put it this way, we aren't going to be throwing televisions out of hotel room windows. We are more like the managers of the rock stars, not the rock stars themselves.*" They continued: "*We are all very confident individuals. High achievers... I feel pushed by my peer group to perform to the best of my ability.*" Some people were keen to assure us that "*the Sloaney element is not overwhelming,*" still, there are plenty of Oxbridge grads. One trainee even claimed that "*for private client and rural estates-type work it is really useful if you have connections with someone from a landed estate simply because you develop very long-standing relationships and it is important to be able to empathise with them.*" Most agreed that "*ten years ago it would have been much easier to stereotype. There is more of a mix nowadays.*" Perhaps the most important stereotype to discuss is the idea that Withers is old-school in every sense. If you've already made this assumption then just consider the fact that in 1999, divorce lawyer Diana Parker was elected as the youngest, and first female, senior partner of a major London law firm.

On the social front there aren't many centrally organised events ("*we aren't the types for enforced jollies*"), nevertheless the Christmas party is always a glitzy affair. The football, cricket and hockey teams are popular and "*everyone will go out for a couple of drinks after a session.*" This is a firm people grow fond of and this affection is evidenced by the fact that so many people want to stay on when they qualify. In 2009, 11 of the 19 qualifiers did so: six on permanent contracts, five on fixed-term ones. The economy hurt the firm to an extent. "*There was a round of redundancies, mainly affecting support staff, and a couple of fee earners were encouraged to leave. It was all a bit cloak and dagger; they didn't really announce it... a couple of people just disappeared.*" The property department was also put onto a four-day week earlier in 2009, but overall our sources believed that the situation within the firm was "*not too bad compared to the doom and gloom of the press.*"

And finally...

This is a clever firm with a well-considered business plan. Just like its trouser-shaped office there is more to Withers than first meets the eye: "*From the front it looks like a 12-partner firm doing very crusty work. Look around the corner and it's much bigger and flashier.*"

Wragge & Co LLP

The facts

Location: Birmingham, London

Number of UK partners/solicitors: 111/287

Total number of trainees: 53

Seats: 4x6 months

Alternative seats: Occasionally Brussels secondments,

Extras: Pro bono – various advice schemes

Birmingham's Big Daddy, Wragge recruits lively and accomplished trainees who generally have a whale of a time. Clients, too, love what Wragge has to offer them.

The largest independent firm in Birmingham, Wragge's USP is the capacity to serve FTSE 250 clients that might otherwise consider a London firm from the less expensive environs of England's second city.

Bwragging rights

To simply label Wragge as a strong Birmingham firm would be to understate its achievements. It may not have a sprawl of offices across the country, but it does have a substantial and established London office and its trainees genuinely feel that Wragge is "*the best place to be.*" Look at our favoured barometer of success – the *Chambers UK* rankings – and you'll see a firm with a massive presence regionally and nationally across a very broad spectrum of practices. It wins shedloads of Band 1 rankings in both mainstream and niche practice areas. For more evidence, see *Chambers Client Report's* annual FTSE survey, which ranks law firms by the number of FTSE 100 and 250 clients on their books. Wragge fares very well: only the magic circle, Herbert Smith and a couple of the larger national firms do better. Wragge has the City firmly in its sights and, in addition to its Brum programme, is starting a London-only training contract from 2010.

There's a huge choice of departments available to trainees, from the traditional big-firm panoply of corporate, real estate, litigation and employment, to a decent selection of specialist areas like IT, environment, pensions and competition. These teams are all under one roof in Birmingham, and there's a good range of practices in London too, though they are not divided into so many specialist subgroups. Reflecting the thrust of its business, Wragge stipulates that trainees undertake seats in real estate, litigation and corporate, but this need not be limiting as there are plenty of subgroups that fall under these broad heads, and it's also possible to tick off two of these requirements at once, by doing real estate litigation, for instance.

Band on the one

Real estate is a big practice area at Wragge and the department handles transactional, financing and contentious instructions. Not unexpectedly, the department was hit following the credit crunch, and the majority of the firm's redundancies were made in this area. Trainees hinted that the amount of work available to them did dip, but said: "*There is work there in good times and bad.*" Recently, lawyers tackled a US Congress-approved project to move the American Embassy in London from Mayfair to new, high-security, low carbon footprint premises in Wandsworth. Working with the same developer (Ballymore), Wragge advised on the Snowhill scheme in Birmingham that will see the construction of the city's tallest residential tower, its first five-star hotel and two new office buildings (one of which will be the firm's new home, eventually). It has also been appointed to the legal panel for London's £16bn Crossrail project and panels for numerous real estate investors. Topically, it has also advised several parties on the installation of wind turbines. Trainees see plenty of the normal day-to-day business of real estate practice: "*advising on leases and complex repossessions, serving notices and working on development agreements.*" They also run some smaller projects on their own.

There is "*a really clear line separating corporate and commercial.*" 'Corporate' refers exclusively to M&A work and "*is on a totally different floor with different people to the 'commercial' people.*" There are some real whoppers among the M&A transactions including a €54m share purchase deal between FTSE-listed engineering company Hill & Smith and associated company Zinkinvent; a £32.5m investment by 3i in research company SLR Holdings; the £75m cross-border acquisition of Concentric by Swedish company Haldex; and the creation of a €200m fund to be invested in projects across Europe. These transactions demonstrate Wragge's international reach but for further evidence visit its website and view a map of the world pockmarked by red circles commemorating its cross-border achievements. Assisting Wragge is a network of foreign 'best friend' firms plus its own offices in Brussels, Guangzhou and Munich. And on home soil, what *Chambers UK* ranking does it get for corporate/M&A in the Midlands? Band 1, naturally.

'Commercial' is a pretty broad term and this department incorporates several teams including IT, outsourcing, trade and technology. In the IT group you'll get to grips with complex IT licensing contracts that call for a "*diverse range of skills.*" Aspects of competition law are often brought to bear on the topic. Another function of the department is dealing with the hot potato that is data protection, so if you want to be able to argue about ID cards with some degree of authority, this would be a good place to go. Wragge has, once again, a Band 1 ranking in this discipline.

Patently good

Although not its most prominent practice group, Wragge has a strong IP team whose annual Band 1 ranking is so consistent that it might as well be carved in stone. The team works for a diverse selection of clients from the nanotech/biotech/pharmaceuticals sector plus the telecoms and video games industries. Most notably, lawyers fought the two largest patent actions ever launched in the UK. Limitations on space prevent us from covering these cases fully, so if you want some homework, go and read up on the precedent-setting matters of Nokia v InterDigital and InterDigital Technology Corporation v Nokia. Trainees described work in this department as "*extremely interesting and dynamic.*"

Pensions is "*an area you either love or hate,*" but we failed to detect any haters among the trainees who'd worked in this "*really expanding*" part of the firm. The pensions experience is described as "*very technical work in a very laid-back team.*" Here, trainees hone their drafting skills by day, and by night they get to party: "*The team is great – we go for drinks regularly, there are loads of social events, including karaoke where there were some embarrassing incidents.*" What? No details?

Chambers UK rankings

Administrative & Public Law	Intellectual Property
Advertising & Marketing	Life Sciences
Aviation	Local Government
Banking & Finance	Outsourcing
Banking Litigation	Pensions
Competition/European Law	Pensions Litigation
Construction	Planning
Corporate/M&A	Product Liability
Debt Recovery	Projects, Energy & Natural Resources
Dispute Resolution	Public Procurement
Employment	Real Estate
Environment	Real Estate Litigation
Healthcare	Restructuring/Insolvency
Information Technology	Retail
Insurance	Tax
	Transport

The construction team is still taking on new NQs because, although "*the developer side has been hit hard,*" it has been "*getting a lot of public sector work on the non-contentious side: lots of PFI projects like the Building Schools for the Future scheme, rail stuff, hospital construction and work on the construction of new independent treatment centres for the NHS.*" With such grand-sounding projects on the go, you might think six months would be insufficient time to get to grips with a project, but trainees are able to deal with smaller, discrete tasks and there are plenty of more manageable files for them to look after solo. At the risk of sounding like a stuck record, Wragge gets a Band 1 ranking in both *Chambers UK's* main construction category and its healthcare subcategory.

Wragge puts in the effort with its trainees. It gives them several days of training in a new practice area whenever they move seats, and every week they have a brief review with their supervisors, who help moderate their workload and check for any problems.

Capital questions

The cold, spindly fingers of the recession pinched from the coffers of every firm in one way or another, but they seemed to really scoop up the gold in Birmingham, perhaps due to the double punch of the property downturn and the extended woes of the manufacturing sector. Trainees tell us: "*A lot of the Birmingham firms rely quite heavily on property and development, leaving them pretty exposed. Also, the West Midlands has the highest rate of unemployment in the country; look at businesses like LDV – they closed down.*" With that in mind, Wragge's drop in profits looked more like the result of dismal circumstances than mismanagement. After all, its peers took a beating too. In 2008/09, Wragge's revenue dropped by

17% (from £126m to £104m) and its profits fell by roughly a third. When discussing the inevitable redundancies, trainees confirmed that the two rounds were handled well, that the compensation given was fair and the firm showed "*a real effort to maintain a pyramid shape – seniors have been dismissed too.*" Other measures were taken to protect jobs, including a pay freeze, flexible working and a reduction in the NQ salary.

Looking ahead, most of our sources were of the opinion that "*Wragge is going out there and doing what it always does best: promoting its culture and cost-effectiveness with a big emphasis on long-term relationships.*" It is also "*trying to retain its position in the market.*" Due to the sheer size of the office, "*Wragge is very much a Birmingham law firm and always will be – Birmingham is its hub,*" but there are questions to be asked about its London ambitions. One trainee described London as "*a feeder office,*" but the firm is about to start a London-only training contract, which suggests that a scaling-up of operations in the City is in the pipeline. Several trainees spoke about the office in the capital bringing the firm closer to the major English courts and a few discussed the wisdom of carving out a better position in the London mid-market. But given the firm's strategy of "*offering lower overheads to top FTSE companies*" by doing work in Birmingham, we don't think it is about to alter the status quo..

Building from the ground up

Trainees described an atmosphere that mixes hard work with warm office relations, occasional late nights with frequent parties and social events. There is an active social committee and the firm pays for membership of trainee solicitor societies and the young professionals networking group Birmingham Futures. Additionally, there are always loads of ad hoc social events going on, including sports. The firm has "*a legendary Christmas party*" and its New Beginnings parties (to celebrate the arrival of new starters) sound great. Indeed there's so much packed into the social calendar here that we wonder when trainees ever get a chance to see their non-work friends.

What of the demographics of the trainee group? "*It's hard to stereotype; there's such a spread of people*" and the "*age range is about 22 through to about 31. There are people who are married, and one has a kid. Plenty of people have had careers before.*" One or two trainees, however, raised concerns that "*Wragge used to recruit on per-

sonality but some of the recent trainees have been questionable – a lot quieter and less sociable, but I suppose they work harder.*" Well, perhaps. As a result of its increasing popularity, the firm is targeting really top universities and takes on more of the Oxbridge set than it used to.

And what about NQ retention? In short, Wragge is consistently good at keeping on its qualifiers. In 2009, despite the harshness of the economy 25 of 32 people stayed on. "*The firm has bent over backwards to fit everyone in,*" confirmed one relieved source. But what does that mean for the next few intakes? Although "*a lot of people are happy and proud to be at Wragge because it has gone out of its way to find jobs,*" others "*don't think it's so black and white. Some teams like pensions are taking on a lot of trainees due to business needs, and some of the NQ jobs result from natural wastage, but I think there was an element of making jobs where there weren't any.*" We're loath to criticise a firm that has made the effort to retain so many of its trainees, but some of our more cautious sources were certainly concerned how this would affect subsequent qualifiers. In short it will all depend on the speed and strength of the recovery.

Earlier on, we referred to Wragge's new home in the Snowhill development. Trainees are looking forward to the move (current lodgings are "*pretty cramped*") and the new premises are supposed to be high-spec, but… work on this project was suspended when the developer's funding was hit. At the time we went to press Wragge's lovely new home was a jagged lift shaft surrounded by a latticework of scaffolding with a dormant crane swaying in the wind above. Hopefully over the coming months Brum's residents will be able to regard the ongoing development as a symbol of the recovery in the property market.

And finally...

There are unashamed Wragge & Co fans up and down the country – clients, legal market observers, the firm's own staff... If you too are falling for its charms we recommend you work super-hard on your application.

- **Want to work for Chambers and Partners?** Our research and editorial team is about 90 strong and works on a range of legal guides. If you have good interviewing and writing skills, why not take a look at our website and find out more about us and what we do? Some of our researchers are with us while waiting for a training contract to start. We're especially interested in people who speak foreign languages.

top tip no. 29

Refine Your Search

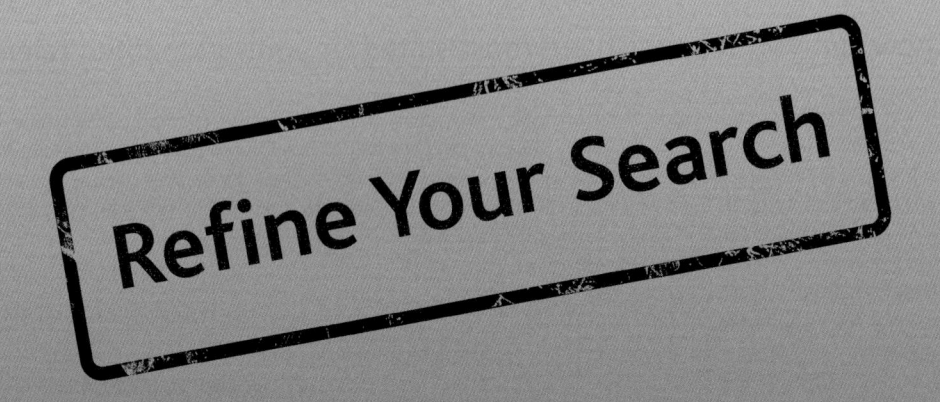

Application and selection methods of the top firms	515
Table of salaries and law school sponsorships	521
Picking a firm for its overseas opportunities	529

Refine your search

We know just how disorienting, disheartening and crazily time consuming it can be to get lost in acres and acres of recruitment material from law firms telling you how they're the best thing since sliced bread. We're sure they are, but how can you tell which are most suited to your undoubted talents?

Snap yourself out of that haze and glance at our crystal clear comparison tables which show you the facts you really want to know, in an instant. Which firms are flashing the cash? Which have moths in their wallets? Which will post you to sunnier climes for a working holiday… ahem, overseas placement? What other carrots are firms prepared to dangle in front of you to secure your signature? Who will pay you to go to law school? And finally, how do you apply?

This section is divided into three easy-to-use reference tables which enable you to narrow down your longlist of target firms. They show at a glance the application and selection procedures of each firm, the number of rival applicants you're likely to compete against for that coveted place, the salaries and benefits on offer, and the locations of overseas seats among those firms that offer them.

Application and selection methods

The table on the following page allows you to compare in seconds how each law firm requires you to apply – whether by a letter crafted in your best joined-up handwriting, by a CV dropped in the post, or online. It shows you what minimum degree is required and how many interviews and/or assessment days you face. Finally, and equally crucially, it gives the number of training contracts available alongside how many applications each firm receives.

Salaries and law school sponsorships

Our table of salaries and law school sponsorships on page 521 reveals the current salaries on offer for first and second-year trainees at each firm plus the salary for newly qualified solicitors. It also gives details of sponsorship and awards available to help you pay for law school, along with information about other benefits once you join the firm, like gym membership, health insurance and financial bonuses.

Overseas seats

The final table on page 530 lists what firms ship trainees out to which international locations, so if you've got a hankering for Hong Kong, a longing for Luxembourg or possibly even a fetish for the Falkland Islands, we'll show you where to apply before you can say: 'Money, tickets, passport!'

Applications and Selection

Firm name	Method of Application	Selection Process	Degree Class	Number of Contracts	Number of Applications
Addleshaw Goddard	See website	Interview + assessment centre	2:1	45-50	1,500
Allen & Overy	Online	Interview	2:1	105	2,500
Anthony Collins	See website	Interview + assessment centre	2:1 preferred	6	700
Ashurst	Online	2 interviews	2:1	55	2,500
Baker & McKenzie	Online	Oral presentation + interview	2:1	38	2,000
Barlow Lyde & Gilbert	Online	Assessment Centre	Not known	15-20	1,500
Beachcroft	Online	Online test + Assessment centre	2:1 preferred	24	Not known
Beale & Company	Application form	Interview + assessment	2:1	Not known	Not known
Berwin Leighton Paisner	Online	Assessment day + interview	2:1	40	1,500
Bevan Brittan	Online	Not known	Not known	Not known	Not known
Bingham McCutchen	Online	Interviews	High 2:1	2	Not known
Bircham Dyson Bell	See website	2 interviews, presentation + assessment	2:1 preferred	7	650
Bird & Bird	Online	Assessment day	2:1	16	900
Bond Pearce	Online	Assessment day	2:1	15-20	Not known
Boodle Hatfield	Online	Interviews + assessment	2:1	6	Not known
B P Collins	Handwritten letter & CV	Interview + selection day	2:1	Not known	Not known
Bristows	Online	2 interviews	2:1 preferred	Up to 10	3,500
Browne Jacobson	Online or CV & covering letter	Telephone interview + assessment centre + interview	Not known	8	700
Burges Salmon	Online	Not known	2:1	20-25	1,500
Capsticks	Application form CV & letter	Interview	2:1	5	200
Charles Russell	Online	Assessment day	2:1	14-21	1,500
Clarke Willmott	Online	Assessment centre	2:1 preferred	10	700
Cleary Gottlieb Steen & Hamilton	CV & covering letter	Usually via vac scheme	High 2:1	10-12	Not known
Clifford Chance	Online	Assessment day + interview	2:1	c.100	2,000
Clyde & Co	Online	Interview + assessments	2:1	24	1,400+
CMS Cameron McKenna	Online	Interview + assessment centre	2:1	60	1,500
Cobbetts	Online	Assessment days	2:1	17	1,000
Coffin Mew	See website	Interview	2:1 (usually)	4-5	400+
Collyer Bristow	Online	Online testing + interview	2:1	Not known	Not known
Covington & Burling	Online	2 interviews	2:1	6	Not known
Cripps Harries Hall	Online	Interview	2:1	8	Up to 750
Davenport Lyons	Online	Interviews	2:1	8	800
Davies Arnold Cooper	See website	See website	2:1	7	Not known
Dechert	Online	Interviews + assessments	2:1	10-15	1,000
Denton Wilde Sapte	Application form	2 interviews + assessments	2:1	25-30	1,500
Dewey & LeBoeuf	Online	2 interviews + assessments	2:1	15	900

Applications and Selection

Firm name	Method of Application	Selection Process	Degree Class	Number of Contracts	Number of Applications
Dickinson Dees	Online	Interview + assessments	2:1	Up to 18	800
DLA Piper	Online	2 interviews + assessments	2:1	85	2,600
Dundas & Wilson	Online	Assessment day	2:1 preferred	35 (12 in London)	300
DWF	Online	2 interviews	2:1	18	800
Edwards Angell Palmer & Dodge	Online	Interview & assessments	2:1	Up to 8	500
Eversheds	Online	Assessment day	2:1	55	3,000
Farrer & Co	Online	Interviews	2:1	10	800
Finers Stephens Innocent	CV & covering letter	2 interviews	2:1	6	800
Fladgate	Application form	Assessment & Interview	2:1	3	Not Known
Foot Anstey	Online	Assessment day	2:1 preferred	15	Not known
Forbes	Handwritten letter & CV	Interview	2:1	4	350+
Ford & Warren	Handwritten letter & CV or email	Interviews + exercise	2:1	4	500
Freeth Cartwright	Online	Interview + selection day	Not known	Not known	Not known
Freshfields Bruckhaus Deringer	Online	2 interviews + written test	2:1	90	2,000
Government Legal Service	Online	Online test + assessment day	2:1	22-30	500+
Halliwells	Online	Group exercise, presentation + interview	2:1	35	1,500
Hammonds	Online	Assessment + interview	2:1	30	1,300
Harbottle & Lewis	CV & letter	Interview	2:1	5	800
HBJ Gateley Wareing	See website	Not known	2:1	Not known	Not known
Henmans	Application form	Assessment day	Not known	3	300
Herbert Smith	Online	Case study + interview	2:1	Up to 100	2,000
Hewitsons	Application form	Interview	2:1	10	850
Higgs & Sons	Online	Interview	2:1 usually preferred	4	250+
Hill Dickinson	Online	Assessment day	Not known	Not known	Not known
Holman Fenwick Willan	Online	2 interviews + written exercise	2:1	12-14	1,000
Howes Percival	Online	Assessment centre	2:1	8	300
Ince & Co	Online	2 interviews + written tests	2:1	15	1,000

Applications and Selection

Firm name	Method of Application	Selection Process	Degree Class	Number of Contracts	Number of Applications
Irwin Mitchell	Online	Assessment centre + interview	Not known	20-25	1,500
Jones Day	CV & letter online	2 interviews	2:1	15-20	1,500
Kirkland & Ellis	CV & letter	Interview	2:1	Not known	Not known
K&L Gates	Online	Assessment day	2:1	Not known	1,000
Latham & Watkins	Online	3 interviews	2:1	15-20	Not known
Lawrence Graham	Application form	Interview	2:1	20-25	800
Laytons	Application form	2 interviews	1 or 2:1 preferred	8	2,000
Lester Aldridge	Letter, CV & application form	Interview & assessment	2:1	6	200
Lewis Silkin	Online	Assessment day	2:1	5	550
Linklaters	Online	2 interviews + assessments	2:1	110	4,000
Lovells	Online	Assessment day + interview	2:1	90	1,500
Macfarlanes	Online	Assessment day	2:1	30	800
Maclay Murray & Spens	Application form	2 interviews + assessments	2:1	30 London/Scotland	150 (London)
Manches	Online	2 interviews	2:1	10	850
Martineau	Online	Half-day assessment centre	2:1	10-12	600
Maxwell Winward	CV & covering letter	2 interviews	2:1	3-4	800
Mayer Brown	Online	Interview + assessments	2:1	30-35	1,000+
McDermott, Will & Emery	Online	Interview + assessment day	Not known	Not known	Not known
McGrigors	Online	Half-day assessment centre	2:1	12-15 (London)	Not known
Memery Crystal	Online	Interview + assessment	2:1	4	180
Michelmores	Online	Interview + assessment day	Usually 2:1	8	200
Mills & Reeve	Online	Assessment day	2:1	20	650
Mishcon de Reya	Online	Not known	2:1	8-12	1,000+
Muckle	Online	Interview + assessment day	2:1	4	120-130
Mundays	Online	Assessment centre + interview	2:1	3	150
Nabarro	Online	Assessment day	2:1	35	1,600
Norton Rose	Online	Interview + group exercise	2:1	55	2,500+
Olswang	Online	Interview + assessments	2:1	24	2,000
O'Melveny & Myers	Online	Interview	Not known	Not known	Not known

Applications and Selection

Firm name	Method of Application	Selection Process	Degree Class	Number of Contracts	Number of Applications
Osborne Clarke	Online	Assessment day	2:1	20	1,000
Pannone	Online	2 interviews	2:1	15	1,300
Paul Hastings	Online	Interview	2:1	4-5	Not known
Penningtons Solicitors	Online	Not known	2:1	8-10	1,000
Pinsent Masons	Online	Assessment day + interview	2:1	60	2,000+
PricewaterhouseCoopers Legal	Online	Not known	2:1	8	Not known
Pritchard Englefield	Application form	Interview	Generally 2:1	3	300-400
Reed Smith	Online	Interview + assessment	2:1	30	1,500
Reynolds Porter Chamberlain	Online	Assessment day	2.1	15	900
Shadbolt	Online	Interview + assessment	Usually 2:1	4	100
Shearman & Sterling	Online	Interview + assessment centre	2:1	15	Not known
Sheridans	CV & letter	2 interviews	2:1	1	Not known
Shoosmiths	Online	Full-day assessment centre	2:1	20	800
Sidley Austin	Application form	Interview(s)	2:1	12	500
Simmons & Simmons	Online	Assessment day	2:1	c. 40	2,000
SJ Berwin	Online	2 interviews	2:1	40	2,000
Skadden	Online	Interview + exercise	2:1	10-12	700
Slaughter and May	Online	Interview	2:1	95 approx.	2,000
Speechly Bircham	Application form	Interview + assessment	2:1	10	800
Stephenson Harwood	Online	Assessment day	2:1	14	Not known
Stevens & Bolton	Online	2 interviews + assessments	2:1	4	200
Taylor Wessing	Online	Assessment centre + interview	2:1	c. 20	700
Thomas Cooper	Online	Interviews	2:1	Not known	Not known
Thomas Eggar	Online	Assessment centre + interview	2:1	8	Not known
Thomson Snell & Passmore	Online	Assessment interview	2:1	5	500
Thring Townsend Lee & Pembertons	Application form & CV	2 Interviews	2:1 preferred	9	150+
TLT	Online	Assessment centre	2:1	Up to 15	600+
Travers Smith	Online	2 interviews	2:1	25	2,000
Trethowans	Letter & application form	Interview + assessment day	2:1	3-4	100+
Trowers & Hamlins	Online	Interviews + assessments	2:1	22	1,600

Applications and Selection

Firm name	Method of Application	Selection Process	Degree Class	Number of Contracts	Number of Applications
Veale Wasbrough	Application form	Interview	2:1 preferred	8-10	Not known
Vinson & Elkins	Online	Interview	2:1	3-4	400
Walker Morris	Online	Interviews	2:1	20	Approx 800
Ward Hadaway	Application form	Assessment centre + interview	2:1	8-10	500+
Warner Goodman	Online	Interview	2:1	2	Not known
Watson, Farley & Williams	Online	Assessment centre + interview	2:1	12-14	700
Wedlake Bell	Application form	2 interviews + open day	2:1	6	Not known
Weil, Gotshal & Manges	Online	Not known	2:1	10	Not known
White & Case	Online	Interview	2:1	30	1,700
Wiggin	Online	2-day selection	2:1	4	500
Wilsons Solicitors	Online or CV	Interview + assessment day	2:1	4	Not known
Winckworth Sherwood	Online	2 interviews	2:1	4	200
Withers	Application form Online	2 interviews + exercises	2:1	16	700
Wragge & Co	Online	Telephone discussion + assessment day	Not known	30	1,000

- **Practical experience can be the most eloquent and essential aspect of your CV:** As a leading human rights lawyer told us, "People always ask me, how do I show an interest in human rights law? But that's the wrong way round. People who are genuinely interested will already be involved."

top tip no. 30

Salaries and Benefits

Firm name	1st Year Salary	2nd year salary	Sponsorship/ awards	Other Benefits	Qualification Salary
Addleshaw Goddard	£35,000 (London) £24,500 (Manch/Leeds)	£36,000 (London) £24,750 (Manch/Leeds)	GDL & LPC: fees + £7,000 (London) or £4,500 (elsewhere)	Corporate gym m'ship, STL, subsd restaurant, pension, pte healthcare	£58,000 (London) £36,500 (Manch/Leeds)
Allen & Overy	£38,000	£42,200	LPC: fees + £7,000 GDL: fees + £6,000 (London), £5,000 (elsewhere)	Pte healthcare, PMI, STL, subsd restaurant, in-house medical facilities, music rooms and gym	£60,000
Anthony Collins	£20,000	£22,000	Not known	Not known	£34,500
Ashurst	£37,000	£41,000	GDL & LPC: fees + £7,500, £500 for first-class degree or LPC distinction, language bursaries	PHI, pension, life ass, STL, gym m'ship	£60,000
Baker & McKenzie	£37,500 + £3,000 'joining bonus'	£40,000	GDL & LPC: fees + maintenance	PHI, life ins, PMI, pension, subsd gym m'ship, STL, subsd restaurant	£59,000
Barlow Lyde & Gilbert	£34,000	£36,000	GDL & LPC: fees + maintenance	Not known	£56,000
Beachcroft	£34,000 (London) £26,000 (Regions)	£37,000 (London) £29,000 (Regions)	GDL & LPC: fees + £5,000	Flexible scheme inc holiday, pension, pte healthcare, EAP	Not known
Beale & Co	£28,000 (London) £23,800 (Regions)	£30,000 (London) £25,500 (Regions)	Not known	STL, discretionary bonus	Competitive
Berwin Leighton Paisner	£37,000	£40,000	GDL & LPC: fees + £7,200	Not known	£58,000
Bevan Brittan	Not known	Not known	GDL & LPC: fees + bursary	Not known	Not known
Bingham McCutchen	£40,000	£45,000	GDL & LPC: fees + £8,000	PHI, travel ins, disability ins, STL, life ass, subsd gym	£100,000
Bircham Dyson Bell	£30,000	£31,000	Not known	Pte healthcare, life ass, STL, PHI, pension, subsd gym	£49,000
Bird & Bird	£35,000	£37,000	GDL & LPC: fees + £5,500	BUPA, STL, subsd sports club m'ship, life cover, PHI, pension, childcare and eyecare vouchers	£55,000
Bond Pearce	£24,000	£25,000	GDL & LPC: fees + £6,000	PHI, BUPA, life ass	Not known
Boodle Hatfield	£32,000	£34,500	GDL & LPC: fees + maintenance	Pte healthcare, life ass, STL, pension, PHI, PMI, conveyancing grant	£48,000
BP Collins	£22,000	£23,000	Not known	Not known	Not known
Bristows	£33,000	£36,000	GDL & LPC: fees + £7,000	Pension, life ass & health ins	£52,500
Browne Jacobson	£24,000	£25,000	GDL & LPC: fees + £5,000	Life ass, PMI, pension	Market rate

Notes: PHI = Permanent Health Insurance; STL = Season Ticket Loan; PMI = Private Medical Insurance; EAP = Employee Assistance Programme

Salaries and Benefits

Firm name	1st Year Salary	2nd year salary	Sponsorship/ awards	Other Benefits	Qualification Salary
Burges Salmon	£30,000	£31,000	GDL & LPC: fees + £7,000	Bonus, pension, pte healthcare, mobile phone, gym m'ship, Xmas gift, life ass	£40,000
Capsticks	£29,000	£30,000	GDL & LPC: financial support	Bonus, pension, PHI, PMI, death-in-service-cover, STL, childcare vouchers	£46,000
Charles Russell	£31,500	£32,500	GDL & LPC: fees + £6,000 (London) £4,500 (Guildford & Cambridge) £3,500 (Cheltenham)	BUPA, PHI, life ass, pension, STL	£55,000
Clarke Willmott	£24,000	£25,500	GDL & LPC: fees	Life ass, pension, gym m'ship, bonus, STL, eyecare & childcare vouchers	£35,000-£37,500 (dependant on location)
Cleary Gottlieb Steen & Hamilton	£40,000	£45,000	GDL & LPC: fees + £8,000	Pension, PHI, disability ins, gym m'ship, BUPA, life ins, childcare vouchers, EAP subsd restaurant	£92,000
Clifford Chance	£37,400	£42,200	GDL & LPC: fees + maintenance	Subsd restaurant, fitness centre, pension, up to 6 weeks' leave on qual	£59,000
Clyde & Co	£35,000	£38,000	GDL & LPC: fees + £7,000 (Lon/Guild) £6,000 (elsewhere)	Interest-free loan on joining, pension, life ass, PMI, subsd gym m'ship, STL	£59,000
CMS Cameron McKenna	£37,500	£41,500	GDL & LPC: fees + up to £7,500	Bonus, gym m'ship, life ass, pension, pte healthcare, STL, care line, subs'd rest, buy-holiday scheme	£59,000
Cobbetts	£23,000	£25,000	GDL & LPC: fees + £5,000 during LPC year	BUPA, gym m'ship, pension, STL, death-in-service cover, counselling	£30,000
Coffin Mew	Competitive	Competitive	LPC: discussed with candidates	Not known	Competitive
Collyer Bristow	£27,500	£31,000	LPC: fees + £4,000	Pension, PMI, life ass, STL	Not known
Covington & Burling	£40,000	£44,000	GDL & LPC: fees + £8,000	Pension, PHI, pte healthcare, life ass, STL	Not known
Cripps Harries Hall	£21,500	£23,500	LPC fees: 50% interest-free loan, 50% bursary	Not known	£37,000
Davenport Lyons	£33,000-£33,666	£34,332-£35,000	No	Pension, STL, client intro bonus, subsd gym m'ship, discretionary bonus, life ass	Not known

Notes: PHI = Permanent Health Insurance; STL = Season Ticket Loan; PMI = Private Medical Insurance; EAP = Employee Assistance Programme

Salaries and Benefits

Firm name	1st Year Salary	2nd year salary	Sponsorship/ awards	Other Benefits	Qualification Salary
Davies Arnold Cooper	£31,000	Not known	GDL & LPC fees + maintenance	PMI, STL	Not known
Dechert	£38,000	£43,000	LPC: fees + £10,000	Not known	£65,000-£73,000
Denton Wilde Sapte	£35,000	£37,000	GDL & LPC: fees + £6,000 (£7,000 in London)	Flexible benefit scheme, STL	£58,000
Dewey & LeBoeuf	£40,000	£45,000	GDL & LPC: fees + £8,500 per year	PMI, PHI, life ass, EAP, private GP service, STL, childcare vouchers, subs'd gym, worldwide travel insurance	£70,000
Dickinson Dees	£19,500	£20,500	GDL & LPC: fees + maintenance	Not known	Not known
DLA Piper	£36,000 (London) £25,000 (other English)	£38,000 (London) £27,000 (other English)	GDL & LPC: fees + up to £7,000	Not known	£58,000 (London) £37,500 (other English)
Dundas & Wilson	£30,000 (London)	£33,500 (London)	GDL & LPC: fees + maintenance	Life ass, PHI, pension, STL, holiday-purchase scheme	Not known
DWF	£24,500	Not known	LPC: fees	Not known	Not known
Edwards Angell Palmer & Dodge	£36,000	£39,000	GDL & LPC: fees + £6,500 (£7,000 in London)	BUPA, STL, subs'd gym, bonus, pension, life ass	£56,000
Eversheds	£35,000 (London) £24,500 (regions)	£37,000 (London)	GDL & LPC: fees + maintenance	Regional variations	£57,000 (London)
Farrer & Co	£32,000	£34,500	GDL: fees + £6,000 & LPC: fees + £6,000	Health & life ins, subsd gym m'ship, STL	£48,000
Finers Stephens Innocent	£30,000	£32,000	GDL & LPC: fees	Pension, PMI, life ins, long-term disability ins, STL, EAP	£47,000
Fladgate	£30,000	Not known	Not known	Pension, PHI, Life ass, STL, gym loan, bonus, PMI	£50,000
Foot Anstey	£19,500	£21,000	LPC: £9,600	Pension	£32,000-£36,000
Forbes	At least Law Soc min	£19,500	Not known	Not known	Highly competitive
Freeth Cartwright	£22,000	Not known	Not known	Not known	Not known
Freshfields Bruckhaus Deringer	£39,000	£44,000	GDL: fees + £6,250 LPC: fees + £6,000 (for BPP accelerated LPC)	Life ass, PHI, pension, interest-free loan, STL, PMI, subsd gym	£59,000
Government Legal Service	£22,900 - £25,200 (London)	£24,250-£27,350	BVC & LPC: fees + £5,000-£7,000 GDL: possibly	Pension, subsd canteen	£32,000-£40,000
Halliwells	£24,000 £32,500 (London)	£25,000 £33,500 (London)	GDL & LPC: fees + £6,500	STL, subsd gym m'ship, life ass	£39,000 £62,000 (London)

Notes: PHI = Permanent Health Insurance; STL = Season Ticket Loan; PMI = Private Medical Insurance; EAP = Employee Assistance Programme

Salaries and Benefits

Firm name	1st Year Salary	2nd year salary	Sponsorship/ awards	Other Benefits	Qualification Salary
Hammonds	£32,000 (London) £22,000 (other)	£35,000 (London) £25,000 (other)	GDL: fees + £4,500 (£6,000 London) LPC: fees + £5,000 (£7,000 London)	Pension, life ass, subsd gym m'ship, STL	£55,000 (London) £34,000 (other)
Harbottle & Lewis	£28,000	£29,000	LPC: fees + interest-free loan	Lunch, STL	£45,000
HBJ Gateley Wareing	£20,000-£22,000	£22,000-£24,000	LPC: fees + £5,000 GDL: fees	Not known	£32,000
Henmans	£22,000	£24,000	Not known	BUPA, Pension, EAP, subs'd cafe, free parking, corp massage	£34,000
Herbert Smith	£37,500	£42,500	GDL & LPC: fees + up to £7,000	Bonus, PHI, PMI, STL, life ass, subsd gym m'ship accident ins, interest-free loan, pension	£60,000
Hewitsons	£23,500	£25,000	None	Not known	£35,000
Higgs & Sons	£21,500	£24,000	Professional Skills Course	PMI, life ass, pension	£32,000
Hill Dickinson	£24,000 (north) £32,000 (London)	£26,000 (north) £34,000 (London)	LPC fees	Not known	Not known
Holman Fenwick Willan	£32,000	£34,000	LPC: fees + £7,000 GDL: fees + £6,000	PMI, PHI, accident ins, subsd gym m'ship, STL	£58,000
Howes Percival	£24,500	£26,500	GDL & LPC: funding + maintenance grant	Pension, PHI	Not known
Ince & Co	£36,000	£39,000	GDL & LPC: fees + £6,000 (London and Guildford), £5,500 (elsewhere)	STL, corporate health cover, PHI, pension, subs'd gym m'ship	£58,000
Irwin Mitchell	£22,450 (outside London)	£24,650 (outside London)	GDL & LPC: fees + £4,500	Healthcare, pension, subsd gym m'ship	Not known
Jones Day	£39,000-£41,000	£45,000-£50,000	GDL & LPC: fees + £8,000	Pte healthcare, sports club m'ship, group life cover, STL	£70,000
K&L Gates	£35,000	£38,000	GDL: fees + £5,000 LPC: fees + £7,000	STL, subs'd gym m'ship, PHI, life ass, bonus, pension	£56,000
Kirkland & Ellis	£40,000	£43,000	GDL & LPC: fees + £7,500	PMI, travel ins, life ass, pension, EAP, gym m'ship	Not known
Latham & Watkins	£41,000	£44,000	GDL & LPC: fees + £8,000	Healthcare & dental scheme, pension, life ass	£96,970
Lawrence Graham (LG)	£32,000	£36,000	GDL & LPC: fees + £6,500 (London) £6,000 (elsewhere)	STL, life ass	£55,000
Laytons	Market rate	Market rate	GDL & LPC: funding considered	Not known	Market rate
Lester Aldridge	£17,250-£17,750	£18,250-£18,750	LPC: funding available	Life ass, pension, flexible benefits, STL	£33,000 - £34,000

Notes: PHI = Permanent Health Insurance; STL = Season Ticket Loan; PMI = Private Medical Insurance; EAP = Employee Assistance Programme

Salaries and Benefits

Firm name	1st Year Salary	2nd year salary	Sponsorship/ awards	Other Benefits	Qualification Salary
Lewis Silkin	£32,000	£34,000	GDL: fees LPC: fees + £5,000	Life ass, critical illness cover, health ins, STL, pension, subsd gym m'ship, bonus	£50,000
Linklaters	£37,400	Not known	GDL & LPC: fees + maintenance	Bonus, life ass, PMI, PHI, pension, gym/health club m'ship, travel ins, STL, and others	£61,500 + bonus
Lovells	£37,000	£42,000	GDL & LPC: fees + maintenance grant	PMI, life ass, PHI, STL, in-house gym, staff rest, in-house dentist, doctor & physio, local retail discounts	£59,000
Macfarlanes	£37,000	£41,500	GDL & LPC: fees + £7,000, prizes for LPC distinction or commendation	Pension, life ass, health, STL, gym sub	£59,000
Maclay Murray & Spens	£32,000 (London)	Not known	Not known	Pension, death-in-service benefit, conveyancing, medical & dental plans, income protection insurance	Not known
Manches	£30,000 (London)	£33,000 (London)	GDL & LPC: fees + £5,000	STL, PHI, pension, BUPA, life ass	£50,000 (London)
Martineau	c.£21,000	c.£22,500	Not known	Not known	£40,000
Maxwell Winward	£29,000	£31,500	GDL & LPC: contribution	STL, PHI	£48,000
Mayer Brown	£37,500	£42,300	GDL & LPC: + £7,000	STL, sports club m'ship, pte healthcare	Not known
McDermott, Will & Emery	£39,000	£43,000	GDL & LPC: fees + maintenance	PMI, dential ins, life ass, EAP, PHI, STL, subsd gym m'ship	£75,000
McGrigors	£32,000 (London)	£37,000 (London)	GDL & LPC: fees + £6,000	PMI, STL, life ass, pension, income protection	£56,000 (London)
Memery Crystal	£26,500	£29,500	GDL & LPC: fees	Life ass, health, STL, gym sub	£54,000
Michelmores	£20,000	£21,000	LPC: fees + prizes for first-class degrees and LPC distinction	Pte healthcare, PHI, subs'd restaurant, subs'd gym, free pkg	£33,000
Mills & Reeve	£23,000	£24,000	GDL & LPC: fees + maintenance	Life ass, pension, bonus, subsd gym & restaurant, STL, PMI	Not known
Mishcon de Reya	£32,000	Not known	GDL & LPC: fees + maintenance	PMI, travel ins, subsd gym m'ship, STL, life ass, pension, doctor, EAP, income protection	Not known
Muckle	£20,000	Not known	LPC: fees + maintenance	Pension, PHI, Life ass	£30,000 to £37,000

Notes: PHI = Permanent Health Insurance; STL = Season Ticket Loan; PMI = Private Medical Insurance; EAP = Employee Assistance Programme

Salaries and Benefits

Firm name	1st Year Salary	2nd year salary	Sponsorship/ awards	Other Benefits	Qualification Salary
Mundays	Not known	Not known	LPC: £7,500 contribution + maintenance of £4,000 paid at month 2 and 7 of LPC	Pension, Private healthcare scheme, death in service scheme, childcare vouchers	Not known
Nabarro	£37,000 (London) £25,000 (Sheffield)	£40,000 (London) £28,000 (Sheffield)	GDL: fees + £6,000 (London) or £5,000 (elsewhere) LPC: fees + £7,000 (London) or £6,000 (elsewhere)	PMI, pension, STL, subsd restaurant, subsd gym m'ship	£57,000 (London) £38,000 (Sheffield)
Norton Rose	£35,700	£40,200	GDL & LPC: funded	Life ass, pte health ins, STL, subsd gym m'ship	Not known
Olswang	£35,000	£39,000	GDL & LPC: fees + £7,000 (London) or £6,500 (elsewhere)	Pension, PMI, life cover, dental scheme, STL, subsd gym m'ship and staff restaurant, PHI	£58,000
O'Melveny & Myers	£39,000	£42,500	GDL & LPC: fees + £7,000	Pension, travel ins, PMI, subs'd gym m'ship, PHI, death in service benefit	Market Rate
Osborne Clarke	Competitive	Competitive	GDL & LPC: fees + maintenance	Pension PMI, STL, PHI, life ass, bonus, subs'd gym m'ship	Competitive
Pannone	£23,000	£23,000	Half grant for LPC fees at COL, Manchester	Not known	£34,000
Paul Hastings	£40,000	£45,000	Funding available	Ptd healthcare, life ass, pension, STL subs'd of gym m'ship	£80,000
Penningtons Solicitors	£30,000 (London)	£32,000 (London)	LPC: fees + £5,000	Pension, life ass, PMI, STL, critical illness cover	£47,000 (London)
Pinsent Masons	£36,000 (London)	£39,000 (London)	GDL & LPC: fees + maintenance	Not known	£63,000 (London)
PricewaterhouseCoopers Legal	£30,000	£35,000	GDL & LPC: fees + maintenance	Not known	Not known
Pritchard Englefield	£22,250	Not known	LPC: fees	Subsd training, luncheon vouchers, PMI, STL	Market rate
Reed Smith	£37,000 (London)	£40,000 (London)	GDL: fees + £6,000 LPC: fees + £7,000	PMI, STL, life ass, pension, bonus, staff conveyancing, subs'd restaurant	£57,000 + bonus (London)
Reynolds Porter Chamberlain	£37,000	£40,000	GDL & LPC: fees + £6,500	Flexible package	£58,000
Shadbolt & Co	£31,000	£35,000	LPC: fee refund when TC starts	Private healthcare, PHI, life ass, paid study leave, STL, bonus, prof m'ships + subs	£52,000

Notes: PHI = Permanent Health Insurance; STL = Season Ticket Loan; PMI = Private Medical Insurance; EAP = Employee Assistance Programme

Salaries and Benefits

Firm name	1st Year Salary	2nd year salary	Sponsorship/ awards	Other Benefits	Qualification Salary
Shearman & Sterling	£39,000	£39,000	GDL & LPC: fees + £7,000	Not known	£73,000
Shoosmiths	Under review	Under review	GDL & LPC: fees + maintenance	Life ass, pension, staff discounts, Christmas bonus, flexible holidays scheme	Under review
Sidley Austin	£39,000	£43,000	GDL & LPC: fees + £7,000	PMI, life ass, subs'd gym m'ship, STL, income protection, pension, subsd restaurant	Not known
Simmons & Simmons	£36,000	£40,000	GDL & LPC: fees + up to £7,500	Not known	£59,000
SJ Berwin	£37,500	£41,500	Not known	Pte healthcare, subsd gym m'ship, life ass, pension, STL, free lunch	£59,000
Skadden	£40,000	£43,000	GDL & LPC: fees + £8,000	Life ass, PMI, PHI, travel ins, subsd gym m'ship and resturant, technology allowance, EAP	Not known
Slaughter and May	£38,000	£43,000	GDL & LPC: fees + maintenance	BUPA, STL, pension, subsd health club m'ship, 24-hour accident cover	£61,000
Speechly Bircham	£32,000-£33,000	£34,000-£35,000	GDL & LPC: fees + maintenance	Not known	£50,000
Stephenson Harwood	£35,000	£40,000	GDL & LPC: fees + maintenance	PMI, BUPA, STL, gym sub	£58,000
Stevens & Bolton	£25,500	£27,500	GDL & LPC: fees + £4,000	PMI, life ass, pension, STL, PHI	Not known
Taylor Wessing	£31,500	£35,000	GDL & LPC: fees + £6,000 (for BPP London)	PMI, PHI, STL, subsd staff restaurant, pension, life ass, EAP	£55,000
Thomas Cooper	£30,000	£33,660	LPC: fees	Health, life ass, pension, STL, gym sub	Not known
Thomas Eggar	Not known	Not known	LPC: 50% grant, 50% loan	Not known	Not known
Thomson Snell & Passmore	Competitive	Competitive	LPC: grant + interest-free loan	Not known	Not known
Thring Townsend Lee & Pembertons	£23,000	£25,000	Not known	PMI, pte healthcare, life ass, subsd restaurant, prof m'ships & subs	£35,000
TLT Solicitors	Not known	Not known	GDL & LPC: fees + maintenance	Flexible package	Not known
Travers Smith	£36,000	£40,000	GDL & LPC: fees + £7,000 (London) or £6,500 (elsewhere)	PHI, PMI, life ass, STL, subsd bistro, health club m'ship	£58,000

Notes: PHI = Permanent Health Insurance; STL = Season Ticket Loan; PMI = Private Medical Insurance; EAP = Employee Assistance Programme

Salaries and Benefits

Firm name	1st Year Salary	2nd year salary	Sponsorship/awards	Other Benefits	Qualification Salary
Trethowans	Not known	Not known	LPC: fees	Pension, death-in-service cover, PHI, bonus, car parking and others	Market rate
Trowers & Hamlins	£35,000	£38,000	GDL & LPC: fees + £6,000	Not known	£55,000
Veale Wasbrough	£23,000	£25,000	GDL & LPC: funding	Not known	£35,000
Vinson & Elkins	£40,000	£42,000	LPC: fees + £7,500	Pension, STL, life ass, priv med & dental	£75,000
Walker Morris	£24,000	£26,000	GDL & LPC: fees + £5,000	Not known	£38,000
Ward Hadaway	£20,000	£20,500	GDL & LPC: fees + maintenance	Death-in-service cover, pension, flexible holiday scheme	£35,000
Warner Goodman	Not known	Not known	See website	Not known	Market rate
Watson, Farley & Williams	£35,000	£40,000	GDL & LPC: fees + £6,500 (London) or £5,500 (elsewhere)	Life ass, PHI, STL, pension, subsd gym m'ship, EAP	Competitive
Wedlake Bell	£29,000	£31,000	LPC: fees + £4,000	Pension, STL, subsd gym m'ship, life ass, PHI	Not known
Weil, Gotshal & Manges	£41,000	Not known	Not known	Not known	Not known
White & Case	£41,000-£42,000	£43,000-£44,000	GDL & LPC: fees + £7,500. Prize for LPC commendation or distinction	PMI, dental ins, life ass, pension, critical illness cover, travel ins, gym m'ship, retail vouchers, STL, green bikes	£72,000
Wiggin	£26,500	£31,500	GDL & LPC: fees + £3,500	Life ass, pte health cover, pension, PHI, subsd gym m'ship	£50,000
Wilsons Solicitors	Market rate	Market rate	LPC: interest-free loan up to £4,500	Pension, life ass, PMI	Not known
Winckworth Sherwood	£27,000	£31,000	GDL & LPC: financial assistance under certain conditions	PHI, STL, life ass, PMI	Not known
Withers	£33,000	£35,000	GDL & LPC: fees + £5,000	Not known	£53,000
Wragge & Co	£25,750 (Birmingham)	£28,750 (Birmingham)	GDL & LPC: funding	Not known	£36,500 (Birmingham) £57,000 (London)

Notes: PHI = Permanent Health Insurance; STL = Season Ticket Loan; PMI = Private Medical Insurance; EAP = Employee Assistance Programme

Picking a firm for its overseas opportunities

The idea of the international law firm is far from new; UK firms have ventured overseas since the 19th century. What has changed is the number of firms with offices overseas and the increasing desire to plant flags all over the globe.

The largest firm worldwide is Clifford Chance, though it still has some way to go to catch up with Baker & McKenzie for the prize for most offices in most countries. There are so many firms with overseas networks that keeping track of which are opening or closing offices in different countries is almost a full-time occupation. Wherever possible, we have mentioned the main changes from the past year in our True Picture reports. What we can't predict is exactly who is going to merge with whom.

The big firms are canny operators. They understand that to survive in a competitive legal market it is necessary to have a network of offices (or relationships with overseas firms) in parts of the world where the economies are growing. China and India are of real interest at present, as are the Middle East and the oil and gas-rich parts of Central Asia. The crash of the world economy accelerated this process with firms becoming ever more determined to invest in developing countries where growth was less affected. They all want to follow the money and build a presence in the jurisdictions that their big business clients are hoping to exploit. Essentially, wherever commercial interests go, so law firms follow. Similarly, when a country begins to look stale, firms start to lose interest and scale back the size of their offices.

The following table summarises exactly where overseas opportunities lie this year. As for international work back in the UK, the nature of a firm's clientele and worldwide office footprint determine what trainees see day to day. At White & Case there is a considerable amount of project finance work conducted in conjunction with Eastern European and Central Asian offices. CMS Cameron McKenna's superb energy practice brings in similar work. At Dewey & LeBoeuf, African LNG deals have flowed from the firm's energy clientele. Trowers & Hamlins' dominance in the Middle East brings work back to London, as does Wiggin's relationship with major film studios in Los Angeles and Lawrence Graham's Indian connections.

If international work interests you then consider whether you would want to remain at home during your training or have the guarantee of an overseas seat. If it is the latter, then pick a firm where you can be certain of securing a foreign posting. The competition at some firms is tough, while at others everyone who wants to go does. The True Picture reports should help you here. One other thing to bear in mind is your ability to speak another language. If you're fluent in Russian you may be collared for Moscow instead of the New York opening you've got your eye on. It also follows that where language skills would be useful – say in Italy – those who possess them prove to be more attractive at a training contract interview. Some firms even actively recruit with language needs in mind. International private client firm Withers, for example, tries to ensure it has at least two fluent Italian speakers in each intake to fill its coveted corporate seat in Milan. Consequently the firm claims to have the largest number of Italian speakers in the City.

Although time abroad gives you experience of working in another jurisdiction, you won't normally practise foreign law. An overseas seat is without doubt a very rewarding and challenging experience. It will usually be taken in an office that is smaller than your home office, and you will normally have greater responsibility. The trick to securing the most popular overseas seats is to wage an effective campaign of self-promotion and to get the prerequisite experience in the UK office before you go.

On arrival in a new country you don't need to worry about feeling isolated as the local lawyers and staff invariably give a warm welcome to newcomers. In some cities with a large influx of UK trainees there is a ready-made social scene and it's likely that the first thing to pop into your inbox will be an invite to meet other new arrivals. In Singapore trainees make the most of the region by jetting off for group weekends on Malaysian or Indonesian islands. In Brussels they hook into the social scene attached to the vast EU machine. Another big plus is the free accommodation provided by the law firms. Usually, trainees are housed in their own apartments in smart areas close to a city's centre. It may be some time before they can afford such plush digs – and domestic help – back home. For more info on life as a trainee in an overseas seat check out our website where we report from the most frequented training locations around the world.

Overseas seats: Who goes where?

Location	Firm
Abu Dhabi	Allen & Overy, Clifford Chance, Clyde & Co, Denton Wilde Sapte, DLA Piper, Norton Rose, Reed Smith, Simmons & Simmons, Trowers & Hamlins, White & Case
Almaty	White & Case
Amsterdam	Allen & Overy, Clifford Chance, Freshfields Bruckhaus Deringer, Linklaters, Norton Rose, Simmons & Simmons, Slaughter and May
Athens	Norton Rose, Thomas Cooper
Auckland/NZ	Slaughter and May
Bahrain	Charles Russell, Norton Rose, Trowers & Hamlins
Bangkok	Allen & Overy, Watson Farley & Williams
Barcelona	Freshfields Bruckhaus Deringer
Beijing	Allen & Overy, Freshfields Bruckhaus Deringer, Linklaters, Norton Rose
Berlin	Freshfields Bruckhaus Deringer, Linklaters
Brussels	Allen & Overy, Arnold & Porter, Ashurst, Baker & McKenzie, Berwin Leighton Paisner, Cleary Gotlieb Steen & Hamilton, Clifford Chance, Dechert, Dickinson Dees, Freshfields Bruckhaus Deringer, Hammonds, Herbert Smith, Linklaters, Lovells, Mayer Brown, Nabarro, Norton Rose, Olswang, O'Melveny & Myers, Sidley Austin, SJ Berwin, Slaughter and May, White & Case
Bucharest	Allen & Overy, Clifford Chance, CMS Cameron McKenna
Budapest	Allen & Overy, CMS Cameron McKenna
Chicago	Baker & McKenzie, Mayer Brown
Cologne	Freshfields Bruckhaus Deringer
Copenhagen	Slaughter and May
Dar Es Salaam	O'Melveny & Myers, Shadbolt
Dubai	Allen & Overy, Ashurst, Clifford Chance, Clyde & Co, Denton Wilde Sapte, Dewey & LeBoeuf, Freshfields Bruckhaus Deringer, Herbert Smith, Holman Fenwick Willan, Linklaters, Lovells, Norton Rose, Pinsent Masons, Reed Smith, Simmons & Simmons, Trowers & Hamlins, Vinson & Elkins
Düsseldorf	Bird & Bird, Freshfields Bruckhaus Deringer, Slaughter and May
Falkland Islands	McGrigors
Frankfurt	Ashurst, Bird & Bird, Clifford Chance, Freshfields Bruckhaus Deringer, Herbert Smith, Linklaters, Lovells, Norton Rose, SJ Berwin, White & Case
Geneva	Charles Russell
Hong Kong	Allen & Overy, Baker & McKenzie, Barlow Lyde & Gilbert, Bingham McCutchen, Cleary Gotlieb Steen & Hamilton, Clifford Chance, Clyde & Co, Freshfields Bruckhaus Deringer, Hammonds, Herbert Smith, Linklaters, Lovells, Mayer Brown, Norton Rose, Morrison & Foerster, O'Melveny & Myers, Orrick, Reed Smith, Simmons & Simmons, Skadden, Slaughter and May, Stephenson Harwood, White & Case
Istanbul	Denton Wilde Sapte
Jakarta	Herbert Smith
Johannesburg	White & Case
Kiev	CMS Cameron McKenna
Luxembourg	Clifford Chance, Slaughter and May

Overseas seats: Who goes where?

Location	Firm
Madrid	Allen & Overy, Ashurst, Baker & McKenzie, Bird & Bird, Clifford Chance, Freshfields Bruckhaus Deringer, Linklaters, SJ Berwin, Slaughter and May
Milan	Allen & Overy, Ashurst, Clifford Chance, Freshfields Bruckhaus Deringer, Linklaters, Norton Rose, SJ Berwin, Slaughter and May, Withers
Moscow	Allen & Overy, Cleary Gotlieb Steen & Hamilton, Clifford Chance, CMS Cameron McKenna, Denton Wilde Sapte, Dewey & LeBoeuf, DLA Piper, Freshfields Bruckhaus Deringer, Herbert Smith, Linklaters, Norton Rose, Salans, Skadden, Vinson & Elkins, White & Case
Munich	Bird & Bird, Clifford Chance, Dechert, Norton Rose, SJ Berwin, Slaughter and May
Muscat	Denton Wilde Sapte
New York	Allen & Overy, Cleary Gotlieb Steen & Hamilton, Clifford Chance, Edwards Angell Palmer & Dodge, Freshfields Bruckhaus Deringer, Linklaters, Mayer Brown, Slaughter and May, Weil Gotshal & Manges, White & Case
Oman	Trowers & Hamlins
Oslo	Slaughter and May
Paris	Allen & Overy, Ashurst, Baker & McKenzie, Cleary Gotlieb Steen & Hamilton, Clifford Chance, Denton Wilde Sapte, Dewey & LeBoeuf, Eversheds, Freshfields Bruckhaus Deringer, Hammonds, Herbert Smith, Holman Fenwick Willan, Linklaters, Lovells, Norton Rose, Simmons & Simmons, SJ Berwin, Slaughter and May, Stephenson Harwood, Thomas Cooper, Travers Smith, Watson Farley & Williams, Weil Gotshal & Manges, White & Case
Piraeus	Clyde & Co, Hill Dickinson, Holman Fenwick Willan, Reed Smith, Watson Farley & Williams
Prague	Allen & Overy, Clifford Chance, CMS Cameron McKenna, Norton Rose, Slaughter and May, White & Case
Riyadh	Freshfields Bruckhaus Deringer, White & Case
Rome	Clifford Chance
São Paulo	Barlow Lyde & Gilbert, Clifford Chance, Linklaters, Mayer Brown
San Francisco	Baker & McKenzie
Shanghai	Allen & Overy, Barlow Lyde & Gilbert, Clifford Chance, Eversheds, Freshfields Bruckhaus Deringer, Linklaters
Silicon Valley	Weil Gotshal & Manges
Singapore	Allen & Overy, Ashurst, Barlow Lyde & Gilbert, Clifford Chance, Clyde & Co, Herbert Smith, Hill Dickinson, Linklaters, Lovells, Norton Rose, O'Melveny & Myers, Stephenson Harwood, Watson Farley & Williams, White & Case
Sofia	CMS Cameron McKenna
Stockholm	Bird & Bird, Slaughter and May
Sydney	Baker & McKenzie, Slaughter and May
Tokyo	Allen & Overy, Ashurst, Baker & McKenzie, Clifford Chance, Freshfields Bruckhaus Deringer, Herbert Smith, Linklaters, Norton Rose, Morrison & Foerster, Simmons & Simmons, Slaughter and May, White & Case
Toronto	Baker & McKenzie
Vienna	CMS Cameron McKenna (client secondment), Freshfields Bruckhaus Deringer
Warsaw	Allen & Overy, Clifford Chance, CMS Cameron McKenna, Linklaters
Washington	Freshfields Bruckhaus Deringer

- **A training partner speaks:** "It's important to be yourself and to know a little about the firm. Please don't tell us what's on the website, and don't overdo it. Likewise, try and read the *FT* or *The Economist* a few times. You should be able to recall basic contract law and something interesting you studied from an academic perspective, but you must understand that law is a business as well."

A-Z of Solicitors

A-Z of Solicitors

- **Things always takes longer than you think:** However long you reckon it will take to complete an application form, double your estimate (and then add some more). You can always go to the pub if you finish early.

top tip no. 32

Addleshaw Goddard

Milton Gate, 60 Chiswell St, London, EC1Y 4AG
Sovereign House, PO Box 8, Sovereign Street, Leeds LS1 1HQ
100 Barbirolli Square, Manchester, M2 3AB
Website: www.addleshawgoddard.com/graduates
Tel: (020) 7606 8855 / (0161) 934 6000
Fax: (020) 7606 4390 / (0161) 934 6060

Firm profile
As a major force on the legal landscape, Addleshaw Goddard offers extensive and exciting opportunities to all its trainees across the entire spectrum of commercial law, from employment and banking to real estate, corporate finance, intellectual property, employment, PFI and litigation. As a trainee with this firm, you'll be a key member of the team from day one. Whether based in the London, Leeds or Manchester office (or out on secondment), you'll work closely with blue-chip clients within a supportive yet challenging environment, and be part of a structured training programme designed to ensure your success – now and in the future.

Main areas of work
The firm has four main business divisions: Finance and Projects, Contentious and Commercial, Corporate and Real Estate. Within these divisions as well as the main practice areas it also has specialist areas such as sport, intellectual property, employment and private client services such as trusts and tax.

Trainee profile
Graduates who are capable of achieving a 2:1 and can demonstrate commercial awareness, motivation and enthusiasm. Applications from law and non-law graduates are welcomed, as are applications from students who may be considering a change of direction. We also have a diversity access programme for applicants on GDL or LPC with less conventional academic backgrounds. Further details can be found on our website.

Training environment
During each six-month seat, there will be regular two-way performance reviews with the supervising partner or solicitor. Trainees have the opportunity to spend a seat in one of the firm's other offices and there are a number of secondments to clients available. Seated with a qualified solicitor or partner and working as part of a team, enables trainees to develop the professional skills necessary to deal with the demanding and challenging work the firm carries out for its clients. Practical training is complemented by high-quality training courses provided by both the in-house team and external training providers.

Sponsorship & benefits
GDL and LPC fees are paid, plus a maintenance grant of £7,000 (London) or £4,500 (elsewhere in the UK). Benefits include corporate gym membership, season ticket loan, subsidised restaurant, pension and private healthcare.

Vacation placements
Places for 2010 – 90; Duration – 1, 2 or 3 weeks (over Easter and the summer); location – all offices; Apply by 31 January 2010.

Partners 178
Associates 500+
Trainees 91

Contact
The Graduate Recruitment Team
grad@addleshawgoddard.com

Selection procedure
Interview, assessment centre

Closing date for 2012
31 July 2010

Application
Training contracts p.a. 45-50
Applications p.a. 1,500
% interviewed 10%
Required degree grade 2:1

Training
Salary
1st year
London £35,000
Leeds/Manchester £24,500
2nd year
London £36,000
Leeds/Manchester £24,750
Holiday entitlement
25 days
% of trainees with
a non-law degree p.a. 45%

Post-qualification
Salary
London £58,000
Leeds/Manchester £36,500
% of trainees offered job
on qualification (2006) 80%

Other offices
London, Leeds, Manchester

Allen & Overy LLP

One Bishops Square, London E1 6AD
Tel: (020) 3088 0000 Fax: (020) 3088 0088
Email: graduate.recruitment@allenovery.com
Website: www.allenovery.com/careeruk

Firm profile
Allen & Overy LLP is an international legal practice with approximately 5,000 people working across 31 major centres worldwide. The firm's client list includes many of the world's top businesses, financial institutions and governments.

Main areas of work
Banking, corporate, international capital markets, dispute resolution, tax, employment and benefits and real estate. Allen & Overy Partners frequently lead the field in their particular areas of law and the firm can claim both an enviable reputation amongst clients and unrivalled success in major deals.

Trainee profile
You will need to demonstrate a genuine enthusiasm for a legal career and Allen & Overy. The firm looks for a strong, consistent academic performance and you should have achieved or be predicted at least a 2:1 degree (or equivalent). At Allen & Overy you will be working in a team where you will use your initiative and manage your own time and workload, so evidence of teamwork, leadership and problem solving skills are also looked for.

Training environment
Allen & Overy offers a training contract characterised by flexibility and choice. The seat structure ensures that you get to see as many parts of the firm as possible and that your learning is hands-on, guided by an experienced associate or Partner. Your choice of a priority seat is guaranteed when you begin your training contract. Given the strength of the firm's International Finance Practice, trainees are required to spend a minimum of 12 months in at least two of the three core departments of banking, corporate and international capital markets. The firm now offers its trainees the option of completing a litigation course. This means that trainees will no longer need to spend time in the firm's dispute resolution or employment departments to gain their contentious experience if they are sure their interests lie elsewhere. There are also opportunities for trainees to undertake an international or client secondment during their final year of training.

Vacation placements
Allen & Overy offers 65 vacation placements across the year. The winter placement is for finalists and graduates who should apply from 1 October to 31 October 2009. Summer placements are for penultimate year undergraduates who should apply from 1 October 2009 to 17 January 2010. Remuneration: £250.00 per week.

Benefits
Private healthcare, private medical insurance, in-house medical facilities, interest-free season ticket loan, free in-house gym, subsidised staff restaurants, multi-faith prayer rooms and music rooms.

Sponsorship & awards
GDL and LPC course fees are paid in full along with contributions towards your maintenance costs. For the Allen & Overy LPC in London, a £7,000 maintenance grant is provided. For the GDL, £6,000 is provided in London and £5,000 elsewhere. Financial incentives are also offered to future trainees achieving a first class undergraduate degree or a distinction in the LPC.

Partners 450*
Associates 2302*
London Trainees 240
*Denotes world-wide number

Contact
Graduate Recruitment

Method of application
Online application form

Selection procedure
Interview

Closing date for 2012
Non Law candidates
17th Jan 2010
Law candidates
31st July 2010

Application
Training contracts p.a. 105
Applications p.a. 2,500
% interviewed p.a. 8-10%
Required degree grade 2:1 (or equivalent)

Training
Salary
1st year (2009) £38,000
2nd year (2009) £42,200
Holiday entitlement 25 days
% of trainees with a non-law degree p.a. 45%
% of trainees with a law degree p.a. 55%
No. of seats available in international offices
34 seats twice a year;
11 client secondments

Post-qualification
Salary (2009) £60,000
% of trainees offered job on qualification 83%
% of partners who joined as trainees over 50%

International offices
Abu Dhabi, Amsterdam, Antwerp, Bangkok, Beijing, Brussels, Bratislava, Budapest, Bucharest (associated office), Dubai, Dusseldorf, Frankfurt, Hamburg, Hong Kong, London, Luxembourg, Madrid, Mannheim, Milan, Moscow, Munich, New York, Paris, Prague, Riyadh (associated office), Rome, Sao Paulo, Shanghai, Singapore, Tokyo, Warsaw

Anthony Collins Solicitors LLP

134 Edmund Street, Birmingham, B3 2ES
Tel: (0121) 200 3242   Fax: (0121) 212 7442
Website: www.anthonycollins.com

Firm profile
Anthony Collins Solicitors is a full service commercial and private client law firm advising businesses, not-for-profit organisations, local authorities, public sector bodies and individuals throughout the UK.

The firm has adopted seven themes which represent the outworking of its mission and the focus for delivering its service: adult health and social care, children and young people, entertainment and leisure, enterprise, housing, transforming communities and faith communities.

Trainee profile
Academically the firm asks that you have, or are on course for, at least a 2:1 degree and a minimum of 320 UCAS points and that you have the potential to successfully complete the legal practice course.

Further, the firm seeks applicants who combine a strong academic record with innovative thinking, not to mention a compassionate and caring approach to clients and an appreciation of their needs and concerns.

Training environment
During each of the 4 seats of your training contract you will be appointed a supervisor who will provide regular feedback and you will also receive formal feedback through an appraisal system that takes place in middle and at the end of each seat. Regular, informal meetings with a supervisor and appraiser also ensure that you are able to discuss and raise any concerns or feedback that you may have.

During each seat of your training contract you will be appointed a supervisor who will provide you with regular feedback and you will also receive formal feedback through an appraisal system that takes place in the middle and at the end of each seat. Additionally, regular formal and informal (review) meetings with your supervisor and appraiser also ensures that you are able to discuss and raise any concerns or feedback that you may have.

As part of your training contract with Anthony Collins Solicitors, you will attend the Professional Skills Course (PSC), which covers the compulsory subjects of finance and business skills, client care and professional standards, and advocacy and communication skills in addition to your own chosen electives.

Partners 21
Assistant solicitors 71
Total trainees 16

Contact
Deborah Taylor (HR Officer)
(0121) 212 7485
deborah.taylor@anthonycollins.com

Selection procedure
Graduate testing session - half a day, structured interview - two hours, assessment centre - one day (all of the above take place in the firm's offices)

Closing date
The firm invites applications two years in advance of your preferred intake date and run up to two recruitment processes each year; whilst there is no formal deadline for applications, it is preferable that they are received by July 31 of each year i.e. for September 2010 applications, applications to be received by 31 July 2009

Application
Training contracts p.a. 6 (on average)
Applications p.a. 700
% interviewed 10%
Required degree grade 2:1 preferred

Training
Salary
1st year £20,000
2nd year £22,000
Holiday entitlement 23 days

Post-qualification
Salary £34,500
% of trainees offered job on qualification (2007-08) 90%

Ashurst LLP

Broadwalk House, 5 Appold St, London EC2A 2HA
Tel: (020) 7638 1111 Fax: (020) 7638 1112
Email: gradrec@ashurst.com
Website: www.ashurst.com

Firm profile
Ashurst LLP is an elite law firm advising corporates and financial institutions, with core businesses in mergers and acquisitions, corporate and structured finance. The firm's strong and growing presence around the world is built on extensive experience in working with clients on the complex international legal and regulatory issues relating to cross-border transactions.

Main areas of work
Corporate; employment, incentives and pensions; energy, transport and infrastructure; EU and competition; international finance; litigation; real estate; tax; and technology and commercial.

Trainee profile
To become an Ashurst trainee you will need to show common sense and good judgement. The firm needs to know that you can handle responsibility because you will be involved in some of the highest quality international work on offer anywhere. The transactions and cases you will be involved in will be intellectually demanding, so Ashurst looks for high academic achievers who are able to think laterally. But it's not just academic results that matter. Ashurst wants people who have a range of interests outside of their studies. And they want outgoing people with a sense of humour who know how to laugh at themselves.

Training environment
Your training contract will consist of four seats. For each, you will sit with a partner or senior solicitor who will be the main source of your work and your principal supervisor during that seat. Seats are generally for six months. Anything less than that will not give you sufficient depth of experience for the responsibility Ashurst expects you to take on. The firm asks trainees to spend one seat in the Corporate Department and one seat in the International Finance Department. Trainees spend their two remaining seats in the firm's other practice areas, on secondment to a client or on secondment to an overseas office.

Benefits
Private health insurance, pension, life assurance, interest-free season ticket loan, gym membership and 25 days holiday per year during training. Other benefits can be found on the 'benefits and salaries' section of the firm's website.

Vacation placements
Places for 2010: A two-week Easter placement scheme primarily aimed at final-year non-law undergraduates and all graduates. Two three-week summer placement schemes primarily aimed at penultimate-year law undergraduates. Remuneration £275 p.w. Closing date 31 January 2010.

Sponsorship & awards
GDL and LPC funding plus maintenance allowances of £7,500 per annum. LPC distinction and first class degree awards of £500. Language tuition bursaries.

Partners 220
Assistant Solicitors 785
Total Trainees 106

Contact
Stephen Trowbridge
Graduate Recruitment and Development Manager

Method of application
Online

Selection procedure
Interview with Graduate Recruitment and Development Manager followed by interview with two Partners

Closing date for 2012
31 July 2010

Application
Training contracts p.a. 55
Applications p.a. 2,500
% interviewed p.a. 10%
Required degree grade 2:1

Training
Salary (2009)
First year
£37,000
Second year
£41,000
Holiday entitlement 25 days
% of trainees with a non-law degree 54%
Number of seats abroad available p.a. 10

Post-qualification
Salary (2009) £60,000
% of trainees offered job on qualification (2009) 80%

Overseas offices
Abu Dhabi, Brussels, Dubai, Frankfurt, Hong Kong, Madrid, Milan, Munich, New Delhi, New York, Paris, Singapore, Stockholm, Tokyo, Washington DC

Baker & McKenzie LLP

100 New Bridge Street, London EC4V 6JA
Tel: (020) 7919 1000 Fax: (020) 7919 1999
Email: london.graduate.recruit@bakernet.com
Website: www.mutliplyingyourpotential.co.uk

Partners 84
Assistant Solicitors 217
Total Trainees 78

Contact
Justine Beedle

Method of application
Online application form

Selection procedure
Candidates to give a short oral presentation based on the facts of a typical client problem, interview with two partners, meeting with an associate

Closing date for 2012
Non-law 18 Feb 2010
Law 31 July 2010

Application
Training contracts p.a. 38
Applications p.a. 2,000
% interviewed p.a. 10%
Required degree grade 2:1

Training
Salary
1st year (2009) £37,500 + £3,000 'joining bonus'
2nd year (2009) £40,000
Holiday entitlement 25 days
% of trainees with a non-law degree p.a. Approx 50%
No. of seats available abroad p.a. Variable
post-qualification
Salary (2009) £59,000
% of trainees offered job on qualification (2009) 78%

Firm profile
Baker & McKenzie LLP is a leading global law firm based in 69 locations across 39 countries. With a presence in virtually every important financial and commercial centre in the world, the firm's strategy is to provide the best combination of local legal and commercial knowledge, international expertise and resources.

Main areas of work
Corporate; dispute resolution; banking; EU, competition and trade; employment; intellectual property; information technology and commercial; pensions; tax; projects; property; structured capital markets. In addition the firm has cross-departmental practice groups, such as media and communications, insurance and reinsurance, business recovery and environmental law.

Trainee profile
The firm is looking for trainee solicitors who are stimulated by intellectual challenge and want to be 'the best' at what they do. Effective communication together with the ability to be creative and practical problem solvers, team players and a sense of humour are qualities which will help them stand out from the crowd.

Training environment
Four six-month seats which include a corporate and a contentious seat, usually within the firm's highly regarded dispute resolution department. There is also the possibility of a secondment abroad or to a client. During each seat you will have a meeting to discuss individual seat preferences. In addition, you will receive formal and informal reviews to discuss your progress. Your training contract commences with a highly interactive and practical induction programme which focuses on key skills including practical problem solving, interviewing, presenting and the application of information technology. The firm's training programme includes important components on management and other business skills, as well as seminars and workshops on key legal topics for each practice area. There is a Trainee Solicitor Liaison Committee which acts as a forum for any new ideas or raises issues which may occur during your training contract. Trainees are actively encouraged to participate in a variety of pro bono issues and, outside office hours, there is a varied sporting and social life.

Benefits
Permanent health insurance, life insurance, private medical insurance, group personal pension, subsidised gym membership, season ticket loan, subsidised staff restaurant.

Vacation placements
London Summer Placement - Places for 2010: 30; Duration: 3 weeks; Remuneration (2009): £270 p.w.; Closing date: 31 January 2010.

International Summer Placement - Places for 2010: 3-5; Duration: 8-12 weeks divided between London and an overseas office; Remuneration (2009): £270 p.w.; Closing date: 31 January 2010.

Barlow Lyde & Gilbert LLP

Beaufort House, 15 St Botolph Street, London EC3A 7NJ
Tel: (020) 7247 2277 Fax: (020) 7071 9000
Email: grad.recruit@blg.co.uk   Website: www.blg.co.uk

Partners 86
Vacancies 15-20
Trainees 41
Total staff 711

Contact
Caroline Walsh
Head of Graduate Recruitment & Trainee Development

Method of application
Online application form

Selection procedure
Assessment Centre

Closing date for 2012
31 August 2010

Application
Training contracts p.a.
15-20
Applications p.a. 1,500
% interviewed p.a. 10%

Training
Salary
1st year £34,000 (2009)
2nd year £36,000 (2009)
Holiday entitlement
5 weeks
post-qualification
Salary £56,000 (2009)
Trainees offered job
on qualification (2009)
90%

Offices
London, Oxford, Manchester, Hong Kong, Shanghai, Singapore, São Paulo

Firm profile

Barlow Lyde & Gilbert LLP ("BLG") is a pre-eminent international law firm with an unrivalled reputation within major industry sectors including financial services, professional practices, aerospace, shipping, commodities, energy, construction, and healthcare, particularly where clients in those sectors also require insurance and reinsurance market expertise. The firm's Insurance and Reinsurance Practice is one of the largest in the world, providing services of unparalleled breadth across the sector. BLG was named "Best Law Firm" to the global insurance industry at Reactions London Market Awards 2009. BLG is also renowned for its Commercial Litigation and Arbitration Practice, providing an extensive range of high-value, multi-jurisdictional dispute resolutions to clients from many different industries across the world. The firm scooped "Litigation Team of the Year" at the Legal Week Awards in 2005, and again at both The Lawyer Awards and the Legal Business Awards in 2006. BLG's non-contentious expertise spans corporate, commercial, employment, pensions, insolvency, property, outsourcing, technology, and insurance risk transactions. The firm has over 80 partners and more than 200 lawyers in its offices in London, Singapore, Oxford, Manchester, and São Paulo, together with its affiliated undertakings in Hong Kong and Shanghai. BLG was named "one to watch" in the Best Companies Guide 2009.

Trainee profile

The firm recruits 15-20 trainees a year. It looks for intelligent and motivated graduates with good academic qualifications and excellent communication skills. Trainees must be able to work independently or in a team, and are expected to display common sense and initiative. An appreciation of the client's commercial interests is essential.

Training environment

During your training contract you will have six-month seats in four different practice areas. The firm always try to accommodate a trainee's preference for a particular type of work. There are opportunities to spend time in its other offices, on secondment with clients or on exchange programmes with overseas law firms. A capable trainee will deal regularly with clients from an early stage in his or her training, subject to supervision. All trainees are expected to undertake and assist in practice development and client care. Successful candidates will enjoy a wide variety of social and sporting events at BLG, ensuring that trainees have the chance to meet and stay in contact with employees from across the firm.

Work placement scheme

An increasing number of the firm's trainees come through its summer vacation schemes. Whether you are a law or non-law student, the firm will introduce you to life in a City law firm. You can even choose which department you want to spend time in. The closing date for applications is 31 January 2010. The firm also runs open days and drop-in days throughout the year. Full details on these are available from the website - www.blg.co.uk.

Whether you wish to apply for an interview day or a vacation scheme, please apply via the firm's website at www.blg.co.uk. The closing date for interview days is 31 August 2010.

Sponsorship & awards

A maintenance grant is provided and law school fees are paid in full.

Beachcroft LLP

100 Fetter Lane, London EC4A 1BN
Tel: (020) 7242 1011 Fax: (020) 7831 6630
Email: trainee@beachcroft.co.uk
Website: www.beachcroft.com

Firm profile
Beachcroft LLP is one of the largest commercial firms in the UK, with a turnover of over £121m. The firm has over 1,500 people working from eight offices and it serves the broadest range of clients. This means the firm offers exceptional career opportunities for ambitious people who want to become leaders in their field.

Beachcroft is one of the largest law firms to obtain the 'Investors in People' award across all of its offices. The firm values its people and works with them to help them achieve excellence in legal knowledge and commercial understanding alike. The firm's working culture of mutual respect has led it to be seen as both a friendly firm – and one that literally means business.

Main areas of work
From routine insurance claims management to 'trusted adviser' work for major national and international organisations, the firm delivers integrated legal services to clients in six main industry groups; financial institutions, health and public sector, real estate, technology and telecommunications, industrial goods and services, and consumer goods and services.

Trainee profile
You're bright, articulate, inquisitive and adaptable. But what makes you right for Beachcroft is an unpretentious but real interest in the work, a respect for others, and ambitions to be a leader in your field. People from varied backgrounds convert to law with Beachcroft; the firm finds their experience an asset.

Training environment
The firm's aim is to develop its future leaders – not just to provide legal training. That's why its programme is tailored to ensuring that its trainees acquire the skills and knowledge that will enable them to lead its business in the future. The firm offers a programme that identifies individual skills and talents and directs these to parts of its business where they will develop and thrive. It goes without saying that the firm's scheme delivers the required SRA elements for qualification as a solicitor, but its programme also includes business and personal skills training modules, coaching groups and varied internal placements as swell as secondments with top clients. The firm offers support through individual mentors and challenge trainees with high quality work. It's all about attracting, nurturing and retaining the best talent.

Benefits
A flexible benefits package where you can personalise your rewards – 'buying' or 'selling' options such as pension entitlement and private healthcare. Additional benefits include well woman and man checks, free eye test, employee assistance programme, travel loans, discounted insurance, a bikes-to-work scheme and many other fringe benefits.

Vacation placements
Summer: June (apply by 1 March).

Partners 140
Assistant Solicitors 738
Total Trainees 62

Contact
Carrie Daniels
Trainee Recruitment Officer
Email: trainee@beachcroft.co.uk

Method of application
Apply online at www.beachcroft.com

Selection procedure
Online psychometric testing and assessment centre

Closing date
1 August each year

Application
Training contracts per annum 24
Required degree 2:1 preferred

Training
Salary
1st year, regions
£26,000 p.a.
2nd year, regions
£29,000 p.a.
1st year, London
£34,000 p.a.
2nd year, London
£37,000 p.a.
Holiday entitlement - 25 days
% of trainees with a non-law degree p.a. - 45%
Beachcroft provides payment for GDL, LPC and £5,000 bursary.

Offices
Birmingham, Brussels, Leeds*, Bristol*, Manchester*, Winchester, Newcastle, Dublin
(*training offices)

Beale and Company Solicitors LLP

Garrick House, 27-32 King Street, Covent Garden, London, WC2E 8JB
Tel: (020) 7240 3474   Fax: (020) 7240 9111
Email: h.kapadia@beale-law.com
Website: www.beale-law.com

Firm profile

Beale and Company is a specialist niche practice based in London, Bristol and Dublin. With the firm ranked as a leading practice for Technology and Construction Professional Negligence and Construction in London; and for Professional Negligence generally in the Regions, it provides the perfect opportunity for trainees to explore their legal capabilities in a range of challenging areas. It combines the cut and thrust of a practice focussed on providing the best service to clients who are nationally and internationally recognised leaders in their fields with the community and balance that the ethos of a smaller firm embodies. With an active participation in a European Network of law firms, and a regular international dimension to the matters handled, trainees are able to experience a diversity of legal issues.

Main areas of work

The firm specialises in: construction, professional negligence; dispute resolution; insurance; IT; corporate and commercial; employment; health and safety; and property (domestic and commercial) together with some private client work.

Trainee profile

The firm is looking for candidates with a strong academic background (having obtained or being predicted a 2:1 honours degree in any subject), and a real interest in pursuing a career in the law. Trainees need to be commercial, motivated and analytical. A candidate should have the ability to work as a team player and have the initiative to be involved in the strategy and management of a matter from an early stage so as to achieve the most from the training experience.

Training environment

The two year training contract will include six month seats in the key areas of the practice, two of which will be within the Dispute Resolution Department. There may be opportunities to spend time in a different office within the firm, or to go on secondment to clients. Trainees also enjoy a number of social and sporting activities throughout the year, both internally and within the local business community.

Benefits

The firm's benefits include: holiday entitlement; interest free loan for a season ticket for travel; discretionary annual bonus and a competitive salary.

Partners 13
Assistant Solicitors 25
Trainees 8

Contact
Mrs Heidi Kapadia

Method of application
Application form

Selection procedure
Interview and assessment

Closing date for 2010/2011
Not applicable

Training
Salary
1st year, £28,000 (London)
1st year, £23,800 (Regions)
2nd year, £30,000 (London)
2nd year, £25,500 (Regions)

Berwin Leighton Paisner

Adelaide House, London Bridge, London EC4R 9HA
Tel: (020) 7760 1000 Fax: (020) 7760 1111
Email: traineerecruit@blplaw.com   Website: www.blplaw.com

Firm profile
Berwin Leighton Paisner LLP is a premier, full-service City law firm, with particular strengths in real estate, corporate, finance, tax and a strong litigation and dispute resolution capability. The firm's open and friendly culture, combined with a strong commitment to career development means that it has become a magnet for quality staff. BLP has been named as "Most Upwardly Mobile Firm" in the Legal Week's survey of City lawyers and was included in the Sunday Times Top 100 Companies To Work For 2009.

Main areas of work
The full range of real estate work including investment, development, planning, construction, property finance, litigation and funds. Traditional corporate finance areas of M&A, equity capital markets and investment funds, as well as outsourcing, EU, competition, IT, telecoms and employment. An active Banking and Capital Markets Team with a growing securitisation capability, a Project Finance Team that is expanding internationally, and an Asset Finance Team. Strong and growing Corporate Tax Team, Intellectual Property, Commercial Litigation, and Insurance/Reinsurance Team. The firm is widely recognised for its expertise in a number of industry sectors, including real estate, hotels, leisure and gaming, defence, energy, utilities and retail.

LPC+
All trainees study at the College of Law for both the GDL and LPC. The firm runs the UK's first tailor-made LPC Course, called the LPC+ where tutors are joined by BLP lawyers and trainers who help to deliver some of the sessions, using BLP precedents and documents, discussing how theory is applied to real cases and transactions.

Trainee profile
The firm is looking for intelligent, energetic, positive and hard-working team players who have an interest in business and gain a sense of achievement from finding solutions.

Training environment
BLP is an exciting, ambitious, dynamic and entrepreneurial firm. When recruiting trainees, the focus is on quality rather than quantity. As a result, trainees are rewarded with a high degree of responsibility and involvement underpinned by an exceptional standard of training and support. BLP won the LawCareers.net "Best Trainer-Large City firm" award in 2009 and has always worked hard to provide the right environment for people to grow. Employees believe that BLP is a genuinely innovative and friendly firm with a refreshing lack of hierarchy, the open-door policy is something that trainees value tremendously. The trainee induction covers the practical aspects of working in a law firm, from billing to client care. There is technical training for each department, with weekly skills sessions and seminars for trainees as well as professional skills courses.

Vacation placements
Places for 2010: Assessment centers held during December, January and February at the firm's London office, applications accepted online before 31 January 2010 (at www.blplaw.com). Easter vacation scheme, one week, aimed at final year law students and those at a later stage of legal education/ employment. Summer vacation scheme, two weeks, aimed at those in their penultimate year and above (law and non-law).

Sponsorship
CPE/GDL and LPC+ fees paid and £7,200 maintenance p.a.

Partners 190
Assistant Solicitors 380
Total Trainees 80

Contact
Claire England

Method of application
Online application form

Selection procedure
Assessment day & partner interview

Closing date for 2012/2013
31 July 2010

Application
Training contracts p.a. 40
Applications p.a. 1,500
% interviewed p.a. 5%
Required degree grade 2:1

Training
Salary
1st year (2009)
£37,000
2nd year (2009)
£40,000
Holiday entitlement 25 days
% of trainees with a non-law degree p.a. 40%
No. of seats available abroad p.a. 1

Post-qualification
Salary (2009) £58,000
% of trainees offered job on qualification (March 2009) 83%
% of assistants who joined as trainees (2008) 47%
% of partners who joined as trainees (2008) 30%

Offices
London, Brussels, Paris, Abu Dhabi, Moscow, Singapore, preferred firms network in over 65 countries

Bevan Brittan

Kings Orchard, 1 Queen Street, Bristol, BS2 0HQ
Tel: (0870) 194 3050 Fax: (0870) 194 8954
Email: hr.training@bevanbrittan.com
Website: www.bevanbrittan.com

Partners 48	
Total Trainees 31	
Contact	HR and Training (0870) 194 3050
Method of application	Online application
Closing date for 2012	31 July 2010
Post-qualification	% of trainees offered job on qualification (2009) 71%
Other offices	Birmingham, London

Firm profile
Bevan Brittan has firmly established itself as a truly national law firm and continues to attract high profile national clients and challenging, groundbreaking work. The firm is nationally recognised for its expertise in providing legal advice to clients in both the public and private sectors and is notable for being one of the very few practices whose work is equally strong in both sectors.

Main areas of work
The firm is structured around three primary areas of the UK economy: health, communities and local government and major corporates. The firm operates in cross departmental teams across these markets, harnessing the full range of skills and experience needed to provide top quality legal advice in the context of specialist knowledge of both the sector concerned and the client's business. Areas of work covered include corporate, commercial, commercial litigation, projects, employment, medical law and personal injury, property and construction.

Trainee profile
Bevan Brittan recognises that the firm's success depends upon a team of lawyers dedicated to service excellence. Its success is maintained by attracting and retaining enthusiastic, bright people with sound common sense, plenty of energy and the ability to work and communicate well with others.

Training environment
During each six-month seat, the core of your training will be practical work experience in conjunction with an extensive educational programme. Together the training is aimed at developing attitudes, skills and legal and commercial knowledge essential for your career success. You are encouraged to take on as much work and responsibility as you are able to handle, which will be reviewed on a regular basis with your supervising Partner. The firm is friendly and supportive with an open-door policy along with a range of social, sporting and cultural activities.

Vacation placements
Places available for 2010: 24 across the three offices. Closing date: 31st March 2010.

Sponsorship & awards
Bursary and funding for GDL and LPC.

Bingham McCutchen (London) LLP

41 Lothbury, London, EC2R 7HF
Tel: (020) 7661 5300 Fax: (020) 7661 5400
Email: graduaterecruitment@bingham.com Website: www.bingham.com

Firm profile

Bingham's London team of 40 high-flying finance, litigation and corporate lawyers is dedicated to providing a seamless and responsive service to international financial institution clients. The firm's London office capabilities have been carefully shaped to meet the complex needs of a demanding client segment. Through practical experience and in-depth study of the legal and business issues facing these clients, the firm's London lawyers provide counsel in an intelligent, savvy, forceful and focused way. Members of Bingham's London office have represented institutions and funds in precedent-setting workouts and restructurings in the UK and across Europe, including BAA, Cheyne Finance, Concordia Bus, Elektrim, Emap, Focus DIY, Gate Gourmet, Golden Key, The Icelandic Banks, Jarvis, Kremikovtzi, Lehman Brothers, Level One, Marconi, Northern Rock, Parmalat, Queens Moat Houses, Sea Containers, The UK homebuilders and Whistlejacket. The financial restructuring practice in London is closely integrated with the firm's restructuring and insolvency practice in the United States, Tokyo and Hong Kong, leading The International Who's Who of Business Lawyers to name Bingham as 'Global Insolvency and Restructuring Law Firm of the Year' in 2006 and 2007. London lawyers also have extensive experience in the areas of finance, litigation, corporate, tax and financial services regulatory.

With nearly 1,000 lawyers in 12 offices spanning the United States, the United Kingdom and Asia, Bingham focuses on serving clients in complex financial transactions, high-stakes litigation and a full range of sophisticated corporate and technology matters.

Main areas of work

Bingham's London office capabilities include financial restructuring, finance, litigation, corporate, tax and financial services regulatory.

Trainee profile

The firm is looking for top quality candidates who can demonstrate an exceptional academic record combined with evidence of extra-curricular achievement. Prospective trainees will show initiative, be solution driven and seek to be part of a challenging yet friendly environment.

Training environment

The firm currently recruits two trainee solicitors a year. The training contract consists of four six-month seats, rotating between the following practice areas: financial restructuring, finance, corporate and litigation. Trainees also have the opportunity to spend one of their second year seats in the firm's Hong Kong office. The intimate nature of the London office means that you will benefit from a bespoke training programme with a high level of partner involvement. With the firm's small team approach, you will assume responsibilities from day one.

Benefits

The firm offers an extensive compensation programme for trainees. As well as a highly competitive salary, the firm offers private health insurance, travel insurance, long term disability insurance, season ticket loan, life assurance, a critical illness scheme and subsidised gym membership. A discretionary bonus is also payable.

Sponsorship & awards

LPC fees and maintenance grant of £8,000 per annum. PgDL fees and maintenance grant of £8,000 per annum.

Assistant solicitors 25
Total Trainees 4

Contact
Vicky Anderson, Human Resources Manager.
(020) 7661 5300

Method of application
Online application via firm website at www.bingham.com or via CV Mail

Selection procedure
Currently face to face interviews

Closing date for 2012
31 July 2010

Application
Training contracts p.a. up to 2
Required degree grade:
High 2:1 from a leading university and excellent A-levels

Training
Salary
1st year £40,000
2nd year £45,000
Holiday entitlement
25 days

Post-qualification
Salary (2009) £100,000

Overseas offices
Boston, Hartford, Hong Kong, Los Angeles, New York, Orange County, San Francisco, Santa Monica, Silicon Valley, Tokyo, Washington

Bircham Dyson Bell LLP

50 Broadway, London SW1H 0BL
Tel: (020) 7227 7000 Fax: (020) 7222 3480

Firm profile
Bircham Dyson Bell is a leading London law firm. The firm's approach and track record has enabled it to attract and retain some of the most talented people in the profession. This is achieved through the breadth and variety of work that the firm does. As part of the firm's commitment to providing a high level of service, it has been accredited with the Law Society's Lexcel quality mark and are one of the first law firms to be awarded ISO 14001, the internationally recognised standard for Environmental Management Systems. The firm is a leading member of Lexwork International, a network of 34 mid-sized independent law firms with over 1,700 lawyers in major cities across North America and Europe.

Main areas of work
Bircham Dyson Bell is recognised as having leading departments in the charity, private client, parliamentary, planning and public law fields. The firm also has strong corporate, commercial, employment, litigation and real estate teams.

Trainee profile
Applications are welcome from both law and non-law students who can demonstrate a consistently high academic record. The firm is looking for forward thinkers with a practical outlook and lots of initiative to join in the firm's friendly, hard-working environment. If you're focused, positive and a confident leader, get in touch. Many of the firm's current trainees have diverse interests outside law.

Training environment
The firm's training is designed to produce its future partners. To achieve this they aim to provide a balance of both formal and practical training and will give early responsibility to those who show promise. The two-year training contract consists of four six-month seats during which you will work alongside partners and other senior lawyers, some of whom are leaders in their field. As the firm practises in a wide variety of legal disciplines, trainees benefit from a diverse experience. Trainees undergo specific technical training in each seat in addition to the mandatory Professional Skills Course (PSC). Great emphasis is also placed on soft skills training and development so when you qualify you have the breadth of skills required to be an excellent solicitor.

Benefits
Bonus scheme, group health care, life assurance, pension scheme, on site subsidised café, season ticket loan and corporate rate gym membership

---

Partners 49
Fee Earners 118
Total Trainees 14

Contact
Graduate Recruitment Team
(020) 7227 7000

Method of application
Please visit the firm's website,
www.bdb-law.co.uk

Selection procedure
Two interviews with members of the Graduate Recruitment Team, comprising a number of partners, associates and HR. In addition you will be required to complete a verbal reasoning test, in-tray exercise and presentation

Closing date for 2012
31 July 2010

Application
Training contracts p.a. 7
Applications p.a. 650
% interviewed p.a. 8%
Required degree grade:
2:1 or above degree preferred

Training
Salary
1st year (1 October 2009)
£30,000
2nd year (2009) £31,000
Holiday entitlement
25 days

Post-qualification
Salary £49,000
% of trainees offered job on qualification (2009) 40%

Bird & Bird

15 Fetter Lane, London EC4A 1JP
Tel: (020) 7415 6000 Fax: (020) 7415 6111
Website: www.twobirds.com

Firm profile

Bird & Bird is an international law firm that operates on the basis of an in-depth understanding of key industry sectors, including: aviation and aerospace, financial services, communications, electronics, energy, IT, life sciences, media and sport. The firm is proud to be working with some of the world's most innovative and technologically advanced companies, each of which depend on cutting-edge legal advice to meet their business objectives.

The firm is ambitious and it manages to combine a resilient business approach with a hugely supportive attitude to its employees. With offices in Beijing, Bratislava, Brussels, Budapest, Düsseldorf, Frankfurt, The Hague, Helsinki, Hong Kong, London, Lyon, Madrid, Milan, Munich, Paris, Prague, Rome, Shanghai, Singapore, Stockholm, Warsaw and close ties with firms in other key centres in Europe, Asia and the United States, the firm is well placed to offer its clients local expertise within a global context.

The firm is proud of its friendly, stimulating environment where individuals are able to develop first class legal, business and interpersonal skills. It has an open and collegiate culture reflected in its good retention rate and assistant involvement. The way the firm is structured also means that there is a very strong international perspective to its culture - integrated teams working for cross-border clients as well as a range of international sport and social activities enables this.

At Bird & Bird, there is a genuine commitment to acting as a responsible employer and also as a proactive member of its local and wider international communities. The firm has a full programme of corporate social responsibility initiatives and policies in place, which fall under three broad areas, people, community and environment.

Main areas of work

Aviation and aerospace, banking and finance, commercial, construction and engineering, corporate finance, dispute resolution, employment, energy and infrastructure, clean technology, EU and competition, restructuring and insolvency, intellectual property, IT, communications, life sciences, media, private equity and venture capital, real estate, sport and tax.

Trainee profile

The firm recognises that its lawyers are its most important asset and that is why the firm recruits strong graduates capable of developing expert legal skills and commercial acumen. A certain level of intelligence and common sense is a prerequisite (the firm looks for excellent A levels and a strong 2.1), but more importantly it looks for well-rounded individuals who will fit in.

The firm's trainee solicitors are outgoing, articulate team-players, willing to work hard when called upon and genuinely interested in progressing their careers. The firm aims to recruit people who will stay with the firm and therefore seek candidates who have a long-term interest in Bird & Bird and the sectors and areas of legal practice it focuses on.

Training environment

The firm's trainees take on responsibility from day one and enjoy varied and challenging work for industry-shaping clients. If you become a trainee with the firm, you will be given the chance to excel.

The firm runs a business skills development programme to provide you with the basic building blocks for your future development within the business of law. The firm is still personal enough for its trainees to make their mark in the firm's friendly, stimulating work place.

Trainees will spend six months in three of the following practice areas: corporate, commercial, employment, banking, tax, intellectual property, dispute resolution and real estate.

Trainees are encouraged to join the number of sports teams at the firm and to attend various social events.

Partners 213*
Assistant Solicitors 492*
Total Trainees 35 in London
*denotes worldwide figures

Contact
Lynne Walters, Graduate & Trainee Manager
lynne.walters@twobirds.com

Method of application
Online application form via the firm website.

Selection procedure
Insight and selection days in February 2010 for Summer placements and August 2010 for Training Contracts.

Closing date for 2012
31 July 2010 for law and non-law students.

Application
Training contracts p.a. 16
Applications p.a. 900
% interviewed p.a. 10%
Required degree grade 2:1

Training
Salary
1st year (2009) £35,000
2nd year (2009) £37,000
Holiday entitlement
25 days
% of trainees with a non-law degree p.a. Varies

Post-qualification
Salary (2009) £55,000
% of trainees offered job on qualification (2009) 100%

Overseas offices
Beijing, Bratislava, Brussels, Budapest, Düsseldorf, Frankfurt, The Hague, Helsinki, Hong Kong, London, Lyon, Madrid, Milan, Munich, Paris, Prague, Rome, Shanghai, Singapore, Stockholm, Warsaw

Bond Pearce LLP

3 Temple Quay, Temple Back East, Bristol, BS1 6DZ
Tel: 0845 415 0000   Fax: 0845 415 6900
Email: sam.lee@bondpearce.com
Website: www.bondpearce.com

Vacancies 15
Trainees 24
Partners 80
Total staff 650
Contact
Samantha Lee
Method of application
Electronic application form
Selection procedure
Assessment days
Closing date
31 July 2010
Application
Training contracts p.a. 15-20
Required degree grade 2:1
Training
Salary
1st year £24,000
2nd year £25,000
Holiday entitlement
25 days
Offices
Bristol, Plymouth, Southampton, London, Aberdeen

Firm profile

With aspirations to become a top five national business law firm this is an exciting time to be thinking about joining Bond Pearce. The firm's recent growth has been based on forging strong client relationships, providing effective business solutions and recruiting high calibre people across the firm.

Outstanding client service is something the firm is passionate about, as it helps to build and reinforce relationships, improve the timeliness of advice and encourage teamwork. The result: commercial legal advice that is proactive rather than simply reactive. According to the most recent Chambers FTSE survey the firm is ranked as the joint-leading choice, regionally, for FTSE 100 clients.

Main areas of work

The firm's particular strengths lie in its sector expertise and much of its work lies at the cutting edge of developments in key sectors such as energy, retail, financial services, real estate and the public sector. The firm boasts an impressive portfolio of clients which includes, for example: Lloyds TSB, BBC, QBE Group, RWE Npower Plc, Carnival Plc, Associated British Ports, English Heritage, The Crown Estate, MoD, Barclays Bank, Royal Mail, Kingfisher, B&Q, Virgin Group, Chemring Group, Carlsberg, Marks & Spencer.

Trainee profile

The firm is looking for individuals who are capable of combining great legal knowledge with a sound commercial focus; people who are driven, creative and have a genuine enthusiasm for both the law and the firm's business and individuals with a natural ability in dealing with people.

Training environment

You couldn't ask for a better start to your legal career. The firm offers a first class training and development programme ensuring that you qualify with the best possible legal, business and personal skills. The firm has worked hard to create a culture that encourages, inspires and challenges. The Graduate Team, consisting of partners, associates and HR provide all the support and encouragement that you need to see you through your two years with the firm. Structured over four seats the firm offers a good range of practice areas for you to train and qualify into.

The firm's trainees are an integral part of the business and right from the start of your training contract you will enjoy early responsibility and exposure to high profile clients at the most senior level.

When & how to apply

Applications for a training contract should be made by 31 July 2010. You can apply using the firm's application form on the graduate pages of the website. The closing date for the summer vacation scheme is 9 April 2010.

Vacation placements

Two weeks in June/July.

Sponsorship & awards

Full GDL and LPC £6,000 maintenance grant for both.

Boodle Hatfield

89 New Bond Street, London, W1S 1DA
Tel: (020) 7629 7411 Fax: (020) 7629 2621
Email: traineesolicitors@boodlehatfield.com
Website: www.boodlehatfield.com

Firm profile
Boodle Hatfield is a highly successful medium-sized firm which has been providing bespoke legal services for more than 275 years. They still act for some of their very first clients and are proud to do so. The firm has grown into a substantial practice, serving the full spectrum of commercial and private clients, both domestically and internationally.

Main areas of work
The ethos of facilitating private capital activity and private businesses underpins the work of the whole firm. The interplay of skills between five major areas – private client and tax, property, family, corporate and litigation – makes Boodle Hatfield particularly well placed to serve these individuals and businesses.

Trainee profile
The qualities the firm looks for in its trainees are commitment, flexibility and the ability to work as part of a team. Students with 2.1 or above and high A levels should apply.

Training environment
Trainees spend six months in up to four of the firm's main areas: property, corporate, family, private client and tax, and litigation. Boodle Hatfield is well known for the high quality of its training. All trainees are involved in client work from the start and are encouraged to handle their own files personally as soon as they are able to do so, with the appropriate supervision. The firm's trainees therefore have a greater degree of client contact than in many firms with the result that they should be able to take on more responsibility at an early stage. Trainees are given formal appraisals every three months which are designed as a two-way process and give trainees the chance to discuss their progress and to indicate where more can be done to help in their ongoing training and development.

Benefits
Private healthcare, life assurance, season ticket loan, pension scheme, enhanced maternity pay, conveyancing grant, permanent health insurance, employee assistance line, childcare vouchers, cycle to work scheme, give as you earn scheme.

Vacation placements
Two week placement between June and September, for which 10 students are accepted each year. Applicants should apply via the application form on the website at www.boodlehatfield.com.

Sponsorship & awards
LPC and GDL plus maintenance grant.

Partners 28
Assistant Solicitors 28
Total Trainees 13

Contact
Bethan Quinn
(020) 7079 8103

Method of application
Online application

Selection procedure
Interviews with the Training Principal, a Partner and the HR Director plus an ability test in verbal reasoning

Closing date for 2012
See website

Application
Training contracts p.a. 6
Required degree grade 2:1

Training
Salary
1st year £32,000
2nd year £34,500
Holiday entitlement
25 days

Post-qualification
Salary £48,000

Regional offices
Oxford

B P Collins

Collins House, 32-38 Station Road, Gerrards Cross SL9 8EL
Tel: (01753) 889995 Fax: (01753) 889851
Email: jacqui.symons@bpcollins.co.uk
Website: www.bpcollins.co.uk

Firm profile
B P Collins was established in 1966, and has expanded significantly to become one of the largest and best known legal practices at the London end of the M4/M40 corridors. At its offices in Gerrards Cross, the emphasis is on commercial work, including corporate/commercial work of all types, commercial conveyancing and general commercial litigation. Alongside this there is a highly respected private client department specialising in tax planning, trusts, charities, wills and probates, and an equally successful family law team.

Main areas of work
Corporate/commercial, employment, IT/IP, civil and commercial litigation, commercial conveyancing, property development, private client and family law.

Trainee profile
Most of the partners and other fee-earners have worked in London at one time or another but, tired of commuting, have opted to work in more congenial surroundings and enjoy a higher quality lifestyle. Gerrards Cross is not only a very pleasant town with a large number of high net worth private clients but it is also a convenient location for serving the extremely active business community at the eastern end of the Thames Valley including West London, Heathrow, Uxbridge, Slough and Windsor. The firm therefore looks for trainees who are likely to respond to this challenging environment.

Training environment
The firm aims to have eight trainee solicitors at different stages of their training contracts at all times. Trainees serve five months in four separate departments of their choice. The final four months is spent in the department in which the trainee intends specialising. The firm has a training partner with overall responsibility for all trainees and each department has its own training principal who is responsible for day to day supervision. There are regular meetings between the training principal and the trainee to monitor progress and a review meeting with the training partner midway and at the end of each departmental seat. The firm also involves its trainees in social and marketing events including football and cricket matches, and other sporting and non-sporting activities.

Partners 19
Assistant Solicitors 28
Total Trainees 8

Contact
HR Manager Mrs Jacqui Symons

Method of application
Handwritten covering letter & CV

Selection procedure
Screening interview & assessment day

Closing date for 2011
31 May 2010

Application
Required degree grade 2:1, A & B 'A' level grades.

Training
Salary
1st year £22,000
2nd year £23,000

Bristows

100 Victoria Embankment, London EC4Y 0DH
Tel: (020) 7400 8000 Fax: (020) 7400 8050
Email: info@bristows.com
Website: www.bristows.com

Firm profile
Bristows is a medium-sized firm that handles the kind of work that might normally be associated with only the very largest firms. Established more than 170 years ago, the firm has built up a client list that includes leading businesses from a variety of sectors, whether global corporations, growing start-ups, charities or financial institutions. Working with so many ambitious organisations, the firm is often advising on issues that shape entire industries and on which a company's future might depend. For example, advising on whether the business is entitled to launch a new product or assisting a client to buy a rival business.

Main areas of work
Bristows might be known as one of the foremost intellectual property firms in the UK, but this only tells part of the story. The firm's lawyers are also recognised as leading authorities in a wide variety of other legal disciplines and as a firm offer a true breadth of expertise. These are our core practice areas: intellectual property-including patent, trademarks and brand protection; information technology; privacy and data protection; regulatory; EU and competition; advertising, marketing and promotion; corporate; commercial disputes; employment; real estate; product liability; tax; publishing and media.

Trainee profile
The size of the firm makes this an ideal environment for trainees. As part of a small intake, the trainees work alongside the partners dealing directly with clients right from the start. There's plenty of responsibility but this is matched by an extremely supportive and friendly culture so you're never far from encouragement and advice when you need it. The firm recognises that its reputation as a leading city law firm is entirely down to the individuals who work here, so it places great stock in attracting talented people and doing all it can to make sure they enjoy life at Bristows.

Training environment
Each year the firm has between 10-12 graduates join its team. The firm is extremely selective because its looking for the people who will be its future partners. As part of such a small and high calibre intake you'll have every chance to shine and the firm will give you real responsibility earlier than you might expect. During the two years' training, you'll spend time in each of the firm's main departments, developing your skills and knowledge. You'll also work closely with its partners, something which is guaranteed to speed up the learning process. Part of this training may also involve a secondment to one of a number of leading clients. With the international spread of its clients, the probability of overseas travel is high, especially following qualification.

Benefits
Life Assurance, pension scheme; private medical insurance, permanent health insurance, eye care, health assessment, employee assistance programme, cycle to work scheme, childcare voucher scheme, season ticket loan.

Placement schemes
The firm runs placement schemes which give you the chance to work at Bristows over Easter, Summer or Winter. It's a great chance to assess whether law as a career, and Bristows as a firm, are for you. The kind of things you'll find yourself doing will include research, drafting documents, attending meetings and you might also go along to court hearings.

Sponsorship & awards
GDL and LPC fees paid in full, plus a maintenance grant of £7,000 for each.

Partners 28
Assistant Solicitors 56
Total Trainees 15

Contact
Trainee Recruitment & Training Officer

Method of application
Online

Selection procedure
2 individual interviews

Closing date for 2012
31 January 2010 for February interviews,
31 July 2010 for August interviews

Application
Training contracts p.a.
Up to 10
Applications p.a. 3,500
% interviewed p.a. 6%
Required degree grade
2:1 (preferred)

Training
Salary
1st year (2009) £33,000
2nd year (2009) £36,000
Holiday entitlement
4 weeks
% of trainees with
a non-law degree p.a. 86%

Post-qualification
Salary (2009) £52,500
% of trainees offered job
on qualification (2008) 60%
% of assistants (as at 5/6/06)
who joined as trainees 46%
% of partners (as at 01/08/07)
who joined as trainees 33%

Browne Jacobson

Nottingham, Birmingham, London
Tel: (0115) 976 6000 Fax: (0115) 947 5246
Email: traineeapplications@brownejacobson.com
Website: www.brownejacobson.com/trainees.aspx

Firm profile
Browne Jacobson is one of the largest full service commercial law firms in the Midlands with regional and national reach through its offices in Nottingham, Birmingham and London.

With around 500 people, Browne Jacobson is large enough to attract some of the best talent in the country, but small enough to foster a supportive and flexible working environment. The firm's people are the key to its success and it has a track record of attracting and retaining outstanding people. This was recognised by the Lawyer HR Awards 2008 when the firm picked up the Graduate Recruitment Campaign of the Year Award.

Browne Jacobson focuses on long-term relationships that are friendly, flexible and straightforward, both with its people and its clients. The firm's modern, progressive working environment and its friendly and open culture mean that its people enjoy working here so they stay. This allows good working relationships to develop and provides consistency for clients. It's a simple tactic yet one that works; a large proportion of the firm's client base has been with the firm for a number of years.

Main areas of work
The firm has a long established and nationwide reputation in all areas of its commercial, public sector, health and insurance practices and is recognised as regional heavyweight for corporate, property, public enquiry, litigation and professional risk work.

Trainee profile
Browne Jacobson is looking for talented law and non-law graduates who can bring with them enthusiasm, commitment, client focus and a flexible and friendly attitude.

Training environment
Trainees start with a comprehensive induction programme, a fast track professional skills course and then go onto a trainee development programme. They spend four periods of six months in some of the principle areas of the firm, gaining an overview of the practice. Trainees get great training, a friendly and supportive working environment, and real career opportunities. They are also given quality work and exposure to clients from early on, but are supported in achieving results and recognised for their contribution.

Sponsorship & awards
LPC/PGDL tuition fees paid, plus maintenance grant for LPC/PGDL of £5,000.

Open days
Browne Jacobson run open days in the spring - application deadline for 2010 open days is 17 March 2010. Apply online or by CV and covering letter.

Benefits
Life assurance, income protection insurance, pension, private medical insurance and corporate discounts.

Partners 68
Associates 47
Assistant Solicitors 72
Total Trainees 20
Total Staff 500

Contact
Zena Comrie, HR Executive

Method of application
Apply online at www.brownejacobson.com/trainees.aspx or by CV and covering letter

Selection procedure
Telephone interview, assessment centre and partner interview

Closing date
31 July 2010 for 2012 training contracts

Application
Training contracts p.a. 8
Applications p.a. 700
% interviewed p.a. 8%

Training
Salary
1st year (2009) £24,000
2nd year (2009) £25,000
Holiday entitlement 25 days
% of trainees with a non-law degree p.a. 40%

Post-qualification
Salary Market Rate
Holiday entitlement 25 days
% of trainees offered a job on qualification (2008) 62.5%

brownejacobson

Burges Salmon

Narrow Quay House, Narrow Quay, Bristol BS1 4AH
Tel: (0117) 902 2766 Fax: (0117) 902 4400
Email: katy.main@burges-salmon.com
Website: www.burges-salmon.com

Firm profile
Burges Salmon is proof that law doesn't have to mean London.

Based in Bristol, the firm's turnover has more than tripled in recent years as it continues to win prestigious clients out of the hands of City rivals. Clients such as Orange, the Ministry of Defence and Virgin Mobile rely on its legal expertise and in doing so have helped cement the firm's reputation for creative, lateral thinking. Burges Salmon's primary asset is its people. Trainees benefit from supervision by lawyers who are leaders in their field with a formidable depth of experience. All this against the backdrop of Bristol: a city with a quality of life you would be hard pressed to find anywhere else in the UK.

Main areas of work
Burges Salmon provides national and international clients such as The Crown Estate, Discovery Channel and Chanel with a full commercial service through five main departments: corporate and financial institutions; commercial; property; private client and wealth structuring; and disputes, environment and planning.

Trainee profile
Burges Salmon lawyers are hard working, motivated individuals with a strong academic background and enthusiasm for a career in law. Candidates must be commercially aware and possess excellent communication skills.

Training environment
Trainees play a vital role in shaping the future of the firm and Burges Salmon invests a great deal of time and resource into training and development. Training is personalised to suit each individual, and the six seat structure allows the opportunity to experience a wider range of practice areas before making a decision on qualification. This dedication to trainees is demonstrated by a high retention rate, which is well above the industry average.

Vacation placements
Burges Salmon runs two open days in February and offers 40 two-week vacation placements during the summer. Individuals visit two departments of their choice supervised by a Partner or senior solicitor, and attend court visits and client meetings. Current trainees run skills training sessions, sports and social events. Remuneration: £250 per week.

Sponsorship and awards
The firm pays GDL and LPC fees at the institution of your choice. Maintenance grants of £7,000 are paid to LPC students, and £14,000 to students studying for both the GDL and LPC (£7,000 p.a.).

Benefits
Annually reviewed competitive salary, 24 days paid annual leave, qualification leave, bonus scheme, pension scheme, private health care membership, life assurance, mobile phone, Christmas gift, corporate gym membership, sports and social club.

Partners 69
Assistant Solicitors 345 Total
Trainees 43

Contact
Katy Main, Recruitment Manager

Method of application
Employer's application form available on website

Selection procedure
Penultimate year law students, final year law and non-law students, recent graduates and those considering a change of career are considered for open days, vacation placements and/or training contracts.

Closing date for 2012
31 July 2010

Application
Training contracts p.a. 20-25
Applications p.a. 1,500
% interviewed p.a. 10%
Required degree grade 2:1

Training
Salary
1st year (2009) £30,000
2nd year (2009) £31,000
Holiday entitlement 24 days
% of trainees with
a non-law degree p.a. 50%

Post-qualification
Salary (2008) £40,000
% of trainees offered job
on qualification (2009) 91%
% of assistants who joined as trainees (2009) 50%
% of partners who joined as trainees (2009) 30%

Capsticks

77-83 Upper Richmond Road, London SW15 2TT
Tel: (020) 8780 2211   Fax: (020) 8780 4811
Email: career@capsticks.com
Website: www.capsticks.com

Firm profile
Capsticks is the leading provider of legal services to the healthcare sector and has over 100 lawyers focusing on healthcare across its offices in London and Birmingham. The firm has ambitious plans for further growth, both in its core market and by promoting its broader capability and expanding private sector client base.

Main areas of work
The firm acts for a wide range of healthcare clients, including NHS Trusts and Health Authorities, the NHSLA, regulatory bodies, charities and independent healthcare providers. The firm's main practice areas are clinical law, corporate/commercial, dispute resolution, employment and property.

Trainee profile
The firm is committed to recruiting the best people to maintain its market leading position. The firm recruits five trainee solicitors each year and welcomes applications from candidates who are either on course for or have achieved at least a 2.1 (or equivalent) in their undergraduate degree. The firm expects candidates to be committed to a career in healthcare law and to be able to demonstrate they are highly driven, but well rounded, team players, with good problem solving and communication skills.

Training environment
The firm's broad range of practice areas and healthcare clients enables it to give its trainees an opportunity to experience a wide variety of legal work. Trainees are therefore able to acquire an in-depth knowledge of both healthcare law and the healthcare industry, in addition to developing the skills that any good lawyer needs.

The training contract is designed to give trainees maximum exposure to the work of the firm and trainees undertake seats in all of the firm's practice areas, including clinical law, corporate/commercial, dispute resolution, employment and property.

Benefits
Bonus scheme, 25 days holiday, pension contribution, permanent health insurance, private medical insurance, death in service benefit, childcare voucher scheme and season ticket loan.

Vacation placements
The firm's vacation scheme runs from the end of June through to the middle of August and placements last for two weeks each. In order to be eligible for the 2010 vacation scheme you should be looking to secure a training contract with the firm in September 2012. The firm welcomes applications for a place on its 2010 vacation scheme between 15 November 2009 and 26 February 2010. Further details are available from the website.

The firm encourages all prospective trainee solicitors to participate in the vacation scheme as this is their primary means for selecting future trainee solicitors.

Sponsorship & awards
The firm offers its future trainees financial support for both the Graduate Diploma in Law and the Legal Practice Course.

Partners 34
Assistant Solicitors 74
Total Trainees 10
Other Fee-earners 33

Contact
HR department,
career@capsticks.com

Method of application
Application form, CV and covering letter

Selection procedure
Interview with Partner and Director of HR

Closing date for 2012
13 August 2010

Application
Training contracts p.a. 5
Applications p.a. 200
% interviewed p.a. 7%
Required degree grade
2:1 or above

Training
Salary
1st year £29,000 p.a.
2nd year £30,000 p.a.
Holiday entitlement
25 days p.a.
% of trainees with a
non-law degree p.a. 40%

Post-qualification
Salary (2009)
£46,000 p.a.
% of trainees offered job
on qualification (2009) 80%

Charles Russell LLP

5 Fleet Place, London, EC4M 7RD
Tel: (020) 7203 5000 Fax: (020) 7203 5307
Website: www.charlesrussell.co.uk

Firm profile
Charles Russell LLP is a leading legal practice, providing a full range of services to UK and international businesses, governments, not-for-profit bodies, and individuals. It has eight offices: two in London, Cheltenham, Guildford, Cambridge, Oxford, Geneva and Bahrain. The practice is known for its client care, high quality, expertise and friendly approach. The strategy is simple – to help clients achieve their goals through excellent service. Experienced in carrying out cross-border corporate and commercial work, the practice also provides clients with access to 150 recommended law firms across the world as part of the two major legal networks, ALFA International and the Association of European Lawyers. The practice's lawyers and staff are highly motivated and talented people and many are ranked as leaders in their fields. The practice's commitment to training and development and strong team spirit is a key ingredient to being known as a friendly practice to work with and work at.

Main areas of work
75% of the Practice's work is commercial. Principal areas of work include corporate/commercial, litigation and dispute resolution, intellectual property, employment and pensions, real estate, technology, media, communications and sport, healthcare, charities, private client and family.

Trainee profile
Trainees should be balanced, rounded achievers with an excellent academic background and outside interests.

Training environment
The practice recruits a small number of trainees for its size each year. This allows trainees to undergo the best possible training. Trainees spend six months in four of the following training seats – corporate/commercial, employment/pensions, family, litigation and dispute resolution, private client and real estate. Secondments to clients are also often available. Wherever possible the practice will accommodate individual preferences. You will be seated with a partner/senior solicitor. Regular appraisals are held to discuss progress and direction. Trainees are encouraged to attend extensive in-house training. The PSC is taught both internally and externally. Trainees are encouraged to take on as much responsibility as possible. A social committee organises a range of activities from quiz nights through to sporting events.

Benefits
BUPA; PHI; Life Assurance; pension; season ticket loan; 25 days holiday plus additional day for house moves.

Sponsorship & awards
The practice pays for course fees whilst you are at law school and also offers a grant per academic year of £6,000 to London trainees, £4,500 to Guildford and Cambridge trainees, £3,500 to Cheltenham trainees.

Partners 101
Other fee-earners 232
Total trainees 39
Total staff 615

Contact
trainee.recruitment@charlesrussell.co.uk

Method of application
Online application via the website

Selection procedure
Assessment days to include an interview & other exercises designed to assess identified performance criteria

Closing date for 2011/12
31st July 2010

Application
Training contracts for 2011: 14
2012: 21
Applications p.a.
Approx 1,500
% interviewed p.a. 7%
Preferred degree grade 2:1

Training
Salary (London)
1st year (2009) £31,500
2nd year (2009) £32,500
Holiday entitlement
25 days + additional day for house moves

Post-qualification
Salary (2009) £55,000

Regional offices
Also offers training contracts in its Cheltenham (2 places) Guildford (3 places) offices and Cambridge (1 place).

Clarke Willmott LLP

138 Edmund Street, Birmingham, B3 2ES
Tel: (0845) 209 1729   Fax: (0845) 209 2516
Email: heather.cooper@clarkewillmott.com
Website: www.clarkewillmott.com/trainees

Firm profile

Clarke Willmott LLP is a UK law firm with a national reputation in key commercial and private client services. With 74 Partners and approximately 500 people in total, the firm operates from five locations: Bristol, Birmingham, Taunton, Southampton and London (serviced office).

The firm's lawyers are, first and foremost, business advisers whose objectives are to help clients achieve their goals and to enhance the value of their opportunities. The firm takes a straightforward, proactive approach, and has helped enterprises of all sizes and at all stages of the business lifecycle navigate a range of complex legal issues with positive results. Above all the firm understands that its clients are not looking for more legal advice, they are looking for more business. The firm sees it as its role to help them achieve it.

Main areas of work

Services include corporate, commercial, real estate and construction, business recovery, dispute resolution and insolvency, employment, health and safety, intellectual property, personal injury, insurance, property and private capital as well as a range of services to private clients. The firm has specialist industry experience in real estate (development, investment, social housing, construction and urban regeneration), retail, sport, agriculture, renewable energy and private client.

Trainee profile

The firm recruits commercially aware trainees who can demonstrate a clear commitment to a career in law. Clarke Willmott looks for trainees who have a confident, energetic approach and who have the ability to work and communicate well with others. Applications are welcomed from both law and non-law graduates, with ideally a 2:1 degree.

Training environment

Trainees complete four six-month seats, providing a wide range of practical experience and skills in contentious and non-contentious work. Individual preference is sought and will be balanced with the firm's needs. Trainees work closely with partners and solicitors in a supportive team structure, and have regular reviews to ensure they are reaching their potential. Training in both legal and non-legal areas is provided to meet the needs of the individual trainee and the Professional Skills Course is undertaken in-house.

Sponsorship & benefits

Life assurance, group personal pension, gym membership, performance related bonus, funding for the GDL and LPC, occupational sick pay, season ticket loans, eyecare vouchers, childcare vouchers, and cycle to work scheme.

Partners 74
Solicitors 135
Trainees 19

Contact
Heather Cooper, Graduate Recruitment Manager

Method of application
Online application form

Selection procedure
Assessment centre

Closing date for 2012
31 July 2010 (interviews September 2010)

Application
Training contracts p.a.: 10
Applications p.a. c. 700
% interviewed p.a. 10%
Preferred degree grade 2:1

Training
Salary
1st year (2009) £24,000
2nd year (2009) £25,500
Holiday entitlement
25 days

Post-qualification
Salary (2009) £35,000-£37,500 (dependant on location)
% of trainees offered job on qualification (2009) 79%

Regional offices
Birmingham, Bristol, Southampton, Taunton, London

*clarke willmott

Cleary Gottlieb Steen & Hamilton LLP

City Place House, 55 Basinghall Street, London, EC2V 5EH
Tel: (020) 7614 2200 Fax: (020) 7600 1698
Email: longraduaterecruit@cgsh.com
Website: www.cgsh.com/careers/london

Firm profile

Cleary Gottlieb is one of the leading international law firms, with 12 closely integrated offices located in major financial and political centres around the world. For more than 60 years, the firm has been pre-eminent in shaping the globalisation of the legal profession. Its worldwide practice has a proven track record for innovation and providing advice of the highest quality to meet the domestic and international needs of its clients.

Main areas of work

Core practice groups in London are mergers and acquisitions, private equity, financing, and debt and equity capital markets (IPOs), plus additional self-standing practices in competition, tax, international litigation and arbitration, financial regulation, intellectual property and information technology.

Trainee profile

Cleary looks for candidates who are enthusiastic about the practice of law in a challenging and dynamic international setting. Whilst academic excellence is a pre-requisite, the firm places particular emphasis on recruiting candidates that they and their clients will enjoy working with. A sense of humour is as important as the ability to think critically and creatively about cutting-edge legal issues.

Training environment

By limiting its graduate intake to just 10-12 trainees a year, Cleary is able to offer bespoke training that is individually tailored to the interests, experience and aptitudes of the individuals that join them. The firm does not believe that the transition from trainee solicitor to associate occurs overnight on qualification, but rather that the transition should be a smooth and gradual one. It therefore encourages its trainee solicitors to accept increased responsibility as soon as they are ready to do so. With appropriate levels of supervision, trainees operate as lawyers of the firm from the day that they join.

Benefits

Health club membership, BUPA private healthcare cover (personal and family), life insurance of twice annual salary, long-term disability insurance, employer pension contribution, employee assistance programme and subsidised staff restaurant.

Vacation schemes

The firm's London office offers 35 vacation places each year (five in winter, ten in spring and ten in each of two summer schemes). The firm actively encourages all candidates that are seriously considering applying for a trainee solicitor position to undertake a vacation placement with the firm. Applications for winter vacation placements should be received by November 15. The deadline for spring and summer vacation scheme applications is January 28.

Sponsorship & awards

Cleary funds the LPC for all future trainee solicitors. For non-law graduates, the firm also funds the GDL. A maintenance grant of £8,000 is paid for each year of professional study.

Trainees 17
Partners 198
(16 in London)
Total Staff 2500
(200 in London)

Contact
Graduate Recruitment

Method of application
Cover letter and CV

Selection procedure
Future trainees are primarily selected from among those having completed a vacation scheme with the firm

Closing date for 2012
July 31 2010

Application
Training contracts p.a. 10-12
Required degree grade
High 2:1

Training
Salary
1st year £40,000
2nd year £45,000

Post-qualification
Salary £92,000

Overseas offices
New York, Washington DC, Paris, Brussels, Moscow, Frankfurt, Cologne, Rome, Milan, Hong Kong and Beijing

Clifford Chance

10 Upper Bank Street, Canary Wharf, London, E14 5JJ
Tel: (020) 7006 3003 Fax: (020) 7006 3563
Email: Recruitment.London@CliffordChance.com
Website: www.cliffordchance.com/gradsuk

Firm profile
Clifford Chance is a leading international law firm delivering innovative and practical legal solutions to corporate, institutional, and government clients around the world.

Trainee profile
At Clifford Chance there is interest in your potential to become a first-class business lawyer. Intellectual curiosity and communication, analytical and team-working skills are all valuable attributes that the firm looks for during its selection process. However, it's also interested in you as an individual; what motivates you and which personal qualities, insights and experiences you can bring to the firm.

Training environment
Each seat will bring you into contact with new clients and colleagues, and you can expect to work on a variety of deals and projects, both large and small, as you build your portfolio of skills.

Benefits
As well as a competitive salary, you'll enjoy: a subsidised restaurant; free use of fitness centre, swimming pool, squash courts and wellness centre; the option of up to six weeks' leave on qualification and a pension.

Vacation placements
See website for details.

Sponsorship & awards
Fees for GDL and LPC covered. Maintenance is also provided, please refer to website for details.

Employer of Choice for Law 2009, The Times Graduate Recruitment Awards.

London office
Partners 220
Lawyers 859
Trainees 210

Contact
Recruitment London (020) 7006 3003

Method of application
Online at www.cliffordchance.com/gradsuk

Selection procedure
Verbal reasoning test, group exercise, case study, competency-based interview

Application
Training contracts p.a. Around 100
Applications p.a. 2,000
% interviewed p.a. 33%
Required degree grade 2:1

Training
Salary
1st year £37,400
2nd year £42,200
Holiday entitlement 25 days
% of trainees with a non-law degree p.a. 40%
No. of seats available abroad p.a. 92 (46 in each six month seat)

Post-qualification
Salary £59,000
% of trainees offered job on qualification (2008) 81%

Overseas offices
Abu Dhabi, Amsterdam, Bangkok, Barcelona, Beijing, Brussels, Bucharest, Budapest, Dubai, Düsseldorf, Frankfurt, Hong Kong, Kyiv, London, Luxembourg, Madrid, Milan, Moscow, Munich, New York, Paris, Prague, Riyadh (co-operative office), Rome, São Paulo, Shanghai, Singapore, Tokyo, Warsaw, Washington DC

Clyde & Co

51 Eastcheap, London EC3M 1JP
Tel: (020) 7623 1244 Fax: (020) 7623 5427
Email: theanswers@clydeco.com   Website: www.clydeco.com/graduate

Firm profile
With roots in international trade, Clyde & Co LLP's main objective is to help clients do business in over 120 countries around the globe. The firm values entrepreneurialism, commercial problem solving, excellence and the freedom to be an individual. Clients value the firm's hands on, innovative approach. The firm's lawyers know their industries, their clients, and most importantly understand the commercial realities of business. Availability and responsiveness are key in the firm's core industries and these characteristics have become part of the mindset of a Clyde & Co lawyer.

The firm has expanded rapidly in recent years and is a dominant player in the insurance, reinsurance, international litigation, shipping, aviation, transport, international trade and energy, and commodities sectors. Clyde & Co has one of the largest Litigation practices in the UK.

Main areas of work
Aviation and Aerospace, Corporate/Commercial, Dispute Resolution, EC/Competition, Energy, Trade and Commodities, Insurance and Re-insurance, Real Estate, Shipping, Transport and Logistics.

Trainee profile
The firm is looking for graduates with excellent academic records, outgoing personalities and keen interests. Trainees need to have the social skills that will enable them to communicate effectively and build relationships with clients and colleagues. The ability to analyse problems, apply common sense and provide solutions to situations are all qualities the firm seeks. Ultimately Clyde & Co recruits to retain and they are seeking candidates who will remain with the firm beyond qualification.

Training environment
You will gain early responsibility and be supported through close personal supervision and day-to-day coaching complemented by a wide range of training courses. You will undertake four six-month seats in London and Guildford, which will cover both transactional and contentious work. You may also choose to be seconded to one of the firm's overseas offices or have the opportunity for a client secondment.

Benefits
An optional £1,000 interest free loan on joining, pension, life assurance, private medical insurance, subsidised gym membership, interest-free season ticket loan and coffee shop.

Legal work experience
The firm runs two-week summer vacation schemes for 20 students. The dates for the 2010 schemes are 21 June to 2 July and 19 July to 30 July. Applications are made online and the closing date is 31 January 2010. For more details please visit the website at www.clydeco.com/graduate.

Sponsorship & awards
GDL and LPC fees paid plus a maintenance grant of £7,000 in London/Guildford and £6,000 elsewhere.

Partners 160
Assistant Solicitors 700
Trainees 48

Contact
Kate Wild
Trainee Solicitor Recruitment Manager

Method of application
Online via website
www.clydeco.com/graduate

Selection procedure
Assessment session with Graduate Recruitment followed by interview with 2 partners
Closing date for 2012
31 July 2009

Application
Training contracts p.a. 24
Applications p.a. 1,400 +
% interviewed p.a. 10%
Required degree grade 2:1

Training
Salary
1st year (2009) £35,000
2nd year (2009) £38,000
(Reviewed annually)
Holiday entitlement 25 days
% of trainees with
a non-law degree p.a. 50%

Post-qualification
Salary (2009) £59,000

Overseas offices
Abu Dhabi, Caracas, Doha, Dubai, Hong Kong, San Francisco, Moscow, Nantes, New York, Paris, Piraeus, Rio de Janeiro, Shanghai, Singapore, and associate offices in Bangalore, Belgrade, Mumbai, Riyadh and St Petersburg

CMS Cameron McKenna LLP

Mitre House, 160 Aldersgate Street, London EC1A 4DD
Tel: (0845) 300 0491 Fax: (020) 7367 2000
Email: gradrec@cms-cmck.com Website: www.cmstalklaw.com

Firm profile
CMS is the leading European organisation of law and tax firms with more offices across Europe than any other firm. CMS brings together nine unique firms including CMS Cameron McKenna, which operates in the UK and across Central and Eastern Europe. The firm advises on a wide range of transactions and issues, and has developed many long-term relationships throughout the business world, meaning that the firm's clients benefit from working with teams that really understand their issues and concerns.

Main areas of work
The firm's clients benefit from an extensive range of tailored services, delivered through offices in the UK, Central Europe, North America and Asia. The firm's services include banking and international finance, corporate, real estate, commercial, energy projects and constructions, insurance and re-insurance.

Trainee profile
The firm looks for high achieving team players with good communication, analytical and organisational skills. You will need to show initative and be able to accept personal responsibility, not only for your own work, but also for your career development. You will need to be resilient and focused on achieving results.

Training environment
The firm is highly supportive and puts no limits on a trainee's progress. It offers four six-months seats over a period of two years. You will be awarded a priority seat when you start your training contract and will undertake a compulsory seat in these areas: corporate or banking, and a contentious seat. To develop you and your legal skills even further, you can expect to be seconded to a client or spend time in one of their international offices. In each seat you will be allocated high quality work on substantial transactions for a range of government and blue-chip clients. The three compulsory modules of the Professional Skills Course will be completed on a fast track basis during the trainee induction. This enables trainees to be effective and participate on a practical level as soon as possible. The Professional Skills Course is complimented by a comprehensive in-house training programme that continues up to qualification and beyond.

Vacation placements
Places for 2010: 60 over spring and summer. Duration: 2 weeks. Remuneration: £250pw. Closing date for applications: 31 January 2010.

Benefits
Annual bonus, gym membership/subsidy, life assurance, pensions scheme with firm contributions, private healthcare, season ticket loan, confidential care line, subsidised restaurant and 25 days holiday with options to buy a further five days.

Sponsorship & awards
GDL and LPC sponsorship is provided. London trainees will be required to undertake their LPC at BPP Law School London where the firm will pay their fees and provide a maintenance grant of up to £7,500. Further details will be supplied on offer of a Training Contract.

Partners 138
Assistant Solicitors 603
Total Trainees 120

Contact
Graduate Recruitment Team
(0845) 300 0491

Method of application
Online application form
www.cmstalklaw.com

Selection procedure
Online application form and psychometric test, Interview and presentation, analysis exercise, group exercise, partner interview

Closing date
31 July 2010

Application
Training contracts p.a. 60
Applications p.a. 1,500
% interviewed p.a. 35%
Required degree grade 2:1

Training
Salary
1st year (2009) £37,500
2nd year (2009) £41,500
Holiday entitlement
25 days + option of flexible holidays
% of trainees with a non-law degree p.a. 50%
No. of seats available abroad p.a. Currently 12

Post-qualification
Salary (2009) £59,000
% of trainees offered job on qualification (2008) 83%

Cobbetts LLP

58 Mosley Street, Manchester M2 3H2
Tel: (0845) 165 5100
Email: gr8training@cobbetts.com
Website: www.cobbetts.com/graduate

Firm profile
Cobbetts is a top 40 law firm with offices in the UK's most exciting commercial centres, Birmingham, Leeds, London and Manchester. The firm continues to place high-quality and long-term relationship building with clients at the forefront of its strategy for success. This leads to a requirement for talented individuals with first-class legal expertise and the people skills to really deliver value to both the firm and its clients. The firm's varied client base gives its trainees the opportunity to get involved in the legal work of PLCs, mid-sized corporates, financial institutions, public sector and not for profit clients. Working in a firm with a reputation for quality work and innovation, and surrounded by business focused, forward thinking individuals, trainees have the perfect opportunity to make their mark in a growing and successful legal business. The firm employs around 680 people (inc. 36 trainee solicitors) across the offices. Training contracts are offered in Birmingham, Leeds and Manchester.

Main areas of work
Cobbetts operates through a number of flexible service teams based on work type and managed across seven areas of practice: banking, commercial, corporate (including business restructuring), dispute resolution, employment, private capital and real estate. Cobbetts' legal expertise spans many industry sectors, especially banking and finance, leisure, retail, IT, media and regeneration.

Trainee profile
The firm looks for high academic achievers who show potential to offer something above and beyond the undertaking of legal work. Individuals must demonstrate the confidence and commitment to thrive in a strong client centred commercial environment and have a desire for responsibility early in their training. The firm welcomes applications from students of any discipline who are in the penultimate year or final year of study and from those who have already graduated.

Training environment
Trainee solicitors are supervised by partners and solicitors who have the expertise to turn trainees into confident and capable newly qualified solicitors. Trainees are supervised through five five-month seats to gain a broad depth of experience in the firm's core and specialist areas of law including corporate, real estate and dispute resolution. Depending on business needs, opportunities may also arise for a trainee to spend time on secondment at client or partner organisations.

Trainees are also developed through activities with students who have been offered a contract with the firm and through the firm's structured CSR initiatives. Trainees are supported with development before their training contract through the buddy scheme and LPC+ in conjunction with the College of Law, and during their training contract via practice area induction workshops and the PSC. In addition, once trainees qualify, they will undergo the Cobbetts NQ programme and gain benefit from "Springboard", the firm's structured legal training programme in their first two years of qualification.

Benefits
Opportunity to join the BUPA healthcare scheme after three months, gym membership, social club, pension scheme, season ticket travel loan, death in service and counselling service. In addition to annual holiday entitlement, employees are also entitled to a free day's holiday for moving house and wedding day and have an option to buy or sell additional holidays.

Sponsorship & awards
GDL and LPC fees paid. Maintenance grant of £5000 during LPC year.

Partners 90
Other fee earners 245
Total Trainees 36

Contact
Paul Kendall
(0845) 165 5053
gr8training@cobbetts.com

Method of application
Online application form

Selection procedure
Assessment days

Closing dates
Training contracts 2012: 31 July 2010
Easter and Summer vacation schemes 2010: 14 February 2010

Application
Training contracts p.a. 17
Applications p.a. 1,000
% interviewed p.a. 10%
Required degree grade 2:1

Training
Salary for each year of training
1st year £23,000
2nd year £25,000
(both reviewed annually)
Holiday entitlement
Starting at 23 days

Post-qualification
Salary NQ £30,000
Reviewed annually

% of trainees offered job on qualification 68%

Other offices
Birmingham, Leeds, London

Coffin Mew LLP

Fareham Point, Wickham Road, Fareham PO16 7AU
Tel: (01329) 825617 Fax: (01329) 825619
Email: sarajlloyd@coffinmew.co.uk
Website: www.coffinmew.co.uk

Firm profile

Coffin Mew LLP offers an exceptional training opportunity. The firm is rapidly expanding to become one of the larger southern regional firms with major offices located in the cities of Portsmouth and Southampton and just off the M27 Motorway at Fareham. The firm is in the enviable position of operating a balanced practice offering top quality commercial and private client services in approximately equal volume and is particularly noted for a number of niche practices with national reputations.

Main areas of work

The firm is structured through nine core departments: corporate and corporate finance, commercial services, employment, commercial litigation, property litigation, personal injury, property; family and trust/probate. Niche practices (in which training is available) include intellectual property; insolvency; finance and business regulation; social housing; and medical negligence.

Trainee profile

The firm encourages applications from candidates with very good academic ability who seek a broad based training contract in a highly progressive and demanding but friendly and pleasant environment.

Training environment

The training contract is usually divided into six seats of four months each which will include a Property Department, a Litigation Department and a Commercial Department. The remainder of the training contract will be allocated after discussion with the trainee concerned. The firm aims, when possible to ensure that the trainee spends the final period of his or her training contract in the department in which he or she hopes to work after qualification.

Sponsorship & awards

LPC funding available by discussion with candidates.

Vacation placements

Open Week in July each year; applications for the 2010 Open Week are accepted between 1 November 2009 and 31 March 2010. For further details see the firms website.

Partners 27
Associates 16
Assistant solicitors 26
Total trainees 10

Contact
Mrs Sara Lloyd
Practice Manager

Method of application
Please see firm's website

Selection procedure
Interview

Closing date for July 2012
31 July 2010 (not before January 1 2010)

Application
Training contracts p.a. 4/5
Applications p.a. 400+
% interviewed p.a. 5%
Required degree grade 2:1 (save in exceptional circumstances)

Training
Salary
1st year
Competitive market rate
2nd year
Competitive market rate
Holiday entitlement currently 24 days
% of trainees with a non-law degree p.a. 40%

Post-qualification
Salary Competitive market rate
% of trainees offered job on qualification (2009) 60%
% of assistants who joined as trainees 25%
% of partners who joined as trainees 20%

Collyer Bristow LLP

4 Bedford Row, London, WC1R 4DF
Tel: (020) 7242 7363 Fax: (020) 7405 0555
Email: recruitment@collyerbristow.com
Website: www.collyerbristow.com

Partners 32
Trainees 6
Total Staff 130

Contact
Jonathan Demeuse
HR Advisor

Method of application
Online application form

Selection procedure
Online testing & interview

Training
Salary
1st year (2009) £27,500
2nd year (2009) £31,000
(Both reviewed annually)

Firm profile
London and Geneva based, the firm celebrates the breadth and diversity of its client base which includes multinationals, public and private companies, businesses and partnerships, public sector organisations and a substantial private client practice. Many of the firm's lawyers have trained and qualified with the firm and share their diverse experiences, outlooks and expertise with the firm's clients. The firm is famous for its ground-breaking in-house art gallery and is passionate in its support for the contemporary arts.

Main areas of work
The firm advises a diverse range of businesses and individuals on challenges of all shapes, sizes and complexity and offers top quality legal advice in private client, family, property, company commercial and dispute resolution.

Trainee profile
The firm is looking for individuals who are able to demonstrate a strong academic performance having gained a 2.1 or at least on track to achieve this. Successful candidates will be motivated individuals who possess strong commercial awareness, common sense and an ability to understand the client's business needs.

Training environment
You will spend six months in four of the firm's five key practice areas working with a range of people from senior Partners to more recently qualified solicitors. The firm has a mentoring, training and appraisal programme which nurtures the development of your technical expertise and client advisory skills. You will be encouraged at an early stage to take responsibility for your own files and to participate in managing the client's work.

Benefits
25 days holiday, pension, private medical insurance, life assurance and season ticket loan.

Sponsorship & awards
Full LPC funding and maintenance grant of £4,000.

Covington & Burling LLP

265 Strand, London WC2R 1BH
Tel: (020) 7067 2000 Fax: (020) 7067 2222
Email: graduate@cov.com
Website: www.cov.com

Firm profile
Covington & Burling LLP is a leading international law firm founded in Washington DC that has over 700 lawyers in offices in Beijing, Brussels, London New York, San Francisco, San Diego, Silicon Valley and Washington. Covington London is dynamic and growing. The firm opened its London office in 1988, and now offers services to clients over a wide range of practice areas from its modern offices next to the Royal Courts of Justice.

Main areas of work
The principal practice groups in Covington's London office are corporate, dispute resolution, life sciences, and technology and media. The demarcation between these areas is not rigid and solicitors frequently work across several practice groups. In particular, lawyers in the corporate and dispute resolution groups often draw on Covington's vast regulatory experience in areas such as food and drug, communications, and new technologies. At a firm level, practice and industry groups work closely together across all offices. Household names for which the London office acts include Microsoft, the Business Software Alliance, QUALCOMM, Giorgio Armani, Bacardi, Benetton, Harley-Davidson, AstraZeneca, Procter & Gamble, Merck, GlaxoSmithKline, Schering-Plough and Johnson & Johnson.

Trainee profile
The firm is looking for outstanding students who are committed to providing quality legal advice in an imaginative way, so that it can maintain its ability to respond to the evolving needs and expectations of clients. The firm looks for team players, but above all else, it looks for intellectual distinction, imagination and integrity. The firm is looking for consistently high academic performers that have or expect to achieve a minimum of 2:1 degree in any discipline. In return the firm believes it can offer more challenging and dynamic opportunities for Covington lawyers.

Training environment
The firm splits the two year period into four six-month seats rotating between practice areas. All trainees will spend six months in the corporate and dispute resolution practice areas. Currently, the other seats are in the life sciences, employment, tax and information technology/intellectual property practice areas. A secondment to the in-house Legal Department of a client may also be possible. The size of the programme means that the firm is able to adopt a flexible approach, accommodating your wishes wherever possible.
You will sit and work closely with a senior associate or partner who will supervise your work during each training seat. In addition to their supervisors, trainees have the opportunity to work with other lawyers in the practice group relevant to their training seat. Much of the firm's work is cross-boarder in nature, and often trainees work with associates and partners in the Brussels and US offices. Their limited number helps ensure that the firm's trainees receive high quality, meaningful work in a supportive and open environment.

Benefits
Pension, income protection, private health cover, life assurance and season ticket loan.

Vacation placements
24 places during summer vacation. Closing date for applications 28 February 2010.

Sponsorship & awards
GDL and LPC fees paid. Maintenance grant of £8,000 per annum.

Partners: 213
Associate Lawyers & Other
Fee-earners: 566
Total Trainees London:
2009   11
2010   12
2011   12

Contact
Graduate Recruitment Manager
(020) 7067 2098
graduate@cov.com

Method of application
Online Application Form
See website www.cov.com
selection procedure
1st & 2nd interview

Closing date for 2012
31 July 2010

Application
Training contracts p.a. 6
Required degree grade 2:1

Training
Salary:
1st year   £40,000
2nd year   £44,000
(subject to review)
Holiday entitlement 25 days

Overseas offices
Beijing, Brussels, New York, San Francisco, San Diego, Silicon Valley, Washington

COVINGTON
COVINGTON & BURLING LLP

Cripps Harries Hall LLP

Wallside House, 12 Mount Ephraim Road, Tunbridge Wells TN1 1EG
Tel: (01892) 506006 Fax: (01892) 506360
Email: graduates@crippslaw.com
Website: www.crippslaw.com

Firm profile
A leading regional law firm and one of the largest in the South East, the firm is recognised as being amongst the most progressive and innovative regional practices.

The firm's organisation into client-focused, industry sector groups promotes a strong ethos of client service and ensures the firm's solicitors are not only excellent legal practitioners but also experts in specialist business sectors. The firm is regarded by many businesses, institutions and wealthy individuals as the natural first choice among regional law firms. Although long-established, the firm's profile is young, professional, forward-thinking, friendly and informal.

The firm achieved the Lexcel quality mark in January 1999, the first 'Top 100' firm to do so. In 2008 the firm was awarded one star status in the Sunday Times Best Companies to work for accreditation.

Main areas of work
Commercial 18%, dispute resolution 18%, private client 26%, property 38%.

Trainee profile
Individuals who are confident and capable, with lively but well organised minds and a genuine interest in delivering client solutions through effective and pragmatic use of the law; keen to make a meaningful contribution both during their contract and long term career with the firm.

Training environment
The firm offers a comprehensive induction course, a well structured training programme, frequent one to one reviews, regular in-house courses and seminars, good levels of support and real responsibility.

The training programme is broader than most other firms and typically includes six seats in both commercial and private client areas. Trainees usually share a room with a partner or an associate and gain varied and challenging first hand experience.

Sponsorship awards
Discretionary LPC funding: Fees – 50% interest free loan, 50% bursary.

Partners 39
Assistant Solicitors 61
Total Trainees 16

Contact
Jim Fennell
Head of HR & Development

Method of application
Application form available on website

Selection process
One interview with Managing Partner and Head of Human Resources

Closing date for 2012
31 July 2010

Application
Training contracts p.a. 8
Applications p.a. Up to 750
% interviewed p.a. 6%
Required degree grade 2:1

Training
Salary
1st year (2009) £21,500
2nd year (2009) £23,500
Holiday entitlement 25 days
% of trainees with a non-law degree p.a. 37%

Post-qualification
Salary (2009) £37,000
% of trainees offered job on qualification (2009) 60%
% of assistants/associates (as at 1/5/09) who joined as trainees 52%
% of partners (as at 1/5/09) who joined as trainees 22%

Davenport Lyons

30 Old Burlington Street, London W1S 3NL
Tel: (020) 7468 2600 Fax: (020) 7437 8216
Email: mmardner@davenportlyons.com
Website: www.davenportlyons.com

Firm profile
A leading law firm focused on delivering value and practical commercial advice to its clients nationally and internationally across a broad range of industries. With a 48 Partner strong practice, over 70 fee earners and supporting operational functions, the firm is commercially focused, based in the luxurious surroundings of Mayfair. Coupled with the firm's desire to retain its warm and friendly environment, Davenport Lyons is the ideal place to start your career as a successful solicitor.

Main areas of work
The firm provides comprehensive legal advice from its 12 specialist departments covering: corporate; dispute resolution; contentious rights; media; corporate tax; private client; property; licensing; employment; matrimonial; insolvency and reconstruction; and intellectual property.

Trainee profile
Davenport Lyons is looking for candidates with excellent academic qualifications (2:1 and above, good A level results) and interesting backgrounds, who are practical and can demonstrate good business acumen. Candidates should have a breadth of interests and foreign language skills are an advantage. In short, the firm is looking for well-rounded individuals.

Training environment
The training programme consists of four six-month seats. During each seat trainees receive mid and end of the seat reviews, and each seat has a dedicated trainee supervisor. Davenport Lyons has an on-going in-house training and lecture programme. The firm prides itself on offering interesting, hands-on training with trainees being encouraged to develop their own client relationships and to handle their own files under appropriate supervision, therefore being treated as junior fee earners. The firm aims to make its training contract informative, educational, practical, supportive and, let us not forget, as enjoyable as possible.

Benefits
Season ticket loan; client introduction bonus; contribution to gym membership; discretionary bonus; 23 days holiday; life assurance; Employee Support Programme; pension and private health scheme.

Vacation placements
A limited number of places are available on the Summer Vacation Scheme, which runs during July and August. Remuneration is £200 per week.

Sponsorship & awards
The firm does not offer financial assistance.

Partners 48
Fee Earners 50
Total Staff 207
Trainees 16

Contact
Marcia Mardner
Human Resources Director
Michael Hatchwell
Training Partner

Method of application
Apply online at
www.davenportlyons.com.

Selection procedure
Interviews

Closing date for 2012
31 July 2010

Application
Training contracts p.a. 8
Applications p.a. c.800
% interviewed p.a. 8.6%
Required degree grade 2:1, AAB at A Level (320+ UCAS Points)

Training
Salary
1st Year trainee
£33,000 - £33,666
2nd Year trainee
£34,332 - £35,000
Holiday entitlement 23 days
% of trainees with a non-law degree p.a. 70%

Post-qualification
% of trainees offered job on qualification
(2008) 75%

Office
London

Davies Arnold Cooper LLP

6–8 Bouverie Street, London EC4Y 8DD
Tel: (020) 7936 2222 Fax: (020) 7936 2020
Email: gradrecruit@dac.co.uk
Website: www.dac.co.uk

Partners 74
Total Fee-earners 227
Total Trainees 17
Total Staff 380

Firm profile
Davies Arnold Cooper LLP is an international law firm particularly known for its dispute resolution and real estate expertise. It advises in relation to specialist areas of law, including insurance, real estate, construction, employment and product liability, and has a leading Hispanic practice. The firm has offices in London, Manchester, Madrid and Mexico City.

Main areas of work
Dispute resolution: 65%; real estate: 35%.

Trainee profile
The world of law is vast and peculiarly technical and you need to demonstrate that you will be up to the job intellectually. The firm looks for intellect (a UCAS tariff of 300, excluding General Studies, a 2:1 or first class degree is usual). The firm also looks for common sense and maturity. It relishes forthright views and social confidence but it doesn't care for arrogance.

Although it may sometimes seem to you that life consists of studying and sitting exams, the firm does look for a bit more. It is impressed by people who push themselves. What you have done with your life so far counts for much more than where you went to school or university. The firm is interested to talk to those who are embarking on law as a second career as it is to see undergraduates.

Training programme & environment
The firm encourages you to take on responsibility as soon as you join and will give you as much as you can handle, although you will always be supervised and never left alone to struggle. You will experience both contentious and non-contentious work and because the firm only takes on up to ten trainees every year, the chances are you will be able to select your preferred seats. There are seven training contract positions available for September 2011. Applications should be made using the firm's application form which is available from the website.

Benefits
Current first year salary is £31,000 with 25 days holiday, private medical insurance and season ticket loan.

Sponsorship & awards
GDL and LPC fees paid plus maintenance grants.

Dechert LLP

160 Queen Victoria Street, London EC4V 4QQ
Tel: (020) 7184 7000 Fax: (020) 7184 7001
Email: application@dechert.com Website: www.dechert.com

Firm profile
Dechert LLP is a dynamic international law firm, with 2,000 people across the USA, Europe and Asia. London is the third largest office, after Philadelphia and New York.

Main areas of work
The London office has particular strengths in investment funds, corporate and securities including private equity, and finance and real estate; and smaller teams in employment, IP, litigation and tax.

Trainee profile
Dechert looks for enthusiasm, intelligence, an ability to find practical solutions, and for powers of expression and persuasion. Graduates from any discipline are welcome to apply.

Training environment
The highly personalised six seat rotation system allows trainees to structure their training contract to their interests and aspirations, and allows ample opportunity for secondments to Brussels, Munich, Paris or the USA as well as to clients. A training contract with Dechert is international from day one, starting with a trip to Philadelphia to take part in the firm-wide induction programme. Your seat plan and professional development are guided by both the firm's Director of Training and by your dedicated trainee partner, who meet with you regularly. Your trainee partner is allocated to you when you start your training contract and acts as a sounding board and a source of support until you qualify.

Vacation placements
Work placement programmes at Easter, and in the summer. The firm's work placement programmes are aimed at penultimate year law students. The closing date for applications is 31 January 2010.

Sponsorship & awards
The firm pays LPC fees plus £10,000 sponsorship.

Partners 35*
Assistant Solicitors 52*
Total Trainees 21*
*denotes London figure

Contact
Graduate Recruitment Manager

Method of application
Online

Selection procedure
An assessment morning or afternoon which includes interviews with partners, associates and recruiters, and written tests

Closing date for 2012
31 July 2010

Application
Training contracts p.a.
10-15
Applications p.a. Approx 1,000
% interviewed p.a. Approx 12%
Required degree grade 2:1 (or capability of attaining a 2:1)

Training
Salary
1st year £38,000
2nd year £43,000
Holiday entitlement 25 days
% of trainees with a non-law degree p.a. Varies
No. of seats available abroad p.a. three in Brussels and others in the US

Post-qualification
Salary c.£65,000 to £73,000 (depending on practice area)
% of trainees offered job on qualification 70%

Overseas offices
Austin, Beijing, Boston, Brussels, Charlotte, Hartford, Hong Kong, Luxembourg, Moscow, Munich, Newport Beach, New York, Paris, Philadelphia, Princeton, San Francisco, Silicon Valley, Washington

Denton Wilde Sapte LLP

One Fleet Place, London EC4M 7WS
Tel: (020) 7242 1212 Fax: (020) 7320 6555
Email: graduaterecruitment@dentonwildesapte.com
Website: www.friendly-firm.com

Firm profile
Denton Wilde Sapte is an international law firm with a network of offices and associate offices spanning the UK, Europe, Middle East, CIS and Africa.

Main areas of work
The firm provides a full range of commercial legal services in the following areas: banking and finance; corporate; dispute resolution; employment and pensions; energy, infrastructure and project finance; EU and competition; real estate and planning; tax; technology, media and telecommunications.

Trainee profile
The firm looks for candidates who are team players with a strong academic and extra curricular record of achievement. Given the diversity of the firm's business, it looks for people with wide-ranging skills, aptitudes and personalities. You will need drive and ambition, with the potential to contribute to the growing success of the firm.

Training environment
As a trainee you will undertake four six-month seats. This will include a contentious seat and a banking seat. You will also have the opportunity to work in one of the firm's international offices or with one of the firm's clients.

You will be given as much responsibility as you can handle, and will be working with the law, with your team and with clients in real business situations.

The firm works hard to maintain a friendly and open environment where ideas are shared and people work together to achieve goals.

Benefits
Flexible benefit scheme including private health insurance and sports club membership allowance. Season ticket loan.

Vacation placements
One week summer scheme open to second, penultimate, final year law students and those who have already completed a law degree. Open days in December open to final year non-law students and those who have already completed a non-law degree. Open day at Easter open to first year law students.

Sponsorship & awards
GDL and LPC tuition fees covered plus £6,000 maintenance grant for each year of study, £7,000 if studying in London.

Partners 180
Fee-earners 600
Total Trainees 70

Contact
Kate Raggett

Method of application
Application form

Selection procedure
First interview; selection test; second interviews and case study

Closing date for 2012
31 July 2010

Application
Training contracts p.a. 25-30
Applications p.a. 1,500
% interviewed p.a. 15%
Required degree grade 2:1

Training
Salary
1st year £35,000
2nd year £37,000
Holiday entitlement 24 days
% of trainees with a
non-law degree p.a. 30%
No. of seats available
abroad p.a. Currently 6

Post-qualification
Salary (2009) £58,000
% of trainees offered job
on qualification (2008) 85%

Overseas offices
Abu Dhabi, Almaty, Amman (associate office), Ashgabat (associate office), Cairo, Doha, Dubai, Istanbul, Kuwait (associate office), Moscow, Muscat, Paris, Riyadh (associate office), St Petersburg (associate firm), Singapore (associate office), Tashkent.

Dewey & LeBoeuf

No 1 Minister Court, Mincing Lane, London, EC3R 7YL
Tel: (020) 7459 5000   Fax: (020) 7444 7379
Email: londongraduate@dl.com   Website: www.dl.com

Firm profile
Dewey & LeBoeuf is a full-service international law firm advising a wide range of clients throughout the United States, Europe, Russia/ the CIS, the Middle East, Asia and Africa.
With more than 1,200 lawyers in virtually all major financial and commercial centers, the firm represents multinational corporations, financial institutions, government agencies and state-owned entities in their most complex legal matters.
The London office of Dewey & LeBoeuf is the firm's largest international office with 46 partners and over 130 legal staff. The majority of the firm's London based partners and associates are English qualified solicitors, and the London office is the natural centre of some of the firm's most interesting and diverse work.

Main areas of work
Banking, mergers and acquisitions, corporate finance, project finance, dispute resolution, arbitration, intellectual property and information technology, EU/ competition, tax, real estate, environmental and employment. The firm also possesses leading industry experience in sectors including insurance, energy and utilities, environment and banking.

Trainee profile
Dewey & LeBoeuf is looking for dynamic, internationally minded, versatile individuals who demonstrate commercial awareness and a genuine enthusiasm for the law. The firm wants people who are dedicated to delivering excellent advice and client service. Language skills are desirable but not essential.

Training environment
The firm emphasises learning through one-on-one interaction with its partners and experienced associates. Trainees are encouraged to see and experience as much of the practice as possible and you can expect to be exposed to high quality work with early responsibility. Trainees typically undertake four six-month seats within different practice areas. Six month client secondments, as well as secondments to the firm's International offices in Paris, Moscow and Dubai are also available.
The firm's training programme is comprehensive, and in addition to the professional skills course, covers an induction programme and attendance at internal and external courses. Trainees will also participate in regular training sessions run through its own internal 'Dewey & LeBoeuf University' (DLU), which offers regular seminars on law and practice. Progress and training needs are formally reviewed every three months.

Benefits
The firm offers 25 days holiday per annum, private medical insurance, permanent health insurance, life assurance, employee assistance programme, private GP services, Ride2Work scheme, worldwide travel insurance, season ticket loan, childcare vouchers, and preferential rates for dental care and for gym membership.

Vacation placements
The firm offers one-week spring vacation and two-week summer vacation schemes for penultimate year law undergraduates and graduates of all disciplines. Places for 2010: 20; Remuneration: £400 per week; closing date 31 January 2010. Apply online at www.dl.com.

Sponsorship & awards
Full payment of GDL/LPC fees and maintenance grant of £8,500 provided per annum.

Partners 46
Other lawyers 94
Total Trainees 27

Contact
Gail Sorrell Director of Legal HR

Method of application
Apply online www.dl.com

Selection procedure
Verbal and numerical testing, two interviews with the firm's partners, associates and graduate recruitment team

Closing date for 2012
31 July 2010

Application
Training contracts p.a. 15
Applications p.a. 900
% interviewed p.a. 6%
Required grades AAB at A-level and 2:1 degree or equivalent

Training
Salary
1st year (2009) £40,000
2nd year (2009) £45,000

Post-qualification
Salary (2009) £70,000
% of trainees offered job on qualification (2009) 92%

Offices
Albany, Almaty, Beijing, Boston, Brussels, Chicago, Doha, Dubai, Frankfurt, Hong Kong, Houston, Johannesburg, London, Los Angeles, Madrid, Milan, Moscow, New York, Paris, Riyadh, Rome, San Francisco, Silicon Valley, Warsaw, Washington DC

Dickinson Dees LLP

St. Ann's Wharf, 112 Quayside, Newcastle upon Tyne NE1 3DX
Tel: (0844) 984 1500 Fax: (0844) 984 1501
Email: graduate.recruitment@dickinson-dees.com
Website: www.trainingcontract.com

Firm profile
Dickinson Dees enjoys an excellent reputation as one of the country's leading commercial law firms. Based in Newcastle upon Tyne with additional offices in Tees Valley, York and London the firm prides itself on the breadth of expertise across its 38 practice areas which enables it to offer services of the highest standards to clients. Whilst many of the firm's clients are based in the North, Dickinson Dees works on a national basis for national and internationally based businesses and organisations.

Main areas of work
The firm has 620 employees and is organised into four key departments (Company commercial, commercial property, litigation and wealth management) with 38 cross departmental teams advising on specific areas.

Trainee profile
The firm is looking for intellectually able, motivated and enthusiastic graduates from any discipline who have good communication skills. Successful applicants will understand the need to provide practical, commercial advice to clients. They will share the firm's commitment to self-development and teamwork and its desire to provide clients with services which match their highest expectations.

Training environment
There are relatively few trainees for the size of the practice which ensures a supportive and friendly environment. You will be fully integrated into the firm and involved in all aspects of the firms business. The training contract consists of four seats across the different departments. Trainees sit with their supervisors and appraisals are carried out every three months. The firm has its own Training Department as well as a supportive Graduate Recruitment Team. There are induction courses for each seat move with opportunities for trainees to get involved in the firm's training programme. The firm offers a tailored in-house Professional Skills Course which is run in conjunction with the College of Law.

Work placements
Places for 2010: 40; Duration: 1 week; Remuneration: £200 p.w. The firm's work placement weeks are part of the recruitment process and all applicants should apply online at www.trainingcontract.com. Apply by 31 January 2010 for Easter and Summer placements.

Sponsorship & awards
GDL/LPC fees paid and maintenance grant offered.

Partners 72
Total Staff 620
Total Trainees 36

Contact
Sally Brewis, Graduate Recruitment Adviser

Method of application
Apply online at www.trainingcontract.com

Selection procedure
Aptitude and ability tests, negotiation exercise, personality questionnaire, presentation, interview

Closing date for 2012
31 July 2010

Application
Training contracts are based in Newcastle, Tees Valley and York (up to 18 across the three offices)
Applications p.a. 800
% interviewed p.a. 10%
Required degree grade 2:1 in any subject

Training
Salary
1st year £19,500
2nd year £20,500
Holiday entitlement 25 days
% of trainees with a non-law degree p.a. 50%
No. of seats available abroad p.a. 3
(3-month secondments)

Post-qualification
% of trainees offered job on qualification (2009)
84%(15/17)
% of partners (as at 01/08/09) who joined as trainees 35%

Other offices
Tees Valley, York, London
Brussels (associated office)

DLA Piper UK LLP

3 Noble Street, London, EC2V 7EE
Tel: (0870) 0111 111
Email: recruitment.graduate@dlapiper.com
Website: www.dlapiper.com

Firm profile

DLA Piper are one of the world's largest full service commercial law firms. They now have more than 8,000 employees working from over 60 offices across Europe, Asia, the Middle East and the US. Their current vision is to be the leading global business law firm. Clients include some of the world's leading businesses, governments, banks and financial institutions. This impressive client base coupled with an emphasis on providing high quality service and teamwork, offers a challenging fast-paced working environment.

DLA Piper offers its trainees the opportunity to apply for international secondments to a range of its offices, as well as a number of client secondments.

In 2008 DLA Piper won the prestigious National Graduate Recruitment Awards' 'Diversity Recruitment Award' proving their commitment to recruiting people from a wide variety of backgrounds and ages. This progressive approach to recruitment creates a mix of talents that contributes to their success.

DLA Piper is committed to making sure you feel part of the firm once you accept a training contract with them. Future trainees have access to the website 'Inside DLA Piper' where they can, amongst other things, contact one another via chat forums, and keep up to date with what is going on in the firm wherever they are in the world.

Main areas of work

Corporate; employment, pensions and benefits; finance and projects; intellectual property and technology; litigation and regulatory; and real estate.

Trainee profile

The firm is looking for individuals from either a law or non-law background who have a minimum ABB at A Level (or equivalent) and expect, or have achieved a 2.1 degree classification - however, a strong academic background alone is no longer sufficient. DLA Piper looks for highly motivated and energetic team players with sound commercial awareness, outstanding communication and organisational skills. As well as this, in line with the firm's main focus of work, a keen interest in the corporate world is essential - as is an appetite for life!

Training environment

Following a comprehensive residential induction, trainees complete four six month seats during the course of their training contract. If you want responsibility, the firm will give you as much as you can handle and your progress will be monitored through regular reviews and feedback. The compulsory Professional Skills Course is run in-house and is tailored to meet the needs of the firm's trainees. This combined with on-the-job experience, provides trainees with an excellent grounding on which to build their professional careers.

Summer placements

DLA Piper runs two week summer placement schemes across all of its UK offices. The scheme aims to give a thorough insight into life at the firm. There will be approximately 170 places available for 2010. The closing date is 31 January 2010.

Sponsorship & awards

Payment of LPC and GDL fees plus maintenance grant in both years of up to £7,000.

Partners 1300
Fee-earners 2200
Total Trainees 180

Contact
Sally Carthy, Head of Graduate Recruitment

Method of application
Online application form

Selection procedure
First interview, second interview, assessment afternoon

Closing date for 2011
31 July 2010

Application
Training contracts p.a. 85
Applications p.a. 2,600
% interviewed p.a. 15%
Required degree grade 2:1

Training
Salary (2009)
1st year (London) £36,000
2nd year (London) £38,000
1st year (Regions) £25,000
2nd year (Regions) £27,000
1st year (Scotland) £22,000
2nd year (Scotland) £24,000
% of trainees with a non-law degree p.a. 40%

Post-qualification
Salary (2009)
£58,000 (London)
£37,500 (English Regional offices)
£34,000 (Scotland)

UK offices
Birmingham, Edinburgh, Glasgow, Leeds, Liverpool, London, Manchester, Sheffield

Overseas offices
Austria, Belgium, Bosnia-Herzegovina, Bulgaria, China, Croatia, Czech Republic, France, Georgia, Germany, Hong Kong, Hungary, Italy, Japan, Netherlands, Norway, Poland, Russia, Singapore, Slovak Republic, Spain, Thailand, Ukraine, UAE, USA.

Dundas & Wilson LLP

Northwest Wing, Bush House, Aldwych, London, WC2B 4EZ
Tel: (020) 7240 2401   Fax: (020) 7240 2448
Email: lorraine.bale@dundas-wilson.com

Firm profile
Dundas & Wilson is a leading UK commercial law firm with offices in London, Edinburgh and Glasgow. The firm services a wide range of prestigious clients, including major companies and public sector organisations, throughout the UK and abroad.

Main areas of work
Lawyers are grouped into key areas of expertise including banking and finance, construction and engineering, corporate, corporate recovery, dispute resolution, environment, employment, EU and competition, IP / IT, outsourcing, pensions, planning and transport, projects, property, property finance, public law and Tax.

Trainee profile
D&W are looking for applicants with enthusiasm, commitment, adaptability, strong written and oral communication skills, excellent interpersonal skills, commercial awareness and an aptitude for problem solving and analysis.

Training environment
The two year traineeship is split into four six-month seats. The firm aims to accommodate trainees' preferences when allocating seats as the firm wants to encourage trainees to take an active part in managing their career development.

During the traineeship trainees receive on-the-job training, two day seat training at the beginning of each seat, training in core skills such as drafting and effective legal writing and regular seminars. Trainees receive a formal performance review every three months and are allocated a mentor for each seat.

The firm's open plan environment means that trainees sit amongst assistants, associates, senior associates and Partners – this provides daily opportunities to observe how lawyers communicate both with clients and each other. This type of learning is invaluable and great preparation for life as a fully fledged lawyer.

Benefits
Life assurance, permanent health insurance, group personal pension, season ticket loan, holiday purchase scheme.

Vacation scheme
Dundas & Wilson offers three-week summer placements. To apply, please visit the website and complete the online application form. The closing date is 30 January 2010.

Sponsorship & awards
GDL/CPE and LPC fees paid plus maintenance grant.

Partners 86
Lawyers 300
Trainees 64

Contact
Lorraine Bale

Method of application
Online application

Selection procedure
Assessment day comprising interview, group exercise, occupational personality questionnaire and aptitude tests

Closing date for 2012
31 July 2010

Application
Training contracts p.a. 35 (12 in London)
Applications p.a. 300
% interviewed p.a. 15%
Required degree grade 2:1 preferred

Training
Salary
1st year (Scotland) £19,000
(England) £30,000
2nd year (Scotland) £22,000
(England) £33,500
Holiday entitlement 25 days

Offices
London, Edinburgh, Glasgow

DWF LLP

Bridgewater Place, Water Lane, Leeds, LS11 5DY
5 St Paul's Square, Old Hall Street, Liverpool, L3 9AE
Capital House, 85 King William's Street, London, EC4N 7BL
Centurion House, 129 Deansgate, Manchester, M3 3AA
6 Winckley Square, Preston, PR1 3JJ
Tel: (0161) 603 5000   Fax: (0161) 603 5050

Firm profile

DWF LLP is a leading, full service law firm. The firm provides a full range of legal services to businesses and private clients across the UK.

The firm employs over 970 people, including 125 Partners and with over 500 fee earners, DWF is ranked as the largest in the North West by number of fee earners by independent legal directory Legal 500.

The firm is able to serve clients on a national basis from offices in Leeds, Liverpool, London, Manchester and Preston and internationally through its relationships with law firms around the world. The business continues to expand through a combination of organic growth, lateral hires and other consolidation activity.

The firm prides itself on providing outstanding client service that combines excellent commercial advice with an approachable style.

Main areas of work

DWF provides a full range of legal services: banking and finance, business recovery, corporate, insurance, litigation, employment, pensions, private client and real estate. A full list of these services can be found on the firm's website at www.dwf.co.uk.

DWF also provides legal services across a range of different industries and sectors, and has developed particular expertise in a number of specific areas. To enable clients to benefit from this expertise, the firm has developed a series of sector-focused teams: automotive, education, food, legal expenses, public sector, police law, resourcing and retail and leisure.

Trainee profile

DWF's future depends on recruiting and retaining the right people. DWF only recruit people of the highest quality and are always on the look out for ambitious and driven professionals who are able to add value to their developing team. DWF wants its trainee solicitors to play a part in building on its success. The firm is looking for trainees who enjoy working as part of a busy team, respond positively to a challenge and have what it takes to deliver results for clients. The firm is looking for its Partners of the future and in recent years virtually all of its qualifying trainees have been offered jobs. DWF is an equal opportunities employer and is committed to diversity in all aspects.

Training environment

DWF provides a well structured training programme for all new trainee solicitors which combines the day to day practical experience of working with a Partner, associate or senior solicitor, backed by a comprehensive in-house lecture and workshop programme and the PSC course. You will very quickly become a vital member of the team, being delegated the appropriate level of responsibility from an early stage in your training.

Full supervision is provided and it is the firm's policy for each trainee to sit with a Partner or associate, whilst working for a legal team as a whole. The two year training contract is divided into "seats"; four seats of four months' duration followed by eight months in their chosen area, enabling a detailed period of pre-qualification experience.

Trainees will work in the firm's main departments (banking and finance, business recovery, corporate, insurance, litigation, people, private client and real estate) which gives opportunities to look at specialist areas of work within each department.

Partners 125
Assistant Solicitors 438
Total Trainees 35

Contact
Stephanie Whitaker
Asst. HR Business Partner

Method of application
Online application

Selection procedure
2 stage interview/selection process

Closing date for 2011/2012
31 July 2010

Application
Training contracts p.a. 18
Applications p.a. c. 800
% interviewed p.a. 25%
Required degree grade 2:1

Training
Salary
1st year (2008) £24,500
Holiday entitlement
25 days p.a. minimum + option to buy & sell holidays

Post-qualification
% of trainees offered job on qualification (2009) 100%

Benefits
Flexible benefits scheme including insurance, life assurance, pension and other benefits

Vacation placements
Summer vacation placement schemes across all offices

Sponsorship & awards
LPC funding for tuition fees

Edwards Angell Palmer & Dodge UK LLP

One Fetter Lane, London, EC4A 1JB
Tel: 020 7583 4055
Fax: 020 7353 7377
Email: traineerecruitment@eapdlaw.com
Website: www.eapdlaw.com

Firm profile
EAPD is an international commercial law firm combining the expertise of over 600 lawyers in 30 practice groups, across the US, UK and Hong Kong. The firm offers a full array of legal services to clients worldwide.

Main areas of work
In London, the firm's main practice areas are litigation, regulatory and transactional, insolvency and restructuring and intellectual property. Within these areas the firm has many specialisms including insurance/reinsurance, private equity, employment, public international law, asset recovery, life sciences, trademarks and brand protection.

Trainee profile
The firm seeks engaging and motivated individuals from law or non-law backgrounds with initiative, good commercial sense and who want to make their mark. The trainees work hard and are rewarded with early responsibility and influence over the matters they work on. The firm expects you to have excellent interpersonal skills as you'll be interacting with clients from day one. A strong academic background will give you the analytical skills and rigorous approach needed to provide focussed and effective commercial advice to clients. You should also be adaptable, capable of thinking on your feet and a problem-solver. The firm looks for those who want to get involved in the life of the firm as a whole, socially or through contribution to the various committees. A range of work/life experiences to demonstrate these skills and qualities is key.

Training environment
The firm believes you learn best by doing, getting involved in real work from the start and because of its size in London, it can offer excellent training with high-quality work in a more personal environment. The firm gives trainees the chance to meet clients, be responsible for their own work and join in marketing and client development activities. Trainees spend six months in four of the firm's major practice areas, in addition to opportunities for secondments. Frequent workshops on the tailored training programme help develop the technical skills and knowledge needed in those areas. Regular structured feedback, reviews and constructive advice enable you to fulfil your true potential. A multi-level support network including buddies, partner mentors and the Trainee Recruitment Team, ensures you have the correct level of guidance and support is never overstretched. Any suggestions or concerns can be voiced at a trainee solicitors' committee, which meets quarterly.

The firm won the LawCareers.Net award for best work placement scheme in 2008 and 2009 and was nominated as Best Trainer in 2008 & 2009. The firm is also a frequent category winner in the Lex 100 surveys.

Benefits
Bupa, STL, subsidised gym membership, bonus scheme, pension scheme, life assurance

Vacation placements
The firm offers a structured two-week placement for up to 10 students in June/July of each year. The firm also hosts open days at Easter, Summer and Christmas - check website for dates and details.

Sponsorship & awards
CPE/GDL and LPC funding, plus a maintenance grant of £7,000 (London) / £6,500 (outside London).

Partners 21
Assistant Solicitors 28
Total Trainees 15

Contact
Sarah Warnes 020 7556 4414

Method of application
Online applications only
www.trainee.eapdlaw.com

Selection procedure
Assessment morning plus one interview with two partners/senior associates

Closing date for 2012
30 July 2010

Application
Training contracts p.a. up to 8
Applications p.a. 500
% interviewed p.a. 10%
Required degree grade 2:1

Training
Salary
1st year £36,000
2nd year £39,000
Holiday entitlement 25 days

Post-qualification
Salary £56,000
Summer placements up to 10 p.a.
Open days 4-5 accomodating up to 125 students
Closing date for summer placements 26 February 2010
Closing date for open days check website

Offices
UK-London, US-New York, Boston, Hartford, Providence, Stamford, Washington, West Palm Beach, Wilmington, Madison, Ft Lauderdale, Asia-Hong Kong

Eversheds

1 Wood Street, London, EC2V 7WS
Tel: (0845) 497 9797 Fax: (0845) 497 4919
Email: gradrec@eversheds.com
Website: www.eversheds.com/graduaterecruitment

Firm profile
Eversheds LLP is one of the largest full service international law firms in the world with over 5,000 people and 48 offices in major cities across the UK, Europe and Asia. The firm works for some of the world's most prestigious organisations in both the public and private sector, offering them a compelling mixture of straightforward advice, clear direction, predictable costs and outstanding service.

The firm has recently laid out a strategic plan that will see the firm build on its achievements and grow over the next few years. The firm is looking for highly ambitious and focused trainees to help it achieve its goals.

Main areas of work
Core work: company commercial, litigation and dispute management, real estate, human resources (employment and pensions) and legal systems group.

Trainee profile
Eversheds people are valued for their drive and legal expertise but also for their business advice too. The firm develops the same qualities in its trainees. As a trainee you'll be given as much responsibility as you can handle and will benefit from the firm's hands-on philosophy. The firm takes learning and development very seriously and will help you build the career you want.

Training environment
The firm offers a full well-rounded training programme with the opportunity to focus your technical skills in each of the various practice groups as you rotate through four six-month seats. You will also take part in a full programme of personal and commercial development skills training, including finance and business, communication, presenting, business writing, client care, professional standards and advocacy.

Vacation placements
Please visit the firm's website for details.

Sponsorship & awards
GDL and LPC fees and maintenance grants in accordance with the terms of the firm's offer.

Offices
Abu Dhabi, Amsterdam, Barcelona, Berne, Birmingham, Bratislava, Brussels, Budapest, Cambridge, Cardiff, Copenhagen, Doha, Dublin, Edinburgh, Geneva, Hong Kong, Ipswich, Jeddah, Johannesburg, Kuala Lumpur, Leeds, London, Madrid, Manchester, Milan, Munich, Newcastle, Nottingham, Ostrava, Paris, Port Louis, Prague, Riga, Riyadh, Rome, Shanghai, Singapore, Sofia, Stockholm, Valladolid, Vienna, Vilnius Tallinn, Tirana, Warsaw and Wroclaw. Further details are available on the firm's website.

Partners 300+
Lawyers 1,200+
Total Trainees 125

Contact
gradrec@eversheds.com

Method of application
Apply online at www.eversheds.com/graduatesrecruitment

Selection procedure
Selection days include group and individual exercises, presentations and interview
Closing date: Please visit the firm's website for details

Application
Training contracts p.a. 55
Applications p.a. 3,000
% interviewed p.a. 20%
Required degree grade 2:1 or 300 UCAS points

Training
Salary
1st year London (2008) £35,000
2nd year London (2008) £37,000
Holiday entitlement 25 days
% of trainees with a non-law degree p.a. 45%
No. of seats available abroad p.a. Up to 10

Post-qualification
Salary London (2009) £57,000
% of trainees offered job on qualification (2008) 73%

Farrer & Co LLP

66 Lincoln's Inn Fields, London WC2A 3LH
Tel: (020) 7242 2022 Fax: (020) 7242 9899
Email: training@farrer.co.uk
Website: www.farrer.co.uk

Firm profile
Farrer & Co is a mid-sized London law firm. The firm provides specialist advice to a large number of prominent private, institutional and commercial clients. Farrer & Co has built a successful law firm based on the goodwill of close client relationships, outstanding expertise in niche sectors and a careful attention to personal service and quality.

Main areas of work
The firm's breadth of expertise is reflected by the fact that it has an outstanding reputation in fields as diverse as matrimonial law, offshore tax planning, employment, heritage work, charity law, defamation and sports law.

Trainee profile
Trainees are expected to be highly motivated individuals with keen intellects and interesting and engaging personalities. Those applicants who appear to break the mould – as shown by their initiative for organisation, leadership, exploration, or enterprise – are far more likely to get an interview than the erudite, but otherwise unimpressive, student.

Training environment
The training programme involves each trainee in the widest range of cases, clients and issues possible in a single law firm, taking full advantage of the wide range of practice areas at Farrer & Co by offering six seats, rather than the more usual four. This provides a broad foundation of knowledge and experience and the opportunity to make an informed choice about the area of law in which to specialise. A high degree of involvement is encouraged under the direct supervision of solicitors and partners. Trainees attend an induction programme and regular internal lectures. The training partner reviews trainees' progress at the end of each seat and extensive feedback is given. The firm has a very friendly atmosphere and regular sporting and social events.

Benefits
Flexible benefits scheme, sporting teams/clubs, season ticket loan, 25 days' holiday, group income protection, group life assurance, company doctor, subsidised gym membership, subsidised yoga/pilates, pension scheme, private medical insurance after one year, wellwoman/wellman checks..

Vacation placements
Places for 2010: 30; Duration: 2 weeks at Easter, two schemes for 2 weeks in summer; Remuneration: £260 p.w.; Closing Date: 31 January 2010.

Sponsorship & awards
CPE Funding: Fees paid plus £6,000 maintenance. LPC Funding: Fees paid plus £6,000 maintenance.

Partners 69
Assistant Solicitors 74
Total Trainees 20

Contact
Trainee Recruitment Manager

Method of application
Online via the firm's website

Selection procedure
Interviews with Trainee Recruitment Partner and partners

Closing date for 2012
31 July 2010

Application
Training contracts p.a.10
Applications p.a. 800
% interviewed p.a. 5%
Required degree grade 2:1

Training
Salary
1st year (sept 2009) £32,000
2nd year (sept 2009) £34,500
Holiday entitlement 25 days
% of trainees with non-law degrees p.a. 40-60%

Post-qualification
Salary (2009) £48,000
trainees offered job on qualification (2009) 100%
% of partners (as at July 08) who joined as trainees 57%

Finers Stephens Innocent

179 Great Portland St, London W1W 5LS
Tel: (020) 7323 4000 Fax: (020) 7580 7069
Email: gradrecruitment@fsilaw.com
Website: www.fsilaw.com

Partners 37
Assistant Solicitors 36
Total Trainees 12

Contact
Personnel Department

Method of application
CV & covering letter

Selection procedure
2 interviews with the Training Partners

Closing date for 2012
30 June 2010

Application
Training contracts p.a. 6
Applications p.a. 800
% interviewed p.a. 3%
Required degree grade 2:1

Training
Salary
1st year £30,000
2nd year £32,000
Holiday entitlement 25 days
% of trainees with a non-law degree p.a. 0-50%

Post-qualification
Salary £47,000
% of trainees offered job on qualification (2009) 100%

Firm profile

Finers Stephens Innocent is an expanding practice in Central London, providing a range of high quality legal services to corporate, commercial and private clients. The firm's philosophy includes close partner involvement and a cost-effective approach in all client matters. They have a working style which is unstuffy and informal, but still aspires to the highest quality of output, while offering a sensible work-life balance. The firm is a member of the Meritas international network of law firms.

Main areas of work

Commercial property, company commercial, employment, private client, family, media, defamation. See the website for further details.

Trainee profile

The firm requires academic excellence in all applicants. It also looks for maturity, personality, a broad range of interests, initiative, strong communication skills, and the ability to write clear English, and to think like a lawyer. The firm has for several years given equal consideration to applicants whether applying straight from university or having followed another career previously. Trainees get early responsibility, client contact and close involvement in transactions and litigation matters.

Training environment

Between offering you a training contract and the time you start, the firm aims to keep regularly in touch with you, including offering you some work experience with them. When you start they provide a careful induction programme, after which you complete four six-month seats in different departments, sharing a room with either a Partner or Senior Assistant. The firm has three Training Partners who keep a close eye on the welfare and progress of trainees. There are regular group meetings with trainees, and an appraisal process which enables you to know how you are progressing, as well as giving you a chance to provide feedback on your training. The firm runs a variety of in-house training courses for trainees.

Benefits

25 days holiday; pension; private medical insurance; life insurance; long-term disability insurance; season ticket loan, EAP scheme.

Sponsorship & awards

LPC and CPE course fees.

Fladgate LLP

25 North Row, London, W1K 6DJ
Tel: (020) 7323 4747   Fax: (020) 7629 4414
Email: trainees@fladgate.com   Website: www.fladgate.com

Firm profile
Fladgate LLP is an innovative, progressive and thriving law firm which prides itself on its friendly and professional working environment.

Main areas of work
The firm provides a wide range of legal services to a portfolio of prestigious clients in the UK and overseas, including multinationals, major institutions and listed companies, clearing banks, lenders and entrepreneurs. Fladgate LLP's lawyers have experience in most major areas of practice and the firm combines an accessible and responsive style of service with first-class technical skills and in-depth expertise.

The firm has a strong international dimension based on multi-lingual and multi-qualified lawyers working in London and complemented by access to an extensive network of overseas lawyers. The firm operates specialist teams which serve continental Europe (with an emphasis on the Germanic countries), India, Israel, South Africa, the US and the Middle East.

The firm's three main departments comprise property (which includes separate planning, construction and property litigation teams), corporate (which includes tax, commercial and employment groups) and litigation. These are supported by a number of specialist cross-departmental teams that provide co-ordinated advice on a range of issues.

Trainee profile
Fladgate LLP seeks trainees with enthusiasm, leadership potential and excellent interpersonal skills. You must be able to work both independently and in a team, and will be expected to show common sense and initiative. Awareness of the commercial interests of clients is essential. You will have a minimum of a 2:1 degree, although not necessarily in law, together with three excellent A levels or equivalent. The firm is keen to attract candidates with language skills.

Training environment
Typically, you will complete four six-month seats. Each seat will bring you into contact with new clients and colleagues, and you can expect to gain real hands-on experience of a variety of deals and projects, both large and small. In each seat you will work alongside senior lawyers who will supervise your development and ensure that you are involved in challenging and interesting work. In addition to on-the-job training, each department has a comprehensive training schedule of seminars and workshops covering a range of legal and skills training.

The firm has a modern culture and an open-door policy where trainees are given early responsibility and encouraged to achieve their full potential.

Benefits
Pension, permanent health insurance, life assurance, season ticket loan, sports club loan, private medical.

Partners 44
Assistant Solicitors 29
Total Trainees 6

Contact
Mrs Annaleen Stephens, Senior Human Resources Manager

Method of application
Please apply using the firm's application form. Further information and an application form are available at the firm's website www.fladgate.com

Selection procedure
Assessment day including interview

Closing date for 2011/2012
Apply by 31 July 2010

Application
The firm operates a biennial recruitment programme and will be recruiting for the 2011 and 2012 intakes in Summer 2010.
Training contracts p.a. 3
Required degree grade 2:1

Training
Starting salary £30,000
Holiday entitlement 22-25 days

Post-qualification
Salary £50,000

Foot Anstey

Salt Quay House, 4 North East Quay, Sutton Harbour, Plymouth, PL4 0BN
Tel: (01752) 675000 Fax: (01752) 675500
Email: training@footanstey.com   Website: www.footanstey.com

Firm profile

Foot Anstey is the largest legal firm in Devon, Somerset and Cornwall with substantial offices in Exeter, Plymouth, Taunton and Truro. The firm offers specialist legal advice to businesses, public sector organisations and individuals both regionally and nationally and prides itself in the excellence of advice and service to clients. Foot Anstey has grown rapidly in recent years, doubling in size, since 2005, to a turnover of £20m. The firm was the first in the UK to achieve the Law Society's national award for excellence in practice standards and is both IIP and Lexcel accredited and holds a Legal Services Commission Specialist Quality mark.

The firm recognises that a client focused strategy relies on the attraction and retention of the best lawyers. The firm has successfully attracted top lawyers from London and major regional centres seeking the combination of the quality of life offered by the south west and a high quality of work from an impressive regional and national client portfolio.

Main areas of work

As a full service law firm, Foot Anstey delivers the spectrum of services associated with a major regional law firm. Main areas of work include: agriculture and rural business, banking, charities, clinical negligence, construction, commercial property, company commercial, criminal advocates, dispute resolution, education, employment, family finance and childcare, financial services, insolvency, IT/IP, media and private client. The firm has an extensive range of clients from commercial, public and private sectors, acting for numerous local, regional and national companies and high net worth individuals.

Trainee profile

The firm welcomes applications from all law and non-law graduates who have a strong academic background, exceptional communication skills and the ability to work as part of a dynamic team. Trainees are welcomed into a friendly and supportive environment where they will find the quality and variety of work both challenging and rewarding.

Training environment

The firm's wide range of legal services enable it to offer trainees experience in a wide range of disciplines. Trainees undertake four seats of six months. Individual monthly meetings are held with supervisors and appraisals are conducted halfway through each seat. Regular communication between the trainees and supervisors ensures an open and friendly environment. The Professional Skills Course is taught externally.

Benefits

Contributory pension scheme, 25 days' holiday.

Vacation placements

The deadline for the 2010 summer placement scheme is 31 March 2010.

Sponsorship & awards

£9,600 grant towards LPC and living expenses.

Vacancies 15
Trainees 22
Partners 42
Total Staff 356

Contact
Kelly Cooke
(01752) 675069

Method of application
Apply online at
www.footanstey.com

Selection procedure
Assessment day
application
Training contracts p.a. 15
Required degree grade
2:1 (preferred)

Closing date for 2011/ 2012
31 July 2010

Training
Salary
1st year (2009) £19,500
2nd year (2009) £21,000
Holiday entitlement 25 days

Post-qualification
Salary (2009) £32,000-£36,000
% of trainees offered job on qualification (2009) 66%
% of assistant solicitors who joined as trainees
(as at 30/04/09) 29%
% of partners who joined as trainees (as at 30/04/09) 36%

Offices
Exeter, Plymouth, Taunton & Truro

Forbes

73 Northgate, Blackburn BB2 1AA
Tel: (01254) 580000 Fax: (01254) 222216
Email: graduate.recruitment@forbessolicitors.co.uk

Firm profile

Forbes is one of the largest practices in the north with 35 partners and over 350 members of staff based in nine offices across the north of England. The firm has a broad based practice dealing with both commercial and private client work and can therefore provide a varied and exciting training contract. The firm is however especially noted for excellence in its company/commercial; civil litigation; defendant insurer; crime; family and employment departments. It has a number of Higher Court Advocates and the firm holds many Legal Service Commission Franchises. Underlying the practice is a strong commitment to quality, training and career development – a commitment underlined by the fact that Forbes was one of the first firms to be recognised as an Investor in People and its ISO 9001 accreditation. For applicants looking for a 'city' practice without the associated hassles of working in a city then Forbes could be it. The firm can offer the best of both worlds – a large firm with extensive resources and support combined with a commitment to quality, people and the personal touch.

Main areas of work

Company/commercial, civil litigation, defendant insurer, crime, family and employment services.

Trainee profile

Forbes looks for high-calibre recruits with strong North West connections and good academic records, who are also keen team players. Candidates should have a total commitment to client service and identify with the firm's philosophy of providing practical straightforward legal advice.

Training environment

A tailored training programme involves six months in four of the following: crime, civil litigation, defendant insurer in Leeds or Blackburn, matrimonial, and non-contentious/company commercial.

Partners 35
Assistant Solicitors 53
Total Trainees 15+

Contact
Graduate Recruitment Manager

Method of application
Handwritten letter and CV

Selection procedure
Interview with partners

Closing date for 2012
31 July 2010
If no invite to interview is received by 31/08/10 applicants to assume they have been unsuccesful.

Application
Training contracts p.a. 4
Applications p.a. 350 plus
% interviewed p.a. Varies
Required degree grade 2:1

Training
Salary
1st year At least Law Society minimum
2nd year £19,500
Holiday entitlement
20 days p.a.

Post-qualification
Salary
Highly competitive
% of trainees offered job on qualification (2009) 100%

Ford & Warren

Westgate Point, Westgate, Leeds, LS1 2AX
Tel: (0113) 243 6601 Fax: (0113) 242 0905
Email: Lee.Lewis@forwarn.com
Website: www.forwarn.com

Partners 20
Solicitors 32
Total Trainees 8
Other fee-earners 25
Total staff 158
Contact
Lee Lewis
Method of application
Handwritten letter and CV or email
Selection procedure
Interviews and exercise
Closing date for 2012
31 July 2010
Application
Training contracts p.a. 4
Applications p.a. 500
minimum degree grade 2:1

Firm profile

Ford & Warren is one of the largest single office commercial law firms in the region. With roots in Leeds stretching back almost 200 years, the firm has achieved its present size entirely by generic growth without mergers or acquisitions. The cost effective and quality services have enabled the firm to achieve a national reputation in key industry sectors and specialised areas of work. Areas of particular specialisation include: employment and industrial relations, road and rail transportation, licensed and leisure industry, commercial property, commercial litigation and finance. Ford & Warren has a significant presences in the public sector, particularly in health, education and local authority.

Main areas of work

Employment and industrial relations; road and rail transportation; corporate; insurance and personal injury; commercial property/real estate; public sector; tax and inheritance; matrimonial. The Dispute Resolution/Commercial Litigation Department has five sections: commercial dispute resolution, property litigation, finance litigation, insolvency and debt recovery.

Trainee profile

The firm is looking for hard working, self-reliant and enthusiastic individuals who will make a contribution to the firm from the outset. Applicants must have a strong academic background, a genuine enthusiasm for the law and the social abilities required to work effectively with colleagues and clients. The majority of lawyers practising at the firm joined as trainees.

Training environment

The firm offers seats in employment, commercial litigton, corporate, insurance and personal injury, commercial property and private client. Usually, trainees will undertake four seats of six months, although split seats may sometimes be available. The firm has a comprehensive in-house training programme for all lawyers and the PSC is also provided internally.

Selection procedure

First interviews for 2012 will take place in late 2010 with a Partner and Associate of the firm. Successful candidates are invited to a second assessment interview involving at least one member of the managing board.

Freeth Cartwright LLP

Cumberland Court, 80 Mount Street, Nottingham NG1 6HH
Tel: (0115) 901 5504 Fax: (0115) 859 9603
Email: carole.wigley@freethcartwright.co.uk
Website: www.freethcartwright.co.uk

Firm profile

Tracing its origins back to 1805, Freeth Cartwright LLP became Nottingham's largest firm in 1994 with successful offices now established in Birmingham, Derby, Leicester and Manchester. Whilst Freeth Cartwright LLP is a heavyweight commercial firm, serving a wide variety of corporate and institutional clients, there is also a commitment to a range of legal services, which includes a substantial private client element. This enables it to give a breadth of experience in training which is not always available in firms of a similar size.

Freeth Cartwright is extremely pleased to have been awarded The Sunday Times 100 Best Companies to Work for 2009 status and was also winner of LawCareers.Net Training & Recruitment 2008 award for the 'Best Trainer' category for National/ Large Regional Firms.

Main areas of work

Real estate and construction, commercial services, private client and personal litigation.

Trainee profile

Freeth Cartwright LLP looks for people to bring their own perspective and individuality to the firm. The firm needs people who can cope with the intellectual demands of life as a lawyer and who possess the wider personal skills which are needed in its diverse practice.

Training environment

Freeth Cartwright LLP is committed to providing comprehensive training for all its staff. The firm's training programme is based on in-house training covering technical matters and personal skills, supplemented with external courses where appropriate. The firm endeavours to give the best possible experience during the training period, as it believes that informal training on-the-job is the most effective means of encouraging the skills required in a qualified solicitor. One of the firm's senior partners takes responsibility for all its trainees and their personal development, overseeing their progress through the firm and discussing performance based on feedback. Normally, the training contract will consist of four six month seats in different departments, most of which are available in the firm's Nottingham offices, although it is possible for trainees to spend at least one seat in another location.

Members 78
Assistant Solicitors 34
Total Trainees 17

Contact
Carole Wigley, Senior HR Manager

Method of application
Online application form

Selection procedure
Interview & selection day

Closing date for 2012
30 June 2010

Training
Starting salary (2009) £22,000

Offices
Birmingham, Derby, Leicester Manchester and Nottingham

Freshfields Bruckhaus Deringer

Freshfields Bruckhaus Deringer LLP
65 Fleet Street, London EC4Y 1HS
Tel: (020) 7936 4000 Fax: (020) 7832 7001
Email: uktrainees@freshfields.com
Website: www.freshfields.com/uktrainees

Firm profile
Freshfields is a leader among international law firms. With over 2,700 lawyers in 27 key business centres around the world, the firm provides a comprehensive service to national and multinational corporations, financial institutions and governments.

Main areas of work
Corporate; mergers and acquisitions; banking; dispute resolution; joint ventures; employment, pensions and benefits; asset finance; real estate; tax; capital markets; intellectual property and information technology; project finance; private finance initiative; securities; antitrust, competition and trade; communications and media; construction and engineering; energy; environment, planning and regulatory; financial services; restructuring and insolvency; insurance; investment funds; public international law; arbitration.

Trainee profile
The firm is looking for candidates with proven academic ability, an excellent command of spoken and written English, high levels of drive and determination, good team working skills and excellent organisational ability.

Training environment
The firm's trainees receive a thorough professional training in a very broad range of practice areas, an excellent personal development programme and the chance to work in one of the firm's international offices or on secondment with a client. You'll be working with and learning from one of the most talented peer groups in the legal world, and will get the blend of support and freedom you need to evolve your career.

Benefits
The firm offers a flexible benefits package which includes: life assurance; permanent health insurance; group personal pension; interest-free loan for a season travel ticket; private medical insurance; subsidised gym membership and an interest-free loan when you start.

Vacation placements
Places for 2010: 60; Duration: 3 weeks; Remuneration: £825 (net); Closing Date: 15 January 2010 but apply as early as possible after 1 October 2009 as there may not be places left by the deadline.

Sponsorship & awards
GDL and LPC fees paid plus maintenance grant of £6,000 for those studying the accelerated LPC at BPP Law School in London and £6,250 for those studying the GDL.

Partners 460
Assistant Solicitors 1,682
Total Trainees 195
(London based)

Contact
uktrainees@freshfields.com

Method of application
Online application form

Selection procedure
2 interviews and written test

Closing date for 2012
31 July 2010

Application
Training contracts p.a. 90
Applications p.a. c.2,000
% interviewed p.a. c.12%
Required degree grade 2:1

Training
Salary
1st year £39,000
2nd year £44,000
Holiday entitlement 25 days
% of trainees with a
non-law degree p.a. c.40%
No. of seats available
abroad p.a. c.86

Post-qualification
Salary £59,000
% of trainees offered job
on qualification c.95%

Overseas offices
Abu Dhabi, Amsterdam, Bahrain, Barcelona, Beijing, Berlin, Brussels, Cologne, Dubai, Düsseldorf, Frankfurt, Hamburg, Hanoi, Ho Chi Minh City, Hong Kong, Madrid, Milan, Moscow, Munich, New York, Paris, Rome, Shanghai, Tokyo, Vienna, Washington DC

Government Legal Service

11th Floor, Castlemead, Lower Castle Street, Bristol, BS1 3AG
Tel: 0845 3000 793
Email: glstrainees@tmpw.co.uk
Website: www.gls.gov.uk

Firm profile
The Government Legal Service (GLS) is the collective term for the 2000 lawyers working in the legal teams of over 30 of the largest government departments and agencies. GLS lawyers have one client, the government of the day, which requires advice and support across the entire spectrum of its activities.

Main areas of work
There are many parallels between the GLS' work and that found in private practice. The government employs staff, purchases goods and services, buys and sells land and enters into contracts. GLS lawyers advise and represent the government on a huge range of issues which are often high profile and politically sensitive.

In addition to interpreting existing laws, GLS lawyers also have the opportunity to make new legislation. GLS lawyers are part of the teams that breathe life into the policies pledged by governments. They advise ministers and policy officials on what can (and can't) be done under existing legislation. If new legislation is required, GLS lawyers will help to draft and take it through Parliament in the form of a Bill. They will work closely with policy officials and Ministers and even support Ministers in Parliamentary debates. This type of work is unique to the GLS.

Trainee profile
To join the GLS as a trainee solicitor or pupil barrister, you'll need at least a 2:1 degree (which need not be in law). You must also provide evidence of strong analytical ability, excellent communication and interpersonal skills and motivation for working in public service.

Training environment
The GLS provides a unique and varied training environment for trainees and pupils. Generally, trainee solicitors work in four different areas of practice over a two-year period in the government Department to which they are assigned. Pupil barristers divide their year's pupillage between their Department and chambers. The GLS prides itself on involving trainees and pupils in the full range of casework conducted by their Department. This frequently includes high profile matters and will be under the supervision of senior colleagues.

Benefits
These include professional development opportunities, excellent pension scheme, civilised working hours, generous holiday entitlement and subsidised restaurant facilities.

Vacation placements
Summer 2010 vacation placement scheme; approx 60 places. Duration: 2-3 weeks. Closing date: end of January 2010. Remuneration: £200-£250 pw.

Sponsorship & awards
LPC and BVC fees as well as other compulsory Professional Skills Course fees. Funding may be available for the GDL. The GLS also provides a grant of around £5,000-7,000 for the vocational year.

Total Trainees around 50

Contact
glstrainees@tmpw.co.uk or visit www.gls.gov.uk

Method of application
Online application form and verbal reasoning test

Selection procedure
Half day at assessment centre involving a group discussion exercise, a written exercise and an interview

Closing date for 2012
31 July 2010

Application
Training contracts p.a. 22-30
Applications p.a. 500+
% interviewed p.a. 10%
Required degree grade (need not be in law) 2:1

Training
Salary
1st year salary: £22,900-£25,200
2nd year salary £24,250-£27,350
Holiday entitlement 25 days on entry

Post-qualification
Salary
£32,000-£40,000
% of trainees accepting job on qualification (2008) over 95%

Halliwells

3 Hardman Square, Spinningfields, Manchester, M3 3EB
Tel: (0844) 875 8000 Fax: (0844) 875 8001
Email: ekaterina.clarke@halliwells.com

Firm profile
Halliwells is a large independent commercial law firm with offices in Manchester, London, Sheffield and Liverpool. The firm specialises in providing a full range of legal services to the business community. With clients on a local, national and international level, Halliwells has high aspirations far beyond its regional boundaries. The firm has grown rapidly in recent years and embraces an internal culture of commitment, enthusiasm and reward.

Main areas of work
Corporate (Corporate, Banking, Pensions and Tax), Corporate Recovery, Real Estate (Property, Planning and Licensing), Business Services (Employment and Intellectual Property), Dispute Resolution (Commercial Litigation, Insurance Liability, Regulatory & Environmental and Construction) and Private Client (Family and Trusts & Estates).

Trainee profile
Candidates need to show a good academic ability and exhibit the characteristics necessary to thrive in a commercial environment. But beyond this the firm also seeks individuality, enthusiasm, an analytical mind, ability to put your point across and commitment to a career with Halliwells.

Training environment
Each trainee will have five seats in at least four separate departments. These will usually include commercial litigation, corporate and commercial property. Individual requests from trainees for experience in a particular department will be accommodated wherever possible. Requests for inter-office and client secondments are also encouraged.

The trainee will work within one of the department's teams and be encouraged to assist other team members to help broaden their experience. Specific training appropriate to each department will be given and trainees are strongly encouraged to attend the firm's regular in-house seminars on legal and related topics.

A supervisor will be assigned to each trainee to support their development throughout the seat.

Benefits
25 days annual leave, season ticket loan, subsidised gym membership, life assurance.

Work placements
54 summer placements will be available during summer 2010. The firm operates two schemes at all its four offices, each lasts for two weeks. Schemes commence last week in June. Remuneration is £215 per week. Closing date for applications is 28 February 2010.

Sponsorship & awards
The firm pays GDL fees and LPC fees plus a £6,500 maintenance grant for each course.

Partners 148
Assistant Solicitors 220
Total Trainees 73

Contact
Ekaterina Clarke
(Graduate Recruitment Manager)
ekaterina.clarke@halliwells.com

Method of application
Online application only

Selection procedure
Group exercise, presentation and interview

Closing date for 2012/2013
31 July 2010

Application
Training contracts p.a.
Manchester - 20
London - 6
Liverpool - 6
Sheffield - 3
Applications p.a. 1,500
% interviewed p.a. 9%
Required degree grade 2:1

Training
Salary
1st year (2008) £24,000
(London) £32,500
2nd year (2008) £25,000
(London) £33,500

Post-qualification
Salary (2008) £39,000
(London) £62,000
% of trainees offered job on qualification (2008) 75%

Hammonds LLP

Rutland House, 148 Edmund Street, Birmingham B3 2JR
7 Devonshire Square, Cutlers Gardens, London EC2M 4YH
2 Park Lane, Leeds LS3 1ES
Trinity Court, 16 John Dalton Street, Manchester M60 8HS
Tel: (0800) 163 498   Fax: (0870) 839 3666
Email: traineerecruitment@hammonds.com   Website: www.hammonds.com/trainees

Firm profile
Hammonds is one of Europe's largest corporate law firms and a member of the Global 100. In the UK alone, the firm advises over 200 London Stock Exchange quoted companies and 30 FTSE 100 companies. The firm has offices in London, Birmingham, Leeds, Manchester, Brussels, Paris, Berlin, Munich, Rome, Milan, Madrid, Turin, Beijing and Hong Kong. The firm has 1,200 staff, including 185 Partners, 550 solicitors and 50 trainees. The firm is regarded as innovative, opportunistic and highly successful in the markets in which it operates.

Main areas of work
Corporate; commercial dispute resolution; construction, engineering and projects; employment; EU and competition; finance law (including banking); intellectual property and commercial; media/IT; pensions; property; sports law; tax.

Trainee profile
Hammonds seeks applications from all disciplines for vacation work and training contracts. Consideration given to four elements in trainee selection: strong academic performance (2:1 degree classification), evidence of work experience in the legal sector, excellent communication skills and significant achievement in non-academic pursuits.

Training environment
30 trainee solicitors recruited each year. Trainees undertake six four-month seats during their training contract. Trainees have input in choice of seats and are encouraged to undertake a broad selection of seats to benefit their knowledge on qualification. Trainees benefit from two-tier supervision and challenging work. The firm provides a comprehensive induction programme including on-going departmental training, seminars and workshops throughout the training contract. Trainees undertake formal appraisal meetings with their supervisors during each seat. Hammonds' trainees benefit from exposure to clients, cross-border work and opportunity for seats on secondment. Trainees are involved in all aspects of professional life.

Benefits
Pension, life assurance, subsidised gym membership, interest free season ticket loan and a flexible benefits package.

Vacation placements
Places for 2010: 25 Summer Scheme; Duration: 2 weeks; Remuneration: £230 p.w. (London), £180 p.w. (Leeds, Manchester, Birmingham); Closing Date: 31 January 2010.

Sponsorship & awards
PgDL and LPC fees paid and maintenance grant provided. Maintenance grant presently:
GDL: London, £6,000; Regional, £4,500.
LPC: London, £7,000; Regional, £5,000.

Partners 185
Assistant Solicitors 550
Total Trainees 50

Contact
Graduate Recruitment Team

Method of application
Online application form

Selection procedure
Assessment and interview

Closing date for 2012
31 July 2010

Application
Training contracts p.a. 30
Applications p.a. 1,300
% interviewed p.a. 10%
Required degree grade 2:1

Training
Salary
1st year (2009)
£22,000 regional
£32,000 London
2nd year (2008)
£25,000 regional
£35,000 London
Holiday entitlement 25 days
% of trainees with a non-law degree p.a. 40%
No. of seats available abroad p.a. 6

Post-qualification
Salary (2009)
London £55,000
Other £34,000
% of trainees accepting job on qualification (2009) 60%

Overseas offices
Brussels, Beijing, Paris, Berlin, Munich, Rome, Milan, Turin, Hong Kong, Madrid

Harbottle & Lewis LLP

Hanover House, 14 Hanover Square, London W1S 1HP
Tel: (020) 7667 5000 Fax: (020) 7667 5100
Email: kathy.beilby@harbottle.com
Website: www.harbottle.com

Firm profile
Harbottle & Lewis LLP is a London based commercial law firm providing specialist advice primarily to the media, entertainment and communications industries.

Main areas of work
Main areas of work encompasses all areas of media and entertainment including film, television, broadcasting, sport, music, publishing, computer games, advertising, fashion and theatre and the firm remains unique in having expertise right across these sectors. The firm's work involves the technology, new media and telecoms industries and the firm has done ground-breaking work in connection with the digital exploitation of content and e-commerce generally. The firm's expertise in other areas such as aviation and charities is also widely recognised.

Trainee profile
Trainees will have demonstrated the high academic abilities, commercial awareness, and initiative necessary to become part of a team advising clients in dynamic and demanding industries.

Training environment
The two year training contract is divided into four six-month seats where trainees will be given experience in a variety of legal skills. Seats include employment, corporate, litigation, family, tax and private client, real property, as well as seats working within teams focused on the firm's core industries, such as film, tv, theatre, music and video games. The firm has a policy of accepting a small number of trainees to ensure they are given relevant and challenging work and are exposed to and have responsibility for a full range of legal tasks. The firm has its own lecture and seminar programme in both legal topics and industry know-how. An open door policy and a pragmatic entrepreneurial approach to legal practice provides a stimulating working environment.

Benefits
Lunch provided; season ticket loans.

Sponsorship & awards
LPC fees paid and interest-free loans towards maintenance.

Partners 28
Assistant Solicitors 47
Total Trainees 10

Contact
Kathy Beilby

Method of application
CV & letter by post or email

Selection procedure
Interview

Closing date for 2012
31 July 2010

Application
Training contracts p.a. 5
Applications p.a. 800
% interviewed p.a. 10%
Required degree grade 2:1

Training
Salary
1st year £28,000 (2008)
2nd year £29,000 (2008)
Holiday entitlement
in the first year 23 days
in the second year 26 days
% of trainees with
a non-law degree p.a. 40%

Post-qualification
Salary (2007) £45k

HBJ Gateley Wareing LLP

One Eleven, Edmund Street, Birmingham B3 2HJ
Tel: (0121) 234 0000   Fax: (0121) 234 0079
Email: graduaterecruitment.england@hbj-gw.com
Website: www.hbjgateleywareing.com

Partners 102 (firmwide)
Vacancies 12 (England)
Total Trainees 16 (Midlands)
TotalStaff 575 (firmwide)
Contact
HR Department
Closing date for 2012
Training contracts:
31 July 2010
Vacation placements:
11 February 2010
Training
Salary
1st year £20,000-22,000
2nd year £22,000-24,000
Post-qualification
Salary £32,000
Offices
Birmingham, Dubai, Edinburgh, Glasgow, Leicester, London and Nottingham.

Firm profile
A 102 partner, UK commercial based practice with an excellent reputation for general commercial work and particular expertise in corporate, plc, commercial, employment, property, construction, insolvency, commercial dispute resolution, banking, tax and shipping.

The firm also offers individual clients a complete private client service including FSA-approved financial advice. The firm is expanding (575 employees) and offers a highly practical, commercial and fast-paced environment. HBJ Gateley Wareing has built an outstanding reputation across the UK for its practical approach, sound advice and professional commitment to its clients. The firm is a full range, multi-disciplinary legal business with expertise in many areas.

HBJ Gateley Wareing has an enviable reputation as a friendly and sociable place to work. The firm is committed to equality and diversity across the firm.

Trainee profile
To apply for a placement in England: applications are invited from second year law students and final year non-law students and graduates. Applicants should have (or be heading for) a minimum 2.1 degree, and should have at least three Bs (or equivalent) at A-level. Individuals should be hardworking team players capable of using initiative and demonstrating commercial awareness.

Training environment
Four six-month seats with ongoing supervision and appraisals every three months. PSC taken internally. In-house courses on skills such as time management, negotiation, IT, drafting, business skills, marketing, presenting and writing in plain English.

Benefits
Current trainee offered as a 'buddy' – a point of contact within the firm, library available, invitation to summer party prior to joining.

Vacation placements
Two-week placement over the summer. Deadline for next year's vacation placement scheme is 11 February 2010 and the Closing date for 2012 training contracts is 31 July 2010. Apply online at www.hbjgateleywareing.com. Paper/email applications not accepted.

Sponsorship & awards
GDL/LPC and a LPC maintenance grant of £5,000.

Henmans LLP

5000 Oxford Business Park South, Oxford OX4 2BH
Tel: (01865) 780000   Fax: (01865) 778682
Email: welcome@henmansllp.co.uk
Website: www.henmansllp.co.uk

Firm profile
Henmans LLP is the premier firm in Oxford, with several practice areas ranked as the leading experts in the Thames Valley by commentators. The firm has a national reputation in its specialist areas, handling commercial and personal matters for a wide range of clients both nationally and internationally. The firm also acts for a large number of third sector organisations and insurers.

More than half of its senior lawyers are acknowledged as experts within their fields, so clients are confident of receiving the most authoritative advice available. The firm believes that the best advisers are those who thoroughly understand your concerns, so it works hard to ensure that it has a detailed appreciation of your business or personal questions, and can offer the best possible advice.

Main areas of work
The firm's core service of litigation is nationally recognised for its high quality. The firm also has an excellent reputation for its personal injury, clinical negligence, property, private client and charity work. The breakdown of work is as follows: Professional negligence and commercial litigation: 24%; personal injury: 27%; property: 17%; private client (including family) /charities/ trusts: 25%; corporate/ employment: 10%.

Trainee profile
Commercial awareness, sound academic accomplishment, intellectual capability, IT literacy, able to work as part of a team, good communication skills.

Training environment
Trainees are an important part of the firm's future. The firm is committed to providing a high standard of training throughout the contract. Trainees are introduced to the firm with a detailed induction and overview of its client base. A trainee manual is provided to familiarise the trainee with each department's procedures. Experience is likely to be within the PI, property, professional negligence/ commercial litigation, corporate and private client departments. The firm provides an ongoing programme of in-house education and regular appraisals within its supportive friendly environment. The firm values commitment and enthusiasm both professionally and socially as an integral part of its culture and trainees are encouraged to join in social activities and become involved with the life of the firm.

Benefits
Holiday entitlement 23 days + 2 firm days at Christmas. BUPA, pension, EAP, scheme, free car parking, subsidised cafe, pilates.

Partners 23
Other Solicitors & Fee-earners 53
Total Trainees 6

Contact
Viv J Matthews (Mrs)
MA CH FCIPD
Head of HR

Method of application
Application form on website

Selection procedure
The interview process comprises an assessment day with Head of HR and partners, including an interview, presentation, verbal reasoning test, drafting and team exercise

Closing date for 2012
31 July 2010

Application
Training contracts p.a. 3
Applications p.a. 300

Training
Salary
1st year (2009/10) £22,000
2nd year (2009/10) £24,000
Holiday entitlement 23 days + 2 firm days at Christmas. BUPA, pension, EAP scheme, free car parking, subsidised cafe
% of trainees with a non-law degree p.a. 40%

Post-qualification
Salary (2009) £34,000
% of assistants who joined as trainees 28%
% of partners who joined as trainees 15%

Herbert Smith LLP

Exchange House, Primrose Street, London EC2A 2HA
Tel: (020) 7374 8000 Fax: (020) 7374 0888
Email: graduate.recruitment@HERBERTSMITH.com
Website: www.herbertsmithgraduates.com

Firm profile
Herbert Smith LLP is an international legal practice with over 1,200 lawyers across Asia, Europe and the Middle East. It also has a major focus on emerging markets, including China, India and Russia. This, combined with an alliance with Gleiss Lutz and Stibbe and a network of relationship firms, enables Herbert Smith to provide a seamless, cross-border service on a global level.

Main areas of work
Alongside Herbert Smith's outstanding reputation in dispute resolution and corporate work, the firm has leading practices in finance, real estate, competition and employment, pensions and incentives. It is also acknowledged as a leader in several industry sectors, including the energy and natural resources and financial institutions sectors.

Trainee profile
As well as a strong academic record, applicants require a strong level of commercial awareness and the common sense to be able to make their own way in a large firm. Combine these qualities with a creative and questioning mind, and Herbert Smith will offer you great challenges and rewards.

Training environment
The strength and breadth of the firm's practice areas, including corporate, dispute resolution and finance, guarantee excellent training and development opportunities for trainees. The training process balances contentious and non-contentious work; early responsibility and support. An emphasis is also placed on professional and personal development. Trainees rotate around four six-month seats, including a seat in a specialist area such as IP or competition. Trainees can also apply to go on secondment to a client or to one of the firm's international offices. Herbert Smith's global reach makes this a possibility for many.

Sponsorship & benefits
Herbert Smith offers £5,000 for the GDL outside of London; £6,000 GDL inside London and £7,000 for the LPC. Benefits include 25 days' holiday (rising to 27 after qualification), bonus scheme, gym membership subsidy, life assurance, pension scheme with company contributions, private healthcare, season ticket loan, permanent health insurance.

Vacation placements
Herbert Smith offers a two-week winter vacation scheme, a two-week spring vacation scheme and three two-week summer vacation schemes. The vacation scheme will give you an excellent insight into working life at a leading international City firm. Placements are open to both law and non-law students, and during the two weeks you will be exposed to the highest quality contentious and non-contentious work. You will be treated as one of the team and given real work for real clients.

Partners 256*
Fee-earners 742*
Total Trainees 249*
*denotes worldwide figures

Contact
graduate.recruitment@
herbertsmith.com
020 7374 8000

Method of application
Online at
www.herbertsmithgraduates.com

Selection procedure
Case study and interview

**Closing date for
March 2012/Sept 2012**
31 July 2010

Application
Training contracts p.a. up to 100
Applications p.a. circa 2,000
% interviewed p.a. 30%
Required degree grade 2:1

Training
Salary
1st year £37,500
2nd year £42,500
Holiday entitlement
25 days, rising to 27 on qualification
ratio of law to non-law graduates is broadly equal

Post-qualification
Salary (2009) £60,000
% of trainees offered job on qualification (2009) 74%

Overseas offices
Abu Dhabi, Bangkok, Beijing, Brussels, Dubai, Hong Kong, London, Madrid, Moscow, Paris, Shanghai, Singapore, Tokyo
associated offices
Amsterdam, Berlin, Budapest, Dammam, Frankfurt, Jakarta, Jeddah, Munich, New York, Prague, Riyadh, Stuttgart, Warsaw

Herbert Smith

Hewitsons LLP

42 Newmarket Road, Cambridge CB5 8EP
Tel: (01604) 233233 Fax: (01223) 316511
Email: mail@hewitsons.com (for all offices)
Website: www.hewitsons.com (for all offices)

Firm profile
Established in 1865, the firm handles mostly company and commercial work, but has a growing body of public sector clients. The firm has three offices: Cambridge, Northampton and Milton Keynes.

Main areas of work
Three sections: corporate, property and private client.

Trainee profile
The firm is interested in applications from candidates who have achieved a high degree of success in academic studies and who are bright, personable and able to take the initiative.

Training environment
The firm offers four six-month seats.

Benefits
The PSC is provided during the first year of the training contract. This is coupled with an extensive programme of Trainee Solicitor Seminars provided by specialist in-house lawyers.

Vacation placements
Places for 2010: A few placements are available, application is by way of letter and CV to Caroline Lewis; Duration: 1 week.

Sponsorship & awards
Funding for the CPE and/or LPC is not provided.

Partners 43
Assistant Solicitors 37
Total Trainees 13

Contact
Caroline Lewis
7 Spencer Parade Northampton
NN1 5AB

Method of application
Firm's application form

Selection procedure
Interview

Closing date for 2012
End of August 2010

Application
Training contracts p.a. 10
Applications p.a. 850
% interviewed p.a. 10%
Required degree grade
2:1 min

Training
Salary
1st year £23,500
2nd year £25,000
Holiday entitlement 22 days
% of trainees with a
 non-law degree p.a. 50%

Post-qualification
Salary £35,000
% of trainees offered job
on qualification (2009) 38%

Higgs & Sons

134 High Street, Brierley Hill DY5 3BG
Tel: (01384) 342100 Fax: (01384) 342178
Email: graduaterecruitment@higgsandsons.co.uk
Website: www.higgsandsons.co.uk

Partners 30
Fee Earners 38
Total Trainees 8

Contact
Helena Tonks

Method of application
Online application form

Selection procedure
Interview with trainee committee

Closing date for 2012
18th August 2010

Application
Training contracts p.a. 4
Applications p.a. 250 plus
% interviewed p.a. varies
Required degree grade
preferably 2:1, will consider 2:2

Training
Salary reviewed annually
1st year £21,500
2nd year £24,000
Holiday entitlement
25 days p.a.
Post-qualification
Salary £32,000
% of trainees offered job
on qualification 80%

Firm profile

Founded in 1875, Higgs & Sons is now one of the largest and most respected law firms in the West Midlands, operating out of three offices in Brierley Hill, Stourbridge and Kingswinford and employing over 170 staff. The firm is well recognised in the Legal 500 and Chambers Guide to the Legal Profession.

Higgs & Sons is different from the typical law firm. The firm successfully combines traditional values with an innovative approach to legal problems which has helped to attract an impressive client base whilst also staying true to the local community. Clients and staff alike are attracted to Higgs' ability to offer an all round service in a number of areas. The firm is proud to provide a supportive and friendly working environment within which both colleagues and clients can thrive. The opportunity for career progression is also clear as more than half of the firm's partners trained with the firm.

Main areas of work

For the business client: corporate and commercial, insolvency, employment law, commercial litigation and commercial property.

For the private client: wills, probate, trusts and tax, employment law, personal injury, ULR and clinical negligence, conveyancing, dispute resolution, matrimonial/ family, motoring and private criminal.

Trainee profile

Applications are welcome from law and non law students who can demonstrate consistently high academic records, a broad range of interpersonal skills and extra curricular activities and interests. The firm would like to hear about what you have done to develop your wider skills and awareness. It is looking for people who want to get involved and participate fully in the business.

Candidates will preferably have a 2:1 class degree but graduates with a 2:2 class will be considered.

Training environment

A training contract at Higgs is different from those offered by other firms. There is the unique opportunity to undertake six four month seats in a variety of departments, including a double seat in the department in to which you wish to qualify as you approach the end of your training contract. Throughout the training contract you will receive a mix of contentious and non-contentious work and an open door policy means that there is always someone on hand to answer questions and supervise your work. Regular appraisals take place at the end of each seat and a designated Partner oversees you throughout the duration of your training contract, acting as a mentor. Participation in BTSS events and an active Higgs social environment ensures the work life balance.

Benefits

Private medical insurance, contributory pension, life assurance, 25 days holiday and BTSS Membership.

Sponsorship

Professional Skills Course.

Hill Dickinson

No. 1 Street, Paul's Square, Liverpool, L3 9SJ
Tel: (0151) 600 8000
Email: emma.mcavinchey@hilldickinson.com
Website: www.hilldickinson.com

Firm profile
Hill Dickinson offers the comprehensive range of commercial legal services fromm offices in Liverpool, Manchester, London, Chester, Piraeus and Singapore. It is a top 40 sized practice with over 150 partners and more than 1100 people.

Main areas of work
Hill Dickinson is a major force in insurance and is well respected in the corporate and commercial arena, its marine expertise is internationally renowned and it has award-winning property and construction and employment teams. The firm is widely regarded as a leader in the fields of commercial litigation, healthcare law, clinical negligence, professional risks, intellectual property and wealth management.

The firm is also committed to driving forward its sector offerings in areas such as retail, transport and logistics, the public sector, travel and leisure, energy and media and entertainment.

With a focus on enhancing its international presence, in March 2009, the firm opened a new office in Singapore and in July 2009, it merged with London-based commodities practice Middleton Potts, adding further weight to its global reputation for shipping and transport work.

Clients include multi-national companies, major corporations and UK plcs. insurance companies, UK and foreign banks and financial institutions as well as public and professional bodies and private individuals.

Trainee profile
Commercial awareness and academic ability are the key factors, together with a desire to succeed. Trainees are viewed as the partners of the future and the firm is looking for personable individuals with whom it wants to work.

Training environment
Trainees spend periods of six months in four different practice groups. Trainees are encouraged to accept responsibility and are expected to act with initiative. The firm has an active social committee and a larger than usual selection of competitive sporting teams.

Vacation placements
Four one week schemes. 40 places available for 2010. Apply online by 31 March 2010.

Partners 152
Assistant Solicitors 143
Associates 42
Total Trainees 32

Contact
Emma McAvinchey

Method of application
Online application form

Selection procedure
Assessment day

Closing date for 2012
31st July 2009

Training
Salary
1st year (2009) £24,000
2nd year (2009) £26,000
1st year (London) £32,000
2nd year (London) £34,000
Sponsorship: LPC
Holiday entitlement
25 days

Post-qualification
% of trainees offered job on qualification 70%

Offices
Liverpool, Manchester, London, Chester, Singapore, Piraeus, Greece

Holman Fenwick Willan

Friary Court, 65 Crutched Friars, London, EC3N 2AE
Tel: (020) 7264 8000 Fax: (020) 7264 8888
Email: grad.recruitment@hfw.com

Firm profile
Holman Fenwick Willan is an international law firm and one of the world's leading specialists in maritime transportation, insurance, reinsurance, energy and trade. The firm is a leader in the field of commercial litigation and arbitration and also offers comprehensive commercial advice. Founded in 1883, the firm is one of the largest operating in its chosen fields with a team of over 200 lawyers worldwide, and a reputation for excellence and innovation.

Main areas of work
The firm's range of services include marine, admiralty and crisis management, insurance and reinsurance, commercial litigation and arbitration, international trade and commodities, energy, corporate and financial.

Trainee profile
Applications are invited from commercially minded undergraduates and graduates of all disciplines with good A levels and who have, or expect to receive, a 2:1 degree. Good foreign languages or a scientific or maritime background are an advantage.

Training environment
During your training period the firm will ensure that you gain valuable experience in a wide range of areas. It also organises formal training supplemented by a programme of in-house seminars and ship visits in addition to the PSC. Your training development as an effective lawyer will be managed by the HR and Training Partner, Ottilie Sefton, who will ensure that your training is both successful and enjoyable.

Benefits
Private medical insurance, permanent health and accident insurance, subsidised gym membership, season ticket loan.

Vacation placements
Places for 2010: Dates: 21 June- 2 July; 12 July- 23 July; Remuneration: £250 p.w.; Applications accepted 1 Jan. 2010 - 14 Feb. 2010.

Sponsorship & awards
GDL Funding: Fees paid plus £6,000 maintenance; LPC Funding: Fees paid plus £7,000 maintenance.

Partners 100+
Other Solicitors & Fee-earners 170+
Total Trainees 28

Contact
Marina Farthouat

Method of application
Online application form

Selection procedure
2 interviews & written exercise

Closing date for 2012
31 July 2010

Application
Training contracts p.a. 12-14
Applications p.a. 1,000
% interviewed p.a. 5%
Required degree grade 2:1

Training
Salary (Sept 2009)
1st year £32,000
2nd year £34,000
Holiday entitlement 25 days
% of trainees with
a non-law degree p.a. 50%

Post-qualification
Salary £58,000 (Sept 2009)
% of trainees offered job
on qualification
(Sept 2009) 100% in London

Overseas offices
Brussels, Hong Kong, Paris, Piraeus, Rouen, Shanghai, Singapore, Dubai, Melbourne

Howes Percival LLP

Oxford House, Cliftonville, Northampton NN1 5PN
Tel: (01604) 230400   Fax: (01604) 620956
Email: katy.pattle@howespercival.com
Website: www.howespercival.com

Firm profile

Howes Percival LLP is a leading commercial law firm with offices in Leicester, Milton Keynes, Northampton and Norwich. Last year the firm won the Leicestershire Law Society Firm of the year award and previously has won the UK Regional Firm of the Year at the Legal Business Awards. The firm's working environment is progressive and highly professional and its corporate structure means that fee-earners are rewarded on merit and can progress to associate or partner status quickly. The type and high value of the work that the firm does places it in a position whereby it is recognised as being a regional firm by location only. The firm has the expertise, resources and Partner reputation that match a city firm.

Main areas of work

The practice is departmentalised and the breakdown of its work is as follows: corporate 30%; commercial property 25%; commercial litigation 20%; insolvency 10%; employment 10%; private client 5%.

Trainee profile

The firm is looking for eight well-educated, focused, enthusiastic, commercially aware graduates with a minimum 2:1 degree in any discipline. Howes Percival LLP welcomes confident communicators with strong interpersonal skills who share the firm's desire to be the best.

Training environment

Trainees complete four six-month seats, each one in a different department. Trainees joining the Norwich office will remain at Norwich for the duration of their training contract. Within the East Midlands region, there is the opportunity to gain experience in two of the three East Midlands offices. Trainees report direct to a partner, and after three months and again towards the end of each seat they will be formally assessed by the partner training them. Trainees will be given every assistance by the fee-earners in their department to develop quickly and will be given responsibility as soon as they are ready.

Benefits

Contributory pension scheme. Private health insurance. LPC/GDL/ maintenance grant. Details available upon request.

Vacation placements

Vacation placements are available in June, July and August. Please apply via the online application form found on the trainee page of the firm's website. The closing date is 30 April 2010.

Partners 27
Solicitors 66
Total Trainees 15

Contact
Miss Katy Pattle
HR Officer

Method of application
Online application form

Selection procedure
Assessment centres

Closing date for 2012
31 July 2010

Application
Training contracts p.a. 8
Applications p.a. 300
% interviewed p.a. 10%
Required degree grade 2:1

Training
Salary
1st year £24,500 (Sept 09)
2nd year £26,500 (Sept 09)
Holiday entitlement
25 days p.a.

Post-qualification
% of trainees offered job on qualification (2009) 44%
% of assistants who joined as trainees 24%
% of Partners who joined as trainees 15%

Ince & Co

International House, 1 St Katharine's Way, London E1W 1AY
Email: recruitment@incelaw.com

Firm profile
From its origins in maritime law, the firm's practice today encompasses all aspects of the work areas listed below. Ince & Co is frequently at the forefront of developments in contract and tort law.

Main areas of work
Aviation, business and finance, energy and offshore, insurance and reinsurance, international trade and commodities and shipping.

Trainee profile
Hardworking, competitive individuals with initiative who relish challenge and responsibility within a team environment. Academic achievements, positions of responsibility, sport and travel are all taken into account.

Training environment
Trainees sit with four different partners for six months at a time throughout their training. Under close supervision, they are encouraged from an early stage to meet and visit clients, interview witnesses, liaise with counsel, deal with technical experts and handle opposing lawyers. They will quickly build up a portfolio of cases from a number of partners involved in a cross-section of the firm's practice and will see their cases through from start to finish. They will also attend in-house and external lectures, conferences and seminars on practical and legal topics.

Benefits
STL, corporate health cover, PHI, contributory pension scheme. Well Man/Well Woman health checks, subsidised gym membership.

Vacation placements
Places for 2010: 15; Duration: 2 weeks; Remuneration: £250 p.w.; Closing Date: 31 January 2010.

Sponsorship & awards
LPC/CPE fees, £6,000 grant for study in London & Guildford, £5,500 grant for study elsewhere.

Partners 88*
Senior Associates 32*
Solicitors 118*
Total Trainees 25*
* denotes worldwide figures

Contact
Claire Kendall

Method of application
online at www.incelaw.com

Selection procedure
Interview with HR professional, interview with 2 partners from Recruitment Committee & 3 tests

Closing date for 2012
31 July 2010

Application
Training contracts p.a. 15
Applications p.a. 1,000
% interviewed p.a. 10%
Required degree grade 2:1

Training
Salary
1st year £36,000
2nd year £39,000
Holiday entitlement 25 days
% of trainees with a non-law degree p.a. 55%

Post-qualification
Salary £58,000
% of trainees offered job on qualification (2009) 92%. All accepted!
% of partners (as at 2009) who joined as trainees Approx 70%

Overseas offices
Dubai, Hamburg, Hong Kong, Le Havre, Paris, Piraeus, Shanghai, Singapore

Irwin Mitchell

Riverside East, 2 Millsands, Sheffield S3 8DT
Tel: (0870) 1500 100 Fax: (0870) 197 3549
Email: graduaterecruitment@irwinmitchell.com
Website: www.irwinmitchell.com

Firm profile

Founded in 1912, the firm has grown from strength to strength and today employ more than 2300 people through its office network of major cities within the UK and its two offices in Spain.

Irwin Mitchell Solicitors has grown both organically and through a number of strategic mergers with firms and organisations in tune with the firm's values and culture.

The firm is the largest full service law firm within the UK with its services divided into two main categories; legal services for individuals and those for businesses, institutions and organisations.

As well as being recognised as the leading national personal injury firm in the UK, the firm has also developed a reputation for the delivery of strong commercial services that add real value to businesses, institutions and organisations. Over the last five years the firm as enjoyed substantial growth as its business strategies have reaped rewards.

Main areas of work

Corporate services and private client; insurance; personal injury.

Trainee profile

The firm is looking for ambitious and well-motivated individuals who have a real commitment to the law and who can demonstrate a positive approach to work-life balance. Irwin Mitchell recruits law and non-law graduates and views social ability as important as academic achievement. Irwin Mitchell believes trainees are an investment for the future and endeavours to retain trainees upon qualification. In addition to the firm's training contract vacancies it also runs a work placement scheme giving potential training contract candidates a chance to experience what it is like to be a solicitor within the firm.

Training environment

The firm's training contracts are streamed so that as a trainee you would either undertake a training contract based within the firm's Personal Injury Practice Area, (where you can gain experience in personal injury, clinical negligence, court of protection and personal injury defence) or you would undertake a training contract based within the firm's business and private client practice area (where dependant on office location you could gain experience in departments such as insolvency, commercial litigation, corporate, public law and family). Trainees spend the first year of their training contract undertaking three seats of four months in duration. Having experienced three different areas of law, trainees are then likely to know where they wish to qualify so during the second year trainees undertake a twelve month seat, in the area which they and the firm wish them to qualify into. The firm offers a structured induction programme to trainees joining the practice.

Benefits

Healthcare scheme, contributory pension scheme, subsidised gym membership, away day and Christmas party.

Sponsorship & awards

Payment of PGDL and LPC fees plus a £4,500 maintenance grant.

Partners 136
Assistant Solicitors 210
Total Trainees 51

Contact
Alex Burgess,
Graduate Recruitment Officer
graduaterecruitment@irwinmitchell.com

Method of application
Please visit the firm's website www.irwinmitchell.com and complete the online application

Selection procedure
Assessment centre & interview

Closing date for 2012
31 July 2010

Application
Training contracts p.a. 20-25
Applications p.a. 1,500
% interviewed p.a. 30%
Required degree grade: The firm does not require a specific degree grade
Salary
1st year £22,450
2nd year £24,650
(outside London)
reviewed annually in September
Holiday entitlement
24.5 days
post-qualification
% of trainees offered job on qualification 91%
Overseas/Regional Offices
Birmingham, Leeds, London, Manchester, Newcastle, Sheffield, Glasgow, Madrid & Malaga

Jones Day

21 Tudor Street, London, EC4Y 0DJ
Tel: (020) 7039 5959 Fax: (020) 7039 5999
Email: recruit.london@jonesday.com
Website: www.jonesdaylondon.com

Firm profile
Jones Day operates as one firm worldwide with 2,400 lawyers in 32 offices. Jones Day in London is a key part of this international partnership and has around 200 lawyers, including around 50 partners and 30-40 trainees. This means that the firm can offer its lawyers a perfect combination - the intimacy and atmosphere of a medium sized City firm with access to both UK and multinational clients.

Main areas of work
Principal areas of practice at Jones Day include: corporate finance and M&A transactions; investment funds, private equity and corporate tax planning, banking, capital markets and structured finance, business restructuring, litigation, intellectual property tax and real estate. The London office also has teams of lawyers who are experienced in such areas as competition/antitrust, environmental and employment and pensions law.

Trainee profile
The firm looks for candidates with either a law or non-law degree who have strong intellectual and analytical ability, good communication skills and who can demonstrate resourcefulness, drive, dedication and the ability to engage with clients and colleagues.

Training environment
The firm operates a unique, non-rotational system of training and trainees receive work simultaneously from all departments in the firm. The training is designed to provide freedom, flexibility and responsibility from the start. Trainees are encouraged to assume their own workload, which allows early responsibility, a faster development of potential and the opportunity to compare and contrast the different disciplines alongside one another. Work will vary from small cases which the trainee may handle alone (under the supervision of a senior lawyer) to larger matters where they will assist a partner or an associate solicitor. The firm runs a structured training programme with a regular schedule of seminars to support the thorough practical training and regular feedback that trainees receive from the associates and partners they work with.

Placement schemes
Places for 2009/10: Winter (non-law): closing date 31 October. Spring 2010 (non-law): closing date 31 January. Summer (law): closing date 31 January. Placements last for two weeks with an allowance of £400 per week. Students get to see how the firm's non-rotational training system works in practice by taking on real work from a variety of practice areas. They also get to meet a range of lawyers at various social events.

Benefits
Private healthcare, season ticket loan, subsidised sports club membership, group life cover, salary sacrifice schemes and access to stakeholder pension.

Sponsorship & awards
GDL/PgDL and LPC fees paid and £8,000 maintenance p.a.

Partners approx 50
Assistant Solicitors 90
Total Trainees 30-40

Contact
Jacqui Megson
Graduate Recruitment Manager

Method of application
CV and letter online at www.jonesdaylondon.com

Selection procedure
2 interviews with partners
Closing date for 2012
31 July 2010

Application
Training contracts p.a. 15-20
Applications p.a. 1,500
% interviewed p.a. 12%
Required degree grade 2:1

Training
Salary
1st year (2009) £39,000 increasing to £41,000 after six months
2nd year (2009) £45,000 rising to £50,000 after 18 months
Holiday entitlement
5 weeks

Post-qualification
Salary (2009) £70,000
% of trainees offered job on qualification (2009) 58%

Overseas offices
Continental Europe, Asia, North America, Latin America, Middle East, Asia Pacific

K&L Gates LLP

110 Cannon Street, London, EC4N 6AR
Tel: (020) 7648 9000 Fax: (020) 7648 9001
Email: traineerecruitment@klgates.com
Website: www.klgates.com/europe_recruitment/graduate/

Firm profile
K&L Gates comprises approximately 1,900 lawyers in 33 offices located in North America, Europe and Asia, and represents capital markets participants, entrepreneurs, growth and middle market companies, leading FORTUNE 100 and FTSE 100 global corporations and public sector entities. Whilst the firm's international practice requires lawyers with diverse backgrounds and skills, the firm comes together in its shared values of investment and growth, both for the firm and the individual. The firm is committed to professional development and provides a cutting edge training programme.

Main areas of work
K&L Gates is active in the areas of investment management and related funds work, mergers and acquisitions, private equity, real estate, intellectual property, digital media and sport, travel and leisure, construction, insurance coverage, securities enforcement, environmental matters, litigation and other forms of dispute resolution.

Trainee profile
The firm welcomes applications from both law and non-law students. Law students should generally be in their penultimate year of study and non-law students should be in their final year of study. The firm also welcomes applications from relevant postgraduates or others who have satisfied the 'academic stage of training' as required by the Law Society. You should be highly motivated, intellectually curious, with an interest in commercial law and be looking for comprehensive training.

Training environment
The firm ensures each trainee is given exceptional opportunities to learn, experience and develop so that they can achieve their maximum potential. Trainees spend six month seats in four of the following areas: corporate, dispute resolution and litigation, intellectual property, construction, tax, real estate, employment, pensions and environment. Each trainee sits with a supervisor and is allocated an individual mentor to ensure all round supervision and training. The firm has a thorough induction scheme which includes attendance at the firm's First Year Academy in the US, and has won awards for its career development programme. High importance is placed on the acquisition of business and professional skills, with considerable emphasis on client contact and early responsibility. The training programme consists of weekly legal education seminars, workshops and a full programme of skills electives. Language training is also available. Pro bono and corporate social responsibility activities are also encouraged.

Benefits
25 days holiday per annum, subsidised gym membership, season ticket loan, private health insurance, bonus scheme, life assurance, medicentre membership and pension.

Legal work placements
The firm's formal legal work placement scheme is open to penultimate year law students, final year non-law students, other relevant post graduates or others who have satisfied the 'academic stage of training' as required by the law society.

Sponsorship
GDL funding: fees paid plus £5,000 maintenance grant. LPC funding: fees paid plus £7,000 maintenance grant.

Partners 61
Trainees 16
Total Staff 275

Contact
Hayley Atherton

Method of application
Online at www.klgates.com/europe_recruitment/graduate/ or request a paper application

Selection procedure
Full assessment day

Closing date for 2012
31 July 2010

Application
Training contracts p.a. tbd
Applications p.a. 1,000
% interviewed p.a. 10%
Required degree grade 2:1

Training
Salary
1st year (2009) 35,000
2nd year (2009) 38,000
% of trainees with a non-law degree p.a. Varies

Post-qualification
Salary (2009) £56,000
% of trainees offered job on qualification (2008) 90%

Overseas offices
Anchorage, Austin, Beijing, Berlin, Boston, Charlotte, Chicago, Dallas, Dubai, Fort Worth, Frankfurt, Harrisburg, Hong Kong, Los Angeles, Miami, Newark, New York, Orange County, Palo Alto, Paris, Pittsburgh, Portland, Raleigh, Research Triangle Park, San Diego, San Fransisco, Seattle, Shanghai, Singapore, Spokane/Coeur D'Alene, Taipei, Washington

K&L|GATES

Kirkland & Ellis International LLP

30 St Mary Axe, London, EC3A 8AF
Tel: (020) 7469 2000 Fax: (020) 7469 2001
Website: www.kirkland.com/ukgraduate

Firm profile

Kirkland & Ellis International LLP is a 1,500-attorney law firm representing global clients in offices around the world.

For 100 years, major national and international clients have called upon Kirkland & Ellis to provide superior legal advice and client services. The firm's London office has been the hub of European operations since 1994. Here, approximately 85 lawyers offer detailed expertise to a wide range of UK and international clients.

Main areas of work

The firm handles complex corporate, restructuring, tax, intellectual property, litigation and counselling matters. Kirkland & Ellis operates as a strategic network, committing the full resources of an international firm to any matter in any territory as appropriate.

Trainee profile

Your academic record will be excellent, probably culminating in an expected or achieved 2.1. You will have the initiative, the drive and the work ethic to thrive in the firm's meritocratic culture and arrive with an understanding of the work undertaken in the firm's London office.

Training environment

As one of a select number of trainees, you will be given early responsibility to work on complex multi jurisdictional matters.

The principal focus of your training will be on corporate law with a specialism in private equity. You will complete four, six month seats and obtain training in areas such as banking, arbitration, IP, restructuring and tax. In addition there will be opportunities to undertake an overseas secondment to enable you to experience the international resources and capabilities of Kirkland & Ellis.

Your on the job training will be actively supported by an extensive education programme, carefully tailored to meet your needs.

Benefits

Private medical insurance, travel insurance, life insurance, employee assistance plan, corporate gym membership.

Vacation placements

Places for 2010: up to 14. Duration: 2 weeks. Remuneration: £350 per week. Closing date for applications: 31/01/10.

Sponsorship & awards

GDL and LPC course fees and a maintenance grant of £7,500 p.a.

Partners 624
Assistant solicitors 1522

Contact
Kate Osborne

Method of application
CV and covering letter to include a full % breakdown of degree results per subject

Selection procedure
Interview

Closing date for 2012
31 July 2010

Training
Salary
1st year (2009) £40,000
2nd year (2009) £43,000
Holiday entitlement
25 days

Post-qualification
(currently no data)

Overseas/ regional offices
Chicago, Hong Kong, Los Angeles, Munich, New York, Palo Alto, San Francisco, Washington D.C.

Latham & Watkins

99 Bishopsgate, London, EC2M 3XF
Tel: (020) 7710 1000 Fax: (020) 7374 4460
Email: london.trainees@lw.com
Website: www.lw.com

Firm profile
Latham & Watkins has more than 2,000 lawyers in 27 offices across Europe, America and Asia and the London office advises on some of the most significant and groundbreaking cross-border transactions in Europe. The firm believes that its non-hierarchical management style and 'one firm' culture makes Latham & Watkins unique.

Main areas of work
Corporate, finance, litigation, employment and tax.

Trainee profile
Candidates with a strong academic background, excellent communication skills and a consistent record of personal and/or professional achievement will be rewarded with first class training. The firm is dedicated to diversity and equal opportunity and values originality and creative thinking.

Training environment
Latham & Watkins can provide a very different training experience to that offered by the rest of the elite law firms. Each trainee receives bespoke supervision and outstanding support while being encouraged to recognise that they have their own part to play in the growth and success of the firm. Each trainee also has meaningful responsibility from the outset and significant legal experience on qualification. Trainees may also be given the opportunity to spend one of their four six-month seats in one of the firm's overseas offices.

Benefits
Healthcare and dental scheme, pension scheme and life assurance.

Sponsorship & awards
All GDL and LPC costs are paid and trainees receive a maintenance grant of £8,000 per year whilst studying.

Vacation placements
The firm has a two-week Easter vacation scheme and a two-week summer scheme. Students are paid £300 per week. The deadline for Easter scheme applications is 31st December and the deadline for summer scheme applications is 31st January.

Partners 47
Associates 97
Trainees 24

Contact
Alex Mitchell

Method of application
Online application form at www.lw.com

Selection procedure
3 x 30 minute interviews with a partner and an associate

Closing date for 2012
31 July 2010

Application
Training contracts p.a. 15-20
Required degree grade: 2:1

Training
Salary
1st year (2009) £41,000
2nd year (2009) £44,000

Post-qualification
Salary: £96,970

Overseas/regional offices
Abu Dhabi, Barcelona, Brussels, Chicago, Dubai, Doha, Frankfurt, Hamburg, Hong Kong, London, Los Angeles, Madrid, Milan, Moscow, Munich, New Jersey, New York, Orange County, Paris, San Diego, San Francisco, Shanghai, Silicon Valley, Singapore, Tokyo, Washington DC.

Laytons

Carmelite, 50 Victoria Embankment, Blackfriars, London EC4Y 0LS
Tel: (020) 7842 8000 Fax: (020) 7842 8080
Email: london@laytons.com
Website: www.laytons.com

Firm profile
Laytons is a commercial law firm whose primary focus is on developing dynamic business. The firm's offices in Guildford, London and Manchester provide excellent service to its commercial and private clients who are located throughout the UK. The firm's approach to legal issues is practical, creative and energetic. The firm believes in long-term relationships, they are 'client lawyers' rather than 'transaction lawyers'. The key to its client relations is having a thorough understanding of businesses, their needs and objectives. Working together as one team, the firm is supportive and plays to each other's strengths.

Main areas of work
Corporate and commercial, commercial property (including land development and construction), dispute resolution, debt recovery, insolvency, employment, intellectual property, technology and media, private client and trusts.

Trainee profile
Successful candidates will be well-rounded individuals, commercially aware with sound academic background, and enthusiastic and committed team members.

Training environment
Trainees are placed in four six-month seats, providing them with an overview of the firm's business, and identifying their particular strengths. All trainees have contact with clients from an early stage, are given challenging work, working on a variety of matters with partners and assistant solicitors. Trainees will soon be responsible for their own files and are encouraged to participate in business development and marketing activities. The firm works in an informal but professional atmosphere and its philosophy is to invest in people who will develop and become part of its long-term success.

Vacation placements
Places for summer 2010: 6. Duration: 1 week. Closing Date: 30 April 2010.

Sponsorship & awards
LPC and CPE funding: consideration given.

Partners 32
Associate Partners 6
Assistant Solicitors 24
Total Trainees 15

Contact
Stephen Cates &
Lisa McLean (London)
David McClenaghan (Guildford)
Christine Barker (Manchester)

Method of application
Application form (on website)

Selection procedure
Usually 2 interviews

Closing date for 2012
31 August 2010

Application
Training contracts p.a. 8
Applications p.a. 2,000
% interviewed p.a. 5%
Required degree grade
1 or 2:1 preferred

Training
Salary
1st year (2008) Market rate
2nd year (2008) Market rate
Holiday entitlement
23 days per year

Post-qualification
Salary (2008) Market rate
% of trainees offered job
on qualification (2008) 75%
% of assistants (as at 1/9/08)
who joined as trainees 52%
% of partners (as at 1/9/08)
who joined as trainees 34%

Regional offices
Training contracts are offered in each of Laytons' offices. Apply directly to desired office. See website for further details: www.laytons.com

Lester Aldridge

Russell House, Oxford Road, Bournemouth BH8 8EX
Tel: (01202) 786161 Fax: (01202) 786110
Email: juliet.artal@LA-law.com
Website: www.lesteraldridge.com

Firm profile

Lester Aldridge LLP is a dynamic business providing both commercial and private client services. The firm has highly successful sectors, including asset finance, marine, retail, care sector and fertility.

A key regional player, the firm has an impressive client repertoire supported by the recruitment of outstanding staff.

Lester Aldridge's positioning on the South Coast offers a positive working environment and a great work life balance, whilst providing opportunities to work with first class lawyers, impressive clients, and opportunity for City experience via LA's London office.

Main areas of work

Banking and finance 20%; litigation 30%; private client 24%; commercial property 13%; investments 5%, dispute resolution 15%, real estate 28%.

Trainee profile

Candidates should have a consistently strong academic record, be commercially aware and possess a broad range of interpersonal skills. Applicants should be highly motivated and have a desire to succeed working with teams to advise clients in dynamic and demanding industries.

Training environment

Training contract consists of four six-month seats across the firm (preferences will be accommodated where possible). Direct client involvement is encouraged and each trainee is assigned a mentor to provide guidance and encouragement. Appraisals are carried out with team leaders at the end of each seat, as are regular group meetings with the Managing Partner, to ensure that trainees gain a range of work and experience.

Benefits

Life assurance, pension schemes, flexible benefits. Travel season ticket loan.

Vacation placements

Places for 2010: 8; Duration: 2 weeks; Remuneration: £125 p.w.; Closing Date: 31 March 2010.

Sponsorship & awards

LPC.

Partners 39
Total Trainees 13
Total Staff 250

Contact
Juliet Artal

Method of application
Letter, CV & completed application form

Selection procedure
Interview by a panel of partners as part of assessment and development day

Closing date for 2012
31 July 2010

Application
Training contracts p.a. 6
Applications p.a. 200
% interviewed p.a. 5%
Required degree grade 2:1

Training
Salary
Starting: £17,250 (£500 London weighting) increasing £500 after each seat
Holiday entitlement 22 days
% of trainees with a non-law degree p.a. 20%

Post-qualification
Salary (2009) £33,000-£34,000
% of trainees offered job on qualification (2008) 66%
% of assistants (2008) who joined as trainees 36%
% of partners (2008) who joined as trainees 25%

Offices
Bournemouth (2), Southampton & London

Lewis Silkin LLP

5 Chancery Lane, Clifford's Inn, London EC4A 1BL
Tel: (020) 7074 8000 Fax: (020) 7864 1200
Email: train@lewissilkin.com
Website: www.lewissilkin.com

Partners 51
Assistant Solicitors 76
Total Trainees 10

Contact
Human Resources

Method of application
Online application form

Selection procedure
Assessment day, including an interview with 2 partners, a group exercise, analytical and aptitude test

Closing date for 2012
Please refer to website

Application
Training contracts p.a. 5
Applications p.a. 550
Required degree grade 2:1

Training
Salary
1st year £32,000
2nd year £34,000
Holiday entitlement 25 days

Post-qualification
Salary (2009) £50,000

Firm profile
Lewis Silkin is a commercial firm with 51 partners. What distinguishes them is a matter of personality. For lawyers, they are notably informal, unstuffy...well, human really. They are 'people people'; as committed and professional as any good law firm, but perhaps more adept at the inter-personal skills that make relationships work and go on working. They place a high priority on the excellent technical ability and commercial thinking of their lawyers and also on their relationships with clients. Clients find them refreshingly easy to deal with. The firm has a friendly, lively style with a commitment to continuous improvement.

Main areas of work
The firm has a wide range of corporate clients and provides services through five departments: corporate, employment and incentives, litigation, property, housing and construction, and media, brands and technology. The major work areas are commercial litigation and dispute resolution; corporate services, which includes company commercial and corporate finance; defamation; employment; marketing services, embracing advertising and marketing law; property, construction, technology and communications, including IT, media and telecommunications. They are UK leaders in employment law and have a strong reputation within social housing and the media and advertising sectors.

Trainee profile
They are looking for trainees with keen minds and personalities, who will fit into a professional but informal team.

Training environment
The firm provides a comprehensive induction and training programme, with practical hands-on experience from day one. You will sit with either a partner or senior associate giving you access to day-to-day supervision and guidance. The training contract consists of six four-month seats, working in the firm's five departments and/ or client secondments.

Benefits
These include individual and firm bonus schemes, life assurance, critical illness cover, health insurance, season ticket loan, group pension plan and subsidised gym membership.

Work placements
The two-week work placement scheme which takes place during either June or July, gives participants the opportunity to gain first hand experience of life at Lewis Silkin. Applications should be made via the firm's website between November 2009 and the end of January 2010.

Open days
Open days will be held during spring 2010 to give participants an overview of the firm, its main areas of work and a chance to meet trainees and partners.
Applications should be made between November 2009 and the end of January 2010.

Sponsorship & awards
Funding for GDL and LPC fees is provided plus a £5,000 maintenanceg grant for each.

Lawrence Graham LLP

4 More London Riverside, London, SE1 2AU
Tel: (020) 7379 0000 Fax: (020) 7379 6854
Email: graduate@lg-legal.com
Website: http://graduates.lg-legal.com

Firm profile
LG is a London-based firm delivering a full range of commercial and legal solutions worldwide. Driven by its corporate and real estate practices, the key industry sectors in which the firm operates are financial institutions, real estate, hospitality & leisure, energy, healthcare, publishing and media, support services, technology and the public sector. The firm has strong relationships with law firms around the world, particularly in the US and Asia, as well as offices in Monaco, Dubai and Moscow.

Main areas of work
The firm's four core departments are: business & finance (including corporate/M&A, banking & finance, IT & outsourcing, investment funds, employment, insurance, pensions, EU/competition, housing & local government); real estate (commercial property, planning, construction, environment & health & safety, real estate litigation and finance); dispute resolution (commercial litigation, corporate recovery, insurance & reinsurance disputes, shipping, contentious trusts & estates, corporate investigations); and tax & private capital. Work is often international in its scope.

Trainee profile
The firm is looking for individuals from a variety of backgrounds with refined communication skills who can demonstrate a commitment to a career in the commercial application of law. A strong academic track record with a minimum of 320 UCAS tariff points and a 2:1 degree is a basic requirement. Also required is a good record of achievement in other areas - indicative of the ability to succeed in a demanding career - and evidence of team working skills and the ability to handle responsibility.

Training environment
Under partner supervision trainees will be given early responsibility. Training is structured to facilitate the ability to manage one's own files and interact with clients. In addition to the Professional Skills Course, there are departmental training and induction sessions as well as a two year rolling training programme, designed to develop well-rounded lawyers. Training consists of four six-month seats: real estate, transactional and contentious seat are compulsory. The other seat can be either in tax & private capital or a second in business & finance or real estate.

Benefits
Season ticket loan, life assurance.

Vacation placements
Places for 2010: Duration: 2 weeks during Easter break and 3 x 2 weeks between June and July; Remuneration: £250 p.w; Closing Date: 31 January 2010.

Sponsorship & awards
GDL Funding: Course fees and maintenance grant. £6k outside London, £6.5k in London.
LPC Funding: Course fees and maintenance grant. £6k outside London, £6.5k in London.

Partners 78
Assistant Solicitors 103
Total Trainees 36

Contact
Vicki Baldwin Graduate Recruitment Officer

Method of application
Firm's application form.
For law after 2nd-year results
For non-law after final results

Selection procedure
Interview

Closing date for 2012
31 July 2010

Application
Training contracts 20-25
Applications p.a. 800
Required degree grade 2:1

Training
Salary
1st year (2009) £32,000
2nd year (2009) £36,000
% of trainees with a non-law degree p.a. 40%

Post-qualification
Salary (2009) £55,000
% of trainees offered job on qualification (2009) 52%

Linklaters LLP

One Silk Street, London EC2Y 8HQ
Tel: (020) 7456 2000 Fax: (020) 7456 2222
Email: graduate.recruitment@linklaters.com
Website: www.linklaters.com/ukgrads

Firm profile
Linklaters is a global law firm that advises the world's leading companies, financial institutions and governments on their most important and challenging transactions and assignments. This is an ambitious and innovative firm which aims to become the leading premium global law firm. Its drive to create something new in professional services provides a very special offer to graduates.

Main areas of work
Whilst many law firms have strengths in particular areas, Linklaters is strong across the full range of corporate, financial and commercial law. This makes Linklaters a particularly stimulating place to train as a business lawyer.

Trainee profile
Linklaters people come from many different backgrounds and cultures; by working together to achieve great things for clients, they are encouraged to achieve their own ambitions and potential. With global opportunities, entrepreneurial freedom and world-class training, Linklaters trainees work alongside some of the world's best lawyers on some of the most challenging deals. The firm has high expectations of its trainees, but the rewards – personal and professional as well as financial – are very high indeed.

Training environment
The firm recruits graduates from both law and non-law disciplines. Non-law graduates spend a conversion year at law school taking the Graduate Diploma in Law (GDL). All trainees have to complete the Legal Practice Course (LPC) before starting their training contracts. The firm meets the costs of both the GDL and LPC and provides a maintenance grant for both. The training contract is built around four six-month seats or placements in a range of practice areas. The majority of the firm's trainees have the opportunity to go on international and/or client secondments.

Sponsorship & benefits
GDL and LPC fees are paid in full, plus a maintenance grant. Benefits include profit and performance-related bonus schemes, pension, private medical insurance, life assurance, income protection, in-house healthcare services, family friendly benefits, in-house gym and subsidised health club membership, subsidised staff restaurant, interest-free season ticket loan, holiday travel insurance, time bank scheme, cycle2work and give as you earn.

Vacation placements
Linklaters offers a two-week Christmas Vacation Scheme for final year non-law students, and two Summer Vacation Schemes (four weeks) for penultimate year law students.

Partners 500
Associates 2,200
Trainees 250+*
*(London)

Contact
Charlotte Hart

Method of application
Online application form

Selection procedure
Critical reasoning test, 2 interviews including a commercial case study.

Application
Training contracts p.a. 110
Applications p.a. 4,000
Required degree grade 2:1

Training
Salary
1st year (2009) £37,400
Holiday entitlement 25 days
% of trainees with a
non-law degree p.a. 40%

Post-qualification
Salary £61,500 + discretionary performance-related bonus

Offices
Amsterdam, Antwerp, Bangkok, Beijing, Berlin, Brussels, Dubai, Düsseldorf, Frankfurt, Hong Kong, Lisbon, London, Luxembourg, Madrid, Milan, Moscow, Munich, New York, Paris, Rome, São Paulo, Shanghai, Singapore, Stockholm, Tokyo, Warsaw

Lovells

Lovells LLP, Atlantic House, Holborn Viaduct, London EC1A 2FG
Tel: (020) 7296 2000 Fax: (020) 7296 2001
Email: recruit@lovells.com
Website: www.lovells.com/graduates

Firm profile
Lovells is one of the world's leading international business legal practices with offices in the major financial and commercial centres across Asia, Europe, the Middle East and the US.

Main areas of work
The practice's international strength across a wide range of practice areas gives it an exceptional reputation not only in corporate, dispute resolution and finance, but also for real estate, intellectual property, employment, EU/competition, insurance and tax.

Trainee profile
The practice is looking for people whose combination of academic excellence and specialist knowledge will develop Lovells' business and take it forward. As well as demonstrating strong academic and intellectual ability, candidates should have strong communication and interpersonal skills and a professional, commercial attitude. You should be happy working in a team, yet capable of, and used to, independent action. Above all, candidates should have a single-minded ambition to succeed in a top legal practice.

Training environment
Lovells treats continuous training and development as a priority for both trainee solicitors and qualified lawyers, as clients expect informed, effective legal and business advice from all Lovells lawyers. As a trainee solicitor at Lovells you will participate in an extensive training programme, which covers legal, business and technology skills. The practice is committed to providing you with the highest possible standard of training, so that you will develop into an accomplished legal and business adviser.

Trainees spend six months in four different practice areas to gain as much experience as possible. All trainees spend six months in a Corporate or Finance Group, and six months gaining contentious experience in the firm's Dispute Resolution Practice. In the second year of training, there is the option of spending a seat on secondment either to one of the practice's international offices or the in-house legal team of one of the firm's major clients.

Vacation Placements
The practice offers up to 50 vacation placements over two highly regarded summer schemes. Each scheme lasts three weeks and the application deadline is 31 January 2010.

Benefits
PPP medical insurance, life assurance, season ticket loan, in-house gym, access to dentist, doctor and physiotherapist, subsidised staff restaurant, discounts at local retailers.

Sponsorship
GDL and LPC course fees are paid, and maintenance grants are provided for both the GDL and the LPC.

Partners 365
Assistant Solicitors 1369
Total Trainees 152

Contact
recruit@lovells.com

Method of application
Online application form

Selection procedure
Assessment day: critical thinking test, group exercise, interview

Closing date for 2012/2013
31 July 2010

Application
Training contracts p.a. 90
Applications p.a. 1,500
% interviewed p.a. 25%
Required degree grade 2:1

Training
Salary
1st year (2009) £37,000
2nd year (2009) £42,000
Holiday entitlement 25 days
% of trainees with a non-law degree p.a. 60%
No. of seats available abroad p.a. 25

Post-qualification
Salary (2009) £59,000

International offices
Alicante, Amsterdam, Beijing, Brussels, Budapest, Chicago, Dubai, Düsseldorf, Frankfurt, Hamburg, Hanoi, Ho Chi Minh City, Hong Kong, London, Madrid, Milan, Moscow, Munich, New York, Paris, Prague, Rome, Singapore, Shanghai, Tokyo, Warsaw, Zagreb

Macfarlanes LLP

20 Cursitor Street, London, EC4A 1LT
Tel: (020) 7831 9222 Fax: (020) 7831 9607
Email: gradrec@macfarlanes.com
Website: www.macfarlanes.com

Firm profile
Macfarlanes is a leading law firm in the City of London with a strong international outlook. The firm's success is founded on first-class lawyers, hard work and excellent training at all levels. Much of their work is international, acting in complex cross-border transactions and international disputes. This work is driven by the firm's excellent relationships with leading independent law firms outside the UK.

Main areas of work
The firm has a large corporate, real estate and litigation department and, unusually for a City firm, a significant private client department. They serve a broad range of clients in the UK and overseas, from multinationals, quoted companies and banks to private individuals.

Trainee profile
Trainees need to be highly motivated, high-achieving graduates from any discipline with (or expecting) a strong 2:1 degree or higher, who are looking for top quality work and training in a cohesive firm where everyone's contribution counts and can be seen to count. Macfarlanes needs people who can rise to a challenge and who will relish the opportunities and responsibilities that will be given to them.

Training environment
Anyone joining Macfarlanes cannot expect to lose themselves in the crowd. Because they recruit fewer trainees, each individual is expected to play their part. There are other benefits attached to working in a firm of this size: it helps retain an informal working atmosphere – people quickly get to know one another and are on first name terms across the board. There is the sense of community that comes from working closely together in smaller teams. Everyone at Macfarlanes has a vested interest in getting the best out of each other, including their trainees.

Benefits
Life assurance, pension scheme with company contributions, private healthcare, season ticket loan, subsidised restaurant, gym membership/subsidy, eyecare vouchers and childcare vouchers.

Vacation placements
Places for 2010: 60; Duration: 2 weeks; Remuneration: £250 p.w.; Closing Date: 28 February 2010.

Sponsorship & awards
CPE/GDL and LPC fees paid in full and a £7,000 maintenance allowance.

Partners 75
Assistant Solicitors 147
Total Trainees 55

Contact
Vicki Dimmick

Method of application
Online via website

Selection procedure
Assessment day

Closing date for 2012
31 July 2010

Application
Training contracts p.a. up to 30
Applications p.a. 800
% interviewed p.a. 20%
Required degree grade 2:1

Training
Salary
1st year £37,000
2nd year £41,500
Holiday entitlement 25 days, rising to 26 on qualification
% of trainees with a non-law degree p.a. 65%

Post-qualification
Salary (2009) £59,000
% of trainees offered job on qualification (Sept 2008/March 2009) 96%
% of partners (as at 1/9/09) who joined as trainees 55%

Maclay Murray & Spens LLP

151 St Vincent Street, Glasgow G2 5NJ
Tel: (0141) 248 5011
Website: www.mms.co.uk

Firm profile

Maclay Murray & Spens LLP is a full service, independent, commercial law firm offering legal solutions and advice to clients throughout the UK and beyond. With offices in Aberdeen, Glasgow, Edingburgh and London the firm's objective is to provide a consistently excellent quality of service across the firm's entire service range and from every UK office.

Main areas of work

Banking and finance, capital projects, commercial dispute resolution, construction and engineering, corporate, employment pensions and benefits, EU, competition and regulatory , IP and technology, oil and gas, planning and environmental, private client, property, public sector and tax.

Trainee profile

Applicants should have a strong academic background (minimum 2:1 degree) as well as demonstrate a number of key skills including an inquiring mind and a keenness to learn, commitment, professionalism, determination to see a job through, first class communication skills, the ability to get on with colleagues and clients at all levels, an ability to operate under pressure in a team environment, as well as a sense of humour. The firm welcomes non-law graduates.

Training environment

MMS will provide you with a very broad range of practice experience, including legal writing, drafting, research work, and an element of client contact. This is one of the firm's strengths as a business and a long standing attraction for candidates.

By working as a team member on more complex transactions, you are given the opportunity to gain experience over a broad range of work. You will also be encouraged to meet and work alongside clients from different backgrounds and diverse areas of industry and commerce.

Benefits

At MMS trainees are paid competitive salaries as well as provided with an attractive benefits package. All of the firm's employees receive a combination of fixed and variable holidays totalling 34 days each year. The firm also offers a contributory pension scheme, death in service benefit worth four times your annual salary, support with conveyancing fees, enhanced maternity and paternity pay, income protection insurance and discounted access to medical and dental plans.

Partners 70
Assistant Solicitors 172
Total Trainees 65

Contact
trainee.recruitment@mms.co.uk

Method of application
Application forms only, accessed at www.mms.co.uk/traineeship

Selection procedure
Following an initial interview a number of candidates will be invited to attend a second interview with 2 Partners, where they will also complete a roleplay and research exercise. Offers will be made to the successful candidates very soon after the second interview

Closing date for 2011
London traineeship Monday 10 August 2009
Scottish traineeship October 2009

Application
Training contracts p.a. 30
Applications p.a.
Scotland 300
London 150
Required degree grade 2:1

Training
Salary (2009)
(Scotland) 1st year £17,000
(London) 1st year £32,000
Holiday entitlement All of our employees receive a combination of fixed and variable holidays totalling 34 days per year.

Overseas/regional offices
Aberdeen, Edinburgh, Glasgow, London

Manches

Aldwych House, 81 Aldwych, London WC2B 4RP
Tel: (020) 7404 4433 Fax: (020) 7430 1133
Email: sheona.boldero@manches.com
Website: www.manches.com

Firm profile
Manches is a full-service commercial firm based in London and the Thames Valley with strengths across a range of services and industry sectors. Their current strategy will see a greater concentration and focus on the firm's core industry sectors, while continuing to be market leaders in family law. The firm offers 10 trainee places each September.

Main areas of work
Industry Sectors: Real estate, International wealth protection, retail business, commercial technology.

Legal Groups: Commercial property, commercial litigation, corporate finance, construction, family, trusts & estates, employment, intellectual property, information technology, biotechnology (Oxford and Reading offices only), and environment & planning.

Trainee profile
Manches aims to recruit a broad cross-section of candidates with different ranges of experiences and backgrounds. However, all candidates should demonstrate consistently good academic records, together with cheerful enthusiasm, high levels of commitment, an appreciation of commercial issues, the ability to think for themselves and have warm and approachable social skills. A sense of humour is an asset!

Training environment
The firm gives high-quality individual training. Trainees generally sit in four different seats for six months at a time. The firm's comprehensive induction week, followed by its practically based "learning by doing" training programme enables them to take responsibility from an early stage, ensuring that they become confident and competent solicitors at the point of qualification. Trainees have the opportunity to actively participate in departmental meetings, presentations, client seminars and briefings and they receive regular appraisals on their progress.

Benefits
Season ticket loan, BUPA after six months, permanent health insurance, life insurance, pension after six months.

Vacation placements
Places for 2010: 20 approx.; Duration: 1 week; Closing Date: 15th February 2010; Remuneration: £200 (under review).

Sponsorship & awards
GDL and LPC fees are paid in full together with an annual maintenance allowance (currently £5,000 p.a.).

Partners 59
Assistant Solicitors 65
Total Trainees 20

Contact
Sheona Boldero
sheona.boldero@manches.com

Method of application
Online application form

Selection procedure
1st interview with HR, 2nd Interview with partners.

Closing date for 2012
31 July 2010

Application
Training contracts p.a. 10
Applications p.a. 850
% interviewed p.a. 5%
Required degree grade 2:1 min

Training
Salary
1st year (2009)
London £30,000
2nd year (2009)
London £33,000
Holiday entitlement 24 days

Post-qualification
Salary
London £50,000
% of trainees offered job on qualification (2009) 75%

Martineau

No 1 Colmore Square, Birmingham B4 6AA
35 New Bridge Street, London, EC4V 6BW
Tel: (0870) 763 2000 Fax: (0870) 763 2001
Email: jennifer.seymour@martineau-uk.com
Website: www.martineau-uk.com

Firm profile

Martineau is a dynamic and passionate law firm that combines a commercial and vibrant atmosphere with a personal and caring attitude.

Brand values are based on the three 'i's - integrity, innovation and inspiration. They reflect the working cutlure where they are inspired to deliver innovative solutions to clients, ensuring to exceed their needs, wants and expectations.

Providing national and international advice to its clients, the firm is recognised as market leader in many of its areas of practice and is well known for providing high level expertise.

Martineau look for enthusiastic and committed graduates with good degrees, not necessarily in law, to contribute to its successful practice.

State of the art premises in the heart of Birmingham city centre, coupled with its expanding London office, provide trainees with an ideal base to gain experience in a variety of core and niche practice areas.

As a founder member of Multilaw, an international network of law firms, opportunities also stretch far beyond the UK.

Martineau are also a member of State Law Resources which is a network of independent law firms with a focus on energy and climate across 43 State and Canada.

The firm's commitment to client care and quality is endorsed by the ISO 9001 standard.

Main areas of work

Commercial 27%; corporate 23%; commercial disputes management 22%; property 17%; private client 11%. Focus areas include energy and utilities, education, banking, investment funds and technology.

Trainee profile

Trainees are vital to Martineau future and no effort is spared to give the best possible experience and support to them, whilst treating them as individuals. There is a very high retention rate at the end of training contracts, when trainees are generally offered roles in their preferred departments and specialisms.

Training environment

Martineau aim is to work in partnership with trainees, providing them with mentoring, supervision, support and an exposure to the key areas of the firm's practice. Trainees are actively encouraged to be an integral part of the team delivering legal solutions to its clients whilst benefiting from quality work, flexible seat rotation in a small and friendly team environment. Trainees gain experience in three main areas, corporate, commercial disputes, commercial property and they are then given the opportunity to experience commercial work in areas of their chosen specialism. There are opportunities for Birmingham-based trainees to be exposed to the London scene.

Trainees benefit from a bespoke career development and training programme which is tailored to their personal needs; it covers not only legal technical matters, but also a business and commercial approach which has never been more central to successful professional careers.

In giving training and offering experience that matches the best city firms Martineau offers a rare opportunity for trainees to lay great foundations for their legal career in a fast moving, ever changing but caring environment.

Partners 48
Assistant Solicitors 100
Total Trainees 20

Contact
Jennifer Seymour

Method of application
Online application form
www.martineau-uk.com

Selection procedure
Assessment centre - half day
Closing date for 2012
31 July 2010

Application
Training contracts p.a. 10-12
Applications p.a. 600
% interviewed p.a. 10%
Required degree grade 2:1

Training
Salary
1st year (2008) c. £21,000
2nd year (2008) c. £22,500
Holiday entitlement 25 days
% of trainees with a
non-law degree (2008) 60%

Post-qualification
Salary (2009) £40,000
% of trainees offered job
on qualification (2008) 70%
% of assistants (as at 01/07/09)
who joined as trainees 33%
% of partners (as at 01/07/09)
who joined as trainees 27%

Maxwell Winward LLP

100 Ludgate Hill, London EC4M 7RE
Tel: (020) 7651 0000   Fax: (020) 7651 4800
Email: recruitment@maxwellwinward.com
Website: www.maxwellwinward.com

Firm profile
Maxwell Winward is the successfully established and bedded down firm created by the merger of leading property firm Maxwell Batley and built environment specialists Winward Fearon back in 2007. Two years down the line, the merger has been demonstrably successful, as evidenced by the strengthened breadth and depth of the practice in its key areas and by the full service the firm is able to offer to its clients. The firm has proved itself to be a compelling alternative to larger firms in all aspects of advice provided in the firm's key areas. The firm has a modern focus and a friendly unstuffy ethos where trainees are treated as important members for the team and as future solicitors of the business. Trainees are encouraged to interact with everyone in the firm and become a part of the team from day one. This interaction provides trainees with the best possible opportunity to develop the abilities and skills needed on qualification to become the successful lawyers of the future.

Main areas of work
The firm specialises in Real Estate, Construction (both contentious and non-contentious), Corporate, Company/Commercial, Employment, Projects and Dispute Resolution. As well as acting for several high-profile blue-chip clients, the firm also acts for a number of smaller commercial clients and some high net worth individuals.

Trainee profile
Successful candidates will have at least a 2:1 in any discipline. It is important that candidates are willing to learn and have enthusiasm, common sense, sound judgement and commercial awareness as well as a genuine interest in the firm's specialist areas.

Training environment
The varied nature of the firm's work means that trainees are given a range of experience from all of the different practice areas. The training contract is split into four six-month seats in each of the different practice areas. Whilst trainees are closely supervised, the firm is keen to ensure that they are given valuable practical experience, as much client contact as possible and the responsibility to gradually gain the confidence to tackle matters with little supervision.

The firm arranges internal seminars for trainees in order to give them formal training to complement the day to day experience that comes with assisting on 'real-life' matters.

Benefits
20 days holiday, Season ticket loan, Private health insurance.

Sponsorship & awards
Contribution towards fees and maintenance for GDL and LPC.

Partners 19
Assistant Solicitors 21
Total Trainees 7

Contact
The Practice Manager

Method of application
CV and covering letter

Selection procedure
Two interviews
closing date for 2011 and 2012
01 July 2010

Application
Training contracts p.a. 3-4
Applications p.a. 800
% interviewed p.a. 6%
Required degree grade 2:1

Training
Salary
1st year (2007) £29,000
2nd year (2007) £31,500
Holiday entitlement 20 days

Post-qualification
Salary (2007) £48,000
% of trainees offered job
on qualification (2008) 100%

Mayer Brown[1]

201 Bishopsgate, London EC2M 3AF
Email: graduaterecruitment@mayerbrown.com
Website: www.mayerbrown.com/london

Firm profile

Mayer Brown is a leading global law firm with offices in key business centres across the Americas, Europe and Asia. The firm has approximately 1,000 lawyers in the Americas, 300 in Asia and 500 in Europe. The firm's Asia presence was enhanced by its 2008 combination with Johnson Stokes & Master, the largest and oldest Asia law firm. (In Asia, the firm is known as Mayer Brown JSM.) This unequalled on-the-ground presence in the world's leading markets for legal services enables Mayer Brown to offer clients access to local market expertise on a global basis.

Main areas of work

The firm's lawyers practise in a wide range of areas including corporate, finance, litigation and dispute resolution, real estate, insurance and reinsurance, pensions and employment, competition and trade, tax, intellectual property and information technology. Clients include many of the FTSE and Fortune 500 companies from the worlds of banking, insurance, communications, industrials, energy, construction, professional services, media, pharmaceuticals, chemicals and mining.

Trainee profile

The firm is looking for candidates who not only have a consistently strong academic record including a minimum of a 2.1 degree (predicted or obtained) in any discipline, but also who have a wide range of interests and achievements outside their academic career. Additionally, the firm would like to see innovative candidates who can demonstrate a drive for results, good verbal and written communication skills, and an ability to analyse, with good judgement and excellent interpersonal skills.

Training environment

Mayer Brown advises some of the world's most sophisticated and complex businesses and institutions. You will have the opportunity to work alongside some award-winning teams and individuals. One of the advantages of joining Mayer Brown are the choices available to you. Trainees can tailor their training contract from a range of 27 different seats, including the main practice areas in London (as listed above) and four international secondments (Brussels, two in Hong Kong, New York and São Paulo). If you don't want to stray too far, a wealth of in-house experience is also available via 11 client secondments within the UK. For a large international firm, the London office remains a tightly knit team harbouring an open and inclusive culture. You will nevertheless be given significant opportunities to assist on matters which may be multi-disciplinary, cross-border, complex and high-profile in nature.

Benefits

Benefits include 25 days holiday per annum, an interest free season ticket loan, subsidised sports club membership and membership of private health scheme.

Work experience programmes

Places for 2010: 45. Duration: two weeks at Easter and three weeks in the summer. Experience in two key practice areas plus an programme of seminars and social events, including a trip to our Brussels office.

Sponsorship & awards

The firm will cover the cost of the GDL and LPC fees and provide a maintenance grant of £7,000.

Partners 110
Assistant Solicitors 206
Total Trainees 61

Contact
Isabella Crocker Graduate Recruitment Manager

Method of application
Online application form

Selection procedure
One stage assessment process including an interview, a written exercise, a group exercise and an online verbal reasoning test
Closing date for Sept 2012/March 2013
31 July 2009

Application
Training contracts p.a. approx 30-35
Applications p.a. 1,000+
% interviewed p.a. 10-15%
Required degree grade 2:1

Training
1st year £37,500
2nd year £42,300
Holiday entitlement 25 days
% of trainees with a non-law degree p.a. 50%
No. of seats available abroad p.a. 10

Post-qualification
% of trainees offered job on qualification (2008) 89%

Overseas offices
Bangkok, Beijing, Berlin, Brussels, Charlotte, Chicago, Cologne, Frankfurt, Guangzhou, Hanoi, Ho Chi Minh City, Hong Kong, Houston, London, Los Angeles, New York, Palo Alto, Paris, Sao Paulo, Shanghai and Washington DC.

---

[1] Mayer Brown is a global legal services organisation comprising legal practices that are separate entities ("Mayer Brown Practices"). The Mayer Brown Practices are: Mayer Brown LLP, a limited liability partnership established in the United States; Mayer Brown International LLP, a limited liability partnership incorporated in England and Wales; and JSM, a Hong Kong partnership, and its associated entities in Asia. The Mayer Brown Practices are known as Mayer Brown JSM in Asia.'

McDermott Will & Emery UK LLP

7 Bishopsgate, London EC2N 3AR
Tel: (020) 7577 6900 Fax: (020) 7577 6950
Website: www.mwe.com
Email: graduate.recruitment@mwe.com

Partners 602 (worldwide)
Associate Lawyers & Other Fee-earners 540(worldwide)
Total Trainees 8
Contact Emma Doran
Method of application Apply online at www.mwe.com
Selection procedure Assessment day, written test and one interview with Partners
Closing date for September 2012/ March 2013 30 July 2010
Training Salary 1st year £39,000 2nd year £43,000
Post-qualification Salary £75,000

Firm profile

McDermott Will & Emery UK LLP is a leading international law firm with offices in Boston, Brussels, Chicago, Düsseldorf, Houston, London, Los Angeles, Miami, Milan, Munich, New York, Orange County, Rome, San Diego, Silicon Valley and Washington DC. The firm's client base includes some of the world's leading financial institutions, largest corporations, mid-cap businesses, and individuals. The firm represents more than 60% of the companies in the Fortune 100 in addition to clients in the FTSE 100 and FTSE 250. Rated as one of the leading firms in The American Lawyer's Top 100, by a number of indicators, including gross revenues and profits per Partner.

London Office: The London office was founded in 1998. It is already recognised as being in the top 10 of the 100 US law firms operating in London by the legal media. The firm has around 80 lawyers at present in London, almost all of whom are English-qualified. The firm provides business oriented legal advice to multinational and national corporates, financial institutions, investment banks and private clients. Most of the firm's partners were head of practice at their former firms and are recognised as leaders in their respective fields by the most respected professional directories and market commentators.

Main areas of work

Banking and finance, corporate (including M&A and private equity), dispute resolution, employment (including pensions), energy, EU competition, european telecom, media and technology, information technology, insolvency and restructuring, intellectual property, media and technology, securitisation and structured finance, tax, US securities. London is the hub for the firm's European expansions and the firm coordinates legal advice from here for all multinational clients across Europe and elsewhere.

Trainee profile

The firm is looking for the brightest, best and most entrepreneurial trainees. You will need to convince the firm that you have made a deliberate choice.

Training environment

The primary focus is to provide a practical foundation for your career with the firm. You will experience four seats over the two-year period and a deliberately small number of trainees means that the firm is able to provide a degree of flexibility in tailoring seats to the individual. Trainees get regular support and feedback.

Benefits

Private medical and dental insurance, life assurance, permanent health insurance, season ticket loan, subsidised gym membership, employee assistance programme, 25 days holiday.

Sponsorship & awards

GDL and LPC funding and maintenance grant.

McGrigors LLP

5 Old Bailey, London, EC4M 7BA
Tel: (020) 7054 2500
Email: graduate.recruitment@mcgrigors.com
Website: www.mcgrigors.com

Firm profile

McGrigors has established itself as one of the UK's most dynamic full-service law firms with a team of over 700 people working from offices in London, Edinburgh, Manchester, Aberdeen, Belfast and Glasgow, making it the only firm to operate across all three UK jurisdictions. The firm's work covers the full range of practice areas with firm-wide specialisms in a range of sectors including energy, infrastructure, house-building and regeneration. At the time of writing, McGrigors' client list comprises 35% of the FTSE100 and 40 AIM-listed companies. The firm works with everyone from multinationals to government and local authorities, as well as ambitious SMEs in the public and private sectors.

McGrigors prides itself on its client-friendly approach to business. The firm understands that today's lawyers should be more than just interpreters of the law; they should be commercially-minded business partners. Their lawyers work hard to understand the commercial goals its clients have in mind and then find the most pragmatic ways to achieve them. The firm also recognises that strong relationships are at the heart of good client service; the firm's lawyers invest time in building strong client relations to develop an intuitive understanding of a client's priorities and to ensure that working with McGrigors is a straightforward and enjoyable experience.

Main areas of work

Banking, Projects & Procurement: This team includes leading specialists in finance, infrastructure (including construction) and energy law.
Corporate: A dynamic team with in-depth experience of all kinds of public and private M&A work and renowned capital markets expertise with a particular focus on AIM.
Employment & Pensions: This UK-wide team acts as standalone employment and pensions law adviser to some of the UK's largest businesses as well as providing employment law support as part of the firm's transactional work.
Energy: The team provides breadth and depth, not only in covering all facets of the energy industry from oil & gas to renewables and nuclear, but in covering every practice area.
Litigation & Dispute Resolution: This well-reputed team tackles the full range of commercial disputes with notable specialisms in contentious construction and health & safety advice.
Tax Disputes & Investigations: A market-leading player, McGrigors provides a cutting-edge service to companies and individuals in dispute with the tax authorities.
Real Estate: The team is a leader when it comes to transactions involving property development projects, brownfield and waterfront developments, structured property finance, landlord and tenant work, portfolio management and advising the social housing sector.
Regeneration: One of the first dedicated regeneration teams with the expertise to deliver advice to both public and private sector stakeholders and joint-venture vehicles on the full range of requirements from financing and structuring to managing infrastructure and real estate aspects.

Trainee profile

People who have drive, ability and confidence. Trainees need to prove that they are interested in business, not simply black letter law. In addition, trainees are highly visible throughout the firm and are expected to get actively involved from both a business and social aspect.

Benefits

The firm offers private medical cover, life assurance, pension, 35 days annual leave (including bank holidays) and season ticket loans.

Sponsorship

CPE and LPC fees are paid plus an annual maintenance grant of £6,000 in England. The firm also provides shortfall funding up to £1,000 for those Scottish trainees who receive no or partial funding.

Partners 84*
Assistant Solicitors 248*
Total Trainees 64*
*denotes firm wide

Contact
Margaret-Ann Roy (Scotland & Belfast)
Nadine Harwood (England)

Method of application
Online application

Selection procedure
Half day assessment including interview, presentation and aptitude tests
closing date
30 Jan 2010 for summer scheme
30 July 2010 for 2012 training contracts

Application
No. of training contracts p.a.
12-15 in London
15-20 in Scotland
% interviewed - 15%
Required degree grade realistic estimate of 2.1 or higher

Training
Salary
London 1st year £32,000
         2nd year £37,000
Scotland 1st year £18,000
         2nd year £21,000
Holiday 35 days including bank holidays

Post-qualification
Salary
London (2009/2010) £56,000
Scotland (2009/2010) £31,500
% offered job in 2009 46%

Overseas/regional offices
London, Edinburgh, Glasgow, Aberdeen, Manchester, Belfast & a satellite office in the Falklands -----

Memery Crystal LLP

44 Southampton Buildings, London, WC2A 1AP
Tel: (020) 7242 5905 Fax: (020) 7242 2058
Email: hcowen@memerycrystal.com   Web: www.memerycrystal.com

Firm profile
Memery Crystal LLP is a medium sized city law firm that has grown from strength to strength and is now one of the UK's leading law firms in its specialist areas. The firm's ethos is that people come first, whether they are clients, members of the firm or fellow advisers. This philosophy has enabled the firm to bring out the best in the lawyers who work here and those to whom the firm provides a service have recognised Memery Crystal through numerous awards.

Main areas of work
The firm's main practice areas are company/commercial, dispute resolution and real estate. Within these areas, specialist groups deal with corporate finance, employment, property litigation, tax, insolvency, construction, insurance, corporate crime, regulatory law, digital technology and e-commerce.

Trainee profile
The firm is looking for candidates who have achieved a high standard of education, show a willingness to take on responsibility, are commercially aware, respond to challenges, have the drive and ambition to succeed, and are seeking fulfilment and recognition in their chosen profession.

Training environment
During your training you will have a balance of formal and practical training. Your development will be closely monitored with appraisals carried out every 3 months. You will sit either with a Partner, associate or senior assistant who will monitor your progress on a regular basis. During the course of your training contract, there will be a regular rotation of seats within the firm.

Benefits
The firm provides a bonus scheme, life assurance, health cover, travel insurance, season ticket loan, group pension plan subsidised gym membership and cycle to work scheme.

Vacation placements
There are two one-week vacation places which take place at Easter. Applications should be made via the website by the 31 January 2010.

Sponsorship & awards
Funding for LPC and GDL fees is provided.

Partners 21
Assistant Solicitors 25
Total Trainees 6

Contact
Helen Cowen

Method of application
Online application form

Selection procedure
First interview followed by assessment centre closing date for 2012
31 July 2010 for training

Application
Training contracts p.a. 4
Applications p.a. 180
Required degree grade 2:1

Training
Salary
1st year (2008) £26,500
2nd year (2008) £29,500
Holiday entitlement
25 days p.a.
% of trainees with a non-law degree 40%

Post-qualification
Salary (2008) £54,000

Michelmores LLP

Woodwater House, Pynes Hill, Exeter, EX2 5WR
Tel: (01392) 688 688   Fax: (01392) 360 563   Email: kjt@michelmores.com
Clarges House, 6-12 Clarges Street, London, W1J 8DH
Tel: (020) 7242 5905 Fax: (020) 7242 2058 Website: www.michelmores.com

Partners 41
Total Staff (inc. Partners) 310
Assistant solicitors 76

Contact
Kim Tomlinson
(kjt@michelmores.com)

Method of application
Online application form

Selection procedure
assessment days

Closing date for 2012
1 July 2010

Application
Training contracts p.a.8
Applications p.a. 200
% interviewed - 15%
Required degree grade 2:1
(occasional exceptions)

Training
Salary
1st year (2009) £20,000
2nd year (2009) £21,000
Holiday entitlement
28 days p.a.
% of trainees with a non-law degree 10%
number of seats available abroad 0 (although occasional foreign secondments available)

Post-qualification
Salary (2009) £33,000
% offered job 100%

Firm profile

Michelmores is a dynamic London and Exeter based full service law firm, providing first class service to a wide range of local, national and international clients, including several central government departments. The firm has an established track record of attracting quality recruits at every level and the firm's trainee solicitor retention rate is excellent. Combining state of the art technology in a new purpose built building with a management style which promotes the highest professional standards and an informal atmosphere, the firm has created a great place to work capable of attracting the very best lawyers. The partnership has retained a collegiate style which helps to foster a happy law firm renowned for the enthusiasm of its lawyers, from Managing Partner down to first year trainee. The firm has just been included in The Lawyer 'Rising 50' list of law firms nationally seen as rising stars, and is one of the fastest growing law firms in the country.

Main areas of work

The firm has a good reputation for its work in company commercial law, dispute resolution and commercial property while the firm's Private Client Group (including the firm's Family Team) continues to thrive. The firm also has specialist teams in areas such as projects/PFI, technology, media and communications, construction and medical negligence.

Trainee profile

The firm welcomes applications from both law and non-law graduates. The firm is looking for trainees with a strong academic background who are team players and who genuinely want to share in the firm's success and help it to continue to grow and improve. Common sense and strong inter-personal skills are pre-requisites.

Training environment

As a Michelmores' trainee you will usually spend 6 months in each of the firm's main practice groups (business, property, private client and litigation). You will work closely with your supervisor in each department and will be pleasantly surprised at the level of client exposure, responsibility and client involvement. The firm's trainees are given both the opportunity to handle work themselves (while under supervision) and to work as part of a team. The quality of the firm's training is high. You will be expected to attend relevant in-house training sessions on areas such as marketing, IT skills and time management, and will also be encouraged to attend external conferences, seminars and marketing events. The firm offers the opportunity of spending part of your training contract in the London office.

Sponsorship & benefits

Optional private healthcare, permanent health insurance, payment of LPC fees, subsidised staff restaurant, subsidised gym with fitness assessments and personal training, free parking. Prize for first class degrees and distinction in LPC.

Vacation placements

The firm runs an annual vacation placement scheme in July for one week. The online application form is available on the website. Completed forms should arrive by 28 February 2010.

Mills & Reeve

112 Hills Road, Cambridge CB2 1PH
Tel: (01223) 222336 Fax: (01223) 355848
Email: graduate.recruitment@mills-reeve.com   Web: www.mills-reeve.com/graduates

Firm profile
Mills & Reeve act for commercial organisations; ranging from PLCs to multinationals to start-ups, as well as more than 70 universities and colleges, more than 100 healthcare trusts and NHS bodies, and over 65 local government institutions. The firm also has a national centre of excellence in private client services.

Mills & Reeve has offices in Birmingham, Cambridge, Leeds, London, Manchester and Norwich.

For the sixth year running Mills & Reeve has been listed in the Sunday Times Top 100 Best Companies to Work For, which recognises that the firm puts people at the centre of its business.

Main areas of work
A full-service law firm. Core sectors are: corporate and commercial, banking and finance, technology, insurance, real estate, healthcare, education and private client.

Trainee profile
The firm welcomes applications from both law and non-law disciplines. Candidates should already have or expect a 2.1 degree or equivalent. Trainee solicitors should display energy, maturity, initiative, enthusiasm for their career, a professional approach to work and be ready to accept early responsibility.

Training environment
Trainees complete six four-month seats and are recruited to the Birmingham, Cambridge and Norwich offices. Trainees can temporarily move to another office, to complete a seat not practised in their base office. The firm will support the move with an accommodation allowance.

Trainees work alongside a partner or senior solicitor. Regular feedback is given to aid development. Performance is assessed by a formal review at the end of each seat.

The firm encourages early responsibility. Training is supported by a full induction, in-house training programme developed by the firm's team of professional support lawyers and the professional skills course (PSC).

Job opportunities on qualification are good and a high proportion of trainees remain with the firm.

Benefits
Life assurance, a contributory pension scheme, 25 days holiday, bonus scheme, sports and social club, subsidised staff restaurants and catering facilities, season ticket loan, discounted rate for private medical insurance, corporate gym membership. The firm runs a flexible benefits scheme.

Vacation placements
Applications for two week placements during the summer must be received by 31 January 2010.

Sponsorship & awards
The firm pays the full costs of the CPE/GDL and LPC fees and a maintenance grant during the GDL and LPC.

Partners 90
Assistant Solicitors 354
Total Trainees 46

Contact
Fiona Medlock

Method of application
Online

Selection procedure
Normally one day assessment centre

Closing date for 2012
31 July 2010 for training contracts
31st January 2010 for work placements

Application
Training contracts p.a. 20
Applications p.a. Approx 650
% interviewed p.a. 10%
Required degree grade 2:1

Training
Salary
1st year £23,000
2nd year £24,000
Holiday entitlement
25 days p.a.
% of trainees with a non-law degree 40%

Post-qualification
% of trainees offered job on qualification tbc

Mishcon de Reya

Summit House, 12 Red Lion Square, London WC1R 4QD
Tel: (020) 7440 7000 Fax: (020) 7430 0691
Email: recruitment@mishcon.com
Website: www.mishcon.com

Partners 53
Assistant Solicitors 92
Total Trainees 22

Contact
Ann-Marie Comer, HR Trainee Advisor

Method of application
Online application form

Closing date for 2012
31 July 2010

Application
Training contracts p.a. 8-12
Applications p.a. 1,000+
% interviewed p.a. 5%
Required degree grade 2:1

Training
Salary
1st year £32,000
Holiday entitlement
25 days p.a.
Occasional secondments available

Firm profile

Mishcon de Reya, founded in 1937 is a London based law firm, offering services to companies and individuals. The firm offers every legal service and its expertise covers five areas: analysing risk, protection of assets, managing wealth, resolving disputes and building business.

Main areas of work

Organised internally into four main departments: corporate and employment, dispute resolution, real estate and family, the firm also has a growing number of specialist groups which include: art; betting and gaming; banking and finance; defamation; fraud; immigration; insolvency; IP; private client and public advocacy.

Trainee profile

The firm's trainees are typically high-achieving and intelligent with good interpersonal skills. Strength of character and ability to think laterally are also important.

Training environment

Trainees have the opportunity to gain experience, skills and knowledge from across the firm in four different seats (each six months). These include both contentious and non contentious work. Because of the relatively few training contracts offered, trainees can be exposed to high quality work with early responsibility. Trainees are supported with a training and development programme, in addition to the professional Skills Course. Trainee performance is monitored closely and trainees can expect to receive regular feedback in addition to mid-seat and end-of-seat appraisals.

Benefits

Medical and travel insurance, EAP, subsidised gym membership, season ticket loan, group income protection, life assurance and pension, in-house doctor.

Vacation placements

Places for 2010: 15; Duration: 2 weeks; Expenses: £250 p.w.; Closing Date: 31st January 2010.

Sponsorship & awards

GDL and LPC funding with annual allowance.

Muckle LLP

Time Central, 32 Gallowgate, Newcastle upon Tyne, NE1 4BF
Tel: (0191) 211 7777   Fax: (0191) 211 7788
Email: nsingh@muckle-llp.com   Website: www.muckle-llp.com

Firm profile
Muckle LLP is a leading commercial law firm in the North East of England. The firm has an excellent client base of successful private and public companies, property developers, financial institutions, public sector and educational organisations, which recognise that its innovative commercial skills are a major benefit in enhancing its service delivery to them.

Main areas of work
The firm is divided into five main groups – commercial, property, employment, dispute resolution and private client. The specialist teams within these groups are: banking, business restructuring and insolvency, commercial services, corporate finance, intellectual property and technology, property investment and development, planning, construction, employment, education and private client.

Trainee profile
The firm recruits four trainees a year. The firm is looking to recruit talented individuals who can demonstrate their enthusiasm and desire to become business advisers and a commitment to building their career in the North East. Trainees must have good academic qualifications and communication skills and must be able to work in a team and also independently.

Training environment
The firm runs an excellent training programme that focuses on the trainees' legal, IT, management and business development skills. During your training contract you will experience training within four of the firm's six main service group areas: corporate, commercial, property, employment, dispute resolution and private client. Training is a combination of on-the-job experience, partner mentoring as well as in-house and external courses. Trainees are encouraged to join the social, charitable or graduate recruitment committees.

Benefits
25 days holiday a year and flexible holiday option; pension after six months service; permanent health insurance; life assurance; corporate discounts; wellbeing initiative; salary sacrifice schemes (eg public transport discount).

Sponsorship & awards
LPC fees are paid subject to eligibility and the firm offers a competitive maintenance allowance.

Partners 20
Fee earners 43
Total Trainees 7

Contact
Neena Singh, Graduate Recruitment Co-ordinator 0191 211 7987

Method of application
Apply online via our website www.muckle-llp.com

Selection procedure
Interviews and an assessment day

Closing date for 2010 summer vacation scheme
Tuesday 9th February 2010

Closing date for 2012 training contracts
Saturday 31st July 2010

Application
Training contracts p.a. 80-100
Applications p.a. 120-130
% interviewed p.a. 25%
Required degree grade 2:1

Training
Salary
Starting salary £20,000 with regular reviews throughout training contract
Holiday entitlement
25 days holiday a year and flexible holiday option

Post-qualification
Salary
Salary between £30,000 and £37,000
100% trainees offered job on qualification

Office
Only Newcastle upon Tyne

Mundays LLP

Cedar House, 78 Portsmouth Road, Cobham, Surrey, KT11 1AN
Tel: (01932) 590500   Fax: (01932) 590220
Email: hr@mundays.co.uk
Website: www.mundays.co.uk

Partners 26	
Fee earners 37	
Total Trainees 6	
Contact	
HR Manager	
Method of application	
Online	
Selection procedure	
1 day Assessment Centre, 1 day individual interviews and legal scenario	
Closing date for 2012	
31st August 2010	
Application	
Training contracts p.a. 3	
Applications p.a. 150	
% assessed and interviewed p.a. 13%	
Required degree grade 2:1	
Overseas/ regional offices	
Cobham office (Surrey)	

Firm profile

Mundays is one of Surrey's leading law practices, operating from modern offices in Cobham, with easy access to London and the M25. The practice has grown significantly over the past 10 years. Many of the firm's lawyers have worked in the City but have chosen to relocate to a practice where the firm aims to offer a service as good as (if not better than) competitors in London at more economic rates, while enabling its lawyers to achieve a better work/life balance. The firm offers its diverse range of clients (both corporate and private) comprehensive, responsive and commercial advice, with separate departments working closely together as appropriate.

Main areas of work

The firm is divided into five principal departments: property, corporate/commercial, dispute resolution, private wealth and family. Within these departments we have specialisms in banking, employment, construction, insolvency and intellectual property.

Trainee profile

Candidates will need to demonstrate their confidence, ability to communicate and personality. They are also required to have (or expect to receive) at least a 2.1 degree (applications from law and non-law graduates are welcome) and 3 A levels (AAB or better). We are looking for well-rounded individuals who are keen to develop their career with us as trainees and beyond.

Training environment

At Mundays there is a relaxed, informal working style; Fee-earners have a willingness to share their knowledge and experience in the belief that, with hard work, trainees of today are potentially the firm's partners of the future.

Trainees typically spend periods of six months in each of the corporate/commercial, property and dispute resolution departments; where they spend the fourth period will depend on whether they wish to gain experience of another specialist area. Trainees are encouraged to take on responsibility from the beginning of their training through direct experience of dealing with matters and working alongside fee-earners. Progress is closely monitored and training given to reflect the needs of individual trainees.

Benefits

25 Days annual holiday; Death in Service Scheme at 3x Salary on joining; Pension Scheme at three, four or five percent matching after successful completion of three month probation; Private Healthcare Scheme – eligible to join after successful completion of three month probation; Childcare Voucher Scheme; Cycle to Work Scheme.

Vacation placements

Not offered at this time.

Sponsorship & awards

Mundays will make a contribution of £7,500 towards the cost of the LPC and will offer a maintenance grant of £4000 paid at month 2 and month 7 of LPC.

Nabarro LLP

Lacon House, 84 Theobald's Road, London WC1X 8RW
Tel: (020) 7524 6000 Fax: (020) 7524 6524
Email: graduateinfo@nabarro.com
Website: www.nabarro.com

Firm profile
Nabarro is a major UK law firm renowned for its positive, practical approach. The firm operates across a number of industry sectors and legal disciplines and aims to deliver the highest quality legal advice as clearly and concisely as possible.

Main areas of work
Corporate and commercial law; real estate; IP/IT; projects; PPP; PFI; pensions; employment; dispute resolution; construction and engineering; planning; environmental law; banking, finance and restructuring; insolvency and tax.

Trainee profile
The firm is committed to making the most of diverse skills, expertise, experience, attitudes and backgrounds. Accordingly, there is no typical Nabarro trainee. You will need a strong academic record and, in keeping with clients' needs, the firm also wants you to demonstrate a flexibility of thinking and a flair for creative problem solving that will allow you to provide its clients with the best advice and assistance. The firm is also looking for students who demonstrate a proactive approach, strong interpersonal, entrepreneurial and team working skills and drive and enthusiasm.

Training environment
Trainees undertake six four-month seats to ensure maximum exposure to the firm's core practice areas, as well as the opportunity to spend time in more specialist seats or possibly in Brussels or on secondment to a client. Your development and future seats are discussed with you half way through each seat.

Benefits
Private medical insurance, 26 days holidays, pension, season ticket loan, subsidised restaurant, subsidised gym membership. Trainee salaries are reviewed annually.

Vacation placements
Places for 2010: 65

Duration: 3 weeks between mid June and mid August. Closing date: 8 February 2010.

Nabarro's vacation scheme is an award winning three week scheme offering a comprehensive and structured programme of events. You will be based in one department with an allocated supervisor and buddy who will ensure you gain a good mix of work and an excellent insight into life at Nabarro. The firm recruits the majority of its trainees through its summer scheme.

Sponsorship & awards
Full fees paid for the GDL and LPC plus a maintenance grant: LPC London: £7000, regions £6000. GDL London: £6000, regions £5000. The firm pays full fees retrospectively if you have completed your GDL/ LPC

Partners 130+
Assistant Solicitors 420+
Total Trainees 70

Contact
Jane Drew

Method of application
Online only

Selection procedure
Assessment Day (including interview)

Closing date for 2012
31 July 2010

Application
Training contracts p.a. 35
Applications p.a. 1,600
Required degree grade 2:1

Training
Salary
1st year (2009)
London £37,000
Sheffield £25,000
2nd year (2008)
London £40,000
Sheffield £28,000
Holiday entitlement 26 days

Post-qualification
Salary (2009)
London £57,000
Sheffield £38,000
(reviewed annually)

Overseas offices
Brussels. In Europe the firm has an alliance with GSK Stockmann & Kollegen in Germany, August & Debouzy in France and Nunziante Magrone in Italy.

Norton Rose

3 More London Riverside, London, SE1 2AQ
Tel: (020) 7444 2113 Fax: (020) 7283 6500
Email: grad.recruitment@nortonrose.com
Website: www.nortonrose.com/graduate

Firm profile

Norton Rose LLP is a constituent part of Norton Rose Group, a leading international legal practice offering a full business law services from offices across Europe, the Middle East and Asia. Knowing how Clients' businesses work and understanding what drives their industries is fundamental to the firm. Norton Rose lawyers share industry knowledge and sector expertise across borders, enabling the firm to support clients anywhere in the world. The firm is strong in corporate finance, financial institutions, energy and infrastructure, transport and technology.

Norton Rose Group comprises Norton Rose LLP and its affiliates and has over 1000 lawyers operating from offices in Abu Dhabi, Amsterdam, Athens, Bahrain, Bangkok, Beijing, Brussels, Dubai, Frankfurt, Hong Kong, Jakarta*, London, Milan, Moscow, Munich, Paris, Piraeus, Prague, Rome, Shanghai, Singapore Tokyo and Warsaw.

Main areas of work

Corporate finance; banking; dispute resolution; property, planning and environmental; taxation; competition and regulatory; employment, pensions and incentives; intellectual property and technology.

Trainee profile

Successful candidates will be commercially aware, focused, ambitious and team-orientated. High intellect and international awareness are a priority, and language skills are appreciated.

Training environment

Norton Rose LLP operates an innovative six-seat system. The first four seats (16 months) include one seat in each of the practice's core departments – corporate finance, banking and dispute resolution – plus an optional seat in one of the firm's other, non-core departments – employment, pensions and incentives, tax, competition and EC, intellectual property and technology, or property, planning and environmental. The remaining eight months can be spent in the department in which you wish to qualify, or you can visit a different practice area for four months to help you to decide, and spend the last four months in your qualification seat. Alternatively, from your third seat onwards, you can elect to spend four months in one of the practice's international offices or apply for a client secondment. The practice's flexible seat system makes the transition from trainee to qualified solicitor as smooth as possible. The system has won the practice's trainees' approval, and from their point of view, develops associates with the adaptability and expertise the firm needs for its future.

Benefits

Life assurance, private health insurance (optional), season ticket loan, cycle to work scheme, subsidised gym membership, employee assistance programme, subsidised staff restaurant, eligibility to join the firm's group personal pension scheme.

Placement programmes

Places for 2009: 20 Winter Scheme - duration: two weeks; Places for 2010: 40 Summer Scheme - duration: four weeks; Remuneration: £250 p.w.

Closing Date: 31 October 2009 for Winter Scheme; 31 January 2010 for Summer Scheme. Approximately six open days per year are also held each year.

*With effect from 1 January 2010, Deacons Australia, a leading Australian law firm with offices in Sydney, Melbourne, Brisbane, Perth and Canberra and teams in Singapore and Jakarta, will join Norton Rose Group. The enlarged Group will have over 1800 lawyers in 29 offices worldwide, 700 of whom will be based in Asia Pacific, and will form one of the best-resourced legal practices in the Asia Pacific region.

Partners 274*
Assistant Solicitors 787*
Total Trainees 117
*denotes worldwide figures

Contact
Karen Potts

Method of application
Online only

Selection procedure
Interview and group exercise

Closing date for 2012/12
31 July 2010

Application
Training contracts p.a. 55
Applications p.a. 2,500+ %
interviewed p.a. 9% Required degree grade 2:1

Training
Salary
1st year £35,700
2nd year £40,200
Holiday entitlement 25days % of trainees with a non-law degree p.a. 40% No. of seats available abroad p.a. 22 (per seat move)

Overseas offices
Abu Dhabi, Amsterdam, Athens, Bahrain, Bangkok, Beijing, Brussels, Dubai, Frankfurt, Hong Kong, Jakarta,* London, Milan, Moscow, Munich, Paris, Piraeus, Prague, Riyadh,* Rome, Shanghai, Singapore, Tokyo, Warsaw
*Associated office

Olswang

90 High Holborn, London WC1V 6XX
Tel: (020) 7067 3000 Fax: (020) 7067 3999
Email: traineesolicitor@olswang.com
Website: www.olswang.com/traineesolicitor

Firm profile
Olswang is a leading law firm renowned for its ground-breaking work in the technology, media, communications and real estate industries. Founded in 1981, the firm has grown to a staff of more than 600, including over 90 partners and four European offices.

The firm's sector focus supports the wealth of knowledge and interest among fee earners and attracts a distinct breadth of clients from across industries. The firm represents recognised brands and key industry players, as well as smaller, pioneering companies. These include Brixton plc, eBay, Guardian Media Group plc, ITV, Ladbrokes, MTV Networks Europe, Sony BMG, Tottenham Hotspur FC, UBS, Vectura Group plc and Warner Music International.

The firm continues to be acknowledged as a leading practice in many of its core areas. Olswang has been voted M&A Law Firm of the Year 2008 (M&A Awards), Corporate Team of the Year - Mid Markets 2008 (The Lawyer Awards) and TMT Team of the Year 2009 (Legal Business Awards).

The firm's strong management team and wider partnership is dedicated to its people and is committed to helping everyone realise their own potential. Olswang is proud to be ranked as a top 100 UK employer in the Sunday Times 100 Best Companies to Work for 2009, an achievement gained for the fifth year running.

Main areas of work
The firm's principal practice areas include: corporate; employment; EU and competition; finance; intellectual property; litigation and arbitration; media transactions; real estate; tax; and technology transactions.

Trainee profile
Being a trainee at Olswang is both demanding and rewarding. The firm is interested in hearing from individuals with a 2:1 degree and above or equivalent, exceptional drive and relevant commercial experience. In addition, it is absolutely critical that trainees fit well into the Olswang environment which is challenging, busy, individualistic, meritocratic and fun.

Training environment
Olswang wants to help trainees match their expectations and needs with those of the firm. Training consists of four six-month seats in the corporate, commercial, litigation, finance or real estate groups. You will be assigned a mentor, usually a partner, to assist and advise you throughout your training contract. In-house lectures supplement general training and three-monthly appraisals assess development.

Benefits
Immediately: life cover, medical cover, dental scheme, subsidised gym membership, subsidised staff restaurant, season ticket loan. After six months: pension contributions. After 12 months: PHI.

Vacation placements
Places for 2010: June & July; Duration: 2 weeks; Remuneration: £275 p.w.; 17 students per scheme; Closing Date: 31 January 2010.

Sponsorship & awards
LPC and GDL fees paid in full. Maintenance grant of £7,000 (inside London), £6,500 (outside).

Partners 95
Fee-earners 225
Total Trainees 48

Contact
Sarmini Ghosh
Trainee solicitor recruitment officer

Method of application
Online

Selection procedure
Commercial case study, interview, psychometric test and written exercises

Closing date for 2012
31 July 2010

Application
Training contracts p.a. 24
Applications p.a. 2,000
% interviewed p.a. 4%
Required degree grade 2:1

Training
Salary
1st year (2009) £35,000
2nd year (2009) £39,000
Holiday entitlement 25 days
% of trainees with a non-law degree p.a. 50%

Post-qualification
Salary (2009) £58,000

Overseas offices
Brussels, Berlin

O'Melveny & Myers LLP

Warwick Court, 5 Paternoster Square, London, EC4M 7DX
Tel: (020) 7088 0000 Fax: (020) 7088 0001
Email: graduate-recruitment@omm.com Website: www.omm.com

Firm profile

A top 20 global law firm staffed by over 1,000 lawyers in 14 offices, O'Melveny's clients include many of the world's largest financial institutions, leading private equity houses, investment banks and corporates. The London office is known for its entrepreneurial leadership and its commitment to excellence which underpin its approach to recruitment. The expertise of the team can also draw on the extensive reservoir of know-how and experience within the firm's offices around the world.

Main areas of work

The London office was effectively re-launched in 2004 and offers a full service transactions practice with a focus on private equity fund formation and deals and supported by leading tax, acquisition finance, regulatory, competition/ anti-trusts and IP lawyers. In July 2007 it also established a litigation and arbitration capacity with the hiring of a leading team from Watson, Farley & Williams. Virtually all of our lawyers in London are UK qualified with most having joined from Magic Circle and other leading UK and international law firms.

Trainee profile

The London office is seeking to recruit up to four high calibre graduates for training contracts each year. Successful candidates must be ambitious, have proven academic ability, high levels of drive and determination, good team working skills and sound commercial awareness. The office has a strong entrepreneurial and collegiate style and to date, the majority of our trainees have remained with the firm on qualification.

Training environment

The firm aims to take into account individual preferences when tailoring the training programme subject to the trainee completing the core competencies and subject to the demands of the business. Trainees will usually complete seats with partners or senior lawyers in each of our corporate, finance and funds formation practices and will also be able to obtain contentious experience in our litigation/arbitration practice and possibly in our competition/anti-trust practice (based partly in London and partly in our Brussels office). There will also be opportunities to work with our tax, IP practitioners. The firm has also initiated trainee secondments to its Hong Kong, Singapore, Tokyo and Brussels offices. The firm encourages trainees to be proactive and take responsibility at an early stage. As a firm, O'Melveny & Myers places great importance on training for its lawyers at all levels which it views as key to the firm's ability to offer high quality legal services to its clients and so trainees will participate in the legal and non-legal skills training programme established by the London office. The Professional Skills Course is run by an external provider. Progress of each trainee is monitored with mid and end of seat reviews and feedback is given throughout each seat.

Vacation schemes

The office does run a series of vacation schemes, currently for 2 weeks at a time between June and September. For applications for 2010 Summer vacation schemes, please apply by 1 February 2010. The application process for places on vacation schemes is managed alongside the application procedure for training contracts.

Benefits

5% non contributory pension, travel insurance, private medical insurance, subsidised gym membership, death in service benefit four x annual salary, holiday entitlement 25 days, Permanent Health insurance.

Sponsorship & awards

GDL/LPC tuition fees incurred post recruitment plus a maintenance grant during the GDL/LPC course (currently £7,000 per annum).

Partners 10
Other fee-earners 25+
Trainees 9

Contact
Nicola Matthews
Human Resources Manager

Method of application
www.cvmailuk.com

Selection procedure
Interview process
Closing date for 2012
31 July 2010

Training
Salary
1st year (2008): £39,000
2nd year (2008): £42,500
These are current rates which are reviewed annually

Post-qualification
Market rate

Overseas offices/ regional offices
Beijing, Brussels, Century City, Hong Kong, Los Angeles, Newport Beach, New York, San Francisco, Shanghai, Singapore, Silicon Valley, Tokyo and Washington D.C.

Osborne Clarke

2 Temple Back East, Temple Quay, Bristol BS1 6EG
Tel: (0117) 917 3484
Email: trainee.recruitment@osborneclarke.com
Website: www.osborneclarke.com

Firm profile
Osborne Clarke is one of Europe's most respected and dynamic law firms. The firm's success is the result of delivering excellent business-focused legal advice in an energetic, straightforward and efficient way.

Osborne Clarke advises market leading and high performing organisations on their UK and international legal needs from its City, national and European offices and the Osborne Clarke Alliance.

The firm's main areas of expertise include corporate, finance and property transactions and the full spectrum of business law services, including commercial contracts, employment, pensions, outsourcing and dispute resolution.

Main areas of work
Banking, corporate, employment, pension & incentives, litigation/dispute resolution, property, commercial and tax.

Trainee profile
If you are a highly driven individual with good analytical, communication and organisational skills the firm would like to hear from you. Commercial acumen and the ability to build relationships with clients and colleagues are essential and foreign language skills are an advantage. Ideally, candidates should have grades A - B at A Level or equivalent, as well as a minimum 2:1 degree grade in any discipline. Applications are welcomed from candidates seeking a career change who can demonstrate strong commercial skills.

Training environment
The focus at Osborne Clarke is on developing a high performance culture and the firm's aim is to develop trainees into legal business advisers. The Osborne Clarke trainee development programme offers legal, management and business skills training to develop the professional skills needed to progress as a lawyer in the firm.

The training contract is made up of four seats, each lasting six months in four different practice areas. Three of these seats are usually corporate, property and litigation. Trainees work closely with their training supervisors and fee earners in the department and can expect a high level of responsibility and client contact at an early stage in their training contract. Regular reviews and coaching sessions are held to ensure that trainees are reaching their potential. There are also opportunities for trainees to spend a seat in one of the firm's other offices or on a client secondment.

Benefits
25 days holiday entitlement, life assurance, private medical insurance, permanent health insurance, employer's pension contributions, profit share scheme, interest free season ticket loan, gym discount.

Vacation schemes
The firm's two-week vacation scheme gives candidates the opportunity to experience life and work at Osborne Clarke, and runs throughout the summer in all of the firms UK offices

Sponsorship & awards
The firm provides full funding for GDL and LPC tuition fees plus a maintenance grant for sponsored candidates.

Partners 110
Lawyers 250
Trainees 39

Contact
Zoe Reid, Trainee Recruitment Officer

Method of application
Online application form

Selection procedure
Assessment centre comprises of group exercises, psychometric test, partner interview, written exercise

Closing date for 2012
31 July 2010

Application
Training contracts p.a. 20
Applications p.a. 1,000
% interviewed p.a. 12%
Required degree grade: 2:1, any discipline

Training
1st year Competitive
2nd year Competitive
Holiday entitlement 25 days
% of trainees with a non-law degree p.a. 43%

Post-qualification
Competitive

Offices
Bristol, Cologne, London, Munich, Silicon Valley, Thames Valley

Pannone LLP

123 Deansgate, Manchester M3 2BU
Tel: (0161) 909 3000 Fax: (0161) 909 4444
Email: graduaterecruitment@pannone.co.uk
Website: www.pannone.com

Firm profile
A high-profile Manchester firm continuing to undergo rapid growth. The firm prides itself on offering a full range of legal services to a diverse client base which is split almost equally between private and commercial clients. The firm was the first to be awarded the quality standard ISO 9001 and is a founder member of Pannone Law Group – Europe's first integrated international law group. Pannone was voted 3rd in the Sunday Times '100 Best Companies to Work For' in 2009 and is the highest placed law firm in the survey for the sixth year running.

Main areas of work
Commercial litigation 16%; personal injury 25%; corporate 13%; commercial property 8%; family 8%; clinical negligence 6%; private client 5%; employment 5%; construction 3%; regulatory 6%; residential property 5%.

Trainee profile
Selection criteria include a high level of academic achievement, teamwork, organisation and communication skills, a wide range of interests and a connection with the North West.

Training environment
An induction course helps trainees adjust to working life, and covers the firm's quality procedures and good practice. Regular trainee seminars cover the work of other departments within the firm, legal developments and practice. Additional departmental training sessions focus in more detail on legal and procedural matters in that department. Four seats of six months are spent in various departments and trainees' progress is monitored regularly. Trainees have easy access to support and guidance on any matters of concern. Work is tackled with gusto here, but so are the many social gatherings that take place.

Vacation placements
Places for 2010: 88; Duration: 1 week; Remuneration: None; Closing Date: Easter 19th February 2010, Summer 25 June 2010. Recruitment for training contracts is primarily through vacation placements.

Sponsorship & awards
Half grant for LPC + fees at The College of Law, Manchester.

Partners 110
Assistant Solicitors 103
Total Trainees 36

Contact
Amy Bell

Method of application
Online only

Selection procedure
Individual interview, second interview comprises a tour of the firm & informal lunch

Closing date for 2012
31st July 2010

Application
Training contracts p.a. 15
Applications p.a. 1,300
% interviewed p.a. 7.3%
Required degree grade 2:1

Training
Salary
1st year (2009) £23,000
2nd year (2009) £23,000
Holiday entitlement 23 days
% of trainees with a non-law degree p.a. 33%

Post-qualification
Salary (2009) £34,000
% of trainees offered job on qualification (2008) 93.3%
% of assistant solicitors who joined as trainees 48.51%
% of partners who joined as trainees 22.77%

Paul, Hastings, Janofsky & Walker (Europe) LLP

10 Bishops Square, 8th Floor, London, E1 6EG
Tel: (020) 3023 5100 Fax: (020) 3023 5109
Email: callyarmstrong@paulhastings.com
Website: www.paulhastings.com

Firm profile
With 1,100 lawyers serving clients from 18 worldwide offices, Paul Hastings provides a full range of services to clients around the globe. The firm has established long standing partnerships with many of the world's top financial institutions, Fortune 500 companies and other leading corporations. Paul Hastings represents and advises clients across a full range of practices, industries and regions.

Main areas of work
Paul Hastings' principle practice areas in London are capital markets, corporate, employment, finance, litigation, real estate, restructuring and tax.

Trainee profile
The firm seeks individuals with a wide variety of skills who combine intellectual ability with enthusiasm, creativity and a demonstrable ability to thrive in a challenging environment. The firm expects candidates to have a high level of achievement both at A level (or equivalent) and degree level. This would typically mean an upper second or first class degree and a majority of A grades at A level. The firm recruits both law and non-law graduates.

Training environment
Paul Hastings will provide you with a first class training and development programme, combining on-the-job training and professional courses. The firm will monitor your progress on a formal and informal basis to ensure you receive ongoing training and have the opportunity to give feedback on the programme itself and on those areas that are most important to you.

Trainees spend six months in four of the following practice areas: Capital markets, corporate, employment, finance, litigation, project finance, real estate, restructuring and tax.

Benefits
Private healthcare, life assurance, pension scheme, season ticket loan, gym subsidy.

Sponsorship & awards
Paul Hastings offers sponsorship and maintenance grants.

Vacation placements
Places for 2010: 10; Duration: 2 weeks; Remuneration: £350 per week; Closing date: 28th February 2010.

Partners 21
Assistant Solicitors 47
Total Trainees 11

Contact
Graduate Recruitment

Method of application
online application form available on website

Selection procedure
Interview

Closing date for 2012
31 July 2010

Application
Training contracts p.a. 4-5
Required degree grade 2:1

Training
Salary
1st year (2009) £40,000
2nd year (2009) £45,000
Holiday entitlement
25 days

Post-qualification
Salary (2009) £80,000

Overseas/regional offices
Atlanta, Beijing, Brussels, Chicago, Frankfurt, Hong Kong, London, Los Angeles, Milan, New York, Orange County, Palo Alto, Paris, San Diego, San Francisco, Shanghai, Tokyo, Washington DC

Penningtons Solicitors LLP

Abacus House, 33 Gutter Lane, London, EC2V 8 AR
Tel: (020) 7457 3000 Fax: (020) 7457 3240
Website: www.penningtons.co.uk

Partners 51	
Assistant Solicitors 108	
Total Trainees 18	
* denotes worldwide figures	
Contact	
Andrea Law	
Method of application	
Online via firm's website	
Closing date for 2012	
31 July 2010	
Application	
Training contracts p.a. 8-10	
Applications p.a. 1,000	
% interviewed p.a. 5%	
Required degree grade 2:1	
Training	
Salary	
1st year (2009)	
£30,000 (London)	
2nd year (2009)	
£32,000 (London)	
Holiday entitlement 23 days	
Post-qualification	
Salary (2009) £47,000 (London)	

Firm profile
Penningtons Solicitors LLP is a thriving, modern law firm with a 200-year history and a deep commitment to top quality, partner-led services. Today, the firm is based in London and the South East with offices in London, Basingstoke and Godalming.

Main areas of work
In the business sphere, Penningtons advise on matters relating to all aspects of commercial property, intellectual property, management buy-outs and buy-ins, mergers, acquisitions and joint ventures, as well as dispute resolution. Advice is also given on information technology, business recovery, commercial contracts, agricultural and environmental law, and company secretarial services are offered. The firm helps individuals with advice on property, tax and estate planning, general financial management, the administration of wills and trusts, charities, personal injury, clinical negligence and immigration. Clients often ask Penningtons to advise on both their private and commercial affairs.

Trainee profile
Penningtons seeks high calibre candidates with enthusiasm and resilience. A high standard of academic achievement is expected: three or more good A level passes and preferably a 2:1 or better at degree level, whether you are reading law or another discipline.

Training environment
You will be given a thorough grounding in the law, spending time in three or four of the firm's divisions; commercial property, business services and private individuals. The firm ensures a varied training is given, avoiding too specialised an approach before qualification. Nonetheless, the experience gained in each department gives you a solid foundation, equipping you to embark on your chosen specialisation at the end of your training contract with the firm. Penningtons knows its trainee solicitors are happiest and most successful when busy with good quality work. The firm believes in introducing trainees to challenging cases. The value of giving its trainees responsibility, and allowing direct contact with clients is recognised. However, experienced solicitors are always ready to give support when needed.

Benefits
Life assurance, critical illness cover, pension, private medical insurance, 23 days holiday, interest free season ticket loan, sports and social events.

Vacation placements
The firm offers both summer vacation placements and information days. Applications are accepted from 1 December 2009 to 31 March 2010.

Sponsorship & awards
Full fees and maintenance for the LPC plus a maintenance grant of £5,000.

Pinsent Masons LLP

CityPoint, One Ropemaker Street, London, EC2Y 9AH
Email: graduate@pinsentmasons.com
Website: www.pinsentmasons.com/graduate

Firm profile

Pinsent Masons is a top 15 UK law firm and top 100 law firm internationally, that is committed to sector focussed growth through it's core sector approach. Not constrained by the legacy of many larger commercial practices, this approach aligns the firm to specific business sectors to achieve market-leading positions. The firm is focused on providing a value added service developing a successful and innovative approach to building strong corporate relationships.

With a substantial range of FTSE 100, FTSE 250, Fortune 500 and AIM quoted organisations and public sector clients the firm has an impressive portfolio of clients operating in the global economy. Consequently the firm is constantly looking to extend its own international reach and capabilities. This means you'll be part of a team tackling business issues in some of the world's most dynamic markets. There may also be an opportunity to work overseas through the firm's European Alliance network with 'Salans' or in one of its offices in the Middle East and Asia.

Main areas of work

The firm offers depth, scope and opportunity for it's trainees in a culture of early responsibility and high quality work. As a member of a creative, resourceful and supportive team, you can expect a constant flow of stimulating assignments – developing your legal expertise, market knowledge and commercial vision to deliver commercial legal solutions. Main areas of work include: banking and finance, corporate, dispute resolution and litigation, employment, international construction and energy, outsourcing, technology and commercial, pensions, projects, property, tax, and UK construction and engineering.

Trainee profile

The firm welcomes applications from all backgrounds. Whether your degree is law or non law, there will be no barriers to what you can achieve in the firm's uniquely progressive, meritocratic and open culture. In addition to a strong academic background, the firm is looking for people who can combine a sharp mind with commercial acumen and strong people skills to work in partnership with their clients' businesses.

Training environment

Trainees sit in four seats of six months across the practice areas with supervision from partners and associates. There are also opportunities for trainees to be seconded to clients. There is a supportive team culture which derives from the firms values of; respect and co-operation, ambition and excellence and open and approachable.

In addition to the training required by the Law Societies, the firm offers a broad-ranging and custom-made training programme designed to deliver outstanding technical and management skills that link in with the needs of the business. This is the first stage in the firm's focussed to development programme that supports individuals on their route to partnership.

The firm has an open plan office environment and this no barriers focused approach encourages an informal team atmosphere with a positive focus on work-life balance.

Summer vacation placements

Places for 2010: 100; duration: 2 weeks; Closing Date: 31 January 2010.

Sponsorship & awards

In England, full sponsorship is offered for the GDL and LPC fees, as well as a maintenance grant.
In Scotland, financial assistance is offered for Diploma fees, together with a maintenance grant.

Partners 300+
Lawyers 1,000
Total Trainees 135

Contact
Spencer Hibbert

Method of application
Online application form
www.pinsentmasons.com/graduate

Selection procedure
Assessment day including interview

Closing date for 2012
31 July 2010 (English offices) and 21 October 2010 (Scottish offices)

Application
Training contracts p.a. 60
Applications p.a. 2,000+
Required degree grade 2:1

Training
Salary
1st year £36,000 (London)
2nd year £39,000 (London)
Holiday entitlement 25 days

Post-qualification
Salary (2009) £63,000 (London)

UK offices
London, Birmingham, Bristol, Leeds, Manchester, Edinburgh and Glasgow,

PricewaterhouseCoopers Legal LLP

1 Embankment Place, London, WC2N 6DX
Tel: (020) 7212 1616 Fax: (020) 7212 1570
Website: pwc.com/uk/careers

Firm profile

PricewaterhouseCoopers Legal LLP (PwC Legal) is an independent member of the PricewaterhouseCoopers (PwC) international network of firms. Its services include corporate restructuring, mergers and acquisitions, intellectual property, information technology, immigration, pensions, employment, financial services, banking, commercial contracts, real estate, litigation, private client and environment.

The firm offers domestic and international clients both project-based, specialist legal advice and ongoing general counsel support. And not only does its ambitious growth plans make it an exciting place to launch a legal career; so does its working model, which is unique in the UK legal services market.

PwC Legal can call upon the wider PwC network's specialists when it needs to offer complete, rounded solutions that incorporate multi-disciplinary advice. It often works with PwC tax advisers, human capital consultants, corporate finance experts, actuaries, management consultants and, of course, accountants. And it has access to legal expertise in over 70 countries and immigration expertise in over 112 countries. Thanks to such resources, the firm can deliver a superior client experience that goes beyond just legal services.

Trainee profile

PwC Legal recruits penultimate-year law students and final year non-law students with at least a 2:1 honours degree or equivalent, a 300+ UCAS tariff or equivalent and a keen interest in business law.

Training environment

Trainee solicitors develop into top lawyers in any of the mainstream practice groups: corporate, financial services, banking, litigation, real estate, intellectual property, employment, pensions or immigration. At the same time, exposure to the diverse skill sets of PwC hones strong business advisory skills. Trainees also develop lateral thinking skills, gain practical hands-on experience and help deliver creative solutions. Training includes:

A thorough induction covering core practice groups, client care and time management skills, and IT, research and admin.

Support to gain a professional qualification – trainees take the core modules of the Professional Skills Course (PSC) during their second seat.

A range of electives during the fourth seat to complete the PSC.

Extensive internal training to develop business, management and interpersonal skills.

Exceptional prospects – throughout the training contract and beyond.

Vacation schemes

The firm's paid, three-week summer vacation scheme offers exposure to practice groups and invaluable work experience. Yet another plus point? The scheme is also a good route towards securing a training contract.

Sponsorship & awards

Trainees can apply for a scholarship award to help with the costs of the Graduate Diploma in Law Course and the Legal Practice Course. If successful, they receive the total cost of the tuition and examination fees plus a significant contribution towards living expenses. Details are on the firm's website.

Vacancies 8
Trainees 17
Partners 21
Total staff 170
Work placement Yes

Method of application
Visit pwc.com/uk/careers and complete and submit the online application form

Closing date for 2012
Trainees: July 31 (2010)
Summer vacation scheme March 31 (2010)

Application
Required academic grade 2:1 honours degree in any degree discipline plus at least a 300 UCAS tariff or equivalent

Training
Salary London
1st year (2010) £30,000
2nd year (2010) £35,000

Pritchard Englefield

14 New St, London EC2M 4HE
Tel: (020) 7972 9720 Fax: (020) 7972 9722
Email: po@pe-legal.com
Website: www.pe-legal.com

Firm profile
A niche City firm practising a mix of general commercial and non-commercial law with many German and French clients. Despite its strong commercial departments, the firm still undertakes family and private client work and is renowned for its ever-present international flavour.

Main areas of work
All main areas of commercial practice including litigation, commercial/corporate/ banking (UK, German and French), IP/IT, property and employment, also estate and trusts (UK and off-shore), pensions, charities, personal injury and family.

Trainee profile
High academic achievers with fluent German and/or French.

Training environment
An induction course acquaints trainees with the computer network, online library and finance & administrative procedures and there is a formal in-house training programme during the first week. Four six-month seats make up most of your training. You can usually choose some departments, and you could spend two six-month periods in the same seat. Over two years, you learn advocacy, negotiating, drafting and interviewing, attend court, use your language skills every day and meet clients from day one. Occasional talks and seminars explain the work of the firm, and you can air concerns over bi-monthly lunches with the partners comprising the Trainee Panel. PSC is taken externally over two years. The Social Committee of the firm organises regular parties, French film evenings and quiz nights.

Benefits
Some subsidised training, monthly luncheon vouchers, and eligibility for membership of the firm's private medical insurance scheme as well as an interest free loan for an annual season ticket.

Sponsorship & awards
Full funding for LPC fees.

Partners 22
Assistant Solicitors 13
Other Fee Earners 7
Total Trainees 3

Contact
Graduate Recruitment

Method of application
Standard application form available from Graduate Recruitment or online

Selection procedure
1 interview only in September

Closing date for 2012
31 July 2010

Application
Training contracts p.a. 3
Applications p.a. 300–400
% interviewed p.a. 10%
Required degree grade
Generally 2:1

Training
Salary
1st year (2009) £22,250
Subject to 6 month review
Holiday entitlement 25 days
% of trainees with a non-law degree p.a. Approx 50%

Post-qualification
Salary (2009)
Market rate
% of trainees offered job on qualification (2009) 100%
% of assistants (as at 01/09/09) who joined as trainees 60%
% of Partners (as at 01/09/09) who joined as trainees 20%

Reed Smith

The Broadgate Tower, 20 Primrose Street, London, EC2A 2RS
Tel: +44 (020) 3116 3000 Fax: +44 (020) 3116 3999
Email: graduate.recruitment@reedsmith.com
Website: www.reedsmith.com

Firm profile
Key to Reed Smith's success is its ability to build lasting relationships: with clients and with each other. United through a culture defined by commitment to professional development, team-work, diversity, pro bono and community support, the firm has grown to become one of the 15 largest law firms in the world. Its 23 offices span three continents and London is currently the largest with over 550 people. While the offices benefit from an international framework, each one retains key elements of the local business culture. The team in London has recently consolidated from two premises to one office space in The Broadgate Tower, which boasts fantastic views of the city.

Main areas of work
The firm is particularly well known for its work advising leading companies in the areas of financial services, life sciences, shipping, energy, trade and commodities, advertising, technology and media. It provides a wide range of commercial legal services for all these clients, including a full spectrum of corporate, commercial and financial services, dispute resolution, real estate and employment advice. Much of the work is multi-jurisdictional.

Trainee profile
The firm is looking for individuals with the drive and potential to become world-class business lawyers. They want 'players' rather than 'onlookers' with strong intellect, initiative, the ability to thrive in a challenging profession and the personal qualities to build strong relationships with colleagues and clients.

Training environment
On offer is a four-seat programme in which trainees are able to exercise much influence over the choice and timings of seats. There are many opportunities for secondments to clients and the firm's overseas offices. Trainees also benefit from being able to take a wide range of courses in its award-winning corporate university, developed in partnership with the highly rated Wharton School of the University of Pennsylvania. There are 30 vacancies for training contracts commencing in August 2012 and February 2013.

Benefits
Performance related bonus, pension, life insurance, private health insurance, interest-free season ticket loan, subsidised staff restaurant and staff conveyancing allowance.

Vacation placements
The firm offers up to 20 places each year to applicants who will, on arrival, have completed at least two years of undergraduate study.

Sponsorship & awards
GDL Funding: Fees paid plus £6,000 maintenance. LPC Funding: Fees paid plus £7,000 maintenance

---

Partners 105*
Fee-earners 300*
Total Trainees 41
* denotes UK figures

Contact
Lucy Crittenden

Method of application
Online application form

Selection procedure
Selection exercise, interview, verbal reasoning assessment

Closing date for 2012/2013
31 July 2010

Application
Training contracts p.a. 30
Applications p.a. 1500
% interviewed p.a. 7%
Required degree grade 2:1

Training
Salary
1st year (2009) £37,000
2nd year (2009) £40,000
Holiday entitlement 25 days
% of trainees with a non-law degree p.a. 35%
No. of seats available abroad p.a. 5

Post-qualification
Salary (2009)
£57,000 plus bonus
% of assistants who joined as trainees 43%
% of partners who joined as trainees 45%

Overseas offices
New York, London, Hong Kong, Chicago, Washington DC, Beijing, Paris, Los Angeles, San Francisco, Philadelphia, Pittsburgh, Oakland, Munich, Abu Dhabi, Princeton, N., Wilmington, Dubai, Century City, Piraeus, Richmond, Falls Church, Silicon Valley, Leesburg

Reynolds Porter Chamberlain LLP

Tower Bridge House, St Katharine's Way, London, E1W 1AA
Tel: (020) 3060 6000 Fax: (020) 3070 7000
Email: training@rpc.co.uk
Website: www.rpc.co.uk/training

Partners	64
Assistant Solicitors	185
Total Trainees	30

Contact
Trainee Recruitment Team

Method of application
Online application system

Selection procedure
Assessment days held in September

Closing date for 2012
30/07/2010

Application
Training contracts p.a. 15
Applications p.a. 900
% interviewed p.a. 6%
Required degree grade 2:1

Training
Salary
1st year £37,000
2nd year £40,000
Holiday entitlement 20 days
% of trainees with a non-law degree p.a. Approx 40%

Post-qualification
Salary (2009) £58,000
% of trainees offered job on qualification (2009) 100%
% of assistants (as at 01/05/09) who joined as trainees 28%
% of partners (as at 01/05/09) who joined as trainees 33%

Firm profile
Reynolds Porter Chamberlain LLP is a leading London based practice with over 250 lawyers. Based in the City, the firm work's in an open, collaborative environment designed to bring out the best in its people and to ensure that the service offered to clients is second-to-none. The firm is particularly well known as one of the top insurance and litigation firms in the country, with renowned medical malpractice and professional indemnity practice areas. The firm has a highly rated commercial division which handles the full spectrum of corporate and commercial work for national and multinational companies across several industries.

The firm also has a substantial Dispute Resolution Group, with significant practices in IT, IP, media, employment and insolvency. The Construction Group deals with building disputes and environmental claims, along with building and engineering, major projects and PFI work. The Real Estate Group handles all aspects of commercial real estate work.

Trainee profile
As a trainee you will receive first rate training in a supportive working environment. You will work closely with a partner and will be given real responsibility as soon as you are ready to handle it. At least six months will be spent in four areas of the firm's practice and encouragement will be made to trainees to express preferences for the areas in which they would like to train. In addition to the Professional Skills Course the firm provides a complementary programme of in-house training. When you qualify the firm hopes you will stay and endeavours to place you in the area of law that suits you best.

Training environment
As a trainee you will receive first-rate training in a supportive working environment. You will work closely with a Partner and will be given real responsibility as soon as you are ready to handle it. At least six months will be spent in four areas of the practice and the firm encourages it's trainees to express preferences for the areas in which they would like to train. This will provide a thorough grounding and the chance to develop confidence as you see matters to their conclusion. In addition to the Professional Skills Course the firm provides a complementary programme of in-house training. When you qualify, you will have the choice to remain with the firm and they will endeavour to place you in the area of law that suits you best.

Benefits
The firm feels it is important to offer its employees a creative and competitive benefits package with choice and flexibility. Its full range of benefits can be viewed via the website.

Vacation placements
The firm also runs summer vacation schemes each year to enable prospective trainees to spend time with the firm, getting a feel for the work and atmosphere. Twelve students at a time spend two weeks with us and are integrated as closely as possible with the real working life of the firm. You should get a good idea of whether a career at RPC is right for you.
Places for Summer 2010: 24; Duration: 2 weeks; Remuneration: £275 p/w.; Closing date: 29 January 2010.

Sponsorship & awards
Bursaries are available for the GDL, if applicable, and the LPC. Bursaries comprise course and examination fees and a maintenance grant of up to £6,500. It is requested that all trainees complete their LPC at BPP law.

Shadbolt LLP

Chatham Court, Lesbourne Road, Reigate RH2 7LD
Tel: (0845) 4371000 Fax: (0845) 4371001
Email: recruitment@shadboltlaw.com
Website: www.shadboltlaw.com

Firm profile

Shadbolt LLP is an award-winning, dynamic, progressive firm committed to high quality work and excellence both in the UK and internationally. The atmosphere at the firm is friendly, relaxed and informal and there are various social and sporting activities for staff. The firm comprises a lively and enterprising team with a fresh and open approach to work. The firm's qualified staff have a high level of experience and industry knowledge and some are widely regarded as leading practitioners in their field.

Main areas of work

The firm is well known for its strengths in major projects, construction and engineering and dispute resolution and litigation with established expansion into corporate and commercial, employment, commercial property and IT and e-commerce. The firm provides prompt personal service and its client list includes some of the world's best known names in the construction and engineering industries.

Trainee profile

Applicants must demonstrate that they are self-starters with a strong academic background and outside interests. Leadership, ambition, initiative, enthusiasm and good interpersonal skills are essential, as is the ability to play an active role in the future of the firm. Linguists are particularly welcome, as are those with supporting professional qualifications. The firm welcomes non-law graduates.

Training

Four six month seats from construction and commercial litigation, arbitration and dispute resolution, major projects and construction, employment, corporate and commercial and commercial property. Where possible individual preference is noted. Work has an international bias. There are opportunities for secondment to major clients and work in the overseas offices. Trainees are treated as valued members of the firm, expected to take early responsibility and encouraged to participate in all the firm's activities, including practice development. The firm is accredited by the law society as a provider of training and runs frequent in-house lectures. The PSC is taught externally.

Sponsorship & benefits

Private healthcare, permanent health insurance, group life assurance, paid study leave, season ticket loan, discretionary performance bonus of up to 10% of salary, paid professional memberships and subscriptions, full refund of LPC upon commencement of training contract.

Vacation placements

Places for 2010: 6 to 8; Duration: 2 weeks; Remuneration: £200 p.w.; Closing Date: 28 February 2010; Interviews: March 2010. Please submit the online form no earlier than January 2010.

Partners 21
Snr Assoc/Assoc 19
Total Trainees 6
Total Staff 90

Contact
Andrea Pickett

Method of application
Online application form

Selection procedure
Interview (1) in-tray exercise & group exercise

Closing date for 2012
31 July 2010 (interviews September 2010)

Application
Training contracts p.a. 4
Applications p.a. 100
% interviewed p.a. 20%
Required degree grade 2:1 (occasional exceptions)

Training
Salary
1st year £31,000
2nd year £35,000
Holiday entitlement
20 days rising to 25 on qualification, with opportunity to 'buy' an additional 5 days holiday p.a.
% of trainees with a non-law degree p.a. 50%
No. of seats available abroad p.a. 1

Post-qualification
Salary £52,000
% of trainees offered job on qualification (2009) 0%
% of Snr Assoc/ Assoc (2009) who joined as trainees 0%
% of partners (2009) who joined as trainees 15.78%

Other offices
Reigate, City of London, Paris,
Associated offices:
Bucharest, Dar es Salaam

Shearman & Sterling LLP

Broadgate West, 9 Appold Street, London EC2A 2AP
Tel: (020) 7655 5000 Fax: (020) 7655 5500

Firm profile
Shearman & Sterling LLP is one of New York's oldest legal partnerships, which has transformed from a New York-based firm focused on banking into a diversified global institution. Recognised throughout the world, the firm's reputation, skills and expertise are second to none in its field. The London office, established in 1972, has become a leading practice covering all aspects of English and European corporate and finance law. The firm employs over 200 English and US trained legal staff in London and has more than 1,000 lawyers in 19 offices worldwide.

Main areas of work
Banking, leveraged finance and structured finance. Project finance. M&A. Global capital markets. International arbitration and litigation. Tax. EU and competition. Financial institutions advisory & asset management (legal and regulatory advice to financial instititions and infrastructure providers, both in a retail and wholesale context, and both online and off-line). Executive compensation & employee benefits (sophisticated advice on the design and implementation of compensation and benefits arrangements). Intellectual property. Real estate.

Trainee profile
The firm's successful future development calls for people who will relish the hard work and intellectual challenge of today's commercial world. You will be a self-starter, keen to assume professional responsibility early in your career and determined to become a first-class lawyer in a first-class firm. The firm's two year training programme will equip you with all the skills needed to become a successful commercial lawyer. You will spend six months in each of four practice areas, with an opportunity to spend six months in Abu Dhabi, New York, Hong Kong or Singapore. You will be treated as an integral part of the London team from the outset. The firm will expect you to contribute creatively to all the transactions you are involved in. The firm has an informal yet professional atmosphere. Your enthusiasm, intellect and energy will be more important than what you wear to work. The firm will provide you with a mentor, arrange personal and professional development courses and give you early responsibility.

Sponsorship & awards
Sponsorship for the CPE/ PgDL and LPC courses, together with a maintenance grant of £7,000.

Partners 26
Assistant Solicitors 85
Total Trainees 26

Contact
Rebecca Leitch
Tel: (020) 7655 5088

Method of application
Online at www.shearman.com

Selection procedure
Assessment centre, psychometric test and interview

Closing date for 2012
31 July 2010

Application
Training contracts p.a. 15
Required degree grade 2:1, 340 UCAS points minimum

Training
Salary
1st year (2009) £39,000
2nd year (2009) £39,000
Holiday entitlement
24 days p.a.
% of trainees with non-law degree p.a. 40%
No of seats available abroad 5

Post-qualification
Salary (2009) £73,000
% of trainees offered job on qualification (2009) 64%

Overseas offices
Abu Dhabi, Bejing, Brussels, Düsseldorf, Frankfurt, Hong Kong, Menlo Park, Munich, New York, Paris, Rome, San Francisco, Sao Paulo, Shanghai, Singapore, Tokyo, Toronto, Washington DC

Sheridans

Whittington House, Alfred Place, London, WC1E 7EA
Tel: (020) 7079 0100   Fax: (020) 7079 0200
Email: info@sheridans.co.uk
Website: www.sheridans.co.uk

Firm profile
Sheridans is a full-service law firm with an established reputation for its work in the creative industries. Representing many internationally recognised names in music, film, TV and theatre, it also has a thriving commercial practice offering corporate, private client, dispute resolution, property and employment services.

Main areas of work
ENTERTAINMENT & MEDIA: The music department advises recording artists and recording and management companies on contract negotiation, popular and classical music publishing, merchandising and sponsorship. The film and TV department advises broadcasters, TV and feature film production companies, distribution and sales agents, financiers and talent. Other specialist areas include the theatre, sport, book and magazine publishing, trademarks and domain names, computer games, online and digital media.

DISPUTE RESOLUTION: The firm provides advice and representation in relation to disputes arising in the media and entertainment industries. The disputes typically range from privacy and defamation claims against the national press to rights disputes.

CORPORATE/ COMMERCIAL: The firm advises on commercial contracts, mergers, acquisitions and disposals, management buy-outs and buy-ins, corporate finance, joint ventures, corporate reorganisations, company formations and insolvency.

PROPERTY: Services include the sale and purchase of commercial property, involving investment, leasehold and planning matters, secured lending, building and development schemes and property financing, as well as domestic conveyancing for high net worth individuals.

EMPLOYMENT: The employment practice handles contentious and non-contentious matters, representing both employers and employees, including senior executives.

Trainee profile
Excellent academic background (2.1 and above, good A levels), commercial awareness, great interpersonal skills and an ability to think strategically. Trainees should have an enthusiasm for and a demonstrable commitment to the firm's areas of practice.

Training
The training contract is divided into four six month seats, although trainees are expected to be flexible and assist any department as required. Trainees are given a challenging range of work and exposure to a significant level of responsibility.

Partners 24
Consultants 3
Assistant solicitors 13
Total trainees 2

Contact
Claire Lewis (Training Principal)

Method of application
CV and covering letter, by email to training@sheridans.co.uk (see website)

Selection procedure
2 stage interview process

Closing date for 2012
31 July 2010

Application
Training contracts p.a. 1
Required degree grade 2:1

Training
Salary
1st year competitive with similar firms
2nd year competitive with similar firms
Holiday entitlement
20 days

Post-qualification
Salary Competitive with similar firms
% of trainees offered job on qualification (in last two years) 50%

Shoosmiths

The Lakes, Northampton NN4 7SH
Tel: (0870) 086 3223 Fax: (0870) 086 3001
Email: join.us@shoosmiths.co.uk
Website: www.shoosmiths.co.uk

Firm profile
Shoosmiths is one of the UK's fastest-growing national law firms with offices across the midlands and south of England. The firm is a progressive, forward-thinking law firm with a real spirit of enterprise. The firm really values its people by giving them the freedom, recognition and support to succeed.

Main areas of work
The firm is a full service law firm with numerous practice areas including commercial property, corporate, commercial and dispute resolution.

Trainee profile
You'll be open-minded, flexible, and will be looking to work in a non-hierarchical, open plan environment. You'll also value a life outside of the office. Workwise, you'll care about the quality of service you give to clients (both internal and external) and you'll want to make a real and direct contribution to the firm's success.

Training environment
Trainees are given real work from day one. Experience is built around a practical workload, complemented by technical and business skills training. Over the two years, trainees complete four six-month placements around the firm.

The firm only places one or two trainees in each department which means that you'll be listened to and valued, and will get a good level of access to your supervising Partner and colleagues.

Benefits
Flexible holidays, pension (after three months' service), life assurance, various staff discounts, Christmas bonus.

Vacation placements
The firm offers two-week placements during June and July. Please apply online via the website. The closing date for summer placements will be 5pm, 30 January 2010.

Sponsorship & awards
GDL & LPC funding; the firm pays fees plus a maintenance grant.

Partners 115
Vacancies c20
Total Staff 1400
Total Trainees 33

Contact
Graduate Recruitment

Method of application
Online application form

Selection procedure
Full day assessment centre

Closing date for 2012
See website

Application
Training contracts p.a. 20
Applications p.a. 800
% interviewed p.a. 10%
Required degree grade 2:1

Training
Salary
£tbc
Holiday entitlement
23 days + option to flex

Post-qualification
Salary £tbc

Offices
Birmingham, Northampton, Nottingham, Milton Keynes, Solent, Thames Valley, Basingstoke*, London*, Manchester*
*(not available for TC's or placements)

Sidley Austin LLP

Woolgate Exchange, 25 Basinghall Street, London EC2V 5HA
Tel: (020) 7360 3600 Fax: (020) 7626 7937
Email: ukrecruitment@sidley.com
Website: www.sidley.com

Firm profile
Sidley Austin LLP is one of the world's largest full-service law firms. With approximately 1,700 lawyers practising on four continents (North America, Europe, Australasia and Asia), the firm provides a broad range of integrated services to meet the needs of its clients across a multitude of industries.

Main areas of work
Corporate, competition, corporate reorganisation and bankruptcy, debt and equity capital markets, employment, financial services regulatory, hedge funds, insurance, IP/IT, litigation, real estate and real estate finance, securitisation, structured finance, tax.

Trainee profile
Sidley Austin LLP looks for focused, intelligent and enthusiastic individuals with personality and humour who have a real interest in practising law in the commercial world. Trainees should have a consistently strong academic record and a 2:1 degree (not necessarily in law).

Training environment
The firm is not a typical City firm and it is not a 'legal factory' so there is no risk of being just a number. Everyone is encouraged to be proactive and to create their own niche when they are ready to do so. Trainees spend time in the firm's main groups. In each group trainees will sit with a partner or senior associate to ensure individual training based on 'hands on' experience. You will be encouraged to take responsibility where appropriate. Regular meetings with your supervisor ensure both the quality and quantity of your experience. In addition, there is a structured timetable of training on a cross-section of subjects.

Benefits
Private health insurance, life assurance, contribution to gym membership, interest-free season ticket loan, income protection scheme, pension and subsidised restaurant.

Sponsorship & awards
Tuition fees for the GDL/CPE and the LPC Maintenance grant of £7,000 p.a.

Sidley Austin LLP, a Delaware limited liability partnership which operates at the firm's offices other than Chicago, London, Hong Kong, Singapore and Sydney, is affiliated with other partnerships, including Sidley Austin LLP, an Illinois limited liability partnership (Chicago); Sidley Austin LLP, a separate Delaware limited liability partnership (London); Sidley Austin LLP, a separate Delaware limited liability partnership (Singapore); Sidley Austin, a New York general partnership (Hong Kong); Sidley Austin, a Delaware general partnership of registered foreign lawyers restricted to practicing foreign law (Sydney); and Sidley Austin Nishikawa Foreign Law Joint Enterprise (Tokyo). The affiliated partnerships are referred to herein collectively as Sidley Austin, Sidley, or the firm.

Partners 37
Assistant Solicitors 81
Total Trainees 18

Contact
Lucy Slater,
HR Administrator

Method of application
Application form

Selection procedure
Interview(s)

Closing date for 2012
30 July 2010

Application
Training contracts p.a. 12
Applications p.a. 500
% interviewed p.a. 15
Required degree grade 2:1

Training
Salary
1st year (2009) £39,000
2nd year (2009) £43,000
Holiday entitlement 25 days
% of trainees with a
non-law degree p.a. 50%

Overseas offices
Beijing, Brussels, Chicago, Dallas, Frankfurt, Geneva, Hong Kong, London, Los Angeles, New York, San Francisco, Shanghai, Singapore, Sydney, Tokyo, Washington DC

Simmons & Simmons

CityPoint, One Ropemaker Street, London EC2Y 9SS
Tel: (020) 7628 2020 Fax: (020) 7628 2070
Email: recruitment@simmons-simmons.com
Website: www.simmons-simmons.com/traineelawyers

Firm profile
Dynamic and innovative, Simmons & Simmons has a reputation for offering a superior legal service, wherever and whenever it is required. The firm's high quality advice and the positive working atmosphere in its international network of 20 offices has won admiration and praise from both the legal community and business clients.

Main areas of work
Simmons & Simmons offers its clients a full range of legal services across numerous industry sectors. The firm has a particular focus on the world's fastest growing sectors, namely: energy and infrastructure; financial institutions; life sciences; and TMT. Simmons & Simmons provides a wide choice of service areas in which its lawyers can specialise. These include corporate and commercial; information, communications and technology; dispute resolution; employment and benefits; EU, competition and regulatory; financial markets; IP; projects; real estate; taxation and pensions.

Trainee profile
Simmons & Simmons is interested to find out about your academic successes but will also explore your ability to form excellent interpersonal relations and work within a team environment, as well as your levels of motivation, drive and ambition.

Show evidence of a rich 'life experience' as well as examples of your intellectual capabilities and you will be provided with everything you need to become a successful member of the firm.

Training environment
The training programme at Simmons & Simmons is constantly evolving to build the skills you will need to be successful in the fast moving world of international business. The firm provides experience in a range of areas of law and a balanced approach to gaining the knowledge, expertise and abilities you will need to qualify in the practice area of your choice.

Vacation placements
The firm's internship schemes are one of the primary means of selecting candidates for a career at Simmons & Simmons. Your placement will enable you to gain first-hand experience of a busy and dynamic international law firm, as well as gain exposure to everything from the firm's service areas to the kinds of deals and transactions the firm works on.

Undergraduates usually apply for summer internships in their penultimate year. However, the firm is also happy to offer these internships to final year, international and mature students, graduates and those changing career. The spring internship scheme is a great opportunity for first year law students and penultimate year non-law students to get an in-depth view of the firm at an early stage of your studies. Applications open 01 November 2009.

Simmons & Simmons also runs winter insight workshops aimed specifically at final year non-law students, and non-law graduates. Applications open 01 October 2009. Finally, a series of open days, available to all undergraduates, graduates, mature and international students are run throughout the year.

Sponsorship & awards
The firm will cover your full tuition fees at law school and offer a maintenance allowance of up to £7,500.

Partners 237
Assistant Solicitors 600
Total Trainees 157

Contact
Anna King Graduate
Recruitment Officer

Method of application
Online application, at
www.simmons-simmons.com/graduates
Applications should be made from 01 November, 2009

Selection procedure
Assessment day

Closing date for 2012
31 July 2010

Application
Training contracts p.a. circa 40
Applications p.a. 2,000
% interviewed p.a. 12%
Required degree grade 2:1

Training
Salary
£36,000, 1st and 2nd seat
£40,000, 3rd and 4th seat
Holiday entitlement 25 days
% of trainees with a non-law degree p.a. 50%
No. of seats available abroad p.a. varies

Post-qualification
Salary (2009) £59,000
% of trainees offered job on qualification (2008) 72%

Overseas offices
Abu Dhabi, Amsterdam, Brussels, Doha, Dubai, Düsseldorf, Frankfurt, Funchal, Hong Kong, Lisbon, London, Madrid, Milan, Moscow, Padua, Paris, Rome, Rotterdam, Shanghai, Tokyo

SJ Berwin

10 Queen Street Place, London, EC4R 1BE
Tel: (020) 7111 2268   Fax: (020) 7111 2000
Email: graduate.recruitment@sjberwin.com
Website: www.sjberwin.com

Firm profile

SJ Berwin is an international firm and was founded with the objective of providing outstanding legal advice in a dynamic and different environment. The firm's growth has been fast and furious and in less than 20 years we achieved Top 20 City Firm status. Much of the firm's work is international and clients range from major multinational business corporations and financial institutions to high net-worth individuals. As a result the firm has established a strong reputation in corporate finance.

Main areas of work

SJ Berwin's clients are sophisticated buyers of legal services, principally entrepreneurial companies and financial institutions, whom the firm advises on a comprehensive range of services including: corporate/M&A, commercial, communications, technology, energy and natural resources, employment and pensions, EU and competition, finance, financial markets, intellectual property, investment funds, litigation and dispute resolution, pharmaceutical and life sciences, private equity, real estate, reconstruction and insolvency, retail and tax.

Trainee profile

The firm wants ambitious, commercially minded individuals who seek a high level of involvement from day one. Candidates must have a strong academic record, be on track for, or have achieved, a 2:1 or equivalent in their undergraduate degree, and have demonstrated strong team and leadership potential.

Training environment

The two-year training contract is divided into four six-month seats. Trainees will spend two seats (which may include a seat abroad) within the following areas: finance, mergers and aquisitions, equity capital markets, private equity, venture capital and investment funds. Trainees are given early responsibility and are supported throughout the training contract.

How to apply

The firm welcomes applications from all disciplines and all universities. Applications must be made using the firm's online form available at www.sjberwin.com. The same form can be used to indicate your interest in an open day, a vacation scheme and/or a training contract.

Benefits

25 days holiday, private healthcare, gym membership/subsidy, life assurance, pension scheme, season ticket loan, free lunch.

Partners 175
Assistant Solicitors 400
Total Trainees 83

Contact
Graduate Recruitment Team

Method of application
Online application form

Selection procedure
2 interviews/ case study/ critical reasoning test
Closing date for 2012
31 July 2010
Easter & summer vacation schemes 31 January 2010

Application
Training contracts p.a. 40
Applications p.a. 2,000
10% interviewed p.a.
Required degree grade 2:1

Training
Salary
£37,500, 1st year
£41,500, 2nd year
Holiday entitlement 25 days
% of trainees with a
non-law degree p.a. 50%

Post-qualification
Salary (2010) £59,000
% of trainees offered job
on qualification (2009) 71%

Overseas offices
Berlin, Brussels, Dubai, Frankfurt, Hong Kong, Madrid, Milan, Munich, Paris, Turin

Skadden Arps, Slate, Meagher & Flom (UK) LLP

40 Bank Street, Canary Wharf, London E14 5DS
Tel: (020) 7519 7000 Fax: (020) 7519 7070
Email: graduate.hiring@skadden.com   Website: www.skadden.com/uktraineesolicitors

Partners 29*
Assistant Solicitors 91*
Trainees 8*
*London office

Contact
Kate Harman
Graduate Recruitment Specialist

Method of application
Online application

Selection procedure
A selection event comprising of an interview and a short exercise

Closing date for 2012
31 July 2010

Application
Training contracts p.a. 10-12
Applications p.a. 700
% interviewed p.a. 8%
Required degree grade 2:1

Training
Salary
1st year £40,000
2nd year £43,000
Holiday entitlement 25 days
% of trainees with a
non-law degree p.a. 50%

Overseas offices
Beijing, Boston, Brussels, Chicago, Frankfurt, Hong Kong, Houston, Los Angeles, Moscow, Munich, New York, Palo Alto, Paris, San Francisco, São Paulo, Shanghai, Singapore, Sydney, Tokyo, Toronto, Vienna, Washington DC, Wilmington.

Firm profile
Skadden is one of the leading law firms in the world with approximately 2,000 lawyers in 24 offices across the globe. Clients include corporate, industrial, financial institutions and government entities. The London office is the gateway to the firm's European practice and has some 250 lawyers dedicated to top-end, cross-border corporate transactions and international arbitration and litigation. The firm has handled matters in nearly every country in the greater European region, and in Africa and the Middle East. The firm is consistently ranked as a leader in all disciplines and amongst a whole host of accolades, the firm was recently voted 'Global Corporate Law Firm of the Year' (*Chambers and Partners*), 'Best US Law Firm in London' (*Legal Business*) 'Best Trainer' and 'Best Recruiter' in the US law firm in London category (*Law Careers.Net Training and Recruitment Awards*).

Main areas of work
Lawyers across the European network focus primarily on corporate transactions, including domestic and cross-border mergers and acquisitions, private equity, capital markets, leveraged finance and banking, tax, corporate restructuring and energy and projects. The firm also advise in international arbitration, litigation and regulatory matters.

Trainee profile
The firm seeks to recruit a small number of high-calibre graduates from any discipline to join their highly successful London office as trainee solicitors. The firm is looking for candidates who combine intellectual ability with enthusiasm, creativity and a demonstrable ability to rise to a challenge and to work with others towards a common goal.

Training environment
The firm can offer you the chance to develop your career in a uniquely rewarding and professional environment. You will join a close-knit but diverse team in which you will be given ample opportunity to work on complex matters, almost all with an international aspect, whilst benefiting from highly personalised training and supervision in an informal and friendly environment. The first year of your training contract will be divided into two six month seats where you will gain experience in corporate transactions and international litigation and arbitration. In the second year of your training contract, you will have the opportunity to discuss your preferences for your remaining two seats. The firm also offers the opportunity for second year trainees to be seconded to our Hong Kong or Moscow office for a six month seat.

Benefits
Life insurance, private health insurance, private medical insurance, travel insurance, joining fee paid at Canary Wharf gym, subsidised restaurant, employee assistance programme and technology allowance.

Work placements
Skadden offers the opportunity for penultimate year law and non-law students to experience the culture and working environment of the firm through two week work placements. Placements are paid and take place during Easter and over the course of the summer. The deadline for applications is 12 January 2010 for placements in 2010.

Sponsorship & awards
The firm pays for GDL and LPC course fees and provides a £8,000 grant for each year of these courses.

Slaughter and May

One Bunhill Row, London EC1Y 8YY
Tel: (020) 7600 1200 Fax: (020) 7090 5000
Email: trainee.recruit@slaughterandmay.com (enquiries only)
Website: www.slaughterandmay.com

Firm profile
One of the most prestigious law firms in the world, Slaughter and May enjoys a reputation for quality and expertise. The corporate, commercial and financing practice is particularly strong and lawyers are known for their business acumen and technical excellence. As well as its London, Paris, Brussels and Hong Kong offices, (plus plans to open an office in Beijing), the firm nurtures long-standing relationships with the leading independent law firms in other jurisdictions in order to provide the best advice and service across the world.

Main areas of work
Corporate, commercial and financing; tax; competition; financial regulation; dispute resolution; technology, media and telecommunications; intellectual property; commercial real estate; environment; pensions and employment.

Trainee profile
The work is demanding and the firm looks for intellectual agility and the ability to work with people from different countries and walks of life. Common sense, the ability to communicate clearly and the willingness to accept responsibility are all essential. The firm expects to provide training in everything except the fundamental principles of law, so does not expect applicants to know much of commercial life.

Training environment
Four or five seats of three or six months duration. Two seats will be in the field of corporate, commercial and financing law with an option to choose a posting overseas (either to one of the firm's offices or to a "best friend" firm), or competition or financial regulation. One seat in either dispute resolution, intellectual property, tax or pensions and employment is part of the programme and a commercial real estate seat is also possible. In each seat a partner is responsible for monitoring your progress and reviewing your work. There is an extensive training programme which includes the PSC. There are also discussion groups covering general and specialised legal topics.

Benefits
BUPA, STL, pension scheme, interest free loan, subsidised membership of health club, 24 hour accident cover.

Work experience:
One or two-week work experience schemes are available at Easter, Christmas and during the summer period for those considering a career in law. Please visit the website for full details.

Sponsorship & awards
GDL and LPC fees and maintenance grants are paid.

Partners 130
Associates 471
Total Trainees 182

Contact
The Trainee Recruitment Team

Method of application
Online (via website)

Selection procedure
Interview

Application
Training contracts p.a. Approx 95
Applications p.a. 2,000 approx
% interviewed p.a. 25% approx
Required degree grade Good 2:1 ability

Training
Salary (May 2009)
1st year £38,000
2nd year £43,000
Holiday entitlement
25 days p.a.
% of trainees with a non-law degree Approx 50%
No. of seats available abroad p.a. Approx 30-40

Post-qualification
Salary (May 2009) £61,000
% of trainees offered job on qualification (2009) 96%

Overseas offices
Paris, Brussels and Hong Kong, plus "Best Friend" firms in all the major jurisdictions. Plans to open Beijing office at the end of 2009

Speechly Bircham LLP

6 New Street Square, London, EC4A 3LX
Tel: (020) 7427 6400 Fax: (020) 7353 4368
Website: www.speechlys.com

Firm profile
With over 240 lawyers at its modern City location, the firm is organised around providing intergrated transactional, advisory and disputes services to its three main client markets: business clients, private clients and clients and clients in the real estate and construction sector.

Main areas of work
Business Services: With more than 120 lawyers, teams provide businesses with a comprehensive legal service in areas that include corporate finance; banking; financial services; insolvency; tax; IP; technology; employment; pensions; immigration; data protection and commercial dispute services. Clients operate across a range of sectors that include financial services, pharmaceutical and healthcare, engineering, media, IT, fashion, consumer goods and retail.

Private Client Services: The firm's leading private client practice is ranked as one of the top ten in the world (Chambers Global 2009), and it is the second largest private client group in London (Private Client Practitioner 2008). The firm is widely known for providing a complete service to UK and international wealthy individuals, shareholders, families, trustees, private banks, trust companies and charities which integrates wealth protection, tax and succession planning, family, property, philanthropy and trust and probate litigation.

Real Estate; Construction & Engineering Services: With a team of more than 70 real estate and construction lawyers, legal advice covers commercial property, finance, tax, planning and environmental, sustainability, regeneration, infrastructure, construction, engineering and dispute services. Lawyers advise developers, contractors and consultants as well as occupiers, investors and lenders on a variety of significant real estate investments, developments, urban regeneration schemes and construction projects. Clients are both UK based and international and include blue chip financial institutions, property companies, urban estates, retailers and local authorities.

Trainee profile
Law and non-law graduates capable of achieving a 2.1 degree. The firm seeks candidates with a genuine interest in law who enjoy a collaborative and vibrant environment where they can make a real impact.

Training environment
Speechly Bircham's trainees are regarded as a highly valued part of the team. Training contracts are divided into four six-month seats. Each trainee will be closely supported by a partner or senior solicitor. Emphasis is given to early responsibility and supervised client contact, providing trainees with a practical learning environment. Practical experience is further complemented by comprehensive in-house legal training. Performance reviews are held at the mid point and at the end of each seat to promote development and ensure trainees achieve their potential.

Summer scheme placements
Places for 2010 (20). Unusually the firm offers a three week summer placement scheme giving students an extended opportunity to experience the Speechly Bircham culture, sit in a greater number of practice areas and gain valuable insight into what life in a private practice environment is really like. Feedback is sought from partners and solicitors on a student's performance throughout the scheme, together with end of scheme assessments that include researching and presenting on a current topical issue and undertaking a psychometric test. However, it is not all work and no play and the summer scheme is punctuated by a variety of sports and social events. Applications for 2010 summer placements to be submitted by 12 February 2010.

Sponsorship
GDL and LPC fees paid in full together with a maintenance grant.

Partners 87
Assistant Solicitors 138
Total Trainees 25

Contact
Helen Wiggs
Human Resources Manager

Method of application
Application form (available online)

Selection procedure
Interview and psychometric testing

Closing date for 2012
31 July 2010

Application
Training contracts p.a. 10
Applications p.a. 800
% interviewed p.a. 15%
Required degree grade 2:1

Training
Salary
1st year
£32,000-33,000
2nd year
£34,000-£35,000
Holiday entitlement 25 days

Post-qualification
Salary (2009) £50,000
Holiday entitlement 25 days

Stephenson Harwood

One St Paul's Churchyard, London EC4M 8SH
Tel: (020) 7809 2812 Fax: (020) 7003 8346
Email: graduate.recruitment@shlegal.com
Website: www.shlegal.com/graduate

Firm profile
Stephenson Harwood is an international law firm with over 90 partners and 500 staff worldwide. With a fifth of the firm's people operating out of Asia, the China connection is stronger than ever. And from that first bank client, the firm has today built a formidable strength in the banking and wider financial services sector, accounting for twelve of the firm's top twenty clients. Stephenson Harwood is more than simply a City-based practice. Through its international network of offices and affiliates, it provides clients with quality resources and expert local knowledge in Africa, Asia, Europe, the Middle East and Latin America.

Main areas of work
Corporate (including corporate finance, funds, corporate tax, business technology); employment, pensions, finance; dry and wet shipping litigation; commercial litigation; and real estate.

Trainee profile
The firm looks for high calibre graduates with excellent academic records, business awareness and excellent communication skills.

Training environment
As the graduate intake is relatively small, the firm gives trainees individual attention, coaching and monitoring. Your structured and challenging programme involves four six month seats in areas of the firm covering contentious and non-contentious areas, across any department within the firm's practice groups. These seats include 'on the job' training and you will share an office with a partner or senior associate. In-house lectures complement your training and there is continuous review of your career development. You will have the opportunity to spend six months abroad and have free language tuition where appropriate. You will be given your own caseload and as much responsibility as you can shoulder. The firm plays a range of team sports, offers subsidised membership of a City health club (or a health club of your choice) and has privileged seats for concerts at the Royal Albert Hall and access to private views at the Tate Gallery.

Benefits
Subsidised membership of health clubs, private health insurance, BUPA membership, season ticket loan and 25 days paid holiday per year.

Vacation placements
Places for 2009/2010: 40; Duration: 1-2 weeks; Remuneration: £260 p.w.; Closing Date: 1st November 2009 for Christmas and 15th January 2010 for Easter and Summer.

Sponsorship & awards
Fees paid for GDL and LPC and maintenance awards (if still studying).

Partners 90*
Assistant Solicitors 150*
Total Trainees 31
* denotes world-wide figures

Contact
Ushma Amin (Graduate Recruitment)

Method of application
Online application form only

Selection procedure
Psychometric testing, telephone interviews and assessment centre
closing date for Sept/March 2012
31st July 2010

Application
Training contracts p.a. 14
Required degree grade 2:1

Training
Salary
1st year £35,000
2nd year £40,000
Holiday entitlement 25 days
% of trainees with a non-law degree p.a. 50%
No. of seats available abroad p.a. 8

Post-qualification
Salary £58,000
% of trainees offered job on qualification (2009) 94%

Overseas offices
Paris, Piraeus, Singapore, Guangzhou, Hong Kong, Shanghai

Associated offices
Greece, Kuwait, Croatia, France, Romania

Stevens & Bolton LLP

The Billings, Guildford, Surrey GU1 4YD
Tel: (01483) 302264 Fax: (01483) 302254
Email: julie.bounden@stevens-bolton.co.uk
Website: www.stevens-bolton.co.uk

Firm profile
Stevens & Bolton LLP is a major force in the south east region and the firm's reputation is growing nationally. Its vision is to be the South's top independent law firm – and a great place to work. It was named National/Regional Law Firm of the Year at the 2009 Legal Business Awards and the firm was also named Corporate Law Firm of the Year at the Insider Dealmakers South East awards for the third year running.

Clients include mid-tier businesses (whether quoted or owner managed), household name PLCs and other major international groups and high net worth private clients. Bunzl plc, Hanson Limited, Philips Electronics, Unilever, Kia Motors, Kuoni Travel, Rentokil Initial plc and SABMiller plc are examples of well known companies and brands that entrust their legal work to us.

The firm is a full service law firm and particular features of its approach to client service include the responsiveness of lawyers and strength in depth in all key areas; an emphasis on sound, practical advice aimed at achieving clients' commercial objectives; open, collaborative and friendly relationships with clients and a constructive approach with other advisers; a continuing investment in know how, training and technology to enhance the value of the firm's services. Increasingly its work involves an international element and the firm has established relationships with overseas firms in key jurisdictions.

There are number of active groups in the firm so that everyone is able to contribute ideas in areas such as marketing, profile raising, 'greening the office' and corporate and social responsibility.

Main areas of work
Corporate and commercial, real estate, dispute resolution, employment pensions and immigration, tax and trusts, private client and family.

Trainee profile
The firm would like to hear from you if you have (or expect) a 2:1 or first class degree. Just as important is the kind of person you are. Tell us about your motivations, achievements, interests and hobbies – what gets you out of bed in the morning? Initiative is a quality that the firm looks for too, so think about situations you have been in where your involvement has made a real difference.

Training environment
The firm provides excellent training to all its trainees, with real client contact and responsibility early on. To ensure that trainees get as broad a range of experience as possible you will do six four month seats with the aim of giving you the opportunity (where possible) to spend your final seat in the department you hope to qualify into. All trainees receive regular feedback and appraisals and sit either with a partner or a senior associate.

Benefits
Pension, private healthcare, life assurance, permanent health insurance and an interest free loan for rail travel or car parking.

Sponsorship & awards
The firm will pay the fees for the CPE/GDL and LPC, (if no grant is available), and £4,000 maintenance grant for each course of study.

Vacation placements
The firm will run two programmes each summer of one weeks' duration. Please see the website for further information. Applications are accepted between 1 December 2009 and 31 January 2010.

Partners 30
Associates 52
Total Trainees 8

Contact
Julie Bounden
(01483) 302264

Method of application
Online application form available from website

Selection procedure
Two interviews & other processes

Closing date for 2012
30 September 2010

Application
Training contracts p.a. 4
Applications p.a. 200
% interviewed 15%
Required degree grade 2:1

Training
Salary
1st year (2009) £25,500
2nd year (2009) £27,500
Holiday entitlement 25 days

Overseas/regional offices
Guildford only

Taylor Wessing LLP

5 New Street Square, London, EC4 3TW
Tel: (020) 7300 7000   Fax: (020) 7300 7100
Website: www.taylorwessing.com/graduate

Firm profile

Taylor Wessing offers a full service to its clients providing a powerful source of legal support for commercial organisations doing business in Europe and the emerging markets in Asia and the Middle East. The firm's clients include large and medium size, private and public companies, financial institutions, professional service firms, public sector bodies and wealthy individuals. The firm offers industry-focused advice by grouping together lawyers from different legal areas with in-depth sector experience. The firm's core industries include banking, construction, engineering, fashion, finance, healthcare, infrastructure, leisure, life sciences, media and entertainment, information technology and telecommunications and projects.

Taylor Wessing's 13 international offices are based primarily in Europe's three largest economies with additional offices in China and Dubai. Clients also have the added benefit of the firm's wide network of partner law firms, including most recently, an alliance with BSJP in Warsaw. In Germany, Taylor Wessing is one of the leading law firms, with a team of 280 lawyers.

Main areas of work

The firm's core services underpin the main areas of business activity including: corporate transactions and restructuring, finance, tax, property and construction, intellectual property, commercial contracts, employment and employee benefits, dispute resolution and private client advice.

Trainee profile

High intellectual ability is paramount - the firm seeks a minimum of ABB grades at A level and a 2.1 degree in any discipline. It looks for team players with the potential to build relationships with clients and who have a desire to take on responsibility and make a real impact on the firm's business. Excellent communication skills, energy, ambition, an open mind and a willingness to learn are also key attributes along with the ability to demonstrate a commitment to a career in law.

Training environment

As part of your training programme, you will spend six months in four different practice groups, including a contentious seat and another in one of the firm's corporate or finance areas. There are also secondment opportunities to other offices or one of the firm's clients. All trainees work closely with a number of partners and associates in the practice groups so you will be directly involved in high quality work from the outset. Throughout your training contract you will have ongoing discussions about your interests and how they fit in with the growth and needs of the firm. There is support every step of the way, with regular feedback and appraisals in the middle and at the end of each seat. Not forgetting the essential Professional Skills Course, which is run in-house, along with other training courses as necessary during the two years.

Benefits

Private medical care, life assurance, season ticket loan, pension scheme and employee assistance programme.

Vacation placements

Places for 2010: 30+; Duration: 2 weeks; Remuneration: £250 per week; Closing date: 31 January 2010.

Sponsorship & awards

GDL and LPC fees at BPP London sponsored. A maintenance grant of £6,000 per annum is provided.

Partners 280
Fee-earners 400
Trainees 44 (UK)

Contact
Graduate Recruitment Department

Method of application
Online application form

Selection procedure
Assessment centre and Partner interview

Closing date for 2012
31 July 2010

Application
Training contracts p.a. circa 20
Applications p.a. 700
% interviewed p.a. 30%
Required degree grade 2:1

Training
Salary
1st year £31,500
2nd year £35,000
Holiday entitlement 25 days
% of trainees with a non-law degree p.a. 50%

Post-qualification
Salary £55,000
% of trainees offered jobs on qualification (2009) 63%

Overseas offices
Berlin, Brussels, Cambridge, Dubai, Düsseldorf, Frankfurt, Hamburg, London, Munich, Paris and representative offices in Alicante, Beijing and Shanghai.

Thomas Cooper

Ibex House, 42-47 Minories, London EC3N 1HA
Tel: (020) 7481 8851   Fax: (020) 7480 6097
Email: recruitment@thomascooperlaw.com
Website: www.thomascooperlaw.com

Firm profile
Thomas Cooper is an international law firm and specialises in maritime, trade and finance law. The firm's core areas are: maritime, trade, finance, company and commercial, international arbitration, insurance, oil and gas. The firm was founded in 1825. It has offices in London, Athens, Madrid, Paris, Singapore and Vancouver. The firm's lawyers around the world provide a realistic perspective on the advantages, disadvantages and challenges of different jurisdictions. This enables the firm to give insightful and pragmatic advice to clients and allows it to manage their exposure to risk more effectively.

Main Areas of Work
The firm's core areas are: maritime, trade, finance, company and commercial, international arbitration, insurance, oil and gas.

Trainee Profile
If you are interested in becoming a solicitor you have many possibilities in front of you. The firm's trainees learn by working closely with real experts – and with real characters too. It values trainees because they are vital for the future of the business. Trainees have a broad view of the world, and the firm likes to reinforce this with overseas working. So if you are a well-qualified graduate, and if you are articulate, clear thinking and ambitious, the firm encourages you to apply.

Training Environment
Thomas Cooper has a four-seat trainee programme which is over two years: two seats in shipping, one in defence and personal injury; and one in finance and international trade. These are based in London. Opportunities to do a seat in a non-London office are available dependent upon language skills and team workload.

Benefits
Private medical insurance, permanent health insurance, life assurance, 25 days holiday, pension scheme, loan for dental insurance, season ticket loan and subsidised gym membership. LPC course fees are paid by the firm.

Partners 29
Assistant solicitors 21
Total trainees 7

Contact
Timothy Goode - Managing Partner
Tel: (020) 7481 8851

Method of application
Online application form

Selection procedure
Interviews

Closing date for 2010/2011
2011 applications: 31 July 2010
2012 applications: 31 August 2010

Application
Required degree grade
2:1

Training
Salary
Starting salary for trainees is:
Year 1 £30,000
Year 2 £33,660
25 days holiday

Overseas/ regional offices
Athens, Madrid, Paris, Singapore & Vancouver

Thomas Eggar

The Corn Exchange, Baffins Lane, Chichester PO19 1GE
Tel: (01243) 813129
Email: alice.mcgurk@thomaseggar.com
Website: www.thomaseggar.com

Vacancies 8
Partners 73
Trainees 16
Total Staff 475+

Contact
Alice McGurk

Method of application
On-line
www.apply4law.com/thomaseggar

Selection procedure
CV, assessment centre and interview

Closing date for 2011/2012
31 July 2010

Training
The firm aims to pay the going rate for a firm based in the South. A London weighting is paid to those who undertake seats in the London office.
Required degree grade
2:1 (any discipline)

Other offices
Chichester, Gatwick, London, Worthing, Newbury, Southampton

Firm profile
Thomas Eggar is rated as one of the top 100 law firms in the UK. Based across the South, it is one of the country's leading regional law firms with a staff approaching 500. The firm offers both private client and commercial services to a diverse range of clients, locally, nationally and internationally. It also offers financial services through Thesis, the firm's investment management arm, which is the largest solicitor-based investment management unit in the UK.

Main areas of work
Apart from its strength in the private client sector, the firm handles property, employment, commercial and dispute resolution matters; among its major clients are banks, building societies and other financial institutions, railway and track operators and construction companies, football clubs and sports personalities.

Trainee profile
The firm seeks very able trainees who exhibit good business acumen, with a 2.1 degree in any discipline. Applications can be made up to 31 July 2010 for training contracts to commence in 2011 and 2012. Applications should be online. You should give details of your attachment to the South in your online application. The online application is www.apply4law.com/thomaseggar.

Training environment
Trainees would normally have four seats covering commercial property, commercial, dispute resolution and private client. In order to give good exposure to various specialisations, some of the seats are likely to be in different offices.

Vacation placements
There is a limited summer placement scheme in July and August each year: this runs for five days and can be within any one of our locations. Applications should be made online. Please give details of your accommodation plans in your application. Travel expenses are paid.

Sponsorship & awards
LPC 50% grant, 50% loan.

Thomson Snell & Passmore

3 Lonsdale Gardens, Tunbridge Wells, Kent TN1 1NX
Tel: (01892) 510000 Fax: (01892) 549884
Email: solicitors@ts-p.co.uk
Website: www.ts-p.co.uk

Firm profile
Thomson Snell & Passmore continues to be regarded as one of the premier law firms in the South East. The firm has a reputation for quality and a commitment to deliver precise and clear advice which is recognised and respected both by its clients and professional contacts. It has held the Lexcel quality mark since January 1999. The firm is vibrant and progressive and enjoys an extremely friendly atmosphere. Its offices are located in the centre of Tunbridge Wells and the Thames Gateway and attract clients locally, nationally and internationally.

Main areas of work
Corporate and commercial 9%; employment 5%; dispute resolution 12%; commercial property 10%; residential property 7%; private client 31%; clinical negligence/ personal injury 19%; family 7%.

Trainee profile
Thomson Snell & Passmore regards its trainees from the outset as future assistants, associates and partners. The firm is looking for people not only with strong intellectual ability, but enthusiasm, drive, initiative, strong interpersonal and team-working skills.

Training environment
The firm's induction course will help you to adjust to working life. As a founder member of Law South your training is provided in-house with trainees from other Law South member firms. Your two-year training contract is divided into four periods of six months each. You will receive a thorough grounding and responsibility with early client exposure. You will be monitored regularly, receive advice and assistance throughout and appraisals every three months. The Training Partner will co-ordinate your continuing education in the law, procedure, commerce, marketing, IT and presentation skills. Trainees enjoy an active social life which is encouraged and supported.

Sponsorship & awards
Grant and interest free loan available for LPC.

Partners 38
Solicitors 46
Total Trainees 10

Contact
Human Resources Manager
Tel: (01892) 510000

Method of application
On-line application form available from website

Selection procedure
Assessment interview

Closing date for 2012
31 July 2010

Application
Training contracts p.a. 5
Applications p.a. Approximately 500
% interviewed p.a. 5%
Required degree grade
2:1 (any discipline)

Training
Competitive regional salary
Holiday entitlement 25 days

Post-qualification
% of trainees offered job on qualification 100%

Overseas/regional offices
Network of independent law firms throughout Europe and founding member of Law South

Thring Townsend Lee & Pembertons

6 Drakes Meadow, Penny Lane, Swindon, SN3 3LL
Tel: (01793) 410 800 Fax: (01793) 539 040
Email: solicitors@ttuk.com   Website: www.ttuk.com

Firm profile

With offices in London and the South West, employing nearly 400 staff, Thring Townsend Lee & Pembertons has built a sustainable, growing and successful law business by balancing its commercial and private practices with a strong sector speciality in Agriculture. This top 100 law firm has an impressive national and international client base.

The commitment from the management of the firm to employees, their career development and their non-legal skills training has led to an open and friendly culture and a vibrant work ethic.

Main areas of work

Agriculture: one of the top specialist agriculture teams in the country working as legal panel solicitors for the NFU in the South East.

Commercial property: one of the largest teams in Southern England with an excellent reputation for specialist areas of work.

Corporate and commercial: acting for a wide variety of clients including many national and international household names.

Litigation: a substantial practice with specialists in commercial litigation and claimant professional negligence work. The Insolvency and Corporate Recovery Department is one of the largest in the region and is attracting diverse and complex quality work.

Personal Injury: a niche practice specialising in high value claims for catastrophic brain and spinal injuries and industrial disease.

Family: one of the largest family teams in the region with specialist expertise in collaborative divorce, civil partnerships and divorce for farmers and business owners.

Wills and probate, tax and trusts: specialising in sophisticated capital tax planning, private family trusts, heritage property, business assets and landed estates. Private property: advising individuals and companies including investment landlords and clients resident abroad.

Trainee profile

The firm wants confident, well-rounded individuals who are pro-active, dedicated and commercially aware. It expects a minimum 2:1 degree and strong A-levels but is open to applicants with a 2:2 degree who perhaps have something else to offer.

Training environment

A dynamic learning environment with an equal mix of structure and flexibility to cater for individual needs and career goals.

A structured two-year training contract split into four six-month seats. Trainees gain experience within at least three different practice areas including contentious and non-contentious.

In addition, we offer: dedicated partner supervisor, mid-seat and end-seat appraisal feedback, client management skills development, training courses, social events, competitive salary and benefits package.

Benefits

Three extra concessionary days holiday. Private medical insurance. Private healthcare. Subsidised restaurants. Life Assurance. Paid professional memberships and subscriptions.

Partners 54
Assistant Solicitors 77
Total Trainees 17

Contact
Pat Mapstone (01793) 412 502

Method of application
application form and CV

Selection procedure
1st and 2nd stage interviews, 2nd comprising of an interview with Partner and senior solicitor

Closing date for 2012
31 July 2010

Application
Training contracts p.a. 9
Applications p.a. 150 plus
% interviewed p.a. 20%
Required degree grade
2:1 preferred

Training
Salary: £23,000 (1st year)
        £25,000 (2nd year)
Holiday entitlement
25 days

Post-qualification
Salary £35,000 (dependant on location)
% of trainees offered job on qualification 80%

Overseas/regional offices
Bath, Bristol, London, Swindon

TLT LLP

One Redcliff St, Bristol BS1 6TP
Tel: (0117) 917 7586   Fax: (0117) 917 7649
Email: bee.yazdani@TLTsolicitors.com   Website: www.TLTcareers.com/trainee

Partners 65
Assistant Solicitors 68
Total Trainees 25

Contact
Bee Yazdani, Graduate Resourcer
Tel: 0117 917 7586

Method of application
Online application form at www.TLTcareers.com/trainee

Selection procedure
Application form, telephone screening, verbal & numerical testing, assessment centre
Closing date: 31 July each year

Application
Training contracts: up to 15 p.a.
Applications: circa 600 p.a.
% interviewed: 13% p.a.
Required degree grade:
2:1 or above in any discipline at degree level and a minimum of 300/24 UCAS points at A level

Training
Salary: See website for details
Holiday entitlement: 25 days

Post-qualification
Salary:
See website for details
% trainees offered job on qualification: 80-100%

Offices
London, Bristol, Piraeus (Greece)

Firm profile
TLT LLP is part of a new wave of law firms. A top-100 firm, with 650 people across London, Bristol and Piraeus, Greece, TLT is an award-winning commercial firm, built around the needs of its clients. The firm is progressive in its thinking and in the eyes of the Financial Times, one of Europe's most innovative law firms. In 2008-09, the firm's turnover reached £38 million. Last year alone, TLT gained 400 new commercial clients. Small wonder its seen as a law firm that's going places – and quickly.

Main areas of work
As a full-service law firm, TLT concentrates on providing industry-focused, multi-discipline integrated solutions. The firm's leading strengths are in financial services and leisure, and it has outstanding experience in retail, technology and media, and the built environment. The firm's core legal specialisms are real estate, banking and finance, commercial, corporate, employment, dispute resolution and litigation.

Trainee profile
The firm's trainees are genuinely ambitious, talented and technically impressive. TLT looks for people who stand out. People who embrace team working and share a passion for outstanding client service. And while academic achievement is important, personal qualities and legal work experience count for a lot too.

Training environment
You want first-hand experience of legal practice. You want to gain impressive technical knowledge and invaluable professional skills. You want to be advising clients. And you want expert guidance and unlimited support throughout. Sounds like a big ask, but it's exactly what TLT will give you. From skills workshops to your very own buddy, quality work to client contact, the firm's training contracts have more in them so you get more out of them.

Benefits
The firm offers a full flexible benefits plan. This gives you the opportunity to design your benefits package to meet your lifestyle needs. You'll also be encouraged to get involved in community support work, pro bono legal advice, fundraising activities and environmental initiatives.

Vacation placements
How much can you pick up in a week? With us, a phenomenal amount, especially when you consider the amount of Partner contact you'll enjoy. But it's more than that. The firm has built assessments into the week, which means you won't have to make a separate training contract application or attend an assessment day.

Sponsorship & awards
CPE and LPC fees plus maintenance grant.

Travers Smith LLP

10 Snow Hill, London EC1A 2AL
Tel: (020) 7295 3000 Fax: (020) 7295 3500
Email: graduate.recruitment@traverssmith.com
Website: www.traverssmith.com

Firm profile
A leading City firm with a major Corporate and Commercial Practice. Although less than a quarter of the size of the dozen largest firms, they handle the highest quality work, much of which has an international dimension.

Main areas of work
Corporate law (including takeovers and mergers, financial services and regulatory laws), commercial law (which includes commercial contracts, IT and intellectual property), litigation, corporate recovery/insolvency, tax, employment, EU/competition, pensions, banking and real estate. The firm also offers a range of pro bono opportunities within individual departments and on a firm wide basis. The firm also carries out commercial work for a number of UK charities.

Trainee profile
The firm looks for people who combine academic excellence with common sense; who are articulate, who think on their feet, who are determined and self motivated and who take their work but not themselves seriously. Applications are welcome from law and non-law graduates.

Training environment
Travers Smith has earned a phenomenal reputation in relation to its size. The work they undertake is exciting, intellectually demanding and top quality involving blue-chip clients and big numbers. This means that their trainees gain great experience right from the outset.

The firm has a comprehensive training programme which ensures that trainees experience a broad range of work. All trainee solicitors sit in rooms with partners and assistants, receive an individual and extensive training from experienced lawyers and enjoy client contact and the responsibility that goes with it from the beginning of their training contract.

Benefits
Private health insurance, permanent health insurance, life assurance, corporate health club membership, subsidised bistro, season ticket loan.

Vacation placements
Summer 2010: 3 schemes with 15 places on each; Duration: two weeks; Remuneration: £250; Closing Date: 31 January 2010. The firm also offers a two week Christmas scheme for 15 students.

Sponsorship & awards
GDL and LPC paid in full plus maintenance of £7,000 per annum to those in London and £6,500 per annum to those outside of London.

Partners 65
Assistant Solicitors 154
Total Trainees 48

Contact
Germaine VanGeyzel

Method of application
Online

Selection procedure
Interviews (2 stage process)

Closing date for 2012
31 July 2010

Application
Training contracts p.a. 25
Applications p.a. 2,000
% interviewed p.a. 15%
Required degree grade 2:1

Training
Salary
1st year (2009) £36,000
2nd year (2009) £40,000
Holiday entitlement 25 days

Post-qualification
Salary (2009) £58,000
% of trainees offered job on qualification (2009) 72%

Trethowans LLP

London Road Office Park, London Road, Salisbury Wiltshire, SP1 3HP
Tel: 01722 412512   Fax: 01722 333011
Email: kate.ellis@trethowans.com   Web: www.trethowans.com

Firm profile
Trethowans is a major law firm in the South, advising business and individual clients and has over 130 people, including 23 partners and over 45 lawyers across offices in Salisbury and Southampton. The firm represents international and national household brand names, owner-managed businesses, entrepreneurs and major regional employers across the UK. Service excellence is a priority - clients value the firm's ability to deliver top-quality, expert advice, on time, in a very personable manner and at a competitive price. The firm has expertise across six main industry sectors: property and pensions, healthcare, banking and finance, personal wealth, retail and leisure, media, manufacturing and distribution and agriculture and estates.

Main areas of work
The firm's business lawyers, who specialise in different areas of the law, work together to regularly advise international and national household brand names, owner-managed, entrepreneurial and major regional employers across the UK, Hampshire and Wiltshire. Five of the firm's six teams that advise business clients are rated in the two independent guides to the legal profession, Chambers Guide to the Legal Profession and Legal 500. Legal advice to businesses include: corporate, commercial, commercial property, commercial litigation, employment and licensing.

For individuals the firm's teams of expert lawyers deliver advice in a down-to-earth and approachable manner. The 'Trethowans' personality is particularly important so that individual clients can meet the 'real person' behind the lawyer. Four of the firm's five teams that advise individual clients are also rated in Chambers Guide to the Legal Profession and Legal 500. Legal advice to individuals include: personal injury, private client (Wills, trusts and tax), landed estates, family and residential property.

Trainee profile
Trainees should possess sound academic abilities and be able to demonstrate commercial acumen. Flexibility, ambition and enthusiasm are valued. Candidates should be good communicators and adopt a problem solving approach to client work.

Training environment
Trainee solicitors normally undertake four separate specialist seats, each lasting six months. The firm offers a flexible approach in deciding trainees' seats to suit individual needs, while providing a broad training programme in accordance with the Solicitors Regulation Authority guidelines. Trainees have their own desks and work closely with the supervising fee-earner/Partner to whom they are responsible. They are considered an integral part of each team and become closely involved in the department's work to obtain first-hand legal experience. Each trainee is appraised every six months by their supervisor and the Training Partner. This enables the trainee scheme to be continually evaluated and also ensures that the highest possible standards are maintained. Prospects for trainees are excellent, most trainees are offered a post as an assistant solicitor at the end of their training contract.

Benefits
Incremental holiday entitlement up to 28 days, contributory pension scheme, death in service benefit, PHI scheme, performance-related bonus scheme, car parking, new staff recruitment bonus, childcare voucher scheme.

Sponsorship and awards
Course fees paid for LPC

Partners 23
Assistant Solicitors 20
Total Trainees 7

Contact
Kate Ellis
023 8082 0503

Method of application
Applications by application form (available online) and covering letter

Selection procedure
Two stage process; interview and assessment day

Closing date for 2012
30 July 2010

Application
Training contracts p.a. 3-4
Applications p.a. 100+
% interviewed p.a. 20%
Required degree grade 2:1

Training
Salary: in excess of Law Society minimum
Holiday entitlement 23 days

Post-qualification
Market rate
% of trainees offered position on qualification 100%

Regional offices
Salisbury, Southampton

Trowers & Hamlins LLP

Sceptre Court, 40 Tower Hill, London EC3N 4DX
Tel: (020) 7423 8000 Fax: (020) 7423 8001
Email: hking@trowers.com   Website: www.trowers.com

Firm profile

Trowers & Hamlins is a top 50, full service city law firm offering regional and international opportunities. The firm has UK offices in London, Manchester and Exeter and a long standing presence in the Middle East with offices in Abu Dhabi, Bahrain, Cairo, Dubai and Oman. Although known for its work in the Public Sector and Social Housing, there is far more to the firm than that and it is frequently listed as a key player in the corporate, banking and finance and commercial property sectors.

Main areas of work

Banking and finance, commercial property, corporate, dispute resolution and litigation, employment, housing projects, international, projects and construction, public sector communities and governance, public sector commercial and tax, trusts and pensions.

Trainee profile

The firm recruits twenty-two trainees each year split equally between September and March intakes. Each year the firm recruits one trainee to join the Exeter office and approximately three to join the Manchester office. The firm is naturally looking for an excellent academic record but in addition to this recognises that supplementary skills are required and actively seeks out candidates with exceptional commercial awareness, outstanding communication skills and a genuine passion for the law.

Training environment

The training contract is split into four six month seats. Offering secondment opportunities in the Middle East, Manchester and Exeter alongside seats in a wide range of departments, it is not surprising that trainees gain a varied and interesting experience. Trainees are paired with either a senior solicitor or Partner as their supervisor to ensure that a suitable level of support is provided. Assessment takes place constantly, with trainees completing both a mid seat and end of seat appraisal - providing the opportunity to gain regular feedback and continuously progress.

Responsibility is given from a very early stage with trainees in some departments running files on their own on joining the department. Trainees are encouraged to take as autonomous a role as is possible safe in the knowledge that there is a structured support system in place to provide assistance should they require it.

Training forms an integral part of the training contract with trainee solicitors receiving departmental training every week as part of the Monday Lunchtime Training Programme. In addition to this, further business skills training is provided covering vital skills such as presentation technique and negotiation practice.

Vacation placements

Each summer the firm runs three fortnight long vacation placements which are open to candidates wishing to commence training contracts in September 2012 and March 2013. Online applications should be submitted by 1 March via the firm's website.

Sponsorship & awards

GDL and LPC sponsorship is provided. In addition, those studying for either course will receive a maintenance grant of £6,000. From September 2009 all London based trainees will be required to undertake the LPC at Kaplan Law School.

Partners 106
Assistant Solicitors 179
Total Trainees 39

Contact
Hannah King, Graduate Development Manager

Method of application
Online application form

Selection procedure
Assessment centre, interviews, psychometric tests & practical test

Closing date for 2012
1 August 2010

Application
Training contracts p.a. 22
Applications p.a. 1,600
% interviewed p.a. 4%
Required degree grade 2:1 or higher

Training
Salary (subject to review)
1st year £35,000
2nd year £38,000
Holiday entitlement 25 days
% of trainees with a non-law degree p.a. 50%
No. of seats available abroad p.a. 12

Post-qualification
Salary (2009) £55,000
% of trainees offered job on qualification (2009) tbc%

Offices
London, Exeter, Manchester, Abu Dhabi, Dubai, Oman, Bahrain and Cairo

Veale Wasbrough Lawyers

Orchard Court, Orchard Lane, Bristol, BS1 5WS
Tel: (0117) 925 2020   Fax: (0117) 925 2025
Central Court, 25 Southampton Buildings, Chancery Lane, London, WC2A 1AL
Tel: (020) 3008 6395   Fax: (020) 3043 8889
Email: aparfitt@vwl.co.uk   Website: www.vwl.co.uk

Firm profile
Veale Wasbrough operates from a modern, open-plan and well-equipped office in Bristol and also has a London office in Chancery Lane. The firm believes the quality of the service provided to clients is fundamental to the success and growth of the business and believes the key to success is in the development of high-quality relationships between everyone within the firm and the firm's clients. Consequently the Partners have always made collaborative teamwork and training and development a high priority. Veale Wasborough was one of the first major regional law firms to acquire the Investor in People accreditation in June 1996.

Main areas of work
The firm provides full commercial law services and specialises in six key client sectors: public sector, education and charities, real estate, healthcare, regional corporates and family business. The firm also has two distinctly branded divisions, Augustines Injury Law and Convey Direct.

Trainee profile
The firm recruits 8-10 trainees annually. It is looking for graduates who will become dynamic lawyers, who will make the most of the training opportunities and positively contribute to the future of the firm. Applicants should have proven academic ability, be good team players, with strong communication skills and commercial awareness.

Training environment
The firm offers its trainees early responsibility. It provides four seats of six months in a variety of departments, including Augustines injury law, commercial and projects, commercial litigation, corporate, education, employment, private client and real estate (including construction and property litigation). Trainees therefore benefit from experience in a wide range of practice areas. Many of the firm's present Partners and senior lawyers trained with the firm and are now widely respected experts in their chosen field of specialism.

Sponsorship and awards
Successful candidates may be eligible for sponsorship for the Diploma in Law and/or Legal Practice Course, consisting of a grant for LPC fees and an interest-free loan.

Work experience/ schemes
The firm's summer vacation scheme offers a week's work experience, providing an insight into the day to day workings of a large firm of commercial lawyers as students spend time in different legal teams.

Partners 31
Assistant Solicitors 73
Total Trainees 17

Contact
Angela Parfitt, Recruitment Manager

Method of application
Application form on website

Selection procedure
Interview

Closing date for September 2012
31 July 2010

Application
Training contracts p.a. 8-10
% interviewed (2008) 15%
Required degree grade
Preferably 2:1

Training
1st year £23,000
2nd year £25,000
Holiday entitlement 25 days plus bank holidays

Post-qualification
Salary £35,000
% of trainees offered job on qualification (2008) 100%

Vinson & Elkins

CityPoint, 33rd Floor, One Ropemaker Street, London, EC2Y 9UE
Tel: (020) 7065 6000   Fax: (020) 7065 6001

Firm profile
Vinson & Elkins is one of the largest international law firms and has been repeatedly ranked as the world's leading energy law firm. Founded in Houston in 1917 (and with an office in London for over 30 years), Vinson & Elkins currently has over 750 lawyers with offices in Abu Dhabi, Austin, Beijing, Dallas, Dubai, Hong Kong, Houston, London, Moscow, New York, Shanghai, Tokyo and Washington, D.C.

Main areas of work
Cross-border M&A, private equity, corporate finance and securities advice (including London Main Market and AIM listings and international equity and debt capital markets), banking and finance, international energy transactions, project development and finance transactions, litigation and arbitration.

Trainee profile
The firm is looking for ambitious individuals with strong academic results and sound commercial awareness. The ability to think laterally and creatively is essential, as is a need for common-sense and a willingness to take the initiative.

Training environment
The firm currently offers three to four training contracts commencing each September. These are not run on a rigid seat system, but instead a trainee will gain wide experience in many different areas, working with a wide variety of associates and partners from across the firm.

Whilst the trainees are based in London, the firm is currently regularly seconding its trainees to other offices (particularly its offices in Dubai and Moscow).

Benefits
Private medical and dental, pension, season ticket loan, life assurance.

Vacation placements
Vinson & Elkins views vacation placements as a key part of its recruitment process. For summer 2010 apply by 28 February 2010, by way of online application form.

Sponsorship & awards
The firm pays all LPC course fees and a discretionary stipend (of up to £7,500) to assist with the LPC year.

Partners 9
Assistant Solicitors 17
Total Trainees 7

Contact
Mark Beeley (020) 7065 6046

Method of application
Online Application form

Selection procedure
Interview

Closing date for 2012
31 August 2010

Application
Training contracts p.a. 3-4
Applications p.a. 400
% interviewed p.a. 10%
Required degree grade 2:1

Training
Salary
1st year £40,000
2nd year £42,000
Holiday entitlement 25 days
% of trainees with a
non-law degree p.a. 40%
No. of seats available
abroad p.a. 4

Post-qualification
Salary £75,000
% of trainees offered job
on qualification 80-90%

Overseas, Regional offices
Abu Dhabi, Austin, Beijing, Dallas, Dubai, Hong Kong, Houston, London, Moscow, New York, Shanghai, Tokyo and Washington D.C.

Walker Morris

Kings Court, 12 King Street, Leeds LS1 2HL
Tel: (0113) 283 2500 Fax: (0113) 245 9412
Email: hellograduates@walkermorris.co.uk
Website: www.walkermorris.co.uk

Firm profile
Based in Leeds, Walker Morris is one of the largest commercial law firms in the North, with over 550 people, providing a full range of legal services to commercial and private clients both nationally and internationally.

Main areas of work
CDR, commercial, commercial property, construction, corporate, employment, finance, intellectual property, insolvency, liquor licensing and gaming, PFI/ public sector, planning and environmental, regulatory, sports, tax.

Trainee profile
Bright, articulate, highly motivated individuals who will thrive on early responsibility in a demanding yet friendly environment.

Training environment
Trainees commence with an induction programme, before spending four months in each main department (commercial property, corporate and commercial litigation). Trainees can choose in which departments they wish to spend their second year. Formal training will include lectures, interactive workshops, seminars and e-learning. The PSC covers the compulsory elements and the electives consist of a variety of specially tailored skills programmes. Individual IT training is provided. Opportunities can also arise for secondments to some of the firm's major clients. Emphasis is placed on teamwork, inside and outside the office. The firm's social and sporting activities are an important part of its culture and are organised by a committee drawn from all levels of the firm. A trainee solicitors' committee represents the trainees in the firm but also organises events and liaises with the Leeds Trainee Solicitors Group.

Vacation placements
Places for 2010: 48 over 3 weeks; Duration: 1 week; Remuneration: £250 p.w.; Closing Date: 31 January 2010.

Sponsorship & awards
LPC & PGDL fees plus maintenance of £5,000.

Partners 51
Assistant Solicitors 120
Total Trainees 37

Contact
Neil Lupton

Method of application
Online application form

Selection procedure
Telephone & face-to-face interviews

Closing date for 2012
31 July 2010

Application
Training contracts p.a. 20
Applications p.a. Approx. 800
% interviewed p.a.
Telephone 16%
Face to face 8%
Required degree grade 2:1

Training
Salary
1st year (2009) £24,000
2nd year (2009) £26,000
Holiday entitlement 24 days
% of trainees with a non-law degree p.a.
30% on average

Post-qualification
Salary (2008) £38,000
% of trainees offered job on qualification (2009) 75%
% of assistants (as at 1/7/09) who joined as trainees 55%
% of partners (as at 1/7/09) who joined as trainees 50%

Ward Hadaway

Sandgate House, 102 Quayside, Newcastle upon Tyne NE1 3DX
Tel: (0191) 204 4000 Fax: (0191) 204 4098
Email: recruitment@wardhadaway.com
Website: www.wardhadaway.com

Partners 59
Total Trainees 21
Contact
Graduate recruitment team
Method of application
firm's application form
Selection procedure
Assessment Centre and interview
Closing date for 2012
31 July 2010
Application
Training contracts p.a. 8-10
Applications p.a. 500+
% interviewed p.a. 10%
Required degree grade 2:1
Training
Salary
1st year (2009)
£20,000
2nd year (2009) £20,500
Holiday entitlement 25 days
% of trainees with a non-law degree p.a. Varies
Post-qualification
Salary (2009)
£35,000

Firm profile

Ward Hadaway is one of the most progressive law firms in the North East and is firmly established as one of the region's heavyweights. The firm attracts some of the most ambitious businesses in the region and its client base includes a large number of plcs, new start-ups and well established private companies.

As a business founded and located in the North East, the firm has grown rapidly, investing heavily in developing its existing people, and recruiting further outstanding individuals from inside and outside of the region. The firm is listed in the top 100 UK law firms.

Main areas of work

The firm is divided into five main departments; litigation, property, corporate, commercial and private client, with a number of cross departmental teams. The firm is commercially based, satisfying the needs of the business community in both business and private life. Clients vary from international plc's to local, private clients. The firm is on a number of panels including; the Arts Council, NHS (four panels), English Heritage, Department of Education and the General Teaching Council.

Trainee profile

The usual academic and professional qualifications are sought. Sound commercial and business awareness are essential as is the need to demonstrate strong communication skills, enthusiasm and flexibility. Candidates will be able to demonstrate excellent interpersonal and analytical skills.

Training environment

The training contract is structured around four seats, each of six months duration. At regular intervals, and each time you are due to change seat, you will have the opportunity to discuss the experience you would like to gain during your training contract. The firm will give high priority to your preferences. You will sit with a Partner or Associate which will enable you to learn how to deal with different situations. Your practical experience will also be complemented by an extensive programme of seminars and lectures. All trainees are allocated a 'buddy', usually a second year trainee or newly qualified solicitor, who can provide as much practical advice and guidance as possible during your training. The firm has an active social committee and offers a full range of sporting and social events.

Benefits

25 days holiday (27 after five years service), death in service insurance, contributory pension, flexible holiday scheme.

Vacation placements

Vacation placements run spring/summer between April and July and are of 1 week's duration. Applications should be received by 28 February 2010.

Sponsorship & awards

CPE GDL and LPC fees paid and maintenance grants in accordance with the terms of the firm's offer.

Warner Goodman LLP

Portland Chambers, 66 West Street, Fareham, Hampshire, PO16 0JR
Tel: (01329) 288 121   Fax: (01329) 822 714
8/9 College Place, London Road, Southampton, SO15 2FF
Coleman House, 2-4 Landport Terrace, Portsmouth, PO1 2RG
Email: enquiries@warnergoodman.co.uk   Website: www.warnergoodman.co.uk

Firm profile
Warner Goodman LLP is highly regarded in Hampshire as one of the county's most forward thinking and dynamic firms. The firm values its people highly and invests a lot of time in developing and nurturing their many talents. Work-life balance is respected and a flexible approach for those with caring responsibilities helps the firm retain many high performing fee earners. The firm takes particular pride in delivering professional client friendly services across its six legal disciplines. Advances in e-conveyancing, HIPS and paperless transactions are all exemplified at Warner Goodman.

Main areas of work
The firm is split into six business groups: WG Commercial (which handles all aspects of employment, company commercial, commercial litigation, commercial property, landlord and tennant and licensing), private client; injury and litigation, family, residential conveyancing and financial services.

Trainee profile
The firm seeks to recruit talented bright graduates with a good academic record together with a flair for communication and a common sense approach to business. The firm values an approachable, down to earth attitude. This way the firm can continue its track record in first-rate client service and can continue to put its clients first.

Training Environment
Training will comprise of either four seats of six months duration or occasionally three seats of eight months. Trainees may be asked to work at any of the firm's offices during the training contract giving trainees the opportunity of meeting as many people as possible throughout the firm and amongst the firm's clients, helping trainees to begin to establish their own reputation and following.

Sponsorship & awards
See website.

Partners 13
Total Trainees 4

Contact
Pamela Praine

Method of application
online application form

Selection procedure
Interview

Closing date for 2012
31 July 2010

Application
Average of 2 training contracts per year. Required degree grade 2:1

Training
Training is provided across the firms three offices, and covers each of the practice groups. Input from trainees is sought as to their preferred choice of seat

Post-qualification
Salary at market rate.
% of trainees offered job on qualification (2008) 80%

Regional offices
Fareham, Southampton, Portsmouth

Watson, Farley & Williams LLP

15 Appold Street, London EC2A 2HB
Tel: (020) 7814 8000 Fax: (020) 7814 8017
Email: graduates@wfw.com
Website: www.wfw.com/trainee

Firm profile
Watson, Farley & Williams was founded in 1982 in the City of London. It has since grown rapidly to 91 partners and a total staff of over 550. the firm now has offices in London, New York, Paris, Hamburg, Munich, Rome, Milan, Athens, Piraeus, Singapore, Bangkok.

Watson, Farley & Williams is an international corporate and commercial law firm recognised for its excellence in banking, structured and asset financing, particularly in the transport and energy sectors. Through its international network the firm's lawyers are able to advise in many languages including English, French, German, Greek, Russian, Italian, Thai, as well as advising in US Federal law. The international offices work together, a structure of particular benefit to international clients.

Main areas of work
The firm is divided into five international practice groups: international corporate, international shipping finance, international project and structured finance, international litigation and international tax. These groups are not divided by location but work together internationally. The International Corporate Group is divided into several sub-groups: corporate, employment, EU/competition and commercial property.

Trainee profile
The firm looks to recruit graduates who, in addition to a sound academic background, exhibit enthusiasm, ambition, self-assurance, initiative and an understanding of the commerical world.

Training environment
Each trainee undertakes six four-month seats, one of which will be based in Paris, Piraeus, Singapore or Bangkok. From day one the firm aims to give trainees real experience by sitting them with a partner or a senior assistant.

Each trainee is also likely to have a seat in one of the firm's more specialised areas such as tax, property, employment or EU competition. Trainees undertake professional skills training during their training contract and it also holds regular in-house seminars at which it invites guest speakers and partners to speak.

Benefits
25 days holiday, Income Protection, Life Assurance, Employee Assistance Programme, Pension, Interest Free Season Ticket Loan, £250 towards Sports Club membership, Private Healthcare.

Vacation placements
Places for 2009: 25; Duration: 2 weeks; Remuneration: £250 p.w.; Closing Date: 31st January 2010.

Sponsorship & awards
GDL and LPC fees paid and £6,500 maintenance p.a. (£5,500 outside London).

Partners 91
Total fee-earners 220
Total Trainees 27

Contact
Graduate Recruitment Manager

Method of application
Online application

Selection procedure
Assessment centre & Interview

Closing date for 2012
31 July 2010

Application
Training contracts p.a. 12-14
Applications p.a. 700
% interviewed p.a. 20-30%
Required degree grade
Minimum 2:1 & 300 UCAS points or above

Training
Salary
1st year (2009) £35,000
2nd year (2009) £40,000
Holiday entitlement 25 days
% of trainees with a non-law degree p.a. 50%
No. of seats available abroad p.a. 14

Post-qualification
Salary (2009)
Competitive
% of trainees offered job on qualification (2009) 92%
% of assistants (as at 01/09/09) who joined as trainees 60%
% of partners (as at 1/9/09) who joined as trainees 4%

Overseas offices
New York, Paris, Hamburg, Munich, Rome, Milan, Athens, Piraeus, Singapore, Bangkok

Wedlake Bell

52 Bedford Row, London, WC1R 4LR
Tel: (020) 7395 3000 Fax: (020) 7395 3100
Email: recruitment@wedlakebell.com
Website: www.wedlakebell.com

Firm profile
Wedlake Bell is a medium-sized law firm providing legal advice to businesses and high net worth individuals from around the world. The firm's services are based on a high degree of partner involvement, extensive business and commercial experience and strong technical expertise. The firm has approximately 100 lawyers in central London and Guernsey, and affiliations with law firms throughout Europe and in the United States.

Main areas of work
For the firm's business clients: banking & asset finance; corporate; corporate tax; business recoveries; commercial; intellectual property; information technology; media; commercial property; construction; residential property.

For private individuals: tax, trusts and wealth protection; offshore services; residential property.

Trainee profile
In addition to academic excellence, Wedlake Bell looks for commercial aptitude, flexibility, enthusiasm, a personable nature, confidence, mental agility and computer literacy in its candidates. Languages are not crucial.

Training environment
Trainees have four seats of six months across the following areas: corporate, corporate tax, business recoveries, banking, construction, media and IP/IT, employment, pensions, litigation, property and private client. As a trainee, the firm encourages you to have direct contact and involvement with clients from an early stage. Trainees will work within highly specialised teams and have a high degree of responsibility. Trainees will be closely supervised by a partner or senior solicitor and become involved in high quality and varied work. The firm is committed to the training and career development of its lawyers and many of its trainees continue their careers with the firm, often through to partnership. Wedlake Bell has an informal, creative and co-operative culture with a balanced approach to life.

Sponsorship & benefits
LPC fees paid and £4,000 maintenance grant where local authority grant not available. During training contract: pension, travel loans, corporate gym membership, health insurance and life assurance.

Vacation placements
Places for 2010: 8; Duration: 3 weeks in July; Remuneration: £200 p.w.; Closing Date: End of February, 2010.

Partners 43
Assistant Solicitors 49
Total Trainees 12

Contact
Natalie King

Method of application
Application form

Selection procedure
Two interviews & open day

Closing date for 2012
End of July 2010

Application
Training contracts p.a. 6
Required degree grade 2:1

Training
Salary
1st year £29,000
2nd year £31,000
Holiday entitlement
1st year 23 days
2nd year 24 days
% of trainees with a non-law degree p.a. 50%

Overseas offices
Guernsey

Weil, Gotshal & Manges

One South Place, London EC2M 2WG
Tel: (020) 7903 1074 Fax: (020) 7903 0990
Email: graduate.recruitment@weil.com
Website: www.weil.com

Firm profile

International law firm Weil, Gotshal & Manges has over 1,300 lawyers, including 300 partners, in 20 cities throughout the US, Europe and Asia.

The London office was established in 1996 and has grown to become the second largest of the firm's worldwide offices, with over 110 lawyers, 85% of which are UK-qualified. The London office is the hub of the firm's European practice.

Main areas of work

The firm's Restructuring Practice is recognised as one of the leading practices in its field. The firm has been involved in virtually every major chapter 11 reorganisation case in the US, including Lehmans, Washington Mutual and Pilgrim's Pride, and in major international out-of-court debt restructurings. The London team continues to build on that market-leading reputation across Europe, coordinating international corporate aspects of Lehmans, advising Icelandic bank Kaupstin and various SIC restructurings.

Balanced with its restructuring expertise, it is also one of the leading private equity law firms in London and Europe.

Lawyers in the office advise on all aspects of domestic and cross-border transactional and general corporate issues, including public and private mergers, acquisitions and disposals, demergers and re-organisations, equity capital markets, joint ventures and strategic alliances and corporate governance. Transactional support is provided by specialists in the fields of tax, real estate, commercial contracts, competition, employment/ employee benefits, environment, IP/IT and pensions. The firm offers specialist sector focus across a range of industries including consumer brands, defence, energy, healthcare, technology, media and telecommunications.

Few firms can match the quality and depth of Weil Gotshal's experience in litigation, arbitration and other forms of dispute resolution. The firm helps clients solve their toughest problems in any forum throughout the world and has an impressive track record for winning extremely large and difficult cases.

The firm has an international Finance Practice including bank and institutional lending, acquisition finance (including senior and mezzanine debt), asset finance, derivatives, refinancings and recapitalisations, debt capital markets (including high yield), structured finance, lease financings and securitisation which continues to be among the very best practices in London.

The firm's Antitrust/ Competition Practice is one of the largest, most diversified and highly respected in the legal and business community. The firm provides integrated global counseling, litigation, regulatory and transactional services to a wide range of industries.

Few firms place greater emphasis on pro bono work - the firm's award-winning programme is incredibly varied and upholds the highest standards of public service by the legal community.

Weil Gotshal also invests considerable time and effort in recruiting and retaining exceptional talent, from diverse backgrounds and cultures at all levels.

Vacation placements

Places for 2010 Summer: 15 places. Closing date for applications by online application form: 31 January 2010.

Partners 24
Assistant Solicitors 64
Total Trainees 22

Contact
Jillian Singh

Method of application
online application form

Closing date for 2012
31 July 2010

Application
Training contracts p.a. 10
Required degree grade 2:1

Training
Salary
1st year (2009) £41,000
Holiday entitlement 23 days

Overseas offices
Beijing, Boston, Budapest, Dallas, Dubai, Frankfurt, Hong Kong, Houston, Miami, Munich, New York, Paris, Prague, Providence, Silicon Valley, Singapore, Shanghai, Warsaw, Washington DC, Wilmington

White & Case LLP

5 Old Broad Street, London EC2N 1DW
Tel: (020) 7532 1000 Fax: (020) 7532 1001
Email: trainee@whitecase.com
Website: www.whitecasetrainee.com

	Partners 69 Assistant Solicitors 273 Total Trainees 56
Contact	Ms Jemma Stritch
Method of application	Online application via firm website
Selection procedure	Interview
Closing date for August 2012/ February 2013	31 July 2010
Application	Training contracts p.a. 30 Applications p.a. 1,700 Required degree grade 2:1
Training	Salary £41,000, rising by £1,000 every 6 months Holiday entitlement 25 days All trainees are guaranteed to spend a seat overseas
Post-qualification	Salary £72,000
Overseas offices	Abu Dhabi, Almaty, Ankara, Beijing, Berlin, Bratislava, Brussels, Bucharest, Budapest, Düsseldorf, Frankfurt, Geneva, Hamburg, Helsinki, Hong Kong, Istanbul, Johannesburg, London, Los Angeles, Mexico City, Miami, Moscow, Munich, New York, Palo Alto, Paris, Prague, Riyadh, São Paulo, Singapore, Shanghai, Stockholm, Tokyo, Warsaw, Washington DC

Firm profile

White & Case LLP is a global law firm with more than 2,100 lawyers worldwide. The firm has a network of 35 offices, providing the full range of legal services of the highest quality in virtually every major commercial centre and emerging market. They work with international businesses, financial institutions and governments worldwide on corporate and financial transactions and dispute resolution proceedings. Their clients range from some of the world's longest established and most respected names to many start-up visionaries. The firm's lawyers work on a variety of sophisticated, high-value transactions, many of which feature in the legal press worldwide as the firm's clients achieve firsts in privatisation, cross-border business deals, or major development projects.

Main areas of work

Banking and capital markets; construction and engineering; corporate (including M&A and private equity); dispute resolution (including arbitration & mediation); employment & benefits; energy, infrastructure, project & asset finance; IP, PPP/PFI; real estate; tax; and telecommunications.

Trainee profile

Trainees should be ambitious, creative and work well in teams. They should have an understanding of international commercial issues and have a desire to be involved in high profile, cross-border legal matters.

Training environment

Trainees undertake four seats, each of six months in duration. The firm guarantees that one of these seats can be spent overseas. Regardless of where they work, trainees get a high level of partner and senior associate contact from day one, ensuring they receive high quality, stimulating and rewarding work. Trainees are encouraged to take early responsibility and there is a strong emphasis on practical hands-on training, together with plenty of support and feedback. The firm recruits and develops trainee solicitors with the aim of retaining them on qualification.

Benefits

The firm operates a flexible benefits scheme, through which you can select the benefits you wish to receive. Currently, the benefits include private medial insurance, dental insurance, life assurance, pension, critical illness insurance, travel insurance, retail vouchers, gym membership, season ticket loan and green bikes.

Vacation placements

Places for 2010: 20-25 one-week Easter placements and 40-50 two-week Summer placements available. Remuneration: £350 per week; Closing Date: 31 January 2010.

Sponsorship & awards

GDL and LPC fees paid and £7,500 maintenance p.a. Awards for commendation and distinction for LPC.

Wiggin LLP

10th Floor, Met Building, 22 Percy Street, London, W1T 2BU
Tel: (020) 7612 9612   Fax (020) 7612 9611
The Promenade, Cheltenham GL50 1WG
Tel: (01242) 224114 Fax: (01242) 224223
Email: law@wiggin.co.uk Website: www.wiggin.co.uk

Firm profile
Wiggin are experts in the constantly evolving field of media law. They focus exclusively on media with particular emphasis on film, music, sport, gaming, technology, broadcast and publishing. They are recognised for the uncompromising excellence of their work and an unrelenting determination to deliver the best possible results for their media clients. They have an international reputation for their innovative approach, fresh thinking and cutting edge experience in media law; a sector that is changing with mesmerizing speed. The firm offers a highly personalised relationship, working in partnership with its clients to address the complex legal challenges that the fast evolving media industry presents. They have the knowledge and experience, as well as the commitment and confidence, to deliver straightforward and genuine advice motivated only by the need to achieve the best possible outcome for clients. Based primarily out of their Cheltenham office, and also in London, and with blue-chip clients based all over the World (primarily London and the west coast of America) the firm goes to where clients need them to be.

Main areas of work
Commercial 60%, Corporate 18%, Litigation 22%.

Trainee profile
If you want to experience high profile media issues in a forward thinking environment then contact Wiggin. They're looking for you if you can demonstrate a passion for media and the law, strong academic ability and a commitment to success. One word of warning though, their seats are not for the faint hearted! They need trainees that relish hard work and a challenge. They'll be at the law fairs so come and see what they are all about.

Training environment
Training is split into four seats and these will be allocated from company/commercial, commercial media (2 seats), media litigation, employment, film and property. Although based at the Cheltenham office, you will be meeting clients in London and could end up on a six-month secondment there with the British Phonographic Industry (the record industries trade association).

They don't want you to do the photocopying. Their trainees are encouraged to take an active role in transactions, assume responsibility and deal directly with clients. In-house seminars are held regularly and training reviews are held every three months. You'll get an experience just like your friends in the City but within the exciting and niche area of media law and within a firm small enough to recognise the importance of a personal approach.

Benefits
Life assurance, private health cover, pension scheme, permanent health insurance, gym membership at corporate rates.

Sponsorship & awards
PgDL and LPC fees and £3,500 maintenance p.a.

Partners 16
Assistant Solicitors 22
Total Trainees 8

Contact
Office Manager

Method of application
Online application only –
www.wiggin.co.uk

Selection procedure
Two-day selection

Closing date for 2012
31 July 2010

Application
Training contracts p.a. 4
Applications p.a. 500
% interviewed p.a. 8%
Required degree grade 2:1

Training
Salary
1st year £26,500
2nd year £31,500
Holiday entitlement 20 days + one day per annum up to max 25 days
% of trainees with a non-law degree p.a. 50%

Post-qualification
Salary £50,000
% of trainees offered job on qualification (2009) 60%
% of assistants (as at 2009) who joined as trainees 20%
% of partners (as at 2009) who joined as trainees 19%

Wilsons Solicitors LLP

Steynings House, Summerlock Approach, Salisbury, Wiltshire, SP2 7RJ
Tel: (01722) 412 412   Fax: (01722) 427 610
Email: jo.ratcliffe@wilsonslaw.com
Website: www.wilsonslaw.com

Partners 32
Trainees 9
Total Staff 183

Contact
Mrs J Ratcliffe
jo.ratcliffe@wilsonslaw.com

Method of application
Application via website or CV

Selection procedure
interview and assessment day

Closing dates for
training scheme:
31 March 2010 for training
contract to commence in
September 2011 and 2012

Application
Training contracts p.a. 4
Required degree grade 2:1
Salary
market rate
Holiday entitlement 22 days

Offices
Salisbury, London

Firm profile
Wilsons is ranked as one of the top private client and charity law firms in the country. The firm's 270-year heritage, combined with lawyers who are recognised leaders in their fields, enables the firm to provide a unique combination of skills and experience to wealthy individuals, entrepreneurs, companies, landed estates, trust companies and charities.

Working from the Salisbury and London offices, the firm currently employs 183 people, 61 of whom are lawyers and 32 are partners. The firm prides itself on the quality of its bespoke service delivery. Lawyers are dedicated to ensuring a detailed understanding of clients interests and a seamless working relationship across the different specialities of the practice.

Main areas of work
Private Client: One of the largest private client teams outside of London, its leading practice delivers services which include tax, estate and succession planning, UK and Offshore tax and trusts, Wills, probate and trust administration, litigation and family.
Charities & Education: One of the top five charity practices in the country offering clients corporate and governance advice and both contentious and non-contentious legacy work for the charity.
Company Commercial: The team specialise in employment, commercial property, insolvency, mergers and acquisitions and corporate finance.
Agriculture & Rural Affairs: Many of the firm's clients are substantial land owners and the highly regarded team offer services including property transactions, litigation, tax planning and advice on diversification. The team also specialise in landowner development, working solely for landowners.

Trainee profile
The firm aims to employ the highest quality people. Its reputation relies upon this. The firm places considerable emphasis on teamwork and for this reason it looks for applicants who are clear team players. If quality of life is important to you, the firm would like to meet you.

Training environment
Despite the firm's national and international client base the centre of its operations are situated in Salisbury. During its 270 year history the firm has attracted several senior City lawyers and an enviable client base. This ensures an exceptional quality of work within beautiful surroundings. An open approach to management means information is available across the firm and a flat structure means plenty of potential for positions of responsibility.
A two year training contract enables trainees to samples four disciplines with six monthly seats in different practice areas.

Benefits
Pension (2% in first year, 3% in second year), life assurance (2 times salary), choice of optional benefits and private medical insurance.

Work experience placements
One week available in July at our head office in Salisbury.

Sponsorship & awards
On joining the firm as a trainee the firm can offer you an interest free loan of up to £4,500 for the Legal Practice Course. The firm is committed to your training contract and would hope to retain you once you qualify. If you stay with Wilsons for two years after qualifying the loan will be written off.

Winckworth Sherwood

Minerva House, 5 Montague Close, London, SE1 9BB
Tel: (020) 7593 5000   Fax: (020) 7593 5099
Email: trainees@wslaw.co.uk
Website: www.wslaw.co.uk

Partners 30
Assistant Solicitors 52
Total Trainees 8

Contact
Hugh MacDougald, Training Partner (020) 7593 5149
Heather Cornish (HR) (020) 7593 5077

Method of application
Online application form on website www.wslaw.co.uk

Selection procedure
Two interviews

Closing date for 2012
31 July 2010

Application
Training contracts p.a. 4
Applications p.a. 200
% interviewed p.a. 15%
Required degree grade 2:1

Training
Salary
1st year (2009) £27,000
2nd year (2009) £31,000
Holiday entitlement 24 days + one day at Christmas

Firm profile
Winckworth Sherwood is a dynamic law firm with a commitment to provide clients with more than just legal advice. The firm's diversity is its strength and its lawyers include leading specialists in their fields many with deep personal investment in the firm's clients sectors. This gives trainees a broad exposure to the law as well as a deeper understanding of the sectors which the firm supports. The firm is at the forefront of the private and public sector interface and its modern and collaborative approach enables it to adapt to its clients' individual businesses, providing them with pragmatic solutions to their whole range of requirements. The firm has offices in London, Oxford and Chelmsford although training only takes place at its London office.

Main areas of work
The firm's main specialist areas include real estate, social housing, house building, planning, parliamentary, transport, commercial, ecclesiastical, private client, licensing, dispute resolution and employment. Clients are diverse and include Genesis Housing Group, Barratt, Bellway, Sainsbury's, T Mobile, National Audit bodies, the Rail and Safety Standards Board (RSSB), the Church of England, the Port of London Authority and the Department for Transport.

Trainee profile
The firm requires a strong academic record both at school and university, but it also looks for attributes which demonstrate the potential for making a positive contribution to the firm. It is important to be able to empathise with clients whilst at the same time keeping a clear business head; the firm looks for evidence of these qualities at the outset. The firm is also interested in indications of high achievement in non-academic pursuits. It is a highly individual firm and wants independent, intelligent and personable trainees – not a type. It wants people who, after training, can provide a client with new ideas, bring a fresh approach and help them achieve desired results in a changing legal environment.

Training environment
The firm recruits four trainee solicitors a year; it keeps the number deliberately low to maximise the staff/trainee ratio, so that its trainees are fully involved in all aspects of each department in their two year training period. As a trainee you will rotate through four departments in six month placements or 'seats'. The purpose of each seat is to give you a solid grounding in that area of the law. The firm encourages substantial client contact from the start and you will be involved in all phases of a matter. As a trainee you will usually sit with a partner or senior solicitor and may be given the opportunity to manage your own files, subject to suitable supervision. The firm has a well developed in-house continuing education programme which draws upon the expertise of partners, qualified staff and guest professionals, in which trainees are encouraged to participate.

Benefits
Private health insurance, season ticket loan, life insurance. The holiday allocation is 24 days plus public holidays and one extra day at Christmas.

Sponsorship & awards
Under certain conditions the firm also provides financial assistance to trainees attending the Legal Practice Course (LPC) or Graduate Diploma in Law (GDL).

Withers LLP

16 Old Bailey, London EC4M 7EG
Tel: (020) 7597 6000 Fax: (020) 7329 2534
Email: jaya.louvre@withersworldwide.com
Website: www.withersworldwide.com

Firm profile
Withers LLP is the first international law firm dedicated to the business, personal and philanthropic interests of successful people, their families, their businesses and their advisers.

The firm's mission is to offer a truly integrated legal service to people with sophisticated global wealth, management and business needs.

Main areas of work
The wealth of today's private client has increased in multiples and many are institutions in their own right. The firm has been able to respond to these changing legal needs and offers integrated solutions to the international legal and tax needs of its clients. The firm has unparalleled expertise in commercial and tax law, trusts, estate planning, litigation, charities, employment, family law and other legal issues facing high net worth individuals.

Withers' reputation in commercial law along with its status as the largest Private Client Team in Europe and leading Family Team sets it apart from other City firms.

International exposure at Withers does not mean working in one of the firm's foreign offices, (although trainees can do seats abroad). Much of the work undertaken in London crosses numerous jurisdictions. Currently the firm acts for around a quarter of The Sunday Times Rich List and a significant number of the US 'Forbes' and Asian 'Hurun' Rich Lists.

Trainee profile
Each year the firm looks for a diverse mix of trainees who are excited by the prospect of working with leaders in their field. Trainees must have an excellent academic background and great attention to detail. Team players with leadership potential are of interest to the firm, as is an international outlook and foreign language skills.

Training environment
Trainees spend six months in four different departments. Working in a team with a partner and an assistant solicitor provides autonomy, responsibility and fast development. Buddy and mentor systems as well as on the job training ensure trainees are fully supported from the outset.

Application
Apply online by 31 July 2010 to begin training in August 2012. Interviews usually take place between April and September.

Vacation scheme
The firm runs two week long placements at Easter and over the summer in London and during the Summer in Milan. Apply online by 31 January 2010 for places in 2010. Interviews take place between February and April.

Sponsorship
Fees plus £5 000 maintenance for both the PgDL or CPE and/or LPC are paid.

Partners 111
Total Staff 600
Trainees 36

Contact
Jaya Louvre
Recruitment Manager

Method of application
Application form (available online)

Selection procedure
2 interviews incl. written exercise and presentation

Closing dates for 2012 training scheme:
31 July 2010
2009 vacation placements:
31 January 2010

Application
Training contracts p.a. 16
Applications p.a. 700
% interviewed p.a. 10%
Required grades 2:1, AAB at A-Level

Training
Salary
1st year (2008) £33,000
2nd year (2008) £35,000
Holiday entitlement 23 days
% of trainees with a
non-law degree p.a. 50%

Post-qualification
Salary (2008) £53,000

Offices
London, Milan, Geneva, New York, New Haven, (Connecticut), Greenwich (USA), Hong Kong, BVI

Wragge & Co LLP

55 Colmore Row, Birmingham B3 2AS
Tel: Freephone (0800) 096 9610
Email: gradmail@wragge.com
Website: www.wragge.com/graduate

Firm profile

Wragge & Co is a major UK law firm providing a full service to some of the world's largest and most successful organisations, including 27 FTSE 100 and 22 FTSE 250 companies. It is the only law firm to feature in the Top 50 Best Workplaces in the UK and was named the UK's most client-focused law firm at the 2009 Legal Technology Awards. Working from London or Birmingham on high profile national and international instructions, you will be part of a team passionate about providing the very best client service.

Wragge & Co is a relationship firm, taking time to form lasting relationships with clients to ensure understanding of what makes their businesses tick.

Relationships and excellent client service are two of the firm's driving forces.

To make sure it gets both right, you may find yourself on secondment, experiencing life and work as a client. Relationships within the firm are just as important. The firm is a single team, working together to support colleagues and clients alike. The firm values minimum hierarchy so it is open plan. Everyone has the same space. In fact, being open and honest is one of the firm's most precious values.

Main areas of work

The firm has nationally recognised teams in specialist areas including employment, banking, antitrust, outsourcing, private finance initiatives and regeneration.

This year Wragge & Co was named European High-Tech Law Firm of the Year by Managing Intellectual Property and Employment Team of the Year at the Lawyer Awards.

The firm's core areas of legal advice include corporate, real estate, finance, projects and technology, human resources and dispute resolution. The quality of work is reflected in the firm's client list which includes British Airways, GlaxoSmithKline, Marks & Spencer and E.ON.

Trainee profile

The firm is looking for graduates with some legal or commercial work experience gained either via a holiday job or a previous career. You should be practical, with a common sense and problem solving approach to work, and be able to show adaptability, enthusiasm and ambition.

Vacation placements

Easter and summer vacation placements are offered at Wragge & Co. As part of our scheme you will get the opportunity to experience different areas of the firm, attend client meetings and get involved in real files. You can apply online at www.wragge.com/graduate. The closing date is 31 January 2010.

Training contracts

The firm is currently recruiting for up to 30 training contracts to commence in September 2012/March 2013. You can apply online at www.wragge.com/graduate. The closing date is 31 July 2010.

Partners 112
Qualified Solicitors (excluding partners) 304
Total Trainees 53

Contact
Michelle Byron
Graduate Recruitment Advisor or
Carli Orme Recruitment Officer

Method of application
Applications are made online at www.wragge.com/graduate

Selection procedure
Telephone discussion & assessment day

Closing date
Sept 2012/March 2013: 31 July 2010.

Application
Training contracts p.a. 30
Applications p.a. 1,000
% interviewed p.a. 25%

Training
Salary Birmingham (March 2009)
1st year £25,750
2nd year £28,750
Holiday entitlement 25 days
% of trainees with a non-law degree p.a. Varies

Post-qualification
Salary (2009)
Birmingham £36,500
London £57,000
% of trainees offered job on qualification
(Sept 2009) 83%

The Bar

Barcode	**672**
A career at the Bar	**673**
The Inns of Court	**678**
Practice areas at the Bar	**680**
Chambers reports	**688**

Barcode

Don't let the often curious terms used at the Bar confuse or intimidate you!

Barrister – a member of the Bar of England and Wales
Bench – the judiciary
Bencher – a senior member of an Inn of Court. Usually silks and judges, known as masters of the bench
Brief – the documents setting out case instructions
BPTC – the Bar Professional Training Course. This replaces the BVC (Bar Vocational Course). Successful completion entitles you to call yourself a barrister in non-legal situations (ie dinner parties), but does not of itself give you rights of audience.
BPTC Online – the application system through which applications to Bar school must be made
Cab-rank rule – self-employed barristers cannot refuse instructions if they have the time and experience to undertake the case. You cannot refuse to represent someone because you find their opinions or actions objectionable
Call – the ceremony whereby you become a barrister
Chambers – a group of barristers in independent practice who have joined together to share the costs of practising. Chambers is also the name used for a judge's private office
Circuit – The courts of England and Wales are divided into six circuits: North Eastern, Northern, Midland & Oxford, South Eastern, Western, and Wales & Chester
Clerk – administrator/manager in chambers who organises work for barristers and payment of fees, etc
Counsel – a barrister
Cracked trial – a case that is concluded without a trial. This will be because the defendant offers an acceptable plea or the prosecution offers no evidence. Cracked and ineffective trials (where there is a lack of court time or the defendant or a witness does not attend) frustrate the bench and are considered a waste of money
Devilling – (paid) work done by a junior member of chambers for a more senior member
Employed bar – some barristers do not engage in private practice at chambers, but are employed full time by a company or public body
First and second six – pupillages are divided into two six-month periods. Most chambers now only offer 12-month pupillages, but it is still possible to undertake the two sixes at different sets

FRU – the Free Representation Unit. Any budding barrister should consider membership of this organisation. For more details see page 34
Independent Bar – the collective name for barristers who practise on a self-employed basis
Inns of Court – ancient institutions that alone have the power to 'make' barristers. There was a time when there was a proliferation of them but now there are only four: Gray's Inn, Inner Temple, Lincoln's Inn and Middle Temple. Read more about the Inns on page 678
Junior – a barrister not yet appointed silk. Note: older juniors are known as senior juniors
Junior brief – a case on which a junior is led by a senior. Such cases are too much work for one barrister alone and may involve a lot of research or run for a long time. Ordinarily, junior counsel will not conduct advocacy
Keeping term – eating the dinners in hall required to be eligible for call to the Bar
Mini-pupillage – a short period of work experience spent in chambers
Pupillage – the year of training undertaken after Bar school and before tenancy
Pupillage Portal – this online application system for pupillage replaces the Bar Council's old OLPAS system
Pupilmaster – a senior barrister with whom a pupil sits and who teaches the pupil. The Bar Council is encouraging the term pupil supervisor
QC – one of Her Majesty's Counsel, formerly appointed by the Lord Chancellor. The system fell into abeyance in 2004 and has now been revived with a new, more open appointments system
QLTT – the Qualified Lawyers' Transfer Test allows for the conversion of barristers' qualifications to that of a solicitor
Set – as in a 'set of chambers'
Silk – a QC, so named because of their silk robes
Supervisor – the new name for a pupilmaster
Tenant/tenancy – permission from chambers to join their set and work with them. A 'squatter' is someone who is permitted to use chambers' premises, but is not actually a member of the set. A 'door tenant' is someone who is affiliated with the set, but does not conduct business from chambers' premises

A career at the Bar

Most barristers believe they have the best job in the world. The Bar may be a competitive profession in which the work can be arduous, but the combination of excitement, advocacy, extraordinary experiences, fulfilment and kudos is unique.

Nice work if you can get it

Small wonder then that becoming a barrister is so deeply competitive. The statistics are sobering: the number of candidates starting the BVC rose from 1,407 in 2000/01 to 1,932 in 2006/07, while the total number of first-six pupillages available fell from 695 to 527 in the same period. Hoping to address this over-subscription by raising admission standards for the new Bar Professional Training Course (BPTC), the Bar Council has proposed various changes including an aptitude test which, if it is actually brought in, may affect applicants wishing to start in 2011. The number of enrolments on the BVC had actually already started to fall after peaking in 2007, but the hard fact is that roughly only one in four who commence the course gain pupillage and even fewer gain tenancy. These odds might and probably should discourage the casual applicant, but the average would-be barrister is made of stern stuff and usually has a deep-seated commitment to this branch of the profession.

Will you make it?

So, we've established your vocational drive, but what else helps you make the grade? This is a hard one. Meet enough pupils and barristers and you can see what makes someone successful. The fact that you're gobby/argumentative/confident doesn't mean you'll make it, nor is success guaranteed by ten A*s at A Level and an ability to complete *The Times* crossword in three minutes. Ask a chambers recruiter to define the qualities they look for and they will speak in fairly general terms (academic credentials, people skills, analytical skills, commitment, passion, an ability to express ideas) with the vague caveat that 'you know a good one when you see one'. Perhaps it's best to say that those who thrive at the Bar are people who offer the right traits for their chosen area of practice. Crime is all about guts, personality and advocacy ability, and being to-the-point, down to earth and able to assimilate and recall facts easily is more important than genius. Commercial practice is a more sophisticated game. Brains, commercial acumen and an easy manner with business clients are a must in construction, commercial or Chancery work, while specialisms like tax attract true brainboxes. Advocacy is still important in these areas, but deriving pleasure from crafting a masterpiece of written advice or delivering a phenomenally complex legal argument succinctly is even more so.

By reading the **Chambers Reports** and **Practice Areas at the Bar** you will understand more about the skills required in the Bar's various specialist practices.

Is the cost of training prohibitive?

In a word, yes. The GDL conversion course is quite expensive, the BVC/BPTC is painfully expensive, and many criminal or general common law sets are happy to pay their pupils the Bar Council bare minimum award of £833.33 per month. Some commercial sets make large pupillage awards available, ensuring that they are in line with the salaries of trainee solicitors at big City solicitors' firms; they will even advance funds for the BVC/BPTC year, but unless you've a source of cash, getting to tenancy is a pricey business most commonly funded through bank loans. Read the Funding section on page 77 for more ideas. Of all the potential sponsors out there, the four Inns of Court have the deepest pockets and they make around £4.5m available each year to students.

Huge debts aren't so much of a problem if you'll soon be earning a fat income, but the common perception that all barristers are loaded isn't quite right. Those determined to serve their community will find publicly funded civil, family and criminal work in the midst of a rationalisation by the Legal Services Commission (LSC) that is particularly affecting the availability of instructions at the junior end. Taking some cues from Lord Carter of Coles' 2006 overarching review/shake-up of the provision of publicly funded legal services – and often doing its own thing as well – the LSC's changes, funding cuts and focus on solicitors tendering for contracts as a means of ensuring value for money have caused disquiet at the Bar. Smaller sets are already feeling the pinch. Despite this gloomy description, it is worth remembering that big sets continue to thrive, and each of those fields continue to attract privately paying clients. By contrast, there's no question that the Commercial Bar pays very well. Comm Bar stars can earn £2m or more per year, while pupils who make it to tenancy in good-quality sets can outstrip solicitor colleagues immediately. To give some substance to this comparison, baby juniors in commercial sets can earn from £45,000-£100,000 in their first year alone, while their Criminal Bar contemporaries will be aiming for something like £20,000-

£40,000. Do remember that within each practice at the Bar there are a few Premier League sets and many others in lower divisions: the difference in earnings between the top and the bottom is substantial.

Mini-pupillages

If you're still at university there's plenty you can do to prepare yourself for a shot at the Bar. If there is anything a little *outré* about your CV – you're mature or you have poor A Levels, for instance – getting a First is a really good idea. Applicants with 2:1s are two a penny and a 2:2 will scupper your chances unless you can evidence some pretty remarkable mitigating circumstances or other qualities. In general, chambers are much more interested in your undergraduate performance than what you can muster up on the GDL or BVC/BPTC, but there's never any harm in getting the best grades at every stage. As for post-graduate degrees – a master's from a very good university, either in the UK or abroad – it must be your choice whether to take one or not. All we can say is that many of the Bar's most successful candidates have such a qualification, though by no means all of them. A master's degree is not a silver bullet.

The best way to demonstrate commitment to the Bar is to undertake mini-pupillages – that's barristerspeak for work experience. Whether assessed or unassessed, minis all involve observing barristers in chambers and probably also in court, although the degree of involvement varies hugely from one set to another. A good mini will see you sit in on a pre-trial conference (with the client's permission) and be included in discussions about the law. Don't become fixed on the idea of spending a whole week in chambers, as you may find it easier, more economical and just as beneficial to get a couple of days here and there. Assessed minis are the same, with an added element of paperwork or grading through oral discussion. A typical scenario will see mini-pupils given a set of papers to analyse before producing a piece of written work, which may then be discussed with a supervisor. Some sets only conduct assessed minis or make them a formal part of the recruitment process, but the average outfit recognises that would-be pupils can't go everywhere. During our travels around the Bar this year we met several pupils who hadn't done a mini at their own set.

A mini-pupillage is an important point of contact with a set, an opportunity to show your mettle and create a good impression for a later application. It's also CV and interview fodder: take notes, don't be afraid to ask questions at appropriate moments and be sure to reflect on what was good and bad about your experiences. Recruiters tell us that candidates who simply list or describe legal work experience fall down in comparison with those who can articulate what they've learned from shadowing practitioners. Not all sets offer mini-pupillages, and some will only take students in the final year of academic legal studies (be it degree or GDL), so start off by checking their websites carefully for how and when to apply. In general you should aim for as many as it takes you to decide which areas of practice interest you. Gaining pupillage may be a strictly fair process these days, but personal contacts can still help in obtaining a mini. Apply to an Inn of Court to be assigned a sponsor or if you've started dining at your Inn then start schmoozing.

How to stand out from the crowd

The Bar Council prescribes that BVC/BPTC students must undertake a certain amount of pro bono work. To ensure that you do land something that interests you and adds real weight to a pupillage application form, it is a good idea to investigate the options as soon as possible. You should also heed the advice of the QC who said: "*Do everything you can.*" Get involved with every debating and mooting opportunity, enter mock trial competitions at law school and keep an eye out for essay competitions. The scholarships offered by the Inns are not just a way of funding your education – don't underestimate the capacity of a major prize or award to mark you out from other well-qualified candidates.

Through the Portal

Unless taking time out from academia, most LLB candidates make applications during their final year at university, although in an attempt to snap up the best candidates some of the top commercial sets encourage students to apply in their penultimate year. In 2009 the Bar Council replaced its OLPAS online pupillage application system with a new one called Pupillage Portal. The main aim was to allow applicants to tailor their applications for each of the sets they apply to. While this is an improvement on the old scheme, those who used the system for the first time in 2009 were alarmed by the problems encountered. Hopefully the scheme will run more efficiently second time round. Just as before, the maximum number of sets an applicant can target is 12.

The Pupillage Portal operates just one round per year (as opposed to two under the old system) as it was found that 95% of chambers never made any offers in the second, autumn season of OLPAS. Though participation is voluntary for chambers, if they run their own separate application schemes they must still advertise all vacancies on the Portal website www.pupillages.com and in the Pupillages Handbook. This book is published in March each year to coincide with the National Pupillage Fair in London.

The portal is reasonably easy to use, though drama can be avoided if you fill out all the required details in a Word document and then paste it into the required fields. We found that the site times out after about 30 minutes of inactivity, and in any event you're going to find the process very time consuming so start early. In general, the fields in which you write are generously sized, with a maximum of 350 words allowed for your perfect answers to questions like 'Why do you want to be a barrister?' and

'What areas of law interest you?' You also have 300 words for a 'covering letter' and a further 500 to discuss any further experiences you feel are relevant. In saying all this, do bear in mind that chambers' recruiters can feel quite worn down by excessively long forms. Try to find the right balance between detailed and snappy answers and definitely leave out that one time you went to band camp.

Students can be alerted by e-mail or SMS of the results of their applications, and remember, when you do get good news you have at least two weeks to make a decision. It's important to remember that if you withdraw you cannot reapply in the same year, so save yourself the grief and do your research thoroughly.

It is possible to use the Portal to make a single 'clearing' application. This facility is also used by those who were unsuccessful with all of their 12 first-round applications. The Portal clearing phase allows sets with unfilled vacancies in August to scout for suitable candidates. It is for the sets to make the first move and applicants are advised not to approach them directly. In making a clearing application it's best to keep your parameters as wide as possible to retain your appeal to a broad range of sets. Your application will be accessible to all chambers participating in the clearing process. Clearing opens to chambers around the middle of September and closes in the middle of October. Various deadlines needed to be extended in 2009, but hopefully problems within the system will be rectified by 2010.

Beyond the Portal

Numerous sets recruit pupils outside the Portal machinery because they don't like its format or timetable and feel their interests will be better served by other means. The application method at each non-Portal set will be different; however, all must still advertise vacancies on www.pupillages.com. Some choose to mirror the Portal timetable in their own application procedures, but many don't and this can bring its own problems. The 'exploding offer' phenomenon is a real difficulty: what do you do if a non-Portal set makes you an attractive offer before your 12 Portal applications play out? The decision here must be yours. The good news is that non-Portal sets are generally very good at laying out the specifics of their application process on their websites.

The interview

So you've got an interview – well done. Dress neatly and discreetly with hair tidy, teeth flossed, tie sober, jacket done up. Most chambers will be grading you on standard criteria that include everything from intellect to personality and many publish these guidelines online.

As a rough guide, you can expect your first interview to involve a discussion of the hottest topics in your prospective practice area and some investigation into you and your application form. Remember: you'll face a panel that wants you to stand out. Naturally you should read *The Times'* law supplement every Thursday (you can get it e-mailed), keep your subscription to *Counsel* up to date and maybe even set the Pupillage Portal website as your homepage. Preparation for your interviews should consist of more than boning up on the law; it's important to be clued-up on current affairs too. Finally, think about what isn't on your CV and how you can account for disappointing grades or anything that is missing.

For second interviews expect a larger panel made up of a broader cross-section of people from chambers. While the format of the interviews may vary between sets, the panel will always want to assess the depth of your legal knowledge, your advocacy potential and your strength of character. Weaknesses on your CV will be sniffed out and pursued with tenacity. Don't let them push you around; if you can support your position then stick to it. Resolve is just as necessary for a career at the Bar as receptivity; they want to know that you can fight your corner. Observed one recruiter: *"It is amazing how many people can't stand up for themselves, which is all you want to see."*

Criminal and mixed sets will commonly give you an advocacy exercise, such as a bail application or a plea in mitigation (their basic structures will fit on a post-it, so why not note them down and keep with you at all times). Most, if not all, sets will pose a legal problem of some sort, with the amount of preparation time you are given ranging from ten minutes to a week. If you know that this is going to happen then do take an appropriate practitioner's text unless you know that one will be made available to you. That said, chambers generally aren't looking for faultless knowledge of substantive law, but are trying to get an insight into how your mind works. As one seasoned interviewer explained: *"We are more interested in seeing how a candidate approaches a problem than whether or not they get the right answer."* Other recruiters may not be so forgiving! A second interview is often the time when an ethics question may raise its head. You can prepare by reading the Bar's Code of Conduct, which is available on the Bar Council's website. It's a real page turner. To all rules there are exceptions, but these days sets are pretty good about detailing their procedures online, so with the right research you shouldn't be in for any shocks.

Try, try and try again?

What if you still don't have pupillage by the time you have finished the BPTC? Rather than seeing an enforced year out as a grim prospect, view it as a time to improve your CV and become more marketable. If you are interested in a specialist area of practice consider a master's degree. If the thought of another year in education brings you out in a cold sweat then seek out some useful practical experience. The most obvious answer is to apply for paralegalling and outdoor clerking jobs at solicitors' firms. Although these positions are rarer than hens' teeth, right now, the work you do as a paralegal should teach you how cases actually work and how solicitors – your future clients – operate. As an outdoor clerk you will be in court all the time taking notes. This will give you insight into the procedures and politics of trials. The year might also be spent with an organisation that works in an area related to your legal interest. We have interviewed several lawyers who secured pupillages following a period with a charity or not-for-profit organisation.

Pupillage

If you do gain a pupillage, congratulations! Now the hard work really starts. How the year is divided varies from set to set, but no matter how many pupil supervisors are allotted, the broad division is between the first, non-practising six months and the second, when pupils are permitted to be on their feet in court. During the first six, pupils are tethered to their supervisor, shadowing them at court, conferences and in chambers. They will also likely draft pleadings, advices, skeletons or do research for matters that the supervisor is working on. The nature of the second six will depend on the specific area of practice. At a busy criminal set it can mean court every day, and many civil or commercial sets specialising in areas like employment, PI, construction or insurance will send their pupils out up to three times a week. Some big commercial or Chancery sets actively prefer to keep pupils in chambers throughout the year, either for the purposes of assessment or because the nature of the work means pupils are too inexperienced to take it.

Tenancy

Tenancy is the prize at the end of the year-long interview that is pupillage. Effectively, an offer of tenancy is an invitation from a set to take a space in their chambers as a self-employed practitioner, sharing the services of the clerking and administrative team. How many tenants a set takes on post-pupillage is usually as dependent on the amount of space and work available in chambers as on the quality of the candidates. If you are curious about a set's growth, check to see how many new tenants have joined in recent years by viewing the list of members on its website and compare that against the number of pupillages offered in the same period.

Usually tenancies are awarded after a vote of all members of chambers, after recommendations from a tenancy committee, clerks and possibly also instructing solicitors. Decisions are commonly made in the July of the pupillage year, allowing unsuccessful pupils time to cast around for other tenancy offers or a 'third six' elsewhere. There is evidence to suggest that civil and commercial sets have higher pupil-to-tenant conversion rates than criminal sets. Certainly, it is quite usual for a 12-month criminal pupillage to be followed by a third or subsequent six somewhere other than a pupil's first set. However, plenty of commercial pupils do also find themselves looking for a third six. The general rule is that if a third six is not successful, it is time to look outside the Bar, with it being common for pupils to move to a solicitors' firm, either as an advocate or with a view to qualifying as a solicitor.

Our top five tips

- Keep it personal: Anchor your spiel in your own experiences for a more persuasive application. Eg, only list FRU if you've actually signed out a case.
- Keep it pithy: As Shakespeare once said, brevity is the soul of wit. It should also be the spirit of a pupillage application. Keep it relevant.
- Avoid being trite: Why do you want to be a barrister? Why are you interested in a set? You will be asked to explain yourself, so think what the obvious answer is and then write something more meaningful.
- Write proper: The profession is based upon exact and careful use of the English language, so be eloquent, direct and accurate. One common mistake to remember: 'practice' is the noun; 'practise' is the verb.
- Don't make silly mistakes: Your mantra should be: 'Save, print, check. Save, print, check.' With some sets getting 500 applications, they are itching for a reason to put yours in the bin. Don't give them this one.

And finally...

Few readers will have changed their minds about a career at the Bar after reading these pages. If there's one thing wannabe-barristers have in common it is a firm belief that they are one of the lucky ones who will succeed.

	99-00	00-01	01-02	02-03	03-04	04-05	05-06	06-07	07-08	08-09
BVC applicants	2,370	2,252	2,119	2,067	2,570	2,883	2,917	2,870	2,864	2,540
BVC enrolments	1,490	1,407	1,386	1,332	1,406	1,665	1,745	1,932	1,837	1,749
Students passing the BVC	1,201	1,081	1,188	1,121	1,251	1,392	1,480	1,560	1,720	n/a
First-six pupils	681	695	812	586	518	571	515	527	561	340 (1)
Second-six pupils	704	700	724	702	557	598	567	563	554	482 (1)
Pupils awarded tenancy	511	535	541	698	601	544	531	499	494	287 (2)

Certain figures were unavailable from the Bar Council at the time of going to press. The BVC will be replaced by the Bar Professional Training Course from 2010
(1) Figures from period 1st October 2008-16th June 2009 (2) Figures from period 1st October 2008-12th December 2008

- **Wise words from a QC:** "People will look at our website and see 60-something mostly white faces, mainly from Oxbridge, and think 'I don't stand a chance because I'm not like them'. The message I'd love to get across is: yes you do, we'll give you the same crack of the whip that everyone else gets." The posh boys might get better preparation from their tutors but if you have real talent you shouldn't be afraid to give it a shot – no matter what your background.

top tip no. 33

The Inns of Court

The four Inns of Court appear as oases of calm amid the hustle and bustle of London's legal heartland. Named Lincoln's Inn, Inner Temple, Middle Temple and Gray's Inn, they have many similarities with Oxbridge colleges, not least their libraries, chapels, halls and ancient traditions. So exquisite are some of the locations that they have provided the backdrop for Dickens novels and even Dan Brown schlockbuster *The Da Vinci Code*.

The Inns provide teaching, guidance, scholarships, a social network for members and a calm environment in which to work. Stroll through the Inns and you can practically breathe history. Out in their gardens you can relax with a drink from an on-site bar or play croquet; inside you're surrounded by imposing oil paintings, the austere expressions of past grandees, judges, heads of state and prime ministers gazing out from the wood panelling.

The Inns are the only institutions with the power to 'call' a person to the Bar. Indeed, students must join one of the four Inns before starting their BPTC and, since membership is for life, it's a decision worth mulling over. Although all four provide similar services and facilities, they each have a different flavour and atmosphere, if only due to their differing sizes. Such things are hard to describe, of course, so before picking one take any available opportunity to visit the Inns to see which one most appeals. This is easily done – just call up and ask for a tour. The Inns also produce a wealth of promotional materials/application guides/newsletters all packed with information – soak it up.

At the latest, you'll need to join an Inn before starting the BPTC, but it's a good idea to consider which one much earlier because between them they've got more than £6.6m to give out in scholarships for GDL and BPTC students as well as pupils. The deadlines for scholarship applications are usually in the calendar year before the course begins, so mark your diary once you have perused the detailed information on the Inns' websites or in their hard-copy brochures.

Getting a scholarship is competitive. Applicants face panels of current members (sometimes including judges) who will examine academic records and set challenges to determine on-the-spot presentation and advocacy skills. Achievements such as 'overcoming hardship' are sometimes also considered, as are extra-curricular activities like sporting or musical ability. The top scholarships are the prestigious 'named' scholarships. These can be worth in the region of £15,000. There are also a huge number of smaller awards.

It's advisable to get mini-pupillages and/or other work experience and internships under your belt, especially as there are additional funds to help facilitate these. Check out the Inns' websites or brochures for more information. For students living away from London, there are funds available to help cover transport costs to visit the Inns, and money is available to cover the cost of 'qualifying sessions'. Some of these 'qualifying sessions' are educational, others are purely designed to help students socialise, network and absorb the customs of the Bar. Sessions range from tradition-laden dinners in the Inns' halls to debates, seminars, advocacy weekends or more informal knees-ups in the gardens. During one visit we saw pinball machines being set up by people who would later be dressed as Elvis. Twelve qualifying sessions must be attended if you are to be 'called to the Bar'.

Once a member, a student can be mentored by a practitioner in their chosen field, and there are marshalling schemes whereby students can shadow a judge for a week, observing cases and discussing them at the end of the day. There are educational workshops to polish advocacy skills and seminars discussing areas of law or courtroom technique. Then there are a range of societies for things like drama, music and mooting/debating. All Inns offer mooting at internal, inter-Inn or national level, which we fully recommend you get involved with.

Although this all sounds very exciting, don't get carried away. Ensure that you have this mantra in mind at all times: Securing a Pupillage is Extremely Hard. A BPTC provider is unlikely to turn you away if you've got the cash to spend, but you cannot make your Lord Chief Justice fantasy come true just by completing the course. Even with a much sought-after scholarship, the road to becoming a barrister is neither cheap nor simple. Do remember that the Inns can help you to improve your chances of gaining pupillage, so become adept at networking, study extremely hard and moot, moot, moot.

	Lincoln's Inn	Inner Temple	Middle Temple	Gray's Inn
Contact	Tel: 020 7405 1393 www.lincolnsinn.org.uk	Tel: 020 7797 8250 www.innertemple.org.uk	Tel: 020 7427 4800 www.middletemple.org.uk	Tel: 020 7458 7900 www.graysinn.info
Architecture	The Old Hall was built in 1490 and the larger Great Hall in 1845, the same year as the library. The Stone Buildings are Regency. The largest Inn, it covers 11 acres.	12th-century Temple Church stands opposite the modern Hall built after the original was destroyed in WWII.	Grand. Smoking rooms decked out in oak, Van Dyck paintings and the largest private collection of silver (after the Royal family's). Ornate carvings in the splendid Elizabethan Hall which is tucked down an intricate maze of alleys and narrow streets.	Suffered serious war damage and is largely a 1950s red-brick creation, albeit with its ancient Hall and Chapel intact. Disabled access has recently been improved.
Gardens	Always open, the gardens are especially popular at lunchtimes.	Well kept and stretching down to the Thames. Croquet, chess and giant Connect Four may be played.	Small and award-winning and handy for the bar.	Famous walks good for nearby City Law School students. Restaurant in gardens during summer.
Style	Friendly, international and large.	Sociable, progressive and switched on.	Musical, arty and very sociable. Christmas revels are notorious.	Traditional and, thanks to its smaller size, offers a personal touch.
Gastronomy	Meals in Hall are subsidised for students.	Lunch served every day. Subsidies for students.	Fairly priced, good-quality lunch served daily.	Lunch served in Hall every day. Subsidised rates for students.
Accommodation	14 flats available for students and 3 are let to pupils. All on-site.	Not for students.	Subsidised acccommodation for scholars in Clapham.	Not for students.
Bar	The stylish Members' Common Room has a restaurant and a terrace bar.	The Pegasus Bar has a terraced open-air area. Good for people watching but not a place to go incognito.	Modern bar conveniently located beneath the library and opens onto the lawns. Good for intimate chats in winter.	A walkway between the Hall and the South Square buildings is being rebuilt to house a bar.
Old Members	John Donne Lord Hailsham LC Lord Denning MR Mahomed Ali Jinnah Some 16 British Prime Ministers	Dr Ivy Williams (first woman called to Bar) Bram Stoker Judge Jeffreys of 'Bloody Assizes' M K Gandhi Lord Falconer	Sir Walter Raleigh William Blackstone Charles Dickens	Sir Francis Bacon Lord Birkenhead LC Dame Rose Heibrom (the first female QC, the first female Old Bailey judge and the first female treasurer at an Inn)
Points of Interest	Together with the Royal Navy, Lincoln's Inn takes the Loyal Toast seated. This commemorates a meal with King Charles II when the entire company got too drunk to stand. Inn offers subsidised trips to the Hague, Luxembourg & Strasbourg.	Temple Church includes part of Knights Templar's round church, which was modelled on the Church of the Holy Sepulchre in Jerusalem and used as a film set in *The Da Vinci Code*.	Shakespeare's *Twelfth Night* first performed here. 2008 was the 400th anniversary of the Temple's Charter which granted the freehold of the land to Inner and Middle Temple. Hall has a table from the Golden Hind. Every new barrister signs their name on it.	Shakespeare's *Comedy of Errors* first performed here. Been law teaching on the site of Gray's Inn since the reign of Edward III. The ornate carved screen in the Hall is made from an Armada ship.
Scholarship Interview Process	Panel interview. Scholarship awarded solely on merit then weighted according to financial means.	20-minute interview. GDL scholars entitled to automatic funding for BPTC, but can apply for higher award. Merit and academic excellence prioritised, but all awards (save for the top ones) means tested.	Every applicant interviewed. 15 minute panel interview tests on-the-spot presentation skills.	Shortlisted applicants interviewed by a three-person panel looking for an ability to think on one's feet rather than legal knowledge. Extra-curricular achievements taken into consideration - eg music, sport or overcoming adversity.
Scholarship Money	A total of £1.4m available each year through 240 scholarships.	Entrance awards. GDL: 5 major scholarships and awards totaling £170,000. BPTC: 7 major grants and awards totaling £922,750.	Entrance awards. GDL: around 20 scholarships of up to £10,000. BPTC: around 150 scholarships of up to £18,000. Subsidised accommodation awards. 143 in total, decided first on merit, then need.	Top scholarships awarded on merit. Lesser scholarships awarded then weighted according to means. Awards total £900k Bedingfield – 8 x £17k Prince of Wales – 11 x £14k Others include £10k Hebe Plunkett award for disabled, esp visually impaired.

Practice areas at the Bar

We've summarised the main areas of practice at the Bar to help you work out which you want to try. Read in conjunction with the Chambers Reports, they should help solidify your initial ideas.

The Chancery Bar

In a nutshell

The Chancery Bar is tricky to define. The High Court has three divisions: Family, Queen's Bench (QBD) and Chancery, with cases allocated to the most appropriate division based on their subject matter. What makes a case suitable for the Chancery Division? Historically it has heard cases with an emphasis on legal principles, foremost among them the concept of equity. Put another way, Chancery work is epitomised by legal reasoning. Cases are generally categorised as either 'traditional' Chancery (trusts, probate, real property, charities and mortgages) or 'commercial' Chancery (company law, shareholder cases, partnership, banking, pensions, financial services, insolvency, professional negligence, tax, media, IP). Most Chancery sets undertake both types of work, albeit with varying emphases. The distinction between Chancery practice and the work of the Commercial Bar (historically dealt with in the QBD) is less apparent now. Barristers at commercial sets can frequently be found on Chancery cases and vice versa, though some areas, such as tax and IP, beg specialisation.

The realities of the job

- This is an area of law for those who love to grapple with its most complex aspects. It's all about the application of long-standing legal principles to modern-day situations.
- Barristers must be practical in the legal solutions they offer to clients. Complex and puzzling cases take significant unravelling and the legal arguments/principles must be explained coherently to the solicitor and the lay client. Suave and sophisticated presentation when before a judge is also vital.
- Advocacy is important, but the majority of time is spent in chambers perusing papers, considering arguments, drafting pleadings, skeletons and advices, or conducting settlement negotiations.
- Some instructions fly into chambers, need immediate attention and then disappear just as quickly. Others can rumble on for years.
- Variety is a key attraction. Traditional work can involve human interest; for example wills and inheritance cause all sorts of ructions among families. Commercial Chancery practitioners deal with the blood-on-the-boardroom-table disputes or bust-ups between co-writers of million-selling songs.
- Schedules aren't set by last-minute briefs for next-day court appearances, so barristers need self-discipline and good time management skills.
- The early years of practice feature low-value cases like straightforward possession proceedings in the county court, winding-up applications in the Companies Court and appearances before the bankruptcy registrars. More prominent sets will involve baby barristers as second or third junior on larger, more complex cases.

Current issues

- The Chancery Bar attracts plenty of high-value, complex domestic cases and offshore and cross-border instructions. Russian and Eastern European business affairs are taking up a sizeable amount of court time in the commercial arena, and massive offshore business and private client trusts in the Cayman Islands, the British Virgin Islands, Bermuda and the Channel Islands are increasingly turning to barristers in the field.
- The scope of the Chancery Division means that practitioners get involved in the most enormous commercial and public law matters.

Some tips

- An excellent academic record is essential. Most pupils in leading sets have a First-class degree. You should enjoy the analytical process involved in constructing arguments and evaluating the answers to problems. If you're not a natural essay writer, you're unlikely to be a natural-born Chancery practitioner.
- Don't wander into this area by accident. Are you interested in equity, trusts, company law, insolvency or tax?
- Though not an accurate portrayal of modern practice, Dickens' novel *Bleak House* is the ultimate Chancery saga. Give it a whirl, or watch the DVD.

Read our Chambers Reports on...

Maitland Chambers • Serle Court • 3-4 South Square • 3 Verulam Buildings • Wilberforce Chambers

The Commercial Bar

In a nutshell

The Commercial Bar handles a variety of business disputes. In its purest definition, a commercial case is one heard by the Commercial Court or a county court business court. A broader and more realistic definition includes matters dealt with by both the Queen's Bench and Chancery Divisions of the High Court, and the Technology and Construction Court (TCC). The Commercial Bar deals with disputes in all manner of industries from construction, shipping and insurance to banking, entertainment and manufacturing. Almost all disputes are contract and/or tort claims, and the Commercial Bar remains rooted in common law. That said, domestic and European legislation is increasingly important and commercial barristers' incomes now reflect the popularity of the English courts with overseas litigants. Cross-border issues including competition law, international public and trade law and conflicts of law are all growing in prominence. Alternative methods of dispute resolution – usually arbitration or mediation – are also popular because of the increased likelihood of preserving commercial relationships that would otherwise be destroyed by the litigation process.

The realities of the job

- Barristers steer solicitors and lay clients through the litigation process and advise on strategy, such as how clients can position themselves through witness statements, pleadings and pre-trial 'interlocutory' skirmishes.
- Advocacy is key, but as much of it is paper-based, written skills are just as important as oral skills.
- Commercial cases can be very fact-heavy and the evidence for a winning argument can be buried in a room full of papers. Barristers have to work closely with instructing solicitors to manage documentation.
- Not all commercial pupils will take on their own caseload in the second six. At first, new juniors commonly handle small cases including common law matters like personal injury, employment claims, possession proceedings and winding-up or bankruptcy applications.
- New juniors gain exposure to larger cases by assisting seniors. As a 'second junior' they carry out research and assist the 'first junior' and the QC leading the case. They use the opportunity to pick up tips on cross-examining witnesses and how best to present arguments.
- In time, a junior's caseload increases in value and complexity. Most commercial barristers specialise by building up expertise on cases within a particular industry sector – eg shipping, insurance, entertainment or banking.
- Developing a practice means working long hours, often under pressure. Your service standards must be impeccable and your style user-friendly, no matter how late or disorganised the solicitor's instruction. In a good set you can make an exceedingly good living.

Current issues

- In the past couple of years the commercial litigation market has picked up, not least because of fallout from the financial crisis. Pundits confidently expect to see more disputes across the board, but most especially in relation to insurance, professional negligence and financial institutions. Third-party funding of litigation, and costs risk-sharing arrangements, are now becoming more prevalent and should have an effect on the number of cases brought before the courts.
- Among the biggest cases of 2009 was a multimillion-pound claim by 30,000 people from Côte d'Ivoire against commodities trader Trafigura following exposure to toxic chemicals unloaded from a tanker in 2006. Another leading spat has involved Accenture, which faced a £182m damages claim from Centrica's British Gas division following the alleged failure of an IT system built by Accenture.
- The trend for increased mediation and arbitration continues. One effect of this is that only the big, multi-issue cases tend to reach court, as there are so many other opportunities for dealing with smaller, less complex cases.

Some tips

- Competition for pupillage at the Commercial Bar is fierce. A First-class degree is commonplace and you'll need impressive references.
- Don't underestimate the value of non-legal work experience; commercial exposure of any kind is going to help you understand the client's perspective and motivations.
- Bear a set's specialities in mind when deciding where to accept pupillage – shipping is very different to employment, for example.

Read our Chambers Reports on...

Atkin Chambers • Blackstone Chambers • Crown Office Chambers • One Essex Court • 39 Essex Street • Henderson Chambers • Keating Chambers • 7 King's Bench Walk • Littleton Chambers • Maitland Chambers • Four New Square • Serle Court • 3-4 South Square • 2 Temple Gardens • 3 Verulam Buildings • Wilberforce Chambers

The Common Law Bar

In a nutshell

English common law derives from the precedents set by judicial decisions rather than the contents of statutes. Most common law cases turn on principles of tort and contract and are dealt with in the Queen's Bench Division (QBD) of the High Court and the county courts. At the edges, common law practice blurs into both Chancery and commercial practice, yet the work undertaken in common law sets is broader still, and one of the most appealing things about a career at one of these sets is the variety of instructions available.

Employment and personal injury are the bread and butter at the junior end, and such matters are interspersed with licensing, clinical negligence, landlord and tenant, winding-up and bankruptcy applications, as well as small commercial and contractual disputes. Some sets will even extend their remit to inquests and criminal cases.

The realities of the job

- Barristers tend to engage with a full range of cases throughout their careers, but there is an opportunity to begin to specialise at between five and ten years' call.
- Advocacy is plentiful. Juniors can expect to be in court three days per week and second-six pupils often have their own cases. Small beginnings such as 'noting briefs' (where you attend court simply in order to report back on the proceedings) and masters' and district judges' appointments lead to lower-value 'fast-track' personal injury trials then longer, higher-value, 'multi-track' trials and employment tribunals.
- Outside court, the job involves research, an assessment of the merits of a case and meetings with solicitors and lay clients. The barrister will also be asked to draft statements of claim, defences and opinions.
- Dealing with the volume and variety of cases requires a good grasp of the law and the procedural rules of the court, as well as an easy facility for assimilating the facts of each case.
- Interpersonal skills are important. A client who has never been to court before will be very nervous and needs to be put at ease.
- At the junior end, work comes in at short notice, so having to digest a file of documents quickly is commonplace.
- Acting as a junior on more complex cases allows a younger barrister to observe senior lawyers in court.

Current issues

- The trend for mediation and arbitration of disputes, and the trend for solicitors to undertake more advocacy themselves, have to some extent reduced work at the junior end. However, while solicitor advocates frequently take on directions hearings, they are still rarely seen at trial.
- Conditional fee agreements – especially for PI claims – have definitely affected barristers' remuneration. Ongoing changes to the public funding of legal services are also having an impact. On a more positive note, the growth of third-party funding of cases and increased use of risk-sharing arrangements by solicitors may lead to an increase in the volume of work for barristers.

Some tips

- Though there are a lot of common law sets, pupillages and tenancies don't grow on trees. You'll have to impress to get a foot in the door and then make your mark to secure your next set of instructions.
- If you want to specialise, thoroughly research the sets you apply to.

Read our Chambers Reports on...

Cloisters • Crown Office Chambers • 39 Essex Street • Henderson Chambers • Old Square Chambers • 2 Temple Gardens

The Criminal Bar

In a nutshell

Barristers are instructed by solicitors to provide advocacy or advice for individuals being prosecuted in cases brought before the UK's criminal courts. Lesser offences like driving charges, possession of drugs or benefit fraud are listed in the magistrates' courts, where solicitor advocates are increasingly active. More serious charges such as fraud, supplying drugs or murder go to the Crown Courts, which are essentially still the domain of barristers. In extension, complex cases may go all the way to the Court of Appeal and the Supreme Court. See the diagram of the Criminal Courts of England & Wales on page 98. The average criminal set's caseload incorporates everything from theft, fraud, drugs and driving offences to assaults of varying degrees of severity and murder. Many top-end chambers are also leveraging their forensic analysis and advocacy skills to move into regulatory, VAT tribunal and professional discipline work. A summary of the expanding opportunities at the Crown Prosecution Service is given on page 26.

The realities of the job

- Barristers do need a sense of theatre and dramatic timing, but good oratory skills are only half the story. Tactical sense and great time management are important.
- The barrister must be able to inspire confidence in clients from any kind of background.
- Some clients can be tricky, unpleasant or scary. Some have unfortunate lives, are addicted to alcohol or drugs, have poor housing and little education.
- Barristers will often handle several cases a day, frequently at different courts. Some of them will be poorly prepared by instructing solicitors. It is common to take on additional cases at short notice and to have to cope with missing defendants and witnesses. Stamina and adaptability are consequently a must.
- Sustained success rests on effective case preparation and an awareness of evolving law and sentencing policies.
- Pupils cut their teeth on motoring offences, committals and directions hearings in the mags' courts. By the end of pupillage they should expect to be instructed in their own right and not infrequently make it into the Crown Court.
- Juniors quickly see the full gamut of cases. Trials start small – offences such as common assault – and move onto ABH, robbery and drugs charges. Impressing an instructing solicitor could lead to a role as a junior on a major Crown Court trial.
- Pupils and juniors rely on relationships with instructing solicitors built by seniors and managers.

Current issues

- Being on the Crown Prosecution Service list meant barristers could prosecute as well as defend. On cost-saving grounds, the CPS decided to bring a significant proportion of advocacy in-house by encouraging its own lawyers to develop the required skills. The CPS wants many of its lawyers to develop to become Senior Crown Advocates and handle contested trials in the Crown Court. Quite where an equilibrium between the Bar and CPS prosecutors is reached remains to be seen, but the move has already reduced the amount of work at the junior end. The financial security (albeit not vast riches) offered at the CPS may help it entice barristers from private practice.
- Legal aid cutbacks and the Legal Services Commission's implementation of legal aid reform are also hitting the number of available criminal instructions and their remuneration. The system of fixed fees for work is disliked by many practitioners and many solicitors' firms are being forced out of this area of work, which in turn is affecting barristers' caseloads. If you're willing to accept the likelihood of more limited financial rewards, the legal aid Criminal Bar should still prove irresistible, and our research suggests top sets will ride out the changes with ease.
- Private paying criminal practice is as healthy as ever.

Some tips

- Mini-pupillage experience and plenty of mooting and debating is required before you can look like a serious applicant.
- The Criminal Bar tends to provide more pupillages than other areas, but these don't necessarily translate into tenancies because the market is so competitive. Third and fourth sixes are not uncommon at the Criminal Bar these days, so be prepared for this possibility.
- Be certain that you are suited to this area of practice. Reading a few Rumpole novels is not going to tell you one way or the other; best to gain some direct exposure to the criminal justice system. See page 34 for tips on useful voluntary activities. Such involvement will allow you to look like a serious applicant.

Read our Chambers Reports on...

2 Bedford Row • 2 Hare Court

The Employment Bar

In a nutshell

The Employment Bar deals with any and every sort of claim arising from the relations or breakdown of relations between employees and employers. Disputes are generally resolved at or before reaching an employment tribunal, which deals with cases relating to redundancy; unfair dismissal; discrimination on the grounds of gender, sexual orientation, race, religion or age; workplace harassment; contract claims; and whistle-blowing. Appeals are heard at an Employment Appeal Tribunal (EAT) and high-value claims and applications for injunctions to prevent the breach of restrictive covenants or use of trade secrets are usually dealt with in the county courts or the High Court.

Accessibility is a key aim of the employment tribunal system. Legal representation is not required and only rarely will there be a costs penalty for the unsuccessful party. Such is the emphasis on user-friendliness that employment claims can even be issued online. Applicants making claims will often represent themselves, meaning a barrister acting for a respondent company faces a lay opponent. Nonetheless, many cases are so complex, or worth so much money, that both parties seek specialist legal representation from solicitors and barristers.

The realities of the job

- Most advocacy takes place in employment tribunals or the Employment Appeals Tribunal, where the atmosphere and proceedings are deliberately less formal. Hearings are conducted with everyone sitting down and barristers do not wear wigs.
- Tribunals follow the basic pattern of examination in chief, cross-examination and closing submissions; however, barristers have to modify their style, especially when appearing against someone who is unrepresented.
- A corporate respondent might consider a QC well worth the money, while the applicant's pocket may only stretch to a junior. Solicitor advocates feature prominently in this area of practice.
- Employment specialists need great people skills. Clients frequently become emotional or stressed, and the trend for respondent companies to name an individual (say a manager) as co-respondent means there may be several individuals in the room with complex personal, emotional and professional issues at stake.
- Few juniors limit themselves solely to employment practice; most also undertake civil or commercial cases, some criminal matters. Similarly, few juniors act only for applicants or only for respondents. Seniors' fees mean they act largely for respondents or well-paid execs.
- UK employment legislation mirrors EU law and changes with great rapidity. Cases are regularly stayed while others with similar points are heard on appeal.

Current issues

- High-value claims by employees in the banking sector continue to make headlines.
- Layoffs and bonus disputes resulting from the economic downturn are a key source of claims. Bonus disputes, in particular in the financial sector, are now a hotly debated topic.
- Equal pay cases are another important area that has provided the Bar with a lot of work.
- The advent of Employment Equality (Age) Regulations brought the issue of age discrimination to the fore and various aspects of the law have already been tested, notably in relation to the legal profession.

Some tips

- Get involved with the Free Representation Unit (see page 34). FRU employment law opportunities are varied and no application for pupillage will look complete without some involvement of this kind.
- Practically any kind of temporary or part-time job will give you first-hand experience of being an employee. Not to be underestimated, especially when you consider that as a barrister you will be self-employed.
- High-profile cases are regularly reported in the press, so there's no excuse for not keeping abreast of the area.

Read our Chambers Reports on...

Blackstone Chambers • Cloisters • Littleton Chambers • Old Square Chambers

The Family Bar

In a nutshell

Family law barristers deal with the array of cases arising from marital, civil union or cohabitation breakdown and related issues concerning children. Simple cases are heard in the county courts, while complex or high-value cases are listed in the Family Division of the High Court. Emphasising the importance of this area, UK government stats reveal that around half of divorcing couples have at least one child aged under 16, and together their divorces affect nearly 150,000 children a year. Consequently, a huge amount of court time is allotted to divorce, separation, adoption, child residence and contact orders, financial provision and domestic violence.

The realities of the job

- Financial cases and public and private law children's work each offer their own unique challenges.
- Emotional resilience is required, as is a capacity for empathy, as the work involves asking clients for intimate details of their private life and breaking devastating news to the emotionally fragile. Private law children's cases can sometimes involve serious allegations between parents and require the input of child psychologists. The public law counterpart (care proceedings between local authorities and parents) invariably includes detailed and potentially testing medical evidence.
- For many clients, involvement with the courts is out of the ordinary and they will rely heavily on their counsel to guide them through the process. The law can never fix emotional problems relating to marital breakdown or child issues, but it can palliate a situation.
- The job calls for communication, tact and maturity. Cases have a significant impact on the lives they involve, so finding the most appropriate course of action for each client is important. The best advocates are those who can differentiate between a case and client requiring a bullish approach and those crying out for settlement and concessions to be made.
- Where possible, mediation is used to resolve disputes in a more efficient and less unsettling fashion, requiring a different approach to litigation.
- Teamwork is crucial. As the barrister is the link between the client, the judge, solicitors and social workers, it is important to win the trust and confidence of all parties.
- The legislation affecting this area is comprehensive, and there's a large body of case law. Keeping abreast of developments is necessary because the job is more about negotiating general principles than adhering strictly to precedents.
- Finance-oriented barristers need an understanding of pensions and shares and a good grounding in the basics of trusts and property.
- The early years of practice involve a lot of private law children work (disputes between parents), small financial cases and injunctions in situations of domestic violence.

Current issues

- A few years ago barristers believed that mediation and an increase in solicitor advocates threatened a downturn in work for juniors. Yet, with the exception of children's cases, in which solicitors have always been encouraged to do their own advocacy, the volume of instructions appears to have continued largely unabated, albeit that divorce rates in 2007 dipped slightly to rest at their lowest level for 26 years.
- Big divorces are big news. The wealth and assets involved in cases such as that of Bernie Ecclestone and his wife Slavica far outstrip the reasonable needs of the parties, but precedents for huge payouts have been established and such cases draw significant attention, with the media often being used strategically – just look at Katie and Peter.
- Cases involving the division of assets/child law issues following the breakdown of a civil partnership are beginning to appear.
- Ongoing reform of the legal aid system is hitting the Family Bar hard.

Some tips

- The Family Bar is quite small and competition for pupillage is intense. Think about how you can evidence your interest in family law. See our Pro Bono and Volunteering section on page 34.
- Younger people might find it daunting to advise on mortgages, marriages and children when they've never experienced any of these things personally. Arguably those embarking on a second career, or who have delayed a year or two and acquired other life experiences, may have an advantage.
- Check the work orientation of a set before applying for pupillage, particularly if you don't want to narrow your options too early. For example, some sets specialise only in the financial aspects of divorce.

Public Law at the Bar

In a nutshell

Centred on the Administrative Court, public law cases range from pro bono or legal aid matters for individuals to instructions from government or magic circle firms regarding commercial judicial review. Human rights cases usually relate in some way to the UK's ratification of the European Convention on Human Rights (the Convention) through the Human Rights Act 1998 (HRA). These crop up in criminal and civil contexts, often through the medium of judicial review, a key tool in questioning the decisions of public bodies. Cases concerning community care issues and the provision of social services by local authorities feature heavily, and judicial reviews of immigration decisions make up a chunk of the Administrative Court's case list. Then there are contentious matters such as right-to-life or right to NHS treatment cases. Where an event is deemed to be of great public importance, inquiries are commissioned by the government and then operate independently. The Bloody Sunday Inquiry, the Hutton Inquiry into the death of Dr David Kelly and the Victoria Climbie Inquiry are illustrative. Planning inquiries also feature regularly in a public law set's caseload, dealing with anything from airport expansions to the construction of wind farms. Most public law barristers and sets also work in other areas: some are crime specialists; others have commercial caseloads. For example, criminal barristers will often handle issues relating to prisoners or breaches of procedure by police, and commercial barristers might handle judicial reviews of BIS decisions. A barrister with a local authority clientele will have a wide practice, much of it relating to planning, housing or environmental matters, education, health and children. In reality, even those who do not profess a specialism in public law may also undertake judicial review work.

The realities of the job

- The Administrative Court is inundated, so an efficient style of advocacy is vital. That means cutting to the chase and delivering the pertinent information, case law or statutory regulations.
- Barristers need a genuine interest in the fundamental laws by which we live and the legislative process.
- Public law is a discursive area in which complex arguments are more common than precise answers.
- The combination of real-world scenarios, rarefied legal principle and often complex, emotive cases demands practicality, common sense and the ability to stand back and apply legal intellect.
- Barristers who work on planning inquiries may have to spend periods of time away from home.
- Junior barristers hone advocacy skills early. The 'permissions' stage of judicial review proceedings provides excellent opportunities in the form of short 30-minute hearings. However, reviews tend not to involve juries, witnesses or cross-examination.

Current issues

- The Freedom of Information Act has significantly heightened the ability of pressure groups, individuals and the media to scrutinise the plans, actions and success of public bodies.
- Ongoing changes to legal aid funding will affect public law cases and the livelihoods of barristers.
- There have been many modifications to immigration law, not least in relation to the Highly Skilled Migrant programme. A new points-based immigration system is in operation.
- The interface between terrorism and public law, and between public law and the HRA and the Convention, has become even more acute.
- There are an increasing number of coroners' inquests, with prison and military deaths dominating the field.
- Changes to planning legislation – including the removal of the public inquiry stage in certain high-value developments – have caused controversy.

Some tips

- Getting a public law pupillage is phenomenally competitive. Not only are the highest academic standards required, but many pupils also arrive with significant hands-on experience or related further academic study.
- Public international law appeals to many students but there are few early openings. Traditionally, PIL has been the preserve of academics; the leading names are predominantly sitting or ex-professors at top universities and Foreign Office veterans, with the occasional pure but very experienced barrister thrown in.
- If administrative and constitutional law subjects were not your favourites you should rethink your decision.
- Interesting opportunities are available within the Government Legal Service. See pages 280 and 704.
- A healthy interest in current affairs and knowledge of the latest cases in the news are vital.

Read our Chambers Reports on...

Blackstone Chambers • 39 Essex Street
• 4-5 Gray's Inn Square

Shipping & International Trade at the Bar

In a nutshell

This is such a well-defined specialism at the Commercial Bar it requires its own summary. Shipping and trade work mostly centres upon contract and tort; indeed English case law is awash with examples from the world of shipping. Barristers handle disputes arising from or concerning the carriage of goods or people by sea, air and land, plus all aspects of the financing, construction, use, insurance and decommissioning of the vessels, planes, trains and other vehicles that carry them. There is often a complex international element to such cases, drawing in multiple parties – for example a wrecked vessel might be Greek-owned, Pakistani-crewed, Russian-captained, last serviced in Singapore, carrying forestry products from Indonesia to Denmark, insured in London and chartered by a French company – but English courts are very often the preferred forum for the resolution of such matters, not least because of the worldwide significance of the London insurance market. Trade disputes are often resolved through arbitration conducted in various locations, Paris and London being among the most important.

'Wet' cases deal with problems at sea, while 'dry' cases relate to disputes in port or concerns over the manufacture and financing of vessels. The Bar also has a number of aviation, road haulage and rail specialists, and the sets that dominate these areas also tend to be able to offer commodities trading experts.

The realities of the job

- Cases are fact-heavy and paper-heavy. To develop the best arguments for a case, barristers need an organised mind and a willingness to immerse themselves in the documentary evidence. This can be time-consuming and exhausting.
- There are opportunities for international travel.
- Cases can run on for years and involve large teams of lawyers, both solicitors and barristers. Young barristers work their way up from second or third junior to leader over a number of years. New juniors do get to run their own smaller cases, eg charter party and bills of lading disputes.
- The world of shipping and trade has its own language and customs.
- Solicitor clients will usually work at one of the established shipping firms, but lay clients will be a mixed bag of financiers, shipowners, operators, traders and charterers, P&I clubs, salvors and underwriters.

Current issues

- There is a general downturn in cargo claims due to the increased safety of ships and the success of various conventions such as the International Safety Management Code.
- P&I clubs in particular continue to be increasingly watchful of costs. This has sparked the recent development of instructing barristers directly, cutting out the solicitor middleman.
- Clients are further trying to save money by embracing mediation, although gloomier economic conditions always see a rise in cases going to court.
- Piracy is on the rise, and it's now affecting waters that have ordinarily been considered safe. A good case in point is the Maltese-flagged 'Arctic Sea', which was hijacked in the Baltic Sea in August 2009 as it transported timber from Finland to Algeria. The worldwide rise in piracy has focused minds within the sector and the Kenyan port of Mombasa is poised to become the venue for a special piracy tribunal.

Some tips

- The leading sets are easy to identify. A mini-pupillage with one or more of them will greatly enhance your understanding and chances.
- Despite the prominence of English law, the work calls for an international perspective and an appreciation of international laws. This can be developed within a first or masters' degree and on the BPTC.

Read our Chambers Reports on...

7 King's Bench Walk • Quadrant Chambers

Chambers Reports: introduction

Making an informed choice about where to apply for pupillage isn't easy. Having established the practice area in which you want to specialise, you then need to select your dozen Pupillage Portal scheme sets and consider how many other sets outside the scheme you will apply to. How do you know where you'll fit in and whether a set will be interested in you?

These days the majority of chambers' websites deliver all the pertinent information – not just about their size, nature of work and location, but also about the nature of pupillage and mini-pupillage. Many even carry their full pupillage policy documentation online. Internet surfing can only take you so far though, and there is no substitute for seeing life inside a set during a mini-pupillage. Because it is impossible to do minis at every set, we've done some of the hard work for you.

Since the summer of 2003 we have been calling in on various chambers, taking time to speak with pupils, juniors, QCs, clerks and chief execs. The task is a big one so we visit each of our chosen chambers every second year, merely refreshing the existing Chambers Report for the intervening years. This year's roll call of 24 sets includes nine new features and 15 features reprinted from our 2009 edition. We have tried to visit as many different types of set as possible to give a good sense of the range of areas of practice available. Our visits took us from the grandeur of the Chancery Bar to the more modest surroundings of sets conducting a significant amount of publicly funded work. There should be something to suit most tastes, be they commercial, common law, criminal, IP, tax, or otherwise.

The sets covered this year are all in London, where the majority of chambers (and pupillages) are based, but in your wider research remember that there are some excellent chambers in the regions, mostly in the larger cities of Leeds, Liverpool, Manchester, Birmingham and Bristol. The wild card in our pack is the Government Legal Service, which although not a set operating out of chambers, still offers what we regard as a cracking pupillage. What we have deliberately avoided is poor-quality sets and we make no excuses for our decision to review only the top-ranked organisations. Bear in mind, however, that our selected sets are not the only ones in the Premier League in each practice area. Given the time we would visit many others.

Whichever chambers you do choose, be reassured that the prime aim of recruiters is to find talented applicants and then to persuade them to accept an offer. They do not expect ready-formed barristers to turn up at their door for interview and they gladly make allowances for candidates' lack of knowledge or experience on specific subjects. Much has been said and written about how awful pupillage interviews can be, and how pupillage itself amounts to little more than a year of pain and humiliation. From what we can tell, in an increasingly modern, business-oriented profession that is taking greater notice of what constitutes good HR practice, this is not the norm. Sure, interviews can be challenging, but they are for the most part designed to get the best out of candidates. As for pupillage, it is in the best interests of any set that it should provide a useful and rewarding experience for pupils. Of course, that still doesn't make it a walk in the park for a pupil.

The itinerary for our visits included conversations with members of the pupillage committee, pupilmasters or supervisors, the senior clerk, junior tenants and, most crucially, current pupils. The aim was not merely to get the lowdown on pupillage at each set but also to learn something about each chambers' life and to pick up tips for applicants. To this end we drank endless cups of tea, selflessly munched our way through kilos of biscuits and took numerous guided tours, checking out artwork and libraries along the way. If we've communicated the qualities that make each set unique then we've done our job and it's over to you to make your choices.

Set	Location	Head of Chambers	QCs/Juniors
Atkin Chambers*	London	Nicholas Dennys QC	15/23
2 Bedford Row	London	William Clegg QC	18/51
Blackstone Chambers*	London	Mill QC/Beazley QC	32/42
Cloisters*	London	Robin Allen QC	6/54
Crown Office Chambers*	London	Antony Edwards-Stuart QC	14/71
One Essex Court*	London	Lord Grabiner QC	23/43
39 Essex Street	London	Richard/Wilmot-Smith QC	24/55
Government Legal Service	London	N/a	500
4-5 Gray's Inn Square	London	Appleby QC/Straker QC	14/36
2 Hare Court	London	David Waters QC	16/37
Henderson Chambers	London	Charles Gibson QC	8/30
Keating Chambers	London	John Marrin QC	20/30
7 King's Bench Walk	London	Gavin Kealey QC	19/27
Littleton Chambers	London	Clarke QC/Freedman QC	12/36
Maitland Chambers*	London	Michael Driscoll QC	17/46
Four New Square	London	Jeremy Stuart Smith QC	17/50
Old Square Chambers	London	Cooksley QC/McNeil QC	10/56
Pump Court Tax Chambers	London	Andrew Thornhill QC	9/19
Quadrant Chambers	London	Persey QC/Rainey QC	11/34
Serle Court*	London	Alan Boyle QC	14/37
3/4 South Square	London	Trower QC/Moss QC/Dicker QC	19/25
2 Temple Gardens	London	Benjamin Browne QC	8/48
3 Verulam Buildings*	London	Symons QC/Jarvis QC	18/40
Wilberforce Chambers*	London	Jules Sher QC	22/28

* Sets visited in 2009

Atkin Chambers

The facts

Location: Gray's Inn, London
Number of QCs/Juniors: 15/23 (8 women)
Applications: c. 200
Apply through Pupillage Portal
Pupils per year: 3
Seats: 2x3 and 1x6 months
Pupillage Award: £47,500 (can advance £10,000 for BPTC)

In addition to construction cases, Atkin's official remit covers energy, professional negligence, IT and more besides.

Atkin Chambers is a construction set. No, wait! Keep reading! If the image that immediately springs to mind is all hard hats and builders' bums, you're way off the mark.

No restaurants for the wicked

Just listen to the testimony of a junior in the second year of practice. "*I've had a banking law case where we've been looking to recover some money from a bank that we say was paid wrongfully, a case where we've been looking to resist electricity companies that are coming against the owner of a tiny little restaurant up in North London, and another where a couple have had an acrimonious split. The girlfriend has sued the boyfriend for 30 grand that she says she lent him, and he's counterclaimed a £7,000 holiday that she paid for on his credit card. I was like: 'I thought this was a construction set!'*"

So you see, 'construction' is a useful label to tag onto Atkin for the purposes of things like *Chambers UK* rankings (where it comes in Band 1, naturally), but it's not as easy to define as you might think. "*The solicitors who instruct us know that, but students often see these categories as quite hard and fast.*" Atkin's official remit in fact covers energy, professional negligence, IT and more besides. When you've discounted its technical facets, IT law has more in common with construction than you might think. Be it an office block or a computer, "*it's all about building something. As far as the law is concerned, it's the same thing – contract and tort.*" In fact, many of the really important cases in contract and tort came from construction law. Perhaps a better description for the set is the one a pupilmaster gave us: "*We are commercial coming from the niche.*"

We're not saying that Atkin isn't still heavily invested in 'classic' construction cases – you'll often see its members in the Technology and Construction Court (TCC) acting on high-profile matters. David Sears QC has been representing the architects in a potential claim for professional negligence in connection with the design and supervision for the construction of Wembley Stadium. International arbitration is another hugely important area of work for chambers, with barristers regularly flying out to everywhere from Scotland to Siberia. Many instructions come from the Middle East, India and East Asia and the word from the set is that it is "*punching above its weight getting into China, although it's still tough.*" As if to emphasise Atkin's success in this field, it is one of only two sets to hold the Queen's Award for Enterprise in the International Trade category.

Knowing me, knowing you

Atkin normally takes three pupils per year, but the patter of tiny feet in its corridors was conspicuous by its absence in 2009. The candidates it wanted accepted offers elsewhere – mostly at the magic circle commercial sets – and

Chambers UK rankings

Construction
Energy & Natural Resources
Information Technology
International Arbitration
Professional Negligence

chambers decided that it was better to take no one on at all rather than to offer pupillage just for the sake of it. On discovering this, we asked what Atkin has to offer that the magic circle doesn't. "*Firstly, a specialisation, which I think will become increasingly important with the potential changes in the legal profession and the way barristers and solicitors work,*" replied the head of the pupillage committee, Fiona Parkin. "*It seems to me that the only way the Bar is going to survive is by offering real pockets of specialisation and that's what we provide. Secondly, we are smaller and so you know people – not just to say hello to: you genuinely know everyone that you work with really quite well. I think that makes for a fantastic working environment.*"

Academic excellence is a given to get in here, but of the 12 juniors under ten years' call, five are non-Oxbridge and several don't have First-class degrees, so there's no snobbery. Since we're quoting facts and figures: three of the 12 are from an ethnic minority background and four are female. Ten of them read law at undergraduate level. The further up the set you go, the less diverse it gets: all of the 26 senior juniors and QCs are white, and four are women.

About 20 people get invited to interview in front of a panel of six people. Although it might seem that way, "*it's not meant to be a daunting experience.*" The interview is designed to spot those with an agile mind and is divided into three parts. The first part is "*an opportunity to ask questions about them and why they want to come to this chambers – it's amazing how many people haven't thought about that.*" The second part is a legal problem, usually based in contract and tort. That takes about 15 minutes, then there's a discussion on a topical question that poses a moral dilemma – the right to die, for instance.

Constructive witticism

Pupillage is structured to gradually increase in difficulty as the year goes on. "*You do feel a real sense of progression.*" In the first three months you can expect to see "*a good cross-section of smaller cases with all the basic stuff.*" Pupils generally won't work for anyone apart from their supervisors, although "*if someone is going to the House of Lords or the Court of Appeal, we try to get them along to that as well.*" By Christmas, it's expected that they will have "*a decent grasp of what the issues are*" and be able to start producing work of value (ie something the pupilmaster will actually be able to use). Almost everything pupils do is 'live' with the exception of two assessed written exercises during the first six. If there are problems, "*we won't let them fester;*" chambers tries to get right on top of any niggles before they worsen, which is perhaps why the six-month break option in the pupillage is almost never utilised.

In the second six, it's rare for pupils to develop much of a caseload. Chambers feels that it's more important to learn the job properly; "*there's quite a lot to pick up,*" after all. Atkin does provide advocacy training, however, and there are three advocacy exercises during the year. The first is pupil v pupil, but by the third go they'll be arguing before a big cheese, usually a former member of chambers, possibly even a real High Court judge, "*which is exciting and terrifying in equal measure.*"

There are assessed written exercises. The first is what chambers calls 'panel work'. "*You're given just over five weeks to do six different pieces for six different members of chambers.*" There's just one deadline for all of them, "*so it's up to you to manage your time. You have to make a judgement and think, 'This piece will take four days, this one will take a week' and so on. It's good because it's actually very indicative of how your practice will be.*" Normal pupillage hours are more like 9am to 6pm, but during this period "*you will be working quite late and you will be working weekends.*" Finally, there's The Test, which is a "*quite complex*" fictitious set of instructions. Pupils have a week to produce written advice and a set of pleadings, and essentially "*it's their opportunity to showcase what they've learnt.*"

The tenancy decision is taken shortly afterwards and, in "*an attempt to get into a subjective process as much objectivity as possible,*" the assessed work is the key factor. Pupilmasters produce reports, but these are of lesser importance. The personality of pupils isn't completely disregarded when the decision is taken – they have to be able to "*fly the flag*" and not be a complete embarrassment to the set – but chambers recognises that "*some clients want academic barristers, some want duff-'em-up types and some want people they can go down the pub with.*" You'll find all three breeds here.

With plenty of "*real characters*" among the senior members, it's perhaps not surprising that juniors are exposed to "*some of the funniest conversations I've ever heard*" at tea (every day, 4pm). The youngest members of the set are clearly quite close and will go out for drinks on Friday evenings.

And finally...

From "*piddling little disputes that can be nonetheless quite complex and cutting-edge*" to massive international arbitrations that will make your fortune, the experience that Atkin offers can be as varied as any mainstream commercial set.

2 Bedford Row

The facts

Location: Bedford Row, London
Number of QCs/Juniors: 18/51 (16 women)
Applications: up to 500
Apply through Pupillage Portal
Pupils per year: 4
Seats: 2x6 months
Pupillage award: £22,000

Gritty and workaholic, 2 Bedford Row is one of the Criminal Bar's brightest stars, with a caseload that's equal parts crime, fraud and regulatory.

2 Bedford Row has shot to prominence in relation to crime and fraud cases. Highlights include representing Soho nail bomber David Copeland, Chillingden murderer Michael Stone and Tony Martin, who shot a burglar in his own home, not to mention involvement in the 'Herald of Free Enterprise' prosecution.

Criminally intent

In part, the set's drive can be credited to legendary founder William Clegg QC, who in recent years successfully defended a British paratrooper accused of murdering an Iraqi teenager and helped Barry George secure his acquittal. Between them, members have also appeared for the defence in the 7/7 conspiracy trial, the Jubilee Line fraud and the QPR blackmail trial, as well as for a defendant in the Cheney Pension fraud, in which over £2.8m was stolen. Numerous sportspeople, including Joey Barton when he faced assault charges over a training ground fracas, have used the set and it also has a "*nice sideline acting in road traffic cases for high-profile media types.*" Crime sells papers and so you've probably heard of the trials of hammer killer Levi Bellfield, Mark Dixie, who murdered Croydon model Sally Ann Bowman, and the case of the Polish nursing assistant killed in crossfire between two drug gangs. In fact, as the senior clerk was happy to reflect: "*If you can think of a recent high-profile case, we will probably have been on it...*" and not necessarily for the defence. Chambers is equally skilful in prosecution work and public inquiries, having acted in the Harold Shipman, Victoria Climbie and Stephen Lawrence inquiries.

Proud of the "*brand recognition*" chambers has earned, members are united behind and invested in "*a corporate identity,*" rather than simply engrossed in their own careers. As such, they were in a good position to "*anticipate some ten years ago the challenges facing the Criminal Bar*" and respond by expanding into the regulatory work that now makes up a substantial part of the caseload. Not only is this one of the only criminal sets in the country with a national reputation for health and safety cases, but tenants often work for HMRC, the General Medical Council, the General Optical Council and sports regulatory bodies like The FA. They also defend clients right across the regulatory spectrum, not least in relation to football, an arena in which the set is instructed by seven Premiership clubs. Chambers' prescient diversification has put it several steps ahead of most criminal sets, and a willingness to "*take cues from the way the Commercial Bar has had success*" looks likely to keep it there. Sending juniors on secondment to solicitors, regulatory bodies and HMRC "*generates work and good relations.*"

Chambers UK rankings

Crime
Fraud: Criminal

Health & Safety

Parkinson's law

Pupillage is characterised by *"general crime, serious fraud, some exposure to regulatory work"* and a distinctive system of supervision. During each six, pupils are assigned two supervisors – one junior, one more senior – ensuring experience of *"the full range of work from the smallest to largest cases"* and *"two different sets of opinions and advice."* Pupils like it because *"if your senior supervisor gets stuck on a long trial, you can hop out and go see a two-to-three day-er."* The first months of pupillage are characterised by *"watching and learning: you're in a cocoon and see the more serious cases, how your practice might be in ten years."* It can be high-profile stuff – a source remembered: *"One of my contemporaries helped on the Barry George appeal and I drafted a House of Lords petition."*

> **Chambers and Partners Crime Set of the Year 2009**

Come the second six, *"pupils work like absolute stink."* One enthused: *"I can count on the fingers of one hand the days I've stayed in chambers."* Trips to watch third-sixers in magistrates' courts prepare them for the first *"knee-trembling"* appearance, as do *"short secondments to the solicitors who brief second-six pupils... you start to forge relationships and learn what they want."* After the first day defending a client, *"you're never, ever as well prepared again, although later you realise you could have prepared in four hours what took you 12."* Thereafter the pace is ferocious and pupils can *"earn very well,"* but supervisors remember that they are still in training. *"We try to provide a support network so there is always someone to speak to, whatever the time,"* one explained, pointing out that *"the professional and ethics problems you face in those first months are probably more testing than at any subsequent point."* When a *"client's wife passes a twist of drugs in front of you"* or a *"client changes what they are saying and the solicitor isn't there,"* it's definitely good to have some back-up on the phone.

The set *"takes the training aspect of pupillage very seriously"* and supervisors *"expect pupils to ask for help,"* often inviting them up from the basement library where pupils tend to congregate, to work in their rooms. Said one: *"We want to make sure they're doing alright in work, socially in chambers, and in their own lives."* Pupils use supervisors as their *"first port of call for questions, feedback and advice"* and *"get constant updates on how your work is going."* In-house advocacy training during the second six is *"assessed with the aim of improving performance not marking pupils."* Early sessions take the form of a bail application or plea in mitigation, and these culminate in *"a full-blown, day-long trial with actors playing witnesses in a mock courtroom."* Describing it as *"terrifying but brilliant,"* pupils are observed by up to seven members of chambers while the actors *"really get into role as difficult witnesses, so the artificiality soon evaporates."* Whatever the result, there's plenty of feedback.

Winning ways

The tenancy decision is made in September after a formal interview process that includes an advocacy exercise. References from solicitors help back up a pupil's credentials, as they face a panel of objective juniors and seniors. Pupils are very aware that *"you've got to be outstanding and meet the criteria"* because generally speaking only one person will gain tenancy, although this is not set in stone. *"Having the 2 Bedford Row brand on your CV is a major advantage"* for those who do need to look elsewhere. *"After being here you'll feel confident that your future at the Bar is assured. Whenever you tell people where you're from, they always look at you with more respect."*

"Everyone here has something extra to offer, a bit of personality about them," probably because *"70% of your time is spent with lay clients and if you can't be normal you won't get the work from solicitors."* Chambers isn't fixated on academics in its quest to find *"evidence of a strong human touch"* and excellence in advocacy. As well as straight law graduates, tenants include an ex-police officer, a former tabloid journo and a one-time banker. *"People with 2:2s are considered, if seen in the right context,"* backing up pupils' claims that *"they will give anyone a chance to shine at interview."* Around 90 applicants are invited to a short meet-and-greet with one or two legal questions gently thrown in, and then 18 make it to a second interview, when a more rigorous grilling usually includes something like a plea in mitigation. Candidates must be able to *"coherently articulate why they are drawn to this career and us,"* as well as display the *"surprisingly rare skill of being able to respond on the spot to tricky questions."*

> **And finally...**
>
> The pace of life may be exacting here, but in what is *"a close unit, especially at the junior end,"* pupils can also rely on *"a friendly experience"* and *"a great social muddle,"* whether it's a supervisor inviting them home for dinner with the family or *"someone encouraging you out for a glass of wine."*

Blackstone Chambers

The facts

Location: Temple, London
Number of QCs/Juniors: 32/42 (20 women)
Applications: 200
Apply through Pupillage Portal
Pupils per year: 4-5
Seats: 4x3 months
Pupillage Award: £42,500 (can advance £10,000 for BPTC)

Chambers and Partners Human Rights & Public Law Set of the Year 2009

Jack-of-all-trades and master of, well, all of them, Blackstone Chambers is in a really positive phase.

Considerable economic stress in this period in history

We conducted our interviews with members of Blackstone in the open air this year. Sitting on the set's roof terrace on a blazing hot summer's day with views of Parliament to the left, St Paul's Cathedral to the right and a wide blue sky overhead, it was hard not to come away wanting to write an equally sunny and positive feature. Fortunately, chambers' recent history is as glorious as was the weather. It has succeeded at everything it has turned its hand to: top-tier rankings in *Chambers UK* for an impressive eight practice areas pay testament to that. Now, we said Blackstone was a jack-of-all-trades, but that's not quite true – it doesn't want to spread itself too thin. The best way to view the set is as a three-legged stool, with commercial, employment and public law all of roughly equal importance. *"We want to ensure there is a proper spread of work across all practice areas,"* says chambers director Julia Horner.

The high-profile cases Blackstone has been involved in are numerous, so we'll just mention one from each of its three main areas. A darling of the Bar, Dinah Rose QC acted on R (Binyam Mohamed) v Secretary of State for Foreign and Commonwealth Affairs, seeking disclosure of information regarding the torture of a British resident held in Guantánamo Bay. Other members of Blackstone advised the BBC on its rights and liabilities during the Jonathan Ross/Russell Brand affair, while on the employment side, barristers have successfully defended a couple of law firms in age discrimination cases brought by former partners.

Despite the economic downturn, or perhaps because of it, chambers remains very busy. *"Because of the areas we deal with, and because of the spread that we have, we can shift our balance a little bit as the market demands. Public law is unlikely to disappear and we do an awful lot of regulatory and financial services work. I think we had seven members on the Northern Rock litigation."* The set has been making concerted efforts to expand its competition practice, most recently taking star junior Kieron Beal away from Matrix Chambers.

Go away or we shall taunt you a second time

At the first interview, prospective pupils rock up to Blackstone about 20 minutes early and select one of half a dozen topical subjects on which they will then be grilled. *"Mine was at about the time of the Big Brother racism furore,"* says one pupil, *"and the question I chose was*

Chambers UK rankings

Administrative & Public Law	Immigration
Civil Liberties	Insurance
Commercial Dispute Resolution	Media & Entertainment
Competition/European Law	Professional Discipline
Employment	Public International Law
Environment	Public Procurement
Financial Services Regulation	Sports Law
Fraud: Civil	Telecommunications

about whether OFCOM should require broadcasters to censor live television." Expect a pretty tough ride at this stage and be sure to keep your head. "*You start talking and think you are rolling along nicely, and then all of a sudden you are being cross-examined by seven people.*" Often one member in particular will really lay into you, "*but it's a different person every time. When I arrived here, I couldn't believe how nice the woman who had been heckling me was!*" Coming away from this encounter feeling "*brutalised*" doesn't necessarily mean you're out of the running.

The next stage is a week-long (and potentially partly-funded) assessed mini-pupillage, which includes two days devoted to a piece of set work, plus a look at the live matters the pupil supervisors have on their desks. There's also a trip to court to see advocates in action. Particularly impressive mini-pupils "*are not necessarily the ones who know masses of law, but those who are able to engage with, and talk with clarity about, whatever problem they are presented with.*" Second interviews don't take place until quite late in the summer. By this point, about 15 candidates remain, and "*they mainly want to talk about what you saw in your mini-pupillage and how you felt about it. They are basically trying to assess how keen you are on chambers and whether if they make an offer you're going to accept it.*" Oxford and Cambridge grads naturally do well, but it's worth noting that one of the current pupils not only didn't go to Oxbridge but doesn't have a degree at all: a Certificate of Academic Standing from the Bar Council, plus a glittering previous career with a news agency, was intellectual qualification enough for Blackstone.

A mandate from the masses, not some farcical aquatic ceremony

It's chambers' policy that pupils spend one seat with someone who does a lot of employment law, and one with someone who does a lot of public law. The remaining two seats had been, for one junior, mostly commercial. "*I had to read through a film script to work out which bits were actually the property of the scriptwriter. That was quite fun.*" He also got involved with the Formula 1 'Spygate' case for McLaren. "*That was not only high-profile but a really interesting bit of law.*"

"*Perhaps more is expected from you later on,*" but first-seat work won't be essentially any different from fourth-seat work. For one supervisor at least, "*every last bit of it is live, in the sense that I'm hoping that work product from pupils will be useful to me. Inevitably some of it is low-grade stuff, working out how to present a case. I aim for them to do a draft pleading, or a skeleton argument, or an opinion before I have to, so if they come up with something good I can then incorporate it.*" One pupil found it "*very encouraging*" that a paragraph she had written went out largely unchanged in her second week. Pupils also go along to conferences with clients and see the strategy side of cases.

Chambers runs "*a very detailed advocacy programme,*" and pupils will "*probably do a FRU case or two*" in order to get some experience, but they won't be in court all the time. For juniors, however, it's a different story. "*In terms of getting advocacy experience early on, there's nothing like employment law. You simply don't get that in commercial practice,*" says a junior. Blackstone is keen to ensure that all junior tenants undertake plenty of court work, "*so they get used to cross-examining witnesses and standing in front of any type of judge. That is what will give them the edge in later years.*" Chambers is most definitely "*looking for advocates*" and not "*shrinking violet eggheads.*"

Over the course of the year there are seven written exercises (of which only the post-Christmas ones are assessed) and two advocacy tests. When it comes to deciding tenancy, "*by far the most important views are those of the pupilmasters,*" but having said that, Blackstone is "*a true democracy. I've always been of the view that the closest comparison with chambers is the anarcho-syndicalist collective in Monty Python. It truly is one person, one vote and each person can vote as they see fit.*" In practice, however, it's unheard of for chambers to go against the views of four unanimous pupilmasters. In 2009, there were four pupils. Two of them came from academia and were undertaking truncated pupillages. Of those, one had been offered tenancy, while the other hadn't reached the decision stage yet. As for the two 'regular' pupils, one gained tenancy at the first time of asking, the other was offered a third six at the set.

We dance when we are able

Friday night drinks take place whenever there are mini-pupils in chambers (ie most of the summer) "*and even at other times; three Fridays out of four either someone will be having drinks in their room or everyone will go to the Edgar Wallace.*" Friday fish-and-chip lunches at the Inner Temple are also a tradition.

Blackstone has "*no platonic ideal of a barrister*" and members say that the set is "*remarkably happy considering how diverse we are in terms of personalities. Politically we range from Marxists to some people who are pretty conservative, both big C and small. We've had people stand for parliament for all three major parties.*"

And finally...

If you want further proof of how settled chambers is, take a look at the number of QCs it has. Many of them turned down appointments to the bench to stay in practice. "*No one ever leaves this place.*"

Cloisters

The facts
Location: Temple, London
Number of QCs/Juniors: 6/54 (17 women)
Applications: c. 350
Apply through Pupillage Portal
Pupils per year: 2-4
Seats: 4x3 months
Pupillage Award: £30,000 (can advance £5,000 for BPTC)

Head of chambers Robin Allen QC says: "*You should come here if you want to be a fearless lawyer.*"

Employment, PI and clin neg specialist Cloisters attracts those with a keen interest in the rights of the individual.

Neither tarnished nor afraid

Cloisters' practice has changed quite considerably since it came into existence in the early 1950s. Originally focusing mainly on criminal law, its civil practice gradually grew, especially in the fields of employment, personal injury and clinical negligence. Its founding members were fairly left-wing, and in the old days it "*invariably*" acted for claimants. In fact, senior clerk Glenn Hudson says that once upon a time 90% of its work came from just one firm, Thompsons (the country's largest PI specialist). Chambers' caseload is now far more balanced, and hundreds of solicitors instruct Cloisters on an equal mix of respondent and claimant matters. Approximately 65% of the work that comes to chambers is employment, commercial and regulatory law, 20% is PI and 15% clin neg.

Some time ago, the criminal barristers decided to go their separate ways, mainly to Charter Chambers and Tooks Chambers. Combined with the increase in respondent work, this saw the set drift towards the centre politically, but that doesn't mean it has ditched its original ideals. In a recent talk to some of its interns (what Cloisters now calls mini-pupils in a valiant attempt to sound modern and with-it), head of chambers Robin Allen QC said: "*You should come here if you want to be a fearless lawyer.*" "*That might sound a bit overblown,*" says Anna Beale, a member of the pupillage committee, "*but I think it's probably true. We have a reputation for doing those cutting-edge cases, generally for claimants, and there is a defining feeling that we are all here because we broadly believe in the same things that chambers believes in.*" One of those cutting-edge cases is Abbott & Others v South Tyneside MBC, in which the Employment Appeal Tribunal ruled that 300 low-paid male workers were discriminated against after they failed in a claim over bonuses, while a group of low-paid women with a similar claim succeeded. In another matter, Cloisters is acting for an Orthodox Jewish couple who claim that an automatic security light in their communal accommodation forces them to break their Sabbath rules.

Chambers wants to be regarded as the best in the business for the work that it currently does. It also plans to "*see if we can pick up some of the public law work that we were once so well known for. Ten years ago we were the number-one public law set, ahead of all the others, but with people getting* [judicial] *appointments and retiring, that work has dropped away.*"

Suit you?

Each CV received by chambers gets marked out of 20 by two members. The first ten points are for academic ability (for example, we're told a 2:1 plus a relevant master's would score 6.5). Two extra points are available here for demonstrating outstanding academic ability (coming top in your year, that sort of thing). The second ten points are more subjective and are awarded for various differ-

Chambers UK rankings
Clinical Negligence   Personal Injury
Employment

ent qualities. These are: 'soft' communication skills (having worked in a customer service industry, say a supermarket, would help); advocacy (ie formal presentation skills – ex-teachers or actors would probably score well for this); initiative and independence (are you suited to a self-employed career, can you juggle lots of tasks?) and commitment to the law (past work experience and so on). A final mark is available for "*suitability for Cloisters:*" do you have an interest in the rights of the individual? Get yourself some experience with FRU, we say.

Around 60 people are invited to a first interview. In previous years Cloisters posed a contract and tort-type problem of the type you might find in an exam. After finding that "*a bit too focused on strict legal knowledge,*" it changed things this year. "*We gave them a slightly altered and fictionalised real case and asked them to summarise the main points and challenge the decision.*" Roughly 15 people get through to second interview stage, at which applicants tackle another problem question, "*sometimes related to our practice areas but not always.*" As the question is posed seven days in advance, be prepared for some thorough questioning. Finally, there's a discussion on a topical subject: whether Dwain Chambers should be allowed to compete in the Olympics came up in 2008.

Off the wall

The first six is spent sitting with your supervisor and going to court with them. The second six is when things get really juicy. "*You can expect to be in court with your own cases fairly regularly*" right from the off, and with work still being set by your supervisor, plus a series of assessed exercises to handle, it's fair to say there's "*quite a lot to juggle in the second six.*" Those assessed exercises are vital as the tenancy decision is heavily based on them. In fact, very little weight is given to the reports of the four supervisors – odd, we thought – but Cloisters insists that this method is fairer and that they are trying to move away from "*the old school where everyone just votes on whether they like you or not.*" There are four assessments. The first is a drafting exercise, the second "*an advice with a whole list of things that no one person would ever need to know to research,*" the third is advocacy, and the whole thing concludes with an interview in front of five or six members of chambers who "*all pile in.*" By this point, pupils are probably going to have to work reasonably late to fit everything in. "*I generally leave between 7.30pm and 9.30pm, and am doing weekend work as well – although I'm good about making sure I take one day off a week,*" said a pupil with the second assessment coming up. The hours are much less onerous at the start of pupillage. So is it oral or written skills that count most? The answer depends on what you eventually specialise in. An employment barrister will be in court or tribunal on a weekly basis; a PI specialist on the other hand may find that 80-90% of the time is spent drafting papers and advices.

A word on pro bono. Each barrister does at least five days of pro bono work per year, either at a legal advice centre or for clients who just miss out on legal aid. "*People spend a lot of their effort and time on cases that are very poorly paid, if at all,*" said one pupil. Chambers takes pride in accepting "*cases that are a bit off the wall.*" One such was the lotto rapist case, which Cloisters' Paul Spencer handled on a pro bono basis. It went right up to the House of Lords, and he managed to get the law changed for the benefit of his client, the rapist's victim.

Cloisters but not cloistered

As you might imagine, we get fed a lot of PR at the *Student Guide*, so it was refreshing to find Cloisters relatively free of marketing spin. We notice that the submissions it sends to *Chambers UK* (in which sets try and persuade us why they should be ranked) are some of the most polite we've ever seen; and you might notice that the profiles of members on the website are listed in egalitarian alphabetical order rather than QCs first. The photo of junior Sally Cowen seems to have been taken in a car park. We're not complaining – we think it's terrific that there's a lack of PR BS. During our visit, clerks acknowledged that there are areas in which chambers hasn't done quite as well as it would have liked. They freely admit that "*all chambers are going through the downturn in the work [available to] the Bar.*" And, shock-horror: "*All chambers have internal politics,*" and it's no different here.

One year we dubbed Cloisters 'Bolly Chambers' because of the quantity of champagne that was consumed. Even in these straitened times members "*do like having an excuse to go out together.*" Says a clerk: "*We've lost a couple of people to sets that are very much 'heads down and work' in atmosphere, and privately they have said that's what they miss. It's those little things that you take for granted until you've moved on.*" Juniors share rooms, so there's always someone to bounce ideas off, and if you want proof that Cloisters is a party set, one of the current pupils had come to their first interview straight from Glastonbury. "*They said, 'You've clearly been doing too many of these interviews because you've lost your voice...'*"

And finally...

Cloisters has come a long way from the left-wing, claimant-only set it started out as. In 2009, both pupils took tenancy and will doubtless see the set evolve further.

Crown Office Chambers

The facts

Location: Temple, London
Number of QCs/Juniors: 14/71 (17 women)
Applications: 130
Outside Pupillage Portal Scheme
Pupils per year: Up to 3
Seats: 2x3 + 1x6 months
Pupillage Award: £42,500 (can advance £10,000 for BPTC)

Senior clerk Julian Campbell describes this as "*a forward-thinking traditional set.*"

Crown Office Chambers is the largest common law set at the Bar. Its strong backbone of insurance expertise crosses several fields of practice.

Alien ants

Crown Office Chambers is now approaching its tenth anniversary, having been formed in 2000 through the merger of One Paper Buildings and 2 Crown Office Row. These were two premier insurance sets and "*the watchwords were strength in depth.*" It was felt that since they had such similar practice area footprints, their union would create a 'superset' better able to withstand the slings and arrows of legal fortune. Chambers can look back and say the merger was a good move. Clerks tell us that "*turnover has increased year on year*" (up 15% in 2008/09), and that "*the business of chambers has picked up*" because "*there are enough people specialising in each of our chosen areas that we can offer our clients a range of barristers. If there's a case that requires four or five barristers of different levels, we have the skills all in one chambers.*"

COC doesn't focus on one specific area of practice. Instead, it has identified a number of key sectors in which it is capable. Broadly, these are: construction, insurance, professional negligence, personal injury, health and safety, product liability and clinical negligence. The ambition is simple: "*within five years to have doubled our turnover in all of those.*" The set can justifiably claim to have strength in each of these areas, but looking through the *Chambers UK* rankings over the past few years, we notice that a couple of areas in particular have come to the fore.

The first is personal injury. By the sheer number of instructions received, this is COC's biggest source of instructions.

The set sits in *Chambers UK's* top tier and has a particularly good reputation for industrial disease cases. Members have acted on deafness claims brought by ex-employees of the former vehicle manufacturer British Leyland, and the employers' liability 'Trigger' litigation, which will determine whether employers or insurers should pay for many of the asbestos claims of the past 50 years. Other PI cases of note include one in which a claimant was attacked by a herd of cows while crossing a field in the Lake District, suffering serious injuries. There was a footpath across the field but it was unmarked, and a claim was brought against the farmer in negligence and under the Animals Act. Another was US rock band Alien Ant Farm's $40m claim against a coach operator, one of the largest PI claims in UK history.

With "*fewer but bigger cases*" than PI, construction is the second area to which we draw your attention. Despite COC having fewer members working in this area than Keating and Atkin, our *Chambers UK* colleagues describe it as a thoroughly viable alternative to those specialist construction sets. The star here is Roger ter Haar QC, who has been working on a couple of arbitrations pertaining to a £200m claim arising out of a

Chambers UK rankings

Clinical Negligence	Personal Injury
Construction	Product Liability
Health & Safety	Professional Negligence

telecommunications project on the London Underground and a $50m claim against a state-owned Bulgarian company on behalf of an Arab contractor. And yet even members this senior won't specialise too much. In addition to having built a crack reputation for construction cases, Mr ter Haar is ranked by *Chambers UK* in several other areas.

Martian melodies

There doesn't seem to be much we can tell you about COC's application form that it doesn't tell you itself. You can find the form on its website and you'll see that intellect, work style, people skills, communication, self awareness, commitment and motivation are what you'll be judged on. Chambers operates outside the Pupillage Portal scheme and wants to see something more than "*generic*" answers.

The same goes for the interview process. About 20 people are invited to a first-round interview, and about ten make it to a second, where a typically atypical question might be 'Explain an iPod to a Martian.' It should be obvious from this that oral skills are highly prized. A junior told us: "*I wanted to be a barrister because I wanted to be in court. Now, I know people who want to be barristers because they want to advise on complicated points of law. There are chambers that do one and chambers that do the other.*" COC places emphasis on advocacy, for the early years at least. Said one source: "*Our most junior tenant is in court three or four times a week,*" further honing skills that she had begun to develop in her second six. So, "*if you don't have the ability to be an effective advocate this would not be the chambers for you.*"

"*That doesn't mean there isn't any research or writing bits of advice, because there's that as well.*" Plenty of it by all accounts. Recruits spend the year with four pupilmasters, and in every seat there are two fixed, written assessments, set and marked by a relevant specialist. An assessed advocacy course begins after Christmas, and COC tells us it is looking for a general upward trajectory in the quality of pupils' advocacy skills, rather than stellar performance after stellar performance. Everyone shares the same pupilmasters to ensure fairness of assessment, and these supervisors are selected to give pupils exposure to pretty much all chambers' practice areas. The idea being that it's unwise to put "*all your eggs in one basket.*" Pupils are also encouraged to work for other members of chambers, getting to know more of them by doing so. The tenancy decision is made in July and based partly on the results of the assessments and partly on comments from other members of chambers, but mainly on reports given by pupilmasters. In 2009, the set's sole second-six pupil was offered tenancy.

Back to the future

"*I would describe this as a forward-thinking traditional set,*" says senior clerk Julian Campbell. We asked for clarification of this apparent contradiction in terms. "*We're not a set that would dispense with the Bar's traditions – we like them – but behind the scenes it is run in a very businesslike way.*" An executive committee is the driving force these days: "*It's not practical when you are this size to have all decisions taken by a plenary chambers meeting,*" says a junior. "*That was what happened when I started out, and the meetings would be interminable. People would go on at great length about how much they agreed with each other! The executive committee has made it more efficient.*" It's probably also good that "*as well as being a star at the Bar,*" head of chambers Antony Edwards-Stuart QC "*has good management skills.*" One recent decision of note is an "*affiliation*" with Edinburgh's Compass Chambers. It's the first such tie-up between an English and a Scottish set, and the thinking is that it will help improve the service to insurance industry clients wherever cross-border claims are involved. A business mindset is also reflected in the fact that chambers "*doesn't tolerate second-rate practice, and members are even bearded from time to time. Of course they are self-employed people, but they very much run under a Crown Office Chambers banner, and there is a certain level of expectation because of that.*"

We think chambers' large size really is its defining feature. It has made the push towards a more necessary corporate structure; it has made it possible to carry out a broad range of practice, and it naturally dictates the culture of the place. Members admit that "*to a certain extent you lose the family atmosphere*" of a smaller set, but then knowing what some families are like, is that such a disadvantage? You might not know everyone at COC, but its size does ensure "*there will always be a critical mass of people at about your level doing your thing.*" Equally, there's the space to avoid people you don't get on with. We sense that COC is a broad church with room for both pockets of the old school and the new breed of barrister. Speaking of bonding, bar a couple of the marketing events, pupils are invited to all social functions, from chambers drinks on Thursdays or Fridays to the annual Christmas jolly.

And finally...

Bigger is better for COC. Its six diverse areas of practice give it a solid foundation to withstand whatever the economy and the changing professional environment might throw at it.

One Essex Court

The facts

Location: Temple, London
Number of QCs/Juniors: 23/43 (10 women)
Applications: c. 200
Apply through Pupillage Portal
Pupils per year: 4-5
Seats: 2x3 and 1x6 months
Pupillage Award: £60,000 + earnings (can advance £20,000 for BPTC)

You'll see One Essex Court at the forefront of all kinds of big commercial disputes.

An elite but straightforward set, One Essex Court takes pride in being "*not a formal, suit-wearing place – quite the reverse in fact.*"

Rebels with a cause

The name One Essex Court was first heard in the narrow alleyways and leafy squares of the Temple in 1966, when a group of four barristers and a clerk broke away from a set in Mitre Court. "*Some of them were Catholic, some were Jewish, and in those days the Bar was a lot more English and Establishment. These were people who weren't going to get a place at the leading sets of the time, so they started their own chambers.*"

Current members ascribe OEC's subsequent phenomenal success to the ethos of "*meritocracy*" that was present right from the beginning. It's now a part of the magic circle of commercial sets, although this wasn't cause for boasting during the course of our interviews with members, clerks and pupils – in fact as far as we can remember, the words 'magic circle' didn't crop up once. But nonetheless you'll see chambers at the forefront of all kinds of big commercial disputes, including the Buncefield and Northern Rock litigations and the bank charges test case. Members have also acted on cases such as Esure v Direct Line (in an IP kerfuffle over a mouse-on-wheels logo), Chelsea FC v FC Lyn Oslo (a spat over the signing of John Obi Mikel) and Cable & Wireless v Ofcom (for eight fixed-line operators in an appeal relating to mobile phone termination charges). While other chambers tend to have certain specialist areas, OEC remains very much a set of generalist practitioners.

New senior clerk Darren Burrows is following in the footsteps of two legends in their own lifetimes, Robert Ralphs and Paul Shrubsall, who were instrumental in bringing clerking into the modern era. Since Shrubsall's retirement in 2008 no sweeping reforms have been made, but chambers is increasingly looking to market itself to clients outside the UK. "*That isn't something we've pursued heavily in the past, but we now have good client bases in the Caribbean and the Far East.*" Competition and EU-related work is another growing market that it wants to capitalise on. "*It's a developing area, and one that students are interested in.*" A high demand from solicitors for junior counsel has resulted in chambers "*talking to a number of firms*" about farming juniors out to them for periods of two or three months – "*a mini-secondment if you like.*"

Sanity not vanity

The selection process for pupils begins not with the Pupillage Portal, but "*by going to student law fairs and encouraging people of talent to apply.*" At £60,000, the sum chambers pays pupils is one of the highest at the Bar, "*so that no one can say, I didn't apply because I couldn't afford to.*" More people want to do mini-pupillages than

Chambers UK rankings

Banking & Finance	Fraud: Civil
Commercial Dispute Resolution	Intellectual Property
Company	Internat'l Arbitration
Competition/European Law	Professional Negligence
Energy & Natural Resources	

there are places available, so chambers doesn't insist that you do one. "*If we did, middle class kids with pushy parents who know how to work the system would have a massive advantage.*"

Three members of the pupillage committee read every application. Said one: "*I used to ask myself, 'Is this person cleverer than I am?' If they were, they got an interview. But these days that's virtually everyone, so I have to be a little more critical.*" Academic achievement is "*a necessary but not a sufficient requirement.*" As a junior pointed out: "*My pupilmaster told me 80 Oxbridge Firsts apply each year, and we only interview 40 people!*" So something extra is required, and that something is inevitably subjective. "*Personally, I don't give a toss whether someone's travelled or not – that isn't difficult these days,*" says a QC. "*There was one applicant though, who'd travelled in the second half of his gap year because he had gone door-to-door selling paintbrushes in the first half. I thought that was bloody impressive. It takes more persuasive skill to sell paintbrushes than you'll need with a Commercial Court judge. They have to listen to you whether they like it or not. A bloke on the doorstep can just tell you to f*** off.*"

The pupillage interview consists of a legal problem and a brief chat. Applicants get an hour and a copy of *Chitty on Contracts* to prepare for the problem, to which "*there is no right answer, but we are expecting them to at least see what the issues are.*" How interviewees react to further probing is important. "*We asked a question to one guy and he said: 'That's a very good point, but I'll come back to it later,' which was quite a ballsy thing to do. Of course if he hadn't come back to it, that's just dodging the question and he'd have failed. But he did, and that's good organisation.*" The purpose of the chat is essentially "*to ensure that they're not completely mad.*" As long as you're not round the bend, out to lunch, barking, barmy or generally bonkers, you'll be fine. If you *are* any of these things, there may still be space for you somewhere at the Bar, but you'll have to be exceptionally brilliant for clients to put up with you. Speaking of which, senior clerks are also present at the interview stage to give their opinion on "*whether the applicant is saleable in the market.*" This is a commercial operation, after all.

What the chat is not about is finding out: "*Are they One Of Us?*" Eton-educated members rub shoulders quite happily with those from bog-standard comprehensives (as David Blunkett so charmingly put it), of which there are plenty, including "*one guy whose father runs a market stall in Leicester.*" Three of the four 2008/09 pupils were women, one was non-Oxbridge and one was from an ethnic minority background, although it's fair to say that OEC, like the rest of the Bar, is still predominantly male and white.

Smash and grab

Pupils essentially "*live the daily practice life*" of their pupilmasters, whose styles differ. Some will deal with one case at a time; others will juggle as many matters as they can. Some will regularly leave at 6.30pm; others will stay until 8pm. There is no obligation to work particularly long hours most of the time, but "*if the pressure is on it's good to see that you are committed.*" As a junior told us: "*The occasional late night isn't going to do you any harm. You may even find yourself coming in on a weekend once or twice because you want to be in control. But no one will demand that you do that.*" If you need to leave at 5pm to pick your kids up, that's fine too. During pupillage, everything is live. "*There's nothing you do that's just an exercise. You're never just rehashing some old silk's case that he thinks he really should have won and wants every pupil to re-perform it for him. Everything is going to be used.*" In the second six, pupils will be in court relatively frequently with their own caseload of "*what we call the Robert Ralphs £50 specials*" – road traffic smashes and the like. However, since "*at the junior end most of what we do is written,*" oral and drafting skills are equally important.

After six months the head of the pupillage committee gives pupils "*a fairly candid view*" of whether they are in the running for tenancy. Those who aren't occasionally decide to seek their fortune elsewhere, but are more than welcome to stay for the second six. Obviously it's not an ideal scenario, but it's not the end of the world if you "*stuff up something massively. If the rest of your work is excellent and you're clearly cut out for the Bar, there would be no point throwing you away because of one mistake.*" The whole of chambers votes on tenancy and it's necessary for 75% of the members to be in favour for a motion to be carried. OEC has an excellent record for keeping its pupils on and in 2009 three out of four were offered tenancy.

While not an obligation, pupils are "*almost expected to be the mainstay*" of Friday night drinks. It's generally "*not heavy on work chat. Lord Grabiner will stick his head in every now and then, and when he's there everything's a little more focused on the great man. He'll give us a bit of wisdom and say hello before he heads off for his weekend.*" Pupils are invited to all chambers' events, including the summer party and *The Times Law Awards* (which it sponsors) to make them feel part of the "*OEC family.*"

And finally...

At OEC there is ample proof that brilliance doesn't have to come with a side order of arrogance.

39 Essex Street

The facts

Location: Temple, London
Number of QCs/Juniors: 24/55 (19 women)
Applications: 300+
Apply thorough Pupillage Portal
Pupils per year: Up to 3
Seats: 4 before July
Pupillage award: £40,000 (can advance £8,000 for BPTC)

Anyone who fancies proving their mettle here is advised to do a mini-pupillage. While not mandatory for pupillage applicants, perform well and you can expect it to count in your favour.

Bright, bustling and businesslike, 39 Essex Street is master of its many trades and possessed of an apparently inexhaustible desire for self-improvement.

Still room at the Inn

In the last eight years 39 Essex Street has mushroomed from 30 to nearly 80 barristers, making it one of the larger London sets. Its broad coverage allows it to adopt a contemporary strategy of not only pursuing its core areas but also "*providing connections between them with the aim of being a one-stop shop for clients.*" As it fills its airy premises on the western fringe of the Temple, it has already "*secured accommodation needs for the next ten years.*" Said chambers director Michael Meeson with an acquisitive glint in his eye: "*We're ever-willing to take on new barristers if there's a business need.*"

Many sets advertise broad coverage, few back up the claim as substantially as this one. It has two or more barristers ranked in 16 areas of practice in the latest edition of *Chambers UK*. The "*four genuine trunks of strength*" are common law, environmental and planning, commercial/construction law and public law, and 39 also thrives on the areas of crossover. Construction "*isn't just construction, it brings in environment, planning, regulatory, even nuclear work in extension,*" while "*serving the health industry isn't only clin neg or PI, it's professional negligence and commercial work for the NHS or private providers.*" Multinational conglomerates like Esso and BP instruct members, as do some 85 local authorities.

Away from commercial and common law practice, chambers takes on some eye-catching human rights, immigration, administrative law and local government instructions and costs litigation. Its commitment to pro bono work is evident in links to the Environmental Law Foundation, FRU and Liberty. Certainly the widow of a British serviceman killed in combat was grateful for help at the coroner's inquest that established his death was the result of US friendly fire.

Inspire, aspire, perspire

Some 30 support staff ensure chambers is "*run like an effective business.*" It also means "*the pastoral aspects and structure of pupillage are not left to chance.*" Indeed, pupils praised an "*entirely transparent, well thought-out process*" that starts with their being given a detailed pupillage handbook. They sit with four supervisors in the first nine months, typically two each from the fields of public and private law. As a result they are exposed to anything from "*enormous VAT disputes*" to "*redrafting statutes on education matters,*" from

Chambers UK rankings

Administrative & Public Law	Local Government
Civil Liberties	Personal Injury
Clinical Negligence	Product Liability
Construction	Professional Discipline
Costs Litigation	Professional Negligence
Environment	Tax
Immigration	

common law work where "*you get to grips with the White Book*" to "*construction disputes and immigration cases.*" Our sources laughed at the absurdity of a pupil "*drafting a letter starting Dear Secretary of State,*" but were clearly inspired by the prospect of doing so at some later stage. "*What's great about chambers is that wherever tenancy takes you, the future horizons are broad. In none of its areas is chambers half-hearted, and you look up the food chain in any of them and see barristers doing interesting, sexy work.*"

> **Chambers and Partners Personal Injury Set of the Year 2009**

First-six supervisors take care that their charges handle pleadings and skeleton arguments, rather than running around as a gopher, researching minor points. Their policing role continues into the second six when everything still has to be "*sanctioned by the supervisor.*" Second-sixers go to court a couple of times a week on "*RTAs and credit hire cases,*" with juniors providing support when needed. Pupils love the wealth of advocacy opportunities because it's all about "*developing witness-handling skills, making your mistakes and learning case strategy in a relatively safe environment.*" So much so in fact, that we even heard one source utter the words: "*I really like going to Slough County Court.*" Beyond the commonplace, "*more interesting things pop up.*" One interviewee recalled "*going to the Privy Council, which meant asking a kindly silk where I had to sit.*"

No competition

Predictably, feedback is detailed. As well as responses to each piece of work, pupils receive a formal appraisal and written report at the end of each seat to "*flag problems as you go, so you're not storing up nasty surprises for just before the tenancy decision.*" Unusually, the report also deals with the question of how well pupils have maintained their extra-curricular commitments. The reports are central to the tenancy decision, as are up to four written assessments set by a shadow pupillage committee and completed in the second six. Recalling these, a junior told us: "*They take a lot of hard work – around a week each. One of them was the most difficult legal problem I've ever faced.*" The final hurdle is a tough assessed advocacy session in which pupils demonstrate witness-handling and technical skills to the watching panel while "*supervisors play witnesses with aplomb.*" Pupils say they're entirely satisfied that "*if you meet the objective criteria, you'll be taken on. We're not explicitly or quietly in competition with each other.*" Perhaps proving this, in 2007 two of the three in contention got tenancy, in 2008 the single pupil was not successful while in 2009 both pupils were.

At the pupillage application stage around 30 people attend a first interview. "*You get a case an hour beforehand and are grilled for 20 minutes by a panel of five to assess your legal reasoning.*" The 12 who are summoned back to the second round face a milder "*more traditional, general CV chat.*" Even a brief glance at tenants' CVs reveals that 39 Essex is genuinely open to people of "*all backgrounds, types and skills.*" A number arrived from other careers and our sources told us that "*brains in a vat just don't cut it here*" because "*trawling though paperwork is only half the job – our areas demand broader skills.*"

Taking the biscuit

Work-life balance at chambers isn't so much a vague aim as a rigorously policed policy. Supervisors "*aggressively enforce 9am-to-6pm hours*" for pupils and encourage a "*full hour for lunch.*" Someone who initially doubted the curfew recalled: "*It was 6.04pm on the first day I tried to stay and my supervisor ejected me.*" The set's concern to show pastoral care is also evident in the willingness of juniors to "*make an effort to look after the pupils.*" It might mean "*post-work drinks together,*" a friendly chat at the fortnightly lunch or simply patient forbearance as "*you call up for the nth time saying, 'Aarrgh, I've got this tomorrow – how do I do it?'*" There's also a confidential mentoring system, which sees a senior appointed as an additional point of contact for pupils in need of advice, and often this relationship generates work once tenancy is assured. This is a reasonably casual set on the inside: some of the members we met during our visit wore T-shirts and jeans, and they cheerfully dug into a pile of biscuits as we chatted to them about the set's "*positive atmosphere.*" While munching away, one reflected: "*If I get a complicated, esoteric instruction I have no hesitation in asking anyone about it and I mean anyone.*" Pupils are invited to social events, whether it's the Christmas party for members' children (dressing as an Elf may be required) or the summer garden party.

> **And finally...**
>
> Breadth of excellence and opportunity define a 39 Essex Street pupillage; go to any length to get one.

Government Legal Service (GLS)

The facts

Location: London, Manchester
Number of Barristers: c.500 (c.270 women)
Applications: 200+
Outside Pupillage Portal scheme
Pupils per year: Potentially 15-20
Seats: 2x6 or 3x4 months
Pupillage award: £22,900-£25,200 + BPTC fees and £5,400-£7,600 grant

> Unlike the independent Bar, where pupils must prove their ability to earn money, "*at the GLS they start from the premise you've got to do something wrong not to be employed on qualification.*"

The 500 or so barristers at the GLS have a single client – the government. They advise on the implementation of policy and the implications of European and domestic legislation. The lawyers also provide advocacy in litigation, judicial reviews and other inquiries and tribunals.

Brothers and sisters in law

Over 30 government departments employ lawyers –see page 280– so the subject matter is enormous in scope. Some of the issues our sources had encountered were the freezing of terrorists' assets, supporting a lasting peace in Northern Ireland, advising teams on emergency protocols to deal with animal disease, the implementation of the Gambling Act and prosecuting fraud cases. We could go on all day listing the different topics and areas of law; instead we'll point you to www.gls.gov.uk for detailed info about the available work and which departments offer pupillages.

Applicants are considered alongside those looking to become solicitors with the GLS and some 15-20 of the training places available can potentially be filled by pupils. It is possible to apply to the GLS without committing to either the barrister or solicitor route, as everyone is viewed as a 'trainee'. In some departments "*barristers do much the same job as solicitors,*" and one of our interviewees confessed they had "*a solicitor hat and a barrister hat.*" For further details on the ins and outs of the application process and read the feature on training as a solicitor with the GLS on page 280.

Once assigned to a department, trainees complete two seats of six months or three of four months. All work comes from a designated supervisor, with whom trainees chat about their progress on a weekly basis. "*There's a good deal of autonomy,*" said one source, explaining that while trainees might show complex pieces of work to their supervisors they are "*able to get on with things and liaise with clients directly to a certain extent.*" One seat is usually spent in a prestigious set of chambers working with barristers in private practice. With the work of barristers and solicitors overlapping in the civil service, it's a chance to see the "*more fast-moving*" lifestyle of the independent Bar and "*sit on the other side of the professional fence.*" Our sources said they were treated just like other pupils in chambers and observed "*some superb advocacy.*" Secondments to the Crown Prosecution Service are available in some instances.

The thinker

In certain departments the trainee's work will be predominantly advisory and "*you usually have policy considerations to take into account.*" Recent trainees have advised on the insolvencies of football clubs and the emotive collapse of the Swindon-based Farepak Christmas Club, which lost the hard-earned savings of customers in 2006. Others liaised with counsel to draft Acts of Parliament and pondered the implications of European directives. "*In legal terms,*" explained one academically minded interviewee, "*I'm the one who sits and thinks about thorny issues.*" Contentious work might typically include writing defences, drafting witness statements and orders, instructing investigating officers and advocates on commercial litigation, perhaps against or initiated by the Ministry of Defence, or criminal prosecutions under the Insolvency Act, where much turns on the question of intention to defraud – "*a woolly, difficult area.*"

It's worth pointing out that opportunities for trainees to conduct advocacy are rare, and "*if you want to go to court all the time you probably won't be interested in the GLS.*" The size of legal teams and the even smaller number of barristers mean that "*anything outside the M25 goes to agents.*" Trainees will generally see more of the magistrates' courts than the Crown Court, where government lawyers usually instruct private practice barristers. Our sources didn't feel too hard done by, as there's plenty of scope to develop drafting, interviewing and conferencing skills.

A job for a life

Aside from the quality and broad scope of work, there are other benefits to training with the GLS. Normal work hours "*really are nine to five,*" and "*while they expect you to work hard during the day it's not something that becomes all-encompassing.*" Flexible working is encouraged and everyone has a 30-day holiday allowance. Remember, barristers and pupils in private practice do not get paid holidays. The GLS pays BPTC fees and awards a maintenance grant. It sometimes pays for the GDL year too. There's the security that comes from being an employed barrister without the worry of where the next instruction and pay cheque will come from, and then at the end of your career there's "*a very good pension.*"

There are downsides, of course, one of them being a relatively low salary. Some of our GLS sources thought that attempts to run the service more like a business, and yet not make salaries competitive with those in private practice, smacked of "*the civil service wanting to have its cake and eat it.*" One dedicated public servant had clearly done the maths: "*At the junior level, once you add in pensions and holidays, in terms of financial security you're on par with the civil Bar for a few years. After that they may go miles in front, but they have to sell themselves.*"

Recently it was decided that the period of post-qualification supervision for barristers should be extended by twelve months and eventually everyone will spend two years after qualifying as 'legal officers' on a salary below that of a Grade 7 government lawyer. Some trainees have been left ruing their prospective loss of earnings, but others welcome what is essentially another year of training. The GLS told us the new standardised structure puts trainee barristers and solicitors on more of an equal footing, given the difference in the time it takes to qualify.

So exactly who shuns the long-term financial benefits and freedom of self-employment at the independent Bar? Many have already worked in the private sector, either in law or another career, and most have an interest in politics, even if personal convictions must be kept at arm's length. "*If you don't want to do something because it conflicts with your politics you can protest, but then you might have to resign if you still won't do what is asked.*" The GLS is "*a natural choice*" for someone with a strong interest in pubic and administrative law, but it also attracts people "*who don't have an incredibly specific idea of what they want to do.*" Government lawyers are never in the same place for too long: typically they stay in a department for three years before moving on to another and this produces genuinely capable all-rounders.

And finally...

With trainees dispersed across departments, the Legal Trainee Network makes an admirable effort to get everyone socialising. There's no reason for pupillage to be the lonely and stressful experience it can sometimes turn into at the independent Bar.

4-5 Gray's Inn Square

The facts

Location: Gray's Inn, London
Number of QCs/Juniors: 14/36 (9 women)
Applications: 200+
Apply through Pupillage Portal
Pupils per year: Up to 3
Seats: 4 in first 9 months
Pupillage award: £37,000 (can advance £10,000 for BPTC)

> Over 500 people apply for a mini-pupillage here every year, so check the set's website for details as early as possible.

4-5 Gray's Inn Square combines planning expertise with significant ability in the many facets of public law, judicial review and local government work. It also has an ever-expanding commercial practice.

Inquiring minds

After seven members departed to Matrix Chambers in 2000, this set considered, then dismissed, a merger with Monckton Chambers, subsequently losing a further eight barristers. Left with a 30-strong contingent, it could simply have faded; instead it drew breath and went to work with a vengeance. Today it is a picture of health, and with those past defections rapidly vanishing into ancient history, chambers is sorting out new rooms at 2 Gray's Inn Square to accommodate all the new arrivals.

Nearly half of the membership is involved with public law and planning inquiries, High Court applications for judicial review and complex planning and environmental advice to developers, local authorities and objectors. For some this might be a major wind farm inquiry in Northumbria or preparing for a forthcoming inquiry into the proposal to build a second runway at Stansted airport. If you don't fancy a fleet of Boeing 767s flying over your house all of a sudden, you equally might dislike a high-rise building going up next door. Members were drafted into the major planning inquiry concerning two new Blackfriars Road skyscrapers by the London Borough of Southwark. Naturally the volume of instructions for big developers is slowing as the credit crunch bites deeper, however when the property market is busy, so too are the planning barristers.

You can't underplay the effect that economic and political factors have on planning work; indeed so much of chambers' public law practice is at *"the intersection of policy,* *politics and law."* Basically, if it involves public bodies, 4-5 Gray's Inn Square will get involved, be it judicial review (including human rights issues), employment, social security or mental health tribunals, education, environment or European law. Some 300 local authorities across the country regularly turn to the set across the full spectrum of their legal needs. Chambers has recently been advising around 30 of them on the government's eco-towns plans and many others on proposed changes to the unitary status of local authorities.

Members also acted on the landmark ECHR case concerning retention of fingerprints and DNA samples, and on the challenge to a school's refusal to allow a Sikh pupil to wear a Kara bangle. Some additionally have sports law expertise. This led to involvement in a challenge to the ICC's decision to alter the result of the controversial England v Pakistan 2006 Oval Test. Meanwhile strength in media/defamation issues meant J.K. Rowling turned to chambers over a press intrusion matter. In addition members handle commercial judicial reviews, multi-jurisdictional banking cases and international trade and insurance cases.

Chambers UK rankings

Administrative & Public Law	Local Government
Education	Planning
Environment	Professional Discipline

Smart choices

Proud of its knack for identifying talented applicants, the set recruits with the "*strong presumption that pupils are good enough to be tenants.*" It's no empty boast: only one person hasn't made tenancy in the seven years since the set reduced its annual pupil intake to three at most. Both of the pupils of 2008, and all three in 2009, were successful. The set takes an exacting approach to interviewing candidates, aiming to uncover "*fine analytical skills to go to the heart of a matter and present in a clear, structured framework,*" as well as "*excellent advocacy skills and the ability to be calm, confident and persuasive.*" Around 40 applicants are called to a first-round interview of "*a little discussion about the CV to set people at ease, but mostly questions to probe reasoning.*" The best prospects come back for a second-round day of advocacy, which current pupils remembered as "*the most fulfilling, most completely testing interview*" of any in their experience. Applicants arrive at 9am and are given a bundle of documents from which they must write submissions, before preparing for oral advocacy in front of a panel of up to seven members. Instructed "*not to cite cases,*" non-law graduates needn't worry too much, as the test is one of "*raw ability to reason and present.*" It's undoubtedly a rigorous and "*nerve-wracking*" process, but at the end "*you feel like you've had a good chance to show your stuff.*"

Although carefully structured, pupillage is a busy and demanding year. Pupils sit with up to four supervisors in the nine months before the tenancy decision is made, with these regular switches designed to ensure breadth of experience, not to mention "*exposure to widely different personalities.*" "*The first period is very protected: you're allowed lots of time to do work and told to go home early.*" Following this, there's a clear "*sense of progression, so that you start taking on bigger pieces like whole opinions or skeleton arguments for a supervisor. There's also devilling for other members and you have your own workload as well.*" Different practice areas bring different experiences. The public side might mean "*going to the European Court of Human Rights on a DNA retention case;*" commercial work might equate to "*a heavyweight dispute involving a Kurdistan telecoms company,*" while planning encompasses large and small-scale inquiries, "*perhaps where your supervisor is grilling an expert witness put up to defend an indefensible case by a local authority.*" As an indication of the scope of experiences on offer, one pupil recounted being involved with "*public law-based tribunals, an extradition case, a big compulsory purchase order, mental health reviews and social security tribunals.*"

On the road

Second-six pupils won't be on their feet much unless they take on pro bono instructions. The latter half of pupillage is still designed as a learning experience, learning for example that "*commercial work gives you lots of time to work out a tactical move to wrongfoot the opposition,*" while public sector work "*is very fast-moving and requires a specific skill set to deal with the many people involved in making decisions.*" Regular court visits and trips to inquiries keep things exciting. It might be "*Northumbria one week, Southampton the next,*" in which case "*you're likely to have lunch, dinner and maybe even breakfast with your supervisor.*" This routine also gives an incredible insight into "*the sorts of travel and work pressures of practice proper.*" Pupils may also take a short secondment to a law firm or local authority client.

Pupils are continually informed about their progress as supervisors offer comments "*on a piece-by-piece basis,*" although as time goes by "*if nothing's said it means [your work] is good.*" Whenever pupils do anything for other members "*they fill in a feedback form with a public and private section. You see the public bit*" while the private comments form part of the feedback supervisors provide at three-monthly appraisals and are also taken into consideration at the tenancy decision. Similarly important are three assessed advocacy days that are "*very much like the second-round interview.*" Of course the stakes are higher and the complexity greater. The subjects chosen are deliberately those with which pupils are likely to be unfamiliar, but there's feedback after each day and "*so far as possible, the same people are on the assessing panel, which is good for seeing your development or regression.*"

It's small wonder that pupils feel "*well supported*" and entirely clear about where they stand, despite the "*occasional inevitable moments of pupil paranoia.*" This set thrives on a "*tough, hard-working culture*" but is nevertheless "*very human... there's no dreadful pressure cooker atmosphere.*" Clerks, juniors and even seniors can be relied on to make pupils feel comfortable, particularly at an initial welcome dinner, but also at weekly lunches or occasional drinks. In the summer – weather permitting – chambers lunch takes the form of a picnic in Gray's Inn Gardens. Other notable features of the social calendar are a formal dinner in May and the Christmas party.

And finally...

More so than many sets, this one is deeply committed to its pupils. Successfully negotiate the testing interview process and you'll have every opportunity to embark upon a rewarding practice in planning, commercial and public law.

2 Hare Court

The facts

Location: Middle Temple, London
Number of QCs/Juniors: 16/37 (12 women)
Applications: 300+
Apply through Pupillage Portal
Pupils per year: 2
Seats: 3x4 months
Pupillage award: Min. £24,000

Murder, terrorism, international drug trafficking, fraud, corruption, sexual offences and corporate manslaughter are all in a day's work at 2 Hare Court.

Once upon a time – about eight years ago – 2HC was primarily all about prosecution. The apparent ease with which it has made high-profile defence work an equal part of its caseload says everything about this set's smooth brilliance.

Crime bosses and canoeists

Senior members have recently prosecuted Barry George in the Jill Dando murder retrial; represented criminal mastermind Terry Adams (even the Krays called him Sir, apparently) in trial and confiscation proceedings; prosecuted the Suffolk strangler; and successfully defended both Sean Hoey, the accused in the Omagh bombing case, and Terrence Davison, charged with the murder of Robert McCartney, whose sisters campaigned against the IRA. Then there's the juniors involved in the 21/7 terrorist trial and the Darwin 'forgetful canoeist' case, not to mention head of chambers David Waters' starring role in the criminal prosecution of terrorism defendants including Omar Khyam.

Seeing itself as "*a progressive set in an increasingly competitive market,*" and faced with the uncertainties common to the Criminal Bar, 2HC isn't resting on its laurels. It has moved into areas that suit its skills, and so barristers now regularly prosecute at professional disciplinary tribunals for the General Medical Council and on regulatory matters for organisations like The FA. VAT tribunal work for HMRC is also emerging as a strength. Additionally, individuals shine in licensing and environmental law. It's unlikely that crime will cease to be the mainstay, it's just that the set understands the value of developing these other public law abilities.

Several hundred applicants duke it out for the two pupillages available each year. Candidates face "*questions about a topic they should know about, perhaps a dissertation or specialism, whether law-based or not,*" as well as probing on "*general legal topics.*" The 12 who make it to the second round have 30 minutes to prepare for an advocacy exercise, "*such as an opening for a prosecution.*" The main point is to demonstrate an "*ability to stand up and tell a story*" rather than a grasp of legal proprieties. Pupils who'd navigated the process reflected on how the set "*seemed most interested in your broader skills and experience*" and felt interviews were "*tailored to you, not some pro forma list of questions.*" Perhaps this is because the set is seeking out "*rounded individuals with the capacity to deal one day with an erudite statutory construction in the Court of Appeal, the next day with a difficult client in a magistrates' court.*" Looking at the backgrounds of 2HC tenants, there's no obvious formula for who makes it in. We'd add that the two pupils we met could not have been more different.

Seriously good

Gaining tenancy almost certainly involves a third six, meaning new pupils have senior pupils from whom to

Chambers UK rankings

Crime
Fraud: Criminal
Professional Discipline

take cues. During the long haul, 2HC invests a lot of time and effort in its pupils. As the senior clerk observed: "*We could take on solicitors' magistrates' court lists to secure their Crown Court stuff, but we don't like to treat our pupils that way; we prefer to see them in court on more serious cases*" then "*back in chambers learning social and networking skills, being comfortable with more senior members.*" Raising the pupillage award to £24,000 is one way the set has chosen to support pupils, and a new system of three supervisors in the first year is also designed to "*help them meet more people, get more work, and not face the prospect of a new supervisor and getting on their feet at the same time.*" Similarly, the head of the pupillage committee is working hard to ensure "*supervisors and members of chambers don't overload pupils, because realistically they will never say no to work.*"

The first six involves close observation of both supervisors, learning the ins and outs of court procedures and client-handling skills. Observing certainly isn't boring; indeed the delight on the faces of our interviewees was infectious. "*It's brilliant stuff: we were straight in at the Old Bailey on one murder trial after another. Murders, terrorism, you name it… it's what you've been training for and it's all within touching distance.*" Back in chambers there are fortnightly advocacy exercises, "*when you get feedback there and then,*" and at the end of each seat supervisors will give an appraisal of your performance while in their charge. In the future this process may be handed over to, or supplemented by discussions with, the head of the pupillage committee.

At the end of the first six, a week is spent trailing senior pupils in the magistrates' courts, "*learning the things you'd forgotten and the things you didn't even know you needed to know.*" Emphasising the importance of advocacy in the second six, a mock trial scheme helps prepare pupils, but it's practically the real thing. Staged in the evening at the Old Bailey, a couple of resident judges preside, "*the staff stay on wearing their full regalia*" and "*members of chambers play witnesses,*" (in)advertently revealing that they are "*all complete hams.*" There's also a secondment to the CPS, where pupils "*see the ropes and the sorts of pressures prosecutors are under.*"

Daly life

Life thereafter is all about court – "*the full gamut of magistrates' court appearances, sentences, pleadings and summary trials,*" plus "*maybe a little Crown Court stuff.*" Fielding offers of work for other members, while managing their own practice and impressing a supervisor, the pressure mounts. It's here that supervisors do a good job of "*helping you keep track of what you've done and what you can take on.*" Whether it's taking pleasure in "*getting an acquittal and the clients being grateful*" or even "*losing, but taking satisfaction in performing professionally as a minister of justice,*" pupils had no qualms about working as hard as possible to extract the most from their experiences. The set does look out for them by offering travel expenses for travel outside the M25, "*not charging them clerks' fees or rent during second or third six,*" and perhaps equally importantly "*being just as busy collecting pupils' fees as tenants' fees.*" For those kept on, the third six brings more of the same with a gradual increase in Crown Court work, conducting mentions, plea and directions hearings, sentences, applications to dismiss and legal arguments. Eighteen months is a long time to be a pupil and requires a combination of determination and grace under pressure: those who make the grade do so after the committee has considered feedback from instructing solicitors and judges, and assessed their performance in court and written work. Chambers had not made its decision by the time we went to print in 2009, but in 2008 three new tenancies were awarded; one pupil did not get an offer.

You might think an 18-month-long interview would hamper a pupil's ability to socialise; our sources said otherwise. "*Daly's is the place for a lot of drinks,*" they explained, taking pleasure in the fact that "*if there's a party or an event we'll be invited.*" Given the Criminal Bar's stereotypical reputation for basing social life on alcohol, it was good to hear one add: "*I don't drink heavily and I've never felt out of place.*" Relations between juniors and pupils are good and "*people will always pop by the pupils' room to have a chat.*"

And finally...

"*There's a self-confidence in the place that's justified because of the phenomenal quality of work,*" one source suggested, another remarking on the set's "*flexibility – there's freedom to be yourself.*"

Henderson Chambers

The facts

Location: Temple, London
Number of QCs/Juniors: 8/30 (6 women)
Applications: 200+
Apply through Pupillage Portal
Pupils per year: Up to 3
Seats: 2x6 months (may change to 2x3 + 1x6)
Pupillage award: £42,500 (can advance sum for BPTC)

In the heart of the Temple, Henderson outwardly epitomises the traditional Bar. Step inside and the plasma TV in reception suggests otherwise. Heck, head of chambers Charles Gibson even has an electric drum kit in his room.

Common law set Henderson Chambers has a stellar reputation for health and safety and product liability cases, and is advancing rapidly in fields such as IT, local government and public law, real estate, environment, European law and professional discipline.

On the right track

The contemporary, "*family and community-minded*" world of Henderson Chambers is the product of some 70 years of gradually evolving practice in common law areas. The set now considers itself "*a specialist, but with a wider range of specialisms than other places.*" By "*noting where our strengths are and focusing on them,*" the set has ensured its members gain high-quality instructions in public inquiries, HSE defence, local authority prosecutions and industrial disease litigation. Of late these have included a criminal investigation arising from the Buncefield oil depot explosion and an HSE prosecution against British Waterways, following a double canalside fatality. Well-developed links with rail companies and regulators mean if you can name a recent rail accident inquiry or corporate manslaughter case, Henderson has probably been involved, from the Potters Bar inquest to the Lambrigg and Ufton Nervet rail disasters. Members have also been involved in some of the biggest product liability group actions – the MMR/MR vaccine and Seroxat antidepressant claims, not to mention litigation over food dye Sudan Red 1 and 2007's petrol contamination issues. It is additionally taking on claimant insurance matters.

Such matters may be chambers' most obvious strengths, but it has others, and if breadth of specialisation has become important, so too has "*cross-fertilisation*" between practice areas. By way of example, "*we got our largest ever environment case because the health and safety team at Eversheds referred us to their environment colleagues.*" Another notable case saw barristers acting for a major oil company defending claims brought by Colombian residents alleging that an oil pipe caused nuisance and environmental damage. As well as a healthy stream of solicitors and local authority clients, Henderson is also taking direct instructions from big corporates like BT, Thallis and Network Rail, while head of chambers Charles Gibson QC represented the British government in the Atomic Veterans litigation.

Keeping watch over it all, turbo-charged, entrepreneurial head clerk John White is keen for "*all our practices to develop relations in the communities around their specialisms, whether it's sponsoring an event or running seminars for associations of practitioners.*" A rebrand in late 2009 will see the launch of a new, "*industry-focused*" website, while the entire building is currently undergoing

Chambers UK rankings

Consumer Law
Health & Safety
Information Technology
Product Liability

Professional Discipline
Public Procurement
Real Estate Litigation

major redevelopment, "*so we don't look like the back end of a toilet.*"

Do something that scares you

For juniors, this approach sees them "*spending time with local authorities to understand their work.*" They also gain personal benefit from the increasing variety of instructions that come from investigating the crossover between areas. The emphasis on becoming a rounded practitioner is quite evident, and specialisation is "*actively discouraged before five or six years'* [call]." The court-heavy caseload means "*you're constantly challenged to get your head around new areas*" and sometimes "*you find papers on your desk for something you know nothing about, say an employment tribunal.*" As you might imagine, this is "*sometimes scary*" in the early years.

A straightforward, if equally varied, pupillage does its best to provide as "*friendly and neutral*" a year as possible. Pupils have one supervisor during each six, quarterly appraisals, two or three assessed advocacy exercises in the year ("*something like a plea in mitigation and we perform against each other*") and the certain knowledge that each piece of work completed for other members of chambers will be scrupulously assessed. It's also the case that supervisors "*protect their charges*" for the first quarter before releasing them to work for others. Initially, working closely for supervisors might mean anything from health and safety prosecutions, employment and property litigation, product liability claims, consumer credit issues or large property damage and insurance coverage disputes. When pupils later work under their own steam, they can rely on the "*close relationships*" established during this earlier period; "*your supervisor helps and advises... I know it sounds trite but they're almost like a friend.*" As a result, "*the sense of being assessed fades a bit.*"

Brussels sprouts

Early in the new year, all pupils spend four weeks in Brussels sampling European law from inside a firm of solicitors. This is thanks to a relationship with two associated members who work within US legal giant McDermott Will & Emery/Stanbrook LLP. A month away from the hurly-burly of chambers, a "*fantastic social scene*" and "*exposure to the priorities of clients,*" means pupils tend to return "*relaxed, improved and more rounded.*" The final month of the first six is then spent "*going to proceedings with juniors to explore the courts, meet ushers and get their feet under the table.*" The second six then becomes an advocacy-fest. Said a barrister on the pupillage committee: "*We tell the clerks that a person's career in chambers starts at the beginning of the second six, because if we take them on we want them to hit the ground running with their own clients.*" Pupils gobble up full helpings of "*possession hearings, RTAs, PI cases and property hearings,*" and attend court up to four times a week. Commonly they will additionally work on big cases for their supervisors.

The July tenancy decision is made at "*a long and agonising meeting*" that considers supervisor-penned overviews, feedback from any relevant members of chambers and – to a lesser extent – comments from instructing solicitors. "*We don't tend to consider the state of the market, just whether a person will be an asset and generate work,*" a source explained. One of the two pupils is usually successful and third-sixers arriving from elsewhere also have a decent chance. In 2009, as in 2008, one out of two was offered tenancy, along with one third-sixer.

TGI Friday

Henderson sees itself as a set of "*normal people*" with a distinctive "*family atmosphere.*" Certainly we picked up on a fresh and informal mood the day we visited. "*At five o'clock on a Friday it's impossible to do work; Lauren from reception insists you come for drinks and everyone starts to relax for the weekend.*" The annual Christmas party is a popular event and tenants explained: "*We're particularly good at celebrating notable events like a clerk's 40th birthday.*"

The communal vibe extends to the recruitment process. It's not that the two required interviews aren't rigorous: a 15-minute first round and a 30-minute second round with a panel of senior members both involve "*in-depth discussion*" of set questions and require candidates to "*respond fluently and eloquently, not crumple under pressure.*" The recruiters told us there's also "*an imperceptible quality that you recognise when it's in front of you, some combination of courage, nerves under stress and a well-rounded personality.*" The breadth of chambers' work means "*we'd be vaguely suspicious of anyone who claims too great a love of a specific area without previous experience to back it up,*" so be reasonable and reasoned in any application. Academics aren't the be-all and end-all here because this set sees the Bar as "*a practical profession where you become expert in something via a case not simply for the love of it.*"

And finally...

Henderson offers a commercially minded common law pupillage that presses the fast forward button on court experience and turns out down-to-earth advocates with broad experience. Highly recommended.

Keating Chambers

The facts

Location: Temple, London
Number of QCs/Juniors: 20/30 (13 women)
Applications: 100+
Apply through Pupillage Portal
Pupils per year: 2-4
Seats: 4x3 months
Pupillage award: £42,500 (can advance £15,000 for BPTC)

Sector bible *Keating on Building Contracts* was first authored by Donald Keating QC. Now in its eighth edition, it is still written by members of chambers.

Keating is a heavyweight at the Construction Bar. Its 50 experts take on the biggest domestic and international construction disputes and demonstrate flair in energy, professional negligence and procurement law.

Oil in a day's work

Keating began to specialise in construction in the early 1980s and quickly rose to the top. It now fields barristers in infrastructure projects in the Middle East, transport cases in the Far East and power station disputes in South Africa. Members have recently acted on both sides at the Court of Appeal in Multiplex v Cleveland Bridge (a major Wembley Stadium dispute) and represented Aldi as it brought actions against professionals engaged by its design and build contractor. Given that construction law is "*at the sharp edge of the evolution of contracts and tort law,*" it's no surprise to find chambers' stamp on crucial cases, such as one for Rolls-Royce that has recently provided guidance on the interpretation of joint names insurance and rights of subrogation. The construction sector leads the way in negligence law too: recently members acted in the Channel Tunnel Rail Link case Costain Ltd v Bechtel.

Clients in energy-producing regions have cottoned onto the set's skills. Members are increasingly occupied with foreign business, such as a case over a petrochemical plant in the Slovakia and a $200m dispute arising out of a Middle East oil and gas project. Closer to home E.ON has a multimillion-pound claim relating to contracts for the reprocessing of nuclear waste from European power stations at Sellafield. What's more, while chambers' procurement expertise originally developed out of its construction and engineering PFI and projects work, members are now popping up on major cases in other areas, like the MoD's dispute concerning food supplies for British armed forces worldwide.

Straight to the pint

If Keating's apparently specialist work puts you off, take a moment. Only a handful of its practitioners come from a technical background, and chambers merely expects pupillage applicants to have "*done something which demonstrates commercial interest*" rather than display a deep-seated love of construction law. It's quite common for people to come to the set via a simple desire for a "*general commercial pupillage,*" only later discovering that construction law is "*basically contract and tort with great clients.*" Representing contractors, suppliers and "*the stereotypical hairy-arsed builder*" brings all sorts of unexpected human and legal challenges. "*On a long case you get up close and personal, you basically live with these guys and you have to be able to get on with them,*" explained a seasoned senior who suggested "*rolling up your sleeves and going for a drink goes a long way.*" Junior sources relished the "*robust, straightforward nature*" of clients and the fact "*getting the dispute sorted for them often means something like the ability to pay the school fees.*" Managing expectations and communicating effectively are essential skills.

Chambers UK rankings

Construction	Internat'l Arbitration
Energy & Natural Resources	Professional Negligence

The clients' distinctive real-world approach is at the heart of construction law's technical and academic appeal. Often this means "*you're untangling a massive, tangled ball of wool involving architects, builders, surveyors, employers, contractors and subcontractors*" to determine the extent of a client's involvement, liability or grounds for claim. This requires a head for detail and the ability to process ring binder upon ring binder of information while looking for the salient points. By extension, getting to grips with the technical aspects of cases is an ongoing process; "*you need to find out how things work, so you understand how they've gone wrong.*" The importance of this part of the job is most apparent when you're cross-examining expert witnesses.

Applicants aren't expected to turn up as the finished article, but the interview process is testing. Around 35 are invited to the first round for general questions and a topical discussion (recently the wearing of veils in court and the 42-day detention ruling). The 14 who make the second round are grilled for half an hour: "*Ten minutes of application chat, ten on a mainstream contractual case they've been given beforehand and a ten-minute presentation on a topic of their choice.*" You'll find the set's detailed recruitment criteria online.

Chambers and Partners Construction Set of the Year 2009

Advocating change

Moving pupils between four supervisors over the twelve months is "*less about different types of work as about exposure to different personalities.*" Working closely with supervisors in the first six, pupils draft statements of case, particulars of claim, defences and replies, perhaps writing an opinion on a contractor's liability in a project, and definitely paying close attention as supervisors take matters to court or arbitration. While pupils do some work for other members, "*they're not expected to get around to everyone.*"

In the second six there's masses of court action, often on unrelated subjects – even RTAs provide crucial advocacy experience. Sometimes a "*six or seven-day construction defence case*" will pop up and on these a pupil can be a useful contributor. The emphasis on advocacy in pupillage reflects the cross-examination and court-heavy life of a fully fledged construction barrister. Beyond court visits, Keating arranges three "*assessed (although they don't feel it)*" advocacy exercises at which "*seniors pretend to be judges.*" Additional non-assessed advocacy training was introduced in 2009. Feedback from the exercises contributes to the tenancy decision, along with reports from supervisors and other members. In 2008, a formal feedback session given "*roughly half way through*" was designed to be "*late enough to be informative, but early enough to give pupils a chance to change.*" Its introduction was welcomed by pupils, who'd found it a "*two-way process – you get to say what you need to as well.*" Together with support they'd received from supervisors, it led our interviewees to say: "*The best thing about pupillage here is you feel that you've been given a clear shot to display your skills and become integrated.*" In 2008 the tenancy decision was moved to early July to give unsuccessful applicants a better chance to find a place elsewhere. The set is proud of its record in not only helping people get positions (at the Bar or with solicitors' firms), but also in maintaining good relations with ex-pupils. In 2006 three of four gained tenancy, in 2007 neither of the two pupils did, in 2008 one out of three was successful and in 2009 two of three made the grade.

Making your marquee

Within chambers we detected a warm, unfussy ethos. "*We were integrated socially from the first day. We had a buddy assigned and a group of juniors took us out for drinks,*" said one source. As pupillage progresses, juniors continue to "*provide advice down the pub; they'll say, 'Do x, work for y, avoid z for this.'*" They also get across the message that "*it's in our best interests for pupils to get on [together].*" The group we met described themselves as "*very tight-knit,*" not just "*meeting to polish off the chambers lunch scraps on a Thursday,*" but also enjoying meals at each other's houses. They were clear that "*it's the institution that has allowed this relaxation to exist.*"

That's not to say hard work isn't on the cards: 9am-6pm may be the standard pupil day or "*the norm when you're not too busy, not too slow,*" but there are plenty of times when "*working later, or on the occasional weekend,*" is required. Still, gain tenancy and within a couple of years barristers can expect to earn as much as their contemporaries at the major commercial and Chancery sets.

Broadly speaking, chambers is a sociable place and its annual garden party is a red-letter day in the construction world. In 2009 it also put its weight behind Law Rocks, a charity battle of the bands. With Marcus Taverner QC on lead guitar, the Keating band – Rough Justice – faced off against others from Addleshaw Goddard, BLP, Lovells, Nabarro and CMS Cameron McKenna.

And finally...

A specialism is one of the most valuable things a barrister can possess. At Keating that's exactly what you'll gain.

7 King's Bench Walk

The facts

Location: Temple, London
Number of QCs/Juniors: 19/27 (10 women)
Applications: 150
Apply through Pupillage Portal
Pupils per year: Up to 4, usually 2-3
Seats: 4 in first 9 months
Pupillage award: £45,000 (can advance £10,000 for BPTC)

7KBW's exacting standards make for a demanding pupillage year.

Pre-eminent for insurance and reinsurance, and renowned for its shipping expertise, 7KBW is a compact commercial set cut on classical lines.

Lordy!

Legal history has played out in and around 7 King's Bench Walk. In 1820, resident Serjeant Wilde defended Queen Caroline's life and honour after she was accused of adultery. In the 1850s, legal notables Lord Halsbury and Sir Harry Bodkin Poland occupied rooms here. The modern 7KBW has a proud lineage that goes some way to explain an outside perception that the set is "*starchy and traditional.*" Since its foundation in 1967, this set has produced a string of prominent judges, including the likes of Lords Denning, Mance, Goff, Brandon and Hobhouse. Insiders regard the set's stiff reputation with bemusement, telling us: "*We're not less approachable than some of the 'modern' commercial sets in their new buildings.*" The senior clerks – whose joint experience in chambers totals some 40 years – are also quick to chip in that 7KBW's atmosphere has "*changed beyond all recognition in the last 15 years; we're much friendlier and less stuffy.*" Leaving traditionally exacting standards and a commitment to excellence aside, our sources say: "*What really distinguishes us is our size and the fact that we all practise in the same areas.*" The view is that these factors combine to create a "*tight-knit and collegiate group.*"

The work of the set centres on two areas that are the bedrock of the Commercial Bar – shipping and insurance disputes. Members are well known for Commercial and Admiralty Court shipping cases (whether they relate to finance, shipbuilding or transactional disputes arising from the day-to-day trading of vessels around the world) and the set leapt to prominence in the insurance world via its involvement in the 1990s in the enormous Lloyd's litigation. Looking more broadly at the set's commercial litigation pedigree, you'll find the Barings litigation, arbitrations relating to the Enron and WorldCom corporate collapses, and findings of fraud against KPMG in relation to its US tax avoidance advice. These days, you'll also see members on matters relating to the Buncefield oil depot explosion, the collapse of Northern Rock and disciplinary proceedings against Ernst & Young arising out of its Equitable Life audits.

It's easy to see how 7KBW has developed a reputation worldwide, and this is demonstrated by its involvement in high-end arbitration, such as that for a Middle Eastern government in a major ICC arbitration involving a billion-dollar oil production sharing agreement. General commercial cases in banking and professional negligence also figure prominently, and showing it has an eye for a business opportunity, the set has leveraged its insurance expertise to generate aviation sector instructions. Some members have additionally developed expertise in sports law, recently representing the Rugby Football Union in a dispute with the Premiership clubs, and Formula 1's British American Racing in the 2007 kerfuffle over Jenson Button's service.

Chambers UK rankings

Commercial Dispute Resolution
Insurance
International Arbitration
Professional Negligence
Shipping

Watch and learn

7KBW barristers have a reputation for brilliant technical application of the law. Juniors and pupils gushed about the experience of "*observing brilliant advocates in action*" and "*learning so much about different ways of managing work and approaches.*" The abundance of "*young, ambitious QCs*" also means "*this is a great place to be a junior because of the enhanced levels of work*" that trickle down. Needless to say the earning potential for members is vast.

> **Chambers and Partners Insurance Set of the Year 2009**

So what of the small matter of getting a pupillage? Around 24 applicants are invited to a single-round interview, at which they are grilled on a skeleton argument they have prepared in advance. It is based on a "*pre-supplied, self-contained case that doesn't require in-depth legal knowledge*" and conducted "*more like a Q&A than a formal advocacy exercise.*" This part of the interview assesses "*how well candidates put themselves across on two pages and how well they get to grips with a problem.*" You shouldn't be too surprised to hear that, as in many other top sets, "*often non-law graduates do better than those with law degrees, perhaps because they can take a step back.*" Chambers tells us that "*the stereotype of the bookish student who's not worldly is not what we want;*" however, looking at the CVs of baby juniors it's more than apparent that successful candidates invariably have a flawless academic record and attended an Oxbridge college. We asked some of them what they find so appealing about their work and their answers invariably turned on the intellectual challenges contained within. As one put it: "*There's a lot of law to get your teeth into; it's problem-based work involving pithy questions and seeking out holes in the law.*"

Pupils each sit with four supervisors between October and July. The first stint is for three months and regarded as "*a time to make mistakes and learn.*" Greater importance is placed on a pupil's "*performance trajectory*" over the period than on individual pieces of work. Pupils then spend shorter periods with successive supervisors in a jam-packed six months in which they "*see a cross-section of chambers' specialisms and all facets of cases from advisory to advocacy to settling.*" The expectation is that after the initial three months, pupils will do their utmost to impress supervisors and other members on each piece of work they receive, so it's understandable that they feel some pressure. Typically their work encompasses everything from discrete research assignments to wading through reams of paper to draft pleadings for a QC. At this set "*paper-based advocacy is just as important as court style,*" so don't expect to be out and about on your own. This hadn't put off the pupils we spoke to, who were glad to "*have a good long period where you're learning and applying yourself, taking cues from seniors*" before venturing into court themselves. Second-sixers don't normally appear in court alone until after the tenancy decision is taken.

Everyone's a winner

There's no question that 7KBW's exacting standards make for a demanding pupillage year, but chambers is keen "*not to do anything to add to the pressure,*" and as such "*we don't compare them directly or encourage competition, or have things like advocacy exercises.*" Pupils all work for "*the same four to five senior members, probably QCs*" to ensure fair assessment, and they benefit from regular feedback. Those who don't succeed when it comes to tenancy soon get snapped up by other good sets looking for third-sixers. Those who do stay are fed a rich diet of their own lower-value cases – "*things like advices for P&I clubs and county court trials*" or a position as a second or third junior on "*larger shipping, professional negligence and insurance cases.*" Sometimes they are sent on short secondments to City law firms.

Chambers' focus, and the fact members frequently work together in teams, mean that juniors feel quite comfortable "*popping into anyone's room anytime for help.*" Particularly among those under ten years' call, there is a ready exchange of "*invitations to weddings, birthdays and housewarmings.*" The official social calendar is left in the capable hands of the senior clerks, who take steps to "*help reduce any pressure on pupils by encouraging them to come to functions, buying them drinks and making them feel welcome.*" For the time being, formal gatherings for afternoon tea have fallen out of fashion at 7KBW, though evidently the demand for cakes most afternoons has not!

> **And finally...**
>
> There's something of an air of scholarly detachment here at 7KBW, but that doesn't mean this isn't also a commercially savvy operation. It's one of the very best for commercial litigation, so you'll have to be better than brilliant to get in.

Littleton Chambers

The facts

Location: Inner Temple, London
Number of QCs/Juniors: 12/36 (9 women)
Applications: 120+
Apply through Pupillage Portal
Pupils per year: 2
Seats: 3x4 months
Pupillage award: £40,000 (can advance sum for BPTC)

Since 2006 Littleton has offered tenancy to all eight of its pupils.

Employment, commercial litigation and professional negligence specialist Littleton Chambers is not unique in its desire to be an efficient, modern business, but the strength of its determination is distinctive.

Because they're worth it

Back in the early 90s, Littleton was one of the first sets to appoint a CEO from outside the profession. In 2007, the retiring incumbent was replaced by Gerard Hickie, formerly of L'Oréal, possessed of an MBA, an engineering background and exactly the sort of dispassionate take on the provision of legal services that chambers felt it needed. Littering conversation with terms that might give some old-school clerks a nasty turn – "*I want to increase the value of the business for shareholders, by which I mean barristers,*" and "*we want to build market share*" – Hickie's commercial acumen is clearly taking Littleton places. The last two years have brought a new IT system, new clerks, a series of lateral hires (several poached from close rival Cloisters), a revamped marketing effort that includes a new identity and website, and LUMU: the Littleton Urgent Mediation Unit, for when your mediation just can't wait. The aim is "*to grow by 20-25% in the medium term.*"

Littleton already has well-regarded core expertise in employment and commercial litigation, and this is backed up by expertise in sports law, professional negligence and arbitration/mediation. In 2008, members won a groundbreaking Court of Appeal case involving trade unions unlawfully discriminating against female members, and provided counsel in relation to Dwain Chambers' challenge to his ban under British Olympic Association rules. However, perceiving "*the set was in some ways a sleeping giant,*" management's aim is now to "*maintain our pre-eminence in employment and reputation for punching above our weight in commercial litigation,*" while expanding to roughly 60 barristers.

The human side of the law

The pupillage recruitment process is more than a little concerned with finding candidates with the right people skills as well as intellectual abilities. Around 20% of applicants are invited to a first interview that assesses "*basic advocacy skills and the ability to summarise facts and make judgements*" in a "*testing but not overly bullish*" way. Great academics and pronounced intellect certainly help, but for the dozen or so who reach the second round (an assessed mini-pupillage), it's just as important to show an assured bedside manner. The candidates are set a written assessment – "*there's plenty of time to go to the library*" – which is discussed at the end of the week with a barrister. A further one or two rounds of interviews face the seven or so who make it beyond mini-pupillage.

Pupillage itself is "*very much about commercial litigation and employment,*" with pupils shuttling around three supervisors for four months each. "*I had one* [specialist] *from each*

Chambers UK rankings

Employment

area and a mixed practitioner," a pupil recalled. The two core areas appeal for different reasons. Of commercial litigation, one barrister told us: "*It is less statute-driven and there's more fundamental law. You're dealing with business people who are detached from the issues.*" By comparison, employment law centres on people and workplaces, so it's all about personal relationships breaking down. "*There are more human emotions: often it's people who loathe their boss or the company saying: 'You didn't promote me because I'm black or a woman.'*" And employers are just as prone to emotional responses: "*Often the boss will in turn loathe being accused of being racist, sexist or discriminatory.*" In short, employment practice is "*a complex interrelation of personal and professional legal issues… it's very exciting.*"

Chambers and Partners Employment Set of the Year 2009

Regardless of their area, supervisors tend to be good at "*giving pupils experience of work within their reach.*" Our sources had found "*the first few months were more relaxed; you work 8.30am until 6pm*" and "*your work is closely assessed, much more so than later in the year.*" Rather than taking on their supervisor's work in parallel, pupils cut their teeth on "*a series of set tasks – things like advices and pleadings – from a collection that members contribute to when they have an appropriate case.*" After four months of "*going to court and EAT tribunals with juniors, you get to know the work you'll be doing come the second six.*"

The set "*regards advocacy experience as very important,*" so second-six pupils are off to court once or twice a week, handling "*winding-up petitions in the Companies Court, paperwork for solicitors and small employment cases.*" Littleton's reach means regular trips to Stratford and Croydon are on the cards, with occasional jaunts out to "*Reading, Bury St Edmunds and places like that.*" Said one source: "*You learn first and foremost how long it takes to prepare for even the smallest case at this stage.*" By its nature, employment law is more conducive to early advocacy experience than commercial litigation, but as a junior it's possible to get substantial commercial instructions. For example, one baby junior we spoke to was looking forward to "*a professional negligence construction case that's slated for a 20-day trial.*"

Blah, blah, blah

The set's aim is "*to be constructive in feedback and to sort out problems.*" Said one pupil: "*I was frankly amazed at how seriously they take it. I thought it would be: 'Well done, blah, blah, blah' but my supervisor had taken detailed notes on what I'd done and talked me through them.*" At the end of each seat detailed feedback is given at a meeting attended by "*your old supervisor, your new supervisor, the CEO and the head of the pupillage committee.*" Small wonder, pupils told us: "*These meetings are invaluable; they takes the terror out of the process but you also feel you're getting advice for your career, not just pupillage.*" As well as the appraisals, there are four "*increasingly difficult*" assessed advocacy exercises over the year. Pupils duke it out over an "*anonymised real case: you get bundles and instructions and advocate in front of a member who is sitting as a judge.*" While "*competition kicks in,*" it's still "*very pleasant-natured*" and there's oral feedback afterwards. A written report then goes to the tenancy committee, along with feedback from instructing solicitors and the results of three written assessments, set from January onwards. These are "*scrutinised by an independent member of chambers*" who makes a report. The last weeks before the tenancy decision will also see "*court work scaled back*" and pupil supervisors "*push you to get exposure to more members of chambers,*" so as to make the bid for tenancy more complete. The sole 2009 pupil was offered tenancy, meaning that Littleton has managed to take on eight out of eight since 2006.

Littleton resides in King's Bench Walk in impressive premises that manage to combine the traditional architecture of the Inn with a 1990s extension at the rear. Definitely "*not a ripped denim sort of place,*" members are well dressed. "*We work incredibly hard,*" said one, "*but the culture is a mutually supportive one.*" Littleton tenants are "*very familiar faces*" in the nearby Pegasus Bar, and in the summer they can often be found entertaining clients on one of chambers' three roof terraces. Juniors and clerks' nights out, and even the occasional organised juniors' event, also keep things interesting. Pupils naturally find it hard to forget their status in chambers, but when they join in the post-work drinks "*it's like going out with your friends.*"

And finally…

Pupils and members told us they were proud of the "*openness, approachability and sense of humour*" they feel characterise the set. In part it reflects Littleton's "*collegiate cultural values,*" but equally it is indicative of the heavy employment law caseload.

Maitland Chambers

The facts

Location: Lincoln's Inn, London
Number of QCs/Juniors: 17/46 (10 women)
Applications: 150-200
Outside Pupillage Portal scheme
Pupils per year: 3
Seats: 1x3 months then 6 week seats
Pupillage Award: £45,000 (can advance £11,250 for BPTC)

Maitland is thinking about how it can pitch itself at some of the new universities and says it is "*keen to try and establish links with ethnic student lawyers' associations.*"

"*If you get an offer from Maitland you're not going to say no to it.*" Not some Corleone-style threat, but a pupil's acknowledgment of this set's position at the top of the tree.

An offer you can't refuse

Realistically who's going to say no to a Maitland pupillage offer when there's so much to be gained? For commercial Chancery practice (as opposed to traditional Chancery matters) it stands as the only Band 1-ranked set in *Chambers UK*. That state of affairs has endured pretty much since Maitland was created in 2001, when 13 Old Square and 7 Stone Buildings joined forces. Maitland is also renowned for its property expertise, an area of practice that was bolstered in a second merger in 2004, when the members of 9 Old Square also came on board. At the time, the mergers were seen as "*bold*" – tie-ups between established sets can be a tricky business, especially if there are cultural differences – but they seem to have paid off. "*When I came in seven years ago I could tell to an extent who came from where,*" a clerk told us, "*but now it's really impossible to tell.*" It was probably a wise move to shuffle the members around between the three legacy buildings so that everyone mixed in together.

Chambers receives instructions from around the world and has forged some strong links with offshore tax havens in the Caribbean, the Channel Islands and the Isle of Man. Meanwhile a number of indirect tax law specialists regularly act for Her Majesty's Revenue & Customs. Recent cases of note include Catherine Newman QC's victory on behalf of JD Wetherspoon in a long-running matter in which it was alleged that former property adviser Van de Berg and its managing director had defrauded the pub chain over a period of 16 years. Others involve disputes stemming from the collapse of Farepak, the Christmas hamper savings company. Finally, it might not be typical of instructions received by the set, but we note with interest that one member of chambers advised the producer of *Monty Python and the Holy Grail* in his dispute with the Pythons over royalties and acted on disclosure applications in connection with litigation between the members of Busted.

Bildungsroman

"*From day one you will be keeping up with your supervisor's work.*" Don't panic: chambers recognises what a huge step up from law school pupillage is, and for the first three months pupils sit with one supervisor as they find their feet. From January, they move every six weeks in a quick-fire tour of a variety of practices. Pupils see quite a difference in the way supervisors do things. "*Some will give you work that's separate from what they are doing, and will talk through it with you, but it's never sent out or*

Chambers UK rankings

Agriculture & Rural Affairs	Fraud: Civil
Chancery	Partnership
Charities	Professional Negligence
Commercial Dispute Resolution	Real Estate Litigation
Company	Restructuring/Insolvency

used in court. With others, it's a much more collaborative process where they get a live bit of work and give it to you for three days, then go over it and possibly use it."

While pupils are unlikely to get on their feet in court, there are five advocacy training exercises that begin after Christmas, gradually increasing in difficulty. The first looks at *"the kind of thing that a junior might be doing in a County Court fairly early on in practice,"* while the last might be *"a full-blown contested freezing order application in a commercial context; something that may well be done by a QC."* In one recent exercise, pupils were pitted against each other: *"It was an application to adjourn a trial. We had to prepare for the applicant's side and the respondent's side."* Pupils insisted that this was the only time they had felt themselves to be in direct competition with each other, *"and even then, the person playing the judge was giving us a pretty hard time, so I was more concentrating on him."*

Pupillage here is more a *"personal journey"* than a battle royale, and with the amount of work that chambers is currently receiving, there is room for every pupil who comes up to scratch. In 2009 all three were offered tenancy. When it comes to that decision, performance in the advocacy exercises may be taken into consideration if the pupillage committee is unsure of someone. However, the collective judgement of supervisors over the course of nine months is viewed as a *"pretty reliable way of working out if someone is up to it or not."* Therefore, *"the dominant factor"* in the tenancy decision *"is what the pupil supervisors collectively have made of you."*

Listen and learn

Chambers has recently added *"a couple of slightly more interesting questions"* to its application form. This is an attempt to allow applicants the chance to differentiate themselves, so use that opportunity to the full. Around 30 or 40 go through to a first-round interview, which is less law-centred and more designed to test *"the sort of person they are, because at the end of the day this job is not just about having a decent brain but being able to inspire confidence in clients."* From there, around 15 progress to *"a slightly more intensive and slightly more legally focused"* second-round interview. How to do well? *"It's a combination of being intelligent and being able to distil things to a key point and communicate that point effectively. If you can do that you'll really impress us."* GDL students are at no disadvantage and the majority of younger members of Maitland did not read law at undergraduate level (we note a number of classicists in the ranks).

Chambers worries about recruiting from a wider background. *"People will look at our website and see 60-odd mostly white faces, mainly from Oxbridge, and think 'I don't stand a chance because I'm not like them',"* said a member of the pupillage committee. *"The message I'd love to get across is: yes you do, we'll give you the same crack of the whip that everyone else gets."* To its credit Maitland is thinking about how it can pitch itself at some of the new universities and says it is *"keen to try and establish links with ethnic student lawyers associations."*

Formal afternoon tea takes place daily, and pupils' attendance depends on whether their supervisor goes or not – *"some do, some don't."* Barristers tend to use tea as a sounding board for ideas on their cases, *"which [for a pupil] is very useful. You might get someone very junior talking about a type of small-scale case that we haven't been exposed to so much since all our supervisors are between ten and 15 years' call."* It's for this reason that pupils don't chat much at tea, but they are not alone in this: *"There are plenty of people who have been at chambers for ten years or more who come just to listen."* Work is less often the topic of conversation at chambers drinks every Thursday night. Pupils almost always attend this event as it's a good way to meet members and staff.

And finally...

This weighty, successful set does it all – from disputed wills and personal taxation problems to massive pensions disputes, property litigation, fraud, company law, insolvency and major commercial spats. Make it here and you're made, full stop.

FOUR NEW SQUARE

"The definitive professional negligence set," ……….. "the brand name and the market-leading barristers to go with it."

(Chambers and partners 2008)

"Based in Lincoln's Inn, chambers combines a commitment to achieving and maintaining high standards of advocacy and advice for all clients with the very highest standards of client service. This is reflected in the large awards and guaranteed earnings offered to it's pupils, from whom its junior tenants are regularly recruited."

(Legal 500 2008)

For full details of Chambers' work, individual members' practice profiles and clerking arrangements please visit www.4newsquare.com or contact Lizzy Wiseman on 020 7822 2000 or l.wiseman@4newsquare.com

4 New Square, Lincoln's Inn London WC2A 3RJ
Telephone: 020 7822 2000 Facsimile: 020 7822 2001
Email: barristers@4newsquare.com
DX: 1041 London, Chancery Lane

Four New Square

The facts

Location: Lincoln's Inn, London
Number of QCs/Juniors: 17/50 (17 women)
Applications: 200
Apply through Pupillage Portal
Pupils per year: Up to 4
Seats: 2x3 +1x6 months
Pupillage award: £45,000 (can advance £15,000 for BPTC)

Funky. Fresh. Voraciously ambitious. Can we really be describing a set of chambers? Professional negligence star Four New Square is all these things and more.

Step from the traditional environs of Lincoln's Inn into Four New Square's trendy reception area and several hundred years disappear in an instant.

Style and substance

Huge modern canvases adorn the walls, there are acres of hip stretch-rawhide panelling and a computer for client use that resembles a sci-fi film prop. Such is the evident up-to-the-minute sensibility of this chambers you could almost be in a Soho creative agency. The set aims "*to project a modern image*" and sees itself "*more like a firm of solicitors in our focus on providing a client-oriented service.*" The emphasis on self-presentation doesn't mean Four New Square lacks substance: workaholic tendencies and undisguised ambition ensure that the glitz of the caseload perfectly complements the glamour of the decor. Eye-catching professional negligence instructions flood in from most major (and minor) litigation firms and insurers, occupying almost every member. The massive Accident Group litigation – a multiparty action involving solicitors' negligence – is one case on the go at present, and the members represent a multitude of accountants facing litigation over the film finance advice they gave clients. There's also continued involvement in Wembley stadium disputes, which "*endlessly rumble on,*" while on the product liability side, 4NS barristers represent the government on an atomic test veterans case. Chambers also generates broader commercial work, with members taking an increasing number of commercial, Chancery and insurance cases.

If professional negligence sounds like a narrow field, fear not. Although "*general principles of contract and tort underlie all the work,*" there is "*so much variety because each profession is entirely different.*" Considering that instructions span sectors as diverse as construction, medicine, insurance, reinsurance, law, accountancy, surveying and tax (not to mention the variety within each of these professions), it isn't surprising that "*quickly assimilating information about different professions*" is a both a major challenge and a source of job satisfaction. "*The other day I had to write an advice on a vet's case,*" a pupil told us, "*and I certainly didn't know much about veterinary practice beforehand.*" Possessing the skills to deal as easily with a rough-and-ready construction professional as a phenomenally qualified accountant is crucial.

Smile if you wanna go further

An unassessed mini-pupillage will be helpful, but anyone seriously interested in 4NS should apply before the end of February for one of the paid, assessed minis. There are twelve week-long openings paying £500. Mini-pupils will be given a good steer as to their future chances. They'll either be offered "*a bye through the first-round interview,*" told "*to apply but expect a first-round interview*" or recommended not to apply. A mini is no prerequisite for an application, which at every stage sees candidates assessed according to four main criteria: "*intellectual ability, most prominently displayed via a consistent academic record;*

Chambers UK rankings

| Construction | Product Liability |
| Financial Services Regulation | Professional Negligence |

potential as an advocate; commitment/motivation; and personal qualities – leadership, self-reliance and the like." It's worth noting that academic results carry "*1.5 times the weight of other criteria.*"

Around 70 attend a general first-round interview, up to 28 of which will proceed to the second round to face "*probing but not confrontational or contrived*" questioning on "*moral, ethical or legal issues.*" Applications from construction professionals are not uncommon, but the most important fit is "*with the way in which we work – our client focus and aim to provide brilliant service.*" As such, "*proactive, optimistic, positive*" applicants with "*good people skills and uplifting personalities*" are favoured, so practising a genuine smile could be a good idea.

Chambers and Partners Professional Negligence Set of the Year 2009

4NS fair ground

If the application process is scrupulously fair, pupillage itself is relentlessly so. The year is split into two three-month seats and one of six-months, with supervisors chosen from the "*ten to 14 years' call mark because that gives exposure to advanced work while not being too removed from junior practice.*" These moves give broad experience of "*our core areas of professional negligence and general commercial work,*" as well as "*exposure to more specialist areas, be it Chancery, insurance or construction.*" The first six is about "*shadowing your supervisor, doing what they do in parallel then comparing it together.*" Time after conferences or court visits is spent "*discussing matters so your advocacy skills are tested.*" This "*ongoing process of appraisal,*" is backed up by a three-monthly review system that sees "*pupils assess themselves, then discuss it with their supervisor.*" Supervisors then report to the pupillage committee and its head Ben Hubble goes back to the pupil with more feedback. Small wonder that pupils feel "*at every stage you know what you need to do to improve and how you're performing.*" They also praise the "*teaching mentality*" in chambers.

The second six continues to feature work set by supervisors, and pupils also handle small commercial debt claims, possession hearings, RTAs, simple fast-track trials and employment tribunals. Mortgage work often involves the challenge of "*litigants in person,*" while RTAs are "*good for witness-handling skills.*" There's also likely to be a first taste of professional negligence instructions: "*It tends to be writing advices on cases where maybe the insurer wants a cheaper fee for the pre-court work.*"

If you think the assessment sounds full-on, you haven't heard the half of it. At around the five-month mark, pupils begin to complete three written tasks set one a month by an in-chambers panel. Non-assessed advocacy training is followed up by an assessed moot that takes place either in chambers or an RCJ courtroom before Mr Justice Rupert Jackson, a former silk at the set and now a Court of Appeal judge. This year the audience was restricted to the pupillage committee and supervisors, but was "*still enough to be pretty scary.*" Feedback from all these means of assessment is then considered by the committee that makes the tenancy decision. Chambers is hungry to recruit members, but not to the extent of compromising standards. In recent years, all, none or a couple of pupils have been offered tenancy. Two of the four made the grade in 2008 and three of three in 2009. Depending on the year, third-six applications may or may not fall on fertile ground.

The 4NS work ethic means pupils should expect to put in prodigious effort, despite days being "*fixed around ten hours, including a lunch hour.*" In general, 4NS has a laudable policy of "*fully supporting members' lifestyle choices, whether it's women having children, men wanting to spend more time with their kids or people simply wanting a more flexible existence.*" It's not all work though. A warm welcome helps initiate new arrivals so that "*within three to four weeks you get to know or have spoken to 90% of chambers.*" Junior tenants are also on hand to provide after-work drinks and advice in what genuinely does seem to be a collegiate organisation. Pupils are welcome at all social events, whether it's watching one of the set's horses – Blunham Hill or Joe Twist – or knocking back the Pimm's at the summer barbecue or cultivating clients. When we visited, sore heads were being nursed after a party for 750 clients in Old Billingsgate. For senior clerk Lizzie Wiseman such events are useful "*because we recognise that people often instruct for reasons they don't consciously think about – personal relationships and emotional connections.*" For one source the pleasure was in the novel experience of "*feeling like solicitors might actually want to talk to me.*" You have to suspect that here, the feeling is a common one.

And finally...

Robust, modern and client-focused, Four New Square is a great bet for anyone with the requisite social skills. Get your head around professional negligence and try for an assessed mini.

- **Make full use of sets' websites:** Take note of the identity of any clients mentioned and check which recent cases a set is most proud of. These things will help you at interview. If you get wind of who will be on the interview panel do your homework on them before you submit yourself to a grilling.

top tip no. 34

Old Square Chambers

The facts

Location: Bedford Row, London and Bristol
Number of QCs/Juniors: 10/56 (21 women)
Applications: 300+
Apply through Pupillage Portal
Pupils per year: 2
Seats: 4x3 months
Pupillage award: £35,000 (can advance £10,000 for BPTC)

Arriving at Old Square Chambers on a boiling summer's day, we were greeted by a cheery barrister in T-shirt and sandals. His attire spoke simply of the set's distaste for tradition.

Old and square by name but not nature, this set is very much of the here and now.

United we stand

For decades it has been known as a claimant PI and employment law hothouse, and perceived as *"a left-wing sort of place"* because of its extensive union connections. Yet *"in the last 15 years chambers has diversified so that there's now a 50-50 balance of claimant and respondent work."* Trade union links still account for much of the caseload: recently members acted for the British Air Line Pilots Association against BA and for UNITE member Mrs Grundy in Court of Appeal equal pay disputes. John Hendy QC, who stepped down as head of chambers in 2009, is standing counsel to nearly ten trade unions. Nevertheless, some eight members are on the Treasury's list of juniors and instructions pour in from employers like BT, Ford and Land Rover.

Now occupying tasteful premises at Bedford Row, the large London contingent has plenty of space for *"strategic growth,"* both in its core specialisms and its developing areas of public inquiries, environmental law, clinical negligence, product liability and health and safety. The 14-barrister Bristol arm is growing too and *"may need a new base in a few years."* A surge in disciplinary cases *"as major organisations align their protocols"* has seen the set pull in work from the General Medical Council and the General Dental Council among others; meanwhile there are *"thousands of equal pay disputes across the health sector and far beyond."* Health and safety-based corporate manslaughter instructions and environmental litigation pop up *"as and when,"* and product liability cases are pretty common. Much of 2008 was spent representing claimants in the (epilepsy drug) Sabril group litigation. There are regular instructions from the Prison Officers Association on death or injury in custody inquiries, and chambers has been involved in almost every major rail crash inquiry of recent times.

Making a difference

Old Square ditched chambers tea, formal modes of address and other formalities years ago, but despite its progressive outlook it nevertheless values the *"independence of individuals"* rather than subscribing fervently to the concept of corporate identity. There is a slick website and careful marketing to manage the set's public face; behind it the barristers view themselves as *"independent, very hard-working and mutually respectful,"* coexisting in an *"atmosphere underpinned by an egalitarian attitude."* If you see yourself fitting into this collective-style environment, you'll be pleased to hear that the set has recast its interview process as a two-stage affair, with the aim of *"giving a broader range of people a chance to impress us in person."* Previously only 20 applicants would be interviewed. Last time 40 attended a first-round involving *"five minutes of CV chat, five to ten on a supplied statutory interpretation issue and some probing questioning."* Around five make the 45-minute second round to face *"a

Chambers UK rankings

Employment	Health & Safety
Environment	Personal Injury

problem-based legal scenario with a lot of detail to pick up on." Candidates are asked to treat the panel of three "*as if we're the clients,*" and will then be tested with "*an ethical question arising from the problem.*" Requiring the sort of basic contractual knowledge that any law student will possess, the two per year who are offered pupillage are likely to demonstrate "*clear, client-friendly thinking.*"

The importance placed upon these qualities reflects the need for employment and PI barristers to "*understand the client's perspective.*" These areas often involve dealing with individuals in stressful situations, so people skills are as important as keeping up with ever changing law. Said a new tenant: "*What's great is that you're constantly taking real situations, often involving dramatic events, and applying legal principles to try and find a solution.*" Another barrister spoke of the pleasure in "*making a difference to claimants and to businesses.*" Given this emphasis on well-developed people skills, its not surprising that a number of pupils have already had careers, be they "*former solicitors, accountants, trade union workers or builders.*"

Stress relief

The pupillage has been revamped such that formal assessment is ongoing rather than saved up until one "*fearful session*" at the end of the year. "*We thought, why not acknowledge that it is a stressful year and make it more transparent?*" Pupils are tested in advocacy and written exercises by a three-person panel at the end of each seat taken before the July tenancy decision. "*In the first three [months] they try to give you a supervisor who is sympathetic, to help you settle in and get involved in chambers,*" a pupil explained, adding: "*The first assessment is also more relaxed.*" At the end-of-seat appraisals "*you hear about the positives and negatives in your performance.*" During the second period it is expected that you'll take on work for other members, each piece producing "*feedback that goes to the pupil and to the tenancy committee. There's a one-to-five grading, one being adequate and five outstanding.*" Recruiters are adamant: "*We don't expect fives from day one.*" Pupils tell us: "*You feel they want to see your trajectory of improvement over the year.*"

Supervisors are chosen to reflect "*a spread of personalities and chambers' work.*" Employment and PI are the heart of pupillage: research assignments and notes for clients or conferences are regular tasks, and pupils will learn to draft skeleton arguments and other court documents. In the PI arena, our sources had valued "*learning to draft quickly and succinctly in a way that just isn't taught at law school.*" Once into the second six, pupils are in court up to "*a maximum of three times a week, otherwise they can't keep up with other work.*" It's a steady diet of RTAs and infant approval hearings. The former are "*great for getting your cross-examination skills up to speed. The Highway Code is pretty much your precedent book, and establishing what's happened from different sources is very important.*" Smaller "*two to three-day employment cases*" can also feature, requiring the pupil to perform in front of district judges. Throughout this period supervisors can be relied upon to "*keep an eye out and help you keep juggling all the balls,*" while other members "*take a real interest in what and how you're doing.*" Helpfully, juniors give pupils their phone numbers, so "*there's a stupid-question hotline to get answers to the things you almost dare not ask.*"

Social enterprise

Old Square barristers travel a fair bit. In part this reflects the nature of the work, but also the set's strong connection with the Western Circuit. It is possible for pupils to spend all or part of their year in Bristol, if they so wish, and certainly all must spend a week there. "*The pace of life is very different,*" observed one, adding: "*That's not to say that they don't work hard.*"

There's no doubt about who's got the best deal in chambers' new London home – "*the clerks' room has amazing facilities, with a break-out room and espresso makers.*" Senior clerk Will Meade even gets to watch over his team from a "*Starship Enterprise-style control room.*" Given that chambers tea definitely "*falls into the too-stuffy-for-this-set*" category, get-togethers take the form of monthly drinks. Beyond this, pupils are welcome at chambers' Christmas and summer parties, as well as any client events. Supervisors regularly take them out to lunch and there are always a few people drinking in The Enterprise on a Thursday or Friday night. In 2008 both pupils gained tenancy and apparently there was a lot of congratulatory hugging in the pub that night. It was the same scenario in 2009.

And finally...

Old Square is a poised and purposeful set that offers a kicking PI and employment-focused pupillage.

Pump Court Tax Chambers

The facts

Location: Bedford Row, London
Number of QCs/Juniors: 9/19 (5 women)
Applications: 70+
Outside Pupillage Portal scheme
Pupils per year: 2-3
Seats: Sit with 3 core supervisors
Pupillage award: £40,000 (can advance £8,000 for BPTC)

Allegedly, Albert Einstein once said: *"The hardest thing in the world to understand is income tax."* If he had trouble, what chance do mere mortals have? Pump Court is keen to refute this idea.

After 50 years of practice Pump Court has earned the right to feel it is the litigation tax set of choice. It's also an advisory hothouse, with members offering expertise in every facet of tax law. And we do mean every facet...

Pumped up

The scope of work at this set is broad indeed. There's personal tax planning for individuals, trusts or estates, and employee remuneration cases on share options or pension schemes. Then there's the UK and international tax aspects of corporate M&A, demergers, transfer pricing and structured finance. By contrast, indirect tax work includes VAT, landfill tax and stamp duties on property transactions, not to forget professional negligence disputes involving tax advice. A steady stream of instructions flows in from UK and foreign governments, Big Four accountants and City law firms. When we visited, chambers was about to provide counsel on both sides of a transfer pricing dispute involving a major multinational pharmaceutical company. Other highlights included representing HMRC in a case concerning a Vodafone subsidiary, and Weight Watchers in a VAT dispute, and advising on whether certain decorative items in pubs were 'plant' for capital allowance purposes. One tenant we spoke to had even dealt with *"a case considering whether the sums strippers pay to the clubs they work in should be subject to VAT."*

Tax cases can involve public and European law, even drawing in human rights points. For example, *"the client who paid peanuts for a consignment of cigarettes he believed were duty-paid and has been slapped with a £13m duty bill by the Revenue... it's developed into a human rights case."* What's more, while advisory work is a key aspect of practice, the tough stance adopted by HMRC means *"there's less of a settlement culture than at the Commercial Bar."*

Chambers receives only 70 applications a year and is eager to dispel the 'cloistered academic' perception of tax practitioners. *"There's no one here with two heads,"* one laughed: *"No one wears fob watches, smokes a pipe or wears tweed. Like most of the Commercial Bar we're very aware of being seen to be commercial and modern."* To counter students' misconceptions, chambers offers numerous unassessed mini-pupillages, as well as paid, assessed minis. Participants sit with a silk and will write an opinion. They'll also quickly realise that *"the people are undoubtedly very, very clever."* This need not mean geeky – the members we met were some of the most interesting, articulate and socially switched-on barristers we encountered in our tour of the Inns. However, tax law demands *"rarefied, involved and complex analysis of law,"* suiting people with *"a taste for approaching practice from an academic angle."* There's also the exhilarating pressure of being instructed by *"phenomenally qualified"* tax experts *"who know their stuff inside out, so if they're asking you for a judgement call, it can be very challenging."* So, if *"thinking about rules and principles"* is more to your taste than *"going through a room full of Linklaters' files to find the one operative provision of the one operative contract,"* apply here.

Chambers UK rankings

Tax

The devil's in the detail

Unsurprisingly, recruitment focuses on intellectual rigour, self-discipline and concentration: "*We want stellar individuals… a top First could exhibit this, but it's no requirement.*" The interview process aims to spot "*those who reason clearly, can express themselves and be precise about the small points that make all the difference.*" Around 20 applicants make the first round, which is "*a mix of CV-based interview, assessing competencies and discussion of a legal problem given an hour beforehand.*" Last year eight made it to the second stage – a written assessment. Previous knowledge of tax is not required, and although some commercial orientation can be an advantage, the three pupils who started in 2008 were all straight-through law graduates.

Chambers and Partners Tax Set of the Year 2009

Some pupils come for a full year, and first, second and third sixes are also offered. One tenant we interviewed had arrived via a commercial pupillage for a third six; another had done a three-month stint after several years' practice as a commercial barrister. However long the training, there's an "*initial period with one pupilmaster to protect them and help them find their feet,*" followed by rapidly accelerating work for other members, so that "*towards the end you're spitting pieces out.*" Working with up to five supervisors during the year ensures "*exposure to a broad range of work, whether it's VAT, corporate or personal tax,*" while "*spending weeks with silks, writing an opinion for them and going to court*" offers even more exacting challenges. One pupil who had seen private client income and inheritance tax issues with one supervisor had also enjoyed "*VAT disputes for Oxfam and a Whitechapel art gallery*" with another. Supervisor swapping is made manageable by the paperlight nature of many tax cases: "*Pieces of work are discrete, you can often read all the papers in time for a conference or to write a note, which makes pupillage more close to practice.*"

Pumped for information

Pupils meet with the head of the pupillage committee after six months to gain a sense of their prospects. Assuming all is well, they complete a series of assessments. In each of the past few years, one or two pupils have been taken on as tenants. Two made the grade in 2008 and one in 2009. Chambers recognises "*pupils can't be the finished article*" and instead looks for those with potential. Even during the first couple of years of tenancy, "*you are protected from full exposure to the outside world because the work is so complex and, on the advisory side, the liability can be so great.*" Initially new tenants devil for other members, then take on instructions from "*walk-in clients*" – "*maybe a company director who got the boot and wants help with his payoff.*"

"*About twice the size of other tax sets,*" Pump Court boosted its revenue by 28% in 2008. Prompted by "*an absolute abundance of work,*" it is in the midst of "*a period of strategic growth*" and is spreading into the building next door. Describing the place as a relaxed one where "*there's no strict pecking order,*" juniors are proud of a "*switched-on younger end,*" but also glad of the experience of seniors. At 11am each day, members gather for morning coffee and "*social chit-chat or collaborative discussion of members' legal problems.*" It's "*a great opportunity to say, 'How on earth do I do this?' and have someone else chime in, 'That's new, do x, y and z.'*" Given that tax law is "*an ever-changing field,*" members admit they'd "*be crazy not to tap each other's expertise,*" but the habit emphasises chambers' collegiate feel. Pupils may feel the need to be quieter during morning coffee, but whether it's venturing from their own room to listen in on a supervisor's phone calls or "*knocking on a senior's door to ask for advice,*" they told us: "*People are very generous with their time.*"

And finally…

Bizarrely, Pump Court Tax Chambers is a well-kept secret among students. If you're after a top commercial pupillage, getting in touch with your inner tax lawyer could open up a whole new world of opportunity.

Quadrant Chambers

The facts

Location: Fleet Street, London
Number of QCs/Juniors: 11/34 (6 women)
Applications: 110
Outside Pupillage Portal scheme
Pupils per year: Up to 3
Seats: 2x3 months + 1x6 months
Pupillage award: £40,000 (can advance sum for BPTC)

Quadrant's three-day mini-pupillages are offered at three specific times of the year, each with its own application deadline. See the set's website for details.

Highly successful aviation, shipping and commercial set Quadrant Chambers has its sights set on strategic reinvention.

Zen quadrantism

The glossy splendour of Quadrant's stunning Fleet Street premises – actually four buildings combined into one through architectural sleight of hand – may not apparently speak of ascetic introspection, but chambers is currently all about *"reaching a higher state of excellence."* There's been no attempt to discover collective inner tranquillity in Temple Gardens, instead chambers has brought in management consultants *"to reassess what we do and don't do well"* and purge inefficiencies bequeathed by the past. *"We have the modern buildings, the up-to-date IT system and attitude but the historical clerks-and-barristers staffing structure,"* a senior told us from the comfort of the lotus position. *"So we're bringing in a CEO and an HR person."* Integral to the plan to *"apply business logic"* is *"the major principle that we need to focus on sharing our skills and pulling together as a brand."* This means *"consolidating our position as a leading shipping, aviation, commercial and arbitration set."* It also means drawing out the *"strong work members are doing"* in insurance and reinsurance, energy, banking and finance and international trade and highlighting that to potential new clients.

As it stands, there's little wrong with Quadrant's caseload. Commercial shipping matters abound, with recent prominent cases including a House of Lords judgement on 'The Achilleas' – concerning late redelivery of a chartered ship and consequent loss of profits – that is now the leading case on remoteness of damage. Meanwhile, most members of chambers acted for cargo interests in claims arising out of the wreck of 'MSC Napoli' off the Cornish coast. Aviation is equally strong, whether it's general carriage issues and tour operator disputes, or even liability arising from air crashes or deep vein thrombosis. Advising on the various aviation law and regulatory aspects of easyJet's takeover of GB Airways highlights the set's breadth of expertise in the sector. The number of good general commercial instructions is also growing, some in the banking sector, others relating to sports and media. A member recently represented footballer Matty Holmes against Wolverhampton Wanderers FC in an action arising out of a foul tackle in an FA Cup replay that broke his leg and ended his career. The settlement made it the second most expensive tackle in British football history. Last but not least we should emphasise the set's arbitration experience, not least in relation to insurance, reinsurance and aviation.

Thumbing the breadths

In recent years pupillage has been *"revamped and revitalised,"* as a result of *"a sea change in attitudes towards pupils."* Said one senior: *"We've now got a panel of people who are really committed to making the effort."* Emphasising the extra effort, the set has recently introduced open days for groups of university students and reinstated three-day unassessed mini-pupillages. Neither

Chambers UK rankings

Aviation	Travel
Shipping	

is compulsory for applicants, but both provide an insight into the appeal of a pupillage covering *"everything from international trade and carriage of goods to insurance and aviation."* The rule of thumb is that *"if you're basically interested in anything that involves a contract,"* then Quadrant's general commercial training will be entirely to your taste.

Around 110 people each year make a tilt at the set. The mountain of applications (*"name, gender and age blacked out"*) are thumbed through and marked according to strict criteria, after which 30 people are sent a written assessment to complete and return within five days. Probably *"something like a simple construction case,"* the emphasis is on *"showing clarity of thought and expression, whether the candidate is a law or non-law graduate."* Around 16 will subsequently be invited to a *"tough"* 45-minute interview to be *"quizzed on the written assessment"* and *"discuss a case given out just before interview."* They also face *"an ethical question judging instincts and sensibilities"* and are asked to discuss a topical issue. In 2008 it was whether there should have been an inquest into Princess Diana's death. The style isn't confrontational, it's instead aimed at *"getting past comprehensive preparation to catch people on the topics they haven't discussed with their tutors, mums and partners."* Recruiters insist they aim to *"identify who will be a good lawyer in two years, not who is perfect now."* Having dropped out of the Pupillage Portal system *"to make decisions earlier and before people have to pay Bar School fees,"* Quadrant clearly has an eye for swooping on the best talent, but it's equally happy to take no one if its standards aren't met.

Ship shape

The pupillage experience involves two supervisors in the first six and a single one in the second, when you'll also do work for other members. This arrangement exposes pupils to chambers' main areas of practice. Aviation might involve *"particulars of claim and small discrete tasks,"* but also the challenge of *"going back to basics to learn about an interesting and exciting area."* For one pupil it taught *"so much about being persuasive in written form."* Shipping means charter parties, bills of lading and cargo damage, with our sources gaining from shadowing at conferences and salvage arbitrations. Pupils spending time with supervisors specialising in general commercial litigation might initially research points of law, but in time progress to full sets of papers with a view to presenting advice or drafting claims or defences.

Indicative of the set's desire to improve pupillage, a new system is being introduced whereby one barrister will act as a shadow supervisor for all pupils, setting them exercises throughout the year to provide consistency of assessment. For what it's worth, pupils praised the existing structure (written reports and appraisals from supervisors at the end of each seat), saying: *"You know what you have to work on at each stage."* Several sources spoke of the *"huge emphasis put on feedback throughout the year, from supervisors and other members"* and a defined feeling of being *"let off the leash as time goes by."* A baby-junior remembered: *"I worked 9am to 6pm hours to begin with, but towards the end your supervisor does turn the pressure up a bit. I think they want to see if you will work an evening or a weekend if you need to."*

Paid or court work is delayed until after the July tenancy decision. Initial advocacy experience is gained via assessed exercises of sufficient difficulty that *"tears are sometimes shed."* Attended by members of the pupillage committee and any else who fancies it, these mock cases are presided over by some *"forensically terrifying"* seniors. The assessments are the final piece of a rigorously structured process leading to a decision that *"doesn't leave it to the chance whim of some senior you've never met."* The 2009 decision hadn't been made by the time we went to press, but in 2008 both pupils were offered tenancy. New tenants share a room with a 'godparent' for six months, after which they graduate to their own space.

Lost

On our exhaustive tour of Quadrant's beautiful but piecemeal premises, we quickly became disoriented. Multiple lifts cope with floors at different levels; a junior's eyrie is known as The Frathouse; a conference room resembles a gentleman's club; and there's more plate glass than you could spend an afternoon throwing stones at. Beautiful, yes, confusing, certainly. We wondered if the spacious environs might dissipate social cohesion, but sources enthused about the *"great atmosphere,"* all-inclusive chambers lunches *"whenever there's a good reason"* and gatherings in nearby Daly's Wine Bar most Fridays.

And finally...

In this pragmatic and commercial set, we still sensed a pleasantly informal vibe from its members and staff. *"I came prepared to dislike things in case I didn't get taken on,"* a junior remembered, *"but I've never had a member be anything other than entirely friendly, lovely and down-to-earth."*

Serle Court

The facts

Location: Lincoln's Inn, London
Number of QCs/Juniors: 14/37 (7 women)
Applications: 110+
Outside Pupillage Portal scheme
Pupils per year: 1 or 2
Seats: 4x3 months
Pupillage Award: £45,000 (can advance £15,000 for BPTC)

"When meeting with solicitors my supervisor will always ask if I have anything to add – which is a little thing, but important."

Top commercial Chancery set Serle Court offers a wide range of work in relaxed surroundings.

Roman's army

Serle Court was formed in 2000 through a merger between the Chancery barristers of 13 Old Square and the commercial barristers of 1 Hare Court. The product is a set with strength in a sweep of practice areas. A clerk tells us that "*at the moment, offshore trusts work, lots of fraud work, company insolvency and property are the areas we get most enquiries about. But then sports law and all these other little cases come in as well.*"

This summary tallies well with the set's rankings in *Chambers UK*. Members are acting on one of the biggest shipping fraud cases currently ongoing, Fiona Trust v Privalov. It's a long story, but is essentially a matter brought by the operators of two Russian tanker fleets alleging misappropriation, conspiracy, fraud and bribery against their former president and various other individuals and companies. Keeping it Russo-related, we're told that things are busy in the oligarchy market at the moment, and Roman Abramovich has briefed new head of chambers Alan Boyle QC in fraud matters. Serle Court is ahead of the game in the offshore trusts field: many sets are only just starting to look abroad for work but this one already possesses a number of barristers who often appear in Jersey, the Cayman Islands and elsewhere. As for those other little cases, well, there are plenty of quirky ones to talk about, from the matter of the Jersey accountant claiming to be an illegitimate son of Princess Margaret, to the curious case of the Bishop of Portsmouth, the convent school and the Benedictine nun.

Bacon's buddies

Ye olde lawyer Sir Francis Bacon said that 'reading maketh a full man, conference a ready man, and writing an exact man.' Nowhere does this apply more than in the incredibly complex field of Chancery law and, taking Sir Francis' counsel to heart, pupillage consists of a mix of the three – reading in the form of research, conference in the form of contact with other barristers and solicitors, and writing in the form of drafting.

The proportion of each during the course of the four three-month seats depends largely on the pupilmaster's practice. "*My first supervisor was working on two very big fraud cases,*" said a pupil. That involved researching "*quite a lot of interesting law – jurisdictional questions and the like*" and drafting skeleton arguments and bits of witness statements. By contrast, "*in the second three months I had a supervisor who seemed to have a new set of papers every day. That meant I got a much more regular stream of little things coming in, like contractual disputes and land law.*" As you can see, pupils get exposure to the full breadth of chambers' practice, from commer-

Chambers UK rankings

Banking & Finance	Fraud: Civil
Chancery	Partnership
Commercial Dispute Resolution	Professional Negligence
Company	Real Estate Litigation
Financial Services Regulation	Restructuring/Insolvency

cial and traditional Chancery to property, IP and more. As for conferencing: "*My supervisor has been very good about recognising that I'm there, and when meeting with solicitors he'll always ask if I have anything to add – which is a little thing, but important.*" Being farmed out to several members of chambers is also commonplace. "*It's mostly quite interesting stuff, although occasionally it's one of those negative questions that pupils have to prove: can you go off and prove that there isn't anything on this subject? You'll come back having found nothing and inevitably some document will have been hidden behind the filing cabinet all along,*" joked a pupil.

> **Chambers and Partners
> Client Service
> Set of the Year 2009**

What you won't get is any guarantee of your own caseload. Chambers' attitude to training is simple: "*They're here for a year as a pupil*" and that time is better spent getting to grips with more complex law than going off to court to deal with road traffic accident claims. Although a junior said that "*in practice you tend to get a bit of advocacy*" during the summer after tenancy has been offered, clerks and pupilmasters alike played down the chances of court time. However, a pupil told us that much of the work he had done for supervisors was "*essentially live, which is good for motivational reasons.*" Feedback was described as satisfactory, coming in "*traditional primary school red pen.*" Perhaps the only time it doesn't work quite so well "*is when you do tasks for other members of chambers. You will get an e-mail back saying, 'Thanks very much, very useful,' but that's usually about it.*"

Working hours for pupils are officially 9am to 6pm. It's fair to say that these normally stretch to a little longer than this, but not extortionately so. "*It's very civilised,*" said a pupil, "*I've certainly not been kept hanging around or given unreasonable amounts of work, and there's no doubt that I've been going home well before my supervisors.*"

Stars of the Bar at the bar in the Stars

When chambers moved in to its current premises at 6 New Square, everyone looked forward to coming together under one roof. Best-laid plans being what they are, within a short period of time they ran out of space. Fortunately for would-be tenants the purchase of an annexe has added extra lebensraum, even if it's a little less glamorous than the main building: "*The rooms don't over-look Lincoln's Inn and you're above Wetherspoons.*" Perhaps unsurprisingly, there's a concentration of younger barristers in the annexe, making it, in the words of a pupil, "*the relaxed end of an already relaxed set of chambers.*"

That's definitely Serle Court's style and has been for some time. "*We feel that we have a slightly more relaxed approach to the formalities of life at the Bar,*" says a pupilmaster. "*Ten years ago I think there was clear blue water between us and the rest, although I get the impression that others are catching on now and taking steps to become less stuffy.*" Pupils are actively encouraged to be seen – and heard – at morning coffee or afternoon tea, although "*you might not necessarily wish to hold forth: there are certainly elements of tact involved!*" The Seven Stars is inexplicably more popular than Wetherspoons for an after-work drink, and you'll regularly find "*the usual suspects*" there. There are also football, softball and cricket teams. But, "*whether you're the type of person who likes to socialise over a cup of coffee in the morning, a cup of tea in the afternoon, a glass of wine in the evening, or on the football pitch,*" it's important to meet other members of chambers as, though the ultimate tenancy decision is made by the pupillage committee (as advised by the pupilmasters), a good word from the rest can't hurt. Serle Court has offered tenancy to most of its pupils in the last ten years, so there's no real need for competition between them. In 2009 both made it. Income in the early months of tenancy is usually slow but at least £100K is guaranteed in the first two years.

So who does the set want to recruit as a pupil? Aside from social skills, academic results are hugely important for two reasons. Commercial Chancery is one of the most factually complex areas of the Bar and very intellectually demanding. Secondly, quite simply, chambers now gets about as many people with First-class degrees applying as there are first-interview places and, "*if you're trying to do it fairly, it's very hard to turn away someone with a First in favour of someone with a 2:1.*" It does sometimes happen in exceptional circumstances. Otherwise, we sense there's no specific type. The pupils at the time of our visit were a 20-something law graduate and a 30-something with a PhD in 16th century music.

> ### And finally...
>
> "*Everyone seems happy, and there's a lot of work coming in,*" says a junior. "*I genuinely think Serle Court is a very dynamic place to be at the moment.*" Nice place, very busy. What more is there to say?

3-4 South Square

The facts

Location: Lincoln's Inn, London
Number of QCs/Juniors: 19/25 (7 women)
Applications: 120
Outside Pupillage Portal scheme
Pupils per year: Up to 4
Seats: 6x6 weeks
Pupillage award: £42,500 (can advance £12,500 for BPTC)

This set is best known for its vast insolvency and corporate recovery practice. Its name is so synonymous with this area of law that solicitors suggest it is "*the IBM choice – why would you go anywhere else?*"

Members of 3-4 South Square have left their mark on all the big corporate collapses and restructurings – BCCI, Maxwell, Lloyd's syndicates, Barings, Enron, Marconi, Parmelat, MyTravel, Metronet…

My word is my Bond

…Lehman Brothers, Northern Rock, Landsbanki, Woolworths, Madoff Securities – yes, it's a good time to be in this area of practice. Chambers also has experts in fraud, banking and finance, commercial litigation, company law, insurance and reinsurance and arbitration. While the Insolvency Act is the "*lifeblood*" of the set, a rough 60/40 split between insolvency law and broader commercial matters ensures that pupils will encounter interpretation of contract, property law, trusts, tort and EU law. "*If you can't handle EU law, don't come here,*" advised one interviewee. Fraud is a "*sexy*" area, not least because fraudsters range from the perplexingly normal to "*colourful, famous crooks.*" Pupils say working in this area "*can be a bit like being in a Bond film.*"

It's important to keep clients' business interests in mind at all times. Commercial awareness can be devilishly hard to define, not least when you're trying to show you have it. For a barrister, it's about looking at cases from a fresh perspective and maintaining an awareness of the commercial context. "*In every case you study at law school, and every textbook example, that context will be there, but it can be easily overlooked,*" explained a pupil. Insolvency barristers receive instructions from specialist insolvency practitioners as well as solicitors, and at times they come into contact with some "*very aggressive and difficult*" individuals at personal bankruptcy hearings. Having a real-world view on things is imperative. Equally as important is a healthy interest in raw legal principles, and as one pupil pointed out: "*The Insolvency Act is the second longest statute on the books after the Company Act 2006, which is the other one we specialise in.*" There's no getting around it; if you want pupillage at 3-4 South Square, you're going to have to cover all the bases.

Island life

Supervision is a "*collaborative process*" in which pupils are asked to identify the gaps in their knowledge, so that supervisors can fill them. In this intense year "*you really do hit the ground running.*" "*Difficult stuff is thrown at you from an early stage*" and "*people aren't going to hold your hand – you either sink or swim.*" Pupils complete the same set pieces of work, doing them at different times avoids scrapping for books in the library. "*Chambers really wants you to find out how to work, so pupillage is geared towards letting you make your own decisions.*" Time management, for example, is largely left to the individual. Supervisors will ensure they have access to interesting work, but it's up to them to decide whether they can take it on. "*Everyone makes mistakes,*" but be reassured there are people to ask for advice and support, and "*pupils

Chambers UK rankings

| Banking & Finance | Company |
| Chancery | Restructuring/Insolvency |

are never faced with someone being difficult for the sake of it." It is the supervisors who pupils sit with after Christmas who take the most active role in the tenancy decision.

"*This isn't the place to come if you want to be on your feet in the second six.*" Advocacy skills aren't even formally assessed during pupillage (although it is important to give "*intelligent, lucid responses*" when receiving feedback from supervisors). Adequate advocacy opportunities come in time, and until about eight years' call juniors spend roughly equal amounts of time representing clients alone and being led by seniors. After this, their role becomes more advisory.

> **Chambers and Partners Insolvency/Corporate Restructuing Set of the Year 2009**

The set has a strong international practice, with associate members in Germany, Hong Kong, Singapore, the USA, Australia, South Africa, Scotland and Trinidad and Tobago. One pupil described a "*magical mystery island tour*" taking in "*the British Virgin Islands, Mauritius, the Cayman Islands, the Seychelles, the Isle of Man, Jersey and Guernsey.*" Needless to say, many cases have a trusts element.

Members' hours fluctuate dramatically – some arrive in the wee small hours to catch the Hong Kong traffic, while others work late to fit in with New York. Even for pupils 12-hour days are not unheard of; the average is 9am until 7pm. "*You'll write lots of long opinions and research notes and go through different drafts of one piece of work, but there's also a lot of time thinking about what you've read and staring into space.*" It's important to be able to "*think creatively and logically in order to combat the complexity of the work.*"

Tough cookies

After the first six "*no-hopers are told where they stand and given a choice about staying on or looking for a second six elsewhere.*" The tenancy decision is made in July, when typically two make the cut. Technically, pupils don't compete for tenancy, but we sensed there was a "*combative*" element to the process. As we interviewed them, the pupils engaged in a game of one-upmanship: one had been in court 11 times, visiting the Chancery Division, the Companies Court and the Privy Council. Another, who had been in court only twice, pointed out that he'd written a chapter for a book and several articles during the same period. If there is indeed competition, recent results suggest it's ultimately pointless: in 2008 both pupils were successful while in 2009 no one was taken on as a tenant.

Despite the picture we've painted, 3-4 South Square is by no means a macho set. There's a healthy number of female juniors, and from what we saw, wrap-around cardigans have more currency than sharp suits. At the hub of chambers is a strong administration team run by charismatic senior practice manager Paul Cooklin. "*If you have a technical problem, you go to Yvonne. If you have a pupillage query, you go to Alison. For broader chambers issues, there's Vicky… if you need something typed, you go to Jenny and Julie,*" pupils willingly explained. In this set "*everybody knows your name*" and juniors regularly go for drinks. "*People are very hard-working, but they still know when to take time off.*"

You're advised to take the company law elective on the BVC/BPTC and, if you're considering postgraduate study, the corporate insolvency paper on the BCL. Another new and developing area to consider is restitution law. Chambers takes into account that not everyone has studied that much law by the time they reach interview. "*We don't find setting legal problems very helpful; we prefer to start everyone with an ethics question, for which no prior knowledge is required.*" Interestingly, one of the recruiters admitted: "*Their ethical approach matters quite a lot to us.*" Anyone who impresses in an assessed mini-pupillage (chambers pays £500) is fast-tracked to a second-round interview. Most candidates go through two rounds, with third interviews used when the panel can't decide on someone, perhaps because they've underperformed due to nerves. Successful candidates are invited to a drinks party to meet more of the members.

Insolvency law is fast-paced and challenging, and with companies going bust and individuals teetering on the brink of bankruptcy, you need to be "*thick-skinned and resilient,*" especially in situations that can be "*panicky and stressful for the client.*" After meeting with these pupils, we sensed they were tough cookies.

> **And finally…**
>
> In this slick and ballsy set pupils learn their trade in a challenging and stimulating environment. If you're driven, focused and open-minded, there is every chance to shine; just be prepared for some firm handshakes at interview.

2 Temple Gardens

The facts

Location: Temple, London
Number of QCs/Juniors: 8/48 (18 women)
Applications: 200-250
Apply through Pupillage Portal
Pupils per year: Up to 3
Seats: 3x4 months
Pupillage award: £47,500 (can advance £12,500 for BPTC)

The set offers funded and unfunded mini-pupillages, but don't miss the deadlines for the former: 30 November for the winter season and 15 April for the summer season.

For the commercial and civil law multi-specialists of 2 Temple Gardens, breadth of experience is the name of the game.

From atomic testing to global warming

Chambers has occupied its bijou Temple Gardens residence ever since it was founded just after WWII. It has been a purely civil set since the 1960s, and today it adopts what it calls "*a multi-specialist, practice group approach.*" This strategy was put in place about five years ago and has seen the set "*concentrate on core areas and grow others by a steady drip, drip accumulation.*" As the senior clerk was quick to observe, any of the 50 or so members who now call 2tg home can "*belong to any of the groupings... being in PI doesn't exclude you from media.*"

The set's core areas are thriving under this approach. Its historically strong personal injury practice accounts for nearly 30% of annual revenue and strong relationships with a welter of top insurers means "*about 90% of our work is defendant.*" That said, there's a willingness to "*grow our claimant side a little,*" because "*the clients like barristers to have rounded experience.*" One ongoing highlight is involvement in the "*Trigger litigation concerning asbestos cases... that will probably go all the way to the House of Lords.*" Members are also representing insurer clients in a Buncefield oil depot disaster claim and claimants in the Atomic Test Veterans case against the MoD arising out of 1950s testing. Members' proficiency in clinical and professional negligence also brings in regular instructions from the NHS Litigation Authority and professional bodies such as the Medical Defence Union and the Medical Protection Society. Then there's the growing commercial side, incorporating fraud, banking and finance and commodities cases.

Additionally, an employment practice "*has really kicked on in the last few years.*" Having "*started out predominantly in claimant,*" the set is "*gradually getting work from big banks.*" This might seem like breadth enough, but 2tg can also make credible claim to pronounced skills in public law, media and entertainment and property. The latter involves a "*lot of subsidence, tree root and flooding claims from insurance clients, but also a good landlord and tenant practice.*" With four members on the Treasury panel and ongoing involvement in the inquiry into the murder of a solicitor in Northern Ireland, public law is also buoyant. Meanwhile members in the media and entertainment team have recently acted for The Drifters in a royalty payments case and got involved when the showing of Al Gore's *An Inconvenient Truth* in UK schools became a political hot potato.

New York, Paris, Blackpool

"*Breadth of opportunity was the hook*" for our interviewees and a 2tg pupillage doesn't disappoint. Insurance, PI and banking had been the major experiences of one of our sources, but there is simply no set pattern. Two of the three allocated supervisors feature in the first six, the initial three-month stint being "*slightly more protected.*"

Chambers UK rankings

Clinical Negligence	Professional Discipline
Personal Injury	Professional Negligence

Handling the "*first drafts of court papers and research*" is the norm in the first six, as is accompanying supervisors to conferences, court and client seminars. The focus is on "*generating the skills needed to move into practice,*" and as time goes by "*supervisors will notice pupils contributing more.*" Looking back, juniors told us: "*When you do something complicated and your supervisor is able to use it in later months it is a fantastic feeling.*" Once with their second supervisor, pupils can also expect to take on work for or attend court with other members "*to see new areas and different cases.*" The pupil may be "*purely observing,*" but the payoff is "*getting to chat on the train... it helps expose you to more people before the tenancy decision.*"

Feedback from supervisors comes on a "*piece-by-piece basis*" and they also fill out an end-of-seat report. In the absence of set written assessments, making sure "*there's an organised paper trail*" is important, and members who co-opt pupils to draft pleadings or advices will always fill out a feedback sheet. Once the second six starts, pupils are faced with a flood of advocacy experience, usually requiring them to be in court three times a week. They are fed a diet of RTAs, small insurance cases and even fast-track claims. "*Variety is the greatest feature,*" one pupil enthused, reflecting that "*RTAs help hone your cross-examination skills, while credit hire claims are more about legal analysis and argument.*" The caseload also involves travel, largely in and around London and the South East, with a few jaunts as far as Cardiff or Blackpool. "*Join the Bar, see the world,*" laughed a clerk.

The tenancy decision is made by the end of June, after considering feedback forms, "*input from solicitors or evidence of repeat instructions,*" and the results of several advocacy exercises. 2tg has an excellent record for making tenants, with as many as three a year kept on in the recent past. In 2009 two pupils were successful.

Garden parties

Around 40 pupillage applicants are invited to an appraisal day that includes group activities and a debating exercise. Attendees are also treated to presentations by specialists from different practice areas, making it very much a two-way process. Said one member of the pupillage committee: "*We're aware we compete with other top sets for candidates and we want to show ourselves off.*" Between ten and 15 progress to a more traditional second round for discussion of a legal problem given out half an hour beforehand. Surveying the genuine variety of university backgrounds and career histories of current tenants, the process clearly does successfully focus on "*intellect above all, an ability to persuade and ambition to succeed.*" Displaying the "*maturity and presence to do well in court and with clients*" is perhaps easier for second-careerers, of which there are many, but plenty of law graduates also manage to display such skills.

Commanding fine views of the eponymous gardens, 2tg is spread across multiple floors of its main building and a nearby annexe. Given the separation, you might imagine any sense of cohesion would suffer. Not a bit of it. "*We try to recognise that our members are our assets and it's a mistake not to use them,*" said one tenant describing a "*co-operative ethos.*" While things might be "*full-blooded if they face one another on a case,*" at other times members are "*always available to give advice.*" Said one source: "*Pupils are very much involved in extracurricular activities, we like them to feel they belong.*" Weekly Friday drinks are a perfect time to catch up, and the Christmas party is well attended. If the "*glazed eyes and slow reactions*" we encountered on our visit are anything to go by, the set certainly knows how to organise a knees-up. "*Not that we only do drink-related activities,*" a junior hastened to assure us after recounting tales from the Scottish-themed party held the previous night to celebrate "*a High Court victory in a Scottish coal case.*"

And finally...

Bursting with advocacy and more varied than a stick of rainbow rock, a 2tg pupillage is every flavour of commercial and civil law and a tasty prospect for it.

3 Verulam Buildings

The facts

Location: Gray's Inn, London
Number of QCs/Juniors: 18/40 (10 women)
Applications: 150
Apply through Pupillage Portal
Pupils per year: 3-4
Seats: 4x3 months
Pupillage Award: £42,500 (can advance £15,000 for BPTC)

Chambers is undeniably brilliant in the field of banking and finance disputes.

"*I don't think we're the sort of chambers that looks back.*" We concur: 3VB is a set with the future on its mind.

The magic moment?

For some years now we, among others, have described 3 Verulam Buildings as 'knocking on the door of the magic circle.' As you might expect, its members have something to say about that and as far as they are concerned 3VB is past knocking and is now over the threshold, muddying the carpet and stealing the silver. Or, to put it in the more diplomatic terms of a QC: "*If there is a magic circle we're in it. Our closest competitors in terms of the work we do are Fountain Chambers and One Essex Court, and those are who we come up against most often in court.*" What's more, he says, "*we have more juniors in the commercial litigation tables of Chambers UK than any other set – and bear in mind that they are the people who are pupil supervisors.*" This is undeniable, and a real pool of talent at junior silk and senior junior level means that the future of the set looks bright indeed. We at the *Student Guide* have always been a little sceptical about the whole concept of the magic circle in the first place, but feeling in an investigative mood we canvassed opinion in the corridors of Chambers and Partners. Colleagues described the set as 'clearly a coming force' but stopped short of acclaiming it as a fully paid-up member of the magic circle. Sorry, 3VB. Maybe next year. Smart applicants will, of course, look to the future and realise that the set's pool of talent will come into full bloom when they are juniors. "*That's very exciting because it means the work that people at the bottom of chambers will get led on is only going to get better.*"

Where chambers is undeniably brilliant is in the field of banking and finance disputes. And heck, what an area to excel in right now! 3VB had six members acting for various parties in the recent bank charges litigation, and there have been all manner of instructions relating to the collapse of Lehman Brothers, the failure of the Icelandic banks, problems in the derivatives markets and government-funded rescues all over the world. The set does seem to get its fair share of whatever is blowing through the English courts – it was also extremely active on a number of large insurance/reinsurance disputes that arose from 9/11 and the Equitable Life debacle.

An extensive revamp a couple of years ago makes the moniker 3 Verulam Buildings a bit of a misnomer. Chambers now occupies numbers 1, 2, 4 and 5 as well. "*I suspect we've probably got the best accommodation at the Bar now,*" asserts senior practice manager Nick Hill. Certainly, many sets would envy the fact that not only is everyone at 3VB under one roof, but there is still plenty of room to expand.

Skeleton key

As it isn't the sort of set that has grown through mergers or repeated lateral hires, recruiting the right pupils is very

Chambers UK rankings

Banking & Finance	Insurance
Commercial Dispute Resolution	Media & Entertainment
Financial Services Regulation	Professional Negligence
Fraud: Civil	Restructuring/Insolvency
Information Technology	Telecommunications

important and consequently chambers has put some serious thought into the interview process. The 40 or so applicants who get invited to a first interview can expect a general chat about their CV, their decision to come to the Bar and a current "*legal-ish*" topic (last year it concerned the anonymity of witnesses in criminal trials). Around half will make it through to a second-round interview, which involves the oral argument of a legal problem. "*They make their points and we heckle a bit.*" Hmm, a bit? "*To a realistic degree! We let everyone get well into their stride before we ask any questions and it's always done in a polite way, but it's a thorough testing of abilities and aptitude.*" The problem is sent to interviewees a week in advance. As still happens at some places, 3VB used to spring it on people half an hour beforehand but decided that was "*unrealistic and unfair.*" In another recent innovation at the 'legal problem' stage, chambers also asks for a short skeleton argument to be submitted beforehand. "*We think that's been a distinct improvement... previously we were sometimes rather easily beguiled by people who could talk a good talk, but when it got to pupillage couldn't write a good write.*" By the way, 'short' in this context means about four pages – "*although that doesn't stop some people submitting four pages single-spaced in the smallest possible font.*"

While a mini-pupillage isn't required, chambers does like to see everyone it invites to second interview for at least a day or two at some point before it makes offers. Those who have made it through the process in recent years include not only 'straight through from Oxbridge' types but also a glut of people from Commonwealth universities, former actuaries and lecturers, someone who ran his own business and the former head of Insurance and Prudential Policy at the Financial Services Authority. "*Age or previous career is no boundary.*" Nor is a non-law degree, although as a Pupillage Portal member 3VB feels that the sets outside that system tend to nab the best GDL students early.

Me and my shadow

Pupils sit with four supervisors for three months each in order to see a range of work and types of people. They are also encouraged to work for other members of chambers. The tasks pupils are given are a mix of supervisors' current work and past cases. There are also "*shadow supervisors.*" These are barristers in their first five years of practice who, as well as adding an extra level of pastoral care, "*keep an eye out for pieces of work that it would be useful to show to pupils.*" Four or five advocacy exercises are scheduled for the year. "*We do take notice of how they perform in these, but it's mainly educational – so long as they don't make the same mistake in two exercises.*" A pupil confirmed that this attitude doesn't just apply to the advocacy exercises: "*You're not supposed to make the same mistake twice... but they are very forgiving of the first mistake.*" Chambers "*doesn't kick people out*" after completion of the first six, although if pupils don't look like they're making headway by that stage it's suggested that it might be in their best interests to look elsewhere. In the second six "*the expectations go up,*" work gets more complex, "*the feedback points get finer and more nuanced*" and pupils start to receive their own instructions. "*They definitely make sure you get something, although it's not like a criminal set where you will be constantly in court.*" Chambers has the space to offer tenancy to everyone who comes up to scratch, and in 2009 two out of three took up permanent residence.

A formal afternoon tea isn't quite 3VB's style, but there is a common room that people flit in and out of throughout the day. Also worthy of note are a summer party, an annual dinner and various drinks evenings. "*One of the barristers just made silk so he had a bit of a do.*" Pupils won't actually see much of each other during the day, but do meet up to socialise after office hours.

And finally...

Modern and forward-thinking, 3 Verulam Buildings is a choice pick by anyone's standards.

Wilberforce Chambers

The facts

Location: Lincoln's Inn, London
Number of QCs/Juniors: 22/28 (11 women)
Applications: c. 100
Outside Pupillage Portal scheme
Pupils per year: 2
Seats: 6x2 months
Pupillage Award: £48,000 (can advance £16,000 for BPTC)

> The collapse of Lehman Brothers and Bear Stearns led to some meaty instructions during the early weeks of the financial crisis in 2008.

Back in the 1980s, this set was one of the first to recognise the importance of branding. Accordingly, it renamed itself after one of its most distinguished members, Lord Wilberforce, great-great-grandson of William Wilberforce. It has been growing in size and reputation ever since.

Wilberforce be with you

Wilberforce is a leader among Chancery sets. For 'traditional' Chancery cases it stands alone in the top tier in *Chambers UK*. Possibly its best-known recent success was the headline-making divorce case of Charman v Charman, in which members represented the wife of a fabulously wealthy insurance magnate. Private clients are just one part of the story though. As one of the new breed of Chancery sets, Wilberforce's reach is wide in the commercial sphere, both in relation to Chancery Division cases and those headed for the Queen's Bench Division of the High Court. It is undisputed top dog for pensions matters, and Brian Green QC recently represented the trustees of the Sea Containers 1983 Pension Scheme during the parent company's insolvency.

The set also has a fine reputation for property litigation, professional negligence, fraud, IP and more. In a much-publicised IP case, for example, members represented Lucasfilm, suing one Andrew Ainsworth for copyright infringement. Mr Ainsworth had made some of the original Imperial Stormtrooper helmets and armour for the first *Star Wars* film and had started to sell life-sized replicas. Meanwhile Ian Croxford QC acted for the Ritz Hotel Group during the inquest into the death of Diana, Princess of Wales, while the collapse of Lehman Brothers and Bear Stearns led to some meaty instructions during the early weeks of the financial crisis in 2008. Among other subjects recently touched on by members are feuding oligarchs, the collapse of offshore hedge funds and corruption in the former Zambian government. It's quite a mix.

Analyse this

Now around 50 barristers strong, chambers operates from three buildings on New Square and is actively looking for new premises. Said a source: *"Being under one roof is desirable in itself and will also help to make the set more collegiate."* Although nothing had been decided by the time we went to press, a couple of options were being examined, so this is no idle speculation.

At the same time, the aim is to grow *"a little bit more,"* and the pupillage scheme is certainly going to be a part of this process. Wilberforce has a large number of QCs and *"the ratio of silks to juniors has become somewhat skewed."* Therefore, from 2011 chambers will take three

Chambers UK rankings

Chancery	Intellectual Property
Charities	Pensions
Commercial Dispute Resolution	Professional Negligence
Company	Real Estate Litigation
Fraud: Civil	

pupils per year. Previously it took two as standard, although at the time of our visit just one pupillage applicant had been deemed of a sufficiently high quality to be taken on.

So how are you likely to fare if you put yourself up for consideration? Academic ability is "*a starting point,*" of course, but we also hear from the pupillage committee that it "*doesn't insist on people having a First.*" While this might sound like good news for those who missed out on top grades, be aware that the majority of pupils – and members – do have Firsts. At interview, we're told: "*It's the way in which applicants analyse the set legal problem, and how they put forward their answers, that is crucial.*" Our source on the pupillage committee continued: "*It's very interesting that people who have only just started studying law often do better than some who've been doing law for years but who can prove completely inadequate at doing what a barrister really has to do – legal analysis at very short notice.*" The trend for GDL students to perform better at interview is not unique to this set – many of the commercial and Chancery chambers we visit note the same thing. "*Common sense*" and "*a practical working knowledge of the real world*" are highly desired qualities and it is possible that GDL students, with that extra time behind them, are more likely to display these traits. Interestingly, when we asked if personality was another contributing factor we were told in no uncertain terms: "*No. We have set criteria based on what makes a good barrister, not on who's going to be nice to go to lunch with.*" This strict hiring policy, with its emphasis on fairness, has resulted in an "*eclectic*" mix of tenants. "*We get quiet ones, we get assertive ones. We get people from all walks of life. The only things they have in common are excellent academic results and a high intellect.*" All that said, an analysis of the membership of Wilberforce suggests that unless you have Oxbridge on your CV you're unlikely to make it through the recruitment process.

Chambers and Partners Chancery Set of the Year 2009

Tea and tenancy

"*This pupillage would suit someone who wanted a broad experience of Chancery work.*" Pupils will experience most areas of the set's business over the course of the year by sitting with six supervisors for two months at a time. Each seat naturally offers the chance to develop different skills; for example, "*somebody in the property stream will be in court a lot more than in the private client stream where there is more drafting.*" A pupil's day will tend to mirror their supervisor's. "*Mostly I'll be writing an opinion or doing a statement of case at the same time as my supervisor is doing the same thing live. That keeps the work I'm doing relevant,*" explained the pupil we spoke to. Opportunities for advocacy during the pupillage year are fairly limited. At the end of each seat supervisors prepare a short report bearing a number of criteria in mind – "*was he sufficiently analytical, was he thorough in his research and so on.*" This is "*not done on a strict numbers system*" but is simply a guideline.

People "*do generally reserve judgement on pupils until it's time for the tenancy decision to be made,*" recognising that a pupil in his (or her) first two months is very different from the same pupil six months later. Wilberforce's policy is to offer tenancy to every pupil who meets its exacting standards. "*Other chambers may not want to take two on at once, or say they don't have enough room, but it's our clear policy that we will take pupils on if we consider them to be good enough.*" Unfortunately, in 2009 the sole pupil was not taken on.

"*There isn't the 4 o'clock 'pens down' for tea*" that you might experience at some other sets. Instead chambers drinks take place on a Friday evening and there are also bi-weekly lunches and client events. Plus, said our pupil, "*I have been out with some of the juniors a few times and they are all very nice to me!*" Essentially, "*you can have as much of a social life as you want.*"

And finally...

Wilberforce is looking for the brightest and best so you'll need the analytical skills of Sherlock Holmes and a brain like The Mekon's. We suspect the silver tongue of Barack Obama wouldn't go amiss either.

The True Picture

- **Never give in:** never, never, never, never, in nothing great or small, large or petty, never give in except to convictions of honour and good sense.

    Winston Churchill

top tip no. 35

A-Z of Barristers

- **General advice for life:** Carpe diem; neither a borrower nor a lender be; no one ever went broke by underestimating the intelligence of the American public; carpe noctem; never play cards with anyone called Doc; brevity is the soul of wit; never believe mirrors or newspapers; comparethemeerkat.com; DON'T PANIC; if it looks too good to be true, it probably is; oranges are not the only fruit; courtesy costs nothing; if it ain't broke, don't fix it; faint heart ne'er won fair lady; to err is human, to forgive divine.

top tip no. 36

Atkin Chambers

1 Atkin Building, Gray's Inn, London, WC1R 5AT
Tel: (020) 7404 0102   Fax: (020) 7405 7456
Email: clerks@atkinchambers.com
Website: www.atkinchambers.com

No of Silks	14
No of Juniors	23
No of Pupils	3

Contact
Mr Andrew Burrows
Email: pupillage@atkinchambers.com

Method of application
Pupillage: Pupillage Portal
Mini-pupillage: CV and covering letter to contact

Pupillages (p.a.)
up to 3 funded

Income
(2011/12) expected to be £47,500

Tenancies
six in the last three years

Chambers profile
Atkin Chambers was the first set to specialise in the law relating to domestic and international construction and engineering projects. It has a significant and growing international practice at all levels of seniority. Chambers success in this area has been recognised by the grant of the Queen's Award for Enterprise 2005 in the category of International Trade.

Type of work undertaken
Atkin Chambers is a leader in its field: technology and construction law. Members of Chambers have been involved in many of the largest high profile domestic and international disputes in the fields of construction, technology, power, energy, computers and telecommunications of recent years, both in court and in international and domestic arbitration. Members of Chambers are regular participants as advocates, advisers or tribunals in all forms of alternative dispute resolution.

Pupil profile
Applicants for pupillage should have a first-class degree or a good 2.1 degree. Postgraduate qualifications are viewed favourably but are not essential. Applications from non-law graduates are welcome. Atkin Chambers is committed to applying equal opportunities good practice.

Pupillage
Atkin Chambers takes recruitment to pupillage and tenancy extremely seriously. The pupillage award (anticipated to be £47,500 for 2011/12 – equivalent to the sums paid by other much larger sets of chambers) reflects this.

The Pupillage year is structured to provide all of the Bar Council's training requirements and the additional training Chambers considers is necessary for successful entry into high-quality commercial work of its practice. Atkin Chambers provides its own advocacy training and assessment in addition to that provided by the Inns.

Full and up-to date details of the structure and goals of Atkin Chambers' pupilllage training programme may be reviewed on the website.

Mini pupillages
Six mini-pupillages are offered each year. Mini-pupillages will be offered to candidates who have achieved or have clear potential to achieve the academic standards required for pupilage. Whilst all applications received will be given consideration, applicants are invited to apply by letter with CV by 1 February 2010.

Sponsorship & awards
Three fully funded pupilages of £47,500 per pupil for 12 months are available. Funding for the BVC year by way of drawdown is available.

2 Bedford Row (William Clegg QC)

2 Bedford Row, London, WC1R 4BU
Tel: (020) 7440 8888   Fax: (020) 7242 1738
Email: clerks@2bedfordrow.co.uk
Website: www.2bedfordrow.co.uk

No of Silks 20
No of Juniors 53
No of Pupils 4

Graduate recruitment contact
Stephen Vullo
020 7440 8888

Method of application
Pupillage Portal

Pupillages (p.a.)
12 months 4
Tenancies offered according to ability

Chambers profile

Widely regarded as one of the leading crime sets in the UK, 2 Bedford Row continues to excel in the fields of crime, fraud and regulatory law. Chambers has been described by 'Chambers and Partners' 2008 as a "number-one criminal set" and many of its members are regarded as leaders in their fields.

Type of work undertaken

Chambers has a broad based criminal practice and its members have appeared in some of the most high profile criminal of recent years (in 2008, for example, R v Barry George, R v Levi Bellfield, R v Mark Dixie). In addition, members of Chambers have particular experience in the fields of confiscation/restraint, health and safety, financial services law, sports law, professional regulation/discipline and inquests. Members are frequently instructed to appear before regulatory bodies such as the GMC, the FA, the VAT tribunal and the Police Disciplinary Tribunal.

Pupil profile

Chambers recruits candidates from all backgrounds who display the highest intellectual ability, excellent advocacy skills, sound judgment and a real commitment to criminal law and its related fields. Candidates will also be well rounded individuals who are able to communicate effectively with a wide variety of people.

Pupillage

Chambers offers up to four 12 month pupillages each year. Each pupil will have two pupil supervisors in their first six and a different two in their second six. This ensures that pupils are provided with a thorough grounding in all aspects of Chambers' practice. Chambers also provides structured advocacy training throughout the pupillage year and will pay for pupils to attend the 'Advice to Counsel' and 'Forensic Accountancy' courses.

Mini pupillages

Chambers welcomes applications for mini-pupillage. Please see the website for details.

Funding

Chambers provides a grant of £12,000 to each pupil, paid monthly throughout the year and in addition, guaranteed earnings of £10,000 in second six.

Blackstone Chambers (I Mill QC and T Beazley QC)

Blackstone House, Temple, London EC4Y 9BW   DX: 281
Tel: (020) 7583 1770 Fax: (020) 7822 7350
Email: pupillage@blackstonechambers.com
Website: www.blackstonechambers.com

No of Silks 34
No of Juniors 42
No of Pupils 4 (current)

Contact
Miss Julia Hornor
Chambers Director

Method of application
Pupillage Portal

Pupillages (p.a.)
12 months 4-5
Required degree grade
Minimum 2:1
(law or non-law)

Income
Award £42,500
Earnings not included

Tenancies
Junior tenancies offered in last 3 years 62%
No of tenants of 5 years call or under 9

Chambers profile
Blackstone Chambers occupies large and modern, premises in the Temple.

Type of work undertaken
Chambers' formidable strengths lie in its principal areas of practice: commercial, employment and EU, public law, human rights and public international law. Commercial law includes financial/business law, international trade, conflicts, sport, media and entertainment, intellectual property and professional negligence. All aspects of employment law, including discrimination, are covered by Chambers' extensive employment law practice. Public law incorporates judicial review, acting both for and against central and local government agencies and other regulatory authorities, all areas affected by the impact of human rights and other aspects of administrative law. EU permeates practices across the board. Chambers recognises the increasingly important role which mediation has to play in dispute resolution. Seven members are CEDR accredited mediators.

Pupil profile
Chambers looks for articulate and intelligent applicants who are able to work well under pressure and demonstrate high intellectual ability. Successful candidates usually have at least a 2:1 honours degree, although not necessarily in law.

Pupillage
Chambers offers four (or exceptionally five) 12 month pupillages to those wishing to practise full-time at the Bar, normally commencing in October each year. Pupillage is divided into four sections and every effort is made to ensure that pupils receive a broad training. The environment is a friendly one; pupils attend an induction week introducing them to the Chambers working environment. Chambers prefers to recruit new tenants from pupils wherever possible. Chambers subscribes to Pupillage Portal; applications should be made for the summer season.

Mini pupillages
Assessed mini pupillages are available and are an important part of the application procedure. Applications for mini pupillages must be made by 30 April; earlier applications are strongly advised and are preferred in the year before pupillage commences.

Funding
Awards of £42,500 per annum are available. The pupillage committee has a discretion to consider applications for up to £10,000 of the pupillage award to be advanced during the BVC year. Since Chambers insists on an accessed mini pupillage as part of the overall application procedure, financial assistance is offered either in respect of out of pocket travelling or accommodation expenses incurred in attending the mini pupillage, up to a maximum of £200 per pupil.

Cloisters

Cloisters, 1 Pump Court, Temple, London, EC4Y 7AA
Tel: (020) 7827 4000 Fax: (020) 7827 4100
Email: clerks@cloisters.com
Website: www.cloisters.com

No of Silks 5
No of Juniors 45
No of Pupils 2

Contact
pupillage@cloisters.com

Method of application
Pupillage Portal

Pupillages (p.a.)
2 for 12 months

Chambers profile

Cloisters is a leading set with particular expertise in employment, equality, discrimination and human rights, personal injury and clinical negligence, media and sport, and public and regulatory law. Cloisters is known for its legal excellence, approachability, superb customer service and cost-effectiveness. It recruits only barristers who can offer these qualities.

Type of work undertaken

Cloisters acts for both claimants and respondents in all its practice areas.

Employment and discrimination: Cloisters continues to be at the forefront of this type of law. Recent high-profile cases include: Ahsan v. Watt (HL) – issue estoppel in tribunals, liability of political parties for discrimination; Cadman v. Health & Safety Executive (ECJ) – length of service pay increments; Coleman v. Attridge (ECJ) – discrimination by association.

Personal injury: Cloisters' personal injury team continues to appear in landmark cases and highly complex cases involving large sums. One of their specialisms is in cases involving occupational stress or bullying at work, which contain elements of both personal injury and employment law. Recent high-profile cases include: A v. Hoare (the Lotto Rapist) (HL) – limitation periods; Sarwar v. (1) Ali (2) MIB – highest-ever gross award in a personal injury case of £9.5m; Majrowski v. Guy's and St. Thomas' NHS Trust (HL) – employers' vicarious liability for harassment by employees to other employees at work.

Clinical negligence: In 2007 members of the PI and clinical negligence team and their instructing solicitors secured more than £100m for claimants. The set has the knowledge and experience to handle the full spectrum of work, right up to the multi-million pound catastrophic claims, and regularly appears on such instructions. They handle a full range of cases, including cases worth more than £10m. Recent major cases include: H v. Powys Health Board – highest-ever clinical negligence award of £10.7m.

Sport: Cloisters' sport practitioners handle disciplinary regulations, consultative work, litigation, non-professional sporting activity cases and matters arising from sports and entertainment cases, such as employment or contractual issues. For example, Cloisters has acted for Dwayne Chambers, Sam Allardyce, Status Quo and Frank Warren, among others.

Pupil profile

Chambers welcomes applications from outstanding candidates from all backgrounds and academic disciplines, including lawyers coming late to the Bar.

Pupillage

Chambers offers two twelve month pupillages to those wishing to practise full-time at the Bar, normally commencing in October each year. Each pupil is supervised and the supervisor changes every three months to show the pupil different areas of practice. Second six pupils will be allocated work by clerks subject to availability of work and pupil ability.

Internship programme

Cloisters offers twelve one week internship placements each year. All applicants must have completed at least their first year at university in any subject. The internships are unfunded, but we may pay travel costs in the event that an internee is asked to travel to court outside of London. Internship is not assessed and is not a requirement for applications for pupillage.

Funding

Cloisters offers two funded pupillages each year. Each pupil will receive an award (currently £30,000 per year). Pupils can also ask for an advance.

Crown Office Chambers

Head of Chambers: Antony Edwards-Stuart QC
2 Crown Office Row, Temple, London, EC4Y 7HJ
Tel: (020) 7797 8100   Fax: (020) 7797 8101
Email: mail@crownofficechambers.com
Website: www.crownofficechambers.com

No of Silks 14	
No of Juniors 70	
No of Pupils 2	
Contact	
Matthew Boyle	
Method of application	
Online application form, downloadable from chambers website	
Pupillages (p.a.)	
Up to three per year, 12 months	
£42,500 plus earnings	
Tenancies	
No of tenancies offered in last 3 years 6	

Chambers profile
Crown Office Chambers is one of the foremost sets of chambers specialising in civil common law work. The majority of members undertake at least some personal injury work, and some practise solely in that area. Chambers has an established reputation in other areas including construction, professional negligence, commercial contracts, insurance and product liability. It is not a 'pure commercial' set, and pupils will see a range of work during pupillage.

Pupil profile
Members pride themselves on their professionalism, an astute and business-orientated awareness of the practical needs of solicitors and lay clients, combined with an approachable and unstuffy attitude to their work. Chambers looks for the same in its pupils, all of whom are regarded as having strong tenancy potential. Pupils are expected to display the motivation, dedication and intelligence which are the hallmarks of a first-class barrister. Academically, they should have a first or upper second-class honours degree (not necessarily in law), a flair for oral and written advocacy, and a strong and committed work ethic.

Pupillage
Pupils rotate through three pupil supervisors during the course of the year. In their second six, pupils are briefed to attend County Court hearings on their own, probably at least two or three times per week. Generally these will be small personal injury cases. Pupils receive regular feedback on their work from pupil supervisors and other members of chambers. They also undertake a series of advocacy exercises in front of a panel of four members of chambers and receive extensive feedback after each exercise. There are also two assessed written exercises during the course of pupillage. Tenancy decisions are made in early July.

Mini-pupillage
Mini-pupillages available throughout the year – contact the Mini-Pupillage Administrator via online application form, downloadable from Chambers website.

One Essex Court

Chambers of Lord Grabiner QC, One Essex Court, Temple, London, EC4Y 9AR
Tel: (020) 7583 2000   Fax: (020) 7583 0118
Email: clerks@oeclaw.co.uk   Website: www.oeclaw.co.uk

No of Silks	23
No of Juniors	46
No of Pupils	4

Contact
Joanne Huxley Secretary to the Pupillage Committee

Method of application
Pupillage Portal

Pupillages (p.a.)
4-12 month
Required degree grade
Minimum 2:1
(law or non-law)

Income
Award £60,000

Chambers profile

One Essex Court is a pre-eminent set of barristers' chambers, specialising in commercial litigation. Members provide specialist advice and advocacy services worldwide, which include all areas of dispute resolution, litigation and arbitration.

Type of work undertaken

Chambers' work embraces all aspects of domestic and international trade, commerce and finance. Members of Chambers are recognised specialists in the many diverse fields characterised as commercial disputes, also regularly accepting nominations as arbitrators, mediators and experts. Chambers work includes, but is not limited to: arbitration, banking and finance, civil fraud, commercial litigation, company and insolvency, competition and EU, energy (oil, gas and utilities), financial services, insurance, IP, professional negligence and revenue law.

Pupil profile

Chambers has for many years maintained a policy of active recruitment and expansion and only offers pupillage to those who are thought capable of becoming tenants. Provided a candidate is proven to have the requisite ability, no distinction is drawn between candidates who do and those who do not have a law degree. Pupils at One Essex Court do not compete against one another for a predetermined maximum intake.

Pupillage

Four guaranteed 12 month pupillages are offered per year, each with substantial funding. From the beginning, pupils assist pupil supervisors with their papers, do legal research, draft opinions, pleadings and skeleton arguments. There are substantial opportunities for advocacy in the second six months of pupillage. Chambers subscribes to Pupillage Portal.

Mini-pupillage

Mini-pupillages last for either one or two days. They are not assessed. A mini-pupillage is not a pre-requisite for pupillage although it is encouraged as it can provide a good opportunity both to see how Chambers works and to meet members of Chambers. Please visit Chambers' website for the application process and deadlines.

Funding

Chambers offers each pupil £60,000, supplemented by earnings in the second six. It is understood that this is amongst the highest, if not the highest, remuneration package available to pupils. An advance of the Award is available, upon request, during a prospective pupil's Bar Vocational Course ("BVC") year.

ONE ESSEX COURT

39 Essex Street

39 Essex Street, London, WC2R 3AT
Tel: 020 7832 1111   Fax: 020 7353 3978
Email: clerks@39essex.com   Website: www.39essex.com
82 Kings Street, Manchester, M2 4WQ
Tel: 0161 870 0333   Fax: 020 7353 3978
Email: clerks@39essex.com   Website: www.39essex.com

No of Silks	25
No of Juniors	55
No of Pupils	up to 3
Contact	Pupillage - Charles Cory-Wright QC & Marion Smith clerks@39essex.com 020 7832 1111
Method of application	Pupillage Portal
Pupillages (p.a.)	Up to three

Chambers profile

39 Essex Street is a long established civil set. It currently has 80 members, including 25 QCs. Chambers has several members on each of the Attorney General's A, B and C Panels for civil litigation. Chambers prides itself on its friendly and professional atmosphere. It was described by Chambers & Partners in 2009 as 'An extremely professional outfit, with strong practitioners who offer a good service'. Chambers is fully networked and its clerking and administrative services are of a high standard. Chambers works very hard but it also has extensive social, sporting and professional activities.

Type of work undertaken

Commercial law: commercial regulation; construction and engineering; corporate restructuring; costs; employment; insurance and reinsurance; media, entertainment and sports; oil, gas and utilities; project finance.

Common law: clinical negligence; health and safety; insurance; material loss claims; personal injury; product liability; professional negligence; sports injuries; toxic torts.

Environmental and Planning: compulsory purchase; contaminated land; environmental civil liability; environmental regulation; international environmental law; licensing; marine environment; planning; nuisance; rating.

Public law: central and local government (including education, housing, immigration, prisons and VAT); European law; human rights; judicial review; mental health and community care; parliamentary and public affairs.

Regulatory and Disciplinary: medical; legal; social care and education; financial services; broadcasting, communications and media; sport; transport; health and safety; building and housing; local government standards; licensing.

Pupillage

Chambers takes up to three 12 month pupils a year. During the pupillage year, each pupil will be rotated among four pupil supervisors, covering a broad range of Chambers' work. The pupils will also do a number of assessed pieces of written work for other members of Chambers. There is an in-house advocacy course. Pupils work only 9.00 am to 6.00 pm, Monday to Friday.

Chambers is a member of Pupillage Portal. Applicants should consult the Pupillage Portal timetable.

Mini-pupillage

Mini-pupillage is an important part of Chambers selection process. It is encouraged that anyone who wishes to apply for pupillage at 39 Essex Street apply for mini-pupillage. Due to the limited number of places available, not all applicants will be successful. Applicants should be in their final year before undertaking the BVC, save in exceptional circumstances. Applications are made between 1 September and 30 November. Selection takes place between 1 December and 14 December. The deadline for acceptance of offers is mid-January. Mini-pupillages take place between mid-January until July.

Funding

Each 12 months pupillage comes with an award, currently £40,000. Of this, up to £8,000 may be drawn down during the year before pupillage commences. Awards and offers are all conditional upon passing the BVC. Junior tenants receive an interest free loan of £30,000, which is repaid out of earnings during the first 12 months.

4-5 Gray's Inn Square

Gray's Inn, London, WC1 R 5AH
Tel: (020) 7404 5252   Fax: (020) 7242 7803
Email: clerks@4-5.co.uk
Website: www.4-5.co.uk

Pupillges funded 2
Tenants 54
Tenancies in last 3 years 7
Method of application
Pupillage Portal. Candidates should see Chambers' website for full information
Pupillages (p.a.)
Up to two 12 month pupillages
Annexes
None

Chambers profile

4-5 Gray's Inn Square is a leading set of chambers specialising in a wide range of work, including in particular public law and judicial review, planning and environmental law, commercial law, employment and human rights. A distinctive feature of Chambers is the large number of barristers who practise at the intersection of these various specialisms. Chambers believe its strong reputation owes a lot to this unusual diversity. Chambers is a large set, comprising 54 (15 QCs and 39 junior tenants). and takes a modern and innovative approach to the changing market for legal services. It has well-established links with the academic world and has a number of leading lawyers and academics among its associate tenants. It is fully committed to the Bar's responsibilities as a profession and members of Chambers frequently undertake work in a pro bono capacity. Chambers prides itself on being not only a high-quality set, but a friendly one.

Type of work undertaken

General public law (including judicial review applications for and against local government and human rights challenges); planning and environmental law (including inquiries, statutory appeals and judicial review applications) on behalf of developers and planning authorities, and all aspects of domestic and EU environmental law: employment law (including unfair dismissal, sex, race, disability and other prohibited discrimination and trade union law); commercial law (including fraud, banking, shipping, regulatory work, insurance and reinsurance); professional negligence (including actions involving property, education and solicitors); education (including human rights and discrimination, special educational needs, admissions, exclusions and transport.)

Pupil profile

Chambers has a rigorous selection procedure for pupillage. To obtain a first interview, candidates must show first-class academic ability (though not necessarily a first-class degree) and strong evidence of advocacy potential. Successful interview candidates will be expected to demonstrate exceptional legal problem-solving and advocacy ability.

Pupillage

Pupils will receive a thorough training in the full range of Chambers' work during their pupillage. During the pupillage, pupils will generally be assigned to three or four different members of Chambers (pupil supervisors) to ensure they see the full range of work in which Chambers specialises. There may be some opportunity for pupils to gain advocacy experience by appearing in employment tribunals or in court. To gain additional advocacy experience pupils may take cases for the Free Representation Unit, which can be done both prior to and during pupillage. Chambers pays for all new tenants to attend the annual Advanced International Advocacy Course at Keble College in Oxford.

Mini pupillages

Chambers welcomes applications for mini-pupillages. The deadlines for mini pupillage applications and details of chambers annual open day can be found on our website.

Funding

Chambers normally offers up to two 12-month pupillages, each carrying an award of a minimum of £37,000 with the possibility to draw down up to £10,000 in the BVC year at Chambers' discretion.

2 Hare Court

2 Hare Court, Temple, London EC4Y 7BH
Tel: (020) 7353 5324 Fax: (020) 7353 0667
Email: clerks@2harecourt.com
Website: www.2harecourt.com

No of Silks	16
No of Juniors	36
No of Pupils	4
Contact	Jeremy Benson QC
Method of application	Pupillage Portal
Pupillages (p.a.)	Up to 2 12 month pupillages. Minimum degree 2:1
Tenancies	According to ability
Annexes	None

Chambers profile

Described by the editors of the Chambers and Partners guide as "the current form horse at the criminal bar", 2 Hare Court has long been recognised as one of the UK's leading chambers specialising in criminal, fraud, and regulatory law. "A set of choice for many solicitors" (Legal 500), its first rate reputation is based on a proven track record of high quality client care together with excellence in advocacy and trial management in cases of the utmost gravity and complexity. Chambers counts amongst its members six Treasury Counsel and 19 Recorders of the Crown Court, and a number of former members have become judges in the Crown, Central Criminal and High Courts.

Chambers has a strong tradition of public service with representation on the Bar Council and Criminal Bar Association, and makes a significant commitment to pro-bono work and advocacy training.

Type of work undertaken

The strength and depth of experience amongst its members enables this chambers both to prosecute and defend in all types of criminal work, particularly the more serious and complex matters such as murder, terrorism (including Special Advocates work in closed proceedings), serious fraud, corporate and financial crime, international drug trafficking, serious sexual offences, corruption and organised crime; the cases in which members have appeared read like a who's who of recent criminal litigation.

Its barristers act in healthcare, police and sports disciplinary proceedings, and a number of members have significant practices in the fields of environmental law, VAT tribunal work, licensing and gaming, and health and safety law. They also appear in public inquiries and inquests, and in other jurisdictions (the Caribbean, Iraq, Ireland and mainland Europe, Hong Kong, North Africa, and before the ICC at the Hague, and in the UN's International Criminal Tribunals for Yugoslavia and Rwanda).

Pupil profile

Chambers selects as pupils articulate and well motivated individuals of high intellectual ability who can demonstrate sound judgment and a practical approach to problem solving. Candidates should have at least a 2:1 honours degree.

Pupillage

Chambers offers up to two twelve month pupillages starting in September. The year is divided into two six month periods, and pupils are assigned to a different pupil supervisor every four months to ensure experience in different areas of crime. Chambers pays for the "Advice to Counsel" course and runs its own in-house advocacy training.

Mini pupillages

The programme runs throughout the year with no more than one mini pupil taken each week and two each week in the summer, except between mid-December and mid-January, and throughout August. Applicants must be at least 18 years old and either be studying for a Higher Education qualification or on (or about to start) GDL/CPE or BVC courses. Please see the website for further details of the scheme, the application process and to download an application form.

Funding

12 month pupils will be sponsored through a combination of an award scheme and guaranteed earnings worth £24,000, and you will retain additional earnings, from which no clerks' fees or deductions are taken.

Henderson Chambers

2 Harcourt Buildings, Temple, London EC4Y 9DB
Tel: (020) 7583 9020
Fax: (020) 7583 2686
Email: clerks@hendersonchambers.co.uk
Website: www.hendersonchambers.co.uk

Chambers profile

Henderson Chambers is a leading civil common law/commercial chambers. Chambers has acknowledged expertise in all of its principal areas of practice, and members of Chambers and its pupils are frequently involved in high profile commercial and common law litigation.

Type of work undertaken

Chambers has unrivalled expertise in product liability (which covers a wide range of commercial work including sale of goods and insurance disputes, multi-party pharmaceutical and medical device claims and regulatory and enforcement proceedings) and is consistently rated as the leading set of chambers in this area. Henderson Chambers is also widely recognised for the excellence of its health and safety work.

Members are also noted for their expertise and experience in areas including: employment law, regulatory and disciplinary proceedings, public law and judicial review, personal injury, property law, and technology and construction.

Pupil profile

Chambers looks for individuals who can demonstrate a first class intellect whether via the traditional route of an outstanding higher education record or via proof of success in other professions, in business or in employment. Henderson Chambers is friendly and sociable, and expects candidates to be able to show how they have both worked hard and played hard.

Pupillage

Pupillages are for 12 months, usually with two different pupil supervisors for six months each. Pupils have the opportunity to spend four weeks in Brussels at McDermott Will and Emery in order to experience European practice at first hand. Pupils will attend court regularly during their second six months.

Mini-pupillage

Chambers offers unassessed mini-pupillages. Applications are by way of a CV and covering letter, which should be addressed to Richard Roberts.

Funding

Chambers offers a maximum of three, and usually two, funded twelve-month pupillages with minimum remuneration of £42,500. This consists of an award of £35,000 and guaranteed earnings of £7,500 during the second six months.

No of Silks 8
No of Juniors 32
No of Pupils 2

Contact
Adam Heppinstall (Recruitment Committee secretary)
aheppinstall@hendersonchambers.co.uk

Method of application
Pupillage Portal

Pupillages (p.a.)
1-3 (usually 2) 12 month pupillages offered.
Remuneration for pupillage: £42,500 for 12 months (£35,000 award, £7,500 guaranteed earnings)

Tenancies
5 in the last 3 years.

Keating Chambers

15 Essex Street, London, WC2R 3AA
Tel: (020) 7544 2600
Fax: (020) 7544 2700

Chambers profile

Keating Chambers is a leading commercial set specialising in construction, technology and related professional negligence disputes. Disputes often relate to high-profile projects in the UK and overseas and typically involve complex issues in the law of tort, contract and restitution. Chambers is based in modern premises outside the Temple. In their first years of practice, tenants can expect earnings equivalent to those in other top sets of commercial chambers.

Type of work undertaken

Chambers is involved in disputes of all shapes and sizes: from residential building works to multi-million pound projects for the construction of airports, dams, power stations and bridges. Chambers has been instructed on projects such as Wembley Stadium, the "Gherkin", the Millenium Bridge, the London Eye and the Channel Tunnel. Much of Chambers' work now also includes developing areas such as IT, telecommunications and energy. Chambers acts as advocates in litigation and arbitration throughout the UK and internationally. Some are frequently appointed as mediators, arbitrators, and adjudicators.

Chambers' area of practice is dynamic and challenging. As leaders in the field Chambers are often in cases that are reported in the law reports. Chambers regularly publishes books, articles and journals.

Pupil profile

No specialist or technical knowledge of construction or engineering is required. A thorough understanding of principles of contract and tort law is essential. Criteria are listed on the website.

Pupillage

Pupils are allocated four supervisors over the course of the year ensuring that each pupil sees a variety of work of differing levels of complexity within Chambers. Comprehensive training is provided including a programme of advocacy exercises and provision for attendance at specialist seminars and lectures. For more details, see our website.

Mini pupillages

Chambers offers up to ten funded mini-pupillages lasting one week and 25 unfunded mini pupillages lasting three days. For further details, see website.

Funding

Awards of up to £42,500 are available. Of this, an advance of £15,000 is available during the BVC course.

No of Silks 20
No of Juniors 31
No of Pupils currently 3

Contact
ebrowne@keatingchambers.com

Method of application
Pupillage Portal

Pupillages (p.a.)
Pupillages (p.a.): 4x12 month pupillages available

Tenancies
6 offered in last 3 years.

7 King's Bench Walk

7 King's Bench Walk, Temple, London, EC4Y 7DS
Tel: (020) 7910 8300   Fax: (020) 7910 8464
Website: www.7kbw.co.uk

Chambers profile

7 King's Bench Walk is a leading commercial set of Chambers, with a reputation for excellence and intellectual rigour. The Legal 500 describes it as "One of the Bar's true elite".

Type of work undertaken

Chambers is at the forefront of commercial litigation, specialising in particular in the fields of insurance and reinsurance, shipping, international trade, professional negligence and private international law. Most of its work has an international dimension. Members regularly appear in the High Court (particularly the Commercial Court), the Court of Appeal and the House of Lords, as well as in arbitrations in London and overseas.

Pupil profile

Applicants must have at least a good 2:1, coupled with lively intelligence and strong advocacy skills (both oral and in writing). Chambers encourages applications from all outstanding candidates no matter what their background or academic discipline.

Pupillage

Chambers offers up to four (but typically two or three) twelve month pupillages each year. Pupils will sit with four pupillage supervisors prior to the tenancy decision in July. Pupils will assist their pupil supervisors with their work, and accompany them to hearings. Pupils will, particularly after completion of the first three months of pupillage, also do work for other members of Chambers.

Mini-pupillage

Mini-pupillages are unassessed, and last 3 days. They are offered in three separate periods throughout the year: 1 June to 30 September (excluding August), 1 October to 31 January and 1 February to 31 May. Applications for mini-pupillages during these periods must be received by 31 March, 31 July, and 30 November respectively. Application by way of a CV and covering letter should be made to the Secretary to the Mini-Pupillage Committee. Further details of how to apply may be found on Chambers' website.

Funding

A pupillage award of at least £45,000 will be available for the 2011/12 and 2012/2013 years, of which up to £10,000 may be drawn down during the BVC.

No of Silks 19
No of Juniors 27
No of Pupils up to 4

Contact
Emma Hilliard (pupillage secretary)
Pupillage@7kbw.co.uk

Method of application
Pupillage Portal

Pupillages (p.a.)
Up to 4 12 month pupillages offered.
Required degree grade Minimum 2:1 (law or non-law)
Remuneration for pupillage: at least £45,000

Tenancies
Junior tenancies offered in last 3 years: 6
No of tenants of 5 years call or under: 7

Littleton Chambers

3 King's Bench Walk North, Temple, London, EC4Y 7HR
Tel: (020) 7797 8600   Fax: (020) 7797 8699
Email: clerks@littletonchambers.co.uk
Website: www.littletonchambers.co.uk

No of Silks 12
No of Juniors 36
No of Pupils currently 1

Contact
Samantha Higgins, Chambers Administrator

Method of application
Pupillage Portal

Pupillages (p.a.)
Pupillages (p.a.): 12 month 2 required degree level 2:1 (law or non law)

Tenancies
£40,000

Chambers profile
Littleton Chambers is acknowledged as being a top class set in each of its main practice areas. Its success is based upon both the desire to maintain high professional standards and a willingness to embrace change. It prides itself on the skills of its tenants, not only as advocates and advisers on the law, but also for their analytical and practical skills.

Type of work undertaken
Littleton Chambers specialises in commercial litigation, employment law, professional negligence, sports law, mediation and arbitration.

Pupil profile
Chambers takes a considerable amount of care in choosing its pupils and prefers to recruit its tenants from persons who have completed a full twelve months of pupillage with Chambers. Chambers endeavors to take on pupils who not only have good academic skills, but who also show flair for advocacy and the ability to understand practical commercial issues.

Pupillage
Chambers generally offers pupillage to two people each year.

During your twelve month pupillage you will have the benefit of three pupil supervisors in succession. Your pupil supervisors will provide support and guidance to you throughout your pupillage, ensuring that you understand not only the nuts and bolts of a barristers work, but also the ethical constraints which are such a distinctive feature of Chambers professional life.

After six months pupillage, you will be entitled to take on your own work. Typically, pupils in Littleton Chambers have been briefed once or twice a week. Your pupil supervisor will provide assistance in the preparation of these briefs to ensure that your client receives the best possible service from you.

Mini-pupillage
Assessed mini-pupillage forms part of the pupillage application process. Mini-pupillages are not offered outside of this process.

Funding
Each pupillage is funded (currently £40,000 per year) and, if necessary, it is possible to draw down some of this funding during the year of Bar Finals.

Maitland Chambers

7 Stone Buildings, Lincoln's Inn, London WC2A 3SZ
Tel: (020) 7406 1200 Fax: (020) 7406 1300
Email: clerks@maitlandchambers.com
Website: www.maitlandchambers.com

No of Silks	17
No of Juniors	49
No of Pupils	up to 3

Contact
Valerie Piper
(Pupillage Secretary)
pupillage@maitlandchambers.com

Method of application
See Chambers website from January 2010. Application deadline for pupillage in 2011-12 is 1 February 2010

Pupillages (p.a.)
Up to 3 funded

Income
£45,000 p.a.

Tenancies
5 in last 3 years

Chambers profile

Chambers UK has rated Maitland as the pre-eminent commercial Chancery litigation set every year since 2001.

Type of work undertaken

Maitland is instructed on a very wide range of cases – from major international litigation to county court disputes. Much of the work is done in London, though the set frequently advises and appears for clients in other parts of the United Kingdom and abroad. Barristers are recommended as leaders in their field in commercial Chancery, company, charities, insolvency, media and entertainment, traditional Chancery, property litigation, partnership, pensions, banking, energy, tax, agriculture and professional negligence.

Pupil profile

Academically, Maitland looks for a first or upper second. Pupils must have a sense of commercial practicality, be stimulated by the challenge of advocacy and have an aptitude for and general enjoyment of complex legal argument.

Pupillage

Maitland offers up to three pupillages, all of which are funded. All pupils in chambers are regarded as potential tenants.

Pupils spend their first two to three months in chambers with one pupil supervisor, in order that the pupil can find his or her feet and establish a point of contact which will last throughout the pupil's time in chambers. For the balance of the pupillage year, each pupil will sit with different pupil supervisors, usually for two months at at time. The set believes that it is important for pupils to see all of the different kinds of work done in Chambers so that they can be sure that the Chancery Bar suits them; it also gives different members of chambers the opportunity to assess them. As each member of chambers has a distinctive method of working, dividing the pupillage up in this way helps in developing a pupil's individual approach to work at the Bar.

The Set provides in-house advocacy exercises for pupils during their pupillage. These take the form of mock hearings with senior members of chambers acting as the tribunal. They, together with other members of chambers provide detailed feedback after each exercise. These exercises are both part of the assessment process, and help develop court skills.

Mini pupillages

Applications are considered twice a year with a deadline of 30 April for the period June to November, and 15 November for December to May. Applications should be made with a covering letter and cv (listing undergraduate grades) to the Pupillage Secretary.

Funding

Chambers offers up to three, 12-month pupillages, all of which are funded (£45,000 for pupils starting in October 2011). Up to £11,250 of the award may be drawn down in advance during BVC year or to pay BVC fees.

Four New Square

Four New Square, Lincoln's Inn, London, WC2A 3RJ
Tel: (020) 7822 2000   Fax: (020) 7822 2001
Website: www.4newsquare.com

Chambers profile
Four New Square is a leading commercial and civil set of barristers comprising 67 members, of whom 17 are Queen's Counsel. Chambers acts as specialist advocates and advisers in a wide range of civil disputes and as expert advisers in non-contentious matters. Chambers has a particularly high reputation in the field of professional liability. The leading practitioners' work on the subject, Jackson & Powell on Professional Negligence, was written by Rupert Jackson QC (now Mr Justice Jackson) and John L Powell QC, and continues to be written and edited by members of chambers.

Type of work undertaken
Professional liability, product liability, chancery and commercial law, construction and engineering, insurance and reinsurance, financial services and banking.

Pupil profile
Chambers do not stream its pupils. Each has an equal prospect of securing a tenancy. Selection criteria: evidence of intellectual ability; potential as an advocate; personal qualities such as self-reliance, integrity, reliability and the ability to work effectively with colleagues and clients; motivation. Equal opportunities: Chambers observes a policy of equal opportunities in accordance with the Bar Code of Conduct. All applicants are required to complete the Bar Council Equality Code questionnaire. This is used for monitoring purposes only.

Pupillage
The first six months: You will go to court and attend conferences with your pupil supervisor. You will also assist your pupil supervisor with their written work: carrying out written advisory and drafting work on their current papers and undertaking detailed research on the law. The second six months: During your second six months, you will take on an increasing amount of your own court work. Chambers places a strong emphasis on advocacy and support its pupils in gaining valuable practical experience. You can expect to be in court on your own about once a week up to the tenancy decision and potentially on a more regular basis thereafter. Advocacy: You will also take part in an assessed moot during your first six months. Workshop training sessions are run to help you prepare for the moot, which usually takes place before a former member of Chambers who is now a High Court Judge. Environment: Chambers aims to provide a friendly and sociable atmosphere. Pupils are included in Chambers social events throughout the year.

Mini pupillages
Students considering applying to chambers are encouraged to apply for one of 12 assessed mini pupillages. After an initial review of applications on paper, a number of applicants will be invited for a short interview with two members of chambers. The assessed mini will last for three days with an award of £500. Mini-pupils will be set a piece of assessed work and those judged to be of high calibre will be given an exemption from the first round interviews should they apply.
Chambers understands that not everyone seeking to apply for pupillage will be able to participate in the assessed mini-pupillage programme. Consequently chambers also offers unassessed mini-pupillages. Applications may be made at any time of the year. Unassessed mini –pupillages are granted after a review of an application form by two members of Chambers.

Funding
Funding: Chambers offers up to four 12-month pupillages with awards of £45,000 compromising an award of £37,500 (up to a third which may be drawn down during the BVC year) with further guaranteed second-six-month earnings of £7,500. Chambers also guarantees that the junior tenants will earn a minimum of £150,000 in total, net of Chambers' expenses, during their first three years of tenancy, in addition to their pupillage awards.

No of Silks 17
No of Juniors 50
No of Pupils 3

Contact
Catherine Culley
Tel: (020) 7822 2000
Email:
c.culley@4newsquare.com

Method of application
Online: www.4newsquare.com

Pupillages (p.a.)
Up to 4

Annexes
3, London

FOUR NEW SQUARE

Old Square Chambers

10-11 Bedford Row, London, WC1R 4BU D: 1046 Chancery Lane
Tel: (020) 7269 0300   Fax: (020) 7405 1384
Email: clerks@oldsquare.co.uk
Website: www.oldsquare.co.uk

No of Silks	10
No of Juniors	57
No of Pupils	2

Contact
Ben Cooper
Felicity Schneider

Method of application
Pupillage Portal

Pupillages (p.a.)
2-12 month pupillages

Income
£35,000 (£25,000 award plus £10,000 guaranteed earnings)
Plus additional earnings

Tenancies
4 in last 3 years

Annexes
Bristol

Chambers profile

Old Square Chambers is recognised as a premier set in its core specialist areas of employment and discrimination, personal injury and environmental law. Chambers' defining quality is excellence, both in the specialist legal expertise it has to offer and in the customer-service which it provides. Members and staff have a reputation for being approachable and unstuffy. Many members hold part-time judicial positions, sit on specialist panels, act as mediators, and edit or contribute to leading practitioner texts.

Type of work undertaken

Chambers' strength lies in the depth of experience and expertise in its core practice areas. The Employment and Discrimination Group is widely regarded as one of the foremost in the UK. Work is in all aspects of employment and discrimination law. Clients range from individual employees and directors to major trade unions, private and public sector organisations. Personal Injury work covers all aspects of this wide-ranging and complex field, from employers' liability and road traffic claims to high value head, brain and spinal injury cases, with particular expertise in disaster litigation and multi-party actions. In environmental law, Chambers has been at the forefront of developing litigation in the area of toxic torts. Members appear in high-profile multi-party claims arising from pollution of various kinds. Alongside its core areas Chambers also has expertise in professional discipline, clinical negligence, product liability, public inquiries, health and safety and ADR.

Pupil profile

Chambers assesses candidates on intellectual ability (usually a first or upper second degree will be required), potential as an advocate, interest in Chambers' fields of practice, ability to cope with hard work and pressure and interpersonal skills.

Mini pupillages

Chambers runs a programme of mini-pupillages during the summer. Applications should be made through Chambers' website.

Funding

The current award is £35,000 (£25,000 award plus £10,000 guaranteed earnings). Pupils keep additional earnings from their second six.

Pump Court Tax Chambers

16 Bedford Row, London, WC1R 4EF
Tel: (0207) 414 8080   Fax: (0207) 414 8099
Email: clerks@pumptax.com
Website: www.pumptax.com

No of Silks	9
No of Juniors	19
No of Pupils	2-3 in any given year
Contact	Jonathan Bremner pupils@pumptax.com
Method of application	CV and covering letter (non-Pupillage Portal)
Pupillages (p.a.)	Up to 3 funded
Tenancies	4 in the last 3 years

Chambers profile
Pump Court Tax Chambers is the largest specialist set practising exclusively in tax.

Type of work undertaken
All areas of tax work (both contentious and non-contentious) are covered. On the corporate side, clients typically include the 'Big 4' accountants and 'magic circle' solicitors sending a wide variety of work such as M & A, reconstructions and demergers and structured finance. Chambers' private client work comes from a broad range of sources – city solicitors, accountants, regional firms, chartered tax advisors and IFAs, who act for private individuals, trustees and landed estates. Much of Chambers' work concerns large scale litigation (especially in the field of VAT) and members of chambers regularly appear in the Tax Tribunals, the High Court, the Court of Appeal, the House of Lords and the ECJ.

Pupil profile
Chambers looks for applicants who are intelligent, articulate and well-motivated. Successful candidates will have at least a 2:1 honours degree (although not necessarily in law). Prior experience of studying tax law is not required.

Pupillage
Chambers offers up to three 12 month pupillages (terminable after six months by either party) to those wishing to practise full-time at the Bar. Pupillage normally commences in October each year. Pupils will have at least three pupil supervisors and will also sit with other members of chambers so as to receive a broad training in all aspects of the work of chambers.

Mini pupillages
The programme runs throughout the year. Applications should be made via email to pupils@pumptax.com with accompanying CV and marked for the attention of the Pupillage Secretary.

Funding
Awards of up to £20,000 per six months (£40,000pa) are available. The pupillage committee has discretion to consider applications for up to £8,000 of the pupillage award to be advanced during the BVC year.

Quadrant Chambers (Lionel Persey QC & Simon Rainey QC)

Quadrant House, 10 Fleet Street, London EC4Y 1AU
Tel: (020) 7583 4444 Fax: (020) 7583 4455
Email: pupillage@quadrantchambers.com
Website: www.quadrantchambers.com

No of Silks	11
No of Juniors	35

Contact
Secretary to Pupillage Committee

Method of application
Chambers' application form

Pupillages (p.a.)
1st 6 months 3
2nd 6 months 3
12 months
(Reviewed at 6 months)
Required degree
Good 2:1+

Income
1st 6 months
£20,000
2nd 6 months
£20,000
Earnings not included

Tenancies
Current tenants who served pupillage in Chambers 19
Junior tenancies offered in last 3 years 7
No of tenants of 5 years call or under 9

Chambers profile

Quadrant Chambers is one of the leading commercial chambers. Chambers offers a wide range of services to its clients and is pre-eminent in maritime and aviation law. Quadrant Chambers is placed in the first rank in both specialisms by Chambers Guide to the Legal Profession. In shipping law, seven silks and nine juniors were selected by Chambers, and Chambers concluded that 'these highly commercial barristers are at the forefront of the shipping and aviation field. In both these areas the set had more 'leaders in their field' selected than any other set of chambers. Quadrant Chambers advises on domestic and international commercial litigation and acts as advocates in court, arbitration and inquiries in England and abroad.

Type of work undertaken

The challenging and rewarding work of chambers encompasses the broad range of commercial disputes embracing arbitration, aviation, banking, shipping, international trade, energy oil insurance and reinsurance, professional negligence, entertainment and media, environmental and construction law. Over 70% of chambers work involves international clients.

Pupil profile

Quadrant Chambers seeks high calibre pupils with good academic qualifications (at least a 2.1 degree) who exhibit good written and oral skills.

Pupillage

Chambers offer a maximum of three funded pupillages of 12 months duration (reviewable at six months). Pupils are moved amongst several members of Chambers and will experience a wide range of high quality commercial work. Outstanding pupils are likely to be offered a tenancy at the end of their pupillage. Further information can be found on the website.

Quadrant Chambers will be holding an open day on Wednesday 9th December 2009 designed for those in the second year of their law degree or above. The open day will provide those interested in pursuing a career at the commercial bar with the opportunity to meet members of chambers, learn about life as a barrister and see how chambers works. During the day, members of chambers will give talks on topics such as 'life as a commercial barrister' and will hold workshops on advocacy and interview techniques. Places are limited and will be allocated on a first come, first served basis. Please visit the website for details on how to apply. Chambers is not a member of Pupillage Portal and therefore please consult the website for application timetable.'

Mini pupillages

Mini pupillages are encouraged in order that potential pupils may experience the work of Chambers before committing themselves to an application for full pupillage. Please refer to Chambers' website for more details.

Funding

Awards of £40,000 p.a. are available for each funded pupillage – part of which may be forwarded during the BVC, at the Pupillage Committee's discretion.

Serle Court

Serle Court, 6 New Square, Lincoln's Inn, London WC2A 3QS
Tel: (020) 7242 6105 Fax: (020) 7405 4004
Email: pupillage@serlecourt.co.uk
Website: www.serlecourt.co.uk

Chambers profile
'Refreshingly self-effacing, modern and efficient,' Serle Court is 'an impressive chancery and commercial set that has really been on the move in the last few years' and is 'a first point of call for any client requiring top quality commercial and chancery expertise' 'with tremendous strength across the board.' *Chambers & Partners Guide to the UK Legal Profession 2009*. Serle Court is one of the leading commercial chancery sets with 50 barristers including 14 silks. Widely recognised as a leading set, Chambers is recommended in 21 different areas of practice by the legal directories. Chambers has a stimulating and inclusive work environment and a forward looking approach.

Type of work undertaken
Litigation, arbitration, mediation and advisory services across the full range of chancery and commercial practice areas including: administrative and public law, banking, civil fraud, commercial litigation, company, financial services, human rights, insolvency, insurance and reinsurance, partnership, professional negligence, property, regulatory and disciplinary, trusts and probate.

Pupil profile
Candidates are well-rounded people, from any background. Chambers looks for highly motivated individuals with outstanding intellectual ability, combined with a practical approach, sound sensibility and the potential to become excellent advocates. Serle Court has a reputation for 'consistent high quality' and for having 'responsive and able team members' and seeks the same qualities in pupils.

Pupillage
Pupils sit with different pupil supervisors in order to experience a broad range of work. Two pupils are recruited each year and Chambers offers: an excellent preparation for successful practice; a genuinely friendly and supportive environment; the opportunity to learn from some of the leading barristers in their field; a real prospect of tenancy.

Mini-pupillages
About 30 available each year. Apply online at www.serlecourt.co.uk.

Funding
Serle Court offers awards of £45,000 for 12 months, of which up to £15,000 can be drawn down during the BVC year. It also provides an income guarantee worth up to £100,000 over the first two years of practice.

No of Silks 14
No of Juniors 36
No of Pupils 2

Contact
Kathryn Barry
Tel (020) 7242 6105

Method of application
Chambers application form, available from website or Chambers. Not a member of Pupillage Portal.

Pupillages
Two 12 month pupillages

Tenancies
Up to 2 per annum

3-4 South Square

3-4 South Square, Gray's Inn, London WC1R 5HP
Tel: (020) 7696 9900   Fax: (020) 7696 9911
Email: pupillage@southsquare.com
Website: www.southsquare.com

Chambers profile

Chambers is an established successful commercial set, involved in high-profile international and domestic commercial litigation and advice. Members of Chambers have been centrally involved in some of the most important commercial cases of the last decade including Barings, BCCI, Maxwell, Enron, Marconi, Lehman Brothers, Northern Rock and Kaupthing.

Type of work undertaken

3-4 South Square has a pre-eminent reputation in insolvency and restructuring law and specialist expertise in banking, financial services, company law, professional negligence, domestic and international arbitration, mediation, European Union Law, insurance/reinsurance law and general commercial litigation.

Pupil profile

Chambers seek to recruit the highest calibre of candidates who must be prepared to commit themselves to establishing a successful practice and maintaining Chambers' position at the forefront of the modern Commercial Bar. The minimum academic qualification is a 2:1 degree.

Pupillage

Pupils are welcomed into all areas of Chambers' life and are provided with an organised programme designed to train and equip them for practice in a dynamic and challenging environment. Pupils sit with a number of pupil supervisors for periods of six to eight weeks and the set looks to recruit at least one tenant every year from its pupils.

Mini pupillages

Chambers also offers funded and unfunded mini-pupillages – please see the set's website for further details.

Sponsorship & awards

Currently £42,500 per annum (reviewable annually).

No of Silks 19
No of Juniors 25
No of Pupils 2

Contact
Pupillage Secretary
Tel (020) 7696 9900

Method of application
CV with covering letter

Pupillages (p.a.)
Up to four, 12 month pupillages offered each year

2 Temple Gardens (Chambers of Benjamin Browne QC)

2 Temple Gardens, London, EC4Y 9AY DX: 134 Chancery Lane
Tel: (020) 7822 1200   Fax: (020) 7822 1300
Email: clerks@2tg.co.uk
Website: www.2tg.co.uk

No of Silks 8
No of Juniors 52
No of Pupils 3
Contact
Leanne McCabe
Pupillage Administrator
Method of application
Pupillage Portal (Summer)
Pupillages (p.a.)
Up to three, 12 month pupillages
Award: £47,500

Chambers profile

2tg is regarded as one of the leading commercial and civil law barristers' chambers. The firm specialises in professional negligence, insurance and personal injury and also has significant practices in banking, employment, technology, construction and clinical negligence, alongside strength in private international law.

Pupil profile

Academically, you will need at least a good 2.1 degree to be considered. The firm looks for applicants who work well in teams and have the ability to get on with solicitors, clients and other members of chambers.

Pupillage

Chambers offers one of the most generously funded, well structured and enjoyable pupillages at the Bar. It takes pupillage very seriously: and aims to recruit the best applicants, and to ensure that its pupils have an excellent foundation from which to start a successful career at the Bar.

Pupils have three different pupil supervisors during pupillage, and will also do work for other members of chambers. The aim is for pupils to experience as much of chambers' work as possible during their pupillage year.

Mini pupillages

Chambers welcomes 'mini-pupils'. Generally applicants will only be considered after their first year of a law degree or during CPE. Mini pupillages are a good way to experience life at 2tg first hand. Normally they last for one week. However, two or three day mini pupillages can be arranged. Chambers aims to provide you with a wide range of work during the week. It offers an assessment at the completion of your mini pupillage and encourage you to give feedback too. Chambers also offers help with reasonable expenses (up to £50).

Mini pupillages are usually unfunded but a few funded mini pupillages (maximum £250 per person) are also available.

Funding

Chambers offers up to three, 12 month pupillages, all of which are funded. Its pupillage award for 2011 is £47,500. This is made up of a grant of £35,000, of which up to £12,500 can be taken in the BVC year. The remainder of the grant will be paid in instalments in the first six months of pupillage with a guarantee of earnings during the second six months of £12,500.

3 Verulam Buildings (Christopher Symons QC/John Jarvis QC)

3 Verulam Buildings, Gray's Inn, London WC1R 5NT   DX: LDE 331
Tel: (020) 7831 8441 Fax: (020) 7831 8479
Email: chambers@3vb.com
Website: www.3vb.com

No of Silks	17
No of Juniors	42
No of Pupils	3

Contact
Mr Adam Kramer (Pupillage)
Mr James MacDonald (Mini Pupillage)

Method of application
Pupillage Portal (Pupillage);
CV & covering letter (Mini-pupillage)

Pupillages (p.a.)
12 months 3
Required degree grade 2:1

Income
In excess of £42,500 plus any earnings

Tenancies
Current tenants who served pupillage in Chambers Approx 41
Junior tenancies offered in last 3 years 5
No of tenants of 5 years call or under 11

Chambers profile

Sitting comfortably and spaciously in a newly refurbished and expanded row of buildings in Gray's Inn, 3VB is one of the largest and most highly regarded commercial sets, its members being involved in many of the leading cases, recent examples including the test case on overdraft charges, the $700m Springwell professional negligence litigation, the $600m Honeywell dispute, Rosemary Nelson enquiry, and the substantial Langbar National Grid and Central Bank of Ecuador fraud disputes.

Type of work undertaken

3VB's 17 silks and 42 juniors lead the field in banking and financial services, and are also among the top practitioners in the fields of professional negligence, civil fraud, insurance, arbitration, and company and insolvency. Chambers also has significant expertise in IT and telecommunications, energy, construction, and media and entertainment.

Pupil profile

Commercial practice is intellectually demanding and 3VB seeks the brightest and the best. The typical successful applicant will have a first or upper second class degree (not necessarily in law) from a good university, with good mooting experience and proven experience of the commercial bar (generally through mini-pupillages with us or elsewhere). Many have a Master's degree or other legal or commercial experience.

Pupillage

Chambers seeks to recruit three 12 month pupils each year through the Pupillage Portal process. Chambers are committed to recruiting new tenants from its pupils whenever it can. Although tenancy is offered to all pupils who make the grade, on average two out of three pupils are successful in any one year.

Mini pupillages

Three day mini-pupillages are an important part of Chambers selection procedure and it is strongly encouraged that prospective applicants for pupillage apply for a mini-pupillage (e-mail James MacDonald at minipupillage@3vb.com, attaching a detailed CV).

Funding

For the year 2010/2011, the annual award will be at least £42,500, up to £15,000 of which may be drawn during the BVC year.

Wilberforce Chambers

8 New Square, Lincoln's Inn, London WC2A 3QP
Tel: (020) 7306 0102   Fax: (020) 7306 0095
Email: pupillage@wilberforce.co.uk   Website: www.wilberforce.co.uk

No of Silks	22
No of Juniors	26
Method of application	Online via website
Pupillages (p.a.)	Up to 2 x 12 months
Mini-pupillages	Total of 21 places
Award	£43,000 (2011/2012)
Minimum qualification	2:1 degree
Tenancies in last 3 years	4

Chambers profile

Wilberforce Chambers is a leading Commercial Chancery set of Chambers and is involved in some of the most commercially important and cutting edge litigation and advisory work undertaken by the Bar today. Members are recognised by the key legal directories as leaders in their fields. Instructions come from top UK and International law firms, providing a complex and rewarding range of work for international companies, financial institutions, well-known names, sports and media organisations, pension funds, commercial landlords and tenants, and private individuals. Clients demand high intellectual performance and client-care standards but in return the reward is a successful and fulfilling career at the Bar. Chambers has grown in size in recent years but retains a united and friendly 'family' atmosphere.

Type of work undertaken

All aspects of traditional and modern Chancery work including property, pensions, private client, trust and taxation, professional negligence, general commercial litigation, banking, company, financial services, intellectual property and information technology, sports and media and charities.

Pupil profile

Chambers look to offer two 12 month pupillages. You should possess high intellectual ability, excellent communication skills and a strong motivation to do Commercial Chancery work. You need to be mature and confident, have the ability to work with others and analyse legal problems clearly, demonstrating commercial and practical good sense. Chambers look for people who have real potential to join as tenants at the end of their pupillage. Wilberforce takes great care in its selection process and puts effort into providing an excellent pupillage. There is a minimum requirement of a 2:1 degree in law or another subject, and Wilberforce has a track record of taking on CPE students.

Pupillage

Chambers operates a well-structured pupillage programme aimed at providing you with a broad experience of Commercial Chancery practice under several pupil supervisors with whom you will be able to develop your skills. Wilberforce aims to reach a decision about tenancy after approximately 9-10 months, but all pupils are entitled to stay for the remainder of their pupillage on a full pupillage award.

Mini-pupillages

Wilberforce encourages potential candidates for pupillage to undertake a mini-pupillage in order to learn how Chambers operates, to meet its members and to see the type of work that they do, but a mini-pupillage is not a prerequisite for pupillage. Wilberforce runs three separate mini-pupillage weeks (two in December and one in July). Please visit the website for an application form and for further information.

Funding

Wilberforce offers a generous and competitive pupillage award which is reviewed annually with the intention that it should be in line with the highest awards available. The award is £48,000 for 12 months and is paid in monthly instalments. A proportion of the award (up to £16,000) can be drawn down during the BVC year.

Contacts

The Law Society
113 Chancery Lane,
London WC2A 1PL
Tel: 020 7242 1222
E-mail: contact@lawsociety.org.uk
www.lawsociety.org.uk

Solicitors Regulation Authority
Tel: 0870 606 2555
E-mail: contactcentre@sra.org.uk
www.sra.org.uk

Junior Lawyers Division
The Law Society,
113 Chancery Lane,
London WC2A 1PL
Helpline: 08000 856 131
E-mail: juniorlawyers@lawsociety.org.uk
www.juniorlawyers.lawsociety.org.uk

The Bar Council
289-293 High Holborn,
London WC1V 7HZ
020 7242 0082
www.barcouncil.org.uk

Bar Standards Board
289-293 High Holborn
London WC1V 7HZ
020 7611 1444
www.barstandardsboard.org.uk

Gray's Inn, Education Department
8 South Square, Gray's Inn,
London WC1R 5ET
Tel: 020 7458 7905
E-mail: quinn.clarke@graysinn.org.uk
www.graysinn.info

Inner Temple, Education & Training Department
Treasury Building, Inner Temple,
London EC4Y 7HL
Tel: 020 7797 8208
E-mail: ffulton@innertemple.org.uk
www.innertemple.org.uk

Lincoln's Inn, Students' Department
Treasury Office, Lincoln's Inn,
London WC2A 3TL
Tel: 020 7405 1393
www.lincolnsinn.org.uk

Middle Temple, Students' Department
Treasury Office, Middle Temple Lane,
London EC4Y 9AT
Tel: 020 7427 4800
E-mail: members@middletemple.co.uk
www.middletemple.org.uk

The Institute of Legal Executives
Kempston Manor, Kempston,
Bedfordshire MK42 7AB
Tel: 01234 841000
E-mail: info@ilex.org.uk
www.ilex.org.uk

The National Association of Licensed Paralegals
3.08 Canterbury Court,
Kennington Business Park,
1-3 Brixton Road,
London SW9 6DE
www.nationalparalegals.com

Government Legal Service
GLS Recruiting Team,
11th Floor, Lower Castle Street,
Castlemead,
Bristol BS1 3AG
Tel: 0845 3000 793
E-mail: glstrainees@tmp.com
www.gls.gov.uk

Crown Prosecution Service
50 Ludgate Hill,
London EC4M 7EX
Tel: 020 7796 8000
E-mail: recruitment@cps.gsi.gov.uk
www.cps.gov.uk

The Law Commission
Steel House,
11 Tothill Street,
London SW1H 9LJ
Tel: 020 3334 0200
E-mail: communications@lawcommission.gsi.gov.uk
www.lawcom.gov.uk

Citizens Advice Bureaux
Head Office, Myddelton House,
115-123 Pentonville Road,
London N1 9LZ
Tel: 020 7833 2181
Volunteer Hotline: 08451 264264
www.citizensadvice.org.uk

Legal Services Commission
Head Office, 4 Abbey Orchard Street,
London SW1P 2BS
Tel: 020 7783 7000
www.legalservices.gov.uk

Chartered Institute of Patent Agents
95 Chancery Lane,
London WC2A IDT
Tel: 020 7405 9450
E-mail: mail@cipa.org.uk
www.cipa.org.uk

The Institute of Trade Mark Attorneys
Canterbury House, 2-6 Sydenham Road,
Croydon, Surrey CR0 9XE
Tel: 020 8686 2052
E-mail: tm@itma.org.uk
www.itma.org.uk

The Institute of Chartered Secretaries and Administrators
16 Park Crescent,
London W1B 1AH
Tel: 020 7580 4741
E-mail: info@icsa.org.uk
www.icsa.org.uk

The Law Centres Federation
293-299 Kentish Town Road,
London NW5 2TJ
Tel: 020 7428 4400
E-mail: info@lawcentres.org.uk
www.lawcentres.org.uk

Free Representation Unit
6th Floor, 289-293 High Holborn,
London WC1V 7HZ
Tel: 020 7611 9555
E-mail: admin@freerepresentationunit.org.uk
www.freerepresentationunit.org.uk

The Bar Lesbian & Gay Group
(BLAGG)
www.blagg.org

Lesbian & Gay Lawyers Association
c/o Alternative Family Law,
3 Southwark Street,
London SE1 1RQ
Tel: 020 7407 4007
E-mail: info@blagg.org
www.lagla.org.uk

The Society of Asian Lawyers
c/o Ingram Winter Green Solicitors,
Bedford House, 21A John St,
London WC1N 2BF
E-mail: info@societyofasianlawyers.com
www.societyofasianlawyers.com

Society of Black Lawyers
11 Cranmer Road, Kennington Park,
London SW9 6EJ
Tel: 020 7735 6592
www.blacklawyer.org

The Association of Muslim Lawyers
PO Box 148, High Wycombe,
Bucks HP13 5WJ
E-mail: info@aml.org.uk
www.aml.org.uk

The Association of Women Barristers
187 Fleet Street,
London EC4A 2AT
E-mail: chambers@187fleetstreet.com
www.womenbarristers.co.uk

Group for Solicitors with Disabilities
c/o Judith McDermott,
The Law Society, 113 Chancery Lane,
London WC2A 1PL
Tel: 020 7320 5793
E-mail: Judith.McDermott@lawsociety.org.uk
www.gsdnet.org.uk

LPC Central Applications Board
PO Box 84, Guildford,
Surrey GU3 1YX
Tel: 01483 301282
www.lawcabs.ac.uk

CPE Central Applications Board
PO Box 84, Guildford,
Surrey GU3 1YX
Tel: 01483 451080
www.lawcabs.ac.uk

Pupillage Portal
Technical Assistance
E-mail: enquiries@Pupillageportal.com
www.pupillages.com

Career Development Loans
Tel: (freephone) 0800 585505
www.direct.gov.uk

- **You've read the book:** now try www.chambersstudent.co.uk. There are plenty of additional features on our website to help you keep up to date with what's happening in the profession. We've also prepared many more comparison tables and analysed trends and topical subjects.

If you have feedback for us or career questions please do get in touch via the website.

top tip no. 37